The Philosopher's Way

Thinking Critically About Profound Ideas

JOHN CHAFFEE

CITY UNIVERSITY OF NEW YORK

PEARSON

Prentice Hall

UPPER SADDLE RIVER, NJ 07458

Library of Congress Cataloging-in Publication Data

Chaffee, John
  The philosopher's way : thinking critically about profound ideas / John Chaffee
    p. cm.
  Includes bibliographical references and index
    ISBN 0-13-048069-X
    1. Philosophy. I. Title
  BD21.C49 2005
100—dc22   2004060010

VP, Editorial Director: *Charlyce Jones Owen*
Senior Acquisitions Editor: *Ross Miller*
Assistant Editor: *Wendy Yurash*
Editorial Assistant: *Carla Worner*
Editor-in-Chief, Development: *Rochelle Diogenes*
Development Editor: *Meg Boteon*
VP, Director of Production and Manufacturing: *Barbara Kittle*
Managing Editor: *Joanne Riker*
Production Editor: *Kathleen Sleys*
Production Assistants: *Marlene Gassler, Kristen Sleys*
Marketing Manager: *Kara Kindstrom*
Marketing Assistant: *Jennifer Lang*
Media Project Manager: *Deborah O'Connell*
Prepress and Manufacturing Manager: *Nick Sklitsis*
Manufacturing Buyer: *Christina Helder*
Creative Design Director: *Leslie Osher*
Interior and Cover Design: *Kathryn Foot*
Illustration Specialist: *Bruce Killmer*
Cover Illustration/Photo: *George Holton, Photo Researchers, Inc.*
Cover Image Specialist: *Karen Sanatar*
Director, Image Resource Center: *Melinda Reo*
Interior Image Specialist: *Beth Boyd Brenzel*
Image Permission Coordinator: *Cathy Mazzucca*
Photo Researcher: *Beuara Kathy Ringrose*
Color Scanning Services: *Joe Conti, Greg Harrison, Corrin Skidds, Rob Uibelhoer, Ron Walko*
Composition: *This book set in 10/13 New Baskerville by GGS Book Services, Atlantic Highlands*
Printer/Binder: *Web Crafters*
Cover Printer: *Lehigh Press, Inc.*

For Heide,
Jessie & Joshua

Credits and acknowledgments borrowed from other sources and reproduced, with permission, in this textbook appear on pages 594–601.

Pearson Education LTD.
Pearson Education Australia PTY, Limited
Pearson Education Singapore, Pte. Ltd.
Pearson Education North Asia Ltd

Pearson Education, Canada, Ltd
Pearson Educación de Mexico, S.A. de C.V.
Pearson Education–Japan
Pearson Education Malaysia, Pte. Ltd

10 9 8 7 6
ISBN 0-13-048069-X

> *It is an innovative approach to enabling students to appreciate the value of philosophy and benefit from its study, and I certainly look forward to using it in my courses!*
> CHRISTIAN PERRING, Dowling College

To Know Philosophy is to Love Philosophy.

Professors...

■ *Do your students see themselves as philosophical thinkers?*

■ *Do they come to class having read— and thought about—the text material?*

■ *And do they leave this course inspired to love philosophy like you do?*

Now They Will.

PRENTICE HALL PROUDLY PRESENTS THE PHILOSOPHER'S WAY, TEACHING AND LEARNING CLASSROOM (T.L.C.) EDITION BY JOHN CHAFFEE. This T.L.C. EDITION will ignite students' passion to know more and think more about the profound impact philosophy has on their own lives.

This highly visual T.L.C. EDITION begins with a simple premise: students will not learn what they have not read. THE PHILOSOPHER'S WAY was designed especially to intrigue students to *Read, Think, See, and Do* philosophy—and essentially study smarter and perform better in class.

To Know Philosophy is to
Love Philosophy.

Pique students' curiosity to *read* the text.

This T.L.C. EDITION helps students better understand what they are reading by offering author John Chaffee's insightful explanations throughout the text. Difficult concepts and passages are presented in context with interesting commentary designed to make the reading more meaningful. Mini-biographies, glossaries, and bolded terms appear in context, and full color and interesting visuals including images and icons of today permeate this book from start to finish.

Read

Think

See

Do

are her kindred, and with them she ever lives, when she is by herself and is not let or hindered; then she ceases from her erring ways, and being in communion with the unchanging is unchanging. And this state of the soul is called wisdom?

Cebes: That is well and truly said, Socrates.

Socrates: And to which class is the soul more nearly alike and akin, as far as may be inferred from this argument, as well as from the preceding one?

Cebes: I think, Socrates, that, in the opinion of everyone who follows the argument, the soul will be infinitely more like the unchangeable—even the most stupid person will not deny that.

Socrates: And the body is more like the changing?

Cebes: Yes.

This brief exchange provides a cogent summary of Socrates' metaphysical framework. For Socrates, reality is dualistic, comprised of two dichotomous realms. One realm is changeable, transient, and imperfect, whereas the other realm is unchanging, eternal, immortal. The physical world in which we live—comprised of all that we can see, hear, taste, smell, and feel—belongs to the former realm. All aspects of our physical world are continually changing, transforming, disappearing.

In contrast, the unchanging, eternal, perfect realm includes the intellectual essences of the universe, concepts such as *truth*, *goodness*, and *beauty*. We find examples of these ideal forms in the physical world—for example, we might describe someone as truthful, good, or beautiful. But these examples are always imperfect and limited: it is only the ideal forms themselves that are perfect, unchanging, and eternal.

St. Augustine: *Plato and Christianity*

lato's (and Socrates') metaphysical views were revolutionary:

ST. AUGUSTINE
(354–430)
Christian Philosopher. Augustine's influence on Christian philosophy and theology was unparalleled in the Middle Ages. Augustine's work in philosophy was quite extensive covering many areas such as philosophy of language, philosophy of mind, and the philosophy of religion.

- The existence of an immaterial reality separate from the physical world
- The radical distinction between an immaterial soul and physical body
- The existence of an immortal soul that finds its ultimate fulfillment in union with the eternal, transcendent realm

But these ideas would have died with the decline of Greek civilization had they not been adopted and perpetuated by subsequent cultures. The Roman Empire both conquered and absorbed Greek culture, preserving much of its extraordinary accomplishments in the arts, philosophy, and politics. Plato died in 347 BC, and more than five hundred years later a Roman philosopher named **Plotinus** (AD 205–270) breathed new life into Plato's ideas, spearheading an intellectual movement that came to be known as **Neoplatonism**. Plotinus based his views on Plato's core concepts believing, for example, that "the soul, since it own right and can exist independently of the body,

"This text excels in clarifying difficult philosophical ideas and especially in showing the relevance of philosophy to [students'] everyday lives."
DAVID LOPEZ, American River College

Engage students to *think* philosophically.

Known for his work on critical thinking, author John Chaffee empowers students to *think and rethink* the significance of philosophy by involving them in the philosophical issues through insightful boxed features, integrated readings, and in the narrative itself as they learn to think philosophically.

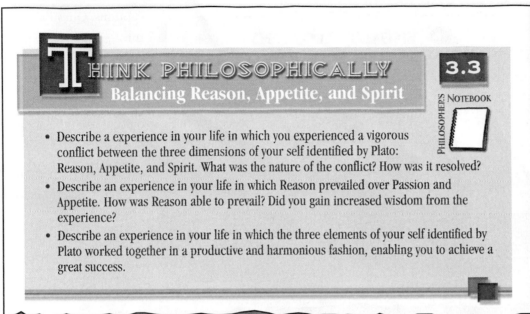

THINK PHILOSOPHICALLY
Balancing Reason, Appetite, and Spirit

PHILOSOPHER'S NOTEBOOK · 3.3

- Describe a experience in your life in which you experienced a vigorous conflict between the three dimensions of your self identified by Plato: Reason, Appetite, and Spirit. What was the nature of the conflict? How was it resolved?
- Describe an experience in your life in which Reason prevailed over Passion and Appetite. How was Reason able to prevail? Did you gain increased wisdom from the experience?
- Describe an experience in your life in which the three elements of your self identified by Plato worked together in a productive and harmonious fashion, enabling you to achieve a great success.

THINK CRITICALLY

PHILOSOPHER'S NOTEBOOK · 3.12

Searching for the Self

Here's an opportunity for you to be a philosophy detective engaged in a "missing person" investigation—looking for your *self*. If Kant is right, you should not be able to find your *self* among the contents of your consciousness. Instead, your *self* should be revealed as the synthesizing principle that unites your experience. Launch a reflective investigation into your *self*, and then describe as clearly as you can what you find. Did you discover your *self*? How would you describe the qualities of your *self*? In what ways is your *self* similar to all other selves? In what ways is your *self* different from all other selves?

> "The questions and exercises for students both clarify concepts and provoke original thought... Students are also encouraged to engage directly with the philosophical problems of the ages."
>
> RANDALL HORTON, San Jacinto College South

To Know Philosophy is to Love Philosophy.

Intrigue students to *see* the significance.

This highly visual T.L.C. EDITION illustrates otherwise difficult concepts with provocative images and photos that appear in context with the text material, and include interesting captions. Questions throughout the text encourage careful consideration of the impact philosophy has on the world today.

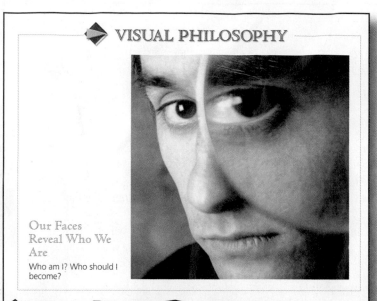

◆ VISUAL PHILOSOPHY

Our Faces Reveal Who We Are

Who am I? Who should I become?

◆ VISUAL PHILOSOPHY

The Faces of Michael Jackson

In what sense does the self change as the body changes? In what sense does the self remain the same?

> " *The author has a gift for making complex philosophical connections understandable.* "
>
> ELIZABETH LAIDLAW, Monroe Community College

Empower students to *do* more than just read.

As students *read, think,* and *see* philosophy more clearly through their text and lectures, they will be equipped to *do* philosophy through a series of activities that engage them in the issues in such a way that gives even difficult concepts meaning. End-of-chapter writing activities include student sample essays to inspire and challenge students' own writing, and Research Navigator™ questions encourage further exploration of key topics online.

Read
Think
See
Do

Students Thinking about Philosophy *Perspectives on the Self*

This chapter has explored the deceptively complex question, "Who Am I?" One of the great ironies of life is that though we have spent our entire waking lives with ourselves, the precise nature of our "self" remains elusive and enigmatic. The philosophers and psychologists we have studied in this chapter have endeavored to unravel the mysteries of consciousness, personal identity, and the soul. It is likely you have found that in studying them you have gained both insight and confusion as your understanding of these issues has deepened and your questions have become more intellectually sophisticated.

This essay is an opportunity to express your own views on the nature of the "self" in a form that is thoughtful and coherent. After reviewing, discussing, and reflecting on the various perspectives regarding the self that you read about and discussed in this chapter, compose a paper which reflects your own synthesis of these issues. Your point of view should be well-reasoned and seek to integrate a variety of different philosophical perspectives. In addition, you should weave into your analysis your own personal reflections and life experiences to illustrate the conceptual points that you are making. One such student synthesis follows, entitled "Perceptions of Self."

Perceptions of Self
Jessie Lange

Years ago my parents met in an elevator in Manhattan and in an instant my existence was made possible. Had my father missed that elevator, had his dentist been running late, he might never have stepped on and seen my mother in her rainbow-striped socks and mini skirt, struggling with a stack of boxes. If she had not smiled, or he had not held the lobby door or gotten up the guts to suggest coffee sometime, or if my mother had not stood next to him on Fifth Avenue and leapt the boundary of timidity to say, "How about right now?" because she knew how easily "sometime" could become "never" as memories of encounters faded and cr...
every...

This essay is an opportunity to express your own views on the nature of the "self" in a form that is thoughtful and coherent. After reviewing, discussing, and reflecting on the various perspectives regarding the self that you read about and discussed in this chapter, compose a paper which reflects your own synthesis of these issues. Your point of view should be well-reasoned and seek to integrate a variety of different philosophical perspectives. In addition, you should weave into your analysis your own personal reflections and life experiences to illustrate the conceptual points that you are making. One such student synthesis follows, entitled "Perceptions of Self."

> *... I think the inclusion of student essays and comments is one of the best features of this text.*

Students need to hear what other students have to say on the new and unfamiliar topic of philosophy. The student essays serve as paradigms for the type of thinking and writing I would expect to find in my students.
Dr. Timothy Davis, **Community College of Baltimore County**

One**Key**

Further Exploration is the Key: **OneKey** offers everything professors and students need—all in one place to-succeed in a truly interactive and collaborative classroom.

For Professors: Whether you are looking for images to show in class, a complete Power Point™ presentation, short video clips to launch lectures, or the complete Instructor's Manual, **OneKey** offers you convenient, easy-to-use resources available online whenever you need them-24-hours a day, 7 days a week.

For Students: In **OneKey**, students have access to a complete on-line study guide including practice quizzes with automatic grading, flashcards, and chapter summaries. **OneKey** also contains relevant and visually dramatic video clips; additional full text primary sources and a reading guide; access to Research Navigator™, our one-stop research site with four databases of reliable sources; material from THE PHILOSOPHY STUDENT WRITER'S MANUAL; and an electronic version of THE PHILOSOPHER'S NOTEBOOK.

OneKey is available in Course Compass™, Blackboard™ or WebCT™. Contact your local Prentice Hall sales representative for a complete demonstration and ordering information.

THE PHILOSOPHER'S NOTEBOOK (0-13-152428-3)

Students are encouraged to maintain a journal of their own philosophical reflections in THE PHILOSOPHER'S NOTEBOOK that accompanies every new copy of **THE PHILOSOPHER'S WAY**. Containing the most important *Think Critically* and *Think Philosophically* activities in the text, THE PHILOSOPHER'S NOTEBOOK is a unique and powerful tool to help students organize their thoughts and ideas on the challenging yet interesting and provocative themes throughout this T.L.C. EDITION.

PRIMARY SOURCE: Philosophical Readings with Commentary CD-ROM

This new CD-ROM, free and automatically bound with THE PHILOSOPHER'S WAY, offers over 100 primary source excerpts, together with instructive commentary on each reading and provocative questions. Organized by philosopher within major historical periods, this CD-ROM is a valuable supplement to the text, offering an extensive array of additional readings. Selections represent a wide and diverse set of philosophers—including American, women, non-Western —and numerous sources from the canon. Additional features include a glossary, philosopher biographies, and an historical timeline. Study questions linked to a website allow students to email their responses to their instructors.

THAT'S NOT ALL! ALSO AVAILABLE:

- **Instructor's Manual with Test Item File** (0-13-048142-4)
- **Prentice Hall Test Manager/Microsoft® Windows** (0-13-048130-0)
- **Common Philosophical Terms** (Packaged with text: 0-13-191547-9)
- **Prentice Hall OneSearch with Research Navigator™** (Packaged with text: 0-13-164874-8)
- **Companion Website™** at *www.prenhall.com/chaffee*

To Know Philosophy is to
Love Philosophy.

BRIEF CONTENTS

CONTENTS

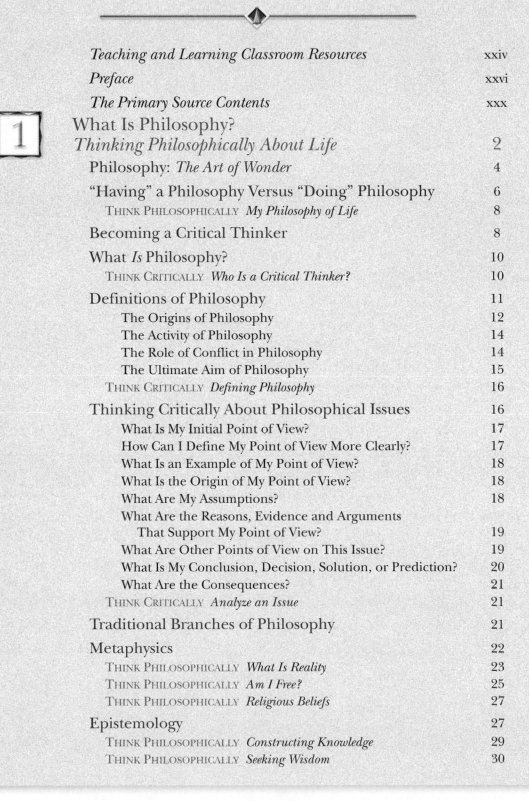

3   Who Am I?
Consciousness, Identity, and the Soul   88

6 What Is Morality?
Constructing an Ethical Theory 270

10   What Is Social Justice?
Creating a Just State   520

VISUAL PHILOSOPHY

Teaching and Learning Classroom Resources

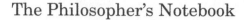

The Philosopher's Notebook

This unique and powerful tool is designed to help readers organize their thoughts and ideas on the challenging, yet interesting and provocative themes throughout *The Philosopher's Way*. Available with every new copy of the text, the notebook includes the most important *Think Critically* and *Think Philosophically* activities from the textbook so that students can record their own philosophical reflections in response to these activities.

Common Philosophical Terms

A useful reference and guide, this glossary includes important terms with definitions that are important to the study of philosophy. See your local Prentice Hall representative for information on how to obtain this supplement for your students.

Instructor's Manual with Test Item File

Prentice Hall Test Generator

Suggestions for teaching, chapter summaries, activities, and a complete test item file organized by chapter make planning lectures and teaching in the classroom easy and effective. The test item file is also available in the *Prentice Hall Test Generator* for IBM and Macintosh formats for creating tests and quizzes electronically.

Media Resources

 ### The Primary Source: Philosophical Readings with Commentary CD-ROM

This collection of over 100 primary source excerpts, together with instructive commentary on each reading and provocative questions. Organized by philosopher within major historical periods, the selections on the CD-ROM represent a wide and diverse set of philosophers and numerous sources from the canon. Additional features include a glossary, biographies, and an historical timeline. Study questions for each reading are linked to a website allow students to email their responses to their instructors. A copy of the CD-ROM is bound into every new textbook.

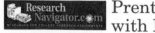 ### Prentice Hall OneSearch with Research Navigator

Prentice Hall's *Research Navigator*™ helps students make the most of their research time. From finding the right articles and journals, to citing sources, drafting and writing effective papers, and completing research assignments, *Research Navigator*™ simplifies and streamlines the entire process. Access to this unique resource is available with every copy of *OneSearch*, a brief guide to evaluating resources on the Internet. See your local Prentice Hall representative for more information about how to obtain copies of this important resource for your students.

Companion Website™

Prentice Hall's exclusive *Companion Website*™ offers unique tools and support that make it easy for students and instructors to integrate this online resource with **The Philosopher's Way**. The website is a study and review resource organized according to the chapters within the text and features chapter quizzes and a variety of learning and teaching modules.

 OneKey

An exciting new resource that offers everything professors and students need—all in one place—to create and succeed in a truly interactive and collaborative classroom. For professors, *OneKey* offers Powerpoint™ presentations, images, video, and all print supplements for use in planning lectures and classroom interactions. For students, *OneKey* offers access to a complete on-line study guide, practice quizzes, flashcards, chapter summaries, additional primary sources and reading guide, and an electronic version of **The Philosopher's Notebook**. *OneKey* offers convenient, easy-to-use resources available online 24 hours a day, 7 days a week.

OneKey is available in Blackboard™ and WebCT™. Contact your local Prentice Hall sales representative for a complete demonstration and ordering information.

PREFACE

I was midway into my freshman year of college—and my very first philosophy course—when I suddenly announced to everyone's astonishment (including my own) that I was changing my major to Philosophy. It didn't concern me that I had never taken a philosophy course, nor even read a philosophy book: somehow I *knew* that I was destined to study this extraordinary discipline. It is a decision I have never regretted. Philosophy has enriched my life in countless ways, both personally and professionally, and I have witnessed it change the lives of many of my own students. I am confident that its study will do the same for you.

We are all the artists of our lives, with our brushstrokes being the choices we make each day as we gradually create our life portraits. Philosophy encourages us to follow Socrates' exhortation to examine our lives and to "know ourselves" so that we can make the most informed choices possible and create the most enlightened portraits. The study of philosophy provides the impetus and the thinking tools to confront the most fundamental questions in life: *Who am I? Who should I become? What is the meaning of my life?* More significantly, philosophy helps us craft an approach to living and develop a reflective attitude towards every aspect of our lives. These are invaluable, life-transforming gifts that only philosophy can provide. On a personal level, philosophy has served as a beacon in my life, helping to illuminate a path for me to follow, while clarifying and informing my choices.

Professionally, philosophy has provided me with a framework for thinking critically and creatively. This has helped me perform my best in every job that I've held, ranging from cabinetmaking to teaching to writing. The study of philosophy trains our minds to think in powerful and analytical ways, enabling us to understand complex issues, reason cogently, and make intelligent decisions. These are foundational abilities that enhance our success in whatever career we choose.

My goal in writing *The Philosopher's Way* is for you to capture the spirit of philosophy, to experience the passion and adventure of engaging in the philosophical exploration of the core dimensions of our lives. In Western culture, philosophy traces its roots to ancient Greece where philosophers like Socrates, Plato, and Aristotle engaged in thoughtful reflection and energetic, rigorous discussions. Your Introduction to Philosophy course is your opportunity to become a part of this philosophical conversation which has spanned millenia, as you engage in philosophical discourse with your professor and your classmates.

This book has been designed to help you become a more accomplished critical thinker and to develop the conceptual abilities and analytical tools needed to think philosophically about important issues such as:

- How do I create an enlightened philosophy of life for myself?
- How do I decide what is the morally right thing to do?
- How can I increase my personal freedom?
- What religious beliefs make the most sense for me?
- How do I determine what's real?
- What should my position be on social issues such as censorship and abortion?
- Is there one ideal political system? What is the role of justice?

- How can I determine which beliefs are true and which are false?
- How can I make informed aesthetic judgments?
- How do I go about creating a meaningful life?

As you read this book, you will encounter not only the ideas of profound thinkers in their own words, but you will also be guided by commentary designed to help you "think" your way through them. You will also be challenged to think deeply about the themes you are studying through innovative activities—Think Philosophically, Think Critically, Visual Philosophy—that will engage you in the process of "thinking philosophically." You will be encouraged to continue your philosophical reflections by keeping a Philosopher's Notebook in which you will express your own thoughtful analyses, relating these ideas to your own life. And you will be given the opportunity to compose your own philosophical papers, for instance a Socratic dialogue in which you defend a principle you would be willing to die for. The book also includes examples written by other aspiring student philosophers.

Philosophy is at the heart of living a meaningful and fulfilling life. The philosopher Bertrand Russell said, "Thought is great, and swift and free, the light of the world and the chief glory of man." The study of philosophy will give your thoughts wings, enabling your spirit to take flight and soar to the to the realms of wisdom and illumination.

Acknowledgments

I have been privileged to work with a stellar team of people at Prentice Hall who are exemplary professionals and valued friends. Charlyce Jones Owen is the publishing soul of this book, a visionary champion who intuited its essence from the beginning and then used her extraordinary talents to ensure that the book fulfilled its potential. Yolanda de Rooy believed in this book throughout its creation and provided the unstinting personal and professional support required in a project of this unique complexity. The multi-talented Ross Miller contributed to every aspect of this book from proposal to publication, and his commitment, creative energy, and friendship were essential ingredients. In addition to lending her wonderfully philosophical name, Rochelle Diogenes did a masterful job in coordinating various editorial dimensions of the project. Kathy Sleys was remarkable in orchestrating the production of this book, like a maestro conducting a symphony, while also demonstrating an impressive talent for researching images to be used. Joanne Riker oversaw the entire production process and ensured the timely publication of a beautiful and complex text. Christina Helder ensured the smooth running of the manufacturing process. Kara Kindstrom is the most creative and enthusiastic marketing manager I have ever encountered, her talents expressed in stunning materials, inspired marketing initiatives, and even the production of philosophical beer! Deb O'Connell did a masterful job of handling all of the media-related activities, ranging from videotaping to the creation of the CD-ROM. Meg Botteon made important editorial contributions, including her excellent work on the chapter summaries. Kathie Foot created an elegant and timeless design for the text; Leslie Osher oversaw the design process and developed the stunning cover. Robert Farrar-Wagner's design for the marketing materials was inventive and memorable. Among her significant marketing related contributions, Theresa Herbst created the outstanding virtual tour for the text. My special thanks go to Carla Worner and Wendy Yurash for their invaluable contributions with respect to reviewers, supplements, and the multitude of other editorial responsibilities required in a project such as this, and thanks also to Jennifer Lang for all of her marketing efforts on behalf of the text. Finally, I would like to extend special acknowledgement to Kathy Boothby-Sestak who first encouraged me to write this text, and whose enthusiastic support helped launch the project.

One of the key features of this text are the chapter-ending essays, and it is with my deepest appreciation that I acknowledge the people who contributed these superb pieces which have so greatly enriched the text: Gina Szeto, Jessie Lange, Andy Snyder, Sonja Tanner, and Sue Martin.

I am grateful to the many scholars and teachers whose thoughtful and detailed comments helped shape *The Philosopher's Way*:

Steve Best, University of Texas; Elizabeth Santana Laidlaw, Monroe Community College; Monica Gerrek, Cleveland State University; Bill E. Lawson, Michigan State University; Christian Perring, Dowling College; Mark Hillringhouse, Passaic County Community College; Merigala Gabriel, Georgia Southern University; Randall Horton, San Jacinto College South; Chris Trogan, John Jay College; David Fox, Montgomery College; David Lopez, American River College; Eric Gampel, CSU Chico; Luis Samuel Gonzalez, Sinclair Community College; Patrice D. Nango, Mesa Community College

Finally, I want to thank my wife Heide and my children Jessie and Joshua for their complete and ongoing love, support, and inspiration. Throughout their lives, Jessie and Joshua have continually taught me the truth of Socrates' statement, "All philosophy has its origins in wonder," for they have been models of both wonder and wisdom. Heide has consistently inspired me to achieve the best of which I'm capable, and provided unwavering support in my efforts to do so. And her extraordinary talents in publishing have provided me with clear professional direction when it was most needed. It is these closest relationships that make life most worth living, and the threads of love that tie us together are woven into the fabric of this book. I also wish to remember my parents, Charlotte Hess and Hubert Chaffee, who taught me lasting lessons about the most important things in life. They will always be with me.

Although this is a published book, it continues to be a work in progress. In this spirit, I invite you to share your experiences with the text by sending me your comments. I hope that this book serves as an effective support for your own philosophical explorations in living an examined life. You can contact me on line at JCthink@aol.com.

John Chaffee

About the Author

John Chaffee, Ph.D., is a Professor of Philosophy at The City University of New York where he has developed a program in Philosophy and Critical Thinking which involves 25 faculty and 3,000 students annually. He is a nationally recognized figure in the area of critical thinking, having authored several leading books, many professional articles and conducted numerous conference presentations and workshops throughout the country. As a pioneer in developing the field of critical thinking, he has received grants from The National Endowment for the Humanities and The Ford Foundation to teach people to think more effectively in all areas of life. He was selected as New York Educator of the Year (1992) and received the Distinguished Faculty Award for Diversity in Teaching in Higher Education (1998). Most recently, he has created a new online community, **www.thinkingworld.com**, which provides people with the opportunity to reflect about important subjects while sharpening their thinking abilities.

THE PRIMARY SOURCE
Philosphical Readings and Commentary

Chapter 1

Chapter 2

Chapter 3

Chapter 4

Chapter 5

SINGLE PC LICENSE AGREEMENT AND LIMITED WARRANTY

The Philosopher's Way

Thinking Critically About Profound Ideas

Thought is great and swift and free, the light of the world, and the chief glory of man.

BERTRAND RUSSELL

Philosophy should be responsive to human experience and yet critical of the defective thinking it sometimes encounters.

MARTHA NUSSBAUM

Philosophy: *The Art of Wonder*

The feeling of wonder is the mark of the philosopher, for all philosophy has its origin in wonder.

—SOCRATES

Philosophy asks the simple question, what is it all about?

—ALFRED NORTH WHITEHEAD

Thus, to sum up our discussion of the value of philosophy; Philosophy is to be studied, not for the sake of any definite answers to its questions since no definite answers can, as a rule, be known to be true, but rather for the sake of the questions themselves; because these questions enlarge our conception of what is possible, enrich our intellectual imagination and diminish the dogmatic assurance which closes the mind against speculation; but above all because through the greatness of the universe which philosophy contemplates, the mind also is rendered great, and becomes capable of that union with the universe which constitutes its highest good.

—BERTRAND RUSSELL

You are about to embark on a thrilling journey: the study of philosophy. Reading this book and taking a philosophy course is likely to be a memorable, life-altering experience for you. Why? One student explains:

> In general, we as people don't usually think critically about the important areas of life, but it's these areas that help us to create a meaningful life. As an individual I was also one of those who didn't take the time to examine, ask questions, and think deeply about different perspectives on serious issues. As a result, studying Philosophy has helped me to become more open-minded and reflective about everything in my life. Some of the topics that we have covered include freedom of choice, moral reasoning, religious beliefs, constructing knowledge and exploring the nature of reality.
>
> —*Tanya Louis*

As Tanya notes, many of us get so caught up in the details and demands of life—deadlines, responsibilities, all the little tasks of living—that we don't make the time to step back and look at the whole picture. Why am I doing the things that I'm doing? In what direction am I headed? What does it all mean? Who am I? Who do I want to become? These questions penetrate the surface of life to confront the deeper currents lying beneath. But to achieve this more profound level of understanding, we need to recognize the need to go beyond the obvious. And we also need to be willing and open-minded enough to do this.

That's the unique mission of philosophy. Philosophy provides us with the motivation and the intellectual abilities required to explore life's most challenging issues. What *is* the meaning of my life? To what extent am I free and responsible for my choices? Facing moral dilemmas, what is the "right" thing to do? What is the relationship between my religious beliefs and other areas of my life? How do I gain genuine knowledge and ascertain truth? These questions, and others like them, are the core questions of life, and philosophy provides the map, compass, and tools needed to explore them.

In what ways will taking this philosophical journey affect your life? Here's one student's analysis:

> Before taking this course I really never explored my thinking abilities: I only explored the obvious. Now that I've almost completed this introductory course to Philosophy, I feel I am more sophisticated in both thought and action. I realize that I react differently to situations; I think twice and evaluate circumstances more closely before I make decisions. Philosophy has helped me in my other courses as it helped me to express myself more clearly in essays and speeches. From taking this course I have grown as a person, and my mind is definitely not what it used to be.
>
> —*Ryan Malley*

VISUAL PHILOSOPHY

Lawrence Olivier
as Hamlet
Philosophy guides us in exploring life's most challenging questions, including "What is the mystery of human existence."

Studying philosophy in a serious and reflective way will *change you as a person.* Learning to think philosophically will inspire you to be more thoughtful, more open-minded, more attuned to the complexities and subtleties of life, more willing to think critically about yourself and all of life's important issues, and less willing to accept superficial interpretations and simplistic answers. It is very tempting for people *not* to think, to remain submerged in reality rather than aware of it, to be carried along by the current of events rather than creating their destiny through thoughtful, independent choices. Philosophy is a training guide for your mind, showing you how to think in clear, analytic, and powerful ways. And as Ryan notes, this high-level, sophisticated thinking will enable you to make thoughtful decisions, communicate more effectively, and grow as a person.

Studying philosophy will help you develop the understanding and insight you will need to make intelligent choices and fulfill your potential as an individual. To use a metaphor, you are an artist, creating your life portrait, and your paints and brushstrokes are the choices you make each day. How do you feel about the portrait you have created so far? Have you defined yourself as the person you always wanted to be, or are you a "work in progress"? Are you achieving your full potential as a human being, "actively exercising your soul's powers"—the ancient Greek definition of happiness (*eudaemonia*)? Do you possess a clear philosophy of life that acts as a guiding beacon, illuminating the whole of your life and showing you the path to wisdom and personal fulfillment? Creating an enlightened self-portrait is your preeminent responsibility in life, and though it is challenging work, it is well worth the effort. Your portrait is your contribution to the world, your legacy to present and future generations.

This is the special power of philosophy: to provide the conceptual tools required to craft a life inspiring in its challenges and rich in its fulfillment. Philosophy is *not* intended to limit your options or dictate your choices. Your responsibility as a student of philosophy is to explore, to reflect, to think critically—and then to create yourself in the image you have envisioned.

"Man is asked to make of himself what he is supposed to become to fulfill his destiny," the theologian **Paul Tillich** wrote. But how do we discover our destiny, the unique meaning of our lives? We must embark on a philosophical journey, a process of self-exploration and discovery, seeking answers to profound questions about our lives and illuminating the mysteries of our existence. Each of us strives to live a life of purpose, to fulfill our unique potential, and to achieve stellar accomplishments. It is the remarkable capability of our minds to reflect deeply and thoughtfully—to *think philosophically*—that enables us to pursue these goals. As the philosopher Bertrand Russell passionately expressed, "Thought is great and swift and free, the light of the world, and the chief glory of man."

"Having" a Philosophy Versus "Doing" Philosophy

To begin our journey of philosophical discovery, we must first distinguish between "having" a philosophy and "doing" philosophy. Every person "has" a philosophy of life—a collection of beliefs that they use to guide their thoughts and actions. For example, you may believe that it's wrong to needlessly kill living things, or you may believe that it's good to be kind to people in difficult circumstances. Such beliefs—and countless others that you have formed over the years of your life—influence the way you see the world and the choices that you make. You may not be aware of all your beliefs—some may be deeply buried in your consciousness—but they can still influence you anyway. For instance, you may instinctively help an elderly person cross the street, without being consciously aware that your action reflects a deeply imbedded belief of yours.

Of course, an individual's philosophy of life can also contain beliefs that are wildly inaccurate, biased, or destructive. For example, racist or sexist beliefs can be factors in a person's philosophy of life—although many people would consider such beliefs to be unenlightened and destructive. Or someone might be convinced that aliens are living among us, planning to take over the human race—a belief that most of us would consider highly questionable.

"Doing" philosophy—thinking philosophically—means thinking critically about your beliefs to ensure that they are the most accurate and enlightened beliefs possible. For example, if your philosophy of life includes stereotyped beliefs

Paul Tillich (1886–1965) Theologian. Influential Christian theologian who maintained that all talk about God is symbolic and sought to broaden the definition of religion by stating it is a person's 'ultimate concern'.

about other races or genders, thinking critically about them would involve asking such questions as:

- What is the factual evidence or reasons for these beliefs? Do I have a compelling rationale for saying that I "know" them to be true?
- How did these beliefs originate? What circumstances gave rise to these beliefs?
- Are these beliefs logical or illogical, rational or irrational?
- If I were a member of this racial group or gender, would I still endorse these beliefs? Why or why not?
- Are there more enlightened, accurate beliefs than mine that I should consider?

Thinking philosophically—"doing" philosophy—involves many advanced forms of thinking that we will be exploring in this book and that you will be developing in your philosophy class. But a productive place to begin is with *your* philosophy of life. The questions included in the following **Think Philosophically** activity are designed to help you articulate some of the basic building blocks of your philosophy of life. You should record your responses in your **Philosopher's Notebook**, which you should keep as you think your way through this book. Or your professor may request that the activity be completed in a form to be handed in or e-mailed. Here is a sample student response to the question, *What role do religious beliefs play in your life?*

> I grew up in the Republic of Ireland, where up until some years ago almost everyone was Catholic. Whether or not everyone practiced their religion, I don't know—people I knew were Catholic—it was just the norm. Even though I don't practice myself, now that I live in America it still seems strange to me that not everybody celebrates Christmas. When I was younger, I was brought to Church every Sunday and all I thought about religious holidays, was that we got time off from school. It wasn't until I was about thirteen years old that I started questioning the Church. In questioning the Church, I was questioning God. "If there is a God, why does he allow famines, wars and even cancer to happen?" I proclaimed myself an atheist.
>
> For some reason, and I'm not sure when this occurred, I changed my mind. Today, I do strongly believe God exists. It's an innate feeling I have. When I think about the wonders of new life—creation—I can't just put it down to science. I don't believe we are just organisms going through the motions of life. I believe we are here for a reason—be it in a position of power or a gift of skill that can affect hundreds of lives, or on a smaller scale, doing one thing in your life that could cause a chain of events. I now believe that I will accomplish things in life that will be **my** reason for being born.
>
> —*Violet Lennon*

You may be wondering that since thinking is a mental activity, why is it necessary to record your thoughts in writing in a Philosopher's Notebook (or its equivalent)? The answer is that writing is a vehicle for creating and communicating your ideas, a catalyst for your intellectual development. The intimate, interactive relationships that connect language, thinking, and writing have been remarked on by many people, including writers Elie Wiesel (*"I write to understand as much as to be understood."*); Annie Dillard (*"I don't know what I think until I see myself write."*); and Leo Tolstoy (*"The relation of word to thought, and the creation of new concepts, is a complex, delicate, and enigmatic process unfolding in our soul."*) The process of writing stimulates your mind, helps shape your thinking, and enlarges your understanding of the world. Just as significantly, writing creates a permanent record—a "snapshot"—of your thinking process at a specific point in time. You can return to your thinking snapshot as often as you wish, evaluate its logic and coherence, and use it as a foundation on which to build a more insightful understanding. Your Philosopher's Notebook can be of your choosing, and, of course, using a computer works just as well and has a number of additional advantages.

Whatever the notebook form, the key to success is developing the discipline and commitment to engage in the process, thinking deeply, and expressing your ideas as clearly and specifically as possible. Once you have established this pattern of thinking and writing, you will find that it will become integrated into your life in a natural and profound way, leading you to deeper insights, creative ideas, and enriched meaning. Make your Philosopher's Notebook an integral part of your life; let it remind you to strive to think well. Expressing your ideas in your Philosopher's Notebook should provide a stimulating, liberating experience and help you formulate and articulate your thinking.

THINK PHILOSOPHICALLY   1.1
My Philosophy of Life

Everybody has a philosophy of life. Identify some of the foundation beliefs that form your philosophy of life, using these questions as a guide. Express your ideas as completely and clearly as you can. Encourage yourself to think deeply and beyond superficialities, to refuse to be satisfied with the first idea that you have, to move to deeper levels.

- What do you most value in life? Why?
- What moral beliefs influence your choices and your behavior toward others? How do you determine the "right" thing to do?
- What role do religious beliefs play in your life? Do you believe in "God"? Why or why not? Is there an afterlife? What is the path to it?
- What gives your life meaning? What is the purpose of your life? What do you hope to achieve in your life?
- How do we find truth? How do you know when you "know" something is true? What is an example of something you know to be true?
- Do you believe that your choices are free? Do you hold yourself responsible for your choices?
- What do you consider to be "beautiful"? Why? What is the function of art? Should "extreme" forms of artistic expression be censored? Why or why not?
- Are all people entitled to basic human rights? Why? What is justice?
- What are other important beliefs in your life?

Becoming a Critical Thinker

Your responses to the previous Think Philosophically activity are a sampler of your "philosophy of life." To "do" philosophy, you have to question, scrutinize, explore, evaluate, analyze, synthesize, and apply these beliefs. You have to use higher-order thinking abilities and sophisticated language skills to determine the worthiness of these beliefs. Becoming a *critical thinker* changes qualitatively the way a person views the world, processes information, and makes decisions.

Who is a "critical thinker"? Traditionally, when people refer to a "critical thinker," they mean someone who has developed a *knowledgeable understanding* of our complex world, a *thoughtful perspective* on important ideas and timely issues, the capacity for *penetrating insight* and *intelligent judgment*, and *sophisticated thinking* and *language* abilities. These goals of advanced understanding have remained remarkably similar for several thousand years. In ancient Greece, most advanced students studied philosophy to achieve "wisdom."

The word *critical* comes from the Greek word for "critic" (*kritikos*), which means to question, to make sense of, to be able to analyze. It is by questioning, making sense of, and analyzing that you examine your thinking and the thinking of others. These critical activities aid us in reaching the best possible conclusions and decisions. The word *critical* is also related to the word *criticize*, which means to question and evaluate. Unfortunately, the ability to criticize is often used destructively, to tear down someone else's thinking. Criticism, however, can also be *constructive*—analyzing for the purpose of developing a better understanding of what is going on. You need to engage in *constructive criticism* as you develop your ability to think critically.

Becoming a *critical thinker* is a total approach to the way we understand our world, and it involves an integrated set of thinking abilities and attitudes that include the following:

- *Carefully analyzing and evaluating your beliefs* to develop the most accurate beliefs possible
- *Viewing situations from different perspectives* to develop an in-depth understanding
- *Supporting viewpoints with reasons and evidence* to arrive at thoughtful, well-substantiated conclusions
- *Critically evaluating the logic, relevance, and validity of information* to construct knowledge of the world
- *Asking penetrating questions at every cognitive level of complexity* to explore important ideas with genuine depth
- *Communicating effectively through speaking and writing* to share ideas and persuade others
- *Engaging in Socratic analysis* through the systematic exchange of ideas with others to explore and learn

The best way to develop a clear and concrete idea of the critical thinker you want to become is to think about people you have known who can serve as critical thinking models. For example, I've been fortunate to have studied with a number of teachers who taught me what it means to be a critical thinker through the example of their lives. I considered them to be brilliant critical thinkers because of the power of their minds and their commitment to excellence. They had a *vision*: a perspective on life that they were always trying to enhance through ongoing curiosity and open-minded exploration. They also modeled a generosity of spirit as they sought to inspire thinking in others.

In some ways, we can view critical thinking as a contemporary reworking of a traditional philosophical perspective. Who would *you* identify as expert critical thinkers? To qualify, the people you identify should have lively, energetic minds and generally display the following qualities:

- *Open-minded:* In discussions they listen carefully to every viewpoint, evaluating each perspective carefully and fairly.
- *Knowledgeable:* When they offer an opinion, it's always based on facts or evidence. On the other hand, if they lack knowledge of the subject, they acknowledge this.
- *Mentally active:* They take initiative and actively use their intelligence to confront problems and meet challenges, instead of simply responding passively to events.
- *Curious:* They explore situations with probing questions that penetrate beneath the surface of issues, instead of being satisfied with superficial explanations.
- *Independent thinkers:* They are not afraid to disagree with the group opinion. They develop well-supported beliefs through thoughtful analysis, instead of uncritically "borrowing" the beliefs of others or simply going along with the crowd.

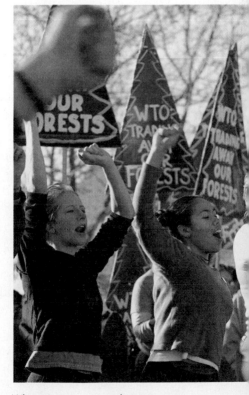

What are some ways that we can develop informed beliefs in order to guide our choices in life?

- *Skilled discussants:* They are able to discuss ideas in an organized and intelligent way. Even when the issues are controversial, they listen carefully to opposing viewpoints and respond thoughtfully.
- *Insightful:* They are able to get to the heart of the issue or problem. While others may be distracted by details, they are able to zero in on the essence, seeing the "forest" as well as the "trees."
- *Self-aware:* They are aware of their own biases and are quick to point them out and take them into consideration when analyzing a situation.
- *Creative:* They can break out of established patterns of thinking and approach situations from innovative directions.
- *Passionate:* They have a passion for understanding and are always striving to see issues and problems with more clarity.

What *Is* Philosophy?

Providing a precise definition of philosophy is not a simple task, in part because of the complex nature of philosophy's mission, and in part because that mission has evolved over time. As we have begun to see, philosophy deals with the most complex, challenging, and profound questions in human life, questions that by their nature resist simple answers. In addition, the scope of philosophy has changed over the centuries. It began in ancient Greece as the "mother of all disciplines," encompassing the entire breadth of inquiry about humans and the universe they inhabit. Over time, as human knowledge expanded, distinct disciplines were established that specialized in understanding various dimensions of human experience. In the natural sciences, physics, biology, chemistry, geology seek understanding of the natural world. The social sciences (psychology, sociology, anthropology, linguistics, political science, economics) seek to analyze, explicate, and propose better models for individual and collective human behavior. Philosophy has retained distinct areas of study that we will explore later in the chapter: *metaphysics, epistemology, ethics, aesthetics, logic,* and *social/political philosophy.* In addition, the evolving role of philosophy has been to continue examining the underlying principles and methodologies of other academic disciplines through the study of "philosophy of science," "philosophical psychology," "medical ethics," and so on.

The actual word *philosophy* is Greek in origin, and it is the composite of two Greek roots: *philein,* a Greek word for "love," and *sophia,* the Greek word for "wisdom." Taken together, they mean "the love or pursuit of wisdom." This definition is a good starting point for understanding the distinctive nature of philosophy. Philosophy is not merely a static compendium of great thoughts of great thinkers—it is an activity that reflects passion, commitment, and intellectual ambition. The ultimate goal of this passionate activity is not mastering a certain amount of information but rather the achievement of "wisdom." What exactly is "wisdom?" Think of several people you know who you would consider to be "wise": what qualities do they possess? It's likely that although they are knowledgeable regarding certain areas of life, it's their ability to *use* and *apply* this knowledge with great intelligence that distinguishes them. They are likely the kind of people who can get to the heart of a complex issue, are able to generate genuinely creative solutions to challenging problems, who exhibit an insightful understanding of what it means to be human. These

THINK CRITICALLY 1.2

PHILOSOPHER'S NOTEBOOK

Who Is a Critical Thinker?

Think about people you know whom you admire as expert thinkers and list some of the qualities these people exhibit that you believe qualify them as "critical thinkers." For each critical thinking quality, write down a brief example involving the person. Identifying such people helps us visualize the kind of people we'd like to emulate. As you think your way through this book, you will be creating a *portrait* of the kind of critical thinker you are striving to become, a *blueprint* you can use to direct your development and chart your progress.

are undoubtedly people who are thoughtful and reflective, who are not afraid to confront the most difficult questions in life, who strive everyday to develop themselves as astute thinkers and honorable individuals. These are people whom you admire and whom you would like to emulate.

Viewing philosophy as the pursuit of wisdom was given eloquent expression by the female philosopher **Perictione**, who is thought to have lived around the time of Plato:

> Humanity came into being and exists in order to contemplate the principle of the nature of the whole. The function of wisdom is to gain possession of this very thing, and to contemplate the purpose of the things that are. Geometry, of course, and arithmetic, and the other theoretical studies and sciences are also concerned with the things that are, but wisdom is concerned with the most basic of these. Wisdom is concerned with all that is, just as sight is concerned with all that is visible and hearing with all that is audible. . . . Therefore, whoever is able to analyze all the kinds of being by reference to one and the same basic principle, and, in turn, from this principle to synthesize and enumerate the different kinds, this person seems to be the wisest and most true and, moreover, to have discovered a noble height from which he will be able to catch sight of God and all the things separated from God in serial rank and order.

In this inspiring passage, Perictione gets right to the heart of being human and the nature of wisdom. Human life has a central purpose—to contemplate the profound essence of the universe, and wisdom is, in her mind, the divine gift we have to accomplish this. While various disciplines such as mathematics and science are concerned with determining specific knowledge of the universe, wisdom has a grander mission: understanding how and why the universe is the way it is, the core principles that underlie and govern the whole of experience.

Although the "wise" people you know may not be professional philosophers, they may very well embody the *spirit* of philosophy that we have been considering in this chapter. This Western concept of philosophy originated in ancient Greece in the work of **Socrates**, **Plato**, and **Aristotle**. We will be exploring their ideas in some depth as we journey through the history of philosophical thinking.

Of course, there have been many important thinkers since Socrates, Plato, and Aristotle, and there were even a number of insightful thinkers before them, the "pre-Socratics" who were known as *Sophos*, wise men and women who posed sophisticated and penetrating questions regarding the essential principles of human life and the natural world. In addition, there have been many significant thinkers in non-Western cultures. Although the primary focus of this text is on Western philosophy, we will also be examining key ideas from philosophers in non-Western cultures.

Definitions of Philosophy

Because of its complex, enigmatic, and profoundly elusive nature, philosophy has resisted being defined in a clear and straightforward way. Over the ages, philosophers and other thinkers have suggested many different definitions of philosophy. Let's engage in some critical thinking by exploring some of the ways people have tried to define the essence of philosophy. As a final stage in the process, you will have an opportunity to fashion your own definition of philosophy.

Socrates probably came closest to capturing the essence of philosophy when he issued a startling challenge that has reverberated through the centuries: *"The unexamined life is not worth living."* The ability to reflect on one's life and one's self is a

Perictione (c. 300 B.C.E.) Ancient Greek Philosopher. Follower of Pythagoras; Maintained wisdom is concerned with all things and those who are able to philosophize concerning all things is wise.

Socrates (469–399 B.C.E.) Ancient Greek Philosopher. Founder of the Western philosophical tradition. Developed method of inquiry called the 'Socratic Dialogue'.

Plato (427?–347 B.C.E.) Ancient Greek Philosopher. Once said that all of Western Philosophy is merely footnotes to Plato. A student of Socrates, Plato wrote many dialogues featuring Socrates as the main character and dealt with many philosophical issues such as morality, politics, metaphysics, and epistemology.

Aristotle (384–322 B.C.E.) Ancient Greek Philosopher. One of most important figures in the history of philosophy because of dividing philosophy into distinct disciplines; major contributions to metaphysics, ethics, and politics; first to attempt to create a system of deductive logic.

distinctly human ability. Humans have the capacity to examine the activity of living, to review our history, reflect on the moment, and project ourselves into the future. Philosophy provides us with the intellectual tools to reflect with clarity and discipline, to critically evaluate the choices we have made, and to use this knowledge to make more enlightened choices in the future. The stakes are high: if we fail to make use of this unique ability to think philosophically about ourselves, then, according to Socrates, our lives have diminished potential. If we are simply existing without reflection or self-examination, then we might just as well have been a turnip.

Let's examine four different dimensions of philosophy:

The **origins** of philosophy

The **activity** of philosophy

The role of **conflict** in philosophy

The **ultimate aim** of philosophy

The Origins of Philosophy

These definitions focus on the *source* of philosophical thinking, the way philosophy encourages us to look both *deeper* and *wider*. Philosophy stimulates us to penetrate beneath the surface of daily experience while seeking a comprehensive, inclusive vision of reality.

- Wonder is the feeling of a philosopher, and philosophy is rooted in wonder.
  —*Plato* (Theaetetus, 155d) *(427–347 B.C.E.), Greek philosopher, student of Socrates and teacher of Aristotle, created a philosophy academy in Athens*

- For it is owning to their wonder that people both now begin and at first began to philosophize.
  —*Aristotle* (Metaphysics, 12, 982b) *(384–322 B.C.E.), Greek philosopher, scientist, logician, and pupil of Plato*

- Philosophy is man's quest for the unity of knowledge: it consists in a perpetual struggle to create the concepts in which the universe can be conceived as a universe and not a multiverse.
  —*William H. Halverson, philosopher*

- The first step toward philosophy is doubt.
  —*Denis Diderot (1713–1784), French writer, philosopher*

- Philosophy traditionally has been nothing less than the attempt to ask and answer, in a formal and disciplined way, the great questions of life that ordinary men put to themselves in reflective moments.
  —Time Magazine *(January 7, 1966)*

The catalyst for thinking philosophically about one's life is often *wonder*, a search for *unity of knowledge*, a desire to answer the *great questions* of life. As Plato and Aristotle observe, philosophy begins with *wonder*, speculation, considering "what if?," asking that powerful question, "why?" Instead of simply accepting life as it presents itself, philosophy seeks to probe beneath the surface, question the familiar, challenge "accepted wisdom." Where can we look for models of philosophical wonder? Children! Young children are brimming over with intellectual energy, blending innate curiosity, passionate convictions, and imaginative speculation: not coincidentally, the essential ingredients required for thinking critically and developing a philosophical perspective on the world. *"Why?"* is perhaps the most penetrating question in human language and thought, and children use it liberally, sometimes driving adults to distraction. Asking *"Why?"* shakes up complacent attitudes, forcing us to expose hidden assumptions and to articulate the rationale for our conclusions. And other questions can help us probe beyond the surface of everyday con-

VISUAL PHILOSOPHY

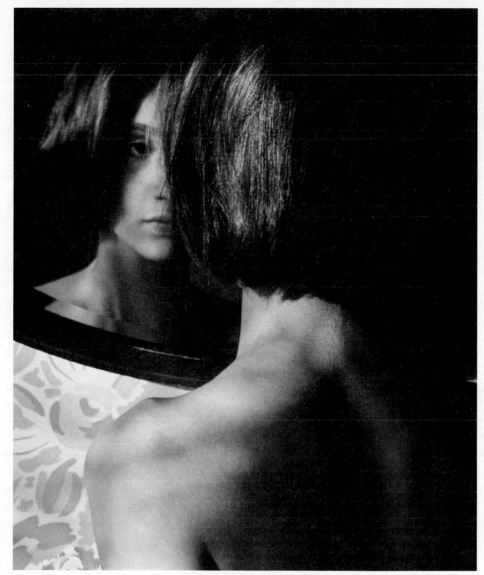

"Philosophy Is Rooted In Wonder," Plato

Where did I come from and where am I going? What is the meaning of my life?

sciousness. Here's a brief sampler provided by my children, Jessie and Joshua, at very young ages. *Why did God create life? What is at the end of space? What happens after forever? Do people still love after they die? Suppose that animals could think just as well as we could, what would the world be like? Imagine that stuffed animals had feelings, how would you treat them? Why are bad people bad?*

Another catalyst for philosophy is the human desire for *synthesis* and *integration*, to "put all of the pieces together." As Halverson observes, this drive toward integration is reflected in our concept of our world as a *uni*verse, the conviction that there are underlying principles of thought and reality that form the structure of our experience. Philosophy has always been driven by the desire to discover these primal principles and then to apply them to make human existence more intelligible. All of us have the responsibility to confront and try to answer these profound questions as we work to craft lives of meaning and purpose.

Søren Kierkegaard

The Activity of Philosophy

These definitions attempt to capture the distinctive nature of *philosophical thinking*. Philosophy is an intellectual process designed to produce insight and meaningful understanding. This process requires a questioning attitude toward every area of experience.

- Philosophy is not a theory but an activity.
  —*Ludwig Wittgenstein (1889–1951), Austrian philosopher*
- Philosophy means liberation from the two dimensions of routine, soaring above the well known, seeing it in new perspectives, arousing wonder and the wish to fly.
  —*Walter Kaufmann (1921–1980), American philosopher*
- Philosophy's first promise is a sense of participation, of belonging to mankind, being a member of society.
  —*Seneca (4 B.C.E.–65 C.E.), Roman philosopher*
- Philosophy is the science which considers the truth.
  —*Aristotle (384–322 B.C.E.), Greek philosopher*
- Philosophy is perfectly right in saying that life must be understood backward. But then one forgets the other clause—that it must be lived forward.
  —*Søren Kierkegaard (1813–1855), Danish philosopher and theologian*

This approach to defining philosophy focuses on the *process* of philosophical thinking. We explored earlier in the chapter the distinction between *having* a philosophy and *doing* philosophy. Most people *have* a philosophy in the form of a set of beliefs they use to guide their choices. Sometimes they are aware of these beliefs; often they are not. Some of these beliefs may be informed and enlightened, others may be ill-informed and ignorant. The only way to develop a well-founded and intelligent philosophy of life is to *do* philosophy: that is, to continually critically evaluate our beliefs by honest questioning, by putting beliefs to the test of experience, and by discussing our beliefs with others, particularly those who disagree with us.

One of the central goals of studying philosophy is to become familiar with this distinctive way of thinking and learning. It involves practicing the conceptual abilities and mental discipline needed to penetrate the surface level of superficial and confused ideas, in order to achieve a deeper understanding of the truth of things. This is a process that, as Seneca notes, introduces us to an intellectual community, inviting us to take part in a philosophical conversation that has been going on for several thousand years. And as Kaufmann observes, engaging seriously in philosophical thought liberates our minds, enabling us to escape from the confines of our limited situations and soar to dizzying heights of comprehension and enlightened awareness. In this regard, Kierkegaard's observation is the most provocative: as important as it is to look backward, exploring and critically evaluating what previously took place, it's equally important that we orient ourselves toward the future, using our philosophical abilities and the knowledge it has produced to chart our courses and make enlightened decisions as we continually create our future.

The Role of Conflict in Philosophy

These definitions probe the *dynamic* nature of philosophical thinking, a process that is *dialectical* in the sense that ideas are continually analyzed in terms of their opposites, with the ultimate goal of creating a more enlightened *synthesis*.

- The beginning of philosophy is the recognition of the conflict between opinions.
  —*Epictetus (ca. 50–120), Greek philosopher*
- Philosophy is a battle against the bewitchment of our intelligence by means of language.
  —*Ludwig Wittgenstein (1889–1951), Austrian philosopher*
- I do not know how to teach philosophy without becoming a disturber of the peace.
  —*Baruch Spinoza (1632–1677), Dutch philosopher*

As Epictetus observes, the philosophical process is powered by conflict, bringing divergent opinions together into a dynamic interaction. Which ideas make most sense? Which are clearer? Best supported? Have greater explanatory power? Are consistent with other beliefs we know to be true? Are most comprehensive? *Why?* As we will see in the next chapter, this ongoing process of comparing and contrasting, analyzing and synthesizing, is at the heart of the Socratic Method, a powerful approach developed and used by Socrates that is characterized by relentless questioning, clear definitions, dialectical analysis, and critical evaluation. It is the process by which we can disentangle complex issues and distinguish more informed ways of thinking from less informed. Language is a key partner of thinking, as Wittgenstein notes: a confused, illogical, and sloppy use of language leads to confused, illogical, and sloppy thinking—and vice versa. Analogously, clarity and precision in our use of language contributes to clarity and precision in our thinking—and vice versa.

In its crusade to enlighten minds and inform choices, philosophy is not confined to the classroom or "ivory towers." The conclusions we reach by thinking philosophically have direct implications for how we live our lives in the real world. And because philosophy is committed to the truth rather than popular opinion, prevailing norms, or conventional wisdom, it means that we may indeed find ourselves, in the words of Spinoza, as "disturbers of the peace." In the case of Socrates, and other truth-seekers like him throughout the centuries, this passion for intellectual integrity and authentic lives had grave personal consequences.

The Ultimate Aim of Philosophy

Finally, these definitions focus on the goal of philosophical thought, which is to improve the quality of our lives by enlightening our minds.

- Philosophy means the complete liberty of the mind, and therefore independence of all social, political, or religious prejudice.
  —*Henri Frederic Amiel (1821–1881), Swiss philosopher*
- Philosophy is the cultivation of the mental faculties; it roots out vices and prepares the mind to receive proper seed.
  —*Cicero (106–43 B.C.E.), Roman orator and statesman*
- Let no young man delay the study of philosophy, and let no old man become weary of it; for it is never too early nor too late to care for the well being of the soul.
  —*Epicurus (340–270 B.C.E.), Greek philosopher*
- The beginning and end of all philosophy is—freedom.
  —*F. W. J. von Schelling (1775–1854), German philosopher and aesthetician*
- Philosophy asks the simple question, what is it all about?
  —*Alfred North Whitehead (1861–1947), English philosopher and mathematician*

Philosophy has grand and lofty aspirations, and this undoubtedly accounts for the fascination and high regard with which it has been held. Just this brief sampling of definitions displays philosophy's exalted aims:

- The complete liberty of the mind
- Independence of all social, political, or religious prejudice
- To root out vices and prepare the mind to receive proper seed
- To care for the well-being of the soul
- Freedom
- Answer the question, "What is it all about?"

Can philosophy really deliver on this ambitious promise? Perhaps a better question is, "Can any other discipline or approach to life do a more effective job than philosophy?" Philosophers—and many others—believe that philosophy is the one best hope we have to discover the truth to these profound questions and intimidating

Defining Philosophy

PHILOSOPHER'S NOTEBOOK

1.3

- Select three of the definitions of philosophy included above that you think are particularly appropriate, and for each one explain in your Philosopher's Notebook what you think the definition means and why you selected it.
- Create your own definition of philosophy (based on your beginning understanding of the discipline) and explain the reasoning behind your definition.

challenges. Philosophy is uniquely qualified, because of the historical scope of its vision and the conceptual and language tools that it employs, to help each person find his or her way to the truth of these issues. Virtually all people desire a liberated mind, an enlightened consciousness, a well-cared-for soul, a rich and fulfilling life. Philosophy provides the equipment you need to construct such a path for yourself: you need only to commit yourself to taking the philosophical journey.

Thinking Critically About Philosophical Issues

ecoming a critical thinker involves developing an integrated set of thinking abilities, language skills, and fundamental attitudes toward oneself and the world. As we noted, a critical thinker is someone who

- *carefully analyzes and evaluates beliefs* to develop the most accurate beliefs possible.
- *views situations from different perspectives* to develop an in-depth understanding.
- *supports viewpoints with reasons and evidence* to arrive at thoughtful, well-substantiated conclusions.
- *critically evaluates the logic, relevance, and validity of information* to construct knowledge of the world.
- *asks penetrating questions at every cognitive level of complexity* to explore important ideas with genuine depth.
- *communicates effectively through speaking and writing* to share ideas and persuade others.
- *engages in Socratic analysis* through the systematic exchange of ideas with others to explore and learn.

A critical thinker is someone who approaches his or her life in an informed and reflective way. This approach is one that you can use in virtually every area of your life as you work to understand your experience and make informed decisions. A critical thinking approach is also appropriate in all the various academic disciplines. Understanding history, psychology, economics, biology, or any other field of study involves much more than mastering that discipline's accumulated knowledge. Genuine understanding means using your critical thinking abilities to understand how each discipline organizes experience, provides explanations, applies concepts, and constructs knowledge. A critical thinking approach to the academic disciplines thus inolves learning how to "think like a historian," "think like a psychologist," and so on.

The same is true of philosophy. "Thinking philosophically"—what we have designated as *doing philosophy*—involves thinking critically about the unique areas of experience with which philosophy is concerned, areas that include the most fundamental questions and issues in human experience. What sets philosophy apart from other academic disciplines is that they all have their roots in philosophy, the "mother" of all disciplines. The same is true for critical thinking—the abilities and attitudes that characterize a critical thinker originated for the most part in philosophical inquiry.

Let's examine this process in action by exploring how a critical thinker approaches a philosophical issue such as *free will*. It is the synthesis of critical thinking with philosophical subjects such as "free will" that leads to "thinking philosophically." The process of learning to think philosophically requires ongoing practice and reflection. The following critical thinking model will help you see philosophical thinking in operation. We will be using the model to think about an important issue that confronts every human being: "Are people capable of choosing freely?"

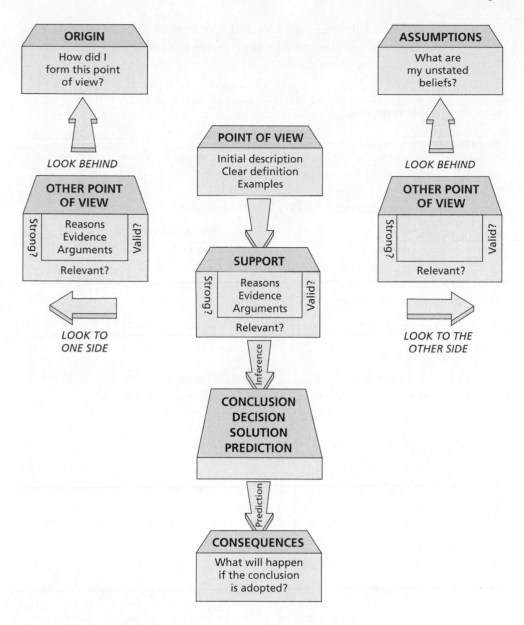

What Is My Initial Point of View?

Reasoning always begins with a point of view. As a critical thinker and aspiring philosopher, you need to take thoughtful positions and express your views with confidence. Using this statement as a starting point, respond in your Philosopher's Notebook as specifically as you can:

- I believe (or don't believe) that people can choose freely because . . .

Here is a sample response:

> I believe that people are capable of choosing freely because when I am faced with choosing among a number of possibilities, I really have the feeling that it is up to me to make the choice that I want to.

How Can I Define My Point of View More Clearly?

After stating your initial point of view, the next step is to define the issues more clearly and specifically. The language that we use has multiple levels of meaning, and it is often not clear precisely what meaning(s) people are expressing. To avoid misunderstandings and sharpen your own thinking, you must clarify the key concepts as early as possible. In this case, the key concept is "choosing freely." Begin by completing the following statement:

- From my point of view, the concept of "choosing freely" means . . .

Here is a sample response:

> From my point of view, the concept of "choosing freely" means that when you are faced with a number of alternatives, you are able to make your selection based solely on what you decide, not because you are being forced by other influences.

What Is an Example of My Point of View?

Once your point of view is clarified, you should provide an example that illustrates your meaning. The process of forming and defining concepts involves the process of *generalizing* (identifying general qualities) and the process of *interpreting* (locating specific examples). Respond to the issue we have been considering by beginning with the following statement:

- An example of a free choice I made (or was unable to make) is . . .

Here is a sample response:

> An example of a free choice I made was deciding what area to major in. There are a number of career directions I could have chosen, but I chose my major entirely on my own, without being forced by other influences.

What Is the Origin of My Point of View?

To fully understand and critically evaluate your point of view, you must review its history. How did the point of view develop? Have you always held this view, or did it develop over time? This sort of analysis will help you understand how your perspective regarding this issue was formed. Respond to the issue of free choice by beginning with the following statement:

- I formed my belief regarding free choice . . .

Here is a sample response:

> I used to believe that everything happened because it had to, because it was determined. Then, when I was in high school, I got involved with the "wrong crowd" and developed some bad habits. I stopped doing schoolwork and even stopped attending most classes. I was on the brink of failing out when I suddenly came to my senses and said to myself, "This isn't what I want for my life." Through sheer willpower, I turned everything around. I changed my friends, improved my habits, and ultimately graduated with flying colors. From that time on I knew that I had the power of free choice and that it was up to me to make the right choices.

What Are My Assumptions?

Assumptions are beliefs, often unstated, that underlie your point of view. Many disputes occur and remain unresolved because the people involved do not recognize or express their assumptions. For example, in the very emotional debate over abortion, when people who are opposed to abortion call their opponents "murderers," they are assuming the fetus, at any stage of development from the fertilized egg onward, is a "human life," because murder refers to the taking of a human life. On the other hand, when people in favor of abortion call their opponents "moral fascists," they are assuming that antiabortionists are merely interested in imposing their narrow moral views on others.

Thus all parties must identify clearly the assumptions that form the foundation of their points of view. They may still end up disagreeing, but at least they will know what they are arguing about. Thinking about the issue that we have been exploring, respond by completing the following statement:

- When I say that I believe (or don't believe) in free choice, I am assuming . . .

Here is a sample response:

> When I say that I believe in free choice, I am assuming that people are often presented with different alternatives to choose from, and I am also assuming that they are able to select freely any of these alternatives independent of any influences.

What Are the Reasons, Evidence, and Arguments That Support My Point of View?

Everybody has beliefs. What distinguishes informed beliefs from uninformed beliefs is the quality of the reasons, evidence, and arguments that support the beliefs. Respond to the issue of free choice by beginning with the following statement:

- There are a variety of reasons, evidence, and arguments that support my belief (or disbelief) in free choice. First . . . Second . . . Third . . .

Here is a sample response:

> There are a variety of reasons, evidence, and arguments that support my belief in free choice. First, I have a very strong and convincing personal intuition when I am making choices that my choices are free. I believe that this intuition is consistent and compelling.
>
> Second, I am able to recognize when I'm not making free choices and distinguish those situations from when I am choosing freely. For example, I know when I'm caving in to external pressures, or sometimes I'll recognize that I'm being manipulated and then make the free choice *not* to be manipulated.
>
> Third, our society is based on the possibility of free choice. Otherwise, we wouldn't be able to hold people responsible for their choices and the consequences of these choices. But we *do* hold people responsible, suggesting that the reality of free choice is an integral part of how humans see themselves. Further, if people were not free, and all of their choices were determined by external forces, then life would have little purpose and there would be no point in trying to improve ourselves. But we *do* believe that life has purpose and we *do* try to improve ourselves, suggesting that we also believe that our choices are free.

What Are Other Points of View on This Issue?

One of the hallmarks of critical thinkers—and philosophers—is that they strive to view situations from perspectives other than their own, to "think empathetically" within other viewpoints, particularly those of people who disagree with their own. If we stay entrenched in our own narrow ways of viewing the world, the development of our minds will be severely limited. Empathetic thinking is the only way to achieve a full understanding of life's complexities. In working to understand other points of view, we need to identify the reasons, evidence, and arguments that have brought people to these conclusions. Respond to the issue we have been analyzing by beginning with the following statement:

- A second point of view on this issue might be . . . A third point . . .

Here is a sample response:

A second point of view on this issue might be that many of our choices are conditioned by experiences that we have had in ways that we are not even aware of. For example, you might choose a career because of someone you admire or because of the expectations of others, although you may be unaware of these influences on your decision. Or you might choose to date someone because he or she reminds you of someone from your past, although you believe you are making a totally free decision. Many psychologists believe that much of our behavior is caused by unconscious influences on our thinking and choices.

A third point of view on this issue might be that our choices are influenced by people around us, although we may not be fully aware of it. For example, we may go along with a group decision of our friends, mistakenly thinking that we are making an independent choice. Or in a more general way, our ways of thinking may have been conditioned by our family and culture over time, so that while we *think* we're making free choices, we're really not.

Of course, simply listening and trying to understand other perspectives is not enough: we need to *respond* to other points of view, explaining why we are unconvinced by these conflicting views and the arguments that support them. Here's a possible response:

I agree that there may sometimes be influences on our thinking and choices of which we are not aware. Sometimes when we look back we can see that our reactions in a given situation were influenced by unconscious motivations or by social conditioning. But I believe that we can escape the influence of these factors by *becoming aware* and choosing to transcend their power over us. This is where critical thinking comes in: using our thinking abilities to understand ourselves and the forces at work on us so that we can make genuinely free choices.

What Is My Conclusion, Decision, Solution, or Prediction?

The ultimate purpose of critical thinking is to reach an informed and successful conclusion, decision, solution, or prediction. With respect to the sample issue we have been considering—determining whether we can make free choices—the goal is to achieve a thoughtful conclusion. This is a complex process of analysis and synthesis in which we consider all points of view; evaluate the supporting reasons, evidence, and arguments; and then construct our most informed conclusion. Respond to our sample issue by using the following statement as a starting point:

- After examining different points of view and critically evaluating the reasons, evidence, and arguments that support the various perspectives, my conclusion about free choice is . . .

Here is a sample response:

After examining different points of view and critically evaluating the reasons, evidence, and arguments that support the various perspectives, my conclusion about free choice is that we are capable of making free choices but that our freedom is sometimes limited. For example, many of our actions are conditioned by our past experience, and we are often influenced by other people without being aware of it. In order to make free choices, we need to become aware of these influences and then decide what course of action we want to choose. As long as we are unaware of these influences, they can limit our ability to make free, independent choices.

What Are the Consequences?

The final step in the reasoning process is to determine the consequences of our conclusion, decision, solution, or prediction. The consequences refer to what is likely to happen if our conclusion is adopted. Looking ahead in this fashion is helpful not simply for anticipating the future but also for evaluating the present. Identify the consequences of your conclusion regarding free choice by beginning with the following statement:

- The consequences of believing (or disbelieving) in free choice are . . .

Here is a sample response:

> The consequences of believing in free choice involve increasing personal responsibility and showing people how to increase their freedom. The first consequence is that if people are able to make free choices, then they are responsible for the results of their choices. They can't blame other people, bad luck, or events "beyond their control." They have to accept responsibility. The second consequence is that although our freedom can be limited by influences of which we are unaware, we can increase our freedom by becoming aware of these influences and then deciding what we want to do. On the other hand, if people are not able to make free choices, then they are not responsible for what they do, nor are they able to increase their freedom. This could lead people to adopt an attitude of resignation and apathy.

Analyze an Issue

Identify an important issue in which you are interested and apply the critical thinking model to analyze it:

- What is my initial point of view?
- How can I define my point of view more clearly?
- What is an example of my point of view?
- What is the origin of my point of view?
- What are my assumptions?
- What are the reasons, evidence, and arguments that support my point of view?
- What are other points of view on this issue?
- What is my conclusion, decision, solution, or prediction?
- What are the consequences?

Traditional Branches of Philosophy

In addition to developing and refining your critical thinking abilities, thinking philosophically also involves studying the ideas of great thinkers who have created coherent frameworks for understanding every dimension of human experience. There is no point in "reinventing the wheel" when brilliant minds have already made significant progress in understanding the most complex and challenging issues in life. So learning to think philosophically involves developing your critical thinking abilities while reading and analyzing the ideas of exceptional philosophers, present and past.

The investigations of philosophers over the centuries in many cultures can be classified by the questions that they explored. Described below are the traditional branches of philosophy, along with some of the central questions that they are endeavoring to answer. Of course, these divisions are somewhat artificial, because philosophical issues and modes of inquiry overlap and interrelate. But there is also value to organizing them into coherent categories.

- Metaphysics
- Epistemology
- Ethics
- Political and social philosophy
- Aesthetics
- Logic and critical thinking

For some people, philosophy has a reputation of being removed from daily life, concerned with abstract questions to which there are no answers and about which

How do the various branches of philosophy encourage us to bring a thoughtful and reflective perspective to every area of experience?

most people don't really care. And philosophers are sometimes stereotyped as impractical dreamers, with their heads in the clouds, separated from the lives and concerns of average people. The truth is that Western philosophy began in ancient Greece as a very practical activity, designed to help people better understand the world around them and to serve as a guide in living enlightened lives. In fact, Socrates spent his days in the public marketplace (the *agora*), discussing philosophical issues with all who were willing, and challenging them to live reflective, virtuous lives. And, after all these centuries, the true spirit of philosophy remains at the core of our lives, helping us make sense of our world and create purposeful lives.

The questions and issues included in the various branches of philosophy are central to how you live your life: the way you think, the choices you make, the way you relate to other people, the issues you analyze, the problems you try to solve. In the pages ahead, we're going to explore the various branches of philosophy in more depth. As part of our analysis, we'll examine responses of students reflecting on how the study of philosophy has influenced their daily lives in practical and profound ways. As you read their passages, consider the ways in which philosophy might help you think more clearly about important issues and make more enlightened choices in your own life.

Metaphysics

Metaphysics involves the study of the most general or ultimate characteristics of reality or existence. It explores issues beyond the physical world such as the meaning of life, the existence of free will, the nature of mind, the fundamental principles of the universe, and the possibility of life beyond death. The philosopher Bertrand Russell (1872–1970) provides the following definition:

> Metaphysics, or the attempt to conceive the world as a whole by means of thought, has been developed, from the first, by the union and conflict of two very different impulses, the one urging men towards mysticism, the other urging them toward science.

Here are some of the questions metaphysics attempts to answer. How would you answer them?

- What is the nature of reality?
- What is the place of humans in the universe?
- Does life have meaning?
- Do we have free wills that enable us to make independent choices?
- How are the mind and body related to each other?
- Is there life after death?
- Does God exist?
- What is the nature of the "self"?

One of the central questions metaphysics addresses is **What is the nature of reality?** Does the world exist independent of our perception of it? Do people experience the same or different realities? Is there an "ultimate" reality in the universe? The following quotes express some well-known perspectives on these questions. Do you agree or disagree with the ideas being presented? Why?

> There is no reality except the one contained within us. That is why so many people live such an unreal life. They take the images outside them for reality and never allow the world within to assert itself.
>
> —*Hermann Hesse (1877–1962), German novelist*

Metaphysics The branch of philosophy that studies the most general or ultimate characteristics of reality or existence, including: the meaning of life, the existence of free will, the nature of mind, the fundamental principles of the universe and the possibility of life beyond death.

We take our shape, it is true, within and against the cage of reality bequeathed us at our birth; and yet it is precisely through our dependence on this reality that we are most endlessly betrayed.

—James Baldwin (1924–1987), American novelist

Here is one student's reflection on the nature of reality:

I think that within me there have always been questions on what is truth and reality. How do I know what is the truth when this world is based on so many beliefs. How can I determine that the world I live in isn't just a dream? Everyone just wants to live their lives by the norms that have been imposed on them. There are so many lies, so many games played by those who have power to manipulate us into believing in false illusions. Like in Plato's Cave, the only way out is to want to see the truth and start living a life based on reality. We need to open our eyes and see the light, see reality, ask questions not just to let our minds get fooled by illogical inputs. We have the potential to create ourselves and not just settle for what is given to us as the truth, or doing what everyone is doing. Plato's story of the cave brings up many philosophical points that are very important to me. He addresses the issue of society's role in our lives. I think that we are all influenced by the thoughts and actions of others; but at the same time, we have the ability to question, draw our own conclusions, and eventually make our own choices. As the philosopher Ludwig Wittgenstein says, *"A thought which is not independent is a thought only half understood."*

—Paula Calle

Plato's Allegory of the Cave, to which Paula refers (and which we explore on page 426), is a powerful metaphor that symbolically portrays the path to intellectual enlightenment. According to Plato, most people do not experience genuine reality: instead they are restricted to seeing images created by others, designed to shape their minds and manipulate their thinking. These issues are particularly relevant in the world today, when so much of our information about the world is filtered through the media. The information presented is always biased in the sense that those in charge have selected what information to include and the particular interpretation, spin, or slant they give it. In many cases, people passively accept the information they are given, placing themselves in jeopardy of attitude manipulation. How can studying philosophy help avoid this danger? By teaching us to critically evaluate the validity and objectivity of information, explore multiple perspectives, and develop independent and well-founded beliefs that we can use to guide our choices.

THINK PHILOSOPHICALLY 1.5
What Is Reality?

PHILOSOPHER'S NOTEBOOK

What is your idea of "reality" and where does it come from? Reflect on your daily media consumption—the hours you spend with a television, a magazine, or online. Do you question what you are viewing, critically evaluating the content and interpretations that are being presented? Or is it easier to simply absorb what you are viewing and hearing without intellectual probing and analysis? Describe one aspect of your view of what's "real" that has likely been influenced by the bias of your source of information. For example, what are your views on other countries in the world and the people who inhabit them?

Another question included in the study of metaphysics is **What is the place of humans in the universe?** Are we the crown jewels of creation or accidents produced by chance events? Is human life qualitatively different from other forms of life? Does the universe display a grand design in which we play a crucial part? A related metaphysical question can be phrased, **Does life have meaning?** Is life's purpose the same for all people, or does each person have to discover his or her own unique purpose? What are the key ingredients of a meaningful life? The following quotes express some perspectives on these questions. Do you agree or disagree with the ideas being presented? Why?

> As soon as man does not take his existence for granted, but beholds it as something unfathomably mysterious, thought begins.
> —*Albert Schweitzer (1875–1965), French humanitarian*

> Out yonder there was this huge world . . . which stands before us like a great eternal riddle.
> —*Albert Einstein (1879–1955), German-American scientist*

> But to live an entire life without understanding how we think, why we feel the way we feel, what directs our actions is to miss what is most important in life, which is the quality of experience itself.
> —*Mihaly Csikszentmihalyi, philosopher*

Another important question for metaphysics is one you began to explore in the last section, namely, **Do we have free wills that enable us to make independent choices?** Or are all of our actions determined by causes beyond our control? In what ways is our freedom limited? Can we increase our freedom by eliminating internal and external constraints? The following quotes express some perspectives on these questions. Do you agree or disagree with the ideas being presented? Why?

> In short, the actions of man are never free; they are always the necessary consequence of his temperament, of the received ideas, and of the notions, either true or false, which he has formed to himself of happiness; of his opinions, strengthened by example, by education, and by daily experience. Man, then, is not a free agent in any one instant of his life.
> —*Paul Henri Thiry, Baron d'Holbach (1723–1789), French philosopher*

> Man is condemned to be free. Condemned, because he did not create himself, yet is nevertheless at liberty, and from the moment that he is thrown into this world, he is responsible for everything he does.
> —*Jean-Paul Sartre (1905–1980), French philosopher*

Here is one student's reflection on the nature of free choice:

> When I first began exploring my freedom, I believed that the only thing limiting my genuine freedom was the external constraint of money: "If only I had more money" I would say on a regular basis. Studying philosophy made me realize that I have been using this statement as a way of escaping from my responsibility. Jean-Paul Sartre wrote, "everything which happens to me is mine." Having read his article on Freedom and Responsibility, I now realize that I can no longer blame my lack of freedom on my lack of money because I have created my situation by the choices I have made. It was my decision to only work part-time, because I wanted to devote most of my time to school and I now accept the responsibility for that. I am also aware that I am capable of changing my situation if I want to. My freedom is not limited to the options which are available to me because I have it in my power to create alternatives and to think of new possibilities to improve my situation.
> —*Jessie Lange*

Many people have naïve and inaccurate beliefs regarding their personal freedom. They often lack awareness of the many ways their freedom is limited, and what they can do to increase their freedom. For example, we often find ourselves in limiting situations, as Jessie describes, which we assume are beyond our control. Yet we have often contributed to creating these circumstances, and we can change them by making different choices. If you find yourself dissatisfied with your financial situation, your social group, your major—or virtually any other area of your life—there are likely alternative choices available that you haven't thought about or considered. Studying philosophy can encourage you to expand your thinking, use your imagination to create new ways of viewing your current reality as well as future possibilities, and stimulate your imagination to create new ideas and alternatives.

Analogously, many people lack awareness of the ways in which we limit our own freedom, through internal constraints that prevent us from making choices that reflect our deepest values and our highest aspirations. Are you unclear about your future goals? Dissatisfied with your current circumstances? Concerned about bad habits or negative elements of your personality? Studying philosophy will give you insight into the dynamics of personal freedom and help you develop the mental discipline required to think clearly and effectively in every area of your life. And your philosophical explorations will also encourage you to take responsibility for your life, liberating you to "know yourself" and fulfill your unique potential as a person.

THINK PHILOSOPHICALLY   1.6
Am I Free?

PHILOSOPHER'S NOTEBOOK

Reflect on some of the limitations to your freedom. Are you locked into situations that present limited opportunities? Have you actively considered making different choices to change those circumstances? Are you passively content to choose from a limited selection of alternatives that are presented to you, instead of using your imagination to create a wide range of possibilities? Is your life limited by self-imposed constraints that result in unsatisfying or destructive choices? Have you explored strategies for removing these constraints so that you can make genuinely free choices?

What is the nature of the "self"? is a question that is also at the core of metaphysical inquiry. Do people have souls? What is a "mind"? What essential qualities make each of us unique? The following quotes express some perspectives on these questions. Related to the nature of the "self" is the question of **How are the mind and body related to each other?** How does the mind influence the body and vice versa? What are the implications of the recent research on the relations between mind and brain? The following quotes express some perspectives on these questions. Do you agree or disagree with the ideas being presented? Why?

Nowhere can man find a quieter or more untroubled retreat than in his own soul.
> —*Marcus Aurelius Antonius (121–180), Roman emperor and philosopher*

Man is nothing else but that which he makes of himself.
> —*Jean-Paul Sartre (1905–1980), French philosopher*

Matter is less material and the mind less spiritual than is generally supposed. The habitual separation of physics and psychology, mind and matter, is metaphysically indefensible.

—*Bertrand Russell (1872–1970), English philosopher*

The soul is that which denies the body. For example, that which refuses to run when the body trembles, to strike when the body is angry, to drink when the body is thirsty.

—*Alain Chartier (1868–1951), French philosopher*

The nature of religious beliefs is also included in metaphysics, addressing such questions as **Does God exist?** If so, what is the nature of God? Is there more than one God? Is God the same for different people? What is God's relation to human events? What is the nature of divine revelation? How can evil be explained? A related area concerns the question **Is there life after death?** Is there life before birth? Is there communication between those who have died and those currently alive? The following quotes express some perspectives on these questions. Do you agree or disagree with the ideas being presented? Why?

The way God has been thought of for thousands of years is no longer convincing; if anything is dead, it can only be the traditional thought of God.

—*Hannah Arendt (1906–1975), German-American philosopher*

The nature of god is a circle whose center is everywhere and whose circumference is nowhere.

—*St. Augustine (354–430), philosopher*

Death is not an event in life; we do not experience death.

—*Ludwig Wittgenstein (1889–1951), Austrian philosopher*

One must take all one's life to learn how to live, and, what will perhaps make you wonder more, one must take all one's life to learn how to die.

—*Seneca (4 B.C.E.–65 C.E.), Roman philosopher*

There is no death, only a change of worlds.

—*Chief Seattle (1786–1866), American Suquamish Indian chief*

Here is one student's reflection on how philosophy influenced her religious beliefs.

Taking this course in Philosophy made me doubt about whether God exists or not. I was brought up in a religious household where my parents as well as my whole family believed that there is a God and that Heaven exists. In the class discussions we had about religion and God I never thought that I would come to the point that I would question myself about God. But I'm glad I was in class that day because from that day on I questioned everything I strongly believed in. From that day on my life is full of WHY that happened. Does an idea really make sense, based on reasons and evidence? Is something "right" or "true" because my parents said so? How do they know the answers in which they believe? If God exists why do people suffer? Why do people die? As you can see, I've questioned everything there is to question. I based this on David Hume *Why Does God Let People Suffer?* and Saint Thomas Aquinas, *Whether God Exists.*

—*Elizabeth Rodriguez*

Studying philosophy is not for the faint-hearted—it requires uncommon courage to be willing to question some of your most closely held beliefs. But as Elizabeth discovered, acting courageously in search of the truth is a liberating and intoxicating experience. Why? Because being willing to question your beliefs puts you in control of your own intellectual destiny. You are no longer dependent on others to tell you what to think and believe—you have taken that authority for yourself. And because you are willing to follow the logic of your own reasoning, you are assured of reaching conclusions that are thoughtful, well-founded, and, most significantly, completely your own. You will have the confidence to discuss your beliefs in the arena of public opinion because you have already scrutinized the validity of your beliefs. And because your commitment is to the truth, rather than someone else's agenda, you are open to revising your beliefs based on clearer thinking or more compelling reasons. Commitment to the truth does, in fact, "set you free," and it gives you an unshakeable sense of intellectual security. You know *what* you believe and you know *why* you believe it. And as Elizabeth discovered, that confidence stimulates you to continue expanding your mind through a process of courageous questioning.

THINK PHILOSOPHICALLY
Religious Beliefs

1.7

PHILOSOPHER'S NOTEBOOK

Reflect on some of your most closely held religious beliefs that you have not really questioned or explored. Why do you think these convictions have been "off limits" for questioning? Can you envision the benefits of putting these beliefs to the test in order to create a rock-solid foundation for your philosophy of life?

Epistemology

Epistemology is the theory of knowledge. It seeks to establish a framework that we can use to construct genuine and accurate understanding. This involves identifying and developing criteria and methodologies for determining what we know and why we know it. Here are some of the questions epistemology attempts to answer. How would you answer them?

- Can we ever really *know* anything?
- What is truth?
- What are the sources of knowledge?
- What justifies our beliefs?
- What is the relation between truth and knowledge?
- How can you increase your wisdom?

The most basic question that epistemology seeks to answer is, **Can we ever really *know* anything?** How do we know when we *don't* know something? What is the difference between "belief" and "knowledge"? Why do some people believe that we're "drowning" in information, but we're "starved" for knowledge? The following quotes express some perspectives on these questions. Do you agree or disagree with the ideas being presented? Why?

> There is no absolute knowledge. And those who claim it, whether scientists or dogmatists, open the door to tragedy. All information is imperfect, we have to treat it with humility. That is the human condition.
>
> —*Jacob Bronowski (1908–1974), British scientist*

Epistemology The branch of philosophy that involves the theory of knowledge, identifying and developing criteria and methodologies for determining what we know and why we know it.

Better know nothing than half-know many things.

> —*Friedrich Nietzsche (1844–1900), German philosopher*

When you know a thing, to hold that you know it; and when you do not know a thing, to allow that you do not know it; that is knowledge.

> —*Confucius (551–479 B.C.E.), Chinese philosopher*

Knowledge, if it does not determine action, is dead to us.

> —*Plotinus (ca. 204–270 B.C.E.), Roman philospher*

The question **What is truth?** is naturally related to epistemology's quest for knowledge. What are the roles of reason and experience in constructing knowledge and determining truth? Does truth evolve or is it unchanging? Can there be different "truths" for different people? The following quotes express some perspectives on these questions. Do you agree with the ideas being presented?

Unless you expect the unexpected you will never find truth, for it cannot be found by search or trail.

> —*Heraclitus (ca. 540–480 B.C.E), Greek philosopher*

Truth is the greatest secret of eloquence and of virtue, the basis of moral authority; it is the highest summit of art and life.

> —*Henri Frederic Amiel (1821–1881), Swiss philosopher*

What is there, then, that can be esteemed true? Perhaps this only, that there is absolutely nothing certain.

> —*René Descartes (1596–1650), French philosopher and mathematician*

The truth is cruel, but it can be loved, and it makes free those who have loved it.

> —*George Santayana (1863–1952), American philosopher*

Here is one student's thoughts about the possibility of achieving true knowledge.

As a result of my exploration of how I construct my knowledge, I have modified my idea of what is actually true knowledge. I had always been aware that there was more than one side to any story of events, but now I realize that even the way in which I receive such information plays an important part in the construction of my knowledge. Bertrand Russell's article helped me realize that we have to make a distinction between appearances and reality. If I receive information about a situation, I now know not to assume that information to be the absolute truth. Not only could the person supplying the information be biased in their reporting of the events, but they could also be mistaken. Even if I undertake to search out the truth for myself, I may still not arrive at the absolute truth. John Locke and George Berkeley both conclude that a lot of what we know is from mental construction. In my analysis of any situation, all I can ever know is the way it appears to me. Through my experiences and previous education, I will already have biases toward certain occurrences and these biases will influence my construction of knowledge. Philosophy has helped me realize that in order to attain true knowledge, I must first evaluate my beliefs. In the future I will endeavor to support my beliefs with thoughtful reasons and compelling evidence. I should also become aware of my perceiving lenses as well as those of the source providing me with information. In doing so, I will not blindly accept any information to be the absolute truth.

> —*Joshua Bartlett*

We're bombarded with information on a daily basis, and much of that information is false, incomplete, and/or biased. Studying philosophy gives you the thinking tools needed to sift through this tangled morass of information and construct knowledge that is clear, insightful, and well supported with reasons and evidence. As Joshua rightly points out, all information is biased in the sense that it reflects the needs and interests of the sources providing it. To construct intelligent knowledge, we need to become aware of the "lenses" through which we and others view the world, lenses that shape and influence our points of view. Additionally, we should never be content with just one point of view. Instead, we should always strive to view situations and issues from a variety of contrasting perspectives to develop a well-rounded and balanced understanding. Unfortunately, many people tend to accept uncritically the information they encounter, lacking both the initiative and thinking tools to analyze and evaluate it.

THINK PHILOSOPHICALLY   1.8
Constructing Knowledge

PHILOSOPHER'S NOTEBOOK

Reflect on your approach to the information you receive from the sources in your life: friends, family, teachers, books, television, newspapers, the Internet, magazines, and so on. How often do you make a special effort to question, analyze, and critically evaluate the information? How often do you tend to simply accept the information in the form it's provided? In what ways would taking a more critical thinking approach to information help you construct well-supported knowledge?

Another question that reflects the central purpose of epistemology and philosophy in general is **How can you increase your wisdom?** Here is one student's reflection on this key question.

> I never realized that my beliefs constitute my philosophy of life, and that my philosophy evolves as time goes on. After taking this class I realize that my beliefs have value and it is important to express them because my beliefs reflect who I am. As Buddha said, *"All that we are is the result of what we have thought. The mind is everything. What we think, we become."* I learned that if you have proofs of what you are saying or what you think, you will be able to support your argument as in the Socratic dialogues. We can use the dialectical method which consists of asking questions in order to understand issues in a deeper, clearer way. This is how you demonstrate how wise you are, and this is what makes you a wiser person. Socrates didn't only help people in ancient Greece—he continues to help people today also.
>
> —Lourdes Cando

Studying philosophy isn't simply an intellectual exercise, a workout for your brain—it's a vehicle for becoming a more enlightened person. This is one of the qualities that distinguishes philosophy from other disciplines—the ideas that you explore, write about, and discuss with others have a direct impact on your life. As you develop insight into yourself and the issues that are central to being human, you are able to make more enlightened choices, to create yourself to be the person you always envisioned you would be.

THINK PHILOSOPHICALLY
Seeking Wisdom

1.9

Think about the areas of your life in which you would like to be able to think more clearly. What impact would developing your understanding have on the choices you make and the person you are?

Ethics

Ethics involves the study of moral values and principles. The study of ethics is derived from the Greek word *ethos*, which refers to moral purpose or "character"—as in "a person of upstanding character." *Ethics* and *morals* are terms that refer to the principles that govern our relationships with other people: the ways we *ought* to behave, the rules and standards that we *should* employ in the choices we make. Here are some questions that ethics attempts to answer. How would you answer them?

- How should we treat other people?
- Is there a "good life" for humans?
- What is the relation between moral values and religion?
- How do we decide on the moral rightness of social issues?

The question of **How should we treat other people?** is central to the study of ethics. Are there universal moral values that apply to all people? Or are moral values relative to cultural norms or personal preferences? What moral principles should we use to guide our decisions? The following quotes express some perspectives on these questions. Do you agree or disagree with the ideas being presented? Why?

> A man is truly ethical only when he obeys the compulsion to help all life which he is able to assist, and shrinks from injuring anything that lives.
>
> —*Albert Schweitzer (1875–1965), French medical missionary and theologian*

Ethics The branch of philosophy that studies moral values and principles: the ways we *ought* to behave, the standards that we *should* employ in our dealings with others.

> There is therefore but one categorical imperative, namely, this: Act only on that maxim whereby thou canst at the same time will that it should become a universal law.
>
> —*Immanuel Kant (1724–1804), German philosopher*

What is good? All that elevates the feeling of power, the will to power, the power itself in man. What is bad? All that proceeds from weakness. What is happiness? The feeling that power increases—that resistance is being overcome.

> —*Friedrich Nietzsche (1844–1900), German philosopher*

Ethics is also concerned with questions related to the purpose of life, such as **Is there a "good life" for humans?** Do we have moral responsibilities to others? Are we our "brothers'" and "sisters'" keepers? What is the ultimate goal of our lives? How can we achieve our moral potential? The following quotes express some

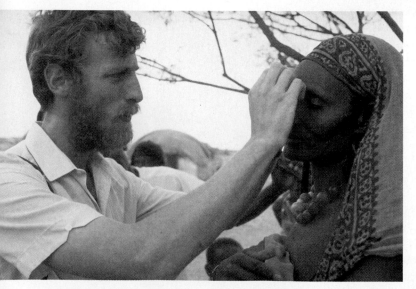

A central question in the study of ethics is "How should we treat other people?" How would you answer this question?

perspectives on these questions. Do you agree or disagree with the ideas being presented? Why?

> Morality is not properly the doctrine of how we may make ourselves happy, but how we may make ourselves worthy of happiness.
> —*Immanuel Kant (1724–1804), German philosopher*

> Morality is the best of all devices for leading mankind by the nose.
> —*Friedrich Nietzsche (1844–1900), German philosopher*

> Live not as though there were a thousand years ahead of you. Fate is at your elbow; make yourself good while life and power are still yours.
> —*Marcus Aurelius Antonius (121–180), Roman emperor and philosopher*

The question of **What is the relation between moral values and religion?** is another issue that has been a focus of ethics throughout history. What role does belief in a divine being play in moral conduct? Does one need to believe in God to be a moral person? Why do different religions agree about many moral values? Why do they disagree? What is the foundation for a humanistic code of ethics? The following quotes express some perspectives on these questions. Do you agree or disagree with the ideas being presented? Why?

> Wherever morality is based on theology, wherever right is made dependent on divine authority, the just immoral, unjust, infamous things can be justified and established.
> —*Ludwig Feuerbach (1804–1872), German philosopher*

> A man may have no religion and yet be moral.
> —*Napoleon Bonaparte (1769–1821), emperor of France*

On a more practical, day-to-day level, ethics is also concerned with **How do we decide on the moral rightness of social issues?** such as capital punishment, euthanasia, lying, human rights, abortion, cloning, pornography, and so on. Slavery was once legal and considered to be morally acceptable by many people in the United States. Were these people morally wrong or did the moral rules change? How can we determine the right views on moral issues that we are confronted with in today's world?

> Morality must grow, it cannot be implanted by precept.
> —*Bertrand Russell (1872–1970), English philosopher*

> Moral feelings are not innate, but acquired.
> —*John Stuart Mill (1806–1873), English philosopher*

Here is one student's analysis regarding the project of developing an accurate moral compass.

> I am striving to live a happy and productive life in which I hope to enhance the lives of others. Before I undertook the reflection of my moral values, I made choices based on if I felt they were the right things to do. I never gave much thought to my decisions, only that they were right for me and that they did not impose on other people. Now that I have studied the ethical principles of several philosophers, I will approach any moral dilemmas I am faced with, with a clearer understanding of *why* I make the choices I do. The teachings of Immanuel Kant have made me realize that I should not consider my actions as affecting only me; that I should also consider the consequences

affecting any other people involved: *"Act so that you treat humanity, whether in your own person or in that of another, always as an end and never as a means only."* In making my decisions, I must also consider that they cannot just be restricted to their effects on my life alone. Kant's Categorical Imperative, *"Act only according to the maxim by which you can at the same time will that it should become a universal law,"* and also John Stuart Mills' moral theory of utilitarianism, are two lessons which I will not forget in my future decision-making. Finally, in whatever choices I make, I am aware that I must take responsibility for the consequences, good or bad.

—*Ed Randall*

Creating yourself to be a wise and knowledgeable person entails developing an enlightened moral compass that will guide your decisions. As Ed observes, people typically rely on what they "feel" is right when faced with challenging moral dilemmas. But how we "feel" is an unreliable moral guide. The only way to ensure that we are making informed and appropriate moral decisions is to develop a clear ethical code that we can use to guide us. Studying philosophy is the most effective way to develop such a code. Over the centuries philosophers have developed a variety of powerful moral systems that are invaluable resources in constructing our own moral codes. Additionally, it is the thinking abilities that we learn and practice when thinking philosophically that are necessary in clarifying complex moral situations and determining the right thing to do. Finally, exploring the ethical dimension of human experience in a thoughtful and disciplined way encourages us to fully accept responsibility for the choices we make and the persons we are. As Socrates noted, when we discuss moral ideas "We are discussing no smaller matter than how we ought to live."

THINK PHILOSOPHICALLY   1.10

Making Moral Decisions

PHILOSOPHER'S NOTEBOOK

Think about some of the particularly confusing and challenging moral decisions that you've had to make in your life. What made these decisions so difficult? Do you believe that you have a clear and accurate moral compass that you can use to guide you when complicated moral dilemmas arise in the future? What are some of the moral areas of your life in which you would like to have a clearer set of values?

Political and Social Philosophy

Political and social philosophy involves the study of social values and political forms of government. It explores the various ways in which people should organize and govern themselves. This involves analyzing the values on which society should be based, and the role of social justice and individual rights. Here are some of the questions that political philosophy attempts to answer. How would you answer them?

- What is the most enlightened form of government?
- What is the nature of justice?

Political and social philosophy
The branch of philosophy that studies social values and political forms of government, including issues regarding the role of social justice and the nature of individual rights.

What is the most enlightened form of government? is naturally one of the core questions of this branch of philosophy. Who has the right to exercise power? What are the limits of the state? The following quotes express some perspectives on these questions. Do you agree or disagree with the ideas being presented? Why?

Politics must conform to the essence and aims of society, not to the passions of rulers. The power of man over man is justifiable only by utility: education and legislation can be effective only when men are convinced that their interests will be served thereby.

Paul Henri Thiry, Baron d'Holbach (1723–1789), French philosopher

It is evident that the state is a creation of nature, and that man is by nature a political animal.

Aristotle (384–322 B.C.E.), Greek philosopher

VISUAL PHILOSOPHY

"The History of Medicine in Mexico, the People Demanding Health"

Social and political philosophy explores questions like "What is the nature of justice?" while aesthetics explores questions like "What is the social purpose of art?"

Political language is designed to make lies sound truthful and murder respectable, and to give an appearance of solidity to pure wind.

—George Orwell (1903–1950), English novelist, essayist

The mode of production of material life determines the general character of the social, political, and spiritual processes of life. It is not the consciousness of men that determines their being, but, on the contrary, their social being determines their consciousness.

—Karl Marx (1818–1883), German political philosopher

A related question but one that has more immediate relevance for most people is **What is the nature of justice?** What individual rights are people entitled to? What is the relationship between the needs of the state and personal liberties? What are the different concepts of justice and how should they be applied?

All virtue is summed up in dealing justly.

—Aristotle (384–322 B.C.E.), Greek philosopher

Justice is the earnest and constant will to render to every man his due. The precepts of the laws are these: to live honorably, to injure no other man, to render to every man his due.

—Justinian I (483–565), emperor of the Byzantine Empire

Aesthetics

 esthetics involves the study of beauty and art. It analyzes efforts to establish standards for beauty in all of its various manifestations. And it explores the nature and purpose of art in human affairs. Here are some of the questions that aesthetics attempts to answer. How would you answer them?

- What is the nature of beauty?
- What is art?

What is the nature of beauty? is a question that has been discussed for thousands of years in most cultures. How do we identify principles of beauty and artistic value? Are there universal standards of beauty, or are they relative to cultural and individual taste? Is there one core concept of beauty or many different concepts? The following quotes express some perspectives on these questions. Do you agree or disagree with the ideas being presented? Why?

Ethics, like natural selection, make existence possible. Aesthetics, like sexual selection, make life lovely and wonderful, fill it with new forms, and give it progress, and variety and change.

—Oscar Wilde (1854–1900), Irish poet, novelist and playwright

Beauty in things exists in the mind which contemplates them.

—David Hume (1711–1776), Scottish philosopher

To feel beauty is a better thing than to understand how we come to feel it. To have imagination and taste, to love the best, to be carried by the contemplation of nature to a vivid faith in the ideal, all this is more, a great deal more, than any science can hope to be.

—George Santayana (1863–1952), American philosopher

Another question aesthetics deals with is **What is art?** What are the proper uses of art? Should art be used for social and political purposes? Should the government be allowed to censor "artistic expression" that it considers to be obscene? The following quotes express some well-known perspectives on these questions. Do you agree or disagree with the ideas being presented? Why?

Aesthetics   The branch of philosophy that studies the nature of beauty and art, exploring whether there are standards for beauty in all its various manifestations.

Art for art's sake is an empty phrase. Art for the sake of the true, art for the sake of the good and the beautiful, that is the faith I am searching for.

—George Sand (1804–1876), French novelist and essayist

I have always believed and still believe that artists who live in and work with spiritual values cannot and should not remain indifferent to a conflict in which the highest values of humanity and civilization are at stake.

—Picasso (1881–1973), Spanish painter and sculptor

Logic and Critical Thinking

Logic and **critical thinking** seek to establish the rules of correct reasoning, clear understanding, and valid arguments. In addition, they identify fallacies—chronic ways in which people use illogical reasoning to reach conclusions. Finally, and more recently, critical thinking has emerged as an integrated attempt to define the thinking processes of the human mind in order to strengthen and improve their functioning. This is a method that can be applied to any discipline as well as to life experience. As we have seen in the section on critical thinking (page 16), becoming a *critical thinker* changes qualitatively the way a person views the world, processes information, and makes decisions. Here are some of the questions that logic and critical thinking seek to answer. How would you answer them?

- What are the logical principles of correct reasoning?
- Why do many people think ineffectively?

What are the logical principles of correct reasoning? expresses the central mission of this branch of philosophy. How can we learn to reason well? How can we distinguish fallacious reasoning from sound reasoning? The following quotes express some perspectives on these questions.

He who will not reason is a bigot; he who cannot is a fool; and he who dares not is a slave.

—William Drummond (1585–1649), Scottish poet and historian

Reason deserves to be called a prophet: for in showing us the consequence and effect of our actions in the present, does it not tell us what the future will be?

—Arthur Schopenhauer (1788–1860), German philosopher

Man has received direct from God only one instrument wherewith to know himself and to know his relation to the universe. He has no other and that instrument is reason.

—Leo Tolstoy (1828–1910), Russian novelist

Reason or a halter.

—Diogenes (d. 320 B.C.E), Greek Cynic philosopher

A more general question in this area of philosophy can be phrased, **Why do many people think ineffectively?** The following quotes express some perspectives on this question.

Most people would rather die than think—in fact they do!

—Bertrand Russell (1872–1970), English philosopher

For every complex question there's a simple answer—and it is clever, neat, and wrong.

—H. L. Mencken (1880–1956), American essayist

Our thinking tends to be hazy, hasty, narrow or sprawling—causal terms for impulsive. Just like anything else, thinking skills require upkeep. If they aren't nourished, they'll fade away.

—David Perkins, American psychologist

Logic The branch of philosophy that seeks to establish the rules of correct reasoning, clear understanding and valid arguments.

Critical thinking The integrated attempt to define the thinking process of the human mind in order to strengthen and improve its functioning. It is a method that can be applied to any discipline as well as to life experience.

Bertrand Russell: *The Value of Philosophy*

BERTRAND RUSSELL
(1872–1970).
British Philosopher. One of the
founders of modern logic. In *The
Principles of Mathematics* (1903) and
with Whitehead in the three volume
Principia Mathematica (1910–1913),
he advanced the view that all of
mathematics could be derived from
logical premises. Also a political
activist, he wrote many popular books
on topics such as religion, ethics, and
marriage.

Bertrand Arthur William Russell (1872–1970), British philosopher, logician, essayist, and social critic, is best known for his work in mathematical logic and analytic philosophy. Along with G. E. Moore, Russell is generally recognized as one of the founders of analytic philosophy. And along with Kurt Gödel, he is also often credited with being one of the two most important logicians of the twentieth century.

Over the course of his long career, Russell made significant contributions, not just to logic and philosophy, but to a broad range of other subjects (including education, politics, history, religion, and science), and many of his writings on a wide variety of topics have influenced generations of general readers. After a life marked by controversy (including dismissals from both Trinity College, Cambridge, and City College, New York), Russell was awarded the Order of Merit in 1949 and the Nobel Prize in Literature in 1950. Also noted for his many spirited antiwar and antinuclear protests, Russell remained a prominent public figure until his death at the age of 97.

In the following selection from his book *The Problems of Philosophy*, Russell addresses the core question that we have considered in this chapter—What is the value of philosophy? The excerpt provides an excellent opportunity to see a philosophical mind at work.

Bertrand Russell,
The Value of Philosophy

Having now come to the end of our brief and very incomplete review of the problems of philosophy, it will be well to consider, in conclusion, what is the value of philosophy and why it ought to be studied. It is the more necessary to consider this question, in view of the fact that many men, under the influence of science or of practical affairs, are inclined to doubt whether philosophy is anything better than innocent but useless trifling, hair-splitting distinctions, and controversies on matters concerning which knowledge is impossible.

This view of philosophy appears to result, partly from a wrong conception of the ends of life, partly from a wrong conception of the kind of goods which philosophy strives to achieve. Physical science, through the medium of inventions, is useful to innumerable people who are wholly ignorant of it; thus the study of physical science is to be recommended, not only, or primarily, because of the effect on the student, but rather because of the effect on mankind in general. Thus utility does not belong to philosophy. If the study of philosophy has any value at all for others than students of philosophy, it must be only indirectly, through its effect upon the lives of those who study it. It is in these effects, therefore, if anywhere, that the value of philosophy must be primarily sought.

But further, if we are not to fail in our endeavour to determine the value of philosophy, we must first free our minds from the prejudices of what are wrongly called "practical" man. The "practical" man, as this word is often used, is one who recognizes only material needs, who realizes that men must have food for the body, but is oblivious of the necessity of providing food for the mind. If all men were well off, if poverty and disease had been reduced to their lowest possible point, there would still remain much to be done to produce a valuable society; and even in the existing world the goods of the mind are at least as important as the goods of the body. It is exclusively among the goods of the mind that the value of philosophy is to be found; and only those who are not indifferent to these goods can be persuaded that the study of philosophy is not a waste of time.

Philosophy, like all other studies, aims primarily at knowledge. The knowledge it aims at is the kind of knowledge which gives unity and system to the body of the sciences, and the kind which results from a critical examination of the grounds of our convictions, prejudices, and beliefs. But it cannot be maintained that philosophy has had any very great measure of success in its attempts to provide definite answers to its questions. If you ask a mathematician, a mineralogist, a historian, or any other man of learning, what definite body of truths has been ascertained by his science, his answer will last as long as you are willing to listen. But if you put the same questions to a philosopher, he will, if he is candid, have to confess that his study has not achieved positive results such as have been achieved by other sciences. It is true that this is partly accounted for by the fact that, as soon as definite knowledge concerning any subject becomes possible, this subject ceases to be called philosophy, and becomes a separate science. The whole study of the heavens, which now belongs to astronomy, was once included in philosophy; Newton's great work was called "the mathematical principles of natural philosophy." Similarly, the study of the human mind, which was a part of philosophy, has now been separated from philosophy and has become the science of psychology. Thus, to a great extent, the uncertainty of philosophy is more apparent than real: those questions which are already capable of definite answers are placed in the sciences, while those only to which, at present, no definite answer can be given, remain to form the residue which is called philosophy.

This is, however, only a part of the truth concerning the uncertainty of philosophy. There are many questions—and among them those that are of the profoundest interest to our spiritual life—which, so far as we can see, must remain insoluble to the human intellect unless its powers become of quite a different order from what they are now. Has the universe any unity of plan or purpose, or is it a fortuitous concourse of atoms? Is consciousness a permanent part of the universe, giving hope of indefinite growth in wisdom, or is it a transitory accident on a small planet on which life must ultimately become impossible? Are good and evil of importance to the universe or only to man? Such questions are asked by philosophy, and variously answered by various philosophers. But it would seem that, whether answers be otherwise discoverable or not, the answers suggested by philosophy are none of them demonstrably true. Yet, however slight may be the hope of discovering an answer, it is part of the business of philosophy to continue the consideration of such questions, to make us aware of their importance, to examine all the approaches to them, and to keep alive that speculative interest in the universe which is apt to be killed by confining ourselves to definitely ascertainable knowledge.

The value of philosophy is, in fact, to be sought largely in its very uncertainty. The man who has no tincture of philosophy goes through life imprisoned in the prejudices derived from common sense, from the habitual beliefs of his age or his nation, and from convictions which have grown up in his mind without the co-operation or consent of his deliberate reason. To such a man the world tends to become definite, finite, obvious; common objects rouse no questions, and unfamiliar possibilities are contemptuously rejected. As soon as we begin to philosophize, on the contrary, we find that even the most everyday things lead to problems to which only very incomplete answers can be given. Philosophy, though unable to tell us with certainty what is the true answer to the doubts which it raises, is able to suggest many possibilities which enlarge our thoughts and free them from the tyranny of custom. Thus, while diminishing our feeling of certainty as to what things are, it greatly increases our knowledge as to what they may be; it removes the somewhat arrogant dogmatism of those who have never travelled into the region of liberating doubt, and it keeps alive our sense of wonder by showing familiar things in an unfamiliar aspect.

Apart from its utility in showing unsuspected possibilities, philosophy has a value— perhaps its chief value—through the greatness of the objects which it contemplates, and the freedom from narrow and personal aims resulting from this contemplation. The life of the instinctive man is shut up within the circle of his private interests: family and friends may be included, but the other world is not regarded except as it may help or hinder what comes within the circle of instinctive wishes. In such a life there is something feverish and confined, in comparison with which the philosophic life is calm and free. The private world of instinctive interests is a small one, set in the midst of a great and powerful world which must, sooner or later, lay our private world in ruins. Unless we can so enlarge our interests so as to include the whole outer world, we remain like a garrison in a beleaguered fortress, knowing that the enemy prevents escape and that ultimate surrender is inevitable. In such a life there is no peace, but a constant strife between the insistence of desire and the powerlessness of will. In one way or another, if our life is to be great and free, we must escape this prison and this strife.

One way of escape is by philosophic contemplation. Philosophic contemplation does not, in its widest survey, divide the universe into two hostile camps—friends and foes, helpful and hostile, good and bad—it views the whole impartially. Philosophic contemplation, when it is unalloyed, does not aim at proving that the rest of the universe is akin to man. . . . In contemplation, on the contrary, we start from the non-Self, and

Bertrand Russell

through its greatness the boundaries of Self are enlarged; through the infinity of the universe the mind which contemplates it achieves some share in infinity.

Thus, to sum up our discussion of the value of philosophy; Philosophy is to be studied, not for the sake of any definite answers to its questions since no definite answers can, as a rule, be known to be true, but rather for the sake of the questions themselves; because these questions enlarge our conception of what is possible, enrich our intellectual imagination and diminish the dogmatic assurance which closes the mind against speculation; but above all because through the greatness of the universe which philosophy contemplates, the mind also is rendered great, and becomes capable of that union with the universe which constitutes its highest good. ■

1.1 Russell, Bertrand: *The Problems of Philosophy*

THINK PHILOSOPHICALLY   1.11
Analyzing Bertrand Russell

In your Philosopher's Notebook, respond in a thoughtful, reflective way to the following questions regarding Bertrand Russell's ideas.

- According to Russell, the "practical" man does not understand that "the goods of the mind are at least as important as the goods of the body." Explain what you think he means by this statement.

- "Philosophy, like all other studies, aims primarily at knowledge. The knowledge it aims at is the kind of knowledge which gives unity and system to the body of the sciences, and the kind which results from a critical examination of the grounds of our convictions, prejudices, and beliefs." Describe some examples of what Russell would consider to be "philosophy" based on this definition.

- One reason that philosophy does not provide definite answers to its questions is that "as soon as definite knowledge concerning any subject becomes possible, this subject ceases to be called philosophy, and becomes a separate science." Explain what Russell means and how this relates to the characterization of philosophy as the "mother of all disciplines."

- A second reason that Russell believes philosophy does not provide definite answers to its questions is that many of its questions "must remain insoluble to the human intellect unless its powers become of quite a different order from what they are now." Identify five such questions and explain why the answers are likely to remain insoluble.

- "The value of philosophy is, in fact, to be sought largely in its very uncertainty. The man who has no tincture of philosophy goes through life imprisoned in the prejudices derived from common sense, from the habitual beliefs of his age or his nation, and from convictions which have grown up in his mind without the co-operation or consent of his deliberate reason. To such a man the world tends to become definite, finite, obvious; common objects rouse no questions, and unfamiliar possibilities are contemptuously rejected. As soon as we begin to philosophize, on the contrary, we find that even the most everyday things lead to problems to which only very incomplete answers can be given." Explain what Russell means in this passage and how it relates to Socrates' admonition, "The unexamined life is not worth living."

- According to Russell, "Philosophy is to be studied, not for the sake of any definite answers to its questions since no definite answers can, as a rule, be known to be true, but rather for the sake of the questions themselves; because these questions enlarge our conception of what is possible, enrich our intellectual imagination and diminish the dogmatic assurance which closes the mind against speculation; but above all because through the greatness of the universe which philosophy contemplated, the mind also is rendered great, and becomes capable of that union with the universe which constitutes its highest good." Explain in your own words what Russell means in this passage.

Can you identify additional reasons for studying philosophy based on your work in this chapter?

Making Connections:
The Search for a Meaningful Life

This first chapter has been designed to introduce you to the discipline of philosophy and to suggest ways that studying philosophy can enrich your life. Studying philosophy is unique, because as you develop your mind by learning how to think philosophically, you are also enlarging yourself as a person—the perspective from which you view the world, the concepts and values you use to guide your choices, and the impact you have on the world as a result of those choices. Learning to think philosophically does not mean simply gaining certain intellectual tools—it involves your personal transformation. Everybody "thinks"—*Homo sapiens* means "thinking man"—but most people don't "think" very well. By learning to think philosophically, you can develop your mind into a powerful, sophisticated resource that will enrich all dimensions of your life. It will initiate a process that transforms the way you view yourself and conduct your business in the world.

We all long to live lives that are meaningful and purposeful, as Viktor Frankl expresses so eloquently in the following passage:

> Man's search for meaning is the primary motivation in his life. This meaning is unique and specific in that it must and can be fulfilled by him alone; only then does it achieve a significance which will satisfy his own will to meaning.

This insight by Dr. Frankl, a psychiatrist and concentration camp survivor, penetrates to the soul of who we are. A well-known Viennese psychiatrist in the 1930s, Dr. Frankl and his family were arrested by the Nazis, and he spent three years in the Auschwitz concentration camp. Every member of his family, including his parents, his siblings, and his pregnant wife, were killed. He himself miraculously survived, enduring the most unimaginably abusive and degrading conditions. Following his liberation by Allied troops, he wrote *Man's Search for Meaning*, an enduring and influential work, which he began on scraps of paper during his internment. Since its publication in 1945, it has been read by millions of people in twenty languages. Its success reflects the hunger for meaning that people are experiencing, trying to answer a question that, in the author's words, "burns under their fingernails." This hunger expresses the pervasive meaning*lessness* of our age, the "existential vacuum," in which many people exist.

Dr. Frankl discovered that even under the most inhumane of conditions, it is possible to live a life of purpose and meaning. But for the majority of prisoners at Auschwitz, a meaningful life did not seem possible. Immersed in a world that no longer recognized the value of human life and human dignity, which robbed them of their will and made them objects to be exterminated, most prisoners suffered a loss of their values. Prisoners who did not struggle against this spiritual destruction lost their feeling of being individuals, beings with a mind, with inner freedom and personal value. Their existence descended to the level of animal life, plunging them into a depression so deep that they became incapable of action. No entreaties, no blows, no threats would have any effect on this apathetic paralysis, underscoring the Russian novelist Fyodor Dostoevsky's observation: "Without a firm idea of himself and the purpose of his life, man cannot live, and would sooner destroy himself than remain on earth, even if he was surrounded with bread."

Dr. Frankl found that the meaning of *his* life in this situation was to try to help his fellow prisoners restore their psychological health. He had to find ways for them

Viktor Frankl discovered that even under the most inhumane of conditions, it is possible to live a meaningful life, defined by the ways we choose to respond to life's challenges. Do you believe that this is true? Why?

to look forward to the future: a loved one waiting for his return, a talent to be used, or perhaps work yet to be completed. These were the threads he tried to weave back into the patterns of meaning in these devastated lives. His efforts led him to the following epiphany:

> We had to learn ourselves, and furthermore we had to teach the despairing men, that it did not matter what we expected from life, but rather what life expected from us. We needed to stop asking about the meaning of life but instead to think of ourselves as those who were being questioned by life, daily and hourly. Our answer must consist not in talk and meditation, but in right action and in right conduct. Life ultimately means taking the responsibility to find the right answer to its problems and to fulfill the tasks which it constantly sets for each individual.

We each long for a life of significance, to feel that in some important way our life has made a unique contribution to the world and to the lives of others. We each strive to create our self as a person of unique quality, someone who is admired by others as extraordinary. We hope for lives characterized by unique accomplishments and lasting relationships that will distinguish us as memorable individuals both during and after our time on earth. Unfortunately, we often don't achieve these lofty goals. To discover the meaning of our lives, we need to understand "who" we are. And we live in an age in which many people are not sure "who" they are or whether in fact their lives have *any* significant meaning whatsoever.

When we are asked such questions as, "Who are you?" or "What is the meaning of your life?" we often lack any idea how to respond. But an even more revealing symptom of our confusion and alienation is the fact that we rarely even *pose* these questions, to ourselves or to others. We are too busy "living" to wonder *why* we are living or *who* the person is that is doing the living. But can we afford to be too busy to find meaning in our lives? *Our lives depend on our answer to this question.* Not our biological lives necessarily, but the life of our *spirit*. We so often cruise along on autopilot—days slipping into weeks, weeks merging into years, years coalescing into a life—without confronting these important questions. If we are to become human in the fullest sense, achieving our distinctive potentials and living a life of significance, we must first have what the theologian Paul Tillich characterized as *"the courage to be."*

There is a terrible price to pay for this loss of wonder and lack of meaning, for such a loss corrodes any life, eating it away from the inside until only a shell remains. The existentialist novelist Albert Camus, expressed it this way:

> To lose one's life is a little thing and I shall have the courage to do so if it is necessary; but to see the meaning of this life dissipated, to see our reason for existing disappear, that is what is unbearable. One cannot live without meaning.

Many people are in fact living with a diminished sense of meaning, and they struggle to fill the void within them by frantically pursuing power, money,

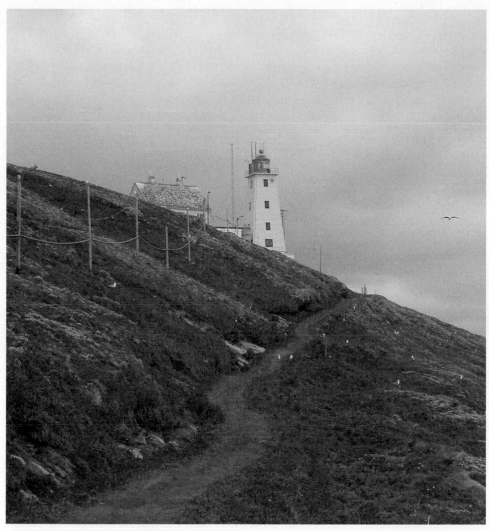

Socrates' statement that "The unexamined life is not worth living" suggests that every person has a responsibility to craft a meaningful life guided by an enlightened personal philopsophy.

pleasure, thrills, mind-altered states, or the latest cultural fad. Yet these compulsive cravings only serve to reveal the *lack* of purpose in their lives, poor substitutes for a life built around authentic purpose and genuine meaning. Dr. Frankl provided an eloquent analysis of the desperate situation in which we find ourselves:

> Modern men and women are caught in an existential vacuum, the total and ultimate meaninglessness of their lives. They lack the awareness of a meaning worth living for. They are haunted by the experience of their inner emptiness, a void within themselves. The existential vacuum is a widespread phenomenon of the 20th century. . . . No instinct tells them what they have to do, and no tradition tells them what they ought to do; soon they will not know what they want to do.

This, then, is the real significance of Socrates' challenge, "The unexamined life is not worth living." Socrates' unambiguous message is that when we live our lives unreflectively, simply reacting to life's situations and not trying to explore its deeper meanings, then our lives have diminished value. When unreflective, we are not making use of the distinctive human capacity to think deeply about important issues and develop thoughtful conclusions about ourselves and our world.

Thinking philosophically in our current world is typically not a simple matter. It's a fast-paced world in which we are bombarded by overwhelming amounts of information and incessant demands on our time. It's not unusual to feel that we are rushing from deadline to deadline, skating on the surface of life, meeting our endless responsibilities, and seeming to be in perpetual motion like hamsters on an exercise wheel. It's difficult to find the time to reflect deeply about important questions and to have in-depth discussions with others regarding significant issues of mutual concern. We're so busy caught up in the process of living that we simply don't make the time or effort to plumb the depths of ourselves, reflect on the meaning of our existence, shape the direction of our lives, and create ourselves as unique and worthy individuals. Yet if we are to take Socrates' challenge seriously, making time to think deeply is exactly what we *must* do if our lives are to have genuine significance.

THINK PHILOSOPHICALLY 1.12
Examining My Life

PHILOSOPHER'S NOTEBOOK

This course in philosophy is going to provide you with a unique opportunity to respond to Socrates' challenge by exploring profound ideas, developing powerful intellectual abilities, and developing as a reflective, insightful thinker. This first chapter has provided you with an introduction to the grand subject of philosophy and is also designed to be a personal invitation for you to begin—or continue—your own personal philosophical journey. Think about the philosophical themes and ideas that you have examined in this chapter, and then write a three-plus-page paper for your Philosopher's Notebook that explains your personal goals for this Introduction to Philosophy course. Discuss the insights you would like to achieve, the ways you would like to develop your mind, the knowledge you would like to achieve.

Concept Review

■ Philosophy, or the love and pursuit of wisdom, is as much a way of living and process of thinking as it is a body of knowledge. Our responsibility as thoughtful, critical citizens is to define for ourselves our own "philosophy of life"—and then to *do* philosophy by continually testing that philosophy against new knowledge and experience.

■ To "do philosophy" effectively requires developing the attributes of *critical thinking*. These attributes include adopting different perspectives, making informed decisions, analyzing complex issues, establishing appropriate goals, communicating effectively, critically evaluating information, asking questions, and exchanging ideas with others (Socratic analysis).

■ Philosophy has its origins in the human capacity for wonder. The activity of philosophy is a rigorous, critical, and honest process of testing and discussing our beliefs. In that activity is implied a conflict, or "dialectic"; in doing philosophy, we continually test ideas and concepts against their opposites, working toward synthesis. That synthesis, or unity, is the ultimate aim of philosophy: to improve the quality of our lives by enlightening and broadening our minds.

■ The traditional branches of philosophy are

■ metaphysics—the study of the ultimate characteristics of reality or existence. (*What is the nature of reality? Does God exist?*)

- epistemology—the study of the construction of knowledge. (*What is truth? Can we ever really know anything?*)
- ethics—the study of moral values and principles. (*How should we treat other people? Is there a "good life" for humans?*)
- political and social philosophy—the study of social values and political forms of government. (*What is the nature of justice? What is the most enlightened form of government?*)

- aesthetics—the study of beauty, art, and taste. (*What is the nature of beauty? What is art?*)
- logic and critical thinking—the study of correct reasoning, clear understanding, and valid arguments. (*What are the logical principals of correct reasoning? Why do many people think ineffectively?*)

There is considerable overlap and nuance between these different categories.

Media Resources

 www.researchnavigator.com

Chapter 1 provides a brief introduction to the major areas of philosophical study. Questions of how and why to do philosophy are posed. For further research on questions of areas that may be most important to you, use the tools available to you in Research Navigator.

As you investigate this topic, consider this question: "What do I want to accept and understand in my own life?"

- **ContentSelect:** search in the philosophy databases using the search terms "meaning of life," "acceptance," and "life."
- **Link Library:** search in the philosophy database under terms "critical thinking" and "belief."
- **New York Times on the Web:** search in the Philosophy database using the search terms "life" and "meaning."

 For additional study resources for this chapter, go to: **www.prenhall.com/chaffee/chapter1**

 The Primary Source: Philosophical Readings and Commentary

Aristotle: *Metaphysics,*
Augustine, St.: *City of God*
d'Holbach, Baron: *The System of Nature*
Descartes, René: *Meditations on First Philosophy*
Epicurus: *Letter to Menoeceus*
Kant, Immanuel: *Fundamental Principles of the Metaphysics of Morals; Prolegomena to Any Future Metaphysics*
Kierkegaard, Søren: *Philosophical Fragments*
Marx, Karl: *The Communist Manifesto*
Nietzsche, Friedrich: *Beyond Good and Evil*
Plato: *The Republic; Theaetetus, Philebus, Sophist, Parmenides, Statesman, Timaeus*
Plotinus: *Enneads*
Rand, Ayn: *Philosophy: Who Needs It?; The Virtue of Selfishness*
Russell, Bertrand: *The Problems of Philosophy*
Sartre, Jean-Paul: *Existentialism Is a Humanism*

That man is wisest who, like Socrates, realizes that his wisdom is worthless.

PLATO

But now the time has come, and we must go away—I to die, and you to live.

SOCRATES

Socrates' Cure for Sleepwalking Through Life

When you reflect on your own personal and intellectual development, you can likely identify key people in your life who stimulated your thinking, challenged your limited perspective, and inspired your spirit to soar to new and unexpected levels. Who are some of these people? How did they stimulate you and enrich your life? Do they continue to influence you, even though you may no longer be in touch with them?

For people living in Athens, Greece, twenty-five hundred years ago, **Socrates** was such a person. Several hundred years previously, the Greek thinker Heraclitus had warned, "One ought not to talk or act as if he were asleep," cautioning against the tendency of many people to live their lives as sleepwalkers: drifting along with life's current, unreflective, unthinking. Socrates embraced Heraclitus's challenge as his life mission, characterizing himself as a "*gadfly*," an annoying, biting insect, attached "to a horse that is large and well-bred but rather sluggish from its size, and needing to be aroused. It seems to me that the god has attached me like that to the state, for I am constantly alighting upon you at every point to rouse, persuade, and reproach each of you all day long."

Centuries later, Socrates is still relevant to us today with the same compelling immediacy that he spoke to his fellow Athenians. Too often we are drowsy sleepwalkers, shuffling through life, submerged in mundane daily tasks, predictable habits, restricted visions of ourselves and who we can be. More than ever we need the gadfly of Socrates to wake us from our dozing, energize our thinking, and open our mind's eye to the depths of our souls and the wonders of the universe. Being shaken awake is not usually a pleasant experience, and Socrates noted, "You are indignant, as drowsy persons are, when they are awakened," tempted initially to "sleep on undisturbed for the rest of your lives." But if we rouse ourselves to full alertness, our minds can become catalysts of creative energy, infusing our lives with vibrant emotions, penetrating ideas, and galvanizing experiences, as expressed in the following student passage:

> Beginning with Socrates' call-to-arms, this course has aided me considerably in my philosophical journey. I have learned to think more critically, to doubt, instead of accepting all that is "intravenously" fed to me through my environment. I discovered what it is to truly make a free decision and what it is to be moral. I read about many intriguing philosophers and their insightful convictions. But most of all I had the opportunity to grow as a person and create my own philosophy on life.
>
> *Danielle Malkusz*

Socrates: *A Model for Humanity*

Socrates, in concert with his student and biographer Plato, shifted the course of Western intellectual history, creating a conceptual framework and method of inquiry that has permeated Western consciousness and culture right up to the present. In fact, the impact of these extraordinary minds is so profound that the renowned twentieth-century philosopher **Alfred North Whitehead** (1861–1947) once observed that the history of Western thought can be seen as "a series of footnotes to Plato."

How is it possible for one or two people to have such a powerful and far-reaching impact? The answer is that throughout human history, there have appeared at pivotal moments extraordinary people that embody an intellectual power, moral character, and creative vision that transcends their current circumstances and sets the standard for generations to come. The philosopher and theologian **Karl Jaspers** (1883–1969) classifies such titanic figures as Socrates, Buddha, Jesus, Moses, and Mohammed as *archetypal* or *paradigmatic* people, individuals who serve as an ideal model for all of humanity. These ideal figures not only embody the breathtaking potential that humans are capable of, but also challenge us to strive and emulate their inspiring vision and sublime level of existence. Jaspers explains:

> A radical change is experienced and demanded (by paradigmatic individuals). They are stirred to their depths, by what we do not know. They express what there is no appropriate way of saying. They speak in parables, dialectical contradictions, conversational replies. . . . Socrates seeks himself and his relation to other men. By his extreme questioning he arouses a real, living certainty that is not mere knowledge of something. He transcends the world without negating it. He forges total knowledge, total judgments, contenting himself with a non-knowledge in which truth and reality are actualized.

Other individuals also have had a profound effect on human culture: in the creative arts, Homer, Mozart, Michelangelo, Beethoven, Shakespeare, Dante, Da Vinci; in philosophy, Confucius, Socrates, Plato, Descartes; in science, Galileo, Newton, Einstein, Marie Curie; in the social sciences, Herodotus, Sigmund Freud, Karl Marx; in politics, Gandhi, Joan of Arc, Elizabeth I, George Washington, Abraham Lincoln, Simón Bolívar, Che Guevara, Martin Luther King, Jr., Nelson Mandela, and so on.

However, this group of archetypal achievers, despite their spectacular talent and awe-inspiring insights, do not represent ethical ideals in the same way that Socrates, Buddha, Jesus, Moses, and Mohammed do. These archetypal figures express the best of humanity, providing inspiring evidence that we are each capable of stellar achievements. They possess a unique charisma combined with a timeless message that touches the souls of people in many different cultures and time periods. They somehow penetrate to the heart of who we are, the primordial desire we each have to create a life that is meaningful and fulfilling. These archetypal individuals serve as life guides, transcendent figures who have achieved an elevated position with respect to all of humanity. Their message to us, embodied in every aspect of their lives, is profound. They are messengers who help us explore the most elemental questions of our lives: Who am I? Who should I become? What is the purpose of my existence?

Alfred North Whitehead (1861–1947) British Mathematician and Philosopher. Collaborated with his student Bertrand Russell on the *Principia Mathematica* and wrote *Process and Reality* about process philosophy which celebrates the changing universe.

Karl Jaspers (1883–1969) German Philosopher and Theologian. Coined the term *Existenzphilosophie*—a forerunner of the term existentialism.

THINK PHILOSOPHICALLY 2.1
Archetypal Figures

Who are some of the influential thinkers and creative artists who have influenced your own intellectual development through exposure to their ideas and creations? After you identify one or two such figures, provide examples of the impact their ideas or lives have had on your own personal, intellectual, or creative development.

A Man of Greece

Here's an opportunity for you to use your imagination. Erase from your mind your entire scientific understanding of the world. Imagine that you and all of the people in your culture explain events in the natural world through superstition, fairy tales, and religion. The sun rises in the morning because it wishes to. Rain needed to grow crops is dependent on the pleasure of the gods. Issues of sickness and health, life and death, reflect unseen spirits living amongst us. Your personal destiny is entirely determined by the position of the planets.

As strange as these beliefs are to our modern consciousness, this was very much the state of affairs in the ancient world. Although understanding of the world progressed in various cultures, it was invariably inhibited by nonscientific factors. For example, the Chinese, Babylonians, Mayans, and Egyptians had developed advanced practical technology in areas such as construction (the pyramids) and astronomy (predicting solar and lunar eclipses), and they had made impressive gains in mathematics. But as the philosopher Paul Strathern (1940–) points out, in every case superstition, myths, and religion infiltrated the processes of reason and observation. For example, Babylonian knowledge of astronomy was intertwined with an unshakeable belief in astrology, and Egyptian advancements in mathematics were permeated with religious superstition.

The ancient Greeks took a fresh view, approaching the natural world using the powerful lenses of *reason* and *observation* to create an intelligible picture of the universe. In so doing, they avoided the limiting effects of superstition, myth, and religion that had influenced other cultures. This new philosophic approach first surfaced between 600 and 500 B.C.E. with a group of "pre-Socratic" thinkers who were particularly interested in identifying the underlying essence of the universe. **Thales** (sixth century B.C.E.) proposed that the primal element of the universe was water; **Anaximenes** (*fl.* c. 550 B.C.E.) suggested it was air, and **Heraclitus** (*fl.* c. 500 B.C.E.) contended that it was fire since "All is change." **Democritus** (c. 460–c. 370 B.C.E.) advanced the prescient view that all matter in the universe was composed of indivisible atoms, and **Pythagoras** (c. 550–c. 500 B.C.E.) was convinced that the fundamental principles of the universe were mathematical relations (a view that foreshadowed the thinking of Albert Einstein a few thousand years later). Although these early efforts were somewhat off the mark, the approach they used, based fundamentally on reason and observation, laid the foundation for Western civilization.

Socrates was an integral participant in the explosion of cultural creativity in the fifth century B.C.E. that was manifested in architecture, politics, art and sculpture, drama, medicine, physics, mathematics, and philosophy. The cumulative advances in the fifth century B.C.E. in Greece are breathtaking in their scope and accelerated evolution, and they formed a cultural foundation for subsequent developments in Western civilization over the next several thousand years.

Socrates (470–399 B.C.E.) was the son of Sophroniscus, a sculptor, and Phaenarete, a midwife, whose careers were to serve as rich metaphors for Socrates throughout his life: as he used the skills of practical wisdom to "shape" the mind and help others "give birth" to new understanding. Unlike the great pre-Socratic thinkers, Socrates was not as concerned with the physics of the natural world as he was with the psychology of the mind. In the words of the Roman philosopher **Cicero** (106–43 B.C.E.) he brought philosophy "out of the clouds and into the market place," into the cities and houses of people. He loved the exploration and interplay of ideas in discussions with others, and it was through these experiences that he developed what has come to be known as the **Socratic Method**. This method used a dynamic approach of questioning and intellectual analysis to draw answers

Thales (c. 585 B.C.E.) Presocratic Philosopher. Considered to be the first philosopher because he introduced a different mode of thinking that relied on reason and observation of nature Argued that the primary substance of the universe was water.

Anaximenes (c. 6th Century B.C.E.) Presocratic Philosopher. Held the belief that air is the one substance out of which the entire universe is formed.

Heraclitus (c. 540–c. 480 B.C.E.) Presocratic Philosopher. The most influential of Presocratic philosophers; maintained all things were in a constant state of flux and that the governing principle of the universe is what he called *logos*.

Democritus (c. mid 5th–4th Century B.C.E.) Presocratic Philosopher. Advanced the doctrine of atomism maintaining that all matter is composed of indivisible atoms in motion.

Pythagoras (c. 570–c. 497) Presocratic Philosopher. Heavily influential on Plato; maintained that the human soul was immortal and transmigrated after death.

Cicero (106–43 B.C.E.) Roman Orator, Lawyer Politician and Philosopher. Brought philosophy to the people by translating Greeks works into Latin.

Socratic Method Investigation of complex issues through a question-and-answer format.

out of people rather than lecture them. The Roman poet and philosopher **Lucretius** (c. 95–52 B.C.E.) pays homage to Socrates' role ("a man of Greece") in creating modern consciousness in the following passage from his great work *On the Nature of the Universe.*

> When human life lay groveling in all men's sight, crushed to the earth under the dead weight of superstition whose grim features glowered menacingly upon mortals from the four quarters of the sky, a man of Greece was first to raise mortal eyes in defiance, first to stand erect and brave the challenge. Fables of the gods did not crush him, nor the lightning flash and the growling menace of the sky. Rather, they quickened his manhood, so that he, first of all men, longed to smash the constraining locks of nature's doors. The vital vigor of his mind prevailed. He ventured far out beyond the flaming ramparts of the world and voyaged in mind throughout infinity. Returning victorious, he proclaimed to us what can be and what cannot: how a limit is fixed to the power of everything and an immovable frontier post. Therefore superstition in its turn lies crushed beneath his feet, and we by his triumph are lifted level with the skies.

The Socratic Midwife

> *Socrates:* Tell me, Euthydemus, have you ever gone to Delphi?
> *Euthydemus:* Yes, twice.
> *Socrates:* And did you observe what is written on the temple wall—"Know thyself"?
> *Euthydemus:* I did.
> *Socrates:* And did you take no thought of that inscription, or did you attend to it, and try to examine yourself, and ascertain what sort of character you are?

THINK PHILOSOPHICALLY 2.2
Know Thyself

Imagine that walking down the street you encountered Socrates, who engaged you in the following exchange:

> *Socrates:* Tell me, did you go to philosophy class this week?
> *You:* Yes, twice.
> *Socrates:* And did your professor mention the philosophical challenge to "Know thyself"?
> *You:* Yes, my professor did.
> *Socrates:* And did you take no thought of that inscription, or did you attend to it, and try to examine yourself, and ascertain what sort of character you are?
> *You:* (Complete your response in your Philosopher's Notebook.)

This excerpt from **Plato**'s dialogue *Xenophon* expresses one of Socrates' central themes, as well as the approach he preferred to communicate his ideas to others. As we discovered in the first chapter, the keystone to Socrates' philosophy was his conviction that "The unexamined life is not worth living." This is the insight that Socrates wants Euthydemus to understand and embrace, but instead of exhorting or "preaching" to him, Socrates uses a sequence

LUCRETIUS
(c. 94–55 B.C.E.)
Roman Philosopher and Poet. In *On the Nature of the Universe* explains the physics of Epicurianism.

PLATO
(427–347 B.C.E.)
An extraordinarily influential Ancient Greek Philosopher. A student of Socrates, Plato wrote many dialogues featuring Socrates as the main character and dealt with a wide range of philosophical issues such as morality, politics, metaphysics, and epistemology.

of carefully crafted questions to help Euthydemus achieve this understanding by means of his own efforts. "Have you ever gone to Delphi?" An innocent enough question. "Did you observe the inscription written on the wall—'Know thyself?'" Socrates begins to focus in on his central point. "Did you take no thought of that inscription, or did you attend to it . . . ?" In other words, Socrates is asking, did you ignore the inscription so as to continue your life as a sleepwalker, or did you use the message as a catalyst to examine who you are and who you want to become? With three brief questions, Socrates has challenged Euthydemus to think about his life in profound terms. In his role as an educational midwife, Socrates is striving to draw out from Euthydemus a reflective insight that he will take seriously and act on.

The Wisest of Men?

> You remember Chaerephon. From youth upwards he was my comrade. . . . Once he went to Delphi and ventured to put this question to the oracle—he asked if there was any man who was wiser than I. The priestess answered that there was no one.
>
> —*Socrates* in The Apology

In ancient Greece, an oracle was a religious shrine where a specially designated priestess would provide answers on behalf of the gods to questions asked by visitors. The most famous oracle was the oracle at Delphi, which was housed in the great temple to Apollo. This temple was the most sacred sanctuary for the ancient Greeks, and they considered it the center of the world, marking the site with a large conical stone, the *omphalos*, meaning navel or center.

For at least twelve centuries, the oracle at Delphi spoke on behalf of the gods, advising rulers, citizens, and philosophers on everything from their sex lives to affairs of state. The oracle was always a woman, her divine utterances made in response to a petitioner's request. Before a prophetic session, the oracle would descend into a basement cell and breathe in the sacred fumes. Then, in a trance, at times in a frenzy, she would answer questions, give orders, and make prophecies. In a fascinating epilogue, archeologists have recently determined that the oracle probably came under the influence of ethylene—a sweet-smelling gas once used as an anesthetic. In light doses, it produces feelings of aloof euphoria and inspirational visions.

The oracle's announcements exerted wide influence, and one of the most famous and admired was that Socrates was the wisest of men, a pronouncement delivered when he was only thirty years old. Yet as the following passage from Plato's dialogue *The Apology* reveals, Socrates did not accept this authoritative statement at face value. Consistent with his commitment to rational investigation, he set out to gather evidence to prove or disprove its truth.

According to the revered Oracle at Delphi, Socrates was pronounced to be the wisest of men; do you agree with her pronouncement? Why?

Plato, *The Apology*

When I heard of the oracle I began to reflect: What can the god mean by this riddle? I know very well that I am not wise, even the smallest degree. Then what can she mean by saying that I am the wisest of men? It cannot be that he is speaking falsely, for he is a god and cannot lie. For a long time I was at a loss to understand his meaning.

Then, very reluctantly, I turned to seek for it in this manner: I went to a man who was reputed to be wise, thinking that there, if anywhere, I should prove the answer wrong, and meaning to point out to the oracle its mistake, and to say, "You said that I was the wisest of men, but this man is wiser than I am." So I examined the man—I need not tell you his name, he was a politician—but this was the result, Athenians. When I conversed with him I came to see that, though a great many persons, and most of all he himself, thought that he was wise, yet he was not wise. Then I tried to prove to him that he was not wise, though he fancied that he was; and by so doing I made him indignant, and many of the bystanders. So when I went away, I thought to myself, I am wiser than this man: neither of us knows anything that is really worthwhile, but he thinks that he has knowledge when he has not, while I, having no knowledge, do not think that I have. I seem, at any rate, to be a little wiser than he is on this point: I do not think that I know what I do not know. Next I went to another man who was reputed to be still wiser than the last, with exactly the same result. And there again I made him, and many other men, indignant. . . .

Athenians, I must tell you the truth: by the god, this was the result of the investigation which I made at the god's bidding: I found that the men whose reputation for wisdom stood highest were nearly the most lacking in it, while others who were looked down on as common people were much more intelligent. . . .

But, my friends, I believe that the god is really wise, and that by this oracle he meant that human wisdom is worth little or nothing. I do not think that he meant that Socrates was wise. He only made use of my name and took me as an example, as though he would say to men; He among you is the wisest who, like Socrates, knows that in truth his wisdom is worth nothing at all. ▪

This passage articulates Socrates' character and philosophy of life in a fashion consistent with all that we know of him. Rather than basking in the glow of the oracle's pronouncement that there is no wiser man than he, Socrates immediately begins thinking critically:

- What does it mean to say "no one is wiser?"
- Is the statement true, particularly since I don't *believe* that I am so wise?
- How can I go about determining the accuracy of the statement?

For Socrates, everything in human experience should be open to critical scrutiny, not in a negative *destructive* way, but in the *constructive* effort to achieve clearer understanding. Socrates is convinced that *reason* is the path to the truth, not opinion or conjecture, and he is willing to follow rational inquiry wherever it might lead—even if it means demonstrating that he is *not* the wisest man! So he embarks on his own experimental exploration, interviewing the people thought to be the wisest in Athens, using his Socratic Method, which we will analyze in the next section.

The results? Under the penetrating analysis of his questioning inquiry, Socrates discovers that those people thought to be wise are unable to articulate their ideas with clarity, logical soundness, and compelling rationale. In fact, it is their smug self-certainty that has inhibited their search for wisdom—they think they've already achieved it! Socrates' search reveals another element of his character: his obvious delight in unmasking pretension, deflating oversized egos, and revealing the emptiness and illogic of unexamined beliefs.

Characteristically, Socrates concludes that his investigations have not "proven" that he is the wisest man—only that he is "a little wiser" than others because he recognizes his lack of *true wisdom*. This echoes the memorable statement by the Chinese philosopher **Confucius** (sixth to fifth century B.C.E.): "He who knows he is a fool is not a great fool."

Socrates was a very complex person, and when we read Plato's dialogues in which he appears as the main character, we need to be attentive to the many layers of meaning, intricate logic, and subtlety, in his nuanced use of language. Interestingly, Socrates left no writing of his own, so all of what we know about him comes through other sources. The richest source of his ideas comes from the *Dialogues*, short dramas

Confucius (551–479 B.C.E.) Chinese Philosopher and Reformer. His teachings are known as Confucianism and are complied in the *Analects*.

written by Socrates' student and disciple, Plato. Although Plato wrote these masterful and enduring *Dialogues* years after Socrates' death, most experts agree that at least the initial Dialogues (*Euthyphro, The Apology, Crito*) are faithful portrayals of Socrates' ideas. As far as Plato's later *Dialogues* are concerned, there are varying opinions regarding the extent to which they express Socrates' views or Plato's views, though there was undoubtedly a great deal of agreement between the two.

The other major source of our knowledge of Socrates comes from another of his students, **Xenophon** (c. 444–357 B.C.E.), a soldier and writer whose best-known work is his *Memorabilia*. In one of his writings he records Socrates asking him, "Where does one go to learn to become an honest man?" When Xenophon is at a loss for words, Socrates responds, "Come with me and I'll show you."

THINK PHILOSOPHICALLY
Wisdom and Humility

2.3

PHILOSOPHER'S NOTEBOOK

In your Philosophy Notebook, think philosophically regarding Socrates' response to the oracle by responding to the following questions:

- How do you think most people would respond to being told that they are the most intelligent person in their community? Why do you think Socrates reacts as he does?

- In another part of the *Apology*, Socrates explains how he interviewed people who were exceptionally talented in one particular area, such as poetry or the arts. He found that these people believed that "because of their poetry (or other talent), they thought that they were the wisest of men in other matters too, which they were not." Describe several examples of people you know who are talented in one area and who believe that they are exceptionally wise in other areas as well.

- Socrates freely admits that after exposing the errors and ignorance of supposedly "wise" people, they were "indignant." This may be something of an understatement, as according to an eyewitness account by Diogenes Laertius, Socrates frequently provoked opponents to attack him with their fists and tear his hair out, "yet he bore all this ill-usage patiently." Why do you think some people had such negative reactions to Socrates' rational inquiries?

- As we noted, Socrates is a very complex individual. Do you think that he really believes that he is only a "little wiser" than others, and that his advantage is solely due to his acceptance of the fact that he is *not* wise? Why or why not? Why is the admission of ignorance the beginning of wisdom?

Xenophon (c. 444–c. 357 B.C.E.) Ancient Greek Philosopher. A student of Socrates. Many of his works deal with the teachings of Socrates and some are said to be based on actual conversations with Socrates. His *Memorabilia of Socrates* attempts to defend the charges of impiety and corrupting the youth that were brought against Socrates.

Dialectic From the Greek word for "to argue" or "converse," a dynamic exchange or method involving contradiction or a technique for establishing an informed conclusion.

The Socratic Method

For Socrates, philosophy was best practiced in conversation with others, and this was an activity that he engaged in with great enthusiasm. "Conversation" did not simply mean "talking"—it was instead a disciplined and investigative give-and-take, probing complex issues in a question-and-answer format. This dynamic exchange of ideas was characterized by Plato as a **dialectic**, which is derived from a Greek word for conversation, and its goal was to achieve a deep, clear, rationally founded understanding of the most significant areas of human experience: knowledge, justice, morality, religion, beauty, goodness, and the traits of good character such as courage and piety.

In most instances, Socrates would begin with a general definition of an important concept, such as justice, and then use his dialectical method to seek an understanding of the *essential nature* of the central concept. To arrive at this point of clarity, Socrates first worked to clear away the debris of inadequate and inconsistent definitions, typically at the expense of his dialogue partner.

In the following passage from Plato's most famous dialogue, *Republic*, Socrates engages with a formidable opponent, **Thrasymachus** (c. 459–c. 400 B.C.E.), a leading Sophist of the day. The **Sophists** were an influential group of traveling educators who, for a fee, would teach people how to argue persuasively. They were, in general, interested in teaching the rhetorical techniques and tricks needed to win an argument at all costs, rather than determining what was "true" or "right" through collaborative investigation. In this sense, they were diametrically opposed to Socrates' quest for genuine knowledge and universal truth. In fact, many Sophists were "relativists" and "skeptics," philosophical views that contend that knowledge is only a matter of opinion, and truth is always relative to a particular context. From this vantage point, universal truth and genuine knowledge simply don't exist: each person or culture determine their own version of "truth" and "knowledge." Relativism and skepticism are philosophical theories that we will explore in great depth in later chapters.

Before the aggressive Thrasymachus bursts onto the scene in the following passage, Socrates has been having a relatively calm and civilized discussion with a number of participants, considering and discarding a variety of efforts to define the essential nature of "justice."

Plato, *The Republic*

While we had been talking Thrasymachus had often tried to interrupt, but had been prevented by those sitting near him, who wanted to hear the argument concluded; but when we paused . . . he was no longer able to contain himself and gathered himself together and sprang on us like a wild beast, as if he wanted to tear us in pieces. Polemarchus and I were scared stiff, as Thrasymachus burst out and said, "What is all this nonsense, Socrates? Why do you go on in this childish way being so polite about each other's opinions? If you really want to know what justice is, stop asking questions and then playing to the gallery by refuting anyone who answers you. You know perfectly well that it is easier to ask questions than to answer them. Give us an answer yourself, and tell us what you think justice is. And don't tell me that it's duty, or expediency, or advantage, or profit, or interest. I won't put up with nonsense of that sort; give me a clear and precise definition."

In stark contrast to the preceding atmosphere of thoughtful exchanges and mutual respect, Plato portrays Thrasymachus as loud, sarcastic, and insulting, often on the verge of physical violence. This should be interesting!

Plato, *The Republic*

I (Socrates) was staggered by his attack and looked at him in dismay. If I had not seen him first I believe I should have been struck dumb; but I had noticed him when our argument first began to annoy him, and so managed to answer him, saying diffidently: "Don't be hard on us, Thrasymachus. If we have made any mistake in the course of our argument, I assure you we have not done so on purpose. For if we were looking for gold, you can't suppose that we would willingly let mutual politeness hinder our search and prevent our finding it. Justice is much more valuable than gold, and we aren't likely to cramp our efforts to find it by any idiotic deference to each other. I assure you we are doing our best. It's the ability that we lack, and clever chaps like you ought to be sorry for us and not get annoyed with us."

Thrasymachus (c. 459–c. 400 B.C.E.) Ancient Greek Sophist. He is distinguished as a teacher of rhetoric and speechwriter in Athens in the fifth century.

Sophists Influential group of traveling educators who would teach rhetoric and oration for a fee. Many Sophists believed truth to be relative.

Notice how clever Socrates is in handling this aggressive assault. Thrasymachus charges like an angry bull, and Socrates deftly steps aside and lets him go galloping past. It's a form of verbal judo that Socrates perfected: instead of meeting aggression with aggression, or backing down in the face of the onslaught, Socrates turns the aggressive energy of his opponent *against* him, leaving Thrasymachus (in this case) looking foolish when Socrates explains, "If we have made any mistake in the course of our argument, I assure you we have not done so on purpose."

Another thing to note is Socrates' exquisite use of **irony**, a form of rhetoric that has at least two conflicting levels of meaning—a literal or obvious level and a hidden or real level. So when Socrates says, "It's the ability that we lack, and clever chaps like you ought to be sorry for us and not get annoyed with us," there are two messages:

- Literal, obvious meaning   You are much more intelligent than we are, so please be patient with us.

- Hidden, real meaning   You *think* you're more intelligent but you're really a pretentious buffoon, which I intend to demonstrate to everyone here.

Socrates was a master of irony and used it to expertly create a false sense of security in his dialogue partners and create the conditions for unmasking their foolishness and ignorance.

Plato, *The Republic*

Thrasymachus laughed sarcastically, and replied, "There you go with your old affectation, Socrates. I knew it, and I told the others that you would never let yourself be questioned, but go on shamming ignorance and do anything rather than give a straight answer."

"That's because you're so clever, Thrasymachus," I replied, "and you know it. You ask someone for a definition of twelve and add, 'I don't want to be told that it's twice six, or three times four, or six times two, or four times three; that sort of nonsense won't do.' You know perfectly well that no one would answer you on those terms. (This person) would reply, 'What do you mean, Thrasymachus; am I to give none of the answers you mention? If one of them happens to be true, do you want me to give a false one?' And how would you answer him?"

"That's not a fair parallel," he replied.

"I don't see why not," I said: "but even if it is not, we shan't stop anyone else answering like that if he thinks it fair, whether we like it or not."

"So I suppose that is what you are going to do," he said; "you're going to give one of the answers I barred."

"I would not be surprised," said I, "if it seemed to me on reflection to be the right one."

"What if I give you a quite different and far better definition of justice? What plea will you enter then?"

"The plea of ignorance: for those who don't know must learn from those who do."

"You must have your joke," said he, "but you must pay your costs as well." (Thrasymachus is having his own "joke" by suggesting that Socrates pay him his customary fee for "instructing" him.)

"I will when I have any cash."

"The money's all right," said Glaucon; "we'll pay up for Socrates. So let us have your definition, Thrasymachus."

"I know," he replied, "so that Socrates can play his usual tricks, never giving us his own views but always asking others to explain theirs and refuting them."

"But what am I to do?" I asked. "I neither know nor profess to know anything about the subject, and even if I did I've been forbidden to say what I think by no mean (insignificant) antagonist. It's much more reasonable for you to say something, because you say you know, and really have something to say. Do please do me a favour and give me an answer, and don't grudge your instruction to Glaucon and the others here."

Glaucon and the others backed up what I had said, and it was obvious that Thrasymachus was anxious to get the credit for the striking answer he thought he could give: but he went on pretending he wanted to win his point and make me reply. In the end, however, he gave in, remarking, "So this is the wisdom of Socrates: he won't teach anyone anything, but goes round learning from others and is not even grateful."

irony   A form of rhetoric that has at least two conflicting levels of meaning—an obvious one and a hidden one.

To which I replied, "It's quite true, Thrasymachus, to say I learn from others, but it's not true to say I'm not grateful. I am generous with my praise—the only return I can give, as I have no money. You'll see in a moment how ready I am to praise any view I think well founded, for I'm sure the answer you're going to give will be that."

Thrasymachus *is* clever enough to recognize Socrates' preference for having others propose ideas and definitions, which he would then critically analyze through relentless, incisive questioning. Socrates' goal was to achieve a deep understanding of essential truths through the process of uncovering unjustified claims to knowledge, exposing logical inconsistencies, and gradually making his discussion partners aware of their *lack* of rational understanding of things they thought they knew. This dialectical analysis of concepts is unique in recorded history, because it is the first systematic use of reason for its own sake in philosophy. And as Thrasymachus rightly notes, it is very difficult to propose and defend a definition of a complex idea like "justice," particularly when faced with the prospect of being carved up by the surgical blade of Socrates' formidable intelligence. Yet despite his wariness and insistence that Socrates be the one to offer a definition of justice, Thrasymachus can't help taking center stage with what he believes to be the truthful definition of justice.

Plato, *The Republic*

"Listen then," (Thrasymachus) replied. "I define justice or right as what is in the interest of the stronger party. Now where is your praise? I can see you're going to refuse it."

"You shall have it when I (Socrates) understand what you mean, which at present I don't. You say that what is in the interest of the stronger party is right; but what do you mean by interest? For instance, Polydamas the athlete is stronger than us, and it's in his interest to eat beef to keep it; we are weaker than he, but you can't mean that the same diet is in our interest and so right for us."

"You're being tiresome, Socrates," he returned, "and taking my definition in the sense most likely to damage it."

"I assure you I'm not," (Socrates) said: "you must explain your meaning more clearly."

"Well then, you know that some states are tyrannies, some democracies, some aristocracies? And that in each city power is the hands of the ruling class?"

"Yes."

"Each ruling class makes laws that are in its own interest, a democracy democratic laws, a tyranny tyrannical ones and so on; and in making these laws they define as 'right' for their subjects what is in the interest of themselves, the rulers, and if anyone breaks their laws he is punished as a 'wrongdoer.' That is what I mean when I say that 'right' is the same thing in all states, namely the interest of the established ruling class; and this ruling class is the 'strongest' element in each state, and so if we argue correctly we see that 'right' is always the same, the interest of the stronger party. . . . Consider how the just man always comes off worse than the unjust. For instance, in any business relations between them, you won't find the just man better off at the end of the deal than the unjust. Again, in their relations with the state, when there are taxes to be paid the unjust man will pay less on the same income, and when there's anything to be got he'll get it all. Thus if it's a question of office, if the just man loses nothing else he will suffer from neglecting his private affairs; his honesty will prevent him appropriating public funds, and his relations and friends will detest him because his principles will not allow him to push their interests. But quite the reverse is true of the unjust man . . . the man . . . who can make profits in a big way: he's the man to study if you want to find how much more private profit there is in wrong than in right. . . . So we see that injustice, given scope, has greater strength and freedom and power than justice; which proves what I started by saying, that justice is the interest of the stronger party, injustice the interest and profit of oneself."

Thrasymachus has presented a forceful definition of "justice" that is consistent with the Sophist's penchant for skepticism regarding universal truths—namely, there *is* no universal definition of justice. Justice is simply what is in the interest of

Lady Justice embodied in sculpture.

the stronger party, the person (or people) who have the authority to *command* what they think is "just" and "right." We can sum up this view with the aphorism, *Might makes right*. And Thrasymachus provides a rationale that on the surface seems to have some intuitive credibility.

When we examine various cultures around the world and throughout history, it is often the case that the most powerful individuals create a form of government that serves their interests, and make laws to ensure that the general populations act in ways that also contribute to their interests. But the real question that Thrasymachus is not addressing is whether we would consider all of these forms of government equally just. In other words, if we compare a tyrannical form of government, such as Nazi Germany under Adolf Hitler or Russia under Joseph Stalin, with democratic forms of government such as Germany today or the United States, would we consider the tyrannies to be as "just" as the democracies? Although it's true that Hitler and Stalin defined what was "right" in their eyes, does that mean that it was *really* "right"? Or was it a *perversion* of what is truly "right" and "just"?

The same logic applies to the other examples Thrasymachus uses: comparing a "just" (honest) person with an "unjust" (dishonest) person in doing business, paying taxes, and going into politics. Thrasymachus' argument is that a dishonest person will come out on top in business deals, cheat on his taxes, and corruptly use his political position to steal for himself and help his friends. But even if all of this is true, does it prove that the dishonest man is a genuine example of a "just" man, simply because he has accumulated more money through dishonest and corrupt behavior? Just the fact that Thrasymachus uses such terms as *just* and *unjust, honest* and *dishonest*, suggests that these concepts have meaning that goes beyond simply exploiting others and stealing money. The question is, how is Socrates going to reveal the problems inherent in the *might makes right* point of view?

Plato, *The Republic*

"Now," I said, "I understand your meaning, and we must try to find out whether you are right or not. Your answer defines 'right' and 'interest' . . . but adds the qualification "of the stronger party.""

"An insignificant qualification, I suppose you will say."

"Its significance is not yet clear; what is clear is that we must consider whether your definition is true. For I quite agree that what is right is an 'interest'; but you add that it is the interest 'of the stronger party,' and that's what I don't know about and want you to consider."

"Let us hear you."

"You shall," said I. "You say that obedience to the ruling power is right and just?"

"I do."

"And are those in power in the various states infallible or not?"

"They are, of course, liable to make mistakes," he replied.

"When they proceed to make laws, then, they may do the job well or badly."

"I suppose so."

"And if they do it well the laws will be in their interest, and if they do it badly they won't, I take it."

"I agree."

"But their subjects must obey the laws they make, for to do so is right."

"Of course."

"Then according to your argument it is *right* not only to do what is in the interest of the stronger party but also the opposite."

"What do you mean?"

"My meaning is the same as yours, I think. Let us look at it more closely. Did we not agree that when the ruling powers order their subjects to do something they are sometimes mistaken about their own best interest, and yet that it is *right* for the subject to do what his ruler enjoins?"

"I suppose we did."

"Then you must admit that it is *right* to do things that are *not* in the interest of the rulers, who are the *stronger* party; that is, when the rulers mistakenly give orders that will harm them and yet (so you say) it is right for their subjects to obey those orders. For surely, my dear Thrasymachus, in those circumstances it follows that it is 'right' to do the opposite of what you say is right, in that the weaker are *ordered* to do what is against the interest of the stronger."

Plato, *The Republic*

In like a bull, out like a lamb. Socrates has clearly dismantled Thrasymachus' position by reducing it to a contradiction. In logical terms, this form of argument is known by the Latin phrase *reductio ad absurdum*, which means "reducing to absurdity," achieved in this case by forcing Thrasymachus to acknowledge that his view of justice results in believing two contradictory definitions:

- Justice, or the right action, is doing what is in the interest of the stronger.
- Justice, or the right action, is doing what is *not* in the interest of the stronger.

How does Socrates put a clever debater like Thrasymachus in such a logically untenable position? He has led Thrasymachus to state the following:

A. Right actions are what is in the interest of the stronger.

B. Obedience to the ruling power is right.

C. Rulers are liable to make mistakes, issuing laws that are not in their interest.

These three claims can lead to a conflict: a ruler could issue a law against his interest (C), and then by B it is right to follow the law, but by A it is not right to follow the law. Thus Thrasymachus must give up one of the three statements.

Of course, the real problem for Thrasymachus is what we noted earlier: defining "right" as whatever the powers that be say "right" is, does not address the question of whether what they say is "right" and "just" is *really* "right" and "just." That's why Socrates is able to force Thrasymachus to acknowledge the self-contradictory nature of his position—because his definition of "right" and "justice" is not based on a clearly defined standard, but instead is "relative" to human desire, which is notoriously inconsistent.

This brief excerpt reveals the intellectual power of the Socratic Method, as well as the formidable logical and interpersonal skills that Socrates brought to each encounter. Based on all we know, he could be an intimidating and infuriating discussion partner—brilliant, devious, capable of biting sarcasm and irony. It's no wonder that people were drawn to him and his conversational performances, and it is also no surprise that those he had made to look foolish often developed an abiding anger toward him, an accumulated enmity that would end up contributing to his death.

Life at the *Agora*

Imagine: it's a beautiful morning and you decide to take a stroll in the *agora*, the bustling, noisy marketplace of your native Athens. Its a large area, on the north side of the hill of the Acropolis and the **agora** is clearly where the action is. Vendors have set up their stalls and are

Does Might Make Right?

Record your responses to the following questions in your Philosopher's Notebook.

- Describe an incident in which you got into an argument with someone with an aggressive discussion style (à la Thrasymachus). What was the outcome? Then describe how you might have adopted Socrates' "bull fighter" or "jujitsu" style in deflecting the aggression and moving the discussion in a more productive direction. How might the outcome have been different?

- There are many instances in everyday experience when people use a *might makes right* philosophy. For example:
  - "Why should you go to bed now? Because I'm your parent and I said so."
  - "I don't want to hear any more questions about my policy—that is, if you want to keep your job. The right thing for you to do is to follow the procedure I gave you."
  - "I gave you a low grade on your Shakespeare paper because your interpretation simply isn't right: it's too far out of what I consider to be the mainstream of scholarly critique."

Describe an incident in which someone has presented you with a *might makes right* philosophy of justice. Then compose a brief dialogue that explains how Socrates might have handled the situation.

Agora   Open marketplace in Athens, a place where crowds would gather for political speech and discussion.

selling everything you might imagine, and then some, as the comic poet Eubulus (*fl.* fourth century B.C.E.) explains:

> You will find everything sold together in the same place in Athens: figs, witnesses to summonses, bunches of grapes, turnips, pears, apples, givers of evidence, roses, medlars, porridge, honeycombs, chickpeas, lawsuits, beestings-puddings, myrtle, allotment machines, lambs, water clocks, laws, indictments.

What draws you to the *agora* is not the fruits, vegetables, or water clocks, however—it's the spirited conversations that are taking place among the citizens. In fact, the word *agora* is derived from the Greek verb *agoreuein*, which means "to speak," "to address," "to harangue," and that's exactly what you're looking for—food for thought. You make your way to the Stoa of Zeus Eleutherios, a shady colonnaded stretch of the *agora*, and there, as expected, you see a crowd of people clustered around several men engaged in an animated discussion. Even above the general din of the market you can hear the audience laughing and offering comments as they listen intently to the conversation. As you move closer, you see that one of the discussants is a handsome youth, beautifully proportioned and very well-dressed, like many of the men and women at the *agora*. The other man is striking because of his physical unattractiveness: his heavily bearded face frames a balding, knobby head, broad snubbed nose, bulging eyes, and protruding lips. This arresting head is set atop a powerfully built, stocky torso, bowed legs, and a paunch that he himself described as "a stomach rather too large for convenience," that he perennially announces he intends to "dance off." He is clothed in a worn and somewhat tattered cloak, in stark contrast to the exquisite fabric adorning many of those at the market.

This remarkable figure is Socrates, known to all in Athens and widely considered to be the wisest man in Greece. You move closer. As soon as you begin hearing his resonant voice, experiencing the charismatic influence of his persona, and considering the clarity and insight of his ideas, all thoughts of his physical appearance disappear. As Socrates' friend Alcibiades once noted (a man whose life Socrates had saved with uncommon valor during a horrific battle with Sparta), Socrates was like the little statues of the Silens that were sold at the stone-carvers' booths—physically ugly in superficial appearance but "on being opened, are found to have images of the gods inside them." It is clear to you why Socrates is so idolized and respected by so many in Athens, particularly the spirited and intellectual young men. Socrates is a crown jewel in your native city, and you have come to learn and be entertained as he wields his brilliant intellect to, as he explained, "find who is wise and who pretends to be wise but isn't," a quest that he vowed to continue into the afterlife.

The *agora* was Socrates' true home—intellectually, emotionally, spiritually—and he loved the crowds and human energy of this social core, as Xenophon explains: "For early in the morning he used to go to the walkways and gymnasia, to appear in the agora as it filled up, and to be present wherever he would meet with the most people." Once teased by his friend Phaedrus for "never setting foot in the country or going outside the city walls," Socrates rejoined, "Look at it my way, my good friend. It is because I love knowledge, and it is the people in the city who teach me, not the country or the trees."

For the Greeks, philosophy was best practiced with others, probing complex issues through a disciplined and investigative give-and-take, an approach perfected by Socrates in the *Agora*.

Socrates' claim that it was "the people in the city who teach me" seems genuine, as one of his recurring themes was his role as an intellectual "midwife," assisting others in the birth of their ideas. The metaphor of "midwife" is particularly appropriate for Socrates, as this was his mother's profession. Here's a sampling of his statements, each exploring a slightly different dimension of this rich metaphor.

> The obstetrics which I practice is the same as that of all midwives, except that they practice on women, while I do so on men. They deal with the body, and I deal with the mind. . . . I myself am empty of wisdom, which is why the god Apollo makes me attend to the wisdom of others, and prevents me from giving birth myself.

> Both I and my mother were endowed by the gods with a midwife's art; she delivered women, but I deliver young men who are noble and fair. . . . The reproach which is often made against me—that I ask questions of others but have not the wit to answer them myself—is very just. The reason is that god compels me to be a midwife, but forbids me to bring forth.

As a midwife, I attend men and not women, and I look after their souls when they are in labor, and not after their bodies; and the triumph of my art is in thoroughly examining whether the thought which the mind of the young man brings forth is a false idol or a noble and true birth. I was really too honest a man to be a politician and live.

THINK CRITICALLY 2.5

Giving Birth to Ideas

Describe in your Philosopher's Notebook an educational experience you have had in which the teacher was able to help you "give birth" to your own knowledge or understanding. The experience could have been part of your schooling or in some other area of your life. What approach did the teacher use to stimulate you to develop your own independent ideas, rather than employing a more traditional, didactic approach? In what way was this approach analogous to that used by Socrates? How could such an approach be used in courses you are currently taking (or have taken)?

The State of Your Soul

For Socrates, the central concern of philosophy, and indeed each one of us, is the state of the "soul"—our **psyche**. What is the soul? It is your core identity, your unique spirit that makes you distinctively *you*. This is your true self, your authentic personality, your distinctive character. Your soul is the source of your deepest thoughts and highest aspirations, the unique life force that shapes and defines itself through choices made on a daily basis. According to Socrates, your soul is "immortal and imperishable, and after death should continue to exist in another world."

Every soul seeks happiness, Socrates believes, and there is a clearly defined path to achieving happiness, though many don't choose to take it. The only people who are truly happy are those who are virtuous and wise, who live reflective, "examined" lives and strive to behave rightly and justly in every area of their lives. These people create souls that are good, wise, and courageous, and as a result they achieve genuine and lasting happiness.

But many people are not happy, because they have not pursued virtue and wisdom. Out of ignorance, they have devoted their lives to accumulating material possessions, indulging themselves in mindless pleasure, enlarging their reputations and inflating their egos, and using their relationships with others to further their own interests. These are the "sleepwalking" individuals in life, the people who are only going through the motions of living. Rather than creating souls of shimmering virtue and dazzling insight, their souls are diseased and corrupted, their lives lacking significance and happiness.

Psyche Your true self or "soul," which is immortal and imperishable.

VISUAL PHILOSOPHY

What Is the State of Your Soul?

Socrates warned the citizens of Athens against "sleepwalking through life." Do you think citizens of our culture run a similar risk of "rushing through life" without taking time to reflect deeply on the meaning of life and the state of their souls?

It is for this reason that Socrates saw himself as a "physician of the soul," seeking to help cure people of the disease of their spirits. Socrates believed that people were not inherently evil, they were simply unaware of how they *ought* to live in order to achieve what they most desire—happiness and fulfillment. In the following passage, taken from the *Apology*, Socrates explains his life mission to the people sitting in judgment of him.

Plato, *The Apology*   Men of Athens, I honour and love you; but I shall obey God rather than you, and while I have strength I shall never cease from the practice and teaching of philosophy, exhorting anyone whom I meet and saying to him after my manner: You, my friend,—a citizen of the great and mighty and wise city of Athens,—are you not ashamed of heaping up the greatest amount of money and honour and reputation, and caring so little about wisdom and truth and the greatest improvement of the soul, which you never regard or heed at all? And if the person with whom I am arguing, says: Yes, but I do care; then I do not leave him or let him go at once; but I proceed to interrogate and examine and cross-examine him, and if I think that he has no virtue in him, but only says that he has, I reproach him with undervaluing the greater, and overvaluing the less. And I shall repeat the same words to everyone I meet, young and old, citizen and alien, but especially to the citizens. . . .

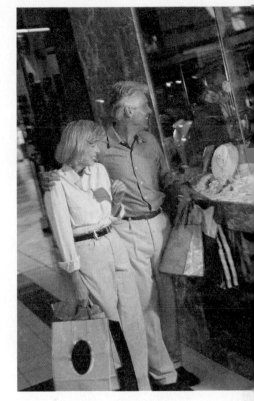

For know that this is the command of the god; and I believe no greater good has happened to this state than my service to the god. For I do nothing but go about persuading you all, old and young alike, not to take thought for your persons or your properties, but first and chiefly to care about the greatest improvement of your soul. I tell you that virtue is not given by money, but that from virtue comes money and every other good of man, public as well as private. This is my teaching.

Socrates' conviction that the improvement of the soul is the central project of philosophy and indeed, the preeminent life project for each one of us, is the foundation of his core teachings:

- *The unexamined life is not worth living.* Socrates was convinced that we have a moral obligation to achieve our full human potential, "actively exercising our soul's powers," which is the Greek definition of happiness (*eudaemonia*). When we live our lives unreflectively, not actively exploring deeper questions such as "Who am I?" and "What is the meaning of my life?" then our lives have diminished value. Yet most disturbing to Socrates was the fact that his fellow citizens so rarely even *posed* these questions, to themselves or to others. They were too busy "living" to wonder *why* they were living or developing a profound understanding of *who* was doing the living. And if Socrates was alive today, it is likely that he would be at least as concerned regarding the "sleepwalking" of people in our culture and world as he was then. The gift of human reason provides us with the extraordinary ability not just to live, but to critically examine our lives in order to make them as productive and worthwhile as possible. If we are to become human in the fullest sense, achieving our distinctive potential and genuine happiness, then we must live "an examined life."

- *The truth lies within each of us.* By living an examined life, we can discover the principles of right thinking and action within us. In our effort to improve our souls and make them more godlike, we need only to apply the divine gift of reason to look deep within ourselves and discover immutable, universal truths. Of course, this process is aided tremendously by engaging in shared explorations with others through dialectical conversations. But the ultimate answers lie within us. Socrates also extends this concept of implicit knowledge to other insights regarding the nature of reality, such as mathematics. In the dialogue *Meno*, he offers a compelling demonstration to his friend Menon to prove that "there is no such thing as teaching, only remembering." He interviews an uneducated Greek slave boy, beginning with the concept of a $2' \times 2'$ square, and then uses a series of skillful questions to successfully elicit some of the basic rules of geometry (for example, If a $2' \times 2'$ space is 4 square feet, what must be the dimensions of an $8'$ space?) Socrates concludes, "Now then, Menon, what do you think? Was there one single opinion which the boy did not give as his own? . . . Then if he did not get them in this life, is it not clear now that he had them and had learnt at some other time?" (*Meno*) Socrates' belief that we each possess implicit knowledge that we can discover through reflective critical analysis of our own minds fits well with his belief in the immortality of the soul: we brought this knowledge with us when our souls entered this life on earth.

- *We should strive for excellence in all areas of life.* As previously mentioned, the Greeks in general and Socrates in particular believed that happiness was a consequence of actively exercising *all* of our soul's powers, and Socrates was a living example of this commitment. History emphasizes the excellence he achieved in developing his intellect and his extraordinary skills as an educator through his ongoing discussions. But he was fully committed to achievement in other areas as well. As a youth Socrates was apprenticed to his father, a sculptor, and according to one tradition, he worked on the masterful *The Three Muses in Their Habits*, which adorned the Acropolis. When the Peloponnesian War broke out with neighboring Sparta, Socrates was drafted into service as a foot soldier (*hoplite*), armed with a shield and a sword. Despite his lowly rank, he distinguished himself with uncommon valor. In the midst of one battle he spied his friend, Alcibiades,

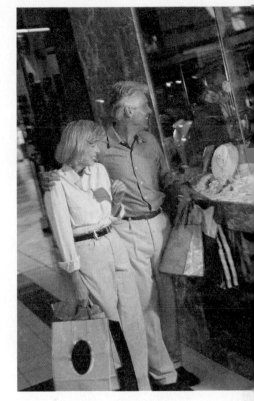

Do you agree with Socrates that "Virtue does not come from wealth, but . . . wealth, and every other good thing which men have, whether in public or in private, comes from virtue." Why?

Socrates believed that we should live examined lives, and strive for excellence in all areas of life, qualities exhibited by the Indian leader Mohandas Gandhi in leading his country to independence. Who would you include as exemplars of these principles?

lying wounded on the ground. He fought his way to him, slung him over his shoulder, and carried him to safety through a mass of armed enemy soldiers. During the battle of Delium, his army broke ranks and retreated before the advancing Spartans. Socrates stood his ground and was the last Athenian soldier to join his comrades. For Socrates, a good and honorable life entailed making full use of all of one's gifts: intellectually, creatively, courageously. And as we shall see, his intellectual and physical courage dominated the final chapter of his life, his trial and execution.

- *No one knowingly does evil.* For Socrates, goodness and wisdom were partners, inextricably connected at their roots. He believed that virtue (**arete**) of the soul is the consequence of knowledge and wisdom (**techne**). It is by determined and clearheaded thinking that we develop an understanding of the rigorous standards of conduct that humans should follow, individually and socially. By training our minds to explore the central questions in life regarding justice, morality, and goodness, we cannot help but become good persons ourselves. Since all people want to be happy, and genuine happiness is the result of living an enlightened, examined life, then people will naturally live morally upright lives so that they can achieve authentic happiness. So why doesn't everyone choose to emulate Socrates' model of virtue and wisdom? Because they are ignorant. They want to be happy, but they are misguided in how to go about achieving this. They believe, like Thrasymachus, that they will become happy by accumulating money, becoming powerful, indulging their senses, or controlling other people. They don't realize that these venal pursuits will not only inhibit their quest for happiness, but also corrupt their souls. Their only hope is to recognize that they need to pursue virtue and wisdom to be genuinely happy, and once they achieve this profound insight, this is the life path that they will choose.

- *"It is better to suffer wickedness than to commit it."* Why be moral? As just noted, Socrates' response is that becoming a moral person is the only way to become a truly happy, psychologically healthy person. Often adages are cliched and empty

Arete   Virtue.

Techne   Wisdom.

of meaning, but for Socrates, the idea that "Virtue is its own reward" contains a substantial measure of truth, a point he expresses in his observation that doing wrong "will harm and corrupt that part of ourselves that is improved by just actions and destroyed by unjust actions." As a thinking individual, you create yourself through the choices that you make much as a sculptor gradually forms a figure through countless cuts of the chisel. If you create yourself as a moral person, you create a person of character and worth, with an acute sense of right and wrong and the power to choose appropriately. But if, out of ignorance, you don't choose to create yourself as a moral person, your soul gradually becomes corrupted. You lose your moral sensitivity, developing a moral blindness that handicaps your ability to see yourself or the world clearly. It is no wonder that Socrates believed that "It is better to suffer wickedness than to commit it." Choosing immorality binds your hands, one loop of thread at a time, until your freedom of movement disappears. Although virtuous people enjoy healthy personalities and spiritual wholeness, immoral people are corrupted at their core, progressively ravaged by a disease of the spirit. And because our soul is immutable and eternal, it is impossible for a virtuous person to ever be harmed by others in any meaningful, lasting sense, and it is for this reason also that, Socrates believes, a virtuous person should have no fear of death.

THINK PHILOSOPHICALLY **2.6**
The Core Teachings of Socrates

PHILOSOPHER'S NOTEBOOK

- When you think about your "self," what image comes to mind? Describe, as best you can, the entity that Socrates refers to as your "soul": that core identity that distinguishes you from every other living creature. Do you think this identity is immortal? Why or why not?

- Socrates posed the following challenge to his fellow citizens: ". . . are you not ashamed of heaping up the greatest amount of money and honour and reputation, and caring so little about wisdom and truth and the greatest improvement of the soul?" Do you think that this challenge is still relevant today? Explain your reasoning.

- Socrates believes that the most important truths already exist within our minds—we need only develop our powers of reflective analysis to discover them. Do you agree with this view? What might be examples of "truths" that exist within every person's mind?

- According to Socrates, no one knowingly does evil. Immoral conduct is always the result of ignorance, and if people are educated regarding the "right" way to act, they will necessarily do it. Do you agree with this view? Have you ever known the "right" thing to do, but suffered from a "failure of will" and ended up doing the wrong thing? If so, how would Socrates analyze your experience?

The Trial and Death of Socrates

Although Socrates lived an exemplary and influential life, if it hadn't been for his trial and ultimate execution, it is very possible that we would not be studying him today. These events were so dramatic and the principles they embodied so profound and timeless, that they elevated Socrates to a near mythic level.

These final extraordinary days in Socrates' life are captured in Plato's dialogue *Apology*, a term that refers to a philosophical defense of an action or viewpoint. At the age of seventy, Socrates finds himself at the court of Athens on trial for his life due to allegations that he has "corrupted the youth" of Athens and that he "does not believe in the gods whom the state believes in, but in other new divinities." As in the case of many political trials of this sort throughout history, these charges were merely a cover for more sinister forces at work. Socrates was indeed unpopular with many influential citizens and political leaders because he had encouraged people throughout his life *not* to blindly accept authority or the pronouncements of self-appointed "wise" people. Instead, in his countless discussions in the *agora*, he insisted by word and example that people think for themselves, and that all ideas be held up to the scrutiny of critical analysis to determine their value and truth. In addition, the aftershocks of the war with Sparta, which Athens had eventually lost, had created political turmoil in which he had inadvertently been caught up. Finally, Socrates was also the target of a vindictive father, Anytus, who was the man behind the charges against him. Several years earlier, the son of Anytus had come to study with Socrates and was so inspired that he decided to pursue philosophy instead of working in the family leather-tanning business. Enraged by his son's decision, Anytus arranged for Meletus, a young, unsuccessful poet with a sarcastic streak, to bring the obviously concocted charges against Socrates. Under Athenian law, Socrates' jury was 501 citizens, a cross-section of the 45,000 free citizens living in Athens.

Let's explore this last and most dramatic chapter in Socrates' life and examine how he applied his philosophical convictions to the greatest challenge he had ever faced. Plato's account of the trial begins at the Court of Justice with an opening statement by Socrates, which is following a statement of the charges against him by his accusers.

Plato, *The Apology*   I cannot tell what impression my accusers have made upon you, Athenians. For my own part, I know that they nearly made me forget who I was, so believable were they; and yet they have scarcely uttered one single word of truth. But of all their many falsehoods, the one which astonished me most was when they said that I was a clever speaker, and that you must be careful not to let me mislead you. I thought that it was most impudent of them not to be ashamed to talk in that way; for as soon as I open my mouth they will be refuted, and I shall prove that I am not a clever speaker in any way at all—unless, indeed, by a clever speaker they mean a man who speaks the truth. If that is their meaning, I agree with them that I am a much greater orator than they. My accusers, then I repeat, have said little or nothing that is true; but from me you shall hear the whole truth. Certainly you will not hear an elaborate speech, Athenians, dressed up, like theirs, with words and phrases. I will say to you what I have to say, without preparation, and in the words which come first, for I believe that my cause is just; so let none of you expect anything else. Indeed, my friends, it would hardly be seemingly for me, at my age, to come before you like a young man with his specious phrases. But there is one thing, Athenians, which I do most earnestly beg and entreat of you. Do not be surprised and do not interrupt with shouts if in my defense I speak in the same way that I accustomed to speak in the market place, at the tables of the moneychangers, where many of you have heard me, and elsewhere. The truth is this. I am more than seventy years old, and this is the first time that I have ever come before a law court; so your manner of speech here is quite strange to me. If I had been really a stranger, you would have forgiven me for speaking in the language and the fashion of my native country; and so now I ask you to grant me what I think I have a right to claim. Never mind the style of my speech—it may be better or it may be worse—give your whole attention to the question, Is what I say just, or is it not? That is what makes a good judge, as speaking the truth makes a good advocate.

These initial remarks reveal a vintage Socrates. Fully aware of Socrates' effectiveness in thinking, reasoning, and persuading, his accusers have attempted to undermine his effectiveness by "warning" the jury not to be misled by his cleverness as a speaker. In logical terms, this is a fallacy known as "poisoning the well," in which the attempt is made to discredit someone's point of view before they even have an opportunity to speak! Socrates recognizes this threat to his credibility, and immediately turns the threat back against his accusers by asserting that his only cleverness is "speaking the truth," and if this is what they mean, then he is indeed "clever." One of the many fascinating qualities of Socrates was the fact that despite the power of his intellect, his language was plain-spoken and direct. He avoided the elaborate and ornate language that the Sophists were prone to use, instead choosing to express himself as clearly as possible. It is for this reason that he asks the court not to object or interrupt him for using his familiar, vernacular form of expression rather than the more formal language customary in the court. Instead, he requests that the court focus solely on the content of what he is saying—is it just or not? After all of those years of conversing with and educating people in every imaginable situation, Socrates cannot resist educating the jury as well, advising them that focusing on the justice of the ideas "is what makes a good judge, as speaking the truth makes a good advocate." In other words, he will speak the truth, they need only concentrate on understanding the justice of his case. "Be careful of Socrates' cleverness." Once again, he has outmaneuvered his opponents with a clearly articulated display of rhetorical artistry.

Socrates then goes on to say,

Plato, *The Apology*

I have to defend myself, Athenians, first against the old false accusations of my old accusers, and then against the later ones of my present accusers. For many men have been accusing me to you, and for very many years, who have not uttered a word of truth; and I fear them more than I fear Anytus and his associates, formidable as they are. But, my friends, those others are still more formidable for they got hold of most of you when you were children, and they have been more persistent in accusing me untruthfully and have persuaded you that there is a certain Socrates, a wise man, who speculates about the heavens, and who investigates things that are beneath the earth, and who can make the weaker reasons appear the stronger. These men, Athenians, who spread abroad this report are the accusers whom I fear; for their hearers think that persons who pursue such inquiries never believe in the gods. Then they are many, and their attacks have been going on for a long time, and they spoke to you when you were at the age most readily to believe them, for you were all young, and many of you were children, and there was no one to answer them when they attacked me. And the most unreasonable thing of all is that I do not even know their names; I cannot tell you who they are except when one happens to be a comic poet. But all the rest who have persuaded you, from motives of resentment and prejudice, and sometimes it may be, from conviction, are hardest to cope with. For I cannot call any one of them forward in court to cross-examine him. I have, as it were, simply to spar with shadows in my defense, and to put questions which there is no one to answer. I ask you, therefore, to believe that, as I say, I have been attacked by two kinds of accusers—first, by Meletus and his associates, and, then, by those older ones of whom I have spoken. And, with your leave, I will defend myself first against my old accusers; for you heard their accusations first, and they were much more forceful than my present accusers are.

Well, I must make my defense, Athenians, and try in the short time allowed me to remove the prejudice which you have been so long a time acquiring. I hope that I may manage to do this, if it be good for you and for me, and that my defense may be successful; but I am quite aware of the nature of my task, and I know that it is a difficult one. Be the outcome, however, as is pleasing to God, I must obey the law and make my defense.

In this passage Socrates is acknowledging the difficulty of overcoming deeply ingrained prejudice. Throughout his life, he contends, there have been those who have spread malicious lies about him, constructing an untrue portrayal of him as one "who speculates about the heavens," "who can make the weaker reasons appear the stronger," and who doesn't "believe in the gods." This prolonged character assassination has been particularly insidious because the young men comprising the

Argument and Persuasion

Imagine that you encounter Socrates emerging from his trial in Athens and he engages you in the following exchange. How would you respond?

Socrates: I had to endure some very unpleasant personal attacks this morning. Fortunately, the power of a well-reasoned argument usually prevails—but not always. Have you ever been in the position of "losing" an argument that you were convinced you were in the right about, because the other person was better equipped to use the persuasive techniques of the Sophists? Can you describe that experience?

You:

Socrates: Why do you think your "opponent" was successful? What techniques of argument did they use against you?

You:

Socrates: If you were confronted with an analogous situation, would you handle it differently? How?

You:

Socrates: One of the attacks against me was trying to "poison my well," attempting to undermine my credibility before I even had an opportunity to make my case. Has this technique ever been used against you? Can you describe it?

You:

Socrates: What do you think is the best way to counter this sort of attack?

You:

Socrates: I have also been the victim of people spreading false and damaging rumors about me. Can you describe a situation in which this has happened to you? Did these rumors influence the opinions of other people toward you?

You:

Socrates: How did you respond to these attacks? How would you respond if they occur in the future?

jury began hearing these lies as children, when their minds were still malleable and their views of the world still being formed. So to judge him fairly, Socrates is warning, they're going to have to think critically by becoming aware of and setting aside their prejudices against him.

One of the most frustrating elements about personal attacks is that the originators tend to create their mischief behind your back rather than confronting you directly, forcing you to "spar with shadows." But Socrates does name one person who, for some reason, conducted a long-running public campaign to ridicule and discredit him: the "comic poet" **Aristophanes** (c. 448–380 B.C.E.), the Greek dramatist who authored such classic plays as *The Birds* and *The Clouds*. For example, in response to Socrates' metaphoric characterization of himself as a "midwife" to men's understanding, Aristophanes contended that too often Socrates produced only a "miscarriage of ideas."

In his play "The Clouds" he even—sarcastically—features Socrates as a major character, a ridiculous airhead with his head "in the clouds." In the following excerpt Aristophanes depicts a country gentleman named Strepsiades visiting Socrates and his pupils at the "Think-shop." Seeing most of the pupils bent over with their noses on the ground, Strepsiades approaches another student:

> **Strepsiades:** What manner of beasts are these? . . . Why are their eyes riveted to the ground?
> **Student:** They are investigating what's under it . . .
> **Strepsiades:** Then why does (that fellow's) rump gaze heavenward?
> **Student:** His secondary interest is astronomy.

Aristophanes' talented wit could certainly make people laugh, and there were undoubtedly those who enjoyed the comic vengeance against someone who had dedicated his life to skewering bloated egos and unmasking pretentious "wise" men in his search for the truth. Although this kind of satire is certainly a legitimate and often harmless form of humor, it can also have a dark side. If you have ever been the target of such ongoing ridicule, you know how hurtful and enraging it can be. And when it is directed against an entire group of people, as is the case of ethnic "jokes" and racial stereotypes, we see the full destructive potential of such "humor."

Socrates continues his defense in the following passage:

Plato, *The Apology*   Let us begin from the beginning, then, and ask what is the accusation which has given rise to the prejudice against me, which was what Meletus relied on when he brought his indictment. What is the prejudice which my enemies have been spreading about me? I must assume that they are formally accusing me, and read their indictment. It would run somewhat in this fashion: Socrates is a wrongdoer who meddles with inquiries into things beneath the earth and in the heavens and who makes the weaker reason appear the stronger, and who teaches others these same things. That is what they say; and in the comedy of Aristophanes (*Clouds*) you yourselves saw a man called Socrates swinging round in a basket and saying that he walked on the air, and prattling a great deal of non-sense about matters of which I understand nothing, either more or less. I do not mean to disparage that kind of knowledge if there is anyone who is wise about these matters. I trust Meletus may never be able to prosecute me for that. But the truth is, Athenians, I have nothing to do with these matters, and almost all of you are yourselves my witnesses of this. I beg all of you who have heard me discussing, and they are many, to inform your neighbors and tell them if any of you have ever heard me discussing such matters, either more or less. That will show you that the other common stories about me are as false as this one.

But the fact is that not one of these is true. And if you have heard that I undertake to educate men, and make money by so doing, that is not true either, though I think that it would be a fine thing to be able to educate men. . . .

Perhaps some of you may reply: But, Socrates, what is the trouble with you? What has given rise to these prejudices against you? You must have been doing something out of the ordinary. All these stories and reports of you would never have arisen if you had not been doing something different from other men. So tell us what it is, that we may not give our verdict in the dark. I think that that is a fair question, and I will try to explain to you what it is that has raised these prejudices against me and given me this reputation. Listen, then: some of you, perhaps, will think that I am joking, but I assure you that I will tell you the whole truth. I have gained this reputation, Athenians, simply by reason of a certain wisdom. But by what kind of wisdom? It is by just that wisdom which is per-haps human wisdom. In that, it may be, I am really wise . . .

You remember Chaerephon. From youth upwards he was my comrade; and also a partisan of your democracy, sharing your recent exile and returning with you. You remember, too, Chaerephon's character—how vehement he was in carrying through whatever he took in hand. Once he went to Delphi and ventured to put this question to the oracle—I entreat you again, my friends, not to interrupt me with your shouts—he asked if there was any man who was wiser than I. The priestess answered that there was no one. Chaerephon himself is dead, but his brother here will confirm what I say.

Astutely, Socrates addresses the common belief "Where there's smoke, there's fire," by undertaking to explain how the campaign to ridicule and discredit him came about. In doing so, he's making use of a very effective discussion strategy, namely, anticipating a potential criticism or counterargument against your posi-tion, and then providing an explanation to counter it.

His explanation is explored earlier in this chapter (pages 50–52). Not con-vinced of the accuracy of the oracle's pronouncement that there was no man wiser than he, Socrates sets out to investigate this claim by interviewing men reputed to be wise. Under the scrutiny of his penetrating questions, he discovers, of course, that these supposed "wise men" are not wise at all. The result of his tenacious ques-tioning and stripping away of arrogance and pretension? His victims and their friends became angry and resentful of Socrates, creating over the years a growing number of people interested in destroying his reputation and ultimately destroying him.

In addition, Socrates had over the years attracted a large number of mainly young disciples who considered him to be "the bravest, most wise and most upright man of our times." Like the son of his chief accuser, Anytus, they sought to emulate him and his questioning techniques, performing the same debunking of false knowledge that their teacher was so fond of. The predictable result was the allega-tion by those unsympathetic to Socrates that he was "corrupting the young."

From this examination, Athenians, has arisen much fierce and bitter indignation, and from this a great many prejudices about me, and people say that I am "a wise man." For the bystanders always think that I am wise myself in any matter wherein I refute another. But, my friends, I believe that the god is really wise and that by this oracle he meant that

Aristophenes (c. 448–385 B.C.E.) Ancient Greek Comic Writer. Commonly satirized the politics, prominent figures, society in general in his comedies. *The Clouds* satirizes Socrates as a person with his head "in the clouds."

Plato, *The Apology*

human wisdom is worth little or nothing. I do not think that he meant that Socrates was wise. He only made use of my name, and took me as an example, as though he would say to men: He among you is the wisest who, like Socrates, knows that in truth his wisdom is worth nothing at all.

Besides this, the young men who follow me about, who are the sons of wealthy persons and have the most leisure, take pleasure in hearing men cross-examined. They often imitate me among themselves; they try their hands at cross-examining other people. And, I imagine, they find plenty of men who think that they know a great deal when in fact they know little or nothing. Then the persons who are cross-examined get angry with me instead of with themselves, and say that Socrates is an abomination and corrupts the young. When they are asked, Why, what does he do? what does he teach? They do not know what to say . . .

What I have told you, Athenians, is the truth: I neither conceal nor do I suppress anything, small or great. Yet I know that it is just this plainness of speech which rouses indignation. But that is only a proof that my words are true, and that the prejudice against me, and the causes of it, are what I have said. And whether you look for them now or hereafter, you will find that they are so.

Having illuminated the accumulated prejudice against him by people whom he has publicly revealed to be "ignorant pretenders to knowledge they don't possess," or those who resent him because of his unvarnished critique of the decadent morals and corrupt political values of many of his fellow citizens, Socrates turns his attention to the matter at hand: the specific charges brought against him by Meletus, the front man for the angry and vindictive tanner, Anytus. It's time for Socrates to demonstrate his Socratic Method to the court, at the expense of Meletus.

Plato, *The Apology*

What I have said must suffice as my defense against the charges of my first accusers. I will try next to defend myself against Meletus, that "good patriot," as he calls himself, and my later accusers. Let us assume that they are a new set of accusers, and read their indictment, as we did in the case of the others. It runs thus. He says that Socrates is a wrongdoer who corrupts the youth, and who does not believe in the gods whom the state believes in, but in other new divinities. Such is the accusation. Let us examine each point in it separately. Meletus says that I do wrong by corrupting the youth. But I say, Athenians, that he is doing wrong, for he is playing a solemn joke by lightly bringing men to trial, and pretending to have zealous interest in matters to which he has never given a moment's thought. Now I will try to prove to you that it is so.

Come here, Meletus. Is it not a fact that you think it very important that the young should be as excellent as possible?

Meletus: It is.

Socrates: Come then, tell the judges who is it who improves them? You care so much, you must know. You are accusing me, and bringing me to trial, because, as you say, you have discovered that I am the corrupter of the youth. Come now, reveal to the gentlemen who improves them. You see, Meletus, you have nothing to say; you are silent. But don't you think that this is shameful? Is not your silence a conclusive proof of what I say—that you have never cared? Come, tell us, my good sir, who makes the young better citizens?

Meletus: The laws.

Socrates: That, my friend, is not my question. What man improves the young, who starts with the knowledge of the laws?

Meletus: The judges here, Socrates.

Socrates: What do you mean, Meletus? Can they educate the young and improve them?

Meletus: Certainly.

Socrates: All of them? Or only some of them?

Meletus: All of them.

Socrates: By Hera, that is good news! Such a large supply of benefactors! And do the listeners here improve them, or not?

Meletus: They do.

Socrates: And do the senators?

Meletus: Yes.

Socrates: Well then, Meletus, do the members of the assembly corrupt the young or do they again all improve them?

Meletus: They, too, improve them.

Socrates: Then all the Athenians, apparently, make the young into good men except me, and I alone corrupt them. Is that your meaning?

Meletus: Most certainly; that is my meaning.

Socrates: You have discovered me to be most unfortunate. Now tell me: do you think that the same holds good in the case of horses? Does one man do them harm and everyone else improve them? On the contrary, is it not one man only, or a very few—namely, those who are skilled with horses—who can improve them, while the majority of men harm them if they use them and have anything to do with them? Is it not so, Meletus, both with horses and with every other animal? Of course it is, whether you and Anytus say yes or no. The young would certainly be very fortunate if only one man corrupted them, and everyone else

To the charge that he has "corrupted the youth of Athens," Socrates responds that with all of the people working to educate and improve young people, how could one individual alone possibly be thought to corrupt them?

did them good. The truth is, Meletus, you prove conclusively that you have never thought about the youth in your life. You exhibit your carelessness in not caring for the very matters about which you are prosecuting me.

Now be so good as to tell us, Meletus, is it better to live among good citizens or bad ones? Answer, my friend. I am not asking you at all a difficult question. Do not the bad harm their associates and the good do them good?

Meletus: Yes.

Socrates: Is there any man who would rather be injured than benefited by his companions? Answer, my good sir; you are obliged by the law to answer. Does nary one like to be injured?

Meletus: Certainly not.

Socrates: Well then, are you prosecuting me for corrupting the young and making them worse, intentionally or unintentionally?

Meletus: For doing it intentionally.

Socrates: What, Meletus? Do you mean to say that you, who are so much younger than I, are yet so much wiser than I that you know that bad citizens always do evil, and that good citizens do good, to those with whom they come in contact, while I am so extraordinarily stupid as not to know that, if I make any of my companions evil, he will probably injure me in some way, and as to commit this great evil, as you allege, intentionally? You will not make me believe that, nor anyone else either, I should think. Either I do not corrupt the young at all or, if I do, I do so unintentionally: so that you are lying in either case. And if I corrupt them unintentionally, the law does not call upon you to prosecute me for an error which is unintentional, but to take me aside privately and reprove and instruct me. For, of course, I shall cease from doing wrong involuntarily, as soon as I know that I have been doing wrong. But you avoided associating with me and educating me; instead you bring me up before the court, where the law sends persons, not for instruction, but for punishment.

What an excellent example of Socrates' ability to slice through confused thinking and emotionally charged generalities to arrive at a clear delineation of the truth! And to do so in such an entertaining way, in a form combining persuasive logic with subtle irony. Socrates begins by engaging Meletus' services in deconstructing the emotionally laden charge that Socrates has been "corrupting the young." Drawing on his years as an educator, Socrates explores the question, "What is the process of shaping a people's thinking and characters?" Meletus quite rightly acknowledges that our development is influenced by numerous people over a long period of time, echoing the African proverb, "It takes a village to raise a child." But if that's the case, Socrates wonders, then how is it possible that he, as a solitary individual, could possibly nullify the influence of all the people the youth of Athens have been taught and influenced by? It's irrational, and defies belief. As Socrates notes: "The young would certainly be very fortunate if only one man corrupted them, and everyone else did them good."

Further, Socrates presses Meletus, what incentive would Socrates have to influence the youth of Athens to be evil rather than good? Creating evil disciples would only end up hurting himself, so it only makes sense to believe that he has been trying to influence people to be good. If he has made mistakes in this quest, they have obviously been unintentional, in which case he should be educated, not punished. But of course the truth is that these are not real charges, they are simply excuses to attempt to hurt Socrates, genuinely "impious" efforts for which he has only contempt:

Plato, *The Apology*

Meletus says that I do wrong by corrupting the youth. But I say, Athenians, that he is doing wrong, for he is playing a solemn joke by lightly bringing men to trial, and pretending to have zealous interest in matters to which he has never given a moment's thought. . . . The truth is, Meletus, you prove conclusively that you have never thought about the youth in your life. You exhibit your carelessness in not caring for the very matters about which you are prosecuting me.

Having demolished the charge of "corrupting the youth," Socrates now addresses the allegation that he "does not believe in the gods whom the state believes in, but in other new divinities."

Plato, *The Apology*

. . . now tell us, Meletus, how do you say that I corrupt the young? Clearly, according to your indictment, by teaching them not to believe in the gods the state believes in, but other new divinities instead. You mean that I corrupt the young by that teaching, do you not?

Meletus: Yes, most certainly I mean that.

Socrates: Then in the name of these gods of whom we are speaking, explain yourself a little more clearly to me and to these gentlemen here. I cannot understand what you mean. Do you mean that I teach the young to believe in some gods, but not in the gods of the state? Do you accuse me of teaching them to believe in strange gods? If that is your meaning, I myself believe in some gods, and my crime is not that of absolute atheism. Or do you mean that I do not believe in the gods at all myself, and I teach other people not to believe in them either?

Meletus: I mean that you do not believe in the gods in any way whatever.

Socrates: You amaze me, Meletus! Why do you say that? Do you mean that I believe neither the sun nor the moon to be gods, like other men?

Meletus: I swear he does not, judges; he says that the sun is a stone, and the moon earth.

Socrates: My dear Meletus, do you think that you are prosecuting Anaxagoras? (*a pre-Socratic philosopher who believed that the entire universe is composed of matter in motion*) You must have a very poor opinion of these men, and think them illiterate, if you imagine that they do not know that the works of **Anaxagoras** of Clazomenae are full of these doctrines. And so young men

Influences on Character

Consider Socrates' central argument regarding education: would you agree that the formation of a person's thinking and character is typically the result of many influences throughout their lives? What influences have shaped your own personal development as an individual? Can you think of an example in which a single individual working in opposition to positive forces was able to corrupt someone? Some people believe that cult leaders are able to exert a brainwashing kind of influence on individuals. Contrast how their techniques for mind control are different from Socrates' method of questioning and dialectical exploration.

learn these things from me, when they can often buy places in the theatre for a drachma at most, and laugh at Socrates were he to pretend that these doctrines, which are very peculiar doctrines, too, were his own. But please tell me, do you really think that I do not believe in the gods at all?

Meletus: Most certainly I do. You are a complete atheist.

Socrates: No one believes that, Meletus, not even you yourself. It seems to me, Athenians, that Meletus is very insolent and reckless, and that he is prosecuting me simply out of insolence, recklessness and youthful bravado. For he seems to be testing me, by asking me a riddle that has no answer. Will this wise Socrates, he says to himself, see that I am joking and contradicting myself? Or shall I outwit him and everyone else who hears me? Meletus seems to me to contradict himself in his indictment: it is as if he were to say, Socrates is a wrongdoer who does not believe in the gods, but who believes in the gods. But that is mere joking.

Now, my friends, let us see why I think that this is his meaning. Do you answer me, Meletus; and do you, Athenians, remember the request which I made to you at the start, and do not interrupt me with shouts if I talk in my usual way.

Is there any man, Meletus, who believes in the existence of things pertaining to men and not in the existence of men? Make him answer the question, my friends, without these interruptions. Is there any man who believes in the existence of horsemanship and not in the existence of horses? Or in flute-playing and not in flute-players? There is not, my friend. If you will not answer, I will tell both you and the judges. But you must answer my next question. Is there any man who believes in the existence of divine things and not in the existence of divinities?

Meletus: There is not.

Socrates: I am very glad that these gentlemen have managed to extract an answer from you. Well then, you say that I believe in divine beings, whether they be old or new ones, and that I teach others to believe in them; at any rate, according to your statement, I believe in divine beings. That you have sworn in your indictment. But if I believe in divine beings, I suppose it follows necessarily that I believe in divinities. Is it not so? It is. I assume that you grant that, as you do not answer. But do we not believe that divinities are either gods themselves or the children of gods? Do you admit that?

Meletus: I do.

Socrates: Then you admit that I believe in divinities. Now, if these divinities are gods, then, as I say, you are joking and asking a riddle, and asserting that I do not believe in the gods, and at the same time that I do, since I believe in divinities. . . . You must have indicted me in this manner, Meletus, either to test me or because you could not find any crime that you could accuse me of with truth. But you will never contrive to persuade any man with any sense at all that a belief in divine things and things of the gods does not necessarily involve a belief in divinities, and in the gods, and in heroes.

But in truth, Athenians, I do not think that I need say very much to prove that I have not committed the crime for which Meletus is prosecuting me. What I have said is enough to prove that. But I repeat it is certainly true, as I have already told you, that I have aroused much indignation. That is what will cause my condemnation if I am condemned; not Meletus nor Anytus either, but that prejudice and suspicion of the multitude which have been the destruction of many good men before me, and I think will be so again. There is no fear that I shall be the last victim.

Socrates wastes no time in demolishing the remaining accusations Meletus has brought against him at the behest of Anytus. He begins by demanding a clear definition of the key concepts under discussion—in this case, the accusation that Socrates is corrupting the young "by teaching them not to believe in the gods the state believes in, but other new divinities instead." In fact, the insistence on "defining your terms" has been a core strategy of philosophy ever since Socrates introduced it. Why is it so important to begin discussions with a clear and precise definition of key terms and concepts? Because those definitions form the bedrock of analysis. If the concepts are permitted to remain vague and ambiguous, it's impossi-

Socrates.

Anaxagoras (500–428 B.C.E.) Presocratic Philosopher. Maintained that what he called Mind (*nous*) was the cause of the ordered universe.

ble to make meaningful progress in the analysis and exploration of those terms. That's exactly why so many discussions and debates go awry, because vague, imprecise definitions encourage each party to "fill in" their own meanings, encouraging miscommunication and conceptual confusion. So Socrates presses Meletus:

Plato, *The Apology*

I cannot understand what you mean. Do you mean that I teach the young to believe in some gods, but not in the gods of the state? Do you accuse me of teaching them to believe in strange gods? If that is your meaning, I myself believe in some gods, and my crime is not that of absolute atheism. Or do you mean that I do not believe in the gods at all myself, and I teach other people not to believe in them either?

Meletus, forced to commit himself to a precise definition of what he means, rather than hiding behind the vague characterization of "corrupting the young by teaching them new divinities," wastes no time in fashioning a semantic noose and hanging himself.

Plato, *The Apology*

I mean that you do not believe in the gods in any way whatever . . . you are a complete atheist.

But Meletus has already acknowledged in his indictment that Socrates believes in some gods—just not the "state-approved" gods. In the same way that Thrasymachus ends up contradicting himself as he struggles to define and redefine "might makes right," so Meletus now finds himself in the position of maintaining that Socrates is a wrongdoer who does not believe in gods, but who believes in the gods. *Reductio ad absurdum!*

Despite administering the coup de grâce to Meletus' feeble argument, Socrates goes on to pursue an intriguing line of reasoning that will foreshadow one of the strongest arguments for the existence of God—the argument by design—used consistently during the past several thousand years. The "argument by design" reasons that

- every dimension of the universe displays design and purpose.
- design and purpose implies a designer who is responsible for creating the design and purpose.
- therefore, God—the supernatural designer—must exist.

Notice how Socrates' line of reasoning echoes the fundamental structure of this argument:

Plato, *The Apology*

Is there any man, Meletus, who believes in the existence of things pertaining to men and not in the existence of men? . . . Is there any man who believes in the existence of horsemanship and not in the existence of horses? Or in flute-playing and not in flute-players? . . . Is there any man who believes in the existence of divine things and not in the existence of divinities?

Socrates concludes this section by noting that although he has conclusively demonstrated his innocence with respect to the charges brought against him, he recognizes those charges are masquerading more sinister forces attempting to destroy him: the anger he has aroused by a lifetime of critically examining the beliefs and values of his fellow citizens, as well as the "prejudice and suspicion of the multitude which have been the destruction of many good men before me, and I think will be so again." This last phrase is a chilling prediction of his soon-to-be-decided fate, a concern underscored by his next sentence, "There is no fear that I shall be the last victim."

Yet despite his belief that he is likely to be found guilty for reasons that had nothing to do with the "official" charges against him, Socrates had no intention of providing the court with an easy way out of the situation they had constructed. He realized that if he promised to cease the philosophical activity that he had practiced for his entire adult life, the court would likely forgo any serious punishment. But he wanted to make clear to them that discontinuing his life work was not an option that he would ever consider. If they were intent on finding him guilty, then they would have to take the responsibility of sentencing him to death.

Plato, *The Apology*

I will never do what I know to be evil, and shrink in fear from what I do not know to be good or evil. Even if you acquit me now, and do not listen to Anytus' argument that, if I am to be acquitted, I ought never to have been brought to trial at all, and that, as it is, you are bound to put me to death because, as he said, if I escape all your sons will be utterly corrupted by practicing what Socrates teaches. If you were therefore to say to me: Socrates, this time we will not listen to Anytus; we will let you go, but on this condition, that you give up this investigation of yours, and philosophy; if you are found following those pursuits again, you shall die. I say, if you offered to let me go on these terms, I should reply: Athenians, I hold you in the highest regard and affection, but I will be persuaded by the god rather than by you; and as long as I have breath and strength I will not give up philosophy and exhorting you and declaring the truth to every one of you whom I meet, saying, as I am accustomed, "My good friend, you are a citizen of Athens, a city which is very great and very famous for its wisdom and strength—are you not ashamed of caring so much for the making of money and for fame and prestige, when you neither think nor care about wisdom and truth and the improvement of your soul?" . . . For know that the god has commanded me to do so. And I think that no greater good has ever befallen you in Athens than my service to the god. For I spend my whole life in going about and persuading you all to give your first and greatest care to the improvement of your souls, and not till you have done that to think of your bodies or your wealth; and telling you that virtue does not come from wealth, but that wealth, and every other good thing which men have, whether in public or in private, comes from virtue. If then I corrupt the youth by this teaching, these things must be harmful; but if any man says that I teach anything else, there is nothing in what he says. And therefore, Athenians, I say, whether you are persuaded by Anytus or not, whether you acquit me or not, be sure I shall not change my way of life; no, not if I have to die for it many times. . . .

Do not interrupt me, Athenians, with your shouts. Remember the request which I made to you, and do not interrupt my words. I think that it will profit you to hear them. I am going to say something more to you, at which you may be inclined to protest, but do not do that. Be sure that if you put me to death, who am what I have told you that I am, you will do yourselves more harm than me. Meletus and Anytus can do me no harm: that is impossible, for I am sure it is not allowed that a good man be injured by a worse. They may indeed kill me, or drive me into exile, or deprive me of my civil rights; and perhaps Meletus and others think those things great evils. But I do not think so. I think it is a much greater evil to do what he is doing now, and to try to put a man to death unjustly. And now, Athenians, I am not arguing in my own defense at all, as you might expect me to do, but rather in yours in order (that) you may not make a mistake about the gift of the god to you by condemning me. For if you put me to death, you will not easily find another who, if I may use a ludicrous comparison, clings to the state as a sort of gadfly to a horse that is large and well-bred but rather sluggish from its size, and needing to be aroused. It seems to me that the god has attached me like that to the state, for I am constantly alighting upon you at every point to rouse, persuade, and reproach each of you all day long. You will not easily find anyone else my friends, to fill my place; and if you are persuaded by me, you will spare my life. You are indignant, as drowsy persons are, when they are awakened, and, of course, if you are persuaded by Anytus, you

Justice and "Mob Mentality"

Can you think of other examples in history in which good men or women have lost their lives as a result of sinister forces and the "mob mentality"? (For example, Jesus, Joan of Arc.) Conduct research on one such person and analyze the similarities to Socrates' situation. Be sure to contrast the "official" reasons why the people were targeted with the "real" reasons they were victimized.

could easily kill me with a single blow, and then sleep on undisturbed for the rest of your lives, unless the god in his care for you sends another to rouse you.

THINK PHILOSOPHICALLY 2.10
Analyzing Socrates

- Explain what Socrates means when he says, "virtue does not come from wealth, but that wealth, and every other good thing which men have, whether in public or in private, comes from virtue." Do you agree with this statement? Why or why not?
- Explain what Socrates means when he says, "Be sure that if you put me to death, who am what I have told you that I am, you will do yourselves more harm than me." Do you agree with this statement? Why or why not?
- Explain why Socrates compares himself to a "gadfly." Identify a person in your life who acts as your own personal Socratic "gadfly," and explain why.
- Identify people in our culture who function as Socratic "gadflies." Select one such person and conduct research to develop more information about him or her that you can share with your classmates.
- Begin thinking about an important principle in your life that you would be willing to risk your life over in a court of law. You will have an opportunity to compose a Socratic dialogue that involves this issue in the final section of the chapter.

Socrates is now ready to make his final statement—his summation—to the court before they pass judgment on him. Although it was common for the accused to plead for mercy and even bring friends and relatives in to induce the sympathy of the judges and jury, Socrates found this sort of conduct distasteful and inappropriate. He felt strongly that the court should render its decision based on a fair and just interpretation of the case against him, a case that he feels was transparently false and laughable.

Plato, *The Apology*   Well, my friends, this, and perhaps more like this, is pretty much what I have to say in my defense. There may be some one among you who will be indignant when he remembers how, even in a less important trial than this, he begged and entreated the judges, with many tears, to acquit him, and brought forward his children and many of his friends and relatives in Court in order to appeal to your feelings; and then finds that I shall do none of these things, though I am in what he would think the supreme danger. Perhaps he will harden himself against me when he notices this: it may make him angry, and he may cast his vote in anger. If it is so with any of you—I do not suppose that it is, but in case it should be so—I think that I should answer him reasonably if I said: My friend, I have relatives too, for, in the words of Homer, "I am not born of an oak or a rock" but of flesh and blood; and so, Athenians, I have relatives, and I have three sons, one of them a lad, and the other two still children. Yet I will not bring any of them forward before you and implore you to acquit me. And why will I do none of these things? It is not from arrogance, Athenians, nor because I lack respect for you—whether or not I can face death bravely is another questions—but for my own good name, and for your good name, and for the good name of the whole state. I do not think it right, at my age and with my reputation, to do anything of that kind. Rightly or wrongly, men have made up their minds that in some way Socrates is different from the mass of mankind. And it will be shameful if those of you who are thought to excel in wisdom, or in bravery, or in any other virtue, are going to act in this fashion. I have often seen men of reputation behaving in an extraordinary way at their trial, as if they thought it a terrible fate to be killed, and as though they expected to live forever if you did not put them to death. Such men seem to me to bring shame upon the state. . . . Those of you, Athenians, who have any reputation at all ought not to do these things, and you ought not to allow us to do them; you should show that you will be much more ready to condemn men who make the state ridiculous by these pitiful pieces of acting, than men who remain quiet.

But apart from the question of reputation, my friends, I do not think that it is right to entreat the judge to acquit us, or to escape condemnation in that way. It is our duty to convince him by reason. He does not sit to give away justice as a favor, but to pronounce judgment; and he has sworn, not to favor any man whom he would like to favor, but to judge according to law. And, therefore, we ought not to encourage you in the habit of breaking your oaths; and you ought not to allow yourselves to fall into this habit, for then neither you nor we would be acting piously. Therefore, Athenians, do not require me to do these things, for I believe them to be neither good nor just nor pious; and, more especially, do not ask me to do them today when Meletus is prosecuting me for impiety. For were I to be successful and persuade you by my entreaties to break your oaths, I should be clearly teaching you to believe that there are no gods, and I should be simply accusing myself by my defense of not believing in them. But, Athenians, that is very far from the truth. I do believe in the gods as no one of my accusers believes in them: and to you and to God I commit my cause to be decided as is best for you and for me.

(He is found guilty by 281 votes to 220.)

Does this photograph of the internment of Japanese citizens in California during World War II illustrate Socrates' characterization of "the prejudice and suspicion of the multitude which have been the destruction of many good men before me, and I think will be so again"? Why?

281 to 220! Looking at this event through our lenses over twenty-five hundred years later, it seems incredible that Socrates could have been found guilty, based on such flimsy, unsubstantiated charges. But the truth is, every culture is vulnerable to powerful emotions that can skew rational judgment. For example, during World War II, irrational fear and ethnic prejudice influenced President Franklin Roosevelt and the U.S. Congress to imprison Japanese American citizens in internment camps for the duration of the war. And several years later, Senator Joseph McCarthy used a widespread fear of Communism to conduct "hearings" that ruined the lives of many innocent citizens, based on unsubstantiated allegations.

When Socrates says, "Rightly or wrongly, many have made up their minds that in some way Socrates is different from the mass of mankind," he is surely speaking the truth. Even in his closing statement, his concern is for the souls of his judges and for Athens in general, for he knows that they will soon regret such an unjust persecution: "And it will be shameful if those of you who are thought to excel in wisdom, or in bravery, or in any other virtue, are going to act in this fashion." He was a person for whom his principles were more important than anything, even his own life.

It is for this reason that Socrates refused to make emotional appeals to the court. Such false appeals have a long and infamous history in human affairs, and they are one of the more popular "fallacies." Fallacies are unsound arguments that are often persuasive because they can appear to be logical and because they usually appeal to our emotions and prejudices. As Socrates points out, appealing to the court for pity or sympathy in order to find him innocent or lessen his punishment is illogical and a violation of their oaths to decide the

Think Critically 2.11

PHILOSOPHER'S NOTEBOOK

Emotional Appeals

Identify some examples of "false appeals to pity" that you have personally experienced: situations in which you or someone else has attempted to override the process of clear thinking by appealing for pity or sympathy. Was the appeal successful? Are there some circumstances in which such appeals are legitimate? Illegitimate?

case based on justice. Although Socrates is convinced that he has proven conclusively that the charges against him are false, he does not want to be found innocent for the wrong—illogical—reasons. For him, a commitment to the principles of clear thinking, logical soundness, and honesty are absolute and unwavering.

In the Athens legal system, once a person was found guilty and a punishment proposed, the convicted person was entitled to propose a lesser punishment. In Socrates case, Meletus and Anytus have asked for the death penalty: an appropriate counterproposal would be on the order of agreeing to exile or paying a substantial fine. Once again, Socrates departs from the norm, and in this instance, it seals his fate.

Plato, *The Apology*

I am not indignant at the verdict which you have given, Athenians, for many reasons. I expected that you would find me guilty; and I am not so much surprised at that as at the numbers of the votes. I certainly never thought that the majority against me would have been so narrow. But now it seems that if only thirty votes had changed sides, I should have escaped. So I think that I have escaped Meletus, as it is; and not only have I escaped him, for it is perfectly clear that if Anytus and Lycon had not come forward to accuse me, too, he would not have obtained the fifth part of the votes, and would have had to pay a fine of a thousand drachmae.

So he proposes death as the penalty. Be it so. And what alternative penalty shall I propose to you, Athenians? What I deserve, of course, must I not? What then do I deserve to pay or to suffer for having determined not to spend my life in ease? I neglected the things which most men value, such as wealth, and family interests, and military commands, and popular oratory, and all the political appointments, and clubs, and factions, that there are in Athens; for I thought that I was really too honest a man to preserve my life if I engaged in these matters. So I did not go where I should have done no good either to you or to myself. I went, instead, to each one of you privately to do him, as I say, the greatest of services, and tried to persuade him not to think of his affairs until he had thought of himself and tried to make himself as good and wise as possible, nor to think of the affairs of Athens until he had thought of Athens herself; and to care for other things in the same manner. Then what do I deserve for such a life? Something good, Athenians, if I am really to propose what I deserve; and something good which it would be suitable to me to receive. Then what is a suitable reward to be given to a poor benefactor who requires leisure to exhort you? There is no reward, Athenians, so suitable for him as a public maintenance in the Prytaneum. It is a much more suitable reward for him than for any of you who has won a victory at the Olympic games with his horse or his chariots. Such a man only makes you seem happy, but I make you really happy; and he is not in want, and I am. So if I am to propose the penalty which I really deserve, I propose this—a public maintenance in the Prytaneum.

Perhaps you think me stubborn and arrogant in what I am saying now, as in what I said about the entreaties and tears. It is not so, Athenians; it is rather that I am convinced that I never wronged any man intentionally, though I cannot persuade you of that, for we have discussed together only a little time. If there were a law at Athens, as there is elsewhere, not to finish a trial of life and death in a single day, I think that I could have persuaded you; but now it is not easy in so short a time to clear myself of great prejudices. But when I am persuaded that I have never wronged any man, I shall certainly not wrong myself, or admit that I deserve to suffer any evil, or propose any evil for myself as a penalty. Why should I? Lest I should suffer the penalty which Meletus proposes when I say that I do not know whether it is a good or an evil? Shall I choose instead of it something which I know to be an evil, and propose that as a penalty? Shall I propose imprisonment? And why should I pass the rest of my days in prison, the slave of successive officials? Or shall I propose a fine, with imprisonment until it is paid? I have told you why I will not do that. I should have to remain in prison, for I have no money to pay a fine with. Shall I then propose exile? Perhaps you would agree to that. Life would indeed be very dear to me if I were unreasonable enough to expect that strangers would cheerfully tolerate my discussions and reasonings when you who are my fellow citizens cannot endure them, and have found them so irksome and odious to you that you are seeking now to be relieved of them. No, indeed, Athenians, that is not likely. A fine life I should lead for an old man if I were to withdraw from Athens and pass the rest of my days in wandering from city to city, and continually being expelled. For I know very well that the young men will listen to me wherever I go, as they do here; and if I drive them away, they will persuade their elders to expel me, and if I do not drive them away, their fathers and kinsmen will expel me for their sakes.

Perhaps someone will say, "Why cannot you withdraw from Athens, Socrates, and hold your peace?" It is the most difficult thing in the world to make you understand why I cannot do that. If I say that I cannot hold my peace because that would be to disobey the god, you will think that I am not in earnest and will not believe me. And if I tell you that no better thing can happen to a man than to discuss virtue every day and the other matters about which you have heard me arguing and examining myself and others, and that an unexamined life is not worth living, then you will believe me still less. But that is so, my friends, though it is not easy to persuade you. And, what is more, I am not accustomed to think that I deserve any punishment. If I had been rich, I would have proposed as large a fine as I could pay: that would have done me no harm. But I am not rich enough to pay a fine unless you are willing to fix it at a sum within my means. Perhaps I could pay you a mina, so I propose that. Plato here, Athenians, and Crito, and Critobulus, and Apollodorus bid me propose thirty minae, and they will be sureties for me. So I propose thirty minae. They will be sufficient sureties to you for the money.

(He is condemned to death by a vote of 361 to 140.)

It's something of an understatement to observe that Socrates' remarks regarding his proposed punishment of death were not well received—eighty men who had voted to find him innocent switched sides to recommend the death penalty! Why? Because Socrates had failed to demonstrate either remorse or respect for the power of the court. It was customary for men facing the death penalty to take extreme measures, pleading for mercy, covering themselves with dirt and tearing their clothes to symbolize their remorse, rolling on the ground while wailing in anguish. Further, they were expected to acknowledge the authority of the court, speaking deferentially and demonstrating their utmost respect. Socrates did none of this. Instead, consistent with his self-proclaimed role as a "gadfly," he revealed the errors of their thinking in convicting him, and warned them against corrupting their souls if they didn't act justly. Rather than propose serious counterpenalties, he recommended that the court award him a special honor for his years of service to Athens and provide him with a pension! Instead of offering to pay a hefty fine, he suggested paying a comparatively miniscule amount (a *minae*), which he asked his friends to increase to 30 minae. In short, Socrates displayed clearly and entertainingly his total contempt for the bogus case that had been brought against him, and his moral disapproval of the role that the judges and jury were playing in the personal vendetta against him. Not surprisingly, the court was not amused, preferring to extinguish the gadfly rather than enduring its ongoing bites.

Despite his unwillingness to adhere to court custom, Socrates does make a compelling case for himself. Why should he be punished if he has "never wronged any man intentionally"? If he has only sought to elevate and enlighten all he came into contact with by having them understand that "an unexamined life is not worth living," why should he propose exile as a punishment, when it would mean, as an old man, wandering strange lands and annoying people who don't know him with his philosophical inquiries? Or why should he propose paying a hefty fine, when it would mean going to prison indefinitely because he did not have the resources to pay for it? And why should he agree to terminate his teaching and philosophical inquiries, because this would mean abandoning his life

What Would I Die For?

Project yourself into Socrates' situation. Knowing that you will face the death penalty unless you can convince the court to be lenient, what would you say in your defense? What counterpenalty would you propose? Would your response be analogous to Socrates'? Why or why not?

work and disobeying the gods he believes have given him a mandate to wake people from their unthinking slumbers? But the judges and jury were in no mood to even hear these questions, much less provide thoughtful responses before passing judgment. Their anger spoke, not their reason, condemning Socrates to death and, ironically, immortality as a martyr to reason and moral principle.

Although many people react to a murder verdict against them with stunned silence, for Socrates it was simply another opportunity to reflect deeply on the human issues that the trial and its outcome provoked.

Plato, *The Apology*

You have not gained very much time, Athenians, and, as the price of it, you will have an evil name for all who wish to revile the state, and they will say that you put Socrates, a wise man, to death. For they will certainly call me wise, whether I am wise or not, when they want to reproach you. If you would have waited for a little while, your wishes would have been fulfilled in the course of nature; for you see that I am an old man, far advanced in years, and near to death. I am saying this not to all of you, only to those who have voted for my death. And to them I have something else to say. Perhaps, my friends, you think that I have been convicted because I was wanting in the arguments by which I could have persuaded you to acquit me, if, that is, I had thought it right to do or to say anything not in arguments, but in impudence and shamelessness—because I would not plead before you as you would have liked to hear me plead, or appeal to you with weeping and wailing, or say and do many other things which I maintain are unworthy of me, but which you have been accustomed to from other men. But when I was defending myself, I thought that I ought not to do anything unworthy of a free man because of the danger which I ran, and I have not changed my mind now. I would very much rather defend myself as I did, and die, than as you would have had me do, and live. Both in a lawsuit and in war, there are some things which neither I nor any other man may do in order to escape from death. In battle, a man often sees that he may at least escape from death by throwing down his arms and falling on his knees before the pursuer to beg for his life. And there are many other ways of avoiding death in every danger if a man is willing to say and to do anything. But, my friends, I think that it is a much harder thing to escape from wickedness than from death, for wickedness is swifter than death. And now I, who am old and slow, have been overtaken by the slower pursuer: and my accusers, who are clever and swift, have been overtaken by the swifter pursuer—wickedness. And now I shall go away, sentenced by you to death; and they will go away, sentenced by truth to wickedness and injustice. And I abide by this award as well as they. Perhaps it was right for these things to be so; and I think that they are fairly measured.

And now I wish to prophesy to you, Athenians, who have condemned me. For I am going to die, and that is the time when men have most prophetic power. And I prophesy to you who have sentenced me to death that a far more severe punishment than you have inflicted on me will surely overtake you as soon as I am dead. You have done this thing, thinking that you will be relieved from having to give an account of your lives. But I say that the result will be very different. There will be more men who will call you to account, whom I have held back, though you did not recognize it. And they will be harsher toward you than I have been, for they will be younger, and you will be more indignant with them. For if you think that you will restrain men from reproaching you for not living as you should, by putting them to death, you are very much mistaken. That way of escape is neither possible nor honorable. It is much more honorable and much easier not to suppress others, but to make yourselves as good as you can. This is my parting prophecy to you who have condemned me.

For those who voted to condemn Socrates to death, his powerful and ominous response must have been disturbing, sowing the first seeds of doubt into what they had just done. Socrates' profound insight into human nature gave him the talent to be an uncanny prognosticator of future events.

You have not gained very much time, Athenians, and, as the price of it, you will have an evil name for all who wish to revile the state, and they will say that you put Socrates, a wise man, to death. For they will certainly call me wise, whether I am wise or not, when they want to reproach you.

Plato, *The Apology*

Socrates seems to understand that despite the people he has annoyed and the enemies he has made, his reputation as a wise and honest man seeking to discover the truth and elevate those around him is secure. And that once the hysteria surrounding his trial has been punctured by his death, the majority of people will come to their senses and recognize the enormous folly—and injustice—of what they have done. This is precisely what happened. Within days following his execution, the city of Athens declared a period of mourning, closing the schools and businesses in honor of their finest citizen. And in an ironic reversal of fortune, his chief accuser, Meletus, was condemned to death, and the chief orchestrator of the trial against him, Anytus the tanner, was banished from Athens. As a crowning tribute, the sculptor Lysippus was commissioned to create a bronze statue that was placed on the Sacred Way.

But Socrates prescience seems to go far beyond the events immediately following his death when he states,

But, my friends, I think that it is a much harder thing to escape from wickedness than from death, for wickedness is swifter than death. And now I, who am old and slow, have been overtaken by the slower pursuer: and my accusers, who are clever and swift, have been overtaken by the swifter pursuer—wickedness. And now I shall go away, sentenced by you to death; and they will go away, sentenced by truth to wickedness and injustice. And I abide by this award as well as they. Perhaps it was right for these things to be so; and I think that they are fairly measured.

Plato, *The Apology*

This last sentence suggests that he understands that his death is necessary in order for his revolutionary beliefs to have their fullest impact on future generations, etching wickedness and righteousness indelibly on the consciousness of mankind. Through death, Socrates rose to archetypal status, his life and death embodying a compelling model for all people to emulate.

THINK PHILOSOPHICALLY 2.13
Analyzing Socrates

Explain what you think Socrates means when he says "it is a much harder thing to escape from wickedness than from death, for wickedness is swifter than death." Can you describe an example of the insight that Socrates was trying to convey?

The painter Jean Louis David's famous painting, "The Death of Socrates," (p. 80) provides a vivid portrayal that imagines the final hours of Socrates' extraordinary life. Surrounded by his grieving family and friends, with the cup of hemlock waiting to be ingested, Socrates is serene, at peace with himself. He reflects on the "prophetic sign" that his been the guiding light in his life, and the comfort it has provided him as he faces death.

"The Death of Socrates," by Jacques Louis David

What are some principles or issues that you would be willing to die for? If you had been convicted unjustly, would you take the opportunity to escape from custody if you could? Why or why not?

Plato, *The Apology*

With you who have acquitted me I should like to discuss this thing that has happened, while the authorities are busy, and before I go to the place where I have to die. So, remain with me until I go: there is no reason why we should not talk with each other while it is possible. I wish to explain to you, as my friends, the meaning of what has happened to me. A wonderful thing has happened to me, judges—for you I am right in calling judges. The prophetic sign has been constantly with me all through my life till now, opposing me in quite small matters if I were not going to act rightly. And now you yourselves see what has happened to me—a thing which might be thought, and which is sometimes actually reckoned, the supreme evil. But the divine sign did not oppose me when I was leaving my house in the morning, nor when I was coming up here to the court, nor at any point in my speech when I was going to say anything; though at other times it has often stopped me in the very act of speaking. But now, in this matter, it has never once opposed me, either in my words or my actions. I will tell you what I believe to be the reason. This thing that has come upon me must be a good; and those of us who think that death is an evil must needs be mistaken. I have a clear proof that that is so; for my accustomed sign would certainly have opposed me if I had not been going to meet with something good.

Confronting death, Socrates is unwavering in his certainty that he has lived a life that is just and true, and he is secure in his confidence that no harm can come to one who has lived such a life. For a just and true individual, death cannot be something to be feared.

And if we reflect in another way, we shall see that we may well hope that death is a good. For the state of death is one of two things: either the dead man wholly ceases to be and loses all consciousness or, as we are told, it is a change and migration of the soul to another place. And if death is the absence of all consciousness, and like the sleep of one whose slumbers are unbroken by any dreams, it will be a wonderful gain. For if a man had to select that night in which he slept so soundly that he did not even dream, and had to compare with it all the other nights and days of his life, and then had to say how many days and nights in his life he had spent better and more pleasantly than this night, I think that a private person, nay, even the great King himself, would find them easy to count, compared with the others. If that is the nature of death, I for one count it a gain. For then it appears that all time is nothing more than a single night. But if death is a journey to another place, and what we are told is true—that there are all who have died—what good could be greater than this, my judges? Would a journey not be worth taking, at the end of which, in the other world, we should be released from the self-styled judges here and should find the true judges who are said to sit in judgment below. . . . And above all, I could spend my time in examining those who are there, as I examine men here, and in finding out which of them is wise, and which of them thinks himself wise when he is not wise. What would we not give, my judges, to be able to examine the leader of the great expedition against Troy, or Odysseus, or Sisyphus, or count-less other men and women whom we could name? It would be an infinite happiness to dis-cuss with them and to live with them and to examine them. Assuredly there they do not put men to death for doing that. For besides the other ways in which they are happier than we are, they are immortal, at least if what we are told is true.

Plato, *The Apology*

And then in an extraordinary moment of personal transcendence, Socrates looks beyond himself and his immanent death to reassure and comfort those close to him. This moment, he explains, was destined by fate and serves a higher purpose than the end of his life. Far from being a tragedy, his death at this moment is the right thing to happen, ordained by the gods and releasing him from the difficulties that are an inescapable part of life. All he asks, as he prepares to drink the hemlock, is that they nurture his sons, treating them in the same way Socrates has treated his friends. And then with calm determination, Socrates embraces his fate, making a final statement that expresses the mystery that each one of us must ultimately confront.

And you, too, judges, must face death hopefully, and believe this as a truth that no evil can happen to a good man, either in life or after death. His fortunes are not neglected by the gods; and what has happened to me today has not happened by chance. I am persuaded that it was better for me to die now, and to be released from trouble; and that was the rea-son why the sign never turned me back. And so I am not at all angry with my accusers or with those who have condemned me to die. Yet it was not with this in mind that they accused me and condemned me, but meaning to do me an injury. So far I may blame them.

Plato, *The Apology*

Yet I have one request to make of them. When my sons grow up, punish them, my friends, and harass them in the same way that I have harassed you, if they seem to you to care for riches or for any other thing more than virtue; and if they think that they are some-thing when they are really nothing, reproach them, as I have reproached you, for not car-ing for what they should, and for thinking that they are great men when really they are worthless. And if you will do this, I myself and my sons will have received justice from you.

But now the time has come, and we must go away—I to die, and you to live. Whether life or death is better is known to God, and to God only. ◼

 Plato, *The Apology*

Making Connections: *Socrates' Legacy*

T his is the only chapter in this book that is devoted to just one philosopher. Why does Socrates merit that distinction, and the careful analysis we have given his life and ideas? Why is he often termed "the father of Western phi-losophy"? Does he deserve this exalted title? Let's examine the evidence so that you can judge for yourself.

- *Socrates was the catalyst for a significant advancement in human consciousness*. Prior to Socrates, thinkers and writers had focused their attention on past events and the physical universe. Taking as his cue the inscription at Delphi, "Know Thyself," Socrates was the first important Western thinker to focus the light of human reason and intelligence on human beings themselves. For the first time in recorded history, humans became the subjects of systematic study—our psyches, our moral aspirations, our relationships with one another, our quest for self-understanding and meaningful lives, our souls. Socrates was in deadly earnest when he announced, "The unexamined life is not worth living."

- *Socrates was an archetypal thinker, a quintessential model of rational inquiry.* Socrates believed in the supreme importance of thinking as well as possible, and for him, everything in human experience was an appropriate subject for exploration and critical analysis. He developed a method of dialectical inquiry that was qualitatively different than anything the world had seen, and which continues to be the bedrock of philosophical thought. Using penetrating questions, Socrates' method insisted on the criteria of logical soundness, clear definitions, consistency, and freedom from self-contradiction. He insisted on

  - establishing clear starting points.
  - viewing issues from multiple perspectives.
  - exploring logical connections and the consequences of beliefs.
  - expressing publicly one's own thinking process and inviting others to respond.
  - being willing to follow the argument wherever it might lead.
  - being open to revising one's opinions based on new insight.

  All of these higher-order intellectual operations have come to be woven into human culture since he taught them over twenty-five hundred years ago.

- *Socrates was committed to making our actions reflect our convictions.* For Socrates, striving to think well meant striving to live well, developing consistent and rigorous standards of conduct and then following through with the choices that we make. For Socrates, there was no distinction between theory and practice, thought and action—in the virtuous person, they are the same. There is an intimate connection between knowledge and virtue, and as we gain intellectual understanding, we should naturally live more enlightened lives.

- *Socrates believed that philosophical inquiry was a social activity.* In contrast to the "ivory tower" dreamer, Socrates found his greatest pleasure engaging in passionate and energetic discussions with others. Socrates was certainly capable of deep, introspective thought. Alcibiades records an incident that occurred when Socrates was in the military. Socrates had arisen early to ponder a particularly difficult problem. He struck a contemplative pose and remained there, oblivious to the world, throughout the day and the following night, to the amazement of his fellow soldiers. But for Socrates, the real testing of one's ideas came through the rough-and-tumble exchanges with others, creating that extraordinary chemistry that results when human minds come into contact with one another.

- *Socrates was a heroic martyr to enlightened thinking and virtuous living.* It wasn't just that he died, but rather that he died *willingly* for the moral principles and values on which his life was constructed. There were numerous ways he could have avoided death, but all of them would have meant betraying his principles and violating his character in some significant way. Not that all great thinkers made the same courageous choice that he did. Some years later, Aristotle, when faced with a similar decision, chose to be exiled from Athens rather than put to death. Galileo, under threat of death from the Catholic Inquisition, recanted his belief that the earth orbits around the sun, and then spent twenty years under house arrest, supposedly doing penance for his "blasphemous" beliefs. But for Socrates, his choice was

Through his influential disciples Plato and Aristotle, Socrates' commitment to rational inquiry became the standard for Western culture and signaled a significant advancement in human consciousness. In addition, as depicted in this 13th century illustration, Aristotle influenced other civilizations as well, serving as the personal tutor to a youthful Alexander the Great.

never in doubt, and he confronted with stirring courage and heart-rending eloquence. As expressed by the writer I. F. Stone, in the prelude of his book *The Trial of Socrates*, "No other trial, except that of Jesus, has left so vivid an impression on the imagination of Western man as that of Socrates."

Socrates' trial, and Plato's literary genius in recreating it with such eloquence and power, epitomizes the eternal struggle between reason and chaos, enlightenment and ignorance, integrity and corruption. I.F. Stone observes near the conclusion of his book,

... His martyrdom, and the genius of Plato, made him a secular saint, the superior man confronting the ignorant mob with serenity and humor. This was Socrates' triumph and Plato's masterpiece. Socrates needed the hemlock, as Jesus needed the Crucifixion, to fulfill a mission.

Socrates seemed to sense that fulfilling his mission on earth meant dying for the beliefs that he had lived for. And it is both his extraordinary life and his memorable death that securely fixes Socrates as an archetypal figure worthy of our thoughtful study and personal emulation.

Students Thinking About Philosophy: *A Socratic Dialogue*

Throughout history people of high moral character have faced punishment, imprisonment, and even death rather than forsake their guiding principles. In Socrates' case, he was unwilling to renounce his commitment to searching for wisdom, examining himself and others, and exhorting others to live virtuously and attend to their souls. Other people have been unwilling to

- renounce their religious beliefs,
- surrender their commitment to personal and political freedom,
- behave in a way that they considered to be immoral.

Think about your deepest convictions for which you would be willing to face imprisonment or death. Imagine yourself in a court setting, similar to Socrates, in which you have one final chance to persuade your accusers that you do not deserve to die, even though you are unwilling to renounce your beliefs. Then compose a Socratic dialogue between yourself and your accusers in which you use penetrating questioning and compelling logic to make your case. Members of the class will act as your jury, deciding whether you have made a strong enough case to survive, or whether you will be condemned.

Your dialogue should be five pages typed and should embody the qualities of Socratic analysis. Included below is a dialogue written by a student who imagines herself as a victim of the Cultural Revolution in China in 1968. She stands accused of subverting the policies of the state, an experience that her father actually experienced. Although her Socratic defense is of a situation in a particular time and place, the themes of freedom of thought and expression are universal.

Socratic Dialogue

Gina Szeto

The Great Proletarian Cultural Revolution was a radical political movement in China that closed schools, slowed production, and virtually severed China's relations with the outside world. Mao Zedong's goals were to rid the schools, the Communist party, the bureaucracy, the army, and the intellectual community of those who opposed him—all of whom he considered "revisionists" determined to lead China back toward middle class capitalism and free enterprise.

Although it was difficult to enter universities before the revolution, I was doing well in school and preparing to take my entrance examination. I was nineteen years old when, in June of 1966, the system of university entrance examinations was halted and the Cultural Revolution closed the doors of learning, jailing the educated and forbidding schooling. The daughter of intellectual parents, I was forced to the countryside—my days filled with a dangerous, relentless pursuit of an education for myself. Although I could not return to school, I began reading books and studying on my own. Most of the books in China were prohibited at the time, so I formed associations with people who smuggled books in and out of closed libraries. As a result of these actions, I am accused of being an anti-revolutionary, a capitalist, a traitor to Red China. These crimes are punishable by death. The year is 1968, the height of the Revolution, and I have been brought before The Court of Justice for trial.

Gina: Two years ago, before the Cultural Revolution began, I was preparing to take my entrance exams. I, like the Red Guards, devoted myself to Mao, never questioning his policies or authority. Since then, my days have been filled with public humiliations and Red Guard raids. My father, like many of yours, has been stoned, beaten, and purged, though I have never seen him act in a way that was disloyal to Mao or China. So why does this country that my father loves so much treat him this way? Why, now that I am at the top of my class, would Mao force me to the countryside and forbid me from learning, from reading, from thinking? I began to question whether my blind devotion to Mao Zedong was more foolish than following the intuitive belief that I, and all Chinese people, had a right to do these things.

I have lived through the failure of the Great Leap Forward, a movement in which millions of our countrymen died because the policies of the party were never questioned. Today, I am living through another movement, larger, more destructive. I will not convince you that I am not guilty of smuggling books out of closed libraries or questioning Mao's policies. I am here today to convince you that I am not a traitor to China. But even more significantly I am here to ask whether a blind adherence to party policies could be more detrimental to China than cultivating a generation to read, think, imagine, and question; to pose questions like What is freedom? What is truth?; and to question how just it is to be incarcerated and put to death for thinking, reading, and learning. I am here today to convince you of our basic right to do these things.

Court: These are questions of a Western mind.

Gina: Too much attention is spent discarding ideas based on criteria that has no relationship to the idea's content. More time needs to be devoted to determining whether the idea is true, if is applicable, and if it is, how it can be put to use. Don't you agree?

Court: In conceiving a Western idea, the assumption is that it will be applied in a Western society, a society that is politically and culturally very different than ours.

Gina: I am in no way implying that we should adopt all political, economic, and social policies endorsed by the West. I am asking if an idea that happens to be Western in origin should be discarded simply because it is Western? What criteria is used to determine the value of an idea?

Court: Mao is the leader of China. His policies and authority should never be questioned, when his authority is questioned, China is questioned, and our society will fall into chaos. This is done for the well being of everyone.

Gina: Is it somewhat naïve to assume that despite countless failed attempts over man's history to resolve the questions of right and wrong, relative and absolute, that only Mao has the answer? The evolution of social and political policies, the constant revision of scientific theories, and the regret, in hindsight, of religious and political actions committed in the name of truth attest to man's, not to mention Mao's, fallibility. Is Mao not also a human, like you and me? Has he, despite his ostensibly good intentions, failed nonetheless? Would he too not suffer if he were tortured, humiliated, and purged in front of his colleagues, family, and friends?

Court: Yes.

Gina: Is it therefore more productive to acknowledge the frailty of the human condition, our uncertainty of our notion of truth, and in so doing, keep our minds, and therefore theories and policies in the public sector, open to progress, flexible in the face of adversity and change? Or is it more productive to construct absolute policies, which are themselves a product of the political and social climate of the time, at the expense of truth, at the expense of our people?

You do not answer because you too have been silently struggling with these questions. Answer: did the Great Leap Forward fail due to a lack of better ideas, because it was impossible to predict the outcome of such ill-conceived policies?

Court: We were not able to question him.

Gina: We were not then, and we cannot now. What are we if we cannot think, rationalize, or question? At the most, animals; at the least, puppets.

Ideas should be judged for the content and efficacy with little regard to their source. New ideas cannot threaten the principles upon which a culture is based if those philosophies are fundamentally true. In science, proof of natural laws, contrary to popular belief, is nearly impossible. Experiments are devised to disprove or rule out theories—it only takes one instance of inconsistent data to invalidate a theory, regardless of its longevity in past investigations. At the same time, numerous instances of data consistent to a hypothesis are not conclusive enough evidence of its truth. If theories in scientific investigations are constantly open to refutation, how can policies that regulate human values, a concept intuitively more subjective and obscure than science, ever be absolute?

Court: Mao has examined all these things for us already. He has taken all the necessary and logical steps to ensure his policies are accurate.

Gina: If we agree that we are a part of and subject to the same complex, covert laws of science, how can an examination of the human condition, our needs, wants, and values, be determined without a thorough, systematic and acute analysis of it? How can we think critically about right from wrong if we are deprived of our ability to read and think? How can we reason for ourselves that Mao is just in depriving us of these intuitively basic rights? How do we know Mao's policies are in fact true? Or more generally, how is any truth found?

Court: It depends.

Gina: Do plants need sunlight to survive?

Court: Yes, plants need the sun to survive.

Gina: How do you know?

Court: From what I see. Plants don't grow well in the dark.

Gina: So you reasoned, from your observation and experience, that plants need sunlight to survive. Observation, experience, and analysis therefore characterize a seemingly mundane inquiry regarding the world we live in. Would you agree that a question concerning a more meaningful aspect of existence, such as "What are fundamental human rights?", might require similar, if not more complex logic to determine? If Mao told us that plants grow best in the dark, don't we have an obligation to investigate that theory? Don't we all have a right to determine truth, however mundane, for ourselves?

Court: Ideally, yes. If everyone sought out to find their "truth" nothing would be accomplished. Immorality would be rampant.

Gina: If one believes that by nature we are corrupt and immoral. A closer and more thoughtful inspection of human nature reveals a universal desire to coexist freely, peacefully, and responsibly. Legislation that takes into consideration these natural inclinations can only produce a community willing to live by those laws. When policies deprive that same community of intuitively basic human rights, like freedom, the community suffers.

Court: How are we depriving them of "intuitively basic human rights"?

Gina: Why were prisons created? As a form of compensation or punishment?

Court: Of course for punishment.

Gina: Why of course?

Court: One's freedom is restricted, one is no longer his own person. He becomes the property of the state, with no voice in society, he no longer exists.

Gina: *"With no voice in society."* So incarceration is not only a physical bondage, but an intellectual one; existence is dependent on a person's ability to not only physically interact with others, but to validate himself intellectually among them.

If a restriction of one's freedom both mentally and physically is considered punishment, freedom, then, in these respects, is considered a good. Is it the natural inclination of all men to exist in this way?

Court: Yes, I suppose.

Gina: Prohibiting books and learning, curtailing education, and forcing youth to the countryside, is a deprivation of freedom both mentally and physically. What have the Chinese people done to warrant such punishment?

Court: They do not know any better.

Gina: If freedom is considered an intuitive good, doesn't going against one's natural inclination produce suffering? Does invoking suffering in others foster loyalty? If a foreign party were capable of overthrowing the existing government, would people who are suffering defend the very government that produces their suffering? Does it seem compassionate to deprive one of an intuitively basic human right?

Court: Survival is not based on compassion.

Gina: True. Then let me ask another question, if the question of compassion is moot, does it seem practical, in terms of survival, to deprive one of their freedom? Meaning, if something similar to the Great Leap Forward were to be proposed today, how could the results, as disastrous as they were, be avoided without the freedom to think or question its effectiveness? In a similar way, how are better policies proposed if one's freedom to think, or freedom to learn, is suppressed?

Court: I don't know.

Gina: Is it more likely that a generation of thinkers educated in history, science, and logic will detect and ultimately rectify unsound economic and social policies, or a generation of illiterate farmers? What is the best defense if and when our country comes under foreign invasion? Is brute force enough or is strategy a necessary component?

Court: Of course strategy is necessary, and Mao will devise those plans.

Gina: And all other proposals are useless. Mao is the brain, and we are his limbs.

Court: It is for the welfare of all.

Gina: If my purpose is simply to exist, to breathe, and not utilize my inherent ability to think, rationalize, or question, then I would rather not live. A sentiment, as you know, shared by the thousands that have committed suicide over the past decade. If this is Mao's purpose for the People's Republic, he would do no worse if more resources were allocated toward building machines and robots, because they will not rebel, they will not fight for the right to be free, because they, unlike us, inherently are not capable of freedom.

Court: How do you know we are free?

Gina: I cannot be certain, philosophically. I can be certain, however, that if I am not free, it is not because Mao Zedong, a man made of flesh and bone, tells me I am not. As much as anyone else tries to repress or contain me by physical means, killing or incarcerating me, they will never defeat me. Defeat only exists when I relinquish my intellectual and emotional judgment to the man you hail the Savior of the People's Republic.

Concept Review

- Socrates, a Greek philosopher who lived twenty-five hundred years ago, created the conceptual framework and method of inquiry for Western consciousness and culture. Among his revolutionary approaches to understanding the social and natural world was to bring philosophy into the marketplace, or *agora*, provoking discussion and debate among people and setting the foundations for academic and political discourse as practiced throughout much of the world today.

- The Socratic Method uses questions and analysis to draw people into an exchange of ideas regarding a central concept, in an attempt to get at the essential nature of that concept. Sometimes coaxing, occasionally sarcastic, and frequently combative, the Socratic Method as practiced by Socrates sought to strip away pretensions, inconsistencies, and false ideas to get at a universal truth.

- Socrates did not leave any writing of his own. What we know of his rhetoric, his style, and his thought has come down to us through the *Dialogues*, a series of dialectical conversations written by Socrates' student Plato.

- Among the opponents of Socrates were the Sophists, educators who believed that "truth" was relative (that is, dependent on context) and "knowledge" merely a matter of opinion.

- Fundamental to Socrates' philosophy is the conviction that every human being has a soul, and that soul is in search of happiness (*eudaemonia*), which is achieved through a life of enlightened thinking and virtuous actions. His core teachings, which speak to this conviction, are

  - "The unexamined life is not worth living."
  - The truth lies within each of us.
  - We should strive for excellence in all areas of life.
  - No one knowingly does evil.
  - "It is better to suffer wickedness than to commit it."

Media Resources

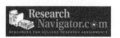 **www.researchnavigator.com**
Chapter 2 examines the life and thoughts of Socrates. It also urges self-reflective thoughts and analysis of the way the world is viewed. For further research on questions on how others have deeply explored the world philosophically and how Socrates has influenced much of human thought, use the tools available to you in Research Navigator.

As you investigate this topic, consider this question: "In what ways have Socrates' ideas implicitly shaped the way you were raised and how is that different from what you think after reading Socrates?"

- **ContentSelect:** search in the Philosophy and Pyschology databases using the search terms "virtue" and "growing up."

- **Link Library:** search in the Philosophy database under terms "intuitionalism" and "Plato."

- **New York Times on the Web:** search in the Philosophy database using the search terms "understanding" and "behavior."

 For additional study resources for this chapter, go to: **www.prenhall.com/chaffee/chapter2**

 The Primary Source: Philosophical Readings and Commentary

Aristophanes: *The Clouds*
Plato: *The Apology; Charmides; Crito; Euthydemus; Euthyphro; Gorgias; Ion; Laches; Phaedo; Protagoras; The Republic*

Who Am I?

Consciousness, Identity, and the Soul

If you would be a real seeker after truth, it is necessary that at least once in your life you doubt, as far as possible, all things.

DESCARTES

The poets and philosophers before me discovered the unconscious. What I discovered was the scientific method by which the unconscious can be studied.

SIGMUND FREUD

Leonardo da Vinci, "De Architectura di Vitruvio" (The Vitruvian Man).
© Scala/Art Resource, NY

Know Thyself?

People travel to wonder at the height of mountains, at the huge waves of the sea, at the long courses of rivers, at the vast compass of the ocean, at the circular motion of the stars, and they pass by themselves without wondering.

ST. AUGUSTINE
Confessions (397–401)

Man is aware of himself, of his past and future, which is death, of his smallness and powerlessness. . . . Man transcends all other life because he is for the first time, life aware of itself.

ERICH FROMM
Man for Himself (1947)

We are unknown, we knowers, ourselves to ourselves; this has good reason. We have never searched for ourselves—how should it then come to pass, that we should ever find ourselves?

FRIEDRICH NIETZSCHE
Genealogy of Morals (1887)

MARCEL PROUST
(1871–1922)
French intellectual and literary figure. Author of several works, including *À la recherché du temps perdu (In Search of Lost Time)* (1913–1922). Satirical and introspective in his work, Proust's central theme involved the affirmation of life.

The cornerstone of Socrates' philosophy was the Delphic Oracle's command to "Know thyself." But what exactly does that mean? Who exactly *is* your "self"? What are the qualities that define it? What differentiates your particular *self* from all others? What is the relation of the *self* you were as a child to the *self* you are now? What is the relation of your *self* to your "body"? How does your *self* relate to other *selves*? What happens to a *self* when the body dies? In what ways is it possible for you to "know" your *self*? In what ways might you never fully know your *self*? What do you mean when you say, "I don't feel like myself today" or when you encourage someone else to "Just be yourself!"

As with many themes and issues in philosophy, the nature of the *self* is a subject that most people take for granted. Many people simply *live*, assuming the existence of their personal self-identity. And when they do think about their *self*, their concerns are typically practical rather than philosophical: How can I make myself happy? How can "I" (shorthand for my "self") develop fulfilling relationships with other selves? How can I improve myself? And so on. Yet when we go searching for our *self* with a philosophical lens, we soon discover that what we thought was a straightforward and familiar presence is in fact elusive, enigmatic, and extraordinarily complex. The French writer **Marcel Proust** captures some of this provocative mystery of the *self* in his novel *In Search of Lost Time* (1913), in which the taste of a madeleine (a kind of cake) provokes memories from his childhood and reflection on the nature of his *self*:

No sooner had the warm liquid mixed with crumbs touched my palate than I stopped, intent upon the extraordinary thing that was happening to me . . . at once the vicissitudes of life had become indifferent to me, its disasters innocuous, its brevity illusory—this new sensation having had on me the effect which love has of filling me with a precious essence; or rather the precious essence was not in me, it WAS me. I had ceased now to feel mediocre, contingent, mortal. Whence could it have come to me, this all-powerful joy? How could I seize and apprehend it? . . . It is plain that the truth I am seeking lies not in the cup but in myself . . . I put down the cup to examine my own mind. It alone can discover the truth. But how? What an abyss of uncertainty, whenever the mind feels overtaken by itself; when it, the seeker, is at the same time the dark region through which it must go seeking and where all its equipment will avail nothing. Seek? More than that: create. It is face to face with something that does not yet exist, to which it alone can give reality and substance, which it alone can bring into the light of day"?

Do you agree with Proust that it is our own minds that "alone can discover the truth"? Why do we experience an "abyss of uncertainty, whenever the mind feels overtaken by itself"? In what sense does our mind "create" the *self* that it is seeking, "face to face with something that does not yet exist, to which it alone can give reality and substance, which it alone can bring into the light of day"?

Developing insight into the nature of the human "self" in general and into your *self* in particular is a daunting task, underscored by the less than successful efforts

VISUAL PHILOSOPHY

Our Faces
Reveal Who
We Are

Who am I? Whom should
I become?

of the best human thinkers for nearly three thousand years. Yet if we are to fulfill Socrates' exhortation to live an examined life, a life of purpose and value, we must begin at the source of all knowledge and significance—our *self*.

 THINK PHILOSOPHICALLY **3.1**
Do I Know Myself?

 PHILOSOPHER'S NOTEBOOK

Answer the following questions regarding your "self" as fully and specifically as you can.

- How would you describe your self?
- What are the qualities that differentiate you from all other selves?
- In what ways has your self changed during the course of your life? In what ways has it remained the same?
- How would you describe the relation of your self to your body?
- How are you able to come to know other selves? Do you think they are similar to or different from you?
- What do you think will happen to your self after you die? If you believe that your self will continue to exist in some form, will you be able to recognize other selves who have died? How?

Did you have difficulty providing in-depth and specific responses to these questions? You should have! The difficulties that you likely encountered are an indication of the philosophical challenges posed by the concept of *self*. As your philo-

This Buddhist funeral dramatizes the profound question, "What happens to the self when the body dies?"

sophical understanding becomes deeper and more sophisticated, your appreciation for the profound nature of these questions will grow as well. Those people who provide simple, ready-made answers to questions like these are likely revealing a *lack* of philosophical understanding. ("Of course I know myself . . . I'm *me*!") So don't be concerned if you find that you are beginning to get confused about subjects like the *self* that you thought you understood—such confusion is the sign of a lively, inquiring mind. As the newspaperman and writer **H. L. Mencken** noted: "To every complex question there's a simple answer—and it is clever, neat, and wrong!"

Your responses also likely reflected the cultural and religious environment in which you were raised. Cultures that originated in Europe have tended to use a common religious and philosophical framework for understanding the "self" that was first introduced by Socrates and Plato in ancient Greece. For example, did your responses reflect the belief that your "self"

- is a unique personal identity that remains the same over time?
- is synonymous with your "soul"?
- is a very different sort of thing from your "body"?
- can be understood by using your reasoning abilities?
- will continue to exist in some form after your body dies?
- is able to connect with other selves in some personal way?

If you found that your responses reflected some (or all) of these beliefs, don't be surprised. These beliefs form the basic conceptual framework for understanding the *self* that has shaped much of Western religious and philosophical thought. So in order to fully appreciate the way our most fundamental views regarding ourselves have been formed, it makes sense for us to return to the birthplace of those views twenty-five hundred years ago, and then to trace the development of these perspectives up to the current century.

H. L. Mencken (1880–1956) American newspaperman, author, and literary and social critic. Born and worked in Baltimore, Maryland; known for humor and biting satire in his work.

Socrates and Plato: *The Soul Is Immortal*

S ocrates was the first thinker in recorded history to focus the full power of reason on the human *self*: who we are, who we should be, and who we will become. Socrates was convinced that in addition to our physical bodies, each person possesses an immortal soul that survives beyond the death of the body. He explored this subject with his friends in the days following his trial and before his sentence of death was executed, a time in his life when the question of immortality no doubt had a special immediacy and significance. The following passage is from Plato's dialogue, *Phaedo*.

Plato, *Phaedo*

> *Socrates:* And were we not saying long ago that the soul when using the body as an instrument of perception, that is to say, when using the sense of sight or hearing or some other sense (for the meaning of perceiving through the body is perceiving through the senses)—were we not saying that the soul too is then dragged by the body into the region of the changeable, and wanders and is confused; the world spins round her, and she is like a drunkard, when she touches change?
>
> *Cebes:* Very true.
>
> *Socrates:* But when returning into herself she reflects, then she passes into the other world, the region of purity, and eternity, and immortality, and unchangeableness, which

are her kindred, and with them she ever lives, when she is by herself and is not let or hindered; then she ceases from her erring ways, and being in communion with the unchanging is unchanging. And this state of the soul is called wisdom?

Cebes: That is well and truly said, Socrates.

Socrates: And to which class is the soul more nearly alike and akin, as far as may be inferred from this argument, as well as from the preceding one?

Cebes: I think, Socrates, that, in the opinion of everyone who follows the argument, the soul will be infinitely more like the unchangeable—even the most stupid person will not deny that.

Socrates: And the body is more like the changing?

Cebes: Yes.

This brief exchange provides a cogent summary of Socrates' metaphysical framework. For Socrates, reality is dualistic, comprised of two dichotomous realms. One realm is changeable, transient, and imperfect, whereas the other realm is unchanging, eternal, immortal. The physical world in which we live—comprised of all that we can see, hear, taste, smell, and feel—belongs to the former realm. All aspects of our physical world are continually changing, transforming, disappearing.

In contrast, the unchanging, eternal, perfect realm includes the intellectual essences of the universe, concepts such as *truth, goodness,* and *beauty.* We find examples of these ideal forms in the physical world—for example, we might describe someone as truthful, good, or beautiful. But these examples are always imperfect and limited: it is only the ideal forms themselves that are perfect, unchanging, and eternal.

Socrates' metaphysical scheme may, at first glance, seem abstract and impractical, but it has a profound impact on the way the *self* is understood. For Socrates, our bodies belong to the physical realm: they change, they're imperfect, they die. Our souls, however, belong to the ideal realm: they are unchanging and immortal, surviving the death of the body. And although a close relationship exists between our souls and our bodies, they are radically different entities.

Our souls strive for wisdom and perfection, and reason is the soul's tool to achieve this exalted state. But as long as the soul is tied to the body, this quest for wisdom is inhibited by the imperfection of the physical realm, as the soul is "dragged by the body into the region of the changeable," where it "wanders and is confused" in a world that "spins round her, and she is like a drunkard." But reason is a powerful tool, enabling the soul to free itself from the corrupting imperfection of the physical realm and achieve "communion with the unchanging."

What is truly remarkable about these ideas is how closely they parallel modern Western consciousness. A finite body, an immortal soul, a perfect, eternal realm with which the soul seeks communion and eternal bliss: all of the basic elements of Western (and some Eastern) religions are present. Even on a secular level, the ideas resonate with modern concepts of the *self:* the notion that the thinking, reasoning *self* and the physical body are radically distinct entities that have a complicated and problematic relationship with one another.

Having described his overall metaphysical vision, Socrates goes on to elaborate his ideas and argue for their plausibility.

Socrates: Yet once more consider the matter in another light: When the soul and the body are united, then nature orders the soul to rule and govern, and the body to obey and serve. Now which of these two functions is akin to the divine? And which to the mortal? Does not the divine appear to you to be that which naturally orders and rules, and the mortal to be that which is subject and servant?

Cebes: True.

Plato, *Phaedo*

Socrates: And which does the soul resemble?

Cebes: The soul resembles the divine, and the body the mortal—there can be no doubt of that, Socrates.

Socrates: Then reflect, Cebes: of all which has been said is not this the conclusion?—that the soul is in the very likeness of the divine, and immortal, and intellectual, and uniform, and indissoluble, and unchangeable; and that the body is in the very likeness of the human, and mortal, and unintellectual, and multiform, and dissoluble, and changeable. Can this, my dear Cebes, be denied?

Cebes: It cannot. ▮

 Plato, *Phaedo*

Although Plato was for the most part committed to the concept of viewing the essence of the self—the soul—as a unified, indissoluble, immortal entity that remains the same over time, he also recognizes the inherent difficulties with this view. In his dialogue *The Symposium*, he cites the views of the female philosopher Diotima, who presents a very different perspective on the nature of the self.

Although we speak of an individual as being the same so long as he continues to exist in the same form, and therefore assume that a man is the same person in his old age as in his infancy, yet although we call him the same, every bit of him is different, and every day he is becoming a new man, while the old man is ceasing to exist, as you can see from his hair, his flesh, his bones, his blood, and all the rest of his body. And not only his body, for the same thing happens to his soul. And neither his manners, nor his dispositions, nor his thoughts, nor his desires, nor his pleasures, nor his sufferings, nor his fears are the same throughout his life, for some of them grow, while others disappear. . . . Thus, unlike the gods, a mortal creature cannot remain the same throughout eternity; it can only leave behind new life to fill the vacancy that is left as it passes away. . . . And so it

◆ VISUAL PHILOSOPHY

The Faces of Michael Jackson

In what sense does the self change as the body changes? In what sense does the self remain the same?

is no wonder that every creature prizes its own offspring, since everything is inspired by this love, this passion for immortality.

This quote penetrates to the core of the problem of personal identity. How is it possible to say that a self remains the same when it is obvious that every self is defined by a process of continual change and evolution? This is visibly apparent in our physical bodies, and contemporary science has revealed that even on the cellular level, old cells are dying and being replaced by new cells on an ongoing basis. In what sense can we say that an infant at the age of six months is the same person at the age of sixty years, when so much of their physical body has changed? And Diotima astutely points out that this same process of continual growth and evolution also defines your "soul." It is analogous to completely renovating an old house, gradually replacing every part of it over time: at what point does it lose its "original" identity and become a "new" house? For Diotima, this dynamic, changing quality of the soul leads her to a very different conclusion than Plato's: unlike the Gods, the human soul is not immortal, though we fervently want it to be. And it is this doomed passion for immortality that inspires the "prizing" of our children. They will become our living legacy as we "leave behind new life to fill the vacancy that is left as it passes away."

THINK PHILOSOPHICALLY 3.2
The Soul and the Self

PHILOSOPHER'S NOTEBOOK

Record your responses to the following questions in your Philosopher's Notebook.

- Compare Socrates' concept of the "soul" with your concept of the *self* which you described in the Think Philosophically activity on page 91. Did you view your "self" as a unified identity that remains the same over time?

  - an indissoluble entity that is immortal and will survive death?
  - an entity that is very different in kind from your physical body?
  - an entity that strives to achieve communion with some ultimate reality?

- In characterizing the relationship between the soul and the body, Socrates explains that the soul uses the body as "an instrument of perception," and that the soul "rules" the body in the same way that the divine rules the mortals. Do you agree with this analysis? Why or why not? How would you characterize the relationship between your soul/*self* and your body?

- Socrates argues that because the soul is of a unified, indissoluble form, we should not be concerned about death because the soul is incapable of being dispersed into nonexistence—it must be eternal. Does this argument address your fears about the potential death of your *self*/soul? Why or why not?

- For Socrates, our physical existence on earth is merely an imperfect reflection of ultimate and eternal reality, and our purpose in life is to achieve communion with this ultimate reality. How do his views compare with your perspective on the purpose of life? Do you believe that our goal in life is to achieve spiritual transcendence and/or intellectual enlightenment? If not, what do you believe is the purpose of your life?

Plato elaborates his concept of the soul (the Greek word is *psyche*) in his later dialogues such as the monumental *Republic* and the *Phaedrus*. In particular, he introduces the idea of a three-part soul/*self* constituted by

- **Reason**—our divine essence that enables us to think deeply, make wise choices, and achieve a true understanding of eternal truths.
- **Physical Appetite**—our basic biological needs such as hunger, thirst, and sexual desire.
- **Spirit or Passion**—our basic emotions such as love, anger, ambition, aggressiveness, empathy.

These three elements of our selves are in a dynamic relationship with one another, sometimes working in concert, sometimes in bitter conflict. For example, we may develop a romantic relationship with someone who is an intellectual companion (Reason), with whom we are passionately in love (Spirit), and whom we find sexually attractive, igniting our lustful appetites (Appetite). Or we may find ourselves in personal conflict, torn between three different relationships, each of which appeals to a different part of our self: Reason, Spirit, Appetite. When conflict occurs, Plato believes it is the responsibility of our Reason to sort things out and exert control, reestablishing a harmonious relationship between the three elements of our selves. Plato illustrates his view of the soul/self in *Phaedrus* with a vivid metaphor: the soul is likened to a winged chariot drawn by two powerful horses: a white horse, representing Spirit, and a black horse, embodying Appetite. The charioteer is Reason, whose task is to guide the chariot to the eternal realm by controlling the two independent-minded horses. Those charioteers who are successful in setting a true course and ensuring that the two steeds work together in harmonious unity achieve true wisdom and banquet with the gods. However, those charioteers who are unable to control their horses and keep their chariot on track are destined to experience personal, intellectual, and spiritual failure. These are themes that we will explore more fully in chapter 4 when we deal with the subjects of human nature and personal freedom.

Plato, *Phaedrus,*
The Chariot Analogy

We will liken the soul to the composite nature of a pair of winged horses and a charioteer. Now the horses and charioteers of the gods are all good and [246b] of good descent, but those of other races are mixed; and first the charioteer of the human soul drives a pair, and secondly one of the horses is noble and of noble breed, but the other quite the opposite in breed and character. Therefore in our case the driving is necessarily difficult and troublesome. Now we must try to tell why a living being is called mortal or immortal. Soul, considered collectively, has the care of all that which is soulless, and it traverses the whole heaven, appearing sometimes in one form and sometimes in another; now when it is perfect [246c] and fully winged, it mounts upward and governs the whole world; but the soul which has lost its wings is borne along until it gets hold of something solid, when it settles down, taking upon itself an earthly body, which seems to be self-moving, because of the power of the soul within it; and the whole, compounded of soul and body, is called a living being, and is further designated as mortal. It is not immortal by any reasonable supposition, but we, though we have never seen [246d] or rightly conceived a god, imagine an immortal being which has both a soul and a body which are

"We will liken the soul to the composite nature of a pair of winged horses and a charioteer:" Do you find Plato's metaphor for the soul to be useful in understanding your *self*? Why?

united for all time. Let that, however, and our words concerning it, be as is pleasing to God; we will now consider the reason why the soul loses its wings. It is something like this.

The natural function of the wing is to soar upwards and carry that which is heavy up to the place where dwells the race of the gods. More than any other thing that pertains to the body [246e] it partakes of the nature of the divine. But the divine is beauty, wisdom, goodness, and all such qualities; by these then the wings of the soul are nourished and grow, but by the opposite qualities, such as vileness and evil, they are wasted away and destroyed. Now the great leader in heaven, Zeus, driving a winged chariot, goes first, arranging all things and caring for all things. [247a] He is followed by an army of gods and spirits, arrayed in eleven squadrons; Hestia alone remains in the house of the gods. Of the rest, those who are included among the twelve great gods and are accounted leaders, are assigned each to his place in the army. There are many blessed sights and many ways hither and thither within the heaven, along which the blessed gods go to and fro attending each to his own duties; and whoever wishes, and is able, follows, for jealousy is excluded from the celestial band. But when they go to a feast and a banquet, [247b] they proceed steeply upward to the top of the vault of heaven, where the chariots of the gods, whose well matched horses obey the rein, advance easily, but the others with difficulty; for the horse of evil nature weighs the chariot down, making it heavy and pulling toward the earth the charioteer whose horse is not well trained. There the utmost toil and struggle await the soul. For those that are called immortal, when they reach the top, [247c] pass outside and take their place on the outer surface of the heaven, and when they have taken their stand, the revolution carries them round and they behold the things outside of the heaven.

But the region above the heaven was never worthily sung by any earthly poet, nor will it ever be. It is, however, as I shall tell; for I must dare to speak the truth, especially as truth is my theme. For the colorless, formless, and intangible truly existing essence, with which all true knowledge is concerned, holds this region [247d] and is visible only to the mind, the pilot of the soul. Now the divine intelligence, since it is nurtured on mind and pure knowledge, and the intelligence of every soul which is capable of receiving that which befits it, rejoices in seeing reality for a space of time and by gazing upon truth is nourished and made happy until the revolution brings it again to the same place. In the revolution it beholds absolute justice, temperance, and knowledge, not such knowledge as has a beginning and varies as it is associated with one [247e] or another of the things we call realities, but that which abides in the real eternal absolute; and in the same way it beholds and feeds upon the other eternal verities, after which, passing down again within the heaven, it goes home, and there the charioteer puts up the horses at the manger and feeds them with ambrosia and then gives them nectar to drink.

Such is the life of the gods; but of the other souls, [248a] that which best follows after God and is most like him, raises the head of the charioteer up into the outer region and is carried round in the revolution, troubled by the horses and hardly beholding the realities; and another sometimes rises and sometimes sinks, and, because its horses are unruly, it sees some things and fails to see others. The other souls follow after, all yearning for the upper region but unable to reach it, and are carried round beneath, [248b] trampling upon and colliding with one another, each striving to pass its neighbor. So there is the greatest confusion and sweat of rivalry, wherein many are lamed, and many wings are broken through the incompetence of the drivers; and after much toil they all go away without gaining a view of reality, and when they have gone away they feed upon opinion. But the reason of the great eagerness to see where the plain of truth is, lies in the fact that the fitting pasturage for the best part of the soul is in the meadow there, and the wing [248c] on which the soul is raised up is nourished by this. And this is a law of Destiny, that the soul which follows after God and obtains a view of any of the truths is free from harm until the next period, and if it can always attain this, is always unharmed; but when, through inability to follow, it fails to see, and through some mischance is filled with forgetfulness and evil and grows heavy, and when it has grown heavy, loses its wings and falls to the earth. ■

Plato

 Plato, *Phaedrus*

Plato believed that genuine happiness can only be achieved by people who consistently make sure that their Reason is in control of their Spirits and Appetites. This harmonious integration under the control of Reason is the essence of Plato's concept of justice, both at the individual level and, as we shall see in chapter 10, at the social and political level as well.

THINK PHILOSOPHICALLY   3.3
Balancing Reason, Appetite, and Spirit
PHILOSOPHER'S NOTEBOOK

- Describe an experience in your life in which you experienced a vigorous conflict between the three dimensions of your *self* identified by Plato: Reason, Appetite, and Spirit. What was the nature of the conflict? How was it resolved?
- Describe an experience in your life in which Reason prevailed over Passion and Appetite. How was Reason able to prevail? Did you gain increased wisdom from the experience?
- Describe an experience in your life in which the three elements of your *self* identified by Plato worked together in a productive and harmonious fashion, enabling you to achieve a great success.

ELIZABETH V. SPELMAN

Barbara Richmond (1940) Professor of the Humanities, Smith College. Prominent figure in both contemporary feminist and African philosophies. Author of several books, including *Inessential Woman: Problems of Exclusion in Feminist Thought* (1988) and *In Repair: The Impulse to Restore in a Fragile World* (2002).

Some contemporary feminist philosophers have criticized Plato for overemphasizing the power and authority of reason, and underemphasizing the importance of the body and emotions. They believe that this view is particularly insidious because Plato—and other traditional philosophers—have tended to identify men with the superior capacity of reason, while relegating women to the "inferior" areas of physical responses and emotions. This perspective is expressed in an excerpt from the essay "Woman as Body" by the philosopher **Elizabeth V. Spelman**.

Elizabeth V. Spelman,
Woman as Body

Plato's Lessons About the Soul and the Body

Plato's dialogues are filled with lessons about knowledge, reality, and goodness, and most of the lessons carry with them strong praise for the soul and strong indictments against the body. According to Plato, the body, with its deceptive senses, keeps us from real knowledge; it rivets us in a world of material things which is far removed from the world of reality; and it tempts us away from the virtuous life. It is in and through the soul, if at all, that we shall have knowledge, be in touch with reality, and lead a life of virtue. Only the soul can truly know, for only the soul can ascend to the real world, the world of the Forms or Ideas.

Plato also tells us about the nature of beauty. Beauty has nothing essentially to do with the body or with the world of material things. *Real* beauty cannot "take the form of a face, or of hands, or of anything that is of the flesh." Yes, there are beautiful things, but they only are entitled to be described that way because they "partake in" the form of Beauty, which itself is not found in the material world. Real beauty has characteristics which merely beautiful *things* cannot have; real beauty

Is an everlasting loveliness which neither comes nor goes, which neither flowers nor fades, for such beauty is the same on every hand, the same then as now, here as there, this way as that way, the same to every worshipper as it is to every other.

Because it is only the soul that can know the Forms, those eternal and unchanging denizens of Reality, only the soul can know real Beauty; our changing, decaying bodies only can put us in touch with changing, decaying pieces of the material world. . . .

Plato's View of the Soul and Body, and His Attitude Toward Women

Plato, and anyone else who conceives of the soul as something unobservable, cannot of course speak as if we could point to the soul, or hold it up for direct observation. At one point, Plato says no mere mortal can really understand the nature of the soul, but one perhaps could tell what it resembles. So it is not surprising to find Plato using many metaphors and analogies to describe what the soul is *like*, in order to describe relations between parts of the soul. For example, thinking, a function of the soul, is described by analogy to talking. The parts of the soul are likened to a team of harnessed, winged horses and their charioteer. The body's relation to the soul is such that we are to think of the body vis-à-vis the soul as a tomb, a grave or prison, or as barnacles or rocks holding down the soul. Plato compares the lowest or body-like part of the soul to a brood of beasts.

But Plato's task is not only to tell us what the soul is like, not only to provide us with ways of getting a fix on the differences between soul and bodies, or differences between parts of the soul. As we've seen, he also wants to convince us that the soul is much more important than the body; and that it is to our peril that we let ourselves be beckoned by the rumblings of the body at the expense of harkening to the call of the soul. And he means to convince us of this by holding up for our inspection the silly and sordid lives of those who pay too much attention to their bodies and do not care enough for their soul; he wants to remind us of how unruly, how without direction, are the lives of those in whom the lower part of the soul holds sway over the higher part. Because he can't *point* to an adulterated soul, he points instead to those embodied beings whose lives are in such bad shape that we can be sure that their souls are adulterated. And whose lives exemplify the proper soul/body relationship gone haywire? The lives of women (or sometimes the lives of children, slaves and brutes).

For example, how are we to know when the body has the upper hand over the soul, or when the lower part of the soul has managed to smother the higher part? We presumably can't see such conflict, so what do such conflicts translate into, in terms of actual human lives? Well, says Plato, look at the lives of women. It is women who get hysterical at the thought of death; obviously, their emotions have overpowered their reason, and they can't control themselves. The worst possible model for young men could be "a woman, young or old or wrangling with her husband, defying heaven, loudly boasting, fortunate in her own conceit, or involved in misfortune or possessed by grief and lamentation—still less a woman that is sick, in love, or in labor." . . .

To anyone at all familiar with Plato's official and oft-reported views about women, the above recitation of misogynistic remarks may be quite surprising. Accounts of Plato's views about women usually are based on what he says in book 5 of the *Republic*. In that dialogue, Plato startled his contemporaries, when as part of his proposal for the constitution of an ideal state, he suggested that

> There is no pursuit of the administrators of a state that belongs to woman because she is a woman or to a man because he is a man. But the natural capacities are distributed alike among both creatures, and women naturally share in all pursuits and men in all. . . .

Well now, what are we to make of this apparent double message in Plato about women? What are we to do with the fact that on the one hand, when Plato explicitly confronts the question of women's nature, in the *Republic*, he seems to affirm the equality of men and women; while on the other hand, the dialogues are riddled with misogynistic remarks? . . . ■

THINK PHILOSOPHICALLY 3.4
Analyzing Elizabeth Spelman

Elizabeth Spelman contends that traditional Western philosophy, beginning with Plato, has tended to view women as more "emotional" than men and thus less able to achieve true knowledge through rational analysis and exploration.

- Do you believe that true knowledge is best achieved through the ability to think logically and rationally? What is the role of emotions—and what the psychologist Daniel Goleman calls "emotional intelligence"—in achieving authentic knowledge? Explain your view and provide examples to support your reasoning.

- Do you think that it is accurate to say, as the author seems to suggest, that in general men are seen as more "logical" and "rational" and women are more "emotional"?

- How would you explain the apparent contradiction in Plato's writings regarding the capacity of women to achieve genuine knowledge and serve in leadership positions?

St. Augustine: *Plato and Christianity*

Plato's (and Socrates') metaphysical views were revolutionary:

- The existence of an immaterial reality separate from the physical world
- The radical distinction between an immaterial soul and physical body
- The existence of an immortal soul that finds its ultimate fulfillment in union with the eternal, transcendent realm

But these ideas would have died with the decline of Greek civilization had they not been adopted and perpetuated by subsequent cultures. The Roman Empire both conquered and absorbed Greek culture, preserving much of its extraordinary accomplishments in the arts, philosophy, and politics. Plato died in 347 B.C.E., and more than five hundred years later a Roman philosopher named **Plotinus** (205–270 C.E.) breathed new life into Plato's ideas, spearheading an intellectual movement that came to be known as **Neoplatonism**. Plotinus based his views on Plato's core concepts believing, for example, that "the soul, since it is a spiritual substance in it own right and can exist independently of the body, possesses a categorical superiority over the body." Plotinus was so fervently committed to his Platonic ideas regarding the imperfection of his physical body, in contrast to the perfection of his eternal soul, that he refused to celebrate his birthday. His reasoning was that he was ashamed that his immortal soul had to be contained in such an imperfect vessel as his body, and that celebrating its birth was a cause for regret, not celebration. Similarly, he refused to have his physical likeness painted or sculpted as he wanted no permanent record of his physical self. His disdain for his body led to his neglect of his physical health, resulting in the loss of his voice and pus-laden sores and abscesses covering his hands and feet. Because he was a teacher with his own school and had a penchant for embracing his students, his physical deterioration ended up driving his students away.

In any case, Plotinus' ideas had a profound influence on the last of the great ancient philosophers, **St. Augustine** (354–430 C.E.), and through him on all of Western consciousness. This extraordinary and far-reaching influence was the result of Augustine integrating the philosophical concepts of Plato with the

Plotinus (205–270 B.C.E.) Roman founder of Neoplatonism, influential in medieval Christian, Islamic, and Renaissance thought. Believed that all being flows from one ultimate and immaterial reality, and that being is expressed in terms of modes of descending order and value: from mind, to soul, to nature.

Neoplatonism Belief that the world emanates from a divine, true being, and that the human soul searches for unity with that divine truth.

tenets of Christianity. Augustine was convinced that Platonism and Christianity were natural partners, going so far as to contend, "If (the Platonists) could have had this life over again with us . . . they would have become Christians, with the change of a few words and statements." He enthusiastically adopted Plato's vision of a bifurcated universe in which "there are two realms, an intelligible realm where truth itself dwells, and this sensible world which we perceive by sight and touch," but then adapted this metaphysic to Christian beliefs. Thus, Plato's ultimate reality, the eternal realm of the Forms, became in Augustine's philosophy a transcendent God. In the same way, Plato's vision of immortal souls striving to achieve union with this eternal realm through intellectual enlightenment became transformed by Augustine into immortal souls striving to achieve union with God through faith and reason. The transient, finite nature of the physical world described by Plato became in Christianity a proving ground for our eternal destinies. Plato's metaphysical framework thus provided philosophical justification for Christian beliefs that might otherwise have been considered farfetched.

Augustine was a complex and fascinating figure. Born to successful parents in northern Africa, he spent much of his youth and young adulthood carousing with friends, indulging in numerous love affairs, and even fathering an illegitimate child. But he also had a powerful and curious intellect, and his explorations ultimately led him to conversion to Christianity when he was thirty-three years old. His personal odyssey is recorded in one of the most extraordinary and compelling books of its kind, his *Confessions*. He spent the remainder of his life in his home country, serving as Bishop of Hippo and writing books and letters that helped shape the theology of Christianity for subsequent centuries.

Like Plato and Plotinus, Augustine believed that the physical body was both radically different from and inferior to its inhabitant, the immortal soul. Early in his philosophical development he describes the body as a "snare" and a "cage" for the soul. He considers the body a "slave" to the soul, and sees their relation as contentious: "The soul makes war with the body." As his thinking matured, Augustine sought to develop a more unified perspective on body and soul. He ultimately came to view the body as the "spouse" of the soul, with both attached to one another by a "natural appetite." He concludes, "That the body is united with the soul, so that man may be entire and complete, is a fact we recognize on the evidence of our own nature." Nevertheless, as for Plato, Plotinus, and all the other Neoplatonists, body and soul remain irreconcilably divided, two radically different entities with diverging fates: the body to die, the soul to live eternally in a transcendent realm of Truth and Beauty.

In melding philosophy and religious beliefs together, Augustine has been characterized as Christianity's first **theologian**, a term derived from the Greek *theos* (God) and *logos* (study of)—the study of God. His ideas defined and shaped the structure of Christianity for the next fifteen hundred years, but by serving as a conduit for Plato's fundamental ideas, Augustine's influence extended beyond Christianity to the cultural consciousness of Western civilization as a whole. We will see his direct impact on the thinking of the next individual we consider, the French philosopher René Descartes. In addition to establishing the groundwork for Descartes' thinking regarding the soul and the body, Augustine also foreshadowed Descartes' theory of knowledge. Engaging in a similar quest for certainty that was to consume Descartes twelve hundred years later, Augustine identified as a first principle, "I am doubting, therefore I am," a statement eerily prescient of Descartes' famous pronouncement, *cogito, ergo sum*—"I think, therefore I am."

St. Augustine of Hippo

ST. AUGUSTINE
(354–430)
Christian philosopher. Augustine's influence on Christian philosophy and theology was unparalleled in the Middle Ages. Augustine's work in philosophy was quite extensive covering many areas such as philosophy of language, philosophy of mind, and the philosophy of religion.

Theology   The study of God or religion.

THINK PHILOSOPHICALLY
Platonic Concepts of the Self

3.5

Though you may not have realized it, many of your fundamental ideas about your *self* have been likely influenced by Plato and Augustine through the cultural consciousness they helped create. Consider your views on the following Platonic concepts:

- There is an immaterial reality that exists separate from the physical world.
- There is a radical distinction between an immaterial soul and physical body.
- There are immortal souls that find their ultimate fulfillment in union with the eternal, transcendent realm (for Augustine, this is God).

In each case, compare and contrast your beliefs with those of Plato and Augustine.

René Descartes: *A Modern Perspective on the Self*

Although Socrates is often described as the "father of Western philosophy," the French philosopher **René Descartes** (1596–1650) is widely considered the "founder of modern philosophy." As profoundly insightful as such thinkers as Socrates, Plato, and St. Augustine were regarding the nature of the *self*, their understanding was also influenced and constrained by the consciousness of their time periods. Descartes brought an entirely new—and thoroughly modern—perspective to philosophy in general and the *self* in particular. Earlier philosophers had focused on exploring the fundamental questions of human existence, such as:

- What is the nature of reality?
- What is the "good life" and how ought we to behave?
- Does God exist? If so, what is God's nature and relation to humankind?
- What is the nature of the soul?
- What is the ideal society?

Although Descartes recognized these as significant questions, he was more concerned with understanding the *thinking process* we use to answer questions such as these. He agreed with the great thinkers before him that the human ability to *reason* constitutes the extraordinary instrument we have to achieve truth and knowledge. But instead of simply *using* reason to try to answer questions, Descartes wanted to penetrate the nature of our *reasoning process* and understand its relation to the human *self*. He was convinced that to develop the most informed and well-grounded beliefs about human existence, we need to be clear about the thinking instrument we are employing. For if our thinking instrument is flawed, then it is likely that our conclusions will be flawed as well.

As an accomplished mathematician (he invented analytic geometry) and an aspiring scientist, Descartes was an integral part of the scientific revolution that was just beginning. (His major philosophical work, *Meditations on First Philosophy*, was published in 1641, the year before Galileo died and Isaac Newton was born.) The foundation of this scientific revolution was the belief that genuine knowledge needed to be based on independent rational inquiry and real-world experimentation. It was no longer appropriate to accept without question the "knowledge"

Descartes applied the geometric method to philosophy.

handed down by authorities—as was prevalent during the religion-dominated Middle Ages. Instead, Descartes and others were convinced that we need to use our own thinking abilities to investigate, analyze, experiment, and develop our own well-reasoned conclusions, supported with compelling proof. In a passage still relevant today, Descartes contrasts the process of learning to construct knowledge by thinking independently with simply absorbing information from authorities.

> For we shall not, e.g., turn out to be mathematicians though we know by heart all the proofs others have elaborated, unless we have an intellectual talent that fits us to resolve difficulties of any kind. Neither, though we may have mastered all the arguments of Plato and Aristotle, if yet we have not the capacity for passing solid judgment on these matters, shall we become Philosophers; we should have acquired the knowledge not of a science, but of history.

René Descartes

But reasoning effectively does not mean simply thinking in our own personal, idiosyncratic ways: that type of commonsense thinking is likely to be seriously flawed. Instead, effective use of "the natural light of reason" entails applying scientific discipline and analytic rigor to our explorations to ensure that the conclusions that we reach have genuine merit.

> So blind is the curiosity by which mortals are possessed, that they often conduct their minds along unexplored routes, having no reason to hope for success . . . it were far better never to think of investigating truth at all, than to do so without a method. For it is very certain that unregulated inquiries and confused reflections of this kind only confound the natural light and blind our mental powers. . . . In (method) alone lies the sum of all human endeavor, and he who would approach the investigation of truth must hold to this rule.

> For to be possessed of good mental powers is not sufficient; the principal matter is to apply them well. The Greatest minds are capable of the greatest vices as well as of the greatest virtues, and those who proceed very slowly may, provided they always follow the straight road, really advance much faster than those who, though they run, forsake it.

 Descartes, René, *Discourse on Method Between Hylas and Philonous*

One of the reasons Descartes is such an influential and enduring figure in philosophy is his willingness to test his reasoning powers to their limit, and to record with absolute candor the results of his explorations. To this end, Descartes typically writes in the first person, inviting us to participate in his reasoning process and compare it with our own. He's saying, in effect: "This is what makes sense to me—do you agree?" In his most well-known work, *Meditations on First Philosophy*, Descartes shares with us his own Philosophical Journal, analogous to the Philosopher's Notebook that you have been encouraged to keep as an integral part of using this text. In an opening passage that virtually every young adult can appreciate, Descartes confesses that he has come to the conclusion that virtually everything he has been taught from authorities and other adults is questionable and likely false. His radical solution? To establish a fresh start on gaining true, well-supported beliefs by simply erasing his endorsement of anything he has previously been taught. What a bold and extraordinary project!

René Descartes,
Mediations on First Philosophy

1. SEVERAL years have now elapsed since I first became aware that I had accepted, even from my youth, many false opinions for true, and that consequently what I afterward based on such principles was highly doubtful; and from that time I was convinced of the necessity of undertaking once in my life to rid myself of all the opinions I had adopted,

Do you agree with Descartes that "If you would be a real seeker after truth, it is necessary that at least once in your life you doubt, as far as possible, all things"?

and of commencing anew the work of building from the foundation, if I desired to establish a firm and abiding superstructure in the sciences. But as this enterprise appeared to me to be one of great magnitude, I waited until I had attained an age so mature as to leave me no hope that at any stage of life more advanced I should be better able to execute my design. On this account, I have delayed so long that I should henceforth consider I was doing wrong were I still to consume in deliberation any of the time that now remains for action. To-day, then, since I have opportunely freed my mind from all cares [and am happily disturbed by no passions], and since I am in the secure possession of leisure in a peaceable retirement, I will at length apply myself earnestly and freely to the general overthrow of all my former opinions.

2. But, to this end, it will not be necessary for me to show that the whole of these are false—a point, perhaps, which I shall never reach; but as even now my reason convinces me that I ought not the less carefully to withhold belief from what is not entirely certain and indubitable, than from what is manifestly false, it will be sufficient to justify the rejection of the whole if I shall find in each some ground for doubt. Nor for this purpose will it be necessary even to deal with each belief individually, which would be truly an endless labor; but, as the removal from below of the foundation necessarily involves the downfall of the whole edifice, I will at once approach the criticism of the principles on which all my former beliefs rested.

Descartes is convinced that committing yourself to a wholesale and systematic doubting of all things you have been taught to simply accept without question is the only way to achieve clear and well-reasoned conclusions. More important, it is the only way for you to develop beliefs that are truly *yours* and not someone else's. He explains, "If you would be a real seeker after truth, it is necessary that at least once in your life you doubt, as far as possible, all things." This sort of thorough-going doubting of all that you have been taught requires great personal courage, for calling into question things like our religious beliefs, cultural values, and even beliefs about your *self* can be, in the short term, a very disruptive enterprise. It may mean shaking up your world, questioning the beliefs of important people in your life, perhaps challenging your image of yourself. Yet there is a compelling logic to Descartes' pronouncement: for if you are *not* willing to question all that you have been asked to accept "on faith," then you will never have the opportunity to construct a rock-solid foundation for your beliefs about the world and your personal philosophy of life. What's more, you will never have the experience to develop the intellectual abilities and personal courage required to achieve your full potential in the future.

This, then, is the beginning of Descartes' quest for true knowledge that leads to his famous first principle: **cogito**, *ergo sum*—"I think, therefore I am." We will be exploring his epistemological odyssey in some detail in the section on Knowledge and Truth (chapters 8 and 9). For now, we're going to focus on Descartes' analysis of the *self*, the theme of this chapter.

Cogito, ergo sum is the first principle of Descartes' theory of knowledge because he is confident that no rational person will doubt his or her own existence as a con-

Cogito   Thinking thing or mind.

scious, thinking entity—*while we are aware of thinking about our self.* Even if we are dreaming or hallucinating, even if our consciousness is being manipulated by some external entity, it is still my *self-aware self* that is dreaming, hallucinating, or being manipulated. Thus, in addition to being the first principle of his epistemology, *cogito ergo, sum* is also the keystone of Descartes' concept of *self.* The essence of existing as a human identity is the possibility of *being aware of our selves*: being self-conscious in this way is integral to having a personal identity. Conversely, it would be impossible to be self-conscious if we didn't have a personal identity of which to be conscious. In other words, having a *self identity* and being *self-conscious* are mutually dependent on one another. Here's how Descartes explains this phenomenon in his *Meditation II.*

Physical body   Material, mortal, nonthinking entity.

Thinking is another attribute of the soul; and here I discover what properly belongs to myself. This alone is inseparable from me. I am—I exist: this is certain; but how often? As often as I think; for perhaps it would even happen, if I should wholly cease to think, that I should at the same time altogether cease to be. I now admit nothing that is not necessarily true. I am therefore, precisely speaking, only a thinking thing, that is, a mind, understanding, or reason, terms whose signification was before unknown to me. I am, however, a real thing, and really existent; but what thing? The answer was, a thinking thing. . . .

But what, then, am I? A thinking thing, it has been said. But what is a thinking thing? It is a thing that doubts, understands [conceives], affirms, denies, wills, refuses; that imagines also, and perceives.

René Descartes,
Meditations on First Philosophy

For Descartes, then, this is the essence of your *self*—you are a "thinking thing," a dynamic identity that engages in all of those mental operations we associate with being a human *self.* For example,

- You *understand* situations in which you find yourself.
- You *doubt* the accuracy of ideas presented to you.
- You *affirm* the truth of a statement made about you.
- You *deny* an accusation that someone has made.
- You *will* yourself to complete a task you have begun.
- You *refuse* to follow a command that you consider to be unethical.
- You *imagine* a fulfilling career for yourself.
- You *feel* passionate emotions toward another person.

But in addition to engaging in all of these mental operations—and many other besides—your *self identity* is dependent on the fact that *you are capable of being aware you are engaging in these mental operations while you are engaged in them.* If you were consistently *not* conscious of your mental operations, consistently *unaware* of your thinking, reasoning, and perceiving processes, then it would not be possible for you to have a *self identity,* a unique essence, a *you.*

But what about your body? After all, a great deal of our self-concept and self-identity is tied up with our physical existence: our physical qualities, appearance, gender, race, age, height, weight, hair style, and so on. Despite this, Descartes believes that your **physical body** is secondary to your personal identity. One reason for this is that he believes you can conceive of yourself existing independently of your body.

THINK CRITICALLY   3.6

PHILOSOPHER'S NOTEBOOK

Seeking After Truth

- Explain your reaction to Descartes' challenge, "If you would be a real seeker after truth, it is necessary that at least once in your life you doubt, as far as possible, all things." Do you agree with this statement? Why or why not? If so, how?

- Describe some important areas of your life in which you would consider yourself to be a "real seeker after truth." Identify several examples of beliefs you had been taught or raised with which you questioned for the purpose of developing your own independent conclusions.

- Describe some important areas of your life in which, in your opinion, you *fell short* of being a "real seeker after truth." Identify several examples of beliefs you have been raised with that you have been reluctant to question. What factors have made it difficult for you to doubt these beliefs? Do you think you will critically analyze them at some point in the future?

René Descartes,
Meditations on First Philosophy

The question now arises, am I anything else besides? I will stimulate my imagination with a view to discover whether I am not still something more than a thinking being. Now it is plain I am not the assemblage of members called the human body; I am not a thin and penetrating air diffused through all these members, or wind, or flame, or vapor, or breath, or any of all the things I can imagine; for I supposed that all these were not, and, without changing the supposition, I find that I still feel assured of my existence. But it is true, perhaps, that those very things which I suppose to be non-existent, because they are unknown to me, are not in truth different from myself whom I know. This is a point I cannot determine, and do not now enter into any dispute regarding it. I can only judge of things that are known to me: I am conscious that I exist, and I who know that I exist inquire into what I am. It is, however, perfectly certain that the knowledge of my existence, thus precisely taken, is not dependent on things, the existence of which is as yet unknown to me: and consequently it is not dependent on any of the things I can feign in imagination.

Nevertheless, even though your body is not as central to your *self* as is your capacity to think and reflect, it clearly plays a role in your self-identity. In fact, Descartes contends, if you reflect thoughtfully, you can see that you have clear ideas of both your *self as a thinking entity* and your *self as a physical body*. And these two dimensions of your *self* are quite distinct.

René Descartes,
Meditations on First Philosophy

And, firstly, because I know that all which I clearly and distinctly conceive can be produced by God exactly as I conceive it, it is sufficient that I am able clearly and distinctly to conceive one thing apart from another, in order to be certain that the one is different from the other, seeing they may at least be made to exist separately, by the omnipotence of God; and it matters not by what power this separation is made, in order to be compelled to judge them different; and, therefore, merely because I know with certitude that I exist, and because, in the meantime, I do not observe that anything else necessarily belongs to my nature or essence beyond my being a thinking thing, I rightly conclude that my essence consists only in my being a thinking thing [or a substance whose whole essence or nature is merely thinking]. And although I may, or rather, as I will shortly say, although I certainly do possess a body with which I am very closely conjoined; nevertheless, because, on the one hand, I have a clear and distinct idea of myself, in as far as I am only a thinking and unextended thing, and as, on the other hand, I possess a distinct idea of body, in as far as it is only an extended and unthinking thing, it is certain that I, [that is, my mind, by which I am what I am], is entirely and truly distinct from my body, and may exist without it.

It is at this point that we can see the pervasive influence of the metaphysical framework created by Socrates and Plato, and perpetuated through the centuries by such thinkers as Plotinus and St. Augustine. Following directly in their footsteps, Descartes declares that the *essential self*—the *self as thinking entity*—is radically different than the *self as physical body*. The *thinking self*—or soul—is a non-material, immortal, conscious being, independent of the physical laws of the universe. The *physical body* is a material, mortal, nonthinking entity, fully governed by the physical laws of nature. What's more, your soul and your body are independent of one another, and each can exist and function without the other. How is that possible? For example, in the case of physical death, Descartes believes (as did Plato, Plotinus, and St. Augustine) that your soul continues to exist, seeking union with the spiritual realm and God's infinite and eternal mind. On the other hand, in cases in which people are sleeping or comatose, their bodies continue to function even though their minds are not thinking, much like the mechanisms of a clock.

René Descartes,
Meditations on First Philosophy

And as a clock, composed of wheels and counter weights, observes not the less accurately all the laws of nature when it is ill made, and points out the hours incorrectly, than when it satisfies the desire of the maker in every respect; so likewise if the body of man be considered as a kind of machine, so made up and composed of bones, nerves, muscles, veins, blood, and skin, that although there were in it no mind, it would still exhibit the same motions which it at present manifests involuntarily, and therefore without the aid of the mind, and simply by the dispositions of its organs. . . .

Thus Descartes ends up with Plato's metaphysic, a **dualistic** view of reality, bifurcated into

- a spiritual, nonmaterial, immortal realm that includes conscious, thinking beings, *and*
- a physical, material, finite realm that includes human bodies and the rest of the physical universe.

In the case of the human *self*, the soul (or mind) and the physical body could not be more different. For example, you can easily imagine the body being divided into various parts, whereas it is impossible to imagine your soul as anything other than an indivisible unity (precisely the point that Socrates makes when he's arguing for the immortality of the soul):

To commence this examination accordingly, I here remark, in the first place, that there is a vast difference between mind and body, in respect that body, from its nature, is always divisible, and that mind is entirely indivisible. For in truth, when I consider the mind, that is, when I consider myself in so far only as I am a thinking thing, I can distinguish in myself no parts, but I very clearly discern that I am somewhat absolutely one and entire; and although the whole mind seems to be united to the whole body, yet, when a foot, an arm, or any other part is cut off, I am conscious that nothing has been taken from my mind; nor can the faculties of willing, perceiving, conceiving, etc., properly be called its parts, for it is the same mind that is exercised [all entire] in willing, in perceiving, and in conceiving, etc. But quite the opposite holds in corporeal or extended things; for I cannot imagine any one of them [how small soever it may be], which I cannot easily sunder in thought, and which, therefore, I do not know to be divisible. This would be sufficient to teach me that the mind or soul of man is entirely different from the body, if I had not already been apprised of it on other grounds.

This dualistic view of the *self* is particularly useful for Descartes, who was faced with a serious conflict in his personal and professional life. As previously noted, Descartes was first and foremost a scientist in his professional life, committed to establishing true knowledge through rigorous reasoning, experimentation, and analysis. Many scientists of the time—physicists, astronomers, biologists—were inclined to view the human *self* in terms of the physical body, governed by the same laws of physics that defined the operation of the rest of the physical universe. However, if the *self* is seen exclusively in terms of the physical body, the *self* is terminated when the body dies. There is no spiritual, immortal soul that continues to exist beyond death. If the *self* is only a physical being, life in any form ends with death. (This philosophical perspective is known as **materialism**, *the view that all aspects of the universe are composed of matter and energy and can be explained by physical laws.*) In addition, because the *self* is governed exclusively by the cause-and-effect laws of the universe, there is no room for free will to exist. You are no more capable of making free choices in your life than the hands of a clock can choose their movements—every choice that you make is determined by previous events.

As a devout Catholic who believed in God, immortal souls, eternal life, and free will, this materialistic view of the world was completely unacceptable to Descartes. However, by advocating a dualistic metaphysic, Descartes was able to maintain both his scientific integrity and his religious convictions. The *physical self* is a part of nature, governed by the physical laws of the universe, and available to scientific analysis and experimentation. At the same time, the *conscious self (mind, soul)* is a

Dualism The view that both material substance (physical body) and immaterial substance (mind or soul) exist.

Materialism The view that all aspects of the universe are composed of matter and energy and can be explained by physical laws.

René Descartes, *Meditations on First Philosophy*

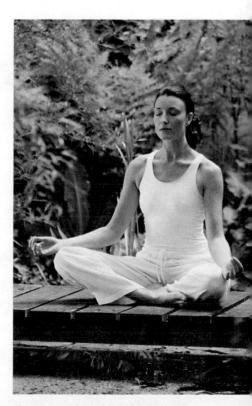

The relationship of the physical self and the thinking self is intimate and complex. Can you think of some examples of this relationship?

part of the spiritual realm, independent of the physical laws of the universe, governed only by the laws of reason and God's will. And because it exists outside of the natural world of cause-and-effect, the conscious *self* is able to exercise free will in the choices it makes.

Although a bifurcated view of the universe solves some immediate problems for Descartes, it creates other philosophical difficulties, most notably the vexing question, "What is the relationship between the mind and the body?" In our everyday experience, our minds and bodies appear to be very closely related to one another. Our thinking and emotions have a profound effect on many aspects of our physical bodies, and physical events with our bodies have a significant impact on our mental lives. For the most part, we experience our minds and bodies as a unified entity, very different from the two different and completely independent substances that Descartes proposes. As the writer and humorist Mark Twain noted, "How come the mind gets drunk when the body does the drinking?" Even Descartes recognized the need to acknowledge the close, intimate relationship between mind and body, as the following passage reveals:

René Descartes,
Meditations on First Philosophy

Nature likewise teaches me by these sensations of pain, hunger, thirst, etc., that I am not only lodged in my body as a pilot in a vessel, but that I am besides so intimately conjoined, and as it were intermixed with it, that my mind and body compose a certain unity. For if this were not the case, I should not feel pain when my body is hurt, seeing I am merely a thinking thing, but should perceive the wound by the understanding alone, just as a pilot perceives by sight when any part of his vessel is damaged; and when my body has need of food or drink, I should have a clear knowledge of this, and not be made aware of it by the confused sensations of hunger and thirst: for, in truth, all these sensations of hunger, thirst, pain, etc., are nothing more than certain confused modes of thinking, arising from the union and apparent fusion of mind and body.

 Descartes, René, *Meditations on First Philosophy*

THINK CRITICALLY

3.7

PHILOSOPHER'S NOTEBOOK

My Body, My Self?

- Describe some of the ways your mind significantly affects your body: for example, when you are anxious, elated, depressed, in love (or lust), and so on.
- Describe some of the ways your body significantly affects your mind: for example, when you are feeling sick, deprived of sleep, taking medications, or finding yourself in a physically dangerous/threatening situation.
- Create your own metaphysical framework for the "*self*" by describing
  - your *self as thinking subject*.
  - your *self as physical body*.
  - your analysis of how these two aspects of your *self* relate to one another.
- Reconsider your views on human souls—what do you believe happens to the *self* after the death of the body? Why do you believe it? What would Descartes think of your views and your justification for them?

Descartes' believed that the "intermingling" point of contact was through the pineal gland, a small gland located at the base of the skull. It was here that he believed that the thinking self connected to the physical brain. Why the pineal gland? Descartes found its physical location appropriate and it had no known biological function at Descartes' time. Ever the scientist, Descartes dissected a variety of animals to learn more about this mysterious gland. Interestingly, Descartes' fascination with the pineal gland is mirrored in the Hindu belief that the pineal gland is the seat of the highest *chakra*, the connection between the individual body and mind to God.

Recognizing the problem of the mind/body relationship in a dualistic system and solving the problem in a satisfactory way are two very different things. Most philosophers agree that Descartes' efforts to provide an integrated model of his concepts of the mind and body were not successful, and it's a problem that has challenged thinkers in every discipline ever since. We will continue our exploration of the mind/body "problem" later in this chapter.

How did Descartes' views regarding the *self* relate to his personal life? In a fascinating way: Descartes was plagued by frail health, a condition that caused him throughout his life to sleep late into the morning. A financial inheritance from his parents meant he didn't have to work. Instead, he devoted his life to study and experimentation, spending much of his time alone, and moving from place to place on a regular basis (he lived in twenty different houses in one twenty-year period). Descartes preferred the company of himself because it provided him the opportunity to fully devote himself to his scientific, mathematical, and philosophical activities, without the distraction of social relationships (although he did find time to father an illegitimate child with a servant). Ironically, it was an error in judgment that hastened the death of his body. Against his better judgment, he accepted the invitation of Queen Christina of Sweden to come to Stockholm and tutor her. Unfortunately, the Queen turned out to be an early riser, depriving Descartes of his beloved sleep. That, combined with the cold and damp climate of Stockholm, led to pneumonia and his premature death at the age of fifty-three, providing him with a first-hand opportunity to test his theory of an immortal soul.

John Locke: *The Self Is Consciousness*

The English philosopher—and physician—**John Locke** (1632–1704) continued exploring the themes Descartes had initiated, both in terms of the nature of knowledge (epistemology) and the nature of the *self*. He shared with Descartes a scientist's perspective, seeking to develop knowledge based on clear thinking, rigorous analysis, and real-world observation and experimentation. However, Locke brought a very different approach to this epistemological enterprise. Descartes believed that we could use the power of reason to achieve absolutely certain knowledge of the world, and then use this rationally based knowledge to understand our world of experience. His extensive work in mathematics served as a model, convincing him that there were absolute truths and knowledge waiting to be discovered by reasoned, disciplined reflection.

Locke's work as a physician, rather than a mathematician, provided him with a very different perspective. The physician's challenge is to gather information regarding the symptoms a patient is experiencing, and then relate these symptoms to his (the physician's) accumulated knowledge of disease. Although a successful doctor uses sophisticated reasoning abilities in identifying patterns and making inferences, his conclusions are grounded in experience. Knowledge, in other words, is based on the careful observation of sense experience and/or memories of previous experiences. Reason plays a subsequent role in helping to figure out the significance of our sense experience and to reach intelligent conclusions.

To sum up: for Descartes, our *reasoning ability* provides the origin of knowledge and final court of judgment in evaluating the accuracy and value of the ideas produced. For Locke, all knowledge originates in our direct *sense experience*, which acts as the final court of judgment in evaluating the accuracy and value of ideas. As a result, Descartes is considered an archetypal proponent of the *rationalist* view of knowledge, whereas Locke is considered an archetypal advocate of the *empiricist* view of knowledge.

JOHN LOCKE
(1632–1704)
British philosopher. In his *Essay Concerning Human Understanding* (1690) Locke lays the groundwork for empiricist philosophy. His theory that the mind is a *tabula rasa*, a blank slate, on which experience writes, challenges the rationalist philosophy that preceded him.

Rationalism The view that reason is the primary source of all knowledge and that only our reasoning abilities can enable us to understand sense experience and reach accurate conclusions.

Empiricism The view that sense experience is the primary source of all knowledge and that only a careful attention to sense experience can enable us to understand the world and achieve accurate conclusions.

Rationalism The view that reason is the primary source of all knowledge.

Empiricism The view that sense experience is the primary source of all knowledge.

These are themes that we will be exploring in depth in chapters 8 and 9, *What Is True? What Is Real?* For now, we will focus on the way in which these contrasting approaches to the world influence their views on the nature of the *self*.

True to his philosophical commitment to grounding his ideas in sense experience, Locke, in his essay entitled "On Personal Identity" (from his most famous work, *Essay Concerning Human Understanding*) engages in a reflective analysis of how we experience our *self* in our everyday lives:

Locke, *On Personal Identity*

To find wherein personal identity consists, we must consider what *person* stands for;—which, I think, is a thinking intelligent being, that has reason and reflection, and can consider itself as itself, the same thinking thing, in different times and places; which it does only by that consciousness which is inseparable from thinking, and as it seems to me, essential to it: it being impossible for any one to perceive without *perceiving* that he does perceive. When we see, hear, smell, taste, feel, meditate, or will anything, we know that we do so. Thus it is always as to our present sensations and perceptions: and by this every one is to himself that which he calls *self*:—it not being considered, in this case, whether the same *self* be continued in the same or divers substances. For, since consciousness always accompanies thinking, and it is that which makes everyone to be what he calls *self*, and thereby distinguishes himself from all other thinking things, in this alone consists personal identity, i.e. the sameness of a rational being: and as far as this consciousness can be extended backwards to any past action or thing, so far reaches the identity of that person; it is the same *self* now it was then; and it is by the same *self* with this present one that now reflects on it, that that action was done.

In this initial passage, Locke makes the following points, implicitly asking the question of his readers, "Aren't these conclusions confirmed by examining your own experiences?"

- To discover the nature of *personal identity*, we're going to have to find out what it means to be a *person*.
- A *person* is a thinking, intelligent being who has the abilities to reason and to reflect.
- A *person* is also someone who considers itself to be the *same* thing in different times and different places.
- *Consciousness*—being aware that we are thinking—always accompanies thinking and is an essential part of the thinking process.
- *Consciousness* is what makes possible our belief that we are the same identity in different times and different places.

Reflect carefully on Locke's points—do you find that his conclusions match your own personal experience? Certainly his first three points seem plausible. What about points 4 and 5? Does *consciousness* always accompany the thinking process? Locke explains: "When we see, hear, smell, taste, feel, meditate, or will anything, we know that we do so. Thus it is always as to our present sensations and perceptions: and by this every one is to himself that which he calls *self*. . . . " Consider what you are doing at this moment: you are thinking about the words on the page, the ideas that are being expressed—are you also aware of yourself as you are reading and thinking? Certainly once the question is posed to you, you're aware of your *self*. Perhaps it's more accurate to say that when you think, you are either conscious of your *self*—or *potentially* conscious of your *self*. In other words, are there times in which you are fully immersed in an activity—such as dancing, driving a car, or playing a sport—and not consciously aware that you are doing so? Analogously, are there times in which you are fully engaged in deep thought—wrestling with a difficult

Do you agree with John Locke that consciousness is what makes possible our belief that we are the same identity in different times and different places?

idea, for example—and not aware that you are doing so? But even if there are times in which you are unreflectively submerged in an activity or thought process, you always have the potential to *become* aware of your *self* engaged in the activity or thought process.

What about Locke's fifth point, that *consciousness* is necessary for us to have a unified self-identity in different times and places? This seems like a point well taken. You consider your *self* to be the same *self* who was studying last night, attending a party at a friend's house two weeks ago, and taking a vacation last summer. How can you be sure it's the same *self* in all of these situations? Because of your *consciousness* of being the same *self* in all of these different contexts.

These points become clearer when we contrast human thinking with animal thinking. It's reasonable to believe that mammals such as chipmunks, dogs, and dolphins are able to see, hear, smell, taste, and feel, just like humans. But are they *conscious* of the fact that they are performing these activities as they are performing them? Most people would say "no." And because they are not *conscious* that they are performing these activities, it's difficult to see how they would have a concept of *self-identity* that remains the same over time and place. So *consciousness*—or more specifically, *self-consciousness*—*does* seem to be a necessary part of having a coherent self-identity. (Some people believe that higher-order mammals such as chimpanzees and gorillas present more complicated cases.) Here is how the psychoanalyst and philosopher **Erich Fromm** (1900–1980) explains this crucial point:

> Man has intelligence, like other animals, which permits him to use thought processes for the attainment of immediate practical aims; but Man has another mental quality which the animal lacks. He is aware of himself, of his past and future, which is death, of his smallness and powerlessness; he is aware of others as friends, enemies, or as strangers. Man transcends all other life because he is for the first time, life aware of itself.

ERICH FROMM
(1900–1980)
German psychologist and humanist philosopher. Author of many works, including *Escape from Freedom* (1941). Taught in Germany, the United States, and Mexico. Fromm praised humans for using their own reason to establish moral codes rather than simply following authoritarian moral values.

THINK PHILOSOPHICALLY
Analyzing John Locke

3.8

Here's an opportunity for you to analyze your own views on the *self*, using Locke's conclusions as a guide:

- How would you define your *personal identity*? How would you define you as a *person*? How would you describe the relationship between the two?
- What do you think are the essential mental qualities that define all *people*?
- What do you think is the relationship between your *consciousness* and your *thinking process*?
- What do you think is the relationship between your *consciousness* and your concept of *self-identity* as something that remains the same in different times and places?

Descartes would agree with Locke's view that a *person*—or *self*—is a thinking, intelligent being that has the abilities to reason and to reflect. And he likely would be sympathetic to Locke's contention that *consciousness* accompanies thinking and makes possible the concept we have of a *self* that remains the same at different times and in different places. But in the following passage, Locke expresses a belief that many people—including Descartes—would likely disagree with. Let's examine his unusual belief regarding the *self*.

Locke, *On Personal Identity*

Consciousness Makes Personal Identity.—But it is further inquired, whether it be the same identical substance. This few (*Locke refers here to Descartes*) would think they had reason to doubt of, if these perceptions, with their consciousness, always remained present in the mind, whereby the same thinking thing would be always consciously present, and, as would be thought, evidently the same to itself. But that which seems to make the difficulty is this, that this consciousness being interrupted always by forgetfulness, there being no moment of our lives wherein we have the whole train of all our past actions before our eyes in one view, but even the best memories losing the sight of one part whilst they are viewing another; and we sometimes, and that the greatest part of our lives, not reflecting on our past selves, being intent on our present thoughts, and in sound sleep having no thoughts at all, or at least none with that consciousness which remarks our waking thoughts,—I say, in all these cases, our consciousness being interrupted, and we losing the sight of our past selves, doubts are raised whether we are the same thinking thing, i.e. the same *substance* or no. Which, however reasonable or unreasonable, concerns not *personal* identity at all. The question being what makes the same person; and not whether it be the same identical substance, which always thinks in the same person, which, in this case, matters not at all: different substances, by the same consciousness (where they do partake in it) being united into one person, as well as different bodies by the same life are united into one animal, whose identity is preserved in that change of substances by the unity of one continued life. For, it being the same consciousness that makes a man be himself to himself, personal identity depends on that only, whether it be annexed solely to one individual substance, or can be continued in a succession of several substances. For as far as any intelligent being *can* repeat the idea of any past action with the same consciousness it had of it at first, and with the same consciousness it has of any present action; so far it is the same personal self. For it is by the consciousness it has of its present thoughts and actions, that it is *self to itself* now, and so will be the same self, as far as the same consciousness can extend to actions past or to come; and would be by distance of time, or change of substance, no more two persons, than a man be two men by wearing other clothes to-day than he did yesterday, with a long or short sleep between: the same consciousness uniting those distant actions into the same person, whatever substances contributed to their production.

As this passage makes clear, Locke is proposing a radically different version of the *self* than the philosophical tradition before him. Plato, Plotinus, St. Augustine, Descartes—they all had agreed that the *self* existed in the form of an immortal, non-material soul that continues to exist following the death of the body. In a fascinating twist, Locke denies that the individual *self* necessarily exists in a single soul or substance. For Locke, the essence of the *self* is its conscious awareness of itself as a thinking, reasoning, reflecting identity. But this in no way means that this *self* is necessarily imbedded in a single substance or soul—it might very well take up residence in any number of substances or souls. Let's see how Locke arrives at the rather surprising conclusion.

In Locke's mind, conscious awareness and memory of previous experiences are the keys to understanding the *self*. In other words, you have a coherent concept of your *self* as a personal identity because you are *aware* of your *self* when you are thinking, feeling, and willing. *And*, you have memories of times when you were aware of your *self* in the past, in other situations—for example, at the party two weeks ago, or your high school graduation several years ago. *But*, as we noted earlier, there are many moments when we are *not* consciously aware of our *self* when we are thinking, feeling, and willing—we are simply, unreflectively, *existing*. What's more, there are many past experiences that we have forgotten or have faulty recollections of. All of which means that during those lapses, when we were not aware of our *self*, or don't remember being aware of our *self*, we can't be sure if we were the same person, the same substance, the same soul! Our personal identity is not in doubt or jeopardy, because we are aware of our *self* (or remember being aware of it). But we have no way of knowing if our personal identity has been existing in one substance (soul) or a number of substances (souls). Let's examine again how Locke explains his reasoning:

But that which seems to make the difficulty is this, that this consciousness being interrupted always by forgetfulness, there being no moment of our lives wherein we have the whole train of all our past actions before our eyes in one view, but even the best memories losing the sight of one part whilst they are viewing another; and we sometimes, and that the greatest part of our lives, not reflecting on our past selves, being intent on our present thoughts, and in sound sleep having no thoughts at all, or at least none with that consciousness which remarks our waking thoughts,—I say, in all these cases, our consciousness being interrupted, and we losing the sight of our past selves, doubts are raised whether we are the same thinking thing, i.e. the same *substance* or no. Which, however reasonable or unreasonable, concerns not *personal* identity at all. The question being what makes the same person; and not whether it be the same identical substance, which always thinks in the same person, which, in this case, matters not at all.

Locke, *On Personal Identity*

So for Locke, personal identity and the soul or substance in which the personal identity is situated are two very different things. Although the idea seems rather strange at first glance, Locke provides a very concrete example to further illustrate what he means:

Personal Identity in Change of Substance—That this is so, we have some kind of evidence in our very bodies, all whose particles, whilst vitally united to this same thinking conscious self, so that we feel when they are touched, and are affected by, and conscious of good or harm that happens to them, are a part of ourselves; i.e. of our thinking conscious self. Thus, the limbs of his body are to every one a part of himself; he sympathizes and is concerned for them. Cut off a hand, and thereby separate it from that consciousness he had of its heat, cold, and other affections, and it is then no longer a part of that which is himself, any more than the remotest part of matter. Thus, we see the substance whereof personal self consisted at one time may be varied at another, without the change of personal identity; there being no question about the same person, though the limbs which but now were a part of it, be cut off.

Locke, *On Personal Identity*

John Locke

It's a rather gruesome example Locke provides, but it makes his point. Every aspect of your physical body (substance) is integrated with your *personal identity*—hit your finger with a hammer and it's *you* that is experiencing the painful sensation. But if your hand is cut off in an industrial accident, your *personal identity* remains intact, although the substance associated with it has changed (you now only have one hand). Or to take another example: the cells of our body are continually being replaced, added to, subtracted from. So it's accurate to say that in many ways you are not the same *physical person* you were five years ago, ten years ago, fifteen years ago, and so on. Nevertheless, you are likely convinced that your *personal identity* has remained the same despite these changes in physical substance to your body. This leads Locke to conclude that our *personal identity* is distinct from whatever substance it finds itself associated with. He continues his provocative analysis with the notions of time-travel, reincarnation, and the end-of-time resurrection.

Locke, *On Personal Identity*

If the same consciousness (which, as has been shown, is quite a different thing from the same numerical figure or motion in body) can be transferred from one thinking substance to another, it will be possible that two thinking substances may make but one person. For the same consciousness being preserved, whether in the same or different substances, the personal identity is preserved. Whether the same immaterial being, being conscious of the action of its past duration, may be wholly stripped of all the consciousness of its past existence, and lose it beyond the power of ever retrieving it again: and so as it were beginning a new account from a new period, have a consciousness that *cannot* reach beyond this new state. All those who hold pre-existence are evidently of this mind; since they allow the soul to have no remaining consciousness of what it did in the pre-existing state, either wholly separate from body, or informing any other body; and if they should not, it is plain experience would be against them. So that personal identity, reaching no further than consciousness reaches, a pre-existent spirit not having continued so many ages in a state of silence, must needs make different persons. Suppose a Christian Platonist or a Pythagorean should, upon God's having ended all his works of creation on the seventh day, think his soul hath existed ever since; and should imagine it has revolved in several human bodies; as I once met with one, who was persuaded his had been the *soul* of Socrates (how reasonably I will not dispute; this I know, that in the spot he filled, which was no inconsiderable one, he passed for a very rational man, and the press has shown that he wanted not parts of learning)—would any one say, that he, being not conscious of any of Socrates' actions or thoughts, could be the same *person* with Socrates? Let any one reflect upon himself, and conclude that he has in himself an immaterial spirit, which is that which thinks in him, and, in the constant change of his body keeps him the same: and is that which he calls *himself*.

The body, as well as the soul, goes to the making of a Man.—And thus may we be able, without any difficulty, to conceive the same person at the resurrection, though in a body not exactly in make or parts the same which he had here,—the same consciousness going along with the soul that inhabits it. But that makes the soul the man, be enough to make the same man. For should the soul of a prince, carrying with it the consciousness of the prince's past life, enter and inform the body of a cobbler, as soon as deserted by his own soul, every one sees he would be the same *person* with the prince, accountable only for the prince's actions: but who would say it was the same *man*? The body too goes to the making the man, and would, I guess, to everybody determine the man in this case, wherein the soul, with all its princely thoughts about it, would not make another man: but he would be the same cobbler to every one besides himself. I know that, in the ordinary way of speaking, the same person, and the same man, stand for one and the same thing.

Uncoupling *consciousness* or *personal identity* from the *soul* or *substance* in which it resides opens up a universe of possibilities. The same *consciousness (person)* can be transferred from one substance to another, and different substances can combine to make one *consciousness* (person). So at the end of time, when all people of faith are resurrected, if the *consciousness* of a prince has assumed the physical body of a cobbler (retaining memories of the prince's past life), Locke maintains that we would still consider him to be the *same person*, in spite of his different physical forms. Conversely, if the *consciousness* of a previous life is *not* maintained, there is no reason to believe that the same *person* has existed in the earlier form. Locke cites—with good humor—the example of a person he knows who claims to have been Socrates in a previous life, though he has no memory of the actions or thoughts of Socrates. Even though, Locke observes (with his tongue firmly planted in his cheek) "he passed for a very rational man, and the press has shown that he wanted not parts of learning," there still is no good reason to believe that this man's consciousness did in fact inhabit the physical body of Socrates. *Consciousness* is the key ingredient needed to unite *self-identity* over time. If you have the same memory of Noah's flood as you did the flood you recently experienced, then you may very well be the same *person* existing in different physical bodies many thousands of years apart.

Consciousness alone unites actions into the same Person.—But though the same immaterial substance or soul does not alone, wherever it be, and in whatsoever state, make the same *man*; yet it is plain, consciousness, as far as ever it can be extended—should it be to ages past—unites existences and actions very remote in time into the same "person," as well as it does the existences and actions of the immediately preceding moment: so that whatever has the consciousness of present and past actions, is the same person to whom they both belong. Had I the same consciousness that I saw the ark and Noah's flood, as that I saw an overflowing of the Thames last winter, or as that I write now, I could no more doubt that I who write this now, that saw the Thames overflowed last winter, and that viewed the flood at the general deluge, was the same *self*,—place that self in what *substance* you please—than that I who write this am the same myself now whilst I write (whether I consist of all the same substance, material or immaterial, or no) that I was yesterday. For as to this point of being the same self, it matters not whether this present self be made up of the same or other substances—I being as much concerned, and as justly accountable for any action that was done a thousand years since, appropriated to me how by this self-consciousness, as I am for what I did the last moment.

Locke, *On Personal Identity*

And just when you think Locke has reached the apex of far-out strangeness in his ideas, he surprises us once again. Imagine that your little finger was hacked off (!) but that your *conscious self* remained with your little finger rather than the rest of your body: then we would have to say that your *self* resides in your little finger, that *you are* your little finger. Fascinating!

Self Depends on Consciousness, not on Substance.—Self is that conscious thinking thing,—whatever substance made up of (whether spiritual or material, simple or compounded, it matters not)—which is sensible or conscious of pleasure and pain, capable of happiness or misery, and so is concerned for itself, as far as that consciousness extends. Thus every one finds that, whilst comprehended under that consciousness, the little finger is as much a part of himself as what is most so. Upon separation of this little finger, should this consciousness go along with the little finger, and leave the rest of the body, it is evident the little finger would be the person, the same person; and self then would have nothing to do with the rest of the body. As in this case it is the consciousness that goes along with the substance, when one part is separate from another, which makes the same person, and constitutes this inseparable self; so it is in reference to the substances remote in time. That with which the consciousness of this present thinking thing *can* join itself, makes the same person, and is one self with it, and with nothing else; and so attributes to itself, and owns all the actions of that thing, as its own, as far as that consciousness reaches, and no further. ■

Locke, *On Personal Identity*

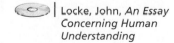

Locke, John, *An Essay Concerning Human Understanding*

THINK PHILOSOPHICALLY
The Conscious Self

3.9

PHILOSOPHER'S NOTEBOOK

- Evaluate Locke's claim that your *conscious self* is not permanently attached to any particular body or substance. Do you agree with this view? Why or why not?

- Do you know anyone personally who has claimed to have lived a past life in another body? If so, do you think they would pass Locke's "test" for determining if their claim is authentic (having a clear memory of the *consciousness* of thinking and behaving as the previous individual)? Have you ever suspected that *your personal identity* lived a previous life? If so, how would Locke evaluate your belief?

- Locke believes that it is our memory that serves to link our *self* at this moment with our *self* in previous circumstances. But people's memories are often faulty. How can we distinguish between accurate memories of our *self* and inaccurate memories? To do so, don't we have to assume that we have a continuous *self* that is performing the evaluation? But since memory is supposed to explain the existence of our *self*, doesn't this mean that Locke's reasoning is circular? Explain your analysis of this dilemma.

David Hume: *There Is No "Self"*

DAVID HUME
(1711–1776)
Scottish philosopher. Hume's philosophy is seen as drawing out the logical consequences of a thoroughgoing empiricism. His skepticism concerning causation, induction, and religion is still widely influential today.

David Hume (1711–1776) continued in the empiricist tradition of John Locke, believing that the source of all genuine knowledge is our direct sense experience. As we have seen, this empiricist approach had led Locke to a number of surprising conclusions regarding the *self*, including the belief that the self's existence is dependent on our *consciousness* of it. In Locke's view, your *self* is not tied to any particular body or substance, and it only exists in other times and places because of our *memory* of those experiences. Using the same empiricist principles as Locke, Hume ends up with an even more startling conclusion—if we carefully examine our sense experience through the process of introspection, we discover that *there is no self*! How is this possible? From Hume's perspective, this astonishing belief is the only possible conclusion consistent with an honest and objective examination of our experience. The following passages are from Hume's essay "On Personal Identity."

Hume, *On Personal Identity*

There are some philosophers, who imagine we are every moment intimately conscious of what we call our SELF *(Hume is referring to Descartes and Locke, among others)*, that we feel its existence and its continuance in existence and are certain, beyond the evidence of a demonstration, both of its perfect identity and simplicity. The strongest sensation, the most violent passion, say they, instead of distracting us from this view, only fix it the more intensely, and make us consider their influence on *self* either by their pain or pleasure. To attempt a farther proof of this were to weaken its evidence; since no proof can be deriv'd from any fact, of which we are so intimately conscious; nor is there any thing of which we can be certain, if we doubt of this.

Unluckily all these positive assertions are contrary to that very experience, which is pleaded for them, nor have we any idea of *self*, after the manner it is here explain'd. For from what impression cou'd this idea be deriv'd? This question 'tis impossible to answer with out a manifest contradiction, and absurdity; and yet 'tis a question, which must necessarily be answer'd, if we wou'd have the idea of self pass for clear and intelligible. It must be some one impression, that gives rise to every real idea. But self or person is not any one impression but that to which our several impressions and ideas are suppos'd to have a reference. If any impression gives rise to the idea of self, that impression must continue invariably the same, thro' the whole course of our lives; since self is suppos'd to exist after that manner. But there is no impression constant and invariable. Pain and pleasure, grief and joy, passions and sensations succeed each other, and never all exist at the same time. It cannot, therefore, be from any of these impressions, or from any other, that the idea of self is deriv'd; and consequently there is no such idea.

According to Hume, if we carefully examine the contents of our experience, we find that there are only two distinct entities, "impressions" and "ideas":

Impressions—Impressions are the basic sensations of our experience, the elemental data of our minds: pain, pleasure, heat, cold, happiness, grief, fear, exhilaration, and so on. These impressions are "lively" and "vivid."

Ideas—Ideas are *copies* of impressions, and as a result they are less "lively" and "vivid." Ideas include thoughts and images that are built up from our primary impressions through a variety of relationships, but because they are derivative copies of impressions, they are once removed from reality.

If we examine these basic data of our experience, we see that they form a fleeting stream of sensations in our mind, and that nowhere among them is the sensation of a "constant and invariable" *self* that exists as a unified identity over the course of our lives. And because the *self* is not to be found among these continually changing sensations, we can only conclude that there is no good reason for believing that the *self* exists. Hume goes on to explain:

But farther, what must become of all our particular perceptions upon this hypothesis? All these are different, and distinguishable, and separable from each other and may be separately consider'd, and may exist separately, and have no need of any thing to support their existence. After what manner, therefore, do they belong to self and how are they connected with it? For my part, when I enter most intimately into what I call *myself*, I always stumble on some particular perception or other, of heat or cold, light or shade, love or hatred, pain or pleasure. I never can catch *myself* at any time without a perception, and never can observe any thing but the perception. When my perceptions are remov'd for any time, as by sound sleep; so long am I insensible of myself, and may truly be said not to exist. And were all my perceptions remov'd by death, and cou'd I neither think, nor feel, nor see, nor love, nor hate after the dissolution of my body, I shou'd be entirely annihilated, nor do I conceive what is further requisite to make me a perfect nonentity. If any one upon serious and unprejudiced reflexion, thinks he has a different notion of *himself*, I must confess I can reason no longer with him. All I can allow him is, that he may be in the right as well as I, and that we are essentially different in this particular. He may, perhaps, perceive something simple and continu'd, which he calls *himself*; tho' I am certain there is no such principle in me.

"I can never catch *myself* at any time without a perception, and never can observe any thing but the perception." Even when we actively look for the *self*, Hume contends, we simply can't find it! All of our experiences are perceptions, and none of these perceptions resemble a unified and permanent self-identity that exists over time. Furthermore, when we are not experiencing our perceptions—as when we sleep—there is no reason to suppose that our *self* exists in any form. Similarly, when our body dies and all empirical sensations cease, it makes no sense to believe that our *self* continues to exist in some form. Death is final. And what of people who claim that they *do* experience a *self* in their stream of perceptions? Hume announces that "I must confess I can reason no longer with him. . . . He may, perhaps, perceive something simple and continu'd, which he calls *himself*; tho' I am certain there is no such principle in me." In other words, as an empiricist, Hume cannot do more that provide an honest description and analysis of his own experience, within which there is no *self* to be found.

But if Hume is right, then why does virtually everybody but Hume believe with certainty that they *do* have a *self-identity* that persists through time and serves to unify their life and give it meaning? After all, it's not enough to say to the rest of the

David Hume
Courtesy of Allen Ramsay/Library of Congress

Hume, *On Personal Identity*

What about dreams? This is self...

?.?....

True empiricist

world—you're wrong and I'm right, and I'm not going to discuss the issue if you insist on disagreeing with me. Let's examine Hume's explanation of the *self* that most people would claim they experience.

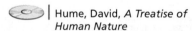

Hume, *On Personal Identity*

But setting aside some metaphysicians of this kind, I may venture to affirm of the rest of mankind, that they are nothing but a bundle or collection of different perceptions, which succeed each other with an inconceivable rapidity, and are in a perpetual flux and movement. Our eyes cannot turn in their sockets without varying our perceptions. Our thought is still more variable than our sight; and all our other senses and faculties contribute to this change; nor is there any single power of the soul, which remains unalterably the same, perhaps for one moment. The mind is a kind of theatre, where several perceptions successively make their appearance; pass, repass, glide away, and mingle in an infinite variety of postures and situations.

There is properly no *simplicity* in it at one time, nor *identity* in different; whatever natural propension we may have to imagine that simplicity and identity. The comparison of the theatre must not mislead us. They are the successive perceptions only, that constitute the mind: nor have we the most distant notion of the place, where these scenes are represented, or of the materials, of which it is compos'd.

The identity, which we ascribe to the mind of man, is only a fictitious one, and of a like kind with that which we ascribe to vegetables and animal bodies. It cannot, therefore, have a different origin, but must proceed from a like operation of the imagination upon his objects.

Our last resource is to . . . boldly assert that these different related objects are in effect the same, however interrupted and variable. In order to justify to ourselves this absurdity, we often feign some new and unintelligible principle, that connects the objects together, and prevents their interruption or variation. Thus we feign the continu'd existence of the perceptions of our senses, to remove the interruption; and run into the notion of a *soul*, and *self*, and *substance*, to disguise the variation. But we may farther observe, that where we do not give rise to such a fiction, our propension to confound identity with relation is so great, that we are apt to imagine something unknown and mysterious connecting the parts, beside their relation; and this I take to be the case with regard to the identity we ascribe to plants and vegetables. And even when this does not take place, we still feel a propensity to confound these ideas, tho' we are not able fully to satisfy ourselves in that particular, nor find any thing invariable and uninterrupted to justify our notion of identity. . . . ■

Hume, David, *A Treatise of Human Nature*

The Buddha uses the *Mudra* (a sacred gesture) to represent the Karmic wheel of birth, death, and rebirth.

What is the *self* we experience according to Hume? A "bundle or collection of different perceptions, which succeed each other with an inconceivable rapidity, and are in a perpetual flux and movement." Humans so desperately *want* to believe that they have a unified and continuous *self* or *soul* that they use their imaginations to construct a *fictional self*. But this fictional *self* is not real; what we call the *self* is an imaginary creature, derived from a succession of impermanent states and events. What is our mind? According to Hume, it's "a kind of theatre, where several perceptions successively make their appearance; pass, repass, glide away, and mingle in an infinite variety of postures and situations."

Comparisons are often made between Hume's concept of the *self* as a unified bundle of thoughts, feelings, and sensations and Buddhism's concept of *anatta* or "no-self." Although there are surface similarities between the two views of the *self*, a deeper analysis reveals significant differences. For Hume, a close examination of our stream of consciousness reveals no *self*, soul, or "I" that exists continually through time. We each create a "fictional *self*" to unify these transient mental events and introduce order into our lives, but this "*self*" has no real existence.

Buddhist doctrine agrees with Hume that the notion of a permanent *self* that exists as a unified identity through time is an illusion. For Buddhists, every aspect of life is impermanent and all elements of the universe are in a continual process of change and transition, a process that includes each "*self*" as well. The *self* can best be thought of as a flame that is continually passed from candle to candle, retaining a certain continuity but no real personal identity. But if the *self* or "I" doesn't refer to a continuous identity, then what does it signify? According to Buddhist philosophy, the *self* is composed of *five aggregates*: physical form, sensation, conceptualization, dispositions to act, and consciousness. Each "*self*" is comprised of the continual interplay of these five elements, but there is no substance or identity beyond the dynamic interaction of these five elements.

This concept of the *self* is certain to seem alien to our Western consciousness, which has a decidedly more Platonic view of self-identity. And, in fact, there was a famous debate regarding these two points of view that occurred in the second century B.C.E., between King Menander, a Greek who ruled northwestern India, and a Buddhist monk Nagasena. Witnessed by five hundred Greeks and thousands of monks, the argument hinged on a chariot simile, though in a much different fashion than that employed by Plato!

Then King Menander went up to the Venerable Nagasena, greeted him respectfully, and sat down. Nagasena replied to the greeting, and the King was pleased at heart. Then King Menander asked: "How is your reverence known, and what is your name?"

"I'm known as Nagasena, your Majesty, that's what my fellow monks call me. But though my parents may have given me such a name . . . it's only a generally understood term, a practical designation. There is no question of a permanent individual implied in the use of the word."

"Listen, you five hundred Greeks and eighty thousand monks!" said King Menander. "This Nagasena has just declared that there's no permanent individuality implied in his name!" Then, turning to Nagasena, "If, Reverend Nagasena, there is no permanent individuality, who gives you monks your robes and food, lodging and medicines? And who makes use of them? Who lives a life of righteousness, meditates, and reaches Nirvana? Who destroys living beings, steals, fornicates, tells lies, or drinks spirits? . . . If what you say is true there's neither merit nor demerit, and no fruit or result of good or evil deeds. If someone were to kill you there would be no question of murder. And there would be no masters or teachers in the (Buddhist) Order and no ordinations. If your fellow monks call you Nagasena, what then is Nagasena? Would you say that your hair is Nagasena?" "No, your Majesty."

"Or your nails, teeth, skin, or other parts of your body, or the outward form, or sensation, or perception, or the psychic constructions, or consciousness? Are any of these Nagasena?" "No, your Majesty."

"Then are all these taken together Nagasena?" "No, your Majesty."

"Or anything other than they?" "No, your Majesty."

"Then for all my asking I find no Nagasena. Nagasena is a mere sound! Surely what your Reverence has said is false!"

Then the Venerable Nagasena addressed the King.

"Your Majesty, how did you come here—on foot, or in a vehicle?"

"In a chariot."

"Then tell me what is the chariot? Is the pole the chariot?" "No, your Reverence."

"Or the axle, wheels, frame, reins, yoke, spokes, or goad?" "None of these things is the chariot."

"Then all these separate parts taken together are the chariot?" "No, your Reverence."

"Then is the chariot something other than the separate parts?" "No, your Reverence."

Milindapanha,
The Simile of the Chariot

Empiricism and the Self

- Perform your own empiricist investigation by examining the contents of your consciousness. What do you find there? Fleeting and temporary sensations, perceptions, and ideas, as Hume describes? Is your *self* anywhere to be found?

- Hume uses the terms *I* and *myself* throughout his writings, words that seem to suggest a continually existing *self-identity* that he is denying. Does Hume contradict himself? Why or why not?

- Descartes' key point was that even if we are dreaming, fantasizing or being deceived, the *act of doubting* proves that I have a *self* that is engaged in the activity of doubting. Is the same true for Hume? By denying the existence of a *self*, is he at the same time *proving* that his *self* exists, the *self* that is engaged in the act of denying? Why or why not?

- If you believe that you have a unifying and conscious *self* that exists through time, but you can't "catch yourself" when you examine your immediate experience, then where does your *self* exist? What is the nature of your *self* if you can't perceive it? (This is precisely the challenge taken up by our next philosopher, Immanuel Kant.)

- Imagine that you were present at the debate between King Menander and the monk Nagasena. How would you critically evaluate the arguments being made by both men? Do you think a chariot is an appropriate simile to the human self? Why or why not? How would you have responded to Nagasena's argument?

- Compare how Plato (in the *Phaedrus*) and Nagasena use the analogy of a chariot to explain the nature of the *self*. What are the similarities? What are the differences?

"Then for all my asking, your Majesty, I can find no chariot. The chariot is a mere sound. What then is the chariot? Surely what your Majesty has said is false! There is no chariot! . . .

When he had spoken the five hundred Greeks cried "Well done!" and said to the King, "Now, your Majesty, get out of that dilemma if you can!" "What I said was not false," replied the King. "It's on account of all these various components, the pole, axle, wheels, and so on, that the vehicle is called a chariot. It's just a generally understood term, a practical designation."

"Well said, your Majesty! You know what the word 'chariot' means! And it's just the same with me. It's on account of the various components of my being that I'm known by the generally understood term, the practical designation Nagasena." ■

Milindapanha,
The Simile of the Chariot

Immanuel Kant: *We Construct the Self*

Brilliant and idiosyncratic, the German philosopher **Immanuel Kant** (1724–1804) helped create the conceptual scaffolding of modern consciousness in the areas of metaphysics, epistemology, and ethics. Kant was alarmed by David Hume's thoroughgoing skepticism, derived from his extreme empiricism: the mind is simply a container for fleeting sensations and disconnected ideas, and our reasoning ability is merely "a slave to the passions." If Hume's views proved true, then humans would never be able to achieve genuine knowledge in any area of experience: scientific, ethical, religious, or metaphysical, including questions such as the nature of our *selves*. For Kant, Hume's devastating conclusions served as a Socratic "gadfly" to his spirit of inquiry, awakening him from his intellectual sleep and galvanizing him to action:

> I admit it was David Hume's remark that first, many years ago, interrupted my dogmatic slumber and gave a completely different direction to my inquiries in the field of speculative philosophy.

Kant was convinced that philosophers and scientists of the time did not fully appreciate the potential destructiveness of Hume's views, and that it was up to him (Kant) to meet and dismantle this threat to human knowledge.

Kant, Prolegomena
to Any Future Metaphysics

Since the origin of metaphysics so far as we know its history, nothing has ever happened which could have been more decisive to its fate than the attack made upon it by David Hume. He threw no light on this species of knowledge, but he certainly struck a spark by which light might have been kindled had it caught some inflammable substance and had its smouldering fire been carefully nursed and developed. . . . However hasty and mistaken Hume's inference may appear, it was at least founded upon investigation, and this investigation deserved the concentration of the brighter spirits of his day as well as determined efforts on their part to discover, if possible, a happier solution of the problem in the sense proposed by him. . . .

But Hume suffered the usual misfortune of metaphysicians, of not being understood. It is positively painful to see how utterly his opponents . . . missed the point of the problem; for while they were ever taking for granted that which he doubted, and demonstrating with zeal and often with impudence that which he never thought of doubting, they so misconstrued his valuable suggestion that everything remained in its old condition, as if nothing happened.

How did Hume's empirical investigations lead him to the unsatisfying conclusion that genuine knowledge—and the *self*—do not exist? Kant begins his analysis at Hume's starting point—examining immediate sense experience—and he acknowledges Hume's point that all knowledge of the world begins with sensations: sounds, shapes, colors, tastes, feels, smells. For Hume, these sensations are the basic data of experience, and they flow through our consciousness in a torrential rushing stream:

> (The sensations in our senses) succeed each other with an inconceivable rapidity and are in a perpetual flux and movement. . . . The mind is a kind of theatre where several perceptions successively make their appearance, pass, re-pass, glide away, and mingle in an infinite variety of postures and situations."

Immanuel Kant

But in reflecting on his experience, Kant observes an obvious fact that Hume seems to have overlooked, namely, *our primary experience of the world is not in terms of a disconnected stream of sensations.* Instead, we perceive and experience an organized world of objects, relationships, and ideas, all existing within a fairly stable framework of space and time. True, at times discreet and randomly related sensations dominate our experience: for example, when we are startled out of a deep sleep and "don't know where we are," or when a high fever creates bizarre hallucinations, or the instant when an unexpected thunderous noise or blinding light suddenly dominates our awareness. But in general, we live in a fairly stable and orderly world in which sensations are woven together into a fabric that is familiar to us. And integrated throughout this fabric is our *conscious self* who is the knowing subject at the center of our universe. Hume's problem wasn't his starting point—empirical experience—it was the fact that he remained fixated on the starting point, refusing to move to the next, intelligible level of experience. Here's how Kant explains the situation:

There can be no doubt that all our knowledge begins with experience. For how should our faculty of knowledge be awakened into action did not objects affecting our sense partly of themselves produce representations, partly arouse the activity of our understanding to compare these representations, and, by combining or separating them, work up the raw material for the sensible impressions into that knowledge of objects which is entitled experience? In the order of time, therefore, we have no knowledge antecedent to experience, and with experience all our knowledge begins.

But though all our knowledge begins with experience, *it does not follow that it all arises out of experience.* (italics added) For it may well be that even our empirical knowledge is made up of what we receive through impressions and of what our own faculty of knowledge (sensible impressions, serving merely as the occasion) supplies from itself. If our faculty of knowledge makes any such addition, it may be that we are not in a position to distinguish it from the raw material, until with long practice of attention we have become skilled in separating it.

This, then is a question which at least calls for closer examination, and does not allow of any off-hand answer:—whether there is any knowledge that is thus independent of experience and even of all impressions of the senses. Such knowledge is entitled *a priori,* and distinguished from the *empirical,* which has its sources *a posteriori,* that is, in experience.

Kant, *Prolegomena to Any Future Metaphysics*

Where does the order and organization of our world come from? According to Kant, it comes in large measure from *us.* Our minds actively sort, organize, relate, and synthesize the fragmented, fluctuating collection of sense data that our sense organs take in. For example, imagine that someone dumped a pile of puzzle pieces on the table in front of you. They would initially appear to be a random collection of items, unrelated to one another and containing no meaning for you, much like the basic sensations of immediate unreflective experience. However, as you began to assemble the pieces, these fragmentary items would gradually begin to form a coherent image that would have significance for you. According to Kant this meaning-constructing activity is precisely what our minds are doing all of the time: taking the raw data of experience and actively synthesizing it into the familiar, orderly, meaningful world in which we live. As you might imagine, this mental process is astonishing in its power and complexity, and it is going on all of the time.

How do our minds know the best way to construct an intelligible world out of a never-ending avalanche of sensations? We each have fundamental organizing *rules* or *principles* built into the architecture of our minds. These dynamic principles naturally order, categorize, organize, and synthesize sense data into the familiar fabric of our lives, bounded by space and time. These organizing rules are *a priori* in the sense that they precede the sensations of experience and they exist independently of these sensations. We didn't have to "learn" these *a priori* ways of organizing and relating the world—they came as software already installed in our intellectual operating systems.

Kant referred to his approach to perception and knowledge as representing a "Copernican Revolution" in metaphysics and epistemology, derived from the breakthrough of the Polish astronomer Copernicus (1473–1543) who was one of the first and most definitive voices asserting that instead of the sun orbiting around the earth, it's actually the reverse—the earth orbits the sun.

In a similar fashion, empiricists like Hume had assumed that the mind was a passive receptacle of sensations, a "theatre" in which the raw data of experience moved across without our influence. According to Hume, our minds conform to the world of which we are merely passive observers. Kant, playing the role of Copernicus, asserted that this is a wrong-headed perspective. The sensations of experience are necessary for knowledge, but they are in reality the "grist" for our mental "mills." Our minds *actively* synthesize and relate these sensations in the process of creating an intelligible world. As a result, the sensations of immediate experience conform to our minds, rather than the reverse. We *construct* our world through these conceptual operations, and as result, this is a world of which we can gain insight and knowledge.

Kant, *Prolegomena to Any Future Metaphysics*

 Kant, Immanuel, *Prolegomena to Any Future Metaphysics*

Hitherto it has been assumed that all our knowledge must conform to objects. But all attempts to extend our knowledge of objects by establishing something in regard to them by means of concepts have, on this assumption, ended in failure. We must, therefore, make trial whether we may not have more success if we suppose that objects must conform to our knowledge. ■

This is a brief overview of Kant's epistemological framework, which we will examine in more depth in chapters 8 and 9 on *What is True? What is Real?*. For now we are interested in how this framework influences Kant's conception of the *self*. Actually, from Kant's standpoint, it's our *self* that makes experiencing an intelligible world possible, because it's the *self* that is responsible for synthesizing the discreet data of sense experience into a meaningful whole. Metaphorically, our *self* is the weaver who, using the loom of the mind, weaves together the fabric of experience into a unified whole so that it becomes *my* experience, *my* world, *my* universe. Without our *self* to perform this synthesizing function, our experience would be unknowable, a chaotic collection of sensations without coherence or significance.

Kant, *Critique of Pure Reason* ■

Sensations would be nothing to us, and would not concern us in the least, if they were not received into our (orderly) consciousness. Knowledge is impossible in any other way. . . . For perceptions could not be perceptions of anything for me unless they could at least be connected together into (my) one consciousness. This principle stands firm *a priori*, and may be called the "transcendental principle of unity" for all the multiplicity of our perceptions and sensations.

The *unity of consciousness* is a phrase invented by Kant to describe the fact that the thoughts and perceptions of any given mind are bound together in a unity by being all contained in *one* consciousness—*my* consciousness. That's precisely what makes your world intelligible to you: it's *your self* that is actively organizing all of your sensations and thoughts into a picture that makes sense to you. This picture is uniquely *your* picture. You are at the center of your world, and you view everything in the world from *your* perspective. For example, think about a time in which you shared an experience with someone but you each had radically different experiences: attending a party, viewing a movie, having a communication misunderstanding. Reflect on the way each person instinctively describes the entire situation from *his* or *her* perspective. *That's* the unity of consciousness that Kant is describing.

Your *self* is able to perform this synthesizing, unifying function because it *transcends* sense experience. Your *self* isn't an *object* located in your consciousness with other objects— your *self* is a *subject*, an *organizing principle* that makes a unified and intelligible experience possible. It is, metaphorically, "above" or "behind" sense experience, and it uses the categories of your mind to filter, order, relate, organize, and synthesize sensations into a unified whole. That's why Kant accords the *self* "transcendental" status: because it exists independently of experience. The *self* is the product of reason, a *regulative principle* because the *self* "regulates" experience by making unified experience possible. Other such "transcendental regulative ideas" include the ideas of *cosmos* and *God*.

> Everything that has its basis in the nature of our powers must be appropriate to, and consistent with, their right employment—if we can only guard against a certain misunderstanding and so discover the proper direction of these powers. We are entitled, therefore, to suppose that transcendental ideas . . . have an excellent, and indeed indispensably necessary, regulative employment, namely, that of directing the understanding towards a certain goal upon which the routes marked out by all its rules converge.
>
> The first (regulative) idea is the "I" itself, viewed simply as thinking nature or soul . . . : in a word, the idea of a simple self-sustaining intelligence. (Reason operates) to represent all determinations as existing in a single subject, all powers, so far as possible, as derived from a single fundamental power, all change as belonging to the states of one and the same permanent being. ■

So where did Hume go wrong, from Kant's standpoint? How could Hume examine his mind's contents and not find his *self*, particularly because, in Kant's view, the *self* is required to *have* intelligible experience? Hume's problem (according to Kant) was that he looked for his *self* in the wrong place! Contrary to what Hume assumed, the *self* is not an object of consciousness, one of the contents of the mind. Instead, the *self* is the transcendental activity that synthesizes the contents of consciousness into an intelligible whole. Because the *self* is not a "content" of consciousness but rather the invisible "thread" that ties the contents of consciousness together, it's no wonder that Hume couldn't find it. It would be analogous to you going to a sporting event and looking in vain to see the "team," when all you see are a collection of players. The "team" is the network of relationships between the individuals that is not visible to simple perception. The "team" is the synthesizing activity that creates a unity among the individuals, much like the *self* creates a unity in experience by synthesizing its contents into an intelligible whole. And because experience is con-

Kant, *Critique of Pure Reason*

 Kant, Immanuel, *Critique of Pure Reason*

Searching for the Self

3.12

Here's an opportunity for you to be a philosophy detective engaged in a "missing person" investigation—looking for your *self*. If Kant is right, you should not be able to find your *self* among the contents of your consciousness. Instead, your *self* should be revealed as the synthesizing principle that unites your experience. Launch a reflective investigation into your *self*, and then describe as clearly as you can what you find. Did you discover your *self*? How would you describe the qualities of your *self*? In what ways is your *self* similar to all other selves? In what ways is your *self* different from all other selves?

Jean Piaget (1896–1980) Swiss developmental psychologist interested in the development of knowledge in persons.

tinually changing, this intelligible picture of the world is being updated on an instantaneous basis.

We can also see Kant's refinement of Descartes' concept of the *self*, which he interprets as a simple, self-evident fact: "I think, therefore I am." Kant was interested in developing a more complex, analytical, and sophisticated understanding of the *self* as a thinking identity. To begin with, Descartes was focusing on one dimension of the thinking process: our ability to reflect, to become aware of our *self*, to be *self-conscious*. But from Kant's standpoint, the thinking *self*—consciousness—has a more complex structure than simple self-reflection. The *self* is a dynamic entity/activity, continually synthesizing sensations and ideas into an integrated, meaningful whole. The *self*, in the form of consciousness, utilizes conceptual categories (or "transcendental rules") such as *substance, cause and effect, unity, plurality, possibility, necessity*, and *reality* to construct an orderly and "objective" world that is stable and can be investigated scientifically. It is in this sense that the *self* constructs its own reality, actively creating a world that is familiar, predictable, and, most significantly, *mine*.

Kant's "Copernican Revolution" accompanied by his comprehensive and penetrating analysis of the central themes of philosophy helped usher in a modern consciousness. In fact, many of his foundational premises have been supported by research in the sciences and social sciences. For example, the renowned developmental psychologist **Jean Piaget** (1896–1980) conducted painstaking empirical research on the way the human mind develops, an interactive process involving both sensory experience and innate cognitive structures. His seminal book *Construction of Reality in the Child* (1950) (published almost 150 years after Kant's death), could very easily have been written by Kant had he been a modern developmental psychologist. Similarly, work in language development by linguists such as Noam Chomsky have also supported the Kantian idea that human experience— such as language abilities—are the product of both exposure to a specific language and innate, *a priori* intellectual rules or categories that are "hard-wired" into each human being.

Kant's dominant influence on Western philosophy and the intellectual framework of modern consciousness was in sharp contrast to his quiet, limited life. Never traveling more than sixty miles from his birthplace in Germany, Kant never married and lived a life of such precise habits that it was said the citizens of his hometown could set their watches based on his daily walks. He was a popular university professor, and his passion for understanding both the universe and human nature is reflected in the inscription he wrote for his tombstone: "The starry heavens above me; the moral law within me."

Sigmund Freud: *There Are Two Selves, One Conscious, One Unconscious*

Our explorations of the *self* have, until this point, focused almost exclusively on the *conscious self*. Of course, Kant's idea of the *self* as a "transcendental unifying principle of consciousness" is certainly not "conscious" in the traditional sense. But nor is it hidden from reflective awareness, if we know where to look for it. This *transcendental self* (or *ego*) is not to be found as an entity *in* consciousness—it is the dynamic organizing principle that makes consciousness possible. One problem with this view of the *self* is that there is nothing *personal* about it. As an abstract organizing principle, it appears to be difficult to distinguish one *transcendental self* from another. As a result, Kant identifies *another* self, the *empirical self* (or *ego*), which includes all of those particular aspects of our *selves* that make us uniquely different people: bodies, memories, personalities, ways of thinking, emotional patterns, and so on. The obvious problem is that this model of consciousness leaves us with *two selves*, leading to some disquieting questions: How do these two *selves* relate to one another? Is one *self* more primary or fundamental than the other? Which *self* is our "true" *self*, our identity, our soul? Are we condemned to be metaphysical schizophrenics? Kant tries mightily to answer these troubling and enigmatic questions, but it's a very difficult challenge.

Sigmund Freud's (1856–1939) view of the *self* leads to an analogous dualistic view of the *self*, though the contours and content of his ideas are very different from Kant's. Freud is not, strictly speaking, a philosopher, but his views on the nature of the *self* have had a far-reaching impact on philosophical thinking, as well as virtually every other discipline in the humanities and social sciences. Naturally, his most dominant influence has been in the fields of psychology and psychoanalysis. Freud's view of the *self* was multitiered, divided among the conscious, preconscious, and unconscious. He explains his psychological model in the following passage from his *An Outline of Psychoanalysis*:

> There is no need to characterize what we call *conscious*: it is the same as the consciousness of philosophers and of everyday opinion. Everything else that is mental is in our view *unconscious*. We are soon led to make an important division in this unconscious. Some processes become conscious easily; they may then cease to be conscious, but can become conscious once more without any trouble: as people say they can be reproduced or remembered. This reminds us that consciousness is in general a very highly fugitive condition. What is conscious is conscious only for a moment. . . . Everything unconscious that can easily exchange the unconscious condition for the conscious one, is therefor better described as "capable of entering consciousness," or as *preconscious*. Experience has taught us that there are hardly any mental processes, even of the most complicated kind, which cannot on occasion remain preconscious, although as a rule they press forward, as we say, into consciousness. There are other mental processes or mental material which have no such easy access to consciousness, but which must be inferred, discovered, and translated into conscious form in the manner that has been described. It is for such material that we reserve the name of the unconscious proper. Thus we have attributed three qualities to mental processes: they are either conscious, preconscious, or unconscious. The division between the three classes is neither absolute nor permanent. What is preconscious becomes conscious, as we have seen, without any activity on our part; what is unconscious can, as a result of our efforts, be made conscious, though in the process we may have an impression that we are overcoming what are often very strong resistances. . . . A lowering of resistances of this sort, with a consequent pressing forward of unconscious material, takes place regularly in the state of sleep and thus brings about a necessary precondition for the formation of dreams.

It is by no means an exaggeration to assert that the concept of the **unconscious** forms the central core in Freud's theory of the structure and dynamics of the human personality. And though the **conscious** *self* has an important role to play in our lives, it is the *unconscious self* that holds the greatest fascination for Freud, and which has the dominant influence in our personalities. Freud's focus on the

---

SIGMUND FREUD

(1856–1939)
Psychologist. Freud founded the school of psychoanalysis which became one of the most influential theories of psychology and therapy in the twentieth century. Especially important was his theory of sub-conscious motivation.

Freudian concepts of the conscious and unconscious
In Freudian psychoanalytic theory, consciousness refers to mental processes of which we are aware; unconsciousness refers to mental processes which are not easily accessible to our awareness.

unconscious self marks a significant departure from previous efforts in philosophy to understand the nature of the *self*. Although Freud is generally given credit for the extensive articulation and subsequent popularization of the concept of the *unconscious*, it was his sincerest conviction that the *unconscious* was not a concept that he invented, but rather a reality characterizing human functioning that he discovered.

> The poets and philosophers before me discovered the unconscious. What I discovered was the scientific method by which the unconscious can be studied.

Essential to an understanding of Freud's conception of the *unconscious* is the psychoanalytic model of "split-level" human functioning. When such a model is employed, human experience is viewed as the product not simply of our *conscious* wishes, desires, and intentions, but also of our *unconscious* wishes and desires. Our behavior is thus seen to be the result of several different levels of functioning, at least one of which we are unaware, as summed up by the psychoanalyst Norman Cameron:

> We are all so organized that we have active infantile and magical processes going on within us, at the same time that we are behaving adequately as mature adults. There is not the slightest possibility of eliminating all these irrational unconscious components. We all operate simultaneously at different levels of maturity and rationality: irrational and often infantile unconscious processes are normal components of everyday behavior and experience.

According to Freud, these two levels of human functioning—the *conscious* and the *unconscious*—differ radically both in their content and in the rules and logic that govern them. The *unconscious* contains basic instinctual drives including sexuality, aggressiveness, and self-destruction; traumatic memories; unfulfilled wishes and childhood fantasies; thoughts and feelings that would be considered socially taboo. The *unconscious* level is characterized by the most primitive level of human motivation and human functioning. At this level, the most basic instinctual drives seek immediate gratification or discharge. Unheedful of the demands and restrictions of reality, the naked impulses at this level are governed solely by the "pleasure principle." As Freud's definitive biographer, Dr. Ernest Jones, explains:

> There reigns in it a quite uninhibited flow towards the imaginary fulfillment of the wish that stirs it—the only thing that can. It is unchecked by any logical contradiction, any causal associations; it has no sense of either time or of external reality. Its goal is either to discharge the excitation through any exit, or, if that fails, to establish a perceptual—if necessary, an hallucinatory—identity with the remembered perception of a previous satisfaction.

Our *unconscious self* embodies a mode of operation that precedes the development of all other forms of our mental functioning. It includes throughout our lives the primitive rock-bottom activities, the primal strivings on which all human functioning is ultimately based. Our *unconscious self* operates at a prelogical and prerational level. And though it exists and influences us throughout our lives, it is not directly observable and its existence can only be inferred from such phenomena as neurotic symptoms, dreams, and "slips of the tongue."

In contrast, the *conscious self* is governed by the "reality principle" (rather than the "pleasure principle"), and at this level of functioning, behavior and experience are organized in ways that are rational, practical, and appropriate to the social environment. Although the ultimate goals of the *conscious self* are the same as the

VISUAL PHILOSOPHY

"The Sleeping Gypsy" by Rousseau

Why did Sigmund Freud believe that "Dreams are the royal road to the unconscious"? What have you learned about yourself by reflecting on your dreams?

The Sleeping Gypsy, Henri Rousseau, 1897, Oil on Canvas, 51" x 6'7", Gift of Mrs. Simon Guggenheim (646.1939). The Museum of Modern Art/Licensed by Scala-Art Resource, NY.

unconscious self—the gratification of needs and the reduction of tensions to optimal levels—the means of achieving these goals are entirely different. Instead of seeking these goals by means that are direct, impulsive, and irrational, the *conscious self* usually takes into account the realistic demands of the situation, the consequences of various actions, and the overriding need to preserve the equilibrium of the entire psychodynamic system. To this end, the *conscious self* has the task of controlling the constant pressures of the *unconscious self*, as its primitive impulses continually seek for immediate discharge.

What is the evidence for this split-level, "two-self" model of functioning? Freud believes that evidence of a powerful *unconscious self* can be found in the content of our dreams, inadvertent "slips of tongue," and techniques—such as free association—used by Freudian psychoanalysts in clinical treatment. However, the most compelling evidence for an *unconscious self* is to be found in pathological, neurotic behavior. From Freud's standpoint, the neurotic symptom has three essential aspects: it is a sign that the balance of forces within the personality system is disturbed; it is a sign that infantile conflicts have been reactivated; and it is itself an attempt at a spontaneous cure, an attempt at adaptation, although the individual may be worse off with his or her neurotic adaptation than without it. For example, an individual who experienced traumatic frustration, conflict, and guilt centering on his toilet training may "adapt" to this potentially threatening situation by compulsively washing his hands several hundred times a day in an effort to assuage his guilt and resolve his emotionally charged conflicts. Although such an adaptation may forestall the disruption of his conscious level of functioning by the anxiety generated by his unconscious conflicts and painful emotions, from the standpoint of normal overall functioning, it could not be considered to be a particularly successful one.

People whose psychological defenses are defective will react to many situations simultaneously at two levels: an adult conscious level, and an infantile unconscious level. Any situation that resembles a traumatic emotional situation of early childhood will call out a repetition of the childhood response at the same time that it calls out the adult response. The adult response is likely to be direct and overt; the childhood response is likely to be covert and derivative. This mingling of different levels of experience may be accomplished without undue stress or trouble, as in the case with normal, well-adjusted behavior and experience. However, it may lead to an exaggerated reaction that is otherwise appropriate, to ambivalent feelings and ambiguous behavior, or to neurotic symptom formation. When this last is the case, the specific form of the symptom will depend both on the person's specific vulnerability and on the situation that disturbs his internal equilibrium.

Because the *unconscious self* plays such an important role in our daily lives (according to Freud), why does it remain inaccessible to conscious awareness? Freud's explanation for this is the psychological activity of "repression," which serves as the theoretical keystone of defensive organizations in both normal and neurotic persons. Although it is thought to be related to the conscious "suppression," repression is assumed to operate at unconscious levels, like most of the psychological defenses. Repression is used to help contain the potentially disruptive aspects of unconscious functioning, and as a consequence it is usually the main defense mechanism for maintaining the ego boundaries necessary for normal conscious functioning. If a deep and inclusive regression to unconscious levels does occur while a person is awake—a situation often referred to as "the return of the repressed"—the effects can be devastating.

The purpose of psychotherapy (the therapeutic method created by Freud) is to enable the patient to acknowledge the conflicts, emotions, and memories at the root cause of his or her disorder. By acknowledging and understanding the traumatized memories, emotions, and conflicts, most of which date back to infancy and early childhood, the individual not only attains a cathartic emotional release, but also is able to resolve basic emotional conflicts that were never before resolved and that lay festering unconsciously as the cause of abnormal maladaptive behavior. As the individual begins to see the reason for the particular symptom or cluster of symptoms that has formed, these symptoms will (in theory) tend to lose their efficacy, as their success lay precisely in the fact that they were unconscious attempts to deal with the specific traumatic contents existing unconsciously. When they and their purpose are disclosed to the individual, they will tend to be discarded as maladaptive forms of behavior, and a normal resolution and adaptation to the repressed and unconscious material will be attained. However, the acknowledgment and affirmation of the patient is not simply an intellectual understanding. Instead, she must recall the original memories with all of their emotional charge and trauma, and work through the emotions involved until she is able to adopt a new and more adaptive attitude both toward the past of childhood and toward her present and future adult life.

THINK PHILOSOPHICALLY
Analyzing Sigmund Freud

3.13

PHILOSOPHER'S NOTEBOOK

Although the contents of the unconscious cannot be observed directly (according to Freud) we can observe them indirectly, like observing footprints in the sand or dusting for fingerprints. There are several areas in which unconscious influences are evident. This is an opportunity for you to look for evidence of unconscious functioning in each of these areas. Record your reflections in your Philosophy Notebook.

- *Slips of the tongue:* Think about a time in which you unexpectedly said what you *really* thought rather than what you intended to say: for example, "I think your new haircut looks *atrocious*" instead of your intended "I think your new haircut looks *attractive*." Do you think this is persuasive evidence for Freud's concept of the unconscious?

- *Dreams:* Describe a particularly disturbing dream, or a recurring dream, that expressed surprising or disturbing themes. What do you think the dream really meant? Do you think the dream is persuasive evidence for Freud's concept of the unconscious?

- *Neurosis:* Describe one sort of neurotic behavior in which you engage. (Don't worry, everyone has at least *one* neurosis!) For example, do you have a compulsion to check and recheck locks? To eat too much or too little? To perform superstitious rituals? To be overly suspicious ("paranoid") about others' intentions? To feel excessively guilty about something? To be chronically depressed? And so on. What do you think is the origin of this neurosis? Do you think this syndrome is persuasive evidence for Freud's concept of the unconscious?

Freud's Topographical model of the mind divided it into systems on the basis of their relationship to consciousness: conscious, preconscious, and unconscious. Freud later developed a Structural model of the mind that divided it according to mental functions: the id, the ego, and the superego. Freud emphasizes the fact that although the Structural model has certain similarities with the earlier Topographical model, the two are not the same. Although the id has virtually the same place as the unconscious in the sense of being the reservoir for the primal instinctual forces responsible for all human motivation, the ego and superego systems consist of aspects that are both conscious and unconscious in the psychoanalytic sense—in other words, they are inaccessible to consciousness except under unusual circumstances. Freud believed that the strength of the Structural model was its ability to analyze situations of mental conflict in terms of which functions are allied with one another and which are in conflict (analogous to the conflicting elements in Plato's division of the soul into Reason, Spirit, and Appetite).

Freud's penetrating and systematic analysis of the complexity of the human mind had a far-reaching impact on modern understanding of our *selves*. However, from a philosophical perspective, there are significant problems with the models of the mind that he developed. Freud's concept of the unconscious is of a "place"—a timeless, unknowable realm—or "entity" that exerts a profound and continual influence on our conscious thoughts, emotions, and behavior. But "where" exactly does this realm exist? "Who" exactly is this entity, and what is its relation to our conscious *self*? Doesn't Freud's model fragment the human mind into a collection of parts, multiple *selves* with enigmatic relationships to one another? Don't we end up with two "I thinks," one conscious and one unconscious?

ALASDAIR MACINTYRE
(1929–)
Communitarian philosopher. Currently teaching at the University of Notre Dame. Author of several works, especially on ethics and moral theory, including *A Short History of Ethics* (1966), *After Virtue* (1981), and *Whose Justice, Which Rationality* (1988).

Seen from another perspective, it's one thing to say that someone is "unconscious" of the true purpose, motive, or intention of their behavior; it's quite another to say that the behavior is "caused" by influences from "the unconscious." According to the philosopher **Alasdair MacIntyre** (1929–) in his book *The Unconscious*, Freud was not merely offering us an instructive model in terms of which conscious thought and behavior could be envisaged. Instead, he was making an existential claim, propounding a hypothesis, asserting that "the world includes an entity hitherto undiscovered," a claim that is unwarranted and conceptually confused.

To put the same point into linguistic terms, the use of "unconscious" as an adjective or as an adverb is quite normal and acceptable in ordinary language. The problem for Freud is that he uses the concept of "unconscious" not only as an adverb and an adjective, but also as a *noun*. As MacIntyre explains it:

> For where Freud uses "unconscious" and "unconsciously" he extends earlier uses of these words; but when he speaks of "*the* unconscious" he invents a new term for which he has to prescribe a meaning and a use. And in this innovation he is curiously dominated by a picture of the mind which he at many points explicitly rejected.

This "picture of the mind" that Freud embraces by his use of "the unconscious" as a noun is that derived from Descartes, who considered the subject as a rational spiritual entity, an entity quite different and distinct from the physical substance of the body. It is this view of the mind that has been described by the philosopher Gilbert Ryle as "the ghost in the machine," and by Jacques Maritain as "the angel in the machine." The new twist that Freud gave it, according to MacIntyre, is that of transferring the notion of the separate substance of the mind from the rational consciousness of Descartes to the irrational unconscious.

> Now Freud clearly does not think of man as possessing this kind of rational self-knowledge in his ordinary consciousness, and in so far as he does not do this he rejects the Cartesian picture of the mind. But Freud retains from the Cartesian picture the idea of the mind as something distinct and apart, a place or a realm which can be inhabited by such entities as ideas. Only he makes dominant not "the conscious" mind but "the unconscious." He introduces "unconscious" as an adjective to describe what we may have hitherto observed but have not hitherto recognized or classified. He introduces "the unconscious" as a noun not to describe, but to explain.

Freud's idea of an existent, spatially located "unconscious" leads to other difficulties as well, including those associated with the Freudian concept of "repression." Repression for Freud clearly refers to a datable event, an occurrence that actually happens when the memory of an experience is denied a place in consciousness and instead relegated to the unconscious. Yet by definition, repression is something of which we are unconscious, and as such is inaccessible to direct observation. As a consequence, we can only infer that something has been "repressed" from subsequent behavior and feelings: for example, neurotic behavior. But the claim that repression has occurred is logically dependent on the fact that certain alleged childhood experiences did in fact take place; yet simply to show that they did take place is not enough to show that repression occurred, and it is indeed difficult to see what would be enough proof. It would therefore appear that no direct empirical evidence can be brought directly to bear on the situation to either validate or falsify the theoretical notions of "repression" and "the unconscious." And if such is the case, then it is indeed untenable to contend that repression is a datable event and that the unconscious is a place in which repressed events exist timelessly, exerting causal influence on our conscious functioning. Because such claims are in principle neither verifiable nor falsifiable, they are therefore empty. Hence any attempt to treat the unconscious as an actual existent realm containing actual repressed mental events, emotions, ideas, and so on will not only run into the traditional problems plaguing any such dualistic conception of human functioning, but also be hard put to produce any empirical evidence in its favor.

Some philosophers—such as Maurice Merleau-Ponty and William Barrett—are convinced that we can develop a model of the human mind—and *self*—that will explain the unconscious dimensions of human experience without falling prey to the philosophical difficulties that Freud encountered in his models. And even some therapists believe that Freud's concept of the *self* is much too restrictive and one-dimensional, such as psychiatrist Dr. **Willard Gaylin** in the following essay, "What You See Is the Real You."

WILLARD GAYLIN

(1925–).
Practicing psychiatrist and psychoanalyst. Educated at Harvard University (A.B., 1947) and Columbia University; cofounder and president of the Hastings Center, which researches ethical issues in the life sciences. Author of several books including *The Rage Within: Anger in Modern Life* (1984) and *The Male Ego* (1992).

Gaylin,
What You See Is the Real You

It was, I believe, the distinguished Nebraska financier Father Edward J. Flanagan who professed to having "never met a bad boy." Having, myself, met a remarkable number of bad boys, it might seem that either our experiences were drastically different or we were using the word "bad" differently. I suspect neither is true, but, rather that the Father was appraising the "inner man," while I, in fact, do not acknowledge the existence of inner people.

Since we psychoanalysts have unwittingly contributed to this confusion, let one, at least, attempt a small rectifying effort. Psychoanalytic data—which should be viewed as supplementary information—are, unfortunately, often viewed as alternative (and superior) explanations. This has led to the prevalent tendency to think of the "inner" man as the real man and the outer man as an illusion or pretender.

While psychoanalysis supplies us with an incredibly useful tool for explaining the motives and purposes underlying human behavior, most of this has little bearing on the moral nature of that behavior.

Like roentgenology *(brain scans)*, psychoanalysis is a fascinating, but relatively new, means of illuminating the person. But few of us are prepared to substitute an X-ray of grandfather's head for the portrait that hangs in the parlor. The inside of the man represents another view, not a truer one. A man may not always be what he appears to be, but what he appears to be is always a significant part of what he is. A man is the sum total of *all* his behavior. To probe for unconscious determinants of behavior and then define *him* in their terms exclusively, ignoring his overt behavior altogether, is a greater distortion than ignoring the unconscious completely.

Kurt Vonnegut has said, "You are what you pretend to be," which is simply another way of saying you are what we (all of us) perceive you to be, not what you think you are.

Consider for a moment the case of the 90-year-old man on his deathbed (surely the Talmud must deal with this?) joyous and relieved over the success of his deception. For 90 years he has shielded his evil nature from public observation. For 90 years he has affected courtesy, kindness, and generosity—suppressing all the malice he knew was within him while he calculatedly and artificially substituted grace and charity. All his life he had been fooling the world into believing he was a good man. This "evil" man will, I predict, be welcomed into the Kingdom of Heaven.

Similarly, I will not be told that the young man who earns his pocket money by mugging old ladies is "really" a good boy. Even my generous and expansive definition of goodness will not accommodate that particular form of self-advancement.

It does not count that beneath the rough exterior he has a heart—or, for that matter, an entire innards—of purest gold, locked away from human perception. You are for the most part what you seem to be, not what you would wish to be, nor, indeed, what you believe yourself to be.

Spare me, therefore, your good intentions, your inner sensitivities, your unarticulated and unexpressed love. And spare me also those tedious psychohistories which—by exposing the goodness inside the bad man, and the evil in the good—invariably establish a vulgar and perverse egalitarianism, as if the arrangement of what is outside and what inside makes no moral difference.

Saint Francis may, in his unconscious, indeed have been compensating for, and denying destructive, unconscious Oedipal impulses identical to those which Attila projected and acted on. But the similarity of the unconscious constellations in the two men matters precious little, if it does not distinguish between them.

I do not care to learn that Hitler's heart was in the right place. A knowledge of the unconscious life of the man may be an adjunct to understanding his behavior. It is *not* a substitute for his behavior in describing him.

The inner man is a fantasy. If it helps you to identify with one, by all means, do so; preserve it, cherish it, embrace it, but do not present it to others for evaluation or consideration, for excuse or exculpation, or, for that matter for punishment or disapproval.

Like any fantasy, it serves your purposes alone. It has no standing in the real world which we share with each other. Those character traits, those attitudes, that behavior—that strange and alien stuff sticking out all over you—*that's the real you!* ■

THINK PHILOSOPHICALLY 3.14
Analyzing Willard Gaylin

- When Gaylin observes the "prevalent tendency to think of the 'inner' man as the real man and the outer man as an illusion or pretender," he clearly has Freud's views regarding the dominant influence of the unconscious in mind. How do you imagine Freud might respond to Gaylin's contention that such a view is false and dangerous?

- Do you have a concept of an "inner self" that the world does not completely see or fully appreciate? If so, how does your "inner self" differ from the "outer self" that is available to others?

- Gaylin states, "A man is the sum total of *all* his behavior. To probe for unconscious determinants of behavior and then define him in their terms exclusively, ignoring his overt behavior altogether, is a greater distortion than ignoring the unconscious completely." Do you think a combined version of your "inner self" and "outer self" is a more accurate version of who you *really* are? Why or why not?

- "The inner man is a fantasy. . . . Like any fantasy, it serves your purposes alone. It has no standing in the real world which we share with each other." People have a tendency to use their "inner people" to explain their mistakes and failures of achievement in life. How would Gaylin respond to those complaints? How would *you* respond to those complaints?

Gilbert Ryle: *The Self Is How You Behave*

The dualistic metaphysic of mind and body initiated by Plato, perpetuated by Descartes, and given an "unconscious twist" by Freud leads, as we have seen, to challenging conceptual questions and vexing enigmas. Some philosophers and psychologists, in an effort to avoid the difficulties of viewing the mind and body as two radically different aspects of the *self*, have decided to simply focus on observable behavior in defining the *self*. Their solution to the mind/body "problem" is to simply deny—or ignore—the existence of an internal, nonphysical *self*, and instead focus on the dimensions of the *self* that we *can* observe. No more inner selves, immortal souls, states of consciousness, or unconscious entities: instead, the *self* is defined in terms of the behavior that is presented to the world, a view that is known in psychology as **behaviorism**.

In philosophy one of the chief advocates of this view is **Gilbert Ryle** (1900–1976), a British philosopher whose book, *The Concept of Mind*, had a dramatic

Behaviorism The view that the "self" is defined by observable behavior.

impact on Western thought. Ryle's behaviorism was a different sort from that of psychology. He thought of his approach as a *logical* behaviorism, focused on creating conceptual clarity, not on developing techniques to condition and manipulate human behavior.

Ryle begins his book by launching a devastating attack on "Descartes' myth," characterizing it as the "official doctrine" that has insidiously penetrated the consciousness of academics, professionals, and average citizens alike. According to Ryle, it's high time that this destructive myth of dualism is debunked once and for all, and replaced with a clearer conceptual and linguistic understanding of the true nature of the *self*.

Ryle, *The Concept of Mind*

There is a doctrine about the nature and place of minds which is so prevalent among theorists and even among laymen that it deserves to be described as the official theory. Most philosophers, psychologists and religious teachers subscribe, with minor reservations, to it's main articles and, although they admit certain theoretical difficulties in it, they tend to assume that these can be overcome without serious modifications being made to the architecture of the theory. It will be argued here that the central principles of the doctrine are unsound and conflict with the whole body of what we know about minds when we are not speculating about them.

The official doctrine, which hails chiefly from Descartes, is something like this. With the doubtful exceptions of idiots and infants in arms every human being has both a body and a mind. Some would prefer to say that every human being has both a body and a mind. His body and his mind are ordinarily harnessed together, but after the death of the body his mind may continue to exist and function.

Human bodies are in space and are subject to the mechanical laws which govern all other bodies in space. Bodily processes and states can be inspected by external observers. So a man's bodily life is as much a public affair as are the lives of animals and reptiles and even as the careers of trees, crystals and plants.

But minds are not in space, nor are their operations subject to mechanical laws. The workings of one mind are not witnessable by other observers; its career is private. Only I can take direct cognizance of the states and processes of my own mind. A person therefore lives through two collateral histories, one consisting of what happens in and to his body, and other consisting of what happens in and to his mind. The first is public, the second private. The events in the first history are events in the physical world, those in the second are events in the mental world.

It has been disputed whether a person does or can directly monitor all or only some of the episodes of his own private history; but, according to the official doctrine, of at least some of these episodes he has direct and unchallengeable cognisance. In consciousness, self-consciousness and introspection he is directly and authentically apprised of the present states and operations of his mind. He may have great or small uncertainties about concurrent and adjacent episodes in the physical world, but he can have none about at least part of what is momentarily occupying his mind.

In these passages Ryle summarizes the essential elements of the dualistic view of the *self*—mind and body as distinct entities—first articulated by Plato and then perpetuated in various incarnations through St. Augustine, Descartes, and others. Under this view, the body is seen as a physical entity, subject to the physical laws of the universe, whereas the mind (soul, spirit) is a nonphysical entity and exempt from the laws of the universe. As a result, the body is mortal and dies, whereas the mind is at least *potentially* able to continue existing beyond the death of the body.

According to Ryle, this dualistic view has serious implications for what we can know and not know. Although each person has direct knowledge of his or her mind, it is impossible for us to have *any* direct knowledge of other minds. Each mind is its own private, personal universe.

Our physical bodies are just the opposite of our minds: our bodies and their movements are available to everyone, including ourselves. Our bodies can be observed, photographed, measured, analyzed, and their movements can be recorded. Although our minds are completely private, our bodies and their movements are completely public.

Analyzed in this fashion, the dualistic division of mind and body seems rather odd, and this is precisely Ryle's point: "It will be argued here that the central principles of the doctrine are unsound and conflict with the whole body of what we know about minds when we are not speculating about them." In other words, although the majority of people assume a mind/body dualism as a general theory, on a practical level we act and speak in a much different fashion. This "ghost in the machine" dualism (Ryle's central metaphor) conflicts directly with our everyday experience, revealing itself to be a conceptually flawed and confused notion that needs to be revised. Ryle continues his argument in the following passages.

Ryle, *The Concept of Mind*

It is customary to express this bifurcation of his two lives and of his two worlds by saying that the things and events which belong to the physical world, including his own body, are external, while the workings of his own mind are internal. This antithesis of outer and inner is of course meant to be construed as a metaphor, since minds, not being in space, could not be described as being spatially inside anything else, or as having things going on spatially inside themselves. But relapses from this good intention are common and theorists are found speculating how stimuli, the physical sources of which are yards or miles outside of a person's skin, can generate mental responses inside his skull, or how decisions framed inside his cranium can set going movements of his extremities.

Even when "inner" and "outer" are construed as metaphors, the problem of how a person's mind and body influence one another is notoriously charged with theoretical difficulties. What the mind wills, the legs, arms and the tongue execute; what affects the ear and the eye has something to do with what the mind perceives; grimaces and smiles betray the mind's moods and bodily castigations lead, it is hoped, to moral improvement. But the actual transactions between the episodes of the private history and those of the public history remain mysterious, since by definition they can belong to neither series. They could not be reported among the happenings described in a person's autobiography of his inner life, but nor could they be reported among those described in someone else's biography of that person's overt career. They can be inspected neither by introspection nor by laboratory experiment. They are theoretical shuttlecocks which are forever bandied from the physiologist back to the psychologist and from the psychologist back to the physiologist.

"Where" precisely is the mind located in Cartesian dualism? Because the mind is conceived to be a nonmaterial entity, this question is problematic. People often use spatial metaphors or images to characterize the mind/soul/spirit: it's the "inner person" somehow contained "within" the body. But as Ryle points out, this way of thinking doesn't make a great deal of conceptual sense. The mind and the body seem connected in complex and intimate ways that spatial metaphors simply don't capture.

And to make matters worse, people tend to "forget" that these are metaphors and instead assume that they are providing an accurate description of the way things are. But this *really* doesn't make conceptual sense. If the mind and body are in reality two radically different substances, then how precisely do they connect to one another? And how could we ever discover such a connection? Neither the personal history of the mind's experiences nor the public history of the body and its movements can describe the moment of their intersection. Each realm—mental and physical—is locked within its own universe, lacking the vocabulary to observe and describe the convergence of these alien worlds with clarity and precision. As

For Ryle, our knowledge of other persons' minds can only be inferential at best.

Ryle observes, these transactional events "can be inspected neither by introspection nor by laboratory experiment. They are theoretical shuttlecocks which are forever bandied from the physiologist back to the psychologist and from the psychologist back to the physiologist." And in Ryle's mind (note the commonly used spatial metaphor!) there are even more serious implications of a dualistic perspective.

Ryle, *The Concept of Mind*

What sort of knowledge can be secured of the workings of a mind? On the one side, according to the official theory, a person has direct knowledge of the best imaginable kind of the workings of his own mind. Mental states and processes are (or are normally) conscious states and processes, and the consciousness which irradiates them can engender no illusions and leaves the door open for no doubts. A person's present thinkings, feelings and willings, his perceivings, rememberings and imaginings are intrinsically "phosphorescent"; their existence and their nature are inevitably betrayed to their owner. The inner life is a stream of consciousness of such a sort that it would be absurd to suggest that the mind whose life is that stream might be unaware of what is passing down it. . . .

On the other side, one person has no direct access of any sort to the events of the inner life of another. He cannot do better than make problematic inferences from the observed behaviour of the other person's body to the states of mind which, by analogy from his own conduct, he supposes to be signalised by the behaviour. Direct access to the workings of a mind is the privilege of that mind itself; in default of such privileged access, the workings of one mind are inevitably occult to everyone else. For the supposed arguments from bodily movements similar to their own to mental workings similar to their own would lack any possibility of observational corroboration. Not unnaturally, therefore, an adherent of the official theory finds it difficult to resist this consequence of his premises, that he has no good reason to believe that there do exist minds other than his own. Even if he prefers to believe that to other human bodies there are harnessed minds not unlike his own, he cannot claim to be able to discover their individual characteristics, or the particular things that they undergo and do. Absolute solitude is on this showing the ineluctable destiny of the soul. Only our bodies can meet.

The privileged knowledge that we have of our own mental *self* means that others are necessarily excluded from any direct understanding of what we're thinking or who we are. Unfortunately the same logic applies to us: we are prevented from having any direct knowledge of other minds/selves/spirits. Although we can observe the bodies and actions of others, we can only make *inferences* regarding the mind that is producing these actions. In fact, there is no way we can be ensured that there even *are* other minds functioning in ways similar to ours. We observe someone waving and smiling at us and we say to ourselves: "When I wave and smile, that means I'm happy to see someone, so that's what this waving and smiling must mean: the mind inside that body is happy to see me. And I'm assuming that there *is* a mind inside that body because the body is acting like I do, and I'm a mind." Of course, we can't really be sure that other minds exist, or that the movement of their bodies really expresses the meaning that we are projecting on to it.

Once again: if you're thinking that this description sounds rather peculiar, this is exactly Ryle's point. In our everyday experience, we act and speak as if we have much more direct knowledge of other minds and what they're thinking without having to go through this tortured and artificial reasoning process. We encounter others, experience the totality of their behavior, and believe that this behavior reveals directly "who" they are and what they're thinking. Ryle goes on to analyze how this apparent conflict between the theory of Cartesian dualism ("the ghost in the machine") and our everyday experience of others is actually the result of confused conceptual thinking, a logical error that he terms a "**category mistake**."

Category mistake Representing the facts or concepts as if they belonged in one logical category when they actually belong in another.

Ryle, *The Concept of Mind*

Such in outline is the official theory. I shall often speak of it with deliberate abusiveness, as "the dogma of the Ghost in the Machine." I hope to prove that it is entirely false, and false not in detail but in principle. It is not merely an assemblage of particular mistakes. It is one big mistake and a mistake of a special kind. It is, namely, a category-mistake. It represents the facts of mental life as if they belonged to one logical type of category (or range of types or categories), when they actually belong to another. The dogma is therefore a philosopher's myth.

I must first indicate what is meant by the phrase "Category-mistake." This I do in a series of illustrations.

A foreigner visiting Oxford or Cambridge for the first time is shown a number of colleges, libraries, playing fields, museums, scientific departments and administrative offices. He then asks "But where is the university? I have seen where the members of the Colleges live, where the Registrar works, where the scientists experiment and the rest. But I have not yet seen the University in which reside and work the members of your University." It has then to be explained to him that the University is not another collateral institution, some ulterior counterpart to the colleges, laboratories and offices which he has seen. The University is just the way in which all that he has already seen is organized. When they are seen and when their coordination is understood, the University has been seen. His mistake lay in his innocent assumption that it was correct to speak of Christ Church, the Bodleian Library, the Ashmolean Museum *and* the University, to speak, that is, as if "the University" stood for an extra member of the class of which these others units are members. He was mistakenly allocating the University to the same category as that to which the other institutions belong. . . .

In the same way that the *university* is a concept expressing the entire system of buildings, curricula, faculty, administrators, and so on, Ryle believes that the *mind* is a concept that expresses the entire system of thoughts, emotions, actions, and so on that make up the human *self.* The *category mistake* happens when we speak about the *self* as something independent of the physical body: a purely mental entity existing in time but not space. According to Ryle, this "self" does not really exist, anymore than the "university" or "team-spirit" exist in some special, nonphysical universe.

This is certainly a compelling argument against Cartesian dualism. However, having made the case for an integrated mind/body perspective on the human *self,* Ryle then focuses his attention primarily on human behavior. From his perspective, the *self* is best understood as a *pattern of behavior,* the *tendency* or *disposition* for a person to behave in a certain way in certain circumstances. And this inevitably leads him to the same difficulties faced by psychologist behaviorists such as John Watson and **B. F. Skinner.**

B. F. SKINNER

(1904–1990)
Philosopher of Psychology. Skinner advanced two important philosophies of psychology, 'radical behaviorism' and 'scientific behaviorism' in which he held the mind itself and unobservable entities in general were not important to scientific explanation.

Ryle, *The Concept of Mind*

To say that a person knows something, or aspires to be something, is not to say that he is at a particular moment in process of doing or undergoing anything, but that he is able to do certain things, when the need arises, or that he is prone to do and feel certain things in situations of certain sorts. . . . Abandonment of the two-world legend involves the abandonment of the idea that there is a locked door and a still to be discovered key. Those human actions and reactions, those spoken and unspoken utterances, those tones of voice, facial expressions and gestures, which have always been the data of all the other students of men, have, after all, been the right and the only manifestations to study. They and they alone have merited but fortunately not received, the grandiose title "mental phenomena." ∎

 Ryle, Gilbert, *The Concept of Mind*

Like the behaviorists before him, Ryle has ended up solving one problem—the conceptual difficulties of Cartesian dualism—but creating another problem just as serious. For example, is the experience of "love" equivalent to the tendency to act in a certain way under certain circumstances? When you say "I am deeply in love with you," is that reducible to a series of behavioral tendencies or dispositions: I will share experiences with you, procreate children, attend you when you are sick, give thoughtful cards and gifts on your birthday, say on a regular basis "I love you," and so on? Although your proposed partner may appreciate your detailed commitments, he or she is unlikely to respond in the passionate, intimate way that you likely hope for. Reducing the complex richness of our inner life and consciousness to a list of behaviors and potential behaviors simply doesn't do the job conceptually for most people.

Ironically, Ryle ends up being his own most incisive critic. He bases his criticism of Cartesian dualism on the premise that "the central principles of the doctrine are unsound and conflict with the whole body of what we know about minds when we are not speculating about them." But exactly the same criticism can be made of Ryle's logical behaviorism: it attempts to define and translate the *self* and the complex mental/emotional richness of the life of the mind into a listing of behaviors (and potential behaviors) that "conflicts with the whole body of what we know about minds when we are not speculating about them." As the Australian philosopher J. J. C. Smart notes, "There does seem to be, so far as science is concerned, nothing in the world but complex arrangements of physical constituents. All except for one place: consciousness." In the final analysis, despite his devastating critique of Descartes' dualism, Ryle hasn't been able to provide a compelling philosophical explanation of Descartes' "I think."

Ryle's denial of inner *selves* causes a difficulty analogous to that engendered by Hume's denial of a similar entity—namely, that Ryle writes, speaks, and acts as if the existence of *their inner selves* is not in doubt. In fact, it's not clear how a person who truly believed what behaviorists say they believe would actually function in life. The philosopher **Brand Blanshard** (1892–1987) provides a biting analysis of the behaviorists' denial of consciousness along with their stated belief that the *self* is the same as bodily behavior.

> Consider the behaviorist who has a headache and takes aspirin. What he means by his "headache" is the grimaces or claspings of the head that an observer might behold. Since these *are* the headache, it must be these he finds objectionable. But it is absurd to say a set of motions . . . is objectionable . . . except as they are associated with the conscious pain. Suppose again, that he identifies the pain with the grimaces and outward movements then all he would have to do to banish the pain would be to stop these movements and behave in a normal fashion. But he knows perfectly well that this is not enough; that is why he falls back on aspirin. In short, his action implies a disbelief in his own theory.

This is not to deny that humans are profoundly influenced by their experiences, that we can in fact control and manipulate human behavior to a certain extent through systematic conditioning, and that these facts have significant implications for the possibility of personal freedom. These are issues that we will explore more thoroughly in chapter 4, "Am I Free? Freedom and Determinism."

THINK CRITICALLY 3.15

PHILOSOPHER'S NOTEBOOK

Self as Behavior

- Think of someone you know and try to describe her solely in terms of her observable behavior. Then analyze your portrait: What aspects of her *self* does your description capture? What aspects of her *self* does your description omit?

- Now think about yourself. Assume the perspective of someone who knows you well and describe your *self* as he might see you, *based solely on your observable behavior*. What aspects of your *self* do you think his description would capture? What aspects of your *self* do you think his portrait of you would omit?

- Identify several of the defining qualities of your *self*: for example, empathetic, gregarious, reflective, fun-loving, curious, and so on. Then, using Ryle's approach, describe the qualities in terms of "a tendency to act a certain way in certain circumstances."

- Analyze your characterizations. Do your descriptions communicate fully the personal qualities of your *self* that you identified? If not, what's missing?

Brand Blanshard (1892–1987) American philosopher. Taught for over 20 years at Swarthmore College. Identified as rationalist philosopher, drawing from classical philosophy, notably Aristotle, in his own work on epistemology.

Materialism: *The Self Is the Brain*

Earlier in the chapter we introduced *materialism,* the philosophical view that all aspects of the universe are composed of matter and energy and can be explained by physical laws. Many philosophers and psychologists view the *self* from a materialistic point of view, contending that in the final analysis mental states are identical with, reducible to, or explainable in terms of physical brain states.

Humans have known since recorded history of the close, intimate relationship between the mind and the body. The health of our bodies, the things we ingest, the experiences we endure—all of these dimensions of our physical *self* have a profound effect on our mental and emotional functioning. Similarly, our emotional states, the way we think about things, our levels of stress, the optimism (or pessimism) we feel—all of these dimensions of our mental *self* have a dramatic impact on our physical condition. As an example, just consider how the single word *heart* is used to display this intimate connection between the emotional and the physical: heartfelt, heartache, heartsick, heartened, large-hearted, heartless, lighthearted, hard-hearted, heartbroken.

Modern science is now able to use advanced equipment and sophisticated techniques to unravel and articulate the complex web of connections that binds consciousness and body together into an integrated *self.* In fact, one of the most dynamic areas of scientific research currently is that devoted to exploring the mind/brain relationships, and the information being developed is fascinating. Scientists are increasingly able to correlate specific areas in the brain with areas of mental functioning, both cognitively and emotionally. Psychotropic drugs are being developed that can influence emotional states such as depression or extreme social anxiety. Brain scans can reveal physical abnormalities that are related to personality disorders. And discoveries are being made in the reverse direction as well, detailing the physical affects of emotional states such as anxiety, depression, anger, pessimism, and optimism on the health and well-being of the body. The assumption of this approach is that to fully understand the nature of the mind we have to fully understand the nature of the brain.

The impressive success of such scientific mind/brain research has encouraged many to conclude that it is only a matter of time before the mental life of consciousness is fully explainable in terms of the neurophysiology of the brain. The ultimate goal of such explorations is to link the *self*—including all of our thoughts, passions, personality traits—to the physical wiring and physiological functioning of the brain. Although such thinkers recognize that achieving such a goal will take time, they are confident that we will progressively develop ways of describing the mind, consciousness, and human experience that are physiologically based. The philosopher **Paul Churchland** articulates such a vision in the following essay. He begins by acknowledging that a simple identity formula—mental states = brain states—is a flawed way in which to conceptualize the relationship between the mind and the brain. Instead, we need to develop a new, neuroscience-based vocabulary that will enable us to think and communicate clearly about the mind, consciousness, and human experience. He refers to this view as "eliminative materialism."

PAUL CHURCHLAND

(1942–)

American philosopher (Ph.D., University of Pittsburgh, 1969); Areas of interest include philosophy of mind, philosophy of science, cognitive neurobiology, epistemology, and perception. Authored several works on mind, including *The Engine of Reason, The Seat of the Soul: A Philosophical Journey into the Brain* (MIT, 1995).

Churchland,
On Eliminative Materialism

The identity theory was called into doubt not because the prospects for a materialist account of our mental capacities were thought to be poor, but because it seemed unlikely that the arrival of an adequate materialist theory would bring with it the nice one-to-one match-ups, between the concepts of folk psychology and the concepts of theoretical neuroscience, that intertheoretic reduction requires. The reason for that doubt was the great variety of quite different physical systems that could instantiate the required functional organization. *Eliminative materialism* also doubts that the correct neuroscientific account of human capacities will produce a neat reduction of our common-sense framework, but here the doubts arise from a quite different source.

As the eliminative materialists see it, the one-to-one match-ups will not be found, and our common-sense psychological framework will not enjoy an intertheoretic reduction, *because our common-sense psychological framework is a false and radically misleading conception of the causes of human behavior and the nature of cognitive activity.* On this view, folk psychology is not just an incomplete representation of our inner natures; it is an outright *mis*-representation of our internal states and activities. Consequently, we cannot expect a truly adequate neuroscientific account of our inner lives to provide theoretical categories that match up nicely with the categories of our common-sense framework. Accordingly, we must expect that the older framework will simply be eliminated, rather than be reduced, by a matured neuroscience.

Historical Parallels

As the identity theorist can point to historical cases of successful intertheoretic reduction, so the eliminative materialist can point to historical cases of the outright elimination of the ontology of an older theory in favor of the ontology of a new and superior theory....

It used to be thought that when a piece of wood burns, or a piece of metal rusts, a spiritlike substance called "phlogiston" was being released: briskly, in the former case, slowly in the latter. Once gone, that "noble" substance left only a base pile of ash or rust. It later came to be appreciated that both processes involve, not the loss of something, but the *gaining* of a substance taken from the atmosphere: oxygen. Phlogiston emerged, not as an incomplete description of what was going on, but as a radical misdescription. Phlogiston was therefore not suitable for reduction to or identification with some notion from within the new oxygen chemistry, and it was simply eliminated from science.

* * *

The concepts of folk psychology—belief, desire, fear, sensation, pain, joy, and so on—await a similar fate, according to the view at issue. And when neuroscience has matured to the point where the poverty of our current conceptions is apparent to everyone, the superiority of the new framework is established, we shall then be able to set about *reconceiving* our internal states and activities, within a truly adequate conceptual framework at last. Our explanations of one another's behavior will appeal to such things as our neuropharmacological states, the neural activity in specialized anatomical areas, and whatever other states are deemed relevant by the new theory. Our private introspection will also be transformed, and may be profoundly enhanced by reason of the more accurate and penetrating framework it will have to work with—just as the astronomer's perception of the night sky is much enhanced by the detailed knowledge of modern astronomical theory that he or she possesses.

The magnitude of the conceptual revolution here suggested should not be minimized: it would be enormous. And the benefits to humanity might be equally great. If each of us possessed an accurate neuroscientific understanding of (what we now conceive dimly as) the varieties and causes of mental illness, the factors involved in learning, the neural basis of emotions, intelligence, and socialization, then the sum total of human misery might be much reduced. The simple increase in mutual understanding that the new framework made possible could contribute substantially toward a more peaceful and humane society. Of course, there would be dangers as well: increased knowledge means increased power, and power can always be misused.

Churchland's central argument is that the concepts and theoretical vocabulary we use to think about our selves—using such terms as *belief, desire, fear, sensation, pain, joy*—actually misrepresent the reality of minds and selves. All of these concepts are part of a commonsense "folk psychology that obscures rather than clarifies the nature of human experience. Eliminative materialists believe that we need to

For Churchland, this couple's emotional connection should be understood with reference to the neurophysiology of the brain.

develop a new vocabulary and conceptual framework that is ground in neuro-science that will be a more accurate reflection of the human mind and self. Church-land proceeds to state the arguments that he believes support his position.

Churchland,
On Eliminative Materialism

Arguments for Eliminative Materialism

The arguments for eliminative materialism are diffuse and less than decisive, but they are stronger than is widely supposed. The distinguishing feature of this position is its denial that a smooth intertheoretic reduction is to be expected—even a species-specific reduction—of the framework of folk psychology to the framework of a matured neuro-science. The reason for this denial is the eliminative materialist's conviction that folk psychology is a hopelessly primitive and deeply confused conception of our internal activities. But why this low opinion of our common-sense conceptions?

There are at least three reasons. First, the eliminative materialist will point to the widespread explanatory, predictive, and manipulative failures of folk psychology. So much of what is central and familiar to us remains a complete mystery from within folk psychology. We do not know what *sleep* is, or why we have to have it, despite spending a full third of our lives in that condition. (The answer, "For rest," is mistaken. Even if people are allowed to rest continuously, their need for sleep is undiminished. Apparently, sleep serves some deeper functions, but we do not yet know what they are.) We do not under-stand how *learning* transforms each of us from a gaping infant to a cunning adult, or how differences in *intelligence* are grounded. We have not the slightest idea how *memory* works, or how we manage to retrieve relevant bits of information instantly from the awe-some mass we have stored. We do not know what *mental illness* is, nor how to cure it.

In sum, the most central things about us remain almost entirely mysterious from within folk psychology. . . .

This argument from explanatory poverty has a further aspect. So long as one sticks to normal brains, the poverty of folk psychology is perhaps not strikingly evident. But as soon as one examines the many perplexing behavioral and cognitive deficits suffered by people with *damaged* brains, one's descriptive and explanatory resources start to claw the air. . . . As with other humble theories asked to operate successfully in unexplored extensions of their old domain (for example, Newtonian mechanics in the domain of velocities close to the velocity of light, and the classical gas law in the domain of high pressures or temperatures), the descriptive and explanatory inadequacies of folk psy-chology become starkly evident.

The second argument tries to draw an inductive lesson from our conceptual history. Our early folk theories of motion were profoundly confused, and were eventually dis-placed entirely by more sophisticated theories. Our early folk theories of the structure and activity of the heavens were wildly off the mark, and survive only as historical lessons in how wrong we can be. Our folk theories of the nature of fire, and the nature of life, were similarly cockeyed. And one could go on, since the vast majority of our past folk conceptions have been similarly exploded. All except folk psychology, which sur-vives to this day and has only recently begun to feel pressure. But the phenomenon of conscious intelligence is surely a more complex and difficult phenomenon than any of those just listed. So far as accurate understanding is concerned, it would be a *miracle* if we had got *that* one right the very first time, when we fell down so badly on all the oth-ers. Folk psychology has survived for so very long, presumably, not because it is basically correct in its representations, but because the phenomena addressed are so surprisingly difficult that any useful handle on them, no matter how feeble, is unlikely to be dis-placed in a hurry. . . .

Churchland's point is that the most compelling argument for developing a new conceptual framework and vocabulary founded on neuroscience is the simple fact that the current "folk psychology" has done a poor job in accomplishing the main reason for their existence—explaining and predicting the commonplace phenom-ena of the human mind and experience. And in the same way that science replaces outmoded, ineffective, and limited conceptual frameworks with ones that can explain and predict more effectively, so the same thing needs to be done in psychology and philosophy of mind. This new conceptual framework will be based on and will integrate all that we are learning about how the brain works on a neurological level.

Although he believes strongly in the logic of his position, Churchland recognizes that many people will resist the argument he is making for a variety of reasons.

Arguments Against Eliminative Materialism

The initial plausibility of this rather radical view is low for almost everyone, since it denies deeply entrenched assumptions. That is at best a question-begging complaint, of course, since those assumptions are precisely what is at issue. But the following line of thought does attempt to mount a real argument.

Eliminative materialism is false, runs the argument, because one's introspection reveals directly the existence of pains, beliefs, desires, fears, and so forth. Their existence is as obvious as anything could be.

The eliminative materialist will reply that this argument makes the same mistake that an ancient or medieval person would be making if he insisted that he could just see with his own eyes that the heavens form a turning sphere, or that witches exist. The fact is, all observation occurs within some system of concepts, and our observation judgments are only as good as the conceptual framework in which they are expressed. In all three cases—the starry sphere, witches, and the familiar mental states—precisely what is challenged is the integrity of the background conceptual frameworks in which the observation judgments are expressed. To insist on the validity of one's experiences, *traditionally interpreted*, is therefore to beg the very question at issue. For in all three cases, the question is whether we should *reconceive* the nature of some familiar observational domain.

* * *

A final criticism draws a much weaker conclusion, but makes a rather stronger case. Eliminative materialism, it has been said, is making mountains out of molehills. It exaggerates the defects in folk psychology, and underplays its real successes. Perhaps the arrival of a matured neuroscience will require the elimination of the occasional folk-psychological concept, continues the criticism, and a minor adjustment in certain folk-psychological principles may have to be endured. But the large-scale elimination forecast by the eliminative materialist is just an alarmist worry or a romantic enthusiasm.

Perhaps this complaint is correct. And perhaps it is merely complacent. Whichever, it does bring out the important point that we do not confront two simple and mutually exclusive possibilities here: pure reduction versus pure elimination. Rather, these are the end points of a smooth spectrum of possible outcomes, between which there are mixed cases of partial elimination and partial reduction. Only empirical research . . . can tell us where on that spectrum our own case will fall. Perhaps we should speak here, more liberally, of "revisionary materialism" instead of concentrating on the more radical possibility of an across-the-board elimination. ▪

Churchland's ultimate concession that the psychology-based conceptual framework currently used by most academic disciplines and popular culture may not end up being completely eradicated and replaced by a neuroscience framework appears to recognize the fundamental differences between the life of the mind and neuroscientific descriptions of the brain's operation. Many people believe that no matter how exhaustively scientists are able to describe the physical conditions for consciousness, this does not mean that the mental dimensions of the *self* will ever be *reducible* to these physical states. Why? Because in the final analysis, the physical and mental dimensions of the *self* are qualitatively different realms, each with its own distinctive vocabulary, logic, and organizing principles. According to this view, even if scientists were able to map out your complete brain activity at the moment you

Churchland,
On Eliminative Materialism

were having an original idea or experiencing an emotional epiphany, that neurobiological description of your brain would provide no clue as to the nature of your personal experience at that moment. Articulating and communicating the rich texture of those experiences would take a very different language and logic.

THINK PHILOSOPHICALLY 3.16
Analyzing Eliminative Materialism

- Explain the reasons why materialists believe that to fully understand the nature of the mind we have to fully understand the nature of the brain.
- Based on your own experience, describe some examples of the close, interactive relationship between the physical dimensions of your *self* and the psychological aspects of your mind and experience.
- Explain why Paul Churchland believes that a close examination of the history of science suggests that we are at the beginning of a conceptual revolution in understanding the nature of the mind.
- Explain the arguments against eliminative materialism. Which arguments do you find most persuasive? Why?

Edmund Husserl and Maurice Merleau-Ponty: *The Self Is Embodied Subjectivity*

EDMUND HUSSERL

(1859–1938)

Philosopher. Husserl founded the field of phenomenology, thereby becoming one of the most influential philosophers of the Twentieth Century. In his *Logical Investigations* (1900–1901) he advocated getting back to things in themselves, that is, objects as they are presented in actual perception.

Philosophers such as the German thinker **Edmund Husserl** (1859–1938) and the French philosopher **Maurice Merleau-Ponty** (1908–1961) take a very different approach to the *self* and the mind/body "problem." From their standpoint, the division between the "mind" and the "body" is a product of confused thinking. The simple fact is, we experience our *self* as a unity in which the mental and physical are seamlessly woven together. This unity is our primary experience of our *selves*, and we only begin to doubt it when we use our minds to concoct abstract notions of a separate "mind" and "body." But these ideas of "mind" and "body" as radically different entities that need to be connected in some way—the "ghost in the machine"—are not real, any more than ghosts or Leprechauns are real. They're mental constructions of our imaginations, not expressions of reality or even accurate descriptions of our experience. As Merleau-Ponty observes, "I live in my body"—there is no mystery of "my body" to be explained. At the basis of our explicit, theoretical knowing, there is an implicit, pretheoretical knowing that includes our lived body and lived-situation in the world. This gives rise to the distinction between the "body as object" on the one hand, and, on the other, the "lived body" that can never be objectified or known in a completely objective sort of way.

For example, when you first wake up in the morning and experience your gradually expanding awareness of where you are and how you feel, what are your first thoughts of the day? Perhaps something along the lines of "Oh no, it's time to get up, but I'm still sleepy, but I have an important appointment that I can't be late for" and so on. Note that at no point do you doubt that the "I" you refer to is a single integrated entity, a blending of mental, physical, and emotional structured around a core identity: your *self*. It's only later, when you're reading Descartes or discussing the possibility of reincarnation with a friend that you begin creating ideas such as independent "minds," "bodies," "souls," or, in the case of Freud, an "unconscious." According to Husserl and Merleau-Ponty, it's these mental creations that result in the apparent mysteries and paradoxes such as the mind/body "problem." But if we honestly and accurately examine our direct and immediate experience of our *selves*, these alleged mysteries, paradoxes, and "problems" fall away. As Merleau-Ponty explains, "There is not a duality of substances but only the dialectic of living being in its biological milieu." In other words, our "living body" is a natural synthesis of mind and biology, and any attempts to divide them into separate entities are artificial and nonsensical.

The underlying question is "What aspect of our experience is the most 'real'?" Is it the experience we have of our *selves* in moments such as when we are first arising, or the experiences we have when we are thinking abstractly with such concepts as "mind" and "body"? From Husserl's and Merleau-Ponty's vantage point, it's the moments of direct, primal experience that are the most real, what they call the *Lebenswelt* or "lived world," which is the fundamental ground of our being and consciousness. To take another example, consider your experience when you are in the midst of activities such as dancing, playing a sport, or performing musically—what is your experience of your *self*? Most likely, you're completely absorbed in the moment, your mind and body functioning as one integrated entity. For Merleau-Ponty, this unified experience of your *self* is the paradigm or model you should use to understand your nature.

This approach to philosophy is known as **phenomenology**, and it is derived from the conviction that all knowledge of our *selves* and our world is based on the "phenomena" of experience. After centuries of elaborate religious and philosophical systems of thought, phenomenology sought to return "to the things themselves" something that many established philosophies had lost sight of. In the words of philosopher **John Bannan**:

Edmund Husserl

> This return was accomplished primarily by beginning with a careful description of *things* as they appear and of the *consciousness* in which they appear—a description sensitive to the richness and complexity that characterize both things and consciousness before they are refined by philosophical analysis. It is this richness, the phenomenologist feels, that previous philosophies have let slip away by attempting to analyze reality as if it were fashioned according to some mechanical, biological, or spiritual model. It is for this reason that Merleau-Ponty argues that "every philosophy should begin with an inventory, a description of consciousness . . . as it appears immediately, the 'phenomenon' of consciousness in all its original variety."

JOHN BANNAN
American philosopher. Ph.D., University of Louvain. Currently teaching at Loyola University Chicago. Primary research interests include Descartes, Merleau-Ponty, Sartre, Levi-Strauss, and French phenomenology. Author of several works, including *The Philosophy of Merleau-Ponty* (1967).

Phenomenologists do not assume that there are more "fundamental" levels of reality beyond that of conscious human experience. Consistent with this ontological (having to do with the nature of *being* or *existence*) commitment is the belief that explanations for human behavior and experience are not to be sought by appeal to phenomena that are somehow behind, beneath, or beyond the phenomena of lived human experience, but instead are to be sought within the field of human experience itself, utilizing terminology and concepts appropriate to this field. And when we examine our *selves* at this fundamental level of direct human experience, we discover that our mind and body are unified, not separate. It is this primal consciousness Merleau-Ponty notes in his book *Phenomenology of Perception*, that is the foundation for our perception of the world and our knowledge about it.

> Consciousness must be reckoned as a *self-contained system of Being*, as a system of *Absolute being*, into which nothing can penetrate and from which nothing can

Phenomenology The study of conscious experience. Phenomenologists do not assume any reality beyond conscious human experience.

MAURICE MERLEAU-PONTY
(1908–1961)
Phenomenologist. In his major work
The Phenomenology of Perception
(1945) Merleau-Ponty argues, like
Husserl, that perception is fundamental
to our knowledge of the world
consciousness is a dynamic form that
actively structures our experience.

escape. On the other side, the whole spatio-temporal world, to which man and the human ego claim to belong as subordinate singular realities, is *according to its own meaning mere intentional Being*, a Being, therefore, which has the merely secondary, relative sense of a Being for a consciousness.

For Merleau-Ponty, everything that we are aware of—and can possible know—is contained within our own consciousness. It's impossible for us to get "outside" of our consciousness because it defines the boundaries of our personal universe. The so-called real world of objects existing in space and time initially exists only as objects of my consciousness. Yet in a cognitive sleight-of-hand, we act as if the space/time world is primary and our immediate consciousness is secondary. This is an inversion of the way things actually are: it is our consciousness that is primary and the space/time world that is secondary, existing fundamentally as the object of our consciousness.

Nor is science exempt from condemnation, according to the phenomenologists, for scientists are guilty of the same flawed thinking as expressed in abstract philosophical and religious theories. Too often scientists treat their abstract theories as if they take precedence over the rich and intuitive reality of immediate lived experience. In cases when the two worlds conflict, scientists automatically assume that the scientific perspective is correct, and the direct experience of the individual wrong. This is the difficulty we pointed out with the concept of the unconscious: it was considered by Freud and many of his followers to be of such supreme authority that no individual's contrasting point of view can measure up to the ultimate truth of the unconscious interpretation. In his *Phenomenology of Perception*, Merleau-Ponty makes the crucial point that these theories couldn't even exist without the primal reality of lived experience to serve as their foundation. And *then* these theories have the arrogance to dismiss this fundamental reality as somehow secondary or derivative.

> Scientific points of view are always both naïve and at the same time dishonest, because they take for granted without explicitly mentioning it, that other point of view, namely that of the consciousness, through which from the outset a world forms itself around me and begins to exist for me.

As a philosophical theory of knowledge, phenomenology is distinctive in the sense that its goal is not to *explain* experience, but rather to *clarify our understanding* of it. A phenomenologist like Merleau-Ponty sees his aim of describing what he sees and then assuming that his description will strike a familiar chord with us, stimulating us to say, "I understand what you're saying—that makes sense to me!" From this perspective, the responsibility of philosophy is not to provide explanations but to seek the root and genesis of meaning, "to reveal the mystery of the world and of reason," to help us think and see things more clearly. For example, to develop a clear understanding of your "being in love," you need to delay using elaborate psychological theories and instead begin by describing the phenomena of the experience in a clear, vivid fashion, trying to uncover the meaning of what you are experiencing. *Then* you can begin developing concepts and theories to help you make sense of the phenomena of "being in love." The danger of using theories prematurely is that you may very well distort your actual experience, forcing it to conform to someone else's idea of what "being in love" means instead of clearly understanding *your* unique experience. Concepts and theories are essential for understanding our *selves* and our world. It's simply a question of which comes first—the concepts/theories or the phenomena of experience that the concepts/theories are designed to explain. For phenomenologists, it's essential that we always begin (and return regularly to) the phenomena of our lived experience. Otherwise, we run the risk of viewing our experience through conceptual or theoretical "lenses" that distort rather than clarify. For instance, in providing a phenomenological analysis of "being in love," you might begin by describing precisely what your immediate responses are: physically, emotionally, cognitively. I'm currently in love and,

- I feel
- I think
- My physical response
- I spontaneously

By recording the direct phenomena of our experience, we have the basic data needed to reveal the complex meaning of this experience, and begin to develop a clearer understanding of what "being in love" is all about, by utilizing concepts and theories appropriate to the reality of our lived experience.

What exactly is "consciousness"? For Merleau-Ponty it is a *dynamic form* responsible for actively structuring our conscious ideas and physical behavior. In this sense it is fundamentally different from Hume's and Locke's concept of the mind as a repository for sensations, or the behaviorists' notion of the mind as the sum total of the reactions to the physical stimuli that an organism receives. Merleau-Ponty's notion of consciousness as a dynamic form that actively organizes and structures our mind and body (our *self*) resembles Aristotle's idea of *soul*, which he conceived of as nothing other than "the form of the body":

> One can no more ask if the body and the soul are one than if the wax and the impression it receives are one, or speaking generally the matter of each thing and the form of which it is the matter; for admitting that the terms unity and existence are used in many senses, the paramount sense is that of actuality. We have then, given a general definition of what the soul is: it is substance expressed as form. It is this which makes a body what it is.

Think Philosophically
Applying Phenomenology

PHILOSOPHER'S NOTEBOOK

Accomplished writers often have a special talent for representing human experience in a rich, vibrant, and textured way. The French novelist **Marcel Proust** is renowned for articulating the phenomena of consciousness in a very phenomenological way. Consider the following descriptions of experiences and analyze their effectiveness from a phenomenological perspective on the *self*. Then compose your own description of an experience from a phenomenological point of view by detailing the phenomena of consciousness.

Waking from Sleep

> When a man is asleep, he has in a circle round him the chain of the hours, the sequence of the years, the order of the heavenly host. Instinctively, when he awakes, he looks to these, and in an instant reads off his own position on the earth's surface the time that has elapsed during his slumbers; but this ordered procession is apt to grow confused, and to break its ranks . . . suppose that he

dozes off in an armchair, for instance, after dinner: then the world will go hurtling out of orbit, the magic chair will carry him at full speed through time and space, and when he opens his eyes again he will imagine that he went to sleep months earlier in another place . . . for me it was enough if, in my own bed, my sleep was so heavy as completely to relax my consciousness; for then I lost all sense of the place in which I had gone to sleep, and when I awoke in the middle of the night, not knowing where I was, I could not even be sure at first who I was; I had only the most rudimentary sense of existence, such as may lurk and flicker in the depths of an animal's consciousness: I was more destitute than a cave dweller; but then the memory—not yet of the place in which I was, but of the various other places where I had lived and might now possibly be—would come like a rope let down from heaven to draw me up out of the abyss of non-being, from which I could never have escaped by myself: but in a flash I would traverse centuries of civilization, and out of a blurred glimpse of oil-lamps, then of shirts with turned-down collars, would gradually piece together the original components of my ego. (Marcel Proust, *In Search of Lost Time 20*)

Recognizing Another Person

But then, even in the most insignificant details of our daily life, none of us can be said to constitute a material whole, which is identical for everyone, and need only be turned up like a page in an account-book or the record of a will; our social personality is a creation of the thoughts of other people. Even the simple act which we describe as "seeing someone we know" is to some extent an intellectual process. We pack the physical outline of the person we see with all the notions we have already formed about him, and in the total picture of him which we compose in our minds those notions have certainly the principal place. In the end they come to fill out so completely the curve of his cheeks, to follow so exactly the line of his nose, they blend so harmoniously in the sound of his voice as if it were no more than a transparent envelope, that each time we see the face or hear the voice it is these notions which we recognize and to which we listen. (Marcel Proust, *In Search of Lost Time 5–6*)

Describing a Previous Relationship

I have said that Albertine had not seemed to me that day to be the same as on previous days, and that each time I saw her she was to appear different. But I felt at that moment that certain modifications in the appearance, the importance, the stature of a person may also be due to the variability of certain states of consciousness interposed between that person and ourselves . . . and each of these Albertines was different, as is each appearance of the dancer whose colours, form, character, are transmuted according to the endlessly varied play of a projected limelight . . . I ought to give a different name to each of the selves who subsequently thought about Albertine; I ought still more to give a different name to each of the Albertines who appeared before me, never the same, like those seas—called by me simply and for the sake of convenience "the sea"—that succeeded one another. (Marcel Proust, *Within a Budding Grove 1010*)

Making Connections: *In Search of the Self*

What is the *self*? We have seen in this chapter that this seemingly innocent question is anything but simple. It's certainly curious that this entity that is so personal and always present to us turns out to be so elusive and enigmatic. It should be some comfort to realize that the greatest minds in history have wrestled with this question without reaching conclusive answers. Is the *self* an immortal soul, distinct from the physical body? Is the *self* simply a receptacle for the stream of sensations moving through our consciousness? Is the *self* defined by its ability to think and reflect? Is the *self* an organizing principle that integrates all of the elements of experience into a personal unity? Are there unconscious dimensions to the *self*? Is the *self* defined by its observable behavior? What is the relationship of consciousness and the physical body? Is the mind/body "problem" the result of confused thinking? Is the *self* identical with the brain or some part of the brain?

Some thinkers have argued that it is a mistake to try to understand the *self* in isolation from others. Instead, we can only be understood in the context of the complex web of social relations that constitute and define us. This was the view of Aristotle, who observed:

> If there were a being who could not live in society or who did not need to live in society because he was self-sufficient, then he would have to either be animal or a god. He could not be a real part of the state. A social instinct is implanted in all people by their nature.

Feminist philosophers have also advocated this point of view, as expressed in the following passage from **Eve Browning Cole's** book *Philosophy and Feminist Criticism: An Introduction*:

> We have already noted the extraordinary isolation of Descartes' metaphysical musings; he cuts off not only the instructions of his perceptive faculties, but also the entirety of his human social surroundings, to seek a certainty accessible only to the lone and insular conscious node "I." A feminist critique of Cartesian method might well begin with just this feature of his project.
>
> The Cartesian ego, rather than being the ground for certainty and the Archimedean point which some philosophers have taken it to be, may in fact be the result of a mistaken abstraction. Feminist philosophers such as Caroline Whitbeck and Lorraine Code have convincingly argued that a preferable starting point for understanding the contents of human consciousness is *the relational self*, the self presented as involved in and importantly constituted by its connectedness to others. Each of us at this moment is connected as it were by invisible threads to an indefinite number of specific other human beings. . . .
>
> Starting with the concept of the relational self would greatly have changed the course of Descartes' meditations. If other persons are not just colorful wallpaper the design of which I contemplate from inside a mental fishbowl but actually part of who I am, then distancing myself from them in thought and supposing that I am the only consciousness in the universe becomes, if not impossible, extremely illogical. What would I hope to accomplish? If on the other had I begin by granting them mentality and humanity, I will proceed by considering the specific ways in which their contributions to my mental life are made.

And, of course, this was the view of Karl Marx who observed "the real nature of man is the totality of social relations." Rather than having a fixed human nature, Marx believed that, "All history is nothing but a continuous transformation of human nature." Humans can only be understood by the cultures in which we live, and the social and economic forces that shape these communities. These themes are the focus of chapter 10, "What Is Social Justice?"

Other philosophers, including existentialists such as Jean-Paul Sartre, believe that human selves are unique in the world because we exist in time, living in a past, present, and future. To truly understand the *self*, it is necessary to grasp the notion

EVE BROWNING COLE
(1952–)
American philosopher. Ph.D., University of California, San Diego (1979). Currently teaching at the University of Minnesota, Duluth. Primary research interests include ancient philosophy, feminist philosophy, ethics, aesthetics, and environmental issues. Author of several books and articles, including *Philosophy and Feminist Criticism* (1993).

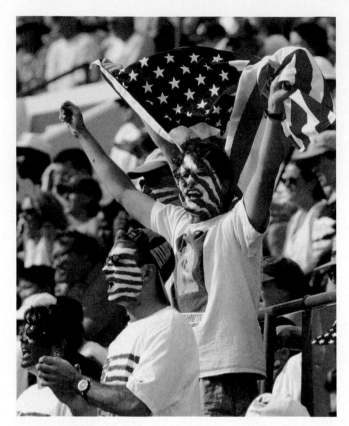

Do you agree with Karl Marx that, "the real nature of man is the totality of social relations"? Why?

that we are continually projecting ourselves into the future. We are not static organisms waiting to be analyzed and dissected—we are dynamic living creatures, changing and evolving on a daily basis, propelled by a future that exists only in our imaginations. As Sartre explains in *Existentialism as a Humanism*:

What do we mean by saying that existence precedes essence? We mean that man first of all exists, encounters himself, surges up in the world—and defines himself afterwards. If man as the existentialist sees him is not definable, it is because to begin with he is nothing. He will not be anything until later, and then he will be what he makes of himself. Thus, there is no human nature, because there is no God to have a conception of it. Man simply is. Not that he is simply what he conceives himself to be, but he is what he wills, and as he conceives himself after already existing— as he wills to be after that leap towards existence. Man is nothing else but that which he makes of himself. . . . But what do we mean to say by this, but that man is of a greater dignity than a stone or a table? For we mean to say that man primarily exists—that man is, before all else, something which propels itself towards a future and is aware that it is doing so.

We will be exploring this perspective on the *self* in depth in chapter 4, "Am I Free? Freedom and Determinism."

These are some of the questions that we have explored in this chapter, and that we will continue to examine throughout this text. But in a larger sense, these are questions that you will continue to explore throughout your life. Your *self* is a wonder, a miracle, an extraordinary creation. When Socrates urged each of us to "Know thyself" and warned that "The unexamined life is not worth living," he was issuing a challenge that requires a lifetime commitment and our mind's best work. But it is in the process of striving to understand our *self* that we may also discover the purpose of our existence and the path to living a productive and fulfilling life.

Students Thinking About Philosophy: *Perspectives on the Self*

This chapter has explored the deceptively complex question, "Who Am I?" One of the great ironies of life is that though we have spent our entire waking lives with ourselves, the precise nature of our "*self*" remains elusive and enigmatic. The philosophers and psychologists we have studied in this chapter have endeavored to unravel the mysteries of consciousness, personal identity, and the soul. It is likely you have found that in studying them you have gained both insight and confusion as your understanding of these issues has deepened and your questions have become more intellectually sophisticated.

This essay is an opportunity to express your own views on the nature of the "*self*" in a form that is thoughtful and coherent. After reviewing, discussing, and reflecting on the various perspectives regarding the *self* that you read about and discussed in this chapter, compose a paper which reflects your own synthesis of these issues. Your point of view should be well-reasoned and seek to integrate a variety of different philosophical perspectives. In addition, you should weave into your analysis your own personal reflections and life experiences to illustrate the conceptual points that you are making. One such student synthesis follows, entitled "Perceptions of Self."

Perceptions of Self

Jessie Lange

Years ago my parents met in an elevator in Manhattan and in an instant my existence was made possible. Had my father missed that elevator, had his dentist been running late, he might never have stepped on and seen my mother in her rainbow-striped socks and mini skirt, struggling with a stack of boxes. If she had not smiled, or he had not held the lobby door or gotten up the guts to suggest coffee sometime, or if my mother had not stood next to him on Fifth Avenue and leapt the boundary of timidity to say, "How about right now?" because she knew how easily "sometime" could become "never" as memories of encounters faded and crumpled phone numbers in wallets slipped unnoticed between the cracks of every day life—if not for everything falling into place: no love, no marriage, no me. When I was two-years-old at a garden party, I made my way precariously across the lawn towards the sparkling rectangle of swimming pool and toppled in. All backs turned, and only one woman saw me. She leapt in with all of her clothing on to pull me free of the suffocating water.

These are the stories of how I was created that circle my consciousness, and that have shaped who I am today, my *self*. It is these stories and experiences that have made me a strong believer in fate: a sensation that things fall into place eventually. This is my perception, this is my overarching belief, and this is myself. Because really, there are so many reasons that none of us should be here, but here we all are, all of these free floating entities miraculously arrived at this place, what Kurt Vonnegut calls "beams of light." Our inner self, our core: invisible and fluctuating and strong. But where do we find this "self"? Where is it contained? And where does it come from? From my experience, it comes partially from our history. From the stories that we have been told that shape what we believe and how we see the world. A chance meeting, a near drowning.

A friend once professed that our self is simply our perceptions. That *all* we are is just a collection of these perceptions: nothing more and nothing less than what we see, smell, taste, touch, and hear. There are moments when this seems valid. In Marcel Proust's *In Search of Lost Time*, the protagonist tastes a madeleine cookie dipped in tea, and is all of a sudden transported, through the taste and texture, to his childhood and everything contained within it. As B. F. Skinner claims, to a certain extent our perspectives on the world are at the mercy of our conditioned responses to our experiences. I walked in a garden one day under trees that came together over the path like a pointed Gothic arch. Or, perhaps, like a small wooden skull overturned on a shelf. I had taken up rowing months before, and all of a sudden trees looked like boats and my present seemed like nothing more than the sum total of all of my past perceptions. What would that arch of trees been before I learned what rowing meant? Perhaps at the age of four or five, I would have looked up on that garden walk and seen an empty tunnel awaiting the clatter of the silver subway in New York City, or the valleys between the humps of cement in Washington Square Park that I ran through on the way home from school. But once I knew the weight of the wooden edge of a boat overturned on my shoulder as I carried it dripping back inside and slid it carefully into its slots, once I had seen the wooden shells all stacked, all in rows, I walked under those trees and they were the enormous ghosts of those overturned boats. My perception, the world as only I see it, myself.

As much as stories, memories of my past, and my sensory perceptions of the world have shaped who I am, I believe that ourselves must be more than *only* our memories and our perceptions, the stories that we have heard and things we have seen. Who we are is also defined by our ability to take these things in, to observe them and to understand where these beliefs and perceptions came from. We are not helpless victims of conditioning because we have the ability to *reason* and to *challenge* our life experience. Only then can we arrive at our true "self," a self that is, to use Kant's term, "created" through contemplation and analysis. For example, many people might see coincidences in life as nothing more than coincidence, and near accidents as nothing more than chance. I have thought about my parent's meeting, about the things in my own life that have fallen into place, and come to the conclusion that there is some order to things. This belief is not solely rational and not solely empirical but rather a combination of Descartes' *rationalism* and Locke's *empiricism*. As humans, we experience life, we think through what we have experienced *because we can*, and we arrive at a conclusion, a belief. It is this belief that is our own and that defines us. Are we always conscious of ourselves? Are we always aware of where our beliefs come from? No, of course not. Often we are caught up entirely in *doing* or we see an arch of trees and the pattern becomes something that we cannot define or put a finger on. However, the potential for examination, consciousness and understanding is always there. The potential to bring to light the forces that have shaped our lives and to examine them critically is what makes us conscious beings.

Making the unconscious conscious, however, is not where self-understanding and growth ends. Once we are able to recognize where our impressions have come from, once we step outside of our selves and become aware of *how* we are seeing the world and *why* we are seeing it as we do, we then have the opportunity to act on this analysis and to make choices that shape and form the selves that we most want to become. Sartre's view of the self is as an entity that is being always projected towards the future, creating and recreating itself as it goes through reflection and choices. When we have acknowledged what has been conditioned, it is this self-consciousness that gives us the freedom to reshape our lives, to envision our ideal future self and to make the choices that will launch us in that direction. Sartre's theory of the human experience is self-perpetuating: the more insight you have into your self the more freedom you have to create who you want to become, and the more freedom you have, the deeper your insights into what it means to create and live a meaningful and fulfilling life.

Many philosophers have suggested that the self is something that is separate from the physical body. That the self is somehow something that lives on after our body fails. While I do not believe the two are entirely separate, I do believe that our spirits do not just disappear with our bodies. One way I define myself is as a writer. I write because it is the best way I know to work through life in an active way, bringing energy to the world around me rather than passing throughout it unthinking, using it as a backdrop for a vacuous existence. I also write to preserve both my own perspective and what I know of the world I live in and the people who are important to me. Like Marcel Proust's endless striving to capture an entire life in a volume (he was still writing on his deathbed), writing is an obsession to capture everything so that it is not lost with the physical self.

For me, the issue of how our selves continue to exist after death is best understood by a belief of the ancient Romans. On a trip to the Vatican Museum in Rome, a guide explained why the Romans created so many tombs and monuments, and carvings dedicated to a single life. The ancients, he said, did not believe in a conventional afterlife, so all that remained after death was non-existence. But if you could capture even a single part of an individual—in art, in writing, in stone—so that years later, centuries later, one person would see that little bit of lost soul, then in that moment of recognition, the person who had died would continue to exist like a flash of light in the settled dust of the universe; a non-entity that flickers on like a light in the dark void of nothingness. Similarly, the Greek Olympians competed not only for a crown, for money, and for fame in their lifetime, but for something far more pressing—immortality: for a way in which to be remembered and so "conquer" death.

Locke goes further than many philosophers in the soul/body issue to make the claim that the self is not even tied to a single being, a single soul, but is rather a consciousness that passes from person to person—from a prince to a cobbler, from one being to another over the centuries. This makes sense in that it is the evolution of humankind, the consciousness and understanding of self that has grown and changed and evolved over thousands of years through interactions, experiences, and the questioning of life's purpose. It is a growth of self-awareness that is the product of philosophic study as ideas pass from one mind to the next.

How do our "selves" fit into a "social" context? Are we defined by our "social" selves? What is a more accurate measure of self—who we *think* we are, or whom others see us as? I believe that our self is not *only* defined by those around us, but the people in our lives certainly impact who we are becoming, and how we see ourselves. You only need to think of the people who have played a key role in your life, changing, in sometimes just a moment, the whole way in which you view the world. And, of course, there are individuals who know better than most who we *are*. These are the people in our lives who recognize us not simply for what we believe we are, but also for what we value about our selves—they see us for what we can become. Like holding up a mirror, these people who take the time and have the insight and empathy to understand enough of the many facets that make up our personalities to allow us to see ourselves more clearly.

I can recall vividly an evening, in which an acquaintance who had at some point become a friend said to me, "You know, it's funny: you're so much different than what I first thought. You were so quiet. I thought you were just this nice quiet person, but you turned out to be not that at all. All of a sudden you just popped out. You're so crazy!" In that instant, I had the bizarre sensation of myself "popping out," springing forth. It is odd to think of it that way, but she was right—that is exactly how it felt. People have images of self: who they want to be; who they want people to think they are; what they think they truly are underneath—hidden away, trapped and unrecognized. But once that "hidden person" emerges, "pops out," it is often not what you might have thought it was. Not as serious, not as profound, but *you*. Comfortably you.

Somehow this friend saw me, recognized me, and held up the mirror. And for the first time, perhaps, I had an almost physical sensation of myself—as though I could see it and feel it, a glowing beam of light before me. Not perfect, not profound, not all that I aspired to be and was moving towards, but me nonetheless. And at the same time, I had a sense of all the other selves around me and thus the smallness and inconsequence of my existence. It was a glimmer of me emerging as something different than what I'd once imagined: a wavering dot on the map, a flash of light somewhere in time, and one of the millions of beams of light being projected towards the future that really shouldn't be here but are here simply because an elevator arrives just when it should, or a pair of hands pulls us from the suffocating waters of non-existence.

Concept Review

- The concept and nature of the *self* has been an ongoing, and evolving, subject of inquiry among philosophers since the time of Socrates. To grapple with the concept of *self* is to begin to explore what it is to know, to believe, to think, to be conscious.

- For Socrates and Plato, the *self* was synonymous with the *soul*. Every human being, they believed, possessed an immortal soul that survived the physical body. Human souls belong to the realm of ideas, the Platonic *ideal*. Plato, in the *Republic* and *Phaedrus*, further defines the soul or self as having three components: Reason, Physical Appetite, and Spirit (or passion). These three components may work in concert, or in opposition; although Reason is always striving toward truth and knowledge, Physical Appetite is often yearning to satisfy basic material needs.

- Neoplatonism, a third-century Roman intellectual movement, was based on the dualistic Platonic concept of an immortal soul within a mortal body. Roman Christians, most notably St. Augustine (354–430 C.E.), connected Platonic and Neoplatonic concepts of a separate and immortal soul with emerging Christian doctrine.

- Early modern European philosophers, including René Descartes (1596–1650), expanded the concept of the "self" to include the thinking, reasoning mind. Descartes and other rationalist philosophers believe the natural world—and human nature—is to be subjected to independent rational inquiry. For Descartes, the act of thinking about the self—of being *self-conscious*—is in itself proof that there is a "*self*" However, Descartes still demonstrates the powerful influence of Platonic thought and Christian theology in his distinction between the physical body (which he believes is material, mortal, and nonthinking) and an immortal, nonmaterial thinking *self*, governed by God's will and the laws of reason.

- John Locke (1632–1704) approached the problem of the *self* from the perspective of an empiricist—someone who believes that sensory experience is the primary source of our knowledge of the world and the *self*. Consciousness—or, more specifically, self-consciousness—of our constantly perceiving *self* is necessary to what Locke called "personal identity," or knowledge of the *self* as a person. However, Locke sharply breaks with the continuous tradition from Plato to Descartes that the *self* is immortal and separate from the body; instead, he argues, our personal identity and the immortal "soul" in which that identity is located are very different entities. Memory—often faulty—is one frail link that connects our "*self*" at any one moment to our "*self*" at any past time.

- David Hume (1711–1776) went radically further than Locke to speculate that there is no "*self*" at all. Our memories and experiences, Hume argued, are made up of *impressions* and *ideas* with no one "constant and invariable," unified identity. When we are not actively perceiving, or conscious of ourselves perceiving, Hume notes, there is no basis for the belief that there is any "self" at all. In a further rupture with earlier philosophy and doctrine, Hume concludes that if there is no "*self*" while the body is living, then there can certainly be no immortal "*self*" or "soul" that goes on after the death of the physical body.

- Immanuel Kant (1724–1804) found Hume's views about the potential for further human development to be alarmingly cynical. In returning to Hume's starting point—that the self is made up of its sensory experiences—Kant speculated that those experiences, far from being random and disconnected, are in fact arranged and given order by the conscious self based on *a priori* organizing rules. If Hume's view of the mind was a kind of passive "theatre" across which random experiences flitted, Kant proposed an actively engaged and synthesizing intelligence that constructed knowledge based on its experiences. This synthesizing faculty—Kant's version of the "*self*"—transcends the senses and unifies experience. In addition, Kant proposed a second "*self*," the *ego*, which consists of those traits that make us each a unique personality.

- Sigmund Freud (1856–1939), the founder of psychoanalysis, proposed a radical new way to consider the *self*. For Freud, the *self* is composed of both rational, thinking consciousness and a more primitive and impulsive unconscious. The conscious self constantly monitors the unconscious—yet the unconscious still bubbles up through slips of the tongue, dreams, and neurotic behaviors.

- The behaviorist approach to the self holds that the "self" is best observed and defined through individual behavior. The great advantage of behavior—unlike an invisible "soul" or transcendent consciousness—is that it can be controlled, observed, collected, and analyzed. How you behave is "who" you are. The behaviorist Gilbert Ryle (1900–1976) attempted to finally discredit what he called "Descartes' myth"—that the soul is independent from the body, a belief Ryle classifies as a "category mistake"—by seeing the *self* as a "pattern of behavior," not some abstraction caught up in a false spatial metaphor. However, Ryle acknowledges that this reconciliation of Cartesian dualism still does not adequately address the nature of the *self*—which is surely more than a collection of observable behaviors.

- Materialism holds that the "*self*" is inseparable from the substance of the brain and the physiology of the body. Contemporary advances in neurophysiology allow scientists to observe the living brain as it works to process information, create ideas, and move through dream states. Philosopher Paul Churchland has worked to resolve the complexities of the relationship between mind and brain through the theory of "eliminative materialism." Churchland argues that "folk psychology," or more traditional "commonsense" ways of understanding psychology, will not find neat and obvious parallels through the discoveries of contemporary neuroscience. In fact, he claims, that "older framework will simply be eliminated" by advances in neuroscience. This new, accurate, objective, and scientifically based understanding of our "selves" will, in Churchland's view, "contribute substantially toward a more peaceful and humane society."

■ Phenomenologists Edmund Husserl (1859–1938) and Maurice Merleau-Ponty (1908–1961) simply dismiss Cartesian dualism as a product of our imagination. The living, physical body and its experiences are all one, a natural synthesis, what Husserl and Merleau-Ponty called the *Lebenswelt* (a German word meaning "lived world"). Phenomenology seeks not to explain experience, but rather to clarify our understanding of it. Jean-Paul Sartre (1905–1980), also a phenomenologist, further developed the concept of the primacy of lived existence through the philosophy of existentialism.

Media Resources

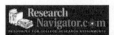 **www.researchnavigator.com**

Chapter 3 explores important questions in metaphysics, or questions of those things that transcend the limits of experience and ordinary knowledge. Hence, important questions about the nature of the self arise in metaphysical inquiry. For further research on questions of the self, use the tools available to you in Research Navigator.

As you investigate this topic, consider this question: "In what ways can our identity, philosophically speaking, transform over our lifetime?"

- **ContentSelect:** search in the Philosophy, Religion, and Sociology databases using the search terms "identity," "self," and "consciousness."

- **Link Library:** search in the Philosophy database under terms "determinism," "free will," and the names "David Hume," "Immanuel Kant," and "John Locke."

- **New York Times on the Web:** search in the Philosophy database using the search terms "consciousness" and "*self*."

 For additional study resources for this chapter, go to:
www.prenhall.com/chaffee/chapter3

 The Primary Source: Philosophical Readings and Commentary

Augustine, St.: *City of God*

Berkeley, George: *Three Dialogues Between Hylas and Philonous*

Descartes, René: *Discourse on Method Rightly Conducting the Reason and Seeking Truth in the Field of Science; Meditations on First Philosophy*

Freud, Sigmund: *An Outline of Psycho-Analysis*

Hume, David: *A Treatise of Human Nature*

James, William: *Does 'Consciousness' Exist?*

Kant, Immanuel: *Critique of Practical Reason; Critique of Pure Reason; Prolegomena to Any Future Metaphysics*

Locke, John: *An Essay Concerning Human Understanding*

Mencius: *Human Nature*

Milindapanha: *The Questions of King Melinda; The Simile of the Chariot*

Plato: *Cratylus; Meno; Phaedo; Phaedrus; Symposium*

Ryle, Gilbert: *The Concept of Mind*

Man is condemned to be free.

JEAN-PAUL SARTRE

*Man is not a free agent
in any one instant of his life.*

BARON D'HOLBACH

Man is condemned to be free. *Condemned, because he did not create himself, yet is nevertheless at liberty, and from the moment that he is thrown into this world, he is responsible for everything he does.*

JEAN-PAUL SARTRE
Man as Self-Creator

The actions of man are never free. . . . Man's life is a line that nature commands him to describe upon the surface of the earth, without his ever being able to swerve from it, even for an instant. . . . Nevertheless, in spite of the shackles by which he is bound, it is pretended he is a free agent, or that independent of the causes by which he is moved, he determines his own will, and regulates his own condition. . . . Man is not a free agent in any one instant of his life.

BARON D'HOLBACH
The System of Nature

Are you free? When people think of "being free," they often conjure up a romantic notion of "getting away" from their concerns and responsibilities, imagining a world where anything is possible and there is plenty of money to pay for it. However appealing this fantasy may be, it is a misconceived and unrealistic notion of freedom. Many thinkers believe that if freedom *is* possible, it makes sense to view it as the process of making thoughtful choices from among the available options, choices that reflect your genuine desires and deepest values, choices that are independent of the influence of external pressures *or* internal forces.

However, other thinkers are convinced that personal freedom is *not* possible, at least in any meaningful sense. They agree with Baron d'Holbach that people *think* that they're free, but in reality this feeling is an illusion. It would be analogous to a puppet believing that it is acting voluntarily, when every movement is controlled by wires wielded by the puppeteer.

Unquestionably, the majority of people *want* to believe that they are free—at least when things are going well. They're attracted to poet William Ernest Henley's notion that "I am the master of my fate; I am the captain of my soul." They're entranced and inspired by the vision of themselves creating a bold, vibrant life through wise choices and principled commitments. At least until things go wrong, mistakes are made, or catastrophes ensue. Then being "the master of one's fate" loses a great deal of its attraction. Instead, people often dive for cover, desperately seeking to blame anything (or any one!) for the failure, underscoring the Chinese proverb, "Success has a thousand fathers, but failure is an orphan."

All of which reveals an important and disturbing element of personal freedom: it is necessarily tied to *personal responsibility*. And personal responsibility is why, on an emotional level, many people are reluctant to embrace the idea of freedom and in fact may actively seek to "escape" from it. If you are committed to the view that your choices are genuinely *free*, then you must accept that you are *responsible* for the outcome of your choices. When you are successful, it is easy to take full responsibility for your success, but when failure occurs, there is a temptation to blame others or forces outside of your control, as expressed by the following common statements (and others like them):

"If only that person hadn't sabotaged my career, I would have . . ."
"If only I had a chance to meet the right person . . ."
"If only I got a break now and then. . . ."
"If only I could get rid of my habitual tendency to _____, I would . . ."
"If only other people were as dependable and caring as I am. . . ."
"If only I had been given the advantages of a different background . . ."
"If only the world had not become so competitive . . ."
"If only I was given the opportunity to show what I could do . . ."

Rather than accepting their role in the choices they made, people tend to believe that *if only* some outside force had not intervened, they would have achieved the goal they set for themselves.

However, whether we are actually free or not is a question that is independent of our personal feelings about our freedom. Whether we are free is a philosophical (and psychological) question that requires thoughtful reflection and rigorous analysis. We need to try to understand the truth about freedom: are we able to make authentically free choices or are our actions determined by factors beyond our control? Given exactly the same conditions or circumstances, could we have chosen otherwise than we did? Are we responsible for the choices we make and their outcomes, or should we be excused from responsibility? These are the central issues that we will explore in this chapter. Of course, as with most philosophical explorations, we will soon see that the questions—and potential answers—are a great deal more complex than the simple conclusion "We're free" or "We're not free." We're going to begin this journey by looking at the mainsprings of human action.

Why Do People Act as They Do?

Everyday we are confronted with the mystery of human action. One person commits an armed robbery, killing a guard in the process. Another person is found to have embezzled large sums of money from the charitable organization that he directed. A firefighter risks her life to save the life of an infant trapped in a burning building. A peaceful protest gets out of control and turns into a violent and destructive altercation. A respected member of the community is accused of abusing the children on the teams that he coached. Two teenagers are accused of murdering their newborn infant and dumping the body in a garbage container. An 84-year-old woman who spent her life cleaning the homes of others donates her life savings—$186,000—to a local college with which she had no previous relationship. In each of these instances, and countless others, we struggle to understand "why" people acted the way they did. Our answers typically depend on our deepest beliefs about the nature of the human self. For example:

- **Human nature:** *"I believe in human nature; people are born with certain basic instincts that influence and determine how they behave."* Based on this view, the actions described above, whether "good" or "evil," are no more than the natural expression of a *universal nature* that is genetically hardwired into every person. From this perspective, we should no more hold people responsible for their destructive actions than we would an animal in the wild that kills in order to survive. There is no possibility of free choice because our actions necessarily follow from our inborn nature, and we cannot be other than we are. Whether you do good or ill in your life is really beyond your control, and you cannot alter your fundamental character.

- **The environment:** *"I believe that people are shaped by their environment, conditioned by their experiences to be the kind of people they are."* From this vantage point, the actions described above are the direct products of the *life experiences* that people have. If the environment in which you developed was deprived or abusive, then these forces shaped a violent individual with little regard for the rights or lives of others. On the other hand, if you were fortunate enough to grow up in a loving and nurturing environment in which kindness and empathy were considered paramount values, then this upbringing shaped who you are. But once again, you cannot be held responsible for how you turned out because you didn't choose your environment; you were a *passive agent* molded by forces beyond your control. And, of course, you are incapable of making free choices. We should no more condemn the embezzler than we should reward the firefighter, because they are each merely products of environments that are ultimately responsible for their behavior.

- **Psychological forces:** *"I believe that people are governed by psychological forces, many of them unconscious, that cause them to think, feel, and act in certain ways."* Based on this point of view, the actions described above are the direct result of deep psychological impulses that have been formed by people's earliest relationships and experiences. Although these people may *think* they are choosing to do the things they are, in reality they are puppets manipulated by unseen psychological strings. The same is true for you. So when the coach sexually abused the children on his teams, he was not actually *choosing* this reprehensible course of action, he was impelled by *psychological forces* over which he had no control. Similarly, your behavior results from psychological motivations, often repressed, that form the basic structure of your personality. Your feelings of freedom are illusory.

- **Social dynamics:** *"I believe that we are social creatures who are greatly influenced by the people around us."* From this perspective, people's behavior results in large measure from the forces exerted by those around them. The need to conform to the prevailing norms, to be accepted by the groups to which you belong, to please those who are close to you, to obey those in positions of authority—these and other social needs determine your behavior and define who you are as an individual. For example, the violent actions of the initially peaceful demonstrators can be understood only by examining the dynamics of *social interaction*. Because the group as a whole is to blame, responsibility is removed from the individuals. In the same way, individuals who act illegally (or immorally) within an organization often seek to be exonerated on the grounds that they were merely acting as cogs in the machine, not independent agents. An extreme version of this occurred after World War II at the Nuremberg trials when many people accused of wartime atrocities explained that they were "only following orders."

THINK PHILOSOPHICALLY　4.1
My Theory of Human Behavior

PHILOSOPHERS NOTEBOOK

Think about some of the actions described at the beginning of this section. How would *you* explain why these people acted in the ways that they did? Which of these theories makes the most sense to you? Do you have your own theory to explain why people behave they way they do?

- A person commits an armed robbery, killing a guard in the process.
- A person embezzles large sums of money from the charitable organization that he directed.
- A firefighter risks her life to save the life of an infant trapped in a burning building.
- A peaceful protest gets out of control and turns into a violent and destructive altercation.
- A respected member of the community is accused of abusing the children on the teams that he coached.
- Two teenagers are accused of murdering their newborn infant and dumping the body in a garbage container.
- An 84-year-old woman who spent her life cleaning the homes of others donates her life savings—$186,000—to provide scholarships at a local college.

If we examine all of these beliefs regarding the nature of human beings, we can see that they have several significant things in common:

- These beliefs represent attempts to explain human behavior in terms of factors that *precede* the action: a universal human nature, past experiences, psychological forces, and social dynamics. In other words, all of these beliefs assume that the "essence" of a person, as defined by the factors identified above, comes *before* the human actions and in fact *causes* these actions to take place.
- As a result, all of these beliefs about the human self have the effect of *removing responsibility* from the individual for his actions. If what you did was the direct result

◆ VISUAL PHILOSOPHY

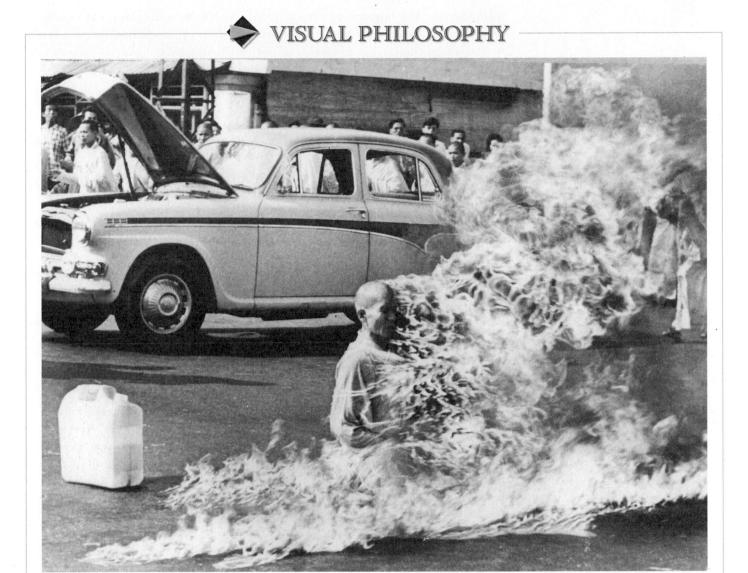

Why Do People Act as They Do?

What is your reaction to this photograph of a monk setting himself on fire? Why do you think he might be acting in such a drastic way? Is this a free choice on his part?

of human nature, past experiences, psychological forces, or social dynamics, then *you cannot be held accountable.* You didn't have a choice; your behavior was outside of your control.

- As a final consequence, these beliefs about the self *limit future possibilities.* If your thoughts, feelings, and actions are caused by forces beyond your control, then you do not have it in your power to change, to alter direction, to improve—any more than a puppet can decide to act independently and contrary to the wishes of the puppeteer.

From a framework rooted in human freedom, these traditional perspectives regarding the nature of people are dangerous and destructive. One of the most passionate and articulate modern exponents of individual freedom is Jean-Paul Sartre. His position is extreme—you are *completely free. You create yourself* entirely through the free choices that you make every day of your life. Though you may try to pretend otherwise, the reality is that you are the originator of your actions, the master of your fate, and the captain of your soul, for better or for worse. You may choose to surrender control of your life to other individuals or organizations, but this is ultimately a free choice that *you make* and for which you are completely responsible. Let's revisit the examples identified above and analyze them from this perspective.

- **Free choice:** *"I believe that people are free to choose their courses of action, and that they should be held responsible for the choices they make."*
    - The person who committed the armed robbery and murdered the guard *freely chose* to steal money and he is completely *responsible*. He was not compelled to act in this fashion: he could have chosen not to steal.
    - The person who embezzled money from the charitable organization which he headed *freely chose* to betray his trusted position out of greed and should be held fully accountable.
    - The heroic firefighter *freely chose* to overcome her natural fear of death and risk her life to save someone else's, and she should be awarded full credit for her heroism.
    - The child abuser *freely chose* to surrender to his destructive sexual impulses and he deserves to be condemned and fully punished.
    - The infant-murdering teenagers *freely chose* to deal with their fear of having an unwanted child by killing it and trying to hide the body (despite having many other alternatives available), and they should be held fully responsible for their choice.
    - The philanthropic senior citizen *freely chose* to donate her money to improve educational opportunities for underprivileged young people rather than spending the money on herself, and she deserves to be praised for her altruism.

From this perspective, each of these people had other alternatives available to them, and they could have made different choices—but they didn't. And so they must be held responsible for the choices that they *did* make. But surely, you might be thinking, I can't be held *completely* responsible for my life. After all, there are many factors outside of my control, people and forces that *do* create obstacles and undermine my efforts. And we are subject to pressures and influences from *within* ourselves: feelings of greed, fear of death, altruistic impulses, sexual compulsions, need for social acceptance, and so on. From the standpoint of Sartre and others who believe in free choice, it is up to us to freely choose the particular impulses, motivations, fears, and desires with which we want to act in accordance. In other words, it is up to you, your *self*. You make the ultimate choice regarding who you want to become and the direction of your life. When you look in the mirror, the person that you see reflected is the person you have created. If you are pleased with who you are and the state of your life, than you have every right to feel proud. On the other hand, if you are dissatisfied with the person you have become and disappointed with the course of your life, then you have to look no further than yourself to determine who is responsible. You must have the courage to accept full responsibility for your situation, but it is within your power to change, to improve yourself and your life through the free choices that you are able to make.

Sartre characterizes humans as the one living creature whose "existence" precedes its "essence." In other words, *you* create your "essence" (your self, soul, or personality) through the free choices that you make in your daily "existence."

> Man first of all exists, encounters himself, surges up in the world—and defines himself afterwards. Man simply *is*—he is what he *wills* to be after that leap towards existence. Man is nothing else but that which he makes of himself.

This is exactly what distinguishes human consciousness from the rest of the animal kingdom: when confronted with a decision situation, we are able to *think about the options* available to us and then *make a free choice* based on our evaluation. And that makes us responsible for our actions, as Sartre makes clear.

> If existence is prior to essence, then man is *responsible* for what he is, it puts every person in possession of himself as he is, and places the entire responsibility for his existence squarely on his shoulders.

Because You Are Free . . .

This discussion of freedom may seem abstract and theoretical to you, and you might be asking yourself: What difference do my beliefs about personal freedom make in my life? The truth is that along with your beliefs about morality and religion, there is perhaps no other belief that has a greater impact on your life. Here are a few examples.

- **Self-improvement:** If you are a person who is constantly striving to improve yourself and the quality of your life, then it is essential that you possess the freedom to make different choices from those you have previously made. Personal freedom is the engine of human change. By using your critical thinking abilities, you can identify appropriate goals and intelligent alternatives; by exercising your freedom, you can choose the goals and alternatives that best meet your needs and fulfill your ideals. On the other hand, an exclusive belief in one of the "nonfreedom" theories (human nature, environmental influences, psychological forces, etc.) undermines and even eliminates the possibility of changing yourself in an independent, autonomous way. Though you may *believe* that the direction in your life is the consequence of autonomous deliberations and choices, the truth is that these deliberations and choices are themselves causally determined by antecedent events or factors. For someone who doesn't believe in the possibility of genuinely free choices, the whole process is causally determined.

- **Morality:** Morality deals with the way we relate to people around us. Societies have developed moral ideals and prohibitions to help their citizens live together in a harmonious and productive fashion. As a result, most societies consider such things as murder, robbery, cheating, stealing, and raping to be "wrong," and they have enacted laws and punishments to discourage antisocial behavior. On the other hand, most societies consider things such as compassion, altruism, sharing in communal responsibilities, and working for the good of everyone as well as yourself to be "right," and encourage this sort of behavior through teaching, exhortation, and example. But none of this makes any sense if you don't believe that people are free to choose among different alternatives. If you believe that people are *not free*, that their actions are caused by genes, past conditioning, or uncontrollable impulses, then they cannot be held responsible for what they do, and there is little point in trying to encourage them to act differently. Without freedom, morality becomes irrelevant. People act the way they are programmed or compelled to act, and that's all there is.

- **Religion:** Most of the world's religions offer a path to an ultimate, spiritual transformation. This spiritual transformation requires devotion and commitment to religious principles and practices so that people can achieve a higher spiritual state on earth and in life after death. But if an individual is *not free* to choose—or not to choose—a spiritual path, then most religions lose their logic and rationale. If your religious actions are completely conditioned by your upbringing or determined by other factors beyond your conscious control, then you can never achieve any spiritual enlightenment through your own efforts. And because enlightenment through free choice is the main purpose of most religions, then they require that individuals have the ability to choose freely in determining their spiritual destiny. In the absence of freedom, religion becomes irrelevant.

- **Social improvement:** We live in an imperfect world, saturated with poverty, discrimination, crime, substance abuse, addictions, war and strife, political repression, environmental pollution, child and spousal abuse, and so on. Many

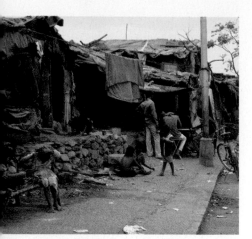

people want to create a better world, but to do so requires the ability to change the past and present by freely choosing to alter the future. But if freedom doesn't exist, then there is no point in even trying to solve social problems and improve society as a whole. Without the possibility of free choice, these problems are destined to take their own course, and all we can do is watch as passive spectators. On the other hand, if freedom *does* exist, then it is our responsibility to envision a better future and to make choices that will help make this future a reality.

- **Raising children:** Whether or not you believe people are capable of free choice can make a dramatic difference in how you approach raising your children. If you believe that people are the product of their circumstances, then you will emphasize external forms of motivation like rewards and punishments; and if you believe that personalities are genetically constructed, you may minimize your involvement in the natural unfolding of who your children are. However, if you believe that your children *are* capable of making free, independent choices, then you will work to educate them regarding the responsibility they have for directing their lives and the importance of thinking critically about their alternatives. With free choice as a framework, you will seek to help them become reflective and principled individuals who make thoughtful decisions and accept the responsibility for their choices. In other words, you will want them to understand the nature of their freedom and to exercise its power wisely.

- **Crime and punishment:** In recent years we have been subjected to a number of high-profile criminal trials. Every trial attempts to answer two basic questions: Did the accused person commit the crime he (or she) is charged with? Did he know what he was doing and make a free choice to do it? If the first question is answered "yes," then the second question becomes pivotal in evaluating a person's guilt and responsibility. But to hold people responsible for what they do, we have to believe that they are capable of making free choices. If people's behavior is caused by other factors, then they couldn't help what they did and it makes no sense to hold them responsible, any more than we should hold a rabid raccoon or a trained pit-bull personally responsible for their attacks. These types of defenses are becoming increasingly prevalent. It used to be that the "insanity defense" was reserved for the most obviously deranged criminal defendants. More recently, however, this type of defense has spread to include such defenses as insanity due to eating junk food like Twinkies, watching violent television, or listening to heavy metal or rap music.

To sum up, whether or not you believe that people are capable of making free choices—independent of habit, past conditioning, genetic heritage, social pressure, or psychological compulsions—will have a significant and far-reaching impact on the way you think and act toward yourself, others, and the world as a whole. The way you live your life is a direct reflection of your deepest held beliefs, and your understanding of the possibility of free choice is one of the cornerstones of your Philosophy of Life. If you end up believing that personal freedom is possible, then having a clear and accurate understanding about your freedom of choice will enable you to create yourself as the kind of person you want to be, and to inspire the best in others as well. As the German poet Rainer Maria Rilke wrote, "We are always becoming the self that we are." On the other hand, if you conclude that personal freedom is limited or nonexistent, then you need to reconcile this belief with other assumptions you make in the living of your life.

Your experience with this Think Philosophically activity on p. 158 may have begun to reveal to you how complex the subject of personal freedom actually is. For example, you might have found that some of your beliefs and assumptions were in apparent conflict with one another; that a conclusion you had previously felt confident about now seemed less certain; and that you ended up the activity more confused about the concepts of "freedom" and "responsibility" than when you began. If so, congratulations! These are healthy signs that you are thinking seriously about these issues and that you are getting below the level of superficial platitudes ("Of course I'm free—I do what I want!") where many people reside. To gain a genuinely sophisticated philosophical understanding of the subject of freedom, you need to first abandon the simplistic notions and cliches that are so prevalent in our culture, and have the courage to openly and honestly explore these crucial yet challenging themes. As you enhance your understanding of freedom, your evolving insights may have a significant impact on your own life.

Our philosophical explorations of freedom will fall into three general areas:

- Some thinkers are convinced that genuine freedom of choice is not possible because all of our decisions and actions are necessarily determined by factors beyond our control. As a result, people are ultimately *not* responsible for anything they do. This view is known as **determinism**, and in its most extreme form, "hard determinism."

- Other thinkers are convinced that genuine freedom of choice is a reality, and that we are fully able to make decisions and initiate actions independently of any influences on our thinking or behavior. This position holds that in precisely the same choice situations an individual "could have done otherwise" had he or she freely chosen to. As a result, people are absolutely responsible for what they do. This view is known as **indeterminism**. Some philosophers make a distinction between "indeterminism" and "libertarianism." For them, all libertarians are indeterminists, but not vice versa. Indeterminism is the position that at least some of our actions are not determined, leaving open the possibility that these undetermined actions are random. The indeterminist need not admit the existence of free will, whereas this is precisely what the libertarian is committed to.

- A third school of beliefs regarding human freedom is called **soft determinism**, or "compatibilism." Soft determinists agree with hard determinists that all events, including human actions are caused. However, soft determinists assert that we can consider human actions "free" if they are the result of internal motivations, not the product of external influences or constraints. These thinkers agree with the determinists that the principle of causality applies universally, and that every explanation of human behavior must also assume the validity of causal laws. However, soft determinists contend that we can still distinguish between actions that are compelled by external constraints and actions that are not. Actions that are externally compelled—for example as the result of threats—are *unfree*. In contrast, actions that are not compelled by external factors are *free*. Freedom means the opposite of compulsion: people are free if they are not impeded from acting on their unimpeded natural desires, even though these natural desires may be causally determined by factors in their personal history.

In addition to these three standard positions, some thinkers are convinced that both determinists and indeterminists each make valid points, but they represent extreme perspectives that need to be synthesized into an integrated whole. A variety of approaches seek to reconcile these two opposing viewpoints, and they are characterized in a variety of ways that we will explore.

THINK CRITICALLY

4.2

PHILOSOPHER'S NOTEBOOK

My Assumptions of Freedom

Think critically about your own assumptions regarding personal freedom by responding to the following questions:

- Do you believe that you can improve yourself by choosing freely to establish goals and make intelligent choices to achieve those goals? If so, do you believe that you are personally responsible for both the positive and "less positive" aspects of yourself? Why or why not?

- Do you believe that people are free to make independent choices in moral situations? Do you accept full responsibility for all of the moral choices you have made, even those you may regret having made? Why or why not?

- If you have religious beliefs, do you believe that you can influence your spiritual growth through the free choices that you make? Do you believe that people who make different religious choices than those prescribed by your religion are in spiritual jeopardy? Why or why not?

- Do you think that the problems of the world can be solved if people make more enlightened choices? Do you think that individuals in each society should be held responsible for the social problems of that society? Why or why not?

- Do you believe that people who commit crimes made free choices to do so? Why or why not? If so, how should they be held responsible for their actions? If not, what should happen to them?

- Do you believe that parents should raise children by encouraging them to think independently and accept responsibility for their choices? Why or why not?

Determinism The view that every event, including human actions, are brought about by previous events in accordance with universal causal laws that govern the world. Human freedom is an illusion.

Indeterminism The view that some events, including human actions, are not necessarily determined by previous events in accordance with universal causal laws. Human freedom is possible.

Soft determinism The view that all events, including human actions are caused. However, we can consider human actions *free* if they are the result of internal motivations, not the product of external influences or constraints.

Determinism: *All Human Actions Are Determined—Freedom Is an Illusion*

The determinist view of human freedom is typically based on the scientific model of the physical universe. Most modern cultures assume that the universe is governed by causal laws that can be discovered and that we can use to predict what will happen in the future. When you set your alarm clock, adjust the thermostat, turn off the light switch, bring an umbrella, turn the key in the ignition of your car, make plans for the evening after the sun disappears—all of these actions, and countless others, are based on your general belief that everything that occurs in the physical world has a cause (or causes) and that by discovering these causal relationships between events, we can predict and influence what will happen in the future. Imagine your surprise if your auto mechanic informed you that there was no cause for your car's difficulties, nor would any cause ever be discovered, so you might as well junk it. Time for a new mechanic, you would likely conclude!

Similarly, when you take vitamins, eat a balanced diet, limit your alcohol intake, take prescribed antibiotics, and get enough sleep—all of these actions, and many others, you are acting on the belief that your physical body is also governed by causal relationships. Again, imagine your surprise if your physician informed you that although you may be feeling ill, there was nothing causing your sickness and so there was absolutely nothing that could be done to improve your health. It's likely that you would seek a second opinion, don't you think?

Those who take a determinist view of personal freedom use these generally accepted areas of causal determinism as a framework for understanding the mainsprings of human action. Their reasoning can be summarized thus:

- Events in the physical universe consistently display well-defined causal connections. There are scientific exceptions to this precise causal determinism at subatomic levels, but it's a scientific perspective generally accepted for the rest of the universe.
- Events in the biological realm also consistently display causal connections, though as we saw in the last chapter, the complex and intimate relationship between the mind and body makes this a much more complicated situation.
- Because humans are a part of the physical universe and the biological realm, it's reasonable to assume that all of our actions (and the choices that initiated the actions) are also causally determined, eliminating the possibility of free choice.

Just as your alarm clock lacks the possibility to choose freely whether it will sound the alarm, so you lack the power to choose freely, because everything that you think, feel, and do is caused by other factors beyond your control. This determinist view has enjoyed passionate support from a wide variety of individuals, including psychologists like B. F. Skinner and Sigmund Freud, and a number of prominent philosophers, including **John Stuart Mill**.

Given the motives which are present to an individual's mind, and given likewise the character and disposition of the individual, the manner in which he will act might be unerringly inferred; that if we knew the person thoroughly, and knew all the inducements which are acting upon him, we could foretell his conduct with as much certainty as we can predict any physical event. . . . No one who believed that he knew thoroughly the circumstances of any case, and the characters of the different persons concerned, would hesitate to foretell how all of them would act. Whatever degree of doubt he may in fact feel, arises from the uncertainty whether he really knows the circumstances, or the character of some one or other of the persons, with the degree of accuracy required; but by no

John Stuart Mill (1806–1873) British Philosopher. Carried on tradition of British empiricists. Wrote on induction and expanded on utilitarianism of Bentham to take into account the quality, not just the quantity, of pleasure when determining the morality of an action.

means from thinking that if he did know these things, there could be any uncertainty what the conduct would be.

—John Stuart Mill

Clarence Darrow

Determinism has worked its way into other aspects of our culture, such as the criminal justice system. For example, in the early part of the twentieth century the dramatic case of Richard Loeb and Nathan Leopold transfixed the United States. These two young men, who were from privileged families and who had attended the best schools, abducted and murdered a fourteen-year-old boy just to experience the thrill of killing someone. The country was outraged at such a cold-blooded and senseless killing, and there was powerful public sentiment to execute the defendants, Loeb and Leopold. Hired to defend them, and save their lives, was the famed attorney, Clarence Darrow. In his famous summation, he passionately employed the determinist argument to convince the jury that the defendants were victims of circumstances beyond their control, not autonomous agents making free choices:

> We are all helpless. . . . This weary old world goes on, begetting, with birth and with living and with death; and all of it is blind from the beginning to the end. I do not know what is was that made these boys do this mad act, but I do know there is a reason for it. I know they did not beget themselves. I know that any one of an infinite number of causes reaching back to the beginning might be working out in these boys' minds, whom you are asked to hang in malice and hatred and injustice. . . .
>
> Nature is strong and she is pitiless. She works in her own mysterious way, and we are her victims. We have not much to do with it ourselves. Nature takes this job in hand, and we play our parts. In the words of old Omar Khayyam, we are:
>
> > But helpless pieces in the game He plays
> > Upon this checkerboard of nights and days:
> > Hither and thither moves, and checks, and slays,
> > And one by one back in the closet lays.
>
> What had this boy to do with it? He was not his own father, he was not his own mother; he was not his own grandparents. All of this was handed to him. He did not surround himself with governesses and wealth. He did not make himself. And yet he is to be compelled to pay.

Darrow was ultimately successful with his argument, and many other defense lawyers have used similar approaches in the decades since.

Most people don't live their lives based on the assumption that all of their thoughts and actions are determined and as a result, unfree. Most people act as if they—and others—have some degree of personal freedom, believing that it makes sense:

- to choose to improve yourself.
- to hold people morally responsible and educate them to be more enlightened.
- to seek to achieve spiritual transformation and enlightenment.
- to work to create a better world.
- to raise children to be thoughtful individuals who accept responsibility.
- to hold wrongdoers responsible and to punish and/or rehabilitate them.

In fact, if we were to closely examine the lives of some of the more vocal exponents of determinism, we might very well find that even they appeared to think and act as if they were capable of free choices for which they were responsible. Nevertheless, people often act on beliefs that turn out to be false (the earth is flat and the center of the solar system; some races are genetically inferior; human sacrifice is necessary to pacify the gods; surgically "bleeding" people is an effective medical treatment for common ailments; emotionally disturbed people should be tortured to drive the demons out of them; and so on). As a result, it makes sense for us to keep an open mind as we explore the theme of freedom, and we should seek to understand the strongest possible case for this position.

Paul Henri Thiry, Baron d' Holbach: *The System of Nature*

One of the most compelling and entertaining defenses of determinism is included in a book by the French philosopher **Paul Henri Thiry**, **Baron d'Holbach**, (1732–1789) entitled *The System of Nature*, a book which was referred to by his critics as "The Atheists' Bible."

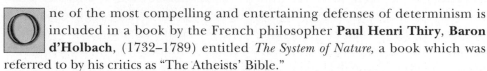

d'Holbach, *The System of Nature*

Motives and the Determination of the Will. In whatever manner man is considered, he is connected to universal nature, and submitted to the necessary and immutable laws that she imposes on all the beings she contains, according to their peculiar essences or to the respective properties with which, without consulting them, she endows each particular species. Man's life is a line that nature commands him to describe upon the surface of the earth, without his ever being able to swerve from it, even for an instant. He is born without his own consent; his organization does in nowise depend upon himself; his ideas come to him involuntarily; his habits are in the power of those who cause him to contract them; he is unceasingly modified by causes, whether visible or concealed, over which he has no control, which necessarily regulate his mode of existence, give the hue to his way of thinking, and determine his manner of acting. He is good or bad, happy or miserable, wise or foolish, reasonable or irrational, without his will being for anything in these various states. Nevertheless, in spite of the shackles by which he is bound, it is pretended he is a free agent, or that independent of the causes by which he is moved, he determines his own will, and regulates his own condition.

However slender the foundation of this opinion, of which everything ought to point out to him the error, it is current at this day and passes for an incontestable truth with a great number of people, otherwise extremely enlightened; it is the basis of religion, which, supposing relations between man and the unknown being she has placed above nature, has been incapable of imagining how man could merit reward or deserve punishment from this being if he was not a free agent. Society has been believed interested in this system; because an idea has gone abroad, that if all the actions of man were to be contemplated as necessary, the right of punishing those who injure their associates would no longer exist. At length human vanity accommodated itself to a hypothesis which, unquestionably, appears to distinguish man from all other physical beings, by assigning to him the special privilege of total independence of all other causes, but of which a very little reflection would have shown him the impossibility. . . .

The keystone of d'Holbach's view is that we are inextricably "connected to universal nature" and so are subject to the "necessary and immutable laws that she imposes on all the beings she contains." In other words, when we consider the natural order, it's clear that humans are woven into the fabric of the universe with countless threads. We fit into the natural world along with all other living beings. And because we assume that all other dimensions of the universe, both physical and biological, are subject to causal laws that necessarily define their natures and relationships, it only makes sense to include ourselves in this natural causal system. Why should humans alone be considered exceptions to immutable laws that govern every other aspect of the universe? We shouldn't, according to d'Holbach, any more than we should believe that certain people are exempt from the law of gravity, or that certain dogs and cats violate the natural order by working out quadratic equations in their minds. We are an integral part of nature in every respect, and so it is only logical to conclude that our states of mind and actions are causally determined in the same way everything else in the universe is.

BARON D'HOLBACH
(1723–1789)
French Philosopher. Major contributor to the Encyclopedia, which brought together ideas from a wide range of eighteenth century scholars. Materialist and unapologetic atheist who mounted several harsh critiques against Christianity.

d'Holbach acknowledges that humans don't believe or act as if their thinking actions are causally determined, and he even cites the arguments for indeterminism that we have already explored. It's true, he observes, that cultural beliefs like religion, morality, and criminal justice are founded on the concepts of personal freedom—it's just that these beliefs are wrong. Simply wanting something to be true doesn't make it true. And if we seek to perpetuate the illusion that we are free agents, then we are similar to actors playing a role, pretending to be someone that we're not—in this case, a free person.

But what about our "will"? Isn't that independent of the causal laws of the universe? Absolutely not, according to d'Holbach!

d'Holbach, *The System of Nature*

The will, as we have elsewhere said, is a modification of the brain, by which it is disposed to action, or prepared to give play to the organs. This will is necessarily determined by the qualities, good or bad, agreeable or painful, of the object or the motive that acts upon his senses, or of which the idea remains with him, and is resuscitated by his memory. In consequence, he acts necessarily, his action is the result of the impulse he receives either from the motive, from the object, or from the idea which has modified his brain, or disposed his will. When he does not act according to this impulse, it is because there comes some new cause, some new motive, some new idea, which modifies his brain in a different manner, gives him a new impulse, determines his will in another way, by which the action of the former impulse is suspended: thus, the sight of an agreeable object, or its idea, determines his will to set him in action to procure it; but if a new object or a new idea more powerfully attracts him, it gives a new direction to his will, annihilates the effect of the former, and prevents the action by which it was to be procured. This is the mode in which reflection, experience, reason, necessarily arrests or suspends the action of man's will: without this he would of necessity have followed the anterior impulse which carried him towards a then desirable object. In all this he always acts according to necessary laws from which he has no means of emancipating himself.

Writing 250 years ago, d'Holbach clearly did not have access to the latest in brain/mind research, but his logic is still clear. Our "will," along with all of the other mental states of consciousness such as "motive," "reflection," and "reason," are reproduced by the chemistry of the brain, and they are necessary products of the brain's interaction with the environment. Certain sets of circumstances in the environment produce one sort of mental response; other sets of circumstances produce a different kind of mental response. In either case, there is not room for personal freedom: the particular mental states—will, motive, reflection, reason, and so on—are determined by necessary causal laws. d'Holbach goes on to provide an example to illustrate his reasoning.

d'Holbach, *The System of Nature*

If when tormented with violent thirst, he figures to himself in idea, or really perceives a fountain, whose limpid streams might cool his feverish want, is he sufficient master of himself to desire or not to desire the object competent to satisfy so lively a want? It will no doubt be conceded, that it is impossible he should not be desirous to satisfy it; but it will be said—if at this moment it is announced to him that the water he so ardently desires is poisoned, he will, notwithstanding his vehement thirst, abstain from drinking it: and it has, therefore, been falsely concluded that he is a free agent. The fact, however, is, that the motive in either case is exactly the same: his own conservation. The same necessity that determined him to drink before he knew the water was deleterious upon this new discovery equally determined him not to drink; the desire of conserving himself either annihilates or suspends the former impulse; the second motive becomes stronger than the preceding, that is, the fear of death, or the desire of preserving himself, necessarily prevails over the painful sensation caused by his eagerness to drink: but, it will be said, if the thirst is very parching, an inconsiderate man without regarding the danger will risk swallowing the water. Nothing is gained by this remark: in this case, the anterior impulse only regains the ascendancy; he is persuaded that life may possibly be longer preserved, or that he shall derive a greater good by drinking the poisoned water than by enduring the torment, which, to his mind, threatens instant dissolution; thus the first becomes the strongest and necessarily urges him on to action. Nevertheless, in either case, whether he partakes of the water, or whether he does not, the two actions will be equally necessary; they will be the effect of that motive which finds itself most puissant; which consequently acts in the most coercive manner upon his will.

This example will serve to explain the whole phenomena of the human will. This will, or rather the brain, finds itself in the same situation as a bowl, which, although it has received an impulse that drives it forward in a straight line, is deranged in its course whenever a force superior to the first obliges it to change its direction. The man who drinks the poisoned water appears a madman; *but the actions of fools are as necessary as those of the most prudent individuals.* (*my italics*) The motives that determine the voluptuary and the debauchee to risk their health are as powerful, and their actions are as necessary, as those which decide the wise man to manage his. But, it will be insisted, the debauchee may be prevailed on to change his conduct: this does not imply that he is a free agent; but that motives may be found sufficiently powerful to annihilate the effect of those that previously acted upon him; then these new motives determine his will to the new mode of conduct he may adopt as necessarily as the former did to the old mode. . . . The errors of philosophers on the free agency of man, have arisen from their regarding his will as the *primum mobile*, the original motive of his actions; for want of recurring back, they have perceived the multiplied, the complicated causes which, independently of him, give motion to the will itself; or which dispose and modify his brain, whilst he himself is purely passive in the motion he receives.

THINK PHILOSOPHICALLY 4.3
Analyzing Baron d'Holbach

Reflect on the way that you make decisions when you have conflicting impulses. For example,

  Whether to have dessert when you're watching your weight

  Whether to date someone you feel ambivalent toward

  Whether to help a friend even though you had other plans

- Do you feel that you are being "pushed" by the stronger force? Why or why not?
- Do you think that you would make the same decision if placed in exactly the same circumstances? Why or why not?
- Do you feel that you are making a "free" choice in these circumstances? If so, how would you try to prove your point to d'Holbach, particularly if you acknowledge that your choice is determined by the strongest force and that you would likely make exactly the same choice in the same circumstances?
- d'Holbach contends that philosophers, speculating on the nature of free choice, have made the mistake of believing that the human *will* is "the original motive of his actions." Instead, d'Holbach believes that we need to go *beyond* the will to identify the factors that cause the will to incline one way or another. The role of the *self* is passive, serving only as a vehicle for the interplay of psychic forces to determine his thoughts, feelings, and actions. How does this analysis compare to your own experience? When you "will" something to result in action—such as rousing yourself when you're resting comfortably—do you have the sense that there are forces *causing* you to will yourself to get up? When this occurs, do you have the sense that your *self* is a passive spectator, a "theatre" (in Hume's terms) for psychic forces? Or are you convinced that your *self* is actively "willing" your actions?

d'Holbach's analysis of this "thirst" example is in response to indeterminists who want to argue that this kind of example proves the existence of free will. The indeterminist's reasoning is something like this: If you place a bowl of water before a thirsty animal like a dog, he will drink. His action is the result of inborn instinct, conditioned behavior, brain chemistry—not free will. *However*, if you present a cold drink to a thirsty human, and then tell her that the drink is poisoned, she will likely *choose freely* not to drink, overriding her instinct to quench her thirst.

Far from proving the existence of free will, d'Holbach believes that the example simply strengthens his case for determinism. The impulse to drink and the impulse not to drink upon discovering that the water is poison are both driven by the same need—self-preservation. And it is this underlying need that causes the individual to drink or not to drink. d'Holbach's model of human functioning is mechanical: each action is the net result of the forces that are driving it. In the case of conflicting forces, it is the strongest ones that will win out. In the case of most rational, well-adjusted people, they will be motivated to refrain from drinking the poisoned water because they don't want to die. This is not a free choice, simply the outcome of their psychological state, undergirded by their brain chemistry. But in the case of people who are emotionally disturbed, who are not thinking clearly, or who are self-destructive, they may very well drink the poisoned water. Again, not because they are choosing freely to, but because that's the direction that their psychological states end up pushing them. That's why d'Holbach is able to conclude that "the actions of the fools are as necessary as the most prudent individuals."

In passages foreshadowing modern theories in psychology, anthropology, and philosophy, d'Holbach goes on to further develop his view that we are completely shaped by social forces beyond our control.

In short, the actions of man are never free; they are always the necessary consequence of his temperament, of the received ideas, and of the notions, either true or false, which he has formed to himself of happiness; of his opinions strengthened by example, by education, and by daily experience. So many crimes are witnessed on the earth only because every thing conspires to render man vicious and criminal; the religion he has adopted, his government, his education, the examples set before him, irresistibly drive him on to evil: under these circumstances, morality preaches virtue to him in vain. In those societies where vice is esteemed, where crime is crowned, where venality is constantly recompensed, where the most dreadful disorders are punished only in those who are too weak to enjoy the privilege of committing them with impunity, the practice of virtue is considered nothing more than a painful sacrifice of happiness. Such societies chastise, in the lower orders, those excesses which they respect in the higher ranks; and frequently have the injustice to condemn those in the penalty of death, whom public prejudices, maintained by constant example, have rendered criminal.

Man, then, is not a free agent in any one instant of his life; he is necessarily guided in each step by those advantages, whether real or fictitious, that he attaches to the objects by which his passions are roused: these passions themselves are necessary in a being who unceasingly tends towards his own happiness; their energy is necessary, since that depends on his temperament; his temperament is necessary, because it depends on the physical elements which enter into his composition; the modification of this temperament is necessary, as it is the infallible and inevitable consequence of the impulse he receives from the incessant action of moral and physical beings.

d'Holbach, *The System of Nature*

In modern psychology, the school of thought d'Holbach is expressing here is known as **behaviorism** because it focuses attention exclusively on the role of the environment in molding our *selves* and conditioning our behavior. The founder of behaviorism, **John Watson** (1878–1958), was famous (or infamous, perhaps) for his statement:

Behaviorism   The view that focuses on the role of the environment in molding our *selves* and conditioning our behavior.

John Watson   (1878–1958) Psychologist. Founder of behaviourism; maintained the field of psychology should only concern itself with the public behaviour of individuals.

Give me a dozen healthy infants, well-formed, and my own specified world to bring them up in and I'll guarantee to take any one at random and train him to become any kind of specialist I might select—doctor, lawyer, artist, merchant-chief, and yes even beggar-man and thief, regardless of his talents, penchants, abilities, vocations, and race of his ancestors.

This is precisely the view that d'Holbach is expressing when he states that human actions are always the result of "received ideas, and . . . of his opinions strengthened by example, by education, and by daily experience." Why would Watson make such a bold claim? To begin with, Watson believed that our behavior is the most important dimension of who we are, our *selves*, Additionally, our behavior can be investigated scientifically in a way that an *inner self* cannot. Behavior can be observed, analyzed, quantified, measured, and described. An organized approach to investigating behavior, under controlled conditions, can be used to generate seemingly precise and objective behavioral *data*. This data can in turn be used to develop theories and principles for understanding why people behave the way they do, which for a behaviorist is the same thing as understanding the human *self*.

For example, imagine that you are dating someone and trying to determine the potential he/she has to be a serious romantic partner. According to Watson, there's no need to try to intuit and analyze their "inner" self: their emotions, motivations, state of mind, future aspirations, or anything else we generally associate with an *inner self*. Instead of chasing these nonobservable and elusive mental entities, we are much better served by focusing exclusively on what is readily available, their external behavior. And we can collect and quantify this data as well: how many times we've gone out, how often they call, how many times they've said "I love you . . . ," and so on. From Watson's standpoint, these actions *are* who they are. There's no thinking, feeling "self" behind the scenes controlling this behavior. As Watson's disciple **B. F. Skinner** (1904–1990) explained, "the self is simply a device for representing a *functionally unified system of responses*," a convenient fiction for representing the sum total of a person's observable behavior.

In addition to focusing on behavior as the defining dimension of the *self*, Watson and Skinner also believed that a person's behavior was a direct result of their experiences, positive and negative. In other words, our actions are the result of *conditioning*, both intentional and accidental. Responses associated with positive results tend to be repeated; responses that have evoked negative consequences tend to be discontinued. To understand the nature of a person, we need only examine their conditioning history, the positive and negative experiences that have shaped the person they have become. Of course, the same is true of your own *self*—"who" you are is the product of the way you have been conditioned throughout your life.

We are concerned, then, with the causes of human behavior. We want to know why men behave as they do. Any condition or event which can be shown to have an effect upon behavior must be taken into account. By discovering and analyzing these causes we can predict behavior; to the extent that we can manipulate them, we can control behavior.

The other main point that d'Holbach argues in the previous passage is that the moral codes and practices of other cultures are not based on universal standards but are instead products of the particular circumstances of that culture. He agrees with some contemporary anthropologists who believe in "cultural relativism"—that the wide diversity of moral beliefs displayed in various cultures means that we have no right to judge other cultures based on our own moral values. These moral values have not been freely chosen by each culture—they are simply the result of the unique circumstances and history of each culture. In the same way that individuals

B. F. Skinner (1904–1990) Philosopher/Psychologist. Skinner advanced two important philosophies of psychology: radical behaviorism and scientific behaviorism, in which he held the mind itself and unobservable entities in general were not important to scientific explanation.

are not responsible for their actions because the actions are causally determine, so cultures also cannot be held responsible for their moral practices, no matter how offensive we may find them, because these practices were not freely chosen. The disturbing implication of d'Holbach's view is that we have no grounds for morally evaluating what we might consider the most barbaric and inhuman regimes such as Nazi Germany or apartheid South Africa. As necessary manifestations of a nonpurposive universe, we can only examine these other cultures by employing understanding, not judgment.

But what about situations in which we choose one of a number of options after careful thought and analysis—doesn't this "prove" that personal freedom is possible? Definitely not, d'Holbach argues.

d'Holbach, *The System of Nature*

Choice Does Not Prove Freedom. In spite of these proofs of the want of free agency in man, so clear to unprejudiced minds, it will, perhaps be insisted upon with no small feeling of triumph, that if it be proposed to any one, to move or not to move his hand, an action in the number of those called indifferent, he evidently appears to be the master of choosing: from which it is concluded that evidence has been offered of free agency. The reply is, this example is perfectly simple; man in performing some action which he is resolved on doing, does not by any means prove his free agency; the very desire of displaying this quality, excited by the dispute, becomes a necessary motive, which decides his will either for the one or the other of these actions. What deludes him in this instance, or that which persuades him he is a free agent at this moment, is, that he does not discern the true motive which sets him in action, namely, the desire of convincing his opponent: if in the heat of the dispute he insists and asks, "Am I not the master of throwing myself out of the window?" I shall answer him, no; that whilst he preserves his reason there is no probability that the desire of proving his free agency, will become a motive sufficiently powerful to make him sacrifice his life to the attempt: if, notwithstanding this, to prove he is a free agent, he should actually precipitate himself from the window, it would not be sufficient warranty to conclude he acted freely, but rather that it was the violence of his temperament which spurred him on to this folly. Madness is a state, that depends upon the heat of the blood, not upon the will. A fanatic or a hero, braves death as necessarily as a more phlegmatic man or coward flies from it.

There is, in point of fact, no difference between the man that is cast out of the window by another, and the man who throws himself out of it, except that the impulse in the first instance comes immediately from without whilst that which determines the fall in the second case, springs from within his own peculiar machine, having its more remote cause also exterior. When Mutius Scaevola held his hand in the fire, he was as much acting under the influence of necessity (caused by interior motives) that urged him to this strange action, as if his arm had been held by strong men: pride, despair, the desire of braving his enemy, a wish to astonish him, and anxiety to intimidate him, etc., were the invisible chains that held his hand bound to the fire.

Imagine that you are engaged in a conversation with d'Holbach, trying to convince him that you are free. "I could throw myself out of that window if I wanted to—it's my choice!" you say. "That proves I'm free!" "Not really," replies d'Holbach. "Your choice is completely determined. If you retain your rationality and sanity, then I can assure you that your forces of self-preservation will prevent you from throwing yourself out of the window. On the other hand, if you are irrational and emotionally disturbed, then these mental forces will compel you to defenestrate yourself. As a third possibility, you may be rational but so intent on proving me wrong that you are willing to sacrifice your life by hurling yourself out of the window. In any case, your action will be necessarily determined by whichever psychic forces are the strongest, not by a free choice on your part."

d'Holbach then goes on to examine a historical example, the curious case of Caius Mutius Cordus (called *Scaevola*, meaning "left-handed," after the loss of his

B. F. Skinner

right hand). Mutius was a Roman warrior who tried to kill Porsenna, king of Etruscans, during their siege of Rome in 508 B.C.E. He accidentally killed a military scripter instead. When brought before Porsenna, he put his right hand in fire and held his hand there until it burned down, to show his determination. Porsenna was so deeply moved by his courage and similar threats of hundreds other Romans waiting to repeat the deed of Mutius that he spared his life and made peace with Rome.

"Surely," you say, "Mutius's deed demonstrates freedom of choice; a person so determined that they are willing to go against all natural impulses to prove a point." "Wrong again," d'Holbach replies. "When Mutius Scaevola held his hand in the fire, he was as much acting under the influence of necessity (caused by interior motives) that urged him to this strange action, as if his arm had been held by strong men: pride, despair, the desire of braving his enemy, a wish to astonish him, and anxiety to intimidate him, etc., were the invisible chains that held his hand bound to the fire."

Are d'Holbach's arguments convincing? Although it's true that he can provide a causal explanation for every action, he runs into a different kind of problem: his theory is not **falsifiable**. In other words, he cannot state conditions under which his theory might be disproved, and then demonstrate sufficient evidence to show that his theory is proved correct. As we saw in chapter 3, this is precisely the same problem **Sigmund Freud** faces with his concept of the unconscious: because *every* human action can be explained in terms of unconscious functioning, it is impossible to

Falsifiable   For a statement to be falsifiable, there must be some way to show under what conditions a theory might be disproved.

Sigmund Freud   (1856–1939) Psychologist. Freud founded school of psychoanalysis which became one of the most influential theories of psychology and therapy in the 20th century, especially theory of subconscious motivation.

Do you agree with d'Holbach that Mutius Scaevola was compelled to hold his hand in the fire by psychological forces rather than choosing freely to do so?

prove the theory true or false. Even a person's passionate denials of unconscious influence are simply taken as evidence of the individual's resistance to acknowledging the domination by their unconscious. Similarly, for the determinist, your—or Mutius Scaevola's—insistence that your action is "free" simply confirms how "unfree" the action is, and how mired in the illusion of freedom you are.

The failure to advance a theory that is falsifiable is a serious though not necessarily mortal blow. In the final analysis, it is still important to determine how well d'Holbach's theory explains the reality of our experience. To this end, d'Holbach goes on to explore another common definition of free choice, namely, the absence of constraint. In other words, people often say an action is free if the action is not being compelled by outside forces, a philosophical position known as "soft determinism" or "compatiblism." Not surprisingly, d'Holbach dismisses this attempt to establish free choice as another misguided effort to avoid accepting causal necessity. What is surprising is his use of Socrates' death as an example to prove his point, an analysis so contrary to Socrates' beliefs regarding the nature of free choice and personal responsibility that Socrates doubtless would have been fascinated—and amused—by d'Holbach's audacity! Socrates' decision to accept the sentence of death rather than cease his teachings or be banished to another country is considered by many (including Socrates, in all likelihood) to be the paradigm of a thoughtful, principled, and *free* choice. For d'Holbach to use this archetypal moment as evidence to support his belief in causal determinism is dramatically ironic.

Absence of Restraint Is Not Absence of Necessity. The partisans of the system of free agency appear ever to have confounded constraint with necessity. Man believes he acts as a free agent, every time he does not see any thing that places obstacles to his actions; he does not perceive that the motive which causes him to will, is always necessary and independent of himself. A prisoner loaded with chains is compelled to remain in prison; but he is not a free agent in the desire to emancipate himself; his chains prevent him from acting, but they do not prevent him from willing; he would save himself if they would loose his fetters; but he would not save himself as a free agent; fear or the idea of punishment would be sufficient motives for his action.

Man may, therefore, cease to be restrained, without, for that reason, becoming a free agent. In whatever manner he acts, he will act necessarily, according to motives by which he shall be determined. He may be compared to a heavy body that finds itself arrested in its descent by any obstacle whatever. Take away this obstacle, it will gravitate or continue to fall; but who shall say this dense body is free to fall or not? Is not its descent the necessary effect of its own specific gravity? The virtuous Socrates submitted to the laws of his country, although they were unjust; and though the doors of his jail were left open to him, he would not save himself; but in this he did not act as a free agent. The invisible chains of opinion, the secret love of decorum, the inward respect for the laws, even when they were iniquitous, the fear of tarnishing his glory, kept him in his prison; they were motives sufficiently powerful with this enthusiast for virtue, to induce him to wait death with tranquility; it was not in his power to save himself, because he could find no potential motive to bring him to depart, even for an instant, from those principles to which his mind was accustomed.

d'Holbach, *The System of Nature*

This is a sophisticated analysis by d'Holbach, foreshadowing important elements of the contemporary discussion regarding free choice. To begin with, d'Holbach distinguishes **"external" constraints** on our free choice from **"internal" constraints**. For the person behind bars and shackled in chains, his freedom of choice is clearly circumscribed. Many choices are not options for him because of his situation: he can't stroll down to Ben and Jerry's for an ice cream cone, take a leisurely walk in the park, or make an appointment for a pedicure. Some philosophers argue that these external constraints are limiting his natural freedom of choice, and when they are removed—for example, upon being released from prison—he is then able

External constraints External forces that limit human freedom such as incarceration, threats, or coercion.

Internal constraints Limits on freedom that are within the individual such as compulsions, obsessions, or uncontrolled anxiety.

to make these free choices. d'Holbach disagrees. Whether in prison or out, the man's actions are still causally determined: it's just that the context has changed. Again he uses an analogy from physics: we may suspend an object in mid-fall by arresting its descent, but as soon as we remove the support, the object will continue to fall. It's the same with humans: the man in prison is not free, and when he gets out of prison he's still not free because his actions are caused by the same inexorable and irresistible forces of nature that cause him to do whatever he does.

But d'Holbach goes on to make the very astute point that it's not just *external* constraints that inhibit our freedom of choice, it's *internal* constraints as well. In the same way that Mutius Scaevola was compelled by internal motivations to hold his hand in the fire, so Socrates was compelled to accept his death sentence. Even though he was not imprisoned and no one was physically coercing him to drink the hemlock to end his life, d'Holbach maintains that Socrates still "did not act as a free agent" because "the invisible chains of opinion, the secret love of decorum, the inward respect for the laws, even when they were iniquitous, the fear of tarnishing his glory, kept him in his prison; they were motives sufficiently powerful with this enthusiast for virtue, to induce him to wait death with tranquility." Socrates' entire history led up to the end of his life, and the choice of his fate was determined by all of the elements of his personality, determining his action in the only way it could have occurred, as d'Holbach contends: ". . . it was not in his power to save himself, because he could find no potential motive to bring him to depart, even for an instant, from those principles to which his mind was accustomed."

THINK PHILOSOPHICALLY 4.4
Do I Choose Freely?

PHILOSOPHER'S NOTEBOOK

- Consider a situation in which you felt you were at a crossroads, having to decide what path to take. d'Holbach argues that whatever choice you made, you *had* to make that choice because of the circumstances and motivations driving your action. Do you agree with this analysis? Why or why not? Do you believe that if you were able to be placed in an identical situation (with no recollection of the initial situation) that you would have the freedom to choose differently, or would your choice be the same? Why or why not?

- Imagine that you are engaged in a discussion with a determinist like d'Holbach over your freedom to choose. If that person says to you, "I know that you would never _____ because of the person you are," and you then go and _____, does that prove that you are capable of free choice? Why or why not?

- How do you think Mutius Scaevola would respond to d'Holbach's suggestion that in holding his hand in the fire, he was not making a free choice?

- How do you think Socrates would respond to d'Holbach's suggestion that in accepting his death sentence, he was not making a free choice?

- It seems as if d'Holbach's brand of determinism is not falsifiable: that because it can be invoked to explain *any* action, it can never ultimately be proved right or wrong. Is this a problem for determinism? Is this also a problem for analogous systems of belief like Freud's unconscious or the predictions of astrology? Why or why not?

If d'Holbach is right, if all that happens in the universe happens out of causal necessity and, as a result, personal freedom is an illusion, then he must deal with the fact that the majority of humans disagree with his analysis and conclusion.

Most people in Western societies are convinced that they have at least some degree of freedom, some power to direct their destiny and make independent choices based on their needs and desires. How does d'Holbach explain this nearly universal belief in freedom? It doesn't seem adequate to simply assert that all of these people are deluded, suffering from a mass illusion of being free. d'Holbach's explanation is that people are not able to recognize the causal necessity of their actions because the human mind is so infinitely complex. This complexity makes a clear causal analysis of their behavior nearly impossible to achieve, and it contributes to the inaccurate belief that free choice is possible. d'Holbach explains:

The Complexity of Human Conduct and the Illusion of Free Agency. It is the great complication of motion in man, it is the variety of his action, it is the multiplicity of causes that move him, whether simultaneously or in continual succession, that persuades him he is a free agent. If all his motions were simple, if the causes that move him did not confound themselves with each other, if they were distinct, if his machine were less complicated, he would perceive that all his actions were necessary, because he would be enabled to recur instantly to the cause that made him act. A man who should be always obliged to go towards the west, would always go on that side; but he would feel that, in so going, he was not a free agent. If he had another sense, as his actions or his motion, augmented by a sixth, would be still more varied and much more complicated, he would believe himself still more a free agent than he does with his five senses.

It is, then, for want of recurring to the causes that move him; for want of being able to analyze, from not being competent to decompose the complicated motion of his machine, that man believes himself a free agent. It is only upon his own ignorance that he founds the profound yet deceitful notion he has of his free agency; that he builds those opinions which he brings forward as a striking proof of his pretended freedom of action. If, for a short time, each man was willing to examine his own peculiar actions, search out their true motives to discover their concatenation, he would remain convinced that the sentiment he has of his natural free agency, is a chimera that must speedily be destroyed by experience. Nevertheless it must be acknowledged that the multiplicity and diversity of the causes which continually act upon man, frequently without even his knowledge, render it impossible, or at least extremely difficult for him to recur to the true principles of his own peculiar actions, much less the actions of others. They frequently depend upon causes so fugitive, so remote from their effects, and which superficially examined, appear to have so little analogy, so slender a relation with them, that it requires singular sagacity to bring them into light. This is what renders the study of the moral man a task of such difficulty; this is the reason why his heart is an abyss, of which it is frequently impossible for him to fathom the depth. . . .

Fatality, is the eternal, the immutable, the necessary order, established in nature; or the indispensable connexion of causes that act, with the effects they operate. Conforming to this order, heavy bodies fall, light bodies rise; that which is analogous in matter reciprocally attracts; that which is heterogeneous mutually repels; man congregates himself in society, modifies each his fellow; becomes either virtuous or wicked either contributes to his mutual happiness, or reciprocates his misery; either loves his neighbour, or hates his companion necessarily, according to the manner in which the one acts upon the other. From whence it may be seen, that the same necessity which regulates the physical, also regulates the moral world, in which every thing is in consequence submitted to fatality. Man, in running over, frequently without his own knowledge, often in spite of himself, the route which nature has marked out for him, resembles a swimmer who is obliged to follow the current that carries him along. He believes himself a free agent, because he sometimes consents, sometimes does not consent, to glide with the stream, which notwithstanding, always hurries him forward; he believes himself the master of his condition, because he is obliged to use his arms under the fear of sinking. . . . ∎

d'Holbach, *The System of Nature*

 d' Holbach, Baron, *The System of Nature*

THINK PHILOSOPHICALLY 4.5
Analyzing Baron d'Holbach

- D'Holbach's core explanation of why people don't readily see and acknowledge their actions are causally determined is because their minds are so complex. Do you find this explanation persuasive? Why or why not?

- Seen from another perspective, could the complexity of the human mind be seen as an argument supporting a belief in free choice? How? Would it be reasonable to argue that d'Holbach is trying to impose an overly simplistic model onto the rich complexity of human experience?

- D'Holbach's entire case for determinism is based on applying a causal model used in understanding the physical universe to the realm of human experience and behavior. How successful do you think this approach is?

- Some philosophers have argued that the concept of "cause" is appropriate for the physical universe but not for human behavior. Instead of "cause," they maintain that we should use the concept "reason," which does not have the same deterministic implications as "cause." Do you think that this criticism of determinism makes sense? Why or why not?

- D'Holbach concludes this essay with a striking metaphor: We are all swimming in the river of the universe, carried along by powerful currents of which we are often unaware. Sometimes we believe we're acting freely by struggling momentarily against the current, but in the end we are simply carried downstream, trying to keep our heads above water. Evaluate the effectiveness of this metaphor in explaining your own experience in life. What metaphor would you use to explain your experience of moving through life?

Indeterminism: *Some Human Actions Are NOT Determined—Freedom Is Possible*

As we have just seen, determinists view all human actions as necessarily caused by preceding events, making any belief in personal freedom a mistaken illusion. In contrast, indeterminists are convinced that at least some human actions are not the necessary result of preceding conditions and that freedom of choice is a genuine possibility, at least in certain circumstances. For example, when you find yourself at a decision crossroads, reflecting on which course of action to take, the indeterminist believes that your choice is at least potentially independent of any external or internal events. *You* choose which path to take, and you are as a result responsible for that choice. If you found yourself in exactly the same situation, you might very well choose another path. In other words, whichever option you choose, there is the conviction that *you could have chosen otherwise.* We are going to explore indeterminism through the eyes of two influential philosophers, William James and Jean-Paul Sartre.

William James: *Believing in Free Will Is More Rational*

WILLIAM JAMES
(1842–1910)
American Pragmatist. With C.S. Pierce, founded the philosophy of Pragmatism. Also contributed to the psychology of religion in *The Varieties of Religious Experience* (1903).

William James (1842–1910) was an American philosopher, psychologist, and medical doctor who wrote books dealing with a variety of subjects including *The Will to Believe, The Varieties of Religious Experience,* and *Pragmatism.* In the following selections, taken from *The Will to Believe,* James mounts a strong offensive for believing in the reality of human freedom.

James begins his defense of free will at precisely the point where determinism is most vulnerable: the criteria for belief. For James, the testimony of our direct, lived experience provides the most compelling grounds for belief, providing there are no sufficiently persuasive intellectual arguments to convince us otherwise. In other words, the fact that most humans live their lives based on the assumption that personal freedom and responsibility are valid concepts is a compelling reason for believing in the reality of these concepts. As we noted, our belief in free choice and personal responsibility infuses our beliefs in self-improvement, morality, religion, social improvement, crime and punishment, and countless other dimensions of our private and public lives. In fact, most aspects of the way we live our lives wouldn't make sense if all our actions were necessarily determined and personal freedom didn't exist.

The question is, are there in fact intellectual grounds for believing that the compelling testimony of our lived experience is mistaken? James thinks not.

The thesis I defend is, briefly stated, thus: *Our passional nature not only lawfully may, but must, decide an option between propositions, whenever it is a genuine option that cannot by its nature be decided on intellectual grounds; for to say, under such circumstances, "Do not decide, but leave the question open," is itself a passional decision,—just like deciding yes or no,—and is attended with the same risk of losing the truth.*

A common opinion prevails that the juice has ages ago been pressed out of the free-will controversy, and that no new champion can do more than warm up stale arguments which everyone has heard. This is a radical mistake. I know of no subject less worn out, or in which inventive genius has a better chance of breaking open new ground,—not, perhaps, of forcing a conclusion or of coercing assent, but of deepening our sense of what the issue between the two parties really is, of what the ideas of fate and free-will imply. . . . Our first act of freedom, if we are free, ought in all inward propriety to be to affirm that we are free. . . .

James, *The Will to Believe*

What a stirring rallying cry for indeterminists, who often seem on the defensive against the mechanistic onslaughts of deterministic arguments: "Our first act of freedom, if we are free, ought . . . to be to affirm that we are free. . . ." But James's affirmation is more than a rallying cry: he is making an epistemological statement about the free-will controversy. His philosophical point is that if free will genuinely exists, then the exercise of it is the strongest evidence for its existence. He has no tolerance for those who are not prepared to commit themselves one way or the other regarding free will, for "not committing" is itself a free choice—just not a very authentic or courageous choice, in James's eyes. If you live your life as though free will exists, then you should come forward and affirm in a loud and clear voice, "I believe that I am able to make free choices." This primal affirmation is itself the ground for believing that your statement is true. The testimony of your direct, lived experience confirms its validity.

This resounding affirmation of free will is the cornerstone of James's overall position, and he next proceeds to lay the foundation of his general argument.

With this much understood at the outset, we can advance. But not without one more point understood as well. The arguments I am about to urge all proceed on two suppositions: first, when we make theories about the world and discuss them with one another, we do so in order to attain a conception of things which shall give us subjective satisfaction; and second, if there be two conceptions, and the one seems to us, on the whole, more rational than the other, we are entitled to suppose that the more rational one is the truer of the two. . . .

James, *The Will to Believe*

James is setting out his basic epistemological criteria for determining truth and knowledge, and his view is remarkably similar to that of phenomenologists such as Edmund Husserl and Maurice Merleau-Ponty who we examined in chapter 3. From this perspective, humans use their intellectual abilities to create concepts and create theories to help them understand and give meaning to their lived experience. When theories conflict with one another, how do we decide which theories are the "best"? In the final analysis, we should endorse those theories that provide the most rational, clearest, complete, and persuasive understanding of our lived experience.

By setting out his basic criteria of evaluation, James is making clear the direction his argument is going to take with respect to free will. Deterministic theories such as those advanced by Baron d'Holbach, B. F. Skinner, and Sigmund Freud are in the final analysis inferior to indeterminist theories because they do an inferior job of helping us understand our lived experience. In fact, as we have seen, and as the determinists openly acknowledge, their theories consistently contradict and clash with our lived experience. Why should we give epistemological precedence to these determinist theories over testimony of our lived experience, which tends to support an indeterminist point of view? We *shouldn't*, James believes. And when people do commit themselves to theories that provide an inadequate account of our experience, they have completely lost sight of the essential purpose of concepts and theories—to help us clarify our experience, not distort it.

James continues to build his case by reviewing the traditional arguments for and against free will.

James, *The Will to Believe*

To begin, then, I must suppose you are acquainted with all the usual arguments on the subject. I cannot stop to take up the old proofs from causation, from statistics, from the certainty with which we can foretell one another's conduct, from the fixity of character, and all the rest. . . . Old-fashioned determinism was what we may call *hard* determinism. It did not shrink from such words as fatality, bondage of the will, necessitation, and the like. Nowadays, we have a *soft* determinism which abhors harsh words, and, repudiating fatality, necessity, and even predetermination, says that its real name is freedom; for freedom is only necessity understood, and bondage to the highest is identical with true freedom. . . .

As we have noted previously, *hard determinists* believe that all events, including human actions, are caused, precluding the possibility of free choice. *Soft determinists* agree with hard determinists that all events, including human actions, are caused. However, soft determinists assert that we can consider human actions "free" if they are the result of internal motivations, not the product of external influences or constraints.

With disdain, James dismisses this as a meaningless distinction, since soft determinists still deny the possibility of free will independent of a causal chain of events. We act the way that we do because we are compelled by internal forces: there is no meaningful sense in which we could have freely chosen "to do otherwise." So for James, "hard" and "soft" determinism are simply variations of the same unacceptable point of view.

James, *The Will to Believe*

Determinism professes that those parts of the universe already laid down absolutely appoint and decree what the other parts shall be. The future has no ambiguous possibilities hidden in its womb: the part we call the present is compatible with only one totality. Any other future complement than the one fixed from eternity is impossible. The whole is in each and every part, and welds it with the rest into an absolute unity, an iron block, in which there can be no equivocation or shadow of turning.

> With earth's first clay they did the last man knead,
> And there of the last harvest sowed the seed.
> And the first morning of creation wrote
> What the last dawn of reckoning shall read.

Indeterminism, on the contrary, says that the parts have a certain amount of loose play on one another, so that the laying down of one of them does not necessarily deter-

William James

mine what the others shall be. It admits that possibilities may be in excess of actualities, and that things not yet revealed to our knowledge may really in themselves be ambiguous. Of two alternative futures which we conceive, both may now be really possible; and the one become impossible only at the very moment when the other excludes it by becoming real itself. Indeterminism thus denies the world to be one unbending unit of fact. It says there is a certain ultimate pluralism in it; and, so saying, it corroborates our ordinary unsophisticated view of things. To that view, actualities seem to float in a wider sea of possibilities from out of which they are chosen; and, somewhere, indeterminism says, such possibilities exist, and form a part of the truth.

Determinism, on the contrary, says they exist *nowhere*, and that necessity on the one hand and impossibility on the other are the sole categories of the real. Possibilities that fail to get realized are, for determinism, pure illusions: they never were possibilities at all. There is nothing inchoate, it says, about this universe of ours, all that was or is or shall be actual in it having been from eternity virtually there. The cloud of alternatives our minds escort this mass of actuality withal is a cloud of sheer deception, to which "impossibilities" is the only name that rightfully belongs.

The issue, it will be seen, is a perfectly sharp one, which no eulogistic terminology can smear over or wipe out. The truth *must* lie with one side or the other, and its lying with one side makes the other false.

The question related solely to the existence of possibilities, in the strict sense of the term, as things that may, but need not, be. Both sides admit that a volition, for instance, has occurred. The indeterminists say another volition might have occurred in its place: the determinists swear that nothing could possibly have occurred in its place. Now, can science be called in to tell us which of these two point-blank contradicters of each other is right? Science professes to draw no conclusions but such as are based on matters of fact, things that have actually happened; but how can any amount of assurance that something actually happened give us the least grain of information as to whether another thing might or might not have happened in its place? Only facts can be proved by other facts. With things that are possibilities and not facts, facts have no concern. If we have no other evidence than the evidence of existing facts, the possibility-question must remain a mystery never to be cleared up.

And the truth is that facts practically have hardly anything to do with making us either determinists or indeterminists. Sure enough, we make a flourish of quoting facts this way or that; and if we are determinists, we talk about the infallibility with which we can predict one another's conduct; while if we are indeterminists, we lay great stress on the fact that it is just because we cannot foretell one another's conduct, either in war or statecraft or in any of the great and small intrigues and business of men, that life is so intensely anxious and hazardous a game. But who does not see the wretched insufficiency of this so-called objective testimony on both sides? What fills up the gaps in our minds is something not objective, not external. What divides us into possibility men and anti-possibility men is different faiths or postulates,—postulates of rationality. To this man the world seems more rational with possibilities in it,—to that man more rational with possibilities excluded; and talk as we will about having to yield to evidence, what makes us monists or pluralists, determinists or indeterminists, is at bottom always some sentiment like this. . . .

In reviewing the traditional positions of determinism and indeterminism, James casts the debate in a fresh light that helps to clarify the underlying issues. There are two ways of viewing the universe:

- A universe of *actualities*, in which no other possibilities exist other than those that occur. If the events of the universe were a story, there is one way and one way only that this story could ever be told. This is the determinist view.
- A universe of *possibilities*, in which no matter what events have occurred in the past, there are still multiple possibilities in the future. If the events of the universe were a story, the past has been written, but we will not be able to write the future until it occurs, because we need to see which of the multitude of possibilities become actualities. This is the indeterminist view.

How can we tell which of these two universes is the "real" universe? Facts won't help, because facts can't tell us anything about possibilities: they can only tell us about other facts. Baron d'Holbach can cite facts about what has occurred previously in the universe, but he cannot marshal any facts to prove that what occurred was the *only* possible sequence of events. Nor can he use facts to predict which of the limitless number of possibilities will end up becoming actualities in the future. And the same argument holds true for other determinists such as B. F. Skinner and Sigmund Freud.

On the other hand, there are no facts that the indeterminist can present to prove that what occurred *wasn't* the only possible sequence of events. Nor can the indeterminist cite facts to prove that the future has more than one set of possibilities that can occur.

But if facts can't decide the issue for us, then what can? James now returns to the original criteria for truth and knowledge that he introduced at the beginning. We choose the theory based on our lived experience: which universe makes the most sense to us, seems the most rational, is consistent with our deepest convictions? Is it a universe *without* possibilities, or a universe *with* possibilities? Determinists claim that it is the former; indeterminists claim it is the latter.

James begins to address this central question—"Which universe is more rational and makes the most sense?"—by exploring (with good humor) the practical implications of each theory.

James, *The Will to Believe*

Nevertheless, many persons talk as if the minutest dose of disconnectedness of one part with another, the smallest modicum of independence, the faintest tremor of ambiguity about the future, for example, would ruin everything, and turn this goodly universe into a sort of insane sand-heap or nulliverse, no universe at all. Since future human volitions are as a matter of fact the only ambiguous things we are tempted to believe in, let us stop for a moment to make ourselves sure whether their independent and accidental character need be fraught with such direful consequences to the universe as these.

What is meant by saying that my choice of which way to walk home after the lecture is ambiguous and matter of chance as far as the present moment is concerned? It means that both Divinity Avenue and Oxford Street are called; but that only one, and that one *either* one, shall be chosen. Now I ask you seriously to suppose that this ambiguity of my choice is real; and then to make the impossible hypothesis that the choice is made twice over, and each time falls on a different street. In other words, imagine that I first walk through Divinity Avenue, and then imagine that the powers governing the universe annihilate ten minutes of time with all that it contained, and set me back at the door of this hall just as I was before the choice was made. Imagine then that, everything else being the same, I now make a different choice and traverse Oxford Street. You, as passive spectators, look on and see the two alternative universes,—one of them with me walking through Divinity Avenue in it, the other with the same me walking through Oxford Street. Now, if you are determinists you believe one of these universes to have been from eternity impossible: you believe it to have been impossible because of the intrinsic irrationality or accidentality somewhere involved in it. But looking outwardly at these universes, can you say which is the impossible and accidental one, and which the rational and necessary one? I doubt if the most ironclad determinist among you could have the slightest glimmer of light on this point. In other words, either universe *after the fact* and once there would, to our means of observation and understanding, appear just as rational as the other. There would be absolutely no criterion by which we might judge one necessary and the other matter of chance. Suppose now we relieve the gods of their hypothetical task and assume my choice, once made, to be made forever. I go through Divinity Avenue for good and all. If,

For the indeterminist, at least some human choices are free in the sense that the choices transcend deterministic influences and whatever choice we make we "could have done otherwise." Do you agree? Why?

as good determinists, you now begin to affirm, what all good determinists punctually do affirm, that in the nature of things I *couldn't* have gone through Oxford Street,—had I done so it would have been chance, irrationality, insanity, a horrid gap in nature,—I simply call your attention to this, that your affirmation is what the Germans call a *Machtspruch*, a mere conception fulminated as a dogma and based on no insight into details. Before my choice, either street seemed as natural to you as to me. Had I happened to take Oxford Street, Divinity Avenue would have figured in your philosophy as the gap in nature; and you would have so proclaimed it with the best deterministic conscience in the world. . . .

And this at last brings us within sight of our subject. We have seen what determinism means: we have seen that indeterminism is rightly described as meaning chance; and we have seen that chance, the very name of which we are urged to shrink from as from a metaphysical pestilence, means only the negative fact that no part of the world, however big, can claim to control absolutely the destinies of the whole. But although, in discussing the word "chance," I may at moments have seemed to be arguing for its real existence, I have not meant to do so yet. We have not yet ascertained whether this be a world of chance or not; at most, we have agreed that it seems so. And I now repeat what I said at the outset, that, from any strict theoretical point of view, the question is insoluble. To deepen our theoretic sense of the *difference* between a world with chances in it and a deterministic world is the most I can hope to do; and this I may now at last begin upon, after all our tedious, clearing of the way.

James's analysis of a concrete example is both ingenious and effective, bringing the core issues in the free-will debate into relief. After gently poking fun at the determinist's phobic reactions to the possibility of chance and ambiguity in the universe, he asks us to visualize two superimposed universes: one in which he chooses to take Divinity Avenue home, and the other in which he opts for Oxford Street. He then asks the determinists: "How can you tell the difference between the selections? Is one more rational than the other? How can you determine which is necessary and which is impossible?" The answer is, James believes, they *can't* tell the difference. They can only tell the difference *after the fact*, once the event has taken place. But, of course, using a theory to explain something that has already occurred typically is not very informative. It is the ability to *predict* events in advance that provides more reliable support for a theory. Many theories confidently proclaim explanations of events after they have taken place, including

- psychological theories ("Unconscious impulses made you . . .").
- astrological theories ("The position of the planets shaped your personality . . .").
- sociological theories ("Social forces molded you into the person you are . . .").
- economic theories ("Economic forces account for your current income level . . .").

But all of these theories are typically much less successful in accurately predicting what is going to occur in the future. Which brings us back to the theories of determinists like d'Holbach. By advancing all-encompassing theoretical explanations for every event that occurs, they are making it impossible to ever assess the truth or falsity of their theories. And if a theory cannot establish clear criteria for evaluating its truth and falsity, then it amounts to little more than what James terms a *Machtspruch*—"a mere conception fulminated as a dogma and based on no insight into details." This conceptual dilemma poses a serious challenge to determinism, but there are additional difficulties that James believes pose an even more devastating threat.

I wish first of all to show you just what the notion that this is a deterministic world implies. The implications I call your attention to are all bound up with the fact that it is a world in which we constantly have to make what I shall, with your permission, call judg-

James, *The Will to Believe*

ments of regret. Hardly an hour passes in which we do not wish that something might be otherwise; and happy indeed are those of us whose hearts have never echoed the wish of Omar Khayyam—

That we might clasp, ere closed, the book of fate,
And make the writer on a fairer leaf
Inscribe our names, or quite obliterate,

Ah! Love, could you and I with fate conspire
To mend this sorry scheme of things entire,
Would we not shatter it to bits, and then
Remould it nearer to the heart's desire?

Now, it is undeniable that most of these regrets are foolish, and quite on a par in point of philosophic value with the criticisms on the universe of that friend of our infancy, the hero of the fable The Atheist and the Acorn,—

Fool! Had that bough a pumpkin bore,
Thy whimsies would have worked no more, etc.

Even from the point of view of our own ends, we should probably make a botch of remodeling the universe. How much more then from the point of view of ends we cannot see! Wise men therefore regret as little as they can. But still some regrets are pretty obstinate and hard to stifle,—regrets for acts of wanton cruelty or treachery, for example, whether performed by others or by ourselves. Hardly any one can remain *entirely* optimistic after reading the confession of the murderer at Brockton the other day: how, to get rid of the wife whose continued existence bored, he inveigled her into a desert spot, shot her four times, and then, as she lay on the ground and said to him, "you didn't do it on purpose, did you, dear?" replied, "No, I didn't do it on purpose," as he raised a rock and smashed her skull. Such an occurrence with the mild sentence and self-satisfaction of the prisoner, is a field for a crop of regrets, which one need not take up in detail. We feel that, although a perfect mechanical to fit to the rest of the universe, it is a bad moral fit, and that something else would really have been better in its place.

To answer the question which universe is more rational and makes more sense—the determinist's or the indeterminist's—James wants us to fully appreciate the implications of a deterministic world, and he does this by analyzing our "judgments of regret." What are "judgments of regret"? Simply the desire that events that have occurred might have occurred differently or with other, more desirable, outcomes. For example, think of mistakes you have made in the past: do you wish you had made different choices, or that the choices you made might have turned out differently? If you had the opportunity, do you imagine that you would select different courses of action? If so, you are experiencing "judgments of regret."

Analogously, consider the human catastrophes that have occurred, both natural and human-made: earthquakes and famines that wreaked havoc on countless lives; diseases such as the bubonic plague, smallpox, and AIDS that have resulted in endless human misery; wars and mindless acts of terror that have left senseless death and destruction in their wake. If you had the power, would you have prevented these calamitous events from occurring? Do you wish they had not occurred, and fervently hope that they will not occur in the future? If so, you are experiencing "judgments of regret."

It is the same with the murderer at Brockton that James describes. How could any sentient being, upon hearing of the accused man's savage murder of his wife, not wish that events had been otherwise, that he had not murdered her? And who among us wouldn't regret *any* such murder of an innocent person that has occurred, and hope that such evil actions would not occur in the future? Such horrendous events violate our moral sense of the way the world *should* be and spur us to hope for a more enlightened future.

VISUAL PHILOSOPHY

The Tragic Explosion of the Space Shuttle Challenger in 1986

Why does William James believe that "judgments of regret," such as those expressed over the tragic explosion of the space shuttle Challenger, are evidence that free will is a reality? Do you agree with his analysis? Why or why not?

But for the determinist, none of these "judgments of regret" and the hopes and desires for the future that emanate from them have any validity or ultimately make any sense. From a determinist point of view, everything that happens in the universe *has* to occur exactly the way in which it does, and the same holds true for the future as well. To think otherwise, to regret an occurrence in the past or hope for an altered future, are ideas and emotions that are futile and illogical.

But for the deterministic philosophy the murder, the sentence, and the prisoner's optimism were all necessary from eternity; and nothing else for a moment had a ghost of a chance of being put into their place. To admit such a chance, the determinists tell us, would be to make a suicide of reason; so we must steel our hearts against the thought.

James, *The Will to Believe*

And here our plot thickens, for we see the first of those difficult implications of determinism and monism which is my purpose to make you feel. If this Brockton murder was called for by the rest of the universe, if it had to come at its preappointed hour, and if nothing else would have been consistent with the sense of the whole, what are we to think of the universe? Are we stubbornly to stick to our judgment of regret, and say, though it *couldn't* be, yet it *would* have been a better universe with something different from this Brockton murder in it? That, of course, seems the natural and spontaneous thing for us to do; and yet it is nothing short of deliberately espousing a kind of pessimism. The judgment of regret calls the murder bad. Calling a thing bad means, if it means anything at all, that the thing ought not to be, that something else ought to be in its stead. Determinism, in denying that anything else can be in its stead, virtually defines the universe as a place in which what ought to be is impossible,—in other words, as an organism whose constitution is afflicted with an incurable taint, an irremediable flaw. The pessimism of a Schopenhauer says no more than this,—that the murder is a symptom; and that it is a vicious symptom because it belongs to a vicious whole, which can express its nature no otherwise than by bringing forth just such a symptom as that at this particular spot. Regret for the murder must transform itself, if we are determinists and wise, into a larger regret. It is absurd to regret the murder alone. Other things being what they are, *it* could not be different. What we should regret is that whole frame of things of which the murder is one member. I see no escape whatever from this pessimistic conclusion, if, being determinists, our judgment of regret is to be allowed to stand at all.

For the determinist, the inescapable conclusion seems to be one of cosmic pessimism. Even though the universe *could* be better than it is if it were to be rid of natural catastrophes and human evil, the universe *never will* be better—or different in any way—than it is. All that happens occurs because it *must* happen in exactly the way in which it does. Recognizing that the universe is necessarily morally flawed and vicious, and that *nothing can ever be done to change it for the better*, necessarily leads a reflective person to a profound feeling of pessimism. We regret, but we recognize that our regrets will always be hopeless. The only "escape" from this sort of cosmic pessimism is through religion, though the escape comes at a very high cost.

James, *The Will to Believe*

The only deterministic escape from pessimism is everywhere to abandon the judgment of regret. That this can be done, history shows to be not impossible. The devil, *quoad existentiam*, may be good. That is, although he be a *principle* of evil, yet the universe, with such a principle in it, may practically be a better universe than it could have been without. On every hand in a small way, we find that a certain amount of evil is a condition by which a higher form of good is bought. There is nothing to prevent anybody from generalizing this view, and trusting that if we could see things in the largest of all ways, even such matters as this Brockton murder would appear to be paid for by the uses that follow in their train. An optimism *quand même*, a systematic and infatuated optimism like that ridiculed by **Voltaire** in his *Candide*, is one of the possible ideal ways in which a man may train himself to look on life. Bereft of dogmatic hardness and lit up with the expression of a tender and pathetic hope, such an optimism has been the grace of some of the most religious characters that ever lived.

Throb thine with nature's throbbing breast,
And all is clear from east to west.

Even cruelty and treachery may be among the absolutely blessed fruits of time, and to quarrel with any of their details may be blasphemy. The only real blasphemy, in short, may be that pessimistic temper of the soul which lets it give way to such things as regrets, remorse, and grief.

Thus, our deterministic pessimism may become a deterministic optimism at the price of extinguishing our judgments of regret.

Voltaire (1694–1778) Enlightenment Author and Philosopher. Rejected the optimism of Pope and Leibniz namely that this is the best of all possible worlds and eveything that happens is for the best and according to God's design; satirizes this position in his work *Candide* (1759).

The religious "solution" to cosmic pessimism for the determinist? Assume that "all things work together for good," and that our perspective is simply too limited to appreciate the grand design of the universe. From this perspective, all of the natural disasters and evil events in the universe have a higher purpose that we can't appreciate because we don't see the role they play in bringing about a greater good. There is no reason to regret anything that occurs, no matter how tragic—we simply need faith that it is part of a grand supernatural design. Similarly, there is no need for us to feel pessimistic—we simply need to maintain the confidence that everything will come out right in the end, exactly the way it was predestined to. Does this approach provide a viable escape for the determinist? James thinks not.

But does not this immediately bring us into a curious logical predicament? Our determinism leads us to call our judgments of regret wrong, because they are pessimistic in implying that what is impossible yet ought to be. But how then about the judgments of regret themselves? If they are wrong, other judgments, judgments of approval presumably, ought to be in their place. But as they are necessitated, nothing else *can* be in their place; and the universe is just what it was before,—namely, a place in which what ought to be appears impossible. We have got one foot out of the pessimistic bog, but the other one sinks all the deeper. We have rescued our actions from the bonds of evil, but our judgments are not held fast. When murders and treacheries cease to be sins, regrets are theoretic absurdities and errors. The theoretic and the active life thus play a kind of seesaw with each other on the ground of evil. The rise of either sends the other down. Murder and treachery cannot be good without regret being bad: regret cannot be good without treachery and murder being bad. Both, however, are supposed to have been foredoomed: so something must be fatally unreasonable, absurd, and wrong in the world. It must be a place of which either sin or error forms a necessary part.

James, *The Will to Believe*

The problem with extinguishing judgments of regret in order to retain an optimistic view that "all things work together for good," is that in a deterministic universe, it is just as impossible to make judgments of approval as it is judgments of regret. Which means that a statement like "all things work together for good" is ultimately meaningless, because the concept of "good" is dependent on a judgment of approval, which can't exist. In other words, if everything that occurs in the universe happens because it *has* to happen, then concepts of regret and approval, evil and good, are irrelevant. Both regret and approval depend on circumstances being different from what they are. But in a determinist universe, circumstances can never be different from what they are.

Determinism, James concludes, fails miserably in explaining the beliefs and convictions of our lived experience, and it is also a perspective that is ultimately self-contradictory and not rational in any meaningful human sense. Which leaves us with indeterminism, in James's opinion, as the only plausible point of view of freedom.

But this brings us right back, to the question of indeterminism. . . . For the only consistent way of representing a pluralism and a world whose parts may affect one another through their conduct being either good or bad is the indeterministic way. What interest, zest, or excitement can there be in achieving the right way, unless we are enabled to feel that the wrong way is also a possible and a natural way—nay, more, a menacing and an imminent way? And what sense can there be in condemning ourselves for taking the wrong way, unless we need have done nothing of the sort, unless the right way was open to us as well? I cannot understand the belief that an act is bad, without regret at its happening. I cannot understand regret without the admission of real, genuine possibilities in the world. Only *then* is it other than a mockery to feel, after we have failed to do our best, that an irreparable opportunity is gone from the universe the loss of which it must forever after mourn. The indeterminism I defend, the free-will theory of popular sense based on the judgment of regret, represents that world as vulnerable, and liable to be

James, *The Will to Believe*

injured by certain of its parts if they act wrong. And it represents their acting wrong as a matter of possibility or accident, neither inevitable nor yet to be infallibly warded off. In all this, it is a theory devoid either of transparency or of stability. It gives us a pluralistic, restless universe, in which no single point of view can ever take in the whole scent; and to a mind possessed of the love of unity at any cost, it will, no doubt, remain forever unacceptable. . . . The great point is that the possibilities are really *here*. Whether it be we who solve them or he working through us, at those soul-trying moments when fate's scales seem to quiver, and good snatches the victory from evil or shrinks nevertheless from the fight, is of small account, so long as we admit that the issue is decided nowhere else than *here* and *now*. *That* is what gives the palpitating reality to our moral life and makes it tingle . . . with so strange and elaborate an excitement. This reality, this excitement, are what the determinists, hard and soft alike, suppress by their denial that *anything* is decided here and now, and their dogma that all things were foredoomed and settled long ago. ∎

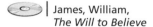

James, William,
The Will to Believe

THINK PHILOSOPHICALLY 4.6
Analyzing William James

- Summarize James's argument that the determinists are unable to permit either judgments of regret or judgments of approval within their theoretical framework. Is this a compelling argument for indeterminism? Why or why not?

- According to James, indeterminism ". . . represents that world as vulnerable, and liable to be injured by certain of its parts if they act wrong. And it represents their acting wrong as a matter of possibility or accident, neither inevitable nor yet to be infallibly warded off." What does this statement mean? Do you agree or disagree with it? Why?

- James returns to his initial epistemological foundation when he states, "The great point is that the possibilities are really *here*. Whether it be we who solve them or he working through us, at those soul-trying moments when fate's scales seem to quiver, and good snatches the victory from evil or shrinks nevertheless from the fight, is of small account, so long as we admit that the issue is decided nowhere else than *here* and *now*." Explain the significance of James grounding his conclusions on the "*here* and *now*." Do you agree with his analysis? Why or why not?

- James believes that our "lived experience" confirms our belief in free will. But what is there in our lived experience to confirm free will? Is it that we do not notice any forces acting on us requiring one choice rather than another? Is that good evidence, or could we simply be blind to the inner springs behind our thinking? Is it that we "feel" free? But again, could that just be that we notice we are not externally constrained, we are able to do what we want, while being blind to the actual inner causes that lead us to have the wants we have? Or does critical reflection give us the means to differentiate genuinely autonomous choices from those choices that are constrained in some way?

- For James, the vibrant energy of our moral lives supports a belief in indeterminism, as he explains: "*That* is what gives the palpitating reality to our moral life and makes it tingle . . . with so strange and elaborate an excitement." Does your experience of your moral life confirm or disconfirm this conclusion? Why?

- Determinists maintain that people believing in free will are deluded and in denial about their lack of freedom. James maintains the reverse: the vitality of our moral lives makes clear that it is determinists who are deluded and in denial about their genuine freedom: "This reality, this excitement, are what the determinists, hard and soft alike, suppress by their denial that *anything* is decided here and now, and their dogma that all things were foredoomed and settled long ago." Who do you think is ultimately deluded and in denial, determinists or indeterminists? Why?

Jean-Paul Sartre: *We Are Condemned to Be Free*

ean-Paul Sartre (1905–1980) was a French philosopher who also expressed his philosophical principles in plays such as *No Exit* and novels such as *Nausea*. Sartre is generally considered to be a chief exponent of modern **existentialism**, a philosophical movement that focuses on human existence as the chief subject of philosophical inquiry. Existentialists assume the reality of human freedom as a basic tenet, and emphasize the challenge and responsibility of all people to create a meaningful existence through the free choices they make. In seeking meaning, existentialists believe that we cannot look outward to a supernatural creator or an intelligible universe: we must look inward, to our own resources and possibilities, as we struggle to create meaning in a world that often seems chaotic and absurd. Sartre's core philosophical text is *Being and Nothingness*, but the following excerpts are taken from a much briefer work, "Existentialism Is a Humanism," which presents a lucid summary of his central beliefs regarding the role of personal freedom in our lives.

In certain respects, Sartre begins his exploration of human freedom where William James leaves off. James makes a compelling case for why believing in the possibility of human freedom is a more rational view of the world than not believing in it. Using the same foundation as James—the testimony of lived experience—Sartre assumes that human freedom is a reality, and then goes on to develop an entire worldview based on this conviction. And while James is most concerned with establishing the possibility of freedom, Sartre's view of freedom is extreme: we are "condemned" to be *totally* free, a radical view of freedom that makes us completely responsible for who we are.

Sartre begins his essay by defining his own view of existentialism.

. . . There are two kinds of existentialists; first, those who are Christian, among whom I would include Jaspers and Gabriel Marcel, both Catholic; and on the other hand the atheistic existentialists, among whom I class Heidegger, and then the French Existentialists and myself. What they have in common is that they think that existence precedes essence, or, if you prefer, that subjectivity must be the starting point.

Just what does that mean? Let us consider some object that is manufactured, for example, a book or a paper-cutter (*letter-opener*): here is an object which has been made by an artisan whose inspiration came from a concept. He referred to the concept of what a paper-cutter is and likewise to a known method of production, which is part of the concept, something which is, by and large, a routine. Thus, the paper-cutter is at once an object produced in a certain way and, on the other hand, one having a specific use; and one can not postulate a man who produces a paper-cutter but does not know what it is used for. Therefore, let us say that, for the paper-cuter, essence—that is, the ensemble of both the production routines and the properties which enable it to be both produced and defined—precedes existence. Thus, the presence of the paper-cutter or book in front of me is determined. Therefore, we have here a technical view of the world whereby it can be said that production precedes existence.

Sartre, Existentialism Is a Humanism

Though it's not initially obvious, Sartre is using this example of producing a letter-opener as a way of illustrating a larger metaphysical framework within which he will situate people. In the production of a letter-opener—or any physical object that is manufactured—there must first be an initial concept of the object and then a production formula for bringing it into existence. Thus, in general terms, we can say that the "essence" of the letter-opener (the initial concept and the production formula) *precedes* its existence. Humans, according to Sartre, are very different from letter-openers, but people often still use this same metaphysical framework as a

Existentialism A philosophical and literary movement that focuses on the uniqueness of each human individual as distinguished from abstract universal human qualities. Defined by Sartre as "existence precedes essence," meaning that humans create themselves through free choices and are responsible for who they are.

model for understanding human development, even though this "essence precedes existence" model is appropriate only for inanimate objects.

Sartre, *Existentialism Is a Humanism*

When we conceive God as the Creator, He is generally thought of as a superior sort of artisan. Whatever doctrine we may be considering, whether one like that of Descartes or that of Leibnitz, we always grant that will more or less follows understanding or, at the very least, accompanies it, and that when God creates He knows exactly what He is creating. Thus, the concept of man in the mind of God is comparable to the concept of paper-cutter in the mind of the manufacturer, and, following certain techniques and a conception, God produces man, just as the artisan, following a definition and a technique, makes a paper-cutter. Thus, the individual man is the realization of a certain concept in the divine intelligence.

When people imagine human existence as being the product of God's creation, Sartre believes they are unwittingly—and mistakenly—using the letter-opener metaphysic to understand human creation. Prior to our physical conception and birth, we "exist" in the omniscient (all-knowing) mind of God, both as a concept and as a formula for production. Thus, just like the letter-opener, our "essence" precedes our "existence;" that is, our *soul* or *spirit* is a reality prior to our physical existence on earth. Our thoughts, ideas, choices, and actions are a direct reflection of our preexisting *soul* or *spirit*.

But according to Sartre, those who believe in a divine Creator are not the only ones guilty of misunderstanding the nature of human existence in such a profound way. There are also those who, while denying the existence of a divine Creator, nevertheless believe that we each possess an essential and universal human nature that precedes our actual historical existence. This essential nature forms the structure of our personalities, and our thoughts, ideas, choices, and action are a direct result of its influence. Thus, this is also a view in which, like the letter-opener, our "essence" precedes our "existence."

Sartre, *Existentialism Is a Humanism*

In the eighteenth century, the atheism of the *philosophes* discarded the idea of God, but not so much for the notion that essence precedes existence. To a certain extent, this idea is found everywhere; we find it in Diderot, in Voltaire, and even in Kant. Man has a human nature; this human nature, which is the concept of the human, is found in all men, which means that each man is a particular example of a universal concept, man. In Kant, the result of this universality is that the wildman, the natural man, as well as the bourgeois, are circumscribed by the same definition and have the same basic qualities. Thus, here too the essence of man precedes the historical existence that we find in nature.

All of these "essence precedes existence" views of human existence are, according to Sartre, irretrievably flawed and confused. In fact, their view of human existence is completely the opposite of what it should be. For Sartre, an accurate view of human experience is based on the principle "existence precedes essence," not the reverse!

Sartre, *Existentialism Is a Humanism*

Atheistic existentialism, which I represent, is more coherent. It states that if God does not exist, there is at least one being in whom existence precedes essence, a being who exists before he can be defined by any concept, and that this being is man, or, as Heidegger says, human reality. What is meant here by saying that existence precedes essence? It means that, first of all, man exists, turns up, appears on the scene, and, only afterward, defines himself. If man, as the existentialist conceives him, is indefinable, it is because at first he is nothing. Only afterward will he be something, and he himself will have made what he will be. Thus, there is no human nature, since there is no God to conceive it. Not only is man what he conceives himself to be, but he is also only what he wills himself to be after this thrust toward existence.

Man is nothing else but what he makes of himself. Such is the first principle of existentialism. It is also what is called subjectivity, the name we are labeled with when charges are brought against us. But what do we mean by this, if not that man has a greater dignity than a stone or table? For we mean that man first exists, that is, that man first of all is the being who hurls himself toward a future and who is conscious of imagining himself as being in the future. Man is at the start a plan which is aware of itself, rather than a patch of moss, a piece of garbage, or a cauliflower; nothing exists prior to this plan; there is nothing in heaven; man will be what he will have planned to be. Not what he will want to be. Because by the word "will" we generally mean a conscious decision, which is subsequent to what we have already made of ourselves. I may want to belong to a political party, write a book, get married; but all that is only a manifestation of an earlier, more spontaneous choice that is called "will." But if existence really does precede essence, man is responsible for what he is. Thus, existentialism's first move is to make every man aware of what he is and to make the full responsibility of his existence rest on him. And when we say that a man is responsible for himself, we do not only mean that he is responsible for his own individuality, but that he is responsible for all men.

JEAN-PAUL SARTRE
(1905–1980)
French Existentialist. Important author, playwright, literary critic and philosopher. In *Being and Nothingness* (1943) envisions the self as a continual project in the world which defines itself through its free choices.

The essential problem with nonexistentialist views of human existence, according to Sartre, is that they focus on our historical existence in the past, not our orientation toward the future. But it is our focus on the future, the way our minds naturally leap ahead imaginatively, that distinguishes our essential natures. It is through imagining a future that we then weigh alternatives and select options to make this imagined future a reality. It is this ongoing projection toward the future that renders us uniquely human, and it is the ability to imagine a nearly limitless number of future paths, and to select from among them, that makes us uniquely free. Although our past experiences and developed personality have set the stage for our moment of choice, it is the beckoning future that defines our spirit.

For example, consider your current state of consciousness. Though you may reflect on your past, it is your future goals and dreams that define your essence. What will you be doing this evening, next week, next year, and beyond? And what actions will you have to take to reach these goals and achieve these dreams? And how can you ensure that the choices you make reflect your authentic self, your deepest values and highest aspirations?

This perspective on human existence is contrary to many common views, which hold that our history defines our present and our future. For example, the view of God as supernatural creator often assumes that each individual's soul is crafted and defined prior to their existence on earth, and so their "essence" precedes their "existence." The same is true, to one degree or another, of the main theories of human behavior that we explored at the beginning of the chapter:

- **Human nature:** *"I believe in human nature; people are born with certain basic instincts that influence and determine how they behave."*
- **The environment:** *"I believe that people are shaped by their environment, conditioned by their experiences to be the kind of people they are."*
- **Psychological forces:** *"I believe that people are governed by psychological forces, many of them unconscious, that cause them to think, feel, and act in certain ways."*
- **Social dynamics:** *"I believe that we are social creatures that are greatly influenced by the people around us."*

Each of these theories is designed to explain who we are by reference to factors that predate the choices we are making. Why do we act the way we do according to these theories? Why do you choose a certain group of friends, select a given career,

Jean Paul Sartre

engage in a romantic relationship, not to mention the countless choices you make on an a daily basis? Because of the influence of

- genetically programmed instincts that comprise our human nature.
- experiential forces that have shaped and molded our personalities.
- deep-seated drives and emotions, of which many we are unaware.
- social pressures from other people.

In all of these instances the underlying assumption is that "essence precedes existence"—that is, factors such as human nature, past experiences, psychological forces, or social dynamics determine who we are and the choices we make. In other words, all of these theories assume that your "essence" as a person, as defined by the factors identified above, comes *before* your actual "existence" in the moment that choices are made and actions are taken.

There are serious consequences to such an "essence precedes existence" framework, as we noted earlier. To begin with, all of these beliefs about the human self have the effect of removing—or diminishing—responsibility from the individual for her actions. If the choices you make, the actions you take, are the direct result of human nature, past experiences, psychological forces, or social dynamics, then you cannot be held responsible (or fully responsible) because these influences were beyond your control. Analogously, an "essence precedes existence" framework limits future possibilities for people. To the extent that our choices and actions are the result of preexistent influences that are beyond our control, to that extent we are limited in our power to think independently and choose freely the directions we want to take in life.

For Sartre, to explain your human essence and the choices you make (which define your existence) in terms of any "essence precedes existence" theory is to place you in the same category as unreflective life forms like moss and cauliflower. But such perspectives, no matter how well intentioned, miss entirely the essence of who you are. You are a thinking being, capable of reflective thought, propelled toward a future of your own creation, making free choices independent of any prior influences. *That's* who you are, a being whose existence from moment to moment precedes your essence, which you are in the process of creating and recreating with every choice you make. Whatever influences are a part of your history—inborn instincts, environmental conditioning, psychological forces, social influences—you have the capacity to separate yourself from them and to make genuinely independent and free choices. Rather than looking at your history in the rearview mirror, you should be looking ahead to the person you are in the process of creating.

The consequence of this radical view of freedom is a radical responsibility. If every choice you make is genuinely free, independent of any historical influence, then you are completely responsible for your choices and their consequences. There is no point in seeking escape from your responsibility by blaming your human nature, past experiences, psychological forces, or social dynamics. You chose freely, therefore your choice is your **responsibility**.

But isn't this a potentially dangerous theory? After all, if we give people unlimited license to choose whatever they want, as long as they accept responsibility for their choices, how can we condemn the actions of evil people like Hitler? When confronted regarding their moral evil, couldn't they respond: "I'm an existentialist: my choices are completely free and I accept responsibility for them. So you have no grounds for condemning me."

This is a serious issue for Sartre, one that we will examine more closely in the next two chapters on *What Is Morality?* But for now we can look briefly at Sartre's approach to dealing with this potentially devastating critique, for he is clearly aware

Responsibility Humans are accountable for their actions which they freely choose.

of its threat. Sartre himself was a person of strong moral principles, which led him to become a fighter for the French Resistance during World War II, following the invasion of France by Nazi Germany. For Sartre, choosing freely and accepting one's responsibility is not a solely individual project: it takes place in a social context, and embodies an enlightened sense of moral responsibility to humanity as a whole.

Sartre, *Existentialism Is a Humanism*

When we say that man chooses his own self, we mean that every one of us does likewise; but we also mean by that that in making this choice he also chooses all men. In fact, in creating the man that we want to be, there is not a single one of our acts which does not at the same time create an image of man as we think he ought to be. To choose to be this or that is to affirm at the same time the value of what we choose, because we can never choose evil. We always choose the good, and nothing can be good for us without being good for all.

. . . If we grant that we exist and fashion our image at one and the same time, the image is valid for everybody and for our whole age. Thus, our responsibility is much greater than we might have supposed, because it involves all mankind. . . . If I want to marry, to have children; even if this marriage depends solely on my own circumstances or passion or wish, I am involving all humanity in monogamy and not merely myself. Therefore, I am responsible for myself and for everyone else. I am creating a certain image of man of my own choosing. In choosing myself, I choose man.

Sartre is invoking a bold blend of **Immanuel Kant** and **Plato** in his effort to save his theory from amorality. Kant founded his ethical theory on what he termed his categorical imperative: "Act as if the maxim of your action were to become by your will a universal law of nature." In other words, Kant is suggesting that the standard we use in making moral decisions is to ask ourselves: "Would I be rationally able to endorse *everyone* making the same choice as I?" For example, if you're contemplating gossiping about someone you don't care for, you would have to support, as a rational requirement, that *everyone* gossip in all comparable situations. Or if you're thinking about purchasing a term paper online and submitting it as your own, you would have to endorse as a rational law *everyone* doing exactly the same thing.

Sartre seems to be trying to attach his theory of free choice to this same "universalizing" concept when he states:

Sartre, *Existentialism Is a Humanism*

When we say that man chooses his own self, we mean that every one of us does likewise; but we also mean by that that in making this choice he also chooses all men. In fact, in creating the man that we want to be, there is not a single one of our acts which does not at the same time create an image of man as we think he ought to be.

When you make a choice, according to Sartre, you are not simply creating and defining yourself as a person—you are also creating and defining your image of the way all humans *should* be. So if you choose to gossip or cheat, you are by implication suggesting that all humans should be gossips and cheats.

Sartre also seems to be drawing on Plato's ethical perspective that no person does evil intentionally. Plato was convinced that when people act immorally it is due to ignorance, because they are unenlightened and don't know better. When you educate people and show them a more enlightened path, they cannot help but take it. Sartre seems to be making the same point when he states, "To choose to be this or that is to affirm at the same time the value of what we choose, because we can never choose evil. We always choose the good, and nothing can be good for us without being good for all." The idea that no one does evil voluntarily is a provocative but also problematic view, for both Plato and Sartre, and we will analyze it further in the next chapters.

Immanuel Kant (1724–1804) German Philosopher. Kant widely regarded as greatest philosopher of modern period. Attempted to synthesize two competing schools of the modern period, rationalism and empiricism, by showing important role both experience and reason play in constructing our knowledge of the world.

Plato (427–347 B.C.E.) Ancient Greek Philosopher. Once said that all of Western Philosophy is merely footnotes to Plato. A student of Socrates, Plato wrote many dialogues featuring Socrates as the main character and dealt with many philosophical issues such as morality, politics, metaphysics, and epistemology.

For now, let's continue our exploration of Sartre's concept of radical freedom. For Sartre, an existentialist perspective illuminates the deeply felt emotions that are an inescapable part of the human condition. Sartre identifies three such fundamental emotions that define our experience when we discover that we are condemned to be free: *anguish*, *abandonment*, and *despair*.

Sartre, *Existentialism Is a Humanism*

First, what is meant by anguish? The existentialists say at once that man is anguish. What that means is this: the man who involves himself and who realizes that he is not only the person he chooses to be, but also a law-maker who is, at the same time, choosing all mankind as well as himself, cannot help escape the feeling of his total and deep responsibility. Of course, there are many people who are not anxious; but we claim that they are hiding their anxiety, that they are fleeing from it. Certainly, many people believe that when they do something, they themselves are the only ones involved, and when someone says to them, "What if everyone acted that way?" they shrug their shoulders and answer, "Everyone doesn't act that way." But really, one should always ask himself, "What would happen if everybody looked at things that way?" There is no escaping this disturbing thought except by a kind of double-dealing. A man who lies and makes excuses for himself by saying "not everybody does that," is someone with an uneasy conscience, because the act of lying implies that a universal value is conferred upon the lie.

Anguish is evident even when it conceals itself. This is the anguish that Kierkegaard called the anguish of Abraham. You know the story: an angel has ordered Abraham to sacrifice his son; if it really were an angel who has come and said, "You are Abraham, you shall sacrifice your son," everything would be all right. But everyone might first wonder, "Is it really an angel, and am I really Abraham? What proof do I have?"

There was a madwoman who had hallucinations; someone used to speak to her on the telephone and give her orders. Her doctor asked her, "Who is it who talks to you?" she answered, "He says it's God." What proof did she really have that it was God? If an angel comes to me, what proof is there that it's an angel? And if I hear voices, what proof is there that they come from heaven and not from hell, or from the subconscious or a pathological condition? What proves that they are addressed to me? What proof is there that I have been appointed to impose my choice and my conception of man on humanity? I'll never find any proof or sign to convince me of that. If a voice addresses me, it is always for me to decide that this is the angel's voice; if I consider that such an act is a good one, it is I who will choose to say that it is good rather than bad.

We commonly think of someone experiencing *distress* as a person in extreme emotional distress, submerged in mental agony, overwhelmed by spiritual torment. Sartre believes that this existential anguish of the soul is a permanent part of the human condition, afflicting all of us even though we may not be consciously aware of it. This profound anguish is a necessary consequence of our freedom: we recognize that we are fully responsible for our choices, that we have no one to depend on for guidance other than ourselves, and that in making choices we are creating an ideal image of humankind. This is a heavy burden, and it takes its toll on us.

Sartre provides a striking example of what he means when he analyzes **Søren Kierkegaard's** concept of "the anguish of Abraham." Commanded by what he takes to be an angel of God, Abraham prepares to sacrifice his only and beloved son, Isaac. But how can Abraham be sure he's doing the right thing? How can he be certain that the angel is really an angel, rather than a satanic apparition or a psychotic hallucination? In the final analysis he *can't* be sure—he has to trust his own judgment. In the context of the Bible, Abraham is generally considered by Christians and Jews as a pillar of spiritual faith, and his willingness to slaughter his son is cited as evidence of his complete devotion to God. But as Sartre suggests, what would we think of someone in today's world threatening to kill their child because they believe an angel commanded them to do so? Would we consider them to be a pillar of faith or emotionally—and dangerously—disturbed?

Søren Kierkegaard (1813–1855) Christian Philosopher. Considered to be first existentialist. Though deeply religious, challenged much of Christian philosophy including the belief that faith could be supported by proofs and reason; maintained true belief in God required an absurd leap of faith for which there is no rational justification.

This is Sartre's point. Throughout our lives we are called on to make difficult decisions in complex circumstances. How can we be sure we're doing the right thing? In the final analysis, we can't be sure. We can't really depend on the advice of others: who is to say that they are right? And even the prevailing norms, moral codes, and holy books that we are familiar with typically provide guidance that is conflicting, ambiguous, or too general to be of practical use.

If we are truly honest with ourselves, we realize the distressing and inescapable fact that we alone have to decide what is the right thing to do, and that there is no one to rely on for advice other than ourselves. The result of this searing insight? A profound, existential anguish. And not only do we shoulder the burden of responsibility for ourselves when we make what we hope are the "right" choices, we are also assuming the responsibility of creating an image for all humankind. And what makes this intimidating responsibility nearly unbearable is the certainty of our uncertainty—we will never be sure that we're doing the right thing.

But what about people who don't seem to be experiencing this overwhelming feeling of anguish, who seem to simply live their lives on the surface, making choices without any apparent sense of profound responsibility. How does Sartre account for these individuals? He believes that they're "in denial."

The Anguish of Abraham

Sartre, *Existentialism Is a Humanism*

Now, I'm not being singled out as an Abraham, and yet at every moment I'm obliged to perform exemplary acts. For every man, everything happens as if all mankind had its eyes fixed on him and were guiding itself by what he does. And every man ought to say to himself, "Am I really the kind of man who has the right to act in such a way that humanity might guide itself by my actions?" And if he does not say that to himself, he is masking his anguish.

Those who deny their experience of existential anguish are striving desperately to escape from their freedom. But their strivings are doomed to failure. We are "condemned to be free," and our freedom is a lifetime sentence. We can try to hide from our freedom, attempt to assign it to others, pretend that our actions are determined by forces beyond our control, claim that we were only following the directions of others— but whatever efforts we make to escape from our freedom, *we are still free* and nothing will ever change this simple fact. Those people who live their lives seeking to deny and escape from their freedom are living lives that are false, diminished, *inauthentic*.

On the other hand, embracing your freedom and experiencing the anguish of your profound responsibility in life does not entail becoming paralyzed with fear, frozen into inaction. Quite the contrary, according to Sartre.

Sartre, *Existentialism Is a Humanism*

There is no question here of the kind of anguish which would lead to quietism, to inaction. It is a matter of a simple sort of anguish that nobody who has had responsibilities is familiar with. For example, when a military officer takes the responsibility for an attack and sends a certain number of men to death, he chooses to do so, and in the main he alone makes the choice. Doubtless, orders come from above, but they are too broad; he interprets them, and on this interpretation depend the lives of ten or fourteen or twenty men. In making a decision he can not help having a certain anguish. All leaders know this anguish. That doesn't keep them from acting; on the contrary, it is the very condition of their action. For it implies that they envisage a number of possibilities, and when they choose one, they realize that it has value only because it is chosen. We shall see this kind of anguish, which is the kind that existentialism describes, is explained, in addition, by a direct responsibility to the other men whom it involves. It is not a curtain separating us from action, but is part of the action itself.

This deep and abiding sense of responsibility should bring out the best in you, encouraging you to be thoughtful and serious about the choices you make. Your life is not trivial: it is your contribution to the human world, your record in history. The self you create, the life that you lead demands your total commitment. This is *your* life—no one else's—and you are responsible for crafting a life of which you can be proud and that will earn the admiration of others. This is Sartre's message. For those who decide to think in limited and myopic ways, to run from their freedom and responsibility, to make choices with only their own selfish needs in mind—these people are living inauthentic lives of diminished value.

Consistent with Sartre's atheistic existentialism is the second profound emotion that he believes is an unavoidable part of the human condition: *abandonment*. Sartre explains:

Sartre, *Existentialism Is a Humanism*

When we speak of abandonment, a term Heidegger was fond of, we mean only that God does not exist and that we have to face all the consequences of this. The existentialist is strongly opposed to a certain kind of secular ethics which would like to abolish God with the least possible expense. . . .

The existentialist, on the contrary, thinks it very distressing that God does not exist, because all possibility of finding values in a heaven of ideas disappears along with Him; there can no longer be an *a priori* Good, since there is no infinite and perfect consciousness to think it. Nowhere is it written that the Good exists, that we must be honest, that we must not lie; because the fact is we are on a plane where there are only men. Dostoevsky said, "If God didn't exist, everything would be possible." That is the very starting point of existentialism. Indeed, everything is permissible if God does not exist, and as a result man feels abandoned, because neither within him nor without does he find anything to cling to. He can't start making excuses for himself.

If existence really does precede essence, there is no explaining things away by reference to a fixed and given human nature. In other words, there is no determinism, man is free, man is freedom. On the other hand, if God does not exist, we find no values or commands to turn to which legitimize our conduct. So, in the bright realm of values, we have no excuse behind us, nor justification before us. We are alone, with no excuses.

When was the last time that you felt abandoned? It's a devastating experience, feeling not just alone, but having been *left alone*. Abandonment is the absence of a caring presence that we had become accustomed to, a caring presence that is suddenly torn away. For Sartre, this is another fundamental emotion of the human condition. Why? Because most of us have been raised to believe that there is an ultimate caring presence to guide, nurture, and take care of us. For many, this caring presence has been a supreme being—"God(s)"—in some form. For others, the caring presence has been a cultural identity that has provided a clear moral framework. For others, it has been a sharply defined natural philosophy that has included universal values independently of religion. All of these caring presences, according to Sartre, provide a false and illegitimate sense of security. When we honestly understand the human predicament, we realize that we are utterly alone, with no one to turn to for support other than ourselves.

Sartre claims that some people try to maintain the moral advantages of God without believing in God's existence. These efforts are doomed to fail. It is not possible to proclaim universal moral values inscribed in the structure of the universe because such a proclamation makes no sense without a supernatural being to authenticate these values. Similarly, we cannot ground values in a universal human nature, because according to Sartre, there is no human nature. Each person creates his or her self through the choices that they make on a daily basis. We must accept our abandonment, forge our own set of values through our free choices, and accept our responsibility.

The final existential emotion that helps define the human condition is *despair*. Sartre explains:

As for despair, the term has a very simple meaning. It means that we shall confine ourselves to reckoning only with what depends upon our will, or on the ensemble of probabilities which make our action possible. When we want something, we always have to reckon with probabilities. I may be counting on the arrival of a friend. The friend is coming by rail or street-car; this supposes that the train will arrive on schedule, or that the street-car will not jump the track. I am left in the realm of possibility; but possibilities are to be reckoned with only to the point where my action comports with the ensemble of these possibilities, and no further. The moment the possibilities I am considering are not rigorously involved by my action, I ought to disengage myself from them, because no God, no scheme, can adapt the world and its possibilities to my will. When Descartes said, "Conquer yourself rather than the world," he meant essentially the same thing.

Sartre, *Existentialism Is a Humanism*

The "despair" that Sartre is referring to is the emotion that results from recognizing that there are many elements in life that are completely outside of our control. No matter how clear our vision, how determined our will, our sphere of influence will always remain limited because of all the factors that we cannot influence. We may train for a career, and then not be able to find a suitable position. We may embark on marriage with great hope, and then have the marriage unravel despite our best efforts. We may develop a detailed, long-term plan for ourselves, and then endure an accident or illness that forces a change of our carefully constructed plans. Although we may begin believing that our freedom of choice is absolute, despair sets in once we realize how limited is our ability to guarantee the consequences of our choices. Does this recognition and the accompanying feeling of despair mean that we should approach life pessimistically, cynical about our power to influence, fearful of what may befall us? Absolutely not!

The doctrine I am presenting is the very opposite of quietism, since it declares, "There is no reality except in action." Moreover, it goes further, since it adds, "Man is nothing else than his plan; he exists only to the extent that he fulfills himself; he is therefore nothing else than the ensemble of his acts, nothing else than his life."

Sartre, *Existentialism Is a Humanism*

Despite the ever-present threat of the unknown, Sartre believes that this recognition of both our absolute freedom and the limitations of our control should spur us to positive action. Why? Because our actions are the only genuine part of ourselves that define our lives. We only truly exist to the extent that we have acted boldly, forcefully, courageously, creatively, and lovingly. Everything else is of little consequence, and for those individuals who choose a life of trivial action, their lives and their selves are also trivialized. Sartre recognizes that his perspective is not going to be very popular.

According to this, we can understand why our doctrine horrifies certain people. Because often the only way they can bear their wretchedness is to think, "Circumstances have been against me. What I've been and done doesn't show my true worth. To be sure, I've had no great love, no great friendship, but that's because I haven't met a man or woman who was worthy. The books I've written haven't been very good because I haven't had the proper leisure. I haven't had children to devote myself to because I didn't find a man with whom I could have spent my life. So there remains within me, unused and quite viable, a host of propensities, inclinations, possibilities, that one wouldn't guess from the mere series of things I've done."
Now, for the existentialist there is really no love other than one which manifests itself in a person's being in love. There is no genius other than one which is expressed in works of art; the genius of Proust is the sum of Proust's works; the genius of Racine is his series of tragedies. Outside of that, there is nothing. Why say that Racine could have written another tragedy, when he didn't write it? A man is involved in life, leaves his impression on it, and outside of that there is nothing. To be sure, this may seem a harsh

Sartre, *Existentialism Is a Humanism*

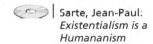 Sarte, Jean-Paul: *Existentialism is a Humananism*

Freedom, Choice, and Responsibility

- Reflect on Sartre's core belief that "existence precedes essence." Do you believe that your *self* (*soul, spirit* or *personality*) already existed before or at the moment of your birth? Or do you believe that you create your *essence* through the choices that you freely make? Explain the reasons for your response.

- Sartre's view of personal freedom is radical and uncompromising: we are "condemned" to be completely free and therefore we are completely responsible. Do you agree with this view? Why or why not?

- A number of factors seem to influence a person's development, including

  environmental experiences and learning

  genetic programming and inborn instincts

  social pressures and cultural socialization

  free choices

  Think about the blending of factors that has produced you as a person. How would you describe your unique "recipe"? Which factors have been most influential in your development? Have some factors had a particularly strong impact in certain areas of your life? How would Sartre respond to the idea that factors other than free choice contributed to your development (if you believe that they have)?

- Sartre believes that many people (perhaps all people to some extent) seek to "escape" from their freedom and responsibility. One indication of such escape attempts is denying the experience of existential emotions such as *anguish*, *abandonment*, and *despair*. Have you ever experienced these emotions in the profound, existential sense that Sartre believes is part of the human condition? Do you think experiencing these emotions is a useful barometer for determining your efforts to escape from your freedom?

- Later in life Sartre became a Marxist and modified his radical views on freedom, arguing that economic and political forces can limit freedom. Should this biographical fact influence our evaluation of these earlier views? Why or why not?

- Some people believe that Sartre's message, while disturbing, is ultimately inspiring and uplifting because of its emphasis on personal freedom and personal responsibility. What is your response to Sartre's basic ideas?

thought to someone whose life hasn't been a success. But, on the other hand, it prompts people to understand that reality alone is what counts, that dreams, expectation, and hope warrant no more than to define a man as a disappointed dream, as miscarried hopes, as vain expectations. In other words, to define him negatively and not positively. However, when we say "You are nothing else than your life," that does not imply that the artist will be judged solely on the basis of his works of art; a thousand other things will contribute toward summing him up. What we mean is that a man is nothing else than a series of undertakings, that he is the sum, the organization, the ensemble of the relationships which make up these undertakings. ■

You are the sum of your actions and accomplishments, not your wishes, dreams, or intentions. It's a harsh message but one that Sartre believes is ultimately uplifting because it encourages people to strive mightily to achieve great things and live a full life. Such a philosophy removes the temptation to remain passively in a fantasy life of "if only." It is the embodiment of the metaphor of you being the artist of your life, encouraging you to make yourself a masterpiece.

Personal Freedom: *Creating a Synthesis*

At the beginning of the chapter we noted that the question of whether we are capable of making free choices was one that becomes progressively more complicated the deeper we delve into it. We have seen that some influential thinkers, such as Baron d'Holbach, believe that personal freedom is an illusion, that all of our actions are necessarily determined by factors outside of our control. Some of these thinkers believe that it is our genetic heritage that plays a dominant role in who we become and the actions we take. Others, such as behavioral psychologists John Watson and B. F. Skinner, believe that we are entirely the products of conditioning experiences that have molded us and determined our actions. Some thinkers, such as Freud, view the locus of control in unconscious instincts and drives that influence us without our even being aware of it. And many believe that who we are is the result of the *interaction* of these various factors. The genetic blueprint with which you begin life—your gender, race, basic temperament, physical qualities—dynamically interacts with environmental factors to gradually shape your development in complex ways. All of these thinkers can be considered *determinists* because they all believe that every choice you make is the necessary consequence of antecedent factors in your experience—a genetic blueprint, conditioning experiences, unconscious drives. There is no room for freedom of choice in these deterministic systems, and any feelings of freedom that we experience are mere illusions, without substance or reality.

And we have also seen that there is an entirely different group of thinkers, such as William James and John Paul Sartre, who are convinced that personal freedom is real, and that we are capable of making free choices independent of any influencing factors beyond our control. These thinkers, *indeterminists*, believe that until cogent evidence to the contrary is presented, we are entitled to put our trust in our belief in freedom (and responsibility) which is so deeply imbedded in our experience as practical beings. We live our lives as if people are free and responsible, at least to some extent. Our core beliefs in morality, religion, self-improvement, social improvement, personal responsibility, criminal and civil justice, child rearing, and many other areas are founded on the conviction that people can make free choices and that they are responsible for the free choices that they make.

Finally, we took note that there is a third perspective on the possibility of human freedom—*soft determinists*—who believe that freedom means the opposite of compulsion: people are free if they are not prevented from acting on their unimpeded natural desires, even though these natural desires may be causally determined by factors in their personal history in accordance with universal laws.

You may recall that William James dismisses soft determinists as thinly disguised determinists because they agree with the fundamental deterministic principles. For the soft determinist, when you choose a major, a person to date, or an item on the menu, you are making a choice that is necessarily determined by factors in your history—you could not choose otherwise. However, if you are not being threatened or coerced to make your choice, then as far as soft determinists are concerned, your choice is free. Most indeterminists agree with James: soft determinism defines free choice in such a narrow, limited way that it is really just a variation of determinism.

So what is the answer? Is personal freedom a reality or an illusion? Are you capable of making genuinely free choices, or are your choices influenced and determined by causal factors woven into your personal history? Perhaps the most enlightened view is one that recognizes that the question is not either/or: rather than people being completely free or completely unfree, perhaps there are *degrees* of freedom and nonfreedom. And that by developing your self-awareness you can *increase your freedom*. Let's explore how we might conceptualize and articulate such a perspective.

Most people have the deep-seated conviction that they are capable of making free choices. But how can we be sure? We are certainly born with a *genetic heritage* that not only determines our gender, race, and physical characteristics, but also influences our personality. For example, studies of identical twins (thus possessing identical genetic "fingerprints") who were separated at birth and reared in different environments have revealed provocative (although complex) results. Years later, despite great differences in their experiences since birth, some twins have exhibited remarkable similarities: identical gestures and senses of humor; the same number (and even names) of children; similar careers and hobbies—all underscoring the influence of genetic factors.

We also know that the *environment* also plays a significant role in shaping people's characters and personalities. Young children are indeed like sponges, absorbing all of the information and influences around them and incorporating these elements into their thinking and behavior. Our attitudes, values, beliefs, interests, ways of relating to others—these and

Hereditary and environmental experiences clearly influence our development. Do you think that we are able to transcend the effects of these influences in order to make free, independent choices? Why?

many other qualities are influenced by family, friends, and culture. This is the process by which positive values such as empathy and commitment get transmitted from generation to generation, and it is also how negative beliefs such as racism and violence are perpetuated.

If your genetic heritage and environmental background are such powerful forces in molding who you are, how is it possible to think that you are capable of making free choices in any meaningful sense? The answer to this enigma is that despite the early influences on your personal development, your mind and your thinking continue to mature. You have not only ongoing experiences, but also the ability to *reflect* on these experiences and *learn* from them. Instead of simply accepting the views of others, you gradually develop the ability to *examine* this thinking and to *decide* whether it makes sense to you and whether you should accept it. So although you might share many beliefs with your parents or the prevailing culture in which you were raised, you likely disagree with many other areas. Although your parents might believe that sex should begin with marriage or that the most important thing about a career is job security, you might have gradually developed very different perspectives on these issues.

The same is true of your personality. Although your genetic background and early experiences might have *contributed* to shaping the framework of your personality, it is up to you to *decide* who your future self will be. For example, your personality may incorporate many positive qualities from your parents as well as some that you dislike—such as a quick temper. But you can decide not to let this temper dominate your personality or be expressed inappropriately. With sufficient determination, you can be successful in controlling and redirecting this temper, though you may have occasional lapses. In other words, you can take a personality tendency formed early in your development and reshape it according to your own personal goals. In the same way, if your early history created qualities of insecurity, shyness, pessimism, insensitivity, passivity, or other qualities that you are unhappy about, you should realize that these traits do not represent a life sentence! You have it within your power to *remold* yourself, creating yourself to be the kind of person that you wish and choose to be. *This is the essence of freedom.* Free choice means dealing with an existing situation, selecting from a finite number of options, and working to reshape the present into the future.

Of course change often doesn't occur immediately. It took a long time for your personality to evolve into its present state, and it's going to take a while for you to reconceptualize and redirect it. It's like changing the course of a large ship: you need to turn the rudder to change course, but the past momentum of the ship makes the turn a gradual process, not a radical change of direction. The same is true with the human personality; meaningful change is a complex process, but by choosing to set the rudder on a new course and maintaining its position, you can change.

Freedom does not, however, involve limitless and unconstrained options—this idea of freedom is a fantasy, not a realistic perspective. Freedom doesn't occur in a vacuum; it always involves concrete options and limited possibilities. In analyzing your personality, you may feel that you too often lack confidence and are beset with feelings of insecurity. In reviewing your personal history you may discover that these feelings stem in part from the fact that your parents were excessively critical and did not provide the kind of personal support that leads to a solid sense of security and self-worth. You might discover other factors in your history that contributed to these feelings as well: painful disappointments such as a divorce or a career rejection. All of these experiences will have influenced who you are, and these historical events cannot now be changed. But the significant question is: *what are you going to do now?* How are you going to respond to the results of these events as embodied in your current thinking and behavior? This is where free choice enters in. Although you can't change what has previously happened, you can control *how you respond* to what happened. You can choose to let these historical influences continue to control your personality, like specters long dead reaching from the grave to influence and entangle the present and future. Or you can choose to move beyond these historical influences, to choose a different path for yourself that transcends their influence and liberates your future. As Viktor Frankl, a psychiatrist who survived the horrors of a Nazi concentration camp, explains in his book *Man's Search for Meaning*:

> Man is not fully conditioned and determined but rather determines himself whether he gives in to conditions or stands up to them. In other words, man is ultimately self-determining. Man does not simply exist but always decides what his existence will be, what he will become in the next moment. No matter what the circumstances we find ourselves, we always retain the last of human freedoms—the ability to choose one's attitude in a given set of circumstances.

 VISUAL PHILOSOPHY

Christopher Reeve Following His Paralyzing Accident

Do you think that Christopher Reeve's life supported Viktor Frankl's belief that "No matter what the circumstances we find ourselves, we always retain the last of human freedoms—the ability to choose one's attitude in a given set of circumstances?" Why?

Increasing Freedom by Eliminating Constraints

F reedom consists of making thoughtful choices that reflect your authentic self: your genuine desires and deepest values. But many forces threaten to limit your freedom and even repress it altogether. The limits to your freedom can come from outside yourself by means of *external constraints*, the restrictions that we discussed in relation to soft determinism.

But limits to your freedom can also come from within yourself—*internal constraints*. Although external factors may limit your freedom—for example, being incarcerated or working in a dead-end job—the more challenging limits are imposed by yourself through internal constraints. For instance, people don't generally procrastinate, smoke, suffer anxiety attacks, feel depressed, or engage in destructive relationships because someone is coercing them. Instead, they are victimizing themselves in ways that they may not be fully aware of.

To remove constraints, you first have to become *aware* that they exist. For example, if someone is manipulating you to think or feel a certain way, you can't begin to deal with the manipulation until you become aware that it exists. Similarly, you can't solve a personal problem such as insecurity or emotional immaturity without first acknowledging that it *is* a problem, and then developing insight into the internal forces that are driving your behavior. Once you have achieved this deeper level of understanding, you are then in a position to *choose* a different path for yourself, using appropriate decision-making and problem-solving approaches. But there is a great deal of ignorance and confusion regarding the nature of free choice. Let's examine what some people consider to be major myths regarding personal freedom.

Myth #1: Freedom means simply making a choice

Many times we make choices that are not free because the choices are compelled by others. For example, if you are threatened with bodily harm by a mugger or an abusive spouse, your choices are made in response to these threats and clearly not free. Similarly, if you are being subjected to unreasonable pressure on the job by someone who has the power to fire you, the choices that you make are obviously constrained by the circumstances. As we have noted, these kinds of limitations on your freedom are known as *external constraints*, because they are external influences that force you to choose under duress. Although hostage tapes, ransom payments, and blackmail threats are extreme examples of this sort of coercion, there are many incipient forms of it as well. The appeal to fear used by political leaders, the subtle manipulations of an acquaintance, the implied threat by a panhandler, the sexual harassment perpetrated by someone in authority—these and countless other instances are testimony to the prevalence of external constraints on your freedom.

The way to free yourself from external constraints is to *neutralize* or *remove* them, so that you can make choices that reflect your genuine desires. For example, if your choices are constrained by an abusive spouse or an unreasonable boss, you have to either change their coercive behavior or remove yourself from the situation in order to achieve genuine freedom. If you believe that your choices are excessively limited by the geographical location in which you live, you might have to move in order to increase your possibilities.

Myth #2: Freedom is limited to choosing from available options

This second myth about freedom interferes with people's capacity to make free choices because it encourages them to passively accept the alternatives presented to them. However, the most vigorous exercise of freedom involves *actively creating* alternatives that may not be on the original menu of options. For example, if you are presented with a project at work, you should not restrict yourself to considering the conventional alternatives for meeting the goals, but should instead actively seek improved possibilities. If you are enmeshed in a problem situation with someone else, you should not permit them to establish the alternatives from which to choose, but you should instead work to formulate new or modified ways of solving the problem. Too often people are content to sit back and let the situation define their choices instead of taking the initiative to shape the situation in their own way. Critical and creative thinkers view the world as a malleable environment that they have a responsibility to form and shape. This liberates them to exercise their freedom of choice to the fullest extent possible.

Myth #3: Freedom means simply "doing what you want"

"No man is free who is a slave to himself." This saying captures the insight that although you may believe that you are making a free choice because you are not the victim of visible *external constraints,* your choice may indeed be *un*free. How is this possible? Because your choice can be the result of *internal constraints,* irrational impulses that enslave you. Even though you may on one level be choosing what you "want," the "want" itself does not express your truest self, your deepest desires and values. Consider the following examples:

How does the theme of this photograph of mother and daughter graduates support the idea that genuine freedom involves *actively creating alternatives* that might not be on the original menu of options?

- You are addicted to cigarettes and have been unable to quit despite many attempts.
- You are consumed by jealousy and find yourself unable to break free of your obsession.
- You can't go to bed without checking all of the locks three times.
- Whenever you think about speaking in front of a group of people you are paralyzed by anxiety, and you perform miserably.
- You have frequent and lasting episodes of depression from which you are unable to rouse yourself and that sap your interest in doing anything.

This is just a small sampling of common behaviors that are clearly "unfree," despite the fact that there are no external threats that are compelling people to make their choices. Instead, in these instances and countless others like them, the compulsions come from *within* the person, inhibiting them from making choices that originate from their genuine self. How can you tell if your choice originates from your genuine self or whether it is the result of an internal constraint? There is no simple answer. You have to think critically about your situation to understand it fully, but here are some questions to guide your reflective inquiry:

- Do you feel that you are making a free, unconstrained choice and that you could easily "do otherwise" if you wanted to? Or do you feel that your choice is in some sense *beyond* your conscious control, that you are "in the grip of" a force that does not reflect your genuine self, a compulsion that has in some way "taken possession" of you?
- Does your choice add positive qualities to your life: richness of experience, success, happiness? Or does your choice have negative results that undermine many of the positive goals that you are striving for?
- If you are asked "why" you are making the choice, are you able to provide a persuasive, rational explanation? Or are you at a loss to explain why you are behaving this way, other than to say, "I can't help myself."

Let's apply these criteria to the example of smoking cigarettes.

- When people are addicted to cigarettes, they usually feel that they are *not* making a free, unconstrained choice to smoke because it is very difficult for them to stop smoking. Instead, they generally feel that they are enslaved by the habit, despite their numerous and determined attempts to quit.

- Smoking cigarettes adds many negative elements to a person's life including health risks to themselves and others near them, stained teeth, and bad breath. On the positive side, people cite reduced anxiety, suppressed appetite, and lessened social awkwardness. But smoking only deals with the symptoms of these problems, not the causes. On balance, the bottom line on smoking is clearly negative.

- Most people who want to stop are at a loss to explain why they smoke, other than to say "I can't help myself."

Using these criteria, habitual smoking clearly seems to be an example of an internal constraint. Of course, although smoking might not be your concern, it is likely that there are other elements of your life that are. Although you might find it easy to advise, "Just say no!" to cigarettes, you might have great difficulty accepting this same simple advice when confronted with an urge for a chocolate eclair, a panicked feeling of insecurity, or a deep depression.

Some internal constraints originate from the expectations of others that we have unconsciously "adopted" as our own. For example, someone in your life may demand exaggerated deference from you, and over time you may internalize this expectation to the point where you actually believe that you are freely choosing to exhibit this self-denying subjugation. But although you may have convinced yourself on a surface level, on a deeper level it is clear that you have surrendered your psychological freedom to the demands of someone else. That's one reason why people have difficulty in breaking out of abusive and destructive relationships: they don't view the relationships as abusive or destructive, and instead may believe that they have freely chosen to be where they are.

This same psychological pattern repeats itself throughout your social life. It is in people's nature to want to be loved, accepted, and respected by others; to fit in with the larger social whole; and to secure the rewards that others can provide. But though you may try to convince yourself otherwise, your choices in response to these pressures and needs are often not truly free because the impetus for these actions does not originate with you; rather, it originates from outside yourself. The key variable is the extent of your *self-awareness*. Free choice demands that you be consciously aware of social pressures and expectations and that you consciously choose how to respond to them. This crucial awareness is often lacking, and so our behavior is the result of external manipulation rather than self-originated choice. The psychologist Erich Fromm provides penetrating insight into this complex phenomenon in his seminal work, *Escape From Freedom*:

Most people are convinced that as long as they are not overtly forced to do something by an outside power, their decisions are theirs, and that if they want something, it is they who want it. But this is one of the great illusions we have about ourselves. A great number of our decisions are not really our own but are suggested to us from the outside; we have succeeded in persuading ourselves that it is we who have made the decision, whereas we have actually conformed with expectations of others, driven by the fear of isolation and by more direct threats to our life, freedom, and comfort.

THINK CRITICALLY

4.8

PHILOSOPHER'S NOTEBOOK

What Are the Limitations to My Freedom?

Making full use of your freedom involves first eliminating the constraints that limit your freedom. Use this thinking activity to begin this self-reflective process, which will prepare you for increasing your freedom.

- Identify some of the important *external constraints* or limitations on your options that are imposed by people or circumstances outside of you. Are there people in your life that actively seek to limit your freedom? Are you locked into situations that present limited opportunities? After identifying some of the significant external constraints, identify ways to diminish their impact on your freedom by either modifying or eliminating them.

- Evaluate the extent to which you are passively content to choose from a *limited selection of alternatives* that are presented to you. Identify several situations to begin actively creating your own possibilities.

- Identify some of the important *internal constraints* in your life using the following criteria to identify behaviors that:
  - you feel are out of your conscious control.
  - add negative results to your life.
  - you cannot provide a rational explanation for.

Even though you may believe that you are making a genuinely free choice, the reality may be that you are making a "pseudo-choice" in response to internal or external constraints. And because you are *unaware* of the influences that are acting on your behavior, you are living the illusion of the puppet who does not see the strings controlling his every movement.

While everybody engages in some pseudo-thinking and pseudo-choosing, the crucial question is to what extent. If you are a person who reflects, reasons, and thinks critically about your beliefs and your choices, then you will be a predominantly *inner-directed* person who is the author of the majority of your thinking and choosing. On the other hand, if you are a person who spends comparatively little time thinking critically about your beliefs and choices, then you will be a much more *other-directed* person who is defined by the expectations of others or inner demons over which you have little control. Genuine freedom requires the will and the capacity to reflect, reason, and think critically about your "self," and in the absence of these abilities, you are in danger of becoming a "pseudo-self."

Jean Grimshaw: *Feminist Analysis of Freedom*

F eminist thought has explored the complexities of freedom in some depth, particularly with respect to the manner in which internal constraints limit the possibility of genuine freedom. In the following reading, the philosopher **Jean Grimshaw** analyzes the ways in which repressive social forces can erode an individual's psychological autonomy and thus create the sort of false desires and pseudo-selves to which Erich Fromm refers. As has been suggested in the previous sections, this is precisely the type of analysis needed to understand our full range of options and to develop the autonomy that is the necessary condition of genuinely free choices.

Issues about women's autonomy have been central to feminist thinking and action. Women have so often been in situations of powerlessness and dependence that any system of belief or programme of action that could count as "feminist" must in some way see this as a central concern. But what is meant by "autonomy" and under what conditions is it possible? This has been an important and contentious question in philosophy. But questions about autonomy, and related questions about self and identity have also been important to feminism, and within feminist thinking it is possible to find radically different ways of thinking about these things. . . .

Jean Grimshaw, *Autonomy and Identity in Feminist Thinking*

Feminist thinking does not, of course, exist in a vacuum, and in thinking about women's autonomy, feminists have drawn on different (and conflicting) approaches to questions about the human self, some of which have a long history. I want to begin by going back to an argument that Aristotle put forward in the *Ethics*, since I think that the point at which his argument breaks down can illuminate the nature of the problem some feminist thinking has faced.

Aristotle's argument concerns the question of what it is that makes an action "voluntary," done of a person's own free will, and in order to answer this question, he distinguished between actions whose origin was "inside" a person, and those whose origin was "outside," which resulted from external influences or pressure or compulsion. He discussed at some length the problems that arise over trying to define ideas such as "compulsion," and in estimating the degree of severity of pressure that could make an action not voluntary. But in this sort of model of autonomy, what defines an action as autonomous is seen as its point of *origin*; it must have an "immaculate conception," as it were, from *within* the self.

Now ultimately I think that it is this definition of "autonomy" in terms of origin and the associated distinction between an "inner" self which can in some way spontaneously generate its "own" actions, and "external" influences which are not "part" of the self, that will need challenging. But I think it is possible to defend the Aristotelian version of autonomy up to a point, provided notions of "inside" and "outside" the self are defined in a certain way. If a person is prevented from doing what they would otherwise intend or desire to do, or if they are coerced into doing what they would *not* otherwise want to desire to do, they are not acting autonomously. Under this interpretation, actions which originate from "inside" the self are those which are seen as in accordance with conscious desires or intentions, and those which originate from "outside" the self are those which one would not do if one were not coerced. The pressure here is to consider the sorts of circumstances which do, in fact, coerce people in these sorts of ways. And, of course, a central concern of feminism has been to identify and fight against the kinds of coercion to which women have been subjected, including things like physical violence and economic dependence.

But it is at this point that an Aristotelian-type argument fails to be able to deal with the most difficult questions about autonomy. The Aristotelian view, as I have interpreted it, "works" only to the extent that it is assumed that there is no problem about what I shall call "the autonomy of desires." Autonomy is defined as acting in accordance with desire (or intention). But what of the desires themselves? Are there *desires* (or intentions) which are not "autonomous," which do not originate from "within" the self, which are not authentic, not really "one's own"?

Grimshaw is delineating here the distinction between *external constraints* and *internal constraints*, which we explored in previous sections. As we have seen, *soft determinists* agree with Aristotle: voluntary choices are those made by an individual that are not the result of external pressures or compulsions. But Grimshaw is asking the same question that many have asked: Can't choices that are not *externally constrained* nevertheless be "involuntary" or "unfree" because they are *internally constrained*? Can we assume that an individual's desires are always autonomous, or is it possible that there are "*desires* (or intentions) which are not 'autonomous,' which do not originate from 'within' the self, which are not authentic, not really 'one's own'?" Grimshaw proceeds to explore the "psychic coercion" that she believes can and does occur, an *internal constraint* that compromises individual autonomy and limits personal freedom.

Jean Grimshaw, *Autonomy and Identity in Feminist Thinking*

Feminist writers have wanted, of course, to indict the various forms of brutality and coercion from which women have suffered. But this brutality and coercion has been seen not merely as a question of physical or "external" coercion or constraint; the force of subjection has also been seen as a psychic one, invading women's very selves. The language of "conditioning," "brainwashing," "indoctrination," and so forth, has been used to describe this force. The female self, under male domination, is riddled through and through with false or conditioned desires. But set against this conditioned, nonautonomous female self are various images of a female self that would be authentic, that would transcend or shatter this conditioning. I want now to look at some of these images of the female self in feminist discourse: my particular examples are from the work of **Mary Daly**, **Marilyn Frye** and **Kate Millett**.

Daly, Frye and Millett all stress the way in which women have been subject to the *power* of men. Much of Daly's book, *Gyn/Ecology* (1979), is an account of the barbarities inflicted on women such as suttee, clitorectomy, footbinding and other forms of mutilation. Millett, in *Sexual Politics* (1977), sees patriarchal power as something so historically all-embracing that it has totally dominated women's lives. Frye, in *The Politics of Reality* (1983) uses the situation of a young girl sold into sexual slavery and then systematically brutalized and brainwashed into a life of service to her captors as an analogy for the situation of all women. And all three writers stress the way in which they see the female self as "invaded" by patriarchal conditioning. Millett writes:

> When in any group of persons, the ego is subjected to such invidious versions of itself through social beliefs, ideology and tradition, the effect is bound to be pernicious. This should make it no very special cause for surprise that women develop group characteristics common to those who suffer minority status and a marginal existence.

Women, she argues, are deprived of all but the most trivial sources of dignity or self-respect. In her discussion of Lawrence's depiction of Connie in *Lady Chatterly's Lover*, what she sees Connie as relinquishing is "self, ego, will, individuality" (243); all those

Mary Daly (1928–) Feminist Theologian and Philosopher. Accuses structures of society from the Church to Christianity and culture itself as embodying and engendering misogyny and patriarchy.

Marilyn Frye Feminist Philosopher. Currently a professor at Michigan State University. Her interests include the philosophy of language and feminist philosophy. She authored *The Politics of Reality: Essays in Feminist Theory*.

Kate Millet (1934–) Feminist Writer and Activist. Her *Sexual Politics* (1970) was highly influential in what is now called the second women's movement.

things which, Millett argues, women had but recently achieved (and for which Lawrence had a profound distaste).

Mary Daly's picture of the way in which women's selves are invaded by patriarchal conditioning is even more striking. She describes women, for example, as "moronized," "robotized," "lobotomized," as "the puppets of Papa". At times she seems to see women as so "brainwashed" that they are scarcely human; thus she describes them as "fembots," even as "mutants." In Millett, Daly and Frye, women are seen primarily as *victims*; the monolithic brutality and psychological pressures of male power have reduced women almost to the state of being "non-persons." And indeed, as Daly sees women as having become "mutants" or "fembots," so Millett sees them as not having been allowed to participate in fully "human" activities, as Frye sees them as simply "broken" and then "remade" in the way that suits her masters.

But behind this victimized female self, whose actions and desires are assumed to be not truly "her own," since they derive from processes of force, conditioning or psychological manipulation; there is seen to be an authentic female self, whose recovery or discovery it is one of the aims of feminism to achieve. The spatial metaphor implicit in the word "behind" is not accidental, since this model of self is premised on the possibility of making a distinction between an "inner" and an "outer" self. Ibsen's Peer Gynt compared his quest for identity to the process of peeling layers off an onion; but after shedding all the "false selves," he found that there was nothing inside, no "core." The sort of spatial metaphor implicit in Peer Gynt's account of himself is also apt in the accounts of self given by Daly, Millett and Frye, except that there *is* assumed to be a "core." This is the clearest in the work of Daly. In *Gyn/Ecology*, discovering or recovering one's own self is seen as akin to a process of salvation or religious rebirth, and Daly writes of what she calls the unveiling or unwinding of the "shrouds" of patriarchy to reveal the authentic female Spirit-Self underneath. And this Self is seen as a unitary and harmonious one. Splits and barriers within the psyche, she argues, as well as those between Selves, are the result of patriarchal conditioning. In the unitary and harmonious female Spirit-Self there will be no such splits. . . .

The paradigm of coercion, writes Frye, is *not* the direct application of physical force. Rather, it is a situation in which choice and action *do* take place, and in which the victim acts under her own perception and judgment. Hence, what the exploiter needs is that

> The will and intelligence of the victim be disengaged from the projects of resistance and escape but that they not be simply broken or destroyed. Ideally, the disintegration and misintegration of the victim should accomplish the detachment of the victim's will and intelligence from the victim's own interests and their attachment to the interests of the exploiter. This will effect a displacement or dissolution of self-respect and will undermine the victim's intolerance of coercion. With that, the situation transcends the initial paradigmatic form or structure of coercion; for if people don't mind doing what you want them to do, you can't really be *making* them do it.

And, she writes:

> The health and integrity of an organism is a matter of its being organized largely towards its own interests and welfare. She is healthy and "working right" when her substance is organized primarily on principles which align it to *her* interests and welfare. Co-operation is essential of course, but it will not do that I arrange everything so that *you* get enough exercise: for me to be healthy, *I* must get enough exercise. My being adequately exercised is logically independent of your being so.

Frye is writing here as if it were possible to distinguish the interests of one self sharply from those of another, and as if, were the effects of male domination to be undone, it would not be too much of a problem for the self to know what its interests were.

In various ways then, underlying much of the work of these three writers is a set of assumptions about the self. First, that it is, at least potentially, a unitary, rational thing, aware of its interests. Second, that "splits" within the psyche should be seen as resulting from the interference of patriarchal or male-dominated socialization or conditioning. Third, that the task of undoing this conditioning is one that can be achieved solely by a rational process of learning to understand and fight against the social and institutional

JEAN GRIMSHAW
Contemporary Feminist Philosopher. Writes on issues surrounding feminism and its relation to philosophy. Author of *Philosophy and Feminist Thinking* (1986) and *Feminist Philosophers: Women's Perspectives on Philosophical Traditions* (1986).

effects of male domination. And implicit in these assumptions about the self, I think, is a conception of autonomy. Frye writes that "left to themselves" women would not want to serve men. Daly writes of unveiling or unwinding the "shrouds" of patriarchy. Millett writes of the individuality and ego that women can discover in themselves once they recognize the effects of their patriarchal socialization. And in all three, what is autonomous (or authentic) is what is seen as originating in some way from *within* the self; what is in some way *untainted* by the conditioning or manipulation to which a woman has previously been subjected.   ■

THINK PHILOSOPHICALLY   4.9
Analyzing Jean Grimshaw

- According to Aristotle, what conditions must be met for an action to be considered "voluntary"? How does this definition relate to the concept of external constraints on freedom that we discussed earlier? Why does the author consider this definition of "autonomy" to be inadequate from a feminist perspective?

- Grimshaw poses the question: "Are there *desires* (or intentions) which are not 'autonomous,' which do not originate from 'within' the self, which are not authentic, not really 'one's own'?" How does this question relate to the following observation from Erich Fromm?

  A great number of our decisions are not really our own but are suggested to us from the outside; we have succeeded in persuading ourselves that it is we who have made the decision, whereas we have actually conformed with expectations of others, driven by the fear of isolation and by more direct threats to our life, freedom, and comfort.

- The authors to whom Grimshaw refers—Daly, Frye, and Millett—all contend that the lack of psychological autonomy experienced by women is due mainly to the repressive forces of male, patriarchal power. What evidence do these thinkers provide to support this contention? Do you agree with their central argument? Why or why not?

- Grimshaw observes that "Ibsen's Peer Gynt compared his quest for identity to the process of peeling layers off an onion; but after shedding all of the 'false selves,' he found that there was nothing inside, no 'core.'" In contrast, the authors referred to by Grimshaw all believe that there is an "authentic female Spirit-Self" at the core of each woman, and that women can discover their "core" by freeing themselves from social and psychological oppression. Do you agree with their conviction regarding the existence of an authentic core self? Do you think this same argument can be extended to include people in general, including men? Why or why not?

Making Connections: *Increasing Your Freedom*

I n this chapter we have explored the major philosophical theories regarding freedom: *hard determinism, soft determinism (or compatibilism), and indeterminism (or libertarianism)*. We have also examined a theoretical perspective that attempts to synthesize the core insights of these different theories. If this synthesizing view of determinism and indeterminism resonates with your own experience, then there are actions people can take to increase their personal freedom. To begin with, you can *make increasing your personal freedom a priority*. Achieving greater freedom for yourself is based on placing a high value on personal freedom. If you are primarily focused on meeting your needs within the existing structure of your life, then maximizing your choices and enlarging the scope of your life may not be a top priority. If you feel dissatisfied with the status quo and long to increase your options and your ability to choose them, increasing your personal freedom will be a very important goal. One strategy is to complete a brief inventory of your life, identifying some of the areas you would like to change, as well as those you are basically satisfied with but would like to enrich. Think about how increasing your personal freedom and making different choices can help you achieve these life goals.

Another initiative you can take in your life is to *explicitly accept your freedom and responsibility*, much in the same way that William James exhorts: "Our first act of freedom, if we are free, ought in all inward propriety to be to affirm that we are free. . . ." Your reaction to responsibility is an effective barometer of your attitude toward freedom. If you are comfortable with your personal responsibility, able openly to admit your mistakes as well as take pleasure in your successes, this is an indication that you accept your freedom. Similarly, if you take pride in your independence, welcoming the opportunity to make choices for which you are solely responsible, this also reveals a willing embracing of your freedom. One strategy in this regard is to create a "responsibility chart" that evaluates your acceptance of responsibility (and freedom) in various areas of your life. On one side of the page describe common activities in which you are engaged ("Decisions at work," "Conflicts with my partner") and on the other side list typical judgments that you make ("I am solely responsible for that mistaken analysis," "You made me do that embarrassing thing and I can't forgive you"). After several days of record-keeping and reflection, you should begin to get an increasingly clear picture of the extent to which you accept (or reject) your personal freedom.

Another approach to increasing your freedom is to *emphasize your ability to create yourself through your free choices*, rather than passively accepting the shaping impact of other forces. Although you may not be fully aware of it, you have your own psychological theory of human nature, which is expressed in how you view yourself and deal with other people. Do you believe that your personality is determined by your genetic history or the environmental circumstances that have shaped you? Or do you believe that people are able to transcend their histories and choose freely? An approach you can pursue is that instead of explaining your (and others') behavior entirely in terms of genes and environmental conditioning, develop the habit of analyzing your behavior in terms of the *choices* you make. Many people have triumphed in life over daunting odds, and many others fail miserably despite having every advantage in life. One key ingredient? An unshakable belief in the ability to influence one's destiny.

An essential dimension of increasing your freedom is to *become aware of the constraints on your freedom*. The key to unlocking your freedom is becoming aware of the external and internal forces that are influencing you. As long as you remain oblivious to external manipulations and internal compulsions, you are powerless to escape from their hold. However, by using your critical thinking abilities, you are able to identify these influences and then neutralize their effect. Developing this awareness is clearly a complex and ongoing process that requires penetrating insight, mature insight, and personal courage. Developing your ability to think philosophically is an essential part of this process. It is by the disciplined practice of critical reflection and thoughtful discussions with others that we gradually become more sophisticated in our understanding of ourselves and our world.

THINK CRITICALLY 4.10

PHILOSOPHER'S NOTEBOOK

Increasing Your Freedom

Select areas of your life in which you would like to be more free: personal habits and behaviors, relationships with others, your career. Make a special effort to become aware of the constraints that are limiting your freedom and the internal messages that are shaping your thinking. Keep a record in your Philosopher's Notebook detailing your efforts and their result. Be sure to allow yourself sufficient time to escape from habitual forms and establish new patterns of thinking, feeling, and choosing. Cultivate the qualities of choosing freely that we explored in this section:

- Make freedom a priority.
- Accept your freedom and responsibility.
- Emphasize your ability to create yourself.
- Become aware of the constraints on your freedom.
- Create new options to choose from.

One final way to increase your freedom is to *create new options to choose from*, instead of simply accepting the options that are presented. Active thinking, like passive thinking, is habit forming. But once you develop the habit of looking beyond the information given, to consistently transcend the framework within which you are operating, you will be increasingly unwilling to be limited by the alternatives determined by others. Instead, you will seek to create new possibilities and actively shape situations to fit your needs. As a strategy, when you find yourself in situations with different choices, make a conscious effort to identify alternatives that are different from those presented. You don't necessarily have to choose the new options you have created if they are not superior to others, but you do want to start developing the habit of using your imagination to look beyond the circumstances as presented.

Students Thinking About Philosophy: *Creating Your Own Synthesis*

As we have seen in this chapter, every person has certain beliefs regarding the possibility of free choice, though these beliefs have not necessarily been critically evaluated. This is an opportunity to express your own view of freedom and determinism in a form that is thoughtful and coherent. After reviewing, discussing, and reflecting on the various perspectives regarding personal freedom, compose a paper that reflects your own synthesis of these issues. Your point of view should be well-reasoned and take into account all of the central arguments regarding whether people are free or not. One such student synthesis follows, entitled "Freedom and Science."

Freedom and Science
Gina Szeto

As William James asserts in his essay, "Will to Believe," when we make theories about the world, we do so in order to attain a conception of things which will give us subjective satisfaction. For example, when discussing the idea of free agency, the world seems more rational with possibilities included to the "possibility man," and more rational with possibilities excluded to the "anti-possibility man."

Most, including myself, want to believe in free will. Without free will, as without God, everything is permissible, as morality, responsibility, and existence itself lose any meaning in a determined universe. At the same time, clinging to free will out of fear of the unknown is like clinging to determinism out of fear of responsibility; we must analyze it objectively, without emotional attachment.

Why determinism gained popularity.

Determinism's rise in popularity paralleled advances in science and genetics. Science was able to reconcile our everyday observations of the world, ourselves, and our behavior with a causal-molecular basis. And in a secular culture so entrenched in the scientific method, determinism was particularly appealing. Everything, from bread-baking to free will, from mood to behavior, had a physical, quantifiable basis. In fact, the acceptance of science was, and continues to be so widespread, that organized religions began to lose their following.

Science reduced us to our molecular constitutions, bundles of nerves and their elements. Even our reasoning ability seemed to be established on the cellular level. For instance, when cells don't receive enough oxygen, they die by necrosis, spewing their molecular contents into their environment. These necrotic cells expel two kinds of molecular components; one is toxic, killing neighboring cells, which then go on to kill other cells, etc., and the other component serves as a warning signal to other neighboring cells, causing them to commit cell suicide, a measure to prevent further cell necrosis. If the molecular conditions for cell-suicide are analogous to human suicide, an injection of the right combination of hormones would invariably illicit suicidal tendencies and eventual death. While the comparison seems remote, we've already begun to see how this may be theoretically possible, having seen how greatly hormone therapy can alter mood and behavior.

Determinist's inability to predict behavior is not evidence for free will.

Since the determinist cannot identify which choices we make are necessarily determined and which might be accidental or the result of free agency, and since the determinist cannot predict people's behavior with precision, the indeterminist claims that free will *must* exist—an argument made not as a proof of free will but as an argument against determinism.

The determinist's inability to predict behavior does not add anything in principle to the free will issue. The determinist does not say that *he* can predict behavior, but that human behavior would be predictable *if* every cause, impulse, and experience could be identified, if their interactions with each other could be ascertained, if the complex causes that move a person could be simplified and broken down. Inability to predict behavior then, is not a flaw of the determinist theory, but rather a flaw in human comprehension. Our inability to predict or determine behavior does not mean it is not predictable in some absolute sense.

Consider the universe as balls on a pool table. On superficial inspection, the balls seem to move at random when hit with the cue ball, making it impossible to predict the direction of any ball. But if it were possible to know the precise angle and point at which the cue ball was struck with the cue, and the precise location of the balls to each other, as a classic example in physics it would be possible to predict with an excellent degree of accuracy in which direction the balls would roll and how they would interact with each other. Even if *we* were unable to make these precise measurements, if the measurements could somehow be determined, would it then be possible to predict the behavior of each ball? Taken to the extreme, would it be possible, at least theoretically in this scenario, for human emotion and behavior to be completely described by comparable mathematical principles?

Why the determinist arguments fall apart.

From a methodological, scientific perspective, the arguments made for determinism are measurable and tangible; they are subjectively satisfying in a culture powered by hard numbers and science. The problem with using science as a basis for any theory is its inability to prove its first hypothesis or premise. Like math or logic, if you accept the first premise, and the resulting conclusions satisfy the conditions of logic, then the argument is sound. But if you question the existence or truth of the first premise, then the entire argument falls apart. For example, if we accept that primordial slime simply showed up, if we don't question its origin, we can use this starting point to develop a scientifically sound theory of determinism based on genetics, the way in which sensory information modifies existing neural connections, thus behavior, etc. However, since science cannot disprove the notion that a God, or an evil genius, was the creator of the primordial slime, or that this God gave human free will in its incipient form as a bacteria, the determinist theory, at least from my perspective, falls apart.

Science constantly revises its own laws in light of new information because science, contrary to popular belief, does not rest on a foundation of absolute truth. Relativity theory, as show by Einstein, is not an absolute description of they way the universe exists, but is rather a more accurate representation of the universe earlier described by Newtonian physics. Using science as a basis for any theory is useful only to the person mindful of its limitations, since its fundamental principles are as subjective as any other human discipline. Science may be able to answer the "how," after accepting the appearance of primordial slime, but at every point in technical achievement, cannot address the philosopher's "why."

Using the analogy of the pool table, was the cue ball randomly dropped from an unknown position, was it thrown in a whirlwind, was it struck by some mysterious deity? Even if it was possible to answer these questions, the answers beg questions, ad infinitum.

The argument against total and complete free will.

Sartre does not claim that with total and complete freedom everything is possible. We are born, he acknowledges, with different constitutions: that is, I am born Chinese and you are born Caucasian. Where we do have complete freedom, he argues, is how we respond to the circumstances presented to us. There is a point when making any decision that we "could have acted otherwise"; that is, we could totally disregard our history, experience, and personality from the decision we're confronted with and nobody could predict with complete certainty which path we would choose. It is possible, I agree, for one to disconnect our decisions from our history, experience, and personality—but only if we act instinctively. Human behavior, however, is commonly regarded as rational as opposed to instinctual.

Why do we act at all? Is the impetus for action, for behavior, not causal? What is the significance of "could have done otherwise" if the alternative is meaningless? Why would I choose one alternative over another if I am more likely to derive benefit from this one, assuming that I desire to derive benefit? Because life is so absurd and random? Is this meaningful? At any moment, I could have done otherwise, but why would I? Why would I go against my inclination, my impulse? Because I reasoned, rationalized it to be so. Why would reason win? Because it is a stronger inclination in my person. Sartre says in deciding, I am free, I am responsible for my decision. One could *decide* to do otherwise, at any moment in time, but what does one do when one *decides*? Is it simply a reaction to a stimulus, reading without understanding, hearing but not listening? We can act instinctively without thought, but we cannot decide to act without thought. The act of deciding involves using a mind (and if science reveals anything meaningful) a mind modified since conception, a product of its genetic constitution, vulnerable and passive to the input it receives, to examine possibilities. At the same time, when Sartre says at any moment I could disregard my history, personality, etc. and decide to do otherwise, he assumes it is possible to disconnect the function of rationality from the mind (at least partly a product of genes and experience) of which it is a member. Is it more reasonable to assume that the function of reason is modified by, and at the same time, modifies the environment of which it is apart, forming a distinct and inseparable relationship with each other?

The use of genetics to support theories of both free will and determinism.

Though science has not proven to be an absolute description of the universe, it has not been proven to be an inaccurate description, and while imperfect, has described human beings and characterized our environment in a subjectively satisfying and consistent way. At the same time, we should be wary when using science as proof of any theory outside of science, especially when discussing free will. We will use it, as we use intuition, psychology, and religion—as a means to discuss theories, to aid our understanding of our universe, ourselves.

Though a superior theory may prove otherwise, we are born with genetic predispositions (i.e., my parents weren't surprised when I came out Chinese and not African). Our first response to our environment is not random, but dependent on this genetic constitution. This first response, which may be prenatal, modifies our genetic program in a unique way (the same stimulus may have a different effect on a different set of genes) so that subsequent responses are a product of both our genes and this response, and so on with subsequent stimuli, products of our environment. As passive receivers of this sensory information, we become a combination of our unique pre-existing genetic program and our environment, at this stage in cognitive development, we act instinctually and not yet rationally. We are determined in this sense because we are born without our consent, with genes we do not choose: we are raised, against our will, in a particular environment, at a specific period in time which confers specific stimuli to our particular genetic program. There is no conscious control, especially before rational function matures, how and when sensory information is received, or the way in which the sensory information is perceived and analyzed. If we agree with this hypothesis, essence begins as a product of factors beyond our control.

If the choices presented to me are determined, my essence is limited by these possibilities. Possibilities exist. I agree with Sartre. But is the freedom to choose these possibilities equal to every man?

As our genetic program responds to, and is modified by its environment, abstraction, reasoning and rationalization develop, as the physical body develops. At some point, and it is difficult to determine when, reasoning and rationalization preside over behavior and action. It's hard to know when, how, and why the mind becomes so modified to take on the qualities of rational thought. At this stage, reasoning works to inhibit or foster the instinct, we become aware of our capacity to control ourselves and our environment through the decisions we make—we become self-aware.

Does the quality of being self-aware create by means unfathomable by scientific and thus human comprehension, and as a consequence of its existence, a novel property to the universe—namely, free will? Why does a body not live, after it's dismembered and sewn back together? Can we quantify this life force the same way we calculate numbers? What is this life force? In the same way, what does it mean to be self-aware, is this a measurable quality? Does self-awareness, reasoning, emerge as a product of the interaction between our experiences and genetic makeup, or is it an autonomous, isolated property that calls upon experience and genes at its discretion? Does it exist as absolute quality or does it exist in degrees? Self-awareness seems to be a property that manifests itself by calling upon experience and genes, but is itself created and influenced by genetics and experience.

If rational thought creates the condition for free will, then we are modified not only by our genes and our environment, but also by this quality of rationalization in an unpredictable way. Following this logic, the development of one's essence then precedes the maturation of rational function, existence: and once self-aware, existence has the capacity to modify essence.

Recognition of genetics as a means of heredity, a scientific basis for rational thought, does not preclude the existence of free will. If free will is a result of rational function, by means unintelligible to human understanding, then the feeling of freedom is not illusory but exists in some indefinable yet absolute sense. (Is the feeling or belief that we are free, or the consideration of incarceration as a universal evil, evidence of the existence of free will?)

The relationship between rationalization, a human function, and existence is that we cannot remove ourselves, our existence, from rational thought—we *are* rational thought. Some people exercise their rational functions more than others as a product of their genes and experience; that is, they are "more free" than others. Rationalization, like any of the five senses, exists in gradations, a notion that justifies, but doesn't excuse our existence. A person may have genuine justifications for their condition—they were born without their consent, with genes and an environment not of their choosing. (We can feel sorry for them.) But they can still be responsible if we believe that reasoning and the exercise of rational thought is our means to freedom. Some people are born into wealth, some are born into poverty. Though more challenging to the impoverished, if American democracy and opportunity is comparable to free will, affluence is possible for every American citizen. So while the poor may have justifications for their circumstances, they cannot deny their freedom. Free will, following this logic, is not handed in whole to every man, but like Aristotle said of the moral virtues, develops with exercise and habituation.

The strength of the free will argument rests on determinism's inability to explain away free will. We may not be able to prove it, but we can't disprove it either. Until we can explain the origins of life force, until we can prove how and why things began, the belief in free will shall continue to exist. And if the belief exists that contemporary human disciplines (i.e., science) reveal something meaningful, however small regarding ourselves and the universe we live in, we can use these insights as a language, as means to communicate our theories about ourselves and the world.

Concept Review

- Philosophical inquiry into the nature of human freedom attempts to define and explain how and why we make choices—are we truly free to choose a course of action, or is there some larger factor that determines what we do and why we do it? If we believe that human behavior is dependent on external forces (such as social dynamics or past psychological trauma), then we cannot ever truly be free to make reasonable choices. However, if we believe that we are the ultimate arbiters of our own actions, solely responsible for the choices we make (whatever their outcome), then we can indeed become truly free.

- Your own beliefs about the nature of personal freedom have a substantial impact on your ability to change and grow as a person, to develop a consistent moral outlook, to relate to a specific spiritual tradition, and to participate in a just and fair society.

- Determinism holds that human behaviors, like all events in the physical world, issue from specific causes that may or may not be within our individual control. There cannot be true freedom, because none of the choices we make are truly "free": our actions are dependent on, or caused by, factors beyond our control. Determinist thinkers include Skinner, Freud, and d'Holbach.

- A determinist view of human freedom further holds that humans are inhibited in their ability to choose freely by both internal and external constraints. External constraints are those imposed by your environment and your circumstances; internal constraints involve limitations to our autonomy that we impose on ourselves.

- Soft determinists assert that we can consider human actions "free" if they are the result of internal motivations, not the product of external influences or constraints. Hard determinists believe that all human actions can be traced to some cause, and therefore no action is truly "free."

- Indeterminism holds that your choices, or at least some of your choices, are made (or can be made) freely. In other words, whichever option you choose, you might still have chosen otherwise.

- William James (1842–1910) argued that indeterminism was the more rational belief about human freedom, as most aspects of the way we live our lives assume that we all have some degree of freedom of choice. James bolstered his argument by pointing out that, in a deterministic universe, neither judgments of approval nor judgments of regret are possible; determinism leads to a radical pessimism that simply does not explain lived human experience.

- Jean-Paul Sartre (1905–1980) argues that we are, in fact, radically free, "condemned to be free." In arguing against the view that "essence precedes existence"—that our choices, our selves, and our actions existed in some cosmic, predetermined realm before we were even born—Sartre posited instead that existence precedes essence. We are oriented toward the future, continually weighing options and considering our choices; that faculty of consideration and choosing is what makes us truly free, in Sartre's view. As a result, however, we are each uniquely and completely responsible for the actions we choose to take.

- Existentialism, the philosophical worldview of Sartre, describes the human response to this radical freedom as anguish, abandonment, and despair. Realizing that we are uniquely responsible for—and alone with—our choices leaves us feeling distressed. Not only can't we ever be completely sure that we are doing the "right" thing, but there is no authority, no "god," to whom to turn for reassurance.

- To increase your personal freedom, you must first explicitly accept your freedom and the responsibility that comes with it. You must accept that you create yourself from your own free choices—you're not merely passive clay in the mold of experience. You must become aware of the constraints on your freedom, analyzing both external manipulations and your internal compulsions. Finally, you must create new options from which to choose.

Media Resources

 www.researchnavigator.com

Chapter 4 focuses on what it is to be free and if we can ever achieve that. Questions of a human nature and its potential influence on our actions raise issues of determined decisions or free will. For further research on questions on self-freedom and potential life influences, use the tools available to you in Research Navigator.

As you investigate this topic, consider this question: "What does it mean to have freedom and based on this, are you free?"

- **ContentSelect:** search in the Philosophy databases using the search terms "essence and existence," "free will and determinism," and "existentialism."

- **Link Library:** search in the Philosophy database under terms "Aquinas" and "Kierkegaard."

- **New York Times on the Web:** search in the Philosophy database using the search terms "freedom" and "self creation."

 For additional study resources for this chapter, go to: **www.prenhall.com/chaffee/chapter4**

 The Primary Source: Philosophical Readings and Commentary

Berkeley, George: *Three Dialogues Between Hylas and Philonous*

d'Holbach, Baron: *The System of Nature*

Freud, Sigmund: *An Outline of Psycho-Analysis*

James, William: *The Will to Believe; Pragmatism*

Kierkegaard, Søren: *Philosophical Fragments*

Mill, John Stuart: *On Liberty*

Sarte, Jean-Paul: *Existentialism is a Humanism*

What Is Morality?
Developing Enlightened Values

One has a moral responsibility to disobey unjust laws…
I agree with St. Augustine that 'an unjust law is no law at all.'
MARTIN LUTHER KING, JR.

Morality differs in every society and is a
convenient term for socially approved habits.
RUTH BENEDICT

Your Moral Compass

The ultimate purpose in studying ethics is not as it is in other inquiries, the attainment of theoretical knowledge; we are not conducting this inquiry in order to know what virtue is, but in order to become good, else there would be no advantage in studying it.

ARISTOTLE

Every day of your life you make moral choices, decisions that reflect your own internal "moral compass." Often we are not aware of the deeper moral values that drive our choices, and we may even be oblivious to the fact that the choices we are making have a moral component. For example, consider the following situations:

- A good friend asks you to provide some "hints" about an upcoming exam that you have already taken.
- You pass a homeless person asking for a "donation."
- A friend confides that she is feeling very depressed and is worried about what she might do.
- You consider purchasing a research paper from an online service that you plan to "customize" and submit as your own.
- You find yourself flirting with your friend's romantic partner.
- You consider donating your time to an organization devoted to helping others, such as Habitat for Humanity.
- Although you've had a few drinks at a party, you still feel sufficiently competent to drive home.
- You find yourself in the middle of a conversation in which a friend is being ridiculed as a "hopeless geek."
- You consider forgoing a party to spend time with a friend going through a difficult period.
- You personally object to the treatment of veal calves, but veal is what is being served by the parents of your romantic partner.
- You were involved in a major mistake at work, and your supervisor asks you to name the people responsible.

These, and countless other situations like them, are an integral part of the choices that we face each day as we shape our lives and create ourselves. In each case, the choices involved share the following characteristics:

- The choices involve your treatment of other people (or animals).
- There may not be one obvious "right" or "wrong" answer, and the dilemma can be discussed and debated.
- There are likely to be both positive and/or negative consequences to yourself or others, depending on the choices that you make.
- Your choices are likely to be guided by "values" to which you are committed and reflect a moral reasoning process that leads to your decisions.
- The choices involve the concept of "moral responsibility."

Philosophy plays a uniquely central role in helping us to develop enlightened values, use informed moral reasoning, and make well-supported conclusions. Although most areas of human study are devoted to describing the world and how people behave, philosophy is concerned with helping people evaluate how the world *ought* to be and what courses of action people *should* take. This was precisely how Socrates envisioned his central mission in life, to remind people of the moral imperative to attend to their souls and create themselves to be individuals of upstanding character and enlightened values.

For I do nothing but go about persuading you all, old and young alike, not to take thought for your persons or your properties, but first and chiefly to care about the greatest improvement of your soul. I tell you that virtue is not given by money, but that from virtue comes money and every other good of man, public as well as private. This is my teaching.

—*Plato*

These next two chapters will introduce you to the ethical theories and moral reasoning central to philosophy. But more than that, your philosophical explorations will provide you with the opportunity to refine and enrich your own moral compass, so that you will be better equipped to successfully deal with the moral dilemmas that we all encounter in the course of living.

What Is Ethics?

 thics and *morals* are terms that refer to the principles that govern our relationships with other people: the ways we *ought* to behave, the rules and standards that we *should* employ in the choices we make. The ethical and moral concepts that we use to evaluate these behaviors include right and wrong, good and bad, just and unjust, fair and unfair, responsible and irresponsible.

◆ VISUAL PHILOSOPHY

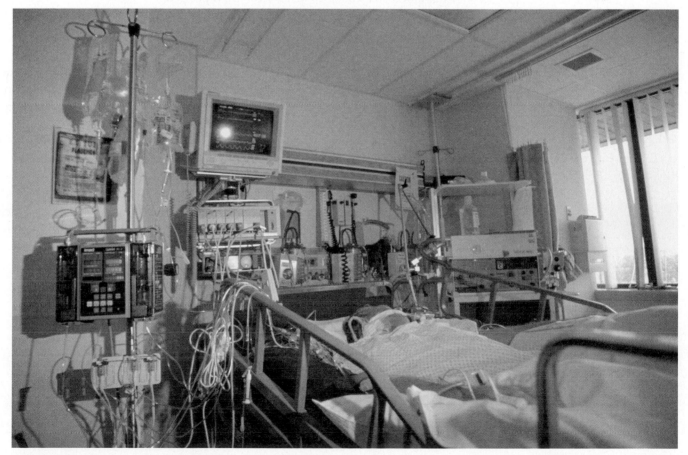

Ethical Dilemmas Are an Unavoidable Part of Life

What is your reaction to this photograph of a comatose patient on life support equipment? Do you believe that medical technology should be used to extend people's lives in all cases? Why?

The study of **ethics** is derived from the ancient Greek word *ethos*, which refers to moral purpose or character—as in "a person of upstanding character." *Ethos* is also associated with the idea of "cultural customs or habits." In addition, the etymology of the word *moral* can be traced back to the Latin word *moralis*, which also means "custom." Thus the origins of these key concepts reflect both the private and the public nature of the moral life: we strive to become morally enlightened people, but we do so within the social context of cultural customs.

Ethical and *moral* are essentially equivalent terms that can be used interchangeably, though there may be shadings in meaning that influence which term is used. For example, we generally speak about medical or business "ethics" rather than "morality," though there is not significant difference in meaning. *Value* is the general term we use to characterize anything that possesses intrinsic worth, that we prize, esteem, and regard highly, based on clearly defined standards. Thus you may *value* your devoted pet, your favorite jacket, and a cherished friendship, each based on different *standards* that establish and define their worth to you. One of the most important value domains includes your *moral* or *ethical* values, those personal qualities and rules of conduct that distinguish a person (and group of people) of upstanding character. Moral values are reflected in such questions as

- Who is a "good person" and what is a "good action"?
- What can we do to promote the happiness and well-being of others?
- What moral obligations do we have toward other people?
- When should we be held morally responsible?
- How do we determine which choice in a moral situation is right or wrong, just or unjust?

Although moral philosophy is certainly interested in the moral customs and practices of various cultures, its true mandate goes beyond simple description to analyzing and evaluating the *justification* and *logic* of these moral beliefs. Are there universal values or principles that apply to all individuals in all cultures? If so, on what basis are these grounded? Are some ethical customs and practices more enlightened than others? If so, what are the reasons or principles upon which we can make these evaluations? Is there a "good life" to which all humans should aspire? If so, what are the elements of such a life, and on what foundation is such an ideal established? These are questions that we will be considering in this chapter and the next, but they are questions of such complexity that you will likely be engaged in thinking about them throughout your life.

THINK PHILOSOPHICALLY 5.1
Who Is a Moral Person?

Think of someone you know whom you consider to be a person of outstanding moral character. This person doesn't have to be perfect—he or she doubtless has flaws. Nevertheless, this is a person you admire, whom you would like to emulate. After fixing this person in your mind, write down in your Philosopher's Notebook the qualities that this person displays that, in your mind, qualifies him or her as a morally upright individual. For each quality, try to think of an example of when the person displayed it. For example:

- **Moral courage:** *Charles is a person in my company who always takes the action he believes is morally "right," even though his point of view may be unpopular with many of the people present. Though he endured criticism, he never flinched or backed down, but instead defended his point of view with compelling reasons and stirring passion.*

If you have the opportunity, ask some people you know to describe their idea of a "moral person," and compare their responses to your own.

Ethics The study of values that govern our moral character and our relationships with other people. Ethical concepts include right and wrong, good and bad, just and unjust, fair and unfair, responsible and irresponsible.

One useful starting point in our explorations is to consider the question, "Who is a moral person?" In the same way that you were able to define the key qualities of a "critical thinker," you can describe the essential qualities of a "moral person."

For millennia, philosophers and religious thinkers have endeavored to develop ethical systems to guide our conduct. But most people in our culture today have not been exposed to these teachings in depth. They have not challenged themselves to think deeply about ethical concepts, nor have they been guided to develop coherent, well-grounded ethical systems of their own. In many cases people attempt to navigate their passage through the turbulent and treacherous waters of contemporary life without an accurate moral compass, relying instead on a tangled melange of childhood teachings, popular wisdom, and unreliable intuitions. These home-grown and unreflective ethical systems are simply not up to the task of sorting out the moral complexities in our bewildering and fast-paced world, contributing to the moral crisis described in the following passage by the writer **M. Scott Peck**:

> A century ago, the greatest dangers we faced arose from agents outside ourselves: microbes, flood and famine, wolves in the forest at night. Today the greatest dangers—war, pollution, starvation—have their source in our own motives and sentiments: greed and hostility, carelessness and arrogance, narcissism and nationalism. The study of values might once have been a matter of primarily individual concern and deliberation as to how best to lead the "good life." Today it is a matter of collective human survival. If we identify the study of values as a branch of philosophy, then the time has arrived for all women and men to become philosophers—or else.

How does one become a "philosopher of values"? By thinking deeply and clearly about these profound moral issues; studying the efforts of great thinkers through the ages who have wrestled with these timeless questions; discussing these concepts with others in a disciplined and open-minded way; and constructing a coherent ethical approach that is grounded on the bedrock of sound reasons and commitment to the truth. In other words, you become a philosopher of values by expanding your role as a *critical thinker* and extending your sophisticated thinking abilities to the domain of moral experience. This may be your most important personal quest. As Socrates emphasized, your values constitute the core of who you are. If you are to live a life of purpose, it is essential that you develop an enlightened code of ethics to guide you.

What Are My Moral Values?

Developing an intelligent moral code that will be your guide to making enlightened ethical choices is an ambitious project best begun with an inventory of your current moral values, a process you can initiate by completing the Think Critically activity 5.2. The purpose of this informal self-evaluation is to illuminate your current moral code and initiate the process of critical reflection. Which of your moral values are clearly articulated and well-grounded? Which are ill-defined and tenuously rooted? Do your values form a coherent whole, consistent with one another, or do you detect fragmentation and inconsistency? Obviously, constructing a well-reasoned and clearly defined moral code is a challenging journey. But if we explore the ideas of great moral philosophers, and think philosophically about the central moral questions, we can make significant progress toward this goal.

Your responses to the questions in this thinking activity reveal your current values. Where did these values come from? Parents, teachers, religious leaders, and other authority figures have sought to inculcate values in your thinking, but friends, acquaintances, and colleagues do as well. And in many cases they have undoubtedly

M. Scott Peck (1937–)
Psychiatrist. Considered an authority on the relationship between religion and science. Much of his work deals with ethical and religious issues.

THINK CRITICALLY

5.2

PHILOSOPHER'S NOTEBOOK

What Are My Moral Values?

You have many values—the guiding principles that you consider to be most important—that you have acquired over the course of your life. Your values deal with every aspect of your experience. The following questions are designed to elicit some of your values. Think carefully about each of the questions, and record your responses in your Philosopher's Notebook along with the reasons you have adopted that value. For example:

"I do believe that we have a moral obligation to those less fortunate than us. Why can a homeless person evoke feelings of compassion in one person and complete disgust in another? Over time, observation, experience, and intuition have formed the cornerstones of my beliefs, morally and intellectually. As a result, compassion and respect for others are moral values that have come to characterize my responses in my dealings with others. As a volunteer in an international relief program in Dehra Dun, India, I was assigned to various hospitals and clinics through different regions of the country. In Delhi, I and the other volunteers were overwhelmed by the immense poverty—thousands of people, poor and deformed, lined the streets—homeless, hungry, and desperate. We learned that over 300 million people in India live in poverty. Compassion, as Buddhists describe it, is the spontaneous reaction of an open heart. Compassion for all sentient beings, acknowledging the suffering and difficulties in the world around us, connects us not only with others but with ourselves."

Also, create your own ethical questions in the space provided. After you have completed this activity, examine your responses as a whole. Do they express a general, coherent, well-supported value system, or do they seem more like an unrelated collection of beliefs of varying degrees of clarity? This activity is a valuable investment of your time because you are creating a record of beliefs that you can return to and refine as you deepen your understanding of moral values.

- Do we have a moral responsibility towards less fortunate people?
- Is it wrong to divulge a secret someone has confided in you?
- Should we eat meat? Should we wear animal skins?
- Is it all right to tell a "white lie" to spare someone's feelings?
- Is it wrong to kill someone in self-defense?
- Should people be given equal opportunities, regardless of race, religion, or gender?
- Is it wrong to ridicule someone even if you believe it's in "good fun"?
- Should you "bend the rules" to advance your career?
- Is it all right to manipulate people into doing what you want if you believe it's for their own good?
- Is there anything wrong with pornography?
- Should we always try to take other people's needs into consideration when we act or should we first make sure that our own needs are taken care of?
- Should parents be held responsible for the misdeeds of their children?

been successful. Although much of your values education was likely the result of thoughtful teaching and serious discussions, in many other instances people may have bullied, bribed, threatened, and manipulated you into accepting their way of thinking. It's no wonder that our value systems typically evolve into a confusing patchwork of conflicting beliefs.

In examining your values you probably also discovered that although you had a great deal of confidence in some of them ("I feel very strongly that animals should never be experimented on in ways that cause them pain because they are sentient creatures just like ourselves"), you felt less secure about other values ("I feel it's usually wrong to manipulate people, although I often try to influence their attitudes and behavior— I'm not sure of the difference"). These differences in confidence are likely related to how carefully you have *examined* and *analyzed* your values. For example, you may have been brought up in a family or religion with firmly fixed values that you have adopted but never really scrutinized or evaluated, wearing these values like a borrowed overcoat. When questioned, you might be at a loss to explain exactly *why* you believe what you do, other than "This is what I was taught." In contrast, you may have other values that you consciously developed, the product of thoughtful reflection and the crucible of experience. For example, doing volunteer work with a disadvantaged group of people may have led to the conviction that "I believe we have a profound obligation to contribute to the welfare of people less fortunate than ourselves."

In short, most people's values are not "systems" at all: they are typically a collection of *general principles* ("Do unto others . . ."), *practical conclusions* ("Stealing is wrong because you might get caught"), and *emotional pronouncements* ("Interracial marriages are wrong because they seem unnatural"). This hodgepodge of

Why do you think some people are willing to suspend their critical thinking abilities and permit their minds to be controlled by cult leaders like Marshall Applewhite, who committed suicide with 39 of his followers on March 28, 1997?

values may reflect the serendipitous way they were acquired over the course of your life, and these values likely comprise your current "moral compass" that you use to guide your decisions in moral situations, even though you may not be consciously aware of it. Your challenge is to create a more refined and accurate compass, an enlightened system of values that you can use to confidently guide your moral decisions.

Think Critically activity 5.3 presents several complex moral decision scenarios. As you think your way through these moral dilemmas, you will probably find yourself appealing to basic moral principles that you typically use to guide your actions. Of course, what makes these examples moral *dilemmas* is the fact that they involve a *conflict* of traditional moral principles.

"The Lifeboat" involves a conflict between the moral beliefs:

- It is wrong to take any innocent life.
- It is right to save *some* lives rather than threaten *all* the lives on board.

"The Whistleblower" involves a conflict between the moral beliefs:

- It is wrong to knowingly jeopardize the health of children.
- It is right to protect the welfare of your family and career.

"The Patient" involves a conflict between the moral beliefs:

- It is wrong to violate the confidentiality of a professional relationship.
- It is right to prevent someone from committing murder.

"The Friend" involves a conflict between the moral beliefs:

- It is wrong to hire someone who is not the best qualified candidate for the job.
- It is right to try to help and support your friends.

What makes each of these examples *dilemmas* is that both of the moral principles that you are appealing to seem ethically sound and appropriate: the problem is that they *contradict* each other. What should you do when this happens? How do you decide which principle is *more* "right"? There is no simple answer to this question, any more than there is to the question, "What do you do when experts disagree?" In both cases, you need to *think critically* to arrive at intelligent and informed conclusions.

Naturally the moral dilemmas described in this Think Critically activity are specifically designed to provoke intense *angst* and vigorous debate, but the situations nevertheless contain elements found in our everyday moral deliberations. For example, though you are unlikely to find yourself in a similar "Lifeboat" situation, you might be faced with the decision of which employees to fire in order to keep your company afloat. And though the "Whistleblower" example may seem extreme, the fact is that employees working for

Making Moral Decisions

The following are several dilemmas that ask you to respond with decisions based on moral reasoning. After thinking critically about each situation, do the following:

- Describe in your Philosopher's Notebook the decision that you would make in this situation and explain the reasons why. Identify the moral value(s) or principle(s) on which you based your decision.
- At the conclusion of the activity, compare the moral values that you used. Did you find that you used the same values to make decisions, or did you use different values?
- Based on this analysis, describe your general conclusions about your own "moral compass."

1. *The Lifeboat:* In 1842 a ship struck an iceberg and sank. There were 30 survivors, crowded into a lifeboat designed to hold just 7. With the weather stormy and getting worse, it was obvious that many of the passengers would have to be thrown overboard or the boat would sink and everyone would drown. Imagine that you were the captain of the boat. Would you have people thrown over the side? If so, on what basis would you decide who would go? Age? Health? Strength? Gender? Size? Survival skills? Friendships? Family?

2. *The Whistleblower:* Imagine that you are employed by a large corporation that manufactures baby formula. You suspect that a flaw in the manufacturing process results in contamination of the formula in a small number of cases, and that this contamination can result in serious illness and even death. You have been told by your supervisor that "Everything is under control," and you have been warned that if you "blow the whistle" by going public, you will be putting the entire company in jeopardy from multi-million-dollar lawsuits. You will naturally be fired and blackballed in the industry, and as the sole provider in your household, your family is depending on you. What do you do? Why?

3. *The Patient:* As a clinical psychologist, you are committed to protecting the privacy of your patients. One afternoon a patient tells you that her husband, a person who has been abusing her physically and mentally for years, has threatened to kill her, and she believes him. You try to convince her to leave him and seek professional help, but she tells you that she has decided to kill him. She is certain that he will find her wherever she goes and feels that she will only be safe when he is dead. What do you do?

4. *The Friend:* As the director of your department, you are in charge of filling an important vacancy. Many people have applied, including your best friend, who has been out of work for over a year and needs a job desperately. Although your friend would likely perform satisfactorily, there are several more experienced and talented candidates who would undoubtedly perform better. You have always prided yourself in hiring the best people, and you have earned a reputation as someone with high standards who will not compromise your striving for excellence. Whom do you hire?

companies that manufacture baby formula, ephedra-based diet supplements, and tobacco products have often found themselves in precisely this moral dilemma. You yourself have likely been in a job situation where telling the truth or objecting to an unethical practice would jeopardize your position or opportunity for advancement. Many therapists, clergy, lawyers, and doctors wrestle daily with issues of confidentiality, analogous to that described in "The Patient," and we all have to deal with the question of under what circumstances is it morally appropriate to break our promises to avoid a greater evil or achieve a greater good. It requires little imagination to identify the issues of "The Friend." There are countless instances in which we are forced to balance our feelings of personal obligation with our objective or professional analysis.

In addition to these kinds of ethical situations, you will also undoubtedly confront other types of moral dilemmas that are at least as problematic. It is probable that at some point in your life you will have to make a "right to die" decision regarding a loved one nearing the end of his or her life. You might also find yourself in a situation in which you are torn between ending a difficult marriage or remaining as a full-time parent of young children. Or you might be tempted to take advantage of an investment opportunity that, although not completely illegal, is clearly unethical. Dealing with complicated, ambiguous moral challenges is an inescapable part of the human condition. Because these situations can't be avoided, you need to develop the insight and conceptual tools to deal with them effectively.

Ethical Theories

Making the best moral decision, doing the "right" thing on a consistent basis, is often a difficult and confusing experience. It's likely that there are times when, wrestling with a moral decision, you're simply not sure what the "right" course of action is. Or looking back on a decision you made, you may now feel that you made a serious mistake, and wonder how you can avoid similar moral errors in the future. And when you discuss—and debate—moral issues with others, you undoubtedly find that people often have different perspectives from yours regarding what is ethically appropriate in a given situation. How do you decide which view is correct?

Making sense out of the confusing and emotionally charged territory of moral experience is the express purpose of moral philosophy. Moral philosophy— ethics—attempts to create coherent theoretical frameworks that we can apply to the moral decisions that we encounter in our daily lives. The ultimate goal of moral philosophy is for us to use these moral theories to accurately calibrate our moral compasses, sharpen our moral intuitions, and refine our moral consciences. In this way, when we are faced with moral decisions and ethical issues, we will be able to choose confidently, with decisions that are wise, enlightened, and justified. We should be able to provide a clear rationale for our decision and cite compelling reasons why our point of view is ethically appropriate. To reach this point of moral confidence, we need to familiarize ourselves with the core theories of moral reasoning that constitute moral philosophy.

Here are the major ethical theories that we will be thinking our way through in this chapter and the next one.

- **Ethical subjectivism**
- **Cultural relativism**
- **Ethical absolutism**
- **Ethical egoism**

- **Utilitarianism**
- **The ethics of duty (Immanuel Kant)**
- **Virtue ethics**
- **Existentialist ethics**
- **The ethics of care**

They are not all mutually exclusive, requiring you to choose only one. In other words, you may find that your own personal moral compass will be informed by a thoughtfully constructive framework that makes use of a number of different theories in a coherent synthesis. In addition, as in previous chapters, we will be looking closely at the original writings of philosophers who are archetypal representatives of each of these approaches, in order to fully understand their point of view and rationale.

Jean-Jacques Rousseau

Ethical Subjectivism: *Each Person Determines What Is Morally Right*

What I feel is right is right. What I feel is wrong is wrong.

—*Jean-Jacques Rousseau*

Does this conversation sound familiar?

Emily: Sometimes it's all right to have a flexible view of morality. For example, I bought, from an online service, a research paper for my History course, and I even got an A- on it. I was totally swamped with work—I don't usually do things like that. And anyway, the professor shouldn't assign paper topics that you can buy papers for.

Jorge: Well, I don't think buying research papers and submitting them as your own is the right thing to do. We're in college to learn, and buying papers defeats the whole purpose of education.

Emily: Yeah, well, that is fine in theory. But what about when you're overwhelmed with work, and your teacher is ready to squash you like a bug if you turn your paper in late. What then?

Jorge: Well, you shouldn't have put yourself in this situation. And trying to get by with cheating is just plain wrong.

Emily: You're being naïve and overly rigid. I know we agree about the important issues: this is just a little disagreement on the fringes, in the "gray" area. In a way, we're both right, it just depends on what your point of view is. You have to go with your inner feeling, what feels right, and this feels OK to me.

Jorge: I guess you're right. Sometimes you do have to be flexible in your morality: what's right for one person may be wrong for someone else—that's just the way it is. As long as you're being true to yourself, then you're morally right. It all depends on your personal feelings. People can have different feelings, but they can't tell you that you're wrong. They simply have different feelings from yours.

The view of morality portrayed in this dialogue is both popular and problematic. It's typically referred to as **ethical subjectivism**, because the ultimate moral authority is considered to be the individual, the "subject." It is a popular view because it embodies some superficially attractive qualities. Many people enjoy the idea that they alone determine what's right and what's wrong in their lives, independent of the views and pressures of others. They also like romantic notions of "being true to myself," or "I have to go with what I truly believe." In addition, awarding each person the moral authority to determine right and wrong, good and evil, seems on the surface to be a tolerant and open-minded approach to the views of others: "I have my moral beliefs; you have your moral beliefs—who is to say which

Jean-Jacques Rousseau
(1712–1778) Enlightenment Philosopher. Maintained society and culture corrupted the inherent goodness of man and restricted the freedom man enjoys in the state of nature; offered up a version of the social contract that was much different than his contemporaries'.

Ethical subjectivism The view that the ultimate moral authority is the individual or the "subject."

Mohandas Gandhi

beliefs are better?" To many people, advocating ethical subjectivism seems to be equivalent to a "live and let live" moral policy. So what's the problem?

Actually, an ethical subjectivist view of morality has some serious philosophical difficulties. For example, consider the following exchange:

Emily: Somebody stole my laptop! I left it on the table here for a minute to get some coffee and now it's gone. Did you see someone take it?

Jorge: Actually, *I* took it. My laptop died yesterday and I needed a new one, so I took yours.

Emily: Are you crazy? Give it back! What were you thinking? How can you be so unethical?

Jorge: Actually, I'm being very ethical. I'm an ethical subjectivist, and I'm simply acting in accordance with my own moral convictions. Remember what you said? In making moral decisions, "You have to go with your inner feeling, what feels right." Well, taking your laptop feels right to me. You have a lot more money than I do, and you can simply buy another laptop. As far as my moral beliefs are concerned, the right thing to do is whatever advances my own interests. And taking your laptop is definitely advancing my own interests.

Emily: Well, in that case, be prepared for a visit from Campus Security, because getting my laptop back is in *my* best interests, even if it means getting you in serious trouble. But before I do that, maybe we should rethink the ethical subjectivism we thought was such a good idea!

Rethink indeed! The fatal flaw of ethical subjectivism is that it does not entail tolerance for the views or interests of others. It simply invests each individual with the moral authority to determine what is morally right and wrong, even if this means violating the rights or interests of others. Stealing a laptop is one example. But so are lying, cheating, mugging, raping, murdering, abusing children, being racist, being sexist, and virtually any other actions that are commonly considered to be "immoral" or "unethical." We can see now that ethical subjectivism does not really mean advocating a "live and let live" point of view, because it does not guarantee a tolerant acceptance of the rights and interests of others. Such tolerance of others would be an ethical value that transcends any individual's point of view. **Mohandas Gandhi**, the man responsible for India's independence and an individual considered by many to be morally enlightened, makes this point clear in the following passage:

> The golden rule of conduct, therefore, is mutual tolerance, seeing that we will never all think alike and we shall see Truth in fragments and from different angles of vision. Conscience is not the same thing for all. Whilst there, it is a good guide for individual conduct, imposition of that conduct upon all will be an insufferable interference with everybody's freedom of conscience.

So although ethical subjectivism is attractive on the surface, it becomes rather unattractive just below the surface. In fact, it is a recipe for moral anarchy, a world in which everyone does whatever they want, even if this means threatening or harming others. Why is ethical subjectivism so popular? Because people who espouse it haven't really thought critically about the implications of their views. When they say things like, "With moral choices, you have to go with your inner feeling, what feels right," or "Everyone is entitled to have their own beliefs," or "You have to be true to yourself,"—they are generally *assuming* a universal principle of tolerance. But once you commit yourself to a universal principle of tolerance—something like the belief that we're entitled to our beliefs *as long as they don't infringe on the rights or interests of others*—we are no longer ethical subjectivists. The ultimate moral authority for beliefs does not reside in the individual. Instead, *all individuals* are answerable to a

Mohandas Gandhi　(1869–1948) Political and Religious Leader. The leader of India's struggle for independence from Britain. Achieved independence through non-violent means and resistance, which was very influential on Martin Luther King Jr. and others.

higher value, namely, the principle of tolerance. And if they violate that principle, then they are morally wrong. And *that* moral belief poses a mortal threat to ethical subjectivism.

What are the roots of ethical subjectivism, and why does it seem to be particularly popular on college campuses and in our culture as a whole? Part of the answer lies in the confusion between **descriptive ethics** (what *is* the case) and **normative ethics** (what *ought to be* the case). Individuals have a diverse array of moral beliefs, which vary from person to person and culture to culture. To say this is to simply *describe* what is the case. But this is very different from saying that this is the way things *ought* to be. Yet this is exactly what ethical subjectivism stands for, the idea that each individual *should* have their own moral beliefs and that these beliefs are by definition *morally right*. According to this view, simply having a sincere moral belief gives that belief a moral authority by definition. But this move from a statement about what *is* the case ("People *have* many different moral beliefs") to a conclusion about what *ought* to be the case ("People *should* have different moral beliefs and they *should* act on these beliefs because they are right for them") is illogical and is known in philosophy as committing "the naturalistic fallacy." The philosopher **John Searle** explains:

> It is often said that one cannot derive an "ought" from an "is." . . . Put in more contemporary terminology, no set of descriptive statements can entail an *evaluative* statement without the addition of at least an evaluative premise. To believe otherwise is to commit the naturalistic fallacy.

Another reason people are drawn to ethical subjectivism—or at least, what they *think* is ethical subjectivism—has to do with a misunderstanding about the nature and logic of moral beliefs. There is a temptation to think that because people have different moral beliefs that these beliefs all have equal value, like matters of taste. The popular statement "Everyone is entitled to their own belief" suggests that no individual person has the right to say to another, "Your belief is wrong—you should believe *this* instead." In fact, it's often considered "bad manners" to question the beliefs of others, and to suggest that their beliefs are confused, unfounded, illogical, or outright wrong. This approach *seems* to be tolerant and democratic, and it often works well for matters of taste. However, as we noted earlier, it's an approach that doesn't work well for moral beliefs. For example, people's tastes in fashion, hairstyle, music, food, slang, and so on vary greatly. And by and large, most people acknowledge—in theory at least—that people are entitled to their individual preferences and that, as the old maxim states, "There is no accounting for taste." In other words, it doesn't make sense for you to say to someone else, "You are *wrong* to wear your hair in a mullet, sport a tattoo, and eat chunky peanut-butter directly from the jar." You might reasonably say, "That's not my style," or "I prefer a different look," but not that a person with different tastes is *wrong*. As evidence, look at a photograph of yourself from four or five years ago: you probably thought at the time that you looked quite stylish—how does it look now? A little embarrassing?

But moral beliefs are very, very different. If someone says "I agree with Hitler—there is only one super-race and all others are inferior," it *does* make sense to disagree and say, "I think your belief is unethical and wrong. On what rationale do you base it?" Similarly, if someone says "I think that the sexual abuse of children is all right," they are not simply stating a personal belief: they are enunciating a general moral value that they believe applies to *everyone*. That's the unique logic of moral beliefs: when I say that something is "right" or "wrong," I am by definition suggesting that it is right or wrong not just for me but for everyone.

In this way we can see that many people naïvely fall into ethical subjectivism because they fail to make a distinction between beliefs about taste and moral

Descriptive ethics An ethical approach that simply represents ethical beliefs without evaluating their accuracy or appropriateness.

Normative ethics An ethical approach that attempts to prescribe what ethical behavior should be accepted or become cultural norms.

John Searle (1932–) Philosopher of Mind. Mills Professor of the Philosophy of Mind and Language at the University of California, Berkeley. Has written influential articles on the philosophy of mind in which he rejects the notion that the mind can be understood as a computer program.

beliefs. You're entitled to have whatever opinion you want about matters of taste without justifying your belief or providing an explanation. But if you are advocating a moral belief, it is your responsibility to explain why you think such a belief should be adopted by others: what are the reasons, evidence, or rationale for such a belief.

This confused notion that "Everyone is entitled to their opinion, and everyone's opinion is equally valuable, no matter how uninformed, illogical, or ignorant," has been encouraged by influences in our culture. Developing informed beliefs about all important issues—moral and otherwise—is an ongoing challenge to our thinking abilities. In thinking about these and any other issues, we should ask ourselves two important questions:

- *What is my opinion about this issue?* Do you believe that human cloning should be pursued? What about whether "profiling" is a legitimate technique for improving public safety?
- *Is my opinion informed by evidence and reasons?* For each of the opinions that you have regarding these (and other) issues, can you answer the question, "*Why* do you have that opinion?" with intelligent and compelling reasons?

The truth is that while opinions are easy to come by, *informed* opinions are much more difficult to find. To express an opinion you merely have to say, "Well, I think . . ." or "I believe . . ." People are more than willing to make such pronouncements on virtually any subject. But to express an *informed* opinion means that you have some idea of what you're talking about: you have *explored* the subject, *examined* different points of view, *evaluated* the supporting reasons and evidence, and *synthesized* your analysis into a cogent and compelling conclusion. You can provide a clear, articulate explanation to the question *"Why do you believe that human cloning should be prohibited?"*

But isn't everyone "entitled to his or her opinion"? Yes and no. Living in a democracy with broad free-speech protections, people are allowed to think and express virtually *any* opinion, no matter how illogical, uninformed, or foolish. But this does not mean that they are entitled to have their uninformed opinions taken seriously, or that their opinions should be given the same consideration as *informed* opinions! We show respect for other people—and ourselves—by challenging them to think critically about their beliefs.

Ethical subjectivism can result in more damage to the social fabric of our lives than simply legitimating ignorant and ill-informed opinions. It can also encourage a sense of social isolation and moral apathy. A recent instance of what has come to be known as "The Kitty Genovese Syndrome" (named after the murder of a young woman in 1964 that was witnessed by 38 neighbors, none of whom made any effort to intervene) occurred in Detroit in 1995 on the Belle Isle Bridge. Deletha Word, a 33-year-old woman, was involved in a minor traffic accident. The enraged 19-year-old male driver of the other car began to beat her mercilessly as a crowd of people gradually assembled to watch. Again, not one person attempted to intervene, and some were even cheering the attacker on. Finally, in desperation to escape her attacker, Deletha Word jumped off the bridge and drowned. One man who jumped off after her in a unsuccessful attempt to save her observed that the crowd was "standing around like people taking an interest in sports." Once again, from the standpoint of ethical subjectivism, these morally indifferent people can be described as morally enlightened individuals, providing that they were doing what they "felt" was right by not "getting involved."

The point is that our moral beliefs, whether openly acknowledged or implicit, have real-world consequences. These beliefs are not simply academic exercises to be discussed in the hermetically sealed environments of college classrooms. A moral philosophy like ethical subjectivism can in fact contribute to the unraveling

◆ VISUAL PHILOSOPHY

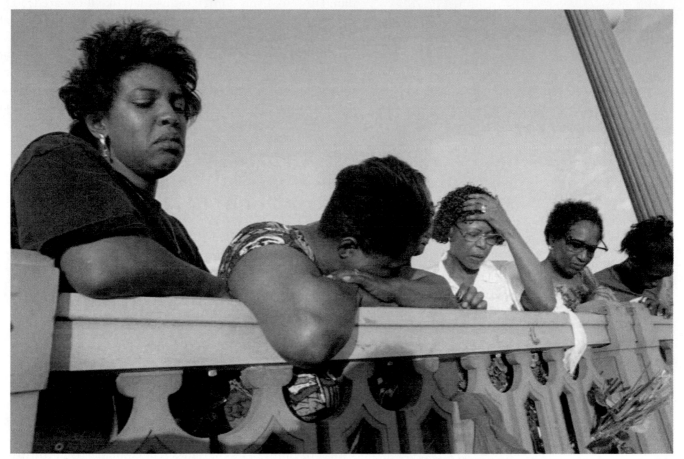

Friends and Relatives of Deletha Word Pray Tuesday,
August 22, 1995 on the Belle Isle Bridge in Detroit

Some people believe that the popularity of a belief in ethical subjectivism in our culture contributes to the kind of moral apathy displayed when a crowd of people watched Deletha Word jump to her death trying to escape an attacker. Do you agree? Why?

of our social fabric and undermining of our sense of community. Rather than viewing ourselves as tied to one another through a sense of social relationships and mutual responsibilities, people can come to see themselves as on their own, obligated to pursue only their own personal interests. They "don't want to get involved," do not consider themselves to be "their brother's (or sister's) keeper." Were this to become a prevalent moral philosophy, the quality of life for all would be greatly diminished.

But is ethical subjectivism in fact the prevalent norm in most cultures? The answer is a clear "no," a fact that casts doubt on its credibility as a moral theory. In all cultures, just because an individual "feels" like raping, robbing, assaulting, or murdering does not mean that the other members of the society believe that the actions are morally justified. Quite the contrary. Such individuals are morally condemned and generally punished for violating the accepted moral norms. And as we shall see in the next session on *ethical relativism,* we also con-

How "Ethically Subjective" Are My Ethics?

5.4

PHILOSOPHER'S NOTEBOOK

- Keeping in mind the issues discussed in this section, how would you respond to someone making the following statements:

  "In moral situations, you have to go with your inner feeling, what feels right."

  "What's right for one person may be wrong for someone else."

  "As long as you are being true to yourself, then you're morally right."

- In your own words, provide a clear definition of ethical subjectivism. What is attractive about this ethical theory? What are the fatal flaws that undermine the credibility of this approach?

- Identify some moral beliefs that an ethical subjectivist might hold but that you consider to be dangerous.

- Consider your own moral beliefs. What is the basis for your beliefs? Do any fall into the category of ethical subjectivism? Which ones? Why?

- Which moral beliefs do you consider to be based on the needs and interests of others rather than simply your personal feelings?

- Identify some moral beliefs that you consider to be self-evident, for instance:

  All people are created equal.

  Abusing children is wrong.

  Human slavery is unethical.

  Then explain why you consider your examples to be self-evident.

Herodotus (c. 5th Century B.C.E.) Ancient Greek Historian. Considered to be the world's first historian. Was interested in the various cultures of the world and maintained no one culture can be considered as superior to another.

Cultural relativism The view that cultural norms determine what is ethically right and wrong.

demn the leaders of countries who we consider to be acting immorally: Adolf Hitler, Idi Amin, Slobodan Milosevic, Saddam Hussein. Even though individuals like these are leaders of countries in which they establish the law of the land based on what they "feel" is right, the majority of the civilized world condemns their policies of genocide, terror, and senseless brutality toward innocent citizens. Whether on an individual level or social level, most people do not consider ethical subjectivism to be an appropriate or enlightened moral philosophy of life.

Cultural Relativism: *Each Culture Determines What Is Morally Right*

For if anyone, no matter who, were given the opportunity of choosing from amongst all the nations of the world the set of beliefs which he thought best, he would inevitably, after careful consideration of their relative merits, choose that of his own country. Everyone without exception believes his own native customs . . . to be the best.

—Herodotus

Human sacrifice, slavery, cannibalism, torture, genocide, child abuse—these, and every other possible atrocity that humans are capable of, have been considered morally "right" in various times and various cultures. In a more neutral category we also find a nearly infinite variety of cultural/moral values related to marriage (the number and age of brides), sexuality (homosexuality, genital mutilation), treatment of children and the elderly, and every other dimension of human experience. This extraordinary diversity of ethical perspectives has led some people to conclude that moral values are nothing more than the mutual agreement of various groups of people and so are relative to each culture's unique context. In other words, if cannibalism, or slavery, or polygamy are common practice in a certain culture, then these practices are *morally right* for that culture. No one outside that culture has the right to criticize or evaluate these beliefs as being "morally wrong." Any culture's moral values are right simply because they are that culture's values.

Cultural relativism is thus ethical subjectivism on a social level. Ethical subjectivism contends that each individual determines what is morally right and wrong. Cultural relativism makes a similar argument with the exception that it is the entire culture—not each individual—that determines what is morally right and wrong. Both ethical theories are driven by the diversity of moral viewpoints that we find in the human species. Because we each have our own unique set of moral values, ethical subjectivism argues that it doesn't make sense to search for universal moral standards that transcend individuals. Analogously, cultural relativism contends that because every culture has its own unique set of moral values, it doesn't make sense to try to identify universal moral standards that transcend all cultures.

One of the most passionate and articulate exponents of cultural relativism is **Ruth Benedict** (1887–1948), an American anthropologist whose book *Patterns of Cultures* (1935) was enormously influential. For Benedict, the term *morality* should be defined as "socially approved customs"—nothing more, nothing less. There are no universal values that we can use to evaluate the moral values of any culture; there are only the moral values that each culture creates.

To a certain extent, Benedict (and other social scientists such as Emile Durkheim, Franz Boas, and William Graham Sumner) were reacting to what they perceived to be the cultural imperialism of the West—the assumption by some that the moral values of Western Europe and America were morally superior to the moral values of more "primitive" cultures. From this perspective, it was the moral "obligation" of Western culture to "educate" the rest of the world regarding these more "enlightened" values.

Many of these thinkers used as a framework the ideas of **Charles Darwin**, whose books *The Origin of the Species* (1859) and *The Descent of Man* (1871) introduced the theory of evolution to explain the biological development of life on earth. Appropriating the general concepts of evolutionary theory without its scientific detail, these Social Darwinists proposed that moral values also had evolved over time in the same way that forms of life had. The moral values of "primitive" cultures represented early stages of moral development, whereas modern Western culture represented the pinnacle of moral evolution.

Benedict and her colleagues viewed Social Darwinism as being culturally arrogant, socially destructive, and factually inaccurate, and they set out to demonstrate this through anthropological research and analysis.

> Early anthropologists tried to arrange all traits of different cultures in an evolutionary sequence from the earliest forms to their final development in Western civilization. But there is no reason to suppose that by discussing Australian religion rather than our own we are uncovering primordial religion, or that by discussing Iroquois social organization we are returning to the mating habits of man's early ancestors.
>
> Since we are forced to believe that the race of man is one species, it follows that man everywhere has an equally long history behind him. Some primitive tribes may have held relatively closer to primordial forms of behavior than civilized man, but this can only be relative and our guesses are as likely to be wrong as right. There is no justification for identifying some one contemporary primitive custom with the original type of human behavior.
>
> —*Ruth Benedict*

For Benedict, the values of any one culture are neither superior nor inferior to those of another—they are all on the same moral plane. Each culture is thought of as a self-contained cultural entity, a social organism in which its values, practices, and belief systems have developed as an integrated whole. It is not possible, nor appropriate, for any culture to judge the moral enlightenment of other cultures. We must accept them as they are and try to understand how they evolved in their unique fashion.

Which perspective is right? Do moral values evolve to higher, more enlightened levels? Are there universal moral standards that can be applied to every culture? Or should we adopt the perspective of cultural relativism and acknowledge that all moral values are equal, no matter how offensive and unacceptable we may personally find them? To answer these crucial ethical questions, we need to let proponents of these views make their strongest possible case, and then engage in critical thinking and philosophical reflection. The following

RUTH BENEDICT
(1887–1948)
American Anthropologist. One of the first prominent women in American anthropology and social science. In *Patterns of Culture* (1945) advocated cultural relativism and attempted to apply individual psychological concepts to whole groups.

Charles Darwin (1809–1882)
Scientist. In *On the Origin of Species* (1859) advanced his theory of evolution and natural selection. Many social scientists picked up on his theory and tried to explain the development of cultures in much the same way.

passages are taken from Ruth Benedict's essay, "Anthropology and the Abnormal." Benedict begins by articulating her central thesis and explaining her rationale.

Benedict, *Anthropology and the Abnormal*

Modern social anthropology has become more and more a study of the varieties and common elements of cultural environment and the consequences of these in human behavior. For such a study of diverse social orders primitive peoples fortunately provide a laboratory not yet entirely vitiated by the spread of a standardized world-wide civilization. Dyaks and Hopis, Figians and Yakuts are significant for psychological and sociological study because only among these simpler peoples has there been sufficient isolation to give opportunity for the development of localized social forms. In the higher cultures the standardization of custom and belief over a couple of continents has given a false sense of the inevitability of the particular forms that have gained currency, and we need to turn to a wider survey in order to check the conclusions we hastily based upon this near-universality of familiar customs. Most of the simpler cultures did not gain the wide currency of the one which, out of our experience, we identify with human nature, but this was for various historical reasons, and certainly not for any that gives us as its carriers a monopoly of social good or of social sanity. Modern civilization, from this point of view, becomes not a necessary pinnacle of human achievement but one entry in a long series of possible adjustments.

Benedict's central thesis is encapsulated in the last two sentences: modern civilization does not embody an evolutionary "pinnacle of human achievement" but is rather "one entry in a long series of possible adjustments." From her perspective, every culture uses its own unique cultural "recipe" to create its social structure and maintain its community. Moral beliefs are an essential ingredient in the recipe, as are customs, rituals, political structures, religious views, and other core beliefs. But it is not possible to say that one recipe is "better" than another–they simply represent different ways people use to organize themselves into social groups. But, someone might object, doesn't the widespread acceptance of Western moral values suggest that these are more perfect embodiments of "social good"? Not at all, counters Benedict. The cultural dominance of Western values, and the concept of "human nature" that goes along with them, simply reflects the fact that these cultures have been successful in conquering less powerful cultures and replacing their indigenous belief systems with Western values. This has created a "false sense of the inevitability" of the "standardized" Western customs and beliefs. Rather than uncritically accepting these standardized values as morally superior, we need to conduct "a wider survey in order to check the conclusions we hastily base upon this near-universality of familiar customs."

In comparing non-Western cultures with Western culture we find obvious differences with respect to social practices involving marriage and religion that can be easily described. But what about the deeper levels of cultural beliefs and values, fundamental conceptual categories like what the culture considers "normal" and "abnormal"? What do we find if we explore and compare these deeper dimensions of their social framework? Results that are quite astonishing. Practices and values that are considered to be categorically "abnormal" in Western culture are found to be functioning productively and harmoniously as perfectly "normal" and even honorable in other cultures. Benedict goes on to provide several

VISUAL PHILOSOPHY

Maniere dont elles S'ENTERRENT toutes vivantes avec le Corps de leurs EPOUX.

Woman Being Buried Alive Along with her Dead Husband at a Funeral Ceremony in the East Indies

Cultural relativists believe that cultural practices (such as that depicted in this engraving) determine what is ethically right and wrong. Do you agree? Why?

provocative examples of such normal/abnormal cultural ways of thinking and behaving.

Homosexuality is an excellent example. . . . A tendency toward this trait in our culture exposes an individual to all the conflicts to which all aberrants are always exposed, and we tend to identify the consequences of this conflict with homosexuality. But these consequences are obviously local and cultural. Homosexuals in many societies are not incompetent, but they may be if the culture asks adjustments of them that would strain any man's vitality. Wherever homosexuality has been given an honorable place in any society, those to whom it is congenital have filled adequately the honorable roles society assigns to them. Plato's *Republic* is, of course, the most convincing statement of such a reading of homosexuality. It is presented as one of the major means to the good life, and it was generally so regarded in Greece at that time. . . .

Benedict, *Anthropology and the Abnormal*

Benedict's point is that although homosexuality is considered as aberrant and even immoral behavior in some cultures, in other cultures it is tolerated and even positively endorsed. This fact seems to suggest that how homosexual behavior is perceived is a direct result of that culture's social "recipe," and it is not linked to any universal human nature. Thus it makes no sense to condemn the practice of homosexuality in a culture that considers it normal behavior, simply because in your culture it is considered abnormal. Benedict goes on to consider a less common, more extreme example of the normal/abnormal phenomenon.

Benedict, *Anthropology and the Abnormal*

The most spectacular illustrations of the extent to which normality may be culturally defined are those cultures where an abnormality of our culture is the cornerstone of their social structure. It is not possible to do justice to these possibilities in a short discussion. A recent study of an island northwest in Melanesia by Fortune describes a society built upon traits which we regard as beyond the border of paranoia. In this tribe the exogamic groups look upon each other as prime manipulators of black magic, so that one marries always into an enemy group which remains for life one's deadly and unappeasable foes. They look upon a good garden crop as a confession of theft, for everyone is engaged in making magic to induce into this garden the productiveness of his neighbors'; therefor no secrecy in the island is so rigidly insisted upon as the secrecy of a man's harvesting of his yams. Their polite phrase at the acceptance of a gift, is "And if you now poison me, how shall I repay you this present?" Their preoccupation with poisoning is constant; no woman ever leaves her cooking pot for a moment untended. Even the great affinal economic exchanges that are characteristic of this Melanesian culture area are quite altered in Dobu since they are incompatible with this fear and distrust that pervades the culture. They go farther and people the whole world outside their own quarters with such malignant spirits that all-night feasts and ceremonials simply do not occur here. They have even rigorous religiously enforced customs that forbid the sharing of seed even in one family group. Anyone else's food is deadly poison to you, so that communality of stores is out of the question. For some months before harvest the whole society is on the verge of starvation, but if one falls to the temptation and eats up one's seed yams, one is an outcast and a beachcomber for life. There is no coming back. It involves, as a matter of course, divorce and the breaking of all social ties.

Now in this society where no one may work with another and no one may share with another, Fortune describes the individual who was regarded by all his fellows as crazy. He was not one of those who periodically ran amok and, beside himself and frothing at the mouth, fell with a knife upon anyone he could reach. Such behavior they did not regard as putting anyone outside the pale. They did not even put the individuals who were known to be liable to these attacks under any kind of control. They merely fled when they saw the attack coming on and kept out of the way. "He would be all right tomorrow." But there was one man of sunny, kindly disposition who liked work and liked to be helpful. The compulsion was too strong for him to repress it in favor of the opposite tendencies of his culture. Men and women never spoke of him without laughing; he was silly and simple and definitely crazy. Nevertheless, to the ethnologist used to a culture that has, in Christianity, made his type the model of all virtue, he seemed a pleasant fellow.

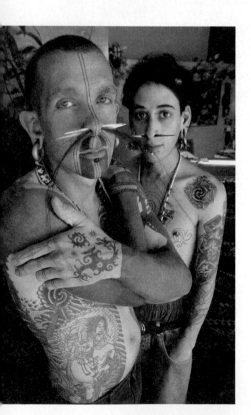

Do you agree with Ruth Benedict's statement that "Morality differs in every society and is a convenient term for socially approved habits"? Why?

What a fascinating example! Living in this Melanesian culture would, for most people, be like living in a world turned upside down. In sharp contrast to the values of kindness, social cooperation, harmonious collaboration, friendships, and family ties that are prized in many cultures, the Melanesians view all of these as dangerously abnormal. Their culture is paranoia personified, as all individuals assume that everyone else is out to do them harm. In this world of seemingly inverted values, the aberrant "crazy" person is the one who has a compulsion to be friendly, trusting, and helpful. Once again, Benedict's point is that moral values that we may assume to be a universal part of our divine or human natures are actually merely the consequence of the social adaptation of particular cultures. But in other cultures, like the Melanesians, these adaptations can take a very different—and equally legitimate—form.

A useful way to understand Benedict's point is to consider the case of language. People are born with a basic linguistic capacity, a genetically transferred ability that is hardwired into our DNA. This linguistic ability allows us to invest sounds with meaning and organize words together into syntactic combinations, giving us the ability to think and communicate. However, the *precise* language one learns is determined by the culture within which one is born. Each language has selected a distinct set of sounds to carry meaning and evolved its own set of grammatical rules to link individual words and ideas together into more complex combinations. Although these various languages seem very different on the surface, most linguists believe that they all reflect an underlying "depth grammar" and meaning-giving abilities.

Anthropologists like Benedict believe that the same is true of cultural customs, belief structures, and moral values. Faced with the need to develop ways to live together and survive as an integrated community, each culture has developed its own specific cultural adaptations. Seen in this way, it makes no sense to say that one culture's adaptations are "better" or "more enlightened" than another's, any more than it makes sense to argue that one language (Russian or Arabic, for example) is superior to another language (French or Chinese).

Thus, according to Benedict, your specific beliefs regarding morality, religion, and every other cultural practice is entirely dependent on an accident of birth. Because humans are so malleable, had you been born in a different culture, you would have ended up with an entirely different cultural identity.

The vast majority of the individuals in any group are shaped to the fashion of that culture. In other words, most individuals are plastic to the molding force of the society into which they are born. In a society that values trance, as in India, they will have supernormal experience. In a society that institutionalizes homosexuality, they will be homosexual. In a society that sets the gathering of possessions as the chief human objective, they will amass property. The deviants, whatever the type of behavior the culture has institutionalized, will remain few in number, and there seems no more difficulty in molding that vast malleable majority to the "normality" of what we consider an aberrant trait, such as delusions of reference, than to the normality of such accepted behavior patterns as acquisitiveness. The small proportion of the number of the deviants in any culture is not a function of the sure instinct with which that society has built itself upon the fundamental sanities, but of the universal fact that, happily, the majority of mankind quite readily take any shape that is presented to them. . . .

THINK CRITICALLY

5.5

PHILOSOPHER'S NOTEBOOK

Cultural Relativism and My Moral Perspective

- When we explored ethical subjectivism in the previous section, we saw that it seems to commit the naturalistic fallacy—trying to derive an "ought" from an "is." Can the same criticism be leveled against cultural relativism?

- Critics of cultural relativism have contended that it is self-contradictory. On the one hand, cultural relativists want to assert that there are absolutely *no* universal moral values that apply to all cultures. On the other hand, they seek to maintain that, as a universal value, members of one culture have no right to evaluate the moral values of another culture. Do you think this criticism of cultural relativism is valid? Why or why not?

- Cultural relativism seems to assume that in most cultures, the majority of people agree about basic moral values. Although this may be true in smaller, simpler cultures, this seems untrue with large, complex, modern cultures. How would a cultural relativist go about determining the prevailing view on moral values in a culture that is deeply divided? Is this a fatal flaw?

- The history of civilization includes individuals who stood alone against the prescribed moral values of their culture which they considered to be immoral. Who are some of these individuals? Why do so many people admire them? How would cultural relativism view these individuals: as courageous heroes and heroines or as abnormal deviants? Does this pose a problem for cultural relativism? Why?

- Several years ago a family that had immigrated to Minnesota was caught in a clash of cultural values. Consistent with cultural practices in his home country, the father of two daughters, aged 13 and 14, arranged marriages for them with two men in their thirties. The twin marriage ceremonies was an event of great celebration, with many friends and relatives attending. The day after the ceremony, the two young "brides" went to local law enforcement authorities, complaining about their situation. Their parents were arrested and charged with child endangerment and the two "grooms" were charged with statutory rape. All four adults stated that it never occurred to them that they were doing anything wrong. Nevertheless, they were convicted. How would Ruth Benedict analyze this event? How would you analyze this event?

Benedict, *Anthropology and the Abnormal*

Benedict concludes that because one's moral and religious beliefs are contingent on one's specific cultural experience, there can be no universal moral values that apply to all cultures. What we think of as moral values are simply the customs—the approved ways of thinking and behaving—that each culture has determined to be "right." Trying to find additional meaning in the concept of "moral values" is a lost cause.

Benedict, *Anthropology and the Abnormal*

 Benedict, Ruth, *Anthropology and the Abnormal*

We recognize that morality differs in every society and is a convenient term for socially approved habits. Mankind has always preferred to say, "It is morally good," rather than "It is habitual," and the fact of this preference is matter enough for a critical science of ethics. But historically the two phrases are synonymous. ■

THINK PHILOSOPHICALLY
Analyzing Ruth Benedict
5.6

- What is your personal reaction when you learn about moral values and practices in other cultures that are very different from your own? Do you agree with Benedict that we should strive to be nonjudgmental and simply accept these contrasting moral codes as different but equal to our own? Why or why not?

- In addition to variations in moral beliefs *between* different cultures, Benedict believes that the same relativistic principles apply to different time periods *within* the same culture. For example, 200 years ago in the United States, human slavery was not only legal, it was also considered by many (including a number of the country's "founding fathers") to be morally acceptable and even laudatory. In other words, in 1780 slavery *was* morally right. What is your reaction to this perspective? On what reasoning do you base your point of view?

- Benedict states that the statement "It is morally good" is equivalent to "It is habitual." Are these two statements equivalent in meaning? If not, identify the ways in which these two statements differ in meaning.

Ethical Absolutism: *Some Moral Values Are Universal and Apply to All Individuals and Cultures*

Ethical absolutism contends that at least some moral values apply to every individual and every culture in every time period. This is in sharp contrast to ethical relativism, which includes the two ethical theories we just considered:

- Ethical subjectivism: All moral values are relative to the individual.
- Cultural relativism: All moral values are relative to the specific culture.

Ethical absolutism The view that at least some moral values are universal and apply to all individuals and cultures.

Ethical relativism The view that all moral values are relative to the individual or specific culture.

For the ethical absolutist, a moral value such as "Human slavery is wrong" applies to all individuals and cultures. It doesn't matter if some individuals—or many individuals—believe that slavery is ethically acceptable: for the ethical absolutist, these individuals *must* be wrong because prohibiting slavery is a universal value. Analogously, it doesn't matter if human slavery is an integral component of a culture's social and economic fabric: slavery is morally wrong, and this moral evaluation is independent of whatever customs and moral practices a particular culture holds. Finally, for the ethical absolutist, the period of time being evaluated does not matter—human slavery is morally wrong today and it was also morally wrong 200 years ago in the United States.

Which view is right? Are moral values relative to an individual or specific culture? Or are they universal, applying to all humans in all cultures and all time periods? In the previous Think Critically activity we suggested some difficulties that a moral relativist faces. In the following reading, the philosopher **W. T. Stace** (1886–1967) examines some of these difficulties at some length, while also considering the arguments for ethical absolutism. Stace begins by providing a very clear and succinct analysis of the ethical absolutist perspective.

> **W. T. STACE**
> (1886–1967)
> British Philosopher. *The Concept of Morals* provides a lucid analysis of moral theories and a compelling defense of ethical absolutism.

Ethical Absolutism

Stace, *The Concept of Morals*

According to the absolutists there is but one eternally true and valid moral code. This moral code applies with rigid impartiality to all men. What is a duty for me must likewise be a duty for you. And this will be true whether you are an Englishman, a Chinaman, or a Hottentot. If cannibalism is an abomination in England or America, it is an abomination in Central Africa, notwithstanding that the African may think otherwise. The fact that he sees nothing wrong in his cannibal practices does not make them for him morally right. They are as much contrary to morality for him as they are for us. . . . There is not one law for one man or race of men, another for another. There is not one moral standard for Europeans, another for Indians, another for Chinese. There is but one law, one standard, one morality, for all men. And this standard, this law, is absolute and unvarying.

Moreover, as the one moral law extends its dominion over all the corners of the earth, so too it is not limited in its application by any considerations of time or period. That which is right now was right in the centuries of Greece and Rome, nay, in the very ages of the cave man. That which is evil now was evil then. If slavery is morally wicked today, it was morally wicked among the ancient Athenians, notwithstanding that their greatest men accepted it as a necessary condition of human society. Their opinion did not make slavery a moral good for them. It only showed that they were, in spite of their otherwise noble conceptions, ignorant of what is truly right and good in this matter.

Stace then goes on to address the central thesis of Ruth Benedict and other cultural relativists—namely, the diversity of moral values and customs from culture to culture.

Stace, *The Concept of Morals*

The ethical absolutist recognizes as a fact that moral customs and moral ideas differ from country to country and from age to age. This indeed seems manifest and not to be disputed. We think slavery morally wrong, the Greeks thought it morally unobjectionable. The inhabitants of New Guinea certainly have very different moral ideas from ours. But the fact that the Greeks or the inhabitants of New Guinea think something right does not make it right, even for them. Nor does the fact that we think the same things wrong make them wrong. They are *in themselves* either right and wrong. What we have to do is to discover which they are. What anyone thinks makes no difference. It is here just as it is in matters of physical science. We believe the earth to be a globe. Our ancestors may have thought it flat. This does not show that it *was* flat, and it is *now* a globe. What it shows is that men having in other ages been ignorant about the shape of the earth have now learned the truth. So if the Greeks thought slavery morally legitimate, this does not indicate that it was for them and in that age morally legitimate, but rather that they were ignorant of the truth of the matter.

This is a crucial point that Stace is making: the ethical absolutist believes that at least some moral values are independent of human belief and practice, just as the physical facts of the universe are independent. But what are the grounds for the independent status of moral values? We discover the truth of the physical universe through scientific investigation. How can we discover the truth about moral values?

That is precisely the problem that most ethical theories are designed to solve, theories that we will be considering in these two chapters. Stace continues his analysis.

Stace, *The Concept of Morals*

The ethical absolutist is not indeed committed to the opinion that his own, or our own, moral code is the true one. Theoretically at least he might hold that slavery is ethically justifiable, that the Greeks knew better than we do about this, that ignorance of the true morality lies with us and not with them. All that he is actually committed to is the opinion that, whatever the true moral code may be, it is always the same for all men in all ages. His view is not at all inconsistent with the belief that humanity has still much to learn in moral matters. If anyone were to assert that in five hundred years the moral conceptions of the present day will appear as barbarous to the people of that age as the moral conceptions of the middle ages appear to us now, he need not deny it. If anyone were to assert that the ethics of Christianity are by no means final, and will be superseded in future ages by vastly nobler moral ideals, he need not deny this either. For it is of the essence of his creed to believe that morality is in some sense objective, non manmade, not produced by human opinion; that its principles are real truths about which men have to learn—just as they have to learn about the shape of the world—about which they may have been ignorant in the past, and about which therefore they may well be ignorant now.

Stace then proceeds to provide a similarly lucid account of ethical relativism, beginning with his belief that the motivation that powers these movements is a reaction *against* ethical absolutism. In fact, as we saw, it was Ruth Benedict and her colleagues' opposition to what they saw to be Western cultural imperialism—the view that Western values were superior to all others and should be universally adopted by all cultures—that helped shape her cultural relativist perspective.

Stace, *The Concept of Morals*

Any ethical position which denies that there is a single moral standard which is equally applicable to all men at all times may fairly be called a species of ethical relativity. There is not, the relativist asserts, merely one moral law, one code, one standard. There are many moral laws, codes, standards. What morality ordains in one place or age may be quite different from what morality ordains in another place or age. The moral code of Chinamen is quite different from that of Europeans, that of Africans quite different from both. Any morality, therefore, is relative to the age, the place, and the circumstances in which it is found. It is in no sense absolute.

Stace goes on to emphasize a crucial dimension of ethical relativism, namely, that it is not simply providing a *descriptive account* of the diverse moral values of various cultures—it is also providing a *normative endorsement* of these values. Ethical relativism, in other words, is stating that each culture's moral values, whatever they may be, *are* morally right.

Stace, *The Concept of Morals*

This does not mean merely —as one might at first sight be inclined to suppose—that the very same kind of action which is *thought* right in one country and period may be *thought* wrong in another. This would be a mere platitude, the truth of which everyone would have to admit. Even the absolutist would admit this—would even wish to emphasize it—since he is well aware that different peoples have different sets of moral ideas, and his whole point is that some of these sets of ideas are false. What the relativist means to assert is, not this platitude, but that the very same kind of action which *is* right in one country and period may *be* wrong in another. And this, far from being a platitude, is a very startling assertion. . . . Moral right *means* what people think morally right. It has no other meaning.

At this point you might be finding that your views regarding moral values are becoming more confused rather than more clear. This is a perfectly natural process. Why? Because when people form views uncritically—as many do when it comes to moral values—their conclusions may not reflect their best thoughtful, insightful analysis. For example, you might believe that all values are relative to specific individuals or cultures, a misguided "live and let live" perspective, without fully appreciating the disturbing and unintended consequences of such a view. Or you might believe that you have a universal code in hand, derived from religion or respected authority such as the Ten Commandments, the Book of Mormon, or the Qur'an. But such moral codes pose problems of their own; what do we do when universal moral codes conflict? What is the justification for asserting that *our* moral code is the one, true universal set of values to which everyone ought to adhere? In short, once you begin the process of philosophical examination of the core issues of virtually any area of life experience, the initial effect is likely to be one of confusion, as you begin to appreciate the complexity of the situation. This questioning doubt and confusion is the engine that drives philosophical inquiry, and it stands in distinct contrast to the unreflectively simplistic views of nonphilosophical understanding. But be assured that as you continue your critical analysis of moral values—and other areas of philosophical investigation—that you are in the process of developing an informed understanding and building a solid foundation for your views, which you will be able to explain and justify through compelling analysis.

How do we decide which moral theory is correct: ethical relativism or ethical absolutism? We need to think critically, exploring and evaluating the rationale for each view, and come to an intelligent conclusion. To this end, Stace proceeds to critically evaluate the arguments supporting each of these ethical points of view.

Arguments in Favor of Ethical Relativity

Stace, *The Concept of Morals*

. . . the first (argument) is that which relies upon the actual varieties of moral "standards" found in the world. It was easy enough to believe in a single absolute morality in older times when there was no anthropology, when all humanity was divided clearly into two groups, Christian peoples and the "heathen." . . . Greater knowledge has brought greater tolerance. We can no longer exalt our own morality as alone true, while dismissing all other moralities as false or inferior. The investigations of anthropologists have shown that there exist side by side in the world a bewildering variety of moral codes. On this topic endless volumes have been written, masses of evidence piled up. Anthropologists have ransacked the Melanesian islands, the jungles of New Guinea, the steppes of Siberia, the deserts of Australia, the forests of central Africa, and have brought back with them countless examples of weird, extravagant, and fantastic "moral" customs with which to confound us. We learn that all kinds of horrible practices are, in this, that, or the other place, regarded as essential to virtue. We find that there is nothing, or next to nothing, which has always and everywhere been regarded as morally good by all men. Where then is our universal morality? Can we, in the face of all this evidence, deny that it is nothing but an empty dream?

This argument, taken by itself, is a very weak one. It relies upon a single set of facts—the variable moral customs of the world. But this variability of moral ideas is admitted by both parties to the dispute, and is capable of ready explanation upon the hypothesis of either party. The relativist says that the facts are to be explained by the non-existence of any absolute moral standard. The absolutist says that they are to be explained by human ignorance of what the absolute moral standard is. And he can truly point out that men have differed widely in their opinions about all manners of topics including the subject-matters of the physical sciences—just as much as they differ about morals. And if the various different opinions which men have held about the shape of the earth do not prove that it has no one real shape, neither do the various opinions which they have held about morality prove that there is no one true morality.

Thus the facts can be explained equally plausibly on either hypothesis. There is nothing in the facts themselves which compels us to prefer the relativistic hypothesis to that of the absolutist. And therefore the argument fails to prove the relativist conclusion. If that conclusion is to be established, it must be by means of other considerations.

In the conflict between ethical relativism and ethical absolutism, this is a very important point that Stace is making. We saw that Ruth Benedict rested her entire argument for ethical relativism on the broad diversity of moral values across cultures, using this basic argument form:

- Ethical values vary from culture to culture and time period to time period in a bewildering and conflicting array of moral codes.
- Therefore, there are no universal values that exist independently—all moral values are relative to a specific culture and are "right" for that culture.

But ethical absolutism doesn't dispute the descriptive facts of cultural variation in moral values: it's in the *interpretation* of this data where the conflict lies. For the ethical relativist, this cultural diversity suggests the normative conclusion that there are no absolute moral values that can be applied to all cultures. But as we noted on page 225, this "leap of logic" commits the naturalistic fallacy: simply describing a situation provides no evidence for concluding that this is the way things *should* be. And this is the ethical absolutist's point: yes, there is a diversity of moral values across cultures; but this simply means that some cultures are not as morally enlightened as others because they have not accepted certain universal moral values that apply to all individuals, in all cultures, in all time periods.

Stace then goes on to consider a second argument for ethical relativity, which is in the form of a critique of ethical absolutism. The form of the argument is something like this:

- Ethical absolutists have never been able to establish a solid foundation or justification on which a universal set of values can be built.
- Therefore, there is no such foundation or justification for universal values, so we must conclude that all moral values are relative.

Stace, *The Concept of Morals*

(Another) argument in favor of ethical relativity . . . consists in alleging that no one has ever been able to discover upon what foundation an absolute morality could rest, or from what source a universally binding moral code could derive its authority.

If, for example, it is an absolute and unalterable moral rule that all men ought to be unselfish, from whence does this *command* issue? For a command it certainly is, phrase it how you please. There is no difference in meaning between the sentence "You ought to be unselfish" and the sentence "Be unselfish." Now a command implies a commander. An obligation implies some authority which obliges. Who is this commander, what is this authority? Thus the vastly difficult question is raised of *the basis of moral obligation.* Now the argument of the relativist would be that it is impossible to find any basis for a universally binding moral law; but that it is quite easy to discover a basis for morality if moral codes are admitted to be variable, ephemeral, and relative to time, place, and circumstance.

Naturally, simply because a universally accepted set of moral values has not yet been developed does not mean that it *won't* be developed at some point in the future. And it also doesn't mean that such a moral code hasn't already been developed but has not yet been universally accepted. Nevertheless, the challenge to provide a compelling rationale is central for ethical absolutism. Traditional attempts to provide such a foundation have often been religious in nature, embedding the moral code within the metaphysic of a specific religion. In these cases, the universal authority for the moral values is typically divine or supernatural in nature: for example, "Killing is wrong because God prohibits it." But the fact that there are so many different religions with divergent codes of ethics tends to put this approach back in the ethical relativism quandary, namely, "Who is to say that *this* religion, along with its moral code, is the one true approach that should be universally accepted?" We will consider the key issues regarding the philosophy of religion in chapter 7, but for now we are interested in approaches to ethical absolutism that are not dependent on accepting specific religious beliefs (that is, a *secular* approach to moral values).

To sum up, these are the two arguments in favor of ethical relativism:

- The fact that moral values vary widely from culture to culture, age to age. *But*, inferring from this descriptive statement of fact that this moral relativism represents the way morality *ought* to be viewed commits the naturalistic fallacy.
- The fact that no system of moral values has yet been universally accepted. *But*, although this is the central challenge confronting ethical absolutism, the fact that such a moral system has not yet been universally accepted doesn't mean that it shouldn't be or that it won't be at some point in the future.

William James

Having considered arguments supporting ethical relativism, it's time to explore arguments critical of this view. Stace articulates several serious concerns with the ethical relativist position. The first argument is analogous to a point of view articulated by **William James** in his analysis of whether there is the possibility that we can make free choices. Those thinkers committed to determinism contend that all human actions are caused by influences beyond any person's control. Indeterminists counter that even though our actions may be subject to the effects of influences, we nevertheless retain the ability to make free choices independent of these influences, choices for which we are personally responsible. Which view is right? Are we free or not free? James frames his answer by stating what he considers to be the criteria we should use to evaluate theories and determine what is true.

> The arguments I am about to urge all proceed on two suppositions: first, when we make theories about the world and discuss them with one another, we do so in order to attain a conception of things which shall give us subjective satisfaction; and second, if there be two conceptions, and the one seems to us, on the whole, more rational than the other, we are entitled to suppose that the more rational one is the truer of the two. . . .

James's point is that humans use their intellectual abilities to create concepts and develop theories to help them understand and give meaning to their lived experience. When theories conflict with one another, how do we decide which theories are the "best"? In the final analysis, we should endorse those theories that provide the most rational, complete, and persuasive understanding of our lived experience. Stace employs analogous epistemological criteria to the questions of "Are moral values relative or absolute? Which theory is correct?"

Stace, *The Concept of Morals*

Ethical relativity, in asserting that the moral standards of particular social groups are the only standards which exist, renders meaningless all propositions which attempt to compare these standards with one another in respect of their moral worth. And this is a very serious matter indeed. We are accustomed to think that the moral ideas of one nation or social group may be "higher" or "lower" than those of another. . . . We habitually compare one civilization with another and judge the sets of ethical ideas to be found in them to be some better, some worse. The fact that such judgments are very difficult to make with any justice, and that they are frequently made on very superficial and prejudiced grounds, has no bearing on the question now at issue. The question is whether such judgments have any *meaning*. We habitually assume that they have.

William James (1842–1910)
American Pragmatist. With C.S. Peirce, founded the philosophy of Pragmatism. Also contributed much to the psychology of religion in *The Varieties of Religious Experience* (1903).

But on the basis of ethical relativity they can have none whatever. For the relativist must hold that there is no *common* standard which can be applied to the various civilizations judged. Any such comparison of moral standards implies the existence of some superior standard which is applicable to both. And the existence of any such standard is precisely what the relativist denies. . . .

What is true of comparisons between the moral standards of different races will also be true of comparisons between those of different ages. It is not unusual to ask such questions as whether the standard of our own day is superior to that which existed among our ancestors five hundred years ago. And when we remember that our ancestors employed slaves, practiced barbaric physical tortures, and burnt people alive, we may be inclined to think that it is. At any rate we assume that the question is one which has meaning and is capable of rational discussion. But if the ethical relativist is right, whatever we assert on this subject must be totally meaningless. For here again there is no common standard which could form the basis of any such judgments.

This in its turn implies that the whole notion of moral *progress* is sheer delusion. Progress means an advance from lower to higher, from worse to better. But on the basis of ethical relativity it has no meaning to say that the standards of this age are better (or worse) than those of a previous age. For there is no common standard by which both can be measured. . . .

In the same way that James argues that humans live their lives based on the assumption that they are capable of making free choices, so Stace is arguing that we live our lives based on the assumption that *there are* absolute moral standards that are independent of individual or group preferences. It is because of our belief in absolute moral standards that we believe we are justified in making moral judgments, such as:

- The genocidal actions of Adolf Hitler and Slobodan Milosevic were morally reprehensible.
- Terrorist activities in which innocent lives are taken are morally indefensible.
- Cultures that systematically abuse children are morally inferior.

If ethical relativism is true, then we would not be able to make these judgments of moral evaluation. But *we do* make these sorts of moral evaluations all of the time, and we believe that we are justified in doing so. Let's apply the epistemological criteria suggested by William James and W. T. Stace in evaluating which view of moral values makes most sense: ethical relativism or ethical absolutism.

    Criteria #1   Which theory provides the most *subjective satisfaction*?

    Criteria #2   Which theory provides the *more rational* explanation?

James and Stace want to argue, with good reason, that because we believe that we are justified in making moral evaluations and comparisons of other cultures, a belief in ethical absolutism is going to provide us with more *subjective satisfaction*, and will provide a more *rational* explanation of the world. Otherwise, if we commit ourselves to ethical relativism, then we must conclude that our judgments of moral evaluation and comparison are illegitimate. And this *does not* provide us with as much subjective satisfaction or as rational an explanation of the world as that provided by ethical absolutism.

The same principle applies in evaluating moral values in different time periods and the possibility of moral progress. The fact is that most people believe that the barbaric treatment of mentally ill people in past centuries (to "drive the demons out of them") was morally inferior to the treatment of them today. And that practices such as slavery, human sacrifice, cannibalism, the burning of witches and widows, and the subjugation of women are morally inferior to current, more enlightened practices. Yet, if ethical relativism is accurate, then such moral comparisons are not valid and the concept of moral progress is an illusion—conclusions that are

VISUAL PHILOSOPHY

Satirical Illustration Depicting a Scene from a
Nineteenth-Century Mental Institution.

Do you agree with the contention of cultural relativists that we cannot evaluate the practices of other cultures (such as the treatment of the mentally ill) as being either inferior or superior to any others? Why?

simply not consistent with our assumptions and beliefs about the world. In James's terms, these relativist conclusions provide less subjective satisfaction and present a less rational explanation than an absolutist perspective.

But a further difficulty with ethical relativism is just as serious as its inconsistency with our general epistemological framework. Ethical relativism contends that moral values are determined by "the group." But who precisely is "the group"? Ethical relativists assume that in most cultures, the majority of people agree about basic moral values. Although this may be true in smaller, simpler cultures, this seems untrue with large, complex, modern cultures. How would the ethical relativist determine the prevailing view on moral values in a culture that is deeply divided? What is the rationale for delimiting smaller groups within larger groups? Stace addresses these concerns in the following passage:

Stace, *The Concept of Morals*

But even if we assume that the difficulty about defining moral groups has been surmounted, a further difficulty presents itself. Suppose that we have not definitely decided what are the exact boundaries of the social group within which a moral standard is to be operative. And we will assume—as is invariably done by relativists themselves—that this group is to be some actually existing social community such as a tribe or nation. How are we to know, even then, what actually *is* the moral standard within that group? How is anyone to know? How is even a member of the group to know? For there are certain to be within the group—at least this will be true among advanced peoples—wide differences of opinion as to what is right, what wrong. Whose opinion, then, is to be taken as representing *the* moral standard of the group? Either we must take the opinion of the majority within the group, or the opinion of some minority. If we rely upon the ideas of the majority, the results will be disastrous. Wherever there is found among a people a small band of select spirits, or perhaps one man, working for the establishment of higher and nobler ideals than those commonly accepted by the group, we shall be compelled to hold that, for that people at that time, the majority are right, and that the reformers are wrong and are preaching what is immoral. We shall have to maintain, for example, that Jesus was preaching immoral doctrines. . . . Moral goodness will have to be equated always with the mediocre and sometimes with the definitely base and ignoble. If on the other hand we say that the moral standard of the group is to be identified with the moral opinions of some minority, then what minority is this to be? We cannot answer that it is to be the minority composed of the best and most enlightened individuals of the group. This would involve us in a palpably vicious circle. For by what standard are these individuals to be judged the best and the most enlightened? There is no principle by which we could select the right minority. And therefore we should have to consider every minority as good as every other. And this means that we should have no logical right whatever to resist the claim of the gangsters of Chicago—if such a claim were made—that their practices represent the highest standards of American morality. It means in the end that every individual is to be bound by no standard save his own.

THINK CRITICALLY   5.7

PHILOSOPHER'S NOTEBOOK

Ethical Relativism and My Moral Values

- Reflect on your own views regarding moral values. Do you live your life assuming that there are some universal moral values that apply to all cultures in all time periods? If so, identify which moral values these are. If not, explain how you would deal with someone whose moral values included hurting you.

- Imagine that you were engaged in a discussion with an ethical relativist. How would you use James's and Stace's criteria of "subjective satisfaction" and "rational explanation" to argue against their views.

- Consider the universal values that you identified in the first question (if you did, in fact, identify any). What is your foundation for these values, your justification for believing that these values apply not just to you but to other people as well, even though they may not agree with you? If you cited religious beliefs as part of your rationale, can you provide a justification for these values that is not based on religion?

- Imagine that you agree with the ethical relativists, believing that moral values are based entirely on group consensus. How would you go about identifying groups in your college or workplace? Which groups would qualify and which groups wouldn't? If the members of each group were not in complete accord, how would you recommend determining the group's values? What would you say to the "minority opinions" in each group?

- Do you agree with Stace that if people became convinced that ethical relativism was indeed true, that this would gradually have the effect of eroding their moral values to what we generally think of as less sophisticated, less enlightened levels? Why or why not?

Stace's final concern regarding ethical relativism is less philosophical and more practical, posing the question, "What would be the effect on human thinking and behavior if people genuinely adopted a relativist perspective, not just on a theoretical level but in their day-to-day lives?" The consequences would be dire, Stace is convinced, resulting in moral chaos. After all, if morality is truly rootless and subjective and not tied to any universal foundation, then every sort of action would be morally permissible. And once people come to understand and accept this, Stace believes that there is the risk that this will result in the *de*volution of moral values to more primitive, barbaric, and selfish levels. Nor would people be inspired to try to elevate themselves, to become more enlightened, if all moral values (or what are traditionally thought of as immoral values) are of equal validity.

Stace, *The Concept of Morals*

Finally, not only is ethical relativity disastrous in its consequences for moral theory, it cannot be doubted that it must tend to be equally disastrous in its impact upon practical conduct. If men come really to believe that one moral standard has nothing special to recommend it, they might as well then slip down to some lower and easier standard. It is true that for a time, it may be possible, to hold one view in theory and to act practically

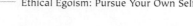

upon another. But ideas, even philosophical ideas, are not so ineffectual that they can remain forever idle in the upper chambers of the intellect. In the end they seep down to the level of practice. They get themselves acted on. . . .

Ethical Egoism: *Pursue Your Own Self-Interest*

For every man by natural necessity desires that which is good for him.

—*Thomas Hobbes*

The achievement of his own happiness is man's highest moral purpose.

—*Ayn Rand*

The conceptual flaws and logical self-contradictions of ethical relativism have led many philosophers to conclude that it is untenable as an ethical theory. And as W. T. Stace points out, if we abandon ethical relativism, then we are left within some form of ethical absolutism: the notion that at least some moral values are universal and binding on all humans. However, within the general framework of ethical absolutism, there are many possible theories. The first that we shall explore is **ethical egoism**, the belief that the highest moral value for all humans is to pursue their own happiness. This does not mean that you should necessarily be selfish, seeking to take more than your share in life. Rather, it simply expresses the view that all things being equal, your needs and interests should take precedence over the needs and interests of others. For the ethical egoist, "Looking out for #1" is not something to be ashamed about—in fact, it is the best way for you to act in a morally enlightened manner. Nor does it entail being an *egotist*—a person who is arrogant, boastful, and obsessed with his or her self. Instead, the ethical egoist may have friendly, harmonious, and productive relationships with others. It's just that in the final analysis, when our needs and interests are in conflict or competition with those of others, it is our moral obligation to take care of our own needs and interests first. For the ethical egoists, this is a moral value that is binding on all humans.

The ethical egoists recognize that such a view runs counter to the prevailing moral values of many cultures, in which the venerated moral values include altruism, self-sacrifice, empathy, communal responsibility, love, social responsibility to those in need, and a willingness to sacrifice our own needs for the good of the group. Nevertheless, the ethical egoists are convinced that these traditional moral values represent a skewed and unhealthy perspective on how humans ought to think and behave.

One of the first coherent expressions of the ethical egoist perspective is found in Plato's *Republic*, his monumental exploration of the nature of justice. **Plato** was not himself, strictly speaking, an ethical egoist, but he gives voice to this view through the person of Glaucon, who tries to convince Socrates that pursuing our own self-interest is our natural condition, and rather than denying this fact, we should embrace it. Glaucon uses a story, "The Myth of Gyges," to make his point.

Glaucon: First, I will state what is commonly held about the nature of justice and its origin; secondly, I shall maintain that it is always practiced with reluctance, not as good in itself, but as a thing one cannot do without; and thirdly, that this reluctance is reasonable, because the life of injustice is much the better life of the two—so people say. . . . Accordingly, I shall set you an example by glorifying the life of injustice with all the energy that I hope you will show later in denouncing it and exalting justice in its stead. Will that plan suit you?

Socrates: Nothing could be better, I replied. Of all subjects this is one on which a sensible man must always be glad to exchange ideas.

Good, said Glaucon. Listen then, and I will begin with my first point: the nature and origin of justice.

Plato, *The Republic,*
The Myth of Gyges

Ethical egoism The view that we act morally when we pursue our own self-interest.

PLATO

(427–347 B.C.E.)
Ancient Greek Philosopher. It was once said that all of Western Philosophy is merely footnotes to Plato. A student of Socrates, Plato wrote many dialogues featuring Socrates as the main character and dealt with many philosophical issues such as morality, politics, metaphysics, and epistemology.

What people say is that to do wrong is, in itself, a desirable thing; on the other hand, it is not at all desirable to suffer wrong, and the harm to the sufferer outweighs the advantage to the doer. Consequently, when men have had a taste of both, those who have not the power to seize the advantage and escape the harm decide that they would be better off if they made a compact neither to do wrong nor to suffer it. Hence they began to make laws and covenants with one another; and whatever the law prescribed they called lawful and right. This is what right or justice is and how it came into existence; it stands half-way between the best thing of all—to do wrong with impunity—and the worst, which is to suffer wrong without the power to retaliate. So justice is accepted as a compromise, and valued, not as good in itself, but for lack of power to do wrong; no man worthy of the name, who had that power, would ever enter into such a compact with anyone; he would be mad if he did. That, Socrates, is the nature of justice according to this account, and such the circumstances in which it arose.

Glaucon begins his case for ethical egoism with a proposed analysis of the origins of "justice." The version he is presenting has come to be known as the **social contract theory** of political development. This view of humans assumes that we are by nature solitary, aggressive, and competitive. It is in our nature to promote our own interests over those of others, and even inflict harm on them if it will advance our desires. However, although it is our nature to inflict harm in order to advance ourselves, we realize that in such a lawless world we ourselves are vulnerable to being victimized by others. As a result, we enter into a social agreement with others, promising not to hurt or take advantage of them if they won't hurt or take advantage of us. This "compromise," as Glaucon terms it, is not ideal, but it's the best we can do under the circumstances. It would be much preferable to us if we could simply exert our own will and desires on others without fear of reprisals or counterattacks.

Glaucon's next point in his argument for ethical egoism is that although people have freely entered into a social contract to escape the danger and instability of the "state of nature," they do so reluctantly. Abiding by the laws of the social contract runs counter to our nature to dominate and exploit others for our own personal advancement. And if we had an opportunity to break these laws without suffering negative consequences, *all of us* would leap at the opportunity to do so. And such behavior would be morally appropriate, because we would simply be acting in accord with our universal nature.

Plato, *The Republic,*
The Myth of Gyges

The next point is that men practice it against the grain, for lack of power to do wrong. How true that is, we shall best see if we imagine two men, one just, the other unjust, given full license to do whatever they like, and then follow them to observe where each will be led by his desires. We shall catch the just man taking the same road as the unjust; he will be moved by self-interest, the end which it is natural to every creature to pursue his good, until forcibly turned aside by law and custom to respect the principle of equality.

Now, the easiest way to give them that complete liberty of action would be to imagine them possessed of the talisman found by Gyges, the ancestor of the famous Lydian. The story tells how he was a shepherd in the King's service. One day there was a great storm, and the ground where his flock was feeding was rent by an earthquake. Astonished at the sight, he went down into the chasm and saw, among other wonders of which the story tells, a brazen horse, hollow, with windows in its sides. Peering in, he saw a dead body, which seemed to be of more than human size. It was naked save for a gold ring, which he took from the finger and made his way out. When the shepherds met, as they did every month, to send an account to the King of the state of his flocks, Gyges came wearing the ring. As he was sitting with the others, he happened to turn the bezel of the ring inside his hand. At once he became invisible, and his companions, to his surprise, began to speak of him as if he had left them. Then, as he was fingering the ring, he turned the bezel outwards and become visible again. With that, he set about

Social contract theory The view that the main reason people agree to form political communities is out of necessity, because life in a prepolitical "state of nature" would be, though preferable, extremely difficult.

testing the ring to see if it really had this power, and always with the same result: according as he turned the bezel inside or out he vanished and reappeared. After this discovery he contrived to be one of the messengers sent to the court. There he seduced the Queen, and with her help murdered the King and seized the throne.

Now suppose there were two such magic rings, and one were given to the just man, the other to the unjust. No one, it is commonly believed, would have such iron strength of mind as to stand fast in doing right or keep his hands off other men's goods, where he could go to the market-place and fearlessly help himself to anything he wanted, enter houses and sleep with any woman he chose, set prisoners free and kill men at his pleasure, and in a word go about among men with the powers of a god. He would behave no better than the other; both would take the same course. Surely this would be strong proof that men do right only under compulsion; no individual thinks of it as good for him personally, since he does wrong whenever he finds he has the power. Every man believes that wrongdoing pays him personally much better, and according to this theory, that is the truth. Granted full license to do as he liked, people would think him a miserable fool if they found him refusing to wrong his neighbors, or to touch their belongings, though in public they would keep up a pretence of praising his conduct, for fear of being wronged themselves. So much for that. . . . ■

Plato, *The Republic*

THINK PHILOSOPHICALLY   5.8
Analyzing the Myth of Gyges

- Do you think that most people will break laws and violate traditional moral values if they're confident that they won't be caught? Identify one example that would support this thesis (for example, the looting that takes place during riots) and another example that contradicts it (returning a lost wallet that only you know you found).

- When you hear about someone who could have cheated or lied for their own benefit but refused to, do you consider them, in Glaucon's words, "a miserable fool"? Why or why not?

- If you found yourself in possession of the Ring of Gyges, identify three "immoral" things you might do by making yourself invisible that you ordinarily wouldn't do (for example, walking into a sold-out concert for which you couldn't buy tickets).

- Glaucon states that, "What people say is that to do wrong is, in itself, a desirable thing; on the other hand, it is not at all desirable to suffer wrong, and the harm to the sufferer outweighs the advantage to the doer." Socrates believes just the opposite, stating that "It is better to suffer wickedness than to commit it," and contending that doing wrong "will harm and corrupt that part of ourselves that is improved by just actions and destroyed by unjust actions." Identify which viewpoint you believe makes most sense, and explain your reasons for believing so.

Ethical egoism should not be confused with **psychological egoism**, a theory that purports to describe the way humans necessarily behave. According to psychological egoism, we are driven to pursue our own self-interest by our inborn human nature—we cannot do otherwise. We form reciprocal relationships with one another out of necessity, not because we are impelled to be empathetic, charitable, or loving. Everything we do can ultimately be traced to our pursuing our own self-interest. Even when it appears we are doing something selfless or self-sacrificing, the real reason is to give ourselves pleasure or satisfaction.

Some members of the contemporary field of "sociobiology" (a blending of sociology and biology) have added their support to the concept of psychological egoism. For example, **E. O. Wilson** has argued in his book *On Human Nature* that

Psychological egoism   The view that we are compelled by our psychological makeup to always pursue our own self-interest above all else.

E. O. Wilson   (1929–)
Sociobiologist. Considered to be the founder of the field of Sociobiology which attempts to explain social behavior on the basis of biology.

humans are genetically programmed to seek their own self-interest. According to Wilson, apparent acts of altruism are really designed to perpetuate the evolutionary survival of family members or even the species as a whole. Survival is the only purpose of so-called moral values.

> Can the cultural evolution of higher ethical values gain a direction and momentum of its own and completely replace genetic evolution? I think not. The genes hold culture on a leash. . . . Human behavior—lie the deepest capacities for emotional response which drive and guide it—is the circuitous technique by which human genetic material has been and will be kept intact. Morality has no other demonstrable ultimate function.

There are serious challenges to the theory of psychological egoism, which we will explore later in the chapter in the work of philosopher James Rachels. For now, however, we are interested in the theory of ethical egoism, which holds that although it may be possible for humans to act in a way that sacrifices their own self-interests, *it is immoral to do so*. The core belief of ethical egoism is that it is our moral obligation to pursue our own self-interest as our first priority, and when we fail to do so, our behavior is ethically inappropriate. One individual who has given a passionate defense of this view is the novelist and essayist **Ayn Rand**.

> **AYN RAND**
> (1905–1982)
> American Novelist. Advocated a moral theory known as ethical egoism which holds one should always act according to one's own self-interest and defends the 'virtue of selfishness.'

Ayn Rand: *Rational Egoism*

Ayn Rand (1905–1982) is best known for her novels *The Fountainhead* and *Atlas Shrugged*, and her ethical philosophy of individualism and "the virtue of selfishness" which they embody. Rand agrees with the sociobiologists that the chief function of morality is to extend our evolutionary survival. But rather than simply articulate a *descriptive* theory regarding the way humans are constructed, Rand is also proposing a *normative* theory that expresses the way humans ought to behave. From her standpoint, it is our moral duty to pursue our own self-interest. The "virtues" of altruism and compassion that traditional ethical theories and religions recommend are actually vices, because they encourage people *not* to pursue their own self-interest as their top priority. The following excerpt is from Rand's book *The Virtue of Selfishness*.

Rand, *The Virtue of Selfishness*

In popular usage, the word "selfishness" is a synonym of evil; the image it conjures is of a murderous brute who tramples over piles of corpses to achieve his own ends, who cares for no living being and pursues nothing but the gratification of the mindless whims of any immediate moment.

Yet the exact meaning and dictionary definition of the word "selfishness" is: *concern with one's own interests*.

This concept does *not* include a moral evaluation; it does not tell us whether concern with one's own interests is good or evil; nor does it tell us what constitutes man's actual interests. It is the task of ethics to answer such questions.

The ethics of altruism has created the image of the brute, as its answer, in order to make men accept two inhuman tenets: (a) that any concern with one's own interests is evil, regardless of what these interests might be, and (b) that the brute's activities are *in fact* to one's own interest (which altruism enjoins man to renounce for the sake of his neighbors).

For a view of the nature of altruism, its consequences and the enormity of the moral corruption it perpetrates, I shall refer you to *Atlas Shrugged*—or to any of today's newspaper headlines. What concerns us here is altruism's *default* in the field of ethical theory.

There are two moral questions which altruism lumps together into one "package-deal" (1) What are values? (2) Who should be the beneficiary of values? Altruism substitutes the second for the first; it evades the task of defining a code of moral values, thus leaving man, in fact, without moral guidance.

Altruism declares that any action taken for the benefit of others is good, and any action taken for one's own benefit is evil. Thus the *beneficiary* of an action is the only criterion of moral values—and so long as that beneficiary is anybody other than oneself, anything goes.

Hence the appalling immorality, the chronic injustice, the grotesque double standards, the insoluble conflicts and contradictions that have characterized human relationships and human societies throughout history, under all the variants of the altruist ethics.

Observe the indecency of what passes for moral judgments today. An industrialist who produces a fortune, and a gangster who robs a bank are regarded as equally immoral, since they both sought wealth for their own "selfish" benefit. A young man who gives up his career in order to support his parents and never rises beyond the rank of grocery clerk is regarded as morally superior to the young man who endures an excruciating struggle and achieves his personal ambition. A dictator is regarded as moral, since the unspeakable atrocities he committed were intended to benefit "the people," not himself.

Observe what this beneficiary-criterion of morality does to a man's life. The first thing he learns is that morality is his enemy: he has nothing to gain from it, he can only lose; self-inflicted loss, self-inflicted pain and the gray, debilitating pall of an incomprehensible duty is all that he can expect. He may hope that others might occasionally sacrifice themselves for his benefit, as he grudgingly sacrifices himself for theirs, but he knows that the relationship will bring mutual resentment, not pleasure—and that, morally, their pursuit of values will be like an exchange of unwanted, unchosen Christmas presents, which neither is morally permitted to buy for himself. Apart from such times as he manages to perform some act of self-sacrifice, he possesses no moral significance: morality takes no cognizance of him and has nothing to say to him for guidance in the crucial issues of his life; it is only his own personal, private, "selfish" life and, as such, it is regarded either as evil or, at best, *amoral*.

Since nature does not provide man with an automatic form of survival, since he has to support his life by his own effort, the doctrine that concern with one's own interests is evil means that man's desire to live is evil—that man's life, as such, is evil. No doctrine could be more evil than that.

Yet that is the meaning of altruism, implicit in such examples as the equation of an industrialist with a robber. There is a fundamental moral difference between a man who sees his self-interest in production and a man who sees it in robbery. The evil of a robber does *not* lie in the fact that he pursues his own interest, but in *what* he regards as to his own interest; *not* in the fact that he pursues his values, but in *what* he chooses to value; *not* in the fact that he wants to live, but in the fact that he wants to live on a subhuman level.

If it is true that what I mean by "selfishness" is not what is meant conventionally, then *this* is one of the worst indictments of altruism: it means that altruism *permits no concept* of a self-respecting, self-supporting man—a man who supports his life by his own effort and neither sacrifices himself nor others. It means that altruism permits no view of men except as sacrificial animals and profiteers-on-sacrifice, as victims and parasites—that it permits no concept of a benevolent coexistence among men—that it permits no concept of *justice*.

If you wonder about the reasons behind the ugly mixture of cynicism and guilt in which most men spend their lives, these are the reasons: cynicism, because they neither practice nor accept the altruist morality—guilt, because they dare not reject it.

To rebel against so devastating an evil, one has to rebel against its basic premise. To redeem both man and morality, it is the concept of "*selfishness*" that one has to redeem.

The first step is to assert *man's right to a moral existence*—that is: to recognize his need of a moral code to guide the course and the fulfillment of his own life. . . . The reasons why man needs a moral code will tell you that the purpose of morality is to define man's proper values and interests, that *concern with his own interests* is the essence of a moral existence, and that *man must be the beneficiary of his own moral actions*.

Since all values have to be gained and/or kept by men's actions, any breach between actor and beneficiary necessitates an injustice: the sacrifice of some men to others, of the actors to the non-actors, of the moral to the immoral. Nothing could ever justify such a breach, and no one ever has. . . .

The Objectivist ethics holds that the actor must always be the beneficiary of his action and that man must act for his own *rational* self-interest. But his right to do so is derived from his nature as man and from the function of moral values in human life—and, therefore is applicable *only* in the context of a rational, objectively demonstrated and validated code of moral principles which define and determine his actual self-interest. It is not a license "to do as he pleases" and it is not applicable to the altruists' image of a "selfish" brute nor to any man motivated by irrational emotions, feelings, urges, wishes or whims. . . . Just as the satisfaction of the irrational desires of others is *not* a criterion of moral values, neither is the satisfaction of one's own irrational desires. Morality is not a contest of whims.

It's a provocative thesis that Rand is defending, and she expresses her view with unrepentant passion. "Selfishness" is not evil—"altruism" is evil. Traditional views of what is morally good and right have inverted the true nature of moral values. Why? Because people who are weak fear and envy the strong individualists in our world. They resent their independence, their passion, their creative visions. These parasitic "second-handers" constrain the strong individualists by creating a perverse system of morality that villainizes the true individual and celebrates the weak altruist devoted to self-sacrifice and misplaced compassion. The pursuit of self-interest—which nature intended us to strive for—is branded as immoral "selfishness," whereas the unnatural denial of self-interest is considered to be a saintly virtue. According to Rand, this violates the natural order, the primal impulses we have been equipped with to insure our survival.

Rand, *The Virtue of Selfishness*

Ethics is an *objective, metaphysical necessity of man's survival*—not by grace of the supernatural nor of your neighbors nor of your whims, but by the grace of reality and the nature of life.

This perverse morality of the weak and parasitic "second-handers" has a deadening, debilitating effect on the general population, for it discourages them from fulfilling their potential greatness by binding them with the need to devote themselves to promoting the good of others.

Rand, *The Virtue of Selfishness*

Observe what this beneficiary-criterion of morality does to a man's life. The first thing he learns is that morality is his enemy: he has nothing to gain from it, he can only lose; self-inflicted loss, self-inflicted pain and the gray, debilitating pall of an incomprehensible duty is all that he can expect.

Rand, Ayn, *The Virtue of Selfishness*

Rand is careful to point out, however, that the ultimate moral value of pursuing one's self-interest means pursuing one's *rational* self-interest. What this means is that the code of ethics that each person is expected to create on his or her own must be an "objectively demonstrated and validated code of moral principles which define and determine his actual self-interest. It is not a license 'to do as he pleases.'" In other words, pursuing your self-interest means creating a value system that is not destructive to yourself, nor is it unnecessarily destructive to others. From Rand's point of view, it is not rational to claim that narcotic use and excessive drinking are your moral values, because these inhibit living a productive, fulfilling life that is truly in your self-interest. Similarly, it is irrational to declare that stealing from others will be your defining moral value in pursuing your self-interest, because such behavior is the antithesis of a strong, independent person achieving his or her creative potentials. Other people are not our enemies, and it is likely that we will have friendly and productive relationships with many people. But we should never sacrifice our self-interest for the sake of others because such immoral behavior enslaves us to the group will and prevents us from achieving our greatest goals.

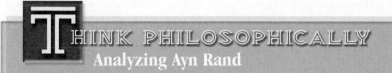

THINK PHILOSOPHICALLY 5.9
Analyzing Ayn Rand

- Rand contends that endorsing altruism as a moral value necessarily means condemning the pursuit of ones' own self-interest. Do you agree with this point? Why or why not? Provide an example to support your conclusion.

- In her analysis, Rand equates the terms *self-interest* and *selfishness*. Do they really mean the same thing? Can't you pursue your own self-interest without being selfish? Provide an example to support your response.

- Rand states, "An industrialist who produces a fortune, and a gangster who robs a bank are regarded as equally immoral, since they both sought wealth for their own selfish benefit. A young man who gives up his career in order to support his parents and never rises beyond the rank of grocery clerk is regarded as morally superior to the young man who endures an excruciating struggle and achieves his personal ambition." Critically evaluate these examples. Can you provide parallels to contemporary figures or people in your own life?

- After endorsing the very sensible notion that every person must "recognize his need of a moral code to guide the course and fulfillment of his own life," Rand goes on to say "The reasons why man needs a moral code will tell you that the purpose of morality is to define man's proper values and interests, that *concern with his own interests* is the essence of a moral existence, and that *man must be the beneficiary of his own moral actions*." Critically evaluate the logic of this position.

- In Rand's influential novel *The Fountainhead*, the central character is Howard Roark, a gifted architect who lives only for his work and himself. Roark personifies Ayn Rand's moral ideal. When his designs for a huge public works project are modified—and in his mind adulterated—without his permission, he undertakes to destroy the completed structures. Facing criminal charges, he attempts to defend himself by explaining his philosophy of life to the court, in which he includes the following statement:

  > But the mind is an attribute of the individual. There is no such thing as a collective brain. There is no such thing as a collective thought. An agreement reached by a group of men is only a compromise or an average drawn upon many individual thoughts. It is a secondary consequence. The primary act—the process of reason— must be performed by each man alone.

  Is this really the way the thinking and reasoning process works in humans? Is it really a completely individual process? Or are collaborations with others often necessary to achieve our highest potential? Include an example in your response.

- According to Rand, "Altruism is the doctrine which demands that man live for others and place others above self." Do you agree with this statement? Why or why not? Include an example with your response.

James Rachels: *Egoism Is a Flawed Theory*

he views of Glaucon (illustrated in the *Ring of the Gyges* myth) and Ayn Rand represent a complex blending of psychological egoism (people necessarily act in their own self-interest) and ethical egoism (people *should* always strive to act in their own self-interest). These views have naturally been attacked by those who believe that egoism does not represent human's natural inclinations (psychological egoism), nor should it be endorsed as a moral value (ethical egoism). The contemporary philosopher **James Rachels** provides a systematic critique of both of

JAMES RACHELS

(1941–2003)
American Moral Philosopher. Wrote influential articles on applied ethics and especially the ethical issues surrounding euthanasia. Author of *The Elements of Moral Philosophy* (4th ed. 2002) a significant and widely used introductory textbook to ethics.

these views in the following article, "Egoism and Moral Skepticism." Rachels begins his analysis by critiquing Glaucon's contentions directly, placing them in the larger context of traditional moral assumptions and values.

James Rachels,
Egoism and Moral Skepticism

Our ordinary thinking about morality is full of assumptions that we almost never question. We assume, for example, that we have an obligation to consider the welfare of other people when we decide what actions to perform or what rules to obey; we think that we must refrain from acting in ways harmful to others, and that we must respect their rights and interests as well as our own. We also assume that people are in fact capable of being motivated by such considerations, that is, that people are not wholly selfish and that they do sometimes act in the interests of others.

Both of these assumptions have come under attack by moral skeptics, as long ago as by Glaucon in Book II of Plato's *Republic*. Glaucon recalls the legend of Gyges, a shepherd who was said to have found a magic ring in a fissure opened by an earthquake. The ring would make its wearer invisible and thus would enable him to go anywhere and do anything undetected. Gyges used the power of the ring to gain entry to the Royal Palace where he seduced the Queen, murdered the King, and subsequently seized the throne. Now Glaucon asks us to determine that there are two such rings, one given to a man of virtue and one given to a rogue. The rogue, of course, will use his ring unscrupulously and do anything necessary to increase his own wealth and power. He will recognize no moral constraints on his conduct, and, since the cloak of invisibility will protect him from discovery, he can do anything he pleases without fear of reprisal. So, there will be no end to the mischief he will do. But how will the so-called virtuous man behave? Glaucon suggests that he will behave no better than the rogue: "No one, it is commonly believed, would have such iron strength of mind as to stand fast in doing right or keep his hands off other men's goods, when he could go to the market-place and fearlessly help himself to anything he wanted, enter houses and sleep with any woman he chose, set prisoners free and kill men at his pleasure, and in a word go among men with the powers of a god. He would behave no better than the other; both would take the same course."* Moreover, why shouldn't he? Once he is freed from the fear of reprisal, why shouldn't a man simply do what he pleases, or what he thinks is best for himself? What reason is there for him to continue being "moral" when it is clearly not to his own advantage to do so?

These skeptical views suggested by Glaucon have come to be known as *psychological egoism* and *ethical egoism*, respectively. Psychological egoism is the view that all men are selfish in everything that they do, that is, that the only motive from which anyone ever acts is self interest. On this view, even when men are acting in ways apparently calculated to benefit others they are actually motivated by the belief that acting in this way is to their own advantage, and if they did not believe this, they would not be doing that action. Ethical egoism is, by contrast, a normative view about how men *ought* to act. It is the view that, regardless of how men do in fact behave, they have no obligation to do anything except what is in their own interests. According to the ethical egoist, a person is always justified in doing whatever is in his own interests, regardless of the effect on others.

Clearly, if either of these views is correct, then "the moral institution of life" (to use Butler's well-turned phrase) is very different from what we normally think. The majority of mankind is grossly deceived about what is, or ought to be, the case, where morals are concerned.

The Republic of Plato, translated by F. M. Cornforde (Oxford, 1941), p. 45

Following this succinct summary of egoism theories (both psychological and ethical), Rachels next proceeds to review and critique the arguments commonly advanced for psychological egoism.

James Rachels,
Egoism and Moral Skepticism

Psychological egoism seems to fly in the face of the facts. We are tempted to say: "Of course people act unselfishly all the time. For example, Smith gives up a trip to the country, which he would have enjoyed very much, in order to stay behind and help a friend with his studies, which is a miserable way to pass the time. This is a perfectly clear case of unselfish behavior, and if the psychological egoist thinks that such cases do not occur then he is just mistaken." Given such obvious instances of "unselfish behavior," what reply can the egoist make? There are two general arguments by which he might try to show that all actions, including those such as the one just outlined, are in fact motivated by self-interest. Let us examine these in turn:

The first argument goes as follows. If we describe one person's action as selfish, and another person's action as unselfish, we are overlooking the crucial fact that in both cases, assuming that the action is done voluntarily, *the agent is merely doing what he most wants to do*. If Smith stays behind to help his friend, that only shows that he wanted to help his friend more than he wanted to go to the country. And why should he be praised for his "unselfishness" when he is only doing what he most wants to do? So, since Smith is only doing what he wants to do, he cannot be said to be acting unselfishly.

This argument is so bad that it would not deserve to be taken seriously except for the fact that so many otherwise intelligent people have been taken in by it. First, the argument rests on the premise that people never voluntarily do anything except what they want to do. But this is patently false; there are at least two classes of actions that are exceptions to this generalization. One is the set of actions which we may not want to do, but which we do anyway as a means to an end which we want to achieve; for example, going to the dentist in order to stop a toothache, or going to work every day in order to be able to draw our pay at the end of the month. These classes may be regarded as consistent with the spirit of the egoist argument, however, since the ends mentioned are wanted by the agent. But the other set of actions are those which we do, not because we want to, nor even because there is an end which we want to achieve, but because we feel ourselves *under an obligation* to do them. For example, someone may do something because he has promised to do it, and thus feels obligated, even though he does not want to do it. It is sometimes suggested that in such cases we do the action because, after all, we want to keep our promises; so, even here, we are doing what we want. However, this dodge will not work: if I have promised to do something and if I do not want to do it then it is simply false to say that I want to keep my promise. In such cases we feel a conflict precisely because we do *not* want to do what we feel obligated to do. It is reasonable to think that Smith's action falls roughly into this second category: he might stay behind, not because he wants to, but because he feels that his friend needs help.

But suppose we were to concede, for the sake of the argument, that all voluntary action is motivated by the agent's wants, or at least that Smith is so motivated. Even if this were granted, it would not follow that Smith is acting selfishly or from self-interest. For if Smith wants to do something that will help his friend, even when it means forgoing his own enjoyments, that is precisely what makes him *un*selfish. What else could unselfishness be, if not wanting to help others? Another way to put the same point is to say that it is the *object* of a want that determines whether it is selfish or not. The mere fact that I am acting on *my* wants does not mean that I am acting selfishly; that depends on *what it is* that I want. If I want only my own good, and care nothing of others, then I am selfish; but if I also want other people to be well-off and happy, and if I act on *that* desire, then my action is not selfish. So much for this argument.

The argument and counterarguments Rachels is making here can be summarized in this way:

Egoist Argument #1   Whatever choices people make, they are always doing what they most want to do. So if one person wants to sacrifice a trip to the country to help his friend study, and another person doesn't, both choices are equally selfish because both people are doing what they most want to do.

Counterargument #1   We often do things we don't want to do because we have made a promise or feel an obligation. For example, we may have promised our friend, "We will help you study whenever you need us," and now feel that we have to honor that promise even though we would much rather go to the country. This is very different from the person who chooses *not* to honor his promise to his friend, and instead goes to the country instead of helping his friend study.

Counterargument #2   Even if we derive some satisfaction from giving up our trip to the country to help our friend, this is precisely what it means to act "unselfishly"—acting to promote someone else's interests, not just our own. In contrast, the person who breaks his promise and goes to the country is acting only to promote his own interest. The criteria for determining if an action is "selfish" or "unselfish" is the *object* or *consequence* of the action, not the satisfaction it brings the person initiating it.

Rachels then goes on to consider a second argument for psychological egoism.

James Rachels,
Egoism and Moral Skepticism

The second argument for psychological egoism is this. Since so-called unselfish actions always produce a sense of self-satisfaction in the agent* and since this sense of satisfaction is a pleasant state of consciousness, it follows that the point of the action is really to achieve a pleasant state of consciousness, rather than to bring about any good for others. Therefore, the action is "unselfish" only at a superficial level of analysis. Smith will feel much better with himself for having stayed to help his friend—if he had gone to the country, he would have felt terrible about it—and that is the real point of the action. According to a well-known story, this argument was once expressed by Abraham Lincoln.

Mr. Lincoln once remarked to a fellow-passenger on an old-time, mud-coach that all men were prompted by selfishness in doing good. His fellow-passenger was antagonizing this position when they were passing over a corduroy bridge that spanned a slough. As they crossed this bridge they espied an old razor-backed sow on the bank making a terrible noise because her pigs had got into the slough and were in danger of drowning. As the old coach began to climb the hill, Mr. Lincoln called out, "Driver, can't you stop just a moment?" Then Mr. Lincoln jumped out, ran back, and lifted the little pigs out of the mud and water and placed them on the bank. When he returned, his companion remarked: "Now, Abe, where does selfishness come in on this little episode?" "Why, bless your soul, Ed, that was the very essence of selfishness. I should have had no peace of mind all day had I gone on and left that suffering old sow worrying over those pigs. I did it to get peace of mind, don't you see?"†

This argument suffers from defects similar to the previous one. Why should we think that merely because someone derives satisfaction from helping others this makes him selfish? Isn't the unselfish man precisely the one who *does* derive satisfaction from helping others, while the selfish man does not? If Lincoln "got peace of mind" from rescuing the piglets, does this show him to be selfish, or, on the contrary, doesn't it show him to be compassionate and good-hearted? (If a man were truly selfish, why should it bother his conscience that *others* suffer—much less pigs?) Similarly, it is nothing more than shabby sophistry to say, because Smith takes satisfaction in helping his friend, that he is behaving selfishly. If we say this rapidly, while thinking about something else, perhaps it will sound all right; but if we speak slowly, and pay attention to what we are saying, it sounds plain silly.

Moreover, suppose we ask *why* Smith derives satisfaction from helping his friend. The answer will be, it is because Smith cares for him and wants him to succeed. If Smith did not have these concerns, then he would take no pleasure in assisting him; and these concerns, as we have already seen, are the marks of unselfishness, not selfishness. To put the point more generally: if we have a positive attitude toward the attainment of some goal, then we may derive satisfaction from attaining that goal. But the *object* of our attitude is *the attainment of that goal*; and we must want to attain the

Abraham Lincoln

*Or, as it is sometimes said, "It gives him a clear conscience," or "He couldn't sleep at night if he had done otherwise," or "he would have been ashamed of himself for not doing it," and so on.
†Frank C. Sharp, *Ethics*, New York, 1928, pp. 74–75. Quoted from the Springfield (Ill.) *Monitor* in the *Outlook*, vol. 56, p. 1059.

goal *before* we can find any satisfaction in it. We do not, in other words, desire some sort of "pleasurable consciousness" and then try to figure out how to achieve it; rather, we desire all sorts of different things—money, a new fishing-boat, to be a better chess-player, to get a promotion in our work, etc.—and because we desire these things, we derive satisfaction from attaining them. And so, if someone desires the welfare and happiness of another person, he will derive satisfaction from that; but this does not mean that this satisfaction is the object of his desire, or that he is in any way selfish on account of it.

It is a measure of the weakness of psychological egoism that these insupportable arguments are the ones most often advanced in its favor. Why, then, should anyone ever have thought it a true view? Perhaps because of a desire for theoretical simplicity: In thinking about human conduct, it would be nice if there were some simple formula that would unite the diverse phenomena of human behavior under a single explanatory principle, just as simple formulae in physics bring together a great many apparently different phenomena. And since it is obvious that self-regard is an overwhelmingly important factor in motivation, it is only natural to wonder whether all motivation might not be explained in these terms. But the answer is clearly No; while a great many human actions are motivated entirely or in part by self-interest, only by a deliberate distortion of the facts can we say that all conduct is so motivated. This will be clear, I think, if we correct three confusions which are commonplace. The exposure of these confusions will remove the last traces of plausibility from the psychological egoist thesis.

Having successfully countered (in his mind) the arguments advanced by psychological egoism, Rachels now wants to expose the underlying confusions that account for the persistence of this view over the centuries. There are three such confusions:

Confusion #1:   *It is false* to believe that "selfishness" means the same thing as "self-interest."

Confusion #2:   *It is false* to say that every action is done *either* from self-interest or from other-regarding motives.

Confusion #3:   *It is false* to assume that a concern for one's own welfare is incompatible with any genuine concern for the welfare of others.

The first is the confusion of selfishness with self-interest. The two are clearly not the same. If I see a physician when I am feeling poorly, I am acting in my own interest but no one would think of calling me "selfish" on account of it. Similarly, brushing my teeth, working hard at my job, and obeying the law are all in my self-interest but none of these are examples of selfish conduct. This is because selfish behavior is behavior that ignores the interests of others in circumstances in which their interests ought not to be ignored. This concept has a definite evaluative flavor; to call someone "selfish" is not just to describe his action but to condemn it. Thus, you would not call me selfish for eating a normal meal in normal circumstances (although it may surely be in my self-interest); but you would call me selfish for hoarding food while others about are starving.

The second confusion is the assumption that every action is done *either* from self-interest or from other-regarding motives. Thus, the egoist concludes that if there is no such thing as genuine altruism then all actions must be done from self-interest. But this is certainly a false dichotomy. The man who continues to smoke cigarettes, even after learning about the connection between smoking and cancer, is surely not acting from self-interest, not even by his own standards—self-interest would dictate that he quit smoking at once—and he is not acting altruistically either. He *is*, no doubt, smoking for the pleasure of it, but all that this shows is that undisciplined pleasure-seeking and acting from self-interest are very different. This is what led Butler to remark that "The thing to be lamented is, not that men have so great regard to their own good or interest in the present world, for they have not enough."

James Rachels,
Egoism and Moral Skepticism

The last two paragraphs show (*a*) that it is false that all actions are selfish, and (*b*) that it is false that all actions are done out of self-interest. And it should be noted that these two points can be made, and were, without any appeal to putative examples of altruism.

The third confusion is the common but false assumption that a concern for one's own welfare is incompatible with any genuine concern for the welfare of others. Thus, since it is obvious that everyone (or very nearly everyone) does desire his own well-being, it might be thought that no one can really be concerned with others. But again, this is false. There is no inconsistency in desiring that everyone, including oneself *and* others, be well-off and happy. To be sure, it may happen on occasion that our own interests conflict with the interests of others, and in these cases we will have to make hard choices. But even in these cases we might sometimes opt for the interests of others, especially when the others involved are our family or friends. But more importantly, not all cases are like this: sometimes we are able to promote the welfare of others when our own interests are not involved at all. In these cases not even the strongest self-regard need prevent us from acting considerately toward others.

Once these confusions are cleared away, it seems to me obvious enough that there is no reason whatever to accept psychological egoism. On the contrary, if we simply observe people's behavior with an open mind we may find that a great deal of it is motivated by self-regard, but by no means all of it; and that there is no reason to deny that "the moral institution of life" can include a place for the virtue of beneficence.

Having dispensed with psychological egoism to his satisfaction, Rachels next turns his attention to ethical egoism—the theory that we *ought* to pursue our own self-interest. According to this view—advocated by Ayn Rand—even if we have the ability to act altruistically, the morally correct thing to do is act in our own self-interest.

James Rachels,
Egoism and Moral Skepticism

The ethical egoist would say at this point, "Of course it is possible for people to act altruistically, and perhaps many people do act that way—but there is no reason why they *should* do so. A person is under no obligation to do anything except what is in his own interests."* This is really quite a radical doctrine. Suppose I have an urge to set fire to some public building (say, a department store) just for the fascination of watching the spectacular blaze: according to this view, the fact that several people might be burned to death provides no reason whatever why I should not do it. After all, this only concerns *their* welfare, not my own, and according to the ethical egoist the only person I need think of is myself.

*I take this to be the view of Ayn Rand, in so far as I understand her confusing doctrine.

Of course, Ayn Rand would not be pleased with Rachel's example. She would likely respond that she is advocating *rational* egoism—choices in ones self-interest that can be supported by cogent reasons and compelling evidence. Setting fires on a whim and other acts of senseless violence are clearly *irrational* actions. In fact, Rand delineated the values she believed were integral to being a rational person:

- *Be independent.* Live by the work of your own mind.
- *Have integrity.* Don't sacrifice your convictions to the opinions of others.
- *Be honest.* Don't fake reality.
- *Be just.* Neither seek nor give that which is unearned or undeserved.

These hardly seem to be the values of the pyromaniac that Rachels seems to have in mind when he thinks of an ethical egoist. But even assuming that the ethical egoist is committed to a doctrine of rationality that prevents monstrous actions, the doctrine still faces several serious objections, including the question of whether it is logically consistent. Rachels remarks:

James Rachels,
Egoism and Moral Skepticism

The rational egoist, then, cannot advocate that egoism be universally adopted by everyone. For he wants a world in which his own interests are maximized; and if other people adopted the egoistic policy of pursuing their own interests to the exclusion of his interests, as he pursues his interests to the exclusion of theirs, then such a world would be impossible. So he himself will be an egoist, but he will want others to be altruists.

But of course, because the ethical egoist believes that pursuing one's self-interests is a universal moral value, he *must* recommend that others follow the same mandate, regardless of the consequences. Rand seems to believe that as long as everyone follows the principles of rationality, that conflicts in self-interest will work themselves out in a harmonious fashion. This confidence is in part based on the belief that the central purpose of government is to protect each individual's right to personal liberty in a way that doesn't infringe on the rights of others. However, even given this basic framework, many areas of potential conflict may still exist between people actively seeking their own self-interest. Ethical egoism does not appear to have any conceptual tools to resolve these conflicts between competing interests.

In addition to its purported logical inconsistency, critics of ethical egoism find its lack of natural empathy and caring for others to be particularly disturbing. The entire approach seems to be so cold, calculating, impersonal—in a word, nonhuman. And the fact that it presents itself as an "ethical" theory is seen as being particularly offensive. Rachels expresses this disdain and outrage toward ethical egoism in the passage on page 256.

THINK PHILOSOPHICALLY   5.10
Analyzing James Rachels

- Recall a time in which you acted in a way that you consider to be unselfish or altruistic: for example, you honored an obligation to a friend even though you would have rather done something else, or you voluntarily sacrificed something of yours to help someone else. How would you respond to a psychological egoist's contention that what you did "wasn't really unselfish" because "you were only doing what you wanted to do"?

- Rachels maintains that "wanting" to help someone when it conflicts with our own self-interest is precisely what we mean when we say someone is "unselfish." Do you agree? Why or why not?

- In the anecdote recounted in the article, Abraham Lincoln contends that his efforts to help free the piglets was motivated by self-interest, and so was really a "selfish" action. Do you agree? Why or why not?

- Some philosophers contend that psychological egoism is flawed because it is not "falsifiable"—that is, there is no way to test the theory because it explains *all* human behavior in terms of self-interest. As a result, there are no standards or tests we can use to distinguish selfish from unselfish behavior, and so the theory is conceptually useless. How would you analyze this objection to psychological egoism?

- Is "selfishness" the same thing as acting in one's "self-interest"? Why or why not? If not, provide examples of each concept.

- In your view, does Rachels successfully undermine Ayn Rand's version of ethical egoism? Why or why not?

- Rachels concludes his critique of ethical egoism with an expression of personal contempt and disapproval: "Indeed, a man without any sympathy at all would scarcely be recognizable as a man; and that is what makes ethical egoism such a disturbing doctrine in the first place." Do you find this to be a persuasive argument? Why or why not?

- Would you consider yourself to be an ethical egoist? If so, why? If not, why not?

So a non-egoist will accept "It would harm another person" as a reason not to do an action simply because he cares about what happens to that other person. When the egoist says that he does *not* accept that as a reason, he is saying something quite extraordinary. He is saying that he has no affection for friends or family, that he never feels pity or compassion, that he is the sort of person who can look on scenes of human misery with complete indifference, so long as he is not the one suffering. Genuine egoists, people who really don't care at all about anyone other than themselves, are rare. It is important to keep this in mind when thinking about ethical egoism; it is easy to forget just how fundamental to human psychological makeup the feeling of sympathy is. Indeed, a man without any sympathy at all would scarcely be recognizable as a man; and that is what makes ethical egoism such a disturbing doctrine in the first place.

Morality and Religion

One of the traditional roles of most religions is to provide moral guidelines for believers in that religion. As we saw in our brief overview of religions earlier in the chapter, and as you can no doubt attest to in your own experience, the supernatural/metaphysical dimensions of a religion are intertwined with implications regarding how we should conduct ourselves during this life on earth. To achieve salvation, Nirvana, eternal life, a relationship with the divine, or any other spiritual end-point, we need to live our lives in accordance with certain principles and values.

This relationship between religion and morality is a natural one for several reasons. First, the core purpose of many religions is to serve as a means to achieve ultimate spiritual transformation. And such a spiritual quest necessarily involves what we think, feel, and do. The way we live our lives becomes a vehicle for achieving ultimate spiritual transformation, and our religion provides us with the ethical roadmap.

Second, religion provides a metaphysical grounding for morality. If a person or people develop an ethical system and instruct us to abide by its principles, we can legitimately ask, "Why should I follow your principles? What gives you special legitimacy over any other person to determine ethical guidelines?" However, if an ethical system is grounded in a supernatural creator or what is thought to be a fundamental principle of the universe, then the ethical system speaks with a special authority. "Why should I follow these principles? Because God (or some other metaphysical authority) endorses these principles." That removes moral values from the level of human-to-human debate and raises it to a spiritual level.

But the relationship between religion and morality also presents a fascinating philosophical question that was first articulated by Plato in his dialogue, the *Euthyphro*, when he posed the question, "Do the gods love piety because it is pious, or is it pious because they love it?" In other words, is a moral value "good" or "right" because God *commands* it to be so, or is the moral value "good" or "right" *independently* of God's commands (though it is presumably *consistent* with divine moral values). You may be asking yourself, "What difference does it make? If it's right, it's right!" Actually, the answer to this seminal question turns out to make quite a profound difference in our approach to both religion *and* ethics.

For example, imagine that you hear about a barbaric murder that has been committed. The murderer, who freely

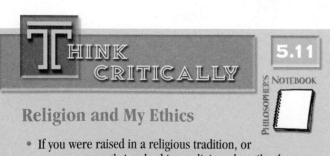

THINK CRITICALLY

Religion and My Ethics

- If you were raised in a religious tradition, or you are currently involved in a religion, describe the ethical principles and values that are endorsed by your religion. Do you personally agree with all of these ethical beliefs? Why or why not?

- If participants in your religion were to be asked, "Why do you believe these ethical beliefs should be accepted by others?" what would be the response?

admits his action, announces that "God commanded me to do it: I had no choice." If you believe, in response to Plato's question, that a moral value is "good" or "right" simply because God commands it to be, then you have to at least admit the possibility that the murderer was acting in an ethically appropriate way. On the other hand, if your response to Plato's question is that a moral value is "good" or "right" independently of any of God's commands, then you leave open the possibility of saying something along the lines of, "This barbaric murder is morally deplorable: it violates the ethical principles of virtually every civilized society, and it doesn't matter what 'God' or 'Gods' you think commanded it: what you did was immoral in the worst possible sense. And it is unthinkable that any supernatural deity would condone such an action."

In short, if you ascribe to what in philosophy and religion is known as the **divine command theory**, what is morally right and good (or wrong and evil), is defined simply by God's will. Our independent moral sense of right and wrong, good and bad, is irrelevant. Here are several examples of divine commands. The first is taken from the Old Testament in the Bible, the second from the Qur'an.

According to Divine Command Theory, we act morally when we do what God commands us to do, such as following the Ten Commandments held by Moses in this statue by Michelangelo.

> And God spoke all these words, saying,
> I am the Lord your God, who brought you out of the land of Egypt, out of the house of bondage.
> You shall have no other gods before me.
> You shall not make for yourself a graven image. . . . you shall not bow down to them or serve them; for I the Lord your God am a jealous God, visiting the iniquity of the fathers upon the children to the third and the fourth generation of those who hate me, but showing steadfast love to thousands of those who love me and keep my commandments.
>
> —*Exodus 20: 1–4*

> It is not righteousness that you turn your faces towards East or West; but it is righteousness to believe in God and the Last Day and the Angels, and the Book, and the Messengers; to spend of your substance, out of love for Him, for your kin, for orphans, for the needy, for the wayfarer, for those who ask; and for the freeing of captives; to be steadfast in prayers, and practice regular charity; to fulfill the contracts which you made; and to be firm and patient in pain (or suffering) and adversity and throughout all periods of panic. Such are the people of truth, the God-conscious.
>
> —*The Holy Qur'an, 2:177*

Divine commands are not intended to be questioned, critically evaluated, or negotiated by the audience for whom they are intended: the commands are intended to be obeyed—period. Such a religious/ethical point of view clearly invites the possibility of disturbing situations, as we noted in citing the example of the murderer who claims to be following God's command. Once critical judgment is suspended, there is also the danger of individuals becoming vulnerable to manipulative leaders—as we see in the case of cults in which people lose their autonomy and sometimes their lives (for example, the mass suicides/murders of the People's Temple or the Branch Davidian cults). On a social level, the belief that it is our spiritual responsibility to suspend our intellectual independence and follow divine commands can lead to bloody and destructive wars and persecutions.

One of the more provocative examples of divine command theory is the story of Abraham and his son, Isaac, from the Old Testament. Abraham is revered as a spiritual exemplar for Judaism, Christianity, and Islam. Yet, as recorded in the following

Divine command theory The view that we act morally when we do what God commands us to do.

passage, Abraham seemed prepared to murder his only and beloved son, Isaac, for the sole reason that God commanded him to.

> After these things God tested Abraham, and said to him, "Abraham!" And he said, "Here am I." He said, "Take your son, your only son Isaac, whom you love, and go to the land of Mori'ah, and offer him there as a burnt offering upon one of the mountains of which I shall tell you." So Abraham rose early in the morning, saddled his ass, and took two of his young men with him, and his son Isaac; and he cut the wood for the burnt offering, and arose and went to the place of which God had told him. On the third day Abraham lifted up his eyes and saw the place afar off. Then Abraham said to his young men, "Stay here with the ass; I and the lad will go yonder and worship, and come again to you." And Abraham took the wood of the burnt offering, and laid it on Isaac his son, and he took in his hand the fire and the knife. So they went both of them together. And Isaac said to his father Abraham, "My father!" And he said, "Here am I, my son." He said, "Behold, the fire and the wood; but where is the lamb for a burnt offering?" Abraham said, "God will provide himself the lamb for a burnt offering, my son" So they went both of them together.
>
> When they came to the place of which God had told him, Abraham built an altar there, and laid the wood in order, and bound Isaac his son, and laid him on the altar, upon the wood. Then Abraham put forth his hand, and took the knife to slay his son. But the angel of the Lord called to him from heaven, and said, "Abraham, Abraham!" And he said, "Here am I." He said, "Do not lay your hand on the lad or do anything to him; for now I know that you fear God, seeing you have not withheld your son, your only son, from me." And Abraham lifted up his eyes and looked, and behold, behind him was a ram, caught in a thicket by his horns; and Abraham went and took the ram, and offered it up as a burnt offering instead of his son. So Abraham called the name of that place The Lord will provide; as it is said to this day, "On the mount of the Lord it shall be provided."
>
> And the angel of the Lord called to Abraham a second time from heaven, and said, "by myself I have sworn, says the Lord, because you have done this, and have not withheld your son, your only son, I will indeed bless you, and I will multiply your descendants as the stars of heaven and as the sand which is on the seashore."
>
> *—Genesis 22: 1–18*

In this chilling and disturbing account (who could not be touched by Isaac's trusting question, "but where is the lamb for a burnt offering?"), the ethical implications have reverberated for centuries. Within the divine command religions for whom Abraham is considered a patriarch and prophet, his willingness to murder his son at God's command is endorsed as revealing Abraham's great faith. But to people outside of the divine command framework, disturbing questions are raised:

- How could Abraham (and others, by implication) be sure that it was the voice of God and not the voice of Satan or mental illness? This is what Jean-Paul Sartre refers to as "the anguish of Abraham."
- Because God is omniscient, and presumably knows precisely what is in Abraham's heart and mind, why does he need to test his faith in this uniquely barbaric way?
- What kind of God would command a believer to murder an innocent person, simply to demonstrate his uncritical willingness to follow His command without question?
- Following this incident, how would Isaac view his father and his father's God?
- How would you react to what seemed to be a divine command that violated your personal sense of moral rightness?

Thomas Aquinas: *Natural Law Ethics*

Natural law ethics The ethical theory based on the view that universal moral values can be discovered in nature by using the faculty of reason.

 s we noted, the divine command theory responds to Plato's provocative question ("Do the gods love piety because it is pious, or is it pious because they love it?") with the response that something is "good" or "right" simply because God commands it to be so. Responding to Plato's question with the converse response—namely, that God loves the "good" and "right" *because* it is good and right, *not* simply because God commands it—leads to an entirely different view of the relationship between religion and moral principles. This alternative view, traditionally known as **natural law ethics**, contends that there are universal moral values

VISUAL PHILOSOPHY

Detail of "Apotheosis of St. Thomas of Aquinas," by Zurbaran, 1631

According to Natural Law Ethics, championed by St. Thomas Aquinas pictured in this painting, universal moral values can be discovered in nature by using the faculty of reason. Can you identify any universal moral laws that you believe are grounded in human nature?

which people can discover by using their rational, intellectual and emotional capabilities. For those who believe in God, it is reasonable to assume that such moral principles are consistent with God's nature, because God is good and in creating us, God ensured that we were implanted with the "divine spark," the gift of reason. However, the net effect of this view is that whatever is morally "good" and "right" exist independently of God's commands and can be discovered by people using their gift of reason.

There have been centuries of energetic efforts to provide a foundation for moral principles, a grounding that will remove it from the grip of divine command theory, social conditioning, and the shadowland of inscrutable mystery. It was the ancient Greeks who first elaborated this approach by making a distinction between nature (*physis*) and convention (*nomos*). The social conventions of a society are the customs and beliefs, laws, and tastes that are peculiar to that society. That is why when you examine the numerous cultures in the world, past and present, you find a spectacular diversity in the social fabrics of each society: you are observing the social conventions that are relative to each individual society.

Nature, however, embodies the vast realm of truth that exists on a deeper level than social conventions that exist on the surface. These "natural truths" are *not* relative to each society: they are constant from culture to culture, and from age to age. These truths are rooted in the fundamental *nature* of what it means to be human. According to this view, there is a *natural law* that is based on humanity's essential nature and that is universal and binding on all people. We can discover these natural moral truths through reason and reflection, and they have been articulated in the greatest legal and moral philosophies and theological systems of Western culture (and other world cultures as well). The challenge for each individual and culture is to discover this immutable natural law that underlies the specific conventions of any society. It is an effort that the religious thinker St. Thomas Aquinas devoted his life to, and that America's founding fathers sought to articulate in the Declaration of Independence and Constitution. "We hold these truths to be self-evident that all men are created equal, that they are endowed by their Creator with certain inalienable rights. . . ."

To discover the specifics of the natural law, we need to develop an in-depth understanding of the essential nature of men and women, not simply as they currently *are*, but as they could be if they were fully morally developed. What are the basic requirements of human fulfillment? What are the most enlightened values that humans can aspire to? What are the norms of conduct that foster the most meaningful and productive society? What are the conditions that maximize an individual's freedom and personal growth? What are the moral responsibilities that we have to each other as members of an interdependent human community?

To answer these difficult questions, many people turn to religion. After all, if we are indeed God's creations (whatever your religion's conception of God), designed in God's image, then it makes sense that by understanding our true nature we will be following the path of both moral *and* spiritual enlightenment. In fact, it would be shocking if there was *not* an essential identity between the ethics of our religion and our natural

THINK CRITICALLY 5.12

PHILOSOPHER'S NOTEBOOK

Natural Law and My Beliefs

- Identify three ethical principles that you personally believe reflect "natural laws" that are self-evident and that all people ought to ascribe to. If you don't personally believe that there are any such principles, then identify three such ethical principles that are incorporated into one or more religions (such as the Golden Rule).

- For each of the ethical principles that you just identified, describe a moral situation in which the principle would guide you in making an ethically appropriate decision.

- Aquinas ties his natural law ethic to a comprehensive religious theology. However, Aristotle argued that a belief in God is not necessary for the existence of natural law. Which point of view do you agree with? Why?

- "We hold these truths to be self-evident that all men are created equal, and that they are endowed by their Creator with certain inalienable rights, and that among these are life, liberty, and the pursuit of happiness." So begins the Declaration of Independence. Would this statement have the same authority if the phrase "endowed by their Creator" were replaced by the phrase "entitled by natural law"? Why or why not?

moral intuitions. By following what Thomas Aquinas described as the "dictates of reason," he believes we are able to discover God's ethic encoded in our human nature, in the same way that we are able to display the mysteries of the physical universe through the study of science. In other words, we can use our critical thinking abilities to reveal the essential moral nature of people, the ideal image of fulfilled human potential—and then use this image to inform our moral choices and guide our personal development.

Thomas Aquinas (1225–1274) is one of the most significant Christian thinkers of the medieval period. His systematic development of natural law theory was both innovative and influential, especially on the development of ethical theory in the Catholic Church. His most important work is *The Summa Theologica*, in which he attempts to integrate key elements of **Aristotle's** thinking with Christian theology. Aquinas's metaphysic includes a hierarchy of laws: *Eternal Law* (the uncreated reason of God that guides the universe); *Divine Law* (the law that directs humans to a vision of God and eternal blessedness); *Natural Law* (the moral laws derived from Divine Law that humans can discover through reason); and *Human Law* (the legislation and custom that govern cultures). In an ideal world, human laws would be faithful reflections of natural law, which is directly based on divine law. Of course, the world is not ideal, and human laws are often poor replicas of natural law.

Quoting Aristotle, Aquinas views the purpose of laws to "make men good by habituating them to good works." This is the mainspring of Aristotle's ethical theory: people become virtuous by acting virtuously, and that is why education and proper laws are necessary to help citizens develop virtuous habits. Thus Aquinas portrays human lawgivers as responsible for creating virtuous laws that reflect (or "partake in") the natural law, which in turn reflects the divine law. Of course, medieval society in Western Europe at the time Aquinas was writing was very different from today's world—it was dominated by the Catholic Church, and the rulers—typically kings—were seen to be the representatives of God on earth. Nevertheless, even given this rigid, hierarchical, religiously permeated society, Aquinas recognized that human laws could be "tyrannical" and "perversions" of virtuous laws. Which leads to the question, "What is a citizen's responsibility when confronted with human laws that she considers to be unjust and immoral?" Individuals such as Gandhi and Dr. Martin Luther King, Jr., believe that in these circumstances civil disobedience is an appropriate response to protest unjust laws.

Natural law ethics confronts the same challenges as all general ethical theories: first, what precisely *are* the ethical principles, and second, how are these general principles translated into specific, concrete ethical guidelines that are useful to us in making complex moral decisions in our lives? Aquinas's first effort is not particularly helpful: *"good is to be done and pursued, and evil is to be avoided."* This is, presumably, the purpose of any ethical theory. The salient question is, naturally, what exactly is "good" and "evil"? Next, he cites inborn instincts that we find in all animals: "sexual intercourse, education of offspring, and so forth." Again, this is not ethically instructive, for some of the vexing questions ethical theories must deal with is *when* and *where* such inborn behaviors as sexual intercourse or aggression are ethically appropriate. Finally, Aquinas asserts that natural law (as reflected in our natural inclinations) inspires us to know the truth about God and to live in society with others. And to live harmoniously in society with others, we need to "shun ignorance" and "avoid offending those among whom one has to live, and other such things regarding the above inclination." This seems to be more akin to common sense and social customs, rather than ethical principles. Of course, Aquinas spells

ST. THOMAS AQUINAS
(1225–1274)
Medieval Philosopher/Theologian. Heavily influenced by both Aristotle and the Catholic Church. Sought to synthesize philosophy and theology and offered detailed and systematic works on the nature of man, God, and the universe.

Aristotle (384–322 B.C.E.) Ancient Greek Philosopher. One of the most important figures in the history of philosophy because of his division of philosophy into distinct disciplines and his extensive contribution to each of these divisions including being the first to attempt to create a system of deductive logic, and his empirical work in biology, not to mention his contributions to metaphysics, ethics, and politics.

VISUAL PHILOSOPHY

Dr. Martin Luther King, Jr., Being Arrested and Led Away by Police

In the tradition of natural law ethics, Dr. Martin Luther King, Jr., believed that "one has a moral responsibility to disobey unjust laws." Do you agree? Why?

DR. MARTIN LUTHER KING, JR.
(1929–1968)
American Civil Rights Activist. Major figure of the American Civil Rights Movement. Winner of Nobel Peace Prize. Advocated effecting social and political change through non-violent means and resistance.

out his concept of natural law in other passages in *The Summa Theologica*, but his struggles in this passage underscore the difficulty of translating general principles into specific precepts.

From the Birmingham jail, where he was imprisoned as a participant in nonviolent demonstrations against segregation, **Dr. Martin Luther King, Jr.**, wrote in longhand the passages from the remarkable letter that follows. It was his response to a public statement of concern and caution issued by eight white religious leaders of the South. Like Thomas Aquinas, King believed that there was a natural law containing universal moral principles by which a society could be judged. There are occasions when our commitment to natural law demands civil disobedience against unjust laws, as Dr. King contends in these excerpts from "Letter from a Birmingham Jail: April 16, 1963."

King,
Letter from a Birmingham Jail

. . . You express a great deal of anxiety over our willingness to break laws. This is certainly a legitimate concern. Since we so diligently urge people to obey the Supreme Court's decision of 1954 outlawing segregation in the public schools, at first glance it may seem rather paradoxical for us consciously to break laws. One may well ask: "How can you advocate breaking some laws and obeying others?" The answer lies in the fact that there are two types of laws: just and unjust. I would be the first to advocate obeying just laws. One has not only a legal but a moral responsibility to obey just laws. Conversely, one has a moral responsibility to disobey unjust laws. I would agree with St. Augustine that "an unjust law is no law at all."

Now, what is the difference between the two? How does one determine whether a law is just or unjust? A just law is a man-made code that squares with the moral law or the law of God. An unjust law is a code that is out of harmony with the moral law. To put it in the terms of St. Thomas Aquinas: An unjust law is a human law that is not rooted in eternal law and natural law. Any law that uplifts human personality is just. Any law that degrades human personality is unjust. All segregation statutes are unjust because segregation distorts the soul and damages the personality. It gives the segregator a false sense of superiority and the segregated a false sense of inferiority. Segregation, to use the terminology of the Jewish philosopher Martin Buber, substitutes an "I-it" relationship for an "I-thou" relationship and ends up relegating persons to the status of things. Hence segregation is not only politically, economically and sociologically unsound, it is morally wrong and awful. Paul Tillich said that sin is separation. Is not segregation an existential expression of man's tragic separation, his awful estrangement, his terrible sinfulness? Thus it is that I can urge men to obey the 1954 decision of the Supreme Court, for it is morally right; and I can urge them to disobey segregation ordinances, for they are morally wrong.

Let us consider a more concrete example of just and unjust laws. An unjust law is a code that a numerical or power majority group compels a minority group to obey but does not make binding on itself. This is difference made legal. By the same token, a just law is a code that a majority compels a minority to follow and that it is willing to follow itself. This is sameness made legal.

Let me give another explanation. A law is unjust if it is inflicted on a minority that, as a result of being denied the right to vote, had no part in enacting or devising the law. Who can say that the legislature of Alabama which set up that state's segregation laws was democratically elected? Throughout Alabama all sorts of devious methods are used to prevent Negroes from becoming registered voters, and there are some counties in which, even though Negroes constitute a majority of the population, not a single Negro is registered. Can any law enacted under such circumstances be considered democratically structured?

Sometimes a law is just on its face and unjust in its application. For instance, I have been arrested on a charge of parading without a permit. Now, there is nothing wrong in having an ordinance which requires a permit for a parade. But such an ordinance becomes unjust when it is used to maintain segregation and to deny citizens the First Amendment privilege of peaceful assembly and protest.

I hope you are able to see the distinction I am trying to point out. In no sense do I advocate evading or defying the law, as would the rabid segregationist. That would lead to anarchy. One who breaks an unjust law must do so openly, lovingly, and with a willingness to accept the penalty. I submit that an individual who breaks a law that conscience tells him is unjust and who willingly accepts the penalty of imprisonment in order to arouse the conscience of the community over its injustice, is in reality expressing the highest respect for law.

Of course, there is nothing new about this kind of civil disobedience. It was evidenced sublimely in the refusal of Shadrach, Meshach and Abednego to obey the laws of Nebuchadnezzar, on the ground that a higher moral law was at stake. It was practiced superbly by the early Christians, who were willing to face hungry lions and the excruciating pain of chopping blocks rather than submit to certain unjust laws of the Roman Empire. To a degree, academic freedom is a reality today because Socrates practiced civil disobedience. ∎

King, Dr. Martin Luther, Jr.,
Letter from Birmingham Jail

THINK PHILOSOPHICALLY   5.13
Analyzing Dr. Martin Luther King, Jr.

- King compares his strategy of civil disobedience to the approach of Socrates in trying to rouse the citizens of Athens from their lethargic slumbers. In what ways do you think this comparison is apt?

  > Just as Socrates felt that it was necessary to create a tension in the mind so that individuals could rise from the bondage of myths and half-truths to the unfettered realm of creative analysis and objective appraisal, we must see the need for nonviolent gadflies to create the kind of tension in society that will help men rise from the dark depths of prejudice and racism to the majestic heights of understanding and brotherhood.

- King quotes the theologian Reinhold Niebuhr in observing that "groups tend to be more immoral than individuals." Do you agree with this statement? Why or why not?

- The heart of King's philosophical argument is based on an appeal to universal values—a natural law—that transcends all cultures and time periods. Explain what you consider to be the strengths of this argument. Then identify some potential questions or problems that such a view must confront.

  > One has not only a legal but a moral responsibility to obey just laws. Conversely, one has a moral responsibility to disobey unjust laws. I would agree with St. Augustine that "an unjust law is no law at all." . . . To put it in the terms of St. Thomas Aquinas: An unjust law is a human law that is not rooted in eternal law and natural law.

On Becoming an Ethical Person

The following essay, "The Disparity Between Intellect and Character," is by **Robert Coles**, a professor of psychiatry and medical humanities at Harvard University, who has focused much of his work on the moral development of people, especially children. In this essay he explores the question of how someone can be intellectually knowledgeable about ethics and yet not act ethically or be an ethical person, as well as what responsibility the college community has to encourage students to become more ethically enlightened.

Coles, *The Disparity Between Intellect and Character*

Over 150 years ago, Ralph Waldo Emerson gave a lecture at Harvard University, which he ended with the terse assertion: "Character is higher than intellect." Even then, this prominent man of letters was worried (as many other writers and thinkers of succeeding generations would be) about the limits of knowledge and the nature of a college's mission. The intellect can grow and grow, he knew, in a person who is smug, ungenerous, even cruel. Institutions originally founded to teach their students how to become good and decent, as well as broadly and deeply literate, may abandon the first mission to concentrate on a driven, narrow book learning—a course of study in no way intent on making a connection between ideas and theories on one hand and, on the other, our lives as we actually live them.

Students have their own way of realizing and trying to come to terms with the split that Emerson addressed. A few years ago, a sophomore student of mine came to see me in great anguish. She had arrived at Harvard from a Midwestern, working-class background. She was trying hard to work her way through college, and, in doing so, cleaned the rooms of some of her fellow students. Again and again, she encountered classmates who apparently had forgotten the meaning of *please*, or *thank you*—no matter how high their Scholastic Assessment Test scores—students who did not hesitate to be rude, even crude toward her.

One day she was not so subtly propositioned by a young man she knew to be a very bright, successful premed student and already an accomplished journalist. This was not the first time he had made such an overture, but now she had reached a breaking point. She had quit her job and was preparing to quit college in what she called "fancy, phony Cambridge."

The student had been part of a seminar I teach, which links Raymond Carver's fiction and poetry with Edward Hopper's paintings and drawings—the thematic convergence of literary and artistic sensibility in exploring American loneliness, both its social and its personal aspects. As she expressed her anxiety and anger to me, she soon was sobbing hard. After her sobs quieted, we began to remember the old days of that class. But she had some weightier matter on her mind and began to give me a detailed, sardonic account of college life, as viewed by someone vulnerable and hardpressed by it. At one point, she observed of the student who had propositioned her: "That guy gets all A's. He tells people he's in Group I (the top academic category). I've taken two moral-reasoning courses with him, and I'm sure he's gotten A's in both of them—and look at how he behaves with me, and I'm sure with others."

She stopped for a moment to let me take that in. I happened to know the young man and could only acknowledge the irony of his behavior, even as I wasn't totally surprised by what she'd experienced. But I was at a loss to know what to say to her. A philosophy major, with a strong interest in literature, she had taken a course on the Holocaust and described for me the ironies she also saw in that tragedy—mass murder of unparalleled historical proportion in a nation hitherto known as one of the most civilized in the world, with a citizenry as well educated as that of any country at the time.

Drawing on her education, the student put before me names such as Martin Heidegger, Carl Jung, Paul De Man, Ezra Pound—brilliant and accomplished men (a philosopher, a psychoanalyst, a literary critic, a poet) who nonetheless had linked themselves with the hate that was Nazism and Fascism during the 1930s. She reminded me of the willingness of the leaders of German and Italian universities to embrace Nazi and Fascist ideas, of the countless doctors and lawyers and judges and journalists and schoolteachers, and, yes, even members of the clergy—who were able to accommodate themselves to murderous thugs because the thugs had political power. She pointedly mentioned, too, the soviet Gulag, that expanse of prisons to which millions of honorable people were sent by Stalin and his brutish accomplices—prisons commonly staffed by psychiatrists quite eager to label those victims of a vicious totalitarian state with an assortment of psychiatric names, then shoot them up with drugs meant to reduce them to zombies.

I tried hard, toward the end of a conversation that lasted almost two hours, to salvage something for her, for myself, and, not least, for a university that I much respect, even as I know its failings. I suggested that if she had learned what she had just shared with me at Harvard—why, *that* was itself a valuable education acquired. She smiled, gave me credit for a "nice try," but remained unconvinced. Then she put this tough, pointed, unnerving question to me: "I've been taking all these philosophy courses, and we talk about what's true, what's important, what's *good*. Well, how do you teach people to *be* good?" And she added: "What's the point of *knowing* good, if you don't keep trying to *become* a good person?"

I suddenly found myself on the defensive, although all along I had been sympathetic to her, to the indignation she had been directing toward some of her fellow students, and to her critical examination of the limits of abstract knowledge. Schools are schools, colleges are colleges, I averred, a complaisant and smug accommodation in my voice. Thereby I meant to say that our schools and colleges these days don't take major responsibility for the moral values of their students, but, rather, assume that their students acquire those values at home. I topped off my surrender to the *status quo* with a shrug of my shoulders, to which she responded with an unspoken but barely concealed anger. This she expressed through a knowing look that announced that she'd taken the full moral measure of me.

ROBERT COLES
Contemporary professor of psychiatry and medical Humanities at Harvard. Pulitzer Prize winner. His more than 1,200 articles and 55 books deal with issues in child psychiatry.

Suddenly, she was on her feet preparing to leave. I realized that I'd stumbled badly. I wanted to pursue the discussion, applaud her for taking on a large subject in a forthright, incisive manner, and tell her she was right in understanding that moral reasoning is not to be equated with moral conduct. I wanted, really, to explain my shrug—point out that there is only so much that any of us can do to affect others' behavior, that institutional life has its own momentum. But she had no interest in that kind of self-justification—as she let me know in an unforgettable aside as she was departing my office: "I wonder whether Emerson was just being 'smart' in that lecture he gave here. I wonder if he ever had any ideas about what to *do* about what was worrying him—or did he think he'd done enough because he'd spelled the problem out to those Harvard professors?"

She was demonstrating that she understood two levels of irony: One was that the study of philosophy—even moral philosophy or moral reasoning—doesn't necessarily prompt in either the teacher or the student a determination to act in accordance with moral principles. And, further, a discussion of that very irony can prove equally sterile—again carrying no apparent consequences as far as one's everyday actions go.

When that student left my office (she would soon leave Harvard for good), I was exhausted and saddened—and brought up short. All too often those of us who read books or teach don't think to pose for ourselves the kind of ironic dilemma she had posed to me. How might we teachers encourage our students (encourage *ourselves*) to take that big step from thought to action, from moral analysis to fulfilled moral commitments? Rather obviously, community service offers us all a chance to put our money where our mouths are; and, of course, such service can enrich our understanding of the disciplines we study. A reading of *Invisible Man* (literature), *Tally's Corners* (sociology and anthropology), or *Childhood and Society* (psychology and psychoanalysis) takes on new meaning after some time spent in a ghetto school or a clinic. By the same token, such books can prompt us to think pragmatically about, say, how the wisdom that Ralph Ellison worked into his fiction might shape the way we get along with the children we're tutoring—affect our attitudes toward them, the things we say and do with them.

Yet I wonder whether classroom discussion, *per se*, can't also be of help, the skepticism of my student notwithstanding. She had pushed me hard, and I started referring again and again in my classes on moral introspection to what she had observed and learned, and my students more than got the message. Her moral righteousness, her shrewd eye and ear for hypocrisy hovered over us, made us uneasy, goaded us.

She challenged us to prove that what we think intellectually can be connected to our daily deeds. For some of us, the connection was established through community service. But that is not the only possible way. I asked students to write papers that told of particular efforts to honor through action the high thoughts we were discussing. Thus goaded to a certain self-consciousness, I suppose, students made various efforts. I felt that the best of them were small victories, brief epiphanies that might otherwise have been overlooked, but had great significance for the students in question.

"I thanked someone serving me food in the college cafeteria, and then we got to talking, the first time," one student wrote. For her, this was a decisive break with her former indifference to others she abstractly regarded as "the people who work on the serving line." She felt that she had learned something about another's life and had tried to show respect for that life.

The student who challenged me with her angry, melancholy story had pushed me to teach differently. Now, I make an explicit issue of the more than occasional disparity between thinking and doing, and I ask my students to consider how we all might bridge that disparity. To be sure, the task of connecting intellect to character is daunting, as Emerson and others well knew. And any of us can lapse into cynicism, turn the moral challenge of a seminar into yet another moment of opportunism: I'll get an A this time, by writing a paper cannily extolling myself as a doer of this or that "good deed"!

Still, I know that college administrators and faculty members everywhere are struggling with the same issues that I was faced with, and I can testify that many students will respond seriously, in at least small ways, if we make clear that we really believe that the link between moral reasoning and action is important to us. My experience has given me at least a measure of hope that moral reasoning and reflection can somehow be integrated into students'—and teachers'—lives as they actually live them. ▪

- We opened this chapter with the following quote from Aristotle:

  > The ultimate purpose in studying ethics is not as it is in other inquiries, the attainment of theoretical knowledge; we are not conducting this inquiry in order to know what virtue is, but in order to become good, else there would be no advantage in studying it.
  >
  > —*Aristotle*

  How would Robert Coles respond to this quote? How do *you* respond to this quote?

- How do you explain the fact that morally evil people can be highly educated in terms of ethics and religion? In other words, how do you account for the "gap" that sometimes occurs between knowledge *of* ethics and *being* an ethical person?

- If you were in Robert Coles' position, what would have been *your* response to the student's concerns regarding the disconnect between ethics and education?

- Do you think colleges have a moral obligation to help students become more ethical individuals? Why or why not?

- If you were teaching a course in ethics, what would be your major goals for the course? For example, in addition to exposing students to the major ethical theories in philosophy, would you also want to encourage students to become more thoughtful and enlightened moral individuals?

- Explain how the following thinkers would respond to the student's concern that colleges do not teach students to become more ethical people: Ruth Benedict, Ayn Rand, James Rachels.

Making Connections: *Your Moral Compass Revisited*

ou began this chapter thinking about your "moral compass," the values that you use to analyze moral situations and make ethical choices. Much of this chapter has been devoted to considering and critically evaluating some of the more popular ethical beliefs that are often held by people who do not fully appreciate their shortcomings and difficulties. For example, many people espouse, at least some of the time, a form of *ethical subjectivism*, believing that moral principles are a matter of personal preference. On closer scrutiny, however, we discovered that this ethical theory has serious consequences that many people may not fully appreciate. Ethical subjectivists have no right to judge or critique the moral values of others, no matter what those values might be. This is clearly unacceptable to most people, who want to be able to condemn the abuse of children, the persecution of innocent people, or prohibitions against incest. Further, ethical subjectivists have no right to criticize those who would take advantage, steal from, or hurt others, because ethical subjectivism makes no provision for a principle of tolerance, "live and let live." And for analogous reasons, cultural relativism is ultimately unacceptable to most people. We want to be able to legitimately disagree with the moral practices of other cultures with which we have strong disagreements. Whether it's the atrocities of Nazi Germany, the unspeakable massacres in Rwanda, the brutal subjugation of women in Taliban-ruled Afghanistan, or the exploitation of children working in sweat shops for pennies a day, we want the ethical legitimacy to say, "This practice is wrong, you should develop a more enlightened set of values."

We also considered *ethical egoism* as a moral theory and discovered that pursuing your own self-interest is not incompatible with taking the needs of others into consideration. But if *all* we are concerned with is our own interests, to the exclusion of others, we found that such a view takes a very limited and self-absorbed view of human relationships, a view that is ultimately unsatisfactory for many people.

Having thus considered and highlighted the serious flaws of ethical subjectivism, cultural relativism, and ethical egoism, we are now in a position to begin considering ethical theories that do take the interests of others into account in a vital way. *Natural law ethics* was the first such theory we considered, and we also explored *divine command theory*. However, it is in the next chapter that we will begin our explorations of traditional ethical theories in earnest, becoming familiar with all of the major moral perspectives that have been developed over the centuries. Yet as Robert Coles points out in his essay, there is no guarantee that studying ethical theory will necessarily result in our becoming more ethical individuals. Becoming a morally enlightened person, however that idea is defined, requires not just an insightful moral compass, but also the commitment to use this compass to navigate our way through the storms and shoals of our moral lives.

Concept Review

- The terms *ethics* and *morals* describe how we *ought* to behave, and the rules and standards we *should* employ in the choices we make. The philosophical study of ethics and morals seeks to analyze and evaluate how different patterns of ethics have evolved and are applied by individuals as well as groups and cultures.

- Descriptive ethics is used to describe and analyze current moral and ethical beliefs and behaviors of an individual or a group. Normative ethics analyzes what *ought* to be the moral and ethical beliefs and choices of an individual or group.

- The theory of ethical subjectivism holds that each individual determines what is morally right or wrong, that he or she should determine their own best course of action by following their own moral compass. Some believe that ethical subjectivism can lead to social isolation and moral apathy, a sort of "every man for himself" attitude.

- Cultural relativism is the social correlative to ethical subjectivism. Cultural relativism holds that each culture has its own inherent moral and ethical beliefs, and that people who do not belong to that culture have no "right" to judge or evaluate those beliefs. Although some cultural relativists (including Ruth Benedict and Franz Boas) worked from the perspective of postcolonialist critics, seeking to undo the "civilizing" damage wrought by imperialist Western cultures on non-Western colonized societies, cultural relativism can be very damaging if it simplistically overlooks injustice.

- The converse of relativism is ethical absolutism, which holds that some moral and ethical values apply to all peoples in all circumstances. Although ethical absolutism acknowledges—through descriptive ethics—that different individuals and groups hold different moral and ethical principles, the ethical absolutist (unlike the ethical relativist) does not then hold those beliefs as *normative*—applicable to all people everywhere. However, there is no one "universal code" toward which ethical absolutists can point in support of their perspective. Absolutists argue, based on our own lived experience, that most people conduct themselves *as though there were* such a universal code. Most people, for example, believe that murder is "wrong," and that coming to the aid of someone in distress is "right."

- Ethical egoism is the belief that acting in your own best personal interests is the most ethical and moral way to conduct your life. Ethical egoists find that such traditional community values as altruism, empathy, and social responsibility to those in need actually erode both the personal and the common good. Novelist Ayn Rand went one step further with her theory of rational egoism, which holds that altruism and compassion encourage people to *not* pursue their own self-interest, which should be the highest virtuous motivation. She is careful to point out, however, that to act in one's self-interest implies a responsibility to act *rationally*, not to simply satisfy whatever impulses you might be feeling at any particular moment.

■ Many individuals and groups set their moral and ethical compass by a specific religious doctrine, in what is known as the divine command theory. Such people believe that what is morally "right" or "wrong" is determined by whatever god(s) they worship. In contrast, natural law ethics holds that there is an eternal, true "human nature" that provides a written moral code for all human beliefs as to what actions are "right" and what are "wrong." There is a long tradition in many religions of working to connect this innate, "natural" facility for determining right and wrong with a divine and unchanging moral principle.

Media Resources

www.researchnavigator.com
Chapter 5 examines some ways of determining a code of ethics. What comprises a moral code is explored as well. Some theorists believe ethics are subjective and others believe they are objective or determined by a God. For further research on questions about ethics and morals, use the tools available to you in Research Navigator.

As you investigate this topic, consider this question: "How have I determined my code of ethics and am I justified if I fail to act on this?"

● **ContentSelect:** search in the Philosophy database using the search terms "intention," "morals," "will," and "virtue."

● **Link Library:** search in the Philosophy database under terms "applied ethics" and "values."

● **New York Times on the Web:** search in the Philosophy database using the search terms "morality" and "ethical."

 For additional study resources for this chapter, go to:
www.prenhall.com/chaffee/chapter5

 The Primary Source: Philosophical Readings and Commentary

Aristotle: *Nicomachean Ethics*
Benedict, Ruth: *Anthropology and the Abnormal*
James, William: *The Will to Believe*
King, Martin Luther, Jr.: *Letter from Birmingham Jail*
Plato: *The Republic*
Rachels, James: *Elements of Moral Philosophy*
Rand, Ayn: *The Virtue of Selffishness; Philosophy: Who Needs It*

6 What Is Morality?
Constructing an Ethical Theory

Two things fill the mind with ever new and increasing admiration and awe, the oftener and more steadily we reflect on them: the starry heavens above and the moral law within.

IMMANUEL KANT

We are not concerned to know what goodness is, but how we are to become good men, for this alone gives the study (of ethics) its practical value.

ARISTOTLE

Nature has placed mankind under the governance of two sovereign masters, pain *and* pleasure. *It is for them alone to point out what we ought to do, as well as to determine what we shall do.*

JEREMY BENTHAM

The imperative of duty may be expressed thus: Act as if the maxim of thy action were to become by thy will a universal law of nature.

IMMANUEL KANT

There is no way for a man to escape from this world. It is in this world that . . . he must realize himself morally.

SIMONE DE BEAUVOIR

The first part of our explorations into the moral realm—chapter 5—introduced moral theories in which the individual is preeminent. For *ethical subjectivism*, it is the individual who is the ultimate arbiter of moral values, whereas in *cultural relativism*, it is collections of individuals who make these determinations. In *ethical egoism* and Ayn Rand's *rational egoism*, it is *my* interests that are most important—while everyone else's interests are a distant second. Other people do not play a significant part in the moral reasoning process, except to the extent that they can assist me in achieving my goals.

But of course, when most people think about the moral life, they are usually referring to how we ought to treat others and the challenge of becoming a virtuous, authentic person. Rather than calculating how we can advance our own interests, morality typically challenges us to help others achieve their interests, even if it means sacrificing what we want. Morality also involves the human project of creating ourselves to be people of moral value, making morally enlightened choices. This chapter examines the major ethical theories in which these themes are preeminent, including:

- Utilitarianism
- The ethic of duty (Immanuel Kant)
- Virtue ethics
- Existentialist ethics
- The ethics of care

Utilitarianism The view that we should act to promote the greatest amount of happiness (and create the least amount of suffering possible) for the greatest number of people.

Utilitarianism: *The Greatest Good for the Greatest Number*

Ethical egoism, with its exclusive focus on each individual's self-interest, is an unsatisfactory moral theory for many people. They wonder if this is really the most sublime ethical goal to which we should each aspire—always promoting our own interests as our primary priority. It certainly doesn't seem to be a very inspiring vision of the purpose of life, the grand potential of human existence, or the essence of the human community. In fact, some critics contend, if we apply William James's criteria for evaluating theories—subjective satisfaction and rationality—ethical egoism seems misconceived at a fundamental level. It simply doesn't provide an adequate explanation for the complexity and richness of our moral life. And ethical egoism's attempt to nullify and discredit powerful nonselforiented experiences such as altruism and love that invest our lives with profound meaning appears to them to be misguided. As a result, many philosophers have attempted to develop ethical systems that do justice to certain widespread moral sentiments while also attempting to elevate people to higher levels of moral awareness—to bring out the moral "best" in them.

This was certainly the goal of **Jeremy Bentham** (1748–1832) and **John Stuart Mill** (1806–1873), the two dominant thinkers who created and refined an ethical theory that came to be known as **utilitarianism**. Bentham was a lawyer, philosopher, and social reformer who was outraged by the abuses spawned by the Industrial Revolution in England. New scientific manufacturing techniques had initiated a profound change in England's economy. The creation of factories that could produce manufactured goods quickly and cheaply initiated a population shift from farms and rural locations to cities where the factories were located. These people became a new class of "workers" who found themselves in fierce competition for jobs that were often repetitious, dangerous, poorly paid, and dehumanizing. It was common for workers as young as twelve to toil fifty or sixty hours a week at machines in poorly lit, noisy, unventilated factories—for wages that could barely sustain the family. Bentham didn't simply want to create an elegant ethical theory—he wanted to effect social change by reforming the legal system and creating a more enlightened society that would benefit all members. He was remarkably successful in this quest, a testimony to the force of his personality and the power of his ideas.

Bentham grounded his theory in **hedonism**, a term derived from the Greek root *hedone*, which means "pleasure." Hedonism was a theory first identified with **Aristippus** (430–350 B.C.E.), a Greek philosopher who believed that the meaning of life is pleasure, pure and simple. Aristippus argued that if you observe people and what motivates them, it's clear that they seek to enjoy pleasure and avoid pain. Therefore, he concluded, the purpose of life must be to achieve as much intense, sensual pleasure as possible.

Jeremy Bentham developed utilitarianism for the purpose of effecting social change, such as ending the use of children as factory workers. Is child labor still an ethical problem in the world?

Epicurus (341–270 B.C.E.), another Greek thinker, was the next major figure to advocate hedonism as a way of life. Unlike Aristippus, who made no distinction between different types of pleasure, Epicurus believed that there were "higher" pleasures—such as intellectual pursuits—and "lower" pleasures—such as physical gratifications. Only the higher pleasures could provide optimal pleasure and peace of mind, as he describes in the following passage.

> Thus when I say that pleasure is the goal of living I do not mean the pleasures of libertines or the pleasures inherent in positive enjoyment, as is supposed by certain persons who are ignorant of our doctrine or who are not in agreement with it or who interpret it perversely. I mean, on the contrary, the pleasure that consists in freedom from bodily pain and mental agitation. The pleasant life is not the product of one drinking party after another or of sexual intercourse with women or of the seafood and other delicacies afforded by a luxurious table. On the contrary, it is the result of sober thinking—namely, investigation of the reasons for every act of choice and aversion and elimination of those false ideas about the gods and death which are the chief source of mental disturbances.

Epicurus truly lived his philosophy. He created a school—"The Garden" he called it—in which everyone was invited to stop by, socialize, eat and drink well, and discuss philosophy. It was a serene retreat from the noisy bustle of Athens, and what made it even more remarkable was the fact that all people were welcome and treated as equals: women, merchants, slaves, prostitutes, as well as the wealthy and educated men who controlled Athenian society.

Fascinatingly enough, this idyllic Garden was founded on principles that, two thousand years later, Jeremy Bentham would have appreciated. Bentham was committed to social equality, democracy, public education, and a universal improvement in the public welfare. He was also a hedonist, believing that humans are not

Hedonism   The view that pleasure is the only thing truly of value. Some hedonists emphasize the "higher" pleasures such as intellectual pursuits.

Epicurus   (341–327 B.C.E.) Ancient Greek Philosopher. Advanced the view in ethics that pleasure is the one sole good and pain is the one sole bad and that one should not seek out pleasures solely but devote oneself to also avoiding pain.

Aristippus   (c. 435–c. 395 B.C.E.) Ancient Greek Philosopher. Follower of Socrates; Believed happiness consists in pleasure and is commonly associated with the ethical doctrine of Hedonism.

only necessarily governed by pleasure and pain (**psychological hedonism**), but also *should* be governed by pleasure and pain (**ethical hedonism**). But Bentham takes a very different path from Aristippus and Epicurus, who saw hedonism as a *personal* philosophy: the purpose of life is for each of us to seek the greatest pleasure for ourselves. Bentham takes this basic framework and then expands it to a *social* philosophy. The argument that Bentham makes is that in order for each of us to achieve maximum pleasure, it is in our interest to live in a society in which *everyone* has an opportunity to achieve genuine pleasure for themselves as well. And to achieve that, we need to create a democratic society based on the principles of social justice and personal opportunity, rights that are enforced by the authority of the law. Thus, it's in our *self*-interest to help people fulfill their own *self*-interest. The moral guide for our actions thus becomes what he termed the *principle of utility: Act always to promote the greatest happiness for the greatest number.* It's an ingenious approach, and one that was surprisingly effective for him. Let's examine his reasoning firsthand.

Bentham,
An Introduction to the Principles of Morals and Legislation

The Principle of Utility

Nature has placed mankind under the governance of two sovereign masters, *pain* and *pleasure*. It is for them alone to point out what we ought to do, as well as to determine what we shall do. On the one hand the standard of right and wrong on the other the chain of causes and effects, are fastened to their throne. They govern us in all we do, in all we say, in all we think; every effort we can make to throw off our subjection will serve but to demonstrate and confirm it. In words a man may pretend to abjure their empire: but in reality he will remain subject to it all the while. The *principle of utility* recognizes the subjection, and assumes it for the foundation of that system, the object of which is to tear the fabric of felicity by the hands of reason and of law. Systems which attempt to question it, deal in sounds instead of sense, in caprice instead of reason, in darkness instead of light.

In this famous and provocative passage with its arresting metaphor of "two sovereign masters, *pain* and *pleasure*," Bentham articulates the philosophical foundation for utilitarianism. It's a foundation that combines both psychological egoism and ethical egoism: the experiences of pain and pleasure determine what we "shall" do, as well as what we "ought" to do. It's reasonable to ask: if pain and pleasure "govern us in all we do, in all we say, in all we think," then what is the point of exhorting people to adopt a utilitarian perspective that is based on seeking pleasure and avoiding pain? In other words, if our behavior is causally determined, then what sense does it make to encourage people to make ethically enlightened choices, a capacity that presumes that we are able to escape the causal web of determinism to make free choices independent of it?

Bentham's apparent response is ingenious. Although it is true that our thinking and behavior are *in general* dominated by the irresistible influences of pleasure and pain, we have the freedom to make *specific choices* within this general framework. In seeking pleasure and avoiding pain, people often make choices that are short-sighted, uninformed, unnecessarily cruel, and exploitative. The results of such ignorant and unenlightened choices are evident in the deplorable social conditions that we find in societies in which classes of people are mistreated and abused. However, through the power of education, people have the opportunity to become more informed and insightful, and make choices that reflect a more enlightened ethical standard. For Bentham, that ethical standard is "the principle of utility"— promoting the greatest happiness for the greatest number of people. The principle of utility recognizes the dominating power of pleasure and pain, and seeks to harness and direct this power to more enlightened social ends. Systems of thought—

Psychological hedonism The view that all human desire is necessarily directed to achieving pleasure and avoiding pain.

Ethical hedonism The moral view that human desire and action *ought* to be directed to achieving pleasure and avoiding pain.

whether they be ethical, legal, or political—that fail to recognize and respect the sovereign mastery of pleasure and pain in human affairs do so at their own peril: they "deal in sounds instead of sense, in caprice instead of reason, in darkness instead of light." Bentham goes on to further articulate the principle of utility and its role in shaping human thinking and behavior.

Bentham,
An Introduction to the Principles of Morals and Legislation

But enough of metaphor and declamation: it is not by such means that moral science is to be improved.

The principle of utility is the foundation of the present work; it will be proper, therefore, at the outset to give an explicit and determinate account of what is meant by it. By the principle of utility is meant that principle which approves or disapproves of every action whatsoever, according to the tendency which it appears to have to augment or diminish the happiness of the party whose interest is in question; or what is the same thing in other words, to promote or to oppose that happiness. I say of every action whatsoever; and therefore not only of every action of a private individual, but of every measure of government.

By utility is meant that property in any object, whereby it tends to produce benefit, advantage, pleasure, good, or happiness (all this in the present case comes to the same thing) or (what comes again to the same thing) to prevent the happening of mischief, pain, evil, or unhappiness of the party whose interest is considered: if that party be the community in general, then the happiness of the community: if a particular individual, then the happiness of that individual.

The interest of the community is one of the most general expressions that can occur in the phraseology of morals: no wonder that the meaning is often lost. When it has a meaning, it is this. The community is a fictitious *body*, composed of the individual persons who are considered as constituting as it were its *members*. The interest of the community then is, what?—the sum of the interests of the several members who compose it. . . .

An action then may be said to be conformable to the principle of utility, or, for shortness' sake, to utility (meaning with respect to the community at large) when the tendency it has to augment the happiness of the community is greater than any it has to diminish it.

Bentham was determined to give his ethical approach a "scientific" grounding, an objective credibility that would compel social change by persuading people of its truth. Although many ethical philosophies focus on the moral enlightenment of the individual, Bentham's priority was to effect social change by replacing the existing legal system with more socially progressive laws. He wanted people to believe that the principle of utility represented a rational, practical way of thinking that was based in reality—not some abstract philosophical doctrine that was disconnected from real-world problems.

To this end, Bentham makes a special effort to define the principle of utility in clear, practical terms: the principle endorses all actions that "tend to produce benefit, advantage, pleasure, good, or happiness," or, on the other hand, to "prevent the happening of mischief, pain, evil, or unhappiness." Bentham is confident that this will appeal to individuals—after all, who wouldn't readily acknowledge that they seek to secure happiness and avoid pain? But he wants individuals to see that this is a principle with far-reaching social implications, not just personal consequences, embracing "the happiness of the community" as well as "the happiness of the individual." So, although it is important for individuals to seek their own happiness in accordance with the principle, it is equally important for *governments* to abide by the same principle for the community as a whole.

Bentham,
An Introduction to the Principles of Morals and Legislation

A measure of government (which is but a particular kind of action, performed by a particular person, or persons) may be said to be conformable to or dictated by the principle of utility, when in like manner the tendency which it has to augment the happiness of the community is greater than any which it has to diminish it. . . .

Considered objectively, Bentham questions, what is the "community" other than the sum total of the members that comprise the community? And if the individuals are intent in seeking happiness, it is only logical for them to seek the greatest happiness of the general community that they comprise, because each is an integral part of it. And as a personal bonus, if the members of a community create a legal system and ethical policies designed to bring about the greatest happiness for the greatest number of people, this will be an environment that will be most conducive to each individual achieving the maximum personal happiness. Does Bentham's "social math" make sense? That's certainly a question worth exploring. But on a practical level, it was an argument that found a receptive audience, resulting in a progressive revision in social laws and educational policies.

How precisely does one go about calculating the "greatest happiness" in applying the principle of utility? Here we see Bentham's scientific aspirations in full force.

Bentham,
An Introduction to the Principles of Morals and Legislation

The Hedonistic Calculus

Pleasures, then, and the avoidance of pains, are the *ends*, which the legislator has in view: it behooves him therefore to understand their *value*. Pleasures and pains are the *instruments* he has to work with: it behooves him therefore to understand their force, which is again, in other words, their value.

To a person considered *by himself*, the value of a pleasure or pain considered *by itself*, will be greater or less, according to the four following circumstances:

1. Its *intensity*.
2. Its *duration*.
3. Its *certainty* or *uncertainty*.
4. Its *propinquity* or *remoteness*.

These are the circumstances which are to be considered in estimating a pleasure or a pain considered each of them by itself. But when the value of any pleasure or pain is considered for the purpose of estimating the tendency of any *act* by which it is produced, there are two other circumstances to be taken into the account; these are,

5. Its *fecundity*, or the chance it has of being followed by sensations of the *same* kind: that is, pleasures, if it be a pleasure: pains, if it be a pain.
6. Its *purity*, or the chance it has of *not* being followed by sensations of the *opposite* kind: that is, pains, if it be a pleasure: pleasures, if it be a pain.

These two last, however, are in strictness scarcely to be deemed properties of the pleasures or the pain itself; they are not, therefore, in strictness to be taken into the account of the value of that pleasure or that pain. They are in strictness to be deemed properties only of the act, or other event, by which such pleasure or pain has been produced; and accordingly are only to be taken into the account of the tendency of such act or such event.

To a *number* of persons, with reference to each of whom the value of a pleasure or a pain is considered, it will be greater or less, according to seven circumstances: to wit, the six preceding ones: viz.

1. Its *intensity*.
2. Its *duration*.
3. Its *certainty* or *uncertainty*.
4. Its *propinquity* or *remoteness*.
5. Its *fecundity*.
6. Its *purity*.

And one other; to wit:

7. Its *extent*; that is, the number of persons to whom it *extends*; or (in other words) who are affected by it.

To take an exact account then of the general tendency of any act, by which the interests of a community are affected, proceed as follows. Begin with any one person of those whose interests seem most immediately to be affected by it: and take an account,

1. Of the value of each distinguishable *pleasure* which appears to be produced by it in the *first* instance.

2. Of the value of each *pain* which appears to be produced by it in the *first* instance.

3. Of the value of each *pleasure* which appears to be produced by it *after* the first. This constitutes the *fecundity* of the first *pleasure* and the *impurity* of the first *pain*.

4. Of the value of each *pain* which appears to be produced by it after the first. This constitutes the *fecundity* of the first *pain*, and the *impurity* of the first *pleasure*.

5. Sum up all the values of all the *pleasures* on the one side, and those of all the *pains* on the other. The balance, if it be on the side of pleasure, will give the *good* tendency of the act upon the whole, with respect to the interests of that *individual* person; if on the side of pain, the *bad* tendency of it upon the whole.

6. Take an account of the *number* of persons whose interests appear to be concerned; and repeat the above process with respect to each. *Sum up* the numbers expressive of the degrees of *good* tendency, which the act has, with respect to each individual, in regard to whom the tendency of it is *good* upon the whole: do this again with respect to each individual, in regard to whom the tendency of it is *bad* upon the whole. Take the *balance*; which, if on the side of *pleasure*, will give the general *good tendency* of the act, with respect to the total number or community of individuals concerned; if on the side of *pain*, the general *evil tendency*, with respect to the same community.

It is not to be expected that this process should be strictly pursued previously to every moral judgment, or to every legislative or judicial operation. It may, however, be always kept in view: and as near as the process actually pursued on these occasions approaches to it, so near will such process approach to the character of an exact one.

Although there is a certain undeniable logic to Bentham's hedonistic calculus, the most obvious question is, "Will it work?" After all, simply because an elaborate system makes sense on paper is not reason to believe that it can be usefully applied to the extraordinarily complex world of lived experience. The Think Critically activity 6.1 describes an example based on an incident that occurred in 1989 in Springfield, Missouri.

If you ran into difficulty in applying Bentham's "scientific" calculus, you are likely not alone. There are certain basic difficulties with his approach that are intrinsic to the method itself. For example:

- What counts as a "unit of pleasure" (or pain)? Bentham provides a name for each unit: a "hedon." But what exactly does that refer to? In his definition of the principle of utility, Bentham equates the following terms for "pleasure," stating confidently "all this in the present case comes to the same thing":

  pleasure   happiness   good   benefit   advantage

  Similarly, he equates the following terms for "pain":

  pain   mischief   evil   unhappiness

THINK CRITICALLY 6.1

PHILOSOPHER'S NOTEBOOK

Hedonistic Calculus and Ethical Controversy

Imagine that you are a member of a student group at your college that has decided to stage the controversial play *The Normal Heart* by Larry Kramer. The play is based on the lives of real people and dramatizes their experiences in the early stages of the AIDS epidemic. It focuses on their efforts to publicize the horrific nature of this disease and to secure funding from a reluctant federal government to find a cure. The play is considered controversial because of its exclusive focus on the subject of AIDS, its explicit homosexual themes, and the large amount of profanity contained in the script. After lengthy discussion, however, your student group has decided that the educational and moral benefits of the play render it a valuable contribution to the life of the college.

While the play is in rehearsal, a local politician seizes upon it as an issue and mounts a political and public relations campaign against it. She distributes selected excerpts of the play to newspapers, religious groups, and civic organizations. She also introduces a bill in the state legislature to withdraw state funding for the college if the play is performed. The play creates a firestorm of controversy, replete with local and national news reports, editorials, and impassioned speeches for and against it. Everyone associated with the play is subjected to verbal harassment, threats, crank phone calls, and hate mail. The firestorm explodes when the house of one of the key spokespersons for the play is burned to the ground. The director and actors go into hiding for their safety, rehearsing in secret and moving from hotel to hotel.

Your student group has just convened to decide what course of action to take. Analyze the situation using the six criteria of the hedonistic calculus, and then conclude with your decision and the reasons that support your decision.

VISUAL PHILOSOPHY

Censorship

The hedonist goal of pursuing pleasure sometimes conflicts with social and political policy. What areas of personal pleasure do you think should be controlled or censored by the government? Why?

But does it make sense to believe that each of these categories can be reduced to one, homogeneous category? And what about different kinds of pleasurable experiences, for example: Falling in love? Enjoying a good meal? Earning a degree? Dancing the night away? Triumphing in sports? Engaging in quiet meditation? Helping out a grateful friend? Soaking in a hot bath? Having your child say 'I love you'? Listening to your favorite music? There are nearly limitless experiences that provide pleasure, and in many cases, each with their own distinctive kinds of pleasure. Trying to compare them would seem to be akin to comparing apples, oranges, pizza, ice cream, and pop tarts.

- Even if you could define a "hedon," is the formula that Bentham suggests really workable? Applying it would seem to be a rather complex operation. Of course, you could enlist the help of computers in your calculations—an option that wasn't available to Bentham! But simply because a model like the hedonistic calculus "seems" to be logical, scientific, and objective, does that mean it really is? Or does such a model create a false sense of scientific objectivity that is not reflected in the reality of lived experience?

However, if we abandon the "scientific" version of the hedonistic calculus, and instead use it as a guide for "rough" calculations, it can provide some insight and guidance. For example, in the case of the staging of *The Normal Heart* cited above, you might pose the following questions in deliberating what to do.

1. How would you describe the potential pleasure/happiness of
   - following through on your principles and staging the play?
   - demonstrating to the politicians and others that you won't be intimidated by their threats?
   - staging a play that you believe has an important social message?

2. How would you describe the potential *pain/unhappiness* of
- verbal harassment, crank calls, hate mail?
- the threat of enduring physical injury or the destruction of your property?
- having the legislature cut funding for the college?
- potential sanctions (such as withdrawing your financial aid) that the college might impose?

3. When you consider *all* of the people involved—members of the cast, fellow students, college administrators, members of the community, (even) politicians—do you think on balance that staging the play would result in more pleasure/happiness for the greatest number of people, or more pain/unhappiness? Whatever your conclusion, that would be the ethically correct thing to do, in accordance with the principle of utility.

In reasoning through the previous Think Critically example (based on the principle of utility), it may have felt rather odd to focus only on consequences in order to determine a moral course of action. That's because, when engaging in moral reasoning, we generally appeal to principles, values, and motivations, asking ourselves questions such as:

- What is the just and honorable course of action?
- What would a "good" person do?
- What choices would be consistent with maintaining my integrity?

But the hedonistic calculus leaves minimal room for the inclusion of such factors as principles, values, and motivations: it's mainly consequences that matter, to be determined by logical calculations. Bentham recognizes that this is going to strike some people as peculiar, and he attempts to address their anticipated concerns in the following passage.

Motives

With respect to goodness and badness, as it is with everything else that is not itself either pain or pleasure, so is it with motives. If they are good or bad, it is only on account of their effects: good, on account of their tendency to produce pleasure, or avert pain: bad, on account of their tendency to produce pain, or avert pleasure. Now the case is, that from one and the same motive, and from every kind of motive, may proceed actions that are good, others that are bad, and others that are indifferent. . . .

It appears then that there is no such thing as a sort of motive which is a bad one in itself: nor, consequently, any such thing as a sort of motive which in itself is exclusively a good one. And as to their effects, it appears too that there are sometimes bad, at other times either indifferent or good, and this appears to be the case with every sort of motive. *If any sort of motive then is either good or bad on the score of its effects, this is the case only on individual occasions, and with individual motives*, and this is the case with one sort of motive as well as with another. *If any sort of motive then can, in consideration of its effects, be termed with any propriety a bad one*, it can only be with reference to the balance of all the effects it may have had of both kinds within a given period, that is, of its most usual tendency.

Bentham,
An Introduction to the Principles of Morals and Legislation

Bentham, Jeremy, *An Introduction to the Principles of Morals and Legislation*

Consistent with his ethical framework, Bentham contends that motives and intentions are morally neutral—it's the consequences of these motives and intentions that determine their moral goodness or badness. For example, sexual desire within the context of a consensual relationship may be morally positive, whereas sexual desire expressed as forcible rape would be considered morally negative. Of course, certain motivations—such as lust and cruelty—are more likely to end up with morally negative results than such motivations as sympathy and kindness. But in the final analysis, it's the consequences, not the motivations or intentions that determine moral values.

Analogously, when we evaluate the consequences of an action, it doesn't really matter what the intentions of the person were. Suppose you are rescued from a car wreck by a passing motorist. According to utilitarian reasoning, that action of a person hoping for fame and a reward is just as morally positive as that of a person motivated only by altruism.

Despite its potential flaws and limitations, Bentham's utilitarian theory was a stunning contribution to philosophical thought, and it had the added benefit of improving the lives of many people in concrete and significant ways. Nevertheless, it was a system of thought that had the potential to be strengthened and refined, a task bequeathed to **John Stuart Mill** by Bentham. The relationship between these two men was quite extraordinary and certainly unique. Mill's father, James, was by all accounts a cold, emotionally distant father, raising his children through fear, intimidation, and criticism. Young John was saved from a completely repressive childhood by Bentham's befriending of his father, James, who became a convert to utilitarianism. Bentham and James Mill shared the conviction that all children were born with the same intellectual capacity, and that through proper education they could become intellectually accomplished individuals. They decided to use young John Stuart Mill as a test case for their theories and devised a rigorous educational plan for him: Greek and arithmetic at the age of three; Latin, geometry, and algebra at eleven; logic and philosophy at twelve. His education was so all-consuming that it left no time for friends or normal childhood activities. The emotional pressures of this skewed upbringing must have been enormous, and the consequences were devastating: an emotional breakdown at the age of twenty that lasted for several years, and recurring bouts of depression that lasted throughout his life.

Yet on an intellectual level Bentham's and James Mill's plan succeeded brilliantly, for John Stuart Mill was an authentic genius who brought a powerful and creative vision to Bentham's utilitarianism as well as many other areas of inquiry. One of Mill's most serious reservations regarding Bentham's version of utilitarianism was his (Bentham's) failure to distinguish between various kinds of pleasures. For Bentham, the hedonistic calculus did not distinguish between spending an evening at the local tavern swilling beer versus spending an evening at the opera sipping champagne. One simply counted up the hedons and made the utilitarian calculations. Mill is greatly offended by this leveling of pleasures. He was convinced that the "higher" pleasures—activities that were intellectual, literary, aesthetic, philosophical—were greatly to be preferred over the "lower" physical pleasures. Mill's vivid and provocative characterization of this issue earned him a place in philosophical folklore, as he issued his own resounding version of Socrates' challenge, "The unexamined life is not worth living."

Mill, *Utilitarianism*
It is better to be a human being dissatisfied than a pig satisfied; better to be Socrates dissatisfied than a fool satisfied. And if the fool, or the pig, are of a different opinion, it is because they only know their own side of the question. The other party to the comparison knows both sides. . . .

This is really the heart of Mill's argument, as he states elsewhere:

Mill, *Utilitarianism*
The comparison of the Epicurean life to that of beasts is felt as degrading, precisely because a beast's pleasures do not satisfy a human being's conceptions of happiness. Human beings have faculties more elevated than the animal appetites, and when once made conscious of them, do not regard anything as happiness which does not include their gratification.

JOHN STUART MILL
(1806–1873)
British Philosopher. Carried on tradition of British Empiricists. Wrote on induction and expanded on utilitarianism of Bentham to take into account the quality, not just the quantity, of pleasure when determining the morality of an action.

Although, as we saw, Epicurus did in fact consider more elevated pleasures to be of greater value, that did not prevent critics from lumping him into the same category as hedonists who failed to make any distinction between "higher" (intellectual, aesthetic, contemplative) pleasures and "lower" (physical, sensual) pleasures. Mill is determined to make sure that he is not vulnerable to the same criticism, suggesting his explicit revision of utilitarianism.

Mill, *Utilitarianism*

It is quite compatible with the principle of utility to recognize the fact, that some *kinds* of pleasure are more desirable and more valuable than others. It would be absurd that while, in estimating all other things, quality is considered as well as quantity, the estimation of pleasures should be supposed to depend on quantity alone.

If I am asked, what I mean by difference of quality in pleasures, or what makes one pleasure more valuable than another, merely as a pleasure, except it being greater in amount, there is but one possible answer. Of two pleasures, if there be one to which all or almost all who have experience of both give a decided preference, irrespective of any feeling of moral obligation to prefer it, that is the more desirable pleasure. If one of the two is, by those who are competently acquainted with both, placed so far above the other that they prefer it, even though knowing it to be attended with a greater amount of discontent, and would not resign it for any quantity of the other pleasure which their nature is capable of, we are justified in ascribing to the preferred enjoyment a superiority in quality, so far outweighing quantity as to render it, in comparison, of small account.

This, of course, is a question that must be dealt with in attempting to establish a hierarchy of pleasure. *On what basis* does one declare that the so-called "higher" pleasures have more intrinsic worth than the "lower" pleasures? What is the justification for asserting that the pleasure of drinking an expensive Beaujolais is inherently superior to the pleasure derived from a six-pack of beer? Or that listening to Mozart provides higher quality pleasure than popular music? Or that the joy of attending the opera outclasses attending a sporting event? Mill's response is that the only way to do this is to observe and speak to people who have experienced both "higher" and "lower" pleasures, and ask them which they prefer. Mill is confident that the "higher" pleasures will consistently triumph.

Mill, *Utilitarianism*

Now it is an unquestionable fact that those who are equally acquainted with, and equally capable of appreciating and enjoying, both, do give a most marked preference to the manner of existence which employs their higher faculties. Few human creatures would consent to be changed into any of the lower animals, for a promise of the fullest allowance of a beast's pleasures; no intelligent human being would consent to be a fool, no instructed person would be an ignoramus, no person of feeling and conscience would be selfish and base, even though they should be persuaded that the fool, the dunce, or the rascal is better satisfied with his lot than they are with theirs. They would not resign what they possess more than he for the most complete satisfaction of all the desires which they have in common with him. If they ever fancy they would, it is only in cases of unhappiness so extreme, that to escape from it they would exchange their lot for almost any other, however, undesirable in their own eyes. A being of higher faculties requires more to make him happy, is capable probably of more acute suffering, and certainly accessible to it at more points, than one of an inferior type; but in spite of these liabilities, he can never really wish to sink into what he feels to be a lower grade of existence. . . .

Do you agree with John Stuart Mill's conviction that the "higher" pleasures are superior to the "lower" pleasures? Why?
Sir John Everett Millais, P.R.A., British 1829–1896. Peace Concluded 1856. Oil on canvas. 46 x 36 in. (116.84 x 91.44 cm) The Minneapolis Institute of Arts, The Putnam Dana McMillian Fund. (69.48)

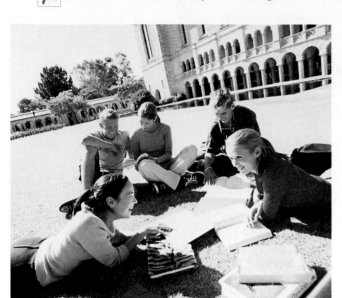

How would you compare the pleasures of pursuing a college education with the pleasures of attending parties? Do you think one type of pleasure is superior? Why?

Mill, *Utilitarianism*

This is certainly a provocative assertion of Mill, and it's one that requires a great deal of careful analysis and investigation. But Mill goes on to say that even if you doubt that the more "elevated" activities provide a qualitatively superior form of pleasure than the less refined activities, nevertheless it is incontrovertible that it is much better to live in a society in which the majority of people pursue the "higher" pleasures, than a society dominated by the physical, sensual pleasures.

I have dwelt on this point, as being a necessary part of a perfectly just conception of Utility or Happiness, considered as the directive rule of human conduct. But it is by no means an indispensable condition to the acceptance of the utilitarian standard; for the standard is not the agent's own greatest happiness, but the greatest amount of happiness altogether; and if it may possibly be doubted whether a noble character is always the happier for its nobleness, there can be no doubt that it makes other people happier, and that the world in general is immensely a gainer by it. Utilitarianism, therefore, could only attain its end by the general cultivation of nobleness of character, even if each individual were only benefited by the nobleness of others, and his own, so far as happiness is concerned, were a sheer deduction from the benefit. But the bare enunciation of such an absurdity as this last, renders refutation superfluous.

THINK PHILOSOPHICALLY   6.2
Applying Utilitarianism

PHILOSOPHER'S NOTEBOOK

- Describe a moral decision involving other people that you made recently. Using Bentham's hedonistic calculus as a general guide, calculate what would have been the morally correct choice to make based on the principle of utility. How does this conclusion compare with the choice you actually made?

- Now analyze that same decision using Mill's distinction of "higher" and "lower" pleasures. What ethical conclusion does this method result in? Do you agree with Mill that "higher" pleasures have intrinsically greater value than "lower" pleasures? Why or why not? Use examples to support your conclusion.

- One major criticism of utilitarianism is its potential conflict with the principle of justice: that is, treating an individual unjustly so long as this leads to more overall happiness. For example, suppose the government is planning to execute a person they know to be innocent for the purpose of "setting an example." Create a scenario in which the utilitarians would have to support such an execution.

- In ancient Rome, innocent people—especially Christians—were slaughtered in the Coliseum for the entertainment and pleasure of thousands of people. How would the utilitarians analyze this situation?

- Explain why Mill believes that in calculating the greatest good for the greatest number of people that it is essential that you "be as strictly impartial as a disinterested and benevolent spectator."

- What do you think about only judging the consequences of actions to determine their moral worth, without reference to an individual's moral values, intentions, or motivations. Describe what role evaluating consequences plays in your moral reasoning? What other factors come into play in your efforts to "do the right thing"?

As a final act, Mill reviews the major themes he has been discussing and then weaves them together into his revised version of utilitarianism.

Mill, *Utilitarianism*

According to the Greatest Happiness Principle, as above explained, the ultimate end, with reference to and for the sake of which all other things are desirable (whether we are considering our own good or that of other people), is an existence exempt as far as possible from pain, and as rich as possible in enjoyments, both in point of quantity and quality; the test of quality, and the rule for measuring it against quantity, being the preference felt by those who in their opportunities of experience, to which must be added their habits of self-consciousness and self-observation, are best furnished with the means of comparison. This, being, according to the utilitarian opinion, the end of human action, is necessarily also the standard of morality; which may accordingly be defined, the rules and precepts for human conduct, by the observance of which an existence such as has been described might be, to the greatest extent possible, secured to all mankind, and not of them only, but, so far as the nature of things admits, to the whole sentient creation. . . .

Peter Singer: *Utilitarianism and Animal Rights*

PETER SINGER
(1946–)
Moral Philosopher. Important figure in the field of applied ethics. Heavily influenced by utilitarianism. In his major work, *Animal Liberation* (1975), argues that animals have equal moral status with humans such that to continue to use animals for science and food is a form of prejudice akin to racism or sexism.

Mill's concluding sentence in the passage above makes clear that he believes that the principle of utility should be applied not only to humans but to nonhuman animals as well, ". . . the whole sentient creation." Similarly, Bentham fervently believed that animals as well as humans of all races should be included in the moral community.

The Australian philosopher **Peter Singer** has given this point of view a modern voice, arguing that reason requires that the principle of utility be equally applied to all animals capable of experiencing suffering. The following passages are taken from his influential book, *Animal Liberation*.

Singer, *Animal Liberation*

All Animals Are Equal . . . *or why the ethical principle on which human equality rests requires us to extend equal consideration to animals too*

"Animal Liberation" may sound more like a parody of other liberation movements than a serious objective. The idea of "The Rights of Animals" actually was once used to parody the case for women's rights. When Mary Wollstonecraft, a forerunner of today's feminists, published her *Vindication of the Rights of Woman* in 1792, her views were widely regarded as absurd, and before long an anonymous publication appeared entitled *A Vindication of the Rights of Brutes*. The author of this satirical work (now known to have been Thomas Taylor, a distinguished Cambridge philosopher) tried to refute Mary Wollstonecraft's arguments by showing that they could be carried one stage further. If the argument for equality was sound when applied to women, why should it not be applied to dogs, cats, and horses? The reasoning seemed to hold for these "brutes" too; yet to hold that brutes had rights was manifestly absurd. Therefore the reasoning by which this conclusion had been reached must be unsound, and if unsound when applied to brutes, it must also be unsound when applied to women, since the very same arguments had been used in each case.

* * *

. . . *The principle of the equality of human beings is not a description of an alleged actual equality among humans: it is a prescription of how we should treat human beings.* Jeremy Bentham, the founder of the reforming utilitarian school of moral philosophy, incorporated the essential basis of moral equality into his system of ethics by means of the formula: "Each to count for one and none for more than one." In other words, the interests of every being affected by an action are to be taken into account and given the same weight as the like interests of any other being. A later utilitarian, Henry Sidgwick, put the point this way: "The good of any one individual is of no more importance, from the point of view (if I may say so) of the Universe, than the good of any other." More recently the leading figures in contemporary moral philosophy have shown a great deal of agreement in specifying as a fundamental presupposition of their moral theories some similar require-

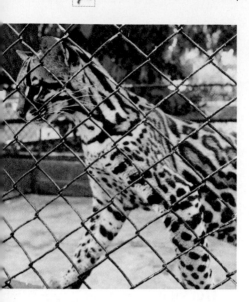

ment that works to give everyone's interests equal consideration—although these writers generally cannot agree on how this requirement is best formulated.

It is an implication of this principle of equality that our concern for others and our readiness to consider their interests ought not to depend on what they are like or on what abilities they may possess. Precisely what our concern or consideration requires us to do may vary according to the characteristics of those affected by what we do: concern for the well-being of children growing up in America would require that we teach them to read; concern for the well-being of pigs may require no more than that we leave them with other pigs in a place where there is adequate food and room to run freely. But the basic element—the taking into account of the interests of the being, whatever those interests may be—must, according to the principle of equality, be extended to all beings, black or white, masculine or feminine, human or nonhuman.

* * *

. . . Speciesism—the word is not an attractive one, but I can think of no better term—is a prejudice or attitude of bias in favor of the interests of members of one's own species and against those of members of other species. It should be obvious that the fundamental objections to racism and sexism made by Thomas Jefferson and Sojourner Truth apply equally to speciesism. If possessing a higher degree of intelligence does not entitle one human to use another for his or her own ends, how can it entitle humans to exploit nonhumans for the same purpose?

Many philosophers and other writers have proposed the principle of equal consideration of interests, in some form or other, as a basic moral principle; but not many of them have recognized that this principle applies to members of other species as well as to our own. Jeremy Bentham was one of the few who did realize this. In a forward-looking passage written at a time when black slaves had been freed by the French but in the British dominions were still being treated in the way we now treat animals, Bentham wrote:

> The day may come when the rest of the animal creation may acquire those rights which never could have been withholden from them but by the hand of tyranny. The French have already discovered that the blackness of the skin is no reason why a human being should be abandoned without redress to the caprice of a tormentor. It may one day come to be recognized that the number of legs, the villosity of the skin, or the termination of the *os sacrum* are reasons equally insufficient for abandoning a sensitive being to the same fate. What else is it that should trace the insuperable line? Is it the faculty of reason, or perhaps the faculty of discourse. But a full-grown horse or dog is beyond comparison a more rational, as well as a more conversable animal than an infant of a day or a week or even a month old. But suppose they were otherwise, what would it avail? The question is not, Can they *reason*? Nor, Can they *talk*? But, Can they *suffer*?

In this passage Bentham points to the capacity for suffering as the vital characteristic that gives a being the right to equal consideration. The capacity for suffering—or more strictly, for suffering and/or enjoyment or happiness—is not just another characteristic like the capacity for language or higher mathematics. Bentham is not saying that those who try to mark "the insuperable line" that determines whether the interests of a being should be considered happen to have chosen the wrong characteristic. By saying that we must consider the interests of all beings with the capacity for suffering or enjoyment Bentham does not arbitrarily exclude from consideration any interests at all—as those who draw the line with reference to the possession of reason or language do. The capacity for suffering and enjoyment is *a prerequisite for having interests at all*, a condition that must be satisfied before we can speak of interests in a meaningful way. . . .

Racists violate the principle of equality by giving greater weight to the interests of members of their own race when there is a clash between their interests and the interests of those of another race. Sexists violate the principle of equality by favoring the interests of their own sex. Similarly, speciesists allow the interests of their own species to override the greater interests of members of other species. The pattern is identical in each case.

Most human beings are speciesists . . . ordinary human beings—not a few exceptionally cruel or heartless humans, but the overwhelming majority of humans—take an active part in, acquiesce in, and allow their taxes to pay for practices that require the sac-

rifice of the most important interests of members of other species in order to promote the most trivial interests of our own species.

* * *

Although, . . . the view that animals are automata was proposed by the seventeenth-century French philosopher Rene Descartes, to most people, then and now, it is obvious that if, for example, we stick a sharp knife into the stomach of an unanesthetized dog, the dog will feel pain. That this is so is assumed by the laws in most civilized countries that prohibit wanton cruelty to animals. . . .

Do animals other than humans feel pain? How do we know? Well, how do we know if anyone, human or nonhuman, feels pain? We know that we ourselves can feel pain. We know this from the direct experience of pain that we have when, for instance, somebody presses a lighted cigarette against the back of our hand. But how do we know that anyone else feels pain? We cannot directly experience anyone else's pain, whether that "anyone" is our best friend or a stray dog. Pain is a state of consciousness, a "mental event," and as such it can never be observed. Behavior like writhing, screaming, or drawing one's hand away from a lighted cigarette is not pain itself; nor are the recordings a neurologist might make of activity within the brain observations of pain itself. Pain is something that we feel, and we can only infer that others are feeling it from various external indications. . . .

If it is justifiable to assume that other human beings feel pain as we do, is there any reason why a similar inference should be unjustifiable in the case of other animals?

Nearly all the external signs that leads us to infer pain in other humans can be seen in other species, especially the species most closely related to us—the species of mammals and birds. The behavioral signs include writhing, facial contortions, moaning, yelping or other forms of calling, attempts to avoid the source of pain, appearance of fear at the prospect of its repetition, and so on. In addition, we know that these animals have nervous systems very like ours, which respond physiologically as ours do when the animal is in circumstances in which we would feel pain: an initial rise of blood pressure, dilated pupils, perspiration, and increased pulse rate, and, if the stimulus continues, a fall in blood pressure. Although human beings have a more developed cerebral cortex than other animals, this part of the brain is concerned with thinking functions rather than with basic impulses, emotions, and feelings. These impulses, emotions, and feelings are located in the diencephalon, which is well developed in many other species of animals, especially mammals and birds. . . .

* * *

It may be objected that comparisons of the sufferings of different species are impossible to make and that for this reason when the interests of animals and humans clash the principle of equality gives no guidance. It is probably true that comparisons of suffering between members of different species cannot be made precisely, but precision is not essential. Even if we were to prevent the infliction of suffering on animals only when it is quite certain that the interests of humans will not be affected to anything like the extent that animals are affected, we would be forced to make radical changes in our treatment of animals that would involve our diet, the farming methods we use, experimental procedures in many fields of science, our approach to wildlife and to hunting, trapping and the wearing of furs, and areas of entertainment like circuses, rodeos, and zoos. As a result, a vast amount of suffering would be avoided.

So far I have said a lot about inflicting suffering on animals, but nothing about killing them. This omission has been deliberate. The application of the principle of equality to the infliction of suffering is, in theory at least, fairly straightforward. Pain and suffering are in themselves bad and should be prevented or minimized, irrespective of the race, sex, or species of the being that suffers. How bad a pain is depends on how intense it is and how long it lasts, but pains of the same intensity and duration are equally bad, whether felt by humans or animals.

The wrongness of killing a being is more complicated. I have kept, and shall continue to keep, the question of killing in the background because in the present state of human tyranny over other species the more simple, straightforward principle of equal consideration of pain or pleasure is a sufficient basis for identifying and protesting against all the major abuses of animals that human beings practice. Nevertheless, it is necessary to say something about killing.

Just as most human beings are speciesists in their readiness to cause pain to animals when they would not cause a similar pain to humans for the same reason, so most human beings are speciesists in their readiness to kill other animals when they would not kill human beings. . . .

This does not mean that to avoid speciesism we must hold that it is as wrong to kill a dog as it is to kill a human being in full possession of his or her faculties. The only position that is irredeemably speciesist is the one that tries to make the boundary of the right to life run exactly parallel to the boundary of our own species. Those who hold the sanctity of life view do this, because while distinguishing sharply between human beings and other animals they allow no distinctions to be made within our own species, objecting to the killing of the severely retarded and the hopelessly senile as strongly as they object to the killing of normal adults.

To avoid speciesism we must allow that beings who are similar in all relevant respects have a similar right to life—and mere membership in our own biological species cannot be a morally relevant criterion for this right. Within these limits we could still hold, for instance, that it is worse to kill a normal adult human, with a capacity for self-awareness and the ability to plan for the future and have meaningful relations with others, than it is to kill a mouse, which presumably does not share all of these characteristics; or we might appeal to the close family and other personal ties that humans have but mice do not have to the same degree; or we might think that it is the consequences for other humans, who will be put in fear for their own lives, that makes the crucial difference; or we might think it is some combination of these factors, or other factors together.

Whatever criteria we choose, however, we will have to admit that they do not follow precisely the boundary of our own species. We may legitimately hold that there are some features of certain beings that make their lives more valuable than those of other beings; but there will surely be some nonhuman animals whose lives, by any standards, are more valuable than the lives of some humans. A chimpanzee, dog, or pig, for instance, will have a higher degree of self-awareness and a greater capacity for meaningful relations with others than a severely retarded infant or someone in a state of advanced senility. So if we base the right to life on these characteristics we must grant these animals a right to life as good as, or better than, such retarded or senile humans.

This argument cuts both ways. It could be taken as showing that chimpanzees, dogs, and pigs, along with some other species, have a right to life and we commit a grave moral offence whenever we kill them, even when they are old and suffering and our intention is to put them out of their misery. Alternatively one could take the argument as showing that the severely retarded and hopelessly senile have no right to life and may be killed for quite trivial reasons, as we now kill animals.

Since the main concern of this book is with ethical questions having to do with animals and not with the morality of euthanasia I shall not attempt to settle this issue finally. I think it is reasonably clear, though, that while both of the positions just described avoid speciesism, neither is satisfactory. What we need is some middle position that would avoid speciesism but would not make the lives of the retarded and senile as cheap as the lives of pigs and dogs now are, or make the lives of pigs and dogs so sacrosanct that we think it wrong to put them out of hopeless misery. What we must do is bring nonhuman animals within our sphere of moral concern and cease to treat their lives as expendable for whatever trivial purposes we may have. At the same time, once we realize that the fact that a being is a member of our own species is not in itself enough to make it always wrong to kill that being, we may come to reconsider our policy of preserving human lives at all costs, even when there is no prospect of a meaningful life or of existence without terrible pain.

I conclude, then, that a rejection of speciesism does not imply that all lives are of equal worth. While self-awareness, the capacity to think ahead and have hopes and aspirations for the future, the capacity for meaningful relations with others and so on are not relevant to the question of inflicting pain—since pain is pain, whatever other capacities, beyond the capacity to feel pain, the being may have—these capacities are relevant to the question of taking life. It is not arbitrary to hold that the life a self-aware being, capable of abstract thought, of planning for the future, of complex acts of communication, and so on, is more valuable than the life of a being without these capacities. ∎

Singer, Peter, *Animal Liberation*

THINK PHILOSOPHICALLY 6.3
Analyzing Peter Singer

- How does the author, Peter Singer, define "speciesism"? In what way is this concept based on the principles of utilitarianism, both in terms of the principle of utility and the principle of equality?

- According to Singer, "Most human beings are speciesists" because they "take an active part in, acquiesce in, and allow their taxes to pay for practices that require the sacrifice of the most important interests of members of other species in order to promote the most trivial interests of our own species." Explain whether you agree with Singer's conclusion, supporting your analysis with reasons and examples.

- According to Singer, the principle of equality demands that it is our moral obligation to avoid inflicting needless pain on animals, any more than we would inflict it on humans, and that if we followed this principle "we would be forced to make radical changes in our treatment of animals that would involve our diet, the farming methods we use, experimental procedures in many fields of science, our approach to wildlife and to hunting, trapping and the wearing of furs, and areas of entertainment like circuses, rodeos, and zoos. As a result, a vast amount of suffering would be avoided." Do you agree with Singer's conclusion? Why or why not?

- Singer's application of the principle of equality to the subject of killing has resulted in some of his more controversial suggestions, such as the passage below. How would you respond to Singer regarding these issues. How do you think he would respond to your points?

  > This argument cuts both ways. It could be taken as showing that chimpanzees, dogs, and pigs, along with some other species, have a right to life and we commit a grave moral offence whenever we kill them, even when they are old and suffering and our intention is to put them out of their misery. Alternatively one could take the argument as showing that the severely retarded and hopelessly senile have no right to life and may be killed for quite trivial reasons, as we now kill animals.

- Has reading and reflecting on Singer's article influenced your views on the way we treat animals in our society? If so, what are some areas in which society should reconsider its treatment of nonhuman animals?

Immanuel Kant: *Moral Duty Is Based on Reason*

Two things fill the mind with ever new and increasing admiration and awe, the oftener and more steadily we reflect on them: the starry heavens above and the moral law within.

—Immanuel Kant

For the utilitarians Jeremy Bentham and John Stuart Mill, the locus of morality is to be found almost entirely in the *consequences* of our actions. What makes an action good or evil is determined by evaluating the amount of happiness (or unhappiness) it produces in the people affected. It is for this reason that such ethical theories as utilitarianism are known as **consequentialist** theories. From this perspective, you construct a moral code and evaluate the relative moral value of action through empirical research. Should you choose to tell a

Consequentialism The view that an action's consequences determine its moral value.

IMMANUEL KANT
(1724–1804)
German Philosopher. Kant widely
regarded as greatest philosopher
of modern period. Based his moral
philosophy on the principle of reason,
developing the highly influential
concept of the "Categorical
Imperative."

lie to protect a decent person's reputation from getting ruined? You simply apply the hedonistic calculus to determine whether lying or telling the truth will bring about the greatest happiness for the greatest number of people.

For **Immanuel Kant** (1724–1804), determining the moral value of an action by assessing its consequences could not be more wrongheaded. Kant was a **deontologist**, a person with an ethical perspective that holds that it is the principle of *duty* that determines the moral value of actions, not the consequences. Deontology is derived from the Greek word *deon*, which means "duty" or "that which is obligatory." Deontologists are intent on discovering the moral duties that all people in all situations should follow. Should you choose to tell a lie to protect a decent person's reputation from being ruined? If the deontologist concludes that telling the truth is a universal duty that all people are obligated to follow (as Kant does), then lying is morally wrong regardless of the consequences.

We examined some of the specifics of Kant's life when we explored his views on the "self" in chapter 3. What makes Kant such a towering figure in modern philosophy (although he barely topped five feet in real life) was the extraordinary influence he had in so many areas of philosophy: metaphysics, epistemology, and ethics. In fact, the noted American philosopher William Barrett once observed, "Kant can justly be called the father of modern philosophy, for out of him stem nearly all the still current and contending schools of philosophy." Kant's views are stunning in their depth, comprehensiveness, and compelling rationales.

Why was Kant so certain that moral value needed to be based on using our rational faculties to discover moral laws that would be universally binding on all people? Because he was convinced that all other potential foundations for morality were irretrievably flawed. For example, suppose we attempt to ground our moral beliefs in right and wrong in our feelings, impulses, or desires—what Kant calls *inclinations*. How can these possibly serve as a consistent and reliable moral guide? These personal inclinations are so subjective that they vary wildly from person to person, culture to culture. Even inclinations that are generally considered admirable—sympathy, empathy, love, caring—are hopeless candidates for establishing a universally binding system of ethical values. Should you choose to tell a lie to protect a decent person's reputation from getting ruined? If you rely on your personal inclinations to instruct you, it's clear that whatever your conclusion, some people will agree (based on their inclinations) and others will disagree (based on their inclinations). There's simply no way to determine with absolute certainty what the morally right choice is. Similarly, if we try to apply the utilitarian approach to the same moral question, we run into the same difficulty. In assessing lying in that situation (or in any situation for that matter), people will likely arrive at different calculations of "the greatest happiness for the greatest number."

What we need, Kant is convinced, is a grounding for morality that is *beyond* the everyday experience of personal inclinations. We need to develop a *metaphysic of morals* that will stand independently of any particular moral belief or custom. Observing the way people make moral choices simply tells us *what* they are doing—it sheds no light on what they *should* be doing. That can only be established by discovering the necessary and universal laws of moral conduct, laws that are **a priori**. A law that is *a priori* is one that we can be certain is true independently of its application to actual empirical experience. And there is only one way that we can discover such necessary and universal moral laws, Kant believes, and that is through the faculty of reason.

Deontology The ethical view that moral value is determined by fulfilling one's duty.

A priori Prior to experience. Often used to describe a proposition, argument, or value that we can be certain is true without empirical verification, something derived from pure reason.

Thus the moral worth of an action does not lie in the effect expected from it, nor in any principle of action which requires to borrow its motive from its expected effect. For all these effects—agreeableness of one's condition, and even the promotion of the happiness of others—could have been also brought about by

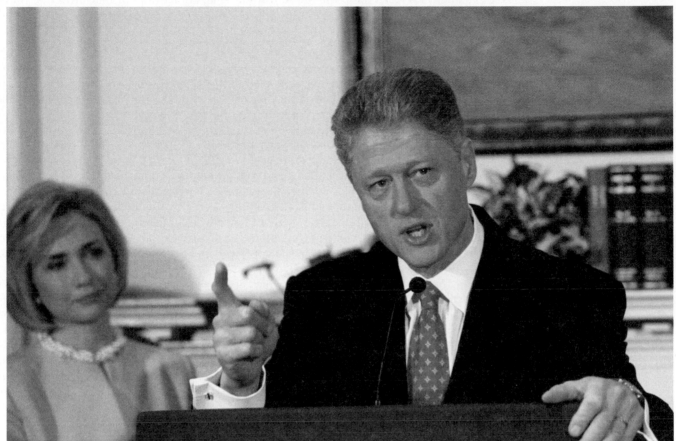

Bill Clinton Denies Relations with Monica Lewinsky

Do you agree with Immanuel Kant that lying is wrong in all circumstances? What are some situations in which you believe lying might be ethically justified? Why? How do you think Kant would respond to these "exceptions" to telling the truth?

other causes so that for this there would have been no need of the will of a rational being; whereas it is in this alone that the supreme and unconditioned good can be found. The preeminent good which we call moral can therefore consist in nothing else than *the conception of law* in itself, which certainly is only possible in a rational being, in so far as this conception, and not the expected effect, determines the will.

However, to fully appreciate the binding and compelling nature of our universal moral obligations, Kant believes that we must first understand the human "will." It's not enough for people to be told or even understand what their moral obligations are—they need to *choose* to respond to these moral laws. For example, even if you are persuaded that it's morally wrong to lie to protect someone's reputation, you need to *will* yourself to make this choice. There are many times when people *know* what the morally right thing to do is—they simply don't do it, they don't *will* it.

So for Kant, fulfilling your potential as a moral person involves both

- developing a clear understanding of the necessary and universal moral laws that apply to all people in all circumstances, *and*
- developing the "good will" to actually follow these laws.

We can discover these universal laws by using our ability to reason thoughtfully and logically. And it is through our recognition and acceptance of ourselves as rational beings that we develop the "good will" to make choices in our daily lives that reflect these universal duties. But to fully appreciate Kant's complex and compelling views, we need to let him speak for himself.

Kant, *Fundamental Principles of the Metaphysics of Morals*

Nothing can possibly be conceived in the world, or even out if it, which can be called good without qualification, except a Good Will. Intelligence, wit, judgment, and the other *talents* of the mind, however they may be named, or courage, resolution, perseverance, as qualities of temperament, are undoubtedly good and desirable in many respects; but these gifts of nature may also become extremely bad and mischievous if the will which is to make use of them, and which, therefore, constitutes what is called *character*, is not good. It is the same with the *gifts of fortune*. Power, riches, honor, even health, and the general well-being and contentment with one's condition which is called *happiness*, inspire pride, and often presumption, if there is not a good will to correct the influence of these on the mind, and with this also to rectify the whole principle of acting, and adapt it to its end. The sight of a being who is not adorned with a single feature of a pure and good will, enjoying unbroken prosperity, can never give pleasure to an impartial rational spectator. Thus, a good will appears to constitute the indispensable condition even of being worthy of happiness.

There are even some qualities which are of service to this good will itself, and may facilitate its action, yet which have no intrinsic unconditional values, but always presuppose a good will, and this qualifies the esteem that we justly have for them, and does not permit us to regard them as absolutely good. Moderation in the affections and passions, self-control and calm deliberation are not only good in may respects, but even seem to constitute part of the intrinsic worth of the person; but they are far from deserving to be called good without qualification, although they have been so unconditionally praised by the ancients. For without the principles of a good will, they may become extremely bad, and the coolness of a villain not only makes him far more dangerous, but also directly makes him more abominable in our eyes than he would have been without it.

A good will is good, not because of what it performs or effects, not by its aptness for the attainment of some proposed end, but simply by virtue of the volition; that is, it is good in itself, and considered by itself is to be esteemed much higher than all that can be brought about by it in favor of any inclination, nay even of the sum total of all inclinations. Even if it should happen that, owing to special disfavor of fortune, or the niggardly provision of a stepmotherly nature, this will should wholly lack power to accomplish its purpose, if with its greatest efforts it should yet achieve nothing, and there should remain only the good will (not, to be sure, a mere wish, but the summoning of all means in our power), then, like a jewel, it would still shine by its own light, as a thing which has its whole value in itself. Its usefulness or fruitlessness can neither add to nor take away anything from this value. It would be, as it were, only the setting to it the attention of those who are not yet connoisseurs, but not to recommend it to true connoisseurs, or to determine its value.

Immanuel Kant

It's an inspired argument that Kant is making to ground his moral system in the concept of the "good will." He asks us to consider all the qualities of mind and temperament that we normally value: intelligence, wit, judgment, courage, resolution, perseverance. In the service of a will that is evil, these qualities are stripped of their moral value. Similarly, "gifts of fortune" such as power, riches, honor, health, and happiness—if they characterize the life of a person with a morally deficient will, they become instruments of evil rather than good. Kant's point is that it is the "good will" that is the irreducible source of moral value. Other qualities and characteristics that we normally associate with moral goodness are derivative, depending for their moral value on the goodness of the will exercising them. For Kant, even if the good will is ineffectual, unable to achieve its intended goals, it is nevertheless "like a jewel, it would still shine by its own light, as a thing which has its whole value in itself."

Kant realizes that this is a unique and in some ways counterintuitive notion of "will," and so goes on to analyze this keystone concept further.

Kant, *Fundamental Principles of the Metaphysics of Morals*

. . . The will is a faculty to choose *that only* which reason independent of inclination recognizes as practically necessary, that is, as good. But if reason of itself does not sufficiently determine the will, if the latter is subject also to subjective conditions (particular impulses) which do not always coincide with the objective conditions, in a word, if the will does not *in itself* completely accord with reason (which is actually the case with men), then the actions which objectively are recognized as necessary are subjectively contingent, and the determination of such a will according to objective laws is *obligation*, that is to say, the relation of the objective laws to a will that is not thoroughly good is conceived as the determination of the will of a rational being by principles of reason, but which the will from its nature does not of necessity follow.

The conception of an objective principle, in so far as it is obligatory for a will, is called a command of (reason), and the formula of the command is called an Imperative.

Even though the "will" is the only human faculty capable of being purely and irreducibly good, Kant observes that it is often contaminated by "inclinations" (desires, motives) that result in actions that are *not* good. The will is vulnerable, in other words, to the emotions and desires that form the lifeblood of human experience. Sometimes these emotions and desires are morally good, and they influence the will in a positive direction. Often, however, emotions and desires can be morally misdirected, resulting in willed choices that are morally lacking or even evil. For example, reflecting on your life, you can likely recall choices you willed with great determination that turned out to be moral mistakes that you later regretted. The bottom line is that though the "good will" is the mainspring of moral goodness, it is a force that needs to be directed by reason. It is the human ability to reason and reflect that makes possible the creation of moral ideals that we can then will into existence through the choices we make. These moral ideals function as *commands*, exhorting us to strive for moral excellence in our lives. These ideas are *imperatives* that create a sense of moral *obligation* in determining the direction of our actions. How do we determine, through reason, the precise nature of these moral imperatives? This question leads us to the heart of Kant's metaphysic of morals.

Kant, *Fundamental Principles of the Metaphysics of Morals*

All imperatives are expressed by the word *ought* (or *shall*), and thereby indicate the relation of an objective law of reason to a will which from its subjective constitution is not necessarily determined by it (an obligation). They say that something would be good to do or to forbear, but they say it to a will which does not always do a thing because it is conceived to be good to do it. That is practically *good*, however, which determines the will by means of the conceptions of reason, and consequently not from subjective causes, but objectively, that is, on principles which are valid for every rational being as such. It is distinguished from the *pleasant* as that which influences the will only by means of sensation from merely subjective causes, valid only for the sense of this or that one, and not as a principle of reason which holds for every one.

The ability to think rationally provides us with the insight and authority to determine what we *ought* to do, according to Kant. But even when reason has provided us with moral clarity in a situation calling for a choice to be made, our will is often a reluctant or completely unwilling partner. We have all experienced the conflict—sometimes agonizing conflict—between our feelings of moral obligation and our lack of will power to fulfill obligations by making the morally right choices.

To understand how we can strengthen the "good will" in all of us, to encourage it to fulfill its moral obligations, we need to better understand the moral imperatives to which it is expected to respond.

Kant, *Fundamental Principles of the Metaphysics of Morals*

Now all *imperatives* command either *hypothetically* or *categorically.* The former represent the practical necessity of a possible action as means to something else that is willed (or at least which one might possibly will). The categorical imperative would be that which represented an action as necessary of itself without reference to another end, that is, as objectively necessary.

Since every practical law represents a possible action as good, and on this account, for a subject who is practically determinable by reason as necessary, all imperatives are formulae determining an action which is necessary according to the principle of a will good in some respects. If now the action is good only as a means *to something else,* then the imperative is *hypothetical;* if it is conceived as good *in itself* and consequently as being necessarily the principle of a will which of itself conforms to reason, then it is *categorical.*

Thus, the imperative declares what action possible by me would be good, and presents the practical rule in relation to a will which does not forthwith perform an action simply because it is good, whether because the subject does not always know that it is good, or because, even if it knows this, yet its maxims might be opposed to the objective principles of practical reason.

Accordingly the hypothetical imperative only says that the action is good for some purpose, *possible* or *actual.* In the first case it is a *problematical,* in the second an *assertorial* practical principle. The categorical imperative which declares an action to be objectively necessary in itself without reference to any purpose, that is, without any other end, is valid as an *apodictic* (practical) principle.

Kant distinguishes two kinds of moral imperatives: *hypothetical* imperatives and *categorical* imperatives. **hypothetical imperatives** embody the logical form, *If _____, then _____.* Here are some examples:

- *If* you want to be morally just, *then* you should strive to remove your personal feelings from your judgments.
- *If* you want to be charitable, *then* you should help those less fortunate than you.
- *If* you want to go to Heaven, *then* you should follow the Ten Commandments.

Each of these imperatives is considered a hypothetical imperative because the action being commanded is seen only as a means to something else. You should

- remove your personal feelings.
- help those less fortunate.
- follow the Ten Commandments.

And if you take these actions, *then* you will

- be morally just.
- be charitable.
- go to Heaven.

Hypothetical imperative A moral maxim that does not express a value that one should pursue independently. Instead, the action being commanded by the maxim is seen only as a means to something else.

Categorical imperative A maxim that commands moral obligation independently of experience or consequences. It is derived from pure reason and always carries overriding value.

Maxim A moral law.

None of the actions being commanded are considered to be *intrinsically* good, to be good *in themselves.* Instead, they are good *only* as a means to something else.

Categorical imperatives are very different, because they command actions that are intrinsically good, *not* actions that are good as a means to something else. They prescribe ways of acting that all rational beings are morally required to follow. But how exactly do we discover categorical imperatives, those moral laws or **maxims**, that command us to fulfill moral obligations that are both necessary and universal? What reason-based moral law could possibly meet these standards? Kant identifies one supreme "categorical imperative" that he believes fulfills this requirement, a universal and necessary moral law that has been a prime element of many modern ethical theories since he first articulated it.

Kant, *Fundamental Principles of the Metaphysics of Morals*

Finally, there is an imperative which commands a certain conduct immediately, without having as its condition any other purpose to be attained by it. This imperative is *categorical.* It concerns not the matter of the action, or its intended result, but its form and the principle of which it is itself a result; and what is essentially good in it consists in the mental disposition, let the consequence be what it may. This imperative may be called that of *morality.* . . .

When I conceive a hypothetical imperative, in general I do not know beforehand what it will contain until I am given the condition. But when I conceive a categorical imperative, I know at once what it contains. For as the imperative contains besides the law only the necessity that the maxims* shall conform to this law, while the law contains no conditions restricting it, there remains nothing but the general statement that the maxim of the action should confirm to a universal law, and it is this conformity alone that the imperative properly represents as necessary.

There is therefore but one categorical imperative, namely, this: *Act only on that maxim whereby thou canst at the same time will that it should become a universal law.*

Since the universality of the law according to which effects are produced constitutes what is properly called *nature* in the most general sense (as to form)—that is, the existence of things so far as it is determined by general laws—the imperative of duty may be expressed thus: *Act as if the maxim of thy action were to become by thy will a universal law of nature.*

*A "maxim" is a subjective principle of action, and must be distinguished from the *objective principle, namely, practical law. The former contains the practical rule set by reason according to the conditions of the subject (often its ignorance or its inclinations), so that it is the principle on which the subject acts; but the law is the objective principle valid for every rational being, and is the principle on which it* ought to act—that is an imperative.)*

Kant's formulation of his categorical imperative is conceptually revolutionary. Previous moral theories had tended to focus on

- the *content* of a moral action (e.g., "Thou shalt not kill.").
- the *consequences* of an action ("Act to bring about the greatest happiness for the greatest number of people.").
- the *intent* of an action ("Love God and love your neighbor.").
- the *character* of the person initiating the action ("Act as a virtuous person would act.").

In contrast, Kant focuses on the *logical form* of moral maxims. A moral action is one that a rational person can consistently *universalize* as a moral law applicable to all rational creatures. What determines the moral value of an action is not its content, consequences, intention, or the character of the individual acting—it is whether it is logically consistent for the action to be practiced by *all* women and men. For example, should you choose to tell a lie to protect a decent person's reputation from being ruined? Kant's categorical imperative mandates that we ask—and try to answer—the following question to determine what to do: "Is it logically consistent to will that all people in all comparable circumstances tell a lie to protect a decent person's reputation?" If we apply this standard, Kant believes the answer is clear: it is morally wrong to tell a lie in these (or any other) circumstances. Why? Because if we endorsed the moral rightness of telling a lie, then we would never have reason to believe people when they assured us they were telling the truth. For all we know, they might be lying to protect someone's reputation (or some other "worthy" reason) *and* they would be confident that they were taking the morally correct action. But if lying becomes a "morally correct" action, then the concept of "telling the truth" loses all meaning and value. It's precisely because "telling the truth" is often difficult and disturbing that the concept has moral value. But if telling the truth and *not* telling the truth (lying) *both* can be morally right, then both concepts become meaningless. And that would result in a very chaotic—and unlivable—world indeed, because we would never be able to

If you were to apply Kant's Categorical Imperative, what conclusion would you come to regarding the moral justification of owning a "gas guzzling" car? Why?

The Categorical Imperative and My Moral Compass

Using Kant's categorical imperative as a guide, analyze the following moral dilemmas to determine what the morally right course of action is. Be sure to explain your reasoning along with explaining your conclusion.

- Mired in a deep depression in which you believe that your life has no meaning and that there is no reason for going on, you contemplate suicide.

- Financial reverses have put you on the verge of bankruptcy and personal financial ruin. Your only hope is to borrow money, but you also know that there is virtually no chance that you will be able to repay the borrowed funds.

- You have been told that you possess a great talent in _____, and you are confident that you could fulfill your unique potential and accomplish great things in this area. But you are also lazy: the prospect of making the kind of commitment in time and energy to realize your talent seems daunting. Why not continue to enjoy the simple, relaxed pleasures of life rather than working so hard?

- Fortune has been good to you and you are financially very comfortable. You realize that many others are less fortunate than you, but your attitude is, "I wish them well, but they have to improve their lives on their own. I became a success by my own efforts—let them do the same."

depend on the accuracy of what anyone said to us. As a result, telling a lie to protect someone's reputation fails the test of the categorical imperative, because if we attempt to universalize it—to *will* that everyone take the same action in similar circumstances—the result is logically inconsistent and so morally wrong.

Kant's "metaphysic of morals" is based on the concept that humans are first and foremost rational creatures, and as such we are necessarily committed to the belief in *logical consistency*. For rational creatures, it is offensive and unacceptable to promote beliefs that are logically *in*consistent—for example, the statements:

- "Telling the truth is the morally right thing to do."
- "Not telling the truth is the morally right thing to do."

That's why, when we universalize an action as commanded by the categorical imperative, if the result of our universalized action ("Telling a lie") is logically inconsistent in the real world, then it must be morally wrong.

But suppose a person says: "It's all right for me to lie in this situation, but I'm *different*—special, unique, superior—from everyone else, and so I don't have to universalize this action to determine its moral value. And if only *I* choose to lie, while everyone else is telling the truth, then the result will not be chaos or logical inconsistency.

Kant's response is that to believe that you are *different* from others—special, unique, superior—is an irrational belief. Reason insists that we be *impartial* in evaluating the needs and perspectives of people, and when we do this, it is apparent that as rational creatures, all people share the same intrinsic worth. To claim that you are special, unique, or superior simply because *you are you* is logically absurd.

Let's explore some moral dilemmas to which Kant applies the categorical imperative. But before reading Kant's analysis of these moral situations, why don't you first do the Think Critically activity 6.4, and then compare your perspective with Kant's.

Now let's examine Kant's analysis of these same moral situations.

Kant, *Fundamental Principles of the Metaphysics of Morals*

- A man reduced to despair by a series of misfortunes feels wearied of life, but is still so far in possession of his reason that he can ask himself whether it would not be contrary to his duty to himself to take his own life. Now he inquires whether the maxim of his action could become a universal law of nature. His maxim is: From self-love I adopt it as a principle to shorten my life when its longer duration is likely to bring more evil than satisfaction. It is asked then simply whether this principle founded on self-love can become a universal law of nature. Now we see at once that a system of nature of which it should be a law to destroy life by means of the very feeling whose special nature it is to impel to the improvement of life would contradict itself, and therefore could not exist as a system of nature; hence that maxim cannot possibly exist as a universal law of nature, and consequently would be wholly inconsistent with the supreme principle of all duty.

From Kant's perspective, applying the categorical imperative to the situation of a person contemplating suicide renders a clear moral conclusion: suicide is morally wrong. Why? Not because it violates God's law or because it would be a waste of a human life. Instead, Kant believes it is wrong because it is logically inconsistent, involving belief in the following two contradictory propositions:

> "Suicide would be an act of self-love, because I am convinced that continuing my life is likely to bring me more evil than satisfaction."
>
> "By its nature, self-love seeks to perpetuate and improve my life."

In addition to Kant's analysis, we can also imagine the difficulties associated with universalizing suicide as a morally correct action whenever people became convinced that the balance of their lives was likely to be more unhappy than happy. Such a morally endorsed value would likely result in an increased suicide rate in addition to other negative social consequences.

Kant, *Fundamental Principles of the Metaphysics of Morals*

- Another finds himself forced by necessity to borrow money. He knows that he will not be able to repay it, but sees also that nothing will be lent to him unless he promises stoutly to repay it in a definite time. He desires to make this promise, but he has still so much conscience as to ask himself; Is it not unlawful and inconsistent with duty to get out of a difficulty in this way? Suppose, however, that he resolves to do so, then the maxim of his action would be expressed thus: When I think myself in want of money, I will borrow money and promise to repay it, although I know that I never can do so. Now this principle of self-love or of one's own advantage may perhaps be consistent with my whole future welfare; but the question now is, is it right? I change then the suggestion of self-love into a universal law, and state the question thus: How would it be if my maxim were a universal law? Then I see at once that it could never hold as a universal law of nature, but would necessarily contradict itself. For supposing it to be a universal law that everyone when he thinks himself in a difficulty should be able to promise whatever he pleases, with the purpose of not keeping his promise, the promise itself would become impossible, as well as the end that one might have in view in it, since no one would consider that anything was promised to him, but would ridicule all such statements as vain pretenses.

Kant's analysis of this moral dilemma is analogous to the earlier situation in which we applied the categorical imperative to the question of telling a lie to protect someone's reputation. In this circumstance, the question is whether it's morally acceptable to make a promise that we know we will be unable to keep, in order to avoid financial ruin. Kant's reasoning is clear and unambiguous: intentionally breaking a promise is necessarily immoral. If we apply the categorical imperative by universalizing the action of intentionally breaking promises, we can readily see that this would destroy the entire concept of "promises." If breaking a promise is morally acceptable whenever a person believes it is justified, we would never have any reason to believe any promise that was made to us. And without a belief in "commitment" that is symbolized by promises, our entire social fabric would unravel.

Kant, *Fundamental Principles of the Metaphysics of Morals*

- A third finds in himself a talent which with the help of some culture might make him a useful man in many respects. But he finds himself in comfortable circumstances and prefers to indulge in pleasure rather than to take pains in enlarging and improving his happy natural capacities. He asks, however, whether his maxim of neglect of his natural gifts, besides agreeing with his inclination to indulgence, agrees also with what is called duty. He sees then that a system of nature could indeed subsist with such a universal law, although men (like the South Sea islanders) should let their talents rest and resolve to devote their lives merely to idleness, amusement, and propagation of their species—in a word, to enjoyment; but he cannot possibly *will* that this should be a universal law of nature, or be implanted in us as such by a natural instinct. For, as a rational being, he necessarily wills that his faculties be developed, since they serve him, and have been given him for all sorts of possible purposes.

This moral dilemma proposed by Kant is fascinating, as it reflects a very modern consciousness involving the moral value of fulfilling one's human potentials. Kant acknowledges the likelihood that even if we universalize the action of choosing a life of self-indulgent enjoyment over hard work and achievement of one's potentials, life in some form would continue, as it does with cultures based on more hedonistic principles. But from a *rational* point of view, intentionally universalizing such a principle of moral action is unthinkable. As rational beings, Kant maintains, we necessarily believe that fulfilling our human potential is a morally appropriate course of action, one that provides our lives with meaning and a sense of purpose.

Kant, *Fundamental Principles of the Metaphysics of Morals*

- A fourth, who is in prosperity, while he sees that others have to contend with great wretchedness and that he could help them, thinks: What concern is it of mine? Let everyone be happy as Heaven pleases, or as he can make himself; I will take nothing from him nor even envy him, only I do not wish to contribute anything to his welfare or to his assistance in distress! Now no doubt, if such a mode of thinking were a universal law, the human race might very well subsist, and doubtless even better than in a state in which everyone talks of sympathy and good-will, or even takes care occasionally to put it into practice, but, on the other side, also cheats when they can, betrays the rights of me, or otherwise violates them. But although it is possible that a universal law of nature might exist in accordance with that maxim, it is impossible to *will* that such a principle should have the universal validity of a law of nature. For a will which resolved this would contradict itself, inasmuch as many cases might occur in which one would have need of the love and sympathy of others, and in which, by such a law of nature, sprung from his own will, he would deprive himself of all hope and the aid he desires.

Kant's final example deals with the moral sentiments such as empathy, love, caring, sympathy. But Kant's endorsement of the emotions has a logical, not an emotional, foundation. Why is it morally wrong to believe in a selfish, self-absorbed view of our relationships with others? Because it is very likely that there will be times in which we will need and profit from the sympathy and love of others. And if we have already endorsed a detached, lack of caring for others as a universal value, then we ourselves will be victimized by our own moral value. Thus, such a moral belief contradicts our own self-interest. Of course, although many people would doubtless agree with Kant's conclusion regarding the need to endorse such sentiments as sympathy, love, and concern for other's welfare as moral values, many would also question whether the moral authority of these values is one based purely on the logic of self-interest. Nevertheless, this is Kant's position, and it is certainly consistent with his entire moral system.

Interestingly enough, Kant extends his metaphysic of morals to include another version of the categorical imperative that seems much more consistent with traditional moral values involving our relationships with others. *"Act as to treat humanity, whether in thine own person or in that of any other, in every case as an end withal, never as means only."* Again, Kant's fundamental concept here is strikingly modern: Because all people possess the same *intrinsic value*, a value that is defined by an ability to understand their options and make autonomous choices, we should always act in a way that respects their inherent dignity as rational agents. Although it's permissible to treat every other element of our experience as a potential *means to an end* (including animals, in Kant's view), we should never treat people instrumentally, as a means to some end we want to achieve. Imagine, for example, that you want to sell something: Is it all right to manipulate people's feelings so that they will buy? Or suppose that your friend is planning to do something that you don't think is in her best interests: Is it permissible to manipulate her thinking indirectly so that she will make a different choice? According to Kant, both of these actions are morally wrong because you are not treating the people involved as "*ends*," rational agents who are entitled to make their own choices. Instead, you are treating them as "*means*" *to an end*, even though you may believe that your manipulation is in their best interests. The morally right thing to do is to tell them exactly what you are thinking and then give them the opportunity to reason through the situation and make their own choices.

Now I say: man and generally any rational being *exists* as an end in himself, *not merely as a means* to be arbitrarily used by this or that will, but in all his actions, whether they concern himself or other rational beings, but be always regarded at the same time as an end. All objects of the inclinations have only a conditional worth; for if the inclinations and the wants founded on them did not exist, then their object would be without value. But the inclinations themselves, being sources of want, are so far from having an absolute worth for which they should be desired that, on the contrary, it must be the universal wish of every rational being to be wholly free from them. Thus, the worth of any object which is *to be acquired* by our action is always conditional. Beings whose existence depends not on our will but on nature's, have nevertheless, if they are irrational beings, only a relative value as means, and are therefore called *things*: rational beings, on the contrary, are called *persons*, because their very nature points them out as ends in themselves, that is, as something which must not be used merely as means, and so far therefore restricts freedom of action (and is an object of respect). These, therefore are not merely subjective ends whose existence has a worth *for us* as an effect of our action, but *objective ends*, that is, things whose existence is an end in itself—an end, moreover, for which no other can be substituted, which they should subserve *merely* as means, for otherwise nothing whatever would possess *absolute worth*; but if all worth were conditioned and therefore contingent, then there would be no supreme practical principle of reason whatever.

If then there is a supreme practical principle or, in respect of the human will, a categorical imperative, it must be one which, being drawn from the conception of that which is necessarily an end for everyone because it is *an end in itself*, constitutes an *objective* principle of will, and can therefore serve as a universal practical law. The foundation of this principle is: *rational nature exists as an end in itself*. Man necessarily conceives his own existence as being so; so far then this is a *subjective* principle of human actions. But every other rational being regards its existence similarly, just on the same rational principle that holds for me; so that it is at the same time an objective principle from which as a supreme practical law all laws of the will must be capable of being deduced. Accordingly the practical imperative will be as follows: *So act as to treat humanity, whether in thine own person or in that of any other, in every case as an end withal, never as means only.* . . .

The conception of every rational being as one which must consider itself as giving all the maxims of its will universal laws, so as to judge itself and its actions from this point of view—this conception leads to another which depends on it and is very fruitful, namely, that of a *kingdom of ends*.

By a *kingdom* I understand the union of different rational beings in a system by common laws. Now since it is by laws that ends are determined as regards their universal validity, hence, if we abstract from the personal differences of rational beings, and likewise from all the content of their private ends, we shall be able to conceive all ends combined in a systematic whole (including both rational beings as ends in themselves, and also the special ends which each may propose to himself), that is to say, we can conceive a kingdom of ends, which on the preceding principles is possible. ▪

Kant, *Fundamental Principles of the Metaphysics of Morals*

 Kant, Immanuel, *Fundamental Principles of the Metaphysics of Morals*

It's a glorious vision of Kant's, the idea of a "kingdom of ends" in which every person is always treated as a person of intrinsic worth. Such a "kingdom" would be governed by laws that ensure the "universal validity" of all people, a harmonious community based on the unassailable rationality of the categorical imperative. Is such a "kingdom of ends" possible? It's a question well worth exploring in chapter 10 when we consider social and political philosophy.

THINK PHILOSOPHICALLY 6.5
Analyzing Immanuel Kant

- One criticism of Kant's ethical philosophy is that, like other deontology theories, it overemphasizes abstract principles of justice and rationality over subjective emotions such as empathy and love. Do you feel that this criticism is justified? Why or why not? Do you think that Kant's second formulation of the categorical imperative helps address some of these concerns?

- Kant's starting point in his ethical analysis is the rational, autonomous individual, from whom he builds toward rationally ordered relationships with other members of the community. Other thinkers, like the German philosopher G. W. F. Hegel, initiate their analysis from the community, because they believe that we are fundamentally social beings who naturally exist in a complex web of interconnected relationships. From this vantage point, resting an ethical philosophy on each solitary individual is the exact opposite of the approach that should be taken. Which starting point for an ethical theory makes the most sense to you: the individual or the community? Explain your rationale and provide examples from your own life.

- Some people contend that Kant's idea of evaluating moral actions independent of their consequences makes little sense. For example, the family hiding Anne Frank from the Nazis during World War II would have been compelled by Kant's interpretation of the categorical imperative to answer truthfully when asked by the Gestapo, "Are you hiding any Jews in your house?" Do you think this is a valid criticism? How do you think Kant might respond to this criticism (for example, employing the second formulation of the categorical imperative)? Can you think of other examples in which rigidly applying the categorical imperative could result in consequences that most people would consider to be "immoral"?

- Some critics of Kant have contended that his approach is unable to provide ethical guidance when two moral principles are in conflict. For example, the Anne Frank example can be seen as involving a conflict between the principles "Do not lie" and "Do not let innocent persons be harmed if you can prevent it." How do you think Kant would respond to this objection?

- People with "fanatical" beliefs pose another difficulty for Kant. Couldn't a Kantian terrorist claim he was acting on the basis of the moral imperative to "Destroy all people who don't believe in my 'true' religion"? How would you go about countering such a contention?

- The philosopher **Friedrich Nietzsche** voiced contempt for Kant's moral theory because he believed that using rational duty as the sole criterion for conduct promoted mindless conformity among people. Instead, he believed that individuals must follow their natural passions and instincts for life: otherwise, they are doomed to become faceless members of the human "herd." In *Twilight of the Idols* he observes: "(Virtue) must be our own invention, our most necessary self-expression. . . . The fundamental laws of self-preservation and growth demand . . . that everyone invent his own virtue, his own categorical imperative. A people perishes when it confuses its duty with duty in general." Do you think Nietzsche's point has merit? Support your analysis with specific examples from contemporary culture.

- Kant's moral system is based on the assumption that all people have the ability to understand their ethical options, reason clearly, and make autonomous choices. Yet, as we found in exploring the nature of human freedom in chapter 4, people often don't understand all their options and/or reason clearly, thus inhibiting their ability to make autonomous choices. Do you think this is a valid criticism of Kant? Why or why not? Could Kant's approach to ethics be adapted to take this point into consideration? If so, how?

Frederich Nietzsche (1844–1900) German Philosopher. One of the first existentialist philosophers who challenged the foundation of traditional morality and Christianity.

Yet Kant was not simply concerned with our moral responsibilities toward others: he was equally as interested in the moral responsibilities that we have toward ourselves. In a passage that is eerily prescient of modern psychological theory, Kant makes the claim that we cannot love others more than we love ourselves: In other words, that a healthy self-esteem is necessary to act in a morally enlightened fashion toward others.

> The greatest love I can have for another is to love him as myself. I cannot love another more than I love myself. . . . Our duties towards ourselves (therefore) constitute the supreme condition and the principle of all morality. . . . He who transgresses against himself loses his manliness and becomes incapable of doing his duty toward his fellows.

One final point needs to be underscored. Some people have tended to view Kant's formulations of the categorical imperative as no more than formalized statements of the Golden Rule: "Do unto others as you would have them do unto you." Kant was aware of such efforts, even while he was alive, and he vigorously rejected all such attempts to reduce the categorical imperative to the Golden Rule.

> Let it not be thought that the common: *quod tibi non vis fieri*, ("Do not do unto others what you would not have them do to you.") etc. could serve here as the rule of principle . . . it cannot be a universal law, for it does not contain the principle of duties to oneself, nor of the duties of benevolence to others (for many a one would gladly consent that others should not benefit him, provided only that they might be excused from showing benevolence to them), nor finally that of duties of strict obligation to one another, for on this principle the criminal might argue against the judge who punishes him, etc.

As admirable as the intent of the Golden Rule may be, Kant finds it insulting that anyone would confuse this imprecise principle with the rational clarity of the categorical imperative. In the span of a few sentences, Kant reels off three ways in which the Golden Rule is conceptually inferior to the categorical imperative.

- First, the Golden Rule makes no mention of the duties we have toward ourselves, to regard ourselves well and strive to fully develop our personal human potential.
- Second, the Golden Rule does not ensure feelings of kindness, consideration, and benevolence to others. Why not? Imagine a person who cares only for himself, lacking any interest in others or desire to have others treat him well. For him the Golden Rule simply means, "I'll leave you alone if you leave me alone,"—hardly the foundation of an enlightened moral philosophy. In contrast, the categorical imperative expects such benevolent sentiments to flourish in our efforts to treat others as ends, not simply as means to an end.
- Third, the Golden Rule has the potential for perverting what ought to be understood as rationally based, clearly defined duties toward others. For example, the prisoner before the judge might invoke the Golden Rule to ask for freedom, "because if I were judge I would grant you freedom." Again, this is not a moral outcome that the Golden Rule was created to endorse, nor is it an outcome that would be permitted under the categorical imperative.

Aristotle: *Virtue Ethics and Becoming a Virtuous Person*

> We are not concerned to know what goodness is, but how we are to become good men, for this alone gives the study (of ethics) its practical value.
>
> —*Aristotle*

Virtue ethics believes in the possibility of universal moral values, but it has a decidedly different approach than utilitarianism and deontology. As we discovered, utilitarianism, as articulated by Bentham and Mill, evaluates moral actions based primarily on their consequences: morally good actions are those that

Virtue ethics The ethical theory that focuses on the moral quality of individuals rather than their actions.

bring the greatest amount of happiness to the greatest number of people. We don't need to be overly concerned about the *intentions* of the person making a moral choice—we simply need to apply the hedonic calculus (or something like it) to determine the moral value of the action. So, for example, if a wealthy individual makes a generous contribution to a university for the express purpose of funding scholarships for needy students, we can safely conclude that this is a morally good action, as it is likely to bring happiness to many deserving students. It really doesn't matter if the donor is revealing a generous spirit, engineering a tax break, trying to get elected to public office, or trying to convince a judge to commute his prison sentence on an embezzlement conviction—the positive consequences are sufficient for the utilitarian to conclude that the action is "morally good."

For deontologists like Kant, the moral reasoning is quite different, focusing on the *logic* of the moral action. Is the moral choice one that could be rationally universalized? Is making a generous donation for needy student scholarships the sort of action that could be endorsed as a universal maxim? Many people, particularly needy students, would answer with a resounding "Yes!" to such a question. Are the motivations of the donor relevant to the moral goodness of the action, as far as the deontologist is concerned? Not necessarily, although the issues are more complex than first appears, as we will see shortly.

However, for advocates of virtue ethics, the ethical framework for analysis and evaluation of moral actions stands in sharp contrast. From this ethical perspective, it is not the moral quality of the *action* that is paramount: it is instead the moral quality of the *person* that is fundamental. To evaluate the moral value of the scholarship donation, we have to explore the motivations of the *donor*: was the gift made as an expression of generosity, from a desire to promote the social good, out of a feeling of empathy for those less fortunate? If so, then the action has moral worth, because it reflects the virtuous character of the individual making the donation. However, if the gift is made for cynical or manipulative reasons—to get elected, reduce jail time, or simply to avoid paying taxes, then the moral value of the donation is questionable. Because the action does not spring from a virtuous character, the moral worth of the action is diminished or even eliminated entirely.

The towering Greek philosopher **Aristotle** (384–322 B.C.E.) was a passionate exponent of virtue ethics, as were many of the early Greek philosophers. Aristotle was a student of Plato's, founded his own school (The Lyceum), wrote prodigiously on a staggering variety of topics, and even tutored a young boy who was to become Alexander the Great. Aristotle set the tone of the virtue ethics approach with his observation that in exploring the moral dimension of experience, "We are discussing no small matter, but how we ought to live," a sentiment that echoed Socrates' commitment to moral action.

For Aristotle and other believers in virtue ethics, it is the cultivation of a virtuous *character* that is the goal of ethics, to *become* a virtuous person. The assumption is that genuinely virtuous people will act in morally principled ways as a natural expression of their moral goodness. And these moral actions will in turn strengthen their virtuous nature.

Aristotle, *The Nicomachean Ethics*

But the virtues we acquire by first exercising them, as is the case with all the arts, for it is by doing what we ought to do when we have learnt the arts that we learn the arts themselves; we become, for example, builders by building and harpists by playing the harp. Similarly it is by doing just acts that we become just, by doing temperate acts that we become temperate, by doing courageous acts that we become courageous. . . . It is by acting in such transactions as take place between man and man that we become either just or unjust. It is by acting in the face of danger and by habituating ourselves to fear or courage that we become either cowardly or courageous.

The concept of *character*, as a "virtuous character," is derived from the Greek word *charakter*, a term that itself comes from the word *charassein*, which means "to make sharp" or "to engrave." And in a sense that is precisely how we form our characters, by gradually etching their outlines and dimensions through the moral choices that we make every day of our lives. Your *moral character* refers to the integrated totality of your moral traits and dispositions, the ways in which you habitually respond when confronted with moral choices. Your character typically displays consistency and coherence, because it has been created gradually, inscribed over the totality of your life. This doesn't mean that you can't change or refine your character, only that such changes and refinements are likely to take time as you alter your personal self-portrait by making different choices.

Do you agree with Aristotle that we develop virtuous traits—such as generosity—by developing the habit of generosity in our actions? Why?

THINK PHILOSOPHICALLY 6.6
What Is My Moral Character?

PHILOSOPHER'S NOTEBOOK

Reflect on the nature of your own moral character: how do you think others view you? Identify ten "moral character" terms that you think others might use to identify you (for example, compassionate, loyal, courageous, altruistic, just, patient, friendly, truthful, temperate). Then describe several moral situations in which you had an opportunity to display these qualities.

Aristotle's particular brand of virtue ethics has had a dominating impact on moral thinking for several thousand years. Aristotle's major work in this area is *The Nicomachean Ethics*, named after his son Nicomachus. Let's explore his central ethical themes as expressed in this enduring treatise, beginning with his view on the ultimate goal for which all humans strive.

As all knowledge and moral purpose aspires to some good, what is in our view the good at which the political science aims, and what is the highest of all practical goods? As to its name there is, I may say, a general agreement. The masses and the cultured classes agree in calling it happiness, and conceive that "to live well" or "to do well" is the same thing as "to be happy." But as to the nature of happiness they do not agree, nor do the masses give the same account of it as the philosophers.

Aristotle, *The Nicomachean Ethics*

Aristotle was a scientist by inclination and training, and so he grounded his inquiry into ethics on empirical observations: What *are* the ultimate aims that people strive for in life? Most people would state that their preeminent goal is to "be happy" and to "live well." Yet people have many different notions of precisely what "being happy" and "living well" actually mean. For Aristotle, one thing that it definitely *doesn't* mean is the hedonistic notion of seeking sensual, unrefined pleasure, which he considered to be "a life fit only for cattle" (foreshadowing Mill's warning centuries later against the bankruptcy of a life lived as "a contented pig.")

Aristotle, *The Nicomachean Ethics*

Ordinary or vulgar people conceive (the good) to be pleasure, and accordingly approve a life of enjoyment. . . . Now the mass of men present an absolutely slavish appearance, as choosing the life of brute beasts, but they meet with consideration because so many persons in authority share (such) tastes.

For Aristotle, as for Socrates, devoting your life to acquiring such things as wealth, fame, or public success is as limited a life as seeking pleasure: these goals do not reflect the talents and values that define the human soul. Despite their popularity among people, pleasure, wealth, fame, success are superficial and transient and will never be able to bring deep and lasting fulfillment.

Aristotle, *The Nicomachean Ethics*

The life of money-making is in a sense a life of constraint, and it is clear that wealth is not the good of which we are in quest; for it is useful in part as a means to something else. . . . But (the love of fame) appears too superficial for our present purpose; for honor seems to depend more upon the people who pay it than upon the person to whom it is paid, and we have an intuitive feeling that the good is something which is proper to a man himself and cannot be easily taken away from him.

But if these common values in human affairs do not embody "living well," then what does? Aristotle believes that to answer this question, we need to understand the true nature of human "happiness."

Aristotle, *The Nicomachean Ethics*

We speak of that which is sought after for its own sake as more final than that which is sought after as a means to something else; we speak of that which is never desired as a means to something else as more final than the things which are desired both in themselves and as means to something else; and we speak of a thing as absolutely final if it is always desired in itself and never as a means to something else.

It seems that happiness pre-eminently answers to this description, as we always desire happiness for its own sake and never as a means to something else, whereas we desire honor, pleasure, intellect, and every virtue, partly for their own sakes (for we should desire them independently of what might result from them) but partly also as being means to happiness, because we suppose they will prove the instruments of happiness. Happiness, on the other hand, nobody desires for the sake of these things, nor indeed as a means to anything else at all. If we define the function of Man as a kind of life, and this life as an activity of soul, or a course of action in conformity with reason, if the function of a good man is such activity or action of a good and noble kind, and if everything is successfully performed when it is performed in accordance with its proper excellence, it follows that the good of Man is an activity of the soul in accordance with virtue or, if there are more virtues than one, accordance with the best and most complete virtue. But it is necessary to add the words "in a complete life." For as one swallow or one day does not make a spring, so one day or a short time does not make a fortunate or happy man.

Inasmuch as happiness is an activity of the soul in accordance with complete or perfect virtue, it is necessary to consider virtue, as this will perhaps be the best way of studying happiness. . . .

In this rich, insightful passage, Aristotle points out that though we desire pleasure, wealth, fame, and success, we desire them mainly because we hope that they will bring us happiness. Similarly, people often strive to achieve virtues such as honor and intellectual insight, though again the ultimate aim is to be happy.

Happiness, for Aristotle, is expressed in the Greek word *eudaemonia*, which means "actively exercising your soul's powers." What exactly does this mean? It means that achieving happiness necessarily involves fulfilling your distinctive function as a human being, living your life in accordance with reason and virtue. This constitutes the "good life" for you and every other human being.

Aristotle

For Aristotle, every element of the universe has an ultimate goal or purpose, a *raison d'etre* (reason for being). This view of the universe is known as **teleological**, a philosophical perspective in which all things are understood in terms of their unique end, purpose, or goal, as Aristotle explains:

> Every art and every scientific inquiry, and similarly every action and purpose, may be said to aim at some good. Hence the good has been well defined as that at which all things aim.

Aristotle, *The Nicomachean Ethics*

The natural principle that drives the teleology of the universe is **entelechy**, a principle that reveals that all events occur according to a natural design. In humans, our entelechy is embodied in our souls, which exist as the "form" of our bodies. What makes the human soul distinctive is its capacity to reason, reflect, and make choices. Thus, achieving your unique purpose in life, and experiencing genuine happiness in the process, means choosing to permit your soul to reach its full potential, to exercise its full powers in accord with reason and virtue (which is based on reason). Fulfilling your human potential is a lifelong project, not a one-time occurrence. As Aristotle so eloquently observes, creating a "complete life" is an evolving process, "For as one swallow or one day does not make a spring, so one day or a short time does not make a fortunate or happy man."

All of these considerations lead Aristotle to conclude that "happiness is an activity of the soul in accordance with complete or perfect virtue." But to understand what this means, we need to develop a clear and concrete sense of what Aristotle has in mind with the term *virtue*.

> Virtue or excellence being twofold, partly intellectual and partly moral; intellectual virtue is both originated and fostered mainly by teaching; it therefore demands experience and time. Moral virtue, on the other hand, is the outcome of habit, and accordingly its name is derived by a slight deflexion from habit. From this fact it is clear that no moral virtue is implanted in us by nature; a law of nature cannot be altered by habituation. . . . It is neither by nature then nor in defiance of nature that virtues are implanted in us. Nature gives us the capacity of receiving them, and that capacity is perfected by habit. . . . But the virtues we acquire by first exercising them, as is the case with all the arts, for it is by doing what we ought to do when we have learnt the arts that we learn the arts themselves; we become, for example, builders by building and harpists by playing the harp. Similarly it is by doing just acts that we become just, by doing temperate acts that we become temperate, by doing courageous acts that we become courageous. . . . It is by acting in such transactions as take place between man and man that we become either just or unjust. It is by acting in the face of danger and by habituating ourselves to fear or courage that we become either cowardly or courageous. It is much the same with our desires and angry passions. Some people become temperate and gentle, others become licentious and passionate, according as they conduct themselves in one way or another way in particular circumstances. In a word moral states are the results of activities corresponding to the moral states themselves. It is our duty therefore to give a certain character to the activities, as the moral states depend upon the differences of the activities. Accordingly the difference between one training of the habits and another from early days is not a light matter, but is serious or rather all-important. . . .

Aristotle, *The Nicomachean Ethics*

When it comes to virtues, Aristotle distinguishes two distinct categories: "intellectual" and "moral." Intellectual virtues include qualities such as wisdom, knowledge, rationality, clarity of understanding, and cognitive intelligence. Aristotle believes that intellectual virtues are developed through teaching and practice over time. For example, that is the express purpose of your education, from Kindergarten to the present—to stimulate and guide you to develop a basic framework of

Teleological The view that everything has a design or purpose.

Entelechy The principle that reveals that all events occur according to a natural design. All elements of the universe embody a distinctive essence or potential the purpose of which is to achieve full expression.

The three theological virtues, Faith, Hope and Charity.

knowledge, as well as the sophisticated thinking and language abilities needed to communicate and use this knowledge in productive ways. The fact that you can analyze a work of literature, apply a psychological theory, explain the roots of modern consciousness, discuss the implication of the Internet on human affairs, solve a quadratic equation, understand the biochemistry of Alzheimer's disease, interpret a modern painting, or perform any other of a countless number of intellectual operations—all these abilities reflect intellectual virtues you have developed through your educational experiences.

Moral virtues are somewhat different in nature, and they include qualities such as being temperate, just, courageous, compassionate, generous, friendly, and truthful. Moral virtues are also developed over time, but unlike intellectual virtues that require a great deal of formal instruction, Aristotle believes that moral virtues are mainly developed through consistent and ongoing practice. Becoming a compassionate person necessarily involves engaging in ongoing acts of compassion toward other deserving people. Gradually, acting compassionately becomes a habitual way of thinking and behaving, an important element in the shaping of your character. People who know you *expect* you to be compassionate in appropriate situations because this virtue reflects an intrinsic part of "who" you are.

Certainly this reasoning of Aristotle's seems to make sense on a surface level: "moral states are the result of activities corresponding to the moral states themselves." It's difficult to argue with the argument that you become courageous by acting courageously; honest by acting honestly, and so on. But this formulation also leads immediately to serious questions: What precisely is meant by moral virtues such as *compassion, courage, honesty*? And assuming that we can clearly define these moral virtues, how do we motivate people (and ourselves) to emulate these qualities in our daily lives? Particularly because moral choices often involve agonizing conflicts between competing desires? And how do we encourage people (and ourselves) to commit to these moral virtues over a long period of time, to shape their characters to include them as constitutive elements? Even Aristotle recognizes that simply *knowing* what a moral virtue is or the ethical correct course of action is no guarantee that a person is going to *will* themselves to make the morally enlightened choice.

Aristotle, *The Nicomachean Ethics*

Our ability to perform such actions is in no way enhanced by knowing them since the virtues are characteristics (that is, fixed capacities for action, acquired by habit).

Aristotle clearly recognizes the need to address these questions, because after all, it seems almost tautological to observe that "you become moral by being moral." Let's examine how he approaches this apparent dilemma.

Aristotle, *The Nicomachean Ethics*

But it may be asked what we mean by saying that people must become just by doing what is just and temperate by doing what is temperate. For if they do what is just and temperate, they are *ipso facto* proved, it will be said, to be just and temperate in the same way as, if they practice grammar and music, they are proved to be grammarians and musicians. . . .

But actions in accordance with virtue are not, for example, justly or temperately performed (merely) because they are in themselves just or temperate. It is necessary that the agent at the time of performing them should satisfy certain conditions, that is, in the first place that he should know what he is doing, secondly that he should deliberately choose to do it and to do it for its own sake, and thirdly that he should do it as an instance of a settled and immutable moral state. If it be a question whether a person possesses any art, these conditions, except indeed the condition of knowledge, are not taken into account; but if it be a question of possessing the virtues, the mere knowledge is of little or no avail, and it is the other conditions, which are the results of frequently performing just or temperate actions, that are not of slight but of absolute importance.

Accordingly deeds are said to be just and temperate, when they are such as a just or temperate person would do, and a just and temperate person is not merely one who does these deeds but one who does them in the spirit of the just and the temperate. . . .

For Aristotle, the experience of acting morally (compassionately, courageously, truthfully, and so on) only counts as an authentic moral action if the following conditions apply. The person acting should

- *know* what he/she is doing. In other words, if you are acting compassionately, you should be aware of what the moral virtue of compassion is and be aware that you are acting that way.
- *deliberately choose* to do it and to *do it for its own sake*. In other words, the compassionate action doesn't really count if the person is not *willing* to do it intentionally. If it's an accidental or unconscious action, it may still have beneficial consequences for the person on the receiving end, but it will not help the person acting to develop compassion as a habitual part of their moral character.
- do it as an example of a *settled and immutable moral state*. In other words, authentic moral choices should reflect an established and committed moral character. If the compassionate act is merely a random action inconsistent with the person's underlying character, there is no reason to think that the choice reflects a genuine moral virtue, or that we can expect more such compassionate acts on a regular basis.

This further articulation of his position may help Aristotle address some of the questions regarding his ethical approach, but still unarticulated is how we go about defining moral virtues in a precise and persuasive way. Aristotle responds to this challenge with his famous doctrine of the Golden Mean, a moral philosophy that is based on the concepts of temperance (moderation), self-discipline, and balance (an approach analogous to "The Middle Way" practiced in Buddhism).

Aristotle, *The Nicomachean Ethics*

First of all, it must be observed that the nature of moral qualities is such that they are destroyed by defect and by excess. We see the same thing happen in the case of strength and of health . . . excess as well as deficiency of physical exercise destroys our strength, and similarly, too much and too little food and drink destroys our health; the proportionate amount, however, produces, increases, and strengthens it. The same applies to self-control, courage, and the other virtues: the man who shuns and fears everything becomes a coward, whereas a man who knows no fear at all and goes to meet every danger becomes reckless. Similarly, a man who revels in every pleasure and abstains from none becomes self-indulgent, while he who avoids every pleasure like a boor becomes what might be called insensitive. Thus we see that self-control and courage are destroyed by excess and deficiency and are preserved by the mean.

Again the scientist in Aristotle influences him to reason from the physical world to the moral world. How do we determine the appropriate amount of physical exercise in which to engage, or the right amount of food and drink to ingest? We reason away from the extremes until we arrive at the optimal amount to promote health and happiness. The danger, Aristotle believes, lies in the extremes: too much (or too little) exercise, food, or drink can be destructive. Thus we need to avoid the extremes and focus on the ideal balance between them. But we can't use the same rigid standard for everyone: we need to evaluate each situation on its own merits. The ideal amount of exercise (or food or drink) for one person is likely to be very different than for another.

The same principles apply to determining moral virtues. For example, let's take a concept like seeking sensuous pleasure. For many of the hedonists, the "good life" consists in trying to maximize the amount of pleasure that you are receiving. Aristotle, however, believes that this attitude is ruinous. An excessive focus on sensuous pleasure leads to a life of self-indulgence and dissipation. At the other extreme, peo-

VISUAL PHILOSOPHY

Finding the Golden Mean

If Aristotle were to speak at your college, what advice do you think he would give to students regarding how best to achieve happiness and "the good life"?

ple who deny themselves any sensuous pleasure are ascetic and often self-righteous boors. The virtuous ideal is the mean between these two extremes: people who fully appreciate sensuous pleasures, but who integrate these pleasures into their lives in healthy and harmonious ways through the exercise of self-discipline and intelligent judgment. Aristotle goes on to elaborate this way of thinking.

Aristotle, *The Nicomachean Ethics*

Every science then performs its function well, if it regards the mean and refers the works which it produces to the mean. This is the reason why it is usually said of successful works that it is impossible to take anything from them or to add anything to them, which implies that excess or deficiency is fatal to excellence but that the mean state ensures it. Good artists too, as we say, have an eye to the mean in their works. But virtue, like Nature herself, is more accurate and better than any art; virtue therefore will aim at the mean;—I speak of moral virtue, as it is moral virtue which is concerned with emotions and actions, and it is these which admit of excess and deficiency and the mean. Thus, it is possible to go too far, or not to go far enough, in respect of fear, courage, desire, anger, pity, and pleasure and pain generally, and the excess and the deficiency are alike wrong; but to experience these emotions at the right times and on the right occasions and towards the right persons and for the right causes and in the right manner is the mean or the supreme good, which is characteristic of virtue. Similarly there may be excess, deficiency, or the mean, in regard to actions. But virtue is concerned with emotions and actions, and here excess is an error and deficiency a fault, whereas the mean is successful and laudable, and success and merit are both characteristics of virtue.

It appears then that virtue is a mean state, so far at least as it aims at the mean.

Again, there are many different ways of going wrong; for evil is in its nature infinite, to use the Pythagorean figure, but good is finite. But there is only one possible way of going right. Accordingly, the former is easy and the latter difficult; it is easy to miss the mark but difficult to hit it. This again is a reason why excess and deficiency are characteristics of vice and the mean state a characteristics of virtue.

For good is simple, evil manifold.

Virtue then is a state of deliberate moral purpose consisting in a mean that is relative to ourselves, the mean being determined by reason, or as a prudent man would determine it. It is a mean state firstly as lying between two vices, the vice of excess on the one hand, and the vice of deficiency on the other, and secondly because, whereas the vices either fall short of or go beyond what is proper in the emotions and action, virtue not only discovers but embraces the mean.

Although Aristotle's Golden Mean approach has a certain commonsense appeal, it's an approach that also raises serious questions. For example, if the ideal virtue—the mean state—varies from person to person, situation to situation, how can we know for certain if we are "hitting the mark," particularly because Aristotle describes how difficult such moral accuracy is? And in the case of conflicting opinions regarding what "hitting the mark" actually means, what standard can we use to decide? One person's pleasure may be another person's self-indulgence and another person's exaggerated self-denial. Or as the twentieth-century philosopher **Bertrand Russell** noted in a famous declension:

I am firm.   You are stubborn.   He is pigheaded.

Aristotle tries to address this concern by introducing two proposed criteria: "Virtue then is a state of deliberate moral purpose consisting in a mean that is relative to ourselves, the mean being determined by reason, or as a prudent man would determine it." But this only delays the problem: how precisely do we determine what "reason" is advising or who a "prudent man" is?

Aristotle's alternative response to this question is to provide a more concrete and detailed description of each of the virtues, with the hope that his analysis will resonate with us, that our experience with these concepts of ideal virtues will be consistent with his own. From this point of view, the ultimate determinant of what is morally virtuous is determined by each individual, using his/her accumulated experience and ability to reason to define his/her own personal Golden Mean. As you think through Aristotle's analysis of these moral virtues, ask yourself whether his concepts are consistent with your own; and if not, why not.

But first, Aristotle wants to point out that not all behaviors or emotions are appropriate for a Golden Mean analysis: some things are just vices, pure and simple.

But it is not every action or every emotion that admits of a mean state. There are some whose very name implies wickedness, as for example, malice, shamelessness, and envy, among emotions, or adultery, theft, and murder, among actions. All these, and others like them, are censured as being intrinsically wicked, not merely the excesses or deficiencies of them. It is never possible then to be right in respect of them; they are always sinful. Right or wrong in such actions as adultery does not depend on our committing them with the right person, at the right time or in the right manner; on the contrary it is sinful to do anything of the kind at all. It would be equally wrong then to suppose that there can be a mean state or an excess or deficiency in unjust, cowardly or licentious conduct; for, if it were so, there would be a mean state of an excess or of a deficiency, an excess of an excess and a deficiency of a deficiency. But as in temperance and courage there can be no excess or deficiency because the mean is, in a sense, an extreme, so too in these cases there cannot be a mean or an excess or deficiency, but, however the acts may be done, they are wrong. For it is a general rule that an excess or deficiency does not admit of a mean state, nor a mean state of an excess or deficiency.

But it is not enough to lay down this as a general rule; it is necessary to apply it to particular cases, as in reasonings upon actions, general statements, although they are broader, are less exact than particular statements. For all action refers to particulars, and it is essential that our theories should harmonize with the particular cases to which they apply. We must take particular virtues then from the catalogue of virtues.

Aristotle, *The Nicomachean Ethics*

Bertrand Russell (1872–1970) British Philosopher. One of the founders of modern logic. In *The Principles of Mathematics* (1903) and with Whitehead in the three volume *Principia Mathematica* (1910–1913) advanced the view that all of mathematics could be derived from logical premises. Also a political activist and wrote many popular books on topics such as religion, ethics, and marriage.

In regard to feelings of fear and confidence, courage is a mean state. On the side of excess, he whose fearlessness is excessive has no name, as often happens, but he whose confidence is excessive is foolhardy, while he whose timidity is excessive and whose confidence is deficient is a coward.

In respect of pleasures and pains, although not indeed of all pleasures and pains, and to a less extent in respect of pains than of pleasures, the mean state is temperance, the excess is licentiousness. We never find people who are deficient in regard to pleasures; accordingly such people again have not received a name, but we may call them insensible.

As regards the giving and taking of money, the mean state is liberality, the excess and deficiency are prodigality and illiberality. Here the excess and deficiency take opposite forms; for while the prodigal man is excessive in spending and deficient in taking, the illiberal man is excessive in taking and deficient in spending.

(For the present we are giving only a rough and summary account of the virtues, and that is sufficient for our purpose; we will hereafter determine their character more exactly.)

Aristotle then proceeds to perform a comparable analysis with respect to attitudes toward money, honor and dishonor, the expression of emotions, truthfulness, and even a sense of humor! The following chart summarizes his analysis of the various virtues and vices considered in this passage:

Deficiency/Vice	Mean/Virtue	Excess/Vice
Cowardice	Courage	Foolhardiness
Inhibition	Temperance	Overindulgence
Stinginess	Generosity	Profligacy
Shabbiness	Magnificence	Vulgarity
Standoffishness	Friendliness	Obsequiousness
Shyness	Proper pride	Vanity
Celibacy	Monogamy	Promiscuity
Dullness	Well-roundedness	Wildness
Maliciousness	Righteous indignation	Envy
Sarcasm	Truthfulness	Boastfulness
Boorishness	Wittiness	Buffoonery
Shamelessness	Modesty	Shamefacedness

Being virtuous is a difficult and complicated process, according to Aristotle. Take something like generosity: what is the Golden Mean, the ideal virtuous state? Giving the "right amount" to the "right persons" at the "right time" and for the "right cause." It's no wonder that he ends on the cautionary note that "it is rare and laudable and noble to do well."

Aristotle, *The Nicomachean Ethics*

It has now been sufficiently shown that moral virtue is a mean state, and in what sense it is a mean state; it is a mean state as lying between two vices, a vice of excess on the one side and a vice of deficiency on the other, and as aiming at the mean in the emotions and actions.

That is the reason why it is so hard to be virtuous; for it is always hard work to find the mean in anything, for example, it is not everybody, but only a man of science, who can find the mean or center of a circle. So too anybody can get angry—that is an easy matter—and anybody can give or spend money, but to give it to the right persons, to give the right amount of it and to give it at the right time and for the right cause and in the right way, this is not what anybody can do, nor is it easy. That is the reason why it is rare and laudable and noble to do well.

For Aristotle, a virtuous life—the way that we ought to live—involves a balanced and harmonious integration of the various behaviors, values, emotions, and attitudes, in accordance with the Golden Mean. But all virtues are not equal, according to Aristotle. The most virtuous life is one devoted to intellectual reflection and contemplation, and it is this life that leads to the greatest possible human happiness, as Aristotle describes in the following passage:

We said that happiness is not a habit or trained faculty. If it were, it would be within the reach of a man who slept all his days and lived the life of a vegetable, or of a man who met with the greatest misfortunes. As we cannot accept this conclusion we must place happiness in some exercise of faculty, as we said before. But as the exercises of faculty are sometimes necessary (*i.e.* desirable for the sake of something else), sometimes desirable in themselves, it is evident that happiness must be placed among those that are desirable in themselves, and not among those that are desirable for the sake of something else: for happiness lacks nothing; it is sufficient in itself. . . .

Now, the exercise of those trained faculties which are proper to him is what each man finds most desirable; what the perfect man finds most desirable, therefore, is the exercise of virtue. Happiness, therefore, does not consist in amusement; and indeed it is absurd to suppose that the end is amusement, and that we toil and moil all our life long for the sake of amusing ourselves. We may say that we choose everything for the sake of something else, excepting only happiness; for it is the end. But to be serious and to labour for the sake of amusement seems silly and utterly childish; while to amuse ourselves in order that we may be serious, as Anacharsis says, seems to be right; for amusement is a sort of recreation, and we need recreation because we are unable to work continuously. Recreation then, cannot be the end; for it is taken as a means to the exercise of our faculties. . . .

But if happiness be the exercise of virtue, it is reasonable to suppose that it will be the exercise of the highest virtue; and that will be the virtue or excellence of the best part of us. Now, that part or faculty—call it reason or what you will—which seems naturally to rule and take the lead, and to apprehend things noble and divine—whether it be itself divine, or only the divinest part of us—is the faculty the exercise of which, in its proper excellence, will be perfect happiness . . . this consists in speculation or theorizing. . . .

. . . It follows that the exercise of reason will be the complete happiness of man, *i.e.* when a complete term of days is added; for nothing incomplete can be admitted into our idea of happiness. But a life which realized this idea would be something more than human; for it would not be the expression of man's nature, but of some divine element in that nature—the exercise of which is as far superior to the exercise of the other kind of virtue, as this divine element is superior to our compound human nature. If then reason be divine as compared with man, the life which consists in the exercise of reason will also be divine in comparison with human life. Nevertheless, instead of listening to those who advise us as men and mortals not to lift our thoughts above what is human and mortal, we ought rather, as far as possible, to put off our mortality and make every effort to live in the exercise of the highest of our faculties; for though it be but a small part of us, yet in power and value it far surpasses all the rest. And indeed this part would even seem to constitute our true self, since it is the sovereign and the better part. It would be strange then, if a man were to prefer the life of something else to the life of his true self. Again, we may apply here what we said above—for every being that is best and pleasantest which is naturally proper to it. Since, then, it is the reason that in the truest sense is the man, the life that consists in the exercise of the reason is the best and pleasantest for man—and therefore the happiest.

Aristotle, *The Nicomachean Ethics*

Do I Have a Virtuous Character?

- Identify and describe several moral decisions you have made recently. Then analyze the moral criteria that you used to make your decision: Did you focus on the *consequences* of the choice? Or on a moral *rule* that has objective authority? Or did you try to make a choice that reflects what a *virtuous person* would do? Or did you use a blending of all three ethical approaches, or another one of your own choosing?

- Do you agree with Aristotle that the ultimate goal all people strive for is happiness? Why or why not? Describe your concept of "happiness." How does it compare and contrast with that of Aristotle's notion of *eudaemonia*: "actively exercising your soul's powers in accord with virtue and reason"?

- Examine the Golden Mean virtues that Aristotle identifies as displayed in the chart on page 308. Do you agree with his formulations? What changes would you suggest? Create three more moral virtues in the same format:

  Vice (deficient)   Virtue (the mean)   Vice (excess)

- Identify and describe someone you believe to have a virtuous character. What virtuous qualities do they display on a consistent basis? How would you describe your own moral character? What moral virtues do you believe are prominent in your character? Which moral virtues would you like to strengthen?

This is truly a lovely and inspiring vision: living a life based on the mind's best work, its ability to reason, reflect, and contemplate. Such a life enables us to touch the divine, realize our "true self," and achieve the greatest possible happiness.

In the final analysis, the great strengths of Aristotle's ethical vision are tied inevitably to its flaws. Aristotle presents us with a grand and inspiring vision of "the Good Life," a life devoted to fulfilling our most sublime potential as humans in a life that is founded on reason and virtue. He conceives of it as a rich life, which integrates all of the significant dimensions of human ability in an integrated and harmonious whole. And it is a life in which its defining essence, the human soul, strives to soar to transcendent heights, achieving the glorious final end that nature intended.

But an ethical vision drawn on this large a scale cannot help but be imprecise, a risk that Aristotle fully understands and a risk that he is fully prepared to accept. We will leave him with the last word.

Aristotle, *The Nicomachean Ethics*

But let us first agree that any discussion on matters of action cannot be more than an outline and is bound to lack precision. . . . And if this is true of our general discussion, our treatment of particular problems will be even less precise, since these do not come under the head of any art which can be transmitted by precept, but the agent must consider on each different occasion what the situation demands, just as in medicine and in navigation. But although this is the kind of discussion in which we are engaged, we must do our best. ▪

Aristotle,
Nicomachean Ethics

Relations Among Utilitarianism, Deontology, and Virtue Ethics

The three major moral theories that we have considered to this point—utilitarianism, Kantian deontology, and virtue ethics—each have a different focus in defining and evaluating moral values:

- Utilitarianism   Moral value is determined by the *consequences* of actions: the greatest happiness for the greatest number.
- Deontology   Moral value is determined by following the moral rules (*maxims*) prescribed by reason.
- Virtue ethics   Moral value is determined by cultivating a virtuous *character*.

However, when we turn an analytical lens to the way these theories actually function in human experience, we see that they are much more closely related than first appears. The truth is that in the practical application of each of these theories the moral elements of *consequences, maxims,* and *character* are dynamically interrelated. For example, in virtue ethics, it is by the repeated and habitual choosing of morally enlightened *actions* that we develop the habits of thought and patterns of behaving that gradually shape our moral character. And the moral virtues themselves reflect *moral maxims* that serve as guides. A virtuous person may possess the quality of "compassion," which means, in practical terms, responding in an empathetic, compassionate manner in appropriate circumstances. And the virtue of "compassion" is displayed through action. Simply because people announce that they are compassionate doesn't mean that they *are* in fact compassionate. It is only when they *act* in a compassionate manner that their pronouncements of virtue have genuine meaning, as Aristotle explains:

Moral virtue, on the other hand, is the outcome of habit, and accordingly its name is derived by a slight deflexion from habit. From this fact it is clear that no moral virtue is implanted in us by nature; a law of nature cannot be altered by habituation. . . . it is neither by nature then nor in defiance of nature that virtues are implanted in us. Nature gives us the capacity of receiving them, and that capacity is perfected by habit. . . . But the virtues we acquire by first exercising them. . . .

The same dialectical relationships between *consequences*, *maxims*, and *character* are also found in utilitarian theory. After all, expecting to act consistently to promote the principle of utility assumes that their characters are sufficiently virtuous to provide an ongoing desire to do so. In his essay "On Liberty," Mill explicitly recognizes this intimate connection between virtue and action:

> There is nothing which makes (the virtuous person) so much a blessing to (other members of society) as the cultivation of disinterested love of virtue. And consequently . . . (utilitarianism) enjoins and requires the cultivation of the love of virtue up to the greatest strength possible, as being above all things important to the general happiness.

For Mill, cultivating a virtuous and benevolent character is a crucial element in becoming a "good" person in the fullest sense. Embodying the utilitarian spirit means more than simply applying the hedonic calculus in an impersonal, mechanical fashion. Instead, the principle of utility implies a genuine concern for others and a desire to enrich the lives of those less fortunate. For Mill, we don't simply desire happiness in a self-absorbed quest—we also desire to become virtuous people.

> Now it is palpable that (people) do desire things which, in common language, are decidedly distinguished from happiness. They desire, for example, virtue and the absence of vice, no less really than pleasure and the absence of pain. The desire of virtue is not as universal, but it is as authentic a fact, as the desire of happiness. . . . But does the utilitarian doctrine deny that people desire virtue, or maintain that virtue is not a thing to be desired? The very reverse. It maintains not only that virtue is to be desired, but that it is to be desired disinterestedly.

Mill believes that it is the power of reflection that enables us to analyze the consequences of our moral choices and then use this information to refine our basic moral character to become more habitually virtuous, which will better enable us to apply the principle of utility in our daily lives. But this entire process is driven by a love of virtue, which motivates us to become more virtuous.

Finally, we find these same interconnections between *consequences*, *maxims*, and *character* in the deontology of Immanuel Kant. In fact, Kant (as we saw), begins his foundational ethical work with an impassioned description of "the good will" as an essential dimension of any enlightened morality.

> Nothing can possibly be conceived in the world, or even out of it, which can be called good without qualification, except a Good Will. Intelligence, wit, judgment, and the other *talents* of the mind, however they may be named, or courage, resolution, perseverance, as qualities of temperament, are undoubtedly good and desirable in many respects; but these gifts of nature may also become extremely bad and mischievous if the will which is to make use of them, and which, therefore, constitutes what is called *character*, is not good. . . . Thus, a good will appears to constitute the indispensable condition even of being worthy of happiness.

Without a fully developed and authentically grounded "good will," there is no reason to think that people will use the categorical imperative or any other moral maxim. Such moral rules depend for their efficacy on the desire of people to actually abide by these rules. Exhorting others about their moral "duty," the need to employ reason to universalize their proposed moral choices, or the obligation to treat others as ends, not simply as means—all of these potentially powerful moral ways of thinking are empty and useless in the absence of the "good will" required to implement them. Thus the moral maxims of the deontologist require a virtuous character to passionately and consistently employ them. As Kant noted in the "Introductory Observations" to his *Lectures on Ethics*,

> Ethics is sometimes described as the theory of virtue. . . . A man who complies with coercive laws is not necessarily virtuous. To be virtuous man must, to be sure, respect the law and be punctilious in his observance of human rights, but virtue goes beyond this, to the disposition from which the action . . . arises.

However, a word of caution is in order. Although there are undeniable areas of overlap and connection between the major ethical theories, there are also significant areas of conflict as well. Each ethical theory identifies different fundamental values and they thus have different priorities in terms of which values take precedence: utility, maxims, or virtue. Thus in analyzing complex ethical situations, each theory is likely to provide a very different analysis in terms of moral reasoning, and may end up with very different conclusions regarding the ethically appropriate course of action. For example, take the case of an individual who was convicted of committing a heinous murder when he was younger, and, having served a significant portion of his sentence, is now eligible for parole. What is the ethically appropriate course of action? For *utilitarians* like Bentham and Mill, the decision would depend on determining whether his release would result in the greatest happiness (and least unhappiness) for the greatest number of people. For those believing in *virtue ethics* like Aristotle, they might seek to determine whether the individual has truly reformed his character into one embodying the qualities of virtue. For *deontologists* like Kant, the application of one or more formulations of the categorical imperative would provide ethical guidance.

As a result, each of the theories could reach different conclusions regarding whether it was ethically appropriate to grant the individual parole. And even when the theories reached the same conclusions, it is likely that they would employ very different forms of moral reasoning to reach the same recommendation. Many times people want to say that they believe "a little bit of every theory" and then try to "blend" them all together. But this temptation should be avoided. When we understand ethical theories in-depth—not superficially—we realize that each theory provides a complex and distinctive way of analyzing moral choices that cannot be simply "blended" into other equally complex and distinctive types of moral analysis. Thinking philosophically about ethics involves critically evaluating the complex reasoning and serious arguments produced by conflicting theories.

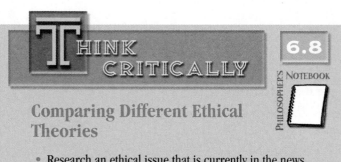

THINK CRITICALLY 6.8 PHILOSOPHER'S NOTEBOOK

Comparing Different Ethical Theories

- Research an ethical issue that is currently in the news, assembling several articles or opinion pieces that provide a well-rounded and in-depth perspective on the issue.
- Perform an in-depth analysis from each of the three moral perspectives that we have explored in this chapter—utilitarianism, virtue ethics, deontology—making sure that you reach a clear and specific conclusion/recommendation for each theory.
- Compare the various conclusions and forms of moral reasoning between the three theories. Which ethical perspective do you find to be most compelling? Why? Which ethical perspective do you find to be least compelling? Why?

Existentialist Ethics: *Living an Authentic Life*

The question is not what am I to believe, but what am I to do?

—*Søren Kierkegaard*

irtue ethics, as embodied in Aristotle, shifts the moral emphasis from generalities like the hedonic calculus and the categorical imperative to the moral character of the individual—how do you become a virtuous person? Existentialism is another philosophical approach that places the individual at the center of ethical analysis, though in a much different way than virtue ethics. For existentialism the question is not "Who is a virtuous person?" but rather "How do I live my life authentically?" Rather than trying to inscribe virtuous traits onto your character through habitual repetition, as Aristotle recommends, existentialism is focused on investing your life with meaning through the free choices that you make.

Søren Kierkegaard, Jean-Paul Sartre, Simone de Beauvoir, and Albert Camus are a disparate group of thinkers who share a common commitment to placing the living, concrete individual at the center of all philosophical analysis. Existentialism rose up as a passionate response against a world in which the intrinsic value of the solitary individual was increasingly becoming crushed by the dehumanizing forces of industrial development, the increased pressures to conform to homogeneous social standards, the so-called objective frameworks of modern science. Existentialists saw (and continue to see) the cumulative effect of these influences to be the profound *alienation* of the individual. Instead of viewing their work as a personal expression of their individual talents, average individuals become "cogs in the machine," alienated from the process and products of their labor. Instead of crafting themselves to be unique and creative individuals, they become one of the "masses," lumped together with a legion of nameless, faceless people indistinguishable from each other. And instead of viewing themselves as the "crowning jewel" of creation, advancements in science have drained their life spirit, viewing them simply as biological organisms, psychological constructs, historical incidentals, specks in the universe. What can the individual know? He is hopelessly subjective. What value can the individual possess? She is simply an infinitesimal molecule in the cosmic organism.

It was in response to this pervasive diminishment of the individual that existentialist thinkers began to shout, "Enough!" For these thinkers, the starting point for all knowledge and inquiry of the universe, both human and scientific, is subjective human experience: "Truth is subjectivity," Kierkegaard announced, and Sartre echoed this sentiment with the statement, "We must begin from the subjective." *Nothing* is more important than the concrete individual. Without this living, feeling, experiencing person there would be no technology, no social culture, no science or scientific knowledge. Rather than pushing the individual to the margins of the universe, the individual *must* be returned to the central position of honor and focus. The most pressing questions of the cosmos are *not*

- How do we create more efficient technology?
- How do we develop a more smoothly running social machine?
- How do we construct more sophisticated—and less humanized—scientific knowledge?

Instead, the most immediate questions *are*

- What is the purpose of my life?
- What choices should I make?
- To what values should I commit myself?
- How do I become authentic?

Compared to these distinctly "human" questions, the very questions that Socrates and other early thinkers posed as central to human existence, all other concerns pale.

One of the first existentialist voices was the enigmatic and brilliant Danish philosopher **Søren Kierkegaard** (1813–1855). Kierkegaard was outraged by the destruction of individual values, repulsed by what he considered to be the hypocrisy of political and religious leaders, and despairing of all the individuals who had permitted their souls to become pedestrian and mediocre. His scathing attacks on these "inauthentic" values still reverberate today.

SØREN KIERKEGAARD
(1813–1855)
Christian Philosopher. Considered to be first existentialist. Though deeply religious, challenged much of Christian philosophy including the belief that faith could be supported by proofs and reason; maintained true belief in God required an absurd leap of faith for which there is no rational justification.

Let others complain that the age is wicked; my complaint is that it is wretched, for it lacks passion. Men's thoughts are thin and flimsy like lace, they are themselves pitiable like lacemakers. The thoughts of their hearts are too paltry to be sinful. For a worm it might be regarded as a sin to harbor such thoughts, but not for a being made in the image of God. Their lusts are dull and sluggish, their passions sleepy. They do their duty, these shopkeeping souls, but they clip the coin a trifle . . . : they think that even if the Lord keeps ever so careful a set of books, they may still cheat Him a little. Out upon them! This is the reason my soul always turns back to the Old Testament and to Shakespeare. I feel that those who speak there are at least human beings: they hate, they love, they murder their enemies, and curse their descendants throughout all generations, they sin.

Kierkegaard counted Socrates as his philosophical mentor, and for both thinkers the care of the soul is paramount in human existence: *everything* else is secondary. We need to cultivate our souls, committing ourselves passionately to the quest of truth and personal authenticity. We need to fully recognize and accept our personal responsibility in creating ourselves through the choices we make. We need to invest our lives with meaning through our own efforts, fulfilling our unique potential through the power of our minds and the talents of our spirits. These are the core values of the existentialist ethic.

The antithesis of this passionate commitment to creating the "project" of our individual lives is to succumb to the social forces of conformity, permitting the expectations of others to seep into our consciousness, causing us to become weak and insignificant, a tiny inconsequential part of a larger whole. Kierkegaard explains the pernicious and utterly false view that "the crowd" is the ultimate reality to which we should strive to bend our wills, sacrifice our individuality, and become absorbed.

Kierkegaard,
*On the Dedication
to 'That Single Individual'*

There is a view of life which holds that where the crowd is, the truth is also, that it is a need in truth itself, that it must have the crowd on its side. There is another view of life; which holds that wherever the crowd is, there is untruth, so that, for a moment to carry the matter out to its farthest conclusion, even if every individual possessed the truth in private, yet if they came together into a crowd (so that "the crowd" received any *decisive*, voting, noisy, audible importance), untruth would at once be let in.

For "the crowd" is untruth. Eternally, godly, christianly what Paul says is valid: "only one receives the prize," [I Cor. 9:24] not by way of comparison, for in the comparison "the others" are still present. That is to say, everyone can be that one, with God's help—but only one receives the prize; again, that is to say, everyone should cautiously have dealings with "the others," and essentially only talk with God and with himself—for only one receives the prize; again, that is to say, the human being is in kinship with, or to be a human is to be in kinship with the divinity. The worldly, temporal, busy, socially-friendly person says this: "How unreasonable, that only one should receive the prize, it is far more probable that several combined receive the prize; and if we become many, then it becomes more certain and also easier for each individually." . . . But the eternal, which vaults high over the temporal, quiet as the night sky, and God in heaven, who from this exalted state of bliss, without becoming the least bit dizzy, looks out over these innumerable millions and knows each single individual; he, the great examiner, he says: only one receives the prize; that is to say, everyone can receive it, and everyone ought to become this by oneself, but only one receives the prize. Where the crowd is, therefore, or where a decisive importance is attached to the fact that there is a crowd, *there* no one is working, living, and striving for the highest end, but only for this or that

Do you agree with Søren Kierkegaard that people are too willing to sacrifice their individuality to "the crowd," to surrender their identities to the forces of social conformity? What are some examples of this behavior in modern culture?

earthly end; since the eternal, the decisive, can only be worked for where there is one; and to become this by oneself, which all can do, is to will to allow God to help you—"the crowd" is untruth.

Kierkegaard introduces this passage with the theme that he will repeat throughout: "The crowd is untruth." Although there are many people who contend just the opposite—that reality lies in social groups and organizations—Kierkegaard is convinced that "only one receives the prize." Not that he means this in terms of competition with others—when we compare ourselves with others we are by definition letting "the crowd" mentality penetrate our psyches. No, "only one receives the prize" is a mental state, in which you view your project on earth as striving to achieve "your" prize, the prize that only *you* can achieve. "The crowd" cannot help you in this quest, you must reach your goal by means of your own individual resources.

> A crowd—not this or that, one now living or long dead, a crowd of the lowly or of nobles, of rich or poor, etc., but in its very concept—is untruth, since a crowd either renders the single individual wholly unrepentant and irresponsible, or weakens his responsibility by making it a fraction of his decision. . . . The untruth is first that it is "the crowd," which does either what only *the single individual* in the crowd does, or in every case what *each single individual* does. For a crowd is an abstraction. . . .

Kierkegaard,
*On the Dedication
to 'That Single Individual'*

The concept of "the crowd" is a state of consciousness for the individual, not necessarily corresponding to a particular group of people. It's the automatic inclination to view yourself and your life only in terms of others: a family member, an employee, a member of a religion, and so on. When you view yourself *only* as a member of a social group, you implicitly deny your individuality, your unique human distinctness. In so doing you surrender your autonomy, permitting the crowd to make decisions for you, enabling you to temporarily escape from your personal responsibility for your choices. Of course, as Sartre makes clear in chapter 4, this "escape" is an illusion, for you are fully responsible for surrendering your ability to make free choices to the crowd, and you are fully responsible for anything that the crowd chooses to do. For Kierkegaard, surrendering ourselves to the crowd is *inauthentic* and the height of immorality. Moral action begins with "respecting what it means to be human," and concludes with acting on the truth that "everyone can be the one."

Technology has exacerbated the human tendency to subsume themselves to the crowd. In Kierkegaard's time, the power of printed publications like newspapers made it easier for clever leaders to manipulate the thinking of the citizens, fashioning them into a docile crowd to do their bidding. In our day and age, this power to anonymously manipulate large numbers of people has increased exponentially through the electronic mediums of television and the Internet. And the crowd is always vulnerable to the manipulations of "untruths," because untruths play on people's emotions and appeal to their innate desires. Truth, on the other hand, requires thought, understanding, reflection, insight, and critical analysis. In contrast, untruth requires "no previous knowledge, no schooling, no discipline, no abstinence, no self-denial, no honest self-concern, no patient labor!" Untruths are brain candy for the masses, telling them what they want to hear, manipulating them to think and feel precisely what the manipulators want them to. It is in this sense that the crowd, thinking itself strong, is really weak, a herd of unthinking and easily controlled animals, pushed and prodded, stumbling down preordained paths with smiles on their simple faces.

VISUAL PHILOSOPHY

Manipulation by the Media

Identify some of the ways that the media (print, television, Internet, radio) is able to manipulate the thinking and behavior of people. Why are people vulnerable to these "untruths"?

Kierkegaard,
*On the Dedication
to 'That Single Individual'*

One cannot say that, again with the help of the press, "the truth" can overcome the lie and the error. O, you who say this, ask yourself: Do you dare to claim that human beings, in a crowd, are just as quick to reach for truth, which is not always palatable, as for untruth, which is always deliciously prepared, when in addition this must be combined with an admission that one has let oneself be deceived! Or do you dare to claim that "the truth" is just as quick to let itself be understood as is untruth, which requires no previous knowledge, no schooling, no discipline, no abstinence, no self-denial, no honest self-concern, no patient labor! No, "the truth," which detests this untruth, the only goal of which is to desire its increase, is not so quick on its feet. Firstly, it cannot work through the fantastical, which is the untruth; its communicator is only a single individual. And its communication relates itself once again to the single individual; for in this view of life the single individual is precisely the truth.

But Kierkegaard believes there is hope. It is a hope that is ignited every time a person rejects the sleeping unreflection of the crowd mentality and insists on being "a single individual," rejecting the mindless tyranny of the crowd and replacing it with the eternal life of the authentic individual. This is the ethical ideal to which every person should aspire.

> A crowd is indeed made up of single individuals; it must therefore be in everyone's power to become what he is, a single individual; no one is prevented from being a single individual, no one, unless he prevents himself by becoming many. To become a crowd, to gather a crowd around oneself, is on the contrary to distinguish life from life; even the most well-meaning one who talks about that, can easily offend a single individual. But it is the crowd which has power, influence, reputation, and domination—this is the distinction of life from life, which tyrannically overlooks the single individual as the weak and powerless one, in a temporal-worldly way overlooks the eternal truth: the single individual. ■

Kierkegaard,
*On the Dedication
to 'That Single Individual'*

 Kierkegaard, Søren,
That Individual

The dehumanizing domination of "the crowd," in which uncritical masses of people look outward to political and religious leaders, as well as popular culture, to tell them "who" to be, reflects what Kierkegaard calls "the abstract principle of leveling." With the annihilation of individuality, people are reduced to abstractions, labels, and categories defined by age, race, marital status, career, socioeconomic status, nationality, educational level, and gender. The net effect of removing the unique and rich qualities from each individual is to place all people on the same abstract level. This is true alienation, and as Kierkegaard describes it in *The Present Age*, it is profoundly immoral.

> The present age tends toward a mathematical equality in which it takes so and so many to make one individual. Formerly the outstanding individual could allow himself everything and the individual in the masses nothing at all. Now everyone knows that so and so many make an individual, and quite consistently people add themselves together (it is called joining together, but that is only a polite euphemism) for the most trivial purposes. Simply in order to put a passing whim into practice a few people add themselves together, and the thing is done—they dare to do it . . . the individual no longer belongs to God, to himself, to his beloved, to his art or to his science; he is conscious of belonging in all things to an abstraction to which he is subjected by reflection. . . .
>
> The abstract principle of leveling . . . like the biting east wind, has no personal relation to any individual, but has only an abstract relationship which is the same for everyone. There no hero suffers for others, or helps them; the taskmaster of all alike is the leveling process, which itself takes on their education. And the man who learns most from the leveling and himself becomes greatest does not become an outstanding man or hero—that would only impede the leveling process, which is rigidly consistent to the end; he himself prevents that from happening because he has understood the meaning of leveling: he becomes a man and nothing else, in the complete equalitarian sense.

We can now more fully appreciate Kierkegaard's pronouncement, "Truth is subjectivity." For several centuries new discoveries in every branch of science have emboldened certain scientists and philosophers to maintain that the rational and empirical concepts and methodologies of science are "objective" and therefore "truer" and "more real" than the subjective experiences of humans. For Kierkegaard and other existentialists, this notion is dangerous and delusionary. All scientific thought is rooted in the concrete immediacy of lived human experience, without which it wouldn't exist. The world in which each individual lives is infinitely more "real" than any scientific abstraction. Your thoughts and emotions, your quest to understand the purpose of your life and death, your desire to shape your existence through freely originated choices, your passionate commitment to truth, honesty, and authenticity—these are the building blocks of the human universe. Scientific thought simply reflects an abstracted version of the ground of its reality—to argue that it is more "real" than the direct experience of the living individual who gave rise to it makes as little sense as assuming that a sophisticated computer is "more real" than the individual human mind that created it, or that a motion picture is "more real" than the life experiences upon which it is based. Kierkegaard makes this point eloquently in his *Concluding Unscientific Postscript*:

> All logical thinking employs the language of abstraction. . . . It is easier to indulge in abstract thought than it is to exist. . . .
>
> The difficulty that inheres in existence, with which the existing individual is confronted, is one that never really comes to expression in the language of abstract thought, much less receives an explanation. . . . Abstract thought ignores the concrete and the temporal, the existential process, the predicament of the existing individual arising from his being a synthesis of the temporal and the eternal situated in existence. . . .
>
> Existing is ordinarily regarded as no very complex matter, much less an art, since we all exist; but abstract thinking takes rank as an accomplishment. But to really exist . . . that is truly difficult.

Kierkegaard, Søren, *Concluding Unscientific Postscript*

To "really exist," for Kierkegaard, is a lifelong challenge and evolutionary process. He identifies "Three Stages on Life's Way" through which every person must pass in order to become an authentic individual and "really exist."

- *Aesthetic Stage*   This is the stage of life in which people are absorbed in pursuing the beautiful and pleasurable dimensions of life, living for the moment, led by emotions and sensuous passions. Although powerfully seductive, a life devoted to simply pursuing pleasurable experience after pleasurable experience is ultimately dissatisfying. Kierkegaard describes his own experience in the aesthetic stage as a vain search for anchorage on a "boundless sea of pleasure," an existence in which he had "tasted the fruit of the tree of knowledge . . . but the pleasure did not outlast the sea of pleasure." Kierkegaard concludes that a hedonistic life devoted solely to the pursuit of pleasure is devoid of genuine meaning and ultimately filled with emptiness and dread.

- *Ethical Stage*   Dissatisfaction with the excesses of the aesthetic stage typically motivates people to seek a life guided by moral standards and ethical values. Moral codes provide people with a structure that was lacking in the aesthetic stage. Such codes provide them with a clear listing of "dos" and "don'ts," of values to live by, of virtuous people to aspire to. But for Kierkegaard, this stage is ultimately unsatisfactory as well. Too often people look outside themselves for moral guidance, and define themselves in terms of the values of others, "the crowd." The ethical stage is a necessary but transitory stage in an individual's quest for ultimate meaning, an authentic existence that can only be realized in the *religious stage*. In fact, as far as ethical beliefs are concerned, Kierkegaard contends, "The important thing is not what you may think is precisely right or wrong. What matters is that you choose to have an opinion at all on what is right or wrong."

- *Religious Stage*   Unlike the previous life stages, which are characterized by a distinct set of beliefs and behavior that are easily identifiable, the religious stage is characterized by a highly personal, subjective, and nonrational "leap of faith." And because it is beyond reason and objective analysis, it is impossible by its nature to communicate it in any precise fashion. For Kierkegaard this is the realm of *subjective truth*, an existence in which people become profoundly aware of their individuality and relationship to the divine. This is an area of Kierkegaard's thought that we will examine more fully in the next chapter, "What Is Religion?"

THINK PHILOSOPHICALLY

Analyzing Søren Kierkegaard

6.9

NOTEBOOK

- For Kierkegaard, the moral goal in life is to achieve *authenticity*, a state in which you fully and honestly accept your existential predicament: your freedom to choose your destiny, your independence of outside groups or individuals in defining your "self," your willingness to confront the uncertainties of the cosmos—including death and the meaning of life—with courage and resilience. With this as a criteria, evaluate to what extent you are living what Kierkegaard would consider an "authentic" life.

- Reflect on the forces that existentialists believe have alienated modern men and women, including the increasing dominance of technology; the complex size and structures of many businesses, bureaucracies, and social organizations; the manipulation by the media. In what ways have these forces affected you and the way you see yourself? For example, do you sometimes feel that you are being treated more as a Social Security number or a statistic than as a human being? Do you sometimes feel that it's difficult to forge meaningful relationships with other people in the professional or social groups of which you are a member? Have you felt disconnected from the jobs that you have had, being treated like a "cog" in a machine, or an impersonal paper-pusher?

- Consider society as a whole. To what extent do you believe that Kierkegaard's and Socrates' condemnations are on target?

  > Let others complain that the age is wicked; my complaint is that it is wretched, for it lacks passion. Men's thoughts are thin and flimsy like lace, they are themselves pitiable like lacemakers. The thoughts of their hearts are too paltry to be sinful. For a worm it might be regarded as a sin to harbor such thoughts, but not for a being made in the image of God. Their lusts are dull and sluggish, their passions sleepy. They do their duty, these shopkeeping souls. . . . (Kierkegaard)

  > You, my friend,—a citizen of the great and mighty and wise city of Athens,—are you not ashamed of heaping up the greatest amount of money and honour and reputation, and caring so little about wisdom and truth and the greatest improvement of the soul, which you never regard or heed at all? (Socrates)

- Evaluate Kierkegaard's analysis of how the abstraction of "the crowd" has usurped the concrete, living individual as the foundation of modern society. Do you agree with his analysis? Why or why not? Provide examples from your life and your experience with society to support your view.

- Do you agree with Kierkegaard that there has been a "leveling" of the individual: that you are seen by others primarily in terms of abstract categories rather than as a uniquely valuable individual? Why or why not?

Jean-Paul Sartre's (1905–1980) approach to ethics was based on the same fundamental themes as Kierkegaard's, though he was writing nearly a century later in a very different world. We explored Sartre's views in some detail in chapter 4, "Am I Free?" As with Kierkegaard, Sartre believes that becoming an authentic individual is the ethical ideal we should strive to achieve. And authenticity means fully accepting the fact that we are "condemned to be free," completely responsible for every action we take in life. We create ourselves through our daily choices, and those choices are free: we are without excuse.

Atheistic existentialism, which I represent, is more coherent. It states that if God does not exist, there is at least one being in whom existence precedes essence, a being who exists before he can be defined by any concept, and that this being is man, or, as

JEAN-PAUL SARTRE

(1905–1980)
French Existentialist. Important author, playwright, literary critic and philosopher. In *Being and Nothingness* (1943) envisions the self as a continual project in the world created through free choices.

Sartre,
Existentialism Is a Humanism

Heidegger says, human reality. What is meant here by saying that existence precedes essence? It means that, first of all, man exists, turns up, appears on the scene, and, only afterward, defines himself. If man, as the existentialist conceives him, is indefinable, it is because at first he is nothing. Only afterward will he be something, and he himself will have made what he will be. Thus, there is no human nature, since there is no God to conceive it. Not only is man what he conceives himself to be, but he is also only what he wills himself to be after this thrust toward existence.

Man is nothing else but what he makes of himself. Such is the first principle of existentialism. It is also what is called subjectivity, the name we are labeled with when charges are brought against us. But what do we mean by this, if not that man has a greater dignity than a stone or table? For we mean that man first exists, that is, that man first of all is the being who hurls himself toward a future and who is conscious of imagining himself as being in the future.

But if existence really does precede essence, man is responsible for what he is. Thus, existentialism's first move is to make every man aware of what he is and to make the full responsibility of his existence rest on him. And when we say that a man is responsible for himself, we do not only mean that he is responsible for his own individuality, but that he is responsible for all men. . . .

For Sartre, our choices are entirely free, and we can depend only on ourselves to determine the "right" choice to make. Because God does not exist, and there are no absolute moral codes that apply to all people, this means that there are no reliable guidelines to instruct us as to what we should do. We are alone, abandoned in a callous and uncaring universe, with only ourselves as resources.

But isn't this a potentially dangerous theory? After all, if we give people unlimited license to choose whatever they want, as long as they accept responsibility for their choices, how can we condemn the actions of evil people like Hitler and Stalin? When confronted regarding their moral evil, couldn't they respond: "I'm an existentialist: my choices are completely free and I accept responsibility for them. So you have no grounds for condemning me." This is a potentially devastating issue for Sartre, and he is clearly aware of its threat. Sartre himself was a person of strong moral principles, which led him to become a fighter for the French Resistance during World War II, following the invasion of France by Nazi Germany. For Sartre, choosing freely and accepting one's responsibility is not a solely individual project: it takes place in a social context, and embodies an enlightened sense of moral responsibility to humanity as a whole.

Sartre, *Existentialism Is a Humanism*

When we say that man chooses his own self, we mean that every one of us does likewise; but we also mean by that that in making this choice he also chooses all men. In fact, in creating the man that we want to be, there is not a single one of our acts which does not at the same time create an image of man as we think he ought to be. To choose to be this or that is to affirm at the same time the value of what we choose, because we can never choose evil. We always choose the good, and nothing can be good for us without being good for all.

. . . If we grant that we exist and fashion our image at one and the same time, the image is valid for everybody and for our whole age. Thus, our responsibility is much greater than we might have supposed, because it involves all mankind. . . . if I want to marry, to have children; even if this marriage depends solely on my own circumstances or passion or wish, I am involving all humanity in monogamy and not merely myself. Therefore, I am responsible for myself and for everyone else. I am creating a certain image of man of my own choosing. In choosing myself, I choose man.

In an effort to save his theory from charges of amorality, Sartre is invoking a bold blend of Immanuel Kant and Plato. Kant, as we saw on page 292, founded his ethical theory on what he termed his categorical imperative: "Act as if the maxim of your action were to become by your will a universal law of nature." In other words, Kant is suggesting that the standard we use in making moral decisions is to ask ourselves: "Would I be rationally able to endorse *everyone* making the same choice as I?" For example, if you're thinking about purchasing a term paper online and submitting it as your own, you would have to endorse as a rational law *everyone* doing exactly the same thing. Sartre seems to be trying to attach his theory of free choice to this same "universalizing" concept when he states:

Sartre, *Existentialism Is a Humanism*

When we say that man chooses his own self, we mean that every one of us does likewise; but we also mean by that that in making this choice he also chooses all men. In fact, in creating the man that we want to be, there is not a single one of our acts which does not at the same time create an image of man as we think he ought to be.

When you make a choice, according to Sartre, you are not simply creating and defining yourself as a person—you are also creating and defining your image of the way all humans *should* be. So if you choose to cheat in school, you are by implication suggesting that all humans should act exactly the same way. It's a fascinating approach to ethical choice, combining a belief in absolute freedom with a Kantian responsibility to universalize our choices with an implicit endorsement that all men and women make the choice that you are making.

Jean-Paul Sartre

Despite the surface similarities, however, Sartre believed that his approach to ethics was fundamentally different from Kant's. For Kant, obeying the categorical imperative is an absolute duty grounded on the primacy of reason: we are in essence rational creatures, so we cannot help but recognize our responsibility to universalize our choices with logical consistency. For Sartre, there are no absolute moral standards or duties that transcend the individual: our choices rest solely on our own shoulders, guided by our own spontaneous and unfettered ability to choose freely. Yet if this is truly the case, what is Sartre's rationale for contending that when we choose for ourselves we implicitly "choose for all men"?

Sartre also seems to be invoking Plato's ethical perspective that no person does evil intentionally. Plato was convinced that people act immorally due to ignorance. When you educate people and show them a more enlightened path, they cannot help but take it. Sartre seems to be making the same point when he states, "To choose to be this or that is to affirm at the same time the value of what we choose, because we can never choose evil. We always choose the good, and nothing can be good for us without being good for all."

Sartre realized that many people are terrified by the prospect of such absolute freedom and complete responsibility. Their response is to flee, to escape from this life sentence of freedom and responsibility. This refusal to accept responsibility creates *inauthenticity*. Inauthentic individuals deny their freedom, attempt to surrender their freedom to others, passively let outside forces shape their lives, or pretend that the formation of their characters was beyond their control. They lack the courage to accept themselves as self-creators, creating a false image of themselves that they present to the world as real, a mask concealing their weak and trembling selves. And they refuse to acknowledge their awesome responsibility of legislating for all humankind by the choices that they make.

Sartre, *Existentialism Is a Humanism*

The existentialists say at once that man is anguish. What that means is this: the man who involves himself and who realizes that he is not only the person he chooses to be, but also a law-maker who is, at the same time, choosing for all mankind as well as himself, cannot help escape the feeling of his total and deep responsibility. Of course, there are many people who are not anxious; but we claim that they are hiding their anxiety, that they are fleeing from it. Certainly, many people believe that when they do something, they themselves are the only ones involved, and when someone says to them, "What if everyone acted that way?" they shrug their shoulders and answer, "Everyone doesn't act that way." But really, one should always ask himself, "What would happen if everybody looked at things that way?" There is no escaping this disturbing thought except by a kind of double-dealing. A man who lies and makes excuses for himself by saying "not everybody does that," is someone with an uneasy conscience, because the act of lying implies that a universal value is conferred upon the lie.

All such efforts to escape from freedom and responsibility are doomed, because we are "condemned" to be free. Our efforts to escape succeed only in creating inauthentic selves with no hope of living meaningful lives. The only way to live a genuinely authentic life is to embrace your freedom, acknowledge your responsibility, and face the profound existential emotions of abandonment, anguish, and despair with uncommon courage. (These are the views of the "early" Sartre: the "later" Sartre, influenced by Marxism, qualified his extreme notion of freedom.)

Sartre provides a real-world example to illustrate the general framework that he is proposing. His example is set during World War II, after Nazi Germany had invaded France. A certain percentage of the French population became "collaborators," cooperating with the occupying Germans, whereas others continued to fight against the Germans in the French Resistance, of which Sartre himself was a member. But before describing the example, he first provides us with a memorable restatement of his central thesis regarding human freedom.

Sartre, *Existentialism Is a Humanism*

That is the idea I shall try to convey when I say that man is condemned to be free. Condemned, because he did not create himself, yet, in other respects he is free; because, once thrown into the world, he is responsible for everything he does. The existentialist does not believe in the power of passion. He will never agree that a sweeping passion is a ravaging torrent which fatally leads a man to certain acts and is therefore an excuse. He thinks that man is responsible for his passion. . . .

To give you an example which will enable you to understand abandonment better, I shall cite the case of one of my students who came to see me under the following circumstances: his father was on bad terms with his mother, and, moreover, was inclined to be a collaborationist; his older brother had been killed in the German offensive of 1940, and the young man, with somewhat immature but generous feelings, wanted to avenge him. His mother lived alone with him, very much upset by the half-treason of her husband and the death of her older son; the boy was her only consolation.

The boy was faced with the choice of leaving for England and joining the Free French Forces—that is, leaving his mother behind—or remaining with his mother and helping her to carry on. He was fully aware that the woman lived only for him and that his going-off—and perhaps his death—would plunge her into despair. He was also aware that every act that he did for his mother's sake was a sure thing, in the sense that it was helping her to carry on, whereas every effort he made toward going off and fighting was an uncertain move which might run aground and prove completely useless; for example, on his way to England he might, while passing through Spain, be detained indefinitely in a Spanish camp; he might reach England or Algiers and be stuck in an office at a desk job. As a result, he was faced with two very different kinds of action: one, concrete, immediate, but concerning only one individual; the other concerned an incomparably vaster group, a national collectivity, but for that very reason was dubious, and might be interrupted en route. And, at the same time, he was wavering between two kinds of ethics. On the one hand, an ethics of sympathy, of personal devotion; on the other, a broader ethics, but one whose efficacy was more dubious. He had to choose between the two.

Who could help him choose? Christian doctrine? No. Christian doctrine says, "Be charitable, love our neighbor, take the more rugged path, etc., etc." But which is the more rugged path? Whom should he love as a brother? The fighting man or his mother? Which does the greater good, the vague act of fighting in a group, or the concrete one

Two soldiers of the Free French Forces.

of helping a particular human being to go on living? Who can decide *a priori*? Nobody. No book of ethics can tell him. The Kantian ethics says, "Never treat any person as a means, but as an end." Very well, if I stay with my mother, I'll treat her as an end and not as a means; but by virtue of this very fact I'm running the risk of treating the people around me who are fighting, as means; and, conversely, if I go to join those who are fighting, I'll be treating them as an end, and, by doing that, I run the risk of treating my mother as a means.

What makes this a fascinating example is that it involves choosing between two morally desirable outcomes: the personal value of staying with a loved one who needs us versus the social value of fighting to defeat a terrible enemy who has occupied one's homeland and threatens increasingly monstrous evil. Sartre's point is that there are no moral codes that will instruct him in clear and unambiguous terms what the morally "right" choice is. This is something he must decide for himself. Moral codes and rules are too general to provide guidance in specific situations like this. Whichever alternative he chooses can be justified on moral grounds as a "good" thing, but there is no way of determining the "best" choice outside of his own independent thinking and thoughtful action. His choice is totally free and he is completely responsible for it.

Does that mean that we should trust our moral "instincts," our ethical "emotions," our "conscience?" Sartre thinks not.

If values are vague, and if they are always too broad for the concrete and specific case that we are considering, the only thing left for us is to trust our instincts. That's what this young man tried to do; and when I saw him, he said, "In the end, feeling is what counts. I ought to choose whichever pushes me in one direction. If I feel that I love my mother enough to sacrifice everything else for her—my desire for vengeance, for action, for adventure—then I'll stay with her. If, on the contrary, I feel that my love for my mother isn't enough, I'll leave."

But how is the value of a feeling determined? What gives his feeling for his mother value? Precisely the fact that he remained with her. I may say that I like so-and-so well enough to sacrifice a certain amount of money for him, but I may say so only if I've done it. I may say "I love my mother well enough to remain with her" if I have remained with her. The only way to determine the value of this affection is, precisely, to perform an act which confirms and defines it. But, since I require this affection to justify my act, I find myself caught in a vicious circle.

Sartre, Existentialism Is a Humanism

Sartre contends that our moral instincts, emotions, "conscience" are notoriously unreliable and difficult to interpret. We discover which instinct or emotion is stronger by what alternative we choose, but then it is too late to use this instinct or emotion as a guide. That's why Sartre describes this sort of reasoning as a "vicious circle." What's more, it's often difficult to discern the "strength" of emotions and instincts when they are in conflict with one another, and it is also difficult to differentiate "authentic" emotions from "false" emotions. The net result? We cannot discover moral guidance by trying to follow our moral instincts and emotions, any more than we can look to external moral codes for moral direction.

What about seeking the guidance of wise and morally upright people? This approach isn't going to work either, according to Sartre.

You will say, "At least, he did go to a teacher for advice." But if you seek advice from a priest, for example, you have chosen this priest; you already knew, more or less, just about what advice he was going to give you. In other words, choosing your adviser is involving yourself. The proof of this is that if you are a Christian, you will say, "Consult a priest." But some priests are collaborating, some are just marking time, some are

Sartre, Existentialism Is a Humanism

Sarte, Jean-Paul,
Existentialism Is a Humanism

resisting. Which to choose? If the young man chooses a priest who is resisting or collaborating, he has already decided on the kind of advice he's going to get. Therefore, in coming to see me he knew the answer I was going to give him, and I had only one answer to give: "You're free, choose, that is invent." No general ethics can show you what is to be done, there are no omens in the world. The Catholics will reply, "But there are." Granted—but, in any case, I myself choose the meaning they have. ■

Sartre's point is that we cannot rely on other people for moral instructions because by selecting the person we are going to for advice we ourselves are already making the choice of which alternative to select. We know what their values and biases are, and we can be fairly certain of what advice they will be giving us. It's the same in nonmoral circumstances. Suppose you are engaged in a romantic relationship and are trying to decide whether to remain or break up. You undoubtedly have a pretty good idea what each of your friends or family will advise you to do, so by selecting the individuals you will ask for advice, you are already reflecting which choice you really want to make. In the final analysis, this is your choice and your choice alone, for which you are fully responsible.

Another powerful voice for existentialism is **Simone de Beauvoir** (1908–1986). A philosopher and novelist, she had an intimate and enduring relationship with Jean-Paul Sartre that spanned most of their adult lives. As revealed in the following excerpt from her book *Ethics of Ambiguity*, de Beauvoir brought a distinct but complementary perspective to the ethical questions that existentialism confronts.

> **SIMONE DE BEAUVOIR**
> (1908–1986)
> Feminist Philosopher. Influenced by existentialism. In *The Second Sex* (1949) espoused view that women, historically subordinate to men, have been relegated to the category of the Other Sex.

de Beauvoir, *Ethics of Ambiguity* ■

There is no way for a man to escape from this world. It is in this world that—avoiding the pitfalls we have just pointed out—he must realize himself morally. Freedom must project itself toward its own reality through a content whose value it establishes. An end is valid only by a return to the freedom which established it and which willed itself through this end. But his will implies that freedom is not to be engulfed in any goal; neither is it to dissipate itself vainly without aiming at a goal. It is not necessary for the subject to seek to be, but it must desire that there *be* being. To will oneself free and to will that there be *being* are one and the same choice, the choice that man makes of himself as a presence in the world. We can neither say that the free man wants freedom in order to desire being, nor that he wants the disclosure of being by freedom. These are two aspects of a single reality. And whichever be the one under consideration, they both imply the bond of each man with all others.

In this passage de Beauvoir grapples with the mystery of freedom, which, like Sartre, she considers to be radical in nature and central to human experience. Freedom is the source of all value in human experience: as it projects itself outward through intention and action, it confers value. So, for example, when you choose to pursue your education in college, you are at the same time conferring value on your choice. This pursuit has value to you not because someone else *says* it's important, but because you *chose* to pursue it as an end. At the same time, de Beauvoir maintains that the act of choosing freely also reveals a desire on our part that there be a world in which our choices can have meaning, a world populated with other freely choosing agents.

de Beauvoir, *Ethics of Ambiguity*

This bond does not immediately reveal itself to everybody. A young man wills himself free. He wills that there be being. This spontaneous liberality which casts him ardently into the world can ally itself to what is commonly called egoism. Often the young man perceives only that aspect of his relationship to others whereby others appear as enemies. In the preface to *The Inner Experience* Georges Bataille emphasizes very forcefully that each individual wants to be All. He sees in every other man and particularly in those whose existence is asserted with most brilliance, a limit, a condemnation of himself. "Each consciousness," said Hegel, "sees the death of the other." And indeed at every moment others are stealing the whole world away from me. The first movement is to hate them. But his hatred is naïve, and the desire immediately struggles against itself. If I were really everything there would be nothing beside me; the world would be empty. There would be nothing to possess, and I myself would be nothing. If he is reasonable, the young man immediately understands that by taking the world away from me, others also give it to me, since a thing is given to me only by the movement which snatches it from me. To will that there be being is also to will that there be men by and for whom the world is endowed with human significations. One can reveal the world only on a basis revealed by other men. No project can be defined except by its interference with other projects. To make being "be" is to communicate with others by means of being.

Our freedom, which defines our existence, only has meaning in relationship to others who are exercising their freedom of choice. Even when the initial impulse of someone is to control and dominate everything—in the same way that an immature person may seek to have the world revolve entirely around *him*—there is the rapid realization that we need other people in order for our own lives to have meaning. Even when others make choices that challenge or interfere with our own choices, we recognize that the only way we can define ourselves as humans is through our interaction with others.

This truth is found in another form when we say that freedom cannot will itself without aiming at an open future. The ends which it gives itself must be unable to be transcended by any reflection, but only the freedom of others can extend them beyond our life. I have tried to show in *Pyrrhus and Cineas* that every man needs the freedom of other men and, in a sense, always wants it, even though he may be a tyrant; the only thing he fails to do is to assume honestly the consequences of such a wish. Only the freedom of others keeps each one of us from hardening in the absurdity of facticity. And if we are to believe the Christian myth of creation, God himself was in agreement on this point with the existentialist doctrine since, in the words of an anti-fascist priest, "He had such respect for man that He created him free." ∎

de Beauvoir, *Ethics of Ambiguity*

We need other people to become fully human, and this is the existential basis for morality. The essence of being human is to be continually exercising our freedom of choice, projecting ourselves into the future, transcending ourselves, continually evolving. This is only possible through our interplay with others, who are striving to achieve the same significance for themselves through the choices they make. If we were completely alone, solitary in an empty world, our dynamic humanity would become hardened into "thingness," sapped of its life and spirit.

In defining his freedom-based ethic, Sartre argued that in choosing for ourselves we are choosing for all men. De Beauvoir provides a compelling rationale for this view by displaying the intimate and essential connection that we have to all men and women: our existence can only have meaning in relationship to the existence of others. Our freedom to choose can only exist in relation to the freedom of choice exercised by others. Thus the choices we make as we define who we are must necessarily reflect the kinds of choices that we believe all men and women should make, for we are connected to one another in ways that are profound and inescapable.

Albert Camus (1913–1960) was a friend and associate of Jean-Paul Sartre and Simone de Beauvoir. Camus was a French writer of powerful plays and novels with existentialist themes, including such well-known works as *The Stranger* and *The Plague*. One of Camus' most haunting works is his essay *The Myth of Sisyphus*, an analysis of human existence based on the ancient Greek myth. Sisyphus is condemned by the gods to eternally push a huge stone up a hill in Hades, only to watch

ALBERT CAMUS
(1913–1960)
Existentialist. Winner of the Nobel Prize in Literature in 1957; wrote many novels, including *The Stranger* and *The Plague* (1942). Dealt with what he felt was the absurd situation of human beings due to fact that the world is essentially irrational, yet humans have an intense desire to rationalize it.

it roll all the way down the slope once he nears the top. For Camus, Sisyphus' fate is emblematic of the human condition. Our lives are doomed to the same sort of *absurd* existence, living our lives in an "unintelligible and limited universe" devoid of intrinsic meaning. We make choices and engage in activities with the inescapable specter that they are ultimately without purpose. Yet Camus believes that, even in the midst of an absurd world, meaning is possible through critical reflection and courageously free choices.

Here is Camus' account of the myth, followed by his thoughts regarding the implications of the myth for human existence. As we will see, Camus believes that "There is but one truly serious philosophical problem, and that is suicide," and he also believes that even in the face of a universe that lacks ultimate purpose or meaning, suicide is a betrayal of existentialist ethics. The greatest challenge for each of us is to discover meaning in an absurd world, a conviction revealed even more explicitly in the following comment:

> To lose one's life is a little thing and I shall have the courage to do so if it is necessary; but to see the meaning of this life dissipated, to see our reason for existing disappear, that is what is unbearable. One cannot live without meaning.

Camus, *The Myth of Sisyphus*

The gods had condemned Sisyphus to ceaselessly rolling a rock to the top of a mountain, whence the stone would fall back of its own weight. They had thought with some reason that there is no more dreadful punishment than futile and hopeless labor.

If one believes Homer, Sisyphus was the wisest and most prudent of mortals. According to another tradition, however, he was disposed to practice the profession of highwayman. I see no contradiction in this. Opinions differ as to the reasons why he became the futile laborer of the underworld. To begin with, he is accused of a certain levity in regard to the gods. He stole their secrets. Aegina, the daughter of Aesopus, was carried off by Jupiter. The father was shocked by that disappearance and complained to Sisyphus. He, who knew of the abduction, offered to tell about it on condition that Aesopus would give water to the citadel of Corinth. To the celestial thunderbolts he preferred the benediction of water. He was punished for this in the underworld. Homer tells us also that Sisyphus had put Death in chains. Pluto could not endure the sight of his deserted, silent empire. He dispatched the god of war, who liberated Death from the hands of her conqueror.

It is said that Sisyphus, being near to death, rashly wanted to test his wife's love. He ordered her to cast his unburied body into the middle of the public square. Sisyphus woke up in the underworld. And there, annoyed by an obedience so contrary to human love, he obtained from Pluto permission to return to earth in order to chastise his wife. But when he had seen again the face of this world, enjoyed water and sun, warm stones and the sea, he no longer wanted to go back to the infernal darkness. Recalls, signs of anger, warnings were of no avail. Many years more he lived facing the curve of the gulf, the sparkling sea, and the smiles of earth. A decree of the gods was necessary. Mercury came and seized the impudent man by the collar and, snatching him from his joys, led him forcibly back to the underworld, where his rock was ready for him.

You have already grasped that Sisyphus is the absurd hero. He is, as much through his passions as through his torture. His scorn of the gods, his hatred of death, and his passion for life won him that unspeakable penalty in which the whole being is exerted toward accomplishing nothing. This is the price that must be paid for the passions of this earth. Nothing is told us about Sisyphus in the underworld. Myths are made for the imagination to breathe life into them. As for this myth, one sees merely the whole effort of a body straining to raise the huge stone, to roll it, and push it up a slope a hundred times over; one sees the face screwed up, the cheek tight against the stone, the shoulder bracing the clay-covered mass, the foot wedging it, the fresh start with arms outstretched, the wholly human security of two earth-clotted hands. At the very end of his long effort measured by skyless space and time without depth, the purpose is achieved.

The punishment of Sisyphus.

Then Sisyphus watches the stone rush down in a few moments toward that lower world whence he will have to push it up again toward the summit. He goes back down to the plain.

It is during that return, that pause, that Sisyphus interests me. A face that toils so close to stones is already stone itself! I see that man going back down with a heavy yet measured step toward the torment of which he will never know the end. That hour like a breathing-space which returns as surely as his suffering, that is the hour of consciousness. At each of those moments when he leaves the heights and gradually sinks toward the lairs of the gods, he is superior to his fate. He is stronger than his rock.

If this myth is tragic, that is because its hero is conscious. Where would his torture be, indeed, if at every step the hope of succeeding upheld him? The workman of today works everyday in his life at the same tasks, and his fate is no less absurd. But it is tragic only at the rare moments when it becomes conscious. Sisyphus, proletarian of the gods, powerless and rebellious, knows the whole extent of his wretched condition: it is what he thinks of during his descent. The lucidity that was to constitute his torture at the same time crowns his victory. There is no fate that can not be surmounted by scorn.

* * *

If the descent is thus sometimes performed in sorrow, it can also take place in joy. This word is not too much. Again I fancy Sisyphus returning toward his rock, and the sorrow was in the beginning. When the images of earth cling too tightly to memory, when the call of happiness becomes too insistent, it happens that melancholy arises in man's heart: this is the rock's victory, this is the rock itself. The boundless grief is too heavy to bear. These are our nights of Gethsemane. But crushing truths perish from being acknowledged. Thus, Oedipus at the outset obeys fate without knowing it. But from the moment he knows, his tragedy begins. Yet at the same moment, blind and desperate, he realizes that the only bond linking him to the world is the cool hand of a girl. Then a tremendous remark rings out: "Despite so many ordeals, my advanced age and the nobility of my soul make me conclude that all is well." Sophocles' Oedipus, like Dostoevsky's Kirilov, thus gives the recipe for the absurd victory. Ancient wisdom confirms modern heroism.

One does not discover the absurd without being tempted to write a manual of happiness. "What! by such narrow ways—?" There is but one world, however. Happiness and the absurd are two sons of the same earth. They are inseparable. It would be a mistake to say that happiness necessarily springs from the absurd discovery. It happens as well that the feeling of the absurd springs from happiness. "I conclude that all is well," says Oedipus, and that remark is sacred. It echoes in the wild and limited universe of man. It teaches that all is not, has not been, exhausted. It drives out of this world a god who had come into it with dissatisfaction and a preference for futile suffering. It makes of fate a human matter, which must be settled among men.

All Sisyphus' silent joy is contained therein. His fate belongs to him. His rock is a thing. Likewise, the absurd man, when he contemplates his torment, silences all the idols. In the universe suddenly restored to its silence, the myriad wondering little voices of the earth rise up. Unconscious, secret calls, invitations from all the faces, they are the necessary reverse and price of victory. There is no sun without shadow, and it is essential to know the night. The absurd man says yes and his efforts will henceforth be unceasing. If there is a personal fate, there is no higher destiny, or at least there is but one which he concludes is inevitable and despicable. For the rest, he knows himself to be the master of his days. At that subtle moment when man glances backward over his life, Sisyphus returning toward his rock, in that slight pivoting he contemplates that series of unrelated actions which become his fate, created by him, combined under his memory's eye and soon sealed by his death. Thus, convinced of the wholly human origin of all that is human, a blind man eager to see who knows that the night has no end, he is still on the go. The rock is still rolling.

I leave Sisyphus at the foot of the mountain! One always finds one's burden again. But Sisyphus teaches the higher fidelity that negates the gods and raises rocks. He too concludes that all is well. This universe henceforth without a master seems to him neither sterile nor futile. Each atom of that stone, each mineral flake of that night filled mountain, in itself forms a world. The struggle itself toward the heights is enough to fill a man's heart. One must imagine Sisyphus happy. ∎

 Camus, Albert, *The Myth of Sisyphus*

THINK PHILOSOPHICALLY 6.10
Analyzing Albert Camus

PHILOSOPHER'S NOTEBOOK

- For Camus, Sisyphus is the *absurd hero* because of "his scorn of the gods, his hatred of death, and his passion for life." His existence is absurd because he pays for his passions by suffering "that unspeakable penalty in which the whole being is exerted toward accomplishing nothing." Why do you think Camus considers Sisyphus to be a "hero"? If Sisyphus is a model for human existence, how does Camus believe that we can also become heroes? Why do you think Camus believes that Sisyphus, at these moments of consciousness, "is superior to his fate . . . stronger than his rock"?

  > It is during that return, that pause, that Sisyphus interests me. A face that toils so close to stones is already stone itself! . . . That hour like a breathing-space which returns as surely as his suffering, that is the hour of consciousness. At each of those moments when he leaves the heights and gradually sinks toward the lairs of the gods, he is superior to his fate. He is stronger than his rock.

- For Camus, "Crushing truths perish from being acknowledged," liberating us to discover meaning and happiness. "Ancient wisdom confirms modern heroism" in the remarkable words of Oedipus, "Despite so many ordeals, my advanced age and the nobility of my soul make me conclude that all is well." What does Camus believe we have to do, as modern men and women living in an absurd world, in order for us to also conclude that "all is well"?

- Camus believes that despite his eternal torment, Sisyphus is joyful because "His fate belongs to him." "The universe henceforth without a master seems to him neither sterile nor futile. Each atom of that stone, each mineral flake of that night filled mountain, in itself forms a world. The struggle itself toward the heights is enough to fill a man's heart. One must imagine Sisyphus happy."

Reflect on your own life: even if you were to conclude that there is no benevolent God nor ultimate purpose to life, do you think that your life could still be meaningful and happy? Why or why not?

The Ethics of Care

> The epithets *sociable, good-natured, humane, merciful, grateful, friendly, generous, beneficent,* or their equivalents, are known in all languages, and universally express the highest merit, which *human nature* is capable of attaining.
> —*David Hume,* An Enquiry Concerning the Principles of Morals

NEL NODDINGS

(1929–)

American Feminist Philosopher. Writes on issues surrounding ethics and the philosophy of education. In *Caring: A Feminine Approach to Ethics and Moral Education* (1984) and *Women and Evil* (1989) argues ethics should be founded on caring and interpersonal relationships.

Ethics of care Ethical theory that considers the needs and interests of others to be the primary focus of moral reasoning.

The major ethical theories we have considered to this point—hedonism, utilitarianism, deontology (Kantism), existentialist ethics—all tend to focus on the person contemplating a moral choice—in other words, *you.* Certainly the interests of others and the impact of your choices on them is a relevant consideration in your moral deliberations (in the case of utilitarianism it is the major focus), but *you* are the agent who is center stage.

But there is another ethical tradition that considers the needs and interests of others to be the primary focus of moral reasoning. The term **ethics of care** is sometimes used to designate this loose confederation of theories that emphasize the role of others in our moral relationships, and includes such diverse people as Jesus, David Hume, and Nel Noddings.

Nel Noddings (b. 1929) is a contemporary American philosopher who has devoted her work to the concept of "care ethics," which holds sympathy and caring to be the most important virtues. Noddings believes that morality is rooted in "natural caring," a primal emotional response. Our moral obligations are not created through the rational logic of the categorical imperative or the calculations of the utilitarian calculus: our moral obligations are instead created by the *caring response*. Noddings articulates her views on the caring response in the following passages from her work *Caring: A Feminine Approach to Ethics and Moral Education*.

What Does it Mean to Care?

Our dictionaries tell us that "care" is a state of mental suffering or of engrossment: to care is to be in a burdened mental state, one of anxiety, fear, or solicitude about something or someone. Alternatively, one cares for something or someone if one has a regard for or inclination toward that something or someone. If I have a regard for you, what you think, feel, and desire will matter to me. . . .

When I look at and think about how I am when I care, I realize that there is invariably this displacement of interest from my own reality to the reality of the other. . . . I am suggesting that we do not see only the direct possibilities for becoming better than we are when we struggle toward the reality of the other. We also have aroused in us the feeling, "I must do something." When we see the other's reality as a possibility for us, we must act to eliminate the intolerable, to reduce the pain, to fill the need, to actualize the dream. When I am in this sort of relationship with another, when the other's reality becomes a real possibility for me, I care. Whether the caring is sustained, whether it lasts long enough to be conveyed to the other, whether it becomes visible in the world, depends upon my sustaining the relationship or, at least, acting out of concern for my own ethicality as though it were sustained.

Noddings,
Caring: A Feminine Approach to Ethics and Moral Education

The act of *caring*, for Noddings, involves a full-fledged empathy that is both cognitive as well as emotional. In Noddings' terms, there is a "displacement of interest from my own reality to the reality of the other," moving us out of our unconscious absorption in our own frame of reference to that of another. When we "care" in this deep and meaningful way, "the other's reality becomes a real possibility for me," a reality that we connect to on an existential level. Of course, the act of caring does not necessarily entail action—it is a *prelude* to action. For example, you may encounter someone who has just experienced a personal tragedy, which in turn evokes a caring response in you—"your heart goes out to her"—and yet you may take no overt action. Or, as is frequently the case, your caring response may be a prelude to action, motivating you to offer to the person words of comfort and support, share your own similar experiences, or place a consoling hand on her arm. As Nodding expresses it: "Whether the caring is sustained, whether it lasts long enough to be conveyed to the other, whether it becomes visible in the world, depends upon my sustaining the relationship. . . ."

In this latter case, one in which something has slipped away from me or eluded me from the start but in which I strive to regain or to attain it, I experience a genuine caring for the self. This caring for self, for the *ethical* self, can emerge only from a caring for others. But a sense of my physical self, a knowledge of what gives me pain and pleasure, precedes my caring for others. Otherwise, their realities as possibilities for my own reality would mean nothing to me. When we say of someone, "He cares only for himself," we mean that, in our deepest sense, he does not care at all. He has only a sense of that physical self—of what gives him pain and pleasure. Whatever he sees in others is preselected in relation to his own needs and desires. He does not see the reality of the other as a possibility for himself but only as an instance of what he has already determined as self or not-self. Thus, he is ethically both zero and finished. His only "becoming" is a physical becoming.

Noddings,
Caring: A Feminine Approach to Ethics and Moral Education

The caring response, Noddings believes, is originally directed toward others. Once we have developed the ability to empathize with others, welcoming "their reali-

Do you agree with Nel Noddings that acting ethically involves the "caring" response in which there is a "displacement of interest from my own reality to the reality of the other"? Why?

ties as possibilities for me," we are then equipped to direct this same caring toward ourselves in our desire to cultivate our own ethically enlightened character. But if a person has not developed the ability to genuinely care for others, then they cannot really care for themselves in an ethical sense. They lack the understanding of what empathetic caring is all about. They are absorbed in themselves, submerged in their own reality, living in a dualistic universe that is divided between "self" and "not-self." Such a person "does not see the reality of the other as a possibility for himself but only as an instance of what he has already determined as self or not-self." As a result, the potential for ethical growth does not exist, only physical, sensual growth—hedonistic attempts to maximize his own pleasures and diminish his pains. This morally empty existence is "both zero and finished."

According to Noddings, we can be generally caring people and yet not behave in a caring way in a given situation. Even when well-intentioned, if we are intent on imposing our own ideas *before* attempting to achieve a deep and empathetic understanding of what the other person is thinking and feeling—then we are not "caring" in an authentic way. To achieve genuine caring, we have to bracket our own immediate reactions to the situation and make every effort to understand and appreciate *their* reactions to the situation. Then we are in a position, through genuine caring, to "struggle together."

Noddings,
Caring: A Feminine Approach to Ethics and Moral Education

Apprehending the other's reality, feeling what he feels as nearly as possible, is the essential part of caring from the view of the one-caring. For if I take on the other's reality as possibility and begin to feel its reality, I feel, also, that I must act accordingly; that is, I am impelled to act as though in my own behalf, but in behalf of the other. Now, of course, this feeling that I must act may or may not be sustained. I must make a commitment to act. The commitment to act in behalf of the cared-for, a continued interest in his reality throughout the appropriate time span, and the continual renewal of commitment over this span of time are the essential elements of caring from the inner view.

As I think about how I feel when I care, about what my frame of mind is, I see that my caring is always characterized by a move away from self. Yet not all instances of caring are alike even from the view of one-caring. Conditions change, and the time spanned by caring varies. While I care for my children throughout our mutual lifetimes, I may care only momentarily for a stranger in need. The intensity varies. I care deeply for those in my inner circles and more lightly for those farther removed from my personal life. Even with those close to me, the intensity of caring varies; it may be calm and steady most of the time and desperately anxious in emergencies. . . .

I reject the notion of universal caring—that is, caring for everyone—on the grounds that it is impossible to actualize and leads us to substitute abstract problem solving and mere talk for genuine caring. Many of us think that it is not only possible to care for everyone but morally obligatory that we should do so. We can, in a sense that will need elaboration, "care about" everyone; that is, we can maintain an internal state of readiness to try to care for whoever crosses our path. But this is different from the caring-for to which we refer when we use the word "caring." If we are thoughtful persons, we know that the difference is great, and we may even deliberately restrict our contacts so that the caring-for of which we are capable does not deteriorate to mere verbal caring-about. . . .

Genuine caring suggests *acting* on our feelings. When we "take on the other's reality as a possibility and begin to feel its reality," the next natural step is to try to do something to express our caring *because it feels as if we're doing it for ourselves* because the boundary between our "self" and the other "self" is being erased. Of course, as Noddings points out, we need to *commit* ourselves to action if our caring is going to be expressed and sustained in a meaningful way.

Noddings makes the further point that not all caring is alike: caring varies from person to person, relationship to relationship. Appropriate caring toward one person, would be inappropriate caring toward another. In addition, Noddings believes that *universal caring* is an empty concept. On a practical level, it's impossible to genuinely care for more than a finite number of people. Those who claim to "care for everyone" are "merely talking" or retreating into abstract analyses. What could it possibly mean to say that you "care for everyone," the vast majority of whom you don't know personally and will never meet? The only possible meaning is that *if* you were to meet them, *then* you would be prepared to enter into a caring relationship with them. Otherwise, "caring for everyone" is simply an empty use of language.

Noddings goes on to advance the idea that to qualify as a moral response, two types of "caring" must be present. The foundation of morality is the natural caring that occurs in humans toward children, parents, and other close family members. Such natural caring may also extend to intimate romantic relationships, as well as close friendships. But the *natural caring* in all of these instances is not, Noddings believes, *ethical caring*. Ethical caring necessarily involves natural caring but takes it one step further, directing your caring toward individuals to whom you do not naturally experience caring feelings. Thus, caring for a homeless individual, coming to the aid of a stranger in need, donating your time to a soup kitchen—all of these would qualify as ethical actions. Although they assume the existence of natural caring, they extend beyond it to include people we wouldn't naturally care about.

From Natural to Ethical Caring

David Hume long ago contended that morality is founded upon and rooted in feeling—that the "final sentence" on matters of morality, "that which renders morality an active virtue—this final sentence depends on some internal sense or feeling, which nature has made universal in the whole species. For what else can have an influence of this nature?"

What is the nature of this feeling that is "universal in the whole species"? I want to suggest that morality as an "active virtue" requires two feelings and not just one. The first is the sentiment of natural caring. There can be no ethical sentiment without the initial, enabling sentiment. In situations where we act on behalf of the other because we want to do so, we are acting in accord with natural caring. A mother's caretaking efforts in behalf of her child are not usually considered ethical but natural. Even maternal animals take care of their offspring, and we do not credit them with ethical behavior.

Recognizing that ethical caring requires an effort that is not needed in natural caring does not commit us to a position that elevates ethical caring over natural caring. **Kant** has identified the ethical with that which is done out of duty and not out of love, and that distinction in itself seems right. But an ethic built on caring strives to maintain the caring attitude and is thus dependent upon, and not superior to, natural caring. The source of ethical behavior is, then, in twin sentiments—one that feels directly for the other and one that feels for and with that best self, who may accept and sustain the initial feeling rather than reject it.

Does this distinction between "natural caring" and "ethical caring" make sense? A number of philosophers have criticized Noddings for suggesting that she artificially limits the concept of ethical caring. Does her view mean, for example, that a self-sacrificing action directed toward a friend doesn't count as an "ethical action," because it is the product of natural caring? That seems rather silly, and at serious variance from common understanding of moral motivations and actions.

The ethical "North Star" for Noddings is an *ethical ideal*: the image of the best of ourselves when we are caring and being cared for, deeply and authentically. It is this ethical ideal that we strive for when we experience the call of moral obligation, the "I must." She believes this to be in sharp contrast with ethical approaches

Noddings,
Caring: A Feminine Approach
to Ethics and Moral Education

David Hume (1711–1776) Scottish Philosopher. Hume's philosophy seen as drawing out logical consequences of a thoroughgoing empiricism. His skepticism concerning causation, induction, and religion is widely influential in the history of philosophy and contemporary philosophy.

Immanuel Kant (1724–1804) German Philosopher. Kant widely regarded as greatest philosopher of modern period. Attempted to synthesize two competing schools of the modern period, rationalism and empiricism, by showing important role both experience and reason play in constructing our knowledge of the world.

based on general principles, either specific pronouncements like "Thou shalt not . . . ," or more general principles like Kant's categorical imperative ("Act only on that maxim whereby thou canst at the same time will that it should become a universal law"). Her criticism of such universalizing principles is that they are unworkable in practical terms. Every moral situation is unique, with its own special circumstances. We cannot assume that other people will confront moral choices that are sufficiently similar to our own for the maxim to have meaning.

Noddings,
Caring: A Feminine Approach to Ethics and Moral Education

We shall discuss the ethical ideal, that vision of best self, in some depth. When we commit ourselves to obey the "I must" even at its weakest and most fleeting, we are under the guidance of this ideal. It is not just any picture. Rather, it is our best picture of ourselves caring and being cared for. It may even be colored by acquaintance with one superior to us caring, but, as I shall describe it, it is both constrained and attainable. It is limited by what we have already done and by what we are capable of, and it does not idealize the impossible so that we may escape into ideal abstraction. . . .

Let me say here, however, why it seems preferable to place an ethical ideal above principle as a guide to moral action. It has been traditional in moral philosophy to insist that moral principles must be, by their very nature as moral principles, universifiable. If I am obligated to do X under certain conditions, then under sufficiently similar conditions you also are obligated to do X. But the principle of universifiability seems to depend, as Nietzsche points out, on a concept of "sameness." In order to accept the principle, we should have to establish that human predicaments exhibit sufficient sameness, and this we cannot do without abstracting away from concrete situations those qualities that seem to reveal the sameness. In doing this, we often lose the very qualities or factors that gave rise to the moral question in the situation. That condition which makes the situation different and thereby induces genuine moral puzzlement cannot be satisfied by the application of principles developed in situations of sameness.

But can't the same kind of criticism be leveled against Noddings? After all, what does it actually mean to advise others to emulate an ideal that represents the best of themselves caring and being cared for? Isn't that formulation so general and open to so many subjective interpretations that it is virtually useless as a moral standard? And how does such an ethical recommendation differ from Kant's second version of the categorical imperative: "So act as to treat humanity, whether in thine own person or in that of any other, in every case as an end withal, never as means only." Isn't this simply a more articulate formulation of the kind of ethical values Noddings is promoting?

She then goes on to discuss the real-world limits to ethical caring.

Noddings,
Caring: A Feminine Approach to Ethics and Moral Education

Our obligation is limited and delimited by relation. We are never free, in the human domain, to abandon our preparedness to care; but, practically, if we are meeting those in our inner circles adequately as ones-caring and receiving those linked to our inner circles by formal chains of relation, we shall limit the calls upon our obligation quite naturally. We are not obliged to summon the "I must" if there is no possibility of completion in the other. I am not obliged to care for starving children in Africa, because there is no way for this caring to be completed in the other unless I abandon the caring to which I am obligated. I may still choose to do something in the direction of caring, but I am not obliged to do so. ∎

Noddings is advancing the very sensible idea that our ability to form caring relationships is not infinite. We have limited time, limited energy and, as a result, a finite ability to engage in genuinely caring relationships. It's important for us to acknowledge this reality, and choose judiciously those individuals with whom we wish to form authentic caring relationships.

However, critics of Noddings have suggested that there are troubling implications to her insistence that to speak meaningfully of "caring" necessarily entails the possibility of engaging in a direct caring relationship with that person. Such a rigid definition of ethical caring leads her to make statements like "I am not obliged to care for starving children in Africa, because there is no way for this caring to be completed in the other." Such a statement is likely to make many people morally queasy in its apparent callous insensitivity. We might well ask: Isn't it possible that this exclusive emphasis on personal, caring relationships will encourage many people to become morally apathetic toward larger ethical issues? Shouldn't we feel, in some meaningful sense, morally "obliged" to do what we can to reduce the pain and suffering of the millions of people outside of our own limited and familiar world? And shouldn't we strive to encourage others to enlarge their concept of the moral community rather than provide them with a rationale for shrinking their moral community and feeling ethically upright as they do?

THINK PHILOSOPHICALLY 6.11
Analyzing Nel Noddings

PHILOSOPHER'S NOTEBOOK

- The ethics of care is based on *empathy*, a complex intellectual and emotional identification with another person. Think of a recent situation in which you felt empathy toward someone else, and describe what the experience felt like as specifically as you can.
- Reflect on several of the moral decisions that you have made recently. What role has the ethics of care played in your moral reasoning?
- In your own words, explain what you think Noddings means by the concept of "grasping the reality of the other as a possibility for myself."
- Do you agree with Noddings' distinction between "natural caring" and "ethical caring"? Why or why not? What is your reaction to Noddings' statement that "I am not obliged to care for starving children in Africa, because there is no way for this caring to be completed in the other unless I abandon the caring to which I am obligated"?

Making Connections: *Choosing to Be a Moral Person*

An individual can possess a comprehensive understanding of moral concepts and approaches and *not* be a moral person. How is that possible? Just as people can possess an array of critical thinking abilities and yet choose not to use them, so people can be a walking compendium of moral theory and yet not choose to apply it to their lives, as we saw in Robert Coles' essay at the conclusion of the previous chapter. To achieve an enlightened moral existence in your own life, you need to *choose* to be a moral person struggling to live a moral life. You need to *value* morality, to aspire to an enhanced moral awareness, to exert the motivation and commitment required to reach this lofty but reachable goal.

Once you have developed a clear understanding of your moral code, the struggle has just begun. Becoming a morally enlightened person—a person of character and integrity—is a hard-won series of accomplishments, not a one-time award like winning an Oscar. Every day confronts you with new choices and unexpected challenges, many of which you cannot possibly anticipate. With your moral compass in hand to guide you, you need to commit yourself to making the choices that best express your moral philosophy of life. As a reflective critical thinker, you will be conscious of the choices you are making and the reasons you are making them, and you will learn from experience, refining your code of ethics and improving your moral choices through self-exploration. Achieving moral enlightenment is an ongoing process, but it is a struggle that cannot be avoided if you are to live a life of purpose and meaning, created by a self that is authentic and, as Aristotle would say, "great-souled."

The psychologist **Abraham Maslow** (1908–1970) conducted a comprehensive study of the qualities of what he considered to be self-actualized people and found that people with healthy human personalities also had strong moral characters. According to this research, morally mature, psychologically healthy people think, decide, and act in accordance with *thoughtfully developed moral standards*; are *open-minded* about their moral beliefs; defend them with *reasoned argument* when they are challenged; and change or modify them when they are shown to be false or unjustified. Their conclusions are based on their own *reflective analysis*, rather than being unquestioning "children of their culture." And they are fully committed to *living their values*, recognizing that ethics is not an intellectual game: it's a light that guides their moral growth and personal evolution.

These considerations provide a convincing answer to the question: *"Why be moral?"* As it turns out, becoming a moral person helps you become a psychologically healthy person; promoting the happiness of others frequently enhances your own happiness. Often adages are clichéd and empty of meaning, but in this case, "Virtue is its own reward," contains a substantial measure of truth, a point noted by Socrates in his observation that doing wrong "will harm and corrupt that part of ourselves that is improved by just actions and destroyed by unjust actions." As a free individual, you create yourself through the choices that you make much like a sculptor gradually forms a figure through countless cuts of the chisel. If you create yourself as a moral person, you create a person of character and worth, with an acute sense of right and wrong and the power to choose appropriately. But if you *don't* choose to create yourself as a moral person, you gradually become corrupted. You lose your moral sensitivity, developing a moral blindness that handicaps your ability to see yourself or the world clearly. It is no wonder that Socrates believed that "It is better to suffer wickedness than to commit it." You gain true power when you possess the unfettered and unrestrained ability to choose freely. Choosing immorality binds your hands, one loop of thread at a time, until your freedom of movement disappears. In the same way that substance abusers gradually surrender their freedom of choice to their destructive cravings, so immoral people have only the illusion of genuine freedom in their lives. Moral people enjoy healthy personalities and spiritual wholeness, whereas immoral people are corrupted at their core, progressively ravaged by a disease of the spirit.

Students Thinking About Philosophy:
Analyzing Moral Choices in a Film or Novel

Films and novels can be excellent vehicles for applying ethical theories and thinking through complex moral situations. For example, the existentialist philosophers we examined in this chapter all wrote creative works to elaborate their ideas and also point out existentialist themes in literature written by others. In contrast to the simple, bare-bones moral examples that are typically found in textbooks, films and novels can present moral choices as we often experience them: multileveled, entangling, unstructured, and ambiguous.

For this assignment, select a film or novel with which you are familiar that provides a rich moral context for analysis. Focus on one or two of the characters and think philosophically about the moral choices that they are making, addressing questions such as

- What are the moral choices that the character(s) is (are) making?
- How do they justify their choices? To what moral theories or principles are they appealing?
- How would various moral theories evaluate their choices? How would *you* evaluate their choices? What is your moral reasoning in reaching this conclusion?

The author of the following essay wrote about a film called *A Simple Plan*, directed by Sam Raimi, and adapted from the novel by Scott B. Smith. Because many people may not be familiar with it, a summary of the plot is included below.

An endless white landscape of rolling hills and snow-blanketed forests. A lonely acoustic score playing in the background. A vision of rural simplicity portrayed in hushed tones. The stillness is about to shatter. Brothers Hank (Bill Paxton), an accountant at a small-town feed store, and Jacob (Billy Bob Thornton), an unemployed, hygienically challenged dim bulb, accompanied by Jacob's "town drunk" pal Lou (Brent Briscoe), stumble across a downed plane in the brush containing a corpse and a sack containing four million dollars—surely the aftermath of a drug deal, they conclude. Greed overcomes good sense, and the three agree to hide the money for a year and keep the secret to themselves, believing in their innocence that if no one claims it, they'll be safe in spending it. A simple plan indeed, and it doesn't take long for it to go all to hell as the lure of wealth tears at kinship and friendship, and the ruthless machinations of impetuous partners leave a body count in its wake. Bridget Fonda is Hank's surprisingly resourceful wife, Sarah, whose initial hesitation gives way to cold-blooded plotting. As the nightmare of unintended consequences unfolds, Hank keeps killing to protect his family's stake in the American dream, the secrets of his earlier murders, and his sense of himself as normal "despite everything I've done that might make it seem otherwise." Although stunned by his own actions, Hank keeps drifting back to the rationale he and Sarah share: he had to do it, it wasn't his fault.

[Amazon.com]

A Simple Hell

Joshua Bartlett

Imagine that you happened upon four million dollars and you were reasonably sure that you would be able to keep it without anyone knowing: what would you do? This is the choice facing the main characters in *A Simple Plan*. The central character in the film is Hank, a seemingly average "everyman" who is underemployed in a dead-end job at a local feed store. He considers himself "happy" by his father's definition because he has a steady job, a wife who loves him, and the respect of members of the community. His first response to discovering the money is to return it because otherwise, he reasons, it would be stealing. His brother Jacob and Jacob's no-account pal Lou disagree with a string of rationalizations: It's not really "stealing" because it's probably already stolen money that no-one will miss; it's like "finding a treasure"; "nobody will get hurt"; and keeping the money "is the American dream." Hank is quickly convinced on the condition that he be the one to keep the money for six months to see if anyone comes looking for it. Would you be tempted to make the same ethical choice as Hank? It seems like an innocent enough option, but in the film, events quickly overtake Hank and his "simple plan" as he begins a rapid descent into a moral inferno of his own creation.

According to the writer Henry David Thoreau, the majority of people lead quiet lives of desperation, a claim that still seems relevant 150 years later as illustrated in this film. Out of fear of our own mortality and insignificance, as a way to find meaning in our lives and in the universe, we find something to cling to, to give us a false sense of meaning, security, and comfort. But when confronted with the possibility for more, when the stability is challenged, the desperate voice emerges. As a commentary on the state of the human condition and a society constructed around materialism, power, and wealth, *A Simple Plan* depicts human nature's response to itself and its own creation.

Were Hank's actions symptoms of a discontented life of which he himself was not conscious? And if he was discontented, was this discontent a result of a lack of material wealth, or his perception of what material wealth would bring? Friedrich Nietzsche wrote in his *Genealogy of Morals* that "the oppressed, downtrodden whisper among themselves. Let us be unlike those evil ones. Let us be good. And the good shall be he who does not do violence, does not attack or retaliate, who . . . altogether asks very little of life—like us, the patient, the humble, the just ones . . . this means nothing more than We weak ones are, in fact, weak. It is a good thing that we do nothing for which we are not strong enough." From a certain perspective, perhaps a perverse one, the film seems to validate this depiction of humanity.

The film begins with Hank's narration of his current life: "Without realizing it, I had all the things of a good life." Was Hank's good life the result of non-action, of his lack of power to do or be anything more, as Nietzsche claims? Or was his "good" life truly a product of his natural state of being and intentional, reflective choices? The movie seems to substantiate the former. While the film depicts Hank as happy, morally upstanding, and content with his life, when faced with the chance for more, he acts aggressively. The bold choices he makes run directly counter to his supposed moral principles as he devises his "simple plan," an action that raises suspicion regarding the sincerity of his moral beliefs. Perhaps he was a man who never experienced suffering or sadness, and thus had never been given the impetus for reflection and introspection. Perhaps the image of Hank as a "good man" was a one-dimensional façade that he himself didn't realize. Perhaps he was a man good at following rules, but never questioning why he should follow them or why they exist. Perhaps Hank's moral convictions were a result of others' commands, not his personal introspection, a result of the compact people have made with each other over time, leaving less room for intellectual analysis regarding certain behaviors. In short, perhaps his carefully cultivated "goodness" is a sham, the result of weakness not choice. In this case, the sequence of increasingly duplicitous, manipulative, and violent actions that he takes reveal his raw, genuine self. Is he thus immoral for following his intuitive inclinations, or as Nietzsche might say, for exerting his "will to power"?

As we witness Hank's radical transformation from "good" man to "evil," at least in conventional terms, the film challenges us with the questions "What is happiness?" and "Is money the ends or the means to happiness?" It asks us to consider whether the purpose of money to serve as a utility has taken on greater significance in the lives of those its purpose it was to serve, and at a devastating cost to human value. Money, some would argue, gives us freedom. We need money, this would imply, to transcend the restriction that living in a society governed by money imposes. Yet, like Hank, many people spend the majority of their time working in unsatisfying careers in order to spend a minority of their time doing what they really want. They dread the drudgery of their daily existence, impatiently waiting for Friday. Doesn't this seem profoundly contradictory? And isn't this the reason why we tend to empathize with Hank, Jacob, and Lou when they pursue their dreams of financial and personal liberation by keeping the money they have discovered?

Money, it seems, is not a cause of unhappiness, nor of the division and social stratification of peoples, but money has served as a means to create those classes, and has given the conscience psychological reassurance of the existence of the inequities among those people. The utility of money, and the belief in its ability to affect the human psyche in a profound way, has fostered those qualities of human nature that result in human suffering and conflict, resulting in the present state of the human condition, and the pervasive unhappiness that exists therein. Many would argue that the United States, the richest country in the world, also holds one of the highest standards of living in the world, a statement that would seem to contradict the idea that masses of money lead to suffering. But on closer inspection, does the above statement reveal anything regarding human happiness? Are the majority of Americans truly happy, are the majority of the affluent happy? Should this be taken as a symptom of the perversion of money's utility?

How can we evaluate Hank's moral reasoning? Although self-interest motivates him, he can hardly be said to act in the rational self-interest advocated by ethical egoists such as Ayn Rand. It never occurs to him that taking possession of money that is not rightfully his is likely to create more problems than it solves. Unlike Gyges, he doesn't act with impunity; even though the knowledge of what he has done is shared by his wife, there is ultimately no evidence to be used against him. Hank believes that keeping the money will ensure his happiness, but it ultimately condemns him to a life of misery. On the surface, Hank's desire to keep the money can be said to illustrate Hobbes' comment that "Every man by natural necessity desires that which is good for him": however, the money ends up being far from good for Hank and those he cares about. Apparently, people aren't always the best judges of what is truly good for themselves.

For the utilitarian, according to Mill, "the standard of what is right in conduct is not the agent's own happiness, but that of all concerned." When Hank is persuaded by Jacob and Lou that they can keep the money and no one else will be either hurt or inconvenienced by their gain, he does not consider the "greater good" in any way; he considers only the smallest possible circle, which includes only those on the scene and their immediate families. There is no real thought about whose money it actually is and what its return might mean to the rightful owners. Hank wants to believe that it is drug money, but he does not know this for a fact. Sarah investigates the matter because knowing the origin of the money is important to her; knowing will ease her mind in terms of whether or not it ought to be kept. If it is "safe" to keep, all the better. That it turns out to be ransom money taken during a kidnapping/murder makes her ill at ease, but the report that the bills are unmarked and, therefore, untraceable, makes keeping the money the practical thing to do. Hank and Sarah are convinced that the pleasure which keeping the money will give them will outweigh any pain or guilt that might have been caused. This is the type of pseudo-reasoning that Hank requires to justify his actions. He needs to believe that he is acting for the best despite the increasing evidence that he is not. That's why, after he commits the first murder, he pleadingly asks Sarah, "Just tell me you would have done the same thing in those circumstances," a request which she answers with silence. Potential consequences not related to his own security rarely figure into Hank's decision making. He is acting instinctively, not reflectively, driven by his increasing obsession with the money.

For the deontologist, duty is the basis of morality. For Immanuel Kant, one must always act according to the Categorical Imperative regardless of possible consequences: can we rationally will that our actions become universal law? Are we treating others as ends in themselves, not as means to some other purpose? Hank seems decidedly non-Kantian. From his narration at the film's end, it is clear that he is remorseful and disgusted with the way in which he has acted; one would hardly expect one who is regretful to will those same actions to be universalized. More conspicuously however, Hank consistently treated himself and his family as ends and every other person as means, even his brother Jacob. If he had followed either of Kant's formulations of the Categorical Imperative, he never would have caused the human carnage and moral depravity that weighs on his soul.

Which brings us back to the original question: given the opportunity to keep the four million dollars, what would we do? The applicability of the film to its audience is expressed in the ease with which most people can relate to the critical decisions made by the characters in the film. Entrenched in the subconscious of mainstream America, it seems, is the tacit belief in the ability of money to deliver happiness. At the same time, the audience recognizes that money and its single-minded pursuit has the power to destroy happiness, to devalue humanity and corrupt human values. The film's creators seem to have hit upon a fundamental insight regarding human nature, laying bare a universal response to the seduction of money and vividly displaying how the values of our society have shaped us.

Concept Review

- Utilitarianism, as framed by Jeremy Bentham and John Stuart Mill, is a socially conscious approach to hedonism that holds that the greatest good is to promote happiness and alleviate suffering. A society in which all people have the opportunity to pursue the higher pleasures, and which works to promote social justice, would conform to the principle of utility: *Act always to promote the greatest happiness for the greatest number.*

- Bentham's "hedonistic calculus" attempts to quantify the pursuit of pleasure and the avoidance of pain as demonstrated both by individuals and societies. He describes each unit of pleasure or pain as a "hedon." To calculate the "greatest happiness" in applying the principle of utility, Bentham requires that six factors of a pleasure or pain be considered: its intensity, duration, certainty or uncertainty, propinquity or remoteness, fecundity, and purity. In the case of pleasures or pains experienced by a group of people, the extent of the circumstance must also be considered. Because it is difficult, however, to determine what exactly constitutes a "hedon," or to make distinctions between different kinds and degrees of "pleasure" or "pain," the hedonistic calculus can create a false sense of scientific objectivity; its exclusive focus on consequences, rather than also taking into account intentions or motivations, also creates difficulties in using it to determine real-world conduct and evaluate real-world actions.

- John Stuart Mill refined Bentham's utilitarian theory by qualifying different kinds and degrees of "hedons" (units of pleasure) as being either "higher" levels of pleasure or "lower" levels of pleasure. The higher levels of pleasure are intellectual, literary, aesthetic, and philosophical, and much to be encouraged among individuals and societies. The pursuit of these higher pleasures "is necessarily also the standard of morality," according to Mill; a society that pursues and encourages the "higher" pleasures is therefore a more ethically sound and morally correct society.

- Both Mill and Bentham were revolutionary for their time in expanding their principle of utility (their call for a society that works for the pleasure and against the suffering of its participants) to include all sentient beings, including animals. In contemporary philosophy the ethicist Peter Singer has worked to make even more explicit the link between a society's treatment of animals and its potential for fair and humane treatment of all human beings. Singer's concept of "speciesism" holds that humanity's willingness to allow the suffering of some species in order to make the lives of people easier and more pleasurable is morally wrong; that no one species has the right to subject another to suffering.

- If utilitarianism focuses on the consequences of actions to determine their moral and ethical soundness, deontologist ethics (such as those held by Immanuel Kant) focus instead on the notion of duty or obligations as the measure of ethically correct conduct. For a deontologist, moral value is determined by following the moral maxims prescribed by reason. Kant believed that the work of philosophy was to uncover those moral laws that should be universally binding on all people, laws that are *a priori* (that is, laws that are true independently of actual empirical experience). Once we understand these universal laws, we then need to exercise the "good will" necessary to *choose* to follow those laws as we determine the best course of action.

- Kant distinguished between two types of moral imperatives: hypothetical imperatives and categorical imperatives. Hypothetical imperatives are actions that are "good" only as a means to something else; they are not "good" in and of themselves. Categorical imperatives command actions that are intrinsically good and prescribed actions that all rational beings are morally required to follow. Kant's conceptions of moral maxims is revolutionary in that it focuses on the logical form of moral maxims, rather than the content, consequences, or intention of the action, or the character of the acting agent. Using reason to determine a categorical imperative, we see that an action is morally right because it is logically consistent (or, conversely, morally wrong because it is logically inconsistent). Kant also holds that these moral maxims apply to the duties we have toward ourselves as individuals, as well as toward others in the society in which we live.

- Virtue ethics holds that the character or moral quality of the person performing an action determines the moral value of that action. An action undertaken for morally worthy motives is in itself a virtuous action; an action that has worthy consequences that is undertaken for morally suspect reasons cannot be considered a virtuous action, however beneficial the consequences. The goal of virtue ethics is to develop a morally principled character. Aristotle laid the groundwork for virtue ethics in *The Nicomachean Ethics*.

- Aristotle's view of the world is teleological, in that it holds that everything has a unique end, purpose, or goal. Driving that teleology is entelechy, or the principle that a hidden natural design governs all things and motivates them to fully express their essence or potential. According to this teleological view, Aristotle believes that it is natural for all humans to strive to realize their full potential as reasonable, happy, virtuous people.

■ Aristotle divides virtues into two broad categories: intellectual and moral. Intellectual virtues are developed through education, social interactions, and practice. Moral virtues are also developed through modeling and practice. However, learning to identify and execute moral actions requires the exercise of free will to make the morally enlightened choice. To truly act morally, a person needs to know why he or she is acting, deliberately choose to take the morally correct action, and perform the action for its own sake (rather than, for example, in hopes of a reward). The accumulation of these moral actions gradually builds a consistent moral character. Aristotle's "Golden Mean" defines this consistent moral character as founded on temperance, self-discipline, and balance.

■ Existentialist ethics holds that an authentic life is lived according to the free choices that you make. For Søren Kierkegaard, the individual's recognition of choice—and responsibility for those choices—is paramount. Rather than succumbing to the values of "the crowd," it is through the exercise of our own free will that we invest our lives with meaning and develop our own, internally consistent, moral values. Jean-Paul Sartre's ethics also reinforce the primacy of the individual in the absence of a "God" or other universalizing moral force, but underscores that the moral choices we make are not just for ourselves in isolation, but for all humankind. This tremendous sense of responsibility leads many to attempt to escape what Sartre defines as being "condemned to be free;" those attempts to escape lead to inauthentic lives. Simone de Beauvoir elaborated on the relationship between free choice and the establishment of moral values; our freedom, which defines our existence, only has meaning in relationship to others who are exercising their freedom of choice. For Albert Camus, most of us live in a way that is "unintelligible and limited" until we make free choices that are courageous and work to discover meaning in an otherwise absurd universe.

■ The ethics of care, associated with the work of feminist philosopher Nel Noddings, holds that our individual ethical actions are motivated by what she defines as a "caring response" rooted in "natural caring." We arrive at our moral values as much through the emotions as through cognitive reasoning, and our moral actions are prompted by empathy and relationship. Unless we have developed the capacity to be empathetic, we cannot genuinely act in a caring way toward ourselves. Because these actions are determined by the establishment of a caring relationship with another individual, there can be no genuine "universal caring"; you cannot genuinely "care" for someone if you have not established an empathetic relationship with them. Noddings goes on to distinguish between natural caring and ethical caring. Natural caring involves relationships that we as humans feel for family members, children, and some romantic liaisons; ethical caring involves broadening your sense of care to those toward whom you would not naturally have a feeling of care (such as a stranger in need).

Media Resources

 www.researchnavigator.com
Chapter 6 concentrates on the theories of morality that coincide with what and how we perceive of ethics. For further research on questions on theories of how we discovery or create and apply moral values, use the tools available to you in Research Navigator.

As you investigate this topic, consider this question: "What type of ethical theory reflects reality most accurately and does my moral code fit best with this?

● **ContentSelect:** search in the Philosophy databases using the search terms "ethical theory," "feminist ethics," and "virtues."

● **Link Library:** search in the Philosophy database under terms "ethics," "virtue ethics," and "utilitarianism."

● **New York Times on the Web:** search in the Philosophy database using the search terms "fairness" and "morally justified".

 The Primary Source: Philosophical Readings and Commentary

Aristotle: *Nicomachean Ethics*
Bentham, Jeremy: *An Introduction to the Principles of Morals and Legislation*
Camus, Albert: *Absurdity and Suicide; The Myth of Sisyphus*
Epictetus: *The Enchiridion; Discourses*
Hume, David: *An Inquiry Concerning Human Understanding*
Kant, Immanuel: *Fundamental Principles of the Metaphysics of Morals*
Kierkegaard, Søren: *Concluding Unscientific Postscript; That Individual*
Nietzsche Friedrich: *Beyond Good and Evil*
Singer Peter: *Animal Liberation*
Sarte, Jean-Paul: *Existentialism Is a Humanism*
de Spinoza, Benedict: *Ethics*

 For additional study resources for this chapter, go to:
www.prenhall.com/chaffee/chapter6

7 What Is Religion?
Exploring Ways of Being Religious

I contemplate the order of nature in the hope of finding God, and I see omnipotence and wisdom; but I also see much else that disturbs my mind and excites anxiety.

SØREN KIERKEGAARD

Therefore some intelligent being exists by whom all natural things are directed to their end; and this being we call God.

SAINT THOMAS AQUINAS

Your Religious Beliefs

If we take the world's enduring religions at their best, we discover the distilled wisdom of the human race.

HOUSTON SMITH

He who never visits thinks his mother is the only cook.

AFRICAN PROVERB

You very possibly were brought up in a religious tradition that has influenced your life in a variety of ways. If organized religion was part of your upbringing, it likely helped demarcate the major life passages for members of your family including birth, coming of age, marriage, and death. You may have attended religious services or other forms of religious observance on a regular basis. And at those religious observances you probably prayed, meditated, sang, chanted, read from a holy book, or listened to a religious leader speak about important themes. The teachings of your religion, contained in holy books and interpretations of these holy books, very likely provided moral guidelines to follow as you navigated your life. And these same teachings may have provided answers to some of life's most enduring and disturbing mysteries: What is the meaning of my life? Is there some form of continued existence after death? What path should I take to achieve spiritual enlightenment? If you were not raised in an organized religion, you probably encountered religion in a less formal and structured way.

When we explore the religions of the world, we are struck by both their similarities and their differences. On the surface level, the totality of religions form a dizzying mosaic of beliefs, practices, houses of worship, forms of prayer, sacred music, holy writings, religious artifacts, and all of the other external attributes that are readily apparent. However, if we move past these surface qualities to the fundamental themes and motivations that constitute the *raison d'être* (reason for being) of these religions, we soon begin to detect common themes and analogous structures.

To begin your explorations into the philosophy of religion, it is valuable to share your experiences with religion with the experiences of those of your classmates. To this end, complete the following Think Philosophically activity, which is followed by excerpts from several students' writing in response to the same questions.

THINK PHILOSOPHICALLY 7.1
My Religious Beliefs

As you respond to the following questions, express your ideas thoughtfully and articulately. If you have no religious beliefs at this time, respond to these questions with reference to a religion with which you are familiar.

- What is your definition of religion? What do you think is the purpose of religion?
- How would you describe your religious beliefs? Does it include a belief in "God"? If so, describe your concept of God.
- What was the origin of your religious beliefs (or lack of religious beliefs)? If your beliefs are different from those you were raised with, explain what caused you to change your religious views.
- What religious activities do you engage in (for example, worship, prayer, meditation, communion, singing, chanting, liturgy)?
- Describe the role that religious leaders and "holy books" play in your religion.
- Describe some of the "symbols" and "myths" of your religion.
- How does your religion view religions that are different?

Having come from a family that is half-Christian and half-Jewish meant that, as a child, I grew up celebrating both Jewish and Christian festivals. I enjoyed celebrating Hanukkah and Christmas as well as Easter and Passover. To me religion today seems more than ever significant to our daily lives. It is how we worship a Higher Being, and it is how, through that higher being, that we can continue to mature and progress along each of our paths. For me the purpose of religion is not only to worship a higher Being through prayer in a church or a mosque or through meditation, but to worship through the daily work activities, to, through love, develop ourselves and our other relationships. Religion for me is a way of developing a closer connection with the spiritual world and with our soul. Religion gives a sense of comfort and stability as well as a sense that we are not all alone; that we have a purpose in this earthly life. I believe in the presence of God, not as a physical and idealized being who is depicted as an old wise man with a white beard, to whom one not only prays and asks for help or forgiveness, but rather a spiritual being who lives within everyone of us and works through us. I believe we act spiritually when we love, when we contribute of ourselves to others, and when we become useful in a willing and honest way. That is when the higher spiritual being works through us.

—*Dorothea Kuhnemann-Crow*

I am a practicing Nichiren Daishonin Buddhist, which is one of the Japanese Buddhisms started in the Kamakura periods by Nichiren. All Japanese Buddhisms originally came from India through China circa 600 C.E. After his studies in different fields of Japanese Buddhism, the mystic law he had attained was Nam-myoho-renge-kyo, which was the most important law to save people from sufferings in the latter days of the law since Shakamuni's death. Nichiren Daishonin had taught us throughout his life based on Shakamuni's teachings that every single person has a Buddha nature within himself/herself and that he/she can definitely become a Buddha in the same way that Shakamuni had attained Buddhahood. Each individual is a significant performer in society. Nichiren Daishonin Buddhism teaches us that we already have infinite possibilities in our lives and we can bring them out through chanting Nam-myoho-renge-kyo, the essence of the law. Practicing this Buddhism is not something special that you do away from reality. It is for you to fully understand the joy of living and wonderfulness of life through everyday life.

—*Yuko Sento*

A Room with Many Doors: Each moment in life is like walking into a room with many doors. We as individuals have the right to choose which door to go through. Each door leads to a different destination and I believe religion to be our guideline in helping us decide the right doors to choose. In Northern Ireland, where I grew up, religion was more of a political/social identity rather than a faith you followed. In my town you were either a Catholic or a Protestant. This determined which school you went to, which clubs you could get into, and most importantly, whom you could talk to. The Catholic faith in which I was raised told me what doors to go through, but did not always tell me why. In my parish asking "Why?" was not an option; you just agreed and that was that. As I grew up I began to question why some of these doors were off-limits and others were not.

—*Mairead Nixon*

I lived in a Greek neighborhood and almost everyone was Greek Orthodox. I sought comfort and found it in the clean feeling the church had to offer and the smell of the cold marble floors that invited me. One summer I visited Jerusalem and it was there that I realized the importance of God and the diminished importance of a formal religion. Jerusalem is divided into four quarters, three of

Buddhist monk in meditation

The Wailing Wall with the Dome of the Rock in the background.

them being religious ones. There is the Muslim Quarter, the Jewish Quarter and the Christian Quarter. All of them have historical ties to the city and all of them strongly believe their religion is the "right one." I witnessed the Jews pray to a wall (the Wailing Wall), the Muslims worshiping a rock (the Dome of the Rock), and the Christians proclaiming all non-Christians to be condemned to hell. This made me thoroughly examine my beliefs in the religion I had grown up with. It was then that I chose to believe in a God with no physical ties (church, wall or rock) but strictly on a spiritual level. I need nothing symbolic of Him to reassure me of my belief in Him and I don't need to sanction others to prove my will to Him. For it was then that I understood that nothing physical or verbal could ever remotely come close to his meaning to me.

—*Michelle Anagnostopoulos*

I come from a family where religion was important only to the older generation and it did not occupy too much 'space' in my thinking. I learned one prayer from my grandmother, who believed that I needed at least this knowledge to be able to get in touch with God. This prayer was at the time the only religious 'item' in my baggage with which I set out in the big world. So I had to ask myself what religion meant to me, apart from the only prayer I inherited. I got a little help when I started studying philosophy and encountered one of the pantheists, Baruch Spinoza. According to Spinoza, God is nature; God is everything surrounding us. It sounded to me like a religion that I had already acquired. Could it be as simple as this? Some say that God is love. I believe in their God then, since this view, this piece also fits in the religion-belief puzzle I try to put together in order to get a picture that will make sense to me and will also say something about who I am. But then I return to the point where I have to ask myself: do I have a religion, a God? Can I call belief in life, in myself, a religion? If I had to answer a general question whether I am religious or not, whether I believe in God or not, I would probably answer with a "no." I am still searching and maybe this search will last forever. Looking now into that baggage with which I set out in the big world as a child, I still find that one prayer, but not many other things that would fall into the religion category. I am content "religion-less"; however, I feel open-minded enough to welcome a "real" God into my life if I encounter him/her on my journey.

—*Szilvia Kelemen*

Philosophy of Religion

hat is the purpose of studying the philosophy of religion? Perhaps it's best to begin with what such study is *not* about. The purpose of studying the philosophy of religion is *not* designed to

- transform you into an atheist or agnostic.
- convert you from being an atheist or agnostic to a belief in God or gods.
- undermine your religious beliefs or "convert" you to another religion.
- engage you in emotional arguments with classmates over which is the one "true" religion.

Instead, the philosophy of religion *is* designed to

- develop your ability to think philosophically regarding the religious dimension of experience.
- critically evaluate the reasons, evidence, and arguments with respect to religion, both pro and con.
- expand, enrich, and deepen your understanding of other religions in the world.
- encourage you to reflect on the nature and foundation of your own religious beliefs.

Philosophy and religion have had a volatile and at times contentious relationship with one another. As we saw in chapter 2, when we examined the pre-Socratic thinkers, religion was a precursor to philosophy as well as organized science. Early religions tended to be rooted in mythology and superstition, encouraging a world-view that initially inhibited the development of philosophy and science as independent disciplines based on reason, systematic inquiry, and empirical/logical validation. This was, in Western culture, the beginning of a long and uneasy relationship among philosophy, science, and religion, a competition over what each considered to be their legitimate domains of expertise. Over the centuries, the "highlight" reel of these mutual tensions would include

- the execution of Socrates for allegedly not believing in the conventional gods of the time (in addition to "corrupting" the youth of Athens).
- the threatened execution of Galileo for asserting the same "blasphemous" truth as Copernicus. Because he publicly recanted this belief, announcing that the earth (and, symbolically, humankind) formed the center of the solar system, he was able to have his death sentence commuted to a 20-year house arrest. (However, he was reported to have muttered on leaving the Inquisition Tribunal, "But still the earth circles the sun.")
- the uproar over the publication and subsequent dissemination of Charles Darwin's *Origin of the Species*, which contended that all life forms on earth have evolved from simpler origins through a process of "natural selection."

But seen through a modern lens, many people believe that there is *in principle* no necessary and compelling reason philosophy, science, and religion can't coexist

 VISUAL PHILOSOPHY

The Sun Circles the Earth?

Why did the Catholic church persecute scientists like Galileo for suggesting that the earth circles the sun and not vice versa? What accounts for the tension that has existed between science and religion?

(relatively) peacefully. It's only when one of the three disciplines intentionally encroaches on one or both of the other areas that problems may arise. For example:

- If philosophy decrees, as the logical positivists did, that religious statements have no "truth value" because they cannot be verified empirically
- If science proclaims, as scientific materialists have, that only physical matter exists in the universe: entities such as souls, spirits, or gods are simply concocted fantasies
- If religion announces, as many religions have, that the conclusions of philosophy and science should be automatically dismissed if they appear to conflict with religious truths

Unfortunately, it is too often the loudest, most strident, and least-informed voices that capture the headlines and people's attention. In contrast, a solid group of serious, reflective, and informed philosophers, scientists, and religious leaders believe that we should be using these three frameworks to achieve a more integrated, synthesized, and enlightened view of the entirety of human experience. Many philosophers have had strong religious convictions, including Immanuel Kant, René Descartes, William James, and Søren Kierkegaard. And many scientists have likewise believed in the compatibility of science and religion, including Charles Darwin and **Albert Einstein**, as he reveals in his essay "Religion and Science":

> It is easy to see why the churches have always fought science and persecuted its devotees. On the other hand, I maintain that the cosmic religious feeling is the strongest and noblest motive for scientific research. Only those who realize the immense efforts and, above all, the devotion without which pioneer work in theoretical science cannot be achieved are able to grasp the strength of the emotion out of which alone such work, remote as it is from the immediate realities of life, can issue. What a deep conviction of the rationality of the universe and what a yearning to understand, were it but a feeble reflection of the mind revealed in this world, Kepler and Newton must have had to enable them to spend years of solitary labor in disentangling the principles of celestial mechanics! Those whose acquaintance with scientific research is derived chiefly from its practical results easily develop a completely false notion of the mentality of the men who, surrounded by a skeptical world, have shown the way to kindred spirits scattered wide through the world and the centuries. Only one who has devoted his life to similar ends can have a vivid realization of what has inspired these men and given them the strength to remain true to their purpose in spite of countless failures. It is cosmic religious feeling that gives a man such strength. A contemporary has said, not unjustly, that in this materialistic age of ours the serious scientific workers are the only profoundly religious people.

So, as you approach the philosophy of religion, make a special effort to do so with an open mind. A person's religious beliefs are an intensely personal affair. It is natural that many people feel inclined toward the religion with which they were raised because, just like their culture, it's the one with which they are most familiar. However, the unique character of religion makes it especially important that we strive to transcend the relatively limited religious perspective with which we were raised. Religions purport to offer definitive answers to the most profound and challenging questions in life, and they often require that we accept a great deal of their authority on "faith" rather than rigorous critical examination. In addition, many religions consider themselves to be the "one true religion," setting them on an unavoidable collision course with all of the other "one true religions." So, although religions have traditionally resulted in some of the grandest and most sublime contributions to human culture—enlightened ethical systems, extraordinary art and architecture, deeply meaningful spiritual experiences—religions have also created some of the most devastating and destructive chapters in human history—wars, per-

ALBERT EINSTEIN

(1879–1955)
Physicist. Advanced the theories of special and general relativity which had a profound impact on many areas of human interest, especially on the philosophy of science. Was very concerned with the relationship between science, religion and ethics.

Albert Einstein

secution, and religious discrimination. One need only look at current events across the world to see displayed the strife, barbarity, and human catastrophe perpetrated in the name of "religion."

Thus, these frequently occurring elements of the religious experience can be a potent recipe for unleashing the most primal and destructive impulses of the human experience:

- Proposing definitive answers to the most profound and challenging questions in life.
- Asking adherents to accept a great deal on authority and "faith" rather than rigorous critical examination.
- A conviction by many religions that they are the "one true religion" and that it is their responsibility to "convert" others to their way of thinking—or persecute and murder them.

Our only hope to avoid getting pulled into this destructive vortex is to make extraordinary efforts to be ecumenical in our perspectives, transcending our own biases and religious tendencies. We need to honestly and openly seek to understand the religious experience in its deepest dimensions, endeavoring with intellectual empathy to appreciate the many ways of being religious with which we are unfamiliar. In this regard, it is helpful to remind ourselves that the reason we believe one religion rather than another (or believe in *no* religion) is often due to *an accident of birth*. In short, we need to think critically and philosophically at the highest possible levels to navigate our way through the emotional minefield of religion.

But "forewarned is forearmed." If we *are* aware of the course we must steer, and we *do* consistently embody the values of openness, empathy, critical scrutiny, objectivity, tolerance, and a willingness to grow in our understanding—*then* exploring the philosophy of religion can be one of the most rewarding endeavors in which we can engage. And if we as individuals can become more enlightened and less myopic regarding religion, then we can share this more informed perspective with others who have not had the same opportunity to think philosophically about these issues. And by so doing we can elevate their understanding in an effort to create a more peaceful, tolerant world.

In addition to exposing us to the extraordinary variety of religions and ways of being religious, studying the philosophy of religion helps us develop conceptual lenses for understanding the religious phenomenon, including questions such as

- What is the nature of various religious experiences, and how do they differ from one another?
- What is the relationship between religious beliefs and our everyday lives?
- How do various religions define the meaning and ultimate purpose of human life?
- Are there compelling proofs or evidence for the existence of God (or Gods)?
- If you believe in an all-powerful, all-good supernatural Being, how is it possible to account for the existence of evil in the world?
- What is the relationship between faith and reason?
- What are the reasons, evidence, and arguments for religious beliefs, both pro and con?

THINK CRITICALLY

7.2

PHILOSOPHER'S NOTEBOOK

My Concept of Religion

Describe your concept of religion as specifically as possible. Where did the concept originate for you? How has it evolved as you have matured? Explain the reasons or experiences that support your concept.

Evaluate your concept of religion by answering the following questions, which are designed to help you develop a sufficiently broad and precise concept of religion:

- Does your definition reduce religion to what you happen to be acquainted with by accident of birth and socialization?
- Does your definition reflect a bias on your part—positive or negative—toward religion as a whole, or toward a particular religion?
- Does your definition limit religion to what it has been in the past, and nothing else, or does your definition make it possible to speak of emerging forms of religion?

Compare your definition of religion to the definitions of other students in your class. What are the similarities? What are the differences? How do you explain these similarities and differences?

These are very complex issues that require rigorous philosophical analysis to make sense of them. And there are many thinkers who have thought deeply about these issues whose ideas we can profit from as we pursue our own religious explorations.

Religions of the World

One of the dilemmas of thinking philosophically about religion (and the religious experience) is that, in order for philosophical analysis to be meaningful, it requires a basic understanding of the subject—in this case, religion. However, as we noted previously, many people have an in-depth understanding of only the religion in which they were raised. Knowledge of other religions tends to be fragmentary and anecdotal. This is true even on the level of professional philosophical analysis. Many writings in the philosophy of religion are based almost entirely on the dominant religions of Western culture—Christianity and Judaism—with their belief in a transcendent, supernatural creative spirit—God. However, this approach omits the religions of the majority of the world's population. And in a world that is becoming increasingly globalized in every way, such an approach to understanding the complex phenomenon of religion seems narrow and provincial.

Naturally, it is not feasible to include an in-depth analysis of all the major religions of the world within the scope of this chapter, but it is possible to provide a brief overview of some of these religions. You can explore further those religions you find of particular interest through other publications, including the excellent text on which much of the following material is based: *Living Religions* by Mary Pat Fisher. The religions we will be briefly "visiting" are the following:

- Indigenous Sacred Ways
- Buddhism
- Hinduism
- Taoism
- Judaism
- Christianity
- Islam

Following our review of these religions, we will engage in a more traditional philosophical analysis of the religious experience, enriched by a more comprehensive understanding of the varieties of religious experience.

Indigenous Sacred Ways

In contrast to the major religions of the world that have spread across geographical boundaries from their original points of origin, **indigenous religions** have for the most part remained tied to the original people and location from which they developed. Making up approximately four percent of the world population, these indigenous religions include Australian aborigines; Native Americans (Navajo, Hopi, Zuni, Lakota, Cheyenne, Iroquois); Inuit; Saami; African (Dagara, Dahomey, Ibo, Efe, Kung, Yoruba, Kikuyu) and others located in isolated pockets around the world. These religions are practiced by the original inhabitants of lands now controlled by larger political systems and dominated by one or more of the major world religions. For the most part, indigenous religions practice sacred ways and a spiritual way of life that has remained virtually unchanged for centuries. They have had to resist the extreme socialization and conversion pressures from around them by maintaining an insulating barrier to protect their ancient ways. Rather than relying on writ-

Indigenous religions Religions that have remained tied to the original people and location from which they developed. For the most part, indigenous religions practice sacred ways and a spiritual way of life that has remained virtually unchanged for centuries.

ten texts or holy books, indigenous religions pass their core beliefs and secret practices down by an oral tradition entrusted to spiritual leaders.

Indigenous religions are fully integrated into the lives of those practicing them, rather than being discrete and separate activities. This includes a profound respect for their natural environment, which they tend to view as dynamic and alive. For indigenous people, religion, life, and the environment are all part of one integrated reality. They seek to maintain balance and harmony between all dimensions of their lives by developing *right relationships* with everything that exists: the unseen world of spirits, the land and weather, the people and creatures, and the power within.

Inuit Shaman wooden mask.

Relationships with Spirit

For indigenous religions, the spirit world is central, the source of awesome power that influences every aspect of life. Establishing and maintaining a *right relationship* with the spirit world is of paramount importance. Many indigenous religions worship a Supreme Spirit whom they view as the Sacred Creator of the cosmos. Other religious views include a complex spirit world that includes unseen powers at work in the natural world or located in sacred places. The Supreme Spirit or Great Power is thought to be mysterious but all-powerful, penetrating into every element of the world, as described in the following passage by an Inuit **shaman** (a "medicine person" specially trained to communicate with the spirit world):

A power that we call Sila, which is not to be explained in simple words. A great spirit, supporting the world and the weather and all life on earth, a spirit so mighty that (what it says) to mankind is not through common words, but by storm and snow and rain and the fury of the sea—all the forces of nature that men fear. But Sila has also another way of (communicating); by sunlight and calm of the sea, and little children innocently at play, themselves understanding nothing. . . . When all is well Sila sends no message to mankind, but withdraws into endless nothingness, apart.

Maintaining harmonious relationships with the spirits of ancestors is another significant theme in many indigenous religions. Indigenous people tend to view themselves not as individuals but as integral members of a spiritual community of those both living and dead. Ancestors continue to serve as important guides, helpers, and influences, and they are revered and worshiped.

Kinship with All Creation

For participants in indigenous religions, everything in the world is alive. The physical world is considered to be fully animate and spiritually interconnected with all life-forms in the universe. This spiritually dynamic view of the world is expressed in the following passage by Josiah Young, describing how in African traditional religion, both the visible and invisible realms are filled with spiritual forces:

The visible is the natural and cultural environment of which humans, always in the process of transformation, are at the center. The invisible connotes the numinous field of ancestors, spirits, divinities, and the Supreme Being, all of whom, in varying degrees, permeate the visible. Visible things, however, are not always what they seem. Pools, rocks, flora, and fauna may dissimulate invisible forces of which only the initiated are conscious.

This spiritual view of "mother earth" encourages an ecological philosophy of the environment, in which human life is intended to interlock and mesh with the natural world, thus preserving the harmony and balance between people and their

Shaman A "medicine person," a man or woman, who has undergone spiritual ordeals and can communicate with the spirit world to help the people in indigenous traditions.

home, the natural world. Respect is due to all living creatures, and when trees are felled or animals are killed for food, one must explain one's intentions and ask for forgiveness. An elder of the Onondaga Nation Wolf Clan, **Oren Lyons**, explains this intimate, spiritual relationship with the natural world:

> [The indigenous people's] knowledge is profound and comes from living in one place for untold generations. It comes from watching the sun rise in the east and set in the west from the same place over great sections of time. We are as familiar with the lands, rivers and great seas that surround us as we are with the faces of our mothers. Indeed we call the earth Etenoha, our mother, from whence all life springs. . . . We do not perceive our habitat as wild but as a place of great security and peace, full of life.

Spiritual Specialists

In most indigenous religions the average person has limited contact with the spirit world. Instead, this task is typically entrusted to spiritual specialists: priests, priestesses, and shamans. The spirit world is considered to be dangerous in the same way that a lightning bolt is both awesome and lethal. Only those who have undergone extensive training and preparation are thought to be able to act as intermediaries between this world and the unseen world. These spiritual specialists see themselves as human vessels for conducting spiritual communication and power. Preparing themselves for this role involves rituals of self-purification and self-emptying, applying the sacred knowledge that has been handed down for generations, from previous spiritual specialists.

In many indigenous religions, the spiritual specialists include shamans, who are able to channel spiritual power and use it to heal physical, psychological, and spiritual problems. In addition to healing, shamans are sometimes thought to have powers that extend to controlling the weather, communicating with the spirit world, and making prophecies. But in all cases, spiritual specialists consider themselves simply as conduits for the spiritual power, as the Native American **Black Elk** explains:

> Of course it was not I who cured. It was the power from the outer world, and the visions and ceremonies had only made me like a hole through which the power could come to the two-leggeds. If I thought that I was doing it myself, the hole would close up and no power could come through.

In many instances, connecting with the spiritual world involves entering an altered state of consciousness, initiated by techniques such as drumming, singing, dancing, meditation, and hallucinogenic drugs. Once on their way, the specialists' journey to the spirit world is often experienced as an arduous spiritual quest through the unseen world, a journey preserved in various cultural myths such as the story of Orpheus' journey through the Underworld. Completing their journey, they return to the world of the seen and bring spiritual power and sacred knowledge.

Group Observances

A final dimension of indigenous religions are the group rituals that bind the community together in a shared participation in their spiritual life. These collective rituals include dances, ritual dramas, ritual purifications, pilgrimages to sacred sites, and, though undertaken individually, vision quests. The rituals typically occur at prescribed times or at defining moments in the life cycle: birth, naming, puberty, marriage, and death. The rituals constitute essential threads in the social fabric: they affirm the social bonds with each other, they honor the sacred, and they represent the group's harmony with the universe.

Oren Lyons (1930–) Native American. Elder of the Onondaga Nation Wolf Clan and professor of American Studies at the State University of New York, Buffalo, is active in many areas including native people's rights and environmental issues.

Black Elk (1863–1950) Native American. Considered to be a holy man of the Oglala Lakota. In *Black Elk Speaks* (1932) he recounted to poet John Neihardt the traditions and history of the Lakota in hopes of preserving them.

Ritual dramas, replete with masks and costumes, reenact the creation stories and the sacred history of the group; ritual dances commemorate transitions from one life stage to another; and pilgrimages to sacred sites are designed to pay homage to the sacred but also to absorb spiritual energy from the site. One common purification ritual among Native Americans is the "sweat lodge" (*inipi*), a handmade sauna with great symbolic meaning, as described by **Leonard Crow Dog**:

What role does ceremony play in various religions?

> The *inipi* is probably our oldest ceremony because it is built around the simplest, basic, life-giving things: the fire that comes from the sun, warmth with out which there can be no life; *inyan wakan*, or *tunka*, the rock that was there when the earth began, that will still be there at the end of time; the earth, the mother womb; the water that all creatures need; our green brother, the sage; and encircled by all these, man, basic man, naked as he was born, feeling the weight, the spirit of endless generations before him, feeling himself part of the earth, nature's child, not her master.

One common coming-of-age ritual is the *vision quest*, when, after ritual purification and secret instructions, a young boy or girl is sent off to spend up to four days alone in a sacred location, to discover insights from the spirits regarding their purpose in life, and to seek help in their life-journey. The indigenous Mexican leader **Tlakaelel** describes one type of vision quest:

> You stay on a mountain, desert, or in a cave, isolated, naked, with only our sacred things—the things that you have gained, in the years of preparation—your eagle feathers, your pipe, your *copal* (tree bark used as incense). You are left alone four days and four nights without food and water. During this time when you are looking for your vision, many things happen. You see things move. You see animals that come close to you. Sometimes you might see someone that you care about a lot and they're bringing water. You feel like you're dying of thirst, but there are limits around you, protection with hundreds of tobacco ties. You do not leave this circle.

Buddhism

Buddhism is one of four of the major religions of the world that is based on the life and teachings of one individual (the others are Confucianism, Christianity, and Islam). It is also a nontheist religion that does not believe in a supernatural God or Creator. Instead, the "ultimate transformation" to which Buddhists aspire is to escape the world of suffering through our own efforts until we finally achieve Nirvana (the ultimate egoless state of bliss).

The originator of Buddhism, **Siddhartha Gautama**, was born about 563 B.C.E., in the foothills of the Himalayas in India. In many respects, the **Buddha**—a title meaning "Enlightened One," which he later acquired—must have seemed an unlikely individual to create what has become one of the great world religions. He was born into a wealthy and prestigious family, his father a regional chief of a powerful clan. He lived a privileged and pampered existence: fine clothes, white umbrellas for shade, a mansion for each season, the company of female musicians, a harem of dancing girls, and a wife who bore him a son. Despite his insulation from the harsh realities of life most people faced, he nevertheless began to question the value and meaning of his opulent existence. According to legend, he

Leonard Crow Dog (1942–) Native American. Important figure in the American Indian Movement of the 1960's and 1970's.

Tlakaelel Native Mexican. Name means "Counselor to the Council"; a leader of the Mexican Indigenous People.

Siddhartha Gautama (c. 563 B.C.E.) Founder of Buddhism. After much spiritual searching set forth the basic tenets of Buddhism, The Four Noble Truths of Suffering and The Eightfold Path of Liberation, earning the title of Buddha, or "Enlightened One".

Buddha Title meaning "Enlightened One."

gained insight into the realities of life by encountering the "four sights" that changed the direction of his life:

- A bent old man—representing the suffering of old age
- A sick person—representing the suffering of illness
- A dead person—representing the impermanence of life
- A monk—representing the quest for eternal rather than temporal pleasure

These sights reportedly had such a profound effect on him that at the age of twenty-nine, Prince Siddhartha renounced his hedonistic lifestyle and his position as heir to his father's throne, abandoned his wife and family, shaved his head and embarked on a spiritual quest dressed only in a coarse robe. Leading a homeless life of poverty, he initially sought to achieve spiritual truth by means of the traditional Brahamanic Hindu methods of meditation. Disappointed and unfulfilled, he next attempted a life of extreme ascetic self-denial for a period of six years that involved naked exposure to heat and cold, a bed of brambles, and severe fasting. He finally became disillusioned with a self-denying approach to spirituality, and instead decided to pursue a path of deep meditation. Sitting beneath a now-famous fig tree at Gaya one night, he experienced a Supreme Enlightenment, which transformed him into a "Buddha," an enlightened being. This spiritual epiphany led to his developing the core beliefs on which Buddhism is founded: the Four Noble Truths about suffering; the Eightfold Path for liberation from suffering; The Wheel of Birth and Death; and Nirvana. He began a wandering ministry that was to last forty-five years, gathering disciples—the **sangha**—and teaching the truths of reality—the **dharma**—which revealed the path for each person's state of spiritual evolution. Near death at the age of eighty, he bequeathed his final words to his followers:

> You must be your own lamps, be your own refuges. . . . A monk becomes his own lamp and refuge by continually looking on his body, feelings, perceptions, moods, and ideas in such a manner that he conquers the cravings and depressions of ordinary men and is always strenuous, self-possessed, and collected in mind.

The Four Noble Truths of Suffering

The foundation for Buddha's religious philosophy is contained in the Four Noble Truths of Suffering, from which all other dimensions of his thinking flow.

1. *Life inevitably involves suffering, is imperfect and unsatisfactory.* Suffering and frustration—**dukkha**—is an unavoidable part of living: physical pain, sickness, grief, unfulfilled desires, and ultimately death. Happiness is fleeting, with unhappiness its constant shadow. Even the "self" is an impermanent illusion. In a view that foreshadows that of David Hume, what we view as our continual "I" is really a perpetually transient bundle of fleeting sensations, impressions, ideas, and feelings. The metaphor often used for the Buddhist concept of the self is that of a flame being passed from candle to candle in continual movement.

2. *Suffering originates in our desires.* Desires are wishes for things to be different than they are. We wish for good health, riches and fame, eternal life, perpetual happiness, permanence and security, and many other things as well. But none of these wishes can be achieved in a permanent fashion because life and the universe are essentially impermanent. And because our wishes are continually thwarted and events in the world are beyond our control, frustration and suffering are unavoidable.

3. *Suffering will cease if all desires cease.* The only certain and final way to escape from suffering—*dukkha*—is by removing desire. This can only be achieved by realizing and accepting the fact that there is no unique, separate, perma-

Sangha The spiritual community of followers of the Buddha.

Dharma In Buddhism, the doctrine or law, as revealed by the Buddha; also the correct conduct for each person according to his or her level of awareness. In Hinduism, moral order, righteousness, religion.

Dukkha According to the Buddha, a central fact of human life, variously translated as discomfort, suffering, frustration, or lack of harmony with the environment.

nent, immortal "self." Once we understand that our "self" is simply an impermanent flow of energy tied to the larger energies of the cosmos, we are freed to realize that desires and suffering are irrelevant. As the Buddhist monk Ajahn Sumedho explains:

> When you open the mind to the truth, then you realize there is nothing to fear. What arises passes away, what is born dies, and is not self—so that our sense of being caught in an identity with this human body fades out. We don't see ourselves as some isolated, alienated entity lost in a mysterious and frightening universe. We don't feel overwhelmed by it, trying to find a little piece of it that we can grasp and feel safe with, because we feel at peace with it. Then we have merged with the Truth.

In practical terms, accepting the nonexistence of a permanent self encourages us to live happily and fully in the moment, liberated from self-centeredness and full of compassion for others.

4. *There is a way to realize this state: the Noble Eightfold Path.* Extinguishing desire and suffering is a process that can be achieved by following the guidelines embodied in the Noble Eightfold Path, devoted to pursuing morality, focus, and wisdom.

The Eightfold Path of Liberation

The Noble Eightfold Path is a systematic philosophy of life that enables people to gradually free themselves from desire and suffering and achieve the ultimate peace of Nirvana. This process typically extends over multiple lifetimes, as we are caught in the perpetual cycle of death and rebirth. Once again, the "self" is not a permanent, immortal entity, but is akin to a flame being passed from moment to moment, lifetime to lifetime. The Noble Eightfold Path includes:

- *Right understanding:* Developing a deep, profound understanding of the Four Noble Truths through mental discipline and mental purity.
- *Right thought and motives:* Transcending the limitations of self-centeredness by eliminating unwholesome emotions and intentions, and freeing us to live in a clear and open fashion.
- *Right mindfulness:* Living fully in each moment with complete attention and concentration.
- *Right meditation:* Meditating to quell the unruly and restless mind, transforming it into a quiet pool in which the true nature of everything is clearly reflected. The meditation master Achaan Chah observes:

What roles do dress and costumes play in various religions?

> Try to be mindful, and let things take their natural course. Then your mind will become still in any surroundings, like a clear forest pool. All kinds of wonderful, rare animals will come to drink at the pool, and you will clearly see the nature of all things. You will see many strange and wonderful things come and go, but you will be still. This is the happiness of the Buddha.

The Wheel of Birth and Death

The Wheel of Birth and Death is the Buddhist framework for explaining the ongoing quest of each life to ascend the planes of existence and achieve Nirvana by following the Four Noble Truths and the Eightfold Path of Liberation. The philosopher Mary Pat Fisher explains this complex framework in the following passage:

> Buddhist teachings about rebirth are slightly different from those of Hindu orthodoxy, for there is no eternal soul to be reborn. In Buddhism, one changing state of being sets another into motion: every event depends on a cause. The

central cause in this process karma (Pali: *kamma*)—our acts of will. These influence the level at which that personality-developing process we think of as "me" is reborn. The impressions of our good and bad actions help to create our personality moment-by-moment. When we die, this process continues, passing on the flame to a new life on a plane that reflects our past *karma*.

There are thirty-one planes of existence, interpreted as psychological metaphors by some Buddhists. Whether metaphors or metaphysical realities, these include hells, "hungry ghosts" (beings tormented with unsatisfied desires), animals, humans, and gods. Like the lower levels, the gods are imperfect and impermanent. Round and round we go, life after life, caught in this cycle of *samsara* (worldly phenomena), repeatedly experiencing aging, decay, suffering, death, and painful rebirth, unless we are freed into Nirvana, which is beyond all the cause-and-effect-run planes of existence.

Nirvana

Nirvana is the ultimate state to which all human life aspires. The word itself refers to the extinguishing of a flame from lack of fuel, an image consistent with the metaphor of human life as a flame that is continually being passed from candle to candle. Unlike most religions that devote significant attention to the ultimate goal of spiritual transformation, the Buddha had very little to say about Nirvana. This is in part due to its nature: it symbolizes nothingness, the end of desire and suffering, escape from the inexorable cycle of the Wheel of Birth and Death. According to the Buddha, entering Nirvana means achieving "quietude of heart," "Where there is nothing, where naught is grasped, there is the Isle of No-beyond. Nirvana do I call it—the utter extinction of aging and dying," "the unborn . . . undying . . . unsorrowing . . . stainless, the uttermost security from bonds." The unique energy that we term the "self" is absorbed into the general cosmic energy, entering a deathless, peaceful, unchanging state that is beyond description and understanding. The *Dhammapada*, a collection of short sayings attributed to Buddha, provides this poetic description of Nirvana:

> No suffering for him
> who is free from sorrow
> free from the fetters of life
> free in everything he does.
> He has reached the end of his road . . .
>
> Like a bird invisibly flying in the sky
> he lives without possessions,
> knowledge his food, freedom his world,
> while others wonder . . .
>
> He has found freedom—
> peaceful his thinking, peaceful his speech,
> peaceful his deed, tranquil his mind.

Nirvana   The ultimate egoless state of bliss in Buddhism; the extinction of the self.

Hinduism

Hinduism is the term used to designate the complex mosaic of religious beliefs and practices of the vast majority of the people of India. As one of the oldest living religions in the world, Hinduism is unique in that it had no single founder but evolved over a period of four thousand years, its history interwoven with religious and cultural movements. Other religions that originated on the Indian subcontinent include Buddhism, Jainism, and Sikhism.

The word *Hindu* is derived from the Sanskrit word *sindu*, which means river, Hindu referring to the Indus river. An alternative label preferred today is **Sanatana Dharma**. *Sanatana* means "eternal religion," reflecting the belief that these religious ways have always existed, and *Dharma* embodies a holistic approach to both personal spiritual fulfillment and social harmony. Although there are literally millions of deities in Sanatana Dharma, followers believe that they are all manifestations of a single God assuming different forms. As expressed in a passage from the holy writings of Sanatana Dharma, referred to as the **Vedas**,

> The feeling of thee and thine is the outcome of knowledge I and mine come from ignorance. Knowledge makes one feel: O God! Thou art the Doer and I am thy instrument. O God! To thee belongs all-body, mind, house, family, all living.
>
> An ignorant person says God is there—very far, the man of knowledge knows that god is right here, very near in the heart, that he has assumed all forms and dwells in all hearts as their controller.
>
> Behind all of the manifestations of divinity is one unseen reality that exists beyond human understanding, continuously creating and sustaining everything that exists, encompassing all time and space.

The Vedas are a collection of ancient hymns in four parts, the last being the **Upanishads**, which include the teaching of highly realized spiritual masters, the **rishis**, who explain the path to spiritual transformation. The *Upanishads* are thought to have developed between 600 and 400 B.C.E., about the same time as Gautama Buddha, the founder of Buddhism (c. 563–483 B.C.E.), lived on the Indian subcontinent. It is not surprising that these two world religions share certain common themes, though there are significant differences as well.

Contemplation of the Luminous Self

As with the teachings of the Buddha, spiritual enlightenment can only be achieved by turning one's attention inward to discover a transcendent reality from within. The *rishis* explain in the *Upanishads* that the bodily senses are made for looking outward and are easily enticed by sensory pleasures and worldly spectacles. But these sensations are fleeting and impermanent, passing away when one dies, and obscure the search for the infinite, everlasting reality. This unseen but all-pervading reality they called **Brahman**, the Unknowable. From Brahman originate the multiplicity of all forms, including humans, and thus Brahman can be discovered in the soul (*atman*) within ourselves, as explained in this *Upanishad* passage:

> In the beginning there was Existence alone—One only, without a second. He, the One, thought to himself: Let me be many, let me grow forth. Thus out of himself he projected the universe, and having projected out of himself the universe, he entered into every being. All that is has its self in him alone. Of all things he is the subtle essence. He is the truth. He is the Self. And that . . . THAT ART THOU.

Reincarnation

Central to all forms of Sanatana Dharma is the doctrine of **reincarnation**, the belief that the soul leaves the dead body and enters a new one, being born over and over in countless bodies. Whether the body is that of an animal or other life form, the self remains constant. But rebirth as a human being is a precious and rare opportunity for the soul to advance toward its ultimate goal of liberation from rebirth and merging with the Absolute Reality.

What roles do holy places of worship play in various religions?

 The Upanishads

Sanatana Dharma The "eternal religion" of Hinduism.

Vedas Ancient scriptures revered by Hindus.

Upanishads The philosophical part of the Veda in Hinduism, intended only for serious seekers.

Rishis A Hindu sage.

Brahman The impersonal Ultimate Principle in Hinduism.

Reincarnation The belief that the soul leaves the dead body and enters the new one, being born over and over in countless bodies.

Karma

Progress toward a merging with Absolute Reality is the result of **karma**, which refers to one's actions as well as the consequences of one's actions. Every action we take, even every thought we have—whether good or evil—shapes our present and also our future. The ultimate goal of creating ourselves through good choices is to escape from the *karmic* wheel of birth, death, and rebirth, which is called **samsara**. To escape from *samsara* is to achieve **moksha**, or liberation from the limitations of space, time, and matter through realization of the immortal Absolute. Many lifetimes of upward-striving incarnations are required to reach this transcendence of earthly miseries. This desire for liberation from earthly existence is also one of the underpinnings of Buddhism, analogous to the Buddhist concept of *Nirvana* or *satori*, enlightenment through the realization of ultimate truth.

Yogic Practices

Spiritual seekers are generally encouraged to engage in disciplines that clear the mind and support a state of serene, detached awareness. This desired state of balance, purity, and peacefulness of mind is described as *sattvic*, in contrast with active, restless states or lethargic dull states. The practices for increasing *sattvic* qualities are known collectively as **yoga**, from the Sanskrit word for "union" (in this case the union of body, mind, and spirit). The physical and psychic practices of yoga are extremely ancient, dating back as long ago as the Neolithic Age. By 200 B.C.E., a yogi named Patanjali (or perhaps a series of people taking the same name) had described a coherent system for attaining the highest consciousness. Patanjali distinguishes eight "limbs" of the yogic path to making the mind absolutely clear and increasing the body's supply of life energy (*prana*): moral codes (the *yamas* and *niyamas*), physical conditioning (*asana*), breath control (*pranayama*), sense control (*pratyahara*), concentration (*dharana*), meditation (*dhyana*), and the state of peaceful spiritual absorption (*samadhi*).

Fire Sacrifices

Ritual animal sacrifice around a fire was an essential part of ancient Sanatana Dharma practice, which has survived in various forms to the modern day. The practice of fire sacrifice is based on the idea that generous offerings to a deity will be rewarded by some specific results. Over time elaborate fire sacrifice rituals were created, controlled by **Brahmins** (priests) involving **mantras** (sacred chants) and sacred actions. The cumulative purpose of these practices was to invoke the breath behind all of existence, the Absolute, the Supreme Reality.

Castes

Because sacrifices involved communion with the gods, priests who performed the public sacrifices had to be carefully trained and maintain high standards of ritual purity, and these Brahmins came to constitute a special class of individuals. According to ancient practice, the orderly working of society included a clear division of labor among four occupational groups, which later became entrenched as **castes**. The *Brahmins* were the priests and philosophers, specialists in the life of the spirit. *Kshatriyas* formed the next group, the nobility of kings and warriors whose function was to guard and preserve the society. The economic specialists—farmers and merchants—were called *vaishyas*. The *Shudra* were the manual laborers and artisans. Finally, even lower than these original four castes were those "outcastes" who came to be considered "untouchables," carrying on work such as removing human wastes and corpses and working with leather from the skins of dead cows—occupations

Karma In Hinduism and Buddhism, our actions and their effects on this life and the lives to come.

Samsara The continual round of birth, death, and rebirth in Hinduism and Buddhism.

Moksha In Hinduism, liberation of the soul from illusion and suffering.

Yoga A systematic approach to spiritual realization, one of the major Hindu philosophical systems.

Brahmins Priests or members of the priestly caste in Hinduism.

Mantras A sound or phrase chanted to evoke the sound vibration of one aspect of creation or to praise a deity.

Castes Social class distinctions on the basis of heredity or occupation.

that made their bodies and clothing abhorrent to others. Over time caste membership became hereditary and a rigidly enforced element in Indian society. The caste system was attacked by the great Indian leader Mahatma Gandhi, and in 1948 the stigma of "untouchability" was legally abolished, though many caste distinctions still linger in modern India, including an aversion to marriage across caste lines.

Taoism

At the time that India was giving birth to Hinduism and Buddhism, East Asia saw the creation of Taoism and Confucianism (in China) and Shinto (in Japan). On the surface, Taoism and Confucianism appear very different. Confucianism, based on the teachings of Master K'ung (Confucius), developed an organized code of moral conduct and political organization that evolved over centuries into the guiding principles of Chinese life. It is a philosophy primarily concerned with ways of training wise and altruistic public servants, and educating people to achieving a better life on earth. Taoism, on the other hand, is a way of life inspired from the rhythms of the natural phenomena. For example, the Taoist martial arts were originally borrowed from nature, imitating the movement of wild animals as they attack and defend. It is believed that if somebody studies natural phenomena closely, he/she can discover valuable indications as to the best approach to various life circumstances. Taoism promotes a constant interaction with our environment and the importance of being aware of it.

Tao is believed to be the first cause of the universe. It is the "unnamable" and "eternally real" force that flows through life, and each believer's goal is to become one with the Tao. Although Tao can be translated as "path" or "the way," it is basically indefinable. Reality cannot be named or known through language, logic, or concepts—it must be experienced. Tao refers to a power that envelops and flows through all things, living and nonliving. The Tao regulates natural processes and balances the universe. It embodies the harmony of opposites as expressing a transcendent unity: there would be no love without hate, no light without dark, no male without female. The Tao surrounds everyone and therefore everyone must listen to find enlightenment. Its ubiquitous yet paradoxical nature is expressed in the following passage from the *Tao-te Ching*:

> There is a thing confusedly formed,
>
> Born before heaven and earth.
>
> Silent and void
>
> It stands alone and does not change,
>
> Goes round and does not weary.
>
> It is capable of being the mother of the world.
>
> I know not its name
>
> So I style it "the way."
>
> I give it the makeshift name of "the great."

The founder of Taoism is believed by many to be **Lao-Tsu** (604–531 B.C.E.). According to tradition, Lao-Tsu was a curator of the royal library of the Chou dynasty who was searching for a way that would avoid the constant feudal warfare and other conflicts that were disrupting society during his lifetime. The result was his composing a book of five thousand characters known as the *Tao-te Ching* (quoted above). The book's central philosophy is a practical concern with improving harmony in life, attuning oneself to the natural energies of the cosmos by being receptive and quiet.

Brahmin priests light the sacred fire.

Lao Tsu (604–531 B.C.E.) Founder of Taoism. Name means the Old Master; Believed to be the author of the *Tao-te-Ching*, translated as the "Classic of the Way and Virtue", which lays down the fundamental beliefs of Taoism.

The taoist Yin-Yang symbol

Taoists do not pray to a Supreme Being; instead, they seek answers to life's problems through inner meditation and observation. For the Taoist, time is cyclical, not linear as in Western thinking. The entire cosmos is a manifestation of an impersonal self-generating energy called *ch'i*. This force has two aspects whose interplay causes the ever-changing phenomena of the universe. *Yin* is the dark, receptive, "female" aspect; *Yang* is the bright, assertive, "male" aspect. The Yin is considered to be the breath that formed the earth, whereas the Yang is the breath that formed the heavens. These two forces symbolize the pairs of opposites that are seen throughout the universe, such as good and evil, light and dark, male and female. Wisdom lies in recognizing the ever-shifting, but regular and balanced, patterns of movement of Yin and Yang and moving along with them. The Tao is this creative rhythm of the universe. According to Lao-Tzu:

> Humans model themselves on earth,
> Earth on heaven,
> Heaven on the way,
> And the way on that which is naturally so.

Taoists follow the art of *wu-wei*, which is to let nature take its course, rather than trying to impede it. To take a metaphor from the natural world, one should allow a river to flow toward the sea unimpeded, instead of erecting a dam that would interfere with its natural flow. Analogously, we should be like flowing water ourselves, bypassing and gently wearing away obstacles rather than aggressively attacking them, effortlessly moving through life without struggling, leaving all accomplishment behind without trying to hold on to them. Flowing water is a Taoist metaphor for being, as Lao-Tzu observes:

> Water is the softest thing on earth,
> Yet its silken gentleness
> Will easily wear away the hardest stone.
> Everyone knows this;
> Few use it in their daily lives.
> Those of Tao yield and overcome.

This is the Taoist paradox of nonaction—*wu-wei*—which entails taking no intentional or invasive action contrary to the natural flow of things. *Wu-wei* is spontaneous, creative activity proceeding from the Tao, letting the Tao take its course. In fact, Lao-Tzu taught that all straining, all striving are not only vain but also counterproductive. We need to discern and follow the natural forces, as a butcher whose knife always stays sharp because he lets his hand be guided by the makeup of the carcass, finding the spaces between the bones where a slight movement of the blade will glide through without resistance. Even when difficulties arise, the Taoist does not panic and take unnecessary action. This is a philosophy that should be practiced on a social and political level as well, as Lao-Tzu writes:

 Lao-Tzu, *Tao Te Ching*

> The Tao abides in non-action,
> Yet nothing is left undone.
> If kings and lords observed this,
> The ten thousand things would develop naturally.
> If they still desired to act,
> They would return to the simplicity of formless substance.
> Without form there is no desire.
> Without desire there is tranquillity.
> In this way all things would be at peace.

The Taoist approach embodies a love of nature and an occasional retreat to it from the cares of the world to rest and heal. Taoism also inspires an intense affirmation of physical life: health, well-being, vitality, longevity, and even immortality. Traditionally, the Taoists have experimented with herbal medicine and pharmacology, greatly advancing these arts; they developed principles of macrobiotic cooking and other healthy diets; and they developed systems of gymnastics, massage, and martial arts (including *T'ai-chi ch'uan*) to keep the body strong and youthful. Taoism can perhaps best be summed up in a quote from one of its early sages, Chuang Tzu:

> To regard the fundamental as the essence, to regard material things as coarse, to regard accumulation as deficiency, and to dwell quietly alone with the spiritual and the intelligent—herein lie the techniques of Tao of the ancients.

Judaism and Christianity

These religions will always be intertwined in their belief in a transcendent, all-powerful, monotheistic Creator/God, as revealed in the scriptures of the Old Testament. Yet these two religions are also destined to remain radically divided over the issue of whether **Jesus** was in fact the long-awaited Messiah—and Son of God—prophesied in the Old Testament. For Christians, a divine Jesus—the Christ—is the core of their religion. For most Jews, Jesus is not viewed as divine, and is instead seen as either a prophet of a still-to-come Messiah, or merely a man with no special religious status.

The theological frameworks of Judaism and Christianity have historically dominated Western culture. And because prominent thinkers and rulers in the Middle Ages such as Emperor Constantine, St. Augustine, and St. Thomas Aquinas also shared a love of Greek culture and thought, Christianity and Platonism have also tended to frame most of the philosophical questions regarding the philosophy of religion, including:

- What are "proofs" for the existence of God?
- What is the nature of God? What are God's attributes?
- What is the relationship between humans and God?
- What is the relation between faith and reason in developing one's religious beliefs?
- In a universe created by an all-powerful, perfect God, how does one account for the existence of evil?
- What is the nature of life after death, the immortality of the soul, the possibilities of spiritual transcendence, resurrection, and salvation?

Of course, some of these questions—and questions like them—apply to other of the world religions with varying degrees of relevance, but the fact is that these questions grew directly out of a Christian/Platonist metaphysical framework, and they are specifically tailored to explore issues within this framework. Despite this, it is important for us to make a special effort to explore these and comparable philosophical questions with all of the world's major religions, thinking philosophically about the rich diversity of religious experience.

Judaism

The precise origins of the Jewish people and the Jewish religion are unclear. Aside from the accounts in the Old Testament (the *Tanakh* in Hebrew) the history of the "Children of Israel" has not yet been confirmed by references of other cultures at the time or by archeological records. No mention of the Israelites appears in other sources until about 1230 B.C.E., although biblical narrative and genealogies place the first patri-

Jewish religious items

Jesus (1–33) Founder of Christianity. Believed by Christians to be the Son of God; During his three-year ministry before his crucifixion advanced an ethic that was egalitarian rather than one that was based on privilege.

arch of the Israelites, Abraham, at about 1700 to 1900 B.C.E. It is also unclear precisely who the Israelites were, though it is likely that because of frequent moving and inter-marrying they were an ethnic mixture of Hebrew, Aramaean, and Canaanite.

The Chosen People

Judaism is both an ethnic designation and a religion. It is possible for people who are not ethnically Jewish to convert to the Jewish religion, which typically occurs in cases of intermarriage. What is distinctive regarding Judaism as a religion is the con-viction that the Jews have been "chosen" by God to have a unique and enduring relationship with Him. They believe that God entered into a living covenant with the Jewish people, a continuing dialogue in which in exchange for their exclusive devotion and obedience, God would "choose" them to enjoy special consideration and protection. But the history of the Israelites in the Old Testament is one in which they repeatedly failed to keep their end of the covenant, worshiping a variety of other gods, and leading an angry God to punish them by being defeated by other cultures and dispersed around the world. As in the contentious conflict that often occurs in families, the Israelites always repent and a stern but loving paternalistic God then forgives them.

In the last several thousand years, the Jews have been singled out for persecu-tion in many cultures around the world, culminating in the genocide perpetrated by Adolph Hitler and Nazi Germany, which resulted in the deaths of over six mil-lion Jews in what has come to be known as the Holocaust. Following World War II, the United Nations created the political state of Israel, partitioning Palestine into two areas, one to be governed by the Jews and the other by the Arabs. The state of Israel instituted the "Law of Return," in which all Jews from around the world are invited to immigrate and settle what Jews consider to be their "homeland." The relationship between Israel and its Arab neighbors was and is, as of the writing of this book, primarily hostile in nature.

Religious Stories, Holidays, and Rituals

There is no single founder of Judaism on which its religious beliefs are based, nor is there a central leader or theological governing body for the religion. Also, in con-trast to most of the world religions, Judaism is not interested in converting others to its faith, a result of its overlap as an ethnic group and the group's self-image as "the chosen people."

Much of the religion is based on key events in Jewish history as recorded in the Old Testament, as well as the religious holidays and rituals based on these events. These events serve as moral paradigms, symbolically rich stories that have contin-ued relevance to our contemporary lives. These include:

- The creation story (there are actually two slightly different versions in Genesis, the first book of the Old Testament).
- Adam and Eve's adventures in the Garden of Eden.
- Noah and the great flood.
- Abraham and the founding of the Israelites through his son, Isaac, whom he later was willing to execute as a sacrifice at God's command.
- Abraham and the founding of the Arab race through his son Ishmael (by the Egyptian slave Hagar).
- The bondage and Exodus from Egypt, led by Moses; the delivery of the Ten Commandments to Moses; and ultimate deliverance to the "promised land" of Palestine after forty years of wandering in the wilderness.
- The reign of King Solomon and the building of the Temple of Jerusalem.

- The confrontation between the young shepherd David and the giant warrior Goliath and David's subsequent ascension as King of the Israelites.
- The words and warnings of the Prophets throughout Jewish history, as well the lives of memorable individuals such as Job, whose faith was tested by God through a series of misfortunes.

Of course, these same biblical stories from the Old Testament form an important part of the teachings of Christianity, but they are not at the heart of that religion. Holidays that have grown out of these events include the observation of the Sabbath (the seventh day on which God rested after the creation); Passover, symbolizing the Israelites' delivery out of Egypt; Rosh Hashanah, signaling the anniversary of creation and the beginning of a new year; Yom Kippur, a day of atonement; Hanukkah, or Feast of Lights, commemorating the war against the Maccabees; and Purim, the Feast of Lots, recalling the exploits of Queen Esther.

What roles do coming-of-age rituals play in various religions?

Core Religious Beliefs

Jewish religious beliefs have evolved over time, and even today embody a wide diversity ranging from highly orthodox to liberal, from legalistic to mystical. Nevertheless there are certain core beliefs that are common threads through all of this diversity. First and foremost is monotheism, a belief in one Creator God, all-powerful and all-loving, ever-present, as David sings in Psalm 139: 7–10.

> Where can I escape from Your spirit?
> Where can I flee from Your presence?
> If I ascend to Heaven, You are there:
> If I descend to Sheol (the underworld),
> You are there too.
>
> If I take wing with the dawn
> To come to rest on the western horizon,
> Even there Your hand will be guiding me.
> Your right hand will hold me fast.

A second pillar of Jewish faith follows directly from the belief in a Creator God, namely, we should be utterly devoted to God. The central prayer in any Jewish religious service and the inscription on the *mezuza* at the doorpost of every traditional Jewish home is the *Shema Israel*, taken from Deuteronomy 6: 4–9.

> Hear, O Israel! The Lord is our God, the Lord alone. You shall love the Lord your God with all your heart and with all your soul and with all your might. Take to heart these instructions with which I charge you this day. Impress them upon your children. Recite them when you stay at home and when you are away, when you lie down and when you get up. Bind them as a sign on your hand and let them serve as a symbol on your forehead; inscribe them on the doorposts of your house and on your gates.

Divinely inspired laws that cover every aspect of Jewish social, communal, and religious life are a third core element of Jewish religious faith. These laws have been codified in the *Torah*, which has a variety of meanings. In its purest form, the Torah refers to the first five books of the Old Testament (the Pentateuch). But the term is also used to designate the entire Old Testament, as well as the entire body of Jewish teaching and traditional practices. These teachings have evolved over time through the ongoing study and writings of Jewish scholars.

The Messiah

"Messiah" generally means "the anointed one" or "the Christ," and it was the Hebrew name for the promised deliverer of humankind. The concept of Messiah combines the Hebrew ideal of a Davidic King with the priestly tradition exemplified by Moses. The greatest hope of the religious Jews throughout the ages has been the hope of the Messiah, a Jewish man who is to bring peace on earth and set Israel at the head of the nations. The Messiah is also seen as the "Anointed One" of God who would one day come to redeem his people from oppression at the beginning of an era of world peace.

According to Jewish scholars, the coming of the Messiah is foretold throughout the Old Testament through a multitude of signs and predictions that present a complex and not always consistent portrait. Many of these predictions appear consistent with the life of Jesus, including those listed below with Old Testament references. The Messiah would

- be born in Bethlehem (Micah 5:2)
- be born of a virgin (Isaiah 7:14)
- be a descendent of David (Jeremiah 23:5)
- be a "light to the Gentiles" (Isaiah 49:7)
- speak in parables (Psalm 78.2)
- heal the blind, deaf, and lame (Isaiah 35:5)
- enter Jerusalem riding on a donkey (Zechariah 9:9)
- be betrayed (Psalm 41:9)
- die among criminals (Isaiah 53:9, 12)
- have his hands and feet pierced (Psalm 22:16)
- rise from the dead (Isaiah 53: 11,12)

On the other hand, prophecies regarding the Messiah that did not seem to be fulfilled in the person of Jesus included restoring the Kingdom of David, restoring the Temple that had been destroyed, gathering all of the exiles, reestablishing Israel by supernatural power, and leading the world to perfection. To complicate the situation even more, a number of other individuals have claimed to be the Jewish Messiah, including, a few years before the birth of Jesus, a Jew from Egypt who led thirty thousand men to the Mount of Olives, with the intent of forcibly taking Jerusalem from the Romans. He was intercepted by the forces of the Roman procurator, and the ancient historian Josepheus reports that the Egyptian fled, leaving many of his unfortunate followers to be killed in battle.

The concept of the Messiah has been the sustaining hope of the Jewish people for thousands of years. And the birth, life, and death of Jesus of Nazareth turned out to be a defining moment in the development of the Jewish religion. Frustration and Messiah-hopes were running high, as Israel was suffering under the heavy hand of Roman rule and taxation. For those Jews who believed that Jesus was the long-anticipated Messiah, fulfilling many of the prophetic details, Jesus became the beginning of a new religion, Christianity. However, for those Jews who believed that Jesus was not in fact the prophesied Messiah, Jesus became merely another individual falsely claiming to be the long-awaited savior of the Jewish people.

Christianity

Of course, it is with the crucifixion of Jesus that Christianity begins. If the intention of his execution was to discredit the idea that Jesus was the Jewish Messiah, it was an action that spawned profound and unintended consequences. Actually, Christianity doesn't really begin with the death of Jesus, but several days *after* Jesus' crucifixion when, according to biblical accounts, a number of women closest to Jesus (including Mary Magdalene) went to his tomb to anoint his body. Through a series of events and encounters they and the other disciples, and later increasing numbers of people, became utterly convinced that Jesus was alive, albeit present in the world in a very different manner than he had been before. They took this victory over death as God's vindication of what Jesus had been teaching and demonstrating in the three years he had been with them. Now, from a dispirited and fearful remnant who had been in hiding following his execution, this tiny group of followers became an exuberant and energetic movement. "He is risen!" they announced to all who would hear and fanned out to announce this "good news" (the meaning of the word *gospel*). At once the Jesus movement began to multiply, first in Palestine, then in neighboring regions, then in every part of the Roman Empire and eventually throughout much of the world. In the extraordinary impact of this obscure Jewish teacher and prophet who lived for only thirty-three years in a remote outpost of the Roman Empire we see, as in the cases of Muhammad, Buddha, and Confucius, the extraordinary ability of one individual with a powerful message to alter history and literally change the world for subsequent generations.

An artist's depiction of Jesus

The Life and Teachings of Jesus

Jesus was born in humble surroundings in Bethlehem in Palestine, an event that is now celebrated around the world. Little is known of his life growing up, other than he worked as a carpenter. At the age of twelve he was found by his parents discussing the Torah with the rabbis, and "all who heard him were amazed at his understanding and his answers." When challenged by his parents, he replied, "Did you not know that I must be in my Father's house?"—a response that Christians interpret as revealing his sense of mission, his knowledge of Jewish tradition, and the close personal relationship between Jesus and God.

All of this changed when, at the age of thirty, he appeared at the Jordan river to ask an idiosyncratic prophet named John the Baptist to baptize him. Citing the prophecies of the revered Jewish prophet Isaiah regarding the coming of the Kingdom of God, John had been calling people to repent of their sins and then be spiritually purified and sanctified by immersion in the river. Apparently recognizing Jesus' spiritual uniqueness, John initially resisted Jesus' request to baptize him, feeling that he was not worthy to perform such a ceremony, but Jesus insisted and the Bible records:

> When he came up out of the water, immediately he saw the heavens opened and the Spirit descending upon him like a dove; and a voice came from heaven. "Thou art my beloved Son; with thee I am well pleased."
>
> —*Mark 1: 10–11*

This event seems to signal the beginning of his three-year ministry and is interpreted by Christian believers as a consecration as the Son of God and the Messiah. Following his baptism, the Bible records that Jesus retreated to the wilderness for forty days, where he was tempted by Satan to use his divine power for secular ends, but he refused. Following this retreat, Jesus began gathering disciples, a core group of followers that ultimately numbered twelve. Jesus asked them to leave all their possessions and human attachments to follow him, urging them and others to focus on the spiritual rewards of the next life rather than the physical comforts and riches of this life:

> Is not life more than food, and the body more than clothing? Look at the birds of the air; they neither sow nor reap nor gather into barns, and yet your heavenly Father feeds them. Are you not of more value than they? And which of you by being anxious can add one cubit to his span of life?
>
> *—Matthew 6: 25–27*

Jesus presents God as paternal, a loving Father who will take care of those who love Him and want to follow the path of righteousness. Jesus' message was to reveal this path, through words and actions, so that all could achieve spiritual perfection and salvation in preparation for life after death. He makes clear that each person's relationship with God is intensely personal, nurtured through worship, reflection, and personal prayer. God will always respond to sincere requests: "Ask, and it will be given you; seek, and you will find; knock, and it will be opened to you." (Matthew 7:7)

During the three years of his ministry, Jesus traveled around Palestine preaching, often with vivid parables, and, according to the biblical account, performing miracles. Among the miracles ascribed to Jesus are healing the sick and disabled, casting devils out of the possessed, restoring the dead to life, walking on water, cleansing lepers, and feeding five thousand people with just a few loaves and fish. The Bible describes Jesus as performing these miracles without fanfare, and they were widely interpreted as confirming his special spiritual status and possible divinity.

Jesus preached a radical ethic, in sharp contrast to the elitist and hierarchical framework created by religious leaders of the time. Jesus surprised and angered these religious leaders by focusing his attention on the most despised and disinherited people of the day, including the poor, the outcasts, the prostitutes, and even the most despised people of the day, the tax collectors. What's more, Jesus preached that in the next life, the favored individuals would include the poor in spirit, the meek, the mourners, the seekers of righteousness, the pure in heart, the merciful, the peace-makers, and those who are persecuted for the sake of righteousness and of spreading the gospel. He lived this radically egalitarian vision, welcoming women as equals in a male-dominated society, and spending much of his time with the social "outcasts."

In addition to complete devotion to God, the core of Jesus' message was a love and devotion to others: "These two commandments I give unto you, that you love God with all your heart and that you love your neighbor as yourself." (Mark 10:27) This core message represented a clear break with the "eye for an eye" ethic of the Old Testament, replacing it with "turning the other cheek" to those who seek to harm us. Jesus explicitly acknowledged this break in saying, "You have heard that it was said to the men of old . . ." and is intent on making clear his new vision of the path of righteousness:

> Love your enemies and pray for those who persecute you, so that you may be sons of your Father who is in heaven; for he makes his sun rise on the evil and on the good and sends rain on the just and on the unjust.
>
> *—Matthew 5: 44–45*

This selfless devotion is expected to be extended not only to our family and friends, but to our neighbors and those in need whom we don't know personally. In fact, Jesus made clear that in extending ourselves to the less fortunate in society, we are symbolically worshiping God:

Then the righteous will answer him, "Lord, when did we see thee hungry and feed thee, or thirsty and give thee drink? And when did we see thee a stranger and welcome thee, or naked and clothe thee? And when did we see thee sick or in prison and visit thee?" And the King will answer them, "Truly, I say to you, as you did it to one of the least of these my brethren, you did it to me."

—Matthew 25: 37–40

Jesus often communicated his message through *parables*, stories about ordinary life that can be interpreted in powerfully symbolic ways, serving as a compelling lesson on how to stay on the path to righteousness. One of the classic parables is that of the Good Samaritan.

A man was going down from Jerusalem to Jericho, and he fell among robbers, who stripped him and beat him, and departed, leaving him half dead. Now by chance a priest was going down that road; and when he saw him he passed by on the other side. So likewise a Levite, when he came to the place and saw him, passed by on the other side. But a Samaritan, as he journeyed, came to where he was; and when he saw him, he had compassion, and went to him and bound up his wounds, pouring on oil and wine; then he set him on his own beast and brought him to an inn, and took care of him. And the next day he took out two denarii and gave them to the innkeeper, saying "Take care of him; and whatever more you spend, I will repay you when I come back," Which of these three, do you think, proved neighbor to the man who fell among the robbers?

—Luke 10:30–36

Like most of Jesus' parables, this one can be interpreted on a number of levels. On the surface, it exhorts us to help those in need, even if they are strangers. But deeper interpretation demands the uncovering of additional levels. At this time in history, there was such animosity between the Israelites and the Samaritans that in combining the words "Good" and "Samaritan" Jesus was asking his audience to consider the inconceivable. The real point of the parable is the challenge of extending love to those we consider to be our enemies without the expectation that it will be reciprocated. Thus the underlying purpose of many of the parables is for the listeners to realize how their own opinions and behaviors must be questioned in order to understand the intentions of God. People must confront their deepest doubts and biases as they become aware of the meaning of God's message and begin to think and act in new ways. Many of Jesus' parables have passed into the cultural vocabulary, including the following:

- A wise man builds his house on a rock; a fool on sand (Matthew 7:24–27, Luke 6:47–49)
- New wine in old wineskins (Matthew 9:17, Mark 2:22, Luke 5: 37, 38)
- You reap what you sow (Matthew 13: 3–23, Mark 4: 2–20, Luke 8: 4–15)
- The lost sheep (Matthew 18: 12–14, Luke 15: 3–7)
- The prodigal son (Matthew 21: 28–32)

Occasionally the parables were used to make some very explicit and disturbing points, as the following:

The kingdom of heaven is like a dragnet cast into the sea that brings in a haul of all kinds. When it is full, the fishermen haul it ashore; then, sitting down, they collect the good ones in a basket and throw away those that are of no use. This is how it will be at the end of time: the angels will appear and separate the wicked from the just to throw them into the blazing furnace where there will be weeping and grinding of teeth.

—Matthew 13: 47–50

Parable of the Lost Sheep

VISUAL PHILOSOPHY

"The Good Samaritan" by Delacroix

What is the religious message of the parable of The Good Samaritan? What are the roles of parables, stories, and myths in various religions?

Although the Jews were expecting the Messiah to provide immediate relief from their current oppressed state under Roman rule, Jesus made clear on numerous occasions that the kingdom of God that he was promising was a spiritual kingdom that would be fully realized only in the future. By devoting themselves to God and following the path of righteousness, they could become spiritually transformed in this life and prepare themselves for eternal life at the end of time.

> Every one who drinks of this water will thirst again, but whoever drinks of the water that I shall give him will never thirst: the water that I shall give him will become in him a spring of water welling up to eternal life.
>
> —*John 4: 13–14*

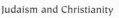

In some passages Jesus seems to foretell the apocalyptic end of the world when he would return to earth and God's glory would be fully manifested.

> Then will appear the sign of the Son of man in heaven, and then all the tribes of the earth will mourn, and they will see the Son of man coming on the clouds of heaven with power and great glory: and he will send out his angels with a loud trumpet call, and they will gather his elect from the four winds, from one end of heaven to the other.
>
> —*Matthew 24: 29–31*

The Jewish leaders of the day found Jesus' egalitarian ethic and his apparent claims to divinity to be religiously disturbing and politically threatening. These leaders included the Pharisees (the shapers of rabbinic Judaism), the Sadducees (the priests and upper class), and the Scribes (specially trained laymen who copied the written law and formulated the oral law of Judaism). Jesus seemed to view his message as being in the spirit and tradition of Mosaic law, but he had complete contempt for what he considered to be the artificial legalism and hypocrisy of the religious hierarchy. At one point, according to Matthew, Jesus' disciples were castigated by the Pharisees and scribes for not washing their hands before eating. Jesus responded with a blistering attack:

> Alas for you, scribes and Pharisees, you hypocrites! You who are like whitewashed tombs that look handsome on the outside, but inside are full of dead men's bones and every kind of corruption. In the same way you appear to people from the outside like good honest men, but inside you are full of hypocrisy and lawlessness.
>
> —*Matthew 23: 27–28*

Jesus' direct challenge of the ruling clique's authority made them understandably apprehensive about the growing following he was gathering. By proclaiming a Reign of God that was immanent, Jesus was undercutting the symbolic basis of their authority. They were also worried that the Romans might interpret his grass-roots movement as a threat to the empire, and decided that rather than risk a possibly bloody Roman crackdown, they themselves would have to take action. Jesus was arrested and turned over to the Roman authorities who, after some indecision, executed him by a torture in the manner reserved for those found to be subversive to the imperial order. Jesus was crucified, and his followers scattered and fled. A minor incident in the long saga of Rome—and Judaism—seemed to be over: until Jesus' close circle of friends and disciples became convinced that he had in fact been resurrected from the dead.

Who Was Jesus?

The ultimate validity of Christianity hinges on this question. Christianity has based its entire theology on the belief that Jesus was divine, the Son of God, made incarnate in human form to make salvation available to all who believe in him and his message. However, if one concludes that Jesus may have been a very wise and charismatic figure, but was *not* divine, then the foundation of Christianity is seriously undermined.

According to the Gospel of Mark, Jesus himself once posed this question to his immediate followers: "Who do people say that I am?" he asked. His followers offered several answers. Some people, they reported, thought he was another Elijah, the Jewish prophet who was expected to return to earth just before the end of the world. Others thought he was some other prophet. Then Jesus asked Peter, one of his first disciples, the same question. Peter responded by telling Jesus that he was the "Messiah," the ambiguously defined figure most of his fellow Jews were hoping would soon appear and help them overcome the captivity and religious persecution they were suffering under the Roman Empire.

What is the role of religious statues and icons in various religions?

Jesus told Peter he was right. But the next lines in the story suggest that Peter's answer, far from solving the question of Jesus' identity, instead deepened it. For Jesus went on to state that he would soon have to go to Jerusalem, the religious and political capital of his captive nation, and that there he would meet his death. At this point Peter disagreed with his master and rabbi. There was no place in his thinking, or in that of most of his contemporaries, for a Messiah who would be defeated and die. It was a contradictory scenario. One could fail and die, and thus obviously not be the Messiah, or one could triumph and therefore manifestly be the long-awaited one. But the combination seemed bizarrely incongruous.

Of course, Peter and other Christians came to believe that it was not Jesus' intention to establish a physical kingdom on earth at that time, but rather to initiate the creation of spiritual kingdom on earth. The establishment of God's Kingdom will come at the apocalyptic end of the world, when Jesus returns triumphantly to fight the final battle of Armageddon and pass eternal judgment on the souls of all who have lived.

Islam

There is no god but God, and Muhammad is his Messenger" is the defining core of the Islam religion. In contrast to most religions, Islam sees itself as intrinsically connected to two of the other great monotheistic world religions: Judaism and Christianity. Islam views its founder, **Muhammad** (570–632), as the last in a line of great prophets who have included Abraham, Moses, and Jesus, divinely inspired messengers who have exhorted people to worship the one true God, as expressed in the first chapter, **Sura**, of Islam's holy book, the **Qur'an**:

> Say ye: We believe
> In God, and the revelation
> Given to us, and to Abraham
> Isma'il, Isaac, Jacob,
> And the Tribes, and that given
> To Moses and Jesus, and that given
> To (all) Prophets from their Lord:
> We make no difference
> Between one and another of them:
> And we bow to God in surrender.

According to Islamic teaching, monotheism has always been the one true religion, even before the advent of the prophet Muhammad and the birth of Islam. When humans strayed into polytheistic beliefs, God would send prophets to exhort them to return to a pure monotheism, or face dire consequences. However, Islam considers Muhammad to be the final prophet, receiving messages meant for all people in all times, and the Qur'an is considered to be the final Word of God, the "Seal of the Prophets," the ultimate divine authority. It supersedes previous teachings by the prophets in the Old Testament and the teachings of Jesus, because it is the direct, unchanged, untranslated word of God.

Who exactly was Muhammad and how did he come to receive the Qur'an? Muhammad (the name means "the praised one" in Arabic) was a man born into a poor clan who was raised by his uncle after the deaths of his father, mother, and grandfather. He began working as a shepherd, and then on to managing caravans

Muhammad (570–632) Founder of Islam. Believed to be the last of the great prophets from Abraham to Jesus and to have received the uninterpreted, divine word of God.

Sura　A chapter of the Qur'an.

Qur'an　The holy book of Islam.

for an intelligent, wealthy woman named Khadijah, whom he eventually married when he was twenty-five and Khadijah was forty. At the age of forty, Muhammad was on a spiritual retreat when the angel Gabriel appeared in human-like form, exhorting him to "recite" the Word of God. Three times Muhammad demurred, protesting that he was uneducated and not fit to transmit such a holy message. Finally, Muhammad cried out: "What shall I recite?" and the angel began dictating the first words of what became the Islamic holy book, the Qur'an.

> Proclaim! (or Recite!)
> In the name
> Of thy Lord and Cherisher,
> Who created—
> Created man, out of
> A (mere) clot
> Of congealed blood:
> Proclaim! And thy Lord
> Is Most Bountiful,—
> He Who taught
> (The use of) the Pen,—
> Taught man that
> Which he know not.

A page from the Qur'an.

Muhammad continued to receive these revelations over the next twenty-three years, and Muslims believe that when recited, the passages have an unsurpassed lyrical beauty and power. The fact that Muhammad was, in his own words, "unlettered," is taken by Muslims as evidence that the Qur'an is the direct Word of God. Initial sections of the Qur'an are striking affirmations of the unity of God and the terrible consequences for those who do not respond to God's message. Later sections deal with the social and political lives or ethics of the Muslim community. The Qur'an is designed to be recited in a solemn tone, and Muhammad exhorted followers to "Weep, therefore, when you recite it." He described the process of receiving the Qur'an in the following way:

> Revelation sometimes comes like the sound of a bell; that is the most painful way. When it ceases I have remembered what was said. Sometimes it is an angel who talks to me like a human, and I remember what he says.

The Qur'an was kept alive through an oral tradition during the life of Muhammad and even beyond his death in C.E. 632. A single authoritative written text was compiled in 650 by a council of religious elders. The written version is divided into 114 *suras* (chapters). The first *sura* is the *Fatiha*, which expresses the essence of the Qur'an:

> In the name of God, Most Gracious, Most merciful,
> Praise be to God.
> The Lord of the Worlds;
> Most Gracious, Most Merciful;
> Master of the Day of Judgment.
> Thee do we worship.
> And Thine aid we seek.
> Show us the straight way,
> The way of those on whom
> Thou has bestowed Thy Grace
> Those whose portion
> Is not wrath,
> And, who go not astray.

The Qur'an is considered to be deeply symbolic, with multiple layers of meaning that require great scholarly effort to reveal. The message of the Qur'an is spiritually inspiring but also contains vivid warnings. For those who choose to follow Allah, they are insured an afterlife in Paradise of splendid pleasures. However, for those who do not embrace and submit themselves to Allah, they will be called to account at The Last Judgment and they will suffer the terrifying torments of hell.

Muhammad's divine revelations and message was not welcomed by the aristocratic leaders (the *Qurayshites*) in Mecca, the city in which he lived. In fact, he was actively persecuted by them, protected only by the influence of his wife and uncle. Ultimately, he escaped to a neighboring city, Medina, where in addition to continuing his Qur'an recitations, he also developed a constitution for the city that was to later serve as a model for Islamic social administration. There followed a period of warfare between Mecca and Medina, in which Muhammad took an active role. In 630 Muhammad returned triumphantly to Mecca with an overwhelming number of followers, taking charge of the city and instituting Islam as the religion. Muhammad died in 632, leaving no clear instructions for who should succeed him, and the net result was a division into two groups of Muslims, the *Sunni* and the *Shi'a*, a division that continues to this day.

The Five Pillars of Islam

Zakat Spiritual tithing in Islam.

The Qur'an, which incorporates both the early and later revelations received by the Prophet Muhammad from Allah through the angel Gabriel throughout a period of twenty-three years, reveals the central patterns of worship known as the Five Pillars of Islam. The Five Pillars is also known as the *outer practice* of Islam. It is set forth in the *Shari'ah*, the "straight path" of the Divine law. Its main purpose is to bring remembrance of God into every aspect of daily life and practical ethics into the fabric of society. The Five Pillars spells out the way of Muslim life and its purposes. It allows a Muslim to know where he stands, who he is, and who God is.

The First Pillar concerns the private life of Muslims in their direct relationship with God, embodied in Islam's creed: "There is no God but Allah, and Muhammad is his Prophet." This is the foundation-stone of Islam, incorporating both a monotheistic belief in God and the recognition that while Muhammad is not divine, he is the last and greatest Prophet of God. Although Islam believes that there might be many *names* for God, it is a religion built on the firm conviction that there is only *one* God, and it is our responsibility to *submit totally* to God's will in every dimension of our lives. The Second Pillar of Islam is the performance of a continual round of prayers, a response to the natural yearning of the human heart to pour forth its love and gratitude towards its Creator. Regular prayer also keeps a Muslim's life in proper perspective, reminding him to submit himself to God's will as rightfully sovereign over his life. A Muslim should pray five times daily—upon rising, at noon, in mid-afternoon, after sunset, and before retiring. The Third Pillar is **zakat**, the giving of alms, which occur once a year. There are always those who possess more material things than others, and Islam tries to bring a balance to this situation by asking those who have much to help lift the burden of those who have less. The Fourth Pillar is the observance of *Ramadan*, the

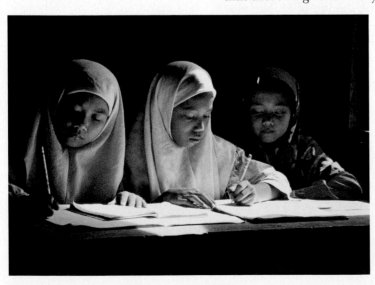

What is the role of education in various religions?

holy month in the Arabian calendar. This was the period in which Muhammad received his initial commission as a prophet and ten years later made his historic sojourn from Mecca to Medina. To commemorate these two occasions, those who are strong and sufficiently healthy fast during the entire month. From dawn-to-sunset Muslims do not eat, drink, have sexual intercourse, or smoke. Fasting underscores man's dependence upon God and, by experiencing what it is like to feel hunger and suffering, helps make him more compassionate. The Fifth Pillar is **hajj**, the pilgrimage to Mecca. Once in a lifetime a Muslim is expected, if physical and economic conditions permit, to make this journey to Mecca where God's ultimate revelation was first disclosed. Here again, similar to fasting during Ramadan, the purpose is to heighten the pilgrim's devotion to God and to His revealed will.

Hajj The holy pilgrimage to Mecca, for Muslims.

Muslims who weave the Five Pillars of Islam into their daily lives lead a life that is intensely devoted to their faith. Islam allows a Muslim to experience his spiritual faith as a long journey that gets ever more deeper as he manages to approach Allah's presence within his own daily activities and within himself.

Sufism

As with many religions, Islam has a tradition of mysticism—*Sufism*—which is separate from the mainstream practices of Islam. Sufism, which has been described as the mystical, inner pathway of Islam, derives its name from *tasawwuf*, an Arabic word meaning "to dress in wool." Sufists believe that to experience the Divine, one must give up feelings of ego as well as thoughts of self, an act called *fana*. In the words of one Sufist, it is necessary to "die before you die,"—in other words, you need to die to yourself so that nothing remains but the One:

> What's in your head—toss it away! What's in your hand—give it up! Whatever happens—don't turn away from it. . . . Sufism is the heart standing with God, with nothing in between.

> —*Abu Sa'id Abu al-Khayr*

In Sufism, the way to become one with God, The Unity of Being, goes through the obligatory practices of prayer, fasting, charity, and pilgrimage. However, there are additional methods for believers to find their path to spiritual understanding of the Beloved. Poetry, dance, chant, and contemplation are all part of the divine experience, as are interpretations of dreams and visions. The fascinating Sufi order of the whirling dervishes in Turkey emphasize dance as an important part of *dhikr*, the ceremony whose purpose is to find unity with God and in repeated worship of His name. Khwajah 'Abdallah al-Ansari, a Sufi author who lived in the eleventh century and became a saint after his death, wrote the following poem, which captures the spiritual, loving essence of Sufism:

> For some time I would seek Him yet would find my self
> Now I seek my self and find Him
> Love arrived and became like my blood within veins and skin
> Until it emptied me and filled me with the Beloved.
> The Beloved has completely taken possession of the parts of my body.
> A name is given by me to me, and the rest is all Him.

As we learned at the beginning of this chapter, a thoughtful exploration of the philosophy of religion does not ask us to undermine our own beliefs. Rather, by thinking critically about the common themes that connect various dimensions of religious inquiry, we come to a better understanding of our shared humanity. In the following

Whirling dervishes performing their mesmerising dance ritual.

essay, written in response to the previous Think Critically activity, student Dorothea Kuhnemann-Crow reflects on what other faiths can teach her about her own beliefs.

Kuhnemann-Crow,
Common Threads

In order to explore the meaning of religion as a whole, it is essential to look, without judgment, at other religions simultaneously. I was surprised to find that the several religions I have so far explored share many aspects that reflect a common human nature; aspects such as the common need to reach an altered state of consciousness through meditation, often accompanied by physical and emotional suffering, love and compassion, and the aspect of death and life after death.

Altered States of Consciousness

The ultimate goal in all religions, including the indigenous sacred practices, is to reach through direct experience, an altered state of consciousness. Why so? I believe it is in our common human nature to seek for a sense of unity within ourselves and with God. To reach such a state, each religion has found different means, whether it be through symbolic rituals, prayers or meditations, to express a common goal in which one's own spirit can enter into an identity with the Divine Being or Supreme Creator.

The Australian Aborigines used their own sacred practices to keep, on a daily basis, in spiritual contact with their ancestors, who are known as the supreme creators of everything, including their next generation. The Buddhists, Taoists, and Confucianists sit for days to years in order to achieve wisdom or wakefulness. However, this philosophy of wisdom and enlightenment is not only emphasized through meditation but through daily activities: finding oneself with the flow of the universe in nature and within one's own community.

The religious Jews as well as Muslims not only structure their daily lives with prayer and meditation in order to reach a state where they feel personally closer to their God, but they also choose once a year to fast (Muslims during the month of Ramadan and Jews during Yom Kippur). They say, "fasting makes one think and reflect" to the point where the act of fasting becomes physically painful and unbearable. Only then can one reach the transition point where one can more easily separate oneself from the physical world and be connected with a higher realm closer to God. Therefore, fasting not only teaches self-discipline but allows one to develop a stronger faith in one's creator.

I reflected on the idea of fasting a little further and realized that each founder of the main world religions has actually gone through a similar stage of spiritual retreat until they reached wisdom or received their revelations. Siddhartha (Buddha) chose to leave and isolate himself from his own family and community. He too, examined other religious paths and then sat to meditate and also fast until the true nature of reality and of the universe was revealed to him. When asked who he was, he said "I am awake."

Lao Tzu, the founder of Taoism, also chose to leave society in order to achieve greater personal solitude; without his solitude, he wouldn't have returned with the 5,000 characters, later known as Tao-te Ching or "The Way of the Universe and its Power," which was then revealed to him.

Both Muhammad, the founder of Islam, and Jesus, the founder of Christianity, chose to go through a period of spiritual retreat. Muhammad frequently visited a cave to seek out deeper solitude. When the right time came, the heavens opened to him as it did to Jesus Christ. But, the voice of Allah dictated to him, through the archangel Gabriel, what later became known as the Qur'an. For Jesus, after forty days and forty nights in the wilderness without food and very little sleep, God empowered him with his spirit and declared him to be his unique Son whom he chose for messianic ministry.

Why is it in our human nature to isolate ourselves from our own communities when we need greater personal solitude or when we wish to connect with a higher realm? Furthermore, why do all religions encourage us to suffer in one form or another, whether it be through fasting, meditation or deeper solitude? To me it becomes clear when I realize that it simply is in our nature to be, on a daily basis, entangled with earthly matters (insurance, car, family, education, money). Sometimes we become so immersed with such matters that we forget to take care of ourselves or set aside time to be by ourselves

Jesus alone in the desert with the wild birds and beasts being tempted by the Devil.

in quiet reflection. Thus, we lose control and we are no longer able to look at life as a whole. Taoists suggest to let the true nature of life take its course. That is, to go with the flow and not against it. In order to reach a sense of unity, inner peace and right conduct for each person's state of evolution, a periodic separation from the physical world is necessary; a period in which one should reflect but mostly be perceptive, and a period that would allow one to put the puzzle of life back together.

Love, Empathy, and Compassion

Jesus teaches his disciples that his own Son-ship is a son-ship of suffering. To be his disciples they too have to leave everything they have and submit to suffering and death as the fate and love of the Son of God. In other words, loving God with heart, soul and mind and one's neighbor as oneself.

Taoists, similarly to Buddhists and Confucianists, aim their long enduring practice of sitting meditation, which often demands tremendous amounts of patience and self-discipline, to reach a better and clearer understanding of the way of the universe and its power. This attempt to achieve wisdom and enlightenment, if practiced, will not only bring about the restoration of themselves but of the entire society; as a result people will develop more compassion for others, they will learn to listen and open their hearts to each other instead of seeking to be the dominant or the most well-known among all.

The Kabbalist Jews direct their religious practice toward the discovery of the meaning of evil in the world and the suffering that follows as a result, by tracing evil back to the stages in the "Tree of Life" where it was manifested already within the process of creation. Similar to Taoists, Kabbalists say that bringing about the awareness and the will to work with or restore the existing evil in the universe and the evil within ourselves, will bring about, with the help of the coming Messiah, a repair or restoration to the evil and the suffering in the universe. This in turn will bring only love and joy.

Finally, a Muslim who fasts during the month of Ramadan claims that the hardship of fasting sensitizes compassion, because after such an experience he will be apt to listen more carefully the next time he is approached by someone in need.

Why then are love, empathy and compassion so essential for all religions? Christians learn to love their neighbors as they love themselves. Muslims express their compassion for their brothers by the yearly giving of alms (one of the Five Pillars of Islam) where the wealthy donate a certain percentage of their income to those in greater need. Jews are known for leading a communal lifestyle where everyone is considered part of a loving and supportive family. Buddhists, Confucianists and Taoists teach about wisdom and compassion through meditative processes, which primarily aim at reversing self-seeking and cultivating perfect cleanliness of thought and body. Indigenous peoples, through their sacred practices, learn to not only be compassionate to each other but to every single living being within nature and the cosmos.

I believe that the aspect of loving our neighbor and our supreme creator as well as we love ourselves is taught in all religions because it reflects our true nature as human beings. Love brings people together rather than alienating them. However, it is in our nature to do the opposite as well. Alienation has almost always been the cause of one person or an entire nation trying to be superior to another, either because of ethnic differences or religious differences.

Life and Death

Throughout the centuries people of all religious backgrounds have been concerned with life on earth, yet interestingly enough, many religions also share a common view about death and life after death. This view is that death is not the end of life's journey. Our soul and spirit continues to live in the spiritual world.

Australian Aborigines as well as the Far-Eastern religions view life and death as a continual cycle. Australian Aborigines believe that the spirit never dies. It returns to what they call the "spirit place" where the spirit becomes part of the next generation of ancestors preparing for and creating the next generation to come.

Buddhists understand this continuous cycle of life and death through *Karma*—our act of will. According to them every event depends on a cause. Therefore, one changing

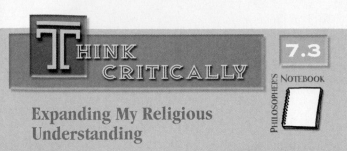

Expanding My Religious Understanding

- Reflect on the religions that we reviewed in this chapter (indigenous, Buddhism, Hinduism, Taoism, Judaism, Christianity, Islam) as well as other religions with which you are familiar. Identify several common themes that you find to be particularly significant.
- Explain as best you can the reasons these themes resonate with you, and describe how these themes might relate to your life. Provide specific examples.

state of being sets another into motion; and when we die this process will continue in life after life—until we reach *Nirvana*.

Taoists view the cycle of life and death simply as phases in which the end resolves in all-embracing continuum. For Confucianists, Heaven is considered far more important than Earth. Heaven is comprised of the ancestors who hold control over the earth's welfare. To keep a continuous relationship between earth and Heaven, the earthly inhabitants are to never stop worshiping their ancestors.

Islam, Judaism and Christianity share similar views of life after death and the difference between Heaven and Hell. Upon death each person will be judged not only according to the good or bad things they have done ethically, but by how faithful that person was to God's laws. Thus, their souls will repair either to Heaven or to Hell. Heaven is commonly described as being the land of boundless fertility, lush fruit and vegetation. Hell, on the other hand, is typically portrayed as being filled with darkness, boiling liquids, and the devil's fire splitting everything into pieces. A sinner in Islam, although placed in Hell, will always have the chance to improve and gradually move to a better stage, and maybe even leave Hell.

Part of the reason death, and life after death, concerns people of all religious backgrounds is, I believe, because it is in our nature to ask such questions about life after death, especially when it concerns our own lives. Many of us naturally fear death, but at the same time feel that death doesn't become the end of our journey. Many believe, including myself, that beyond our earthly world exists another more spiritual realm. What this realm is comprised of has always been difficult to describe in words, and will always depend on one's own religious beliefs.

Learning about other religions has clarified my understanding of religion as a whole, because I now better understand why the different religions formed and how they developed the way they did. I realize that the main goals of each religion are often analogous yet approached differently. Religion still continues to provide a way for us to connect with the spiritual world and with our souls or "true selves." Moreover, it helps many of us to better structure our daily lives and gives us the sense that we have a purpose or certain mission to accomplish in this earthly world. Each religion has enriched my religious beliefs as a whole, as well as my perspective on the world. ∎

Thinking Critically About Religion

Our just-completed survey of some of the great religions of the world has been primarily *descriptive* in nature: trying to get a sense of how each religion approaches spirituality and the religious experience. We now turn our attention to *thinking critically* about religions and the religious experience. What exactly does this mean? Thinking critically about religion entails examining the epistemological foundations for religious beliefs, the cogency and coherence of their metaphysics, the intelligibility and appropriateness of their ethical systems. Thinking critically involves asking—and trying to answer—significant questions about issues that all religions must answer, including

- the validity of religious claims.
- the experience of the holy.
- the relation of religion to everyday life.
- the issues of death, immortality, and human destiny.
- arguments for and against the belief in a supernatural Creator.
- the problem of "evil" in a cosmos created by a perfect Being.
- the relationship of faith and reason.

How Valid Are Religious Claims?

Although religions are woven into the fabric of virtually every culture, this does not necessarily mean that religious claims are valid. In fact, many philosophers have argued that all religions are simply human creations that lack any metaphysical reality. We shall consider two such thinkers in this section—Friedrich Nietzsche and Mary Daly—and later the views of Bertrand Russell.

Friedrich Nietzsche: *God Is Dead*

Friedrich Nietzsche (1844–1900) was a German philosopher whose writings were enigmatic, passionate, poetic, disturbing, inspiring, and open to varied interpretations. He was in many ways an outsider with respect to his culture, his philosophical tradition, and his personal life. At the heart of his philosophy, he glorified the individual self in all of its power and nobility. For Nietzsche, all of life is governed by a primal force, the *will to power* —"the will to grow, spread, seize, become predominant"—that is manifest in all living things. The *will to power* finds its highest expression in humankind in our universal desire to control others and impose our values on them. Thus the ultimate moral good is an individual's striving to exert his or her *will to power* to the fullest possible extent.

This conviction set Nietzsche at odds with the prevailing Christian and Judeo-Christian morality of his time (and to a certain extent, our time as well), which trumpeted the virtues of compassion, self-sacrifice, meekness, humility, pity, dependency, and a denial of self. He found these qualities to be a gross violation and perversion of the natural life principle of *will to power*. For Nietzsche, these traditionally "good" values were in fact contemptible, destructive, and socially toxic. Why? Because these so-called virtues were in fact the product of a conspiracy of the weak and powerless designed to constrain the strong and powerful individuals in a web of moral restrictions. Instead of encouraging individuals to fulfill their glorious potential through the unrestrained expression of their *will to power*, this perverted moral code of the weak and powerless exhorted people to serve and devote themselves to others, particularly the weak and incompetent. For Nietzsche, the pervasive domination of this Christian "slave morality" perpetrated by the decadent, sheeplike herds of resentful weaklings was an evolutionary catastrophe. He was convinced that humans were destined to evolve to higher forms of being, the *ubermensch* (the "overman"), but that this "slave morality"—with its values of humility, self-sacrifice, compassion, and equality—was threatening to weaken the human spirit and prevent the best and strongest individuals from becoming strong and dominant. The Judeo-Christian slave morality represented a moral *de*volution in its rejection of the ancient virtues of nobility and devotion to the growth of self rather than subjugation to others. As he exclaims in his book *Daybreak*:

> How the overall moral judgments have shifted! The great men of antique morality, Epictetus for instance, knew nothing of the now normal glorification of thinking of others, of living for others; in the light of our moral fashion they would have to be called downright immoral, for they strove with all their might *for* their ego and *against* feeling with others (that is to say, with the sufferings and moral frailties of others). Perhaps they would reply to us: "If you are so boring or ugly an object to yourself, by all means think of others more than yourself! It is right you should."

For Nietzsche, the role of the overman is to *create* values, not to conform to the decadent and life-denying values of the slave morality. Ironically, he considered Jesus to be a supreme example of the overman, an individual of great power, influence, and originality. However, he considered the religion and moral system that was based on Jesus' life and teachings to be a distorted version of his true message ("The last Christian died on the cross," he said). Christianity is a religion that warns against the sins of ambition, pride, and domination, precisely those qualities that Nietzsche found to be the purest expression of the *will to power*. He found obscene the Christian concepts of devoting ourselves to God, becoming empty vessels for God's will, pursuing the values of loving our neighbors, and humbly caring for the meek. For Nietzsche, devoting ourselves to God is a wasted effort because, as he declared, "God is dead." Not literally dead, of course: what he meant was that the concept of God as an all-powerful dominant entity was being eroded by modern consciousness, the evolving influence of scientific progress, and the increasing faith in humankind's abilities to solve humankind's problems without divine intervention. In one of the most memorable passages in contemporary philosophy, Nietzsche articulates his prophecy of the death of God in the form of a parable:

> *The madman.*—have you not heard of the madman who lit a lantern in the bright morning hours, ran to the market place, and cried incessantly: "I seek God! I seek God!"—As many of those who did not believe in God were standing around just then, he provoked much laughter. Has he got lost? asked one. Did he lose his way like a child? asked another. Or is he hiding? Is he afraid of us? Has he gone on a voyage? Emigrated?—Thus they yelled and laughed.
>
> The madman jumped into their midst and pierced them with his eyes. "Whither is God?" he cried; "I will tell you. *We have killed him*—you and I. All of us are his murderers. But how did we do this? How could we drink up the sea? Who gave us the sponge to wipe away the entire horizon? What were we doing when we unchained the earth from its sun? Whither is it moving now? Whither are we moving? Away from all suns? Are we not plunging continually? Backward, sideward, forward, in all directions? Is there still any up or down? Are we not straying as through an infinite nothing? Do we not feel the breath of empty space? Has it not become colder? Is not night continually closing in on us? Do we not need to light lanterns in the morning? Do we hear nothing as yet of the noise of the gravediggers who are burying God? Do we smell nothing yet of the divine decomposition? Gods, too, decompose. God is dead. God remains dead. And we have killed him."

The implications of the death of God are profound: no longer can humans depend on a supernatural being to provide purpose to their lives and a moral code to live by. We can no longer consider ourselves "children of God," our supernatural "father," needing his forgiveness to cleanse us of "original sin." Nietzsche believes it is now up to we humans to create meaning in life and a moral code to live by. The brave and fearless overmen welcome this challenge: the weak and insecure "undermen" fear and resist it.

> The greatest recent event—that "God is dead," that the belief in the Christian god has become unbelievable—is already beginning to cast its first shadows. . . . The event itself is far too great, too distant, too remote for the multitude's capacity for comprehension even for the tidings of it to be thought of as having *arrived* as yet. Much less may one suppose that many people know as yet *what* this event really means—and how much must collapse now that (the possibility of) faith has been undermined because it was built upon this faith (in God's existence), propped up by it, grown into it; for example, the whole of our morality.

The weak "doglike" people seek to establish a social order in which everyone is considered equal, whether they are or not. The slave mentality envies and resents these superior individuals. The weak yearn to be like them, but they lack the strength and determination, so they first deny that *anyone* is superior. In his strikingly original narrative, *Thus Spoke Zarathustra*, a combination of prose and poetry "spoken" as a character based on a Persian prophet, Nietzsche give voice to this idea.

> You higher men learn this from me: in the market place nobody believes in higher men. And if you want to speak there, very well! But the mob blinks: "We are all equal." "You higher men"—thus blinks the mob—"there are no higher men, we are all equal, man is man; before God we are all equal."
>
> Before God! But now this God has died. And before the mob we do not want to be equal. You higher men, go away from the market place!

This "marketplace" mentality inhibits individuals' pursuit of excellence, and leads to the creation of a slave morality that is designed to completely submerge the individual in tradition, conformity, and devotion to the "greater good." But because the group is based on fear and insecurity, it is distrustful of outsiders in any form, and it demands unthinking allegiance to the will of the group. Rather than the open, honest and natural expression of each individual's *will to power*, this life-affirming instinct becomes a perverted surrender to the group identity. As he notes in *Towards a Genealogy of Morals*, the individual is lost, a human sacrifice to fear and weakness.

> The slaves' revolt in morals begins with this, that *ressentiment* itself becomes creative and gives birth to values: the *ressentiment* of those who are denied the real reaction, that of the deed, and who compensate with an imaginary revenge. Whereas all noble morality begins out of a triumphant affirmation of oneself, slave morality immediately says No to what comes from outside, to what is different, to what is not oneself: and *this* No is its creative deed. This reversal of the value-positing glance—this *necessary* direction outward instead of back to oneself—is of the nature of *ressentiment*: to come into being, slave morality requires an outside world, a counterworld; physiologically speaking, it requires external stimuli in order to react at all: its action is always at bottom a reaction.

Nietzsche ties together these themes in the following passages from his book, *Beyond Good and Evil*. For Nietzsche, the value-creating *ubermensch* exists "beyond" good and evil: proud, fierce, courageous, bold, independent, glorious, noble. She is the master of morality, not its victim. She has been able to overcome her own doubts and weaknesses, vanquishing obstacles in the path to full development as an individual.

Nietzshe,
Beyond Good and Evil

Refraining mutually from injury, violence, and exploitation and placing one's will on a par with that of someone else—this may become, in a certain rough sense, good manners among individuals if the appropriate conditions are present (namely, if these men are actually similar in strength and value standards and belong together in *one* body). But as soon as this principle is extended, and possibly even accepted as the *fundamental principle of society*, it immediately proves to be what it really is—a will to the *denial* of life, a principle of disintegration and decay.

Here we must beware of superficiality and get to the bottom of the matter, resisting all sentimental weakness: life itself is *essentially* appropriation, injury, overpowering of what is alien and weaker; suppression, hardness, imposition of one's own forms, incorporation and at least, at its mildest, exploitation—but why should one always use those words in which a slanderous intent has been imprinted for ages?

Even the body within which individuals treat each other as equals, as suggested before—and this happens in every healthy aristocracy—if it is a living and not a dying body, has to do to other bodies what the individuals within it refrain from doing to each other: it will have to be an incarnate will to power, it will strive to grow, spread, seize, become predominant—not from any morality or immorality but because it is *living* and because life simply *is* will to power. But there is no point on which the ordinary consciousness of Europeans resists instruction as on this: everywhere people are now raving, even under scientific disguises, about coming conditions of society in which "the exploitative aspect" will be removed—which sounds to me as if they promised to invent a way of life that would dispense with all organic functions. "Exploitation" does not belong to a corrupt or imperfect and primitive society: it belongs to the *essence* of what lives, as a basic organic function; it is a consequence of the will to power, which is after all the will of life.

If this should be an innovation as a theory—as a reality it is the *primordial fact* of all history: people ought to be honest with themselves at least that far. ▪

For Nietzsche, the cardinal Christian values of refraining from injury, violence, and exploitation are not intrinsically negative—among superior individuals they may actually be viewed as "good manners." The problem comes when these values are elevated to a universal status, dominating the relations between all people—weak and strong—in all circumstances. When universalized, these values of compassion, kindness, and empathy have the cumulative effect of denying life and the fundamental principle that powers all life—the *will to power*. Although conventional society condemns "exploitation" as an evil, Nietzsche views it a necessary consequence of the *will to power* that is essential for the survival of the species. Evolutionary development is based on strong individuals making full use of their powers, unconstrained by a false and corrosive belief in equality.

THINK PHILOSOPHICALLY 7.4
Analyzing Friedrich Nietzsche

PHILOSOPHER'S NOTEBOOK

- Nietzsche grounds his religious and moral philosophy on what he considers to be a basic principle found at the core of life—"an incarnate will to power, it will strive to grow, spread, seize, become predominant—not from any morality or immorality but because it is *living* and because life simply *is* will to power." Do you agree with this characterization of a basic life force? Why or why not?

- What does Nietzsche mean by his arresting pronouncement that "God is dead"? What are his reasons for coming to this conclusion?

- Exploitation and domination are natural consequences of the *will to power*, according to Nietzsche. Rather than see them as "immoral" we should recognize them as essential attributes of the strong and noble individual. Critically evaluate this view and provide an example of your perspective.

- Because the majority of individuals are weak, insecure, and lacking in determination, Nietzsche believes that they conspire to create a system of values to drag down superior individuals and keep them in check. Have you ever personally experienced a situation in which you distinguished yourself in some way, only to find yourself the target of envy and criticism from others? If so, does this experience support Nietzsche's thesis regarding the "slave morality"?

- What are the implications of Nietzsche's views? In other words, suppose the majority of individuals took his exhortations to heart and became superior "overmen," seeking to dominate and exploit those around them. What would be the result?

MARY DALY

(1928–)
Feminist Theologian and Philosopher. Accuses structures of society, from the Church to Christianity and culture itself, as embodying and engendering misogyny and patriarchy.

Mary Daly: *Patriarchal Religion Is Destructive*

Many feminists believe that the major religions of the world express the sexist perspectives of the men who created them, and that these perspectives have helped create sexist societies in which women are consistently discriminated against and exploited. **Mary Daly** is a leading feminist philosopher who gives a passionate and powerful voice to this view. From her perspective, all societies and their institutions are "patriarchal"—that is, they are structured around the archetype of the "father," who symbolizes the ultimate power and authority. Women are required to find their place within this male-dominated perspective, and it generally leaves them with less power, less status, and often in the role of victims. For Daly, virtually all religions are simply expressions of this patriarchal reality and the only way for women to effect meaningful change is to revolutionize the entire social/political system, including perspectives on religion. Anything less may simply lead to reforms and modifications, but will not change the structure and character of the patriarchal system. Daly expands on these themes in her article, "The Leap Beyond Patriarchal Religion."

Mary Daly,
*The Leap Beyond
Patriarchal Religion*

Radical feminism, the becoming of women, is very much an Otherworld Journey. It is both discovery and creation of a world other than patriarchy. Some observation reveals that patriarchy is "everywhere." Even outer space and the future have been colonized. As a rule, even the more imaginative science fiction writers (seemingly the most foretelling futurists) cannot/will not create a space and time in which women get far beyond the role of space stewardess. Nor does this situation exist simply "outside" women's minds, securely fastened into institutions which we can physically leave behind. Rather, it is also internalized, festering inside women's heads, even feminist heads.

The journey of women *becoming*, then, involves exorcism of the internalized Godfather, in his various manifestations (His name is legion). It involves dangerous encounter with these demons. Within the Christian tradition, particularly in medieval times, evil spirits have sometimes been associated with the Seven Deadly Sins, both as personifications and as causes. A "standard" and prevalent listing of the Sins is, of course, the following: pride, avarice, anger, lust, gluttony, envy, and sloth. I am contending that these have all been radically misnamed, that is, inadequately and even perversely "understood" within Christianity. These concepts have been used to victimize the oppressed, particularly women. They are particularized expressions of the overall use of "evil" to victimize women. The feminist journey involves confrontations with the demonic distortions of evil.

Why has it seemed "appropriate" in this culture that a popular book and film (*The Exorcist*) center around a Jesuit who "exorcises" a girl-child who is "possessed"? Why is there no book or film about a woman who exorcises a Jesuit? Within a culture possessed by the myth of feminine evil, the naming, describing, and theorizing about good and evil has constituted a web of deception, a Maya. The journey of women becoming is breaking through this web—a Fall into free space. It is reassuming the role of subject, as opposed to object, and naming good and evil on the basis of our own intuitive intellection. . . .

Wanted: "God" or "The Goddess"?

For some feminists concerned with the spiritual depth of the movement, the word "God" is becoming increasingly problematic. . . . This by no means indicates a movement in the direction of "atheism" or "agnosticism" or "secularism," as these terms are usually understood. Rather, the problem arises precisely because of the spiritual and mythic quality perceived in the feminist process itself. Some use expressions such as "power of being." Some reluctantly still use the word "God" while earnestly trying to divest the term of its patriarchal associations, attempting to think perhaps of the "God of the philosophers" rather than the overtly masculist and oppressive "God of the theologians." But the problem becomes increasingly troublesome, the more the "God" of the various Western philosophers is subjected to feminist analysis. "He"—"Jahweh"—still often hovers behind the abstractions, stunting our own thought, giving us a sense of contrived doublethink. The word "God" just may be inherently oppressive.

Indeed, the word "Goddess" has also been problematic, but for different reasons. Some have been worried about the problem of "crossing." *(Note: The author defines "crossing" as "a notable tendency among oppressed groups to attempt to change or adapt the ideological tools of the oppressor, so that they can be used against him and for the oppressed.")* However, that difficulty appears more and more as a pseudo-difficulty

Venus, Roman Goddess of love and beauty

when it is recognized that "crossing" is likely to occur only when one is trying to work *within* a sexist tradition. For example, Christian women who in their "feminist liturgies" experiment with referring to "God" as "she" and to the Trinity as "The Mother, the Daughter, and the Holy Spirit," are still working within all the boundaries of the same symbolic framework and the same power structure. Significantly, their services are at the same place and time as "the usual," and are regarded by most of the constituency of the churches as occasional variations of "business as usual."

As women who are outside the Christian church inform ourselves of evidence supporting the existence of ancient matriarchy and of evidence indicating that the Gods of patriarchy are indeed contrived, pale derivatives and reversals of the Great Goddess of an earlier period, the fear of mere "crossing" appears less appropriate and perhaps even absurd. There is also less credibility allowable to the notion that "Goddess" would function like "God" in reverse, that is, to legitimate an oppressive "female-dominated" society, if one is inclined to look seriously at evidence that matriarchal society was not structured like patriarchy, that it was non-hierarchical. . . .

THINK PHILOSOPHICALLY 7.5
Analyzing Mary Daly

In the "Prolegomena" (an essay that introduces a longer work) to her article, Daly makes 23 statements that are not in the form of a traditional philosophical argument: instead they are more reminiscent (in a *very* different context) of Martin Luther nailing his 95 Theses against the Catholic Church to the cathedral door in 1517 at Worms in Germany. Daly doesn't simply want to make academic points—she wants people to sit up and take notice, to feel her passion and anger, to take action. Included below are several of her central points. In each case think critically about the point being made by providing reasons and examples to support both a "pro" and a "con" view of the statement.

6. The myths and symbols of Christianity are essentially sexist. Since "God" is male, the male is God. God the Father legitimates all earthly Godfathers, including Vito Corleone, Pope Paul, President Gerald Ford, the Godfathers of medicine (e.g. the American Medical Association), of science (e.g. NASA), of the media, of psychiatry, of education, and of all the "ologies".

7. The myth of feminine evil, expressed in the story of the Fall, is reinforced by the myth of salvation/redemption by a single human being of the male sex. The idea of a unique divining incarnation in a male, the God-man of the "hypostatic union," is inherently sexist and oppressive. Christology is idolatry.

11. There is an inherent dynamic in the women's revolution in Judeo-Christian society which is Antichurch, whether or not feminists specifically concern ourselves with churches. This is so because the Judeo-Christian tradition legitimates patriarchy—the prevailing power structure and prevailing world view—which the women's revolution leaves behind.

16. Since Christian myths are inherently sexist, and since the women's revolution is not about "equality" but about power, there is an intrinsic dynamic in the feminist movement which goes beyond efforts to reform Christian churches. Such efforts eventually come to be recognized as comparable to a Black person's trying to reform the Ku Klux Klan.

20. The women's movement is a new mode of relating to the self, to each other, to men, to the environment—in a word—to the cosmos. It is self-affirming, refusing objectification of the self and of the other.

22. Entrance into radical feminist consciousness involves recognition that all male-dominated "revolutions," which do not reject the universally oppressive reality which is patriarchy, are in reality only reforms. They are "revolutions" only in the sense that they are spinnings of the wheels of the same senescent system.

Clearly, it would be inappropriate and arrogant to try to "explain" or "interpret" this experience of another person. I can only comment that many women I know are finding power of being within the self, rather than in "internalized" father images. As a philosopher, my preference has been for abstractions. Indeed I have always been annoyed and rather embarrassed by "anthropomorphic" symbols, preferring terms such as "ground and power of being" (Tillich), "beyond subjectivity and objectivity" (James), "the Encompassing" (Jaspers), or the commonly used "Ultimate Reality," or "cosmic process." More recently I have used the expression "Intransitive Verb." Despite this philosophical inclination, and also because of it, I find it impossible to ignore the realm of symbols, or to fail to recognize that many women are experiencing and participating in a remythologizing process, which is a new dawn. ■

The Experience of the Holy

The goal of many religions is to achieve some kind of ultimate transformation through a direct encounter with the holy, divine, sacred, or transcendent spiritual reality. This type of direct encounter can take a variety of forms, mirroring the varieties of religious experience. But the most intense form of encounter is *mystical* in nature. Virtually every religion has at least one dimension of it that aspires to a personal encounter with the holy through a mystical experience, including

- *Indigenous religions:* the spiritual encounters of *shamans*, priests, and priestesses with the spirit world
- *Hinduism:* the goal of attaining spiritual realization through yogic practices and meditation
- *Buddhism:* the quest for transcending the self and ultimately achieving Nirvana through "right meditation" and other steps in the Eightfold Path
- *Taoism:* the goal of becoming intimately attuned to the natural energies of the cosmos through meditation and *wu-wei*
- *Judaism:* the mystical traditions of the *Kabbalah*
- *Christianity:* the goal of "communal mysticism" in which God, Jesus, or the Holy Spirit enters your self and transforms you
- *Islam:* the mystical traditions of the Sufis who use asceticism, fasting, and dancing to achieve unity of being

Although such mystical experiences are intensely personal, participants generally claim to have experienced a loss of self-identity, a merging with the holy, a transcendence of space and time, a spiritual impact that changes them in profound ways.

The following essay entitled "Mysticism" by the philosopher and psychologist **William James** is taken from his influential book *The Varieties of Religious Experience* (1902), and it explores some of the core elements of mystical experiences. James begins by defining precisely what he means by the term *mysticism*, identifying what he considers to be four defining qualities—"marks"—of "mystical states of consciousness."

WILLIAM JAMES
(1842–1910)
American Pragmatist. With C.S. Pierce, founded the philosophy of Pragmatism. Also contributed much to the psychology of religion in *The Varieties of Religious Experience* (1902).

William James, Mysticism, *The Varieties of Religious Experience*

What does the expression "mystical states of consciousness" mean? How do we part off mystical states from other states?

The words "mysticism" and "mystical" are often used as terms of mere reproach, to throw at any opinion which we regard as vague and vast and sentimental, and without a base in either facts or logic. For some writers a mystic is any person who believes in thought-transference, or spirit-return. Employed in this way, the word has little value: there are too many less ambiguous synonyms. So, to keep it useful by

William James

restricting, I will . . . propose to you four marks which, when an experience has them, may justify us in calling it mystical. . . . In this way we shall save verbal disputation, and the recriminations that generally go therewith.

- *Ineffability.*—The handiest of the marks by which I classify a state of mind as mystical is negative. The subject of it immediately says that it defies expression, that no adequate report of its contents can be given in words. It follows from this that its quality must be directly experienced; it cannot be imparted or transferred to others. In this peculiarity mystical states are more like states of feeling than like states of intellect. No one can make clear to another who has never had a certain feeling, in what the quality or worth of it consists. One must have musical ears to know the value of a symphony; one must have been in love one's self to understand a lover's state of mind. Lacking the heart or ear, we cannot interpret the musician or the lover justly, and are even likely to consider him weak-minded or absurd. The mystic finds that most of us accord to his experience an equally incompetent treatment.

- *Noetic quality.*—Although so similar to states of feeling, mystical states seem to those who experience them to be also states of knowledge. They are states of insight into depths of truth unplumbed by the discursive intellect. They are illuminations, revelations, full of significance and importance, all inarticulate though they remain; and as a rule they carry with them a curious sense of authority for after-time.

- *Transiency.*—Mystical states cannot be sustained for long. Except in rare instances, half an hour, or at most an hour or two, seems to be the limit beyond which they fade into the light of common day. Often, when faded, their quality can but imperfectly be reproduced in memory; but when they recur it is recognized; and from one recurrence to another it is susceptible of continuous development in what is felt as inner richness and importance.

- *Passivity.*—Although the oncoming of mystical states may be facilitated by preliminary voluntary operations, as by fixing the attention, or going through certain bodily performances, or in other ways which manuals of mysticism prescribe; yet when the characteristic sort of consciousness once has set in, the mystic feels as if his own will were in abeyance, and indeed sometimes as if he were grasped and held by a superior power. Mystical states, strictly so called, are never merely interruptive. Some memory of their content always remains, and a profound sense of their importance. They modify the inner life of the subject between the times of their recurrence.

These four characteristics are sufficient to mark out a group of states of consciousness peculiar enough to deserve a special name and to call for careful study. Let it then be called the mystical group.

What is remarkable about James's definition of "mystical states of consciousness" is its blending of rational analysis and nonrational ways of knowing. Thus he compares the mystical experience to that of being in love or the aesthetic appreciation of music: one needs to "directly experience" all of these phenomena to understand their true qualities. No amount of rational analysis or explication will be an adequate substitute.

At the same time, James wants us to use our rational faculties to map out the topography of mysticism, revealing the fundamental contours and landmarks, so that we can discuss the concept of "mystical states of consciousness" intelligently. Hence his descriptive criteria: ineffability, **noetic** quality, transiency, and passivity. For James, we can use these benchmarks to distinguish mystical states from non-mystical states, and they also provide us with a general sense of the qualities of mystical experience. Of course, the only way to fully appreciate "mystical states of consciousness" is to have the direct experience of them. James then goes on to critically evaluate the credibility, authenticity, and "warrant for truth" of mystical states.

Noetic Pertaining to the intellect or mind.

William James,
The Varieties of Religious Experience, Mysticism

My next task is to inquire whether we can invoke (mystical experience) as authoritative. Does it furnish any *warrant for the truth* of the twice-borness and supernaturality and pantheism which it favors? I must give my answer to this question as concisely as I can.

In brief my answer is this—and I will divide it into three parts:—

- Mystical states, when well developed, usually are, and have the right to be, absolutely authoritative over the individuals to whom they come.

- No authority emanates from them which should make it a duty for those who stand outside of them to accept their revelations uncritically.

- They break down the authority of the non-mystical or rationalistic consciousness, based upon the understanding and the senses alone. They show it to be only one kind of consciousness. They open out the possibility of other orders of truth, in which, so far as anything in us vitally responds to them we may freely continue to have faith.

I will take up these points one by one.

- As a matter of psychological fact, mystical states of a well-pronounced and emphatic sort *are* usually authoritative over those who have them. They have been "there," and know. It is vain for rationalism to grumble about this. If the mystical truth that comes to a man proves to be a force that he can live by, what mandate have we of the majority to order him to live in another way? We can throw him into a prison or a madhouse, but we cannot change his mind—we commonly attach it only the more stubbornly to its beliefs. It mocks our utmost efforts, as a matter of fact, and in point of logic it absolutely escapes our jurisdiction. Our own more "rational beliefs" are based on evidence exactly similar in nature to that which mystics quote for theirs. Our senses, namely, have assured us of certain states of fact, but mystical experiences are as direct perceptions of fact for those who have them as any sensations ever were for us. The records show that even though the five senses be in abeyance in them, they are absolutely sensational in their epistemological quality, if I may be pardoned the barbarous expression,—that is, they are face to face presentations of what seems immediately to exist.

    The mystic is, in short, *invulnerable*, and must be left, whether we relish it or not, in undisturbed enjoyment of his creed. Faith, says Tolstoy, is that by which men live. And faith-state and mystic state are practically convertible terms.

- But I now proceed to add that mystics have no right to claim that we ought to accept the deliverance of their peculiar experiences, if we are ourselves outsiders and feel no private call thereto. The utmost they can ever ask of us in this life is to admit that they establish a presumption. They form a consensus and have an unequivocal outcome; and it would be odd, mystics might say, if such a unanimous type of experience should prove to be altogether wrong. At bottom, however, this would only be an appeal to numbers, like the appeal of rationalism the other way; and the appeal to numbers has no logical force. If we acknowledge it, it is for "suggestive," not for logical reasons: we follow the majority because to do so suits our life.

    But even this presumption from the unanimity of mystics is far from being strong . . . the classic religious mysticism, it now must be confessed, is only a "privileged case." It is an *extract*, kept true to type by the selection of the fittest specimens and their preservation in "schools." It is carved out from a much larger mass: and if we take the larger mass as seriously as religious mysticism has historically taken itself, we find that the supposed unanimity largely disappears. . . .

    Once more, then, I repeat that non-mystics are under no obligation to acknowledge in mystical states a superior authority conferred on them by their intrinsic nature.

- Yet, I repeat once more, the existence of mystical states absolutely overthrows the pretension of non-mystical states to be the sole and ultimate dictators of what we may believe. As a rule, mystical states merely add a supersensuous meaning to the ordinary outward data of consciousness. They are excitements like the emotions of love or ambition, gifts to our spirit by means of which facts already objectively before us fall into a new expressiveness and make a new connection with our active life. They do not contradict these facts as such, or deny anything that our senses have immediately seized. It is the rationalistic critic rather who plays the part of denier in the controversy, and his denials have no strength, for there never can be a state of facts to which new meaning may not truthfully be added, provided the mind ascend to a more enveloping point of view. It must always remain an open question whether mystical states may not possibly be such superior points of view, windows through which the mind looks out upon a more extensive and inclusive world. The difference of the views seen from the

Morocco, woman performing a Guedra, a Tuareg Blessing dance

different mystical windows need not prevent us from entertaining the supposition. The wider world would in that case prove to have a mixed constitution like that of this world, that is all. It would have its celestial and its infernal regions, its tempting and its saving moments, its valid experiences and its counterfeit ones, just as our world has them; but it would be a wider world all the same. We should have to use its experiences by selecting and subordinating and substituting just as is our custom in this ordinary naturalistic world; we should be liable to error just as we are now; yet the counting in of that wider world of meanings, and the serious dealing with it, might in spite of all the perplexity, be indispensable stages in our approach to the final fullness of truth. ▪

James, William, *Mysticism*

THINK PHILOSOPHICALLY
Analyzing William James

7.6

PHILOSOPHER'S NOTEBOOK

- Have you ever had a "mystical experience," religious or otherwise? If so, did it meet the four "marks" that James identifies?

- In attempting to assess the "warrant for truth" of mystical states, James concludes that, "Mystical states, when well developed, usually are, and have the right to be, absolutely authoritative over the individuals to whom they come." In other words, as outsiders, we should presume the authenticity of mystical claims of others, and not try to denigrate or undermine their legitimacy. Do you agree with this point? Why or why not?

- Although James believes that we should acknowledge the potential authenticity of mystical states, we are under no obligation to "accept their revelations uncritically." In other words, we still have a responsibility to think philosophically about the mystical claims of others, even while recognizing the reality of these experiences for those having them. Does this point make sense to you? Why or why not?

- James's final point is his most important, from an epistemological standpoint. By accepting the potential authenticity of mystical experiences, we are acknowledging that there are epistemologically legitimate states of consciousness other than the "rationalistic, non-mystical" state, and that this recognition opens out "the possibility of other orders of truth, in which, so far as anything in us vitally responds to them we may freely continue to have faith." And by including mystical states in our worldview, James believes that we create a vision of a wider, more inclusive world. What is your evaluation of James's view? What other authentic "states of consciousness" might you include in the world in addition to "rationalistic states" and "mystical states"?

ST. THOMAS AQUINAS
(1225–1279)
Medieval Philosopher/Theologian. Heavily influenced by both Aristotle and the Catholic Church. Sought to synthesize philosophy and theology and offered detailed and systematic works on the nature of man, God, and the universe.

St. Augustine (354–430) Christian Philosopher. Unparalleled influence on Christian philosophy and theology in Middle Ages. Augustine's work covered many areas such as philosophy of language, philosophy of mind, and the philosophy of religion.

St. Anselm (1033–1109) Philosopher of Religion. In his most famous work the *Prosolgion* attempts to prove the existence and certain attributes of God, most notably that God is something than which nothing greater can be thought.

Origen (c. 185–c.254) Christian Philosopher. Wrote commentaries on Scripture and believed they could be understood in three ways: literally, morally, and spiritually.

Ways of Seeking Spiritual Enlightenment

The search for ultimate spiritual reality can take an astonishing variety of forms, as we have seen. Yet we can also group these quests for spiritual enlightenment into several broad categories. One such category is that of *direct spiritual encounter* or *personal experience*, which we explored in considering William James's essay on mysticism, as well as in our overview of religions earlier in the chapter. Those who experience such direct spiritual encounters report them to be powerful and transformational, with a sublime intensity that transcends any literal description. For participants, these forms of spiritual experience provide a compelling rationale for their particular religious commitment.

A second category of spiritual quest involves using the human *faculty of reason* to discern religious truths. This was the position of many of the great medieval thinkers such as **Thomas Aquinas**, **St. Augustine**, **St. Anselm**, and **Origen**. As we saw in Aquinas's natural law ethic (in chapter 5), such a perspective assumes that God (in the sense of some ultimate spiritual reality or Creator) imbued humans with the "spark of reason," a divine attribute that enables us to achieve authentic spiritual insight through the thoughtful, reflective application of our rational capacities. For example, in addition to the natural law ethic that Aquinas believed to be discoverable through reason, he also believed that we could establish the existence of God through rational "proofs." In addition, many religions cite actual occurrences in the world that, using our reasoning capabilities, we can interpret to be evidence for God's existence or purpose. These "revelations" of God include the lives of spiritual figures (Abraham, Jesus, Muhammad, Buddha), holy books that are believed to be divinely inspired (such as the Bible, the Qur'an, the Rig Veda) "mighty acts of God," miracles, and prophecies.

A third form of quest for spiritual enlightenment involves *religious faith*, a personal commitment that people make to a religious belief, even though conclusive proof or evidence is lacking. The concept of religious faith is complex, and we shall explore some of its dimensions in the section immediately following this one.

Seeking Spirituality Through Reason: *"Proofs" for God*

Among the various "proofs" for the existence of God through the centuries, the most popular and enduring are *cosmological* arguments. The ancient Greeks were the first to refer to the world as a *cosmos*, an ordered system that contrasts with a disordered, random *chaos*. The insight that the universe is a coherent, intelligible whole, governed by orderly principles and knowable through rational inquiry, constituted a tremendous leap forward in Western thought. For many of the Greeks, the ultimate governing principle of the universe was *Logos*, the cosmic Reason or Intelligence that stood behind, governed, and permeated all aspects of the world. But for the Greeks, *Logos* was not typically conceived of as a personal God or Creator. That particular connection was made by medieval thinkers such as Augustine and Aquinas, who integrated the Greek metaphysic with Christian theology. And it was this unique intellectual marriage that gave rise to a number of the prominent arguments for God's existence. We shall examine three such "cosmological" arguments, so termed because they each take as their starting point the orderly, coherent, intelligible nature of the cosmos.

The first cosmological argument that we shall consider is the *argument from contingency*, which in the broadest sense means "dependency." The logic of this argument goes something like this: when we examine the universe we see that everything that exists and occurs is dependent on something else. However, for the universe to exist as it does, there must be some ultimate reality that is necessary, not contingent. This ultimate reality is God. Aquinas provides, in the following passage from his towering work, *Summa Theologica*, three different formulations of this argument involving the concepts of motion, causality, and contingency (he subsequently provides two additional proofs for God's existence, bringing the total to five proofs).

Cosmological Arguments for God

- Arguments from contingency
  Argument from motion
  Argument from causality
  Argument from contingency/possibility
- Argument from perfection
- Argument from design
- Argument from moral choice
- Argument from moral justice

VISUAL PHILOSOPHY

Creation of the World

Some people believe that God's existence can be established by one or more "proofs," while others believe that God's existence can never be proved as a scientific fact. How would you evaluate the following traditional proofs for God's existence?

Thomas Aquinas,
Summa Theologica

The existence of God can be shown in five ways.

The first and more manifest way is the argument from motion. It is certain, and evident to our senses, that in the world some things are in motion. Now whatever is in motion is put in motion by another, for nothing can be in motion except it is in potentiality to that towards which it is in motion; whereas a thing moves inasmuch as it is in act. For motion is nothing else than the reduction of something from potentiality to actuality. But nothing can be reduced from potentiality to actuality, except by something in a state of actuality. Thus that which is actually hot, as fire, makes wood, which is potentially hot, to be actually hot, and thereby moves and changes it. Now it is not possible that the same thing should be at once in actuality and potentiality in the same respect, but only in different respects. For what is actually hot cannot simultaneously be potentially hot; but it is simultaneously potentially cold. It is therefore impossible that in the same respect and in the same way a thing should be both mover and moved, i.e. that it should move itself. Therefore, whatever is in motion must be put in motion by another. If that by which it is put in motion be itself put in motion, then this also must needs be put in motion by another, and that by another again. But this cannot go on to infinity, because then there would be no first mover, and, consequently, no other mover; seeing that subsequent movers move only inasmuch as they are put in motion by the first mover; as the staff moves only because it is put in motion by the hand. Therefore it is necessary to arrive at a first mover, put in motion by no other; and this everyone understands to be God.

The logic of this argument is straightforward: when we examine the universe, we observe that, as Heraclitus noted, "All is change," as everything is continually moving, evolving, changing. Each state of change is the result of a prior state, which is the result of a prior state, and so on. It is rational for us to assume (the proof argues) that at some point, there is an ultimate, unchanging source of all change: that source is God.

The second argument mirrors the first, substituting the concept of "causation" for "motion."

The second way is from the nature of the efficient cause. In the world of sense we find there is an order of efficient causes. There is no case known (neither is it, indeed, possible) in which a thing is found to be the efficient cause of itself; for so it would be prior to itself, which is impossible. Now in efficient causes it is not possible to go on to infinity, because in all efficient causes following in order, the first is the cause of the intermediate cause, and the intermediate is the cause of the ultimate cause, whether the intermediate cause be several, or only one. Now to take away the cause is to take away the effect. Therefore, if there be no first cause among efficient causes, there will be no ultimate, nor any intermediate cause. But if in efficient causes it is possible to go on to infinity, there will be no first efficient cause, neither will there be an ultimate effect, nor any intermediate efficient causes; all of which is plainly false. Therefore it is necessary to admit a first efficient cause, to which everyone gives the name of God.

Thomas Aquinas,
Summa Theologica

Both of these arguments rest on Aquinas's assumption that there must be an unchanging source of change or a "first cause" of all causal events because the alternative would be an "infinite regress," which is metaphysically and epistemologically unacceptable. Our understanding *demands* that there be a beginning point whether it's an unchanging source of change or a "first cause" of all causal events. But is this necessarily so? Why can't we simply accept that the universe is eternal, that things have been moving and that causal events have been occurring forever? And even if we *do* accept the necessity of an unchanging source of change or a "first cause" of the universe's existence, why must we assume that such a beginning point is "God"? Perhaps it was simply some impersonal principle or phenomena at the origin of things, something beyond our limited ability to comprehend—other than "God."

Another objection that has been raised against the "first cause" argument is that its conclusion ("Therefore God must be the First Cause") is contradicted by it's premise ("Every event must be caused"). As Bertrand Russell expresses it in his essay "Why I Am Not a Christian" that begins on page 391, "If everything must have a cause, then God must have a cause. If there can be anything without a cause, it may just as well be the world as God, so there cannot be any validity in that argument."

The third argument of Aquinas is slightly more complex. Everything in the universe appears to be contingent, a possibility. But if something is *possible*, it means that it is not *necessary* that it exist. It might just as easily have *not* existed, and in fact, at one point it didn't exist. But if everything in the universe is only possible, and not necessary, then at some point everything in the universe would not have existed, because that is what it means to be "possible"—not existing at some point. But because the universe *does* exist, it's rational to assume (according to the proof) that there is a Being that is a necessary (not merely contingent) Being that does not depend on anything else for its existence. That Being is God. However, this argument is going to be vulnerable to the same objections we noted have been raised against the first two arguments.

The third way is taken from possibility and necessity, and runs thus. We find in nature things that are possible to be and not to be, since they are found to be generated, and to corrupt, and consequently, they are possible to be and not to be. But it is impossible for these always to exist, for that which is possible not to be at some time is not. Therefore, if everything is possible not to be, then at one time there could have been nothing in existence. Now if this were true, even now there would be nothing in existence, because that which does not exist only begins to exist by something already existing. Therefore, if at one time nothing was in existence, it would have been impossible for anything to

Thomas Aquinas,
Summa Theologica

have begun to exist; and thus even now nothing would be in existence—which is absurd. Therefore, not all beings are merely possible, but there must exist something the existence of which is necessary. But every necessary thing either has its necessity caused by another, or not. Now it is impossible to go on to infinity in necessary things which have their necessity caused by another, as has been already proved in regard to efficient causes. Therefore we cannot but postulate the existence of some being having of itself its own necessity, and not receiving it from another, but rather causing in others their necessity. This all men speak of as God.

Aquinas's fourth argument is even more problematic because it is based on accepting a Platonic metaphysic, a metaphysic that many philosophers have rejected over the centuries for reasons we will explore in chapter 8, "What Is Real? What Is True?" Aquinas argues that everything that we encounter in life is, to a greater or lesser extent, a particular example of some eternal form. Thus things that we describe as "true," "good," and "noble" are simply imperfect representations of the eternal forms of "truth," "goodness," and "nobility," which cause them to have these qualities. In the same way, there must exist a being that is the ultimate cause of all such good and perfect qualities, and this being is God.

Thomas Aquinas,
Summa Theologica

The fourth way is taken from the gradation to be found in things. Among beings there are some more and some less good, true, noble, and the like. But "more" and "less" are predicted of different things, according as they resemble in their different ways something which is in the degree of "most," as a thing is said to be hotter according as it more nearly resembles that which is hottest; so that there is something which is uttermost being; for the truer things are, the more truly they exist. What is most complete in any genus is the cause of all in that genus; as fire, which is the most complete form of heat, is the cause whereby all things are made hot. Therefore there must also be something which is to all beings the cause of their being, goodness and every other perfection; and this we call God.

Aquinas's fifth argument introduces the second major type of cosmological arguments, the *argument from design*. This argument begins with the observation that the universe is orderly and apparently purposeful or *teleological* (from the Greek *telos*, meaning purpose or end). It is rational to assume (according to this proof) that this order and purposefulness did not simply happen by accident, but is the product of an intelligent Creator: namely, God.

Thomas Aquinas,
Summa Theologica

The fifth way is taken from the governance of the world. We see that things which lack intelligence, such as natural bodies, act for an end, and this is evident from their acting always, or nearly always, in the same way, so as to obtain the best result. Hence it is plain that not fortuitously, but designedly, do they achieve their end. Now whatever lacks intelligence cannot move towards an end, unless it be directed by some being endowed with knowledge and intelligence; as the arrow is shot to its mark by the archer. Therefore some intelligent being exists by whom all natural things are directed to their end; and this being we call God. ■

Aquinas, Thomas, *Summa Theologica*

The design argument was further developed and refined almost six hundred years later by the theologian **William Paley** (1743–1805), who begins his analysis with a vivid image.

William Paley,
Natural Theology

In crossing a heath, suppose I pitched my foot against a *stone*, and were asked how the stone came to be there; I might possibly answer, that, for any thing I knew to the contrary, it had lain there for ever: nor would it perhaps be very easy to show the absurdity of this answer. But suppose I had found a *watch* upon the ground, and it should be inquired how the watch happened to be in that place; I should hardly think of the answer which I had before given, that, for any thing I knew, the watch might have always been there. Yet why should not this answer serve for the watch as well as for the stone? why is it not as admissible in the second case, as in the first? For this reason, and for no other, viz. that, when we come to inspect the watch, we perceive (what we could not discover in the stone) that its several parts are framed and put together for a purpose, *e.g.* that they are so formed and adjusted as to produce motion, and that motion so regulated as to point out the hour of the day; that, if the different parts had been differently shaped from what they are, of a different size from what they are, or placed after any other manner, or in any other order, than that in which they are placed, either no motion at all would have been carried on in the machine, or none which would have answered the use that is now served by it. To reckon up a few of the plainest of these parts, and of their offices, all tending to one result:—We see a cylindrical box containing a coiled elastic spring, which, by its endeavour to relax itself, turns round the box. We next observe a flexible chain (artificially wrought for the sake of flexure), communicating the action of the spring from the box to the fusee. We then find a series of wheels, the teeth of which catch in, and apply to, each other, conducting the motion from the fusee to the balance, and from the balance to the pointer; and at the same time, by the size and shape of those wheels, so regulating that motion, as to terminate in causing an index, by an equable and measured progression, to pass over a given space in a given time. We take notice that the wheels are made of brass in order to keep them from rust; the springs of steel, no other metal being so elastic; that over the face of the watch there is placed a glass, a material employed in no other part of the work, but in the room of which, if there had been any other than a transparent substance, the hour could not be seen without opening the case. This mechanism being observed (it requires indeed an examination of the instrument, and perhaps some previous knowledge of the subject, to perceive and understand it; but being once, as we have said, observed and understood), the inference, we think, is inevitable, that the watch must have had a maker: that there must have existed, at some time, and at some place or other, an artificer or artificers who formed it for the purpose which we find it actually to answer; who comprehended its construction, and designed its use. ◼

 Paley, William,
The Teleological Argument

Although some thinkers have found the design argument to be persuasive, others have raised objections. To begin with, can't we accept the fact that there is a certain *order* in the universe without concluding that this order is the result of *intelligent design*? Perhaps the order that we see simply evolved randomly, or perhaps the universe is governed by certain impersonal principles (such as the ancient Greek concept of *Logos*) that are expressed in the orderliness of the universe that we perceive. Neither possibility entails that we accept the existence of "God" as a supernatural creator or designer. Some thinkers have argued that the universe is actually *poorly* designed, with many elements that don't work as well as they could have if an intelligent designer had created them. Or as Bertrand Russell expresses it in "Why I Am Not a Christian,"

> When you come to look into this argument from design, it is a most astonishing thing that people can believe that this world, with all the things that are in it, with all its defects, should be the best that omnipotence and omniscience have been able to produce in millions of years. I really cannot believe it. Do you think that, if you were granted omnipotence and omniscience and millions of years in which to perfect your world, you could produce nothing better that the Ku Klux Klan or the Fascists?

A third version of the cosmological argument is the *argument from morality*. It takes as its beginning point the reality of the deeply ingrained sense of morality that humans possess, and reasons that the most rational way to account for this moral sense is to assume the existence of a supremely moral mind—namely, God. This argument can be focused in a number of different ways. Natural law ethicists see a broad agreement among the major ethical systems of the world, embodied in writings as diverse as the Tao of Lao-Tse, the Ten Commandments, the Hindu Code of Manu, the Analects of Confucius, the Dharma of Buddha, and the Qur'an of Islam.

WILLIAM PALEY
(1743–1805)
British Theologian. In *Natural Theology* (1802), developed the Argument from Design that argues for the existence of God by showing the high level of order in the world and saying such a design could only be the result of an intelligent designer, God.

How do we account for these apparently universal moral principles? The most reasonable explanation (this proof argues) is that they are derived from a single divine source: God.

Another focus of this moral argument is to observe the nature of the moral sense in humans, the deep-seated conviction that we have a profound obligation to choose what is "right" and "good" and to avoid what is "wrong" and "bad." This sense of moral obligation is accompanied by the conviction that we have the capacity to choose freely in creating an honorable, virtuous life. What is the most plausible explanation for these powerful, deeply ingrained feelings and convictions? A supreme moral authority—God—who has instilled this moral sense in humans, along with the ability to reason and the freedom to choose that renders such moral decisions meaningful.

A final focus of the moral argument for God's existence was proposed by **Immanuel Kant**, and is somewhat more intricate. For Kant, morality is grounded mainly in our ability to reason: hence his supreme moral principle, the categorical imperative, that we explored in the previous chapter: *Act on the principle that you can will to be a universal law of nature.* But Kant also believes that our ability to reason gives us the ability to clearly recognize the "highest good," the *summum bonum*, a concept that integrates the balanced harmony of moral goodness and personal happiness. We have the absolute conviction that people who live virtuous, morally upright lives should be rewarded by happiness, whereas those who lead evil, immoral lives should endure misery and suffering. However, we also observe that at least in this current life on earth, such a harmonious balance often does not exist: virtuous people can endure great misery and unhappiness, whereas immoral people can be successful and even seem to be relatively happy. For Kant, our ability to reason demands that this seemingly unfair state of affairs be corrected, and this can only occur in an afterlife in which virtue will be rewarded and evil punished. Such a future life of rational justice can only be created by a supreme being: God. Kant explains this view in more detail in the following selection from his *Critique of Practical Reason* entitled "God as a Postulate of Practical Reason."

IMMANUEL KANT

(1724–1804)
German Philosopher. Is widely regarded as greatest philosopher of modern period. Attempted to synthesize two competing schools of the modern period, rationalism and empiricism, by showing important role both experience and reason play in constructing our knowledge of the world.

Immanuel Kant,
Critique of Practical Reason,
God as a Postulate
of Practical Reason

The moral law led, in the foregoing analysis, to a practical problem which is assigned solely by pure reason and without any concurrence of sensuous incentives. It is the problem of the completeness of the first and principal part of the highest good, viz. Morality; since this problem can be solved only in eternity, it led to the postulate of immortality. The same law must also lead us to affirm the possibility of the second element of the highest good, i.e., happiness proportional to that morality; it must do just as disinterestedly as heretofore, by a cause adequate to this effect, i.e., it must postulate the existence of God as necessarily belonging to the possibility of the highest good (the object of our will which is necessarily connected with the moral legislation of pure reason). We proceed to exhibit this connection in a convincing manner.

Kant has complete confidence in the capacity of our rational abilities to describe the structure of reality. Because we are able to contemplate the "highest good" for humans in a clear and compelling way, we must assume the existence of those things that make such a "highest good" possible. In the section preceding this passage, Kant has argued that this means assuming that we have immortal souls: otherwise, the concept of achieving the "highest good" would make no sense for humans. In this section, he is arguing that the "highest good" entails the idea of people being happy in direct proportion to their moral goodness: we believe such a formula to be a rational necessity. And because a direct correlation between happiness and moral goodness does not occur in this life, reason demands that we assume (or *postulate*) that this correlation will occur in the next life. And this means postulating the existence of God.

Immanuel Kant

Happiness is the condition of a rational being in the world, in whose whole existence everything goes according to wish and will. It thus rests on the harmony of nature with his entire end and with the essential determining ground of his will. But the moral law commands as a law of freedom through motives wholly independent of nature and of its harmony with our faculty of desire (as incentives). Still, the acting rational being in the world is not at the same time the cause of the world and of nature itself. Hence there is not the slightest ground in the moral law for a necessary connection between the morality and proportionate happiness of a being which belongs to the world as one of its parts and as thus dependent on it. Not being nature's cause, his will cannot by its own strength bring nature, as it touches on his happiness, into complete harmony with this practical principle. Nevertheless, in the practical task of pure reason, i.e., in the necessary endeavor after the highest good, such a connection is postulated as necessary: we *should* seek to further the highest good (which therefore must be at least possible). Therefore also the existence is postulated of a cause of the whole of nature, itself distinct from nature, which contains the ground of the exact coincidence of happiness with morality. This supreme cause, however, must contain the ground of the agreement of nature not merely with actions moral in their form but also with their morality as the motives to such actions, i.e., with their supposition of a supreme cause of nature which has a causality corresponding to the moral intention. Now a being which is capable of actions by the idea of laws is an intelligence (a rational being), and the causality of such a being according to this idea of laws is his will. Therefore, the supreme cause of nature, in so far as it must be presupposed for the highest good, is a being which is the cause (and consequently the author) of nature through understanding and will, i.e., God. As a consequence, the postulate of the possibility of a highest derived good (the best world) is at the same time the postulate of the reality of a highest original good, namely, the existence of God. Now it was our duty to promote the highest good; and it is not merely our privilege but a necessity connected with duty as a requisite to presuppose the possibility of this highest good. This presupposition is made only under the condition of the existence of God, and this condition inseparably connects this supposition with duty. Therefore, it is morally necessary to assume the existence of God. ∎

Immanuel Kant,
Critique of Practical Reason,
God as a Postulate of Practical Reason

Kant, Immanuel, *Critique of Practical Reason*

As we noted previously, the various "arguments" for God's existence have been widely analyzed and criticized over the centuries by various philosophers. Perhaps the most entertaining evaluation of some of these arguments was offered by **Bertrand Russell** (1872–1970) in his essay, "Why I Am Not a Christian."

The Existence of God

Bertramd Russell,
Why I Am Not a Christian

To come to this question of the existence of God: it is a large and serious question, and if I were to attempt to deal with it in any adequate manner I should have to keep you here until Kingdom Come, so that you will have to excuse me if I deal with it in a somewhat summary fashion. You know, of course, that the Catholic Church has laid it down as a dogma that the existence of God can be proved by the unaided reason. That is somewhat curious dogma, but it is one of their dogmas. . . . The arguments and the reasons were set out at great length, and the Catholic Church felt that they must stop it. Therefore they laid it down that the existence of God can be proved by the unaided reason and they had to set up what they considered were arguments to prove it. There are, of course, a number of them, but I shall take only a few.

The First-Cause Argument

Perhaps the simplest and easiest to understand is the argument of the First Cause. (It is maintained that everything we see in this world has a cause, and as you go back in the chain of causes further and further you must come to a First Cause, and to that First Cause you give the name of God.) That argument, I suppose, does not carry very much weight nowadays, because, in the first place, cause is not quite what it used to be. The philosophers and the men of science have got going on cause, and it has not anything like the vitality it used to have; but, apart from that, you can see that the argument that there must be a First Cause is one that cannot have any validity. I may say that when I was a young man and was debating these questions very seriously in my mind, I for a long time accepted the argument of the First Cause, until one day, at the age of eighteen, I read John Stuart Mill's Autobiography, and I there found this sentence: "My father taught me that the question 'Who made me?' cannot be answered, since it immediately suggests the further question 'Who made God?' " That very simple question showed me, as I still think, the fallacy in the argument of the First Cause. If everything must have a cause, then God must have a cause. If there can be anything without a cause, it may just as well be the world as God, so that there cannot be any validity in that argument. It's exactly of the same nature as the Hindu's view, that the world rested upon an elephant and the elephant rested upon a tortoise; and when they said, "How about the tortoise?" the Indian said, "Suppose we change the subject." The argument is really no better than that. There is no reason why the world could not have come into being without a cause; nor, on the other hand, is there any reason why it should not have always existed. There is no reason to suppose that the world had a beginning at all. The idea that things must have a beginning is really due to the poverty of our imagination. Therefore, perhaps, I need not waste any more time upon the argument about the First Cause.

The Argument from Design

The next step in this process brings us to the argument from design. You all know the argument from design: Everything in the world is made just so that we can manage to live in the world, and if the world was ever so little different, we could not manage to live in it. That is the argument from design. It sometimes takes a rather curious form; for instance it is argued that rabbits have white tails in order to be easy to shoot. I do not know how rabbits would view that application. It is an easy argument to parody. You all know Voltaire's remark, that obviously the nose was designed to be such as to fit spectacles. That sort of parody has turned out to be not nearly so wide of the mark as it might have seemed in the eighteenth century, because since the time of Darwin we understand much better why living creatures are adapted to their environment. It is not that their environment was made to be suitable to them but they grew to be suitable to it, and that is the basis of adaptation. There is no evidence of design about it.

When you come to look into this argument from design, it is a most astonishing thing that people can believe that this world, with all the things that are in it, with all its defects, should be the best that omnipotence and omniscience have been able to produce in millions of years. I really cannot believe it. Do you think that, if you were granted omnipotence and omniscience and millions of years in which to perfect your world, you could produce nothing better than the Ku Klux Klan or the Fascists? Moreover, if you accept the ordinary laws of science, you have to suppose that human life and life in general on this planet will die out in due course: it is a stage in the decay of the solar system; at a certain stage of decay you get the sort of conditions of temperature and so forth which are suitable to protoplasm and there is life for a short time in the life of the whole solar system. You see in the moon the sort of thing to which the earth is tending—something dead, cold, and lifeless.

. . . Of course I know that the sort of intellectual arguments that I have been telling you about are not what really moves people. What really moves people to believe in God is not any intellectual argument at all. Most people believe in God because they have been taught from early infancy to do it, and that is the main reason.

Russell includes in his essay a number of reasons why he does not believe in the Christian religion, including:

Bertrand Russell,
Why I Am Not a Christian

- I must say that I think all this doctrine, that hell-fire is a punishment for sin, is a doctrine of cruelty.
- It seems to me that the people who have held to it (Christianity) have been for the most part extremely wicked. . . . In the so-called ages of faith, when men really did believe the Christian religion in all its completeness, there was the Inquisition, with its tortures; there were millions of unfortunate women burned as witches; and there was every kind of cruelty practiced upon all sorts of people in the name of religion.

- You find as you look around the world that every single bit of progress in humane feeling, every improvement in the criminal law, every step toward the diminution of war, every step toward better treatment of the colored races, or every mitigation of slavery, every moral progress that there has been in the world, has been consistently opposed by the organized churches of the world. I say quite deliberately that the Christian religion, as organized in its churches, has been and still is the principal enemy of moral progress in the world.

Russell concludes his essay with the following humanist "call to arms."

Religion is based, I think, primarily and mainly upon fear. It is partly the terror of the unknown and partly, as I have said, the wish to feel that you have a kind of elder brother who will stand by you in all your troubles and disputes. Fear is the basis of the whole thing—fear of the mysterious, fear of defeat, fear of death. Fear is the parent of cruelty, and therefore it is no wonder if cruelty and religion have gone hand in hand. . . .

    Science can teach us, and I think our own hearts can teach us, no longer to look around for imaginary supports, no longer to invent allies in the sky, but rather to look to our own efforts here below to make this world a fit place to live in, instead of the sort of place that the churches in all these centuries have made it.

Bertrand Russell,
Why I Am Not a Christian

 Russell, Bertrand, *Why I Am Not a Christian*

 VISUAL PHILOSOPHY

World Trade Center
9/11

Why does Bertrand Russell believe that historically "cruelty and religion have gone hand in hand." Do you agree? Why?

Evaluating Arguments for Religion

- Reflect on the three cosmological argument's for existence that we explored in this section:
  - The argument from contingency
  - The argument from design
  - The argument from morality

Evaluate each of the arguments in terms of how persuasive you find it. What are its strongest points? What are its weakest points?

- Evaluate Bertrand Russell's critique of the first cause argument and the argument from design. Do you agree with his analysis? Why or why not?

- How would you respond to the question, "Do you believe in God?" If you would respond "Yes," describe what arguments you would use to explain the rationale for your belief. If you would respond "No," describe the reasoning you would use to explain your conclusion.

- Create an argument for the existence (or nonexistence) of God that is different from those we examined in this section. Try the argument out on someone you know and describe their reactions. Did they find the argument persuasive? Why or why not?

- Russell believes that, overall, religion has been a negative force in human experience. Imagine that you were engaged in a discussion with him: compose a Socratic dialogue that examines his criticisms of organized religion.

We want to stand upon our own feet and look fair and square at the world—its good facts, its bad facts, its beauties, and its ugliness; see the world as it is and be not afraid of it. Conquer the world by intelligence and not merely by being slavishly subdued by the terror that comes from it. The whole conception of God is a conception derived for the ancient Oriental despotisms. It is a conception quite unworthy of free men. When you hear of people in church debasing themselves and saying that they are miserable sinners, and all the rest of it, it seems contemptible and not worthy of self-respecting human beings. We ought to stand up and look the world frankly in the face. We ought to make the best we can of the world and if it is not so good as we wish, after all it will still be better than what these others have made of it in all these ages. A good world needs knowledge, kindliness, and courage; it does not need a regretful hankering after the past or a fettering of the free intelligence by the word uttered long ago by ignorant men. It needs a fearless outlook and a free intelligence. It needs hope for the future not looking back all the time toward a past that is dead, which we trust will be far surpassed by the future that our intelligence can create.

Seeking Spirituality Through Faith

For people who are not believers in a particular religion, all of the proofs and evidence religions offer for their religious truths are likely to fall far short of absolute certainty. For example, the "proofs" for the existence of God that we just considered might be viewed as suggestive by many people, but they are hardly air-tight arguments. Similarly, appeal to divinely inspired holy books may carry a certain weight, but there are a number of holy books—which one are we to consider to be the one "true" holy book? And why? The same reasoning applies to historical religious figures: There are many such figures throughout history—on what grounds can we determine the one individual to whom we should commit ourselves? And naturally, the same is true for appeals to miracles, mighty acts of God, prophecies, and the like—how can we be sure these events actually happened as described?

Nor is the evidence of personal spiritual experience helpful to providing incontrovertible proof. As William James notes, although such religious experiences may have great currency for those experiencing them, these experiences have virtually no legitimacy for those who have *not* shared the experiences. And even for those who have had such experiences, questions are likely to remain: how can I be sure this was an authentically religious experience and not some other altered state of consciousness? How can we be certain the voices we are hearing are from God and not from somewhere else?

And yet, despite the lack of absolutely certain proof, many people still choose to commit themselves to religious beliefs, often with great fervor and determination. Why? In a word, "faith." For many religious believers, traditional proofs and evidence may play a role in their religious beliefs, but in the final analysis it is the power of faith that forms the core of their commitment, echoing the writer in the New Testament, "We walk by faith and not by sight." What is faith exactly? It is a form of knowing that is fundamentally different than objective, rational analysis, one that transcends traditional categories of thought and language. For many religions, faith is based on experiencing a relationship with a supernatural force or Creator. It is analogous in some ways to having an authentically loving relationship with another person. It would be pointless to try and subject the relationship to an exhaustive, rational analysis, or to attempt to "prove" the reality of the relationship with objective measures or logical arguments. Instead, we have "faith" in the other person and our relationship to them; we "know" truths about the relationship that cannot be fully articulated in language.

At the same time, faith necessarily involves risk. It is the very absence of conclusive, demonstrable proof that makes room for faith, for if we were objectively certain in our beliefs, faith would be unnecessary. Faith necessarily entails the possibility of our being wrong, whether it is regarding religion or regarding love. Yet in spite of the risk, there is nevertheless a primal urge in many people to *believe*, to *have faith* in the reality of something larger than themselves.

Perhaps the most passionate voice for religious faith is **Søren Kierkegaard** (1813–1855), the Danish philosopher who is widely considered to be the father of modern existentialism. In the following excerpts from his essay "The Leap of Faith and the Limits of Reason," he argues that to fully understand human existence, we must recognize the limits of reason and be prepared to make a "leap of faith" toward belief and commitment when such a leap is required.

> **SØREN KIERKEGAARD**
> (1813–1855)
> Christian Philosopher. Considered to be the first existentialist. Though deeply religious, challenged much of Christian philosophy including the belief that faith could be systematic and supported by proofs and reasons; maintained true belief in God required an absurd leap of faith for which there is no rational justification.

Kierkegaard,
The Leap of Faith and the Limits of Reason

But what is this unknown something with which the Reason collides when inspired by its paradoxical passion, with the result of unsettling even man's knowledge of himself? It is the Unknown. It is not a human being, insofar as we know what man is; nor is it any other known thing. So let us call this unknown something: *God*. It is nothing more than a name we assign to it. The idea of demonstrating that this unknown something (God) exists could scarcely suggest itself to the Reason. For if God does not exist it would of course be impossible to prove it; and if he does exist it would be folly to attempt it. For at the very outset, in beginning my proof, I will have presupposed it, not as doubtful but as certain (a presupposition is never doubtful, for the very reason that it is a presupposition), since otherwise I would not begin, readily understanding that the whole would be impossible if he did not exist. But if when I speak of proving God's existence I mean that I propose to prove that the Unknown, which exists, is God, then I express myself unfortunately. For in that case I do not prove anything, least of all an existence, but merely develop the content of a conception. Generally speaking, it is a difficult matter to prove that anything exists; and what is still worse for the intrepid souls who undertake the venture, the difficulty is such that fame scarcely awaits those who concern themselves with it. The entire demonstration always turns into something very different from what it assumes to be, and becomes an additional development of the consequences that flow from (our) having assumed existence, whether I move in the sphere of palpable sensible fact or in the realm of thought. I do not, for example, prove that a stone exists, but that some existing thing is a stone. The procedure in a court of justice does not prove that a criminal exists, but that the accused, whose existence is given, is a criminal . . .

For Kierkegaard, trying to prove that God "exists" is a pointless endeavor, as he observes: "For if God does not exist it would of course be impossible to prove it; and if he does exist it would be folly to attempt it." Why folly? Because "proof" involves reasoning, and our reasoning powers are limited when it comes to the metaphysical. The best that we can do is acknowledge these limits and recognize that beyond the powers of reason lies the Unknown. In addition, it is virtually impossible to "prove" that anything exists, especially God. Our only realistic goal is to "develop the content of a conception" of God. But how can we do this if our reasoning abilities are by definition not capable of describing the Unknown (God)? Kierkegaard believes that we must take an entirely different approach.

Søren Kierkegaard

Kierkegaard,
The Leap of Faith
and the Limits of Reason

. . . between God and his works there exists an absolute relationship; God is not a name but a concept. Is this perhaps the reason that his (essence involves existence)? The works of God are such that only God can perform them. Just so, but where then are the works of God? The works from which I would deduce his existence are not immediately given. The wisdom of God in nature, his goodness, his wisdom in the governance of the world—are all these manifest, perhaps, upon the very face of things? Are we not here confronted with the most terrible temptations to doubt, and is it not impossible finally to dispose of all these doubts? But from such an order of things I will surely not attempt to prove God's existence; and even if I began I would never finish, and would in addition have to live constantly in suspense, lest something so terrible should suddenly happen that my bit of proof would be demolished. From what works then do I propose to derive the proof? From the works as apprehended through an ideal interpretation, i.e., such as they do not immediately reveal themselves. But in that case it is not from the works that I prove God's existence. . . .

And how does God's existence emerge from the proof? Does it follow straightway, without any breach of continuity? Or have we not here an analogy to the behaviour of these toys, the little Cartesian dolls? As soon as I let go of the doll it stands on its head. As soon as I let it go—I must therefore let it go. So also with the proof for God's existence. As long as I keep my hold on the proof, i.e., continue to demonstrate, the existence does not come out, if for no reason than that I am engaged in proving it: but when I let the proof go, the existence is there. But this act of letting go is surely also something; it is indeed a contribution of mine. Must not this also be taken into the account, this little moment, brief as it may be—it need not be long, for it is a *leap*. However brief this moment, if only an instantaneous now, this "now" must be included in the reckoning. . . .

 | Kierkegaard, Søren,
Philosophical Fragments

For Kierkegaard, any attempt to prove God's existence by reasoning from the observed features of the universe—cosmological arguments—are destined to fail as well. Why? Because we can never be certain that an unexpectedly terrible event might occur that would demolish our carefully constructed arguments from design, contingency, or morality. So it is not God's actions that we use as a basis for inferring His existence: instead, it is an "ideal interpretation" of God that we use, an imaginative construction of His nature. But such an ideal construction already *presupposes* God's existence, so we are not really proving anything.

Then how do we achieve a confidence in God's existence? We must *let go* of our efforts to "prove" His existence with logical, rational means, and instead simply let the reality of his existence become manifest. But this act of letting go is difficult: we naturally strive for objective certainty, demonstrable proof that will satisfy the demands of reason. To let go of this compulsion requires an act of will, a *leap* of faith in God's reality. And when we truly let go of our rational efforts, our faith is rewarded by our experiencing the reality of God's existence in nonrational or suprarational ways. We can again see the analogy with nurturing a loving relationship: we need to "let go" of our need to analyze every dimension of the relationship in order for the authentic emotions to be released and suffuse our shared experiences.

Kierkegaard provides a fuller explication of his view in another book, *Concluding Unscientific Postscript*, in which he articulates the stark contrast between "objective knowing" (logical, rational) and "subjective knowing" (personal, passionate, experiential). For Kierkegaard, we can only achieve genuine understanding of God through subjective knowing.

Kierkegaard,
Concluding Unscientific Postscript

When the question of truth is raised in an objective manner, reflection is directed objectively to the truth, as an object to which the knower is related. Reflection is not focused upon the relationship, however, but upon the question of whether it is the truth to which the knower is related. If only the object to which he is related is the truth, the subject is accounted to be in the truth. When the question of the truth is raised subjectively, reflection is directed subjectively to the nature of the individual's relationship; if only the mode of this relationship is in the truth, the individual is in the truth even if he should happen to be thus related to what is not true. Let us take as an example the knowledge of God. Objectively, reflection is directed to the problem of whether this object is the true God; subjectively, reflection is directed to the question whether the individual is related to a something *in such a manner* that his relationship is in truth a God-relationship. On which side is the truth now to be found? Ah, may we not here resort to a mediation, and say: It is on neither side, but in the mediation of both? Excellently well said, provided we might have it explained how an existing individual manages to be in a state of mediation. For to be in a state of mediation is to be finished, while to exist is to become. Nor can an existing individual be in two places at the same time—he cannot be an identity of subject and object. When he is nearest to being in two places at the same time he is in passion; but passion is also the highest expression of subjectivity.

For Kierkegaard, "objective knowing" can never achieve a genuine understanding of God, because it treats God as an object to be proved and understood—an impossible task, given the limits of our reasoning capacities. "Subjective knowing," on the other hand, enables us to establish a *relationship* with God, a connection founded on *passion*, not dispassionate rational understanding. The objective knowing of reason can provide the illusion of understanding God, but this way of knowing will always be an approximation, an idealized and distorted intellectual construction. Only by surrendering ourselves to subjective knowing, through the leap of faith, can we achieve true knowledge of God through a personal relationship.

◆ VISUAL PHILOSOPHY

Michelangelo, "The Creation of Adam"

Why does Kierkegaard believe that achieving genuine knowledge of God involves a passionate "leap of faith"? Do you agree with his analysis? Why?

Kierkegaard,
Concluding Unscientific Postscript

The existing individual who chooses to pursue the objective way enters upon the entire approximation-process by which it is proposed to bring God to light objectively. But this is in all eternity impossible, because God is a subject, and therefore exists only for subjectivity in inwardness. The existing individual who chooses the subjective way apprehends instantly the entire dialectical difficulty involved in having to use some time, perhaps a long time, in finding God objectively; and he feels this dialectical difficulty in all its painfulness, because every moment is wasted in which he does not have God. . . .

It is at this point, so difficult dialectically, that the way swings off for everyone who knows what it means to think, and to think existentially; which is something very different from sitting at a desk and writing about what one has never done, something very different from writing *de omnibus dubitandum* and at the same time being as credulous existentially as the most sensuous of men. Here is where the way swings off, and the change is marked by the fact that while objective knowledge rambles comfortably on by the way of the long road of approximation without being impelled by the urge of passion, subjective knowledge counts every delay a deadly peril, and the decision so infinitely important and so instantly pressing that it is as if the opportunity has already passed.

THINK PHILOSOPHICALLY   7.8
Analyzing Kierkegaard

- Do you agree with the view Kierkegaard expresses in the following passage, that our powers of reason are limited when it comes to understanding or encountering a supernatural being (God)? Why or why not?

  But what is this unknown something with which the Reason collides when inspired by its paradoxical passion, with the result of unsettling even man's knowledge of himself? It is the Unknown. It is not a human being, insofar as we know what man is; nor is it any other known thing. So let us call this unknown something: *God*.

- As he expresses in the following passage, Kierkegaard believes that we must let go of our rational efforts to prove God's existence in order to *experience* God's existence. Does this analysis make sense to you? Why or why not?

  So also with the proof for God's existence. As long as I keep my hold on the proof, i.e., continue to demonstrate, the existence does not come out, if for no reason than that I am engaged in proving it: but when I let the proof go, the existence is there.

- For Kierkegaard, arguments for God's existence from a cosmological point of view are disturbing, not reassuring. Why do you think he believes this to be the case? Do you agree with his perspective? Why or why not?

  I contemplate the order of nature in the hope of finding God, and I see omnipotence and wisdom; but I also see much else that disturbs my mind and excites anxiety. The sum of all this is an objective uncertainty.

- Paradoxically, it is this "objective uncertainty" produced by reason's attempt to prove God's existence that makes it possible to experience the reality of God through the passion of faith. Explain in your own words Kierkegaard's reasoning in the following passage, which concludes with a stunning metaphor.

  Without risk there is no faith. Faith is precisely the contradiction between the infinite passion of the individual's inwardness and the objective uncertainty. If I am capable of grasping God objectively, I do not believe, but precisely because I cannot do this I must believe. If I wish to preserve myself in faith I must constantly be intent upon holding fast the objective uncertainty, so as to remain out upon the deep, over seventy thousand fathoms of water, still preserving my faith.

Although we normally think of a search for "truth" in terms of objective understanding, Kierkegaard believes that when it comes to God, it is subjective, inward understanding that brings us closer to true understanding. In fact, he believes that objective analysis of God is destined to end in uncertainty, an uncertainty that we cannot help but find to be profoundly disturbing. But it is this "objective uncertainty" that fuels the passion of our subjective knowledge of God, an essential truth that is grounded in a passionate faith.

Kierkegaard,
Concluding Unscientific Postscript

The truth is precisely the venture which chooses an objective uncertainty with the passion of the infinite. I contemplate the order of nature in the hope of finding God, and I see omnipotence and wisdom; but I also see much else that disturbs my mind and excites anxiety. The sum of all this is an objective uncertainty. But it is for this very reason that the inwardness becomes as intense as it is, for it embraces this objective uncertainty with the entire passion of the infinite. In the case of the mathematical proposition the objectivity is given, but for this reason the truth of such a proposition is also an indifferent truth.

But the above definition of truth is an equivalent expression for faith. Without risk there is no faith. Faith is precisely the contradiction between the infinite passion of the individual's inwardness and the objective uncertainty. If I am capable of grasping God objectively, I do not believe, but precisely because I cannot do this I must believe. If I wish to preserve myself in faith I must constantly be intent upon holding fast the objective uncertainty, so as to remain out upon the deep, over seventy thousand fathoms of water, still preserving my faith. ■

Kierkegaard, Søren,
Concluding Unscientific Postscript

The Problem of Evil

Three centuries before the birth of Christ, the Greek philosopher Epicurus posed the following challenge regarding God and the existence of evil in the universe:

> God either cannot or will not prevent evil. If God cannot prevent evil, then God is limited in power. If God will not prevent evil, then God is limited in benevolence. But if God is not limited in either power or benevolence, why is there evil in the world?

The existence of evil in the world poses a serious threat to religion in general, and the concept of an all-loving, all-powerful God in particular. When human catastrophes happen, it is common for people to wonder, "How could God let this happen?" There are two general categories of evil in the world. The first is *natural evil*: the human calamities that are the result of natural disasters: earthquakes, hurricanes, tornadoes, disease, crop-destroying droughts and pestilence, starvation, and other aspects of the natural order that end up destroying lives and crushing human hopes. The second category is *moral evil*, the pain, suffering, and death inflicted by humans upon humans through evil actions: murder, rape, physical abuse, theft, psychological torture, child abuse, warfare, genocide, discrimination, persecution, and other examples of human malevolence. Although these two types of evil are distinct, they are also related in complex ways. For example, starvation and poverty are often the result of human policies as well as natural disasters, and the failure of wealthy cultures to share their resources increases the death and disease in less affluent cultures.

Questions regarding the existence of God and God's nature apply to both kinds of evil. Regarding natural evil, it seems reasonable to ask: Why does God permit natural disasters to occur, with the loss of life and property of innocent people? If God is all-powerful (omnipotent), God should be able to exert some minimal planning and control to prevent hurricanes, earthquakes, disease, and other natural catastrophes from harming innocent people. And if God is all-benevolent, wouldn't God want to prevent such senseless disasters from occurring?

Some people wonder, if God is all-powerful and all-loving, why does God permit evil like natural disasters to occur. What do you think?

With respect to moral evil, it seems reasonable to ask: Why did God create humans with such primal, destructive impulses that result in such evil actions? Couldn't God have created everyone with a sufficiently moral nature to prevent such evil? Couldn't humans have been created with the ability to make free choices while still retaining a basic decency and empathy? And why does God permit the creation of such human monsters as Stalin and Hitler, or serial killers and child abusers? Again, if God is omnipotent, preventing human evil on this scale should not be all that difficult, and if God is all-loving, God should certainly want to prevent this kind of unnecessary human suffering. The obvious responses to this dilemma include

- God does not exist, at least as a personal Creator involved in human affairs.
- God is not all-powerful, and so is unable to influence events in the world.
- God is not all-loving, and so is not interested in preventing evil in the world.

JOHN HICK

(1922–)

Philosopher of Religon. Wrote extensively on many issues on the philosophy of religion including the problem of evil, the concept of the after-life, and the nature of religious belief. Holds the belief that every religion is speaking about the same ultimate reality.

For people with a fervent belief in religions based on a supreme, omnipotent, all-loving Creator—such as Judaism, Christianity, and Islam—none of these alternatives are attractive. As a result, many thinkers have tried to construct alternative metaphysical/theological frameworks that will reconcile the existence of a Creator God with the existence of evil in the universe. The name of this field of inquiry is **theodicy**, which comes from the Greek words *theos* (God) and *dike* (righteous), which together mean the justification of God's goodness in the face of the fact of evil. In the following essay, the theologian **John Hick** (b. 1922) reviews some of the traditional theodicy theories and also presents his own approach to this complex and disturbing issue.

John Hick,
Philosophy of Religion,
God Can Allow Some Evil

To many, the most powerful positive objection to belief in God is the fact of evil. Probably for most agnostics it is the appalling depth and extent of human suffering, more than anything else, that makes the idea of a loving Creator seem so implausible and disposes them toward one or another of the various naturalistic theories of religion.

As a challenge to theism, the problem of evil has traditionally been posed in the form of a dilemma; if God is perfectly loving, he must wish to abolish evil; and if he is all-powerful, he must be able to abolish evil. But evil exists; therefore God cannot be both omnipotent and perfectly loving. . . .

Theodicy, as many modern Christian thinkers see it, is a modest enterprise, negative rather than positive in its conclusions. It does not claim to explain, nor to explain away, every instance of evil in human experience, but only to point to certain considerations which prevent the fact of evil (largely incomprehensible though it remains) from constituting a final and insuperable bar to rational belief in God.

In indicating these considerations it will be useful to follow the traditional division of the subject. There is the problem of *moral evil* or wickedness; why does an all-good and all-powerful God permit this? And there is the problem of the *nonmoral evil* of suffering or pain, both physical and mental: why has an all-good and all-powerful God created a world in which this occurs?

Christian thought has always considered moral evil in its relation to human freedom and responsibility. To be a person is to be a finite center of freedom, and (relatively) free and self-directing agent responsible for one's own decisions. This involves being free to act wrongly as well as to act rightly. The idea of a person who can be infallibly guaranteed always to act rightly is self-contradictory. There can be no guarantee in advance that a genuinely free moral agent will never choose amiss. Consequently, the possibility of wrongdoing or sin is logically inseparable from the creation of finite persons, and to say that God should not have created beings who might sin amounts to saying that he should not have created people.

Theodicy A defense of the justice or goodness of God in the face of doubts or objections arising from the phenomena of evil in the world.

This thesis has been challenged in some recent philosophical discussions of the problem of evil, in which it is claimed that no contradiction is involved in saying that God might have made people who would be genuinely free and who could yet be guaranteed always to act rightly. A quotation from one of these discussions follows:

> If there is no logical impossibility in a man's freely choosing the good on one, or on several occasions, there cannot be a logical impossibility in his freely choosing the good on every occasion. God was not, then, faced with a choice between making innocent automata and making beings, who, in acting freely, would sometimes go wrong: there was open to him the obviously better possibility of making beings who would act freely but always go right. Clearly, his failure to avail himself of this possibility is inconsistent with his being both omnipotent and wholly good.*

A reply to this argument is suggested in another recent contribution to the discussion.[†] If by a free action we mean an action which is not externally compelled but which flows from the nature of the agent as he reacts to the circumstances in which he finds himself, there is, indeed, no contradiction between our being free and our actions being "caused" (by our own nature), and therefore, being in principle predictable. There is a contradiction, however, in saying that God is the cause of our acting as we do but that we are free beings in relation to God. There is, in other words, a contradiction in saying that God has made us so that we shall of necessity act in a certain way, and that we are genuinely independent persons in relation to him. If all our thoughts and actions are divinely predestined, however free and morally responsible we may seem to be ourselves, we cannot be free and morally responsible in the sight of God, but must instead be his helpless puppets. Such "freedom" is like that of a patient acting out a series of posthypnotic suggestions: he appears, even to himself, to be free, but his volitions have actually been predetermined by another will, that of the hypnotist, in relation to whom the patient is not a free agent.

*J.L. Mackie, "Evil and Omnipotence," *Mind* (April, 1955), p. 209. A similar point is made by Antony Flew in "Divine Omnipotence and Human Freedom," *New Essays in Philosophical Theology*. An important critical comment on these arguments is offered by Ninian Smart in "Omnipotence, Evil and Supermen," *Philosophy* (April, 1961), with replies by Flew (January, 1962) and Mackie (April, 1962).
[†]Flew, in *New Essays in Philosophical Theology*.
[‡]As Aquinas said, ". . . nothing that implies a contradiction falls under the scope of God's omnipotence." *Summa Theologica*, Part I. Question 25, article 4.

Hick's analysis in this passage relates directly to the discussion of freedom in chapter 4. If God formed our characters in the process of creating us to ensure that we always chose the morally right alternative, we could not be considered as genuinely free. Even though we might not be limited by external constraints, our actions would have already been limited by God through internal constraints. Genuine freedom, we concluded in chapter 4, means making choices that are truly autonomous, independent of both external and internal constraints.

A different objector might raise the question of whether or not we deny God's omnipotence if we admit that he is unable to create persons who are free from the risks inherent in personal freedom. The answer that has always been given is that to create such beings is logically impossible. It is no limitation upon God's power that he cannot accomplish the logically impossible, since there is nothing here to accomplish, but only a meaningless conjunction of words[‡]—in this case "person who is not a person." God is able to create beings of any and every conceivable kind; but creatures who lack moral freedom, however superior they might be to human beings in other respects, would not be what we mean by persons. They would constitute a different form of life which God might have brought into existence instead of persons. When we ask why God did not create such beings in place of persons, the traditional answer is that only persons could, in any meaningful sense, become "children of God," capable of entering into a personal relationship with their Creator by a free and uncompelled response to his love.

We may now turn more directly to the problem of suffering. Even though the major bulk of actual human pain is traceable to man's misused freedom as a sole or part cause, there remain other sources of pain which are entirely independent of the human will, for example, earthquake, hurricane, storm, flood, drought, and blight. In practice, it is often

John Hick,
Philosophy of Religion,
God Can Allow Some Evil

impossible to trace a boundary between the suffering which results from human wickedness and folly and that which falls upon mankind from without. Both kinds of suffering are inextricably mingled together in human experience. For our present purpose, however, it is important to note that the latter category does exist and that it seems to be built into the very structure of our world. In response to it, theodicy, if it is wisely conducted, follows a negative path. It is not possible to show positively that each item of human pain serves the divine purpose of good; but, on the other hand, it does seem possible to show that the divine purpose as it is understood in Judaism and Christianity could not be forwarded in a world which was designed as a permanent hedonistic paradise.

An essential premise of this argument concerns the nature of the divine purpose in creating the world. The skeptic's assumption is that man is to be viewed as a completed creation and that God's purpose in making the world was to provide a suitable dwelling place for this fully formed creature. Since God is good and loving, the environment which he has created for human life to inhabit is naturally as pleasant and comfortable as possible. The problem is essentially similar to that of a man who builds a cage for some pet animal. Since our world, in fact, contains sources of hardship, inconvenience, and danger of innumerable kinds, the conclusion follows that this world cannot have been created by a perfectly benevolent and all-powerful deity.*

Christianity, however, has never supposed that God's purpose in the creation of the world was to construct a paradise whose inhabitants would experience a maximum of pleasure and a minimum of pain. The world is seen, instead, as a place of "soul-making" in which free beings grappling with the tasks and challenges of their existence in a common environment, may become "children of God" and "heirs of eternal life." A way of thinking theologically of God's continuing creative purpose for man was suggested by some of the early Hellenistic Fathers of the Christian Church, especially Irenaeus. Following hints from St. Paul, Irenaeus taught that a man has been made as a person in the image of God but has not yet been brought as a free and responsible agent into the finite likeness of God, which is revealed in Christ.† Our world, with all its rough edges, is the sphere in which this second and harder stage of the creative process is taking place.

This conception of the world (whether or not set in Irenaeus's theological framework) can be supported by the method of negative theodicy. Suppose, contrary to fact, that this world were a paradise from which all possibility of pain and suffering were excluded. The consequences would be very far-reaching. For example, no one could ever injure anyone else: the murderer's knife would turn to paper or his bullets to thin air; the bank safe, robbed of a million of dollars, would miraculously become filled with another million dollars (without this device, on however large a scale, proving inflationary); fraud, deceit, conspiracy, and treason would somehow always leave the fabric of society undamaged. Again, no one would ever be injured by accident: the mountain-climber, steeplejack, or playing child falling from a height would float unharmed to the ground; the reckless driver would never meet with disaster. There would be no need to work, since no harm could result from avoiding work; there would be no call to be concerned for others in time of need or danger, for in such a world there could be no real needs or dangers.

To make possible this continual series of individual adjustments, nature would have to work by "special providences" instead of running according to general laws which men must learn to respect on penalty of pain or death. The laws of nature would have to be extremely flexible: sometimes gravity would operate, sometimes not; sometimes an object would be hard and solid, sometimes soft. There could be no sciences, for there would be no enduring world structure to investigate. In eliminating the problems and hardship of an objective environment, with its own laws, life would become like a dream in which, delightfully but aimlessly, we would float and drift at ease.

One can at least begin to imagine such a world. It is evident that our present ethical concepts would have no meaning in it. If, for example, the notion of harming someone is an essential element in the concept of a wrong action, in our hedonistic paradise there could be no wrong actions—nor any right actions in distinction from wrong. Courage and fortitude would have no point in an environment in which there is, by definition, no danger or difficulty. Generosity, kindness, the *agape* aspect of love, prudence, unselfishness, and all other ethical notions which presuppose life in a stable environment, could

---

*This is the nature of David Hume's argument in his discussion of the problem of evil in his *Dialogues*, Part XI.
†See Irenaeus's *Against Heresies*, Book IV, Chapters 37 and 38.

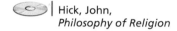

not even be formed. Consequently, such a world, however well it might promote pleasure, would be very ill adapted for the development of the moral qualities of human personality. In relation to this purpose it would be the worst of all possible worlds.

It would seem, then, that an environment intended to make possible the growth in free beings of the finest characteristics of personal life, must have a good deal in common with our present world. It must operate according to general and dependable laws; and it must involve real dangers, difficulties, problems, obstacles, and possibilities of pain, failure, sorrow, frustration, and defeat. If it did not contain the particular trials and perils which—subtracting man's own very considerable contribution—our world contains, it would have to contain others instead.

To realize this is not, by any means, to be in possession of a detailed theodicy. It is to understand that this world, with all its "heartaches and the thousand natural shocks that flesh is heir to," an environment so manifestly not designed for the maximization of human pleasure and the minimization of human pain, may be rather well adapted to the quite different purpose of "soul-making."

At this point, theodicy points forward in two ways to the subject of life after death.

First, although there are many striking instances of good being triumphantly brought out of evil through a man's or a woman's reaction to it, there are many other cases in which the opposite has happened. Sometimes obstacles breed strength of character, dangers evoke courage and unselfishness, and calamities produce patience and moral steadfastness. But sometimes they lead, instead, to resentment, fear, grasping selfishness, and disintegration of character. Therefore, it would seem that any divine purpose of soul-making which is at work in earthly history must continue beyond this life if it is ever to achieve more than a very partial and fragmentary success.

Second, if we ask whether the business of soul-making is worth all the toil and sorrow of human life, the Christian answer must be in terms of a future good which is great enough to justify all that has happened on the way to it. ▪

Hick, John,
Philosophy of Religion

THINK PHILOSOPHICALLY 7.9
Analyzing John Hick

- Do you think that the problem of evil poses a threat to the possibility of a God who is omnipotent and all-loving? Explain your reasoning.

- Hick maintains that if God interfered with the creation or development of people that we would be like "helpless puppets" or patients "acting out a series of posthypnotic suggestions" because it would undermine free choice. Do you agree with this reasoning? For example, aren't individuals already born with inherited traits that influence their personality development and subsequent choices? Couldn't God simply prevent the creation of truly evil individuals without affecting the freedom of the vast majority of people?

- Hick also maintains that if God prevented natural disasters from occurring it would mean negating all of the laws of science. Do you agree with this reasoning? For example, couldn't God have created a scientifically orderly world in which natural disasters did not cause such human catastrophes?

- According to Hick, the sorrows, tragedies, and disappointments of this world are necessary ingredients in "soul-making." Do you agree with this way of thinking? How have the tragedies in your life influenced you? Might some disasters be positive influences, whereas others are simply destructive?

- Because there is not enough time on this earth for our souls to become sufficiently enlightened, Hick believes that this suggests there must be an afterlife in which this process is continued. Does this reasoning make sense to you? Why or why not?

- Does the problem of evil in the world influence your thinking about religion? Why or why not? If you have a belief in God, how do you reconcile the existence of evil with your concept of God?

Making Connections: *Reflections on Philosophy of Religion*

t the beginning of this chapter you were asked to respond to a number of questions, including

- What is your definition of religion?
- What do you think is the purpose of religion?
- What are your religious beliefs?
- How do you view other religions?
- What is the relationship of religion to your daily life?

In reflecting on the various issues that you have explored in this chapter—through readings, writing assignments, class discussions, and personal reflection—how would you respond to these questions now? These questions do not assume that you believe that any religious beliefs are ultimately true. Religion is an integral dimension of virtually every culture, but you may believe that religion can claim no metaphysical reality, only cultural reality.

The philosopher **Frederick Streng** defines religion as "a means toward ultimate transformation." What precisely does he mean by that? He explains in the following passage:

> The term "ultimate" points to what a religious person holds to be "real," to what has such significance that people define their lives on its terms. Whatever is "ultimate" is that without which life would be meaningless and dead because of such common human experiences as physical death, unfulfilled hopes, and the discomfort derived from a sense of not belonging. In this context, the "ultimate" is a power or force in man's life that is recognized by the religious person to undergird, to condition, to encompass life. This appears in the form of words, actions, social relations, and states of consciousness: and its distinguishing mark is that it is so real that one recognizes its power to have been effective before as well as after one has become conscious of it. This is recognized as the reality that (who) establishes a whole and integrated person who then exists in a mutually beneficial relation with other people and with nature.

Religion, in sum, provides a framework for human life, helping us address the most profound and challenging questions that we encounter as existing beings:

- What is the meaning and purpose of my life?
- What is my destiny, both as an individual and as a member of a community of individuals?
- How ought I to conduct my life? What values should I live by?
- What happens to me when I die? What is the relation of death to life?

These questions, and others like them, are situated at the core of our consciousness, whether or not we are explicitly aware of them at any given moment. It is these questions that our souls yearn to comprehend, and it is to these questions that religion attempts to provide answers. Of course, as thinking individuals, we are not supposed to be satisfied with just *any* answers, in order to make us feel better—we want the *right* answers. And that's why it is so essential that we think philosophically about the religious experience, bringing our critical judgment to bear in trying to understand things that may very well lie beyond the scope of reason. Nevertheless, we want to

Frederick Streng (1933–1993)
Philosopher of Religion. Offers a definition of religion that views not as knowledge that is about new concepts or simply information, but as a means towards transformation of the self.

develop the most informed and intelligent understanding of the religious experience that we can. And to do this we need to make full use of *all* the capabilities of our minds. How do we achieve this authentic understanding of the ultimate? Streng explains:

> The term "transformation" implies that human life necessarily presents all of us a comprehensive task. This task may be variously conceived; one may speak of it as the quest for salvation, enlightenment, perfection, fulfillment, or joy, but the distinctively religious claim is that it cannot be escaped. In using the phrase "toward . . . transformation," then, we refer not only to "conversion experiences" especially prominent in prophetic (Western) religious traditions but also to significant changes that may happen either suddenly or slowly, individually or communally, in people's lives. Put more vividly, the claim is that one is threatened by illusion, but that he can move toward truth: by death, but that he can move toward life; by chaos, but that he can move toward meaning; by self-destruction, but that he can move toward an abundant life. These are, no doubt, concerns of the non-religious man as well. But the non-religious man fails (or refuses) to acknowledge the fundamental and comprehensive character of these tasks. He thinks of his humanity simply as given; the religious man insists that authentic humanity, although conditioned, must nevertheless be attained, released, or granted. Put more strongly, in the eyes of the religious man, one who fails to undertake this fundamental and comprehensive task is not merely threatened, inconvenienced, or condemned—he is, as yet, only potentially human. Some religious communities even say that he is sub-human.

As you reflect on your own religious evolution, consider the impact on your thinking—and your life—of the religions and philosophical issues that you explored in this course.

Students Thinking About Philosophy: *Analyzing the Concept of "God"*

When people think about and discuss religion, they tend to focus on the specific beliefs of a specific religion or religions. However, we have seen in this chapter that there are philosophical issues that transcend specific religions and their beliefs, including

- the validity of religious claims.
- the experience of the holy.
- the relation of religion to everyday life.
- the issues of death, immortality, and human destiny.
- arguments for and against the belief in a supernatural Creator.
- the problem of "evil" in a cosmos created by a perfect Being.
- the relationship of faith and reason.

For this assignment, select a philosophy of religion topic, addressing an issue that many or most religions must deal with, rather than an issue related to any one particular religion. In the following student essay, the author analyzes the concept of "God." "I believe in God." is a common enough statement that, in one form or another, has been repeated countless times throughout history and in all parts of the world. But what precisely does this statement mean? Who or what is the "God" that is being referred to? In what ways can we be said to "know" about God? What are God's qualities or attributes? What are the conceptual challenges to understanding God? How does such a belief in God inform people's lives and influence their decisions?

If I Were God, If God Was Us: An Analysis of the Concept of "God"

Andy Snyder

Believing in God or not: what's the difference? Whether it's a decision or a way of life, beliefs about ultimate things must ultimately matter. Otherwise, we would not say there was a belief at all, in any meaningful sense. In what ways can we be said to "know" about God, and how does such a belief in God inform people's lives and influence their decisions? It is not possible to address these questions in a short paper with respect to actual religions: there are simply too many religions and concepts of God(s). But we *can* approach these questions from a philosophical point of view, exploring such questions in terms of their meaning, logic, and limits.

What Do You Believe In?

Philosophically, there are two distinct approaches for attempting to define the concept of God. The first is a *descriptive* approach, which attempts to distinguish the concept of "God" from everything else in the universe. For example, we might say that God is eternal, beyond space and time, uncreated, all-knowing , all-powerful, and morally perfect. However, if God is beyond space and time, then how could we possibly learn directly about these attributes of God? Certainly not from our thinking or experience, since these are both bounded by space and time. In other words, how do we come to understand something that is entirely foreign and alien to us and our categories of thinking? One way many faith traditions and individual believers deal with this difficulty is to focus on *the effects* or "works" of God—the creation of the universe, for example, or the moral/spiritual nature of humans—and then make inferences about the source of these effects. For example: If God created the universe, then God must be beyond space and time, all powerful, and uncreated. We can also look at human beings as manifestations of God's creation. If we describe God as the creator and designer of everything in the universe, including ourselves, then God is the source of knowledge about humanity. Perhaps understanding God could help us understand our own lives and their meaning. As the product of God's purpose, humanity should offer some reflection of God's likeness; we should expect some relation between the maker and the made.

Philosophers of many faith traditions have wondered not only if creation reveals anything about the creator, but whether any created finite world could reveal anything about the infinite. The issue is similar to concerns of whether God includes the world or is also independent of it. If God were only the world, then it would be difficult to distinguish the world from God, but also to explain why some see God and others don't. Likewise, if God is beyond space and time, then it's tough to imagine how God could be experienced or distinguished from the rest of the natural universe.

How Could You Believe That?

There are similar questions that arise in the context of identifying God or a religious tradition which concern recognition and reason. A person might say that they know about God through revelation, but they would have to know enough about God already to know it was God's revelation. In order to trust that a revelation is truly from God, the content of it must already be known. It might be said that the experts of a tradition decide its doctrines, but then who decides on the experts? Could the experts select themselves or does everyone decide who has authority (and if the experts are so much better why trust the rest)?

William James argued that the individual mystic has authority over the interpretation of their experience. Kierkegaard seems to claim that the religious community to which a believer belongs in some way decides their concept of God (but again who decides which community they belong to). He also claims that the individual's passion is more important in decisions of truth: a person who worships an idol passionately can be said to have a more "truthful" understanding of God than someone who intellectually apprehends the concept of "God" but has no passionate worshipful relationship with that God. The pragmatists question whether a belief is such without the corresponding action, while others note that a person could very well have a belief in God but do nothing because of it. Does someone really believe in God if they have not been changed in the least by that belief? Certainly, if one thought that God executed justice, they would want to act justly. Belief in a just God should at least prompt attempts at justice in a "true" believer. A person might believe that God exists, but that God doesn't care about them or what they do. Would this person really be said to share a belief with someone who thinks that God is genuinely concerned for the world? Also, part of sharing beliefs with others in a religious tradition is that you believe that a certain type of lifestyle or practice is indeed the right way to live.

We want a person to be able to refer to God or direct a prayer without needing an exact description of God. For example, I might be totally wrong about what God is like but still desire to pray to the God of Abraham, Isaac, and Jacob. The fact that God appeared to this person or did a certain thing can be descriptions themselves. Instead of the descriptive story, Saul Kripke offers an account where a name is ostensibly bestowed. Yet, it is doubtful that somebody could ostensibly define God.

Certain actions or conduct could be used like descriptions to identify whether a person had a belief. For example: "This person expresses the belief that they should love their neighbor." Yet, a person could be following "right" or "good" conduct but not intentionally with the right accompanying beliefs. There might not be any reason for the action; we could not then compare it to the actions of religious believers. In response, it could be argued that if one thought they were not perfect, they would never try to be. There are in fact many people that don't think we could ever act perfectly, but perhaps might *think* we could always be believing correctly. As Kierkegaard argues, it is more important to believe passionately than to believe correctly. A distinction must also be made between having a bad concept and worshiping a "bad god." It's one thing to have an ill-formulated concept, but quite another to be aiming at illness. Additionally, there could be no direct connection between action and intent, belief, or desire. A believer might not actually practice anything because of their belief. They might have the same conduct as would be expected or called for from the belief, but not actually connect the two; they may have entirely different reasons for what they do or claim no reason at all. If they follow a practice or ritual but have a different mental state, then it might not be the same practice.

A Causal Approach

The second general philosophical approach for defining the concept of God is that of *causal or historical contact*. Either the doctrines of a religion constitute a unique tradition or the uniqueness of the religion is the causal chain leading from the origin. For example, according to the descriptive perspective, a person who shares the same beliefs and practices with a believer of a different tradition would actually not thereby differ in tradition. The causal perspective, however, might consider people to belong to the same religion even if they in fact have very different beliefs because they are a part of the same causal chain.

Even if God were present to a person, it is questionable whether all of the properties of God would be readily accessible and whether God could be uniquely identified in contrast to the space-time framework in which we would experience God. There is, however, the possibility of pointing to an interior experience and claiming that God is in fact the cause of this experience or an object perceived in experience. Thus, after having a religious experience a person might say that the intentional content or "this" associated with the experience was in fact God. Without being located in space or time, God could still be identified or distinguished within a person's experience.

There would need to be clarification about what happens if a tradition is not active. Certainly the causal theory would have more trouble explaining how a tradition resurfaces after thousands of dormant years, but the descriptive theory would have to give some reasons why it should be considered the same one. A tradition could cease, but another later established with the exact doctrines. Would the participants have different beliefs? If a tradition resurfaces, is it the same one even though there is no continued existence? If a given religious tradition has no adherents at a point in time, it can't be said to have been passed down from generations, so there is a causal gap. It dropped out of touch if not out of reach. There could also be disagreement amongst people of the same faith tradition. They may consent to a dominant value system without internalizing its values or accepting them as legitimate. People could very well accept the name and group identity but not concur on all doctrines. This kind of dilemma can be seen in some conflicts between traditional faiths and contemporary culture (for example, although many faith traditions proscribe birth control methods, many members of such faiths use or practice birth control in their personal lives).

The likely resolution to many of our dilemmas will be that a tradition/belief can be identified by using aspects of either a causal or descriptive theory. Traditions are complex, and there will be cases where the two are in tension. For instance, if the doctrines are changeable by members or leaders then the very tradition itself could differ from its original essence. There will always be debate about whether it is a changed tradition or whether it is the same since there has always been the handing down of it and memory from which it was changed. Each theory offers a different perspective on religious traditions and beliefs. The causal theory would allow people to worship the same God who had very different ideas about God or allow us to pray to a Being we don't know much about. The descriptive theory keeps us from the worry that God didn't really appear as or do what we think. Hopefully, they will both help us think about our beliefs.

Concept Review

- The philosophy of religion seeks not to indoctrinate, "convert," or assert the legitimacy of one religion over another. Rather, the philosophy of religion explores the reasons for and nature of religious belief across cultures and societies. Studying the philosophy of religion allows for a deeper and richer understanding of the variety of religious traditions and faith practices around the world, as well as an appreciation for the similarities among those traditions and practices.

- Indigenous sacred traditions are practiced by about four percent of the world's population and are at greatest risk (along with the languages and other cultural traditions of these people) of being lost by the greater homogenization of world culture. Although each indigenous nation has its own faith traditions and spiritual practices, they have in common an oral tradition; a deep connection with the natural world; a belief in a great or supreme "spirit" that infuses and animates all creation; practices that keep deceased ancestors in close contact with the living; spiritual practitioners or shamans who mediate between the quotidian and the spirit worlds; and group rituals that provide structure, coherence, and a sense of time to the community.

- Buddhism is a nontheist religion that originated in India in the fifth century B.C.E. Buddhists believe that the Four Noble Truths explain the human condition: life inevitably involves suffering (*dukkha*); suffering originates in our desires; suffering will cease if desiring ceases; the way to realize this liberation from desire is through the Noble Eightfold Path. This "path," or *dharma*, prescribes a way of living moderately and deliberately that eventually leads to enlightenment, or Nirvana. The Noble Eightfold Path consists of right view, right intention (or understanding), right speech, right action, right livelihood, right effort, mindfulness, and concentration. We are continually reborn into this world to work on our *dharma*, until finally we reach the state of liberation from worldliness that is described as Nirvana.

- Hinduism, or Sanatana Dharma, is a religious system that originated in India four thousand years ago. The world's oldest living religion, Hinduism is practiced by hundreds of millions of people on the Indian subcontinent and around the world. Although there are millions of deities in Sanatana Dharma, adherents believe that they are all manifestations of one true God. The ancient sacred texts of Sanatana Dharma are collectively know as the Vedas, and are written in Sanskrit. The varieties and practices of this vast and ancient religion are complex and innumerable, but in general believers in Sanatana Dharma believe that the soul passes through innumerable incarnations (and is reincarnated after physical death) before it ever reaches a human manifestation; as humans, souls have the opportunity through their words and actions (*karma*) to finally release themselves from the endless cycle of birth and death (*samsara*) and achieve true liberation (*maksha*) and union with the Divine. Many different kinds of disciplines and practices, such as yoga and puja, have developed as ways of contemplating the link between the human self and divinity. Other ancient customs and practices, such as the caste system, have been challenged by modernity.

- Taoism originated in China around the fifth century B.C.E. Tao (the Chinese word for "the way") seeks meaning and purpose in the natural world and emphasizes a healthy and balanced lifestyle as a way of creating spiritual peace. The founder of Taoism is traditionally believed to be the sage Lao-Tse, whose collection of analects, the *Tao-te-Ching*, describes the often paradoxical wisdom of this belief system.

- Judaism is an ancient monotheistic religion whose origins are unclear. Judaism is both an ethnic designation and a religion, and the Jewish faith holds that the Jewish people have been specially "chosen" by God. Much of Jewish faith and tradition is based on the history of the Israelite people as recorded in the *Tanakh*, or Old Testament books of the Bible. The fundamental tenets of the Jewish faith are an utter belief in and devotion to a single God; the eventual coming of a "Messiah" or deliverer who will redeem and restore the Israelites to Israel; and a long, rich tradition of ethics and philosophical inquiry into what it means to live a good and moral life.

- Christianity has its roots in Judaism, but Christians believe that the Messiah arrived some two thousand years ago in the person of Jesus of Nazareth. The historical Jesus was a Jewish teacher and prophet whose radical views on social justice challenged local religious and government authorities. Only in the decades after his death did a strong and growing conviction among his followers that this Jesus did, in fact, fulfill the scriptural prefigurations of the Messiah did "Christianity" begin to take hold as a faith tradition quite distinctive from Judaism.

- Islam is the last of the three great monotheistic traditions, and like Judaism and Christianity, holds that there is but one God. Like the Jews and the Christians, Islam believes in the prophets of the Old Testament (Abraham, Moses), but traces its founding to the revelations delivered to Muhammad in the sixth century. Muslims believe that Muhammad is the last prophet of God (Allah), and their holy scripture, the Qur'an, was dictated to Muhammad by God himself. The core tenets of the Islamic faith are known as the Five Pillars of Islam: there is only one God, and his name is Allah; a continual round of daily prayers keeps the mind focused on and submitted to God's will; *zakat*, or the giving of alms, demonstrates care for God's community on earth; observance of Ramadan underscores man's reliance on God; and a *hajj* or pilgrimage to Mecca should be undertaken once in one's lifetime.

■ Many philosophers have sought to challenge the validity of religious claims. Friedrich Nietzsche held that humans were motivated by the "will to power," a fundamental drive that is contrary to (and even perverted by) the tenets of Christianity and Judaism, which require meekness and modesty. He railed against what he described as the "slave morality" of Christianity, which weakened the human spirit and stunted the development of the *ubermensch*, or "overman." In declaring "God is dead" Nietzsche was issuing a challenge: think for yourself, dare to create meaning in your own life, rather than blindly obeying an abstraction.

■ Feminist philosopher and theologian Mary Daly's critique of Christianity (and other major religions of the world) points out the secondary or subjugated position of women both in the traditional scriptures of these faith traditions and in the societies who have based legal and ethical systems on some distortion of those faith traditions. If women are to develop a fully realized spirituality, they need to collectively and individually recognize, critique, and replace those symbolic structures that are so deeply rooted in patriarchal religious traditions that it has become impossible to conceive of a new spiritual way of being without relying on those symbols and languages.

■ The philosophy of religion also seeks to understand how religion is psychologically and intellectually experienced by its believers. Mysticism is common to faith traditions around the world and throughout time. In seeking to analyze mysticism from a reasonable, philosophical standpoint, William James identified four "marks" of "mystical states of consciousness": ineffability, noetic quality, transiency, and passivity.

■ Thinkers, theologians, and philosophers from different faith traditions have sought to objectively find proof, using the faculty of reason, for their respective beliefs. Cosmological arguments, first advanced by the ancient Greeks, hold that there is a greater *Logos* or universal Reason or Intelligence that designed and orders the universe. The great Catholic theologian Thomas Aquinas provided five "proofs" for the existence of God: arguments from contingency, arguments from perfection, arguments from design, arguments from moral choice, and arguments from moral justice.

■ Kierkegaard, among others, argues that to try to find a reasoned, scientific "proof" for God (or any religious belief) is ultimately futile because of the nature of faith itself. Faith cannot be analyzed, dissected, or quantified; as he notes, "if God does not exist it would of course be impossible to prove it; and if he does exist it would be folly to attempt" to prove his existence. Kierkegaard finds that it is only through "subjective" knowing (personal, passionate, experiential, and brave)—a "leap of faith"—that we can "know" if there is a God or not.

■ All faith traditions attempt to explain, justify, or qualify the presence of "evil" in the world. Philosophers examine two broad categories of evil: "natural evil," such as the human calamities that result from natural disasters; and "moral evil," or the suffering deliberately inflicted by human beings upon other humans (or animals, or the environment). The attempt by philosophers and theologians to reconcile the possibility of a munificent, creating God with the presence of evil is called theodicy. For many thinkers in this tradition—both religious and secular—the role of human choice and free will in creating, avoiding, or alleviating evil is paramount.

Media Resources

 www.researchnavigator.com

Chapter 7 enters into the realms of religious beliefs and manifestoes. It also examines a number of problems that arise within these realms, such as the problems of evil and free will, plurality of religious beliefs, and patriarchal domination. For further research on questions about the philosophies and underlying religion, use the tools available to you in Research Navigator.

As you investigate this topic, consider this question: "Assuming there is a higher being or Reality, are religious experiences of the same Reality or are there many Realities but only one type of experience?"

- **ContentSelect:** search in the Philosophy databases using the search term "god" and the Religion database using the search terms "religious experience" and "one god."

- **Link Library:** search in the Philosophy database under terms "religion" and "holy."

- **New York Times on the Web:** search in the Philosophy database using the search terms "experiences" and "god."

 For additional study resources for this chapter, go to:
www.prenhall.com/chaffee/chapter7

The Primary Source: Philosophical Readings and Commentary

Anselm, St.: *Proslogion*

Aquinas, Thomas: *Summa Theologica*

Augustine: *City of God; The Confessions of St. Augustine*

Aurelius, Marcus: *Meditations*

Bhagavad Gita: *The Bhagavad Gita*

Boethius: *The Consolation of Philosophy*

Buddha: *The Fire Sermon; From the 'Diamond Sutra' (The Vagrakkhedika); The Heart Sutra; Verses from the Sanskrit Dharmapada*

Confucius: *The Analects*

Hick, John: *Philosophy of Religion*

Hume, David: *Dialogues Concerning Natural Religion*

James, William: *Mysticism*

Jaspers, Karl: *Philosophy of Existence*

Kant, Immanuel: *Critique of Practical Reason*

Kierkegaard, Søren: *Philosophical Fragments*

Lao Tzu: *Tao Te Ching*

Paley, William: *The Teleological Argument*

Plotinus: *The Enneads*

Russell, Bertrand: *Why I Am Not a Christian*

The Upanishads

What Is Real? What Is True?
Discovering Reality
and Constructing Knowledge (Part 1)

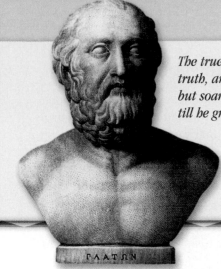

The true lover of knowledge naturally strives for truth, and is not content with common opinion, but soars with undimmed and unwearied passion till he grasps the essential nature of things.

PLATO

Cogito ergo sum.
I think, therefore I am.

RENÉ DESCARTES

Metaphysics and Epistemology

"Reality" and "Truth" are two of the most misunderstood and misused words in the English language. Think about the many ways that you use these terms, and that you hear them used, in our culture. Can you detect any core meanings for these terms? Or do you simply have a collection of diverse examples with some very general resemblance, such as

- "Reality" refers to things the way they really are.
- "Truth" refers to those statements that are one hundred percent accurate.

If you're having difficulty getting a clear grasp on these rich and complex concepts, don't despair: philosophers have been discussing—and sometimes arguing—over the meaning of these terms for several thousand years, without yet reaching a definitive agreement!

In philosophy, questions regarding the nature of reality fall under the category of **metaphysics**, which, as we saw in the first chapter, involves the study of the most general or ultimate characteristics of existence. Metaphysics explores issues beyond the physical world, such as the meaning of life, the existence of free will, the nature of mind, the fundamental principles of the universe, and the possibility of life beyond death. We can trace the origins of the term back to the Greek philosopher Aristotle (384–322 B.C.E.) who wrote on a vast range of topics. One set of writings, the *Physics* (from the Greek word *physika* "of nature"), deals with subjects pertaining to the natural world. Another set of writings, which he sometimes referred to as "first philosophy" or "wisdom," deals with subjects that are more abstract and theoretical than those dealt with in the *Physics*. In time, this set of writings became known as "the books after the books on nature" (in Greek *ta meta ta physika biblia*), which eventually became shortened to *Metaphysics*. Metaphysics deals with a variety of important philosophical questions which include those listed below. We have already explored a number of these questions in the preceding chapters.

- What is the nature of reality?
- What is the place of humans in the universe? (chapters 6 and 7)
- Does life have meaning? (chapters 6 and 7)
- Do we have free wills that enable us to make independent choices? (chapter 4)
- How are the mind and body related to each other? (chapter 3)
- Is there life after death? (chapters 3 and 7)
- Does God exist? (chapter 7)
- What is the nature of the "self"? (chapter 3)

In fact, the only question that we haven't yet fully explored is the first one: "What is the nature of reality?" When philosophers ask this question, they are typically trying to discover "the way the world really is." Although the world has a certain *appearance* to us, many philosophers (and scientists) believe that the *reality* of the world is something very different. This leads to such questions as

- What is the ultimate "stuff" or "substance" of the universe?
- What aspects of the universe are eternal and unchanging?
- What aspects of the universe change and what principles govern this change?

Metaphysics Most generally, the philosophical investigation of the nature, constitution, and structure of reality.

414

- How did substances come into being?
- What is the relation of the material and the nonmaterial dimensions of the universe? (for example, the relations between our minds and our bodies, or God and ourselves?)

In philosophy, questions regarding the nature of Truth fall under the category of **epistemology**, which, as we saw in the first chapter, involves the study of knowledge. The term *epistemology* is derived from the Greek *episteme*, "knowledge," and *logos*, "explanation." It seeks to establish a framework that we can use to construct genuine and accurate understanding, and this entails identifying and developing criteria and methodologies for determining what we know and why we know it. Here are some of the questions epistemology attempts to answer:

- Can we ever really *know* anything?
- How do we know when we *don't* know something?
- What is the difference between *belief* and *knowledge*?
- Is truth possible?
- What are the roles of reason and experience in constructing knowledge and determining truth?
- Does truth evolve or is it unchanging?
- Can there be different "truths" for different people or is "truth" the same for all?

Metaphysics and epistemology are interdependent, and answering the questions in the one area frequently involves answering the questions in the other area. For example, determining the ultimate "substance" of the universe; whether it's eternal or subject to change; the relation of the material to the immaterial—none of these questions can be answered without addressing the questions of knowledge and truth that are a part of epistemology. So as we think our way through the next two chapters, we will be addressing both metaphysical and epistemological issues in an integrated context, exactly the way they naturally occur, rather than trying to impose an artificial separation. We can see this approach clearly illustrated in the following essay by the British philosopher **Bertrand Russell**, which analyzes the philosophical concepts of "appearance" and "reality" from the standpoints of both metaphysics and epistemology.

> **BERTRAND RUSSELL**
> (1872–1970)
> Twentieth century British Philosopher. One of the founders of modern logic. In *The Principles of Mathematics* (1903) and with Whitehead in the three volume *Principia Mathematica* (1910–1913) advanced the view that all of mathematics could be derived from logical premises. Also a political activist, he wrote many popular books on topics such as religion, ethics, and marriage.

Bertrand Russell,
The Problems of Philosophy

Chapter 1: Appearance and Reality

Is there any knowledge in the world which is so certain that no reasonable man could doubt it? This question, which at first sight might not seem difficult, is really one of the most difficult that can be asked. When we have realized the obstacles in the way of a straightforward and confident answer, we shall be well launched on the study of philosophy—for philosophy is merely the attempt to answer such ultimate questions, not carelessly and dogmatically, as we do in ordinary life and even in the sciences, but critically after exploring all that makes such questions puzzling, and after realizing all the vagueness and confusion that underlie our ordinary ideas.

In daily life, we assume as certain many things which, on a closer scrutiny, are found to be so full of apparent contradictions that only a great amount of thought enables us to know what it is that we really may believe. In the search for certainty, it is natural to begin with our present experiences, and in some sense, no doubt, knowledge is to be derived from them. But any statement as to what it is that our immediate experiences make us know is very likely to be wrong. It seems to me that I am now sitting in a chair, at a table of a certain shape, on which I see sheets of paper with writing or print. By turning my head I see out of the window buildings and clouds and the sun. I believe that the sun is about ninety-three million miles from the earth; that it is a hot globe many times bigger than the earth; that, owing to the earth's rotation, it rises every morning, and will continue to do so for an indefinite time in the future. I believe that, if any other normal person comes into my room, he will see the same chairs and tables and books and papers as I see, and that the table which I see is the same as the table which I feel pressing against my arm. All this seems to be so evident as to be hardly worth stating, except in answer to a man who doubts whether I know anything. Yet all this may be reasonably

Epistemology The study of the nature of knowledge and justification.

What is appearance? What is reality?

doubted, and all of it requires much careful discussion before we can be sure that we have stated it in a form that is wholly true.

To make our difficulties plain, let us concentrate attention on the table. To the eye it is oblong, brown and shiny, to the touch it is smooth and cool and hard; when I tap it, it gives out a wooden sound. Any one else who sees and feels and hears the table will agree with this description, so that it might seem as if no difficulty would arise; but as soon as we try to be more precise our troubles begin. Although I believe that the table is "really" of the same colour all over, the parts that reflect the light look much brighter than the other parts, and some parts look white because of reflected light. I know that, if I move, the parts that reflect the light will be different, so that the apparent distribution of colours on the table will change. It follows that if several people are looking at the table at the same moment, no two of them will see exactly the same distribution of colours, because no two can see it from exactly the same point of view, and any change in the point of view makes some change in the way the light is reflected.

For most practical purposes these differences are unimportant, but to the painter they are all-important: the painter has to unlearn the habit of thinking that things seem to have the colour which common sense says they "really" have, and to learn the habit of seeing things as they appear. Here we have already the beginning of one of the distinctions that cause most trouble in philosophy—the distinction between "appearance" and "reality," between what things seem to be and what they are. The painter wants to know what things seem to be, the practical man and the philosopher want to know what they are; but the philosopher's wish to know this is stronger than the practical man's, and is more troubled by knowledge as to the difficulties of answering the question.

To return to the table. It is evident from what we have found, that there is no colour which preeminently appears to be *the* colour of the table, or even of any one particular part of the table—it appears to be of different colours from different points of view, and there is no reason for regarding some of these as more really its colour than others. And we know that even from a given point of view the colour will seem different by artificial light, or to a colour-blind man, or to a man wearing blue spectacles, while in the dark there will be no colour at all, though to touch and hearing the table will be unchanged. This colour is not something which is inherent in the table, but something depending upon the table and the spectator and the way the light falls on the table. When, in ordinary life, we speak of *the* colour of the table, we only mean the sort of colour which it will seem to have to a normal spectator from an ordinary point of view under usual conditions of light. But the other colours which appear under other conditions have just as good a right to be considered real; and therefore, to avoid favouritism, we are compelled to deny that, in itself, the table has any one particular colour.

The same thing applies to the texture. With the naked eye one can see the grain, but otherwise the table looks smooth and even. If we looked at it through a microscope, we should see roughnesses and hills and valleys, and all sorts of differences that are imperceptible to the naked eye. Which of these is the "real" table? We are naturally tempted to say that what we see through the microscope is more real, but that in turn would be changed by a still more powerful microscope. If, then, we cannot trust what we see with the naked eye, why should we trust what we see through a microscope? Thus, again, the confidence in our senses with which we began deserts us.

The *shape* of the table is no better. We are all in the habit of judging as to the "real" shapes of things, and we do this so unreflectingly that we come to think we actually see the real shapes. But, in fact, as we all have to learn if we try to draw, a given thing looks different in shape from every different point of view. If our table is "really" rectangular, it will look, from almost all points of view, as if it had two acute angles and two obtuse angles. If opposite sides are parallel, they will look as if they converged to a point away from the spectator; if they are of equal length, they will look as if the nearer side were longer. All these things are not commonly noticed in looking at a table, because experience has taught us to construct the "real" shape from the apparent shape, and the "real" shape is what interests us as practical men. But the "real" shape is not what we see; it is something inferred from what we see. And what we see is constantly changing in shape as we, move about the room; so that here again the senses seem not to give us the truth about the table itself, but only about the appearance of the table.

Similar difficulties arise when we consider the sense of touch. It is true that the table always gives us a sensation of hardness, and we feel that it resists pressure. But the sensation we obtain depends upon how hard we press the table and also upon what part of the body we press with; thus the various sensations due to various pressures or various parts of the body cannot be supposed to reveal *directly* any definite property of the table, but at most to be signs of some property which perhaps *causes* all the sensations, but is not actually apparent in any of them. And the same applies still more obviously to the sounds which can be elicited by rapping the table.

Thus it becomes evident that the real table, if there is one, is not the same as what we immediately experience by sight or touch or hearing. The real table, if there is one, is not *immediately* known to us at all, but must be an inference from what is immediately known. Hence, two very difficult questions at once arise; namely, (1) Is there a real table at all? (2) If so, what sort of object can it be?

It will help us in considering these questions to have a few simple terms of which the meaning is definite and clear. Let us give the name of "sense-data" to the things that are immediately known in sensation: such things as colours, sounds, smells, hardnesses, roughnesses, and so on. We shall give the name "sensation" to the experience of being immediately aware of these things. Thus, whenever we see a colour, we have a sensation *of* the colour, but the colour itself is a sense-datum, not a sensation. The colour is that *of* which we are immediately aware, and the awareness itself is the sensation. It is plain that if we are to know anything about the table, it must be by means of the sense-data—brown colour, oblong shape, smoothness, etc.—which we associate with the table; but, for the reasons which have been given, we cannot say that the table is the sense-data, or even that the sense-data are directly properties of the table. Thus a problem arises as to the relation of the sense-data to the real table, supposing there is such a thing.

The real table, if it exists, we will call a "physical object." Thus we have to consider the relation of sense-data to physical objects. The collection of all physical objects is called "matter." Thus our two questions may be re-stated as follows: (1) Is there any such thing as matter? (2) If so, what is its nature?

The philosopher who first brought prominently forward the reasons for regarding the immediate objects of our senses as not existing independently of us was **George Berkeley** (1685–1753). His *Three Dialogues between Hylas and Philonous, in Opposition to Sceptics and Atheists*, undertake to prove that there is no such thing as matter at all, and that the world consists of nothing but minds and their ideas. Hylas has hitherto believed in matter, but he is no match for Philonous, who mercilessly drives him into contradictions and paradoxes, and makes his own denial of matter seem, in the end, as if it were almost common sense. The arguments employed are of very different value: some are important and sound, others are confused or quibbling. But Berkeley retains the merit of having shown that the existence of matter is capable of being denied without absurdity, and that if there are any things that exist independently of us they cannot be the immediate objects of our sensations.

There are two different questions involved when we ask whether matter exists, and it is important to keep them clear. We commonly mean by "matter" something which is opposed to "mind," something which we think of as occupying space and as radically incapable of any sort of thought or consciousness. It is chiefly in this sense that Berkeley denies matter; that is to say, he does not deny that the sense-data which we commonly take as signs of the existence of the table are really signs of the existence of *something* independent of us, but he does deny that this something is non-mental, that it is neither mind nor ideas entertained by some mind. He admits that there must be something which continues to exist when we go out of the room or shut our eyes, and that what we call seeing the table does really give us reason for believing in something which persists even when we are not seeing it. But he thinks that this something cannot be radically different in nature from what we see, and cannot be independent of seeing altogether, though it must be independent of *our* seeing. He is thus led to regard the "real" table as an idea in the mind of God. Such an idea has the required permanence and independence of ourselves, without being—as matter would otherwise be—something quite unknowable, in the sense that we can only infer it, and can never be directly and immediately aware of it.

Other philosophers since Berkeley have also held that, although the table does not depend for its existence upon being seen by me, it does depend upon being seen (or otherwise apprehended in sensation) by *some* mind—not necessarily the mind of God, but more often the whole collective mind of the universe. This they hold, as Berkeley does,

George Berkeley (1685–1753) Irish Philosopher. With Locke and Hume one of the three great British Empiricists. In *Treatise Concerning the Principles of Human Knowledge* (1710), defends an idealist position which maintains there exists no matter, only sensible objects whose essence is to be perceived.

Gottfried Leibniz (1646–1716)
German Philosopher. Prominent figure
in the rationalist tradition. Maintained
that the world, as created by God, is
the best of all possible worlds.

chiefly because they think there can be nothing real—or at any rate nothing known to be real except minds and their thoughts and feelings. We might state the argument by which they support their view in some such way as this: "Whatever can be thought of is an idea in the mind of the person thinking of it; therefore nothing can be thought of except ideas in minds; therefore anything else is inconceivable, and what is inconceivable cannot exist."

Such an argument, in my opinion, is fallacious; and of course those who advance it do not put it so shortly or so crudely. But whether valid or not, the argument has been very widely advanced in one form or another; and very many philosophers, perhaps a majority, have held that there is nothing real except minds and their ideas. Such philosophers are called "idealists." When they come to explaining matter, they either say, like Berkeley, that matter is really nothing but a collection of ideas, or they say, like **Gottfried Leibniz** (1646–1716), that what appears as matter is really a collection of more or less rudimentary minds.

But these philosophers, though they deny matter as opposed to mind, nevertheless, in another sense, admit matter. It will be remembered that we asked two questions; namely, (1) Is there a real table at all? (2) If so, what sort of object can it be? Now both Berkeley and Leibniz admit that there is a real table, but Berkeley says it is certain ideas in the mind of God, and Leibniz says it is a colony of souls. Thus both of them

 VISUAL PHILOSOPHY

How Do We Know
What Is Real?

How does this picture illustrate
Bertrand Russell's characterization
of "the strangeness and wonder
lying just below the surface even
in the commonest things of daily
life"?

answer our first question in the affirmative, and only diverge from the views of ordinary mortals in their answer to our second question. In fact, almost all philosophers seem to be agreed that there is a real table. They almost all agree that, however much our sense-data—colour, shape, smoothness, etc.—may depend upon us, yet their occurrence is a sign of something existing independently of us, something differing, perhaps, completely from our sense-data whenever we are in a suitable relation to the real table. Now obviously this point in which the philosophers are agreed—the view that there is a real table, whatever its nature may be is vitally important, and it will be worth while to consider what reasons there are for accepting this view before we go on to the further question as to the nature of the real table. Our next chapter, therefore, will be concerned with the reasons for supposing that there is a real table at all.

Before we go farther it will be well to consider for a moment what it is that we have discovered so far. It has appeared that, if we take any common object of the sort that is supposed to be known by the senses, what the senses *immediately* tell us is not the truth about the object as it is apart from us, but only the truth about certain sense-data which, so far as we can see, depend upon the relations between us and the object. Thus what we directly see and feel is merely "appearance," which we believe to be a sign of some "reality" behind. But if the reality is not what appears, have we any means of knowing whether there is any reality at all? And if so, have we any means of finding out what it is like?

Such questions are bewildering, and it is difficult to know that even the strangest hypotheses may not be true. Thus our familiar table, which has roused but the slightest thoughts in us hitherto, has become a problem full of surprising possibilities. The one thing we know about it is that it is not what it seems. Beyond this modest result, so far, we have the most complete liberty of conjecture. Leibniz tells us it is a community of souls: Berkeley tells us it is an idea in the mind of God; sober science, scarcely less wonderful, tells us it is a vast collection of electric charges in violent motion.

Among these surprising possibilities, doubt suggests that perhaps there is no table at all. Philosophy, if it cannot answer so many questions as we could wish, has at least the power of asking questions which increase the interest of the world, and show the strangeness and wonder lying just below the surface even in the commonest things of daily life. ▪

THINK PHILOSOPHICALLY 8.1
How Do I Know What Is "Real"?

PHILOSOPHER'S NOTEBOOK

- After reading this article, look closely at a piece of furniture that is within your field of vision: Is the piece of furniture *real*? How do you *know* if it's real or not? Explain your reasoning for both responses.
- Russell analyzes the table near him in terms of its color, texture, and shape, and concludes:

  > Thus it becomes evident that the real table, if there is one, is not the same as what we immediately experience by sight or touch or hearing. The real table, if there is one, is not *immediately* known to us at all, but must be an inference from what is immediately known.

  Do you agree with Russell's conclusion? Why or why not?
- Russell goes on to observe: "Hence, two very difficult questions at once arise; namely, (1) Is there a real table at all? (2) If so, what sort of object can it be?" Explain how you would respond to these two questions, and explain the reasoning for your conclusions.
- Russell's article emphasizes the significance of the philosophical distinction between *appearances* (what things seem to be) and *reality*, (what they are). After "thinking philosophically" about these issues, do you see the world around you in a new light? Explain your response and the reasons for it.

Plato: *Reality Is the Eternal Realm of the Forms*

PLATO

(427–347 B.C.E.)
Ancient Greek Philosopher. It was once said that all of Western Philosophy is merely footnotes to Plato. A student of Socrates, he wrote many dialogues featuring Socrates as the main character and dealt with many philosophical issues such as morality, politics, metaphysics, and epistemology.

Plato's view of knowledge (epistemology) and reality (metaphysics) are intimately intertwined. The thinkers before Plato—collectively known as the "pre-Socratic philosophers" (i.e., "before" Socrates) had wrestled with the apparent contradiction between the eternal and the finite, the immutable and the changing. Was reality in a constant state of flux, as the enigmatic **Heraclitus** (c. 500 B.C.E.) believed? "All is change" and "Change alone is unchanging," Heraclitus declared, and if we examine the physical world in which we live, that certainly seems to be the case. Nothing in the world remains static: life forms are continually being born, aging, and dying; even the physical aspects of the universe are in a continual state of change. But if all is flux, then how can we ever hope to achieve permanent, universal knowledge? "It is in changing that all things find repose," Heraclitus announced, but this suggests that other than acknowledging that change is the defining attribute of the cosmos, we must abandon attempts to discover certain knowledge. Heraclitus did believe that the *Logos* is the defining *form* of the universe, the deeper "nature" behind natural, changing events. But the *Logos* is not accessible to us. We cannot see it, hear it, touch it, or—most significantly—*know* it, except through flashes of unexpected insight. "Unless you expect the unexpected you will never find truth, for it is hard to discover and hard to attain." Truth and knowledge are hidden and elusive, and cannot be captured through systematic study. For Heraclitus, "You cannot step into the same river, for other waters are continually flowing on." And with those flowing waters goes any possibility of achieving knowledge in any meaningful sense.

Parmenides (fl. fifth century B.C.E.), an accomplished mathematician and another pre-Socratic thinker, had a different view from Heraclitus, positing a necessary, static, unchanging unity running throughout all of what is in flux. He assumed that reality must necessarily be eternal and unchanging: therefore the changing world of our experience cannot be real: it is an illusion! What *is* real is "Being," which is a single coherent reality, "The One." *Being* is perfect, complete, permanent, and unchanging—it's what *is*. "It is the *being* of the visible cosmos, immobilized, and to a great extent purified, but still clearly recognizable." Parmenides reasons: "How could *being* perish? How could it come into being? If it came into being, it is not; and so too if it is about to be at some future time." But like Heraclitus, Parmenides does not believe that we can achieve extensive knowledge of "The One" in areas other than mathematics.

What is the relation of "Being" to "change"? Parmenides seems to have believed that everything is somehow one, although just what is meant by one could be either holistic or a plurality somehow held together. This is Being, or what is. Read as a holistic unity, it is difficult to comprehend the relation of Being to beings, or the particular things (like ourselves) that seem to partake of it. In what remains of his poem (as with Heraclitus, only fragments of Parmenides' writings have survived), Parmenides characterizes Being as imperishable, indivisible, and unchanging, but if the unity of Being is understood instead as the holding-together of a plurality, then Being must include perishing, division, and change within itself. Being can then be pictured not simply as some form of perfect sphere, but rather the unity that binds all things—the living and dead, the changing and the static, the finite and the infinite—together. Just how this dialectical unity holds such remarkable opposites together is what Parmenides asks us to think about further.

Plato's solution to this monumental conflict between reality-as-change and reality-as-eternal was both brilliant and problematic. Plato simply created the idea of "Two Worlds." One world, the world of *Becoming*, is the world we are familiar with,

These three models represent conceptions of the physical universe by three early Greek thinkers: Homer, Anaximander and Hecataeus. How would you analyze them?

the physical world we inhabit. This world is continually changing, evolving, disappearing. This "Becoming" reality is taken in through our senses, and it is impossible to develop any genuine knowledge of it, for we can merely describe its changing nature as it appears to us. This is the world of "appearance."

The other world, the world of "reality," is much different. This is the world of "Being," a realm that is eternal, unchanging, and knowable through the faculty of reason. Plato doesn't suggest that the everyday world of Becoming is an illusion: it's just that this physical world of changing sensation is "less real" than the timeless world of Being. But what does the eternal world of Being contain, what is its relation to the mutable world of Becoming? It is populated with *Forms*, Plato's the cornerstone of Plato's metaphysics and epistemology.

What precisely are **Forms**? The word *form* itself derives from the Greek word *eidos*, which is variously translated as idea, archetype, or essence. Plato considers Forms to be the ideal archetypes or essences of everything that exists. We can think of them as the perfect ideals of every meaningful object and idea. For example, there is an ideal Form for horses—the essence of what we mean when we use the term *horse*. This Form would include all of the essential qualities that constitute being a "horse," attributes that the tyrannical schoolmaster Thomas Gradgrind gets a terrified student, Bitzer, to enumerate in this passage from Charles Dickens's novel *Hard Times*.

> "Bitzer," said Thomas Gradgrind. "Your definition of a horse."
>
> "Quadruped. Graminivorous. Forty teeth, namely twenty-four grinders, four eye-teeth, and twelve incisive. Sheds coat in the spring; in marshy countries sheds hoofs, too. Hoofs hard, but requiring to be shod with iron. Age known by marks in mouth." Thus (and much more) Bitzer.
>
> "Now girl number twenty," said Mr. Gradgrind, "you know what a horse is."

Of course, Plato's ideal Form of "horse" would also include aesthetic qualities (physical beauty), functional qualities (strength, endurance, speed), and any other attributes that constitute the ideal, perfect idea of "horse."

For Plato, the Form of "horse," actually exists in the timeless and eternal world of Being. Although the form for "horse"—and other Forms—do not exist in a material sense, they do exist independently of the minds of people. And, Plato believes, we can discover these Forms through disciplined study based on developing our ability to reason in an enlightened fashion. That is to say, we can become familiar with the Form of "horse," and in so doing we have knowledge of the ideal pattern that we can use to understand and evaluate all of the actually existing horses in the world. For Plato, the relationship between the ideal Form of "horse," and the multitude of actual, existing horses, is complex and central to Plato's thought. He says that the actually existing horses *participate* in the ideal Form of horse. What exactly does "participate" mean? That's exactly the question that Plato's student Aristotle posed to Plato, and not receiving a satisfactory response, Aristotle vigorously criticized Plato's views:

> It is hard, too, to see how a weaver or a carpenter will benefit in regard to his own craft by knowing this (a form), or how the man who has viewed the Idea itself will be a better doctor or general thereby. For a doctor seems not even to study health in this way, but the health of man, or perhaps rather the health of a particular man; it is individuals that he is healing.

Plato uses other terms to elaborate this idea of "participation," including "to reflect," "to resemble," "to share in." But the precise nature of the Forms to the world of particulars is still ambiguous in Plato's writings.

Heraclitus (c. 540–c. 480 B.C.E.) Presocratic Philosopher. The most influential of Presocratic philosophers; maintained all things were in a constant state of flux and that the governing principle of the universe is what he called *logos*.

Parmenides (c. 515 B.C.E.) Presocratic Philosopher. Maintained only knowledge of "that which is" is possible and not of "that which is not" which led him to the belief that reality must be changeless and undifferentiated since if it were not then it would involve "that which is not."

Form In metaphysics, especially Plato's and Aristotle's, the structure or essence of a thing as contrasted with its matter.

The world of the ancient Greeks was comprised primarily of islands and seas, thus leading them to infer that the whole earth floated on water. What led later Europeans to infer that the earth was flat?

One way to think about how the two worlds relate is conceptually: the ideal Form is the ultimate *concept* of the object or idea. Such a concept is defined by its boundaries: including, in the case of "horse," the qualities enumerated by young Bitzer. The actual horses in the world can then be seen as *examples* or *instances* of the concept. If someone tries to pass off a donkey or zebra as a horse, we will be able to disqualify these pretenders, providing that we have developed knowledge of the Form/concept. "That's not a horse because it lacks the following necessary qualities . . ."

There are many different kinds of Platonic Forms: geometrical, mathematical, and logical relations (triangularity, equivalence, identity); human virtues (goodness, wisdom, courage); sensible properties (roundness, redness); and abstract concepts (justice, beauty, virtue, truth). In the sensible, day-to-day world of living, we see only imperfect examples of these perfect, eternal Forms, and the world of our senses can never yield authentic knowledge, only unsubstantial, changeable opinions.

It is in his doctrine of the Forms that we see the intersection of Plato's metaphysics and his epistemology. The existence of the Forms as transcendent, eternal archetypes enables Plato to distinguish genuine knowledge from mere, ill-informed opinion. We develop opinions through the simple experience of living and observing the world. But these opinions reflect the transitory nature of human life and so can never achieve the status of universal knowledge. Such knowledge only comes from knowledge of the eternal Forms, through our ability to use our reasoning abilities, as he describes:

> That which is apprehended by intelligence and reason is always in the same state, but that which is conceived by opinion with the help of sensation and without reason is always in a process of becoming and perishing and never really is.

Scientific knowledge, in every area of human experience, consists of apprehending the necessary and universal truths of that discipline. For example, gaining knowledge of various forms of government requires developing a grasp of the fundamental concepts of the discipline, as well as the principles and laws that characterize it. Thus, we must use our reasoning capacities to go beyond the world of appearance and opinion, to grasp the essence of the Forms that define that discipline.

> The true lover of knowledge naturally strives for truth, and is not content with common opinion, but soars with undimmed and unwearied passion till he grasps the essential nature of things.

Plato's metaphysical view enables him to achieve his epistemological goals, employing clear rational criteria to distinguish unsubstantiated and transient *opinion,* from the eternal realm of *knowledge.* Even when our opinions happen to be accurate, this does not mean we have achieved knowledge.

> Haven't you noticed that opinion without knowledge is blind—isn't anyone with a true but unthinking opinion like a blind man on the right road?

Plato's metaphysical doctrine of the Forms provides him with a rational grounding for true knowledge, which enables him to escape from the snare of relativism and "unanchored" changeable opinions.

The Divided Line

Plato provides a visual analogy to illustrate the corresponding levels in his metaphysics and epistemology, which is reproduced in Figure 8.1. Levels C and D represent the world of Appearance, the Visible World in which we live our lives. Despite our best efforts, the highest form of knowing that we can achieve in this world is

	Metaphysics		Epistemology			
Being	Higher Forms e.g. Wisdom	Level A	Understanding	Knowledge		INTELLIGIBLE WORLD
	Lower Forms e.g. Human form	Level B	Reasoning			
Becoming	Sensible Objects e.g. Socrates	Level C	Perception	Opinion		VISIBLE WORLD
	Images e.g. Socrates' reputation	Level D	Imagination			

Figure 8.1 Plato's Divided Line

Opinion. This is the world of Becoming, where everything is continually changing, evolving, disappearing, reappearing. The lowest level of Knowing and Being (Level D) is that of images produced by the human faculty of Imagination. This is the level of illusion, composed of unsubstantiated beliefs, transitory images, and fragmentary impressions that are received uncritically. For example, as we saw in *The Apology* in chapter 2, Socrates acknowledged that there were many different images of who he was, conflicting perspectives of his character and reputation. He saw his challenge to be clarifying these unsubstantiated views of him, but realized the difficulty of his task in a realm where people state their opinions without trying to provide compelling reasons and evidence. Plato was convinced that much of what people consider to be "knowledge" in the world is actually at this lowest level of opinion, but that they deceive themselves into thinking that their unsupported impressions have genuine merit.

The next level in Plato's hierarchy of metaphysics and epistemology is Level C, that of Perception, which is effected by means of our five senses. Unlike the images produced by the imagination, perceptions have a grounding in the actual world in which we live. We see, hear, touch, taste, and smell things on an ongoing basis. Thus, Socrates was an actual, physical human being whom people in Athens could experience directly. But although the beliefs about the world based on our perceptions are more substantial than those produced by our imaginations, these perceptual beliefs still fall far short of knowledge. As we shall see, our perceptions are typically fragmentary and incomplete, and the conclusions that we reach based on them are typically subjective and biased. For example, although many people in Athens had seen, heard, and spoken to Socrates over a period of fifty years, people still had a diverse variety of perspectives on him. And, of course, the same principle applies in our lives. For example, interview a number of people who have witnessed the same event and you'll likely hear a wide variety of different perceptions. Ask a number of people their opinion of the President, and you will no doubt receive many different points of view. Compare people's opinions with respect to a movie they saw or a college class they took, and you will no doubt find a range of different perceptions. When people's perceptions conflict, how can we tell which are "true" and rise to the level of Knowledge? That's the challenge of epistemology, and Plato believed that it was impossible to achieve at this level of metaphysics and epistemology.

According to Plato, the realm of human experience where knowledge exists is Level B, the level of the "Lower" Forms. Lower forms are those universals that we find exemplified in our physical world. For example, Socrates was a man who was an example of the universal form of "Human Being." And for us to understand the essence of Socrates, we need to use our reasoning ability to develop a clear idea of what it means to be a human being: what are the essential qualities that constitute this Form. Of course, Socrates isn't the only example of this form: all human beings illustrate or "participate" in the form of Human Being. And this Form qualifies as "Knowledge," according to Plato, because it represents a form of knowing that is universal and unchanging, unlike the transitory perceptions and images of Levels C and D.

The highest realm of Knowledge in Plato's metaphysics and epistemology is that of the "Higher" Forms, Level A. Universals such as Truth, Beauty, the Good, Justice are all examples of Higher Forms. Like the Lower Forms, the Higher Forms represent universals that are unchanging and eternal. The difference is that the Higher Forms refer to abstract ideals rather than actual physical objects in the world. Thus, although many people considered Socrates to illustrate the form of Wisdom by being a wise man, "wisdom" is not the essence of a physical object in the world that we can experience. It—like truth, beauty, justice, and the Good—exists on a much higher intellectual level, and understanding these ideals requires a lifetime of rational exploration and reflection. There are few people who can achieve this supreme understanding of these highest Forms. When you reach this exalted level of understanding, you "directly apprehend" these supreme, absolute Forms.

Plato's Theory of Innate Ideas

Plato's belief that genuine knowledge can only be achieved through our reasoning abilities means that in epistemological terms he is a *rationalist*. In contrast, philosophers who, like Aristotle, believe that we can gain true knowledge through our sense experience, are known as *empiricists* (though Aristotle was, like Plato, also seeking universal knowledge). As we will see in the pages ahead, this division between **rationalism** and **empiricism** has endured since first introduced by Plato and Aristotle, and it has remained one of the core issues in epistemology.

One of the strongest arguments that rationalists advance to support their view that genuine knowledge is based on reason, not sense experience, is that humans seem to possess knowledge that could not possibly be derived solely from our experiences in the world. For example, the principles of mathematics and logic have for the most part been developed independently of experience. And although these principles can be *applied* to objects and events in the world, their truth is not dependent on these objects or events. In the dialogue the *Meno*, Plato uses a dramatic example to illustrate this very point. Socrates is discussing his belief in the immortality of the soul with Meno, along with his conviction that each soul begins life with essential knowledge. Such knowledge is *latent* in the sense that it requires experience to activate it, but it is in no way dependent on experience for its existence or truth. We need only to remember or "recollect" this knowledge for it to be brought to consciousness and used by us. Such knowledge is considered to be *innate* because it is present at birth. How can the existence of such knowledge be demonstrated? Socrates' solution is ingenious. He calls over an illiterate slave boy and presents him with the following problem: Socrates draws on the ground a square two feet by two feet (four feet square) and asks the boy to draw a second square that is exactly twice the size of the first square. The boy's first idea is to double the sides of the square to four feet by four feet, but he sees immediately that this solution is wrong. Through careful questioning, Socrates guides the boy through a systematic solution and geometric proof of the problem. Each step of the way, the boy seems to "know" the correct response, though he has never been taught any form of mathematics. Socrates then reflects on the entire process and its implications for innate knowledge:

Plato

Rationalism The position that reason has precedence over other ways of acquiring knowledge, or, more strongly, that it is the unique path to knowledge.

Empiricism The position that the senses (and sense experience) are primary in acquiring knowledge.

Socrates: What do you think, Meno? Has he, in his answers, expressed any opinion that was not his own?

Meno: No, they were all his own.

Socrates: And yet, as we said, he did not know a short time ago?

Meno: That is true.

Socrates: So these opinions were in him, were they not?

Meno: Yes.

Socrates: So the man who does not know has within himself true opinions about the things that he does not know?

Meno: So it appears.

Socrates: These opinions have now just been stirred up like a dream, but if he were repeatedly asked these same questions in various ways, you know that in the end his knowledge about these things would be as accurate as anyone's.

Meno: It is likely.

Socrates: And he will know it without having been taught but only questioned, and find the knowledge within himself?

Meno: Yes.

Socrates: And is not finding knowledge within oneself recollection?

Meno: Certainly.

Socrates: Must he not either have at some time acquired the knowledge he now possesses, or else have always possessed it?

Meno: Yes.

Socrates: If he always had it, he would always have known. If he acquired it, he cannot have done so in his present life. Or has someone taught him geometry? For he will perform in the same way about all geometry, and all other knowledge. Has someone taught him everything? You should know, especially as he has been born and brought up in your house.

Meno: But I know that no one has taught him.

Socrates: Yet he has these opinions, or doesn't he?

Meno: That seems indisputable, Socrates.

Socrates: If he has not acquired them in his present life, is it not clear that he had them and had learned them at some other time?

Meno: It seems so.

Socrates: Then that was the time when he was not a human being?

Meno: Yes.

Socrates: If then, during the time he exists and is not a human being he will have true opinions which, when stirred by questioning, become knowledge, will not his soul have learned during all time? For it is clear that during all time he exists either as a man or not.

Meno: So it seems.

Socrates: Then if the truth about reality is always in our soul, the soul would be immortal so that you should always confidently try to seek out and recollect what you do not know at present—that is, what you do not recollect?

Meno: Somehow, Socrates, I think that what you say is right.

Socrates: I think so too, Meno.

Plato, *The Meno*

Where does this knowledge come from? Plato's theory is that each soul existed in a perfect world before birth where such knowledge was learned, as he explains:

For as all nature is akin, and the soul has (already) learned all things, there is no difficulty in learning all the rest, if a man is strenuous and does not faint; for all enquiry is but recollection.

Plato, *The Meno*

THINK CRITICALLY

8.2

PHILOSOPHER'S NOTEBOOK

Is Knowledge Innate?

- Do you find Socrates' example of the slave boy's "recollection" of geometric principles that he has not been explicitly taught to be persuasive? Why or why not? Can you think of an alternative explanation for the slave boy's "knowledge"? What else might be going on besides recollection when we see the correctness of the claim that to double the area of square we should use the length of the original diagonal for the new sides.

- Reflect on your own intellectual development. Can you identify knowledge of which you became aware that you did not learn from experience? For example, your belief in the scientific law of cause and effect. Although you may experience events connected to other events, there is nothing in experience that "teaches" you that this connection is a necessary one. Other examples might include your knowledge of logic, mathematics, language, moral principles, or religious insight.

- Imagine that you disagreed with Socrates' concept of innate knowledge learned in a previous perfect world before birth. Explain how you would go about trying to convince Socrates that he was wrong.

- If you believe that there is innate knowledge independent of experience, and you reject Socrates' idea of a perfect world where immortal souls exist before birth, then how would you explain the origin of these innate ideas—in other words, where did they come from?

Most philosophers—as well as psychologists, anthropologists, and linguists—who believe in some sort of innate knowledge *do not* accept these metaphysical beliefs of Plato. Instead, they tend to believe that such innate knowledge is simply part of the biological/cognitive "software" that humans come programmed with. But jettisoning Plato's metaphysical "perfect world" where immortal souls learn their innate knowledge leaves the core argument he is making in this passage untouched: how *do* we acquire knowledge that cannot be accounted for by sense experience if it is not innate and known through reason?

Plato's Allegory of the Cave: The Journey from Ignorance to Knowledge

For Plato, ascending to the realm of the Forms to achieve genuine knowledge is a challenging, arduous process. Most people are submerged in the shadowy world of illusion and mere opinion, completely unaware of their own lack of enlightenment. It is possible for people to move from ignorance to rationally based knowledge and wisdom, but it requires willingness, dedication, and wise teachers as guides. Plato used a variety of metaphors to describe this intellectual journey of discovery. The most powerful and enduring metaphor is "The Allegory of the Cave," which has become a touchstone of Western thinking. The allegory communicates in rich and symbolic terms the journey through the various stages of knowledge, which echo the metaphysical and epistemological structure of the Divided Line analogy:

Plato's Divided Line Structure

Metaphysics	Epistemology
Higher Forms	Wisdom, intellectual enlightenment
Lower Forms	Rationally based knowledge
Sensible objects	Informed opinion
Images	Ignorance, mere opinion, illusion

Plato, *The Republic*

Socrates: Imagine men to be living in an underground cavelike dwelling place, which has a way up to the light along its whole width, but the entrance is a long way up. The men have been there from childhood, with their neck and legs in fetters, so that they remain in the same place and can only see ahead of them, as their bonds prevent them turning their heads. Light is provided by a fire burning some way behind them, and on a higher ground, there is a path across the cave and along this a low wall has been built, like the screen at a puppet show in front of the performers who show their puppets above it.

Glaucon: I see it.

Socrates: See then also men carrying along that wall, so that they overtop it, all kinds of artifacts, statues of men, reproductions of other animals in stone or wood fashioned in all sorts of ways, and, as is likely, some of the carriers are talking while others are silent.

Glaucon: This is a strange picture, and strange prisoners.

Socrates: They are like us, I said. Do you think, in the first place, that such men could see anything of themselves and each other except the shadows which the fire casts upon the wall of the cave in front of them?

Glaucon: How could they, if they have to keep their heads still throughout life?

Socrates: And is not the same true of the objects carried along the wall?

Glaucon: Quite.

Socrates: If they could converse with one another, do you not think that they would consider these shadows to be the real things?

Glaucon: Necessarily.

Socrates: What if their prison had an echo which reached them from in front of them? Whenever one of the carriers passing behind the wall spoke, would they not think that it was the shadow passing in front of them which was talking? Do you agree?

Glaucon: By Zeus, I do.

Socrates: Altogether then, I said, such men would believe the truth to be nothing else than the shadows of the artifacts?

Glaucon: They must believe that.

Socrates: Consider then what deliverance from their bonds and the curing of their ignorance would be if something like this naturally happened to them. Whenever one of them was freed, had to stand up suddenly, turn his head, walk, and look up toward the light, doing all that would give him pain, the flash of the fire would make it impossible for him to see the objects of which he had earlier seen the shadows. What do you think he would say if he was told that what he saw was foolishness, that he was now somewhat closer to reality and turned to things that existed more fully, that he saw more correctly? If one then pointed to each of the objects passing by, asked him what each was, and forced him to answer, do you not think he would be at a loss and believe that the things which he saw earlier were truer than the things now pointed out to him.

Socrates

Glaucon: Much truer.

Socrates: If one then compelled him to look at the fire itself, his eyes would hurt, he would turn round and flee toward those things which he could see, and think that they were in fact clearer than those now shown to him.

Glaucon: Quite so.

Socrates: And if one were to drag him thence by force up the rough and steep path, and did not let him go before he was dragged into the sunlight, would he not be in physical pain and angry as he was dragged along? When he came into the light, with the sunlight filing his eyes, he would not be able to see a single one of the things which are now said to be true.

Glaucon: Not at once, certainly.

Socrates: I think he would need time to get adjusted before he could see things in the world above; at first he would see shadows most easily, then reflections of men and other things in water, then the things themselves. After this he would see objects in the sky and the sky itself more easily at night, the light of the stars and the moon more easily than the sun and the light of the sun during the day.

Glaucon: Of course.

Socrates: Then, at last, he would be able to see the sun, not images of it in water or in some alien place, but the sun itself in its own place, and be able to contemplate it.

Glaucon: That must be so.

Socrates: After this he would reflect that it is the sun which provides the seasons and the years, which governs everything in the visible world, and is also in some way the cause of those other things which he used to see.

Glaucon: Clearly that would be the next stage.

Socrates: What then? As he reminds himself of his first dwelling place, of the wisdom there and of his fellow prisoners, would he not reckon himself happy for the change, and pity them?

Glaucon: Surely.

Socrates: And if the men below had praise and honours from each other, and prizes for the man who saw most clearly the shadows that passed before them, and who could best remember which usually came earlier and which later, and which came together and thus could most ably prophesy the future, do you think our man would desire those rewards and envy those who were honoured and held power among the prisoners, or would he feel, as Homer put it, that he certainly wished to be "serf to another man without possessions upon the earth" and go through any suffering, rather than share their opinions and live as they do?*

Glaucon: Quite so, I think he would rather suffer anything.

Socrates: Reflect on this too. If this man went down into the cave again and sat down in the same seat, would his eyes not be filled with darkness, coming suddenly out of the sunlight?

Glaucon: They certainly would.

Socrates: And if he had to contend again with those who had remained prisoners in recognizing those shadows while his sight was affected and his eyes had not settled down—and the time for this adjustment would not be short—would he not be ridiculed? Would it not be said that he had returned from his upward journey with his eyesight spoiled, and that it was not worthwhile even to attempt to travel upward? As for the man who tried to free them and lead them upward, if they could somehow lay their hands on him and kill him, they would do so.

Glaucon: They certainly would.

Socrates: This whole image, my dear Glaucon, must be related to what we said before. The realm of the visible should be compared to the prison dwelling, and the fire inside it to the power of the sun. If you interpret the upward journey and the contemplation of things above as the upward journey of the soul to the intelligible realm, you will grasp what I surmise since you were keen to hear it. Whether it is true or not only the god knows, but this is how I see it, namely that in the intelligible world the Form of the Good is the last to be seen, and with difficulty; when seen it must be reckoned to be for all the cause of all that is right and beautiful, to have produced in the visible world both the light and the fount of light, while in the intelligible world it is itself that which produces and controls truth and intelligence, and he who is to act intelligently in public or in private must see it.

Glaucon: I share your thought as far as I am able.

Socrates: Come then, share with me this thought also: do not be surprised that those who have reached this point are unwilling to occupy themselves with human affairs, and that their souls are always pressing upward to spend their time there, for this is natural if things are as our parable indicates.

Glaucon: That is very likely.

Socrates: Further, do you think it at all surprising that anyone coming to the evils of human life from the contemplation of the divine behaves awkwardly and appears very ridiculous while his eyes are still dazzled and before he is sufficiently adjusted to the darkness around him, if he is compelled to contend in court or some other place about the shadows of justice or the objects of which they are shadows, and to carry through the contest about these in the way these things are understood by those who have never seen Justice itself?

Glaucon: That is not surprising at all.

Socrates: Anyone with intelligence would remember that the eyes may be confused in two ways and from two causes, coming from light into darkness as well as from darkness into light. Realizing that the same applies to the soul, whenever he sees a soul disturbed and unable to see something, he will not laugh mindlessly but will consider whether it has come from a brighter life and is dimmed because unadjusted, or has come from greater ignorance into greater light and is filled with a brighter dazzlement. The former he would declare happy in its life and experience, the latter he would pity, and if he should wish to laugh at it, his laughter would be less ridiculous than if he laughed at the soul that has come from the light above.

Glaucon: What you say is very reasonable.

---

*The Odyssey 11, 489–90, where Achilles says to Odysseus, on the latter's visit to the underworld, that he would rather be a servant to a poor man on earth than king among the dead (trans. note).

Socrates: We must then, if these things are true, think something like this about them, namely that education is not what some declare it to be; they say that knowledge is not present in the soul and that they put it in, like putting sight into blind eyes.

Glaucon: They sure say that.

Socrates: Our present argument shows that the capacity to learn and the organ with which to do so are present in every person's soul. It is as if it were not possible to turn the eye from darkness to light without turning the whole body; so one must turn one's whole soul from the world of becoming until it can endure to contemplate reality, and the brightest of realities, which we say is the Good.

Glaucon: Yes.

Socrates: Education then is the art of doing this very thing, this turning around, the knowledge of how the soul can most easily and most effectively be turned around; it is not the art of putting the capacity of sight into the soul; the soul possesses that already but it is not turned the right way or looking where it should. This is what education has to deal with. ▪

 Plato, *The Republic*

 VISUAL PHILOSOPHY

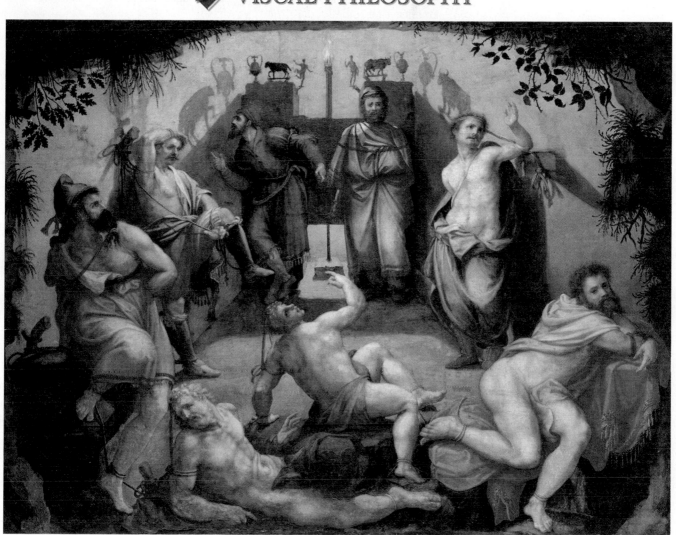

The Quest for Truth

In "Plato's Allegory of the Cave," how are the projected images similar to the images we see on television, publications, or the Internet? How can we achieve a "truer" understanding of the world?

THINK PHILOSOPHICALLY   8.3
Analyzing Plato's Allegory of the Cave

PHILOSOPHER'S NOTEBOOK

- Explain how the images projected on the back wall of Plato's cave are similar to the images we perceive on the television, or the images that are communicated through newspapers, magazines, and books. Why do the people in Plato's cage believe that the perceptual images they are viewing projected on the wall are "real"? Why do people who view television and read information sources uncritically tend to believe that what they are viewing is "real"?

- Explain why recognizing that the perceptions we encounter in our daily lives are often incomplete, inaccurate, and distorted is essential to beginning our journey from the dark depths of ignorance toward the illumination of understanding.

- In Plato's allegory, discarding ignorant beliefs and embracing the truth can be a disturbing process, as we are forced to see things objectively, illuminated as they really are, rather than shrouded in the shadows of bias and distortion. Describe an experience in which achieving a knowledgeable, truthful insight was a disturbing experience for you.

  - Education then is the art of doing this very thing, this turning around, the knowledge of how the soul can most easily and most effectively be turned around; it is not the art of putting the capacity of sight into the soul; the soul possesses that already but it is not turned the right way or looking where it should. This is what education has to deal with.

  Plato believes that the view of knowledge embodied in the Allegory of the Cave has profound and far-reaching implications for education. Explain what you believe Plato means by saying that genuine education involves, "turning one's whole soul from the world of becoming until it can endure to contemplate reality" *instead of* "putting the capacity of sight into the soul." Describe two examples from your own educational experience, one which involved "turning your whole soul towards reality" and another in which you attempted to "put the capacity of sight into your soul."

- Evaluating your life as a whole, at what stage in Plato's allegory would you place yourself? Why?

Aristotle: *Reality Is the Natural World*

ARISTOTLE
(384–322 B.C.E.)
Ancient Greek Philosopher. One of the most important figures in the history of philosophy because of his division of philosophy into distinct disciplines and his extensive contribution to each of these divisions including being the first to attempt to create a system of deductive logic, and his empirical work in biology, not to mention his contributions to metaphysics, ethics, and politics.

Aristotle (384–322 B.C.E.) was a devoted—and brilliant—student in Plato's Academy, and although he shared many philosophical convictions with his esteemed teacher, he also ended up having serious disagreements. Aristotle and Plato were both intent on determining the nature of reality, and they both agreed that genuine knowledge must be universal. But Aristotle was very disturbed at Plato's metaphysical dualism, his sharp division between

- the perfect world of Being constituted by the eternal Forms, and
- the imperfect world of Becoming, the sensible world of experience in which we live our lives, a world that is merely a pale reflection of the world of Being.

Aristotle was concerned that the net result of this division would be to devalue the world of experience as something "less real" and unworthy of serious, systematic study. He feared that Plato's metaphysic would, in his words, push people toward

otherworldliness, to a chasm between the actual and the ideal . . . (which means) that discussion of what is can never amount to more than a "likely story," and knowledge of what *ought to be* has little or no relevance to pressing moral, political and social problems.

This philosophical perspective was completely unacceptable to Aristotle, who was as much a scientist (he is often called "the father of science") as a philosopher: a great biologist, physicist, political theorist, and ethicist. Aristotle was focused on *this* world, committed to understanding it in all of its rich and complex splendor, and using this knowledge to improve the quality of life both individually and socially. As a philosophical naturalist, he was convinced that reality consists of the natural world, and that this natural world follows orderly principles and laws that we can use to understand it. For Aristotle, there *is* no separate, supernatural reality, such as Plato's world of Being and its eternal Forms. This sort of speculation is not only misguided, it is dangerous, because it deflects people from achieving genuine knowledge based on the actual facts of *this* world. Genuine knowledge, he argued, is derived through scientific exploration—careful observation, collection of data, systematic classification—not highly abstract and unprovable theories and speculation. Aristotle was convinced that Plato's epistemology was fatally flawed because Plato was never able to provide an intelligible account of the way the physical dimensions of this world "participate" in the eternal Forms. "Participation," Plato's keystone concept, was for Aristotle "a mere empty phrase and a poetic metaphor."

VISUAL PHILOSOPHY

Aristotle Teaching an Anatomy Class

Unlike Plato, why did Aristotle believe that genuine knowledge was based primarily in scientific observation and analysis, not a quest for an eternal realm of Forms.

For Aristotle, this same naturalistic orientation extended to human beings themselves. As we saw, Plato's metaphysical belief in the world of Being and the eternal Forms is tied to

- his belief in an immortal soul separate from the physical body.
- an existence before birth in which the soul is exposed to universal truths, which need only be "recollected" in this life.
- the ability of the soul to ascend to the world of Being through rational inquiry and enlightenment.
- the continued existence of the soul after death.

Aristotle categorically rejects all of these intertwined metaphysical beliefs. From his perspective, there is indeed a human soul, but it cannot be separated from the body. We are entirely creatures of nature, just as all forms of life are. We are unique because of our ability to reason, but beyond that there is no other reality than this world, either before birth or after death. Metaphysics is not the study of nonphysical realms or entities—it is the study of the natural world, and the study of humans as an integral and inseparable part of the natural world.

Forms

Like Plato, "forms" are an important part of Aristotle's metaphysic—with one significant difference. While Plato believed that Forms (with a capital "F") embodied the highest order of reality in a timeless, transcendent realm knowable only through reason, Aristotle believed that forms (with a lowercase "f") were embedded in physical objects, existing completely within the natural order. Every "thing" that exists has both a material element and a formal element, and although we can separate these two in thought, they cannot be separated in reality. For example, "mortality" is a formal—or essential—aspect of living things. But although we can separate "mortality" and "living things" intellectually, they cannot be separated in reality. "Mortality"—or any formal element in nature—cannot exist independently, on its own. For Aristotle, this was Plato's fundamental mistake, believing that formal elements of things could be abstracted and then elevated to a transcendent status of ultimate reality. Or as Aristotle expressed it, we must take care not to mistake "intellectual analysis" for "ontological status." And this is true for all of Plato's forms: Redness, Roundness, Justice, Beauty—although we can distinguish these concepts in our mind, they can't really *exist* on their own. They can only *exist* as a formal aspect of some material object: a *red* apple, a *round* ball, a *just* law, a *beautiful* sunset.

Matter

Thus, in Aristotle's metaphysical system, there are two basic categories of things:

- Matter (in Greek, *hyle*), which refers to the common "stuff" that makes up the material universe
- Form, which refers to the essence of a thing, that which makes it what it is

Taken together, *matter* and *form* combine to create *formed matter* or *substance*—that is, all of the familiar things we see in the universe. For example, a piece of wood is composed of matter and certain formal elements that give the piece of wood shape, color, and texture. A craftsperson can take a number of pieces of wood and create a bed, reflecting the formal elements of design that he imposed on the wood. Similarly, a sculptor takes a block of marble (which itself embodies both matter and form), and then shapes it into a sculpture, reflecting the formal design she had in her mind.

Thus for Aristotle, matter and form require each other in order to exist. Matter provides the opportunity for formal elements to shape it into a purposeful design.

Or in the case of living things, for a potential purposeful design to become actualized. A fertilized human egg has within it the *potential* to become an embryo, and given the right conditions, this potential will become *actualized* into a *reality*.

Entelechy

For Aristotle, purpose through formal design is a basic principle of the universe. "Nature does nothing in vain," because every natural process has a goal. "Nature, like mind, always acts for a purpose, and this purpose is its end. That it should be so is according to nature." **Entelechy** is one of the core concepts on which Aristotle bases his entire philosophy. The word comes from the Greek for "having its end within itself," and Aristotle interpreted it to be a creative drive or inner urge that impels all things to achieve their purpose in life. "Such principles do not all make for the same goal, but each inner principle always makes for the same goal of its own (kind), if nothing interferes." That is, everything in the universe has its own unique purpose to fulfill: an acorn to be an oak tree, a fertilized egg to become a human being. Of course, achieving one's purpose is typically dependent on the right conditions being present: if an acorn isn't planted, or lacks sufficient water and light, its potential won't be actualized.

The same is true on a human level. Aristotle believed that each person has a potential to fulfill, in accordance with his or her own entelechy. In people, the formal element is the *soul*, which gives shape and purposeful direction to the body: ". . . for every part of a living body is an organ of the soul. Evidently then, all such parts are for the sake of the soul, which is their natural end." But the conditions for a person to fulfill her potential are much more complex and challenging than something like an acorn, and people's potentials are often not realized due to inhibiting experiences.

Aristotle believed that, as with every other aspect of nature, the soul is not immortal: it ceases to exist once the matter in which it is embedded (the body) stops functioning. And as we saw in chapter 6, Aristotle believes that there is a "good life" for each of us to aspire to and achieve, a life of balance, fullness, and happiness.

The Four Causes

Aristotle integrated his central metaphysical ideas into a comprehensive framework that he termed *The Four Causes*. The Greek word for cause is *aitia*, which means "the reason for something happening." For Aristotle this meant achieving a complete understanding of a thing. Although Aristotle's concept of cause as "the reason for something happening" *includes* our modern concept of "one event bringing about another event," it also extends far beyond this notion. Aristotle's Four Causes include

- *Material Cause*—the "matter" of which a thing is made.
- *Formal Cause*—the embedded form that gives shape and purpose to the "matter."
- *Efficient Cause*—the "triggering" action that sets the thing in motion.
- *Final Cause*—the ultimate purpose for which a thing exists.

For Aristotle, a complete explanation for *why* something happens necessarily entails addressing all of these "causes," as he explains in his *Metaphysics*:

It is the business of the natural scientist to know about them all . . . (and to) give his answer to the question "why?" in the manner of a natural scientist . . . (by referring to them all—to the matter, the form, the mover, and the purpose).

Entelechy The creative drive or inner urge that impels all things to achieve their purpose in life.

Aristotle, *Metaphysics*

Material Cause

As we have seen, Aristotle considers *matter* to be the basic "stuff" of the universe. However, *matter* requires *form* to shape it into something useful and purposeful. As he explains in the following passage, simply describing the material (wood or bronze) that something like a bed or statue is made of is *necessary* but in no way *sufficient* for providing a comprehensive explanation of the thing in question.

Aristotle, *Metaphysics*   Some people regard the nature and substance of things that exist by nature as being in each case the proximate element inherent in the thing, this being itself unshaped; thus, (according to such a view) the nature of a bed, for instance, would be wood, and that of a statue bronze. (Those who think this way offer) as evidence . . . the fact that if you were to bury a bed, and the moisture that got into it as it rotted gained enough force to throw up a shoot, it would be wood and not a bed that came into being. (According to this view, the bed's) arrangement according to the rules of an art . . . is an accidental attribute, whereas its substance is what remains permanently, and undergoes all these changes.

Formal Cause

As we discussed previously, *form* is the other major element in Aristotle's metaphysical system, representing the embedded shape or purpose of particular *matter*. In the bed and the sculpture, it is the design of the artisan that uses form to shape the material (wood and bronze) into something useful and purposeful. Before that happens, the material is only *potentially* a bed or sculpture. It is not until the artisan crafts the materials "according to the rules of an art" that the potential becomes an *actuality*. The same principle holds true for biological matter, such as flesh and bone, as well. Until nature shapes matter into the *formed matter* of flesh and bone, they exist only as potentials.

Aristotle, *Metaphysics*   What is potentially flesh or bone does not yet have its own nature until it acquires the form that accords with the formula, by means of which we define flesh and bone; nor can it be said at this stage to exist by nature. So in another way, nature is the shape and form of things that have a principle of movement in themselves—the form being only theoretically separable from the object in question.

Efficient Cause

This is the concept that's closest to our modern idea of "cause"—the "triggering event" that sets things in motion or initiates change, transforming a *potential* into an *actuality*. Aristotle terms this immediate cause the "proximate mover." For example, the artisan is the "efficient cause" of the wood being crafted into a bed and the bronze being shaped into a sculpture.

Aristotle, *Metaphysics*   Thus the answer to the question "why?" is to be given by referring to the matter, to the essence, and to the proximate mover. In cases of coming-to-be it is mostly in this last way that people examine the causes; they ask what comes to be after what, what was the immediate thing that acted or was acted upon, and so on in order.

Final Cause

The Final Cause embodies the ultimate purpose of a thing's existence, its reason for being, its *telos* or final goal. For Aristotle, no description of an object is complete until we place it within the entire teleological framework of the universe. Every aspect of the cosmos is purposive, directed toward a goal, defined and driven by its entelechy. In humans, our soul or *psyche* is our entelechy, directing us toward our ultimate purpose in life. However, Aristotle's conception of "soul" or "ultimate purpose" is in no way supernatural: it simply describes our unique purpose within the natural order. As Aristotle observes: "If purpose is present in art, it must also be present in nature."

Aristotle extends this concept of Final Cause to the universe as whole, a cosmological concept that he variously characterizes as "first (Final) cause," "prime mover," and "pure thought, thinking thought." This is *not* a "God" as a Creator, but rather an impersonal teleological principle that permeates the universe as a whole. Aristotle arrives at this conclusion through an intriguing—and famous—argument. If we examine each of the Four Causes, we can see that each one assumes the existence of something that came before. But to avoid what philosophers term an **infinite regress**, we need to posit a First Final Cause.

How does the process of forming an object through glassblowing illustrate Aristotle's concepts of "matter" and the "Four Causes"?

Moreover, it is obvious that there is some first principle, and that the causes of things are not infinitely many either in a direct sequence or in kind. For the material generation of one thing from another cannot go on in an infinite progression (e.g. flesh from earth, earth from air, air from fire, and so on without a stop); nor can the source of motion (e.g. man be moved by air, air by the sun, the sun by Strife, with no limit to the series). In the same way neither can the Final Cause (that is, purposes) recede to infinity—walking having health for its object, and health happiness, and happiness something else: one thing

Aristotle, *Metaphysics*

THINK PHILOSOPHICALLY 8.4
Analyzing Aristotle

- Plato believes that Forms occupy the highest level of reality in the eternal realm of Being. Thus, the perfect Idea of "horse" is the most real element in his metaphysic, that actual horse the least real. Aristotle inverts this hierarchy of reality: the individual horse is the most real element in his metaphysic, whereas the abstract concept of "horse" the least real. Explain which view you find to be most intelligible and the reasons why.

- Aristotle was severely critical of Plato's concept of "participation"—Plato's concept for explaining the way individual things reflect their perfect Forms ("a mere empty phrase and a poetic metaphor"). Do you agree with his critique? How do you think Plato would defend himself?

- Plato believed that the human soul is immortal, existing before birth and continuing after death. Aristotle believed that the soul is a natural phenomenon that gives form and purpose to the body, but ceases to exist after the body dies. Which view of the soul do you find most compelling? Why?

- Aristotle believed that the entire universe is purposeful, both individually and collectively. Do you agree with his contention? Explain why or why not and provide an example to support your perspective.

- Although Aristotle does not believe in a supernatural Creator or God, he does conclude that there must be a "first (Final) cause," a "prime mover," "pure thought, thinking thought." Evaluate the cogency of Aristotle's idea and the reasoning he uses to reach this conclusion.

Infinite regress A philosophical kind of argument purporting to show that a thesis is defective because it generates an infinite series when either no such series exists or were it to exist, the thesis would lack the role (e.g., of justification) that it is supposed to play.

always being done for the sake of another. And it is just the same with the Formal Cause (that is, the essence). For in the case of all intermediate terms of a series which are contained between a first and last term, the prior term is necessarily the cause of those which follow it; because if we had to say which of the three is the cause, we should say "the first." At any rate it is not the last term, because what comes at the end is not the cause of anything. Neither, again, is the intermediate term, which is only the cause of one (and it makes no difference whether there is one intermediate term or several, nor whether they are infinite or limited in number). But of series which are infinite in this way, and in general of the infinite, all the parts are equally intermediate, down to the present moment. Thus if there is no first term, there is no cause at all. ■

 Aristotle, *The Metaphysics*

The Epistemology of Everyday Life

Plato and Aristotle constructed a framework for thinking about ourselves and the world that profoundly influenced the evolution of thought in Western culture. It is difficult to fully appreciate the extent to which our modern consciousness and the various disciplines devoted to constructing knowledge reflect the concepts and methodologies first introduced by these two towering figures. Before we continue our exploration of other philosophers who have made significant contributions to metaphysics and epistemology, we are going to first take some time to reflect on the role that these areas play in our everyday lives, with particular attention to epistemology.

Though you may not fully realize it, you do have a theory of knowledge, your own epistemology. What does this mean? Simply that you—and everyone else—develops beliefs and constructs knowledge based on certain principles. Of course, this doesn't mean that people necessarily construct the most enlightened beliefs possible—in fact, many times they don't! But that's the purpose of developing the abilities that will enable you to become a sophisticated critical thinker, as we explored in chapter 1. It is these critical thinking abilities that will enable you to develop the most *informed* beliefs and construct the most *enlightened* knowledge of which you are capable. And because you have the advantage of taking an Introduction to Philosophy course, you will be able to integrate these critical thinking abilities into a coherent theory of knowledge—your own epistemology. Before we go any further, let us see these ideas in action in everyday life, and then place these ideas within a larger philosophical context.

Developing Informed Beliefs

Several years ago Reggie Lewis, star basketball player for the Boston Celtics, was diagnosed with a heart condition. A team of renowned cardiologists was assembled to evaluate his condition, and they concluded that he would be risking his life if he continued his basketball career. Not satisfied with this devastating diagnosis, Lewis sought out the opinion of an equally famous cardiologist who assured him that he could safely resume his NBA career. Which doctors should he *believe*? How could he *know* the best course of action? Which perspective was the *true* one? The pressure to continue playing was enormous. The hopes of his family, the team, and millions of his fans rested on his shoulders. Not surprisingly, he chose to believe the latter doctor and began his comeback. Several months later, while practicing in a gym, Lewis collapsed and died.

Reggie Lewis's death underscores the need to develop the thinking tools required to weigh conflicting information accurately, develop informed beliefs, construct a knowledgeable perspective, and discover as true a conclusion as possible. In the same way that you use road maps to guide you to your destination, your belief system constitutes the "map" you use to inform your decisions. If your mental map of the world is reasonably accurate, then it will provide reliable guidance in helping you figure things out and make intelligent decisions. On the other hand, if your mental map is *not* accurate, then the results are likely to be unfortunate and even disastrous. In the case of Reggie Lewis, the map he was using was fatally flawed, and the consequences were tragic.

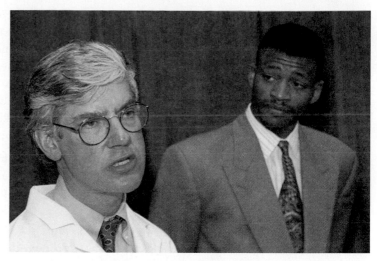

Confronted with conflicting medical advice regarding his heart condition, Reggie Lewis chose the recommendation of those experts who cleared him to play basketball. He died several months later while practicing.

Thankfully, most of our flawed maps don't lead to the dire consequences suffered by Reggie Lewis, although there are probably many times in your life you realize that you barely avoided a tragedy. As critical thinkers, these "near misses" should sober us enough to ask the question: "How can I create a more accurate 'belief map' for myself?" Consider the controversial issue of whether women under 50 years of age should get annual mammograms in order to provide the earliest detection of breast cancer. Although the benefits of mammograms for women *over* 50 is clearly established by research studies—chances of dying from breast cancer are reduced by thirty percent—the benefits for women *under* 50 are uncertain. To resolve this question, an expert panel was formed by the National Institutes of Health. These experts presented their findings in January 1997, concluding that there was not sufficient evidence to recommend routine annual mammograms for women under 50. Their advice: women under 50 should "weigh the risks and benefits of the test and decide for themselves." This conclusion prompted an immediate outcry from other experts in the field, including the American Cancer Society and prominent radiologists. Which expert advice should women follow?

Of course, the thinking dilemmas posed by experts who disagree are not limited to medical situations—we constantly confront conflicting opinions and advice: voluminous and often contradictory financial data; conflicting scientific analyses on environmental concerns such as global warming and overpopulation; contrasting advice from psychologists on how to eradicate that troubling neurosis or nurture the mystery of intimacy. But if we can't accept the recommendations of experts without question, what should we do? How do we decide what to believe?

In philosophy, our efforts to develop accurate beliefs is conceived of as part of a larger quest to achieve knowledge and truth. As we have seen, this area of philosophic analysis is known as *epistemology*, a term that refers to the study of human knowledge: its nature, its sources, its justification. The Greek word *episteme* means "knowledge" and *logos* means "rational discourse," indicating that epistemology is the process of exploring knowledge through analysis and discussion. This is an area of study devoted to the questions of how to develop informed beliefs, construct knowledge, and discover truth. Achieving these epistemological goals is at the heart of thinking philosophically, and your success in these areas will have a profound impact on the quality of your life.

How does this ancient map off the world compare with your map of the world? How can you evaluate the accuracy of your current map of reality, and how can you improve it?

How Informed Are My Philosophical Beliefs?

One of the core elements of thinking philosophically is reflecting thoughtfully on your intellectual development. Make a list of the philosophical themes that you have studied in your Introduction to Philosophy course (your professor may choose to have the class do this as a group). Then, for each of these topics, write a paragraph assessing the relative strength (or weakness) of your beliefs in that area. For example:

> After studying the issues related to developing enlightened values, and exploring a variety of different ethical theories, I believe that I am on my way to developing a thoughtful approach to moral decisions of which I feel confident. Some of my central moral principles include. . . . A recent example of a challenging moral decision in which I applied ethical approach was. . . .

Be sure that your responses are both honest and specific. They represent a rough evaluation of the progress you have made in learning to think philosophically about the most difficult areas of life. This is a journey that you will continue for the rest of your life, and ongoing critical reflection is the tool you can use to chart your growth and ensure that you are on the path you wish to take.

To develop a well-informed set of beliefs that you can use to knowledgeably guide you through life's treacherous currents, you need to combine the critical thinking abilities introduced in the first chapter with the philosophical themes that you have been exploring in subsequent chapters to arrive at informed, intelligent perspectives in every area of life. The tools of critical thinking are powerful, but they need to be integrated with the content of philosophy so that you will be able to

- develop a thoughtful and well-reasoned philosophy of life.
- engage in Socratic analysis and emulate his personal and intellectual virtues.
- develop insight into your "self."
- understand the nature of freedom.
- construct an enlightened ethical perspective.
- develop a thoughtful approach to religion.
- understand the nature of knowledge and truth and how to achieve them.
- develop a sophisticated and integrated view of reality.
- construct an informed perspective on political and social issues.

To initiate this process of evaluating your philosophical beliefs, complete the Think Critically activity 8.5. How did you evaluate your philosophical understanding in these various areas? If you found that you have ample room for growth, you are not alone, and the reason is that we live in a complex, challenging world that is extremely demanding intellectually. Each day we are called on to solve difficult problems, analyze tangled issues, and sift through a tidal wave of information. We are expected to make intelligent decisions, negotiate our way through a jungle of relationships, and communicate our ideas clearly and persuasively. It's no wonder that we often feel overmatched, unable to marshal the thinking abilities needed to succeed in all of these demanding contexts. Here, for example, are a few of the issues that appear daily in the media and about which we, as thoughtful and concerned citizens, ought to develop informed opinions:

On Cloning Humans, "Never" Turns Swiftly Into "Why Not": There has been an enormous change in attitudes since Dolly the lamb became the first animal cloned from a cell taken from an adult. Contrary to early fears of a Brave New World, scientists have become sanguine about the notion of cloning human beings. Some infertility centers are already conducting experiments with human eggs that lay the groundwork for cloning. Ultimately, scientists expect cloning to be combined with genetic enhancement, adding genes to give desired traits.

Arab Americans Protest "Profiling" at Airports: When Dr. Hassan Abbass, a Veterans Affairs Department surgeon, and his wife arrived at the airport to leave for vacation last May 24, they were pulled aside and forced to submit to a careful search before boarding the plane. They became one of thousands of Americans of Middle Eastern heritage who have complained that a secretive and wide-scale "profiling" system sponsored by the government and aimed at preventing air terrorism has caused them to be unfairly selected for extra scrutiny at airports. "Profiling" of this type is being used more frequently in many areas of law enforcement, raising fundamental questions of how a free society balances security fears with civil liberties and the desire to avoid offensive stereotyping.

U.S Reports Disease Link to Gulf War: After years of denying any link between illness and service in the Persian Gulf War, military officials said today that veterans of the conflict were nearly twice as likely as other soldiers to suffer the fatal neurological illness known as Lou Gehrig's disease. The study involved 2.5 million veterans, of which forty cases of the disease have been identified so far. Veterans' groups have long argued that their members are afflicted by unexplained illnesses collectively called Gulf War syndrome. More than 100,000 American service members sent to the region in 1990 and 1991 have reported a range of maladies including fatigue, muscle pain, memory loss, and sleep disorders.

Developing informed beliefs about these and other issues is an ongoing challenge to our thinking abilities. In thinking about these and any other issues, we should ask ourselves two important questions:

What is my belief about this issue? Do you believe that human cloning should be pursued? What about whether "profiling" is a legitimate technique for improving public safety? Is Gulf War illness a genuine health condition?

Is my belief informed by evidence and reasons? For each of the beliefs that you have regarding these (and other) issues, can you answer the question, "*Why* do you have that belief?" with intelligent and compelling reasons?

The fact is that although beliefs are easy to come by, *informed* beliefs are much more difficult to find. To express a belief you merely have to say, "Well, I think . . ." or "I believe. . . ." People are more than willing to make such pronouncements on virtually any subject. But to express an informed belief means that you have some idea of what you're talking about: you have explored the subject, examined different points of view, evaluated the supporting reasons and evidence, and synthesized your analysis into a cogent and compelling conclusion. If someone asks you, "Why do you believe that human cloning should be prohibited?" you can provide a clear, articulate explanation.

The Nature of Beliefs

I t seems to be a natural human impulse to try to understand the world we live in, and beliefs are the conceptual tools humans use to accomplish this. For example, consider the following statements and answer "Yes," "No," or "Not sure" to each.

- A college education will improve your life.
- Alien life forms have visited our planet.
- Every person has a unique purpose in life.
- Developing your mind is as important as taking care of your body.
- You should treat other people the way you would like to be treated.

Your responses to these statements reflect certain beliefs you have, and these beliefs help you explain why the world is the way it is and how you ought to behave. The total collection of your beliefs represents your view of the world, your philosophy of life.

What exactly are "beliefs"? Beliefs represent an interpretation, evaluation, conclusion, or prediction about the world that we endorse as true. For example, the statement

- "I believe that in the play *No Exit*, Jean-Paul Sartre is dramatizing the way other people can force us to acknowledge our personal 'bad faith' and thus create a personal hell on earth"—represents an *interpretation* of that play.
- "I believe that a theory of human choice that allows for freedom of choice makes more sense than a theory that doesn't"—expresses an *evaluation* of rival philosophical theories.

- "I believe that one of the main reasons terrorism has become such a terrible threat is that primitive ways of thinking now have access to the most modern technology of destruction"—expresses a *conclusion* about the problem of world terrorism.
- "If drastic environmental measures are not undertaken to slow the global warming trend, then I believe that the polar ice caps will melt and the earth will be flooded"—represents a *prediction* about events that will occur in the future.

In addition to expressing an interpretation, evaluation, conclusion, or prediction about the world, beliefs also express an endorsement of the truth or accuracy of the beliefs by the speaker or author, based presumably on convincing reasons or evidence. The beliefs you develop in living your life help you explain why the world is the way it is and they guide you in making decisions. But all beliefs are not equal. Some beliefs are certain ("Only women can give birth to babies") because they are supported by compelling reasons. Other beliefs are less certain ("I believe that aliens have visited earth") because the support is not as solid. As you form and revise your beliefs, based on your experiences and your reflection on these experiences, it is important to make them as accurate as possible. The more accurate they are, the better you are able to understand what is taking place and to predict what will occur in the future.

The beliefs you form vary tremendously in accuracy. The idea of *knowing* is one of the ways humans have developed to distinguish beliefs supported by strong reasons or evidence from beliefs for which there is less support. Other beliefs are disproved by evidence to the contrary (such as the belief that men can give birth to babies). This distinction between "believing" and "knowing" can be illustrated by replacing the word *believe* with the word *know* in statements. For example, consider the statements on page 439:

- "I *know* that in the play *No Exit,* Jean-Paul Sartre is dramatizing the way other people can force us to acknowledge our personal 'bad faith' and thus create a personal hell on earth."
- "I *know* that a theory of human choice that allows for freedom of choice makes more sense than a theory that doesn't."
- "I *know* that one of the main reasons terrorism has become such a terrible threat is that primitive ways of thinking now have access to the most modern technology of destruction."
- "If drastic environmental measures are not undertaken to slow the global warming trend, then I *know* that the polar ice caps will melt and the earth will be flooded."

When someone indicates that he or she thinks a belief is completely accurate by saying, "I *know*," your response is often "*How* do you know?" If the person cannot give you a satisfactory answer to this question, you are likely to think to yourself that, "If this person can't explain how they know it, then they don't *really* know it—they're just saying it." In other words, when you say that "you know" something, you mean at least two different things.

1. I think this belief is completely accurate.
2. I can explain to you the reasons or evidence that support this belief.

If either of these standards is not met, we would usually say that the person does not really "know." Or to state it another way, "You can *believe* what is not so, but you cannot *know* what is not so."

We work at evaluating the accuracy of our beliefs by examining the reasons or evidence that support them (known as the *justification* for the beliefs). Your beliefs can be thought of as forming a continuum based on their accuracy and justification. As you learn more about the world and yourself, you try to form beliefs that arc increasingly accurate and justified. Looked at in this way, your beliefs form a range, as pictured:

Beliefs that you know are	Beliefs that you are not sure are	Beliefs that you know are
inaccurate	accurate	accurate
unjustified	justified	justified

Just as temperature is a scale that ranges from cold to hot with many degrees in between, so your beliefs can be thought of as forming a continuum based on their accuracy and justification. As you learn more about the world and yourself, you try to form beliefs that are increasingly more accurate and justified.

Of course, determining the accuracy and justification of your beliefs is a challenging business. How do we assess justification? We generally use a variety of criteria.

- To what extent is the belief supported by sound reasons and compelling evidence derived from reliable sources?
- How effectively does the belief explain what is taking place?
- To what extent is the belief consistent with other beliefs you have about the world?
- How effectively does your belief help you predict what will happen in the future?
- Is the belief falsifiable?

How would you go about proving to a skeptic that you "know" that the earth is round? How might the skeptic respond to your evidence and arguments?

Let's apply these criteria to a sample belief to evaluate the degree of certainty we may ascribe to it:

"I believe that some day I will die because death is the natural end of living."

To what extent is the belief supported by sound reasons and compelling evidence derived from reliable sources?
There is ample evidence that death is a natural and inevitable part of the life process. All living things eventually die, and this has been true for all people in all of history. Certainly there are those who hope that science will find ways to perpetuate eternal life, but at this point there is no compelling reason to believe that this is feasible.

How effectively does the belief explain what is taking place?
This belief does a very effective job of explaining why, every day, many people die, never to live again.

To what extent is the belief consistent with other beliefs you have about the world?
This belief is consistent with the complex web of beliefs that make up biological science, a discipline that details why (among other things) that all living organisms eventually die.

How effectively does your belief help you predict what will happen in the future?
This is a belief that historically has had one hundred percent predictive success. Every person who has lived before us has, at some point, died.

Is the belief falsifiable? This criterion means that we can state conditions—tests— under which the beliefs could be disproved and the beliefs nevertheless *pass* those tests. Why is this important? Because it rules out beliefs that can never be proved or disproved. For example, if you believe that your destiny is related to the positions of the planets and stars (as astrologers do), it is not clear how we could conduct an experiment to determine if the belief is accurate. Because a belief that is not *falsifiable* can never be proved, such a belief is of questionable accuracy. Our sample belief is clearly falsifiable. Unfortunately, if our belief

Evaluating the Accuracy of My Beliefs

State whether you think that each of the following beliefs is

- *completely accurate* (so that you would say, "I know this is the case").
- *generally accurate* but not completely accurate (so that you would say, "This is often, but not always, the case").
- *generally not accurate* but sometimes accurate (so that you would say, "This is usually not the case but is sometimes true").
- *definitely not accurate* (so that you would say, "I know that this is not the case").

After determining the degree of accuracy in this way, explain why you have selected your answer.

Beliefs to be evaluated

- I believe with Socrates that "the unexamined life is not worth living."
- I believe that the *self* is that unifying force that synthesizes our experiences into a personal identity.
- I believe in the existence of a supernatural Creator that I call "God."
- I believe that your astrological sign determines your basic personality traits.
- I believe that people are completely free and so completely responsible for their choices.
- Your example of a belief:

Example: I believe that if you treat other people with respect and consideration, that they will reciprocate and treat you the same way.

> *Degree of accuracy:* Generally, but not completely, accurate.
>
> *Explanation:* Although treating other people with respect and consideration may inspire many people to reciprocate with the same treatment, this is not likely to be true in all cases.

proves true, we won't be there to congratulate ourselves on the accuracy of our belief: we will have to let others perform that function.

Based on these criteria our sample belief that "I believe that some day I will die because this is the natural end of living" seems to be supported with such strong justification that we would likely be comfortable saying, "I *know* that some day I will die. . . ." To view a contrasting situation, use these same criteria to evaluate the following belief:

> *"I believe that though our bodies may die, our spirits or souls continue to exist in some form."*

What differences did you find from the first evaluation? Compare your responses to those of others in the class: did you arrive at different conclusions regarding the relative certainty of the belief? Why or why not?

These criteria, and the two examples we used to illustrate them, constitute some of the epistemological standards we use in everyday life to evaluate our beliefs. We generally term "knowledge" those beliefs that we conclude best meet the criteria. And it is these "I know . . ." beliefs that we consider to be "true." A critical thinking perspective sees knowledge and truth as goals that we are striving to achieve, processes that we are all actively involved in as we construct our understanding of the world. Developing accurate knowledge about the world is often a challenging process of exploration and analysis in which our understanding grows and evolves over a period of time.

Philosophical Foundations of Knowledge

We began this chapter by establishing an epistemological foundation through the ideas of Plato and Aristotle. We then moved on to examining knowledge in a general sense, and exploring critical thinking strategies needed to develop intelligent, informed beliefs. But there are profound questions that underlie these issues that have been the subject of intense philosophical debate since the time of Plato and Aristotle. First and foremost is the question: "Is it possible to have knowledge?" At first glance, that may seem like a silly question with an obvious answer: "Of course we can have knowledge!" But, like most philosophical questions, the obvious answer usually turns out to be simplistic.

We have seen that to qualify as "knowledge," beliefs must be *justified* (supported by compelling reasons and evidence) and *true* (acknowledged to be objectively and universally accurate for all people in all cultures). For example, we have certainly demonstrated that people form beliefs to make sense of their experience, and we have also seen that some beliefs are more "informed" than others—that is, they are more cogent, take more perspectives into consideration, are better justified with reasons and evidence, provide more compelling explanations, are better predictors, and are more consistent with other accepted beliefs. But although these criteria are invaluable in helping to differentiate stronger beliefs from weaker beliefs, they do not ensure that the beliefs in question rise to the level of "knowledge." Simply establishing that one belief is more informed in a particular situation than another belief does not necessarily mean that we have achieved knowledge. For instance, after applying critical thinking criteria, we might come to the conclusion that the belief "Political systems should be based on the concept of equal rights and equal opportunities" is more informed than the belief "Political systems should be based on the concept of a privileged minority controlling the power and material resources." But can we really say that we "know" this to be the case? And how could we demonstrate that our more informed belief should be accepted as a universal truth?

Or to take an example from science: Isaac Newton developed a coherent system of laws to explain the workings of the physical universe, and in general these laws did an excellent job of accounting for observable events in the natural world. Newton's

 VISUAL PHILOSOPHY

Can Knowledge Be Dangerous?

Adam and Eve were expelled from the Garden of Eden for eating the fruit of the Tree of the Knowledge of Good and Evil. Why? Do you believe that some discoveries have made the world a more dangerous place? If so, which ones?

laws were informed and justified, and they certainly seem to be "true," thus qualifying them as "knowledge"—at least until Albert Einstein came along with his theory of relativity. Einstein's theory did an even better job of explaining events in the universe than Newton's did, particularly with respect to such complex phenomena as "light" and "time." Einstein's principles were informed and justified—but were they "true"? Did they rise to the level of knowledge? Many people thought so—at least until the theory of quantum mechanics was introduced to explain events on subatomic levels. And so we see that even in areas such as the hard sciences, where we would expect epistemological issues to be fairly straightforward, concepts such as "truth" and "knowledge" turn out to be extraordinarily slippery and complex.

It is also common for people to confuse "information" with "knowledge." But information is *not* knowledge. Information by itself is inert, discrete, disconnected. It can't become knowledge until the human mind acts on it: analyzing, synthesizing, applying, evaluating, integrating it into a dynamic systems of ideas.

Philosophically, there have been a variety of responses to the question of "Is knowledge possible?"

Skepticism

As you might expect from the name, skeptics do not believe that genuine knowledge can ever be achieved and it is futile to try. **Skepticism** includes positions such as doubting all assumptions until proved, or claiming that no knowledge is possible in any circumstances.

Rationalism

Rationalists believe that knowledge is absolutely possible, and that it can be achieved through the faculty of reason. Although the information we learn through sense experience is useful, genuine knowledge regarding fundamental truths is typically discovered through rational investigation. Such knowledge is said to be *a priori* knowledge, because it is achieved independently of experience by means of rational abilities that are part of our natural intellectual equipment. Some of the most influential rationalists in the history of philosophy include Plato, René Descartes, **Baruch Spinoza**, and Gottfried Leibniz. Rationalists point to systems of knowledge such as mathematics and formal logic as examples of *a priori* knowledge that have been established independently of experience through the faculty of reason. Yet even though mathematics and logic are independent of experience, they are nevertheless extremely powerful tools for explaining the events in experience.

Empiricism

In contrast to rationalists, empiricists believe that, if knowledge is achievable, experience must be the source. Although reason may be a useful tool in helping us organize our experiences, in the final analysis it is the experiences themselves that provide genuine knowledge about the world. Empiricists believe that humans begin their lives with minds that are **tabula rasa**, "blank tablets." It is only by means of their accumulated experiences that the tablets will be inscribed. As a result, all knowledge is *a posteriori* knowledge, meaning knowledge that is based on experience.

Constructivism

As expressed in the epistemology of **Immanuel Kant**, knowledge is the result of the *combination* of our reasoning abilities and our experience. Rather than our minds being the passive recipients of sense experience, Kant believes that our minds

Skepticism The belief that genuine knowledge can never be achieved and it is futile to try. It includes positions such as doubting all assumptions until proved, or claiming that no knowledge is possible in any circumstances.

Baruch Spinoza (1632–1677) Rationalist Philosopher. In his major work the *Ethics*, modeled his philosophical method on that of Euclidean geometry; expounds the view that everything consists of and comes from one primary substance, what Spinoza called God and equated with nature.

Tabula rasa Latin for "blank slate"; the idea that we begin life with a completely "blank" mind open to experiential knowledge.

Immanuel Kant (1724–1804) German Philosopher. Kant widely regarded as greatest philosopher of modern period. Attempted to synthesize two competing schools of the modern period, rationalism and empiricism, by showing important role both experience and reason play in constructing our knowledge of the world.

actively structure these experiences, using rational principles that are part of our natural thinking equipment. Thus **constructivism** is the belief that knowledge is "constructed" by us through our active intellectual activities. *A priori* knowledge is possible, but only in combination with experiences that form its content.

Constructivism The belief that knowledge is "constructed" or made by the mind, which is active and creative.

René Descartes: *Cogito, Ergo Sum*

We were first introduced to this extraordinary philosopher in chapter 3 along with his famous pronouncement, *Cogito, ergo sum* "I think, therefore I am." **Descartes** was a mathematician by training, and he invented analytical geometry. He had a vibrant and wide-ranging intellect, and his influence on modern philosophy and Western thought in general has been profound. In fact, Descartes and Immanuel Kant are generally credited with establishing the intellectual framework for modern Western consciousness, which is still evident today in virtually every academic discipline.

And yet, despite the power and rigor of his thinking, Descartes was able to express his ideas in a very direct and personal way. The best example of this are the *Meditations on First Philosophy* (1641), which are written in the form of a personal journal, even as he explores ideas that people are still discussing and debating today. He begins his Meditation I with the question that virtually every young person has posed to himself or herself at one time or another: suppose every important thing I've been taught in my life to this point has been inaccurate and unreliable—what then? Descartes' response was dramatically unique. He decided to make every effort to dispose of everything he had been taught and start fresh, searching for a foundation point for knowledge that would be absolutely rock-solid—clear, distinct, indubitable.

RENÉ DESCARTES

(1596–1650)
Seventeenth century French Philosopher. Along with Immanuel Kant, Descartes is considered the founder of modern philosophy. In his *Meditations on First Philosophy* (1641) he dealt with issues surrounding skepticism, mind/body dualism, and he applied the geometric method to philosophy. The influence of this work was not only important to the modern period, but is also incredibly influential to this day.

Meditation I
Of the things which may be brought within the sphere of the doubtful

René Descartes,
Meditations on First Philosophy

1. It is now some years since I detected how many were the false beliefs that I had from my earliest youth admitted as true, and how doubtful was everything I had since constructed on this basis; and from that time I was convinced that I must once for all seriously undertake to rid myself of all the opinions which I had formerly accepted, and commence to build anew from the foundation, if I wanted to establish any firm and permanent structure in the sciences. But as this enterprise appeared to be a very great one, I waited until I had attained an age so mature that I could not hope that at any later date I should be better fitted to execute my design. This reason caused me to delay so long that I should feel that I was doing wrong were I to occupy in deliberation the time that yet remains to me for action. To-day, then, since very opportunely for the plan I have in view I have delivered my mind from every care [and am happily agitated by no passions] and since I have procured for myself an assured leisure in a peaceable retirement, I shall at last seriously and freely address myself to the general upheaval of all my former opinions.

2. Now for this object it is not necessary that I should show that all of these are false—I shall perhaps never arrive at this end. But inasmuch as reason already persuades me that I ought no less carefully to withhold my assent from matters which are not entirely certain and indubitable than from those which appear to me manifestly to be false, if I am able to find in each one some reason to doubt, this will suffice to justify my rejecting the whole. And for that end it will not be requisite that I should examine each in particular, which would be an endless undertaking; for owing to the fact that the destruction of the foundations of necessity brings with it the downfall of the rest of the edifice, I shall only in the first place attack those principles upon which all my former opinions rested.

René Descartes

Descartes' attitude is so contemporary that he almost could have written the lyrics to the Paul Simon song, "Kodachrome," which begins, "When I think back on all the crap I learned in high school/ it's a wonder I can think at all." Having had the growing suspicion that much of what he had been taught had been biased, incomplete, or downright wrong, Descartes resolves to try and wipe his epistemological "tablet" clean and begin anew. The "radical doubt" that he is employing is for the positive purpose of establishing a "firm and permanent structure in the sciences," *not* to end up mired in skepticism. In taking this approach Descartes is modeling a very philosophical approach to knowledge first initiated by Socrates, which nonphilosophers often misunderstand. Rather than using doubt *destructively*, to simply disprove and undermine ways of thinking, doubt is used *constructively*, to identify, strengthen, and refine the best beliefs. It is this "trial by fire" that helps us develop beliefs that are tempered and firmly grounded. In the absence of genuine doubt, beliefs are left to exist uncritically and ill-informed. It is also fascinating that Descartes recognized the need to wait until he had reached a level of intellectual maturity before calling into question the beliefs he had acquired growing up, as he wanted to ensure that his beliefs were not still in the process of evolution.

Is it really possible to suspend all of the beliefs we have been brought up with in order to start fresh in constructing our understanding of the world? No, of course not: such a project would surely be impractical, and we would likely retain an abiding faith in many of the beliefs we had come to believe were true. Nevertheless, there is real merit in undertaking a "doubting project" like this, for it encourages us to begin questioning beliefs we may have been unwittingly taking for granted, and it also initiates what will hopefully become a life-long process of critical reflection. And as Descartes is quick to point out, it is not necessary to question every individual belief, simply our core beliefs, such as:

- How is it possible to be certain of what I think I know?
- What is the reason for believing (or not believing) in a God?
- On what basis should I make ethical decisions?
- How do I know that there is a world that exists outside of my experience?

Having identified the general aim of his reflective analysis and established its basic ground rules, Descartes moves on to explore the reliability (and *un*reliability) of our sense experience.

René Descartes,
Meditations on First Philosophy

3. All that up to the present time I have accepted as most true and certain I have learned either from the senses or through the senses; but it is sometimes proved to me that these senses are deceptive, and it is wiser not to trust entirely to anything by which we have once been deceived.

4. But it may be that although the senses sometimes deceive us concerning things which are hardly perceptible, or very far away, there are yet many others to be met with as to which we cannot reasonably have any doubt, although we recognize them by their means. For example, there is the fact that I am here, seated by the fire, attired in a dressing gown, having this paper in my hands and other similar matters. And how could I deny that these hands and this body are mine, were it not perhaps that I compare myself to certain persons, devoid of sense, whose cerebella are so troubled and clouded by the violent vapours of black bile, that they constantly assure us that they think they are kings when they are really quite poor, or that they are clothed in purple when they are really without covering, or who imagine that they have an earthenware head or are nothing but pumpkins or are made of glass. But they are mad, and I should not be any the less insane were I to follow examples so extravagant.

5. At the same time I must remember that I am a man, and that consequently I am in the habit of sleeping, and in my dreams representing to myself the same things or sometimes even less probable things, than do those who are insane in their waking moments. How often has it happened to me that in the night I dreamt that I found myself in this par-

ticular place, that I was dressed and seated near the fire, whilst in reality I was lying undressed in bed! At this moment it does indeed seem to me that it is with eyes awake that I am looking at this paper; that this head which I move is not asleep, that it is deliberately and of set purpose that I extend my hand and perceive it; what happens in sleep does not appear so clear nor so distinct as does all this. But in thinking over this I remind myself that on many occasions I have in sleep been deceived by similar illusions, and in dwelling carefully on this reflection I see so manifestly that there are no certain indications by which we may clearly distinguish wakefulness from sleep that I am lost in astonishment. And my astonishment is such that it is almost capable of persuading me that I now dream.

6. Now let us assume that we are asleep and that all these particulars, e.g. that we open our eyes, shake our head, extend our hands, and so on, are but false delusions; and let us reflect that possibly neither our hands nor our whole body are such as they appear to us to be. At the same time we must at least confess that the things which are represented to us in sleep are like painted representations which can only have been formed as the counterparts of something real and true, and that in this way those general things at least, i.e. eyes, a head, hands, and a whole body, are not imaginary things, but things really existent. For, as a matter of fact, painters, even when they study with the greatest skill to represent sirens and satyrs by forms the most strange and extraordinary, cannot give them natures which are entirely new, but merely make a certain medley of the members of different animals; or if their imagination is extravagant enough to invent something so novel that nothing similar has ever before been seen, and that then their work represents a thing purely fictitious and absolutely false, it is certain all the same that the colors of which this is composed are necessarily real. And for the same reason, although these general things, to wit, [a body], eyes, a head, hands, and such like, may be imaginary, we are bound at the same time to confess that there are at least some other objects yet more simple and more universal, which are real and true; and of these just in the same way as with certain real colors, all these images of things which dwell in our thoughts, whether true and real or false and fantastic, are formed.

7. To such a class of things pertains corporeal nature in general, and its extension, the figure of extended things, their quantity or magnitude and number, as also the place in which they are, the time which measures their duration, and so on.

What we experience through our senses is often incomplete, subjective, and inaccurate. Consider the many times during the day in which you think one thing is happening and it turns out to be something completely different. Or think about those many occasions in which you witnessed an event with others—an accident, a party, a walk downtown—and each person ended up with very different, and perhaps conflicting, perceptions of the experience. Or reflect on optical illusions (such as the "bent" straw in a glass) or the tricks performed by a magician. In all of these cases our sense experience reveals itself to be consistently unreliable, and therefore completely unsuitable for Descartes' "firm and permanent" foundation for knowledge.

But Descartes then takes his radical doubt to the next level, with a provocative suggestion: suppose what we consider to be our entire waking life is instead an illusion? What then? To support the plausibility of this possibility, Descartes first asks us to consider the plight of the mentally ill. Often they are convinced that their deranged perceptions of reality ("they have an earthenware head or are nothing but pumpkins or made of glass") are in fact true: how can we be sure that the same is not true for us? A disturbing notion, certainly. But Descartes recognizes that we need not go to this extreme to doubt the validity of our experience, because we have another and very common altered state of consciousness that makes the same point just as well: dreaming. Think of the times your dream was so vivid and "real" that you woke up sweating and with a pounding heart. When you were fully absorbed in that dream, you were convinced that it was absolutely real—until you woke up. But, Descartes says, how can we be sure that when we believe we are awake we are not actually dreaming? How can we tell the difference? He contends that we can't:

VISUAL PHILOSOPHY

Am I Dreaming or Awake?

How would you respond to Descartes' question of "How can you be sure if you're dreaming or awake?" If we can't be sure, does this mean that we can never really know anything?

René Descartes,
Meditations on First Philosophy

. . . in dwelling carefully on this reflection I see so manifestly that there are no certain indications by which we may clearly distinguish wakefulness from sleep that I am lost in astonishment. And my astonishment is such that it is almost capable of persuading me that I now dream.

This is precisely the premise of the popular and influential film *The Matrix*: people believe that they are living real and authentic lives, when in fact they are suspended in tanks and having their brains stimulated to create a virtually real world.

The Taoist philosopher and mystic Chuang-Tzu (fl. fourth century B.C.E.) makes this same point in the following passage:

> Once upon a time, I, Chuang-Tzu, dreamt I was a butterfly, fluttering hither and thither, to all intents and purposes a butterfly. I was conscious only of following my fancies as a butterfly, and was unconscious of my individuality as a man. Suddenly, I waked, and there I lay, myself again. Now I do not know whether I was then a man dreaming I was a butterfly, or whether I am now a butterfly dreaming I am a man.

But Descartes is not through with his doubting program: in fact, he is just getting ready to ratchet his radical doubt up to a level never before considered in philosophical writing until the moment that he conceived of it. He begins with a preliminary distinction between the relative certainty of the disciplines of arithmetic and geometry (which are independent of sense experience) in comparison with the natural sciences such as physics, astronomy, and medicine (which are dependent on sense experience). But Descartes soon erases the relevance of this distinction with his boldest move yet: the possibility that we are being systematically deceived by supernatural beings.

8. That is possibly why our reasoning is not unjust when we conclude from this that Physics, Astronomy, Medicine and all other sciences which have as their end the consideration of composite things, are very dubious and uncertain; but that Arithmetic, Geometry and other sciences of that kind which only treat of things that are very simple and very general, without taking great trouble to ascertain whether they are actually existent or not, contain some measure of certainty and an element of the indubitable. For whether I am awake or asleep, two and three together always form five, and the square can never have more than four sides, and it does not seem possible that truths so clear and apparent can be suspected of any falsity [or uncertainty].

9. Nevertheless I have long had fixed in my mind the belief that an all-powerful God existed by whom I have been created such as I am. But how do I know that He has not brought it to pass that there is no earth, no heaven, no extended body, no magnitude, no place, and that nevertheless [I possess the perceptions of all these things and that] they seem to me to exist just exactly as I now see them? And, besides, as I sometimes imagine that others deceive themselves in the things which they think they know best, how do I know that I am not deceived every time that I add two and three, or count the sides of a square, or judge of things yet simpler, if anything simpler can be imagined? But possibly God has not desired that I should be thus deceived, for He is said to be supremely good. If, however, it is contrary to His goodness to have made me such that I constantly deceive myself, it would also appear to be contrary to His goodness to permit me to be sometimes deceived, and nevertheless I cannot doubt that He does permit this.

10. There may indeed be those who would prefer to deny the existence of a God so powerful, rather than believe that all other things are uncertain. But let us not oppose them for the present, and grant that all that is here said of a God is a fable; nevertheless in whatever way they suppose that I have arrived at the state of being that I have reached—whether they attribute it to fate or to accident, or make out that it is by a continual succession of antecedents, or by some other method—since to err and deceive oneself is a defect, it is clear that the greater will be the probability of my being so imperfect as to deceive myself ever, as is the Author to whom they assign my origin the less powerful. To these reasons I have certainly nothing to reply, but at the end I feel constrained to confess that there is nothing in all that I formerly believed to be true, of which I cannot in some measure doubt, and that not merely through want of thought or through levity, but for reasons which are very powerful and maturely considered; so that henceforth I ought not the less carefully to refrain from giving credence to these opinions than to that which is manifestly false, if I desire to arrive at any certainty [in the sciences].

11. But it is not sufficient to have made these remarks, we must also be careful to keep them in mind. For these ancient and commonly held opinions still revert frequently to my mind, long and familiar custom having given them the right to occupy my mind against

René Descartes,
Meditations on First Philosophy

my inclination and rendered them almost masters of my belief; nor will I ever lose the habit of deferring to them or of placing my confidence in them, so long as I consider them as they really are, i.e. opinions in some measure doubtful, as I have just shown, and at the same time highly probable, so that there is much more reason to believe in than to deny them. That is why I consider that I shall not be acting amiss, if, taking of set purpose a contrary belief, I allow myself to be deceived, and for a certain time pretend that all these opinions are entirely false and imaginary, until at last, having thus balanced my former prejudices with my latter [so that they cannot divert my opinions more to one side than to the other], my judgment will no longer be dominated by bad usage or turned away from the right knowledge of the truth. For I am assured that there can be neither peril nor error in this course, and that I cannot at present yield too much to distrust, since I am not considering the question of action, but only of knowledge.

12. I shall then suppose, not that God who is supremely good and the fountain of truth, but some evil genius not less powerful than deceitful, has employed his whole energies in deceiving me; I shall consider that the heavens, the earth, colors, figures, sound, and all other external things are naught but the illusions and dreams of which this genius has availed himself in order to lay traps for my credulity; I shall consider myself as having no hands, no eyes, no flesh, no blood, nor any senses, yet falsely believing myself to possess all these things; I shall remain obstinately attached to this idea, and if by this means it is not in my power to arrive at the knowledge of any truth, I may at least do what is in my power [i.e. suspend my judgment], and with firm purpose avoid giving credence to any false thing, or being imposed upon by this arch deceiver, however powerful and deceptive he may be. But this task is a laborious one, and insensibly a certain lassitude leads me into the course of my ordinary life. And just as a captive who in sleep enjoys an imaginary liberty, when he begins to suspect that his liberty is but a dream, fears to awaken, and conspires with these agreeable illusions that the deception may be prolonged, so insensibly of my own accord I fall back into my former opinions, and I dread awakening from this slumber, lest the laborious wakefulness which would follow the tranquility of this repose should have to be spent not in daylight, but in the excessive darkness of the difficulties which have just been discussed.

Thus enters Descartes' "evil genius," perhaps the most influential fictional creation in the history of philosophy. Although Descartes first proposes God as this arch deceiver, he concludes that such thorough-going duplicity would be inconsistent with God's essentially good nature. So the evil genius is born, a powerful device for extending radical doubt to all aspects of experience that we typically accept as incontrovertibly real:

René Descartes,
Meditations on First Philosophy

I shall consider that the heavens, the earth, colors, figures, sound, and all other external things are naught but the illusions and dreams of which this genius has availed himself in order to lay traps for my credulity; I shall consider myself as having no hands, no eyes, no flesh, no blood, nor any senses, yet falsely believing myself to possess all these things . . .

The purpose of this extreme enterprise, Descartes reminds us, is to explicitly recognize and remind himself of the uncertainty of all beliefs based solely on sense experience, and in so doing to "avoid giving credence to any false thing." Naturally, Descartes hopes to achieve "knowledge of truth," but if that is not possible, he at least does not want to continue believing in the truth of things that in fact are corrupted by uncertainty, echoing Socrates' statement, "As for me, all I know is that I know nothing" and Confucius's observation, "He who knows he is a fool is not a great fool."

The closing passage, with its vivid image of an enslaved individual dreaming of freedom, is particularly compelling, as Descartes acknowledges the emotional difficulty of pressing on in his search for certainty. By placing his entire universe in doubt, he recognizes that he is risking the peace of mind that comes from assuming the stability and veracity of one's world. And although his intellect has urged him to destroy the illusion of security through unblinking questioning of all he believes in, on an emotional level he is reluctant to continue the quest, fearful of what he might find. And so, exhausted by his intellectual labors, he falls back into his previous state of consciousness, until he can marshal his courage and energy for another arduous and personally wrenching search for true knowledge. These are surely emotions with which all of us can identify: desirous of finding the truth, yet fearful of what we might discover. And that is precisely why committing ourselves to thinking philosophically in order to achieve an authentic understanding of reality requires uncommon courage.

Meditation II
Of the Nature of the Human Mind; and that it is more easily known than the Body

René Descartes,
Meditations on First Philosophy

1. The Meditation of yesterday filled my mind with so many doubts that it is no longer in my power to forget them. And yet I do not see in what manner I can resolve them; and, just as if I had all of a sudden fallen into very deep water, I am so disconcerted that I can neither make certain of setting my feet on the bottom, nor can I swim and so support myself on the surface. I shall nevertheless make an effort and follow anew the same path as that on which I yesterday entered, i.e. I shall proceed by setting aside all that in which the least doubt could be supposed to exist, just as if I had discovered that it was absolutely false; and I shall ever follow in this road until I have met with something which is certain, or at least, if I can do nothing else, until I have learned for certain that there is nothing in the world that is certain. Archimedes, in order that he might draw the terrestrial globe out of its place, and transport it elsewhere, demanded only that one point should be fixed and immovable; in the same way I shall have the right to conceive high hopes if I am happy enough to discover one thing only which is certain and indubitable.

Refreshed following his debilitating exertions recorded in Meditation I, Descartes is now ready to continue his reflective explorations with renewed energy. Yet a deep sense of unease accompanies his efforts, the result of turning his world upside down through his radical doubt. His metaphor of falling into deep water where one can neither swim nor touch the bottom is particularly apt, as he searches for a single certainty on which he can begin to rebuild the world he has deconstructed.

René Descartes,
Meditations on First Philosophy

2. I suppose, then, that all the things that I see are false; I persuade myself that nothing has ever existed of all that my fallacious memory represents to me. I consider that I possess no senses; I imagine that body, figure, extension, movement and place are but the fictions of my mind. What, then, can be esteemed as true? Perhaps nothing at all, unless that there is nothing in the world that is certain.

3. But how can I know there is not something different from those things that I have just considered, of which one cannot have the slightest doubt? Is there not some God, or some other being by whatever name we call it, who puts these reflections into my mind? That is not necessary, for is it not possible that I am capable of producing them myself? I myself, am I not at least something? But I have already denied that I had senses and body. Yet I hesitate, for what follows from that? Am I so dependent on body and senses that I cannot exist without these? But I was persuaded that there was nothing in all the world, that there was no heaven, no earth, that there were no minds, nor any bodies: was I not then likewise persuaded that I did not exist? Not at all; of a surety I myself did exist since I persuaded myself of something [or merely because I thought of something]. But there is some deceiver or other, very powerful and very cunning, who ever employs his ingenuity in deceiving me. Then without doubt I exist also if he deceives me, and let him deceive me as much as he will, he can never cause me to be nothing so long as I think that I am something. So that after having reflected well and carefully examined all things, we must come to the definite conclusion that this proposition: I am, I exist, is necessarily true each time that I pronounce it, or that I mentally conceive it.

Finally, a point of reference that Descartes believes exists beyond doubt: "I am, I exist, is necessarily true each time that I pronounce it, or that I mentally conceive it." Though everything in the world may be called into question, including the existence of his body and the external world, nevertheless the simple affirmation "I exist" *must* be true each time it is uttered or conceived as a primal statement of personal existence. Yet what precisely does it mean to affirm, "I exist"?

René Descartes,
Meditations on First Philosophy

4. But I do not yet know clearly enough what I am, I who am certain that I am; and hence I must be careful to see that I do not imprudently take some other object in place of myself, and thus that I do not go astray in respect of this knowledge that I hold to be the most certain and most evident of all that I have formerly learned. That is why I shall now consider anew what I believed myself to be before I embarked upon these last reflections; and of my former opinions I shall withdraw all that might even in a small degree be invalidated by the reasons which I have just brought forward, in order that there may be nothing at all left beyond what is absolutely certain and indubitable.

5. What then did I formerly believe myself to be? Undoubtedly I believed myself to be a man. But what is a man? Shall I say a reasonable animal? Certainly not; for then I should have to inquire what an animal is, and what is reasonable; and thus from a single question I should insensibly fall into an infinitude of others more difficult; and I should not wish to waste the little time and leisure remaining to me in trying to unravel subtleties like these. But I shall rather stop here to consider the thoughts which of themselves spring up in my mind, and which were not inspired by anything beyond my own nature alone when I applied myself to the consideration of my being. In the first place, then, I considered myself as having a face, hands, arms, and all that system of members composed on bones and flesh as seen in a corpse which I designated by the name of body. In addition to this I considered that I was nourished, that I walked, that I felt, and that I thought, and I referred all these actions to the soul: but I did not stop to consider what the soul was, or if I did stop, I imagined that it was something extremely rare and subtle like a wind, a flame, or an ether, which was spread throughout my grosser parts. As to body I had no manner of doubt about its nature, but thought I had a very clear knowledge of it; and if I had desired to explain it according to the notions that I had then formed of it, I should have described it thus: By the body I understand all that which can be defined by a certain figure: something which can be confined in a certain place, and which can fill a given space in such a way that every other body will be excluded from it; which can be perceived either by touch, or by sight, or by hearing, or by taste, or by smell: which can be moved in many ways not, in truth, by itself, but by something which is foreign to it, by which it is touched [and from which it receives impressions]: for to have the power of self-movement, as also of feeling or of thinking, I did not consider to appertain to the nature of body: on the contrary, I was rather astonished to find that faculties similar to them existed in some bodies.

6. But what am I, now that I suppose that there is a certain genius which is extremely powerful, and, if I may say so, malicious, who employs all his powers in deceiving me? Can I affirm that I possess the least of all those things which I have just said pertain to the nature of body? I pause to consider, I revolve all these things in my mind, and I find none of which I can say that it pertains to me. It would be tedious to stop to enumerate them. Let us pass to the attributes of soul and see if there is any one which is in me? What of nutrition or walking [the first mentioned]? But if it is so that I have no body it is also true that I can neither walk nor take nourishment. Another attribute is sensation. But one cannot feel without body, and besides I have thought I perceived many things during sleep that I recognized in my waking moments as not having been experienced at all. What of thinking? I find here that thought is an attribute that belongs to me; it alone cannot be separated from me. I am, I exist, that is certain. But how often? Just when I think; for it might possibly be the case if I ceased entirely to think, that I should likewise cease altogether to exist. I do not now admit anything which is not necessarily true: to speak accurately I am not more than a thing which thinks, that is to say a mind or a soul, or an understanding, or a reason, which are terms whose significance was formerly unknown to me. I am, however, a real thing and really exist; but what thing? I have answered: a thing which thinks. . . . What is a thing which thinks? It is a thing which doubts, understands, [conceives], affirms, denies, wills, refuses, which also imagines and feels.

So here it is, the birth of the infamous Cartesian ego that is destined to bedevil philosophers and Western thinking as a whole from its gestation up until the present. Initially, it seems to be an innocent enough creation, and it does provide an apparent escape from the skepticism threatened by the "evil genius." For though the "evil genius" may force us to doubt the existence of our physical bodies, it cannot, by definition, cause us to doubt the existence of our thinking self, the "I think" that "doubts, understands, conceives, affirms, denies, wills, refuses which also imagines and feels." Of course, as we saw in chapter 3, this concept of a pure, thinking self starts us down a slippery slope that leads inevitably to a full-blown dualism of mind and body, with all of its conceptual vexations.

But for the present, we're more concerned with whether Descartes has in fact discovered his philosopher's touchstone, that foundation of absolute certainty upon which he can reconstruct his core beliefs about the world that were swept away by his radical doubt. He begins by addressing the existence of external objects, using a famous example to illustrate his reasoning.

11. Let us begin by considering the commonest matters, those which we believe to be the most distinctly comprehended, to wit, the bodies which we touch and see; not indeed bodies in general, for these general ideas are usually a little more confused, but let us consider one body in particular. Let us take, for example, this piece of wax: it has been taken quite freshly from the hive, and it has not yet lost the sweetness of the honey which it contains; it still retains somewhat of the odour of the flowers from which it has been culled; its colour, its figure, its size are apparent; it is hard, cold, easily handled, and if you strike it with the finger, it will emit a sound. Finally all the things which are requisite to cause us distinctly to recognise a body, are met with in it. But notice that while I speak and approach the fire what remained of the taste is exhaled, the smell evaporates, the colour alters, the figure is destroyed, the size increases, it becomes liquid, it heats, scarcely can one handle it, and when one strikes it, no sound is emitted. Does the same wax remain after this change? We must confess that it remains; none would judge otherwise. What then did I know so distinctly in this piece of wax? It could certainly be nothing of all that the senses brought to my notice, since all these things which fall under taste, smell, sight, touch, and hearing, are found to be changed, and yet the same wax remains.

12. Perhaps it was what I now think, viz. That this wax was not that sweetness of honey, nor that agreeable scent of flowers, nor that particular whiteness, nor that figure, nor that sound, but simply a body which a little while before appeared to me as perceptible under these forms, and which is now perceptible under others. But what, precisely, is it that I imagine when I form such conceptions? Let us attentively consider this, and, abstracting from all that does not belong to the wax, let us see what remains. Certainly nothing remains excepting a certain extended thing which is flexible and movable. But what is the meaning of flexible and movable? Is it not that I imagine that this piece of wax being round is capable of becoming square and of passing from a square to a triangular figure? No, certainly it is not that, since I imagine it admits of an infinitude of similar changes, and I nevertheless do not know how to compass the infinitude by my imagination, and consequently this conception which I have of the wax is not brought about by the faculty of imagination. What now is this extension? Is it not also unknown? For it becomes greater when the wax is melted, greater when it is boiled, and greater still when the heat increases; and I should not conceive [clearly] according to truth what wax is, if I did not think that even this piece that we are considering is capable of receiving more variations in extension than I have ever imagined. We must then grant that I could not even understand through the imagination what this piece of wax is, and that it is my mind alone which perceives it. I say this piece of wax in particular, for as to wax in general it is yet clearer. But what is this piece of wax which cannot be understood excepting by the [understanding or] mind? It is certainly the same that I see, touch, imagine, and finally it is the same which I have always believed it to be from the beginning. But what must particularly be observed is that its perception is neither an act of vision, nor of touch, nor of imagination, and has never been such although it may have appeared for-

René Descartes,
Meditations on First Philosophy

merly to be so, but only an intuition of the mind, which may be imperfect and confused as it was formerly, or clear and distinct as it is at present, according as my attention is more or less directed to the elements which are found in it, and of which it is composed.

Having established the existence of the thinking self, Descartes' next question is "What can the thinking self know that is beyond doubt?" The piece of wax serves his purposes well. From the standpoint of pure sense experience, the piece of wax poses a tangle of contradictions and confusions, as its physical properties change entirely as it is heated or cooled. However, our minds are nonetheless able to maintain a concept of the piece of wax, even as it goes through its various transformations, because its reactions to heat and cold are part of the concept of the wax itself. Therefore, Descartes is confident in saying that although pure sense experience is inadequate to understand the piece of wax, ". . . it is my mind alone which perceives it." How does the understanding mind perceive the piece of wax? Through an "intuition of the mind, which may be imperfect and confused as it was formerly, or clear and distinct as it is at present." And it is this "intuition of the mind" that forms the true foundation for all rationalist thinking and rationalist knowledge. In the case of the piece of wax—and the rest of the external world—our intuitions of the mind provide certain assurance that the external world exists, governed by the laws of mathematics and science. For Descartes, these intuitions of the mind are rationally based, not empirically based, for this is the only way that they could yield clear and certain knowledge.

Then, in Meditation III, Descartes reasons from his first premise—I exist as a thinking thing—to the conclusion that therefore God must exist, because I could not exist without God. Descartes uses both the "cosmological argument" for God, which we analyzed in the previous chapter on philosophy of religion, and also the "ontological argument," which argues (essentially) that God must exist because we have a rational conception of a perfect Being, which necessarily entails God's existence.

Having established (in *his* mind, at least) the existence of God, Descartes next argues that we know by intuition that it is God's very nature to be perfectly good, which means that God would not deceive us. As a result, the world of physical objects and scientific laws must exist precisely the way our intuitions inform us they exist.

René Descartes,
Meditations on First Philosophy

Meditation VI
Of the Existence of Material Things, and of the real distinction between the Soul and Body of Man

Since He has given me a very strong inclination to believe that these ideas (of trees, houses, etc.) arise from corporeal objects, I do not see how he could be vindicated from the charge of deceit, if in truth they proceeded from any other source, or were produced by other causes than corporeal things? (For example, by the evil demon, or in dreams.)

Therefore,

We *cannot be deceived* (whether by the evil demon or whatever else).

. . . I cannot doubt but that there is in me a certain passive faculty of perception, that is, of receiving and recognizing the ideas of sensible things, but this would be useless to me if there were not either in me or in some other thing another active faculty capable of forming and producing these ideas. But this active faculty cannot exist in me [inasmuch as I am a thing that thinks] seeing that it does not presuppose thought, and also that those ideas are often produced in me without my contributing in any way to the same, and often even against my will; it is thus necessarily the case that the faculty resides in some substance different from me in which all the reality which is objectively in the ideas that are produced by this faculty is formally or eminently contained, as I remarked before. And this substance is either a body, that is, a corporeal nature in which there is contained formally [and really] all that which is objectively [and by representation] in those ideas, or it is God Himself, or some other creature more noble than body in which that same is contained eminently. But, since God is no deceiver, it is very manifest that He does not communicate to me these ideas immediately and by Himself, nor yet by the intervention of some creature in which their reality is not formally, but only eminently, contained. For since He has given me no faculty to recognise that this is the case, but, on the other hand, a very great inclination to believe [that they are sent to me or] that they are conveyed to me by corporeal objects, I do not see how He could be defended from the accusation of deceit if these ideas were produced by causes other than corporeal objects. Hence we must allow that corporeal things exist. However, they are perhaps not exactly what we perceive by the senses, since this comprehension by the senses is in many instances very obscure and confused; but we must at least admit that all things which I conceive in them clearly and distinctly, that is to say, all things which, speaking generally, are comprehended in the object of pure mathematics, are truly to be recognized as external objects. ■

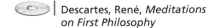 Descartes, René, *Meditations on First Philosophy*

Many philosophers have found these later arguments of Descartes' to be less than convincing, for a variety of reasons. But as a rationalist, Descartes' key point is that we can achieve genuine knowledge through our rational intuition into the nature of beliefs. We can identify those beliefs that are true because they meet the standard of being "clear and distinct;" they are self-evident to our rational intuition, independent of experience. In fact, it is only through the faculty of reason that we can achieve true knowledge: our sense experience on its own can never lead to authentic knowledge independent of our reasoning abilities. As we shall see, this view is the complete opposite of the epistemological views of the British empiricists, for whom knowledge is derived mainly from sense experience.

THINK PHILOSOPHICALLY 8.7
Analyzing Descartes' Radical Doubt

PHILOSOPHER'S NOTEBOOK

- Have you ever had the experience of wondering whether much of what you had been brought up to believe as true was in fact unreliable? If so, identify some of the main beliefs or values that you called into question. Was there a particular event that stimulated this process of doubt and examination? What was the outcome of your reflective questioning?

- Try to replicate Descartes' reflective process. Describe your current situation as you are reading this text, just as he does. Then try to trace his pattern of thinking: Can you imagine that what you think is real is actually a dream? How can you be sure? Haven't you had dreams that were at least as realistic as the current situation in which you now find yourself? Is there any clear criteria you can use to differentiate between when you are dreaming and when you are awake?

- Descartes' "evil genius" bears an uncanny resemblance to the evil forces in the film *The Matrix*. In that film the central character, Neo, is faced with a provocative choice: Does he want to continue existing in a "virtual" world, which is pleasant but unreal, a manipulated reality created by evil forces? Or does he wish to experience the real world, which is unpleasant and dangerous? If you were presented with these alternatives, which would you choose? Why? Is there any resemblance between this type of choice and the one suggested by John Stuart Mill, between being a "contented fool" or a "discontented Socrates"? Why or why not?

- Try to replicate Descartes' foundational starting point, "I think, therefore I am." Does your ability to think convince you, for once and for all, that you exist? What does it mean to you to say, "I exist"? Exactly how would you describe the "I" that exists?

Making Connections: *Searching for Reality*

We began this chapter with Bertrand Russell's essay that poses the central challenge of metaphysics and epistemology:

> Thus what we directly see and feel is merely "appearance," which we believe to be a sign of some "reality" behind. But if the reality is not what appears, have we any means of knowing whether there is any reality at all? And if so, have we any means of finding out what it is like?

Answering these questions, unraveling these riddles, has been a central task of philosophy since its inception. Each of the great thinkers has constructed a unique system of ideas in this grand enterprise. In this chapter we considered the ambitious and carefully reasoned approaches of Plato, Aristotle, and René Descartes. In the next chapter we will continue our explorations by examining the epistemologies and metaphysics of John Locke, Gottfried Leibniz, George Berkeley, David Hume, Immanuel Kant, and Alison Jaggar. You are likely to find that studying these thinkers elucidates some questions while posing other ones. This is the essence of philosophy: an ongoing dialogue between thinkers of all eras grappling with the most profound issues in human existence. This is an intellectually thrilling experience, even though clear and certain answers to these complex issues are typically elusive. As Russell notes at the conclusion of his essay:

> Philosophy, if it cannot answer so many questions as we could wish, has at least the power of asking questions which increase the interest of the world, and show the strangeness and wonder lying just below the surface even in the commonest things of daily life.

Concept Review

- The philosophical study of metaphysics examines issues beyond the physical world such as the meaning of life, the existence of free will, and the fundamental principles of the universe. Metaphysicians attempt to explain the nature of reality itself. The foundations of metaphysics were laid by Aristotle in his *Metaphysics*.

- Philosophical inquiry into the nature of truth is called epistemology. The study of epistemology attempts to describe and explain the nature of knowledge and truth, and whether it is possible to achieve genuine knowledge or perceive an ultimate truth.

- Plato attempted to resolve the conflict between an unchanging, ultimate truth and the everyday flux of our circumstantial lives by proposing two different "worlds": the world of "becoming," of our physical world; and the world of "being," a realm of eternal and unchanging truths that is knowable through the exercise of reason. This world of "being" is populated by ideal "forms," archetypes or essences of everything that exists. In our everyday world of the senses, we experience only imperfect examples of, or "participants" in,

these "forms;" but through careful study, reflection, and reasoning, we can begin to apprehend the true and eternal nature of the forms. Plato's "Allegory of the Cave" is a vivid metaphor for this quest to understand the ultimate essences or truths of things.

- Plato's belief that genuine knowledge of the essential forms can be achieved through "innate" or inborn ideas and the faculty of reason makes him a *rationalist*. In contrast, philosophers who believe that true knowledge is best achieved through sense experience are *empiricists*. This conflict between rationalists and empiricists has both divided and enriched the study of epistemology since the time of Plato and Aristotle.

- Aristotle broke with his teacher Plato's conception of a divided reality. As a philosophical naturalist, Aristotle was devoted to the idea that the nature of reality is best apprehended through close and careful attention to, and study of, sense experience. Whereas Plato believed, for example, in a changing and ultimately mortal human body that was inhabited by an unchanging and immortal soul, Aristotle argued that that the soul cannot be separated from the body; that we as humans are entirely creatures of nature. In Aristotle's metaphysical system, there are two categories of "things": matter (the physicality of things) and form (the essence of a thing). All things contain within themselves their potential, or *entelechy*.

■ Aristotle's metaphysical framework consists of The Four Causes:

- Material cause
- Formal cause
- Efficient cause
- Final cause

■ In our own lives, critical thinking about our own beliefs allows us to establish our own epistemology, our own clearly defined and rational way of achieving knowledge and truth. A belief is an interpretation, evaluation, conclusion, or prediction about our world that we believe is true. Thinking critically about the accuracy and justification of our beliefs—*how* do we know what we know?—helps us to arrive at rational judgments and make better decisions.

■ Philosophers have responded in a variety of ways to the question of whether or not knowledge is possible:

- Skepticism
- Rationalism
- Empiricism
- Constructivism

■ René Descartes established a constructively skeptical approach toward the nature of knowledge, vowing to begin with a "clean slate," or position of radical doubt, and from there objectively evaluate everything he knew or believed to be true. Ultimately, this led him to conceive of the possibility of an "evil genius," an entity that manipulates us into believing that our waking dream is "reality." Descartes only found his way out of this nightmarish possibility through his famous pronouncement, "Cogito, ergo sum" ("I think, therefore I am."), which he believed provided him with a foundation of absolute certainty on which he could construct a system of true beliefs through the power of reason.

Media Resources

www.researchnavigator.com
Chapter 8 pursues ideas on questions of what we can know and how we can know it. It displays a number of influential thinkers' works on these issues for analysis, especially those theories of knowledge acquired before experience. For further research on questions on what it is to have knowledge and belief and how we know things or determine their truth-value, use the tools available to you in Research Navigator.

As you investigate this topic, consider this question: "What is it for me to honestly believe that I know something?"

- **ContentSelect:** search in the Philosophy database using the search term "justified belief," "knowledge," and "belief."

- **Link Library:** search in the Philosophy database under the term "Plato."

- **New York Times on the Web:** search in the Philosophy database using the search terms "mind" and "believe."

 For additional study resources for this chapter, go to: **www.prenhall.com/chaffee/chapter8**

 The Primary Source: Philosophical Readings and Commentary

Aristotle: *Metaphysics; Categories; de Anima; On Interpretation; Physics; Poetics; Posterior Analytics; Prior Analytics; Rhetoric*

Descartes, René: *Discourse on the Method of Rightly Conducting the Reason and Seeking Truth in the Field of Science; Meditations on First Philosophy*

Heraclitus: *Fragments*

Lucretius: *On the Nature of the Universe*

Plato: *The Republic*

Thales: *Fragments*

9

What Is Real? What Is True?
Discovering Reality
and Constructing Knowledge (Part 2)

Let us suppose the mind to be, as we say, a blank tablet (tabula rasa) of white paper, void of all characters, without any ideas; how comes it to be furnished?... To this I answer in one word, from experience.

JOHN LOCKE

There can be no doubt that all our knowledge begins with experience...But though all our knowledge begins with experience, it does not follow that it all arises out of experience.

IMMANUEL KANT

PHRENOLOGY

Empiricism, Rationalism, Kantism

It is indeed an opinion strangely prevailing amongst men, that houses, mountains, rivers, and in a word all sensible objects, have an existence, natural or real, distinct from their being perceived by the understanding.

GEORGE BERKELEY

If we take in our hand any volume; of divinity or school metaphysics, for instance; let us ask, Does it contain any abstract reasoning concerning quantity or number? No. Does it contain any experimental reasoning concerning matter of fact and existence? No. Commit it then to the flames: for it can contain nothing but sophistry and illusion.

DAVID HUME

Plato (427?–347 B.C.E.) Ancient Greek Philosopher. It was once said that all of Western Philosophy is merely footnotes to Plato. A student of Socrates, he wrote many dialogues featuring Socrates as the main character and dealt with many philosophical issues such as morality, politics, metaphysics, and epistemology.

Aristotle (384–322 B.C.E.) Ancient Greek Philosopher. One of the most important figures in the history of philosophy because of his division of philosophy into distinct disciplines and his extensive contribution to each of these divisions including being the first to attempt to create a system of deductive logic, and his empirical work in biology, not to mention his contributions to metaphysics, ethics, and politics.

René Descartes (1596–1650) French Philosopher. Descartes is considered the founder of modern philosophy. In his *Meditations on First Philosophy* (1637) he dealt with issues surrounding skepticism, mind/body dualism, and he applied the geometric method to philosophy. The influence of this work was not only important to the modern period, but is also incredibly influential to this day.

Innate knowledge The knowledge and ideas we were born with.

We began our exploration of metaphysics and epistemology in the previous chapter, examining the influential ideas of **Plato**, **Aristotle**, and **Descartes**. And we also began the process of applying the concepts of epistemology to everyday life, analyzing the process by which we develop informed beliefs and construct knowledge.

This chapter continues this exploration of metaphysics and epistemology, building on the foundation established in chapter 8. Plato and Descartes are rationalists, believing that genuine, universal knowledge is discovered by using our reasoning abilities, independent of sense experience. In this chapter we will initially be examining a number of empiricist philosophers, who believe that genuine knowledge can only be achieved through our sense experience. This was the crux of Aristotle's disagreement with Plato, because he (Aristotle) was convinced that while our reasoning process is indispensable in discerning the formal elements of knowledge and the teleological principles at work in the universe, sense experience is also crucial to constructing knowledge. We will begin this chapter with the group of philosophers known as "British empiricists," which includes John Locke, George Berkeley, and David Hume, exploring and critically evaluating their combined metaphysics and epistemologies. We will then move on to Immanuel Kant, who attempted the monumental task of synthesizing rationalism and empiricism into one comprehensive metaphysical and epistemological system. And finally, we will examine a feminist perspective on epistemology through an essay by philosopher Alison Jaggar.

John Locke: *The Mind Is "Tabula Rasa"*

Let us suppose the mind to be, as we say, a blank tablet (*tabula rasa*) of white paper, void of all characters, without any ideas; how comes it to be furnished? Whence comes it by that vast store, which the busy and boundless fancy of man has painted on it with almost endless variety? Whence has it all the materials of reason and knowledge? To this I answer in one word, from *experience*: in that all our knowledge is founded, and from that it ultimately derives itself.
—*John Locke*, An Essay Concerning Human Understanding, *1689*

This famous passage by **John Locke** (1632–1704) captures his essential perspective on knowledge, an epistemological school of thought that came to be known as empiricism. For Locke and other empiricists, all human knowledge can ultimately be traced back to experiences we have had, transmitted through our five senses. This conviction sets empiricists in direct opposition to the rationalists such as Plato and Descartes. Locke was passionately critical of the rationalist views that

- we enter the world with **innate knowledge** that we come to be aware of through experience.
- we can achieve true knowledge independent of sense experience by using our "rational intuition."

460

Locke was convinced that the rationalist view opened the door to all sorts of metaphysical speculations that were unsupportable and unprovable. He saw himself on a crusade to place philosophy in general, and epistemology in particular, on the firm footing of common sense. How can we have "innate" knowledge of which we are unaware? How can we define "rational intuition" in any precise and meaningful way? When we ask most people how they came to know something, they typically refer to experiences they have had: "I saw it . . . ," "I heard it . . ." and so on. Common sense dictates that we focus on the direct data of experience to discover the source of all knowledge, and thus avoid the speculative pitfalls of rationalism.

Locke expressed his views in the influential work, *An Essay Concerning Human Understanding* (1689), which had a dominant influence in philosophy and other fields in the eighteenth century. The idea for the book came to him following a long and energetic debate with friends over morality and religion when Locke announced, "If we can find out how far the understanding can extend its view; how far it has faculties to attain certainty; and in what cases it can only judge and guess, we may learn to content ourselves with what is attainable by us in this state."

The following passages represent a direct attack on the concept of innate ideas as expressed by Plato and other rationalists.

JOHN LOCKE
(1632–1704).
British Philosopher. In *An Essay Concerning Human Understanding* (1689) Locke laid groundwork for empiricist philosophy. Theory that the mind is a *tabula rasa*, a blank slate, on which experience writes challenges rationalist philosophy that preceded him.

Book I: Chapter II—No Innate Principles in the Mind

1. It is an established opinion amongst some men, that there are in the understanding certain innate principles; some primary notions . . . characters, as it were stamped upon the mind of man; which the soul receives in its very first being, and brings into the world with it. It would be sufficient to convince unprejudiced readers of the falseness of this supposition, if I should only show (as I hope I shall in the following parts of this Discourse) how men, barely by the use of their natural faculties, may attain to all the knowledge they have, without the help of any innate impressions; and may arrive at certainty, without any such original notions or principles. . . .

2. There is nothing more commonly taken for granted than that there are certain principles, both speculative and practical, (for they speak of both), universally agreed upon by all mankind: which therefore, they argue, must needs be the constant impressions which the souls of men receive in their first beings, and which they bring into the world with them, as necessarily and really as they do any of their inherent faculties.

3. This argument, drawn from universal consent, has this misfortune in it, that if it were true in matter of fact, that there were certain truths wherein all mankind agreed, it would not prove them innate, if there can be any other way shown how men may come to that universal agreement, in the things they do consent in, which I presume may be done.

John Locke,
An Essay Concerning
Human Understanding

Locke announces straightaway that he intends to disprove the rationalist idea that there are "certain innate principles; some primary notions . . . characters, as it were stamped upon the mind of man; which the soul receives in its very first being, and brings into the world with it." He believes that the strongest rationalist argument for such innate knowledge is the idea that it is universally present in all humans. If everyone demonstrates an understanding of some law or principle—such as the logical principle "It is impossible for the same thing to be and not to be" (known since the time of Aristotle as the "Law of the Excluded Middle")—then Locke believes that the rationalist will argue that such a principle *must* be innate—otherwise, how did everyone come to acquire knowledge of it, even in the absence of formal education in logic or mathematics? Locke believes that it *is* possible to demonstrate how people could develop such universal knowledge based solely on experience. But he also believes that this rationalist argument of "universality" is even more seriously flawed because there are people who do *not* exhibit this supposedly universal knowledge.

John Locke

John Locke,
An Essay Concerning
Human Understanding

4. But, which is worse, this argument of universal consent, which is made use of to prove innate principles, seems to me a demonstration that there are none such: because there are none to which all mankind give an universal assent. I shall begin with the speculative, and instance in those magnified principles of demonstration, "Whatsoever is, is," and "It is impossible for the same thing to be and not to be"; which, of all others, I think have the most allowed title to innate. These have so settled a reputation of maxims universally received, that it will no doubt be thought strange if any one should seem to question it. But yet I take liberty to say, that these propositions are so far from having an universal assent, that there are a great part of mankind to whom they are not so much as known.

5. For, first, it is evident, that all children and idiots have not the least apprehension or thought of them. And the want of that is enough to destroy that universal assent which must needs be the necessary concomitant of all innate truths: it seeming to me near a contradiction to say, that there are truths imprinted on the soul, which it perceives or understands not: imprinting, if it signify anything, being nothing else but the making certain truths to be perceived. For to imprint anything on the mind without the mind's perceiving it, seems to me hardly intelligible. If therefore children and idiots have souls, have minds, with those impressions upon them, they must unavoidably perceive them, and necessarily know and assent to these truths; which since they do not, it is evident that there are no such impressions. For if they are not notions naturally imprinted, how can they be innate? And if they are notions imprinted, how can they be unknown? . . .

At first glance (and perhaps, even at second glance), you might wonder at the wisdom of Locke's resting his major counterargument to innate ideas on the examples of "children and idiots." But he does. How might Plato and Descartes respond to such an attack? Well, surely they would want to point out that the argument for innate ideas is based on *normal* human development, not *abnormal* exceptions such as idiots (however Locke chooses to define them). Locke observes, "If therefore children and idiots have souls, have minds . . ." Do idiots have minds like most people? Surely not. Do they have souls? That's something for Plato to puzzle out, but as we noted, a belief in innate ideas is in no way dependent on believing in an immortal soul.

Then what about children? They surely have souls and minds, as far as Plato and Descartes are concerned. But isn't it accurate to say that their minds are not yet fully developed? And when they are fully developed, won't they likely demonstrate the same understanding of the Law of Excluded Middle as everyone else (unless they turn out to be idiots)?

But Locke's more serious point is the following:

John Locke,
An Essay Concerning
Human Understanding

. . . To say a notion is imprinted on the mind, and yet at the same time to say, that the mind is ignorant of it, and never yet took notice of it, is to make this impression nothing. No proposition can be said to be in the mind which it never yet knew, which it was never yet conscious of.

What about this point? Is it possible to "know" something and yet not be aware you know it? In other words, does it make sense to say that innate knowledge can exist as *potential* knowledge, waiting to be activated? Have you ever had the experience of reaching an awareness of something and saying to yourself, "I knew that all the time—I just wasn't aware of it!" Clearly there are serious questions for Locke to face, but rather than our posing them, let's turn this task over to a philosopher who was also one of Locke's contemporaries: **Gottfried Wilhelm von Leibniz** (1646–1716). It's a unique opportunity to see two historically influential philosophers square off and lock philosophical horns.

GOTTFRIED WILHELM VON LEIBNIZ

(1646–1716)
German Philosopher. Prominent figure in the rationalist tradition. Invented the infinitesimal calculus. Maintained that the world, as created by God, is the best of all possible worlds.

Leibniz was a rationalist with a very modern notion of innate ideas. Rather than viewing them as being "stamped" on the human mind (Locke's metaphor) in a static, fully formed fashion, Leibniz believes that the human mind at birth contains "inclinations, dispositions, tendencies, or natural potentials" to form these ideas. In a view that is stunningly consistent with modern theories in developmental psychology, cognitive psychology, and linguistics, Leibniz proposed an interactive concept of intellectual development in which, as people mature, their innate tendencies gradually evolve and become fully formed ideas through the mind's interaction with experience. In the following passage, written shortly after the publication of Locke's *Essay Concerning Human Understanding*, Leibniz does a masterful job of turning Locke's arguments against him.

Gottfried Wilhelm von Leibniz,
New Essays on the
Human Understanding

The questions at issue is whether the soul in itself is entirely empty, like the tablet upon which nothing has yet been written (*tabula rasa*), as is the view of Aristotle and the author of the *essay* (Locke), and whether all that is traced on it comes solely from the senses and from experience; or whether the soul contains originally the principles of various notions and doctrines which external objects merely awaken from time to time, as I believe, with Plato and even with the Schoolmen, and with all those who take in this sense the passage of St. Paul (Romans, 2:15) where he remarks that the law of God is written in the heart. . . .

From this there arises another question, whether all truths depend on experience, that is to say, on induction and examples, or whether there are some that have some other basis. For if some events can be foreseen before any trial has been made of them, it is clear that we must here contribute something of our own. The senses, although necessary for all our actual knowledge, are not sufficient to give us the whole of it, since the senses never give anything except examples, that is to say, particular or individual truths. All examples which confirm a general truth, however numerous they may be, are not enough to establish the universal necessity of this same truth; for it does not follow that what has happened will happen again in the same way.

Leibniz believes that sense experience provides no justification for concluding that we can predict that the sun will rise each morning in accordance with a general law of nature. Instead, the notion of "cause and effect" reflects a conceptual structure of the mind.

Leibniz is making the same point to which we referred earlier: by itself, sense experience is incapable of validating any general principles or laws. Take, for example, the principle of "cause and effect." Even though we may see the sun rise each morning (except for cloudy days), sense experience provides no justification for concluding that there is a general law at work that permits us to predict with certainty that the sun will rise in the same way tomorrow, and every day thereafter. To make such a prediction, we need the contribution of the cognitive concept "cause and effect," a concept that is nowhere to be found in our sense experience. In addition to the laws of science, other fields that are dependent on principles of reason that exist independently of sense experience include, according to Leibniz, pure mathematics, logic, ethics, and natural theology.

Gottfried Wilhelm von Leibniz,
New Essays on the
Human Understanding

. . . It would seem that necessary truths, such as are found in pure mathematics, and especially in arithmetic and in geometry, must have principles the proof of which does not depend on examples, nor, consequently, on the testimony of the senses, although without the senses it would never have occurred to us to think of them. This ought to be well recognised; Euclid has so well understood it that he often demonstrates by reason what is obvious enough through experience and by sensible images. Logic also, together with metaphysics and ethics, one of which form natural theology and the other natural jurisprudence, are full of such truths; and consequently their proof can only come from internal principles, which are called innate. It is true that we must not imagine that these eternal laws of the reason can be read in the soul as in an open book, as the edict of the praetor can be read in his *album* without difficulty or research; but it is enough that they can be discovered in us by dint of attention, for which opportunities are given by the senses. The success of experiments serves also as confirmation of the reason, very much as proofs serve in arithmetic for better avoiding error of reckoning when the reasoning is long. . . .

Is our evolving intelligence the result of innate structures or empirical experiences, through "nature" or "nurture"? Like Leibniz and Kant, the prevailing current view is that our evolving intelligence is the product of *both* innate elements and empirical experiences.

Jean Piaget (1896–1980) Swiss developmental psychologist interested in the development of knowledge in persons, which results from the interaction of inate cognitive structures ("schemata") and lived experience.

Noam Chomsky (1928–) Philosopher of Language, Political Activist. Maintains humans possess a type of innate grammar and a "language faculty" that is involved in the acquiring and the use of language.

Claude Levi-Strauss (1908–) Anthropologist and Structuralist. Developed structural anthropology which maintains as man progresses from his natural state to the cultural state he does so according to structures inherent to the brain.

It seems that our able author claims that there is nothing potential in us and nothing even of which we are not at any time actually conscious; but he cannot mean this strictly, or his opinion would be too paradoxical; for acquired habits and the contents of our memory are not always consciously perceived and do not even always come to our aid at need, although we often easily bring them back to mind on some slight occasion which makes us remember them, just as we need only the beginning of a song to remember the song. Also he modifies his assertion in other places by saying that there is nothing in us of which we have not been at least formerly conscious. But besides the fact that no one can be sure by reason alone how far our past apperceptions, which we may have forgotten, may have gone, especially in view of the Platonic doctrine of reminiscence, which, mythical as it is, is not, in part at least, incompatible with bare reason; in addition to this, I say, why is it necessary that everything should be acquired by us through the perceptions of external things, and that nothing can be unearthed in ourselves? Is our soul, then, such a blank that, besides the images borrowed from without, it is nothing? . . . there are a thousand indications that lead us to think that there are at every moment numberless perceptions in us, but without apperception and without reflections; that is to say, changes in the soul itself of which we are not conscious, because the impressions are either too slight and too numerous, or too even, so that they have nothing sufficient to distinguish them one from the other; but, joined to others, they do not fail to produce their effect and to make themselves felt at least confusedly in the mass. ■

These are compelling points that Leibniz is making against Locke's concept of the *tabula rasa*. First, he points out that there are many things that we know—through habit or through our memory banks—that are not immediately before our perception. We can even act on this knowledge without being explicitly aware of it. For example, when an experienced motorist drives a car, she is performing extremely complex calculations and skilled movements while perhaps happily singing a favorite tune and thinking about what she'll be doing later that evening.

But the more penetrating question that Leibniz raises is why should we even try to account for all human knowledge based solely on sense experience, when so much argues against it? Ironically, it's the empirically rooted investigations in the twentieth century that have made such a strong case that the concept of a *tabula rasa* mind is pure fiction. **Jean Piaget's** work in developmental psychology; **Noam Chomsky's** work in linguistics; **Claude Levi-Strauss's** work in anthropology—plus the work of other thinkers has developed exhaustive empirical evidence to suggest that humans come equipped with a whole array of innate conceptual structures that develop and become elaborated through their dynamic interaction with experience. These are points that we will consider more fully when exploring the epistemology of Immanuel Kant, who once again demonstrates his colossal status as a creative and prescient thinker in the history of philosophy. For now, we will move to an analysis of Locke's views on perception and its role in producing knowledge. Locke introduces some provocative ideas in these areas that end up having one significant unintended consequence—the disappearance of the external world.

Locke's Causal Theory of Perception

Locke's epistemology is structured around a theory of perception that very much reflects the scientific worldview of Isaac Newton, a contemporary of his. Newton saw the universe in mechanistic terms, with discrete physical bodies relating to one another by means of particles and masses in motion ("force"). Thus for Locke, there are four independent elements in the knowing process, relating to one another in a mechanically causal fashion:

- The entity or object in the world.
- Sensations (sense data, images, sensory impressions) emitted by the objects via "impulses" and transmitted to our five senses.

- Ideas, which Locke characterizes as "the immediate object of perception, thought, or understanding"—in other words, the images and impressions produced in our minds by the impulses emitted by the objects.
- The human subject, knower, or conscious mind who is able to perceive the ideas in his or her mind and "reflect" on them, thus constructing knowledge.

Although such a theory may seem to have a certain commonsense logic, it contains within itself the conceptual seeds of its own destruction. But let's permit Locke to state his case before we attempt to dismantle it.

Book II—Of Ideas: Chapter I—Of Ideas in General, and Their Original

1. *Idea is the object of thinking.* Every man being conscious to himself that he thinks; and that which his mind is applied about whilst thinking being the ideas that are there, it is past doubt that men have in their minds several ideas,—such as are those expressed by the words *whiteness, hardness, sweetness, thinking, motion, man, elephant, army, drunkenness*, and others: it is in the first place then to be inquired, How he comes by them?

I know it is a received doctrine, that men have native ideas, and original characters, stamped upon their minds in their very first being. This opinion I have at large examined already; and, I suppose what I have said in the foregoing Book will be much more easily admitted, when I have shown whence the understanding may get all the ideas it has; and by what ways and degrees they may come into the mind;—for which I shall appeal to every one's own observation and experience.

2. *All ideas come from sensation or reflection.* Let us then suppose the mind to be, as we say, white paper, void of all characters, without any ideas:—How comes it to be furnished? Whence comes it by that vast store which the busy and boundless fancy of man has painted on it with an almost endless variety? Whence has it all the materials of reason and knowledge? To this I answer, in one word, from EXPERIENCE. In that all our knowledge is founded; and from that it ultimately derives itself. Our observation employed either, about external sensible objects, or about the internal operations of our minds perceived and reflected on by ourselves, is that which supplies our understandings with all the materials of thinking. These two are the fountains of knowledge, from whence all the ideas we have, or can naturally have, do spring.

3. *The objects of sensation one source of ideas.* First, our Senses, conversant about particular sensible objects, do convey into the mind several distinct perceptions of things, according to those various ways wherein those objects do affect them. And thus we come by those ideas we have of yellow, white, heat, cold, soft, hard, bitter, sweet, and all those which we call sensible qualities; which when I say the senses convey into the mind, I mean, they from external objects convey into the mind what produces there those perceptions. This great source of most of the ideas we have, depending wholly upon our senses, and derived by them to the understanding, I call SENSATION.

4. *The operations of our minds, the other source of them.* Secondly, the other fountain from which experience furnisheth the understanding with ideas is,—the perception of the operations of our own mind within us, as it is employed about the ideas it has got;—which operations, when the soul comes to reflect on and consider, do furnish the understanding with another set of ideas, which could not be had from things without. And such are *perception, thinking, doubting, believing, reasoning, knowing, willing*, and all the different actings of our own minds;—which we being conscious of, and observing in ourselves, do from these receive into our understandings as distinct ideas as we do from bodies affecting our senses. This source of ideas every man has wholly in himself; and though it be not sense, as having nothing to do with external objects, yet it is very like it, and might properly enough be called internal sense. But as I call the other SENSATION, so I Call this REFLECTION, the ideas it affords being such only as the mind gets by reflecting on its own operations within itself. . . .

5. *All our ideas are of the one or the other of these.* The understanding seems to me not to have the least glimmering of any ideas which it doth not receive from one of these

John Locke,
An Essay Concerning Human Understanding

Do you agree with Locke's causal theory of perception? Why or why not?

two. External objects furnish the mind with the ideas of sensible qualities, which are all those different perceptions they produce in us; and the mind furnishes the understanding with ideas of its own operations.

Locke goes on to pose a provocative challenge for us in paragraph 5:

John Locke,
An Essay Concerning
Human Understanding

Let any one examine his own thoughts, and thoroughly search into his understanding; and then let him tell me, whether all the original ideas he has there, are any other than of the objects of his senses, or of the operations of his mind, considered as objects of his reflection.

Let's try his suggestion. Examining your own thoughts, what do you find? Locke is confident that the only thing you find will be *images* based directly on your senses, or what he terms your "reflection" on these images, with which he means cognitive operations such as *perception, thinking, doubting, believing, reasoning, knowing, willing*.

We can see right away that this challenge is problematic for Locke. For while you undoubtedly find in your consciousness direct sensory perceptions of your current situation—what you are currently seeing, hearing, touching, tasting, smelling—as well as memories of such experiences, you probably are also discovering all manner of ideas, concepts, and images that go far beyond anything you have directly experienced. Locke might respond that these additional contents of your mind are the results of the cognitive operations listed above: *but this is precisely the rationalist's point!* The rationalist contention is that there is no way we can account for the contents of our mind and the knowledge we have solely by looking at sense experience. We must necessarily introduce mental operations and concepts that *transform* sense experiences into an intelligible world. And because these mental operations and concepts are not to be found in sense experience, we must presume that they are somehow *innate* processes, present (at least potentially) at birth, *and* that these processes are essential for constructing knowledge in any meaningful way.

To further strengthen his case, Locke presents his analysis of the mental development of children. He asks us to imagine a child who has been raised in deprived circumstances, never viewing colors or tasting oysters. Such a child will have no idea of what these sights or tastes would be like.

Locke's challenge: What do you find when you examine the contents of your mind?

John Locke,
An Essay Concerning
Human Understanding

6. *Observable in children.* He that attentively considers the state of a child, at his first coming into the world, will have little reason to think him stored with plenty of ideas, that are to be the matter of his future knowledge. It is by degrees he comes to be furnished with them. And though the ideas of obvious and familiar qualities imprint themselves before the memory begins to keep a register of time or order, yet it is often so late before some unusual qualities come in the way, that there are few men that cannot recollect the beginning of their acquaintance with them. And if it were worth while, no doubt a child might be so ordered as to have but a very few, even of the ordinary ideas, till he were grown up to a man. But all that are born into the world, being surrounded with bodies that perpetually and diversely affect them, variety of ideas, whether care be taken of it or not, are imprinted on the minds of children. Light and colours are busy at hand everywhere, when the eye is but open; sounds and some tangible qualities fail not to solicit their proper senses, and force an entrance to the mind;—but yet, I think, it will be granted easily, that if a child were kept in a place where he never saw any other but black and white till he were a man, he would have no more ideas of scarlet or green, than he that from his childhood never tasted an oyster, or a pine-apple, has of those particular relishes.

Locke's point is that such data are not imprinted on the mind innately, and require sense experience to familiarize an individual with them. But this only states the obvious. The rationalist would contend that it is obvious that the appropriate sense experiences are crucial for normal intellectual development, but that these experiences are in no way sufficient for accounting for the mind's complex development. The only way to do this is to assume, using computer metaphors, innate "hard wiring" and "software" in the human mind which, working in partnership with sense experience, produces an intelligible world and the possibility of knowledge.

Locke then goes on to further analyze the qualities of independent objects and how these qualities relate to the perceiving subject. He distinguishes two types of physical qualities:

- **Primary qualities**, the "properties" of objects that reside in the objects, independent of our perceptions of the object. These include qualities that can be measured: size, shape, and weight.
- **Secondary qualities**, which do not reside within the objects themselves, but instead are the power (or dispositions) of objects to produce sensations in our minds. These would include qualities such as color, smell, texture, and taste.

Book II: Chapter VIII—Primary and Secondary Qualities

8. *Our ideas and the qualities of bodies.* Whatsoever the mind perceives in itself, or is the immediate object of perception, thought, or understanding, that I call idea; and the power to produce any idea in our mind, I call quality of the subject wherein that power is. Thus a snowball having the power to produce in us the ideas of white, cold, and round,—the power to produce those ideas in us, as they are in the snowball, I call qualities; and as they are sensations or perceptions in our understandings, I call them ideas; which ideas, if I speak of sometimes as in the things themselves, I would be understood to mean those qualities in the objects which produce them in us.

9. *Primary qualities of bodies.* Qualities thus considered in bodies are, *First,* such as are utterly inseparable from the body, in what state soever it be; and such as in all the alterations and changes it suffers, all the force can be used upon it, it constantly keeps; and such as sense constantly finds in every particle of matter which has bulk enough to be perceived; and the mind finds inseparable from every particle of matter, though less than to make itself singly be perceived by our senses: e.g. Take a grain of wheat, divide it into two parts; each part has still solidity, extension, figure, and mobility: divide it again, and it retains still the same qualities; and so divide it on, till the parts become insensible; they must retain still each of them all those qualities. For division (which is all that a mill, or pestle, or any other body, does upon another, in reducing it to insensible parts) can never take away either solidity, extension, figure, or mobility from any body, but only makes two or more distinct separate masses of matter, of that which was but one before; all which distinct masses, reckoned as so many distinct bodies, after division, make a certain number. These I call *original or primary qualities* of body, which I think we may observe to produce simple ideas in us, viz. Solidity, extension, figure, motion or rest, and number.

10. *Secondary qualities of bodies. Secondly,* such qualities which in truth are nothing in the objects themselves but power to produce various sensations in us by their primary qualities, i.e. by the bulk, figure, texture, and motion of their insensible parts, as colours, sounds, tastes, &c. These I call *secondary qualities.* To these might be added a *third* sort, which are allowed to be barely powers; though they are as much real qualities in the subject as those which I, to comply with the common way of speaking, call qualities, but for distinction, secondary qualities. For the power in fire to produce a new colour, or consistency, in *wax* or *clay,*—by its primary qualities, is as much a quality in fire, as the power it has to produce in *me* a new idea or sensation of warmth or burning, which I felt not before,—by the same primary qualities, viz. The bulk, texture, and motion of its insensible parts. . . .

15. *Ideas of primary qualities are resemblances; of secondary, not.* From whence I think it easy to draw this observation,—that the ideas of primary qualities of bodies are resemblances of them, and their patterns do really exist in the bodies themselves, but the ideas produced in us by these secondary qualities have no resemblance of them at all. There is nothing like our ideas, existing in the bodies themselves. They are, in the bodies we denominate from them, only a power to produce those sensations in us: and

John Locke,
*An Essay Concerning
Human Understanding*

Many thinkers believe that we must assume the existence of "hard wiring" and "innate software" in the mind which, working in partnership with sense experience, produces an intelligible world.

Primary qualities The "properties" of objects that reside in the objects (such as size, shape, weight), independent of our perceptions of the object.

Secondary qualities Properties that do not reside within the objects themselves, but instead are the power of objects to produce sensations in our mind (such as color, smell, texture, and taste).

Do you think that Locke's distinction between Primary and Secondary qualities makes sense? Why or why not?

what is sweet, blue, or warm in idea, is but the certain bulk, figure, and motion of the insensible parts, in the bodies themselves, which we call so. . . .

17. *The ideas of the primary alone really exist.* The particular bulk, number, figure, and motion of the parts of fire or snow are really in them,—whether any one's senses perceive them or no: and therefore they may be called *real* qualities, because they really exist in those bodies. But light, heat, whiteness, or coldness, are no more really in them than sickness or pain is in manna. Take away the sensation of them; let not the eyes see light or colours, nor the ears hear sounds; let the palate not taste, nor the nose smell, and all colours, tastes, odours, and sounds, *as they are such particular ideas*, vanish and cease, and are reduced to their causes, i.e. bulk, figure, and motion of parts. . . .

This, in a nutshell, is Locke's theory of causal perception, the theoretical scaffolding that frames his empiricist theory. Given his dissatisfaction with rationalism as embodied in Plato and Descartes, combined with a Newtonian view of the universe, it must have seemed indeed like a plausible "commonsense" theory of knowledge. However, as we shall soon see in the writings of George Berkeley and David Hume, the logical consequences of Locke's theory are not at all what he intended, as his theory of causal perception leads inevitably to questioning whether the external world actually exists!

Locke was likely aware that establishing the existence of an external world might prove troublesome, and he does make an effort to reassure us of its existence in the following passages. Interestingly, he emulates Descartes in concluding that "intuition" provides knowledge of ourselves, and "reason" reveals the existence of God. But knowledge of the existence of everything else in the universe can only come through "sensation," as there is "no necessary connection of real existence" between the ideas produced in our minds and the objects that produced them.

John Locke,
An Essay Concerning Human Understanding

Book IV: Chapter XI—Of Our Knowledge of the Existence of Other Things

1. *Knowledge of the existence of other finite beings is to be had only by actual sensation.* The knowledge of our own being we have by intuition. The existence of a God, reason clearly makes known to us, as has been shown.

The knowledge of the existence of *any other thing* we can have only by *sensation*: for there being no necessary connexion of real existence with any *idea* a man hath in his memory; nor of any other existence but that of God with the existence of any particular man: no particular man can know the existence of any other being, but only when, by actual operating upon him, it makes itself perceived by him. For, the having the idea of anything in our mind, no more proves the existence of that thing, than the picture of a man evidences his being in the world, or the visions of a dream make thereby a true history.

But if there is no necessary connection between physical objects and our mental impressions of these objects, then how can we be sure these objects actually exist? After all, our senses often provide partial or inaccurate information to us. Just consider all of those situations in which people experiencing the same event provide very diverse accounts of the experience. Or the times in which you were convinced you had experienced one thing, and it turned out to be something very different. Locke appeals to the persuasiveness of common sense in asserting "the certainty of our senses, and the ideas we receive by them." But is this really convincing?

John Locke,
An Essay Concerning Human Understanding

2. *Instance: whiteness of this paper.* It is therefore the *actual receiving* of ideas from without that gives us notice of the existence of other things, and makes us know, that something doth exist at that time without us, which causes that idea in us; though perhaps we neither know nor consider how it does it. For it takes not from the certainty of our senses, and the ideas we receive by them, that we know not the manner wherein they are produced: v.g. whilst I write this, I have, by the paper affecting my eyes, that idea

produced in my mind, which, whatever object causes, I call white; by which I know that that quality or accident (i.e. whose appearance before my eyes always causes that idea) doth really exist, and hath a being without me. And of this, the greatest assurance I can possibly have, and to which my faculties can attain, is the testimony of my eyes, which are the proper and sole judges of this thing; whose testimony I have reason to rely on as so certain, that I can no more doubt, whilst I write this, that I see white and black, and that something really exists that causes that sensation in me, than that I write or move my hand; which is a certainty as great as human nature is capable of, concerning the existence of anything, but a man's self alone, and of God.

Recognizing that "common sense" may not provide sufficient assurance regarding the external world, Locke brings God in for additional reinforcement: "As to myself, I think God has given me assurance enough of the existence of things without me." But is this really persuasive? Certainly not to those who have doubts in the existence of God!

Locke's next effort is to address Descartes' radical doubt regarding the external world. With barely concealed sarcasm directed toward the "dreamer" Descartes (a reference to Descartes' considering the possibility that our "reality" is actually a dream), Locke once again resorts to the persuasive powers of common sense: "And if our dreamer pleases to try whether the glowing heat of a glass furnace be barely a wandering imagination in a drowsy man's fancy, by putting his hand into it, he may perhaps be wakened into a certainty greater than he could wish, that it is something more than bare imagination." But has Locke missed the entire philosophical point of Descartes' radical doubt?

8. *This certainty is as great as our condition needs.* But yet, if after all this any one will be so sceptical as to distrust his senses, and to affirm that all we see and hear, feel and taste, think and do, during our whole being, is but the series and deluding appearances of a long dream, whereof there is no reality; and therefore will question the existence of all things, or our knowledge of anything. . . . For he that sees a candle burning, and hath experimented the force of its flame by putting his finger in it, will little doubt that this is something existing without him, which does him harm, and puts him to great pain; which is assurance enough, when no man requires greater certainty to govern his actions by than what is as certain as his actions themselves. And if our dreamer pleases to try whether the glowing heat of a glass furnace be barely a wandering imagination in a drowsy man's fancy, by putting his hand into it, he may perhaps be wakened into a certainty greater than he could wish, that it is something more than bare imagination. So that this evidence is as great as we can desire, being as certain to us as our pleasure or pain, i.e. happiness or misery; beyond which we have no concernment, either of knowing or being. . . .

John Locke,
*An Essay Concerning
Human Understanding*

Locke's final effort to put the question of the existence of an external world to rest consists in ridiculing anyone who even has the temerity to *ask* for proof—a very curious position for a philosopher to take! Such an approach is a clear indication of Locke's *lack* of compelling rationale for his position and the problems it engenders. The fact is that his theory of causal perception has created an excruciating dilemma for him. If all knowledge comes from experience, and all we directly know are the mental impressions caused by the sense data emitted by external objects, then there is no way we can ever have direct knowledge of the external world. We are "locked" in a world of our own mental images, with no access to whatever is responsible for producing these images. Locke suggests in some places that our mental impressions are "copies" of external events—"resemblances," he calls them. But how can we ever be sure how accurate the copies are? We lack an external point of reference from which we can compare the objects and the copies. For example, suppose you have a hallucination: how could you tell whether your mental impression correlated to an external object under Locke's

Does putting your finger in the flame prove the existence of an external world?

theory? The same principle holds true for *everything* you perceive: you have no way of determining to what extent your mental impressions reflect an external reality.

Locke,
An Essay Concerning Human Understanding

10. *Folly to expect demonstration in everything.* Whereby yet we may observe how foolish and vain a thing it is for a man of a narrow knowledge, who having reason given him to judge of the different evidence and probability of things, and to be swayed accordingly; how vain, I say, it is to expect demonstration and certainty in things not capable of it; and refuse assent to very rational propositions, and act contrary to very plain and clear truths, because they cannot be made out so evident, as to surmount even the least (I will not say reason, but) pretence of doubting. He that, in the ordinary affairs of life, would admit of nothing but direct plain demonstration, would be sure of nothing in this world, but of perishing quickly. The wholesomeness of his meat or drink would not give him reason to venture on it: and I would fain know what it is he could do upon such grounds as are capable of no doubt, no objection.

Locke, John, *An Essay Concerning Human Understanding*

Locke argues that the qualities we experience—both primary and secondary—must reside in *something*—therefore there must be external substances of which these qualities are a necessary part. But what are these "substances" that we can never directly experience actually like? Locke confesses: such substances are "we know not what," "we have no clear or distinct idea," "nothing but the unknown support of those qualities." Locke's grand empiricist epistemology may have begun with a bang, but it surely ends with a whimper.

THINK PHILOSOPHICALLY 9.1
Analyzing John Locke

PHILOSOPHER'S NOTEBOOK

- Take Locke's challenge again, this time writing out your responses. Carefully examine your own thoughts: can you identify any ideas that did not come from the experiences of sensations or reflections on these experiences?
- Locke believes that it is contradictory to believe that we might possess knowledge of which we are unaware. Do you agree with his position? Why or why not?
- Even though Locke believes that we can only have direct knowledge of the mental images and impressions in our mind, he does not believe this should cause us to doubt the existence of an external world that produces these images and impressions. Do you agree with his analysis? Why or why not?
- Locke provides a number of arguments for the existence of the external world of which we can have no direct knowledge:

    Common sense tells us that the world exists.

    God would not deceive us regarding the existence of the external world.

    People who raise philosophical doubts about the existence of the external world (like Descartes) should place their hand in a fiery furnace to be convinced.

    If we were to doubt such basic convictions as the external world, we would become paralyzed by inaction and perish.

    Do you find any of these arguments for an external world persuasive? Which ones? Why? Can you think of any additional arguments that Locke might use?
- Describe an instance in which you were convinced that you had perceived something that turned out to be very different from what you came to believe actually occurred. How does this sort of experience pose a problem for Locke?
- Describe, in your own words, your own epistemology. How do you think we gain knowledge?

Bishop George Berkeley:
"To Be Is to Be Perceived"

eorge Berkeley (1685–1753) was Ireland's most famous philosopher and was also a bishop in the Anglican Church (hence the title generally attached to his name). He was a remarkable individual, committed to education, particularly in America. He attempted to establish a college for Native Americans and the sons of English planters (it failed for lack of funding) and made important contributions to Harvard, Yale, and Columbia. In honor of his educational contributions, California even established a university in a city named after him—Berkeley.

Berkeley was well versed in the philosophy of John Locke (along with Descartes, Newton, and the other leading thinkers of the time), and Berkeley takes Locke's fundamental ideas to their logical—and astonishing—conclusion. He accepts Locke's basic empiricist perspective: all knowledge comes either through sense experience or by observing our own psychological states and operations (willing, doubting, loving, for example), and this knowledge is represented to us as "ideas." Berkeley follows Locke's definition of ideas as the images, feelings, or sense data that are directly present to our conscious minds, displayed as either vivid sensory or psychological experiences, or the less vivid form of memory and imagination.

But then Berkeley makes a radical departure from Locke's conclusions on two key points:

- Berkeley rejects Locke's distinction between primary qualities (inherent in physical objects) and secondary qualities (dependent on human minds).
- Berkeley rejects Locke's "commonsense" belief in external objects.

The startling result is Berkeley's denial of the existence of any independently existing external world. His reasoning is the logical extension of Locke's principles: because all we know are the ideas we find presented to our conscious minds, then it follows that we can never know a material world that supposedly lies outside of our own personal experiences. Thus, the only things that exist are minds and ideas in the minds. "To be is to be perceived" (*esse est percipi*) is the cornerstone of Berkeley's epistemology, which has come to be known as **subjective idealism**. Objects do not exist independently of consciousness: the only things that exist are conscious minds and the ideas subjectively present to the conscious minds. An apple, for example, is simply an idea in our mind that combines the experiences of roundness, redness, hardness, and sweetness. The word *apple* simply names "recurring patterns" of sense experiences, and nothing else. What most people interpret to be physical objects are actually groups of sense experiences, bundles of sense data that are present to our mind. To the age-old conundrum, "If a tree falls in the forest, does it make a sound?" Berkeley's response is not only doesn't it make a sound, but the tree and the forest don't actually exist independently of someone's perception of them. Berkeley outlines his views in the following passages taken from *A Treatise Concerning the Principles of Human Knowledge.*

GEORGE BERKELEY
(1685–1753)
Irish Philosopher. With Locke and Hume one of the three great British empiricists. In *Treatise Concerning the Principles of Human Knowledge* (1710), defends an idealist position which maintains there exists no matter, only sensible objects whose essence is to be perceived.

For Berkeley, apples exist only in our minds.

1. It is evident to any one who takes a survey of the objects of human knowledge, that they are either ideas actually imprinted on the senses; or else such as are perceived by attending to the passions and operations of the mind; or lastly, ideas formed by help of memory and imagination—either compounding, dividing, or barely representing those originally perceived in the aforesaid ways. By sight I have the ideas of light and colours, with their several degrees and variations. By touch I perceive hard and soft, heat and cold, motion and resistance, and of all these more and less either as to quantity or degree. Smelling furnishes me with odours; the palate with tastes; and hearing conveys

George Berkeley,
A Treatise Concerning the Principles of Human Knowledge

Subjective idealism The belief that only ideas and conscious minds have actual existence.

George Berkeley

sounds to the mind in all their variety of tone and composition. And as several of these are observed to accompany each other, they come to be marked by one name, and so to be reputed as one thing. Thus, for example a certain colour, taste, smell, figure and consistence having been observed to go together, are accounted one distinct thing, signified by the name apple; other collections of ideas constitute a stone, a tree, a book, and the like sensible things—which as they are pleasing or disagreeable excite the passions of love, hatred, joy, grief, and so forth.

2. But, besides all that endless variety of ideas or objects of knowledge, there is likewise something which knows or perceives them, and exercises divers operations, as willing, imagining, remembering, about them. This perceiving, active being is what I call mind, spirit, soul, or myself. By which words I do not denote any one of my ideas, but a thing entirely distinct from them, wherein, they exist, or, which is the same thing, whereby they are perceived for the existence of an idea consists in being perceived.

3. That neither our thoughts, nor passions, nor ideas formed by the imagination, exist without the mind, is what everybody will allow. And it seems no less evident that the various sensations or ideas imprinted on the sense, however blended or combined together (that is, whatever objects they compose), cannot exist otherwise than in a mind perceiving them.—I think an intuitive knowledge may be obtained of this by any one that shall attend to what is meant by the term exists, when applied to sensible things. The table I write on I say exists, that is, I see and feel it; and if I were out of my study I should say it existed—meaning thereby that if I was in my study I might perceive it, or that some other spirit actually does perceive it. There was an odour, that is, it was smelt; there was a sound, that is, it was heard; a colour or figure, and it was perceived by sight or touch. This is all that I can understand by these and the like expressions. For as to what is said of the absolute existence of unthinking things without any relation to their being perceived, that seems perfectly unintelligible. Their *esse* is *percepi*, nor is it possible they should have any existence out of the minds or thinking things which perceive them.

4. It is indeed an opinion strangely prevailing amongst men, that houses, mountains, rivers, and in a word all sensible objects, have an existence, natural or real, distinct from their being perceived by the understanding. But, with how great an assurance and acquiescence soever this principle may be entertained in the world, yet whoever shall find in his heart to call it in question may, if I mistake not, perceive it to involve a manifest contradiction. For, what are the fore-mentioned objects but the things we perceive by sense? And what do we perceive besides our own ideas or sensations? And is it not plainly repugnant that any one of these, or any combination of them, should exist unperceived?

One has to admire Berkeley's self-confidence in his ideas (or his sense of playfulness, perhaps), contending that a belief in an independently existing external world is "an opinion strangely prevailing amongst men," and that the misguided notion that anything should continue to exist unperceived by a mind is an idea that is "plainly repugnant." But the force of his argument clearly has to be reckoned with: accepting Locke's empiricist causal theory of perception, isn't the unavoidable endpoint, *esse est percipi*? Berkeley goes on to attack Locke's idea of "resemblances" directly, arguing in the following passages that it makes no sense to presume that there are things outside of the mind "like" our ideas—for "nothing is like an idea but another idea."

George Berkeley,
A Treatise Concerning
the Principles of Human Knowledge

6. Some truths there are so near and obvious to the mind that a man need only open his eyes to see them. Such I take this important one to be, viz., that all the choir of heaven and furniture of the earth, in a word all those bodies which compose the mighty frame of the world, have not any subsistence without a mind, that their being is to be perceived or known; that consequently so long as they are not actually perceived by me, or do not exist in my mind or that of any other created spirit, they must either have no existence at all, or else subsist in the mind of some Eternal Spirit—it being perfectly unintelligible, and involving all the absurdity of abstraction, to attribute to any single

part of them an existence independent of a spirit. To be convinced of which, the reader need only reflect, and try to separate in his own thoughts the being of a sensible thing from its being perceived . . .

8. But, say you, though the ideas themselves do not exist without the mind, yet there may be things like them, whereof they are copies or resemblances, which things exist without the mind in an unthinking substance. I answer, an idea can be like nothing but an idea; a colour or figure can be like nothing but another colour or figure. If we look but ever so little into our thoughts, we shall find it impossible for us to conceive a likeness except only between our ideas. Again, I ask whether those supposed originals or external things, of which our ideas are the pictures or representations, be themselves perceivable or no? If they are, then they are ideas and we have gained our point; but if you say they are not, I appeal to any one whether it be sense to assert a colour is like something which is invisible; hard or soft, like something which is intangible; and so of the rest.

Berkeley next takes aim at Locke's distinction between "primary" and "secondary" qualities, making the persuasive point that the same arguments apply to both, and that in any case, our mind views them as inextricably tied together, posing the challenge: "But I desire any one to reflect and try whether he can, by any abstraction of thought, conceive the extension and motion of a body without all other sensible qualities."

9. Some there are who make a distinction betwixt primary and secondary qualities. By the former they mean extension, figure, motion, rest, solidity or impenetrability, and number; by the latter they denote all other sensible qualities, as colours, sounds, tastes, and so forth. The ideas we have of these they acknowledge not to be the resemblances of anything existing without the mind, or unperceived, but they will have our ideas of the primary qualities to be patterns or images of things which exist without the mind, in an unthinking substance which they call Matter. By Matter, therefore, we are to understand an inert, senseless substance, in which extension, figure, and motion do actually subsist. But it is evident from what we have already shown, that extension, figure, and motion are only ideas existing in the mind, and that an idea can be like nothing but another idea, and that consequently neither they nor their archetypes can exist in an unperceiving substance. Hence, it is plain that the very notion of what is called Matter or corporeal substance, involves a contradiction in it. . . .

15. In short, let any one consider those arguments which are thought manifestly to prove that colours and taste exist only in the mind, and he shall find they may with equal force be brought to prove the same thing of extension, figure, and motion. Though it must be confessed this method of arguing does not so much prove that there is no extension or colour in an outward object, as that we do not know by sense which is the true extension or colour of the object. But the arguments foregoing plainly shew it to be impossible that any colour or extension at all, or other sensible quality whatsoever, should exist in an unthinking subject without the mind, or in truth, that there should be any such thing as an outward object. . . .

George Berkeley,
A Treatise Concerning
the Principles of Human Knowledge

But doesn't it make sense to assume some sort of independently existing "substance" that is responsible for our mental ideas? Predictably, Berkeley gives a vehement "no!" There are only two ways we can be aware of such substances:

- Through our senses: but because our senses only produce mental ideas, they cannot, by definition, provide any indication of possible external "substances."
- Through reason: but even "the very patrons of matter" (as Berkeley playfully terms Locke and others) admit the lack of necessary connection between mental ideas and external substances.

George Berkeley,
*A Treatise Concerning
the Principles of Human Knowledge*

18. But, though it were possible that solid, figured, movable substances may exist without the mind, corresponding to the ideas we have of bodies, yet how is it possible for us to know this? Either we must know it by sense or by reason. As for our senses, by them we have the knowledge only of our sensations, ideas, or those things that are immediately perceived by sense, call them what you will: but they do not inform us that things exist without the mind, or unperceived, like to those which are perceived. This the materialists themselves acknowledge. It remains therefore that if we have any knowledge at all of external things, it must be by reason, inferring their existence from what is immediately perceived by sense. But what reason can induce us to believe the existence of bodies without the mind, from what we perceive, since the very patrons of Matter themselves do not pretend there is any necessary connexion betwixt them and our ideas?

 Berkeley, George, *A Treatise Concerning the Principles of Human Knowledge*

VISUAL PHILOSOPHY

"Ancient of Days" by William Blake: God Taking the Measure of the Universe

After attempting to prove that the world exists only in our minds and not in reality, Berkeley calls upon a belief in God to guarantee the existence of a world which is real and intelligible. Which line of reasoning do you find to be more compelling? Why?

Berkeley, once again, turns the commonly accepted way of viewing the world on its head, asserting that believing in an external world "must needs be a very precarious opinion; since it is to suppose, without any reason at all, that God has created innumerable beings that are entirely useless, and serve to no manner of purpose."

Finally, Berkeley acknowledges some of the inherent difficulties with his subjective idealist view of knowledge and reality. Although the only things that supposedly exist according to his theory are minds and ideas, how do we account for the fact that we have no control over many of the most vivid ideas (of what appears to be the external world) that we experience? That is, they simply present themselves to our minds? And not only that: these ideas present themselves as a coherent whole, obeying what we observe to be certain regularities that we call the "laws of nature"? Berkeley finally concedes: the things of the world are nothing other than ideas in the mind of God, the "Author of nature," produced by "the will of another and more powerful spirit."

> There is a God, therefore he perceives all things: sensible things do really exist; and if they really exist, they are necessarily perceived by an infinite mind; therefor there is an infinite mind, or God.

THINK PHILOSOPHICALLY 9.2
Analyzing George Berkeley

 PHILOSOPHER'S NOTEBOOK

- What is your reaction to Berkeley's claim that the only things that exist in the universe are minds and ideas that exist in the minds? If you are not comfortable with his eliminating an independently existing external world, how would you go about refuting his ideas?

- Unfortunately, Berkeley's major writings were published after Locke's death. If he had still been alive, how do you think Locke would have responded to Berkeley's criticism of his views?

- Samuel Johnson, a famous English writer who lived at the same time as Berkeley, responded to Berkeley's subjectivist idealism by kicking a stone and sending it flying into the air, while saying, "I refute him thus." Do you think this is a persuasive "argument" by Johnson? Why or why not?

- Berkeley's response to the criticism of common sense by Johnson and others was

  > But after all, say you, it sounds very harsh to say we eat and drink ideas, and are clothed with ideas. I acknowledge it does so—the word idea not being used in common discourse to signify the several combinations of sensible qualities which are called things; and it is certain that any expression which varies from the familiar use of language will seem harsh and ridiculous. But this doth not concern the truth of the proposition, which in other words is no more than to say, we are fed and clothed with those things which we perceive immediately by our senses. The hardness or softness, the colour, taste, warmth, figure, or suchlike qualities, which combined together constitute the several sorts of victuals and apparel, have been shewn to exist only in the mind that perceives them; and this is all that is meant by calling them ideas; which word if it was as ordinarily used as thing, would sound no harsher nor more ridiculous than it. I am not for disputing about the propriety, but the truth of the expression. If therefore you agree with me that we eat and drink and are clad with the immediate objects of sense, which cannot exist unperceived or without the mind, I shall readily grant it is more proper or conformable to custom that they should be called things rather than ideas.

  Imagine that you are Berkeley, and describe the series of perceptions that would constitute Samuel Johnson's kicking the stone.

A somewhat more humorous statement of the same point was made by English writer and priest Ronald Knox (1888–1957), and subsequently quoted by **Bertrand Russell**:

There was a young man who said, "God

Must think it exceedingly odd

If he finds that this tree

Continues to be

When there's no one about in the Quad."

    Reply

Dear Sir:

Your astonishment's odd:

I am always about in the Quad.

And that's why the tree

Will continue to be,

Since observed by

    Yours faithfully,

      GOD

David Hume: *"Commit it (Metaphysics) to the Flames"*

DAVID HUME
(1711–1776)
Scottish Philosopher. Hume's philosophy seen as drawing out logical consequences of a thoroughgoing empiricism. His skepticism concerning causation, induction, and religion is widely influential in the history of philosophy and contemporary philosophy.

The Scottish philosopher **David Hume** (1711–1776) is widely considered to be one of the greatest philosophical skeptics of all time. (In epistemology, skepticism includes positions such as doubting all assumptions until proved, or claiming that no knowledge is possible in any circumstances.) We first ran into his wrecking-ball logic in chapter 3, where he cheerfully maintains that the "self" as a continuous identity through time simply does not exist. Instead, what we consider the "self" is really just a transient bundle of fragmentary sensations that parade across "the stage" of consciousness in a random stream.

Hume's skepticism naturally permeates his general views on epistemology as well. In fact, in the evolution of doubt and skepticism that began with Descartes, and continued on through Locke and Berkeley, Hume can be seen as the final stage, announced with an emphatic exclamation point. As contrary as they are to established beliefs, Hume's views demand to be taken seriously, for they are argued with compelling reasoning and rigorous consistency. Writing two hundred years later, the influential British philosopher Bertrand Russell observed about Hume's skepticism:

To refute him has been, ever since he wrote, a favorite pastime among metaphysicians. For my part, I find none of their refutations convincing; nevertheless, I cannot but hope that something less skeptical than Hume's system may be discoverable.

Descartes championed radical doubt in epistemology, posing the possibility that we are caught in a dream and manipulated by an "evil genius." But Descartes was able to escape (in his own mind, anyway) from this skeptical nightmare by means of reason's *cogito, ergo sum* and the spiritual conviction that God would not permit a universe based on deception and illusion.

Locke took Descartes' radical doubt and applied it to an empiricist framework, concluding that all we can know are the ideas presented to the conscious mind. Hence, there is no evidence that an external world exists independently of the

Bertrand Russell (1872–1970) British Philosopher. One of the founders of modern logic. In *The Principles of Mathematics* (1903) and with Whitehead in the three volume *Principia Mathematica* (1910–1913) advanced the view that all of mathematics could be derived from logical premises. Also a political activist, he wrote many popular books on topics such as religion, ethics, and marriage.

ideas we have of it, and substance is "something we know not what." Locke distinguished "primary qualities" (which reside in the external objects) from "secondary qualities," which reside only in our minds, a distinction that supports the existence of an external world. And to make sure that he avoided the unpalatable possibility of extreme skepticism, Locke also brought God into his epistemology to save the day—or the reality of the external world, anyway. According to Locke, God would not deceive us regarding the existence of an external world. And, he added for good measure, common sense tells us that such a world exists.

Berkeley, proposing an epistemology of subjective idealism, had no patience with two of Locke's three arguments for the existence of an external world. It is impossible to make a clear distinction between primary and secondary qualities, Berkeley contended: they are all ideas that exist only in our minds. And he soundly rejected Locke's commonsense argument for an external reality as being philosophically inconsistent with Locke's empiricist principles. No, Berkeley was convinced that only minds and ideas in minds exist: it is illogical and unsupportable to even consider the existence of an external world. Until . . . just before the external world is to be executed, an order of clemency is received: not from the Governor, but from God. The reality of the external world (and the laws of science, by the way) are preserved because they always exist in the mind of God.

When Hume storms onto the scene, he is outraged at what he considers to be the worst kind of philosophical hypocrisy. There is no empirical or rational evidence for God, he thunders, and so we have no good reason to believe in an external world or the laws of science that are used to organize, explain, and predict events in such a world. Hume ends his monumental work, *An Enquiry Concerning Human Understanding*, with one of the most blistering attacks on God and metaphysics in the history of philosophy:

> When we run over libraries, persuaded of these principles, what havoc must we make? If we take in our hand any volume; of divinity or school metaphysics, for instance; let us ask, Does it contain any abstract reasoning concerning quantity or number? No. Does it contain any experimental reasoning concerning matter of fact and existence? No. Commit it then to the flames: for it can contain nothing but sophistry and illusion.

The following passages from this same work detail his core arguments. In addition to attacking the possibility of knowing an external world, he also takes aim at two principles that are integral to understanding such a world:

- The *principle of universal causation*, which contends that every event has a cause or causes that can be discovered through observation or systematic investigation.
- The *principle of induction*, which contends that, using our understanding of causal relations, we can make justifiable inferences and predictions about future events.

So fasten your philosophical seat belts: here comes David Hume.

Section II—Of the Origin of Ideas

David Hume,
An Enquiry Concerning Human Understanding

Every one will readily allow, that there is a considerable difference between the perceptions of the mind, when a man feels the pain of excessive heat, or the pleasure of moderate warmth, and when he afterwards recalls to his memory this sensation, or anticipates it by his imagination. These faculties may mimic or copy the perceptions of the senses; but they never can entirely reach the force and vivacity of the original sentiment. The utmost we say of them, even when they operate with greatest vigour, is, that they represent their object in so lively a manner, that we could almost say we feel or see it: But, except the mind be disordered by disease or madness, they never can arrive at such a pitch of vivacity, as to render these perceptions altogether undistinguishable. All the colours of poetry, however splendid, can never paint natural objects in such a manner as

According to Hume, the immediate perception of a breathtaking sunset possesses a liveliness and vividness that the memory or imagingation simply cannot duplicate. Do you agree?

David Hume,
An Enquiry Concerning
Human Understanding

to make the description be taken for a real landskip. The most lively thought is still inferior to the dullest sensation.

We may observe a like distinction to run through all the other perceptions of the mind. A man in a fit of anger, is actuated in a very different manner from one who only thinks of that emotion. If you tell me, that any person is in love, I easily understand your meaning, and from a just conception of his situation; but never can mistake that conception for the real disorders and agitations of the passion. When we reflect on our past sentiments and affections, our thought is a faithful mirror, and copies its objects truly; but the colours which it employs are faint and dull, in comparison of those in which our original perceptions were clothed. It requires no nice discernment or metaphysical head to mark the distinction between them.

Here therefore we may divide all the perceptions of the mind into two classes or species, which are distinguished by their different degrees of force and vivacity. The less forcible and lively are commonly denominated Thoughts or Ideas. The other species want a name in our language, and in most others; I suppose, because it was not requisite for any, but philosophical purposes, to rank them under a general term or appellation. Let us, therefore, use a little freedom, and call them Impressions; employing that word in a sense somewhat different from the usual. By the term impression, then, I mean all our more lively perceptions, when we hear, or see, or feel, or love, or hate, or desire, or will. And impressions are distinguished from ideas, which are the less lively perceptions, of which we are conscious, when we reflect on any of those sensations or movements above mentioned.

As an empiricist, Hume wants to differentiate the various elements in our experience, and his empiricist criteria are "lively" and "vivid." "Impressions" refer to those phenomena directly experienced through the senses, or emotions that are directly felt, and they are the most lively and vivid. "Ideas," on the other hand, are the product of our memory or imagination, and they lack the liveliness and vividness of impressions. So, for example, the immediate perceptions of a sweltering hot day or a breathtaking sunset possess a liveliness and vividness that the memory or imagination simply cannot duplicate. Similarly, no one is likely to confuse serenely contemplating the *idea* of love and directly experiencing "the real disorders and agitations of the passion." However, despite their difference in liveliness and vividness, both impressions and ideas are contents of the human mind, and in no way suggest or validate the existence of an external world.

Skeptical Doubts Concerning the Operations of the Understanding Part 1

All the objects of human reason or enquiry may naturally be divided into two kinds, to wit, *Relations of Ideas*, and *Matters of Fact*. Of the first kind are the sciences of Geometry, Algebra, and Arithmetic; and in short, every affirmation which is either intuitively or demonstratively certain. *That the square of the hypotenuse is equal to the square of the two sides*, is a proposition which expresses a relation between these figures. *That three times five is equal to the half of thirty*, expresses a relation between these numbers. Propositions of this kind are discoverable by the mere operation of thought, without dependence on what is anywhere existent in the universe. Though there never were a circle or triangle in nature, the truths demonstrated by Euclid would for ever retain their certainty and evidence.

Matters of fact, which are the second objects of human reason, are not ascertained in the same manner; nor is our evidence of their truth, however great, of a like nature with the foregoing. The contrary of every matter of fact is still possible; because it can never imply a contradiction, and is conceived by the mind with the same facility and distinctness, as if ever so conformable to reality. *That the sun will not rise to-morrow* is no less intelligible a proposition, and implies no more contradiction than the affirmation, *that it will rise*. We should in vain, therefore, attempt to demonstrate its falsehood. Were it demonstratively false, it would imply a contradiction, and could never be distinctly conceived by the mind.

Hume's division of human knowledge into "relations of ideas" and "matters of fact," along with his insistence that every justifiable belief meet the standards of one or the other, has sometimes been referred to in philosophy as "Hume's fork" (as in "fork in the road"). One fork, the "relations of ideas," includes the principles of mathematics and logic, and simple tautologies ("A bachelor is an unmarried man.") These principles are discoverable by reason, without reference to experience, and they do not permit logical contradictions. For example, it doesn't make sense to simultaneously maintain that "A triangle has three sides" and "A triangle *does not* have three sides."

The second fork, "matters of fact," can be confirmed (or disconfirmed) by appeal to our experience. Unlike "relations of ideas," they necessarily involve sense experience, and their statements *do* permit logical contradictions, according to Hume. He believes it does make sense to maintain that "It will be cloudy tomorrow" and "It will *not* be cloudy tomorrow" in the sense that these two statements do not entail a *logical* contradiction.

But Hume is not about to leave things at this level of understanding. He wants to investigate the epistemological foundations of "matters of fact," an exploration that ultimately leads to his radical skepticism regarding empirical knowledge. But for now, he is committed to a completely open and honest inquiry, which he is convinced will "prove useful, by exciting curiosity, and destroying that implicit faith and security, which is the bane of all reasoning and free enquiry." He begins his analysis with what he considers to be a keystone of knowledge, the principle of "cause and effect."

All reasonings concerning matter of fact seem to be founded on the relation of *Cause and Effect*. By means of that relation alone we can go beyond the evidence of our memory and senses. If you were to ask a man, why he believes any matter of fact, which is absent; for instance, that his friend is in the country, or in France; he would give you a reason; and this reason would be some other fact; as a letter received from him, or the knowledge of his former resolutions and promises. A man finding a watch or any other machine in a desert island, would conclude that there had once been men in that island. All our reasonings concerning fact are of the same nature. And here it is constantly supposed that there is a connexion between the present fact and that which is inferred from it. Were there nothing to bind them together, the inference would be entirely precarious. The hearing of an articulate voice and rational discourse in the dark assures us of the presence of some person: Why? Because these are the effects of the human make and fabric, and closely connected with it. If we anatomize all the other reasonings of this nature, we shall find that they are founded on the relation of cause and effect, and that this relation is either near or remote, direct or collateral. Heat and light are collateral effects of fire, and the one effect may justly be inferred from the other.

If we would satisfy ourselves, therefore, concerning the nature of that evidence, which assures us of matters of fact, we must enquire how we arrive at the knowledge of cause and effect.

I shall venture to affirm, as a general proposition, which admits of no exception, that the knowledge of this relation is not, in any instance, attained by reasonings *a priori*; but arises entirely from experience, when we find that any particular objects are constantly conjoined with each other. Let an object be presented to a man of ever so strong natural reason and abilities; if that object be entirely new to him, he will not be able, by the most accurate examination of its sensible qualities, to discover any of its causes or effects. Adam, though his rational faculties be supposed, at the very first, entirely perfect, could not have inferred from the fluidity and transparency of water that it would suffocate him, or from the light and warmth of fire that it would consume him. No object ever discovers, by the qualities which appear to the senses, either the causes which produced it, or the effects which will arise from it; nor can our reason,

David Hume,
An Enquiry Concerning Human Understanding

Hume believes that cause and effect are discovered not by reason but experience.

Hume questions, "Who will assert that he can give the ultimate reason, why milk or bread is proper nourishment for a man, not for a lion or tiger?"

unassisted by experience, ever draw any inference concerning real existence and matter of fact.

This proposition, *that causes and effects are discoverable, not by reason but by experience*, will readily be admitted with regard to such objects, as we remember to have once been altogether unknown to us; since we must be conscious of the utter inability, which we then lay under, of foretelling what would arise from them. Present two smooth pieces of marble to a man who has no tincture of natural philosophy; he will never discover that they will adhere together in such a manner as to require great force to separate them in a direct line, while they make so small a resistance to a lateral pressure. Such events, as bear little analogy to the common course of nature, are also readily confessed to be known only by experience; nor does any man imagine that the explosion of gunpowder, or the attraction of a loadstone, could ever be discovered by arguments *a priori*. In like manner, when an effect is supposed to depend upon an intricate machinery or secret structure of parts, we make no difficulty in attributing all our knowledge of it to experience. Who will assert that he can give the ultimate reason, why milk or bread is proper nourishment for a man, not for a lion or a tiger?

But the same truth may not appear, at first sight, to have the same evidence with regard to events, which have become familiar to us from our first appearance in the world, which bear a close analogy to the whole course of nature, and which are supposed to depend on the simple qualities of objects, without any secret structure of parts. We are apt to imagine that we could discover these effects by the mere operation of our reason, without experience. We fancy, that were we brought on a sudden into this world, we could at first have inferred that one Billiard-ball would communicate motion to another upon impulse; and that we needed not to have waited for the event, in order to pronounce with certainty concerning it. Such is the influence of custom, that, where it is strongest, it not only covers our natural ignorance, but even conceals itself, and seems not to take place, merely because it is found in the highest degree.

But to convince us that all the laws of nature, and all the operations of bodies without exception, are known only by experience, the following reflections may, perhaps, suffice. Were any object presented to us, and were we required to pronounce concerning the effect, which will result from it, without consulting past observation; after what manner, I beseech you, must the mind proceed in this operation? It must invent or imagine some event, which it ascribes to the object as its effect; and it is plain that this invention must be entirely arbitrary. The mind can never possibly find the effect in the supposed cause, by the most accurate scrutiny and examination. For the effect is totally different from the cause, and consequently can never be discovered in it. Motion in the second Billiard-ball is a quite distinct event from motion in the first; nor is there anything in the one to suggest the smallest hint of the other. A stone or piece of metal raised into the air, and left without any support, immediately falls: but to consider the matter *a priori*, is there anything we discover in this situation which can beget the idea of a downward, rather than an upward, or any other motion, in the stone or metal?

And as the first imagination or invention of a particular effect, in all natural operations, is arbitrary, where we consult not experience; so must we also esteem the supposed tie or connexion between the cause and effect, which binds them together, and renders it impossible that any other effect could result from the operation of that cause. When I see, for instance, a Billiard-ball moving in a straight line towards another; even suppose motion in the second ball should by accident be suggested to me, as the result of their contact or impulse; may I not conceive, that a hundred different events might as well follow from that cause? May not both these balls remain at absolute rest? May not the first ball return in a straight line, or leap off from the second in any line or direction? All these suppositions are consistent and conceivable. Why then should we give the preference to one, which is no more consistent or conceivable than the rest? All our reasonings *a priori* will never be able to show us any foundation for this preference.

In a word, then, every effect is a distinct event from its cause. It could not, therefore, be discovered in the cause, and the first invention or conception of it, *a priori*, must be entirely arbitrary. And even after it is suggested, the conjunction of it with the cause must appear equally arbitrary, since there are always many other effects, which, to reason, must seem fully as consistent and natural. In vain, therefore, should we pretend to determine any single event, or infer any cause or effect, without the assistance of observation and experience.

Hume explicitly acknowledges that our belief in the principle of cause and effect is woven into every aspect of our lives, and he provides unique and memorable examples to illustrate this:

- Receiving a letter confirms that your friend is in France.
- Finding a watch on a desert island suggests the previous presence of men.
- Hearing an articulate human voice in the dark convinces us that a person is there.
- Feeling the heat from a fire suggests that the fire is the cause of the heat.

Hume's first goal is to prove conclusively that our belief in cause and effect does not meet the criteria of his first "fork," "relations of ideas." There is no way that reason can inform us of these alleged causal connections between events. To see this, we

VISUAL PHILOSOPHY

Is the Principle of Cause and Effect Unfounded?

David Hume used the example of colliding billiard balls to argue that there is nothing in experience to support a belief in the principle of cause and effect, since every causal event is independent of every other causal event. Do you agree with his reasoning? Why?

need only imagine someone coming across a potential causal relation for the first time to understand that reason is useless in the face of such a situation. Again, Hume provides us with a sparkling example to illustrate his point. Imagine, he proposes, Adam coming across water for the first time: despite his rational faculties, could he possibly be expected to infer from its "fluidity and transparency" that it would suffocate him? Or analogously, that the fire providing light and warmth would consume him? Absolutely not! Experience is required to make such inferences: ". . . nor can our reason, unassisted by experience, ever draw any inference concerning real existence and matter of fact."

Most people have difficulty appreciating this fact because of our familiarity with causally associated events in the world. We know that magnets attract iron, that gunpowder will explode when ignited, and that billiard balls will react in predictable ways when they strike one another. But what of completely new experiences: suppose you were asked to "give the ultimate reason, why milk or bread is proper nourishment for a man, not for a lion or tiger?" Lacking specialized knowledge, you would be at a complete loss to make this causal connection. As a result, we must conclude that the principle of cause and effect cannot be validated through the use of reason.

But Hume is not content to eliminate cause and effect from just one of his two forks of knowledge: he wants to eliminate it from the other fork, "matters of fact," as well, for which he is already laying the conceptual groundwork.

David Hume,
An Enquiry Concerning Human Understanding

The mind can never possibly find the effect in the supposed cause, by the most accurate scrutiny and examination. For the effect is totally different from the cause, and consequently can never be discovered in it. Motion in the second Billiard-ball is a quite distinct event from motion in the first; nor is there anything in the one to suggest the smallest hint of the other. . . . In a word, then, every effect is a distinct event from its cause.

It is apparent where Hume is headed. Not only doesn't reason provide justification for explaining cause-and-effect connections, but experience isn't going to be able to either. When you independently examine a "cause" and an "effect," it is impossible to discover any properties that announce themselves as "causes" or "effects." It is only because these events happen to be conjoined in a particular way that we make the inference that they are causally related. But there is absolutely nothing in our direct observation of these objects and events to provide support for this inference! As a result, failing both "forks" in Hume's test for knowledge, it is not possible for us to say that we have knowledge of cause-and-effect relations in the world. It's a startling conclusion, with far-reaching reverberations. Welcome to Hume's radical skepticism!

Next on Hume's "hit list" is the "principle of induction," the type of reasoning in which we infer: "the water in ice cube trays always turns to ice when I place them in the freezer; so, when I place this new ice cube tray in the freezer, the water will also turn to ice." In other words, the "principle of induction" is the way we predict future events based on past experiences. And because these past experiences are generally based on the principle of cause and effect, it is apparent that Hume is going to discover the same epistemological flaws in the "principle of induction" as he found in that of cause and effect.

David Hume,
An Enquiry Concerning Human Understanding

Skeptical Doubts Concerning the Operations of the Understanding Part 2

. . . As to past *Experience*, it can be allowed to give *direct* and *certain* information of those precise objects only, and that precise period of time, which fell under its cognizance: but why this experience should be extended to future times, and to other objects, which for aught we know, may be only in appearance similar; this is the main question on which I would insist. The bread, which I formerly eat, nourished me; that is, a body of such sensible qualities was, at that time, endued with such secret powers: but does it follow, that other bread must also nourish me at another time, and that like sensible qualities must always be attended with like secret powers? The consequence seems nowise necessary. At least, it must be acknowledged that there is here a consequence drawn by the mind; that there is a certain step taken; a process of thought, and an inference, which wants to be explained. These two propositions are far from being the same. *I have found that such an object has always been attended with such an effect*, and *I foresee, that other objects, which are, in appearance, similar, will be attended with similar effects*. I shall allow, if you please, that the one proposition may justly be inferred from the other: I know, in fact, that it always is inferred. But if you insist that the inference is made by a chain of reasoning, I desire you to produce that reasoning. The connexion between these propositions is not intuitive. There is required a medium, which may enable the mind to draw such an inference, if indeed it be drawn by reasoning and argument. What that medium is, I must confess, passes my comprehension; and it is incumbent on those to produce it, who assert that it really exists, and is the origin of all our conclusions concerning matter of fact.

Hume believes that we have no necessary basis for believing that proper nourishment will contribute to a healthy body.

Hume states his case plainly. Our senses inform us that in the past, eating bread has been associated with our personal nourishment. We commonly believe that eating the bread *caused* our nourishment, but Hume believes we never actually witness the causal connection: we assume it to be there. But now it is apparent how Hume's same form of analysis applies to induction. Because we believe that eating bread has resulted in our healthy nourishment in the past, we believe that continuing to eat other things that resemble bread will nourish our body in the future. But again, Hume queries, where is the actual causal connection that warrants this belief? If we confine ourselves to analyzing our sense experience, such a connection is nowhere to be found. Hume details the "principle of induction":

- *I have found that such an object has always been attended with such an effect,*
- *I foresee, that other objects, which are, in appearance, similar, will be attended with similar effects.*

And then his query:

I shall allow, if you please, that the one proposition may justly be inferred from the other: I know, in fact, that it always is inferred. But if you insist that the inference is made by a chain of reasoning, I desire you to produce that reasoning. The connexion between these propositions is not intuitive.

David Hume,
An Enquiry Concerning Human Understanding

In other words, Hume freely acknowledges that we commonly make such inductive inferences: it is just that when called on to produce the actual connections that warrant such reasoning, we are unable to.

Critics of Hume's skepticism were no doubt quick to confront him with the apparent contradiction between his philosophical beliefs and the assumptions about the world reflected in the way he lived his life, along the lines of: "But Hume, isn't your skepticism refuted by the fact that you live your life as if the principles of cause and effect and induction were legitimate?" Hume's response? As a human being ("an agent") I am comfortable living my life assuming these principles to be warranted. *However*, as a philosopher, it is my responsibility to explore beneath the surface of unreflective existence, "to learn the foundation of this inference." And to this point, "no enquiry has yet been able to remove my difficulty, or give me satisfaction in a matter of such importance."

David Hume,
An Enquiry Concerning Human Understanding

My practice, you say, refutes my doubts. But you mistake the purport of my question. As an agent, I am quite satisfied in the point; but as a philosopher, who has some share of curiosity, I will not say scepticism, I want to learn the foundation of this inference. No reading, no enquiry has yet been able to remove my difficulty, or give me satisfaction in a matter of such importance. Can I do better than propose the difficulty to the public, even though, perhaps, I have small hopes of obtaining a solution? We shall at least, by this means, be sensible of our ignorance, if we do not augment our knowledge.

Hume goes on to elaborate this point in the following passages.

David Hume,
An Enquiry Concerning Human Understanding

Nature will always maintain her rights, and prevail in the end over any abstract reasoning whatsoever. Though we should conclude, for instance, as in the foregoing section, that, in all reasonings from experience, there is a step taken by the mind which is not supported by any argument or process of the understanding; there is no danger that these reasonings, on which almost all knowledge depends, will ever be affected by such a discovery. If the mind be not engaged by argument to make this step, it must be induced by some other principle of equal weight and authority; and that principle will preserve its influence as long as human nature remains the same. What that principle is may well be worth the pains of enquiry.

"Nature will always maintain her rights, and prevail in the end over any abstract reasoning whatsoever." That's an intriguing statement, particularly coming from one of the greatest skeptics of all time. It implicitly recognizes the limits of reason in the face of lived experience ("nature"). Yet though our reasoning ability may not solve all of nature's mysteries, that in no way absolves us of the intellectual responsibility to probe, analyze, and attempt to understand the foundations of knowledge and reality. That is why Hume finds philosophical appeals to "common sense" by thinkers like Locke to be so intellectually hypocritical. Going *beyond* common sense for more compelling explanations is precisely what philosophers are supposed to do! For Hume, the most rigorous and honest application of reason has led him to the conclusion that there is no sound reason to believe in the principles of cause and effect and induction. Instead, we must resign ourselves to the fact that these principles reflect custom and habit, not rational necessity. Nor, in fact, do we have a legitimate philosophical foundation for believing in the existence of an external world, the "self," or God. Does this mean that, lacking such rational evidence for the orderly and intelligible nature of the universe that we should surrender ourselves to lives of quiet despondency? Just the opposite! In a famous passage that concludes his Treatise, Hume happily places his radical skepticism into the larger context of living one's life, acknowledging that after a delightful meal with friends, a few (or perhaps, more than a few) glasses of wine, and a congenial game of backgammon, his disturbing speculations "appear so cold, and strain'd, and ridiculous, that I cannot find in my heart to enter into them any farther."

David Hume,
An Enquiry Concerning Human Understanding

Most fortunately it happens, that since reason is incapable of dispelling these clouds, nature herself suffices to that purpose, and cures me of this philosophical melancholy and delirium, either by relaxing this bent of mind, or by some avocation, and lively impression of my senses, which obliterate all these chimeras. I dine, I play a game of backgammon, I converse, and am merry with my friends; and when after three or four hours' amusement, I wou'd return to these speculations, they appear so cold, and strain'd, and ridiculous, that I cannot find in my heart to enter into them any farther. ∎

Hume, David, *An Enquiry Concerning Human Understanding*

Nevertheless, from a philosophical perspective, we are left with the profound question, "Can Hume's compelling case for skepticism be satisfactorily addressed?" Our next philosopher, Immanuel Kant, believes the answer is a resounding "yes!"

THINK PHILOSOPHICALLY 9.3
Analyzing David Hume

PHILOSOPHER'S NOTEBOOK

- Do you agree with Hume that appealing to the existence of God in order to support the belief that there is an external world (as Locke and Berkeley do) amounts to philosophical hypocrisy? Why or why not?

- Summarize Hume's arguments that it is impossible for us to ever have certain knowledge of the principle of cause and effect, whether we are rationalists or empiricists. Do you agree with his reasoning? Why or why not? Construct an argument to convince Hume that the principle of cause and effect is indeed valid, being sure to provide examples to support your point of view.

- Imagine that you truly believed that the principles of cause and effect and induction were in fact not "knowledge" at all but merely habitual associations. Would this conclusion influence any aspect of your life? Explain why or why not.

- Hume makes a sharp distinction between the skepticism of his philosophical reasoning and the contented optimism of the way he lives his life. What do you think of this "split" between rational/theoretical arguments and lived experience? Do you think that our choices in life should necessarily reflect our epistemological convictions? Describe an example to support your point of view.

- Hume believes that all metaphysical beliefs (that is, any belief not based on direct sense experience) should be "committed to the flames" because it cannot be empirically justified. This would include all beliefs regarding God, human freedom, universal moral laws, and so on. Do you agree with Hume? If not, explain how you would go about rebutting his arguments.

Immanuel Kant: *We Constitute Our World*

We first encountered the brilliant German philosopher **Immanuel Kant** (1724–1804) in chapter 3, where we were introduced to his revolutionary views regarding epistemology and metaphysics. For Kant, the "self" is ultimately viewed as the synthesizing activity at the core of each one of us that integrates all of the disparate elements of experience into *our* experience, *our* world. He identifies this synthesizing "self" as the *"transcendental unity of apperception"*—not a very personal sounding term for an entity that we experience as intensely personal! But Kant is more concerned with constructing a metaphysical framework for the "self" that will account for the phenomena of experience, in particular what he describes as *"the unity of consciousness."*

In the same way that Hume's concept of the "self"—as a transitory stream of sensations moving randomly through the "theater" of our minds—is an integral part of his overall epistemology, so Kant's concept of the "self" is merely one dimension of an intricately and elaborately constructed philosophy that integrates both epistemology and metaphysics in a seamless integration. Kant's thinking is so revolutionary and profound in its implications that philosophies are typically classified as pre-Kantian and post-Kantian. Many of the modern movements in philosophy can trace their intellectual origins to Kant's thought, including existentialism, phenomenology, pragmatism, and linguistic philosophy.

At the time that Kant came onto the scene, the raging controversy in philosophy was between rationalism and empiricism, the twin movements that we have been exploring in these chapters through the philosophies of Plato and Descartes (rationalists) as well as Locke, Berkeley, and Hume (empiricists). Rationalists were con-

IMMANUEL KANT
(1724–1804)
German Philosopher. Kant is widely regarded as greatest philosopher of modern period. Attempted to synthesize two competing schools of the modern period, rationalism and empiricism, by showing important role both experience and reason play in constructing our knowledge of the world.

vinced that genuine knowledge is best achieved through our rational capacities, whereas empiricists were equally certain that all knowledge is derived from sense experience. As we have seen, while the rationalists viewed the human mind as an active agent—reflecting, analyzing, deducing—the empiricists viewed the mind as a passive receiver of impressions and experiences.

Both approaches are vulnerable to serious conceptual problems and challenging questions when it comes to their ability to construct a coherent, compelling theory of knowledge. Once Descartes introduces the "evil genius" as a vehicle for his radical doubt of virtually everything, it's difficult for him to banish the "evil genius" from his epistemological kingdom of rational certainty. And the epistemological regression displayed in the thinking of Locke, Berkeley, and Hume culminates in the depressing conclusion that genuine knowledge of *anything* isn't possible: not of the external world, not scientific laws, not God, not even the "self." It is no wonder that Kant took the measure of this sad state of affairs and described it as "a scandal in philosophy."

But, unlike the other thinkers of his day, Kant also had the insight to fully appreciate the dire threat that Hume's virulent skepticism posed to epistemology and metaphysics in general, and to the "new physics" of science being championed by Isaac Newton and others. If Hume was right, and we are doomed to passively view the impressions and ideas presented to our minds, unable to connect them to each other, to an external world, or to anything else for that matter—then we might as well give up on discovering genuine and certain knowledge in any area of experience. It was the startling recognition of this threat that, in Kant's words, "first interrupted my dogmatic slumber, and gave my investigations in the field of speculative philosophy quite a new direction." Kant describes this intellectually galvanizing experience in the following passages from his *Prolegomena to Any Future Metaphysics* (1783).

Immanuel Kant,
Prolegomena to Any Future Metaphysics

However hasty and mistaken Hume's conclusion may appear, it was at least founded upon investigation, and this investigation deserved the concentrated attention of the brighter spirits of his day as well as determined efforts on their part to discover, if possible, a happier solution of the problem in the sense proposed by him, all of which would have speedily resulted in a complete reform of the science.

But Hume suffered the usual misfortune of metaphysicians, of not being understood. It is positively painful to see how utterly his opponents . . . missed the point of the problem; for while they were ever taking for granted that which he doubted, and demonstrating with zeal and often with impudence that which he never thought of doubting, they so misconstrued his valuable suggestion that everything remained in its old condition, as if nothing had happened.

* * *

Hume started from a single but important concept in Metaphysics, viz., that of Cause and Effect (including its derivatives force and action, etc.). He challenges reason, which pretends to have given birth to this idea from herself, to answer him by what right she thinks anything to be so constituted, that if that thing be posited, something else also must necessarily be posited; for this is the meaning of the concept of cause. He demonstrated irrefutably that it was perfectly impossible for reason to think a priori and by means of concepts a combination involving necessity. We cannot at all see why, in consequence of the existence of one thing, another must necessarily exist, or how the concept of such a combination can arise a priori. Hence he inferred, that reason was altogether deluded with reference to this concept, which she erroneously considered as one of her children, whereas in reality it was nothing but a bastard of imagination, impregnated by experience, which subsumed certain representations under the Law of Association, and mistook the subjective necessity of habit for an objective necessity arising from insight. Hence he inferred that reason had no power to think such, combinations, even generally, because her concepts would then be purely fictitious, and all her pretended a priori cognitions nothing but common experiences marked with a false stamp. In plain language there is not, and cannot be, any such thing as metaphysics at all.

* * *

I openly confess, the suggestion of David Hume was the very thing, which many years ago first interrupted my dogmatic slumber, and gave my investigations in the field of speculative philosophy quite a new direction. I was far from following him in the conclusions at which he arrived by regarding, not the whole of his problem, but a part, which by itself can give us no information. If we start from a well-founded, but undeveloped, thought, which another has bequeathed to us, we may well hope by continued reflection to advance farther than the acute man, to whom we owe the first spark of light.

I therefore first tried whether Hume's objection could not be put into a general form, and soon found that the concept of the connection of cause and effect was by no means the only idea by which the understanding thinks the connection of things a priori, but rather that metaphysics consists altogether of such connections. I sought to ascertain their number, and when I had satisfactorily succeeded in this by starting from a single principle, I proceeded to the deduction of these concepts, which I was now certain were not deduced from experience, as Hume had apprehended, but sprang from the pure understanding. This deduction (which seemed impossible to my acute predecessor, which had never even occurred to any one else, though no one had hesitated to use the concepts without investigating the basis of their objective validity) was the most difficult task ever undertaken in the service of metaphysics; and the worst was that metaphysics, such as it then existed, could not assist me in the least, because this deduction alone can render metaphysics possible. But as soon as I had succeeded in solving Hume's problem not merely in a particular case, but with respect to the whole faculty of pure reason, I could proceed safely, though slowly, to determine the whole sphere of pure reason completely and from general principles, in its circumference as well as in its contents. This was required for metaphysics in order to construct its system according to a reliable method.

Hume's "Trojan Horse" into the bastion of rationalism is his devastating attack on the principle of cause and effect, which we examined in the previous section. Cause and effect is the bedrock principle of science. That's precisely what science attempts to achieve, articulating causal relationships between and among events in order to explain what has occurred in the past, what is happening in the present, and what will take place in the future. If we cannot rely on the power and authenticity of the cause-and-effect principle, then science is an endeavor doomed to epistemological uncertainty. We will never be able to say that we "know" anything for sure about the physical world in which we live (nor, in fact, that there even *is* an external world).

The crux of Hume's critique of rationalism is as follows: when we examine events in the world that *seem* to be causally related, this assumption is in fact unwarranted if we rely solely on our reasoning abilities. Why? Because reason has no right to impose causal connections on events *a priori*—that is, independently of experience. Let's consider two examples that demonstrate this point.

- Imagine that you are introduced to a potential causal relationship regarding which you have no personal experience: for example, the behavior of electrons observed through an electron microscope; a potential chemical

Iron lung used to keep polio victims alive. Kant realized that if Hume's critique went unchallenged, it could have the effect of undermining scientific discovery and progress. If people agreed with Hume's analysis, what would be the effect on efforts to combat diseases like polio?

reaction involving the combining of a number of elements; or the potential effects on cancer cells of a new synthetic hormone. No matter how carefully you explore your *a priori* reasoning abilities independent of empirical experience, you will not be able to find a "rational intuition" that will inform you whether cause-and-effect relations exist.

- On the other hand, reflect on the times that you believed that your "rational intuition" was providing you with cause-and-effect knowledge that turned out to be bogus: for example, superstitious beliefs such as wearing your "lucky" shirt; experiencing an "intuition" regarding a dream you had and the lottery number; or acting on astrological advice. In these and countless other instances, people mistakenly believe that they "know" cause-and-effect relationships via their "rational intuitions," independent of confirming experiences.

To his great credit, Kant unflinchingly acknowledges the strength of these arguments with a vivid metaphor:

Immanuel Kant,
Prolegomena to Any Future Metaphysics

Hence he inferred, that reason was altogether deluded with reference to this concept (*cause and effect*), which she erroneously considered as one of her children, whereas in reality it was nothing but a bastard of imagination, impregnated by experience, which subsumed certain representations under the Law of Association, and mistook the subjective necessity of habit for an objective necessity arising from insight.

Describing the rationalist's attempt to have reason "give birth" to the principle of cause and effect as ". . . a bastard of the imagination, impregnated by experience" is strong language, to be sure! And yet Kant is convinced that to erect a legitimate framework for knowledge, he must begin by addressing directly and honestly Hume's incisive, relentless attack on the scope of reason, which he (Hume) considers to be the "slave of the passions." It is this open-eyed honesty that Kant found lacking in the other thinkers of the day, contemptible behavior that caused him to observe "was positively painful to see how utterly his opponents . . . missed the point of the problem."

Yet as concerned as Kant is to establish an irrefutable theory of knowledge that will serve as a legitimate grounding for modern science, he is just as intent on making sure this epistemological framework also incorporates other *a priori* knowledge. Kant considers such knowledge to be "metaphysical" in the sense that its ultimate justification and truth is based on reason, independent of sense experience, and it includes areas of experience such as

- Mathematics, arithmetic, logic
- Knowledge of the "self"
- The possibility of free will
- Moral principles
- The existence of God

Kant rightly realized that Hume's comprehensive discrediting of the validity and power of reason would prohibit discovering authentic knowledge in these metaphysical areas.

Immanuel Kant,
Prolegomena to Any Future Metaphysics

My object is to persuade all those who think Metaphysics worth studying, that it is absolutely necessary to pause a moment, and, neglecting all that has been done, to propose first the preliminary question, "Whether such a thing as metaphysics be at all possible? . . ."

I therefore first tried whether Hume's objection could not be put into a general form, and soon found that the concept of the connection of cause and effect was by no means the only idea by which the understanding thinks the connection of things a priori, but rather that metaphysics consists altogether of such connections.

For Kant, refuting Hume is not a trivial academic enterprise: it is an intellectual life-and-death struggle to make possible his most deeply held convictions about the universe and man's place in it. This is an intensely personal struggle for Kant, and underlying the extraordinary intellectual edifice that he ends up erecting is a profoundly human passion, revealed in his comment, "If man has the need of any science, then it is the one that can teach him what it means to be human."

Fortunately for Kant, he is not lacking in confidence. Kant viewed Hume's critique as a serious challenge, but more importantly he used it as an intellectual catalyst for his own thinking, a project that he believed to be supremely successful.

But as soon as I had succeeded in solving Hume's problem not merely in a particular case, but with respect to the whole faculty of pure reason, I could proceed safely, though slowly, to determine the whole sphere of pure reason completely and from general principles, in its circumference as well as in its contents. This was required for metaphysics in order to construct its system according to a reliable method.

Immanuel Kant,
*Prolegomena to Any
Future Metaphysics*

 | Kant, Immanuel,
*Progelomena to Any
Future Metaphysics*

To fully understand Kant's "solution," we need to fully appreciate Hume's critique, which was directed not only at rationalism, but at empiricism as well. Recall that Hume established a two-pronged criteria for evaluating attempts to establish genuine knowledge ("Hume's fork"). The first category of knowledge was "relations of ideas," which includes the principles of mathematics and logic, and simple tautologies ("A bachelor is an unmarried man"). These principles are discoverable by reason, without reference to experience, and they do not permit logical contradictions. The force of Hume's argument against rationalism, noted above, was that claims to knowledge *other* than these, such as the principle of cause and effect, were not warranted.

The second category of knowledge, "matters of fact," can be confirmed (or refuted) by appeal to our experience. Unlike "relations of ideas," they necessarily involve sense experience, and their statements *do* permit logical contradictions, according to Hume. However, after careful analysis, Hume concluded that knowledge of such things as the principle of cause and effect are not warranted in this area either. When we investigate our sense experience, we discover that there is absolutely no evidence of causal relations between events. The best that we can say is that we link events by *association* or *habit*, but these connections are not necessary or lawlike, and we cannot legitimately draw inferences or make inductive predictions based on them. Thus, the project of making the universe scientifically intelligible is doomed.

For Kant to effectively commit Hume's critique "to the flames" (Hume's volatile image) and build a compelling theory of knowledge from the ashes, Kant needs to address both "forks" of Hume's attack on the possibility of knowledge. And this is precisely what Kant does through his theory of **transcendental idealism**—an epistemology that describes truths about the world that are both *necessary* and *universal.*

For all his intellectual power, Kant grounds his theory firmly in the world of lived experience. It is an incontrovertible fact that the world of objects exists, that objects are related in lawlike ways that science and common sense can discover (including cause and effect and induction), and that we can develop knowledge about the world that is compelling and verifiable. Yet rationalism and empiricism both run into dead ends, being forced to conclude that all these incontrovertible facts of experience are uncertain and ungrounded. For Kant, this conflict between the evidence of real-world experience and the epistemological skepticism of various theories could mean only one thing: the theories are profoundly flawed. So Kant turned the prevailing trend in epistemology upside down. Instead of questioning whether science could legitimately claim to discover knowledge, Kant initiates his

Transcendental idealism Kant's epistemology that describes truths about the world that are both *necessary* and *universal.*

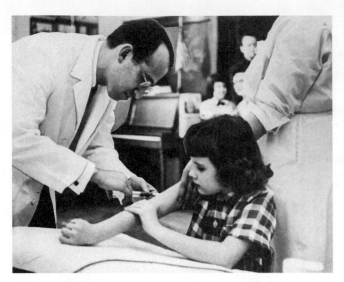

Jonas Salk administering the first polio vaccine. Kant begins with the assumption that the universe is organized in a way that makes scientific knowledge a reality and then poses the question: How is such knowledge possible? What is the nature of the human mind that makes scientific knowledge a reality? How would you respond to this question?

inquiry with the following challenge: science already has discovered knowledge that is necessary, universal, and certain: *How is this possible? What is the nature of the way the human mind works that makes the discovery of such knowledge a reality?*

Thus begins Kant's "Copernican revolution" in epistemology. As we noted in chapter 3, the Polish astronomer Copernicus revolutionized the scientific study of the universe by declaring that the sun was the center of our solar system, around which planets in the system—including Earth— orbited. This was a reversal of accepted belief and directly contradicted the teachings of the Catholic Church, which steadfastly maintained that the Earth was the center of our solar system, placed there by God as a symbol of the spiritual primacy of human life. In analogous fashion, Kant reversed the traditional approach of epistemology, changing the entire perspective. Rather than speculate on how the human mind can somehow connect to or match up with an (ultimately unknowable) external world, Kant decided to investigate precisely *how the human mind constructs a knowable world*. He explains:

Immanuel Kant,
*Prolegomena to Any
Future Metaphysics*

Hitherto it has been assumed that all our knowledge must conform to objects. But all attempts to extend our knowledge of objects by establishing something in regard to them by means of concepts have, on this assumption, ended in failure. We must, therefore, make trial whether we may not have more success if we suppose that objects must conform to our knowledge. ■

". . . if we suppose that objects must conform to our knowledge." This is the core of Kant's revolution. He views the mind as an *active agent* in constructing the world and our knowledge about it. Empiricism, as expressed in the thinking of Locke, Berkeley, and Hume, had viewed the mind as a *passive agent*, a "blank slate" on which is recorded the sounds, images, and other sensations of experience. In *A Treatise of Human Nature*, Hume provides a graphic image to dramatize this view of the mind as passive agent:

(The sensations in our senses) succeeded each other with an inconceivable rapidity and are in a perpetual flux and movement. . . . The mind is a kind of theater where several perceptions successively make their appearance, pass, re-pass, glide away, and mingle in an infinite variety of postures and situations.

From Kant's perspective, this is precisely where the empiricists commit their fatal mistake which culminates in epistemological skepticism and commonsense absurdity. A careful examination of how the mind operates makes clear that as thinking beings, we don't simply "receive" and "record" impressions: instead, we actively select, organize, order, structure, and interpret these sensations, shaping them into an intelligible world about which we can develop insight and knowledge. This is absolutely clear when we observe how science operates. Scientists don't simply record the data of experience: they actively pose questions, develop hypotheses, construct and implement experimental tests, create theories and invent concepts to explain phenomena, continually revise their understanding in light of new information, and countless other thinking operations. It is through the active use of the human mind *in interaction with the data of experience* that science discovers—and constructs—knowledge of the world.

We can see this active operation of the human mind in our daily lives as well. At almost every waking moment of your life, your senses are being bombarded by a tremendous number of stimuli: images to see, noises to hear, odors to smell, textures to feel, and flavors to taste. The experience of all these sensations happening at once creates what the nineteenth-century American philosopher **William James** called "a bloomin' buzzin' confusion." Yet for us, the world usually seems much more orderly and understandable. Why is this so?

In the first place, your sense equipment can receive sensations only within certain limited ranges. For example, there are many sounds and smells that animals can detect but you cannot because their sense organs have broader ranges in these areas than yours do. A second reason you can handle this sensory bombardment is that from the stimulation available, you select only a small amount on which to focus your attention. To demonstrate this, try the following exercise. Concentrate on what you can see, ignoring your other senses for the moment. Focus on sensations that you were not previously aware of and then answer the first question. Concentrate on each of your other senses in turn, following the same procedure.

- What can you *see*? (For example, the shape of the letters on the page, the design of the clothing on your arm.)
- What can you *hear*? (For example, the hum of the air circulator, the rustling of a page.)
- What can you *feel*? (For example, the pressure of the clothes against your skin, the texture of the page on your fingers.)
- What can you *smell*? (For example, the perfume or cologne someone is wearing, the odor of stale cigarette smoke.)
- What can you *taste*? (For example, the aftereffects of a breath mint.)

Compare your responses with those of the other students in the class. Do your classmates perceive sensations that differ from the ones you perceived? If so, how do you explain these differences?

By practicing this simple exercise, you can see that for every sensation on which you focus your attention there are countless other sensations that you are simply ignoring. If you were aware of everything that is happening at every moment, you would be completely overwhelmed. By selecting certain sensations, you are able to make sense of your world in a relatively orderly way. The activity of using your senses to experience and make sense of your world is known as "perceiving," and Kant believed this process is an *active* process of our minds, not passive. When we perceive we actively *select*, *organize*, and *interpret* what is experienced by our senses. Let's continue our exploration of this complex process that forms the foundation of our knowledge of the world.

It is tempting to think, as the empiricists did, that your senses simply record what is happening out in the world as if you were a human camera or voice recorder. You are not, however, a passive receiver of information, a "container" into which sense experience is poured. Instead, you are an active participant who is always trying to understand the sensations you are encountering. As you perceive your world, your experience is the result of combining the sensations you are having with the way you understand these sensations. For example, examine the collection of markings in figure 9.1. What do you see? If all you see is a collection of black spots, try looking at the group sideways. After a while, you will probably perceive a familiar animal.

From this example you can see that when you perceive the world, you are doing more than simply recording what your senses experience. Besides experiencing sensations, you are also

Figure 9.1

William James (1842–1910). American Pragmatist. Following C.S. Peirce, founded the philosophy of Pragmatism. Also contributed to the psychology of religion in *The Varieties of Religious Experience* (1903).

Figure 9.2
Archives of the History of American
Psychology—The University of Akron

actively making sense of these sensations. That is why this collection of black spots suddenly became the figure of an animal—because you were able actively to organize these spots into a pattern you recognized. Or think about the times you were able to look up at the white, billowy clouds in the sky and see different figures and designs. The figures you were perceiving were not actually in the clouds but were the result of your giving a meaningful form to the shapes and colors you were experiencing.

The same is true for virtually everything you experience. Your perception of the world results from combining the information provided by your senses with the way you actively make sense of this information. And because making sense of information is what you are doing when you are thinking, you can see that perceiving your world involves using your mind in an active way. Of course, you are usually not aware that you are using your mind to interpret the sensations you are experiencing. You simply see the animal or the figures in the clouds as if they were really there.

When you actively perceive the sensations you are experiencing, you are usually engaged in three distinct activities:

- *Selecting* certain sensations to pay attention to
- *Organizing* these sensations into a design or pattern
- *Interpreting* what this design or pattern means to you

In figure 9.1, you were able to perceive an animal because you selected certain of the markings to concentrate on, organized these markings into a pattern, and interpreted this pattern as representing a familiar animal.

Of course, when you perceive, these three operations of selecting, organizing, and interpreting are usually performed quickly, automatically, and often simultaneously. Also, you are normally unaware that you are performing these operations because they are so rapid and automatic. Kant understood that we needed to slow down this normally automatic process of perceiving so that we could understand how the process works.

Let's explore more examples that illustrate how you actively select, organize, and interpret your perceptions of the world. Carefully examine figure 9.2. Do you see both the young woman and the old woman? If you do, try switching back and forth between the two images. As you switch back and forth, notice how for each image you are

- *selecting* certain lines, shapes, and shadings on which to focus your attention.
- *organizing* these lines, shapes, and shadings into different patterns.
- *interpreting* these patterns as representing things that you are able to recognize— a hat, a nose, a chin.

Another way for you to become aware of your active participation in perceiving your world is to consider how you see objects. Examine the illustration in figure 9.3. Do you perceive different-sized people or the same-sized people at different distances? When you see someone who is far away, you usually do not perceive a tiny person. Instead, you perceive a normal-sized person who is far away from you. Your experience in the world has enabled you to discover that the farther things are from you, the smaller they look. The moon in the night sky appears about the size of a quarter, yet you perceive it as being considerably larger. As you look down a long stretch of railroad tracks or gaze up at a tall building, the boundary lines seem to come together. Even though these images are what your eyes "see," however, you do not usually perceive the tracks meeting or the building

Figure 9.3

coming to a point. Instead, your mind actively organizes and interprets a world composed of constant shapes and sizes, even though the images you actually see usually vary, depending on how far you are from them and the angle from which you are looking at them.

Examine carefully the engraving pictured in chapter 8 (page 418), entitled "Satire on False Perspective," completed by William Hogarth in 1754. In this engraving, the artist has changed many of the clues you use to perceive a world of constant shapes and sizes, thus creating some unusual effects. By analyzing how the artist has created these unusual perspectives, you gain insight into the way your mind actively takes fragmentary information and transforms it into the predictable, three-dimensional world that is so familiar to you.

So far, we have been exploring how your mind actively participates in the way you perceive the world. By combining the sensations you are receiving with the way your mind selects, organizes, and interprets these sensations, you perceive a world of things that is stable and familiar, a world that usually makes sense to you.

The process of perceiving takes place at a variety of different levels. At the most basic level, the concept of "perceiving" refers to the selection, organization, and interpretation of sensations: for example, being able to perceive the various objects in your experience, such as a basketball. However, you also perceive larger patterns of meaning at more complex levels, as in watching the action of a group of people engaged in a basketball game. Although these are very different contexts, both engage you in the process of actively selecting, organizing, and interpreting what is experienced by your senses—in other words, "perceiving."

To sum up, the cognitive processes of perceiving, developing beliefs, and constructing knowledge involve *both* the data of sense experience *and* what Kant terms the "faculties of the mind." It is through the active *interaction* of these two elements that we are able to "constitute" (Kant's term) an orderly and intelligible world. And it is through the active synthesis of our "self" that this world becomes *my* world, as Kant explains in his *Critique of Pure Reason*:

> Sensations would be nothing to us, and would not concern us in the least, if they were not received into our (orderly) consciousness. Knowledge is impossible in any other way. . . . For perceptions could not be perceptions of anything for me unless they . . . could at least be connected together into (my) one consciousness. This principle stands firm *a priori*, and may be called the "transcendental principle of unity" for all the multiplicity of our perceptions and sensations.

We can now see how rationalism and empiricism created their own epistemological sinkholes because they didn't understand that constituting our world and constructing genuine knowledge involves the ongoing interaction of our thinking activities with sense experience. In science, and everyday life, our approach to making sense of the world is both rational and empirical, a fundamental insight that Kant captured with the memorable phrase, "Thoughts (*concepts*) without content (*sense data*) are empty; intuitions (*of sensations*) without conceptions, blind" (author's italics). Thus, a purely rationalist approach to knowledge is doomed to be "empty" because it fails to appreciate the need for sense experience to provide content for its thinking processes. Conversely, a purely empiricist approach to knowledge is doomed to be "blind," because it fails to understand the need for the structure, order, and interpretation provided by the rational categories of the mind. The only solution, Kant believes, is to recognize the essential role that each partner in the knowing process plays, which he describes in the opening passages of his extraordinary work, *Critique of Pure Reason*.

Immanuel Kant,
Critique of Pure Reason

Introduction: I. Of the Difference Between Pure and Empirical Knowledge

There can be no doubt that all our knowledge begins with experience. For how should our faculty of knowledge be awakened into action did not objects affecting our senses partly of themselves produce representations, partly arouse the activity of our understanding to compare these representations, and, by combining or separating them, work up the raw material of the sensible impressions into that knowledge of objects which is entitled experience? In the order of time, therefore, we have no knowledge antecedent to experience, and with experience all our knowledge begins.

But though all our knowledge begins with experience, it does not follow that it all arises out of experience. For it may well be that even our empirical knowledge is made up of what we receive through impressions and of what our own faculty of knowledge (sensible impressions serving merely as the occasion) supplies from itself. If our faculty of knowledge makes any such addition, it may be that we are not in a position to distinguish it from the raw material, until with long practice of attention we have become skilled in separating it. This, then, is a question which at least calls for closer examination, and does not allow of any off-hand answer:—whether there is any knowledge that is thus independent of experience and even of all impressions of the senses. Such knowledge is entitled *a priori*, and distinguished from the **empirical**, which has its sources *a posteriori*, that is, in experience.

Kant has an astonishing ability to incisively clarify and skillfully unravel what appears to be a hopeless conundrum. Descartes, Locke, Berkeley, Hume—all brilliant thinkers who had nevertheless managed to tie themselves up into philosophical knots, until Kant came along to disentangle them. And like most solutions to seemingly intransigent problems, once illuminated one is tempted to think: "It's so obvious: why didn't someone else think of that before?"

"There can be no doubt that all our knowledge begins with experience." Of course it does! Where else would knowledge originate? If we examine the cases of children who have been raised under experientially or educationally deprived circumstances, they don't "recollect," on their own, a profound understanding of truth and knowledge from the perfect preexistence, as Plato suggests. In fact, they can barely function, think, or communicate. Even the slave boy from whom Socrates elicits "knowledge" of geometric principles has lived a life filled with geometric objects and experiences regarding them, along with the opportunity to discuss and reflect on these sensations and experiences. Knowledge of the world necessarily involves empirical experiences, and to suggest, as the rationalists maintain, that a wealth of *a priori* knowledge about the world is fully evolved in each person's head and completely independent of real-word sense experience seems extremely unlikely.

But the empiricists are no less confused and limited in how they understand the nature of constituting our world and constructing knowledge. *"But though all our knowledge begins with experience, it does not follow that it all arises out of experience."* No, of course it doesn't! Our minds are naturally active: that is what the thinking process is all about, performing complex mental (and linguistic) operations of the information provided through experience so that we can make sense of our world. And at the center of all these complex mental operations is the powerful impetus to *synthesize* everything that is taking place into a "picture" that makes sense to *me*, a picture that is being updated on an instantaneous basis based on new information and further mental processing. What an astonishingly powerful process! How could the empiricists—intelligent, thinking beings who were performing these complex mental operations at the very moment that they were writing that such processes don't exist—fail to see the obvious? Kant has a ready response.

If our faculty of knowledge makes any such addition, it may be that we are not in a position to distinguish it from the raw material, until with long practice of attention we have become skilled in separating it. This, then, is a question which at least calls for closer examination, and does not allow of any off-hand answer:—whether there is any knowledge that is thus independent of experience and even of all impressions of the senses.

Kant, *Critique of Pure Reason*

The reason the empiricists were unable to see the contributions of the human mind to constructing knowledge (and, conversely, the reason why rationalists were unable to fully credit the contributions of sensory experience) was that the world and our understanding of it is presented as an integrated package in which *sensory experience* and the *faculties of the mind* have already created their epistemological synthesis. As a result, we need to make an extraordinary effort to distinguish these two primary contributors to the knowing process "until with long practice of attention we have become skilled in separating it." That was our goal in performing some of the simple perceptual activities in the previous section, trying to slow the perceiving/believing/knowing process down to become aware of the various sensory and thinking components in these processes. Let's try a somewhat different approach that may prove to be even more effective.

Consider the (intentionally) ambiguous photograph in figure 9.4. Describe what you think is going on and what you think will take place next. Now share your responses with other members of the class. Did they have different perceptions of what was taking place and what would happen next? Very likely! How do you account for these differences? Your response might be something like:

- People think differently (a rationalist analysis)
- People have had different experiences (an empiricist analysis)

For Kant, both responses are accurate, and as we will see later in the chapter, modern developmental and cognitive psychology would agree. When you look at the illustration you are gathering sensory information: the lines, the shading, the contours—data that your mind is actively organizing into images that are familiar to you. But your mind is doing something else: it is *interpreting* the resulting images, giving them mean-

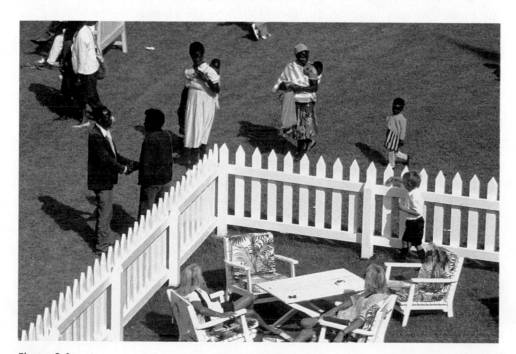

Figure 9.4

ing. But for the most part, you are *un*aware that these processes are taking place, because they are instantaneous and present you with a finished product: an "interpreted image." What's more, if you are like most people, you assume that the interpretation that you are giving to this image is the "right one," that it somehow resides "in" the image, a necessary part of it. It is only when you compare your interpretation with those interpretations of others that you can begin to recognize the contribution of your active thinking process in projecting meaning onto the image. Where do those interpretations come from? Why do people experience the same events—in this case, looking at a simple image—and then register very different interpretations?

- Because people do, in fact, "think" differently. Although we may be using the same fundamental thinking processes, we can use these mental processes to interpret sensations in different ways.
- Because people have, in fact, had different experiences that they draw on in interpreting their experiences in the world. In this illustration, the unique experiences of the viewers contribute to *informing* their interpretations.

Comparing people's different perceptions of the same sensations is like dusting for fingerprints: the fingerprints are there, but you can't "see" them until the right powder is brushed on. One useful image to help understand this knowing process is to realize each one of us views the world through our own unique perceiving/believing/knowing "lenses," which shape and influence every aspect of our experience. These lenses are permanently attached, and they reflect everything that has contributed to the person you are, including your past experiences and your uniquely individual use of your thinking abilities. No two pairs of lenses are exactly alike: they each embody a unique prescription that shapes and organizes each person's view of the world in distinctive ways. In a way, we can view the world we constitute as a dynamic coloring book. Because people have the same basic patterns and categories of thinking, they constitute their worlds in ways that are in basic agreement: I'm sitting in a class in philosophy with x other students discussing Immanuel Kant, and so on. These are the basic outlines of the coloring book, on which there is likely general agreement. (If a student jumped up and shouted, "Get me off this airplane!" we would probably wonder about his psychological stability.) But though we may agree on the basic outlines of life's events, we each "color" in these outlines in very individual ways, reflecting our perceiving lenses.

If we carefully examine the evidence of everyday experience, we see that the world we live in, both individually and collectively, is the product of an active mind interacting with empirical experience. What are the philosophical implications of this insight? That is precisely the question that Kant is attempting to answer, as he explains:

Immanuel Kant,
Critique of Pure Reason

And thus I conclude the analytical solution of the main question which I had proposed: "How is metaphysics in general possible?" by ascending from the data of its actual use, as shown in its consequences, to the grounds of its possibility.

For Kant, metaphysics refers to necessary and universal knowledge that we can discover which is *a priori*—that is, obtained independently of experience. Of course, many empiricists accept the fact that tautologies ("A bald man has no hair") and the principles of formal logic and mathematics can claim a necessary and universal *a priori* truth. But Kant wants to claim another kind of *a priori* knowledge: a *synthetic a priori* knowledge. This is knowledge that is:

- necessary and universally true.
- *a priori*—can be discovered independently of experience.
- *synthetic* in the sense that it provides us with genuine information regarding our experience of the world.

In other words, Kant is suggesting a phenomenological approach to epistemology and metaphysics. He's saying, in effect, "We know things about the world that are necessary and universal—such as the principles of cause and effect and induction—that do not depend on empirical experience. How is this possible?" It is possible because this *synthetic a priori* knowledge of the world reflects the way the human mind operates in constituting the orderly and intelligible world in which we live. The thinking process operates according to certain necessary and universal laws, categories that organize and structure the chaotic sensations of empirical experience. That is the heart of Kant's "Copernican revolution." Instead of trying to understand how to connect our minds to the external world, Kant is proposing that our minds actually *constitute* the world in accordance with certain fundamental *categories of understanding* that are an essential part of every human's thinking process. For example, one such "law" or "category" of the mind is *cause and effect*, which necessarily organizes the world in such a way that we are able to relate events according to this principle. When you (accidentally!) hit your thumb with a hammer, you have no doubt that the hammer blow is causing the excruciating pain in your thumb. Your understanding of this necessary connection is the product of the interaction of this cause-and-effect category of your mind with your experiences in the world. For example, at the age of five when I placed my hand on an iron that my mother had warned me was "hot" ("But it doesn't *look* hot, I reasoned"), the pain

Figure 9.5

alerted me that there was a connection between these events. And as I matured, my mind enabled me to understand the necessary and universal nature of that type of causal connection, as well as many others in the world.

Kant believes that there are twelve such basic categories of the mind, and that one of the goals of metaphysics is to become familiar with these categories so that we can understand how they shape, organize, and constitute our orderly and intelligible world. Other categories include induction, objects, space, and time. And the knowledge that we gain by analyzing these categories is *synthetic a priori* knowledge, because these "transcendental" categories are

- necessary and universally true.
- *a priori*—can be discovered independently of experience.
- *synthetic* in the sense that they provide us with genuine information regarding our experience of the world.

Does this mean that everyone lives in his or her own personal world? Kant believes that the answer to this is "no," because these twelve fundamental categories of the mind are universally present in every person of "normal" cognitive function. In contemporary terms, we might say that they are programmed into the human mind, an essential part of the brain "software" that we come equipped with. It doesn't matter where you were born, given the proper experiences, you will develop an understanding of the necessary, natural law principle of "cause and effect." This doesn't mean that people *apply* the principle correctly in all circumstances (as in the "lucky shirt") but that they have an accurate understanding of what the principle is and how it is supposed to be applied. This approach thus nullifies Hume's contention that we can never "know" that the principle of cause and effect is a true, lawlike relationship: we "know" that principle of cause and effect applies because that's exactly how our mind organizes our experience and constitutes our world. And because this principle is universal and necessary, a part of the mind's thinking equipment with which we are all born, we can be certain of its truth.

The same basic insights apply to Kant's other *a priori* categories of the mind, including "objects," "space," and "time." Kant reasons: we *know* that objects exist independently of our experience of them. How can we be so sure? Where does this certainty come from? Kant believes it comes from our mind, that the concept of an independently existing external object is an *a priori* "rule," "law," or "category" of thought that the mind imposes on the chaotic flux of experience to make the world an orderly and intelligible place.

Empiricists such as Locke, Berkeley, and Hume wondered: how can we ever be sure that the external world exists, because all we encounter are sensations or impressions of this ultimately unknowable world? Kant's approach supersedes their concerns. Because our minds actively constitute the external world, there is no "gap" between mind and object, between our consciousness and the world of which we are conscious. We are dealing with a unified, integrated reality, in which our thinking and the external world it constitutes are necessary partners, inextricably connected one to the other. Because our minds actively *constitute* the world to include external objects that exist independently of our perception of them, we don't have to be concerned about whether these objects actually exist or how our minds connect to or "match up" with the external world. For example, recall Aristotle's image of the soul being the "form" of the body in the same way that a pattern-mold shapes wax in its image. Analogously, the human mind "shapes" the field of sensations into an intelligible and coherent whole. From a Kantian perspective, it makes no sense to question the existence of an external world, because it is the human mind itself that gives shape and form to it, as pattern-mold does to the wax: they are inseparable.

The research in developmental psychology in the twentieth century has provided an empirical foundation for Kant's philosophical analysis. The most influential thinker in this area is Jean Piaget (1896–1980), a Swiss psychologist who used painstakingly careful observations of infants and interviews with young children to trace the cognitive process by which humans constitute their world. In his work *The Child's Construction of Reality*, Piaget details the gradual process by which an infant's mind gradually develops the concepts of "object," "space," "time," "cause and effect," and other foundational ways of organizing experience. In Piaget's version of Kant's "categories," which he calls *schemata*, inherited cognitive structures evolve into more sophisticated and differentiated forms through interaction with experience. Thus an infant playing with an object becomes distressed if the object is covered up, because she has not yet developed the concept of "object" as an independently existing entity. This will only happen later on. Similarly, such relations as cause and effect and induction are grounded in these basic *schemata*, but they need the interaction with empirical experience to gradually evolve into fully formed concepts. The same is true for the concepts of "space," "time," and the other conceptual building blocks of our world: though they exist as *cognitive potentials* in our genetic equipment, they need the ongoing stimulation of experience to reach their fully evolved state. The ultimate result is the world that seems so familiar to us: objects contained in space, bounded by time, and governed by certain lawlike relationships. Yet this entire reality, which we assume to be completely independent of ourselves is in fact, as Kant maintained, constituted by the active structuring of our minds. And because these mental forms—categories or *schemata*—are universally present in normally functioning humans, we all share a common universe, constituted and defined by the same basic qualities and relations.

Jean Piaget used careful observations and interviews with infants and young children to trace the cognitive process by which humans constitute their world.

VISUAL PHILOSOPHY

How Do We Learn Language?

Linguist Noam Chomsky pioneered the theory that learning language involves the interaction of innate mental structures and specific language experiences. How did you learn the language(s) you speak?

We see an analogous model in the development of human language. The linguist Noam Chomsky's (b. 1928) theory, which has gained near universal acceptance among linguists, postulates that humans are born with the innate mental structures that provide for the *potential* of language development. These structures, which he refers to as "depth grammar," make possible the learning of any language. The particular language (or languages) that you learn to speak depends on your specific experiences: namely, the language to which you are exposed. Chomsky's theory is based on the reality that language is much too complex a phenomenon to be learned under a *tabula rasa* empiricist model. At the same time, language abilities will not develop on their own if an individual is not given ongoing experiences with spoken language, undermining the rationalist claim that knowledge exists fully formed at birth. (For those born hearing impaired, "sign language" is the equivalent of a spoken language.)

Finally, research in a variety of disciplines supports the view that although thinking and language begin as distinct processes, they begin to intertwine very early in their evolution, and they quickly become so integrated that it is nearly impossible to disentangle them. Most thinking necessarily involves language and conversely, most language involves thinking. So the fundamental cognitive categories with which we construct our world cannot be fully understood without simultaneously integrating the role of language into the mix.

Two Realities: Phenomenal and Noumenal

Although Kant's transcendental idealism, his Copernican revolution, solves the traditional problems of knowledge posed by rationalism and empiricism, it creates other epistemological challenges. If our experience of the world—our "reality"—is the product of our categories of understanding actively ordering the sensations of experience, the question naturally leaps up: what can we know about the reality that is "outside" of our experience, independent of our perceptions? Kant's answer is

Phenomenal reality Kant's term for the world as we experience it.

Noumenal reality Kant's term for the world that exists beyond our perceptions.

that, from an empirical point of view, this reality is unknowable by us, and he calls it the *ding-an-sich*: "thing-in-itself." There is no way for us to "go beyond" the reality constituted by the categories of our mind as they transform sensations into an intelligible world. Whatever is "out there" by definition transcends our efforts to know and understand. Thus Kant ends up making a radical division between

- **phenomenal reality**—the world as we constitute it and experience it, and
- **noumenal reality**—the world beyond our perceptions, reality "in-itself."

Kant believes that we can achieve knowledge of the noumenal reality: it's just that we can't achieve it through our senses. The noumenal reality can only be known through the application of "pure reason," which in addition to confirming the existence of "objective reality," also gives us knowledge of the possibility

 ## VISUAL PHILOSOPHY

Phenomenal and Noumenal Realities

According to Kant, phenomenal reality is the world as we experience it through our senses. Noumenal reality is the world that exists beyond our perceptions, symbolized in this painting by the rainbow that the blind girl is able to have described to her but is unable to see. What are some things you believe in that exist beyond your sense experience? What is the basis for your belief?

of genuine personal freedom and the existence of a universal moral law (the "categorical imperative"). This is essential for Kant, because, as we saw in chapter 6, he was fervently committed to constructing an ethical system, based on reason, that would have universal authority. And an integral part of such a system is the assumption that individuals are capable of making choices that are genuinely free. Otherwise, if we only act in ways that we are compelled to by forces beyond our control, an ethical system is irrelevant. Kant believed that we could never establish the possibility of genuine personal freedom or the existence of universal moral laws by remaining within phenomenal reality: the world that we constitute simply can't provide that sort of knowledge. It is necessary for us, using the power of pure reason, to go beyond the phenomenal world to the noumenal world.

In addition to the standard transcendental categories of understanding that we use to order sensations into an intelligible world, Kant also identifies three additional transcendental ideas that he believes we use to synthesize experience on a grand scale. These "super" transcendental ideas are "self," "cosmos," and "God," and they help us "bridge the gap" between the phenomenal and the noumenal realms. These "regulative ideas" are also essential for helping us constitute an epistemological framework that is comprehensive and inclusive.

Everything that has its basis in the nature of our powers must be appropriate to, and consistent with, their right employment—if we can only guard against a certain misunderstanding and so discover the proper direction of these powers. We are entitled, therefore to suppose that transcendental ideas . . . have an excellent, and indeed indispensably necessary, regulative employment, namely, that of directing the understanding towards a certain goal upon which the routes marked out by all its rules converge.

Immanuel Kant,
Critique of Pure Reason

* * *

The first (regulative) idea is the "I" itself, viewed simply as thinking nature or soul . . . ; in a word, the idea of a simple self-sustaining intelligence. (Reason operates) to represent all determinations as existing in a single subject, all powers, so far as possible, as derived from a single fundamental power, all change as belonging to the state of one and the same permanent being.

* * *

The second regulative idea of merely speculative reason is the concept of the world in general. . . . The absolute totality of the series of . . . conditions . . . is an idea which can never be completely realised in the empirical employment of reason, but which yet serves as a rule that prescribes how we ought to proceed in dealing with such series. . . . Cosmological ideas are nothing but simply regulative principles, and are very far from positing . . . an actual totality.

* * *

The third idea of pure reason, which contains a merely relative supposition of a being that is the sole and sufficient cause of all cosmological series, is the idea of *God*. We have not the slightest ground to assume in an absolute manner (the existence of) the object of this idea. ■

 Kant, Immanuel,
Critique of Pure Reason

Kant is acknowledging that pure reason does not establish the actual *existence* of "cosmos" or "God," only that these are regulative ideas that are necessary to account for the world as we constitute it. These are universal *a priori* ideas that regulate and make possible the phenomenal world, but because they refer to possibilities that exist in the noumenal world, they can never be empirically verified.

How Do I Construct Knowledge?

For Kant, we constitute our world through the ongoing synthesis of the categories of our mind with the sensations of experience. We have seen in this section that this perceiving is a dynamic process in which we actively select, organize, and interpret sensations in a way that reflects our unique perceiving "lenses." To construct knowledge from the information provided from experience, we must explore many different perspectives on the focus of our attention and take into account the "lenses" of the individuals or organizations that are providing the information—as well as being acutely aware of our own "lenses." This type of organized evaluation of contrasting sources and opinions—"perspective taking"—is an essential strategy of sophisticated thinking and one of the most powerful ways to construct well-supported beliefs and genuine knowledge. To experience this epistemological process in action, let's examine three different media accounts of the assassination of Malcolm X as he was speaking at a meeting in Harlem. As you read through the various accounts, pay particular attention to the different perceptions each one presents of this event. You will note that each account viewed the event through its own perceiving lenses, which shaped and influenced the information the writer selected, the way the writer organized it, his or her interpretations of the event and the people involved, and the language used to describe it. After you have finished reading the accounts, analyze some of the differences in these perceptions by answering the following questions. As you do this, try to begin constructing your own "knowledge" of this event.

- What details of the events has each writer *selected* to focus on?
- How has each writer *organized* the details selected? Remember that most newspapers present what they consider the most important information first and the least important last.
- How does each writer *interpret* Malcolm X, his followers, the gunmen, and the significance of the assassination?
- How has each author used language to express his or her perspective and to influence the reader's thinking?
- After critically evaluating these various sources, compose your own account of this event, as if you were writing for a major news organization. You may integrate additional research that you do into the event.

Three Accounts of the Assassination of Malcolm X

The New York Times: Malcolm X, the 39-year-old leader of a militant Black Nationalist movement, was shot to death yesterday afternoon at a rally of his followers in a ballroom in Washington Heights. The bearded Negro extremist had said only a few words of greeting when a fusillade rang out. The bullets knocked him over backwards. A 22-year-old Negro, Thomas Hagan, was charged with the killing. The police rescued him from the ballroom crowd after he had been shot and beaten. Pandemonium broke out among the 400 Negroes in the Audubon Ballroom at 160th street and Broadway. As men, women and children ducked under tables and flattened themselves on the floor, more shots were fired. The police said seven bullets struck Malcolm. Three other Negroes were shot. Witnesses reported that as many as 30 shots had been fired. About two hours later the police said the shooting had apparently been a result of a feud between followers of Malcolm and members of the extremist group he broke with last year, the Black Muslims.

Life Magazine: His life oozing out through a half dozen or more gunshot wounds in his chest, Malcolm X, once the shrillest voice of black supremacy, lay dying on the stage of a Manhattan auditorium. Moments before, he had stepped up to the lectern and 400 of the faithful had settled down expectantly to hear the sort of speech for which he was famous—flaying the hated white man. Then a scuffle broke out in the hall and Malcolm's bodyguards bolted from his side to break it up—only to discover that they had been faked out. At least two men with pistols rose from the audience and pumped bullets into the speaker, while a third cut loose at close range with both barrels of a sawed-off shotgun. In the confusion the pistol man got away. The shotgunner lunged through the crowd and out the door, but not before the guards came to their wits and shot him in the leg. Outside he was swiftly overtaken by other supporters of Malcolm and very likely would have been stomped to death if the police hadn't saved him. Most shocking of all to the residents of Harlem was the fact that Malcolm had been killed not by "whitey" but by members of his own race.

The New York Post: They came early to the Audubon Ballroom, perhaps drawn by the expectation that Malcolm X would name the men who firebombed his home last Sunday, streaming from the bright afternoon sunlight into the darkness of the hall.

The crowd was larger than usual for Malcolm's recent meetings, the 400 filling three-quarters of the wooden folding seats, feet scuffling the worn floor as they waited impatiently, docilely obeying the orders of Malcolm's guards as they were directed to their seats.

I sat at the left in the 12th row and, as we waited, the man next to me spoke of Malcolm and his followers:

"Malcolm is our only hope," he said. "You can depend on him to tell it like it is and to give Whitey hell."

Then a man was on the stage, saying:

". . . I now give you Brother Malcolm. I hope you will listen, hear, and understand."

There was a prolonged ovation as Malcolm walked to the rostrum past a piano and a set of drums waiting for an evening dance and stood in front of a mural of a landscape as dingy as the rest of the ballroom.

When after more than a minute the crowd quieted, Malcolm looked up and said, "A salaam aleikum (Peace be unto you)" and the audience replied "Wa aleikum salaam (And unto you, peace)."

All people actively construct their understanding of events in the world by actively selecting, organizing, and interpreting sensations in a way that reflects our unique perceiving "lenses."

Bespectacled and dapper in a dark suit, his sandy hair glinting in the light, Malcolm said: "Brothers and sisters . . . " He was interrupted by two men in the center of the ballroom, about four rows in front and to the right of me, who rose and, arguing with each other, moved forward. Then there was a scuffle in the back of the room and, as I turned my head to see what was happening, I heard Malcolm X say his last words: "Now, now brothers, break it up," he said softly. "Be cool, be calm."

Then all hell broke loose. There was a muffled sound of shots and Malcolm, blood on his face and chest, fell limply back over the chairs behind him. The two men who had approached him ran to the exit on my side of the room shooting wildly behind them as they ran.

I fell to the floor, got up, tried to find a way out of the bedlam.

Malcolm's wife, Betty, was near the stage, screaming in a frenzy. "They're killing my husband," she cried. "They're killing my husband."

Groping my way through the first frightened, then enraged crowd, I heard people screaming, "Don't let them kill him." "Kill those bastards." "Don't let him get away." "Get him."

At an exit I saw some of Malcolm's men beating with all their strength on two men. Police were trying to fight their way toward the two. The press of the crowd forced me back inside.

I saw a half-dozen of Malcolm's followers bend over his inert body on the stage, their clothes stained with their leader's blood. Then they put him on a litter while guards kept everyone off the platform. A woman bending over him said: "He's still alive. His heart's beating."

Four policemen took the stretcher and carried Malcolm through the crowd and some of the women came out of their shock long enough to moan and one said: "I don't think he's going to make it. I hope he doesn't die, but I don't think he's going to make it."

I spotted a phone booth in the rear of the hall, fumbled for a dime, and called a photographer. Then I sat there, the surprise wearing off a bit, and tried desperately to remember what had happened. One of my first thoughts was that this was the first day of National Brotherhood Week.

- Why does Kant say that Hume's ideas "first interrupted my dogmatic slumber, and gave my investigations in the field of speculative philosophy quite a new direction"?

- Explain why Kant suggests that his approach embodies a "Copernican revolution" in epistemology. What are the central differences between his epistemology and that of the rationalists and the empiricists?

- Why is the concept of "perceiving lenses" a useful metaphor in illustrating the way in which we actively constitute our world?

- What is the meaning of Kant's famous quote, "Thoughts (concepts) without content (sense data) are empty; intuitions (of sensations) without conceptions, blind"?

- Explain the significance of Kant's observation that "There can be no doubt that all our knowledge begins with experience. . . . But though all our knowledge begins with experience, it does not follow that it all arises out of experience."

- The empiricists concluded that we can never "know" that the principle of cause and effect is valid or that the external world exists independently of our perception of it.
  How does Kant's approach seek to overcome these troubling conclusions?

- What are the phenomenal and noumenal realities, and why does Kant believe in their existence?

- Kant believes that the following transcendental ideas are necessary to explain our experience of the universe: Self, Cosmos, God. Considering each of these "regulative" ideas in turn, analyze whether or not you agree that the idea is required to explain the way we experience the world.

Alison M. Jaggar: *Feminist Epistemology*

The views on epistemology that we have been considering in this chapter are for the most part clearly within the mainstream of traditional philosophical thought. Other perspectives on epistemology, particularly in contemporary thought, present very different points of view on efforts to construct knowledge and discover truth. Among the most vigorous of these newer epistemologies are those that fall under the general category of "feminist" perspectives.

The central point of feminist philosophers in this area is that traditional epistemologies have been selective and biased in their analyses, giving inadequate treatment to theoretical voices that fall outside the philosophical "mainstream," particularly the distinctive perspectives of women. If we are to accept in some form the Kantian view of knowledge, in which the mind is actively engaged in constituting the world and constructing knowledge, it is clear that this process is always susceptible to subjective interpretation. That is the significance of the metaphor of "perceiving lenses" that we introduced earlier in the chapter. We each view the world through lenses with unique prescriptions that shape and influence everything that we perceive, believe, and do. Every aspect of our personal history has contributed to creating our lenses, and we are generally unaware that we are wearing them. Instead, we (mistakenly) assume that the way we see (and constitute) the world is the way the world *is*. It is only when our lenses come into contact with contrasting lenses that we are challenged—and inspired—to critically examine them, evaluating their accuracy and objectivity.

The feminist argument—and it is a compelling one—is that the thinkers who have populated mainstream philosophical thought have shared certain basic assumptions—reflected in their epistemological lenses—which has resulted in an artificially narrow framework for knowledge. In the history of ideas, the voices of individuals who could have provided contrasting perspectives have been systematically repressed, ignored, or never given an opportunity to even speak. However,

Alison M. Jaggar

because the central discussion in the history of ideas is dynamic and ongoing, there is still opportunity for these voices to now be heard and included.

This is the mandate that the philosopher **Alison M. Jaggar** (b. 1942) is operating under in the following essay. Her central thesis is that Western tradition has, for the most part, omitted the entire realm of emotions in the mainstream discussion regarding the nature of knowledge. Instead, Western thinking has focused almost exclusively on the faculty of reason as the instrument for constructing knowledge and discovering truth. And when we consider that Western philosophy was initiated and propelled as a "love of wisdom" this systematic absence and denigration of emotions reveals a particularly jarring irony. Her goal in this paper is to display the central role of emotion in the construction of knowledge, a central premise that she believes every epistemology needs to take into consideration. Reflective analysis reveals that emotions—and their conceptual siblings such as values, motivations, and interests—influence every aspect of the knowing process, in science and everyday life. Emotions motivate and guide our cognitive explorations, influence the knowledge we construct, and are instrumental in evaluating both its certainty and relevance. As a result, emotion demands to be included as an integral partner with reason in the epistemological enterprise.

ALISON M. JAGGAR
Feminist Philosopher. Professor of Women's Studies and Philosophy at University of Colorado, Boulder. Examines contemporary political, ethical, and social issues from a feminist perspective.

I. Introduction: Emotion in Western Epistemology

Alison M. Jaggar,
Emotion in Feminist Epistemology

Within the Western philosophical tradition, emotions have usually been considered potentially or actually subversive of knowledge. From Plato until the present, with a few notable exceptions, reason rather than emotion has been regarded as the indispensable faculty for acquiring knowledge.

Typically, although again not invariably, the rational has been contrasted with the emotional, and this contrasted pair then often linked with other dichotomies. Not only has reason been contrasted with emotion, but it has also been associated with the mental, the cultural, the universal, the public and the male, whereas emotion has been associated with the irrational, the physical, the natural, the particular, the private and, of course, the female.

Although Western epistemology has tended to give pride of place to reason rather than emotion, it has not always excluded emotion completely from the realm of reason. In the *Phaedrus*, Plato portrayed emotions, such as anger or curiosity, as irrational urges (horses) that must always be controlled by reason (the charioteer). On this model, the emotions were not seen as needing to be totally suppressed, but rather as needing direction by reason: for example, in a genuinely threatening situation, it was thought not only irrational but foolhardy not to be afraid. The split between reason and emotion was not absolute, therefore, for the Greeks. Instead, the emotions were thought of as providing indispensable motive power that needed to be channeled appropriately. Without horses, after all, the skill of the charioteer would be worthless.

The contrast between reason and emotion was sharpened in the seventeenth century by redefining reason as a purely instrumental faculty. For both the Greeks, and the medieval philosophers, reason had been linked with value in so far as reason provided access to the objective structure or order of reality, seen as simultaneously natural and morally justified. With the rise of modern science, however, the realms of nature and value were separated: nature was stripped of value and reconceptualized as an inanimate mechanism of no intrinsic worth. Values were relocated in human beings, rooted in their preferences and emotional responses. The separation of supposedly natural fact from human value meant that reason if it were to provide trustworthy insight into reality, had to be uncontaminated by or abstracted from value. Increasingly, therefore, though never universally, reason was reconceptualized as the ability to make valid inferences from premises established elsewhere, the ability to calculate means but not to determine ends. The validity of logical inferences was thought independent of human attitudes and preferences; this was now the sense in which reason was taken to be objective and universal.

The modern redefinition of rationality required a corresponding reconceptualization of emotion. This was achieved by portraying emotions as non-rational and often irrational urges that regularly swept the body, rather as a storm sweeps over the land. The common way of referring to the emotions as the "passions" emphasized that emotions happened to occur or were imposed upon an individual, something she suffered rather than something she did.

The epistemology associated with this new ontology rehabilitated sensory perception that, like emotion, typically had been suspected or even discounted by the Western tradition as a reliable source of knowledge. British empiricism, succeeded in the nineteenth century by positivism, took its epistemological task to be the formulation of rules of inference that would guarantee the derivation of certain knowledge from the "raw data" supposedly given directly to the senses. Empirical testability became accepted as the hallmark of natural science; this, in turn, was viewed as the paradigm of genuine knowledge. Often epistemology was equated with the philosophy of science, and the dominant methodology of positivism prescribed that truly scientific knowledge must be capable of intersubjective verification. Because values and emotions had been defined as variable and idiosyncratic, positivism stipulated that trustworthy knowledge could be established only by methods that neutralized the values and emotions of individual scientists.

Recent approaches to epistemology have challenged some fundamental assumptions of the positivist epistemological model. Contemporary theorists of knowledge have undermined once rigid distinctions between analytic and synthetic statements, between theories and observations and even between facts and values. However, few challenges have been raised thus far to the purported gap between emotion and knowledge. In this paper, I wish to begin bridging this gap through the suggestion that emotions may be helpful and even necessary rather than inimical to the construction of knowledge . . . .

Jaggar's central thesis is that the mainstream epistemology of Western thought has emphasized the role of reason in achieving knowledge and truth, and deemphasized the role of emotions in this process. She notes that this division is not absolute, citing Plato's chariot metaphor in the *Phaedrus*. Although reason was clearly viewed as preeminent by the ancient Greeks, they also believed in the importance of cultivating the "higher" emotions. For example, as we noted in chapter 1, the term *philosophy* is derived from Greek words meaning "love of wisdom," and the early philosophers clearly valued and embodied a passion for understanding. Nevertheless, it is true that in terms of philosophical *approach* and *methodology*, they place their faith in reason as the tool for discovering genuine knowledge, both universal (for example, Plato's "forms") and empirical (Aristotle's natural science).

Jaggar believes that the real split between reason and emotion was spawned by the rise of the "new science," pioneered by thinkers such as Isaac Newton and Galileo. With the focus on making reliable scientific discoveries that could be validated and replicated by other scientists, the spiritual values that dominated the medieval consciousness were intentionally excised. Reason, in the form of experimental design and logical inferences, became the basic tool of science, whereas traditional spiritual values and personal emotions were perceived as threats to the hard-won objective methods of the new science. Jaggar believes that this ill-advised bifurcation of reason and emotion in the epistemology of science has continued to this day, a dualism that has seeped into modern consciousness in much the same way as the mind/body dualism of Descartes.

Alison M. Jaggar,
Emotion in Feminist Epistemology

II. What Are Emotions?

The philosophical question, "What are emotions?" requires both explicating the ways in which people ordinarily speak about emotion and evaluating the adequacy of those ways for expressing and illuminating experience and activity. Several problems confront someone trying to answer this deceptively simple question. One set of difficulties results from the variety, complexity, and even inconsistency of the ways in which emotions are viewed, both in daily life and in scientific contexts. It is in part this variety that makes emotions into a "question" at the same time that it precludes answering that question by simple appeal to ordinary usage. A second difficulty is the wide range of phenomena covered by the term "emotion": these extend from apparently instantaneous "knee-jerk" responses of fright to lifelong dedication to an individual or a cause; from highly civilized aesthetic responses to undifferentiated feelings of hunger and thirst; from background moods such as contentment or depression to intense and focused involvement in an immediate situation. It may well be impossible to construct a manageable account of emotion to cover such apparently diverse phenomena. . . .

III. Emotions as Intentional

Early positivist approaches to understanding emotions assumed that an adequate account required analytically separating emotion from other human faculties. Just as positivist accounts of sense perception attempted to distinguish the supposedly raw data of sensation from their cognitive interpretations, so positivist accounts of emotion tried to separate emotion conceptually from both reason and sense perception. As part of their sharpening of these distinctions, positivist construals of emotion tended to identify emotions with the physical feelings or involuntary bodily movements that typically accompany them, such as pangs or qualms, flushes or tremors; emotions were also assimilated to the subduing of physiological function or movement, as in the case of sadness, depression or boredom. The continuing influence of such supposedly scientific conceptions of emotion can be seen in the fact that "feeling" is often used colloquially as a synonym for emotion, even though the more central meaning of "feeling" is physiological sensation. On such accounts, emotions were not seen as being *about* anything: instead, they were contrasted with and seen as potential disruptions of other phenomena that *are* about some thing, phenomena such as rational judgments, thoughts, and observations. The positivist approach to understanding emotion has been called the Dumb View (Spelman, 1982). . . .

In recent years, contemporary philosophers have tended to reject the Dumb View of emotion and have substituted more intentional or cognitivist understandings. These newer conceptions emphasize that intentional judgments as well as physiological disturbances are integral elements in emotion. They define or identify emotions not by the quality or character of the physiological sensation that may be associated with them, but rather by their intentional aspect, the associated judgment. Thus, it is the content of my associated thought or judgment that determines whether my physical agitation and restlessness are defined as "anxiety about my daughter's lateness" rather than as "anticipation of tonight's performance." . . .

To discern the role of emotion in constructing knowledge, it is essential to develop an intelligent working definition of "emotion." As Jaggar makes apparent, "emotion" is a very complex concept that needs to be analyzed and articulated with care. One dimension of emotion is its "feeling" aspect: the physiological sensation that accompanies the experience of emotion, such as "pangs or qualms, flushes or tremors . . . sadness, depression or boredom." Yet although physiological "feelings" may accompany emotions, they are clearly not the same phenomenon. As Jaggar notes, feelings are "episodic" in the sense that they occur at a given moment in time, whereas emotions are "dispositional" in the sense that they extend over time: "For instance, we may assert truthfully that we are outraged by, proud of or saddened by certain events, even if at the moment we are neither agitated nor tearful." In addition, although people may be unaware of their emotional state—angry, ambivalent, depressed—they are (nearly) always aware of what they are feeling at any given moment in time.

If emotions include but also transcend episodic feelings, what else are they? One perspective—the *cognitivist* point of view—sees emotions as involving intentional judgments as well as physiological sensations. So, for example, you may be *feeling* anxious or agitated—but is the emotion involved related to concern about an upcoming exam or concern about an upcoming romantic date? In other words, an important component in emotions is the *intentional judgment* that is associated with the physiological feeling. We may conclude, for instance, that it is our (intentional) evaluation of an upcoming date that is responsible for the anxiety ("butterflies") we are feeling. Yet as important as "intentional judgments" are for understanding the nature of emotions, we still have not fully accounted for the complex nature of emotional experience.

Alison M. Jaggar,
Emotion in Feminist Epistemology

IV. Emotions as Social Constructs

. . . Mature human emotions can be seen neither as instinctive nor as biologically determined. Instead, they are socially constructed on several levels.

The most obvious way in which emotions are socially constructed is that children are taught deliberately what their culture defines as appropriate responses to certain situations: to fear strangers, to enjoy spicy food or to like swimming in cold water. On a less conscious level, children also learn what their culture defines as the appropriate ways to express the emotions that it recognizes. Although there may be cross-cultural similarities in the expression of some apparently universal emotions, there are also wide divergences in what are recognized as expressions of grief, respect, contempt or anger. On an even deeper level, cultures construct divergent understandings of what emotions are. For instance, English metaphors and metonymies are said to reveal a "folk" theory of anger as a hot fluid contained in a private space within an individual and liable to dangerous public explosion (Lakoff and Kovecses, 1987). By contrast, the Ilongot, a people of the Philippines, apparently do not understand the self in terms of a public/private distinction and consequently do not experience anger as an explosive internal force: for them, rather, it is an interpersonal phenomenon for which the individual may, for instance, be paid (Rosaldo, 1984).

Further aspects of the social construction of emotion are revealed through reflection on emotion's intentional structure. If emotions necessarily involve judgments, then obviously they require concepts, which may be seen as socially constructed ways of organizing and making sense of the world. For this reason, emotions are simultaneously made possible and limited by the conceptual and linguistic resources of a society. This philosophical claim is borne out by empirical observation of the cultural variability of emotion. Although there is considerable overlap in the emotions identified by many cultures (Wierzbicka, 1986) at least some emotions are historically or culturally specific, including perhaps *ennui*, *Angst*, the Japanese *amai* (in which one clings to another, affiliative love), and the response of "being a wild pig," which occurs among the Gururumba, a horticultural people living in the New Guinea Highlands (Averell, 1980, p. 158). Even apparently universal emotions, such as anger or love, may vary cross-culturally. We have just seen that the Ilongot experience of anger is apparently quite different from the contemporary Western experience. Romantic love was invented in the Middle Ages in Europe and since that time has been modified considerably; for instance, it is no longer confined to the nobility. In some cultures, romantic love does not exist at all. . . .

In addition to immediate feelings and intentional judgments, emotions are also constituted by the social context in which they occur. For example, individuals in each culture are taught the appropriate emotional responses to people (strangers, authorities, religious figures, romantic interests) as well as situations (competitive sports, academic achievement, perceived insults). Each culture has its own unique "emotional vocabulary" that members of the culture learn at an early age, and this emotional vocabulary is an essential component in what emotions are all about. This vocabulary is expressed in the concepts and language of the culture, as well as in the actions and attitudes of the members. Jaggar's example of the emotion "romantic love" is pertinent here. Although there is general

According to Alison Jaggar, emotions are in part social constructs, thus accounting for cultural differences in emotional responses to events like marriages.

agreement regarding what this emotional concept means, each culture also tends to define the emotion—and its affiliated attitudes and behavior—in ways that are distinctive to that culture. The net result is that these social influences are integral elements in the construction of human emotions: hence the notion of "emotions as social constructs."

V. Emotions as Active Engagements

Alison M. Jaggar,
Emotion in Feminist Epistemology

We often interpret our emotions as experiences that overwhelm us rather than as responses we consciously choose: that emotions are to some extent involuntary is part of the ordinary meaning of the term "emotion." Even in daily life, however, we recognize that emotions are not entirely involuntary and we try to gain control over them in various ways ranging from mechanistic behavior-modification techniques designed to sensitize or desensitize our feeling responses to various situations to cognitive techniques designed to help us to think differently about situations. For instance, we might try to change our response to an upsetting situation by thinking about it in a way that will either divert our attention from its more painful aspects or present it as necessary for some larger good. . . .

Emotions, then, are wrongly seen as necessarily passive or involuntary responses to the world. Rather, they are ways in which we engage actively and even construct the world. They have both "mental" and "physical" aspects, each of which conditions the other; in some respects they are chosen but in others they are involuntary; they presuppose language and a social order. Thus, they can be attributed only to what are sometimes called "whole persons," engaged in the on-going activity of social life.

Another component of emotions are the conscious decisions we make to engage in them—while pretending that they are natural forces over which we have little control. For example, have you ever had the experience of intentionally "working yourself up" into a state of righteous anger or indignation? And then acting as if it was the situation (a person's inconsiderate behavior, for example) that is responsible?

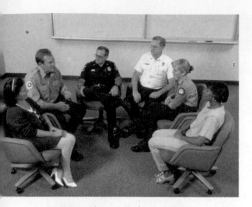

Jaggar points out that emotions are not entirely involuntary and we often try to gain control over them by using a variety of different strategies.

Although the experience of the emotion may appear and feel genuine, it might never have come about if you hadn't made a conscious and active choice to engage the emotion.

VI. Emotion, Evaluation, and Observation

Emotions and values are closely related. . . . Indeed, many evaluative terms derive directly from words for emotions: "desirable," "admirable," "contemptible," "despicable," "respectable," and so on. Certainly it is true (*pace* J.S. Mill) that the evaluation of a situation as desirable or dangerous does not entail that it is universally desired or feared, but it does entail that desire or fear is viewed generally as an appropriate response to the situation. If someone is unafraid in a situation perceived generally as dangerous, her lack of fear requires further explanation; conversely, if someone is afraid without evident danger, then her fear demands explanation; and, if no danger can be identified, her fear is denounced as irrational or pathological. Thus, every emotion presupposes an evaluation of some aspect of the environment while, conversely, every evaluation or appraisal of the situation implies that those who share that evaluation will share, *ceteris paribus*, a predictable emotional response to the situation. . . .

Just as observation directs, shapes, and partially defines emotion, so too emotion directs, shapes, and even partially defines observation. Observation is not simply a passive process of absorbing impressions or recording stimuli; instead it is an activity of selection and interpretation. What is selected and how it is interpreted are influenced by emotional attitudes. On the level of individual observation, this influence has always been apparent to common sense, which notes that we remark very different features of the world when we are happy, depressed, fearful, or confident. . . .

Having articulated a multidimensional definition of "emotions," Jaggar is now ready to examine the implications of this enriched concept of emotions for epistemology. Most philosophers and probably all scientists believe that knowledge originates in sensory experience, through perception. Yet, as we have seen in this chapter, perceiving is an active process, not passive. We are continually selecting, organizing, and interpreting the sensations with which we are presented in our everyday experience, a process that is filtered through our uniquely constructed perceiving "lenses."

Analogously, there is an intimate and interactive relationship between perceiving and emotions. Imagine, for example, that you are waiting patiently in line for a bus, when you feel a vigorous shove from behind: what is your emotion? Annoyance? When you turn around, you see that the "shover" is wearing dark glasses and is holding a cane used for the blind. Now what is your emotion? Sheepish embarrassment? You help the individual onto the bus, guiding him to the last available seat, whereupon the "blind" person takes out a newspaper and begins reading. Now what is your emotional state? Anger? The point is that what we perceive in the world—and our judgments about these perceptions—influence our emotional reactions. And conversely, our emotions have a dramatic influence on what we perceive and how we interpret it. And because our knowledge of the world begins with perceptions, values and emotions are a natural and inseparable part of this knowing process. Jaggar next extends this fundamental insight to the project of constructing scientific knowledge.

Jaggar,
Emotion in Feminist Epistemology

VII. The Myth of Dispassionate Investigation

As we have already seen, Western epistemology has tended to view emotion with suspicion and even hostility. This derogatory Western attitude toward emotion, like the earlier Western contempt for sensory observation, fails to recognize that emotion, like sensory perception, is necessary to human survival. Emotions prompt us to act appropriately, to approach some people and situations and to avoid others, to caress or cuddle, fight or flee. Without emotion, human life would be unthinkable. Moreover, emotions have an intrinsic as well as an instrumental value. Although not all emotions are enjoyable or even justifiable, as we shall see, life without any emotion would be life without any meaning.

Within the context of Western culture, however, people have often been encouraged to control or even suppress their emotions. Consequently, it is not unusual for people to be unaware of their emotional state or to deny it to themselves and others. This lack of awareness, especially combined with a neopositivist understanding of emotion that construes it as just a feeling of which one is aware, lends plausibility to the myth of dispassionate investigation. But lack of awareness of emotions certainly does not mean that emotions are not present subconsciously or unconsciously, or that subterranean emotions do not exert a continuing influence on people's articulated values and observations, thoughts, and actions.

Within the positivist tradition, the influence of emotion is usually seen only as distorting or impeding observation or knowledge. Certainly it is true that contempt, disgust, shame, revulsion or fear may inhibit investigation of certain situations or phenomena. Furiously angry or extremely sad people often seem quite unaware of their surroundings or even of their own conditions; they may fail to hear or may systematically misinterpret what other people say. People in love are notoriously oblivious to many aspects of the situation around them.

In spite of these examples, however, positivist epistemology recognizes that the role of emotion in the construction of knowledge is not invariably deleterious and that emotions may make a valuable contribution to knowledge. But the positivist tradition will allow emotion to play only the role of suggesting hypotheses for investigation . Emotions are allowed this because the so-called logic of discovery sets no limits on the idiosyncratic methods that investigators may use for generating hypotheses.

When hypotheses are to be tested, however, positivist epistemology imposes the much stricter logic of justification. The core of this logic is replicability, a criterion believed capable of eliminating or cancelling out what are conceptualized as emotional as well as evaluative biases on the part of individual investigators. The conclusions of Western science thus are presumed "objective," precisely in the sense that they are uncontaminated by the supposedly "subjective" values and emotions that might bias individual investigators (Nagel, 1968, pp. 33–34).

But if, as has been argued, the positivist distinction between discovery and justification is not viable, then such a distinction is incapable of filtering out values in science. For example, although such a split, when built into the Western scientific method, is generally successful in neutralizing the idiosyncratic or unconventional values of individual investigators, it has been argued that it does not, indeed, cannot, eliminate generally accepted social values. These values are implicit in the identification of the problems that are considered worthy of investigation, in the selection of the hypotheses that are considered worthy of testing and in the solutions to the problems that are considered worthy of acceptance. The science of past centuries provides ample evidence of the influence of prevailing social values, whether seventeenth-century atomistic physics (Merchant, 1980) or nineteenth-century competitive interpretations of natural selection (Young, 1985).

Of course, only hindsight allows us to identify clearly the values that shaped the science of the past and thus to reveal the formative influence on science of pervasive emotional attitudes, attitudes that typically went unremarked at the time because they were shared so generally. For instance, it is now glaringly evident that contempt for (and perhaps fear of) people of color is implicit in nineteenth-century anthropology's interpretations and even constructions of anthropological facts. Because we are closer to them, however, it is harder for us to see how certain emotions, such as sexual possessiveness or the need to dominate others, are currently accepted as guiding principles in twentieth-century sociobiology or even defined as part of reason within political theory and economics (Quinby, 1986). . . .

Positivism views values and emotions as alien invaders that must be repelled by a stricter application of the scientific method. If the foregoing claims are correct, however, the scientific method and even its positivist construals themselves incorporate values and emotions. Moreover, such an incorporation seems a necessary feature of all knowledge and conceptions of knowledge. Therefore, rather than repressing emotion in epistemology it is necessary to rethink the relation between knowledge and emotion and construct conceptual models that demonstrate the mutually constitutive rather than oppositional relation between reason and emotion. Far from precluding the possibility of reliable knowledge, emotion as well as value must be shown as necessary to such knowledge. Despite its classical antecedents and as in the ideal of disinterested inquiry, the ideal of dispassionate inquiry is an impossible dream, but a dream none the less or perhaps a myth that has exerted enormous influence on Western epistemology. Like all myths, it is a form of ideology that fulfils certain social and political functions.

By recognizing that the perceiving process necessarily involves values and emotions, we can see that the dream of some scientists to achieve a pure and objective form of knowledge, "uncontaminated" by human values and emotions, is a doomed enterprise. Because all knowledge originates in perception of experience, and because this perceiving process (and the beliefs that are formed as a result of it) necessarily involve human values and emotions in the complex way we have been analyzing them, scientific knowledge must necessarily involve them as well. And although some members of the scientific community may want to think otherwise, many others readily acknowledge that values and emotions not only motivate scientific inquiry, but also determine the questions it asks, the hypotheses and theories it forms, and the ultimate conclusions it comes to. This is apparent when we examine the history of science and note the dominant influence of the prevailing norms and values of the time. **Thomas Kuhn** (1922–1996) has detailed important dimensions of this evolutionary process in his influential work, *The Structure of Scientific Revolutions*, in which he analyzes the way scientific research is conducted within the prevailing epistemological "paradigm" of the time, whether it's based on a religious worldview, Newton's laws, Einstein's theory of general relativity, or quantum mechanics. For science to operate at optimal efficiency, it must become aware of the integral role of values and emotions in the entire scientific enterprise. Of course, many of the greatest scientists have demonstrated such an understanding, including Albert Einstein in the following passage from his essay "Religion and Science."

Thomas Kuhn American philosopher of science. In *The Structure of Scientific Revolution* (1962, 1970) Kuhn emphasized the discontinuity of scientific progress, characterized by long periods of "normal research" (conducted entirely within the framework of a prevailing theoretical paradigm) that are punctuated by brief and largely inexplicable periods of paradigm-shifting scientific revolution. On this view, there can be no rational grounds for choosing between incommensurable paradigms, each of which solves its own set of problems.

I maintain that the cosmic religious feeling is the strongest and noblest motive for scientific research. Only those who realize the immense efforts and, above all, the devotion without which pioneer work in theoretical science cannot be achieved are able to grasp the strength of the emotion out of which alone such work, remote as it is from the immediate realities of life, can issue. What a deep conviction of the rationality of the universe and what a yearning to understand, were it but a feeble reflection of the mind revealed in this world, Kepler and Newton must have had to enable them to spend years of solitary labor in disentangling the principles of celestial mechanics! Those whose acquaintance with scientific research is derived chiefly from its practical results easily develop a completely false notion of the mentality of the men who, surrounded by a skeptical world, have shown the way to kindred spirits scattered wide through the world and the centuries. Only one who has devoted his life to similar ends can have a vivid realization of what has inspired these men and given them the strength to remain true to their purpose in spite of countless failures. It is cosmic religious feeling that gives a man such strength. A contemporary has said, not unjustly, that in this materialistic age of ours the serious scientific workers are the only profoundly religious people.

THINK PHILOSOPHICALLY

Analyzing Alison M. Jaggar

9.6

PHILOSOPHER'S NOTEBOOK

- Reflect on your study of philosophy to this point. Identify five emotions that you believe play a significant role in thinking philosophically, and explain your rationale. Be sure to include specific examples to illustrate your points.

- Jaggar believes that both philosophy and modern science have artificially separated reason and emotion, and have designated reason as the one true way of achieving knowledge and truth. Do you agree with her reasoning? Why or why not?

- Jaggar identifies the following components of what we mean by the term/concept *emotion*

  A physiological sensation or feeling

  Intentional judgment

  Social construct

  Active engagement/conscious choice

  Select a complex emotion and analyze its structure by explaining how each of these factors contributes to its meaning.

- Jaggar believes that modern science needs to elevate emotions to play a prominent role in every aspect of scientific exploration, though she doesn't provide many concrete examples to examine. Identify one emotion that you believe should be an essential and consistent element in scientific inquiry, and explain (briefly) how this emotion might be better integrated into the process of constructing knowledge.

Making Connections: *Knowledge and Truth*

We have seen in these last two chapters that "knowledge" and "truth" are complex and elusive entities. Although there are compelling reasons to view knowledge and truth as goals toward which we challenge ourselves to strive, many people resist this insight. Either they take refuge in a belief in the absolute, unchanging nature of knowledge and truth, as presented by the appropriate authorities, or they conclude that there is no such thing as knowledge or truth and that trying to seek either is a futile enterprise. In this latter view of the world, known as *relativism*, all beliefs are considered to be "relative" to the person or context in which they arise. For the relativist, all opinions are equal in truth to all others; we are never in a position to say with confidence that one view is right and another view is wrong. Although a relativistic view is appropriate in some areas of experience—for example, in matters of taste such as fashion—in many other areas it is not. Knowledge in the form of well-supported beliefs is often difficult to achieve, but it does exist in some form. Some beliefs *are* better than others, not because an authority has proclaimed them so but because they can be analyzed and evaluated in terms of the criteria we described above.

Philosophers also employ these epistemological criteria, but they also have more theoretically developed theories of truth as well. In general, these theories of truth are bound to the epistemologies of which they are a part. For example, the *correspondence theory of truth* attempts to assess to what extent our beliefs "match up"

Charles Peirce (1839–1914)
Pragmatist. Founder of Pragmatism. Believed that philosophical thinking should be modeled after the scientific method and advanced a type of scientific philosophy.

John Dewey (1859–1952)
Pragmatist. Advocated the epistemology of instrumentalism maintaining that the truth or falsity of any given theory is determined by its practical application.

with reality. This is a theory of truth that makes sense within the epistemologies of the empiricists (Locke, Berkeley, Hume) who were trying to determine the relation between the sensations we experience and the world that is responsible for the sensations. It is also a theory that could be used with rationalist systems of thought (Plato, Descartes) although the "reality" with which they were trying to match our ideas was not empirical but rational in nature.

The *pragmatic theory of truth* was integral to the epistemologies of pragmatist philosophers such as **Charles Peirce**, William James, and **John Dewey**, all of whom believed that "truth" needs to be interpreted in terms of the practical consequences beliefs have in our lives, not the "correspondence" between our ideas and some separate "reality."

The *coherence theory of truth* evaluates the relative truth of beliefs in terms of their relationships with one another. For example, if we consider scientific theories such as the theory of evolution or Einstein's theory of general relativity, the truth of any individual statement can really only be determined by considering it in relation to the theory as a whole: does it "cohere" with the other elements of the theory in a consistent and productive way?

However, a constructivist view of epistemology, first suggested by Immanuel Kant, both transcends and absorbs these traditional theories of truth. For Kant, truth is not a "correspondence" between our ideas and an external reality, but our own system of *a priori* mental categories that we use to constitute reality. And "reality" is the world of our experience that we can know with certainty as "true" for we have constituted it ourselves. Because the categories of our understanding created an integrated reality, we can explore them in terms of their overall "coherence." And because Kant begins with scientific knowledge as an epistemological starting point, one of his central criteria for evaluating the truth of concepts is how adequately they explain the way our world pragmatically "works." Authentic (*synthetic a priori*) knowledge is possible by understanding the nature of the categories of the understanding and how they operate in constructing our experience.

And finally, such thinkers as the feminist Alison M. Jaggar further extend a constructivist view of epistemology by arguing that to understand "knowledge" and "truth," we must take into consideration the concrete personal and social contexts in which they occur.

Students Thinking about Philosophy:
Philosophical Analysis of Popular Culture

The core issues that metaphysics and epistemology are concerned with—Reality and Truth—are at the heart of life. In many ways our existence is framed and motivated by our ongoing efforts to answer the questions "What is real?" and "What is true?" Because these questions are of such central significance, they are explored not just in philosophy, but in other aspects of culture as well, including films, theater, and books. This project will give you an opportunity to bring a philosophical lens to some aspect of culture that addresses the themes of reality and truth. Select a film, play, or novel that you believe focuses on metaphysical and epistemological themes, and write an essay that analyzes the work philosophically. Be sure to make reference to specific philosophers to structure your analysis. The following essay by Sonja Tanner entitled "Philosophy and the 'Desert of the Real,'" takes the film *The Matrix* and engages in just this sort of philosophical exploration, analyzing the film's themes in terms of the ideas of Plato, Descartes, and Kant.

Philosophy and the "Desert of the Real"

Sonja Tanner

Nearly two and a half millennia ago, Plato offered an image of the human condition in which our lives are likened to those of prisoners in a cave, bound by chains to remain where we are and to perceive the stimuli presented to us by hidden forces. One prisoner is described as somehow—mysteriously—being freed from bondage, and undertaking the arduous journey out of the cave and towards the dazzling light of the sun. Upon doing so, this person is able to recognize his former state as one of illusion, as one does when waking up to recognize that what we thought to have transpired was only a dream. Waking up to face reality can be difficult, disorienting and even, in the freed prisoner's case, a dangerous task.

Fast forward into contemporary times and into "The Matrix" where the choice between remaining a prisoner of sensory deception or becoming enlightened as to "true reality" is offered to Neo. Morpheus tells Neo that taking the blue pill will let him return to the matrix—a computer-generated simulation of reality—in which Neo had seemingly been leading a comfortable existence. Taking the red pill would enable Neo to expose the forces behind the illusions, and so to encounter reality. This choice encapsulates several philosophical questions concerning reality and knowledge to which we will now turn. What kind of a choice is this? Can we be sure that taking the red pill would lead to reality, or might this be another simulation thereof? Is there an ethical dimension to this choice—that is, *should* you opt for one over the other? Which pill would you take?

Neo is offered two options, and to many people this means that whichever he chooses he has chosen freely, after all, he could have just as easily chosen the other. But is his choice really a reflection of free will? If we understand free will to refer to the capacity of someone to affect the future through their actions and choices, we can ask whether Neo's choice of the red pill amounts to his controlling the future. Is freedom a matter of having a choice? And is any choice necessarily a free one? Neo has already shown himself to be curious and trusting by following the white rabbit. Does his personality—something which it is extraordinarily difficult for any of us to change—not already influence him in the direction of the red pill?

A further wrinkle is added by two things we learn later. First, Neo has apparently chosen the red pill many, many times before. Second, Neo's actions and choices have been predicted by the Oracle (who, we learn in the second film, is herself part of the program). The more predictable someone's actions and choices are, the more it seems that those choices and actions are chosen for reasons beyond the agent's control. Above the kitchen door Neo enters to find the Oracle baking cookies is written the same imperative as is written above the door at the Delphic shrine which Oedipus visits: Know yourself. Does either Neo or Oedipus know who they are? Would such self-knowledge involve recognition of what may be their own arrogance at thinking themselves above the reaches of fate and determinism? Might being aware of how we are influenced or even determined by such forces lead to having control over them? Neo's encounter with the Oracle raises this question. For Sophocles' Oedipus Rex, about whom an oracle prophesies that he will murder his father and sleep with his mother, it does not seem to matter what course of action is taken: the fated future is accomplished regardless of what choices are made. Indeed, it is precisely through their disbelief in fate and the belief that each can freely forge their own destiny that the futures of Oedipus and Neo are realized. It is only when the Oracle tells Neo not to worry about breaking the vase, that he actually turns around and "accidentally" breaks it.

Regardless of whether or not the choice is a free one, we are compelled to ask whether or not the option is valid. How do we know that the red pill will really lead to reality, and not simply to more deception? Whichever of the two Neo chooses, he must do so from a position of trusting that the choice he is being offered is a valid one. On a very base level, taking any kind of drug should raise questions as to what effect it will have on one's mental and physical condition. Can you believe in whatever is to follow the swallowing of the pill, or is this clouded by the fact that you need a capsule of some unknown chemical in order to have this "experience"? Another way of looking at this choice is whether or not the choice is a rupture in the matrix, or yet another of its illusions.

For the sake of the argument, let's assume that the choice is a valid one. The question then becomes what is it a choice of. After taking the red pill, Neo is shown the true human condition. Like the prisoners in the cave, people in the matrix are enslaved and deceived. Morpheus shows Neo what he calls "the desert of the real," a world in which human bodies are forced to function as batteries—energy sources for the race of machines which keep humans placated by administering electrical signals to their brains. These signals are interpreted by human brains as actual sensory experiences of the outside world when in fact there is no such experience occurring. In other words, in "the desert of the real," the experience of eating a steak, which Cypher fondly recalls, does not involve actual consumption of a slab of beef. It is, rather, a combination of electrical impulses which simulate the taste, texture, smell and resulting fullness of such a meal.

The question is one that has been asked before. Descartes asks us whether or not it is possible that some sort of evil genius is deceiving us to think that the sensory experiences we seem to have are real ones. What if, in other words, we are just brains in a bucket, deceived somehow into thinking that our inner mental states correspond to the outer world? Isn't it entirely possible that I am not truly sitting at my computer typing right now, but only, for example, dreaming that I am? How do I know that I ever wake up—couldn't that too be part of the dream? Unlike Empiricism, which claims that sensory evidence is the most primary and reliable source of knowledge, Descartes and "The Matrix" express a skepticism as to sensory reliability. But then if I can't trust my senses, what can I rely on?

It all depends, as Morpheus says to Neo, on what we mean by the word "real." Morpheus suggests that to the enslaved human bodies, "the real" is nothing other than the electrical impulses interpreted by their brains. For these beings, Berkeley seems to be right: reality is made up of nothing other than the ideas, or sensory qualities I perceive. *A posteriori* knowledge, or knowledge which depends on the senses, would then be our only and most reliable source of knowledge. It does not matter if these qualities don't correspond to the world outside my brain. Assuming Neo's experiences here are to be trusted as more than such electrical impulses—in other words, that his perceptions correspond to a world outside of him and are thus "real" in the ordinary sense of the word, then by what criterion can this distinction between reality and illusion be made? Are Rationalists right in suggesting a *priori* knowledge (knowledge which does not depend on any prior sensory or perceptual experience) not only to exist but also to be our most reliable source of knowledge?

Drawing on both Rationalism and Empiricism, Kant effects what he terms a "Copernican revolution" in understanding reality. Like the shift from thinking of the Earth as occupying a central, stationary and privileged position in the world, around which the sun rotates, to recognizing that the Earth revolves around the sun, Kant suggests that we examine our role as being active in perception. Rather than thinking about how our representations conform to objects in the outer world, we should think of how it is that objects conform to our representations. In other words, reality does not consist simply of objects which our minds passively perceive. Our minds play an active role in how and what we perceive—we *construct* reality—and so inquiry into reality should begin with the mental faculties which allow us to register objects as such. Objects are understood here as phenomenal, or necessarily related to our experience of them, just as our experience of the sun makes it appear to be "rising" or "setting" in a rotation around the Earth, when in fact it is just the other way around. *Noumena*, or objects as they are independent of human perception, are beyond the realm of human experience, and thus also of human comprehension. At least to a degree, we actively shape phenomenal reality, and in order to understand how our experience alters reality, we must explore our own minds: knowing the world, then, requires knowing ourselves. "True reality"—reality understood as independent of our experience of it—or what Neo hopes to experience by swallowing the red pill— is thus not an option for anyone to experience.

The film doesn't so much answer the kinds of questions explored here as it does raise them. While it may seem unlikely that any of us are having a collaborative and interactive hallucination, the questions themselves are worthwhile if we are to know ourselves and the world around us. Having once chosen the red pill, Cypher changes his mind and opts for the pleasant but illusory life—including the hallucinated experience of eating a steak—afforded those comfortably deceived about what reality truly is. Is Cypher wrong to do so? Is choosing the red pill morally better than choosing the blue? In order to answer such questions, we too, face the choice of red or blue pills. Can we trust this choice to be a valid (and even a free) one, or should we be skeptical about ever acquiring true knowledge? The choice seems to be one of living a pleasant but thoroughly manipulated life in "the desert of the real" or of making the steep and rugged ascent out of the cave and into the light of truth. If there is such a thing as freedom, opting for the red pill—the route of philosophy and the questioning of reality, knowledge and ethics—is the only choice which can lead to it.

Concept Review

- John Locke's approach to epistemology is founded on empiricism, or the belief that we achieve knowledge through the experience of the senses (rather than exclusively through inborn, "innate" ideas and the exercise of rational intuition). His contemporary Gottfried Wilhelm von Leibniz did give credence to the concept of "innate ideas," but argued that these innate ideas required experience and education to fully develop. Locke believed that we are all born with an intellectual "blank slate," or *tabula rasa*; Leibniz, to the contrary, pointed out that there are many things that we *do* seem to know innately. Modern work in psychology, anthropology, and linguistics supports Leibniz's contentions.

- For Locke, there are four elements to the process of perceiving or knowing the experiential world:
  - The entity or object in the world.
  - Sensations the entity or object emits through "impulses," and that we detect through our five senses.
  - Ideas, images, and impressions produced in our minds by the "impulses" of objects and entities.
  - The conscious mind that perceives, reflects, and arranges these impulses and ideas.

- According to Locke, these entities and objects are themselves composed of two physical qualities: primary qualities (qualities that do not depend on our perception for their existence); and secondary qualities (the properties of objects to produce sensations in our minds, such as color, smell, texture, and taste). Yet Locke was unable to resolve the nature of the external "substances" in which these emitted qualities must ultimately reside.

■ Bishop George Berkeley's philosophy of "subjective idealism" attempted to resolve the fundamental difficulty with Locke's epistemology by rejecting Locke's distinction between primary and secondary qualities, and Locke's "commonsense" belief in external objects. According to Berkeley, *all* things exist only as minds, or as ideas within minds (*esse est percipi*, "to be is to be perceived"). Ultimately, for Berkeley, all things exist as ideas in the mind of God.

■ David Hume's epistemology is profoundly skeptical, applying Descartes' radical doubt to an empiricist framework. However, he cannot take solace in Descartes' (and Locke's, and Berkeley's) view that ultimately God would not allow us to exist in a universe of illusion and deception. Hume argued—quite forcefully—that there is no empirical or rational evidence for God, and so philosophers who rest on their metaphysical laurels are deceiving not only themselves, but their followers as well, through the worst kind of hypocrisy.

■ In Hume's view, many philosophers and scientists attempted to understand the external world through the principle of universal causation (cause and effect) and the principle of induction (the ability to make predictions based on prior knowledge or experience). To the contrary, for Hume, human knowledge can be divided into two categories ("Hume's fork"): "relations of ideas" and "matters of fact." His epistemology requires every justifiable belief to meet the standards of one or the other branches of this "fork." Causation fails to meet the test of both the "relations of ideas" and "matters of fact," and the principle of induction cannot be supported through a "chain of reasoning." However, Hume acknowledged that his radical skepticism, while his responsibility as a philosopher, did not doom him to a life of confusion and despair; "I dine, I play a game of backgammon, I converse, and am merry with my friends," he wrote.

■ Immanuel Kant sought to resolve the disputes between empiricism and rationalism by refuting Hume's radical skepticism and its bleak conclusions. Kant addressed Hume's "fork" through his theory of "transcendental idealism," which holds that there are truths about the world that are both necessary and universal. Kant's "Copernican revolution" in epistemology was his assertion that science had already discovered such necessary and universal knowledge (such as mathematics); the question he asked was not "how does the human mind come to know an essentially unknowable world," but rather "how does the human mind construct a knowable world?" That is, whereas the empiricists Locke, Berkeley, and Hume conceived of the human mind as a passive *tabula rasa*, Kant argued that the mind is an *active agent* in the construction of knowledge. We come to an understanding of the world through an interaction between the data of sense experience and what Kant describes as "the faculties of the mind" to sort and make sense of that data.

■ Kant's metaphysics describes twelve basic categories of the mind that help us to gain *synthetic a priori* knowledge, which

- is necessary and universally true.
- can be discovered independently of experience (*a priori*).
- provides us with genuine information regarding our experience of the world (*synthetic*).

■ Kant makes a distinction between two kinds of reality: phenomenal reality (the world as we constitute it and experience it) and noumenal reality (the world beyond our perceptions, about which we can achieve knowledge through the application of "pure reason"). Three regulative ideas—self, cosmos, and God—help us to "bridge the gap" between the phenomenal and noumenal realities.

■ Feminist epistemology argues that traditional epistemology is based on a limited set of experiential "lenses," a set of perspectives that has excluded marginal or "othered" voices, experiences, and views (especially those of women). For example, the feminist philosopher Alison M. Jaggar argues that the realm of *emotional* experience has been left out of epistemological analysis. Emotions, she argues, are as important as the senses and reason in shaping our perceptions and understandings of the world.

Media Resources

 www.researchnavigator.com
Chapter 9 delves further into the questions of knowledge, belief, and truth. This chapter focuses on the traditional Philosophies that experience leads to knowledge. For further research on questions how we come to know what we know, use the tools available to you in Research Navigator.

As you investigate this topic, consider this question: "If there are circumstances where I do not trust my experiences to lead me to truth, does this affect the reliability of gaining knowledge from experiences?

● **ContentSelect:** search in the Philosophy database using the search terms "misconception," "empiricism," "metaphysics," and "epistemology."

● **Link Library:** search in the Philosophy database under the term "John Locke."

● **New York Times on the Web:** search in the Philosophy database using the search terms "knowledge" and "mind."

 For additional study resources for this chapter, go to: **www.prenhall.com/chaffee/chapter9**

 The Primary Source: Philosophical Readings and Commentary

Berkeley, George: *A Treatise Concerning the Principles of Human Knowledge*

Hume, David: *An Enquiry Concerning Human Understanding*

Kant, Immanuel: *The Critique of Judgment; Critique of Pure Reason; Prolegomena to Any Future Metaphysic*

Leibniz, Gottfried: *Mondadology*

Locke, John: *An Essay Concerning Human Understanding*

Peirce, Charles Sanders: *The Fixation of Belief; How to Make Our Ideas Clear*

Let the ruling classes tremble at a communist revolution. The workers have nothing to lose but their chains. They have a world to win. Workers of all countries, unite!

KARL MARX

During the time men live without a common power to keep them all in awe, they are in that condition which is called war; and such a war as is of every man against every man…and the life of man (is) solitary, poor, nasty, brutish, and short.

THOMAS HOBBES

Until philosophers are kings, or the kings and princes of this world have the spirit and power of philosophy . . . cities will never have rest from their evils . . . nor the human race . . . and then only will our state behold the light of day.

PLATO, *THE REPUBLIC*

If there were a being who could not live in society or who did not need to live in society because he was self-sufficient, then he would have to either be animal or a god. He could not be a real part of the state. A social instinct is implanted in all people by their nature.

ARISTOTLE, *POLITICS*

Justice is the first virtue of social institutions, as truth is of systems of thought. A theory however elegant and economical must be rejected or revised if it is untrue; likewise laws and institutions no matter how efficient and well-arranged must be reformed or abolished if they are unjust.

JOHN RAWLS, *A THEORY OF JUSTICE*

The only freedom which deserves the name, is that of pursuing our own good in our own way, so long as we do not attempt to deprive others of theirs, or impede their efforts to obtain it.

JOHN STUART MILL, *ON LIBERTY*

A just future would be one without gender. In its social structures and practices, one's sex would have no more relevance than one's eye color or the length of one's toes. No assumptions would be made about "male" and "female" roles.

SUSAN MOLLER OKIN, *JUSTICE, GENDER, AND THE FAMILY*

From each according to his ability, to each according to his need.

KARL MARX

Creating a Just Society

I magine that you were given the project of creating a society based on the principle of justice: how would you go about it and how would you justify your proposed state? This is a question to which you may have given some thought during a recent local or national election. Although your political interest and involvement may typically focus on specific social issues—abortion, affirmative action, government spending, educational issues— political philosophy requires you to question the system as a whole. Of course, if you emigrated from another country with a different political structure, your experiences would give you a very different perspective than those of us who have never lived within a different political regime.

In designing your ideal "just society," you will have to grapple with a number of questions that philosophers and others have been struggling with for thousands of years:

- *Questions of Justice:* What exactly *is* a "just society"? How can we be fair to all the citizens in terms of distribution of wealth, opportunity, and power? (*Distributive Justice*) Should a society treat everyone equally? How should people who have violated society's laws be treated? (*Retributive Justice*) What is the core meaning of the concept of "justice"?

- *Questions of Law:* What is the justification for a society and its laws? Are there "natural laws" on which "civic laws" should be based? Should citizens be expected to obey a society's laws even if they believe the laws to be unjust? When is "civil disobedience" justified?

- *Questions of Public Interest:* Does society have a responsibility to protect and support its less advantaged members? To what extent should individual citizens be expected to sacrifice their individual interests to support the general public interest? To what extent should the state promote the well-being of its citizens through public education, medical services, low-cost housing, welfare support, low-interest loans, and subsidies for businesses? To what extent should the state create and enforce regulations in employee safety, drug and medical safety, ethical practices in business, equal opportunity for citizens?

- *Questions of Duty:* For what obligations and duties are the citizens of the state responsible?

- *Questions of Rights:* To what individual rights are citizens entitled? In addition to the civil rights of a society, are there basic human rights that citizens of all societies are entitled to?

- *Questions of Freedom:* On what basic freedoms is society based? To what individual freedoms should each citizen be entitled? Under what circumstances should personal liberty be limited?

- *Questions of Power and Influence:* How should power be acquired and administered? In what ways can citizens influence the policies and laws?

Responses to these questions form the basic "ingredients" of a sociopolitical community, and because these questions can be answered in many different ways, there have been many different kinds of social/political communities in human history. That is what the study of social and political philosophy is all about: the ways these different themes weave together to form various communities, and the overarching question of whether some communities are more ideal than others. The following Think Philosophically activity gives you an opportunity to reflect on and analyze the ingredients of the society in which we live from *your* perspective (which may be somewhat different from the perspectives of others in the same society). If you have lived in a different social and political system, your professor may ask you to use that society as the subject of your analysis to provide a richer, more varied understanding of these themes for the class as a whole.

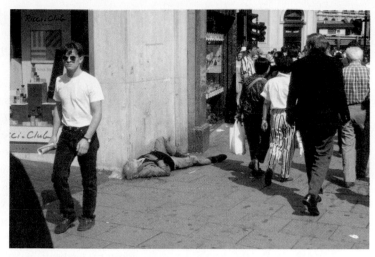

How do people in our society respond to homeless people? What do you think this says about our society?

THINK PHILOSOPHICALLY   10.1
Examining My Society

Reflect on the social and political structure of your society by responding to the following questions:

- *Issues of Justice:* In what ways does your society distribute resources to its citizens? In what ways does it make opportunities for education and to acquire available resources? To what extent are people treated equally? In what ways would you consider your society to be "just"?

- *Issues of Law:* How does your society justify its existence and its laws? To what extent are its "civic laws" based on "natural laws" that are thought to apply to all humans in all societies? To what extent are the laws applied fairly to people, regardless of their wealth, social status, gender, or racial identity? How does your society treat people who disagree with and disobey its laws? How are people who engage in "civil disobedience" treated (for example, those who act disruptively to protest social policies or war policies with which they disagree)?

- *Issues of Public Interest:* In what ways does your society support the well-being of its less advantaged citizens (for example, those who are poor, elderly, unemployed, sick, abused, or neglected)? In what ways are citizens expected to sacrifice their individual interests to support the general interest (for example, paying taxes)? In what ways does your society help those who are unable to help themselves? How does it promote the general good through regulations and economic support?

- *Issues of Duty:* What specific obligations and duties are citizens in your society responsible for performing (for example, serving on juries)?

- *Issues of Rights:* What individual rights do citizens in your society expect to have (for example, the right to practice the religion of their choice)? What rights does your society consider to be "universal" in the sense that they are rights that all people in all societies should enjoy?

- *Issues of Freedom:* What are the basic freedoms that your society guarantees for all of its citizens (for example, freedom to express your views without being arrested or harassed)? In what areas are personal freedoms limited in your society?

- *Issues of Power and Influence:* How is power acquired and administered in your society? What can citizens do to influence social policies and laws?

Social and Political Philosophies

he themes that you explored in the previous Think Philosophically activity are the threads that are woven into the fabric of social/political communities. Since the time of Plato and Aristotle, philosophers and other thinkers have constructed theories to both explain the nature of society and to recommend how an "ideal" society *ought* to be constructed. Thus social and political philosophies are *normative* as well as descriptive, because they embody values that the authors believe should be reflected in an ideal society. This parallels the way that moral theories are designed to both describe the way individuals behave and also how they *ought* to behave. In fact, social/political philosophies involve applying moral values to the context of larger social communities, defined by their common culture and political institutions. Concepts such as "justice," "fairness," "rights," "duties," "equality," and "political freedom" are essentially moral concepts characterizing societies of people. And just like moral concepts that characterize our personal relationships with one another, these moral concepts need to be defined, justified, and critically evaluated. The analysis of moral concepts (and theories) in which we engaged in chapters 5 and 6 thus forms the philosophical foundation for understanding and evaluating social/political theories.

◆ VISUAL PHILOSOPHY

Creating a Just Society

Do you believe that an ideal society should be based on concepts such as justice, fairness, equality, individual rights and duties, and political freedom? What would your ideal society look like?

In this chapter we will explore and critically evaluate the most prominent social/political theories that have been proposed in Western culture. Naturally, these explorations are relevant to understanding non-Western cultures as well, particularly with respect to principles, rights, and freedoms that are thought to be "universal" in nature. Many philosophy books approach this complex and diverse field through various classifications: for example, "Justice," "Justification of the State," "Freedom and Human Rights," and so on. However, the approach of this text is to analyze each social/political theory as a distinct whole, an integrated system in which all the relevant concepts are defined in relation to one another. Our ultimate goal is to develop an in-depth understanding of these core concepts so that we are in a position to develop our own integrated vision of what an ideal society ought to be. This will be a vision that we can use to inform our own actions, as we work to make the society in which we live more enlightened and morally sound. In pursuing this utopian goal, we might aspire to what the philosopher Roderick Firth calls an "Ideal Observer": someone who is knowledgeable, imaginative, objective, and consistent. Such an approach encourages us to conceive of a society that ensures justice for others as well as ourselves.

Plato: *Society Should Be Based on Function and Harmony*

The first comprehensive social theory based on the concept of "justice" was developed by **Plato**, and his vision is fully articulated in his monumental work, *The Republic*. Although his home of Athens had developed a governing structure based on democratic principles, Plato rejected this model as an ideal of a "just" society. (Of course, the right to vote in Athens was reserved for only free men, and excluded women and the large number of slaves and servants that formed the infrastructure of the society.) Why did Plato reject democracy as an ideal form of government? Because he felt that ordinary citizens were too easily swayed by appeals to irrational emotions and illogical arguments. He had witnessed first-hand the destructive power of an irrational group of citizens when they condemned his mentor and friend Socrates to death. For Plato, the unwarranted killing of such a wise and ethically principled person was a profoundly traumatic event that convinced him that the general population could never be trusted to rule with reason and wisdom.

Instead, Plato concluded that an ideal society must be ruled by the wisest and most enlightened of people: the philosopher-kings. These would be people who had dedicated themselves to achieving authentic wisdom through enlightened education and hard work. It was to train such wise leaders (among other reasons) that he created his Academy for philosophical study, a school in which he taught citizens of Athens for the remaining forty years of his life. (Plato's Academy continued for an astonishing 873 years after his death!)

Plato did not believe that all people are created with equal abilities: instead, he believed that each person has unique strengths and talents that must be used in an appropriate way. People, he concluded, fall into one of three general categories:

- Workers (craftsmen, farmers, artisans, shopkeepers)
- Guardians (soldiers, police, fire fighters)
- Philosopher-kings

A just state is one in which all the groups perform their unique functions in exemplary fashion, and all members of society work together harmoniously. Plato

PLATO
(427–347 B.C.E.)
Ancient Greek Philosopher. It was once said that all of Western Philosophy is merely footnotes to Plato. A student of Socrates, Plato wrote many dialogues featuring Socrates as the main character and dealt with many philosophical issues such as morality, politics, metaphysics, and epistemology.

believed that the three types of people correspond to the three fundamental parts of the soul: appetite, spirit, and reason. As we saw in chapter 3, Plato uses the metaphor of a chariot and driver to explain the soul's functioning: the driver is "reason," working to control and direct the two powerful horses, "spirit" and "appetite."

> So the reason ought to rule, having the ability and foresight to act for the whole, and the spirit ought to obey and support it. And this concord between them is effected, as we said, by a combination of intellectual and physical training, which tunes up the reason by intellectual training and tones down the crudeness of natural high spirits by harmony and rhythm.

In a virtuous person, the three elements of the soul function together in a smoothly integrated and productive way. Thus for Plato, the virtuous soul and the just state are mirrors of one another, and they both reflect the "cardinal virtues" characteristic of a good society and a truly happy individual.

Elements of a *Virtuous* Soul	Elements of Soul	Functions	Elements of State	Elements of *Just* State
Wisdom	Reason	Rule	Philosopher-kings	Wisdom
Courage	Spirit	Guard	Guardians	Courage
Temperance	Appetites	Nourish	Workers	Temperance

Justice exists in the state and the individual when all the elements perform their distinctive function and work together as a smoothly articulated and balanced whole. In contrast, injustice occurs when the parts of the state or the individual fail to perform the functions for which they were designed, or they fail to work with the other members in a harmonious way. Plato explores these central themes in the following passage from *The Republic* through an exchange between Socrates and Glaucon:

Plato, *The Republic*

(Socrates) I think that justice is the very thing, or some form of the thing which, when we were beginning to found our city, we said had to be established throughout. We stated, and often repeated, if you remember, that everyone must pursue one occupation of those in the city, that for which his nature best fitted him.

Yes, we kept saying that.

Further, we have heard many people say, and have often said ourselves, that justice is to perform one's own task, and not to meddle with that of others.

We have said that.

This then, my friend, I said, when it happens, is in some way justice, to do one's own job. And do you know what I take to be a proof of this?

No, tell me.

I think what is left over of those things we have been investigating, after moderation and courage and wisdom have been found, was that which made it possible for those three qualities to appear in the city and to continue as long as it was present. We also said that what remained after we found the other three was justice.

It had to be.

And surely, I said, if we had to decide which of the four will make the city good by its presence, it would be hard to judge whether it is a common belief among the rulers and the ruled, or the preservation among the soldiers of a law-inspired belief as to the nature of what is, and what is not, to be feared, or the knowledge and guardianship of the rulers, or whether it is, above all, the presence of this fourth in child and woman, slave and free, artisan, ruler and subject, namely that each man, a unity in himself, performed his own task and was not meddling with that of others.

How could this not be hard to judge?

It seems then that the capacity for each in the city to perform his own task rivals wisdom, moderation and courage as a source of excellence for the city.

It certainly does.

Winston Churchill (British leader, statesman). According to Plato, "Until philosophers are kings, or the kings and princes of this world have the spirit and power of philosophy . . . then only will our state behold the light of day."

You would then describe justice as a rival to them for excellence in the city?

Most certainly.

Look at it this way and see whether you agree: you will order your rulers to act as judges in the courts of the city?

Surely.

And will their exclusive aim in delivering judgment not be that no citizen should have what belongs to another or be deprived of what is his own?

That would be their aim.

That being just?

Yes.

In some way then possession of one's own and the performance of one's own task could be agreed to be justice.

That is so.

Consider then whether you agree with me in this: if a carpenter attempts to do the work of a cobbler, or a cobbler that of a carpenter, and they exchange their tools and the esteem that goes with the job, or the same man tries to do both, and all the other exchanges are made, do you think that this does any great harm to the city?

No.

But I think that when one who is by nature a worker or some other kind of money-maker is puffed up by wealth, or by the mob, or by his own strength, or some other such thing, and attempts to enter the warrior class, or one of the soldiers tries to enter the group of counselors or guardians, though he is unworthy of it, and these exchange their tools and the public esteem, or when the same man tries to perform all these jobs together, then I think you will agree that these exchanges and this meddling bring the city to ruin.

They certainly do.

The meddling and exchange between the three established orders does very great harm to the city and would most correctly be called wickedness.

Very definitely.

And you would call the greatest wickedness worked against one's own city injustice?

Of course.

That then is injustice. And let us repeat that the doing of one's own job by the money-making, auxiliary, and guardian groups, when each group is performing its own task in the city, is the opposite, it is justice and makes the city just.

I agree with you that this is so.

Do you agree with Plato that in the ideal, just state each person performs the duties that he or she is best equipped to?

Plato's theory of the state is both rigid and hierarchical. Once people have been sorted into their respective groups, based on their intrinsic talents, they are expected to remain in those social classes and work toward the good of the entire society. This may entail subsuming their own personal interests and preferences in order that society as a whole may flourish. Although Plato found it acceptable for people to move *within* their social class, he cautioned that trying to move to *another* social class would do harm to society as a whole, contributing to an unjust society. And because society and its citizens have a close, reciprocal relationship with one another, such "wicked" behavior would also threaten the happiness of the citizens.

For many people in the modern era who are committed to **egalitarian** values (everyone is intrinsically equal) and *democratic* principles (all people should have an equal voice in governing), Plato's ideas may seem wrong-headed and even offensive. But it is important to realize that Plato's social and political views are a direct outgrowth of his entire metaphysic and epistemology (which we explored in chapter 8). For Plato's hierarchy is not based on elitist or aristocratic principles, but is rather a hierarchy of wisdom and enlightenment. He believed that all people should strive to achieve a rationally based understanding of the essence of truth and goodness.

Using his "Allegory of the Cave" as a framework, he urged that each person should escape from the enslavement of unreality, and then seek to free the minds of those still submerged in the world of appearances.

If you were a citizen in Plato's ideal state, how would you respond upon receiving the news that you were expected to be a farmer because that career best matched your abilities?

Egalitarian Political view that holds that all citizens are equal.

And you won't go wrong if you connect the ascent into the upper world and the sight of the objects there with the upward progress of the mind into the intelligible realm—that's my guess, which is what you are anxious to hear. The truth of the matter is, after all, known only to God. But in my opinion, for what it is worth, the final thing to be perceived in the intelligible realm, and perceived only with difficulty, is the absolute form of the Good; once seen, it is inferred to be responsible for everything right and good. . . . And anyone who is going to act rationally either in public or private must perceive it. ■

 Plato, *The Republic*

The people who are best equipped to rule are those who have earned the right through the development of their rational intellects. In principle, this system of intellectual merit would not exclude anyone based on gender, race, or social class: the sole criteria would be one's developed wisdom. Of course, the practical application of such an ideal would likely be very different, as everyone in Athens, like now, did not have equal educational opportunities to reach higher stages of enlightenment. Nevertheless, Plato was clear in his belief that women were as qualified as men to be rulers and ought to share the same education as men to prepare them.

Plato believed that for individuals to lead virtuous lives and attain happiness, they needed to conform to their intrinsic natures and fulfill their unique potentials, goals that could only be achieved within the context of a just, rationally ordered state. The natural order is for people of wisdom to lead society, people of courage to protect its interests, and people of temperance to provide the basic nourishing needs of the community. Plato's ideal society is based on the concept of cooperation, a state in which all people fulfill their distinctive functions, fully committed to the general interests of society as a whole.

THINK PHILOSOPHICALLY   10.2
Analyzing Plato's Political Ideas

PHILOSOPHER'S NOTEBOOK

- Plato's concern about democratic forms of government was that many citizens are ill-informed about important issues and vulnerable to being manipulated by those in power. When you examine the current state of affairs in our society, do you believe that there is evidence to support Plato's concern regarding the dangers of democracy? If so, what alternatives would you propose to address these concerns, other than altering the democratic form of government?

- One of the major critiques of Plato's ideas about social justice is that the Athenian system was dependent on a large slave population for its functioning, individuals who are left out of Plato's conception of an ideal state. How do you think Plato would respond to the criticism that his ideas lack validity because of his acceptance of slavery? (The same question can be posed to the founding fathers of America who, like Thomas Jefferson, supported the institution of slavery while advocating "inalienable rights" of life, liberty, and the pursuit of happiness for everyone else.)

- Critically evaluate Plato's basic assumption that people fall into one of three classes: guardians, warriors, or workers. For example, do such natural classes exist? How would one go about determining which group people should be placed in? At what point in a person's life do their abilities become clearly delineated? Is it possible for people to develop abilities later in life that may not have been obvious earlier on? Is their a danger of prematurely classifying people and creating a "self-fulfilling prophecy" for their destinies? Who would make the decision?

- Many people assume "egalitarianism" as a core value today, the idea that every person is created intrinsically equal and that they are entitled to certain basic rights and freedoms. How would you go about defending this point of view to Plato?

Aristotle: *"Every State Is a Community of Some Kind"*

Many theories of social justice begin with the idea that the state is the result of individuals coming together to form an organized society for their mutual benefit. We will see this perspective fully expressed in the upcoming sections in which various philosophers view society as a "social contract" freely entered into by independent and fully informed people.

Aristotle's view is the complete opposite: he believes that "man is a political creature" by nature, and that existing in social communities is our natural state. In fact, we can only exist as fully formed individuals through our social relationships with others. Our self-identity is at its core a social identity, shaped by the network of people who form our social community, and within which we are embedded. This is the argument that Aristotle makes in the following passage from his work, *Politics*.

He who thus considers things in their first growth and origin, whether a state or anything else, will obtain the clearest view of them. In the first place there must be a union of those who cannot exist without each other; namely, of male and female, that the race may continue (and this is a union which is formed, not of deliberate purpose, but because, in common with other animals and with plants, mankind have a natural desire to leave behind them an image of themselves. . . . Out of these two relationships between man and woman . . . the first thing to arise is the family. . . . But when several families are united, and the association aims at something more than the supply of daily needs, the first society to be formed is the village. And the most natural form of the village appears to be that of a colony from the family, composed of the children and grandchildren, who are said to be suckled "with the same milk." . . . When several villages are united in a single complete community, large enough to be nearly or quite self-sufficing, the state comes into existence, originating in the bare needs of life, and continuing in existence for the sake of a good life. And therefore, if the earlier forms of society are natural, so is the state, for it is the end of them, and the nature of a thing is its end. For what each thing is when fully developed, we call its nature, whether we are speaking of a man, a horse, or a family. . . . Hence it is evident that the state is a creation of nature, and that man is by nature a political animal. And he who by nature and not by mere accident is without a state, is either a bad man or above humanity. . . .

Aristotle, *Politics*

Humans are naturally social creatures—"political animals"—in the same way that many other species instinctively form social communities. But humans have abilities that transcend that of other animals. Our ability to use language enables us to think and communicate in complex, symbolic, and abstract ways. (Experiments with higher primates have led some researchers to conclude that higher primates have some ability to think and use language as well.) And these thinking and language abilities enable humans to reflect on their social communities and evaluate them in terms of concepts such as "just" and "unjust," "good" and "evil."

Now, that man is more of a political animal than bees or any other gregarious animals is evident. Nature, as we often say, makes nothing in vain, and man is the only animal whom she has endowed with the gift of speech. And whereas mere voice is but an indication of pleasure or pain, and is therefore found in other animals (for their nature attains to the perception of pleasure and pain and the intimation of them to one another, and no further), the power of speech is intended to set forth the expedient and inexpedient, and therefore likewise the just and the unjust. And it is a characteristic of man that he alone has any sense of good and evil, of just and unjust, and the like, and the association of living beings who have this sense makes a family and a state.

Aristotle, *Politics*

For Aristotle, the fact that the state is "prior to the individual" means that humans can only achieve their full potential through their social existence. In fact,

ARISTOTLE

(384–322 B.C.E.)
Ancient Greek Philosopher. One of the most important figures in the history of philosophy because of his dividing philosophy into distinct disciplines; major contributions to metaphysics, ethics, and politics; first to attempt to create a system of deductive logic.

Aristotle believed that any individual who *can* exist independently of human community must either be a "beast or a god." In addition, the conviction that the state is prior to the individual means that the interests of the individual are secondary to the interests of the entire community, in the same way that the whole body takes precedence over any individual body parts. For humans to achieve their potential, they must work cooperatively with others to achieve virtue for themselves and for their community, "for justice is the bond of men in states, for the administration of justice . . . is the principle of order in political society."

Aristotle, *Politics*

Further, the state is by nature clearly prior to the family and to the individual, since the whole is of necessity prior to the part; for example, if the whole body be destroyed, there will be no foot or hand, except in an equivocal sense, as we might speak of a stone hand; for when destroyed the hand will be no better than that. But things are defined by their working and power; and we ought not to say that they are the same when they no longer have their proper quality, but only that they have the same name. The proof that the state is a creation of nature and prior to the individual is that the individual, when isolated, is not self-sufficing; and therefore he is like a part in relation to the whole. But he who is unable to live in society, or who has no need because he is sufficient for himself, must be either a beast or a god: he is no part of a state. A social instinct is implanted in all men by nature, and yet he who first founded the state was the greatest of benefactors. For man, when perfected, is the best of animals, but, when separated from law and justice, he is the worst of all; since armed injustice is the more dangerous, and he is equipped at birth with arms, meant to be used by intelligence and virtue, which he may use for the worst ends. Wherefore, if he have not virtue, he is the most unholy and the most savage of animals, and the most full of lust and gluttony. But justice is the bond of men in states, for the administration of justice, which is the determination of what is just, is the principle of order in political society. ◼

Aristotle, *The Politics*

Like Plato, Aristotle believes that different people have different potentials to fulfill (their distinctive *entelechy*) and he also agrees that slaves are fulfilling their distinctive purpose in life, a view that people today would find offensive and profoundly immoral. Nor does Aristotle accord women a status comparable to free men.

Although we may find certain dimensions of Plato's and Aristotle's social and political philosophies unacceptable—in particular their endorsement of the inferior status of slaves and women—we must also recognize their lasting contributions to our thinking regarding our social and political lives.

- Both Plato and Aristotle proposed comprehensive sociopolitical theories that were built around the concept of "justice" for the first time in recorded Western history.
- Both Plato and Aristotle affirmed the idea that equals must be treated as equals, a principle that forms the bedrock of many modern concepts of justice. The difference is that many people today believe that *all* people are equal in the most fundamental sense, and that they therefore deserve equal consideration.
- Aristotle articulated the key distinction between **retributive justice** and **distributive justice**, endorsing the notion that wealth and goods should be fairly distributed among the members of society.
- Aristotle also recognized that the poor and disadvantaged members of society required special protection in a just society, to ensure that their basic needs were taken care of.

Retributive justice   Theory of justice dealing with how societies should treat those who violate laws.

Distributive justice   Theory of justice dealing with how society's wealth, opportunity, and power should be distributed.

So as with many circumstances in life, it is helpful for us to retain the core ideas that we find useful and applicable to our thinking about our social and political lives, while discarding the elements (such as slavery) that we find to be morally indefensible and conceptually wrong-headed.

PHILOSOPHER'S NOTEBOOK

- Aristotle believes that humans are first and foremost social creatures who can only fulfill their potential as members of a social community, and that people who could exist independently of human community must be either a "beast or a god." Do you agree? Why or why not?

- According to Aristotle the state is "prior to the individual," suggesting that the public interest of the community takes precedence over the interests of a few individuals. For example, imagine the state wants to construct a new road to alleviate traffic congestion, and that the proposed route runs right through a neighborhood where you and other families have lived for decades. What do you think Aristotle's reaction would be if it was his house that was being demolished? What would your reaction be? Is there a difference in the two reactions? If so, why?

- Aristotle believed that "slaves" were fulfilling their natural function in society by promoting the general interest for all. He also argued that if slaves were freed, they would be unhappy and unable to cope with the challenges of living. Assume that you disagree with Aristotle: what arguments would you make to convince him that his view of slaves is unjust? How might he respond?

- Aristotle also believed that women should not be considered the equals of men, and that fulfilling their potential meant recognizing and accepting their secondary status. Assume that you disagree with Aristotle: what arguments would you make to convince Aristotle that his view is mistaken? How might he respond?

- Justice, for Aristotle, is the result of each person fulfilling his or her natural potential, which would result in a hierarchical but cooperative society. Critically evaluate this definition of "justice."

Thomas Hobbes: *The War of All Against All*

Plato and Aristotle both envisioned an ideal society as one based on the assumption that justice was the natural result of each citizen performing his or her natural function, no matter what their position in the social hierarchy. They grounded their social/political visions in their metaphysical beliefs: Plato's quest for rational enlightenment and wisdom, and Aristotle's belief in the purposeful nature of every dimension of the universe.

The Middle Ages in Europe was dominated by the influence of religion. The ruling monarchs often sought to establish their authority by claiming they ruled by "divine right," supported by the full force of God's will. Thus the state and the rulers came to be seen as an integral part of God's kingdom on earth. As with Plato and Aristotle, this religiously ordained and authoritarian social/political system was rigidly structured and hierarchical. Whether your destiny was to be a slave, serf, landowner, knight, or king, you were expected to embrace your fate willingly and without question, as the natural expression of God's will.

With this as background, we can better appreciate the revolutionary thinking of the seventeenth-century British philosophers Thomas Hobbes, John Locke, and David Hume. Collectively, these thinkers developed views regarding the origins of the state and the nature of social justice that represented a radical departure from the political theories up until that time. Although there were important differences in their philosophical ideas, they all agreed on the following core political beliefs:

- *All members of society are intrinsically equal,* a sharp contrast to Plato and Aristotle's belief that people were naturally *un*equal, based on their natural talents and abilities.

- *Individuals willingly enter into a "social contract" with one another in order to promote a better quality of life for themselves,* the direct opposite of Aristotle's conviction that individuals are naturally social creatures and can only fulfill their unique potential as integral members of the social community.

- *Justice (and other laws) only comes into existence with the formation of the social contract* (Locke has a somewhat different view in this case).

- *Justice is viewed as pursuing the* public interest, *enforced by the authority of the ruling members of the community.* For Plato and Aristotle, on the other hand, justice results from each individual fulfilling his/her special social function in a cooperative fashion.

We begin our analysis of **social contract theory** by exploring the influential ideas of **Thomas Hobbes** (1588–1679). Unlike Aristotle's belief in the original primacy of the social community, Hobbes contends that humans begin in the "state of nature," unconstrained by laws or social agreements. Since Hobbes believes that humans are by nature selfish, destructive, and unprincipled, living in the state of nature is very

THOMAS HOBBES

(1588–1679)
British Philosopher. A thoroughgoing materialist who tried to reconcile free will with materialism. Best known for his social contract theory which advocates the transfer of power to an absolute sovereign.

 VISUAL PHILOSOPHY

War of All Against All

Do you agree with Thomas Hobbes that there is the need for strong, authoritative central government that has the power to maintain control in order to avoid a "war of all against all"? Why?

Social contract theory   The sociopolitical theory that holds that the legitimacy of government is based on an agreement either between the people and their ruler or among the people in a community.

unpleasant indeed: "a war of all against all," is how Hobbes describes it (which mirrored the political unrest that was occurring at this time in England). And the consequence is that our lives in the state of nature are "nasty, brutish and short." What is the remedy? Because humans are capable of reason, they recognize that the only way to improve the quality of their lives is to enter into a cooperative partnership with their competitors, a "social contract" in which they will agree to surrender some of their autonomy to create a safe and productive environment in which to live. This cooperative peace is enforced by laws and a justice system that the individual members have endorsed and ceded power to. And once this central political authority has been established, its actions should not be questioned. Thus the legitimacy of the state is based on the consent of the governed, in the same way that members of an organization might elect a leader to control and direct the group's activities. The following selection is from Hobbes's 1651 work, *Leviathan*, the name of a mythological sea monster symbolizing evil in Christian writings. Hobbes uses this image to symbolize his belief in the need for a strong, authoritative central government that has the power to maintain control and order in the face of political turmoil.

Chapter XIII: Of the Natural Condition of Mankind as Concerning Their Felicity and Misery

Hobbes, *Leviathan*

Nature hath made men so equal in the faculties of body and mind as that, though there be found one man sometimes manifestly stronger in body or of quicker mind than another, yet when all is reckoned together the difference between man and man is not so considerable as that one man can thereupon claim to himself any benefit to which another may not pretend as well as he. For as to the strength of body, the weakest has strength enough to kill the strongest, either by secret machination or by confederacy with others that are in the same danger with himself.

And as to the faculties of the mind, setting aside the arts grounded upon words, and especially that skill of proceeding upon general and infallible rules, called science, which very few have and but in few things, as being not a native faculty born with us, nor attained, as prudence, while we look after somewhat else, I find yet a greater equality amongst men than that of strength. For prudence is but experience, which equal time equally bestows on all men in those things they equally apply themselves unto. That which may perhaps make such equality incredible is but a vain conceit of one's own wisdom, which almost all men think they have in a greater degree than the vulgar; that is, than all men but themselves, and a few others, whom by fame, or for concurring with themselves, they approve. For such is the nature of men that howsoever they may acknowledge many others to be more witty, or more eloquent or more learned, yet they will hardly believe there be many so wise as themselves; for they see their own wit at hand, and other men's at a distance. But this proveth rather that men are in that point equal, than unequal. For there is not ordinarily a greater sign of the equal distribution of anything than that every man is contented with his share.

This is an extraordinary viewpoint being articulated here by Hobbes. Flying in the face of two thousand years of hierarchical thinking, Hobbes uses the tools of reason and common sense to conclude that in general terms, humans are more similar than different, more equal than unequal—physically and intellectually. The proof of this? All people consider themselves to be wiser than all others, pleased with the natural talents they have been awarded. And "there is not ordinarily a greater sign of the equal distribution of anything than that every man is contented with his share." And though they may vary in physical size and strength, weapons and the element of surprise render them an equally lethal threat to one another.

From this equality of ability ariseth equality of hope in the attaining of our ends. And therefore if any two men desire the same thing, which nevertheless they cannot both

Hobbes, *Leviathan*

Thomas Hobbes

enjoy, they become enemies; and in the way to their end (which is principally their own conservation, and sometimes their delectation only) endeavour to destroy or subdue one another. And from hence it comes to pass that where an invader hath no more to fear than another man's single power, if one plant, sow, build, or possess a convenient seat, others may probably be expected to come prepared with forces united to dispossess and deprive him, not only of the fruit of his labour, but also of his life or liberty. And the invader again is in the like danger of another.

And from this diffidence of one another, there is no way for any man to secure himself so reasonable as anticipation; that is, by force, or wiles, to master the persons of all men he can so long till he see no other power great enough to endanger him: and this is no more than his own conservation requireth, and is generally allowed. . . .

Again, men have no pleasure (but on the contrary a great deal of grief) in keeping company where there is no power able to overawe them all. For every man looketh that his companion should value him at the same rate he sets upon himself, and upon all signs of contempt or undervaluing naturally endeavours, as far as he dares (which amongst them that have no common power to keep them in quiet is far enough to make them destroy each other), to extort a greater value from his contemners, by damage; and from others, by the example. So that in the nature of man, we find three principal causes of quarrel. First, competition; secondly, diffidence; thirdly, glory. The first maketh men invade for gain; the second, for safety; and the third, for reputation. The first use violence, to make themselves masters of other men's persons, wives, children, and cattle; the second, to defend them; the third, for trifles, as a word, a smile, a different opinion, and any other sign of undervalue, either direct in their persons or by reflection in their kindred, their friends, their nation, their profession, or their name. Hereby it is manifest that during the time men live without a common power to keep them all in awe, they are in that condition which is called war; and such a war as is of every man against every man. For war consisteth not in battle only, or the act of fighting, but in a tract of time, wherein the will to contend by battle is sufficiently known: and therefore the notion of time is to be considered in the nature of war, as it is in the nature of weather. For as the nature of foul weather lieth not in a shower or two of rain, but in an inclination thereto of many days together: so the nature of war consisteth not in actual fighting, but in the known disposition thereto during all the time there is no assurance to the contrary. All other time is peace.

For most people, equality among people is viewed as a positive and enlightened perspective. But Hobbes sees it differently. Because we all want the same things, and we all have roughly equal abilities and pose equal threats to one another, the result is a free-for-all, a war of all against all. And even when we are not actually engaged in conflict, we are *worried* about being engaged in conflict. This preoccupation with our personal safety precludes the possibility of social cooperation and all of the constructive creations that grow out of such cooperation. It's every person for his/her self, and this results in a very primitive style of living indeed.

Hobbes, *Leviathan*

Whatsoever therefore is consequent to a time of war, where every man is enemy to every man, the same consequent to the time wherein men live without other security than what their own strength and their own invention shall furnish them withal. In such condition there is no place for industry, because the fruit thereof is uncertain: and consequently no culture of the earth; no navigation, nor use of the commodities that may be imported by sea; no commodious building; no instruments of moving and removing such things as require much force; no knowledge of the face of the earth; no account of time; no arts; no letters; no society; and which is worst of all, continual fear, and danger of violent death; and the life of man, solitary, poor, nasty, brutish, and short.

It may seem strange to some man that has not well weighed these things that Nature should thus dissociate and render men apt to invade and destroy one another: and he may therefore, not trusting to this inference, made from the passions, desire perhaps to have the same confirmed by experience. Let him therefore consider with himself: when taking a journey, he arms himself and seeks to go well accompanied; when going to sleep, he locks his doors; when even in his house he locks his chests; and this when he knows there be laws and public officers, armed, to revenge all injuries shall be done him; what opinion he has of his fellow subjects, when he rides armed; of his fellow citizens, when he locks his doors; and of his children, and servants, when he locks his chests. Does he not there as much accuse mankind by his actions as I do by my words? But neither of us accuse man's nature in it. The desires, and other passions of man, are in themselves no sin. No more are the actions that proceed from those passions till they know a law that forbids them; which till laws be made they cannot know, nor can any law be made till they have agreed upon the person that shall make it.

It may peradventure be thought there was never such a time nor condition of war as this; and I believe it was never generally so, over all the world: But though there had never been any time wherein particular men were in a condition of war one against another, yet in all times kings and persons of sovereign authority, because of their independency, are in continual jealousies, and in the state and posture of gladiators, having their weapons pointing, and their eyes fixed on one another; that is, their forts, garrisons, and guns upon the frontiers of their kingdoms, and continual spies upon their neighbours, which is a posture of war. But because they uphold thereby the industry of their subjects, there does not follow from it that misery which accompanies the liberty of particular men.

Do you agree with Hobbes that without laws and police to control us, people would return to a violent state of nature, a "war of all against all"?

Hobbes readily acknowledges that we may never have actually existed in such a "state of nature," but this doesn't matter. We see the reality of people's competitive and destructive natures in the way we behave in current society: we lock our doors, protect our possessions and family, and take consolation in the existence of laws and police to enforce the laws. As Hobbes notes, doesn't each person "accuse mankind by his actions as I do by my words?" In addition, if we look at the history of civilization, we find that it is an unrelenting account of wars, invasions, threats, and destruction. Not that people—or countries—should be blamed for their behavior, according to Hobbes. These competitive and destructive impulses are simply a part of our human nature, wired into our brains since birth. It is only when humans come together to make peace with one another, create laws, and establish a central authority to enforce the laws, that the moral concepts of "justice" and "injustice" come into existence. Before this point is reached, however, "force" and "fraud" are the two cardinal virtues in the war of all against all.

To this war of every man against every man, this also is consequent; that nothing can be unjust. The notions of right and wrong, justice and injustice, have there no place. Where there is no common power, there is no law; where no law, no injustice. Force and fraud are in war the two cardinal virtues. Justice and injustice are none of the faculties neither of the body nor mind. If they were, they might be in a man that were alone in the world, as well as his senses and passions. They are qualities that relate to men in society, not in solitude. It is consequent also to the same condition that there be no propriety, no dominion, no mine and thine distinct; but only that to be every man's that he can get, and for so long as he can keep it. And thus much for the ill condition which man by mere nature is actually placed in; though with a possibility to come out of it, consisting partly in the passions, partly in his reason.

The passions that incline men to peace are: fear of death; desire of such things as are necessary to commodious living; and a hope by their industry to obtain them. And reason suggesteth convenient articles of peace upon which men may be drawn to agreement. These articles are they which otherwise are called the laws of nature, whereof I shall speak more particularly in the two following chapters.

Hobbes, *Leviathan*

Weary from this ongoing conflict, threat, and competition, the rational part of our nature enables us to understand that we need to create a political structure that will enable us to live cooperatively and harmoniously with one another. And so we enter into a "social contract" with others, agreeing to laws and a central governing authority in order to insure peaceful coexistence.

Hobbes, *Leviathan*

Chapter XIV: Of the First and Second Natural Laws, and of Contracts

The right of nature, which writers commonly call *jus naturale*, is the liberty each man hath to use his own power as he will himself for the preservation of his own nature; that is to say, of his own life; and consequently, of doing anything which, in his own judgement and reason, he shall conceive to be the aptest means thereunto.

By liberty is understood, according to the proper signification of the word, the absence of external impediments; which impediments may oft take away part of a man's power to do what he would, but cannot hinder him from using the power left him according as his judgement and reason shall dictate to him.

A law of nature, *lex naturalis*, is a precept, or general rule, found out by reason, by which a man is forbidden to do that which is destructive of his life, or taketh away the means of preserving the same, and to omit that by which he thinketh it may be best preserved. For though they that speak of this subject use to confound *jus* and *lex*, right and law, yet they ought to be distinguished, because right consisteth in liberty to do, or to forbear; whereas law determineth and bindeth to one of them: so that law and right differ as much as obligation and liberty, which in one and the same matter are inconsistent.

And because the condition of man (as hath been declared in the precedent chapter) is a condition of war of every one against every one, in which case every one is governed by his own reason, and there is nothing he can make use of that may not be a help unto him in preserving his life against his enemies; it followeth that in such a condition every man has a right to every thing, even to one another's body. And therefore, as long as this natural right of every man to every thing endureth, there can be no security to any man, how strong or wise soever he be, of living out the time which nature ordinarily alloweth men to live. And consequently it is a precept, or general rule of reason: that every man ought to endeavour peace, as far as he has hope of obtaining it; and when he cannot obtain it, that he may seek and use all helps and advantages of war. The first branch of which rule containeth the first and fundamental law of nature, which is: to seek peace and follow it. The second, the sum of the right of nature, which is: by all means we can to defend ourselves.

From this fundamental law of nature, by which men are commanded to endeavour peace, is derived this second law: that a man be willing, when others are so too, as far forth as for peace and defence of himself he shall think it necessary, to lay down this right to all things; and be contented with so much liberty against other men as he would allow other men against himself. For as long as every man holdeth this right, of doing anything he liketh; so long are all men in the condition of war. But if other men will not lay down their right, as well as he, then there is no reason for anyone to divest himself of his: for that were to expose himself to prey, which no man is bound to, rather than to dispose himself to peace. This is that law of the gospel: Whatsoever you require that others should do to you, that do ye to them. ▪

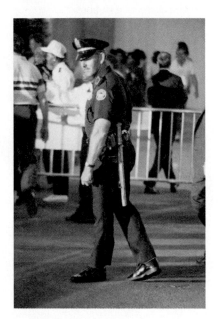

Hobbes believes that people enter into a "social contract" enforced by a central authority to insure everyone's safety. Do you agree that this is the primary motivation of social communities?

 Hobbes, Thomas, *Leviathan*

Thus humans, to extricate themselves from the vicious cycle of war against everyone, agree to seek peace with one another. But it is an uneasy peace, dependent on the consistent intentions of others not to breach the agreement. And so Hobbes is quick to point out that even after agreeing to the social contract, people still retain the right to defend themselves against any and all attacks from their fellow citizens. For Hobbes, the social community is essentially a collection of hostile and untrustworthy individuals, reluctantly drawn together to promote their individual interests. Although cooperative projects with others are pursued to enjoy the mutual benefits such projects produce, it is still prudent for us to keep looking over our shoulders to ensure that we don't make the mistake of being too trustful.

THINK PHILOSOPHICALLY

Analyzing Thomas Hobbes

10.4

PHILOSOPHER'S NOTEBOOK

- In sharp contrast to Aristotle's view that humans are naturally social and political animals, Hobbes believes that being alone is our natural state, and that we form social relationships only out of necessity and personal self-interest. Identify which viewpoint you find more compelling and explain your reasoning.

- Hobbes believes that people are naturally competitive with one another, and that in the absence of laws to keep these impulses in check, we would do whatever it takes to gain wealth, power, and glory. Try to imagine a society in which there were no laws or police or justice system to protect people from one another. Describe what you think would happen to society and our social relationships over the period of a year.

- Have you ever been in a situation in which the normal social rules broke down? For example, in the middle of an out-of-control mob, a panic situation involving other people, or a competitive activity in which people's emotions got out of hand? Describe what it felt like to be in this situation, and analyze its dynamics from Hobbes's point of view.

- Hobbes believes that his rather pessimistic views are supported by our experiences: we take extraordinary precautions to protect ourselves and our possessions, and that when we look at world events, we see ongoing examples of war, oppression, cruelty, competition, hatred, and genocide. Do you think that this is a persuasive argument for Hobbes's view of human nature? Why or why not?

- According to Hobbes, the ideas of "justice" and "injustice" only come into existence when laws are created: they have no natural existence or authority. Do you agree with this perspective? Why or why not?

John Locke: *Life, Liberty, and Property*

John Locke (1632–1704), a younger contemporary of Thomas Hobbes, agreed with him that the concept of a social contract was the most intelligent way to explain the origins of the political state and to justify its authority, an authority derived from the voluntary consent of the governed. But Locke's views were significantly different from Hobbes's views in other respects. To begin with, Locke had a decidedly more optimistic view of human nature than Hobbes. Rather than viewing the "state of nature" as a "war of all against all," Locke believed that humans were governed by certain "natural laws" that made them free, rational, and social creatures. As God's creations, all people are entitled to "inalienable" (that is, nontransferable) rights, including the rights to life, liberty, health, and property. No other person has the authority to threaten or remove any of these God-given rights.

Nevertheless, despite the advantages of living in the "state of nature" as free and independent individuals, humans find it advantageous to come together and form a political state to ensure that their natural rights will be protected by laws and the authority of the government. As with Hobbes, this social contract is freely consented to. For Locke, however, the state is the "servant" of the people, and if the state fails to live up to the terms of the agreement, it can be "dismissed" through revolution. Hobbes disagrees, believing that once contracted for, the authority of the state can never be questioned.

JOHN LOCKE

(1632–1704)
British Philosopher. In *Essay Concerning Human Understanding* (1690) Locke laid groundwork for modern political theory with his concept of "inalienable personal rights."

Locke's views had a profound and far-reaching influence on the political thinking and events of the time. In fact, his fundamental concepts of inalienable rights formed the basis of America's Declaration of Independence as well as its Constitution and Bill of Rights, a relationship we shall explore further in the pages ahead.

The following passages are taken from his influential work, *The Second Treatise of Civil Government*, written in 1690.

Locke,
The Second Treatise of Government

CHAP. II. Of the State of Nature.

Sec. 4. To understand political power right, and derive it from its original, we must consider, what state all men are naturally in, and that is, a state of perfect freedom to order their actions, and dispose of their possessions and persons, as they think fit, within the bounds of the law of nature, without asking leave, or depending upon the will of any other man.

A state also of equality, wherein all the power and jurisdiction is reciprocal, no one having more than another; there being nothing more evident, than that creatures of the same species and rank, promiscuously born to all the same advantages of nature, and the use of the same faculties, should also be equal one amongst another without subordination or subjection, unless the lord and master of them all should, by any manifest declaration of his will, set one above another, and confer on him, by an evident and clear appointment, an undoubted right to dominion and sovereignty. . . .

Sec. 6. But though this be a state of liberty, yet it is not a state of licence: though man in that state has an uncontroullable liberty to dispose of his person or possessions, yet he has not liberty to destroy himself, or so much as any creature in his possession, but where some nobler use than its bare preservation calls for it. The state of nature has a law of nature to govern it, which obliges every one: and reason, which is that law, teaches all mankind, who will but consult it, that being all equal and independent, no one ought to harm another in his life, health, liberty, or possessions: for men being all the workmanship of one omnipotent, and infinitely wise maker; all the servants of one sovereign master, sent into the world by his order, and about his business; they are his property, whose workmanship they are, made to last during his, not one another's pleasure: and being furnished with like faculties, sharing all in one community of nature, there cannot be supposed any such subordination among us, that may authorize us to destroy one another, as if we were made for one another's uses, as the inferior ranks of creatures are for our's. Every one, as he is bound to preserve himself, and not to quit his station wilfully, so by the like reason, when his own preservation comes not in competition, ought he, as much as he can, to preserve the rest of mankind, and may not, unless it be to do justice on an offender, take away, or impair the life, or what tends to the preservation of the life, the liberty, health, limb, or goods of another.

Sec. 7. And that all men may be restrained from invading others rights, and from doing hurt to one another, and the law of nature be observed, which willeth the peace and preservation of all mankind, the execution of the law of nature is, in that state, put into every man's hands, whereby every one has a right to punish the transgressors of that law to such a degree, as may hinder its violation: for the law of nature would, as all other laws that concern men in this world be in vain, if there were no body that in the state of nature had a power to execute that law, and thereby preserve the innocent and restrain offenders. And if any one in the state of nature may punish another for any evil he has done, every one may do so: for in that state of perfect equality, where naturally there is no superiority or jurisdiction of one over another, what any may do in prosecution of that law, every one must needs have a right to do.

John Locke

Notice how idyllic and rational Locke's "state of nature" is when contrasted with Hobbes's violent and perilous war of all against all. Locke's state is one of "perfect freedom to order their actions and dispose of their possessions and persons as they see fit," governed by the "law of nature." It's a state "of equality, wherein all the power and jurisdiction is reciprocal, no one having more than another." Unlike Hobbes, Locke's "state of nature" has a rational structure to it, ordained by God the Creator and manifest in the law of nature "which obliges every one: and reason, which is that law, teaches all mankind, who will but consult it, that being all equal and independent, no one ought to harm another in his life, health, liberty, or possessions." In fact, not only does the law of nature prohibit individuals from harming others, but it exhorts us to actively preserve their well-being.

Yet Locke recognizes that despite the law of nature, some individuals may still invade the rights of others and even try to hurt them. In this case, each person is a government to his or her self, with the right to administer the law of nature and punish the transgressors to protect the innocent and preserve the peace.

But if the "state of nature" is such a utopian paradise, then what is the incentive for people to come together and constitute a formal political state? Locke addresses this question directly:

CHAP. IX. Of the Ends of Political Society and Government.

Locke,
*The Second
Treatise of Government*

Sec. 123. If man in the state of nature be so free, as has been said; if he be absolute lord of his own person and possessions, equal to the greatest, and subject to no body, why will he part with his freedom? why will he give up this empire, and subject himself to the dominion and controul of any other power? To which it is obvious to answer, that though in the state of nature he hath such a right, yet the enjoyment of it is very uncertain, and constantly exposed to the invasion of others: for all being kings as much as he, every man his equal, and the greater part no strict observers of equity and justice, the enjoyment of the property he has in this state is very unsafe, very unsecure. This makes him willing to quit a condition, which, however free, is full of fears and continual dangers: and it is not without reason, that he seeks out, and is willing to join in society with others, who are already united, or have a mind to unite, for the mutual preservation of their lives, liberties and estates, which I call by the general name, property.

Sec. 124. The great and chief end, therefore, of men's uniting into commonwealths, and putting themselves under government, is the preservation of their property. To which in the state of nature there are many things wanting.

First, There wants an established, settled, known law, received and allowed by common consent to be the standard of right and wrong, and the common measure to decide all controversies between them: for though the law of nature be plain and intelligible to all rational creatures; yet men being biassed by their interest, as well as ignorant for want of study of it, are not apt to allow of it as a law binding to them in the application of it to their particular cases.

Sec. 125. Secondly, In the state of nature there wants a known and indifferent judge, with authority to determine all differences according to the established law: for every one in that state being both judge and executioner of the law of nature, men being partial to themselves, passion and revenge is very apt to carry them too far, and with too much heat, in their own cases; as well as negligence, and unconcernedness, to make them too remiss in other men's.

Sec. 126. Thirdly, In the state of nature there often wants power to back and support the sentence when right, and to give it due execution. They who by any injustice offended, will seldom fail, where they are able, by force to make good their injustice; such resistance many times makes the punishment dangerous, and frequently destructive, to those who attempt it.

Sec. 127. Thus mankind, notwithstanding all the privileges of the state of nature, being but in an ill condition, while they remain in it, are quickly driven into society. Hence it comes to pass, that we seldom find any number of men live any time together in this state. The inconveniences that they are therein exposed to, by the irregular and uncertain exercise of the power every man has of punishing the transgressions of others, make them take sanctuary under the established laws of government, and therein seek the preservation of their property. It is this makes them so willingly give up every one his single power of punishing, to be exercised by such alone, as shall be appointed to it amongst them; and by such rules as the community, or those authorized by them to that purpose, shall agree on. And in this we have the original right and rise of both the legislative and executive power, as well as of the governments and societies themselves.

In contemplating the need for a social contract, Locke's "state of nature" suddenly seems less idyllic than initially proposed. In fact, although everyone is equal ("all being kings as much as he, every man his equal") the "greater part" of them are *not* "strict observers of equity and justice." As a result, "this state is very unsafe, very unsecure" and it is "full of fears and continual dangers." It seems that Locke's utopian paradise has become more like Hobbes's jungle. Faced with these unpleasant drawbacks of being a "king" among "kings," individuals reason that it would be in their self-interest to form a political state for the express purpose of ensuring that God's law of nature is effectively administered. Specifically:

- The provisions of the law of nature need to be clearly articulated, because in the "state of nature" people's inherent biases skew their understanding of the law.
- Judges need to be appointed to arbitrate in the case of different interpretations of the law, again because people are "partial to themselves" and "passion and revenge" too often replace rational evaluation.
- There needs to be sufficient power to enforce the law, because offenders rarely accept their punishments passively.

Thus individuals voluntarily enter into a social contract with others, constituting a government (by majority vote) that will effectively carry out these responsibilities, and ensuring that all citizens will receive equal, fair, impartial treatment, and have their fundamental rights (granted under the law of nature) protected.

Locke believed that it was important to create different branches of government that would have distinct powers and responsibilities:

- A legislative branch, to create and interpret laws
- An executive branch, to implement the laws
- A federative branch, responsible for making war and peace

Of course, the first two branches are identical to those of the United States' government, and although Locke believed that judges should play a prominent role in government, he did not propose the judiciary as a distinct branch. This was the unique contribution of **Baron de Montesquieu** (1689–1755) who is often considered the ideological cofounder of the American Constitution along with John Locke.

Thus for Locke, the formation of the social contract is just the beginning of his philosophical thinking, not the culmination as it was for Hobbes. Locke is intent on exploring what form this government should take, what rights it should protect, and what should be justifiable conditions for its dissolution. At the center of his thinking of human rights is the concept of "property," a term that for him extends far beyond the idea of material possessions to include one's body and the products of one's labor (what "he has mixed his labour with").

Baron de Montesquieu (1689–1755) Enlightenment Philosopher. Extensively and systematically studied the social and political affairs of his time and dealt with the themes of toleration, moderation, and freedom in his writings.

Locke,
The Second
Treatise of Government

CHAP. V. Of Property.

Sec. 27. Though the earth, and all inferior creatures, be common to all men, yet every man has a property in his own person: this no body has any right to but himself. The labour of his body, and the work of his hands, we may say, are properly his. Whatsoever then he removes out of the state that nature hath provided, and left it in, he hath mixed his labour with, and joined to it something that is his own, and thereby makes it his property. It being by him removed from the common state nature hath placed it in, it hath by this labour something annexed to it, that excludes the common right of other men: for this labour being the unquestionable property of the labourer, no man but he can have a right to what that is once joined to, at least where there is enough, and as good, left in common for others.

Sec. 28. He that is nourished by the acorns he picked up under an oak, or the apples he gathered from the trees in the wood, has certainly appropriated them to himself. No body can deny but the nourishment is his. I ask then, when did they begin to be his? when he digested? or when he ate? or when he boiled? or when he brought them home? or when he picked them up? and it is plain, if the first gathering made them not his, nothing else could. That labour put a distinction between them and common: that added something to them more than nature, the common mother of all, had done; and so they became his private right. And will any one say, he had no right to those acorns or apples, he thus appropriated, because he had not the consent of all mankind to make them his? Was it a robbery thus to assume to himself what belonged to all in common? If such a consent as that was necessary, man had starved, notwithstanding the plenty God had given him. We see in commons, which remain so by compact, that it is the taking any part of what is common, and removing it out of the state nature leaves it in, which begins the property; without which the common is of no use. And the taking of this or that part, does not depend on the express consent of all the commoners. Thus the grass my horse has bit; the turfs my servant has cut; and the ore I have digged in any place, where I have a right to them in common with others, become my property, without the assignation or consent of any body. The labour that was mine, removing them out of that common state they were in, hath fixed my property in them.

Sec. 51. And thus, I think, it is very easy to conceive, without any difficulty, how labour could at first begin a title of property in the common things of nature, and how the spending it upon our uses bounded it. So that there could then be no reason of quarrelling about title, nor any doubt about the largeness of possession it gave. Right and conveniency went together; for as a man had a right to all he could employ his labour upon, so he had no temptation to labour for more than he could make use of. This left no room for controversy about the title, nor for encroachment on the right of others; what portion a man carved to himself, was easily seen; and it was useless, as well as dishonest, to carve himself too much, or take more than he needed.

Locke's concept of the "right to property" thus represents a core value: we have the right to our own body, meaning the freedom to live our lives and pursue our happiness freely, without arbitrary interference from other individuals or from the state. We also have the right to own property, a significant claim in Locke's time when much of a person's value was defined by the property he owned (or didn't own). Locke was not advocating that everyone should own the *same* amount of property, only that every person be entitled to own *some* property. The amount of property you own depends on your ingenuity and industriousness, qualities that came to be associated with the "Protestant work ethic." And finally, we have the right to reap the benefits that our labor produces. It is a violation of our benefits to be expected to work without receiving a proportionate share of what our labor produces.

Locke's ideas were truly revolutionary when he wrote them, and they remain revolutionary today in many parts of the world. His ideas are surely inconsistent with slavery, as well as the exploitation of underpaid workers. The political leaders in America were very familiar with Locke's writings (along with Montesquieu's) and **Thomas Jefferson** was a particularly avid student of his ideas. This is clear when we compare Locke's declaration of the "inalienable rights of

Thomas Jefferson

THOMAS JEFFERSON
(1743–1826)
American Statesman/Politician. Wrote the Declaration of Independence in 1776. Firm believer in the social contract and the natural rights of humans.

In contrast to Hobbes, John Locke believed that citizens have the right to protest the policies and even dissolve a government which is not insuring the "life, liberty and property" of its citizens.

life, liberty, and the right to own property," with this famous sentence of the Declaration of Independence, composed by Thomas Jefferson:

> We hold these truths to be self-evident, that all men are created equal, that they are endowed by their Creator with certain unalienable Rights, that among these are Life, Liberty and the pursuit of Happiness.

Locke's ideas were also instrumental in shaping the rationale for America's rebellion against the government of England, as we can see in the following passages regarding the conditions for the dissolution of the social contract.

Locke,
*The Second
Treatise of Government*

CHAP. XIX. Of the Dissolution of Government.

Sec. 222. The reason why men enter into society, is the preservation of their property; and the end why they chuse and authorize a legislative, is, that there may be laws made, and rules set, as guards and fences to the properties of all the members of the society, to limit the power, and moderate the dominion, of every part and member of the society: for since it can never be supposed to be the will of the society, that the legislative should have a power to destroy that which every one designs to secure, by entering into society, and for which the people submitted themselves to legislators of their own making; whenever the legislators endeavour to take away, and destroy the property of the people, or to reduce them to slavery under arbitrary power, they put themselves into a state of war with the people, who are thereupon absolved from any farther obedience, and are left to the common refuge, which God hath provided for all men, against force and violence. Whensoever therefore the legislative shall transgress this fundamental rule of society; and either by ambition, fear, folly or corruption, endeavour to grasp themselves, or put into the hands of any other, an absolute power over the lives, liberties, and estates of the people; by this breach of trust they forfeit the power the people had put into their hands for quite contrary ends, and it devolves to the people, who have a right to resume their original liberty, and, by the establishment of a new legislative, (such as they shall think fit) provide for their own safety and security, which is the end for which they are in society. . . .

Locke, John, *The Second
Treatise of Government*

If we compare Locke's passages with the opening paragraphs of the Declaration of Independence, the ideological debt owed to Locke is clear.

Jefferson et al.,
*The Declaration
of Independence: A Transcription*

IN CONGRESS, July 4, 1776.

The unanimous Declaration of the thirteen United States of America,

When in the Course of human events, it becomes necessary for one people to dissolve the political bands which have connected them with another, and to assume among the powers of the earth, the separate and equal station to which the Laws of Nature and of Nature's God entitle them, a decent respect to the opinions of mankind requires that they should declare the causes which impel them to the separation.

We hold these truths to be self-evident, that all men are created equal, that they are endowed by their Creator with certain unalienable Rights, that among these are Life, Liberty and the pursuit of Happiness.—That to secure these rights, Governments are instituted among Men, deriving their just powers from the consent of the governed,—That whenever any Form of Government becomes destructive of these ends, it is the Right of the People to alter or to abolish it, and to institute new Government, laying its foundation on such principles and organizing its powers in such form, as to them shall seem most likely to effect their Safety and Happiness. Prudence, indeed, will dictate that Governments long established should not be changed for light and

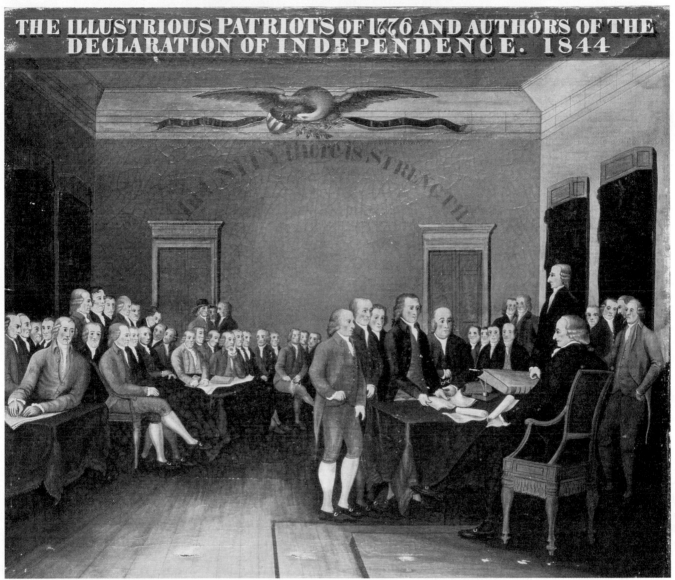

Laying the Cornerstone

What are the key principles of the Declaration of Independence? To what extent do you believe these principles are reflected in our society today?

transient causes; and accordingly all experience hath shewn, that mankind are more disposed to suffer, while evils are sufferable, than to right themselves by abolishing the forms to which they are accustomed. But when a long train of abuses and usurpations, pursuing invariably the same Object evinces a design to reduce them under absolute Despotism, it is their right, it is their duty, to throw off such Government, and to provide new Guards for their future security.—Such has been the patient sufferance of these Colonies; and such is now the necessity which constrains them to alter their former Systems of Government. The history of the present King of Great Britain is a history of repeated injuries and usurpations, all having in direct object the establishment of an absolute Tyranny over these States. To prove this, let Facts be submitted to a candid world.

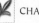

THINK PHILOSOPHICALLY 10.5
Analyzing John Locke

PHILOSOPHER'S NOTEBOOK

- Locke believes that even when people do not live in organized societies with laws and justice systems, they are nevertheless bound by the "law of nature," reflecting God's will. Do you agree with this view? Why or why not? If so, what values and stipulations are a part of the law of nature?

- As the "servant" of the people, Locke believed that the political state should be rebelled against and dissolved if it fails to perform its functions under the social contract. What policies would your government have to adopt for you to support the idea of rebelling against it?

- In some passages Locke's "state of nature" seems to be a utopian paradise; in others, a perilous existence fraught with dangers from others. If a group of people were placed in a situation in which they were living outside the laws of the state (for example, analogous to the novel *Lord of the Flies* or the television show "Survivor" but without rules and cameras), which version of Locke's "state of nature" would be most likely to occur? Why?

- Locke believes that all people retain the right to control their own bodies and are entitled to a fair share of whatever they produce through their own labor. Do you agree with this view? Why or why not? Can you think of any exceptions to this perspective (for example, someone contemplating suicide)?

- Thomas Jefferson changed Locke's statement of inalienable rights from "Life, liberty and property" to "Life, liberty and the pursuit of happiness." How does the meaning of these two formulations differ? Which one do you think is more appropriate for the Declaration of Independence? Why?

David Hume: *There Is No "State of Nature"*

We encountered **David Hume** (1711–1776) and his demolition logic in our explorations of metaphysics and epistemology in chapter 9. Hume took special pleasure in puncturing what he considered to be the overinflated balloons of philosophical speculation, whatever the topic. Social and political philosophy was no exception, and he took dead aim at what he considered to be the fanciful notion of the "state of nature" and the "social contract" that was so much in vogue at the time.

> (Some) philosophers . . . assert . . . that government in its earliest infancy arose from consent, or rather the voluntary acquiescence of the people. . . . They affirm that all men are born equal and owe allegiance to no prince or government, unless bound by the obligation and sanction of a promise. . . .
>
> But would these reasoners look abroad into the world, they would meet with nothing that, in the least, corresponds to their ideas. . . . On the contrary, we find everywhere princes who claim their subjects as their property and assert their independent right of sovereignty, from conquest or succession. We find also, everywhere, subjects who acknowledge this right in their prince. . . . Were you to preach, in most parts of the world, that political connections are founded altogether on voluntary consent or a mutual promise, the magistrate would soon imprison you, as seditious, for loosening the ties of obedience; if your friends did not before shut you up as delirious, for advancing such absurdities. . . . Almost all the governments which exist at present, or of which there remains any record in

DAVID HUME

(1711–1776)
Scottish Philosopher. Hume's philosophy seen as drawing out logical consequences of a thoroughgoing empiricism. His skepticism concerning causation, induction, and religion is widely influential in the history of philosophy and contemporary philosophy.

Jean-Jacques Rousseau

(1712–1778) Enlightenment Philosopher. Maintained society and culture corrupted the inherent goodness of man and restricted the freedom man enjoys in the state of nature; offered up a version of the social contract that was much different from his contemporaries.

history, have been founded originally either on usurpation or conquest or both, without any pretense of a fair consent or voluntary subjection of the people.

"Take a dose of reality!" Hume seems to be saying to these "social contractors," with his typical biting sarcasm. "Look at the governments in the world and their history!" There is absolutely no evidence of people coming together by common consent to form a social contract from some imagined "state of nature." Quite the contrary: the history of political states is one of conquest and succession in which the consent of the governed plays absolutely no role. Even if you were to go to different countries to proclaim that the existing government owes its authority entirely to the voluntary consent of the citizens, you would soon be imprisoned for treason or spirited away by your friends for you own protection. The "state of nature" and "social contract" are no more than the fictional creations of philosopher's overwrought imaginations. They have no basis in reality and as a result are of no practical use in understanding the nature of the state.

John Locke, however, had already anticipated at least a portion of Hume's frontal assault in acknowledging that the "state of nature" may not have actually existed in fact. And even if citizens had never had the opportunity to give their explicit *prior consent* for the existence, authority, and power of the state, they nevertheless have the opportunity to give their *tacit consent* by choosing to live in society and accept the social/political structure that it provides. In other words, by choosing to live in a society, use its services (provisions for property, education, highways), and accept its protections (police, fire, military), you are confirming your voluntary consent to the state. For Locke, this fulfills his conditions for a legitimate government, one that is based on the recognition that because people are "by nature all free, equal and independent, no one can be . . . subjected to the political power of another without his consent."

Does this meet Hume's objections? Hume would likely say "no." For if we interview citizens of various countries—particularly those in authoritarian regimes, which dominated the landscape in Hume's time—it is probable that they would deny they were making a free, voluntary choice to live in that particular political system. In truth, they would probably respond, "What choice do we have?" Of course, the great irony in Hume's case is that he died the year the closest thing to a social contract came into existence: the Declaration of Independence in 1776, and the subsequent Constitution of the United States. In any case, Hume's critique was devastating enough that a serious updating of the social contract theory did not occur until the twentieth century in the person of the philosopher John Rawls.

THINK CRITICALLY

10.6

Government, Law, and Human Nature

The views of Hobbes and Locke regarding the state of nature and social contract theory reflect their views on human nature. Hobbes has a decidedly pessimistic view of human nature in which a government must be formed to protect us from each other. Locke's view of humans is more hopeful: we are governed by innate laws of nature that reflect an intrinsic belief in equality, freedom, and tolerance. Nevertheless, Locke also believes that humans are sufficiently competitive and dangerous to one another that a central government is required to insure social order and protect the intrinsic rights of each individual. The influential French political philosopher **Jean-Jacques Rousseau** (1712–1778) has an even more positive view of humans, believing that we are naturally compassionate toward one another. Although it's true that this natural compassion is repressed or distorted by social conditioning, it nevertheless forms an important part of our human nature.

> It is this compassion that hurries us without reflection to the relief of those who are in distress: it is this which in a state of nature supplies the place of laws, morals, and virtues, with the advantage that none are tempted to disobey its gentle voice: it is this which will always prevent a sturdy savage from robbing a weak child or a feeble old man of the sustenance they may have with pain and difficulty acquired, if he sees a possibility of providing for himself by other means.

Political anarchists have an even more optimistic view of humans—and a commensurately pessimistic view of the need for government. These thinkers are convinced that people are naturally cooperative, much like the instinctive cooperation we see within species of the animal kingdom. From this vantage point, the best form of government is *no* government: the best way to control the socially destructive qualities of some people is to rely on the positive inclinations of the majority, as expressed in the following passage by the Russian anarchist Peter Kropotkin.

> No more laws! No more judges! Liberty, equality and practical human sympathy are the only effective barriers we can oppose to the anti-social instincts of certain among us.

Reflect on the views of human nature proposed by Hobbes, Locke, Rousseau, and Kropotkin. Which view best represents your own view of human nature? To what extent do people need laws and a government to enforce the laws in order to live with one another safely and cooperatively? Explain your reasoning carefully, providing specific reasons and concrete examples to support your point of view.

John Rawls: *"Justice as Fairness"*

JOHN RAWLS

(1921–2002)
American Political Philosopher. Leading figure and major contributor to political philosophy. In *A Theory of Justice* advances view that upon entering the social contract, if everyone is behind a "veil of ignorance," then they would choose a conception of justice as fairness.

Utopia An ideal place, state, or society.

ohn Rawls picked up the torch of social contract theory, which had been discarded for over two hundred years following Hume's withering critique, and gave it a decidedly modern interpretation in his influential book, *A Theory of Justice* (1972). Rawls agreed with Hume that the notion of people living in a "state of nature" and then assembling to enter into a "social contract" were historical fictions. Nevertheless, Rawls believed that we could still make productive use of these concepts by viewing them as theoretical constructs for understanding the nature, purpose, and authority of government and the state. For example, we can pose the question, "If we were living in the 'state of nature' and wanted to enter into an agreement with others to create a social/political community, *what kind of social/political system would we create?*" Imagining ourselves in this situation provides us with the opportunity to identify the values we believe are integral to an enlightened society, and to begin thinking about what form such a society would take. Rather than speculate about what social contract people *actually consented* to, we can entertain the question what type of social/political state we *would consent* to. Once we have constructed a clear model of a **utopian** society, we can then go about the business of trying to reshape our current society into one that more closely approximates our ideal society.

Rawls believes that the primary value of society is that it be based on justice. But his concept of justice is very different than that of Plato and Aristotle, for example, who envisioned a just state as one in which every person happily performed their appropriate function, whether slave, merchant, soldier, or king. For Rawls, the concept of "justice" is necessarily tied to the concept of "fairness." For a society to be truly *just*, it must be truly *fair*. After all, he reasons, wouldn't anyone about to enter into a social contract with others want to be assured that they would be treated fairly with respect to political rights and economic responsibilities? Surely the answer is an emphatic "yes." Who would choose to be a slave, a pauper, an exploited worker, or the target of unfair, discriminatory treatment?

If we assume that all people emerging from the "state of nature" would want to be guaranteed fair treatment and equal opportunities, what is the best way to conceive of what such a state would look like? It is in response to this question that Rawls introduces a simple but powerful concept, "The Veil of Ignorance." Imagine that in devising a utopian society that you had no idea *who* exactly you would be in this new society. Everything about you would be hidden behind a "veil of ignorance" that would conceal your gender, age, race, talents, education, parents—everything that defines you as an individual. In this case, Rawls asks, on what principles would you want this new society to be founded? Rawls is confident that most—perhaps all—people will want to be assured that they will be guaranteed fair treatment and equal opportunities, whatever their situation turns out to be. It is analogous to asking you to divide up a pie for dessert with the proviso that you do not know which piece you will be receiving: you will likely make every effort to ensure that the pieces are exactly equal so that you don't end up getting shortchanged!

In the following passages from *A Theory of Justice*, Rawls explores these themes and also goes on to identify the core principles that a just and fair society will embody.

Rawls, *A Theory of Justice*

The Main Idea of the Theory of Justice

My aim is to present a conception of justice which generalizes and carries to a higher level of abstraction the familiar theory of the social contract as found, say, in Locke, Rousseau, and Kant. In order to do this we are not to think of the original contract as one to enter a particular society or to set up a particular form of government. Rather, the guiding idea is that the principles of justice for the basic structure of society are the original agreement. They are the principles that free and rational persons concerned to further their own interests would accept in an initial position of equality as defining the fundamental terms of their association. These principles are to regulate all further agreements; they specify the kinds of social cooperation that can be entered into and the forms of government that can be established. This way of regarding the principles of justice I shall call justice as fairness.

Thus we are to imagine that those who engage in social cooperation choose together in one joint act, the principles which are to assign basic rights and duties and to determine the division of social benefits. Men are to decide in advance how they are to regulate their claims against one another and what is to be the foundation charter of their society. Just as each person must decide by rational reflection what constitutes his good, that is, the system of ends which it is rational for him to pursue, so a group of persons must decide once and for all what is to count among them as just and unjust. The choice which rational men would make in this hypothetical situation of equal liberty, assuming for the present that this choice problem has a solution, determines the principles of justice.

In justice as fairness the original position of equality corresponds to the state of nature in the traditional theory of the social contract. This original position is not, of course, thought of as an actual historical state of affairs, much less as a primitive condition of culture. It is understood as a purely hypothetical situation characterized so as to lead to a certain conception of justice. Among the essential features of this situation is that no one knows his place in society, his class position or social status, nor does anyone know his fortune in the distribution of natural assets and abilities, his intelligence, strength and the like. I shall even assume that the parties do not know their conceptions of the good or their special psychological propensities. The principles of justice are chosen behind a veil of ignorance. This ensures that no one is advantaged or disadvantaged in the choice of principles by the outcomes of natural chance or the contingency of social circumstances. Since all are similarly situated and no one is able to design principles to favor his particular condition, the principles of justice (for society and government) are the result of a fair agreement or bargain. For given the circumstances of the original position, the symmetry of everyone's relations to each other, this initial situation is fair between individuals as moral persons, that is, as rational beings with their own ends and capable, I shall assume, of a sense of justice. The original position is, one might say, the appropriate initial status quo, and thus the fundamental agreements reached in it are fair. This explains the propriety of the name "justice as fairness": it conveys the idea that the principles of justice are agreed to in an initial situation that is fair. The name does not mean that the concepts of justice and fairness are the same, any more than the phrase "poetry as metaphor" means that the concept of poetry and metaphor are the same.

Rawls believes—along with Hobbes and Locke—that humans are fundamentally *rational* creatures who are interested in using their reasoning abilities to enter into a mutually productive social relationship with others. Hobbes believed this rationally chosen social contract was necessary to curb and control our intrinsic aggressive and destructive impulses. Locke believed that humans entered into a social contract in order to formalize and enforce the divinely inspired "Law of Nature." Rawls has a different perspective. He believes that we should use the idea of the social contract as a conceptual tool for determining how best to construct a fair and just society. And to achieve this end, he suggests that we employ a "veil of ignorance" to develop the fundamental principles of justice on which society should be built. He believes that this process will result in a fair and impartial analysis because the veil will ensure that "no one knows his

Creating a Just Society

We began this chapter with the challenge: "Imagine that you were given the project of creating a society based on the principle of justice: how would you go about it and how would you justify your proposed state?" Using Rawls's concept of the "veil of ignorance," identify what principles of justice you would base your society on in the areas of

- Rights and liberties
- Economic opportunity
- Education
- Allocation of wealth and property
- Health care
- Political representation
- Other areas you believe are important

place in society, his class position or social status, nor does anyone know his fortune in the distribution of natural assets and abilities, his intelligence, strength and the like." And because we can't be sure what social position we will occupy in society, we have no choice but to create a system that will ensure that we are treated fairly and justly no matter *who* we are. It is a fascinating proposal: The Think Critically 10.7 on page 547 gives us the opportunity to try it out.

Of course, Rawls has his own ideas regarding the fundamental principles of justice that ought to form the basis of society that he identifies in the following passages. As you read them, compare your principles of justice with the ones he endorses.

Rawls, *A Theory of Justice*

Two Principles of Justice

I shall now state in a provisional form the two principles of justice that I believe should be chosen in the original position. In this section I wish to make only the most general comments, and therefore the first formulation of these principles is tentative....

The first statement of the two principles reads as follows.

First: each person is to have an equal right to the most extensive basic liberty compatible with a similar liberty for others.

Second: social and economic inequalities are to be arranged so that they are both (a) reasonably expected to be to everyone's advantage, and (b) attached to positions and offices open to all....

By way of general comment, these principles primarily apply, as I have said, to the basic structure of society. They are to govern the assignment of rights and duties and to regulate the distribution of social and economic advantages. As their formulation suggests, these principles presuppose that the social structure can be divided into two more or less distinct parts, the first principle applying to the one, the second to the other. They distinguish between those aspects of the social system that define and secure the equal liberties of citizenship and those that specify and establish social and economic inequalities. The basic liberties of citizens are, roughly speaking, political liberty (the right to vote and to be eligible for public office) together with freedom of speech and assembly; liberty of conscience and freedom of thought; freedom of the person along with the right to hold (personal) property; and freedom from arbitrary arrest and seizure as defined by the concept of the rule of law. These liberties are all required to be equal by the first principle, since citizens of a just society are to have the same basic rights.

The second principle applies, in the first approximation, to the distribution of income and wealth and to the design of organizations that make use of differences in authority and responsibility, or chains of command. While the distribution of wealth and income need not be equal, it must be to everyone's advantage, and at the same time, positions of authority and offices of command must be accessible to all. One applies the second principle by holding positions open, and then, subject to this constraint, arranges social and economic inequalities so that everyone benefits. ∎

 Rawls, John, *A Theory of Justice*

Rawls thus identifies two cardinal principles on which a just society should be based. The first deals with the "basic liberties" of citizens, and he believes that every person should have the maximum amount of freedom that is compatible with the freedom for all. This includes

- voting and being eligible to run for office.
- freedom of speech and assembly.
- freedom of conscience and thought.
- freedom of the person and the right to hold property.
- freedom from arbitrary arrest and seizure.

The second principle deals with economic issues and states that each person should have an equal opportunity to seek careers and economic opportunities. This means that every position should be open to all people, and that the sole criterion for determining which people are selected for these positions is their qualifications.

But this principle also means that all people should have an equal opportunity for the education and training that would enable them to develop the qualifications required. In other words, it is an empty promise to tell people that jobs or careers are open to all qualified candidates, and then not ensure that people have an equal opportunity to *develop* those qualifications.

Rawls is not advocating a social model in which everybody is entitled to exactly the same amount of wealth and income: rather, simply that people have an *equal opportunity* to acquire such wealth and income. And he also recognizes that it is sometimes in the interest of society to have economic *inequalities*. For example, if everyone is going to earn the same amount of salary, no matter how hard they work, there will be little incentive for them to put forth their best effort. It would be analogous to telling students in a class that everyone was going to receive an "A" no matter what their performance in the class. What do you think would be the result of such a policy? Similarly, for a society to achieve its greatest productivity, people should be rewarded for their dedication, ingenuity, and all the other qualities that are a part of being successful.

THINK PHILOSOPHICALLY 10.8
Analyzing John Rawls

- How do Rawls's principles of justice compare and contrast with the principles that you developed in using the "veil of ignorance" to identify principles for *your* ideal society in Think Critically activity 10.7?

- Do you agree with Rawls's idea that everyone should have the greatest amount of political freedom that is compatible with the freedom of all? Why or why not?

- Do you agree with Rawls's idea that economic wealth and income should provide everyone with an equal opportunity to secure all positions? Why or why not? How would you ensure that everyone has a chance to be equally educated or trained for all positions?

- Do you agree with Rawls's idea that there should be economic equalities as long as they benefit society as a whole? Why or why not? Have you ever been in a situation in which there were no incentives for superior performance? If so, how did people respond under those circumstances?

- Do you agree with Rawls's idea that there should be a system of public welfare that insures a basic standard of living for everyone in society, no matter how disadvantaged? Why or why not? Identify some of the challenges of creating and administering such a public welfare system.

- Rawls's colleague at Harvard, the philosopher **Robert Nozick**, believes that liberty and individual rights are so powerful that creating a safety net for less advantaged members of society is illegitimate. The government has no right to transfer property from some individuals (the rich) to other individuals (the poor). Instead, a society should rely on gifts and charity that is freely donated to support needy members of society. This is liberalism in its purest form, and is also characterized as libertarianism. He explains in this passage from his influential book, *Anarchy, State, and Utopia* (1975):

  > Benefits and burdens are distributed justly when society allows every individual the freedom to do what he chooses to do for himself or for others, the freedom to keep what he makes for himself or what others choose to give him, and the freedom to keep what he has or give it to whomever he chooses.

  Critically evaluate Nozick's point of view by citing the reasons that might be used to support it as well as reasons opposed to it. What do you think would be the practical outcome for the less advantaged members of society if Nozick's philosophy was implemented?

Robert Nozick (1938–) Political Philosopher. In *Anarchy, State, and Utopia* (1975) takes a libertarian position and argues that only a "minimal state" is justified.

However, Rawls also recognizes that not everyone is equally talented, and some members of society are at a disadvantage due to disabilities, age, and any number of other variables. So he adds the proviso that any economic inequalities should be for everyone's benefit. In practice, this means that such inequalities as incentives should enrich society as a whole by rewarding excellent performance. And it also means that a public welfare "safety net" should exist to ensure that all members of society are assured of a reasonable quality of life.

To sum up, Rawls's two principles of a just society are:

- Each person should have the greatest amount of political freedom that is compatible with equal freedom for all citizens.
- Economic wealth and income should provide everyone with an equal opportunity to secure all positions. In addition, any economic inequalities (such as incentives for superior performance) should be designed to benefit all people in society, including the least advantaged persons. And the least advantaged persons should be protected by a public welfare safety net that insures a basic standard of living.

KARL MARX

(1818–1883)
German Social Philosopher/Economist. Most important thinker in socialist history. His early philosophical writings and later socio-economic writings laid the groundwork for Communism.

Liberalism Political theory that champions the liberty, rights, and responsibilities of the individual.

Socialism The belief that society's resources belong to all members and should be shared with everyone.

Democracy The belief that all members of a society should have an equal voice in determining its governance.

Capitalism Social organization based on the free-market exchange of goods and services.

Communism Social organization based on communal ownership of resources and communal self-government.

Karl Marx: *Justice Is Based on Need and Ability*

L iberalism is a sociopolitical theory that emphasizes the liberty, rights, and responsibilities of the individual, and as a consequence it is also tied to the concept of "social contract" as reflected in the views of Hume, Locke, and Rawls. For liberalism, a just society is one in which individuals are free to pursue their own interests and achieve their own goals. The role of government is to ensure that individuals' rights are protected so that they can pursue their free choices without interference from others. Modern liberalism, as reflected in the views of philosophers such as John Rawls, recognizes that an individual's freedom of choice may be limited by other factors, such as lack of wealth, inadequate education, and social discrimination. In the previous section, we saw how Rawls attempts to compensate for these inhibiting factors by endorsing a principle of equal economic opportunity, as well as a social welfare safety net for those less advantaged members of society. Nevertheless, the emphasis for liberalism remains on the liberty, rights, and responsibilities of the individual.

Socialism is the sociopolitical philosophy that is the major competitor to liberalism. For socialism, a just society is one in which the wealth and property produced by society belongs to everyone and ought to be shared with everyone. In sharp contrast to liberalism's emphasis on the rights of the individual, socialism takes as its starting point the welfare of the entire community of individuals, and its central theme is captured in Karl Marx's slogan, "From each according to his abilities, to each according to his needs." Liberalism and socialism are the two predominant ideologies in the modern world, and most modern societies are a version of one or the other, or some blending of the two. In general, societies that are characterized as **democratic** and **capitalist** are considered built on the principles of liberalism. In contrast, societies characterized as **Communist** or Marxist are considered built on the principles of socialism.

Karl Marx (1818–1883) is the political theorist who is considered to be the architect of modern socialism, and his views have had a profound and far-reaching impact. Marx grew up in Germany, a philosophy student who aspired to be a philosophy professor. However, his "radical" political views prevented him from pursuing this career, and so he became a political journalist. But his political views continued to cause him problems. In his first position as editor of the *Rhineland Gazette*, he launched a campaign against Christian religion and the Christian state, which resulted in the state censor closing the newspaper down. This same pattern was repeated in subsequent journalistic positions, and he was forced to move throughout Europe as his publications were banned by one government after another. He ultimately settled in London in 1849, where he devoted the rest of his life to writing books and articles on the topics of philosophy, history, politics, and economics that would come to have such an extraordinary impact on the world. Marx fervently believed that ideas should be alive, with real-world consequences, a view captured in his statement that "the philosophers have only *interpreted* the world, in various ways; the point is to *change* it." Marx believed that this change is best accomplished through social and political action. On a personal level, the fact that two of his children died at least in part as the result of poverty and disease doubtless helped fuel his passionate defense of his views.

Marx was drawn to the ideas of **Georg Hegel** (1770–1831), who believed that history unfolds according to certain laws, following a logic that Hegel described as *dialectical.* The dialectical development of historical events means that a current state of affairs (the *thesis*) inevitably creates its opposite (the *antithesis*), which finds ultimate resolution in a state of affairs (the *synthesis*), that both includes and transcends both of these elements. Marx believed that we can see this dialectical movement of history at work in the class struggles that have characterized every historical period. At the time he was writing, he considered the class struggle to be between the *bourgeoisie* and the *proletariat.* The bourgeoisie are those people in control of economic forces: the owners of industrial production (businesses and factories) and the employers of people who work for wages. The proletariat are the wage-earning workers, who typically own no property and who are at the mercy of the owners and employers.

In terms of the dialectic of history, the bourgeoisie represent the *thesis* element, whereas the large angry, disillusioned, and exploited class of workers represent the *antithesis.* Marx believed that it was only a matter of time before the downtrodden proletariat would rise up in revolt against their bourgeoisie exploiters, creating a new economic and social order—the *synthesis*—in which the workers would control the means of production and share equally in the *capital* (goods, services, money) that their efforts produce. This new synthesis would find its social/political form in communism. For Marx, this dialectical process is not speculative: it will necessarily occur because the laws of history are "tendencies working with iron necessity towards inevitable results."

Marx was convinced that the economic structure (in terms of the means of production) of a society is the dominant force that shapes the community's social relationships, political processes, and spiritual values. He states: "The ideas of the ruling class are in every epoch the ruling ideas: The class which has the means of production at its disposal, has control at the same time over the means of mental production." Marx's most famous articulation of his views is to be found in the *Manifesto of the Communist Party*, which he co-authored with **Friedrich Engels** in 1848. The *Manifesto* is a passionate and influential document that merits close scrutiny.

Georg Hegel (1770–1831) German Philosopher. Most influential philosopher of the 19th Century. Wrote extensively on subjects from logic to politics. His dialectical view of the way in which history progresses influenced Marx and many other philosophers that followed him.

FRIEDRICH ENGELS
(1820–1895)
Social Philosopher. Major collaborator with Karl Marx. Co-wrote *The Manifesto of the Communist Party* (1848) with Marx and helped create the foundation of what is now called Marxism.

Marx and Engels,
Manifesto of the Communist Party

A spectre is haunting Europe—the spectre of communism. All the powers of old Europe have entered into a holy alliance to exorcise this spectre: Pope and Tsar, Metternich and Guizot, French Radicals and German police-spies. . . .

Two things result from this fact:

I. Communism is already acknowledged by all European powers to be itself a power.

II. It is high time that Communists should openly, in the face of the whole world, publish their views, their aims, their tendencies, and meet this nursery tale of the spectre of communism with a manifesto of the party itself.

To this end, Communists of various nationalities have assembled in London and sketched the following manifesto, to be published in the English, French, German, Italian, Flemish and Danish languages.

According to Marx and Engels, economic history is best understood as an ongoing struggle between the oppressors and the oppressed—"freeman and slave, patrician and plebeian, lord and serf, guild-master and journeyman"—a fight which inevitably ends "either in a revolutionary reconstitution of society at large, or in the common ruin of the contending classes."

I—BOURGEOIS AND PROLETARIANS

(By *bourgeoisie* is meant the class of modern capitalists, owners of the means of social production and employers of wage labor. By *proletariat*, the class of modern wage laborers who, having no means of production of their own, are reduced to selling their labor power in order to live.) Note by Engels—1888 English edition

The history of all hitherto existing society is the history of class struggles.

Freeman and slave, patrician and plebeian, lord and serf, guild-master and journeyman, in a word, oppressor and oppressed, stood in constant opposition to one another, carried on an uninterrupted, now hidden, now open fight, a fight that each time ended, either in a revolutionary reconstitution of society at large, or in the common ruin of the contending classes.

In the earlier epochs of history, we find almost everywhere a complicated arrangement of society into various orders, a manifold gradation of social rank. In ancient Rome we have patricians, knights, plebeians, slaves; in the Middle Ages, feudal lords, vassals, guild-masters, journeymen, apprentices, serfs; in almost all of these classes, again, subordinate gradations.

The modern bourgeois society that has sprouted from the ruins of feudal society has not done away with class antagonisms. It has but established new classes, new conditions of oppression, new forms of struggle in place of the old ones.

Our epoch, the epoch of the bourgeoisie, possesses, however, this distinct feature: it has simplified class antagonisms. Society as a whole is more and more splitting up into two great hostile camps, into two great classes directly facing each other—bourgeoisie and proletariat.

From the serfs of the Middle Ages sprang the chartered burghers of the earliest towns. From these burgesses the first elements of the bourgeoisie were developed.

The discovery of America, the rounding of the Cape, opened up fresh ground for the rising bourgeoisie. The East-Indian and Chinese markets, the colonisation of America, trade with the colonies, the increase in the means of exchange and in commodities generally, gave to commerce, to navigation, to industry, an impulse never before known, and thereby, to the revolutionary element in the tottering feudal society, a rapid development.

The feudal system of industry, in which industrial production was monopolized by closed guilds, now no longer suffices for the growing wants of the new markets. The manufacturing system took its place. The guild-masters were pushed aside by the manufacturing middle class; division of labor between the different corporate guilds vanished in the face of division of labor in each single workshop.

Meantime, the markets kept ever growing, the demand ever rising. Even manufacturers no longer sufficed. Thereupon, steam and machinery revolutionized industrial production. The place of manufacture was taken by the giant, MODERN INDUSTRY; the place of the industrial middle class by industrial millionaires, the leaders of the whole industrial armies, the modern bourgeois.

Modern industry has established the world market, for which the discovery of America paved the way. This market has given an immense development to commerce, to navigation, to communication by land. This development has, in turn, reacted on the extension of industry; and in proportion as industry, commerce, navigation, railways extended, in the same proportion the bourgeoisie developed, increased its capital, and pushed into the background every class handed down from the Middle Ages.

We see, therefore, how the modern bourgeoisie is itself the product of a long course of development, of a series of revolutions in the modes of production and of exchange. . . .

Marx and Engels begin their *Manifesto*—a word that means a proclamation or declaration of principles—by first describing the social context. This document is being issued by a gathering of Communists who have assembled in London for the express purpose of stating their beliefs and intentions, mobilizing the proletariat of all nations, and warning all governments that a social and economic revolution is coming. History is best understood, they argue, as a sequence of class struggles between the oppressors and the oppressed, a dynamic process that in all cases results either in a "revolutionary reconstitution" of society or the "common ruin" of all parties. The latest incarnation of this class struggle is between the bourgeoisie and the proletariat, the two social groups that have been created and shaped by the evolution of modern industry. The preceding era—the Middle Ages—was a feudal society in which the hierarchy of classes included feudal lords, vassals, guild-masters, journeymen, apprentices, and serfs. The development of improved manufacturing methods, combined with the discovery of new trade markets in America and Asia, fueled an industrial explosion that spelled doom for the previous feudal society. It also created the latest version of class warfare between the owners of these manufacturing and trade industries—the *bourgeoisie*—and the "industrial armies" that they employ—the workers or *proletariat*. In the judgment of the Communists, this economic revolution wreaked havoc on the social relationships, political processes, and spiritual values of nations that it touched and contaminated.

The bourgeoisie, wherever it has got the upper hand, has put an end to all feudal, patriarchal, idyllic relations. It has pitilessly torn asunder the motley feudal ties that bound man to his "natural superiors," and has left no other nexus between people than naked self-interest, than callous "cash payment." It has drowned out the most heavenly ecstacies of religious fervor, of chivalrous enthusiasm, of philistine sentimentalism, in the icy water of egotistical calculation. It has resolved personal worth into exchange value, and in place of the numberless indefeasible chartered freedoms, has set up that single, unconscionable freedom—Free Trade. In one word, for exploitation, veiled by religious and political illusions, it has substituted naked, shameless, direct, brutal exploitation.

The bourgeoisie has stripped of its halo every occupation hitherto honored and looked up to with reverent awe. It has converted the physician, the lawyer, the priest, the poet, the man of science, into its paid wage laborers.

The bourgeoisie has torn away from the family its sentimental veil, and has reduced the family relation into a mere money relation. . . .

Marx and Engels,
Manifesto of the Communist Party

The capitalist economic revolution transformed forever the Middle Ages and the religious-dominated feudal society that existed for nine hundred years (C.E. 600–C.E. 1500) before the Renaissance took root. And while this economic revolution created new possibilities in terms of economic production and international trade, it also destroyed the social fabric and value system that defined the Middle Ages. For Marx and Engels, this is the dialectic of history in action, an inevitable progression in which every social change has both positive and negative aspects to it. So while feudal society had positive social dimensions, it was seriously flawed politically and economically. And in the same way, though capitalism embodies certain progressive aspects, it is also deeply flawed in ways that insure its own destruction and inevitable replacement by a communistic system. Thus it is the economic modes of production that shape and control the social relationships, political processes, and spiritual values of a society.

The bourgeoisie cannot exist without constantly revolutionizing the instruments of production, and thereby the relations of production, and with them the whole relations of society. Conservation of the old modes of production in unaltered form, was, on the

Marx and Engels,
Manifesto of the Communist Party

contrary, the first condition of existence for all earlier industrial classes. Constant revolutionizing of production, uninterrupted disturbance of all social conditions, everlasting uncertainty and agitation distinguish the bourgeois epoch from all earlier ones. All fixed, fast frozen relations, with their train of ancient and venerable prejudices and opinions, are swept away, all new-formed ones become antiquated before they can ossify. All that is solid melts into air, all that is holy is profaned, and man is at last compelled to face with sober senses his real condition of life and his relations with his kind.

The need of a constantly expanding market for its products chases the bourgeoisie over the entire surface of the globe. It must nestle everywhere, settle everywhere, establish connections everywhere.

The bourgeoisie has, through its exploitation of the world market, given a cosmopolitan character to production and consumption in every country. To the great chagrin of reactionaries, it has drawn from under the feet of industry the national ground on which it stood. All old-established national industries have been destroyed or are daily being destroyed. They are dislodged by new industries, whose introduction becomes a life and death question for all civilized nations, by industries that no longer work up indigenous raw material, but raw material drawn from the remotest zones; industries whose products are consumed, not only at home, but in every quarter of the globe. In place of the old wants, satisfied by the production of the country, we find new wants, requiring for their satisfaction the products of distant lands and climes. In place of the old local and national seclusion and self-sufficiency, we have intercourse in every direction, universal inter-dependence of nations. And as in material, so also in intellectual production. The intellectual creations of individual nations become common property. National one-sidedness and narrow-mindedness become more and more impossible, and from the numerous national and local literatures, there arises a world literature.

The bourgeoisie, by the rapid improvement of all instruments of production, by the immensely facilitated means of communication, draws all, even the most barbarian, nations into civilization. The cheap prices of commodities are the heavy artillery with which it forces the barbarians' intensely obstinate hatred of foreigners to capitulate. It compels all nations, on pain of extinction, to adopt the bourgeois mode of production; it compels them to introduce what it calls civilization into their midst, i.e., to become bourgeois themselves. In one word, it creates a world after its own image.

The bourgeoisie has subjected the country to the rule of the towns. It has created enormous cities, has greatly increased the urban population as compared with the rural, and has thus rescued a considerable part of the population from the idiocy of rural life. Just as it has made the country dependent on the towns, so it has made barbarian and semi-barbarian countries dependent on the civilized ones, nations of peasants on nations of bourgeois, the East on the West.

The bourgeoisie keeps more and more doing away with the scattered state of the population, of the means of production, and of property. It has agglomerated population, centralized the means of production, and has concentrated property in a few hands. The necessary consequence of this was political centralization. Independent, or but loosely connected provinces, with separate interests, laws, governments, and systems of taxation, became lumped together into one nation, with one government, one code of laws, one national class interest, one frontier, and one customs tariff.

The bourgeoisie, during its rule of scarce one hundred years, has created more massive and more colossal productive forces than have all preceding generations together. Subjection of nature's forces to man, machinery, application of chemistry to industry and agriculture, steam navigation, railways, electric telegraphs, clearing of whole continents for cultivation, canalization of rivers, whole populations conjured out of the ground—what earlier century had even a presentiment that such productive forces slumbered in the lap of social labor?

We see then: the means of production and of exchange, on whose foundation the bourgeoisie built itself up, were generated in feudal society. At a certain stage in the development of these means of production and of exchange, the conditions under which feudal society produced and exchanged, the feudal organization of agriculture and manufacturing industry, in one word, the feudal relations of property became no longer compatible with the already developed productive forces; they became so many fetters. They had to be burst asunder; they were burst asunder.

According to Karl Marx, "The bourgeoisis . . . created more massive and more colossal productive forces than have all preceding generations together," signaling the end of feudal society and the beginning of the progressive exploitation of the working class. Do you agree with his analysis?

Into their place stepped free competition, accompanied by a social and political constitution adapted in it, and the economic and political sway of the bourgeois class.

For Marx and Engels, the evolution of a feudal society to one based on capitalism, free competition, and free trade is just one more step in the necessary evolution of human history, having profound repercussions. Although they do not explicitly mention the relationship of free trade and capitalism to Renaissance values and intellectual freedom, they do cite the following progressive advancements of capitalism:

- Capitalism has encouraged the invention of consistently superior modes of production (as well as the invention of new products), rather than staying with the "conservation of the old modes of production in unaltered form."
- Capitalism has encouraged the creation of new forms of thinking, replacing the "ancient and venerable prejudices and opinions" of feudal society.
- Capitalism and free trade have encouraged globalization and world literature, a "universal inter-dependence of nations," replacing "national seclusion and self-sufficiency," as well as "national one-sidedness and narrow-mindedness."
- Capitalism has created enormous cities that "rescued a considerable part of the population from the idiocy of rural life."
- Capitalism has "centralized the means of production, and has concentrated property in a few hands," which has resulted in political centralization, replacing a decentralized political structure.
- Capitalism, in the short span of one hundred years, has created "massive" and "colossal" productive forces in the areas of machinery, improved methods of farming, steam navigation, railways, and electric telegraphs.

Thus capitalism, free trade, and free competition remade the world in a very short span of time, creating a new society and culture, controlled economically and politically by the human instruments of capitalism, the bourgeois. The next stage in the evolution of capitalism and its bourgeoisie creators reveals that the seeds for their self-destruction have already been sown—by the same elements that have contributed to their rapid growth and marketplace hegemony.

A similar movement is going on before our own eyes. Modern bourgeois society, with its relations of production, of exchange and of property, a society that has conjured up such gigantic means of production and of exchange, is like the sorcerer who is no longer able to control the powers of the nether world whom he has called up by his spells. For many a decade past, the history of industry and commerce is but the history of the revolt of modern productive forces against modern conditions of production, against the property relations that are the conditions for the existence of the bourgeois and of its rule. It is enough to mention the commercial crises that, by their periodical return, put the existence of the entire bourgeois society on its trial, each time more threateningly. In these crises, a great part not only of the existing products, but also of the previously created productive forces, are periodically destroyed. In these crises, there breaks out an epidemic that, in all earlier epochs, would have seemed an absurdity—the epidemic of overproduction. Society suddenly finds itself put back into a state of momentary barbarism; it appears as if a famine, a universal war of devastation, had cut off the supply of every means of subsistence; industry and commerce seem to be destroyed. And why? Because there is too much civilization, too much means of subsistence, too much industry, too much commerce. The productive forces at the disposal of society no longer tend to further the development of the conditions of bourgeois property; on the contrary, they have become too powerful for these conditions, by which they are fettered, and so soon as they overcome these fetters, they bring disorder into the whole of bourgeois society, endanger the existence of bourgeois property. The conditions of bourgeois society are too narrow to comprise the wealth created by them. And how does the bourgeoisie get over these crises? On the one hand, by enforced destruction of a mass of productive

Marx and Engels,
Manifesto of the Communist Party

Proletariat The class of people who, lacking resources and the means of production, sell their labor.

forces; on the other, by the conquest of new markets, and by the more thorough exploitation of the old ones. That is to say, by paving the way for more extensive and more destructive crises, and by diminishing the means whereby crises are prevented.

The weapons with which the bourgeoisie felled feudalism to the ground are now turned against the bourgeoisie itself.

Like Dr. Frankenstein, Marx and Engels believed that the bourgeoisie have created a monster that they can no longer control, as the forces of capitalism run amok. Free competition, free trade, and the limitless greed of the capitalists creates "the epidemic of over-production." They have created a production machine that is too efficient, the consequence of "too much civilization, too much means of subsistence, too much industry, too much commerce." There simply are not enough buyers for the products. What to do? There are two answers: lay off or fire the workers until production matches demand, or create new markets through aggressive sales and trade initiatives. Capitalism has become an economic system out of control with an appetite for growth that is so rapacious that it is ultimately forced to feed on itself. Capitalism's failure to control the growth of its modes of production has the unintended effect of creating a new class of citizens who will ultimately spell capitalism's downfall—the army of the **proletariat**.

Marx and Engels,
Manifesto of the Communist Party

But not only has the bourgeoisie forged the weapons that bring death to itself; it has also called into existence the men who are to wield those weapons—the modern working class—the proletarians.

In proportion as the bourgeoisie, i.e., capital, is developed, in the same proportion is the proletariat, the modern working class, developed—a class of laborers, who live only so long as they find work, and who find work only so long as their labor increases capital. These laborers, who must sell themselves piecemeal, are a commodity, like every other article of commerce, and are consequently exposed to all the vicissitudes of competition, to all the fluctuations of the market.

Owing to the extensive use of machinery, and to the division of labor, the work of the proletarians has lost all individual character, and, consequently, all charm for the workman. He becomes an appendage of the machine, and it is only the most simple, most monotonous, and most easily acquired knack, that is required of him. Hence, the cost of production of a workman is restricted, almost entirely, to the means of subsistence that he requires for maintenance, and for the propagation of his race. But the price of a commodity, and therefore also of labor, is equal to its cost of production. In proportion, therefore, as the repulsiveness of the work increases, the wage decreases. What is more, in proportion as the use of machinery and division of labor increases, in the same proportion the burden of toil also increases, whether by prolongation of the working hours, by the increase of the work exacted in a given time, or by increased speed of machinery, etc.

Modern Industry has converted the little workshop of the patriarchal master into the great factory of the industrial capitalist. Masses of laborers, crowded into the factory, are organized like soldiers. As privates of the industrial army, they are placed under the command of a perfect hierarchy of officers and sergeants. Not only are they slaves of the bourgeois class, and of the bourgeois state; they are daily and hourly enslaved by the machine, by the overlooker, and, above all, in the individual bourgeois manufacturer himself. The more openly this despotism proclaims gain to be its end and aim, the more petty, the more hateful and the more embittering it is.

The less the skill and exertion of strength implied in manual labor, in other words, the more modern industry becomes developed, the more is the labor of men superseded by that of women.

Marx and Engels believed that the industrial revolution, in addition to causing the migration of people from rural locations to cities, also forced the working class to "sell themselves piecemeal . . . a commodity, like every other article of commerce." This left them—and their children—vulnerable to terrible exploitation at the hands of the owners of capital, the bourgeoisie capitalists.

Differences of age and sex have no longer any distinctive social validity for the working class. All are instruments of labor, more or less expensive to use, according to their age and sex.

No sooner is the exploitation of the laborer by the manufacturer, so far at an end, that he receives his wages in cash, than he is set upon by the other portion of the bourgeoisie, the landlord, the shopkeeper, the pawnbroker, etc.

The lower strata of the middle class—the small tradespeople, shopkeepers, and retired tradesmen generally, the handicraftsmen and peasants—all these sink gradually into the proletariat, partly because their diminutive capital does not suffice for the scale on which Modern Industry is carried on, and is swamped in the competition with the large capitalists, partly because their specialized skill is rendered worthless by new methods of production. Thus, the proletariat is recruited from all classes of the population.

In this exploitative economic system, workers are alienated from the work they are doing, serving as "privates of the industrial army," functioning as "slaves of the bourgeois state" who "are daily and hourly enslaved by the machine."

Capitalism, with its industrialized means of production and voracious appetite for growth, needs an army of workers to run its factories. But these workers are not valued as human beings: they are merely seen as "appendages of the machine." These workers, the proletariat, "must sell themselves piecemeal, are a commodity, like every other article of commerce, and are consequently exposed to all the vicissitudes of competition, to all the fluctuations of the market." And unlike previous eras, when individuals developed expertise in various areas and took pride in the products that they produced, the division of labor has reduced their activities to simple, mindless tasks that have no personal meaning and provide no satisfaction. Instead of taking pride in the crops they have grown, the clothes they have fashioned, the furniture they have built, the bread they have baked, they are now reduced to "repulsive" repetitive tasks in crowded, noisy factories, working excessive hours for low wages. In Marx's terms, they have become profoundly *alienated* from the product of their labor, an alienation that seeps into every area of their lives, as we will see later in the chapter.

Thus the proletariat become objects to be manipulated by the bourgeoisie, at the mercy of market forces, performing tasks that rob them of their sense of human value and self-esteem. To compound their difficulties, the factory tasks have become so unskilled that the work of men is "superseded by that of women," with the consequence that "differences of age and sex have no longer any distinctive social validity for the working class. All are instruments of labor, more or less expensive to use, according to their age and sex." And their exploitation continues once they have been paid, as the other members of the bourgeoisie—the landlords, shopkeepers, pawnbrokers—seek to take advantage of their powerless state.

But although the proletariat are powerless as individuals, they have—potentially—immense power as an organized group. Marx and Engels next describe their idealized vision of the future, as the downtrodden proletariat rise up as a powerful army and take their vengeance on their despised tormenters, the bourgeoisie.

The proletariat goes through various stages of development. With its birth begins its struggle with the bourgeoisie. At first, the contest is carried on by individual laborers, then by the work of people of a factory, then by the operative of one trade, in one locality, against the individual bourgeois who directly exploits them. They direct their attacks not against the bourgeois condition of production, but against the instruments of production themselves; they destroy imported wares that compete with their labor, they smash to pieces machinery, they set factories ablaze, they seek to restore by force the vanished status of the workman of the Middle Ages.

Marx and Engels,
Manifesto of the Communist Party

Marx believed that exploited workers would band together to form ever widening and more powerful unions, culminating in a proletarian revolt. To what extent was his prediction accurate and inaccurate?

At this stage, the laborers still form an incoherent mass scattered over the whole country, and broken up by their mutual competition. If anywhere they unite to form more compact bodies, this is not yet the consequence of their own active union, but of the union of the bourgeoisie, which class, in order to attain its own political ends, is compelled to set the whole proletariat in motion, and is moreover yet, for a time, able to do so. At this stage, therefore, the proletarians do not fight their enemies, but the enemies of their enemies, the remnants of absolute monarchy, the landowners, the non-industrial bourgeois, the petty bourgeois. Thus, the whole historical movement is concentrated in the hands of the bourgeoisie; every victory so obtained is a victory for the bourgeoisie.

But with the development of industry, the proletariat not only increases in number; it becomes concentrated in greater masses, its strength grows, and it feels that strength more. The various interests and conditions of life within the ranks of the proletariat are more and more equalized, in proportion as machinery obliterates all distinctions of labor, and nearly everywhere reduces wages to the same low level. The growing competition among the bourgeois, and the resulting commercial crises, make the wages of the workers ever more fluctuating. The increasing improvement of machinery, ever more rapidly developing, makes their livelihood more and more precarious; the collisions between individual workmen and individual bourgeois take more and more the character of collisions between two classes. Thereupon, the workers begin to form combinations (trade unions) against the bourgeois; they club together in order to keep up the rate of wages; they found permanent associations in order to make provision beforehand for these occasional revolts. Here and there, the contest breaks out into riots.

Now and then the workers are victorious, but only for a time. The real fruit of their battles lie not in the immediate result, but in the ever expanding union of the workers. This union is helped on by the improved means of communication that are created by Modern Industry, and that place the workers of different localities in contact with one another. It was just this contact that was needed to centralize the numerous local struggles, all of the same character, into one national struggle between classes. But every class struggle is a political struggle. And that union, to attain which the burghers of the Middle Ages, with their miserable highways, required centuries, the modern proletarians, thanks to railways, achieve in a few years.

This organization of the proletarians into a class, and, consequently, into a political party, is continually being upset again by the competition between the workers themselves. But it ever rises up again, stronger, firmer, mightier. It compels legislative recognition of particular interests of the workers, by taking advantage of the divisions among the bourgeoisie itself. . . .

Altogether, collisions between the classes of the old society further in many ways the course of development of the proletariat. The bourgeoisie finds itself involved in a constant battle. At first with the aristocracy; later on, with those portions of the bourgeoisie itself, whose interests have become antagonistic to the progress of industry; at all times with the bourgeoisie of foreign countries. In all these battles, it sees itself compelled to appeal to the proletariat, to ask for help, and thus to drag it into the political arena. The bourgeoisie itself, therefore, supplies the proletariat with its own elements of political and general education, in other words, it furnishes the proletariat with weapons for fighting the bourgeoisie.

Further, as we have already seen, entire sections of the ruling class are, by the advance of industry, precipitated into the proletariat, or are at least threatened in their conditions of existence. These also supply the proletariat with fresh elements of enlightenment and progress.

Finally, in times when the class struggle nears the decisive hour, the progress of dissolution going on within the ruling class, in fact within the whole range of old society, assumes such a violent, glaring character, that a small section of the ruling class cuts itself adrift, and joins the revolutionary class, the class that holds the future in its hands. Just as, therefore, at an earlier period, a section of the nobility went over to the bourgeoisie, so now a portion of the bourgeoisie goes over to the proletariat, and in particular, a portion of the bourgeois ideologists, who have raised themselves to the level of comprehending theoretically the historical movement as a whole.

Of all the classes that stand face to face with the bourgeoisie today, the proletariat alone is a genuinely revolutionary class. The other classes decay and finally disappear in the face of Modern Industry; the proletariat is its special and essential product.

The lower middle class, the small manufacturer, the shopkeeper, the artisan, the peasant, all these fight against the bourgeoisie, to save from extinction their existence as fractions of the middle class. They are therefore not revolutionary, but conservative. Nay, more, they are reactionary, for they try to roll back the wheel of history. If, by chance, they are revolutionary, they are only so in view of their impending transfer into the proletariat; they thus defend not their present, but their future interests; they desert their own standpoint to place themselves at that of the proletariat.

The "dangerous class," the social scum, that passively rotting mass thrown off by the lowest layers of the old society, may, here and there, be swept into the movement by a proletarian revolution; its conditions of life, however, prepare it far more for the part of a bribed tool of reactionary intrigue.

Karl Marx

In the condition of the proletariat, those of old society at large are already virtually swamped. The proletarian is without property; his relation to his wife and children has no longer anything in common with the bourgeois family relations; modern industry labor, modern subjection to capital, the same in England as in France, in America as in Germany, has stripped him of every trace of national character. Law, morality, religion, are to him so many bourgeois prejudices, behind which lurk in ambush just as many bourgeois interests.

All the preceding classes that got the upper hand sought to fortify their already acquired status by subjecting society at large to their conditions of appropriation. The proletarians cannot become masters of the productive forces of society, except by abolishing their own previous mode of appropriation, and thereby also every other previous mode of appropriation. They have nothing of their own to secure and to fortify; their mission is to destroy all previous securities for, and insurances of, individual property.

All previous historical movements were movements of minorities, or in the interest of minorities. The proletarian movement is the self-conscious, independent movement of the immense majority, in the interest of the immense majority. The proletariat, the lowest stratum of our present society, cannot stir, cannot raise itself up, without the whole superincumbent strata of official society being sprung into the air.

Though not in substance, yet in form, the struggle of the proletariat with the bourgeoisie is at first a national struggle. The proletariat of each country must, of course, first of all settle matters with its own bourgeoisie.

In depicting the most general phases of the development of the proletariat, we traced the more or less veiled civil war, raging within existing society, up to the point where that war breaks out into open revolution, and where the violent overthrow of the bourgeoisie lays the foundation for the sway of the proletariat.

Hitherto, every form of society has been based, as we have already seen, on the antagonism of oppressing and oppressed classes. But in order to oppress a class, certain conditions must be assured to it under which it can, at least, continue its slavish existence. The serf, in the period of serfdom, raised himself to membership in the commune, just as the petty bourgeois, under the yoke of the feudal absolutism, managed to develop into a bourgeois. The modern laborer, on the contrary, instead of rising with the process of industry, sinks deeper and deeper below the conditions of existence of his own class. He becomes a pauper, and pauperism develops more rapidly than population and wealth. And here it becomes evident that the bourgeoisie is unfit any longer to be the ruling class in society, and to impose its conditions of existence upon society as an overriding law. It is unfit to rule because it is incompetent to assure an existence to its slave within his slavery, because it cannot help letting him sink into such a state, that it has to feed him, instead of being fed by him. Society can no longer live under this bourgeoisie, in other words, its existence is no longer compatible with society.

The essential conditions for the existence and for the sway of the bourgeois class is the formation and augmentation of capital; the condition for capital is wage labor. Wage labor rests exclusively on competition between the laborers. The advance of industry, whose involuntary promoter is the bourgeoisie, replaces the isolation of the laborers, due to competition, by the revolutionary combination, due to association. The development of Modern Industry, therefore, cuts from under its feet the very foundation on

Marx, Karl, *The Communist Manifesto*

which the bourgeoisie produces and appropriates products. What the bourgeoisie therefore produces, above all, are its own grave-diggers. Its fall and the victory of the proletariat are equally inevitable. ▪

Marx and Engels were certain that the dialectical forces of history would cause the ultimate overthrow of capitalism and the bourgeoisie by the proletariat masses, resulting in a new economic, social, political era. This conclusion was seen to be the end result of an inevitable process in which the seeds for the destruction of capitalism were sown at its creation. "What the bourgeoisie therefore produces, above all, are its own grave-diggers. Its fall and the victory of the proletariat are equally inevitable."

Marx and Engels believed that this ultimate conclusion would be the end-product of a sequence of well-defined developmental stages. In the initial stages of capitalism, the proletariat become, as we have noted, exploited and alienated extensions of the bourgeoisie modes of production. As the proletariat grow in numbers, their rage grows as well. They direct this rage not toward the bourgeoisie, but against the instruments of production: "they destroy imported wares that compete with their labor, they smash to pieces machinery, they set factories ablaze, they seek to restore by force the vanished status of the workman of the Middle Ages."

Of course, we know now that such an attack against the instruments of production rarely occurred. However, Marx and Engels were right on one count: in difficult economic times workers often direct their anger toward imported products that threaten their economic well-being, an isolationist tendency that continues to this day. It is typically the "blue-collar" workers who are most vocal in their support of trade barriers to protect their livelihoods.

However, Marx and Engels's vision of the future was more accurate with their vision of the next developmental stage, which involves the potent coalescence of several factors:

- The proletariat increase in number, become concentrated in greater masses, and grow in strength.
- The work of the proletariat becomes more mindless, their wages lower, and their economic stability less secure, reflecting the fluctuations of the commercial crises created by the bourgeoisie.
- Sensing their strength, the proletariat organize into unions and initiate direct confrontations with the bourgeoisie, erupting in occasional riots.
- Improved communication and transportation systems enable the proletariat to organize themselves in ever widening circles of membership.

Marx and Engels were confident that the dialectical forces of history would cause the ultimate overthrow of capitalism and triumph by the workers, resulting in a new economic, social, and political era.

Many of these predictions have in fact occurred in many parts of the world since the time of Marx and Engels. However, in only a few instances have these factors resulted in the "open revolution" and "violent overthrow" of the bourgeoisie and their capitalistic system occurred. Why not?

At least one key assumption made by Marx and Engels appears, in retrospect, to be fatally flawed. They were convinced that the schism between the bourgeoisie and the proletariat would become greater, increasing the distance between the oppressors and the oppressed in every way: economically, socially, and politically. They were convinced that "The modern laborer . . . instead of rising with the process of industry, sinks deeper and deeper below the condition of existence of his own class. He becomes a pauper, and pauperism develops more rapidly than population and wealth." Instead of this scenario occurring, the reverse scenario has occurred in most industrialized countries. Rather than eroding, the economic and social status of the proletariat has often risen, powered by the strength of their unions and the democratic political systems within which they exist. In addition, as we noted in our discussion of Rawls, liberal economies have also intervened to improve the lives of the workers and more disadvantaged members of society through the creation of public education, economic opportunities, avenues of social advancement, the protection of workers through government legislation, and the creation of welfare safety nets to insure a minimum standard of living and health care.

Most disturbingly, in those countries in which genuine revolutions took place—such as Russia, China, North Korea, and Cuba—the idealized rule of the proletariat predicted by Marx and Engels did not occur. Rather than creating classless societies based on the communal rule of the proletariat, the aristocratic and bourgeoisie ruling classes were instead replaced by tyrants and dictators who created violent and repressive regimes that were often many times worse than the ones they overthrew.

THINK PHILOSOPHICALLY 10.9
Analyzing Karl Marx and Friedrich Engels

- Provide brief definitions for liberalism and socialism. Then identify two examples of each kind of society and explain the reasons that you selected them.

- Marx and Engels contend that the economic structure of a society determines its social, political, and spiritual dimensions as well. "The class which has the means of production at its disposal, has control at the same time over the means of mental production." Identify a society with which you are familiar and explain whether you believe that the structure of the society supports and contradicts this thesis.

- Identify the main arguments that Marx and Engels advance against an economic system based on capitalism, free competition, and free trade. Then explain whether you agree or disagree with their point of view and the reasons why.

- Why were Marx and Engels convinced that capitalism would be overthrown by a revolution of the proletariat? Explain the reasons you believe that in general these revolutions never took place. Do you think such revolutions might occur in the future? Why or why not?

  - What constitutes the alienation of labor? First, that the work is *external* to the worker, that it is not part of his nature; and that, consequently, he does not fulfill himself in his work but denies himself, has a feeling of misery rather than well-being, does not develop freely his mental and physical energies but is physically exhausted and mentally debased.

  Marx and Engels believe that alienation from the process and products of one's labor is an inescapable fact of capitalistic societies. This is true in working-class professions as well as so-called white-collar careers in which people work in little cubicles with computerized work stations. Do you think that the majority of people in the United States are alienated from their labor? Why or why not? Do you think that people in socialist or communist societies are less alienated?

- Marx and Engels also believe that alienation from one's labor necessarily leads to a personal, spiritual alienation. Evaluate this claim based on your experiences in contemporary society.

  All these consequences follow from the fact that the worker is related to the *product of his labor* as to an *alien* object. For it is clear on this presupposition that the more the worker expends himself in work the more powerful becomes the world of objects which he creates in face of himself, the poorer he becomes in his inner life, and the less he belongs to himself.

John Stuart Mill: *Justice Is What Promotes the General Welfare*

We first encountered the thinking of **John Stuart Mill** in chapter 6 when we explored the utilitarian perspective on ethics: we determine moral "rightness" or "goodness" by calculating which course of action will bring about the greatest happiness for the greatest number of people (and conversely, which course of action will result in the avoidance of unhappiness for the greatest number of people). Not surprisingly, Mill's views on social justice and liberty are based directly on his ethical theory. Justice on the social and political level is what best promotes the well-being and public interest of the greatest number of citizens. So, for example, does the principle of justice require that a society create a financial and medical "safety net" for its disadvantaged citizens? Mill believes that the answer can be determined with certainty by calculating whether such a policy will maximize social benefits for the majority of citizens, and minimize social harms. The core principle of social justice is, in Mill's terms, the principle of **social utility**.

Mill recognizes that viewing "justice" as being equivalent to "social utility"—that is, calculating the maximum social benefits—does not capture the intuitive conviction and moral passion that most people associate with justice. And so he embarks on a conceptual analysis of justice to demonstrate that the principle of social utility forms the central meaning of the term for most people.

Mill, *Utilitarianism* ■

Chapter 5: On the Connection Between Justice and Utility.

In all ages of speculation, one of the strongest obstacles to the reception of the doctrine that Utility or Happiness is the criterion of right and wrong, has been drawn from the idea of justice. The powerful sentiment, and apparently clear perception, which that word recalls with a rapidity and certainty resembling an instinct, have seemed to the majority of thinkers to point to an inherent quality in things; to show that the just must have an existence in Nature as something absolute, generically distinct from every variety of the Expedient, and, in idea, opposed to it, though (as is commonly acknowledged) never, in the long run, disjoined from it in fact. . . .

Our present object is to determine whether the reality, to which the feeling of justice corresponds, is one which needs any such special revelation; whether the justice or injustice of an action is a thing intrinsically peculiar, and distinct from all its other qualities, or only a combination of certain of those qualities, presented under a peculiar aspect. For the purpose of this inquiry it is practically important to consider whether the feeling itself, of justice and injustice, is *sui generis* like our sensations of colour and taste, or a derivative feeling, formed by a combination of others. And this it is the more essential to examine, as people are in general willing enough to allow, that objectively the dictates of justice coincide with a part of the field of General Expediency; but inasmuch as the subjective mental feeling of justice is different from that which commonly attaches to simple expediency, and, except in the extreme cases of the latter, is far more imperative in its demands, people find it difficult to see, in justice, only a particular kind or branch of general utility, and think that its superior binding force requires a totally different origin.

To his credit, Mill recognizes that for most people, the concept of justice has a uniquely imperative power. It is a concept so fundamental to our way of thinking that it is commonly thought to be a primal instinct. But Mill astutely points out that simply because there are primal emotions associated with the concept of justice is no guarantee that these emotional inclinations or "natural" feelings are enlightened or appropriate. In many cultures past and present, for example, it seemed

Social utility   The principle advanced by utilitarians that justice is produced by the form of government that creates the greatest social benefit for the greatest number of people.

self-evident to citizens that slavery, human sacrifice, or systematic oppression were an essential part of the natural order and so were "just." The problem is, Mill believes, that when beliefs are founded on strong subjective feelings, people tend to believe that they represent "a revelation of objective reality."

Emotions may be powerful, Mill is contending, but emotions often need the guiding light of higher reason to become fully enlightened. One of the major differences between humans and other animals is that we can apply our intellect to arriving at the most enlightened conclusions, whether or not our emotions or instincts are in accord. However, once our reasoning abilities elevate our understanding then our emotions and instincts often follow along behind. For example, once you fully understand the immorality of slavery on an intellectual level, you will likely come to *feel* that slavery is wrong and your instinctive reactions to related issues will probably get reshaped as well. (Mill, by the way, was a passionate abolitionist and supported the Union during the Civil War.)

Mill knows that the idea of calculating the maximum benefits to the general population is not a concept of justice that people are likely to become passionate about. But he wants to argue that if we apply our reasoning ability, this is precisely the conclusion that we will arrive at. But how can we test this idea? Mill proposes the following: let's examine the various common definitions of "justice" and "injustice" and attempt to determine if there is a core meaning—emotional or intellectual or both—that is common to the primary uses of the concept. If there is a common set of qualities that are different than Mill's principle of social utility, then he is willing to accept the conclusion, even though it has the consequence of undermining his entire approach to social justice. Is this likely to happen? A modicum of skepticism would not be misplaced in this instance!

Mill believed that we could define "social justice" by using the hedonistic calculus to calculate what policy brings "the greatest happiness to the greatest number of people." Using this approach, would slavery be considered "just" or "unjust"? Why?

Mill, *Utilitarianism*

To find the common attributes of a variety of objects, it is necessary to begin by surveying the objects themselves in the concrete. Let us therefore advert successively to the various modes of action, and arrangements of human affairs, which are classed, by universal or widely spread opinion, as Just or as Unjust. The things well known to excite the sentiments associated with those names are of a very multifarious character. I shall pass them rapidly in review, without studying any particular arrangement.

In the first place, it is mostly considered unjust to deprive any one of his personal liberty, his property, or any other thing which belongs to him by law. Here, therefore, is one instance of the application of the terms just and unjust in a perfectly definite sense, namely, that it is just to respect, unjust to violate, the legal rights of any one. But this judgment admits of several exceptions, arising from the other forms in which the notions of justice and injustice present themselves. For example, the person who suffers the deprivation may (as the phrase is) have forfeited the rights which he is so deprived of: a case to which we shall return presently. But also,

Secondly; the legal rights of which he is deprived, may be rights which ought not to have belonged to him; in other words, the law which confers on him these rights, may be a bad law. When it is so, or when (which is the same thing for our purpose) it is supposed to be so, opinions will differ as to the justice or injustice of infringing it. Some maintain that no law, however bad, ought to be disobeyed by an individual citizen; that his opposition to it, if shown at all, should only be shown in endeavouring to get it altered by competent authority. . . . Other persons, again, hold the directly contrary opinion, that any law, judged to be bad, may blamelessly be disobeyed, even though it be not judged to be unjust, but only inexpedient, while others would confine the licence of disobedience to the case of unjust laws. . . . Among these diversities of opinion, it seems to be universally admitted that there may be unjust laws, and that law, consequently, is not the ultimate criterion of justice, but may give to one person a benefit, or impose on another an evil, which justice condemns. . . .

Thirdly, it is universally considered just that each person should obtain that (whether good or evil) which he deserves; and unjust that he should obtain a good, or be made to undergo an evil, which he does not deserve. This is, perhaps, the clearest and most emphatic form in which the idea of justice is conceived by the general mind. As it involves the notion of desert, the question arises, what constitutes desert? Speaking in a general way, a person is understood to deserve good if he does right, evil if he does wrong; and in a more particular sense, to deserve good from those to whom he does or has done good, and evil from those to whom he does or has done evil. The precept of returning good for evil has never been regarded as a case of the fulfilment of justice, but as one in which the claims of justice are waived, in obedience to other considerations.

Fourthly, it is confessedly unjust to break faith with any one: to violate an engagement, either expressed or implied, or disappoint expectations raised by our conduct, at least if we have raised those expectations knowingly and voluntarily. Like the other obligations of justice already spoken of, this one is not regarded as absolute, but as capable of being overruled by a stronger obligation of justice on the other side; or by such conduct on the part of the person concerned as is deemed to absolve us from our obligation to him, and to constitute a forfeiture of the benefit which he has been led to expect.

Fifthly, it is, by universal admission, inconsistent with justice to be partial; to show favour or preference to one person over another, in matters to which favour and preference do not properly apply. Impartiality, however, does not seem to be regarded as a duty in itself, but rather as instrumental to some other duty; for it is admitted that favour and preference are not always censurable, and indeed the cases in which they are condemned are rather the exception than the rule. A person would be more likely to be blamed than applauded for giving his family or friends no superiority in good offices over strangers, when he could do so without violating any other duty; and no one thinks it unjust to seek one person in preference to another as a friend, connection, or companion. Impartiality where rights are concerned is of course obligatory, but this is involved in the more general obligation of giving to every one his right. . . .

Nearly allied to the idea of impartiality is that of equality; which often enters as a component part both into the conception of justice and into the practice of it, and, in the eyes of many persons, constitutes its essence. But in this, still more than in any other case, the notion of justice varies in different persons, and always conforms in its variations to their notion of utility. Each person maintains that equality is the dictate of justice, except where he thinks that expediency requires inequality. The justice of giving equal protection to the rights of all, is maintained by those who support the most outrageous inequality in the rights themselves. Even in slave countries it is theoretically admitted that the rights of the slave, such as they are, ought to be as sacred as those of the master; and that a tribunal which fails to enforce them with equal strictness is wanting in justice; while, at the same time, institutions which leave to the slave scarcely any rights to enforce, are not deemed unjust, because they are not deemed inexpedient. . . . Some Communists consider it unjust that the produce of the labour of the community should be shared on any other principle than that of exact equality; others think it just that those should receive most whose wants are greatest; while others hold that those who work harder, or who produce more, or whose services are more valuable to the community, may justly claim a larger quota in the division of the produce. And the sense of natural justice may be plausibly appealed to in behalf of every one of these opinions.

To recapitulate: the idea of justice supposes two things; a rule of conduct, and a sentiment which sanctions the rule. The first must be supposed common to all mankind, and intended for their good. The other (the sentiment) is a desire that punishment may be suffered by those who infringe the rule. There is involved, in addition, the conception of some definite person who suffers by the infringement; whose rights (to use the expression appropriated to the case) are violated by it. And the sentiment of justice appears to me to be, the animal desire to repel or retaliate a hurt or damage to oneself, or to those with whom one sympathises, widened so as to include all persons, by the human capacity of enlarged sympathy, and the human conception of intelligent self-interest. From the latter elements, the feeling derives its morality; from the former, its peculiar impressiveness, and energy of self-assertion.

Mill considers five different meanings of justice, and in each case attempts to demonstrate that they are meanings that do not stand on their own, but instead rely on the principle of social utility (or "expediency" as he calls it) in their actual application.

- *Justice means not depriving someone of his personal liberty, property, or possession which belongs to him by law.* But, Mill notes, there are laws that we consider to be "bad" or "unjust" in our society or other societies. For example, consider societies in which the law permits slavery to exist, an entire group of people are deprived of their liberty and everything else. Mill contends that to brand a law "unjust" we appeal to a principle like that of social utility: the law is unjust because it diminishes the general welfare of that society.

- *Justice means not disobeying any law in society, even if you disagree with it or consider it to be unjust.* This was Socrates' belief: he accepted the judgment against him even though he thought it to be unjust, because he believed that accepting the judgments of a society's legal system was the obligation of citizens who chose to live in a certain society. But there are legitimate perspectives on both sides of this issue: some contend that it is our moral obligation to contest unethical laws because they threaten the general welfare of the state. Others maintain that if laws are not consistently respected and obeyed, then the foundation of the state will be undermined, which will threaten the general welfare of the state. In both cases, the issue turns on the question of social utility.

- *Justice means each person receiving the good or evil that they deserve.* But what is the basis for such a definition? And how is one to determine when someone "deserves" good or evil? And what would be the appropriate amount of good or evil? To answer these questions, we need to appeal to an independent principle, such as the principle of social utility: for example, it is in the interest of the general welfare for there to be a proportionate awarding of rewards and punishments to members of society.

- *Justice means honoring agreements and telling the truth.* But what about examples in which telling the truth will result in great harm coming to innocent people? Or when keeping an agreement that was deceptive in nature will result in the financial ruin of many decent people? Mill notes that this principle can be overridden by other considerations, determined by principles like that of social utility.

- *Justice means acting impartially, not showing preference.* Obviously this is not a meaning that applies in our personal lives, Mill contends, because we are expected to show favor toward our family and friends, providing our action doesn't violate some other duty. And on a social level, such as the judicial system, impartiality is desirable directly because of the principle of social utility: a fair and impartial judicial system is essential in order to promote the general welfare.

- *Justice means treating others with equality.* This is a natural extension of the previous definition. But what exactly does this mean? After all, people are surely not equal to one another; nor are they always deserving of equal treatment. For example, suppose one person is hard-working and conscientious and another is lazy and unreliable: should they both receive equal compensation? Like the other definitions, justice as equality varies from person to person, situation to situation. Ultimately, it is by appealing to principles like that of social utility that people decide when to treat others equally and when to treat them unequally.

In sum, Mill's concept of justice involves two elements:

- A rule of conduct common to all humankind and intended for their good.
- The sentiment that punishment may be suffered by those who infringe upon the rule, because this is in the interest of both individuals and society as a whole.

Thus, according to Mill, both dimensions of justice necessarily involve the principle of social utility, a conclusion that insures the fact that Mill will not have to abandon his life-long utilitarian principles!

Mill then goes on to do a similar analysis for the concepts of "rights," which he defines as follows:

Mill, *Utilitarianism*

When we call anything a person's right, we mean that he has a valid claim on society to protect him in the possession of it, either by the force of law, or by that of education and opinion. If he has what we consider a sufficient claim, on whatever account, to have something guaranteed to him by society, we say that he has a right to it.

But what are the grounds for rights? What exactly is the justification for saying a person "has a valid claim"? According to Mill, it all comes back to the principle of social utility.

Mill, *Utilitarianism*

To have a right, then, is, I conceive, to have something which society ought to defend me in the possession of. If the objector goes on to ask, why it ought? I can give him no other reason than general utility. . . . The interest involved is that of security, to every one's feelings the most vital of all interests. All other earthly benefits are needed by one person, not needed by another; and many of them can, if necessary, be cheerfully foregone, or replaced by something else; but security no human being can possibly do without; on it we depend for all our immunity from evil, and for the whole value of all and every good, beyond the passing moment; since nothing but the gratification of the instant could be of any worth to us, if we could be deprived of anything the next instant by whoever was momentarily stronger than ourselves. . . . Our notion, therefore, of the claim we have on our fellow-creatures to join in making safe for us the very groundwork of our existence, gathers feelings around it so much more intense than those concerned in any of the more common cases of utility, that the difference in degree (as is often the case in psychology) becomes a real difference in kind. . . . The feelings concerned are so powerful, and we count so positively on finding a responsive feeling in others (all being alike interested), that "ought" and "should" grow into "must," and recognised indispensability becomes a moral necessity, analogous to physical, and often not inferior to it in binding force.

 Mill, John Stuart, *Utilitarianism*

The concept of rights in a community of people is essential in order to insure the stability and security of the social order. As Mill points out, lacking basic security, the entire fabric of social relationships may unravel and we risk creating a Hobbes-like state of nature, "a war of all against all." To live in harmony with others, people need the assurance that they have the right to be *protected from* threats such as attacks, robberies, discrimination, as well as the rights to *take action*—such as the right to free speech, education, or working in a career of your choice. And they need to have the confidence that their rights will be enforced by appropriate governmental authorities, thus insuring the general welfare. This need for personal and social security is so deep-seated that the concept of rights takes on powerful emotional associations, and they take on the character of absolute and universal values. But the fact is that the entire group of rights is derived from a profound need for security, which can only be addressed by promoting the general welfare (the principle of social utility).

But while Mill recognizes the need for citizens to feel secure from attack and exploitation, his real passion is for *individual liberty*. The ultimate purpose of government and its laws is to allow individuals to fully realize themselves through their free, unconstrained choices. Mill is convinced that the principle of social utility that forms the foundation of his philosophy—promoting the public welfare for the greatest number of citizens—is best achieved by maximizing the individual liberty of each member of the community. Mill argued this view in the highly influential essay *On Liberty*, to which we will next turn our attention.

Chapter 1: Introductory

Mill, *On Liberty*

The object of this Essay is to assert one very simple principle, as entitled to govern absolutely the dealings of society with the individual in the way of compulsion and control, whether the means used be physical force in the form of legal penalties, or the moral coercion of public opinion. That principle is, that the sole end for which mankind are warranted, individually or collectively, in interfering with the liberty of action of any of their number, is self-protection. That the only purpose for which power can be rightfully exercised over any member of a civilized community, against his will, is to prevent harm to others. His own good, either physical or moral, is not a sufficient warrant. He cannot rightfully be compelled to do or forbear because it will be better for him to do so, because it will make him happier, because, in the opinions of others, to do so would be wise, or even right. These are good reasons for remonstrating with him, or reasoning with him, or persuading him, or entreating him, but not for compelling him, or visiting him with any evil in case he do otherwise. To justify that, the conduct from which it is desired to deter him, must be calculated to produce evil to some one else. The only part of the conduct of any one, for which he is amenable to society, is that which concerns others. In the part which merely concerns himself, his independence is, of right, absolute. Over himself, over his own body and mind, the individual is sovereign.

It is, perhaps, hardly necessary to say that this doctrine is meant to apply only to human beings in the maturity of their faculties. We are not speaking of children, or of young persons below the age which the law may fix as that of manhood or womanhood. Those who are still in a state to require being taken care of by others, must be protected against their own actions as well as against external injury.

John Stuart Mill

"Over himself, over his own body and mind, the individual is sovereign." Mill could not have stated his core belief more clearly. *Whatever* an individual chooses to do is his absolute and irrevocable right, *provided it does not interfere or harm others.* Even if we are convinced that people are acting foolishly, self-destructively, or recklessly, we have no right to intervene and compel them to do otherwise—provided that they pose no threat to others. We may certainly attempt to persuade and reason with them, but beyond that we must respect their autonomy to freely choose. Although Mill's principle is clear and direct, it raises issues that are exceedingly profound and complex. For example, consider the potential implications for issues such as substance abusers, the mentally ill, and those with suicidal tendencies. Should we really stand aside and let them injure or destroy themselves? And what about issues dealing with the expression of unpopular or inflammatory views: is such freedom of speech absolute? What about social issues such as abortion: is that a decision concerned only with a woman's own body and mind, or does it involve a potential threat to another (the fetus)? Mill is well aware of the tangle of issues (excepting abortion) entailed by his view of liberty, and he seeks to disentangle them in his essay.

Mill, *On Liberty*

It is proper to state that I forego any advantage which could be derived to my argument from the idea of abstract right, as a thing independent of utility. I regard utility as the ultimate appeal on all ethical questions; but it must be utility in the largest sense, grounded on the permanent interests of man as a progressive being. Those interests, I contend, authorize the subjection of individual spontaneity to external control, only in respect to those actions of each, which concern the interest of other people. If any one does an act hurtful to others, there is a *primâ facie* case for punishing him, by law, or, where legal penalties are not safely applicable, by general disapprobation. There are also many positive acts for the benefit of others, which he may rightfully be compelled to perform; such as, to give evidence in a court of justice; to bear his fair share in the common defence, or in any other joint work necessary to the interest of the society of which he enjoys the protection;

and to perform certain acts of individual beneficence, such as saving a fellow-creature's life, or interposing to protect the defenceless against ill-usage, things which whenever it is obviously a man's duty to do, he may rightfully be made responsible to society for not doing. A person may cause evil to others not only by his actions but by his inaction, and in either case he is justly accountable to them for the injury. The latter case, it is true, requires a much more cautious exercise of compulsion than the former. To make any one answerable for doing evil to others, is the rule; to make him answerable for not preventing evil, is, comparatively speaking, the exception. Yet there are many cases clear enough and grave enough to justify that exception. . . .

But there is a sphere of action in which society, as distinguished from the individual, has, if any, only an indirect interest; comprehending all that portion of a person's life and conduct which affects only himself, or if it also affects others, only with their free, voluntary, and undeceived consent and participation. When I say only himself, I mean directly, and in the first instance: for whatever affects himself, may affect others through himself; and the objection which may be grounded on this contingency, will receive consideration in the sequel. This, then, is the appropriate region of human liberty. It comprises, first, the inward domain of consciousness; demanding liberty of conscience, in the most comprehensive sense; liberty of thought and feeling; absolute freedom of opinion and sentiment on all subjects, practical or speculative, scientific, moral, or theological. The liberty of expressing and publishing opinions may seem to fall under a different principle, since it belongs to that part of the conduct of an individual which concerns other people; but, being almost of as much importance as the liberty of thought itself, and resting in great part on the same reasons, is practically inseparable from it. Secondly, the principle requires liberty of tastes and pursuits; of framing the plan of our life to suit our own character; of doing as we like, subject to such consequences as may follow: without impediment from our fellow-creatures, so long as what we do does not harm them, even though they should think our conduct foolish, perverse, or wrong. Thirdly, from this liberty of each individual, follows the liberty, within the same limits, of combination among individuals; freedom to unite, for any purpose not involving harm to others: the persons combining being supposed to be of full age, and not forced or deceived.

Mill is quick to point out that even though it may be tempting to ground his concept of liberty by viewing it as an abstract, inalienable "right" (as Locke and Jefferson do), he has no interest in doing so. As noted in the previous section, Mill believes that all notions of "justice" and "rights" are ultimately reducible to the principle of social utility. People should be permitted and encouraged to exercise their full liberty *because this is the best way to promote the general welfare of most citizens*. Mill is convinced that we need to view human potential in the broadest possible way—"the permanent interests of man as a progressive being." Our human identities and possibilities are defined in large measure by our ability to make free choices. It is through unfettered and unconstrained "individual spontaneity" that we create ourselves, shape our destinies, and fulfill our unique potential, both individually and collectively.

Nevertheless, despite this powerful and passionate vision, Mill believes that such freedom does not exist in isolation: it is necessarily accompanied by social responsibilities and obligations toward others. Of course, the most obvious obligation is not to interfere with the free choices of others, and to do so means being punished by legal remedies or being subjected to social disapproval. But in addition, Mill believes that "There are also many positive acts for the benefit of others, which he may rightfully be compelled to perform." Such obligations include participating in the legal process, bearing one's fair share in the common defense of the community, saving a fellow-creature's life, protecting the defenseless against abuse or exploitation, and so on.

The essence of liberty for Mill is the freedoms that ought to naturally accrue to every citizen. Mill identifies three such areas:

- The freedom to think, express, and publish one's opinions on all subjects, including scientific, moral, and religious.
- The freedom to plan one's life and pursue one's goals without interference from others (providing our actions do not cause others harm).
- The freedom to unite with others for any purpose not involving harm to others.

Mill then sums up his views on social liberties with the following memorable and uncompromising statement:

No society in which these liberties are not, on the whole, respected, is free, whatever may be its form of government; and none is completely free in which they do not exist absolute and unqualified. The only freedom which deserves the name, is that of pursuing our own good in our own way, so long as we do not attempt to deprive others of theirs, or impede their efforts to obtain it. Each is the proper guardian of his own health, whether bodily, or mental and spiritual. Mankind are greater gainers by suffering each other to live as seems good to themselves, than by compelling each to live as seems good to the rest.

Mill, *On Liberty*

And he concludes this section with a sobering warning that is as relevant today as in centuries past: in the ongoing tension between the freedom of the individual and the rights of society, there is a perennial tendency to "strengthen society, and diminish the power of the individual." It is our human responsibility to jealously guard the individual liberties (described above) in the face of all efforts to limit or abandon them.

Apart from the peculiar tenets of individual thinkers, there is also in the world at large an increasing inclination to stretch unduly the powers of society over the individual, both by the force of opinion and even by that of legislation: and as the tendency of all the changes taking place in the world is to strengthen society, and diminish the power of the individual, this encroachment is not one of the evils which tend spontaneously to disappear, but, on the contrary, to grow more and more formidable. The disposition of mankind, whether as rulers or as fellow-citizens, to impose their own opinions and inclinations as a rule of conduct on others, is so energetically supported by some of the best and by some of the worst feelings incident to human nature, that it is hardly ever kept under restraint by anything but want of power; and as the power is not declining, but growing, unless a strong barrier of moral conviction can be raised against the mischief, we must expect, in the present circumstances of the world, to see it increase.

Mill, *On Liberty*

Mill goes on to make a compelling case for the absolute guarantee of free speech within a society. There is never justification for the government trying to censor or abridge all people's right to express their opinions with threats or coercion. Even when the majority of people in a society hold a particular view—on politics, religion, or a social issue—it is essential that the rights of the minority individuals be encouraged, not silenced. Mill places the need for these freedoms within the larger context of social utility when he states:

Chapter II: Of the Liberty of Thought and Discussion

Mill, *On Liberty*

But the peculiar evil of silencing the expression of an opinion is, that it is robbing the human race; posterity as well as the existing generation; those who dissent from the opinion, still more than those who hold it. If the opinion is right, they are deprived of the opportunity of exchanging error for truth: if wrong, they lose, what is almost as great a benefit, the clearer perception and livelier impression of truth, produced by its collision with error.

Mill concludes his defense of free expression with four arguments that support his position

Mill, *On Liberty*

The time, it is to be hoped, is gone by, when any defence would be necessary of the "liberty of the press" as one of the securities against corrupt or tyrannical government. No argument, we may suppose, can now be needed, against permitting a legislature or an executive, not identified in interest with the people, to prescribe opinions to them, and determine what doctrines or what arguments they shall be allowed to hear. . . . If all mankind minus one, were of one opinion, and only one person were of the contrary opinion, mankind would be no more justified in silencing that one person, than he, if he had the power, would be justified in silencing mankind. Were an opinion a personal possession of no value except to the owner; if to be obstructed in the enjoyment of it were simply a private injury, it would make some difference whether the injury was inflicted only on a few persons or on many. But the peculiar evil of silencing the expression of an opinion is, that it is robbing the human race; posterity as well as the existing generation; those who dissent from the opinion, still more than those who hold it. If the opinion is right, they are deprived of the opportunity of exchanging error for truth: if wrong, they lose, what is almost as great a benefit, the clearer perception and livelier impression of truth, produced by its collision with error.

We have now recognised the necessity to the mental well-being of mankind (on which all their other well-being depends) of freedom of opinion, and freedom of the expression of opinion, on four distinct grounds; which we will now briefly recapitulate.

First, if any opinion is compelled to silence, that opinion may, for aught we can certainly know, be true. To deny this is to assume our own infallibility. Secondly, though the silenced opinion be an error, it may, and very commonly does, contain a portion of truth; and since the general or prevailing opinion on any subject is rarely or never the whole truth, it is only by the collision of adverse opinions that the remainder of the truth has any chance of being supplied.

Thirdly, even if the received opinion be not only true, but the whole truth; unless it is suffered to be, and actually is, vigorously and earnestly contested, it will, by most of those who receive it, be held in the manner of a prejudice, with little comprehension or feeling of its rational grounds. And not only this, but, fourthly, the meaning of the doctrine itself will be in danger of being lost, or enfeebled, and deprived of its vital effect on the character and conduct: the dogma becoming a mere formal profession, inefficacious for good, but cumbering the ground, and preventing the growth of any real and heartfelt conviction, from reason or personal experience.

Mill continues his analysis by clarifying his concept of free expression, both verbally and in action. The central principle is this: individuals should have the unequivocal right to express their opinions and to act on them *unless their expression harms or poses a threat to others.* The examples he provides are instructive. If a person wants to publish the view "corn-dealers are starvers of the poor," there should be no restriction. However, if such views are expressed to a potentially violent mob in front of the house of a corn-dealer, this ought to be prohibited as it may very well lead to violence against the corn-dealer and his family, in the same way that yelling "Fire!" in a crowded theater may result in injury and even death as people make a panicked rush for the exits.

Mill, *On Liberty*

Chapter III: Of Individuality, as One of the Elements of Well-Being

No one pretends that actions should be as free as opinions. On the contrary, even opinions lose their immunity, when the circumstances in which they are expressed are such as to constitute their expression a positive instigation to some mischievous act. An opinion that corn-dealers are starvers of the poor, or that private property is robbery, ought to be unmolested when simply circulated through the press, but may justly incur punishment when delivered orally to an excited mob assembled before the house of a corn-dealer, or when handed about among the same mob in the form of a placard. Acts of

VISUAL PHILOSOPHY

Individual Liberty Versus Social Welfare

According to John Stuart Mill, "Over himself, over his own body and mind, the individual is sovereign." But what is the appropriate balance when the desires of the individual conflict with the social welfare in cases like the overharvest of natural resources or issues of public safety?

whatever kind, which, without justifiable cause, do harm to others, may be, and in the more important cases absolutely require to be, controlled by the unfavourable sentiments, and, when needful, by the active interference of mankind. The liberty of the individual must be thus far limited; he must not make himself a nuisance to other people. But if he refrains from molesting others in what concerns them, and merely acts according to his own inclination and judgment in things which concern himself, the same reasons which show that opinion should be free, prove also that he should be allowed, without molestation, to carry his opinions into practice at his own cost.

But this legal clarification is much less interesting than Mill's reflection regarding the implications for epistemology and human development in a free society.

That mankind are not infallible; that their truths, for the most part, are only half-truths; that unity of opinion, unless resulting from the fullest and freest comparison of opposite opinions, is not desirable, and diversity not an evil, but a good, until mankind are much more capable than at present of recognizing all sides of the truth, are principles applicable to men's modes of action, not less than to their opinions. As it is useful that while mankind are imperfect there should be different opinions, so is it that there should be different experiments of living; that free scope should be given to varieties of character, short of injury to others; and that the worth of different modes of life should be proved practically, when any one thinks fit to try them. It is desirable, in short, that in things which do not primarily concern others, individuality should assert itself. Where, not the person's own character, but the traditions of customs of other people are the rule of conduct, there is wanting one of the principal ingredients of human happiness, and quite the chief ingredient of individual and social progress. . . .

Mill, *On Liberty*

What a succinct and astute analysis Mill is presenting here. Every individual's perspective, no matter how thoughtful and informed, is ultimately limited. The only way to insure a deep and sophisticated understanding of the world is to enthusiastically welcome diverse points of view, listen carefully to their reasoning, and use them to enlarge our own insight. This is one of the central intellectual activities in developing a critical thinking approach to knowledge, which we have explored in earlier chapters in the book.

Mill concludes this section with a remarkable exhortation to live an examined life in the Socratic tradition, rather than an "ape-like one of imitation."

Mill, *On Liberty*

He who lets the world, or his own portion of it, choose his plan of life for him, has no need of any other faculty than the ape-like one of imitation. He who chooses his plan for himself, employs all his faculties. He must use observation to see, reasoning and judgment to foresee, activity to gather materials for decision, discrimination to decide, and when he has decided, firmness and self-control to hold to his deliberate decision. And these qualities he requires and exercises exactly in proportion as the part of his conduct which he determines according to his own judgment and feelings is a large one. It is possible that he might be guided in some good path, and kept out of harm's way, without any of these things. But what will be his comparative worth as a human being? It really is of importance, not only what men do, but also what manner of men they are that do it. Among the works of man, which human life is rightly employed in perfecting and beautifying, the first in importance surely is man himself. Supposing it were possible to get houses built, corn grown, battles fought, causes tried, and even churches erected and prayers said, by machinery—by automatons in human form—it would be a considerable loss to exchange for these automatons even the men and women who at present inhabit the more civilized parts of the world, and who assuredly are but starved specimens of what nature can and will produce. Human nature is not a machine to be built after a model, and set to do exactly the work prescribed for it, but a tree, which requires to grow and develope itself on all sides, according to the tendency of the inward forces which make it a living thing. . . .

Mill believed that we each have an obligation to create our own unique life path using all of our thinking abilities, rather that living a life of "ape-like imitation" by letting the world choose our path for us. Do you agree?

Mill's concepts of self-determination and human well-being are both classical and contemporary. The ancient Greek concept of happiness—*eudaemonia*—refers to the full exercise of the soul's powers, a concept akin to Mill's notion of each person's responsibility to choose a life plan rather than letting it be chosen for us by others. Such a project can only be undertaken by thinking critically in the fullest sense, using our abilities to observe, reason, judge, discriminate, decide, and commit ourselves to a course of action with steadfastness.

Mill, *On Liberty*

Chapter IV: Of the Limits to the Authority of Society over the Individual

What, then, is the rightful limit to the sovereignty of the individual over himself? Where does the authority of society begin? How much of human life should be assigned to individuality, and how much to society?

Each will receive its proper share, if each has that which more particularly concerns it. To individuality should belong the part of life in which it is chiefly the individual that is interested; to society, the part which chiefly interests society.

Though society is not founded on a contract, and though no good purpose is answered by inventing a contract in order to deduce social obligations from it, every one who receives the protection of society owes a return for the benefit, and the fact of living in society renders it indispensable that each should be bound to observe a certain line of conduct towards the rest. This conduct consists first, in not injuring the interests of one another; or rather certain interests, which, either by express legal provision or by tacit understanding, ought to be considered as rights; and secondly, in each person's bearing his share (to be fixed on some equitable principle) of the labours and sacrifices incurred for defending the society or its members from injury and molestation. These conditions society is justified in enforcing at all costs to those who endeavour to withhold fulfilment. Nor is this all that society may do. The acts of an individual may be hurtful to others, or wanting in due consideration for their welfare, without going the length of violating any of their constituted rights. The offender may then be justly punished by opinion, though not by law. As soon as any part of a person's conduct affects prejudicially the interests of others, society has jurisdiction over it, and the question whether the general welfare will or will not be promoted by interfering with it, becomes open to discussion. But there is no room for entertaining any such question when a person's conduct affects the interests of no persons besides himself, or needs not affect them unless they like (all the persons concerned being of full age, and the ordinary amount of understanding). In all such cases there should be perfect freedom, legal and social, to do the action and stand the consequences.

Although Mill does not believe that a "social contract" was ever voluntarily entered into by members of a society, he nevertheless believes that by choosing to remain in a social community, we commit ourselves to membership and the rights and responsibilities that go along with it. In return for society's protection so that we can live our lives freely, citizens reciprocate this protection by not impeding the rights of others to live freely. In addition, citizens are expected to do their fair share in defending the community from threats to its well-being, whether external or internal. These are expectations for the individual citizens that are enforceable by law. However, Mill believes that there may be other forms of misconduct that detract from the general welfare yet do not rise to the level of legal sanctions. For example, acting rudely, failing to help others in need, speaking to others in an insulting manner—though these and other like behaviors may not merit arrest, fines, or incarceration, the community can nevertheless exercise social control through social disapproval and communal condemnation.

With all other actions, Mill suggests that individuals should, in general, be left alone to pursue their interests and choose their lives. And yet he entertains the intriguing argument that virtually *all* actions we take affect others in some way or other, often negatively. As Mill expresses this point of view: "No person is an entirely isolated being: it is impossible for a person to do anything seriously or permanently hurtful to himself without mischief reaching at least to his near connexions, and often far beyond them." Ought these actions to be condemned as well?

Mill, *On Liberty*

The distinction here pointed out between the part of a person's life which concerns only himself, and that which concerns others, many persons will refuse to admit. How (it may be asked) can any part of the conduct of a member of society be a matter of indifference to the other members? No person is an entirely isolated being; it is impossible for a person to do anything seriously or permanently hurtful to himself, without mischief reaching at least to his near connexions, and often far beyond them. If he injures his property, he does harm to those who directly or indirectly derived support from it, and usually diminishes, by a greater or less amount, the general resources of the community. If he deteriorates his bodily or mental faculties, he not only brings evil upon all who depended on him for any portion of their happiness, but disqualifies himself for rendering the services which he owes to his fellow-creatures generally; perhaps becomes a burthen on their affection or benevolence; and if such conduct were very frequent, hardly any offence that is committed would detract more from the general sum of good. Finally, if by his vices or follies a person does no direct harm to others, he is nevertheless (it may be said) injurious by his example; and ought to be compelled to control himself, for the sake of those whom the sight or knowledge of his conduct might corrupt or mislead.

Mill's argument can be summarized in this way: because our lives are necessarily interwoven with the lives of others in society, virtually all negative actions that we take are liable to have a negative impact on the welfare of others, thus violating Mill's principle of general utility. For example, if you choose to damage or destroy property that you own (closing down a business, for example) you will likely harm those who are benefiting from the business, and you are also diminishing the general resources of the community. Or if you allow your health to deteriorate through neglect, you are causing pain to those who care for you, and you are also diminishing your ability to contribute your fair share to the community. Finally, if you engage in such vices as substance abuse or reckless spending, you are damaging the community by acting as a poor example that might influence others. Do these examples prove that people are never completely free to make autonomous choices, without first taking into account the general welfare of the community?

How does Mill respond to this argument? Although he fully acknowledges that the private choices of individuals often cause pain to those close to them, and perhaps even minimal damage to the community as a whole, Mill doesn't believe that this justifies the state stepping in to impose the principle of general utility. If someone becomes addicted to alcohol or gambling, it may very well be appropriate for friends and acquaintances to express their social disapproval, but that doesn't mean that the person's conduct ought to be seen as illegal. Of course, if a person is drunk while flying a commercial airplane or presiding over a court case, that conduct may merit legal sanctions, because the individual is threatening the welfare of others while performing in an official capacity.

But as a staunch supporter of individual liberty, Mill strongly believes that the greater danger to a community comes from too much interference in the lives of citizens, not too little. In Mill's view, people are much too willing to impose their views and values on others, thus threatening the right to freely live our lives as we wish, a fundamental right to which we are all entitled.

Mill, *On Liberty*

But the strongest of all the arguments against the interference of the public with purely personal conduct, is that when it does interfere, the odds are that it interferes wrongly, and in the wrong place. On questions of social morality, of duty to others, the opinion of the public, that is, of an overruling majority, though often wrong, is likely to be still oftener right; because on such questions they are only required to judge of their own interests; of the manner in which some mode of conduct, if allowed to be practised, would affect themselves. But the opinion of a similar majority, imposed as a law on the minority, on questions of self-regarding conduct, is quite as likely to be wrong as right; for in these cases public opinion means, at the best, some people's opinion of what is good or bad for other people; while very often it does not even mean that; the public, with the most perfect indifference, passing over the pleasure or convenience of those whose conduct they censure, and considering only their own preference. There are many who consider as an injury to themselves any conduct which they have a distaste for, and resent it as an outrage to their feelings; as a religious bigot, when charged with disregarding the religious feelings of others, has been known to retort that they disregard his feelings, by persisting in their abominable worship or creed. But there is no parity between the feeling of a person for his own opinion, and the feeling of another who is offended at his holding it; no more than between the desire of a thief to take a purse, and the desire of the right owner to keep it. And a person's taste is as much his own peculiar concern as his opinion or his purse. It is easy for any one to imagine an ideal public, which leaves the freedom and choice of individuals in all uncertain matters undisturbed, and only requires them to abstain from modes of conduct which universal experience has condemned. But where has there been seen a public which set any such limit to its censorship? or when does the public trouble itself about universal experience? In its interferences with personal conduct it is seldom thinking of anything but the enormity of acting or feeling differently from itself; and this standard of judgment, thinly disguised, is held up to mankind as the dictate of religion and philosophy, by nine-tenths of all moralists and speculative writers. These teach that things are right because they are right; because we feel them to be so. They tell us to search in our own minds and hearts for laws of conduct binding on ourselves and on all others. What can the poor public do but apply these instructions, and make their own personal feelings of good and evil, if they are tolerably unanimous in them, obligatory on all the world? ■

 Mill, John Stuart, *On Liberty*

THINK PHILOSOPHICALLY 10.10
Analyzing John Stuart Mill

PHILOSOPHER'S NOTEBOOK

- In analyzing the concept of justice, Mill distinguishes between the conceptual meaning of the term and the emotions associated with the idea of justice. What is the conceptual meaning of *your* concept of justice? What emotions do you associate with your idea of justice? Are these two dimensions of your notion of justice consistent?

- Identify the five different definitions of justice that Mill describes. Which of these definitions are also a part of your definition of justice? Mill believes that these definitions ultimately depend on the principle of social utility. Do you agree?

- Do you agree with Mill's statement that "Over himself, over his own body and mind, the individual is sovereign"? Why or why not? Identify several examples that would provide clear exceptions to this principle.

- Critically evaluate the following statement:

  The only freedom which deserves the name, is that of pursuing our own good in our own way, so long as we do not attempt to deprive others of theirs, or impede their efforts to obtain it. Each is the proper guardian of his own health, whether bodily, or mental and spiritual. Mankind are greater gainers by suffering each other to live as seems good to themselves, than by compelling each to live as seems good to the rest.

- Do you agree with Mill's concern and warning that there is a perennial tendency to "strengthen society and diminish the power of the individual"? Provide examples from our current culture to support your response.

- Explain what Mill means in the following passage. Do you agree? Why or why not?

  He who lets the world, or his own portion of it, choose his plan of life for him, has no need of any other faculty than the ape-like one of imitation. He who chooses his plan for himself, employs all his faculties. He must use observation to see, reasoning and judgment to foresee, activity to gather materials for decision, discrimination to decide, and when he has decided, firmness and self-control to hold to his deliberate decision.

- John Rawls, whose ideas we encountered earlier in this chapter, articulates the following criticism of a utilitarian approach to social justice. Evaluate his argument.

  Justice is the first virtue of social institutions, as truth is of systems of thought. A theory however elegant and economical must be rejected or revised if it is untrue; likewise laws and institutions no matter how efficient and well-arranged must be reformed or abolished if they are unjust. Each person possesses an inviolability founded on justice that even the welfare of society as a whole cannot override. For this reason justice denies that the loss of freedom for some is made right by a greater good shared by others. It does not allow that the sacrifices imposed on a few are outweighed by the larger sum of advantages enjoyed by many. Therefore in a just society the liberties of equal citizenship are taken as settled; the rights secured by justice are not subject to political bargaining or to the calculus of social interests. The only thing that permits us to acquiesce in an erroneous theory is the lack of a better one; analogously, an injustice is tolerable only when it is necessary to avoid an even greater injustice. Being first virtues of human activities, truth and justice are uncompromising.

Susan Moller Okin: *Justice Must Involve Gender Equality*

For many of the (male) political philosophers—including John Locke and John Stuart Mill—a democratic society is one where the government rests on the freely given consent of the governed. This "free consent" is at the heart of the social contract between the citizens and the government that they constitute and support. But women have legitimately asked where they fit in this equation. Historically, women have been denied equal rights to men in virtually every arena—economic, political, and social—and this inequality persists to this day in many societies. In most instances, the "free consent" of political theories applies only to men, not women.

At the core of this disparity is the distinction between the public and private spheres of life. Women have traditionally been responsible to the area of private life: raising children and maintaining a home. This has enabled men to function freely in the public sphere, pursuing careers and political involvement. Even when women have entered the workforce (as they have increasingly), they are still expected to assume the major responsibility for domestic life. This inhibits their ability to compete equally in the public world, where entrenched attitudes also serve to discriminate against them. For example, even when women perform exactly the same jobs as men, they are typically paid less. And their career advancement is often restricted because it is assumed that they will be primarily responsible for childcare and maintaining a home. Over fifty percent of marriages end in divorce in this country, and in ninety percent of those cases women end up with the primary custody of the children. So for women, in order to achieve a just society, this deep and pervasive inequality based on gender roles must be eradicated and replaced with a social structure that is truly based on equality. This is the only way that they will be able to achieve parity in both economic and political power.

Susan Moller Okin (1946–2004) is a contemporary political philosopher who has written extensively on this subject. The following passages are taken from her book *Justice, Gender, and the Family*.

SUSAN MOLLER OKIN

(1946–2004)

Feminist Political Philosopher. Martha Sutton Weeks Professor of Ethics in Society at Stanford until her recent death. Regarded as one of the most important thinkers in the field of gender and political theory. Author of *Women in Western Political Thought* (1979) and *Justice, Gender, and the Family* (1989).

Okin,
Justice, Gender, and the Family

The United States Supreme Court in the early 1980's.

Introduction: Justice and Gender

We as a society pride ourselves on our democratic values. We don't believe people should be constrained by innate differences from being able to achieve desired positions of influence or to improve their well-being; equality of opportunity is our professed aim. The Preamble to our Constitution stresses the importance of justice, as well as the general welfare and the blessings of liberty. The Pledge of Allegiance asserts that our republic preserves "liberty and justice for all."

Yet substantial inequalities between the sexes still exist in our society. In economic terms, full-time working women (after some very recent improvement) earn on average 71 percent of the earnings of full-time working men. One-half of poor and three-fifths of chronically poor households with dependent children are maintained by a single female parent. The poverty rate for elderly women is nearly twice that for elderly men. On the political front, two out of a hundred U.S. senators are women, one out of nine justices seems to be considered sufficient female representation on the Supreme Court, and the number of men chosen in each congressional election far exceeds the number of women elected in the entire history of the country. Underlying and intertwined with all these inequalities is the unequal distribution of the unpaid labor of the family.

An equal sharing between the sexes of family responsibilities, especially child care, is "the great revolution that has not happened." Women, including mothers of young children, are, of course, working outside the household far more than their mothers did. And the small proportion of women who reach high-level positions in politics, business, and the professions command a vastly disproportionate amount of space in the media, compared with the millions of women who work at low-paying, dead-end jobs, the millions who do part-time work with its lack of benefits, and the millions of others who stay home performing for no pay what is frequently not even acknowledged as work. Certainly, the fact that women are doing more paid work does not imply that they are more equal. It is often said that we are living in a postfeminist era. This claim, due in part to the distorted emphasis on women who have "made it," is false, no matter which of its meanings is intended. It is certainly not true that feminism has been vanquished, and equally untrue that it is no longer needed because its aims have been fulfilled. Until there is justice within the family, women will not be able to gain equality in politics, at work, or in any other sphere.

Susan Moller Okin argues that genuine social and political justice will only be achieved when there is equality in gender roles and responsibilities. Do you agree with her reasoning? Why?

As I argue in detail in chapter 7, the typical current practices of family life, structured to a large extent by gender, are not just. Both the expectation and the experience of the division of labor by sex make women vulnerable. As I shall show, a cycle of power relations and decisions pervades both family and workplace, each reinforcing the inequalities between the sexes that already exist within the other. Not only women, but children of both sexes, too, are often made vulnerable by gender-structured marriage. One-quarter of children in the United State now live in families with only one parent—in almost 90 percent of cases, the mother. Contrary to common perceptions—in which the situation of never-married mothers looms largest—65 percent of the single-parent families are a result of marital separation or divorce. Recent research in a number of states has shown that, in the average case, the standard of living of divorced women and the children who live with them plummets after divorce, whereas the economic situation of divorced men tends to be better than when they were married.

A central source of injustice for women these days is that the law, most noticeably in the event of divorce, treats more or less as equals those whom custom, workplace discrimination, and the still conventional division of labor within the family have made very unequal. Central to this socially created inequality are two commonly made but inconsistent presumptions: that women are primarily responsible for the rearing of children; and that serious and committed members of the workforce (regardless of class) do not have primary responsibility, or even shared responsibility, for the rearing of children. The old assumption of the workplace, still implicit, is that workers have wives at home. It is built not only into the structure and expectations of the workplace but into other crucial institutions, such as schools, which make no attempt to take account, in their scheduled hours or vacations, of the fact that parents are likely to hold jobs.

Now, of course, many wage workers do not have wives at home. Often, they *are* wives and mothers, or single, separated, or divorced mothers of small children. But neither the family nor the workplace has taken much account of this fact. Employed wives still do by far the greatest proportion of unpaid family work, such as child care and housework. Women are far more likely to take time out of the workplace or to work part-time because of family responsibilities than are their husbands or male partners. And they are much more likely to move because of their husbands' employment needs or opportunities than their own. All these tendencies, which are due to a number of factors, including the sex segregation and discrimination of the workplace itself, tend to be cyclical in their effects: wives advance more slowly than their husbands at work and thus gain less seniority, and the discrepancy between their wages increases over time. Then, because both the power structure of the family and what is regarded as consensual "rational" family decision making reflect the fact that the husband usually earns more, it will become even less likely as time goes on that the unpaid work of the family will be shared between the spouses. Thus the cycle of inequality is perpetuated. Often hidden from view within a marriage, it is in the increasingly likely event of marital breakdown that the socially constructed inequality of married women is at its most visible.

This is what I mean when I say that gender-structured marriage *makes* women vulnerable. These are not matters of natural necessity, as some people would believe. Surely nothing in our natures dictates that men should not be equal participants in the rearing of their children. Nothing in the nature of work makes it impossible to adjust it to the fact that people are parents as well as workers. That these things have not happened is part of the historically, socially constructed differentiation between the sexes that feminists have come to call *gender*. We live in a society that has over the years regarded the innate characteristic of sex as one of the clearest legitimizers of different rights and restrictions, both formal and informal. While the legal sanctions that uphold male dominance have begun to be eroded in the past century, and more rapidly in the last twenty years, the heavy weight of tradition, combined with the effects of socialization, still works powerfully to reinforce sex roles that are commonly regarded as of unequal prestige and worth. The sexual division of labor has not only been a fundamental part of the marriage contract, but so deeply influences us in our formative years that feminists of both sexes who try to reject it can find themselves struggling against it with varying degrees of ambivalence. Based on this linchpin, "gender"—by which I mean *the deeply entrenched institutionalization of sexual difference*—still permeates our society. . . .

The Personal as Political

"The personal is political" is the central message of feminist critiques of the public/domestic dichotomy. It is the core idea of most contemporary feminism. Though many of those who fought in the nineteenth and early twentieth centuries for suffrage and for the abolition of the oppressive legal status of wives were well aware of the connections between women's political and personal dominations by men, few pre-1960's feminists questioned women's special role in the family. While arguing for equal rights, such as the vote or access to education, most accepted the prevailing assumption that women's class association with and responsibility for the care of the family was natural and inevitable.

The earliest claims that the personal is political came from those radical feminists of the 1960s and 1970s who argued that, since the family was at the root of women's oppression, it must be "smashed." The anti-family nature of some early radical feminism has been exaggerated and exploited both by antifeminists and by those who have been termed "conservative" or "backlash" feminists. They have focused on it in order to attack all, or all but their own version, of feminism. But most contemporary feminists, while critiquing the gender-structured family, have not attacked all varieties of family. Many advocate that "family" be defined so as to include any intimately connected and committed group, specifically endorsing homosexual marriage; most, certainly, refuse to accept that the choice must be between accepting women's double burden and abolishing the family. We refuse to give up on the institution of the family, and refuse to accept the division of labor between the sexes as natural and unchangeable. More and more, as the extent to which gender is a social construction has become understood, feminists have come to recognize how variable are the potential forms and practices of family groups. The family is in no way inevitably tied to its gender structure, but until this notion is successfully challenged, and nontraditional groupings and divisions of labor are not only recognized but encouraged, there can be no hope of equality for women in either the domestic or the public sphere.

Thus feminists have turned their attention to the politics of what had previously been regarded—and, as I have shown, still is seen by most political theorists—as paradigmatically *non*political. That the personal sphere of sexuality, of housework, of child care and family life *is* political became the underpinning of most feminist thought. Feminists of different political leanings and in a variety of academic disciplines have revealed and analyzed the multiple interconnections between women's domestic

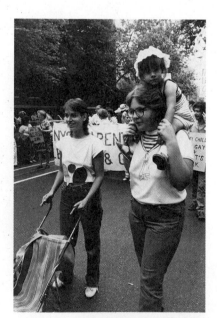

According to Okin, many feminists believe that the traditional gender-structured idea of "family" should be redefined to include "any intimately connected and committed group, specifically endorsing homosexual marriage." Do you agree? Why?

roles and their inequality and segregation in the workplace, and between their socialization in gendered families and the psychological aspects of their oppression. We have strongly and persistently challenged the long-standing underlying assumption of almost all political theories: that the sphere of family and personal life is so separate and distinct from the rest of social life that such theories can justifiably assume but ignore it.

As my argument so far has made clear, however, these feminist arguments have not been acknowledged by most contemporary political theorists writing about justice. In discussing some of the central feminist arguments about the essentially political nature of personal life and of the family in particular, I shall establish that domestic life needs to be just and to have its justice reinforced by the state and its legal system. In the circumstances of the division of labor that is practiced within the vast majority of households in the United States today, women are rendered vulnerable by marriage and especially by motherhood, and there is great scope for unchecked injustice to flourish.

The interconnections between the domestic and the nondomestic aspects of our lives are deep and pervasive. Given the power structures of both, women's lives are far more detrimentally affected by these interconnections than are men's. Consider two recent front-page stories that appeared on subsequent days in the *New York Times*. The first was about a tiny elite among women: those who work as lawyers for the country's top law firms. If these women have children with whom they want to spend any time, they find themselves off the partnership track and instead, with no prospects of advancement, on the "mommy track." "Nine-to-five" is considered part-time work in the ethos of such firms, and one mother reports that, in spite of her twelve-hour workdays and frequent work on weekends, she has "no chance" of making partner. The article fails to mention that these women's children have fathers, or that most of the men who work for the same prestigious law firms also have children, except to report that male lawyers who take parental leave are seen as "wimp-like." The sexual division of labor in the family, even in these cases where the women are extremely well qualified, successful, and potentially influential, is simply assumed.

The next day's *Times* reported on a case of major significance for abortion rights, decided by a Federal Appeals Court in Minnesota. The all-male panel of judges ruled 7 to 3 that the state may require a woman under eighteen years who wishes to obtain an abortion to notify *both* her parents—even in cases of divorce, separation, or desertion—or to get special approval from a state judge. The significance of this article is amplified when it is juxtaposed with the previous one. For it shows us how it is that those who rise to the top in the highly politically influential profession of law are among those who have had the least experience of all in raising children. There is a high incidence of recruitment of judges from those who have risen to partnership in the most prestigious law firms. Other judges are often drawn from the equally highly competitive field of academic law, which also places its greatest demands (those of the tenure hurdle) on lawyers during the child-rearing years, and therefore discriminates against those who participate in parenting. Those who are chosen, therefore, would seem to be those least well informed to make decisions about abortion, especially in cases involving relations between teenage girls and their parents. Here we find a systematically built-in absence of mothers (and presumably of "wimp-like" participating fathers, too) from high-level political decisions concerning some of the most vulnerable persons in society—women, disproportionately poor and black, who become pregnant in their teens, and their future children. It is not hard to see here the ties between the supposedly distinct public and domestic spheres.

This is but one example of what feminists mean by saying the "the personal is political," sometimes adding the corollary "the political is personal." It is because of this claim, of course, that the family became and has remained central to the politics of feminism and to feminist theory. Contemporary feminism poses a significant challenge to the long-standing and still-surviving assumption of political theories that the sphere of family and personal life is sharply distinct from the rest of social and political life, that the state can and should restrain itself from intrusion into the domestic sphere, and

Okin contends that too often women with full-time careers are still expected to assume a disproportionate amount of the responsibility for child-rearing and home-making. Do you agree?

that political theories can therefore legitimately ignore it. In contrast, both challenging and aiming to restructure the public/domestic dichotomy are fundamental to the feminist enterprise.

Conclusion: Toward a Humanist Justice

The family is the linchpin of gender, reproducing it from one generation to the next. As we have seen, family life as typically practiced in our society is not just, either to women or to children. Moreover, it is not conducive to the rearing of citizens with a strong sense of justice. In spite of all the rhetoric about equality between the sexes, the traditional or quasi-traditional division of family labor still prevails. Women are made vulnerable by constructing their lives around the expectation that they will be primary parents; they become more vulnerable within marriages in which they fulfill this expectation, whether or not they also work for wages; and they are most vulnerable in the event of separation or divorce, when they usually take over responsibility for children without adequate support from their ex-husbands. Since approximately half of all marriages end in divorce, about half of our children are likely to experience its dislocations, often made far more traumatic by the socioeconomic consequences of both gender-structured marriage and divorce settlements that fail to take account of it. I have suggested that, for very important reasons, the family *needs* to be a just institution, and have shown that contemporary theories of justice neglect women and ignore gender. How can we address this injustice?

This is a complex question. It is particularly so because we place great value on our freedom to live different kinds of lives, there is no current consensus on many aspects of gender, and we have good reason to suspect that many of our beliefs about sexual difference and appropriate sex roles are heavily influenced by the very fact that we grew up in a gender-structured society. All of us have been affected, in our very psychological structures, by the fact of gender in our personal pasts, just as our society has been deeply affected by its strong influence in our collective past. Because of the lack of shared meanings about gender, it constitutes a particularly hard case for those who care deeply about both personal freedom and social justice. The way we divide the labor and responsibilities in our personal lives seems to be one of those things that people should be free to work out for themselves, but because of its vast repercussions it belongs clearly within the scope of things that must be governed by principles of justice. Which is to say, in the language of political and moral theory, that it belongs both to the sphere of "the good" and to that of "the right."

I shall argue here that any just and fair solution to the urgent problem of women's and children's vulnerability must encourage and facilitate the equal sharing by men and women of paid and unpaid work, of productive and reproductive labor. We must work toward a future in which all will be likely to choose this mode of life. A just future would be one without gender. In its social structures and practices, one's sex would have no more relevance than one's eye color or the length of one's toes. No assumptions would be made about "male" and "female" roles; childbearing would be so conceptually separated from child rearing and other family responsibilities that it would be a cause for surprise, and no little concern, if men and women were not equally responsible for domestic life or if children were to spend much more time with one parent than the other. It would be a future in which men and women participated in more or less equal numbers in every sphere of life, from infant care to different kinds of paid work to high-level politics. Thus it would no longer be the case that having no experience of raising children would be the practical prerequisite for attaining positions of the greatest social influence. Decisions about abortion and rape, about divorce settlements and sexual harassment, or about any other crucial social issues would not be made, as they often are now, by legislatures and benches of judges overwhelmingly populated by men whose power is in large part due to their advantaged position in the gender structure. If we are to be at all true to our democratic ideals, moving away from gender is essential. Obviously, the attainment of such a social world requires major changes in a multitude of institutions and social settings outside the home, as well as within it.

Such changes will not happen overnight. Moreover, any present solution to the vulnerability of women and children that is just and respects individual freedom must take into account that most people currently live in ways that are greatly affected by gender, and most still favor many aspects of current gendered practices. Sociological studies confirm what most of us already infer from our own personal and professional acquaintances: there are no currently shared meanings in this country about the extent to which differences between the sexes are innate or environmental, about the appropriate roles of men and women, and about which family forms and divisions of labor are most beneficial for partners, parents, and children. There are those, at one extreme, for whom the different roles of the two sexes, especially as parents, are deeply held tenets of religious belief. At the other end of the spectrum are those of us for whom the sooner all social differentiation between the sexes vanishes, the better it will be for all of us. And there are a thousand varieties of view in between. Public policies must respect people's views and choices. But they must do so only insofar as it can be ensured that these choices do not result, as they now do, in the vulnerability of women and children. Special protections must be built into our laws and public policies to ensure that, for those who choose it, the division of labor between the sexes does not result in injustice. In the face of these difficulties—balancing freedom and the effects of past choices against the needs of justice—I do not pretend to have arrived at any complete or fully satisfactory answers. But I shall attempt in this final chapter to suggest some social reforms, including changes in public policies and reforms of family law, that may help us work toward a solution to the injustices of gender.

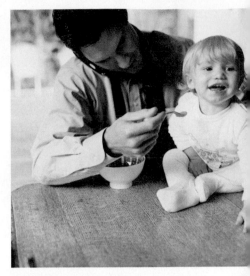

Okin believes that a genuine "humanist justice" would involve doing away with traditional "male" and "female" roles and replacing them with a gender-neutral approach to family responsibilities.

Marriage has become an increasingly peculiar contract, a complex and ambiguous combination of anachronism and present-day reality. There is no longer the kind of agreement that once prevailed about what is expected of the parties to a marriage. Clearly, at least in the United States, it is no longer reasonable to assume that marriage will last a lifetime, since only half of current marriages are expected to. And yet, in spite of the increasing legal equality of men and women and the highly publicized figures about married women's increased participation in the labor force, many couples continue to adhere to more or less traditional patterns of role differentiation. As a recent article put it, women are "out of the house but not out of the kitchen." Consequently, often working part-time or taking time out from wage work to care for family members, especially children, most wives are in a very different position from their husbands in their ability to be economically self-supporting. This is reflected, as we have seen, in power differentials between the sexes within the family. It means also, in the increasingly common event of divorce, usually by mutual agreement, that it is the mother who in 90 percent of cases will have physical custody of the children. But whereas the greater need for money goes one way, the bulk of the earning power almost always goes the other. This is one of the most important causes of the feminization of poverty, which is affecting the life chances of ever larger numbers of children as well as their mothers. The division of labor within families has always adversely affected women, by making them economically dependent on men. Because of the increasing instability of marriage, its effects on children have now reached crisis proportions.

Some who are critical of the present structure and practices of marriage have suggested that men and women simply be made free to make their own agreements about family life, contracting with each other, much as business contracts are made. But this takes insufficient account of the history of gender in our culture and our own psychologies, of the present substantive inequalities between the sexes, and, most important, of the well-being of the children who result from the relationship. As has long been recognized in the realm of labor relations, justice is by no means always enhanced by the maximization of freedom of contract, if the individuals involved are in unequal positions to start with. Some have even suggested that it is consistent with justice to leave spouses to work out their own divorce settlement. By this time, however, the two people ending a marriage are likely to be far *more* unequal. Such a practice would be even more catastrophic for most women and children than is the present system. Wives in any but the rare cases in which they as individuals have remained their husbands' socioeconomic equals could hardly be expected to reach a just solution if left "free" to "bargain" the terms of financial support or child custody. What would they have to bargain *with*?

There are many directions that public policy can and should take in order to make relations between men and women more just. In discussing these, I shall look back to some of the contemporary ways of thinking about justice that I find most convincing. I draw particularly on Rawls's idea of the original position and Walzer's conception of the complex equality found in separate spheres of justice, between which I find no inconsistency. I also keep in mind critical legal theorists' critique of contract, and the related idea, suggested earlier, that rights to privacy that are to be valuable to all of us can be enjoyed only insofar as the sphere of life in which we enjoy them ensures the equality of its adult members and protects children. Let us begin by asking what kind of arrangements persons in a Rawlsian original position would agree to regarding marriage, parental and other domestic responsibilities, and divorce. What kinds of policies would they agree to for other aspects of social life, such as the workplace and schools, that affect men, women, and children and relations among them? And let us consider whether these arrangements would satisfy Walzer's separate spheres test—that inequalities in one sphere of life not be allowed to overflow into another. Will they foster equality within the sphere of family life? For the protection of the privacy of a domestic sphere in which inequality exists is the protection of the right of the strong to exploit and abuse the weak.

Let us first try to imagine ourselves, as far as possible, in the original position, knowing neither what our sex nor any other of our personal characteristics will be once the veil of ignorance is lifted. Neither do we know our place in society or our particular conception of the good life. Particularly relevant in this context, of course, is our lack of knowledge of our beliefs about the characteristics of men and women and our related convictions about the appropriate division of labor between the sexes. Thus the positions we represent must include a wide variety of beliefs on these matters. We may, once the veil of ignorance is lifted, find ourselves feminist men or feminist women whose conception of the good life includes the minimization of social differentiation between the sexes. Or we may find ourselves traditionalist men or women, whose conception of the good life, for religious or other reasons, is bound up in an adherence to the conventional division of labor between the sexes. The challenge is to arrive at and apply principles of justice having to do with the family and the division of labor between the sexes that can satisfy these vastly disparate points of view and the many that fall between.

There are some traditionalist positions so extreme that they ought not be admitted for consideration, since they violate such fundamentals as equal basic liberty and self-respect. We need not, and should not, that is to say, admit for consideration views based on the notion that women are inherently inferior beings whose function is to fulfill the needs of men. Such a view is no more admissible in the construction of just institutions for a modern pluralist society than is the view, however deeply held, that some are naturally slaves and others naturally and justifiably their masters. We need not, therefore, consider approaches to marriage that view it as an inherently and desirably hierarchical structure of dominance and subordination. Even if it were conceivable that a person who did not know whether he or she would turn out to be a man or a woman in the society being planned would subscribe to such views, they are not admissible. Even if there were no other reasons to refuse to admit such views, they must be excluded for the sake of children, for everyone in the original position has a high personal stake in the quality of childhood. Marriages of dominance and submission are bad for children as well as for their mothers, and the socioeconomic outcome of divorce after such a marriage is very likely to damage their lives and seriously restrict their opportunities.

With this proviso, what social structures and public policies regarding relations between the sexes, and the family in particular, would we agree on in the original position? I think we would arrive at a basic model that would absolutely minimize gender. . . . We would also, however, build in carefully protective institutions for those who wished to follow gender-structured modes of life. . . . ▪

Okin, Susan Muller, *Justice and Gender*

- Susan Moller Okin makes the compelling point that in contrast to the democratic ideals of justice and equality, women in our culture (and most others as well) are in fact treated *un*justly and *un*equally. Based on your personal experience, either in this culture or a previous one in which you lived, identify areas in which you believe women have not been treated fairly by the social institutions.

- According to Okin, much of women's unequal status can be traced to their traditional role in the family:

  > . . . the typical current practices of family life, structured to large extent by gender, are not just . . . a cycle of power relations and decisions pervades both family and workplace, each reinforcing the inequalities between the sexes that already exist within the other.

  Explain the reasoning Okin uses to support this position. Do you agree with her?

- As she describes in the following passage, Okin believes that marital divorce and separation (about fifty percent of all marriages) make women and their children extremely vulnerable, both economically and socially. Do you agree with her analysis? Why or why not?

  > It means also, in the increasingly common event of divorce, usually by mutual agreement, that it is the mother who in 90 percent of cases will have physical custody of the children. But whereas the greater need for money goes one way, the bulk of the earning power almost always goes the other. This is one of the most important causes of the feminization of poverty, which is affecting the life chances of ever larger numbers of children as well as their mothers. The division of labor within families has always adversely affected women, by making them economically dependent on men. Because of the increasing instability of marriage, its effects on children have now reached crisis proportions.

- The gender roles for men and women in our culture (and other cultures as well) are not necessary or preordained, according to Okin. Instead, these gender roles are "social constructions," and as a result they can be *re*constructed more justly and equally. What does it mean to say that gender roles are "social constructions"? What are some of the ways that these roles could be "reconstructed"? Explain the meaning of the following passage, which deals with the issue of gender:

  > The sexual division of labor has not only been a fundamental part of the marriage contract, but so deeply influences us in our formative years that feminists of both sexes who try to reject it can find themselves struggling against it with varying degrees of ambivalence. Based on this linchpin, "gender"—by which I mean *the deeply entrenched institutionalization of sexual difference*— still permeates our society. . . .

- What does Okin mean when she says, " 'The personal is political' is the central message of feminist critiques of the public/domestic dichotomy. It is the core idea of most contemporary feminism"? In this regard, evaluate the cogency of the argument that Okin is making in this passage: What are the premises? What is the conclusion? How would you evaluate the truth of the premises? Does the conclusion follow logically from the premises?

  > The family is in no way inevitably tied to its gender structure, but until this notion is successfully challenged, and nontraditional groupings and divisions of labor are not only recognized but encouraged, there can be no hope of equality for women in either the domestic or the public sphere.

- Okin cites two articles that she believes reveal the interconnections—and resulting injustice for women— between the "personal" life of the family and the "public" life of careers and politics. The first article deals with the "mommy track" for women in law firms, and the second describes a court ruling that affirmed the law mandating women under the age of eighteen to notify both parents before getting an abortion. Explain the point Okin is making and analyze her reasoning.

- In the following passage, Okin describes her vision of a truly just society for both men and women. Compare this with your own idea for a just society.

  > I shall argue here that any just and fair solution to the urgent problem of women's and children's vulnerability must encourage and facilitate the equal sharing by men and women of paid and unpaid work, of productive and reproductive labor. We must work toward a future in which all will be likely to choose this mode of life. A just future would be one without gender. In its social structures and practices, one's sex would have no more relevance than one's eye color or the length of one's toes. No assumptions would be made about "male" and "female" roles; childbearing would be so conceptually separated from child rearing and other family responsibilities that it would be a cause for surprise, and no little concern, if men and women were not equally responsible for domestic life or if children were to spend much more time with one parent than the other. It would be a future in which men and women participated in more or less equal numbers in every sphere of life, from infant care to different kinds of paid work to high-level politics.

- Okin believes that the institution of marriage is at the core of many of the inequalities that women experience. Do you agree with her analysis? What suggestions would you make for reforming the institution of marriage?

Making Connections: *An Ideal Society*

This chapter began with the challenge for you to reflect on the social and political "ingredients" that constitute the particular "recipe" of your culture. This activity was designed to encourage you to step back and examine your culture from a more analytical perspective. Since that point, you have had an opportunity to explore the way influential thinkers from the past twenty-five hundred years have grappled with these same issues. And you have likely been constructing in your own mind the kind of ideal society in which you would like to live.

For Plato, such an ideal society would be based on matching the unique talents of each individual to the social responsibilities required for people to live together: Leaders (philosopher-kings), Guardians, and Workers. The central criterion for evaluating a society is how harmoniously and productively do all of its various elements function together. Aristotle endorsed this general approach to constructing an ideal society, founding his theory on the belief that humans are naturally communal animals, and that each person should seek happiness by discovering and fulfilling his or her own unique purpose (*entelechy*). Both Plato and Aristotle rejected the idea that an ideal society is "egalitarian" (the belief that people are intrinsically equal) or "democratic" (the belief that each person should have an equal voice in governing).

Leaping ahead a few thousand years, egalitarianism and democracy *are* the concerns of thinkers such as Thomas Hobbes, John Locke, and John Rawls. Beginning with the concept of a "state of nature"—either real or imagined—these philosophers developed the notion of a "social contract" that individuals voluntarily enter into with one another to ensure their safety and individual rights. What form should such a society take? Rawls suggests that we imagine that we are behind a "veil of ignorance," not knowing who we will be in the new society—what sort of society would we wish for that would guarantee ourselves an equal opportunity regardless of our gender, race, culture, or social pedigree? Rawls suggests it would be a society based on political freedom and equal economic opportunities for all, with a social safety net for less advantaged members of society.

Karl Marx and Friedrich Engels approach the development of an ideal society from the opposite extreme. Rather than focusing on individual rights as primary, as liberalism does, they believed that the needs of the social community taken as a whole were primary. Thus all individuals are expected to willingly contribute whatever talents they have, while all goods and wealth are divided equally among society's members, regardless of their social station in life. Marx and Engels believed that the creation of such a socialist society was inevitable, produced by the inexorable dialectic of historical forces.

John Stuart Mill returned our focus to the concept of individual rights, echoing many of the ideas of John Locke and the founders of the United States, as articulated in the Declaration of Independence and the Constitution. Yet the eloquent and powerful statement that all people are "endowed by their Creator with certain inalienable rights," which include "life, liberty, and the pursuit of happiness" was in seemingly sharp contradiction to the legal existence of slavery in America at this time. The fact is that slaves were seen primarily as "property" and not members of the "moral community" and thus not deserving of these "inalienable rights."

And Susan Moller Okin reminds us that neither have women historically been accorded the same basic human rights as men, even in the United States, where they did not receive the right to vote until the early twentieth century. And even more profoundly, the gender role division that expects women to be responsible for the "personal sphere" of child rearing and homemaking, and men responsible for the "public" sphere of careers and politics, has resulted in unequal treatment of women throughout society. Okin appeals to Rawls's "veil of ignorance" to argue that a truly ideal society would reshape both the private and public spheres so that all responsibilities would be divided in an equal, gender-neutral fashion.

As citizens of a particular society, we each have a solemn responsibility to reflect and think clearly about these critical issues, and to assume our share of the responsibility to help our society become more enlightened, more like the "ideal society" in which we would each like to live. The Students Thinking About Philosophy activity is designed to guide your further explorations toward this end, inviting you to articulate your own personal vision of an ideal society.

Students Thinking About Philosophy: *Designing My Ideal Society*

At the beginning of this chapter, you were asked to reflect on the social and political structure of your society by responding to a number of questions. During the course of this chapter, you have had the opportunity to become acquainted with the major social/political theories and concepts. Using this knowledge, describe your vision of an ideal society by responding to the following questions. Included below is a student essay by Sue Martin that articulates her personal response to this challenge.

- *Issues of Justice:* In what ways will your society distribute wealth to its citizens? In what ways will it make opportunities for education and to acquire wealth available? To what extent will people be treated equally? In what ways will you consider your society to be "just"?

- *Issues of Law:* How will your society justify its existence and its laws? To what extent will its "civic laws" be based on "natural laws" that are thought to apply to all humans in all societies? To what extent will the laws be applied fairly to people, regardless of their wealth, social status, gender, or racial identity? How will your society treat people who disagree with and disobey its laws? How will people who engage in "civil disobedience" be treated (for example, those who act disruptively to protest social policies or war policies with which they disagree)?

- *Issues of Public Interest:* In what ways will your society support the well-being of those less advantaged citizens (for example, those who are poor, elderly, unemployed, sick, abused, or neglected)? In what ways will citizens be expected to sacrifice their individual interests to support the general interest (for example, paying taxes)? In what ways will your society help those who are unable to help themselves? How will it promote the general good through regulations and economic support?

- *Issues of Duty:* What specific obligations and duties will citizens in your society be responsible for performing (for example, serving on juries)?

- *Issues of Rights:* What individual rights will citizens in your society be expected to have (for example, the right to practice the religion of your choice)? What rights will your society consider to be "universal" in the sense that they are rights that all people in all societies should enjoy?

- *Issues of Freedom:* What will be the basic freedoms that your society guarantees for all of its citizens (for example, freedom to express your views without being arrested or harassed)? In what areas will personal freedoms be limited in your society?

- *Issues of Power and Influence:* How will power be acquired and administered in your society? How will citizens be able to influence social policies and laws?

Where Do I Stand?

Sue Martin

There are certain political assumptions I thought were universally accepted since their inception.

My first assumption crumbled during the war in Yugoslavia in the early 1990's when Serbs tried to annihilate Muslim neighbors with whom they had lived for centuries. I had thought it was a truth universally held since the Enlightenment that all people were considered equal under the law, especially in a European nation where different ethnic groups had coexisted since the Middle Ages. I had vaguely heard that Tito had kept disparate groups under fierce control so that they would not attack each other after WWII, but I had assumed that by the 1990's all such ethnic rivalry had died out. The depth of my naiveté was revealed as increasingly horrific stories and photographs of bloodshed, concentration camps and mass graves came out of Yugoslavia. It would never have occurred to me that citizens of the same political state would perpetuate ancient hates rather than work together, yet this is what people in Yugoslavia demonstrated less than a decade ago.

Another assumption I had was that all people born in a country were automatically citizens of that country and therefore equal under the law. Sometime in the 90's I read an essay in The New York Review of Books by an Israeli author who compared Palestinians in refugee camps to Jews in concentration camps. I was stunned. Why were Palestinians being kept behind barbed wire? Why were they not granted full citizenship? How could the Israelis have resorted to the very violation of human rights they themselves had undergone during World War II? The demographic argument that Israel would cease to be a Jewish state if it allowed Palestinians full citizenship made me question the legitimacy, the viability and the fairness of a state based on religion.

On 9/11/01 I lost my assumption that the United States was impregnable. Someone very clever and very organized had achieved a stunning blow to our sense of secure isolation, and we Americans had to admit we were no longer safer than other people. But the question arose why? Why did this attack occur? What was someone trying to tell us? What was someone trying to achieve? I ran to read books on fundamentalism, the history of the Middle East during the twentieth century, anything that might give me clues as to whom we were dealing with and what their motives, goals and mode of operating were. I found a staggering amount of information, too much to be absorbed quickly. Two years later I am still reading all I can on Arab and Islamic history and the relationship between the West and Islam, as well as daily and weekly reports on world events.

When I try to imagine how the world might be improved, I am stymied. What policy or conception should be established first for a livable, just world? How do I weight all the current factors when they so quickly contradict each other? What would be fair, what would work, and where do I stand in this suddenly new world where everyone's purpose, cause and right to exist seem to be in question?

Looking back over the events of the past decade, the first rule I would establish to set up a free yet peaceful society would follow John Stuart Mill's definition of personal liberty: "Over himself, over his own body and mind, the individual is sovereign . . . the only purpose for which power can be rightfully exercised over any member of a civilized community, against his will, is to prevent harm to others." (p. 567) In other words, a person has the right to do anything, provided it does not harm anyone else. This law would theoretically protect us from airplanes used as bombs. The individual's freedom is only bound by how it may infringe on someone else's. That leaves a lot of room to operate in, while protecting us from attack.

Second, I would establish that everyone is equal under the law. I don't think Plato would agree with the idea. According to the dialogue quoted earlier, Plato affirms that, "possession of one's own and the performance of one's own task could be agreed to be justice," implying one should accept one's station and thus not strive for change or demand equal consideration with someone higher in rank before the law.

Aristotle, by contrast, senses the vital importance of law as a means to protect individual rights when he says, "For man, when perfected, is the best of animals, but, when separated from law and justice, he is the worst of all; since armed injustice is the more dangerous, and he is equipped at birth with arms, meant to be used by intelligence and virtue, which he may use for the worst ends. . . . But justice is the bond of men in states, for the administration of justice, which is the determination of what is just, is the principle of order in political society." (p. 530)

Aristotle acknowledges that there can be no order in society without some system of laws, and though he does not directly say so, the quote above leads one to understand that there can be no fair and honest judgement of people accused of breaking the law, if all are not considered equal before the law. As soon as someone puts him or herself above the law, there is always the risk that that person might act cruelly to others without means of being stopped. Aristotle recognizes that people must be stopped if and when they use arms "for the worst ends" and that justice, rather than military force, is the most desirable and effective way to maintain order in an ongoing society.

Mill puts the idea clearly when he says: ". . . [I]t is, by universal admission, inconsistent with justice to be partial; to show favour or preference to one person over another, in matters to which favour and preference do not properly apply." (p. 564)

One major impact of establishing equality before the law is that second-class citizenship cannot occur. Different points of view must be tolerated as well as different ways of life, different practices and beliefs, and dissenters' ideas. Everyone becomes protected from a misuse of power. The Declaration of Independence reflects the concept of equality under the law indirectly when it states that, "Governments . . . [derive] their just powers from the consent of the governed," (p. 542), as society gives power to rulers by electing them, and may transfer it to others at new elections.

I realize, as I look over my initial choices of laws for a just society above, that my perspective is distinctly liberal, that is to say, it concentrates on the liberty, rights and responsibilities of the individual. I believe that socialism to some degree is necessary in the age we live in, for without a collective, centralized effort to provide housing, food, health care and education, our country would be vastly diminished and our conduct inhumane. Rawls's concerns about the economic well-being of people in a society focus on individual development and growth: it is essential that equal opportunities of development should be provided for the realization of individual talents and capacities. In addition, I believe that if people lack financial and physical security (employment, housing and food) they may become desperate and disenfranchised, incapable of participating as responsible citizens. A growing discrepancy between rich and poor, as noted recently in The New York Times, may further contribute to the poor's inability to participate as responsible and able citizens.

Though some people take exception to the mixing of democratic and socialist practices, I do not find a contradiction between giving the individual the right to choose his or her employment, and providing care for someone who requires it. Pragmatically speaking, there is enough money for many social needs in this country, if it is carefully managed, and the constant tension between allowing people liberty at their own risk, and support at the risk of losing autonomy, is, in my opinion, a necessary and a healthy one to maintain. Ben Jonson once said, "A society should be judged on how it treats its poor." The quote has haunted me since I first read it, for no matter what philosophic justification I may give as to why people should find the means to support themselves, the specter of indigent people who cannot, for whatever reason, take care of themselves, cries out to me for some systematic means of help, and our government is the best organization to provide such care because it draws from everyone's revenue accordingly.

Up until now I have considered only the needs of a single society. What about international relations? Of course I accept, as Hobbes says, that, ". . . the first and fundamental law of nature . . . is: to seek peace and follow it. The second, the sum of the right of nature . . . is: by all means we can to defend ourselves." (p. 536). In other words, if one is attacked, one is allowed to defend oneself. Nations, just like people, are entitled to preserve themselves through self-defense. This idea goes far beyond Locke's claim that, "[t]he great and chief end, therefore, of men's uniting into commonwealths, and putting themselves under government, is the preservation of their property." (p. 539) or Marx's view that the proletariat must not be bereft of his relationship to his handiwork (p. 556): "Owing to the extensive use of machinery, and to the division of labor, the work of the proletarians has lost all individual character. . . ." A country is entitled to protect itself against invasion and takeover.

But what happens when an invasion occurs? What right does a country have to stay once it has subdued a country which was attacking it? What if the invading country was not being attacked? I know that from time immemorial countries have taken each other's territories, that is how countries grow, and no one would expect Australia to give the continent back to the Aborigines, or the Brazilians to move to Portugal, but is the taking of someone else's land right? Is it fair? Should England never give Ireland back its northern territory? Should the United States control Iraq's oil production and maintain a sphere of influence over the Middle East? Should there be some kind of international socialism to allow those countries who need more financial, educational, health care and/or business assistance to get it from other countries who have more?

The Communist Manifesto looks rather naive when one realizes that many of its proclamations did not come true. The U.S.S.R. ultimately fell, no world revolution against capitalism occurred, and many workers were glad to become part of the modern world with the benefits it offered. However, the manifesto's global proposal that, "[t]he Proletarians have nothing to lose but their chains. They have a world to win. Proletarians of all countries, unite!" inspires the reader by suggesting that a global cause might unite people as a local or national one once did. Might a world peace movement begin with people across the world exerting pressure on their leaders to negotiate it? Here I may be as naive as Marx, but trade unions emerged as workers realized that there was force in numbers, and perhaps, given the sophisticated world communication that exists now with the Internet, international movements might be generated quickly and easily in keeping with a perception of ourselves not as members of competing nations, but as members of a single species on a fragile planet. John Rawls' notion of a "veil of ignorance" (p. 546) to blind everyone who helps shape the laws of a society, would be useful here as a means to help everyone consider his or her own needs, and thus ensure that important rights be protected.

If one day a global, rather than simply a national identity emerges, should not then nations, like individuals, be considered equal under the law? Should not countries submit to a world council as we now send representatives to Congress? The U.N. has at many times looked like a superfluous collection of diplomats. After centuries in which the stronger nation has dominated the weak, what a change in justice if all nations were held accountable under one "common power," as Mill called it.

The idea of an identity beyond national, religious or historical experience was first proposed by Baruch Spinoza (1632–1677), a Marrano Jew living in Amsterdam during a century of religious wars who conceived of himself, not as Jew or a Dutchman, but as a thinking, rational individual. Is it possible that people today might conceive of themselves beyond their national identities, and thus find common ground, rather than abject strife, with those who do not share their political philosophy?

A geology professor of mine once said the geological time, the process of millions of years by which the earth itself changed, was so slow it could only be conceived of by reminding oneself that what at first appeared impossible—a desert that would become a blooming valley, a mountain that would become a beach, an inland sea bigger than Europe that would become the dry land of mid-America—over time became probable and then possible. So too, perhaps, with civilization. Over periods of time much longer than a lifetime, or even generations, change, growth and understanding can and do occur. I disagree with John Stuart Mill when he says that, "we have natural feelings of justice." (p. 562). I believe we have natural feelings of injustice: impulses for revenge, anger, jealousy, hatred and covetousness. I believe justice is hard won, and once established must be carefully protected and developed to be maintained.

I have a theory that countries develop like individuals. One cannot rush the process, it must unfold. One hopes for good influences, but just as each person's experience will be unique, each country's experience will be unique, and during this slow course of maturation periods of adjustment to the next level of understanding will most often be violent and destructive. How I wish countries as well as individuals believed in Mill's definition of justice: ". . . [I]t is just to respect, unjust to violate, the legal rights of anyone." (p. 563). Sadly, individual and national conduct doesn't often follow Mill's definition. Countries often violate each other's territory with no respect for the other's rights.

What does one do when another nation internally violates a civil right within its own country? Some countries practice female circumcision. Some countries have slaves. Some countries are led by dictators. Does one do nothing unless the action crosses into one's own country? Does one invade the other country to enforce one's own moral code? What constitutes international justice and how should it be monitored?

If only the nations of the world would accept Mill's idea of tolerance: "Mankind are greater gainers by suffering [permitting] each other to live as seems good to themselves, than by compelling each other to live as seems good to the rest." (p. 569). If everybody let other people live the way they wanted, the world would be more peaceful. On the other hand, much of the strife these days seems to go beyond a mere intolerance for someone else's lifestyle. Intolerance may be the pretext for violence, but it is not always the cause, which is often hidden under layers of economic and historical conflict.

Are there certain precepts, despite cultural differences, which nonetheless all must obey for the good of the international body politic? Of course. We could not permit murder, theft, fraud and harassment in any society. Are such precepts always readily accepted and easily enforced? No. Herein lies one tragedy of human existence, that we as countries as well as individuals must struggle to understand what we value most and how best to protect it, though the conflict may take beyond our lifetime to resolve.

How do we begin? First, we have to keep learning about ourselves and each other, which includes hearing sides we don't know about, or don't agree with. Mill writes, ". . . [U]nity of opinion, unless resulting from the fullest and freest comparison of opposite opinions, is not desirable, and diversity not an evil, but a good, until mankind are much more capable than at present of recognizing all sides of the truth . . ." (p. 571). If we shut out the opinions we don't want to hear, we may never understand the other side's point of view and never be able to resolve our differences.

What if the conflict is too great to resolve? Mill writes: "[A] person's taste is as much his own peculiar concern as his opinion or his purse." That is a Western concept of individual freedom. In some countries one may be put to death for voicing one's own taste. How do countries coexist when their philosophies are diametrically opposed?

The night after 9/11, I received an email from my older brother in Los Angeles. He wrote something to the effect of, "We'll find those bastard scum and blast them all to hell!" I remember responding something along the lines of, "Whoever did this will be brought to trial. Let the legal system do its job. If you kill without due process as they did, then we are just as bad as they. The system we are trying to maintain will be weakened."

We are gripped in the middle of a great fear for which forces of strength must be harnessed to fight forces of evil, but where is the evil, and wherein lies our strength? If we lose sight of what makes for a fair society, with a Patriot Act that threatens the civil liberties of Americans even as it justifies overturning those rights in order to search for terrorists, we may lose our rights and the very society we fear is threatened from without.

How does justice begin? With an examination of existing laws, their application or reinterpretation, and perhaps the legislating of new laws if necessary in response to new circumstances. With learning about who's on the other side of a conflict, and why. Suddenly we are part of a global existence and owe it to ourselves to learn as much as we can, on an ongoing basis, about what is happening, what has happened, what legal precedents have been set in our own country and abroad to ensure a free and peaceable society, and how all those brought before the law may be ensured a fair hearing. Without the law, some accepted standard of judgment under which all parties may speak and be considered impartially, I do not see a way of resolving conflict between individuals or nations.

Where do I stand? I stand daunted by the task of trying to understand a world suddenly in such stark and dangerous contention, but eager to try to consider what those before have offered as rules for a just and fair society. Though the prospect is overwhelming, the alternative—to do nothing—is far worse, and so with trepidation, but with hope, I begin.

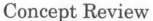

Concept Review

- Philosophers interested in political and social constructions explore questions about the following broad topics: justice, law, public interest, duty, rights, freedom, and power and influence. Social and political philosophies are both *normative*, in that they propose ideal societies, and *descriptive*, in that they offer critical analysis of how a specific political system actually functions (or doesn't!).

- Plato's political philosophy, the first to be based on the concept of "justice," is based on the ideals of "function" and "harmony." Such a society would be ruled by carefully educated "Philosopher-kings," who would preside over a society of Workers, Guardians, and other Philosopher-kings. In an ideal and just state, these three classes of people would function harmoniously together.

- Aristotle believed that humans are inherently "political," gregarious animals who only achieve their individual potential through social interaction. For him, the state is "prior to the individual," meaning that the interests of the community take precedence over the interests of the individual. Like Plato, he proposed a society based on ideals of justice. (It is important to remember, of course, that both Plato and Aristotle lived and wrote in a society that condoned and depended on slavery, and neither Plato nor Aristotle conceived of a "freedom" that would extend to slaves.) Aristotle also articulated a distinction between *retributive* and *distributive* justice, arguing that it is the duty of a just society to take care of its disadvantaged citizens.

- In stark contrast to Aristotle, Thomas Hobbes believed that humans are fundamentally predisposed to selfishness, destruction, and a kind of crude "state of nature" that, when unrestrained by laws or moral discipline, leads to chaos. Because of their ability to reason, however, humans agree to enter into "social contracts," by which they surrender some of their personal autonomy to a governing authority in exchange for protection. The authority of the state is based on the consent of those it governs, and cannot be questioned. Because we are all "equal" in terms of our desires, goals, and cravings, we are all at risk of a "war of all against all"; a strong central authority is needed to keep us from placing our cravings for personal safety above our agreements to cooperate with one another.

- John Locke, a contemporary of Hobbes, took a more optimistic view of human nature. Humans, he said, are governed by certain "natural laws" inherent to us as God's creation. These natural laws include the rights to life, liberty, health, and property. A just society respects and protects each citizen's natural rights; humans willingly enter into social contracts in order to create a just society with a central authority. This ideal state would be composed of three branches of government, each with specific powers and responsibilities: a legislative branch, an executive branch, and a federative (responsible for defense) branch. Unlike Hobbes, Locke believed that the authority of the state could be questioned, challenged, or even changed. His views had a profound influence on the American Revolution.

- David Hume, as might be expected, took violent exception to the idea that people willingly entered into social contracts with one another. Using examples of repressive, violent, and unjust regimes throughout history, Hume argued that political states have little interest in the rights of individual citizens.

- Modern liberalism, as exemplified by John Rawls, agrees with Hume that the concepts of a "state of nature" or a "social contract" were historical fictions. However, these concepts could be used as the theoretical basis of a just and fair political society. For Rawls, the concept of "justice" is inextricably linked to the concept of "fairness." He further suggests that to conceive of a fair and just society, we need to assume a "veil of ignorance" regarding our own standing and situation within that idealized society. If we were to assume such a "veil of ignorance," upon what principles would we want such an ideal or utopian society to be established?

- Rawls's sociopolitical philosophy is considered an exemplar of *liberalism*, in that it is founded on the assumption that all citizens are entitled to equal *opportunities* to achieve their maximum potential. Because economic inequality is a necessary part of such a society (in which people are rewarded according to their efforts, talents, and contributions), Rawls also requires a social welfare "safety net" to provide for those who (for whatever reason) cannot achieve their full potential, or who have fewer resources for doing so.

- Marxism, as articulated by Karl Marx and Friedrich Engels, is a social, economic, and political system based on the socialist ideal of "from each according to his abilities, to each according to his needs." If liberalism privileges the rights and freedoms of the individual, socialism (and communism) emphasize the duty of a society to equally distribute wealth and property among all its citizens.

- Marx and Engels conceived of history as *dialectical*—that is, each historical state of events creates, or leads to, its opposite. In their own time, Marx and Engels believed that struggles between economically privileged classes (the bourgeoisie) and the working classes (the proletariat) formed the key dialectic not only of modern times, but of all recorded history. The resolution of this particular dialectic—its *synthesis*—would result in communism, or a society in which goods, resources, the means of production, and participation in the government would be equally distributed among and held by all members of society.

- For John Stuart Mill, the touchstone for creating a society based on social justice and individual liberty is the concept of social utility. A rational critique of the concept of justice will lead us to understand it as that which calculates and implements the maximum good for the maximum amount of people. He defines five different requirements of justice that each, after a fashion, depend on this concept of social utility:
  - Not depriving someone of his personal liberty, property, or legally owned possessions.
  - Not disobeying any of a society's laws, even if you personally find that law to be unjust.
  - Each person receiving the good or evil that they deserve.
  - Honoring agreements and telling the truth.
  - Acting impartially and without preference.
  - Treating others with equality.

- Although Mill agrees that a harmonious society requires an authority that can guarantee its citizens protection from harm, his foremost concern was for individual liberty. Each individual has the right to freely choose his own conduct; as long as that conduct does not impinge upon the basic rights and freedoms of others, the government has no right to interfere.

- Feminist sociopolitical philosophy focuses on the traditional disparity between the sexes when it comes to social duties and obligations. For most of recorded time, they point out, women have not had the freedom to participate fully and equally in the rights and governance of society. Feminist philosophers such as Susan Moller Okin call for a reconsideration of traditional gender roles to more fully and equitably distribute justice and equality to all members of society.

Media Resources

 www.researchnavigator.com

Chapter 10 considers a variety of governmental and societal possibilities and asks questions about how and if a society should and can be maintained. Inquiries are imposed as to what role community members should play in a society and what type of management, if any, is required. For further research on questions on governmental ethics, justice, and human nature within a social realm, use the tools available to you in Research Navigator.

As you investigate this topic, consider this question: "What are the most important features of a successful society, and how can these be maintained or instated?"

- **ContentSelect:** search in the Criminal Justice, Finance and Economics, and Philosophy databases using the search terms "justice," "labor," and "violence."

- **Link Library:** search in the Philosophy database under the terms "communitarianism," "egalitarianism," and "quality of life" and the Economics database under "capitalism."

- **New York Times on the Web:** search in the Philosophy database using the search terms "justice" and "property."

 For additional study resources for this chapter, go to:
www.prenhall.com/chaffee/chapter10

 The Primary Source: Philosophical Readings and Commentary

Aristotle: *The Politics*

Du Bois, W.E.B.: *The Souls of Black Folks*

Hegel, Georg: *The Philosophy of History: Introduction*

Hobbes, Thomas: *Leviathan*

Locke, John: *The Second Treatise of Government*

Marx, Karl: *The Communist Manifesto*

Mill, John Stuart: *On Liberty; Utilitarianism*

Okin, Susan Moller: *Justice and Gender*

Plato: *The Republic, The Laws*

Rawls, John: *A Theory of Justice*

Smith, Adam: *An Inquiry into the Nature and Causes of the Wealth of Nations*

Wollstonecraft, Mary: *A Vindication of the Rights of Women*

CREDITS

◆

TEXT CREDITS

Chapter 1

p. 11   Perictione, Quoted in *A History of Women Philosophers*, ed. Mary Ellen Waithe (Boston: Martinus Nijhoff, 1987).

p. 17   Illustration, "The Elements of Reasoning Within a Point of View" A modified version of a schema originally devised by Ralph H. Johnson; design and layout by J.A. Blair.

p. 36   Russell, Bertrand. From *The Problems of Philosophy* by Bertrand Russell. Copyright 1912. Reprinted by permission of Oxford University Press.

Chapter 2

p. 47   Karl Jaspers, *Socrates, Buddha, Confucius, Jesus: the Paradigmatic Individuals*, trans. Ralph Manheim, ed. Hannah Arendt (New York: Harcourt Brace Jovanovich, 1962), p. 87.

p. 49   Lucretius, *On the Nature of the Universe*, trans. By Ronald Latham. Baltimore: Penguin Books (1951).

p. 49   Plato, *Xenophon*, From *Plato: Complete Works* John M. Cooper (editor) D.S. Hutchinson (editor) Hackett Publishing Co. (1997).

p. 50   Plato. The Apology from *The Dialogues of Plato*, translated by Benjamin Jowett. Copyright © 1998. Reprinted by permission of Oxford University Press.

p. 53   Plato, *The Republic*, trans. H.D.P. Lee (London: Penguin, 1955), bk 1, sec. 3, lines 336–339.

p. 60   Plato. The Apology from *The Dialogues of Plato*, translated by Benjamin Jowett. Copyright © 1998. Reprinted by permission of Oxford University Press.

p. 67   Aristophanes, The Clouds, in *The Complete Plays of Aristophanes*, trans. Moses Hadas (New York: Bantam, 1962).

p. 83   I.F. Stone, *The Trial of Socrates*, Little, Brown and Co. (1988).

Chapter 3

p. 90   Marcel Proust, *In Search of Time Lost*, Modern Library (2003).

pp. 92; 96   Hamilton, Edith. Plato, copyright © 1961 Princeton University Press, 1989 renewed. Reprinted by permission of Princeton University Press.

p. 98   Spelman, Elizabeth V., "Woman as Body: Ancient and Contemporary Views," was originally published in *Feminist Studies*, Volume 8, Number 1 (Spring 1982): 109–131, by permission of the publisher, Feminist Studies, Inc.

p. 103   Descartes, René. *Rules for the Direction of the Mind and Discourse on Method* from *The Philosophical Works of Descartes, Vol. I*. Reprinted with the permission of Cambridge University Press.

p. 110   John Locke, "On Personal Identity" from *An Essay Concerning Human Understanding* (London: E. Holt, 1690).

p. 111   Erich Fromm, *Escape From Freedom*, Henry Holt & Company (1994).

p. 112   John Locke, "On Personal Identity" from *An Essay Concerning Human Understanding* (London: E. Holt, 1690).

p. 116   Hume, David. "On Personal Identity" from *A Treatise on Human Nature* by David Hume, edited by Sebly-Bigge, L. A. Reprinted by permission of Oxford University Press.

p. 119   From *Milindapanha* (Trenckner ed.).

p. 120   Immanuel Kant, *Prolegomena to Any Future Metaphysics*, trans. Lewis White Beck (Indianapolis: Liberal Arts, 1950), intro., pp. 5–6

p. 121   Hume, David. "On Personal Identity" from *A Treatise on Human Nature* by David Hume, edited by Sebly-Bigge, L. A. Reprinted by permission of Oxford University Press.

p. 122   Immanuel Kant, *Critique of Pure Reason*, 2nd ed., unabridged ed., trans. Norman Kemp Smith (New York: St. Martin's, 1929).

p. 125   Freud, Sigmund. "An Outline of Psychoanalysis" © copyright The Institute of Psychoanalysis and The Hogarth Press for permission to quote from *The Standard Edition of the Complete Psychological Works of Sigmund Freud* translated and edited by James Strachey. Reprinted by permission of Random House Group Limited and W. W. Norton & Co. Inc.

p. 126   Norman Cameron, *Personality Development and Psychopathology* (Boston: Houghton-Mifflin Co, 1963), p. xiii.

p. 126   Ernest Jones, *The Life and Work of Sigmund Freud* (New York: Basic Books, 1953), p. 436.

p. 130 Alasdair MacIntyre, *The Unconscious* (London: Routledge & Kegan Paul Ltds., 1958).

p. 131 Gaylin, Willard. "What You See is the Real You," 10/07/77. Copyright © The New York Times Company. All rights reserved.

p. 133 Gilbert Ryle, *The Concept of Mind* by Gilbert Ryle. Copyright © 1949. Reprinted by permission of Taylor and Francis, UK.

p. 137 Brand Blanshard, "The Limits of Naturalism" from *Contemporary American Philosophy* J. Smith (ed.), (London: Allen and Unwin, 1970).

p. 138 Churchland, Paul M. Pages 43–49 from *Matter and Conscience*, revised edition. Reprinted by permission of MIT Press.

p. 143 John Bannan, *The Philosophy of Merleau-Ponty*, (New York, Harcourt Brace).

p. 143 Maurice Merleau-Ponty, *Phenomenology of Perception* trans. Colin Smith (New York: Routledge & Kegan Paul 1962).

p. 145 Marcel Proust, *In Search of Time Lost*, Modern Library (2003).

p. 145 Aristotle, *De Anima*, trans. W.S. Hett (Cambridge, MA: Harvard University Press, 1936).

p. 146 Marcel Proust, *Within a Budding Grove* (New York: Random House, 1998) 1010.

p. 147 Aristotle, *Politics*, bk. I, ch. II trans. Benjamin Jowett (1896).

p. 147 Eve Browning Cole, *Philosophy and Feminist Criticism* (Paragon House, 1993).

p. 148 Sartre, Jean-Paul. From *Existentialism is a Humanism* trans. Phillip Mairet. Copyright © 1974. All rights reserved. Reprinted by arrangement with Kensington Publishing Corp. *www.kensingtonbooks.com*.

Chapter 4

p. 164 John Stuart Mill, quoted in the introduction to *A Modern Introduction to Philosophy: Readings from Classical and Contemporary Sources*, e. by P. Edwards & Pap (NY: Free Press, 1967).

p. 165 Clarence Darrow, "The Crime of Compulsion," in *Attorney for the Damned*, ed. Arthur Weinberg (New York: Simon and Schuster, 1957)

p. 166 Thiry, Paul Henry, Baron d'Holbach, *The System of Nature*, Vol. I, Chapters 11 and 12, translated by H. D. Robinson (1853). Reprinted by permission of Clinamen Press.

p. 170 J.B. Watson, *Behaviorism* (Chicago: University of Chicago Press 1924, rev. ed.) 1930, p. 104.

p. 170 B.F. Skinner, *Science and Human Behavior* (New York: MacMillan Free Press, 1953) p. 23.

p. 171 Thiry, Paul Henry, Baron d'Holbach, The System of Nature, Vol. I, Chapters 11 and 12, translated by H. D. Robinson (1853). Reprinted by permission of Clinamen Press.

p. 177 William James, *The Will to Believe* (Dover Publications, 1960).

p. 187 Jean-Paul Sartre, *Existentialism is a Humanism* trans. Philip Mairet (World Publishing Company, 1956).

p. 199 Viktor Frankl, *Man's Search for Meaning* (New York: Pocket Books, 1997).

p. 202 Erich Fromm, *Escape From Freedom* (New York: Henry Holt & Co., 1994.

p. 203 Grimshaw, Jean. "Autonomy and Identity in Feminist Thinking" (pp. 90–95) in *Feminist Perspectives in Philosophy*, edited by Morwenna Griffiths and Mary Whitford. Copyright © 1988 by Indiana University Press. Reprinted by permission.

Chapter 5

p. 216 Aristotle. "Nicomachean Ethics" translated by JEC Weldon from *Philosophers Speak for Themselves*, TV Smith, ed. Reprinted by permission of University of Chicago Press.

p. 219 M. Scott Peck, *The Road Less Traveled*, (Touchstone Books, 2003).

p. 224 Mohandas Gandhi, *All Men Are Brothers* (New York: Columbia Univ. Press, 1058), p. 143.

p. 228 Herodotus, *The Histories* (c. 500 B.C.) trans. Aubrey de Selincourt (Harmondsworth, England: Penguin, 172), pp. 219–220.

p. 229 Ruth Benedict, *Patterns of Culture* (Boston: Houghton Mifflin Co., 1958).

p. 230 Ruth Benedict, "Anthropology and the Abnormal" *The Journal of General Psychology* 10 (1934): 59–82. Reprinted with the permission of the Helen Dwight Reid Educational Foundation. Published by Heldrerf Publications, 1319 Eighteenth St. N.W., Washington, DC, Copyright 1934).

p. 235 W. T. Stace, *The Concept of Morals* by W. T. Stace. Copyright 1937 by The Macmillan Company, renewed 1965 by The Macmillan Company. Reprinted by permission of the publisher.

p. 239 William James, *The Will to Believe* (Dover Publications, 1960).

p. 243 Plato, the *Republic*, trans. H.D.P. Lee (London: Penguin, 1955) Book 2, *The Myth of Gyges*.

p. 246 Edmond O. Wilson, *On Human Nature*, (Cambridge: Harvard Univ. Press, 1978, p 167).

p. 246   Ayn Rand, *The Virtue of Selfishness* by Ayn Rand (New York: American Library, 1964).

p. 246   Ayn Rand, *The Fountainhead* by Ayn Rand (New York: Plume, 2002).

p. 250   Rachels, James. "Egoism and Moral Skepticism" from *Moral Problems* copyright © 1972 by James Rachels. Reprinted by permission of the Estate of James Rachels.

p. 257   Exodus 20: 1–4, The Holy Bible, St. James Edition.

p. 257   2:177, The Holy Qu'ran.

p. 258   Genesis 22: 1–18, The Holy Bible, St. James Edition.

p. 263   King, Martin Luther Jr. From "Letter from a Birmingham Jail." Copyright © 1963 by Martin Luther King, Jr., copyright © renewed 1991 by Coretta Scott King. Reprinted by arrangement with the Estate of Martin Luther King Jr., c/o Writer's House as agent for the proprietor, New York, NY.

p. 264   Coles, Robert. "The Disparity Between Intellect and Character." Copyright © 1995 by Robert Coles. First appeared in *The Chronicle of Higher Education*. Reprinted by permission of the author.

Chapter 6

p. 273   Epicurus, *Letter to Menoceceus*, trans. George D. Strodach, quoted in *Hellenistic Philosophy*, ed. Herman Shapiro and Edwin M. Curley (New York: Modern Library, 1965), p. 6.

p. 274   Jeremy Bentham, *An Introduction to the Principles of Moral and Legislation* (London: Wilson & Pickering, 1823), chaps. 1, 2, 4, and 10.

p. 280   John Stuart Mill, "Utilitarianism" from *Utilitarianism* by JSM, (London, NY: Longman, 1907).

p. 283   Singer, Peter. From *Animal Liberation, Second Edition* by Peter Singer. Copyright © 1990 by Peter Singer. Reprinted by permission of the author.

p. 290   Kant, Immanuel. *Fundamental Principles of the Metaphysics of Morals*, translated by T. K. Abbott (London: Longmans, Green, 1907).

p. 299   Immanuel Kant, "Duties to Oneself," in *Lectures on Ethics* (Indianapolis: Hackett, 1775–1780/1963), p. 118.

p. 300   Aristotle, *Nicomachean Ethics* trans. J.E.C. Weldon, in *Philosopohers Speak for Themselves*, ed. T.V. Smith (Chicago: University of Chicago Press, 1934).

p. 311   Kant, Immanuel. *Fundamental Principles of the Metaphysics of Morals*, translated by T. K. Abbott (London: Longmans, Green, 1907).

p. 311   John Stuart Mill, "On Liberty," in *Utilitarianism and Other Writings*, ed. Mary Warnock (New York: Meridian, 1962), p. 189.

pp. 312; 314; 317   Bretall, Robert. From *A Kierkegaard Anthology* copyright 1946 Princeton University Press, 1974 renewed Princeton University Press. Reprinted by permission of Princeton University Press.

p. 318   Swenson, David. *Concluding Unscientific Postscript by Søren Kierkegaard*. Copyright 1941 Princeton University Press, 1969 renewed. Reprinted by permission of Princeton University Press.

p. 319   Sartre, Jean-Paul. From *Existentialism is a Humanism* trans. Phillip Mairet. Copyright © 1974. All rights reserved. Reprinted by arrangement with Kensington Publishing Corp. *www.kensingtonbooks.com*

p. 324   Simone de Beauvoir, *The Ethics of Ambiguity*, Copyright © 1948 by Philosophical Library, Inc. Reprinted by permission of Philosophical Library, Inc., publishers.

p. 326   Camus, Albert. From *The Myth of Sisyphus*, translated by Justin O'Brien, copyright © 1955, 1983 by Alfred A. Knopf. Used by permission of Alfred A. Knopf, a division of Random House, Inc.

p. 329   Noddings, Nel. "Caring: A Feminine Approach to Ethics and Moral Education" copyright © 1984 The Regents of the University of California. Reprinted by permission.

Chapter 7

p. 346   Albert Einstein, "Religion and Science," in Ideas and Opinions, trans. Sonia Bargmann (New York: Crown, 1954).

p. 349   Knud Rasmussen, *Across Arctic America* (New York: G.P. Putnam's Sons, 1927) p. 386.

p. 349   Josiah U. Young III, "Out of Africa: African Traditional Religion and African Theology," in *World Religions and Human Liberation*, Dan Cohn-Sherbok, ed., Maryknoll, (New York: Orbis Books, 1992) p. 93.

p. 350   Jo Agguisho/Oren R. Lyons, spokesman for the Traditional Elders Circle, Wolf Clan, Onondaga Nation, Haudenosaunee, Six Nations Iroquois Confederacy, from the speech to the Fourth World Wilderness Conference, September 11, 1987, p. 2.

p. 350   Quoted in John Neihardt, *Black Elk Speaks* 1932, (Lincoln, Nebraska: University of Nebraska Press, 1961.

p. 351   Leonard Crow Dog and Richard Erdoes, in Joan Halifax, *Shamanic Voices* (New York: E.P. Dutton, 1979) p. 77.

p. 351   Tlakaelel, talk at Interface, Watertown, Massachusetts, April 15, 1988.

p. 352   Muhaparinibbana Sutta, Digha Nikaya, 2.99f, 155–156, quoted in *Sources of Indian Tradition*, William Theodore de Bary, ed., (New York: Columbia University Press, 1958) pp. 110–111.

p. 353   Ajahn Sumedho, cited in Satnacitto Bhikku, ed., *Buddha-nature*, World Wide Fund for nature, London, 1989.

p. 353   Mary Pat Fisher, *Living Religions 5/e* (New Jersey: Prentice Hall) p. 152.

p. 354   *The Dhammapada*, translated by P. Lal. Copyright © 1967. Reprinted by permission of Farrar, Straus and Giroux, L. L. C.

p. 355   *The Upanishads*, trans. Swami Prabhavananda and Frederick Manchester. (New York: Mentor Books, 1957).

p. 355   *Chandogya Upanishad* Walpola Sri Rahula, *What the Buddha Taught* (New York: Grove Press, 1974) p. 17.

p. 357   Lau-tzu, Tao-te Ching, translated by D. C. Lau (London: Penguin, 1963).

p. 358   Lau-tzu, Tao-te Ching, translated by D. C. Lau (London: Penguin, 1963).

p. 358   *The Way to Life: At the Heart of the Tao-te Ching*, trans. Benjamin Hoff (New York/Tokyo: Weatherhill, 1981).

p. 361   Psalm I 39: 7–14, *The Holy Bible* King James Version.

p. 361   Deuteronomy 6: 4–9, *The Holy Bible* King James Version.

p. 363   Mark 1: 10–11, *The Holy Bible* King James Version.

p. 364   Matthew 6:25–27, *The Holy Bible* King James Version.

p. 364   Matthew 5:44–45, *The Holy Bible* King James Version.

p. 365   Matthew 25: 37–40, *The Holy Bible* King James Version.

p. 365   Luke 10: 30–36, *The Holy Bible* King James Version.

p. 365   Matthew 13: 47–50, *The Holy Bible* King James Version.

p. 366   John 4: 13–14, *The Holy Bible* King James Version.

p. 367   Matthew 24: 29–31, *The Holy Bible* King James Version.

p. 367   Matthew 23: 27–28, *The Holy Bible* King James Version.

p. 369   *The Holy Qur'an*, XCVI: 1–5, English translation by Abdullah Yusuf Ali, Durban, R.S.A.: Islamic Propagation Center International, 1946.

p. 375   Friedrich Nietzsche, *Daybreak*, in Philip Novak, *the Vision of Nietzsche* (Vega, 2003) p. 78.

p. 376   Friedrich Nietzsche, *The Gay Science*, trans. Walter Kaufmann (New York: Vintage, 1974) p. 181; 279.

p. 377   Friedrich Nietzsche, *Thus Spoke Zarathustra* in *The Portable Nietzsche* trans. Walter Kaufmann (New York: Vintage/Ebury, 1975) p. 199

p. 377   Friedrich Nietzsche, *Toward a Genealogy of Morals* in *The Portable Nietzsche* trans. Walter Kaufmann (New York: Vintage/Ebury, 1975) p.199.

p. 377   Friedrich Nietzsche, *Beyond Good and Evil*, trans. Walter Kaufmann (New York: Random House, 1966).

p. 379   Daly, Mary. "The Qualitative Leap Beyond Patriarchal Religion." As appeared in *Quest*, vol. 1, no. 4 (Spring 1975). Reprinted by permission of the author.

p. 381   William James, *The Varieties of Religions Experience* (New York: Longman, Green, 1902).

p. 386   Thomas Aquinas, *Summa Theologica* (Benzier Bros. Edition, 1947) Translated by Fathers of the English Dominican Province.

p. 388   William Paley, *Natural Theology*, First published in 1822.

p. 389   Russell, Bertrand. Reprinted with the permission of Simon & Schuster Adult Publishing Group and Taylor and Francis from *Why I Am Not a Christian* by Bertrand Russell. Copyright © 1957 by George Allen & Unwin Ltd. Electronic rights Courtesy of The Bertrand Russell Peace Foundation.

p. 390   Immanuel Kant, *Critique of Practical Reason*, trans. White Beck © 1993. Reprinted by permission of Prentice Hall, Upper Saddle River, NJ.

p. 391   Russell, Bertrand. Reprinted with the permission of Simon & Schuster Adult Publishing Group and Taylor and Francis from *Why I Am Not a Christian* by Bertrand Russell. Copyright © 1957 by George Allen & Unwin Ltd. Electronic rights courtesy of The Bertrand Russell Peace Foundation.

p. 395   Kierkegaard, Søren. From *Philosophical Fragments*, copyright 1936 Princeton University Press, 1962, 1990 renewed. Reprinted by permission of Princeton University Press.

p. 396   Søren Kierkegaard, *Concluding Unscientific Postscript*, trans. David F. Swenson and Walter Lowrie. Copyright 1992 by Howard Hong. Reprinted by permission of Princeton University Press.

p. 400   John Hick, "God Can Allow Some Evil," from *Philosophy of Religion* © 1963. Reprinted by permission of Prentice Hall, Upper Saddle River, NJ.

p. 404   Frederick Streng, et al. *Ways of Being Religious* (Prentice Hall: Upper Saddle River, NJ, 1973).

Chapter 8

p. 415   Bertrand Russell, "Appearance and Reality," reprinted from the *Problems of Philosophy* (Oxford University Press, 1959).

p. 421   Charles Dickens, *Hard Times* (New York: Bantam, 1981).

p. 421	Aristotle, *Metaphysics* in *The Philosophy of Aristotle*, ed. Renford Bambrough (New York: New American Library, 1963).
p. 422	Plato, *Timaeus, 27D–28A*, trans. Benjamin Jowett, in *The Dialogues of Plato, 3rd ed.* (Oxford: Clarendon, 1982).
p. 425	Plato, *The Meno*, trans. G.M.A. Grube (Indianapolis, IN: Hackett, 1976).
p. 426	Plato, From *The Republic*, Book VII, translated by G. M. A. Grube. Copyright © 1974. Reprinted by permission of Hackett Publishing.
p. 430	Aristotle, *Metaphysics*, in W.T. Jones, *the Classical Mind, 2nd ed.* (New York: Harcourt Brace Jovanovich, 1970).
p. 431	Aristotle, *Metaphysics*, trans. W.D. Ross (Oxford: Oxford University Press, 1924).
p. 433	Aristotle, *Metaphysics*, trans. Phillip Wheelwright in *Aristotle* (New York: Odyssey, 1951).
p. 435	Aristotle, *Metaphysics*, trans. Hugh Terdennick (Cambridge, MA: Harvard University Press, 1933).
pp. 445; 449	Descartes, René. Excerpts from "Meditations on the First Philosophy" from *The Philosophical Works of Descartes, Vol. 1*, edited by Elizabeth S. and Ross, G. R. T. Reprinted by permission of Cambridge University Press.
p. 449	From Herbert A. Giles, trans. *Chuang-Tzu: Taoist Philosopher and Chinese Mystic.* (London: George Allen and Unwin, 1961 (1889).

Chapter 9

p. 461	John Locke, *An Essay Concerning Human Understanding*, 1689 ed. A.C. Fraser (Oxford: Clarendon Press, 1894).
p. 463	Gottfried Wilhelm von Leibniz. Reprinted by permission of Open Court Publishing Company, a division of Carus Publishing Company, Peru, IL from *New Essays Concerning Human Understanding* by Gottfried Wilhelm von Leibniz, translated by Alfred Gideon Langley. Copyright 1949.
p. 465	John Locke, *An Essay Concerning Human Understanding*, 1689 ed. A.C. Fraser (Oxford: Clarendon Press, 1894).
p. 471	George Berkeley, *Treatise Concerning the Principles of Human Knowledge* (New York: Bobbs-Merril, 1957) Reprinted by permission of Prentice-Hall, Inc., Upper Saddle River, NJ.
p. 475	George Berkeley, *Three Dialogues Between Hylas and Philonous*, 1713 (New York: Bobbs-Merril, 1957) Reprinted by permission of Prentice Hall, Inc., Upper Saddle River, NJ.
p. 476	Bertrand Russell, *A History of Western Philosophy* (New York: Simon and Schuster, 1945).
p. 477	Hume, David. From *An Enquiry Concerning Human Understanding*, 2nd Edition (1902) by David Hume, edited by Selby-Bigge, LA. Reprinted by permission of Oxford University Press.
p. 486	Immanuel Kant, *Prolegomena to Any Further Metaphysics*, trans. Lewis White Beck © 1957. Reprinted by permission of Prentice Hall, Upper Saddle River, NJ.
p. 490	Hume, David. From *An Enquiry Concerning Human Understanding*, 2nd Edition (1902) by David Hume, edited by Selby-Bigge, LA. Reprinted by permission of Oxford University Press.
pp. 493; 494	Immanuel Kant, *the Critique of Pure Reason*, 2nd ed., unabridged ed., trans. Norman Kemp Smith (New York: St. Martin's, 1929).
p. 497	"The Investigation" @ John Jonik. Reproduced with permission. This cartoon first appeared in *Psychology Today*, February 1984.
p. 502	"On the Assassination of Malcolm X," *The New York Times*, February 22, 1965. Copyright © 1965 The New York Times Company. Reprinted by permission.
p. 502	"Assassination of Malcolm X." *Life*, 2/22/65. Copyright © 1965 Time, Inc. Reprinted by permission.
p. 502	"The Assassination of Malcolm X," *The New York Post*, February 22, 1965. Reprinted by permission.
p. 505	Jaggar, Alison. Reprinted from Alison M. Jaggar, "Love and Knowledge: Emotion in Feminist Epistemology" *Inquiry*, 32:151:176. (*www.tandf.no/inquiry*) by permission of Taylor & Francis AS.
p. 512	Albert Einstein, "Religion and Science," in *Ideas and Opinions*, trans. Sonia Bargmann (New York: Crown, 1954).

Chapter 10

p. 526	Plato, *The Republic*, Bk. IV, VI, VII, trans. G.M.A. Grube (Indianapolis, IN: Hackett.
p. 529	Aristotle, *Politics*, trans. Benjamin Jowett.
p. 533	Thomas Hobbes, *Leviathan* (New York: Hafner, 1926).
p. 538	John Locke, *The Second Treatise of Civil Government* (New York: Hafner, 1947).
p. 544	David Hume, "Of the Original Contract," in Essay, Literary, Moral, and Political (New York: Ward, Lock).
p. 546	Rawls, John. Reprinted by permission of the publisher from *A Theory of Justice* by John Rawls, pp. 11–13, Cambridge, Mass.: The Belknap Press of Harvard University Press, copyright © 1971, 1999 by the President and Fellows of Harvard College.

p. 551   Karl Marx and Friedrich Engels, *Manifesto of the Communist Party*, 1888 ed.

p. 562   John Stuart Mill, *Utilitarianism* (New York: Bobbs-Merrill, 1957).

p. 575   Rawls, John. Reprinted by permission of the publisher from *A Theory of Justice* by John Rawls, pp. 11–13, Cambridge, Mass.: The Belknap Press of Harvard University Press, copyright © 1971, 1999 by the President and Fellows of Harvard College.

p. 576   John Stuart Mill, *On Liberty*, (London: Longmans, 1859).

p. 576   Okin, Susan Moller. From *Justice, Gender and the Family*. Copyright © 1989 by Basic Books, Inc. Reprinted by permission of Basic Books, a member of Perseus Books, L.L.C.

PHOTO CREDITS

Chapter 1

p. 2: Alinari Archives/Corbis/Bettmann; **p. 3 (top, left):** Getty Images Inc.—Hulton Archive Photos; **p. 3 (top, right):** Jerry Bauer Photography; **p. 3 (bottom, left):** Gala/SuperStock, Inc.; **p. 5:** Corbis/Bettmann; **p. 9:** AP Wide World Photos; **p. 13:** Nancy Honey/Getty Images Inc.—Stone Allstock; **p. 14:** National Historical Museum, Frederiksborg/Danish Embassy; **p. 22:** Betsie Van der Meer/Getty Images Inc.—Stone Allstock; **p. 30:** J.C. Francolon/Getty Images, Inc – Liaison; **p. 33:** Diego Rivera (1866-1957). "The History of Medicine in Mexico, The People Demanding Health", 1953. (Detail) Fresco, approx. 7.4 × 10.8 m. Hospital de la Raza, Mexico City, D.F., Mexico. Photo: Art Resource, NY. © 2003 Banco de Mexico Diego Rivera & Frida Kahlo Museums Trust. Av. Cinco de Mayo No. 2, Col. Centro, Del. Cuauhtemoc 06059, Mexico, D.F. Reproduction authorized by the Instituto Nacional de Bellas Artes y Literatura; **p. 37:** Getty Images Inc.—Hulton Archive Photos; **p. 40:** Corbis/Bettmann; **p. 41:** Susan Van Etten/PhotoEdit;

Chapter 2

p. 44: Scala/Art Resource, N.Y.; **p. 45 (top, left):** FPG/Getty Images, Inc. – Taxi; **p. 45 (top, right):** Araldo de Luca/Corbis/Bettmann; **p. 45 (bottom, left):** Fototeca Storica Nazionale/Getty Images, Inc.-Photodisc; **p. 50:** My Studio; **p. 55:** Nevada State Historic Preservation Office; **p. 58:** The Bridgeman Art Library International Ltd.; **p. 60:** Wolf, Hans/Getty Images Inc.—Image Bank; **p. 61:** EyeWire Collection/Getty Images—Photodisc; **p. 62:** Margaret Bourke-White/Getty Images/Time Life Pictures; **p. 65:** Stan Wakefield/Pearson Education/PH College; **p. 69:** Michael Newman/PhotoEdit; **p. 71:** Library of Congress; **p. 75:** Thomas L. Shafer/Acme/Corbis/Bettmann; **p. 80:** Francis G. Mayer/Corbis; **p. 82:** The Bridgeman Art Library International Ltd.;

Chapter 3

p. 88: Reunion des Musees Nationaux/Art Resource, NY; **p. 89 (top, left):** Sheila Terry/Science Photo Library/Photo Researchers, Inc.; **p. 89 (top, right):** Corbis/Bettmann; **p. 89 (bottom):** Leonardo da Vinci, "De Architectura di Vitruvio" (The Vitruvian Man). © Scala/Art Resource, NY; **p. 91:** Photodisc/Getty Images; **p. 92:** Getty Images Inc.—Hulton Archive Photos; **p. 94 (bottom, left):** Getty Images Inc.—Hulton Archive Photos; **p. 94 (bottom, middle):** Frank Edwards/Getty Images Inc.—Hulton Archive Photos; **p. 94 (bottom, right):** Getty Images, Inc.; **p. 96:** Alan Williams © Dorling Kindersley; **p. 97:** Library of Congress; **p. 101:** Photo Courtesy of Historic St. Augustine Preservation Board **p. 102:** Photodisc/Getty Images; **p. 103:** Courtesy of the Library of Congress; **p. 104:** Christopher Zacharow/Stock Illustration Source, Inc.; **p. 107:** Photolibrary.com **p. 111 (top, left):** Corbis/Bettmann; **p. 111 (top, right):** Michael A. Mariant/AP Wide World Photos; **p. 113:** National Library of Medicine; **p. 117:** Allen Ramsay/Library of Congress; **p. 118:** Photodisc/Getty Images; **p. 121:** Library of Congress; **p. 127:** The Sleeping Gypsy, Henri Rousseau, 1897, Oil on Canvas, 51″ × 6′7″, Gift of Mrs Simon Guggenheim (646.1939). The Museum of Modern Art/Licensed by Scala-Art Resource, NY.; **p. 134:** © Dorling Kindersley; **p. 139:** Pearson Education Corporate Digital Archive; **p. 143:** Corbis/Bettmann; **p. 148:** Stone/Getty Images;

Chapter 4

p. 154: Erich Lessling/Art Resource, N.Y.; **p. 155 (top, left):** Reg_Lancaster/Getty Images Inc.—Hulton Archive Photos; **p. 155 (top, right):** The Bridgeman Art Library International Ltd.; **p. 155 (bottom, right):** Cal Vornberger/Peter Arnold, Inc.; **p. 159:** AP Wide World Photos; **p. 161:** Laima Druskis/Pearson Education/PH College; **p. 162:** Rameshwar Das/Government of India; **p. 165:** Library of Congress; **p. 171:** National Library of Medicine; **p. 172:** Gianni Dagi Orti/Corbis/Bettmann; **p. 179:** National Library of Medicine; **p. 180:** Edmond Van Hoorick/Getty Images, Inc.- Photodisc; **p. 183:** Bruce Weaver/AP Wide World Photos; **p. 190:** Reg_Lancaster/Getty Images Inc.—Hulton Archive Photos; **p. 193:** Peter Dennis © Dorling Kindersley; **p. 197:** Ross H. Miller, Ph.D.; **p. 199:** AP Wide World Photos; **p. 201:** Image Bank/Getty Images;

Chapter 5

p. 214: Francis G. Mayer/Corbis/Bettmann; **p. 215 (top, left):** Corbis/Bettmann; **p. 215 (top, right):** Arthur Muray, NY/Vassar College Libraries; **p. 215 (bottom):** Corbis RF; **p. 217:** Mark Richards/PhotoEdit;

p. 220: AP Wide World Photos; p. 223: Library of Congress; p. 224: EMG Education Management Group; p. 227: AP Wide World Photos; p. 231: Hulton-Deutsch Collection/Corbis/Bettmann; p. 232: Catherine Karnow/Corbis/Bettmann; p. 239: Alice Boughton/Library of Congress; p. 241: Hulton Archive/Getty Images; p. 252: Library of Congress; p. 257: Gianni Dagli Orti/Corbis/Bettmann; p. 259: Neil Lukas © Dorling Kindersley, Courtesy of the Museo de Bellas Artes, Seville; p. 262: UPI/Corbis/Bettmann;

Chapter 6

p. 270: Corbis/Bettmann; p. 271 (top, left): North Wind Picture Archives; p. 271 (top, right): Pawel Wojcik © Dorling Kindersley; p. 271 (bottom, right): Stele of Hammurabi—detail of upper part: The sun god dictating his laws to King Hammurabi. Babylonian relief from Susa, c. 1760 BC. (diorite, height of stele c. 2.1 m, height of relief 71 cm). Louvre, Paris, France. Copyright Giraudon/Art Resource; p. 273: Hulton Archive/Getty Images; p. 278: Eric Drooker; p. 281: Sir John Everett Millais, P.R.A., British 1829-1896. Peace Concluded 1856. Oil on canvas. 46 × 36 in. (116.84 × 91.44 cm) The Minneapolis Institute of Arts, The Putna Dana McMillian Fund. (69.48); p. 282: Photolibrary.Com; p. 284: Dewey/EMG Education Management Group; p. 285: Nick Koudis/Getty Images, Inc.-Photodisc; p. 289: Ricardo Watson/Corbis/Sygma; p. 290: Courtesy of the Library of Congress; p. 293: Fotosearch.com, LLC; p. 295: Silver Burdett Ginn; p. 296: © Dorling Kindersley; p. 301: Bill Aron/PhotoEdit; p. 302: Library of Congress; p. 304: Heidi Grassley © Dorling Kindersley; p. 306: The Image Works; p. 314: Phil Schermeister/CORBIS–NY; p. 316: Corbis/Bettmann; p. 321: Reg_Lancaster/Getty Images Inc.—Hulton Archive Photos; p. 322: © Dorling Kindersley, Courtesy of the H Keith Melton Collection; p. 326: Erich Lessling/Art Resource, N.Y.; p. 330: EyeWire Collection/Getty Images—Photodisc; p. 332: P. Pittet/F.A.O. Food and Agriculture Organization of the United Nations;

Chapter 7

p. 340: J. Kershaw © The British Museum; p. 341 (top, left) and 395: Corbis/Bettmann; p. 341 (top, right): Corbis/Bettmann; p. 341 (bottom, left): Geoff Dann © Dorling Kindersley, Courtesy of the Museum of the Order of St John, London; p. 343: Andy Crawford © Dorling Kindersley, Courtesy of the Buddha Padipa Temple, Wimbledon; p. 344: EMG Education Management Group; p. 345: Jim Siebold; p. 346: National Archives and Records Administration; p. 349: Geoff Brightling © Dorling Kindersley; p. 350: EMG Education Management Group; p. 351: Joanna B. Pinneo/Aurora & Quanta Productions Inc; p. 352: Peter Visscher © Dorling Kindersley; p. 353: James Strachan/Getty Images Inc.—Stone Allstock; p. 354: Pearson Education/PH College; p. 355: Robert Francis/Robert Harding World Imagery; p. 357: Eugene Gordon/Pearson Education/PH College; p. 358: Alex Wilson © Dorling Kindersley; p. 359: Stephen Oliver © Dorling Kindersley; p. 361: Paul Chesley/Getty Images Inc.—Stone Allstock p. 363: © Dorling Kindersley; p. 365: Eric Thomas © Dorling Kindersley; p. 366: Victoria & Albert Museum, London/Art Resource, N.Y.; p. 368: Magnus Rew © Dorling Kindersley; p. 369: Laurence Pordes © Dorling Kindersley, Courtesy of The British Library; p. 370: M.Nimsiri/UNEP/Peter Arnold, Inc. p. 371: Jon Spaull © Dorling Kindersley; p. 372: Eric Thomas © Dorling Kindersley; p. 376: Max Alexander © Dorling Kindersley p. 379: John Serafin/SBG/John Serafin; p. 382: Library of Congress; p. 383: Cecile Treal and Jean-Michel Ruiz © Dorling Kindersley; p. 386: The Granger Collection, New York; p. 389: Paul Bricknell © Dorling Kindersley; p. 390: Courtesy of the Library of Congress; p. 392: John Woodcock © Dorling Kindersley; p. 393: AP Wide World Photos; p. 395: National Historical Museum, Frederiksborg; p. 397: Sistine Chapel, Vatican/Canali Photobank Milan/Superstock; p. 400: Philip Wallick/Corbis/Bettmann; p. 401: Library of Congress;

Chapter 8

p. 412: Schuster, Ellen/Getty Images Inc.—Image Bank; p. 413 (top, left): Library of Congress; p. 413 (top, right): CORBIS- NY; p. 413 (bottom, left): Visual Arts Library/Art Resource, NY; p. 416: Brian Cosgrove © Dorling Kindersley; p. 418: CORBIS–NY; p. 420: Jim Siebold; p. 421: Staatliche Antiken-sammlung, Munich, Germany/Bridgeman Art Library, London/SuperStock; p. 422: Karl Shone © Dorling Kindersley; p. 424: Library of Congress; p. 427: Courtesy of the Library of Congress; p. 429: Musee de la Chatrueuse, Douai, France/Bridgeman Art Library/Giraudon/Bridgeman Art Library; p. 431: Kenneth Eward/BioGrafx; p. 433: Matthew Ward © Dorling Kindersley; p. 435: Macduff Everton/Corbis/Bettmann; p. 437 (top): AP Wide World Photos; p. 437 (bottom): SuperStock, Inc.; p. 441: Photo Library International/Corbis/Bettmann; p. 443: Scala/Art Resource, N.Y.; p. 446: Courtesy of the Library of Congress; p. 448: Art Resource/Smithsonian American Art Museum; p. 449: Frank Greenaway © Dorling Kindersley, Courtesy of the Natural History Museum, London; p. 453: Mike Dunning © Dorling Kindersley;

Chapter 9

p. 458: Erich Lessling/Art Resource, N.Y.; p. 459 (top, left): Corbis/Bettmann; p. 459 (top, right): MultiMedia Verlag Werbeagentur; p. 459 (bottom, right): Stockbyte; p. 461: Library of Congress; p. 463: Alistair Duncan © Dorling Kindersley; p. 464: Susan Leavines/Photo Researchers, Inc.; p. 465: Dave King © Dorling Kindersley; p. 466: © Dorling Kindersley; p. 467: Pearson Education/PH College; p. 468: Tim Ridley © Dorling Kindersley; p. 469: © Dorling Kindersley; p. 471: © Dorling Kindersley

Chapter 10

INDEX